MIDDLE EAST CONTEMPORARY SURVEY

Volume XII: 1988

MIDDLE EAST CONTEMPORARY SURVEY
Published for
The Moshe Dayan Center
for Middle Eastern and African Studies
The Shiloah Institute
Tel Aviv University

Other volumes in this series:

Volume I, 1976–77
Volume II, 1977–78
Volume III, 1978–79
Volume IV, 1979–80
Volume V, 1980–81
Volume VI, 1981–82
Volume VII, 1982–83
Volume VIII, 1983–84
Volume IX, 1984–85
Volume X, 1986
Volume XI, 1987

MIDDLE EAST CONTEMPORARY SURVEY

Volume XII
1988

AMI AYALON, HAIM SHAKED
Editors

Barbara Newson, Executive Editor

The Moshe Dayan Center
for Middle Eastern and African Studies
The Shiloah Institute
Tel Aviv University

Routledge
Taylor & Francis Group
LONDON AND NEW YORK

First published 1990 by Westview Press

Published 2018 by Routledge
52 Vanderbilt Avenue, New York, NY 10017
2 Park Square, Milton Park, Abingdon, Oxon OX14 4RN

Routledge is an imprint of the Taylor & Francis Group, an informa business

Typeset in Israel, Graph-Chen Ltd., Jerusalem

Library of Congress Catalog Card Number: 78–648245
ISBN: 0-8133-1044-X
ISSN: 0163-5476

ISBN 13: 978-0-367-00378-4 (hbk)

ISBN 13: 978-0-367-15365-6 (pbk)

About the Series and Editors

Established in 1977, the *Middle East Contemporary Survey* (*MECS*), a unique annual record of political developments in the Middle East, is acknowledged as the standard reference work on events and trends in the region. Designed to be a continuing, up-to-date reference for scholars, researchers and analysts, policymakers, students and journalists, it examines in considerable detail the rapidly changing Middle Eastern scene in all its complexity.

In each volume, the material is arranged in two parts. The first contains a series of essays on broad regional issues and on the overall relations of the region with other parts of the world. Subjects explored in detail include Arab-Israeli and inter-Arab relations, Islamic affairs, Palestinian issues, and the international dimensions of the contending forces in the region. The second part consists of country-by-country surveys of all the Arab states, as well as Iran, Israel, and Turkey. The North African states of Tunisia, Algeria, and Morocco are not covered separately. The emphasis in the second part is on elucidating the inner dynamics of each country's polity and society. Maps, tables, and a detailed index accompany the text.

Ami Ayalon is Senior Lecturer in the Department of Middle Eastern and African History and Senior Research Fellow at the Moshe Dayan Center at Tel Aviv University. **Haim Shaked** is Professor of Middle Eastern and African History and Senior Research Fellow at the Moshe Dayan Center, and Director, Middle East Studies Institute, Graduate School of International Studies, University of Miami.

About the Series and Editors

[illegible]

[illegible]

[illegible]

Preface

The Middle East Contemporary Survey (MECS) is an annual record and analysis of political, economic, military, and international developments in the Middle East. The present volume is the twelfth in a series which provides a continuing, up-to-date reference work recording the rapidly changing events in an exceptionally complex part of the world. Every attempt has again been made to use the widest range of source material and maintain the highest possible academic standards.

Most of the essays in this volume have been researched and written by the members of the Shiloah Institute of the Moshe Dayan Center for Middle Eastern and African Studies at Tel Aviv University. Other contributions have been made by academics and experts from other institutions in Israel and abroad.

This volume covers the year 1988. It witnessed the growth and intensification of the *intifada* in the West Bank and Gaza — a development of profound significance for the Palestinians, the Israelis, and for the region at large — which paved the way for the declaration of Palestinian independence, the concomitant boost in the PLO's international standing, and new movement in the long-stalemated Arab-Israeli peace process. The *intifada* also led to King Husayn's dissociation from the West Bank. Among the other major themes covered in this volume are the sudden termination of the eight-year Iraqi-Iranian War with its domestic and regional repercussions; the Soviet withdrawal from Afghanistan, after nine years of active involvement; the impact of *glasnost* on Moscow's Middle Eastern policy; the ongoing disintegration of Lebanon; and the general elections in Israel, whose results led again to the formation of a National Unity Government.

The period surveyed in this volume, unless otherwise indicated, is from January to December 1988. In order to avoid excessive repetition while at the same time achieving a comprehensive survey of the affairs of each country individually, extensive cross-references have been used.

A.A. & H.S.

Acknowledgments

As editors we are grateful to a large number of contributors who have made this volume possible. First and foremost we recognize the work of the staff of the Moshe Dayan Center and its Shiloah Institute for Middle Eastern and African Studies at Tel Aviv University, whose individual contributions are acknowledged separately.

In the process of preparing this volume we were given much help by Avraham Altman. Barbara Newson's role as executive editor has been indispensable. The exacting work of indexing has been carried out by Ronald Watson. Itamar Rabinovich, elected in 1989 as Dean of the Faculty of Humanities at Tel Aviv University, gave up his editorial role and was succeeded by Ami Ayalon.

At the Dayan Center, Edna Liftman and Amira Margalith, assistants to the Head of the Center, were responsible for the complicated coordination of the production of the volume, and fulfilled a variety of other executive tasks with accuracy, skill, and unflagging care. Others at the Center who must be singled out for special thanks are Lydia Gareh, whose skillful work has been a pillar of the production of *MECS*; Margaret Mahlab, Ilana Grinberg, Margalit Hochman, and the Moshe Dayan Documentation System team, headed by Yigal Sheffi. Ruth Beit-Or prepared the maps for publication, and David Levinson proofread large parts of the volume.

Finally, we would like to express our sincere thanks to Frederick A. Praeger, Barbara Ellington, Carolyn Richards, and the staff of Westview Press for their help in the production and distribution of this volume of *MECS*. The first seven volumes of *MECS* were published by Holmes & Meier. The contribution made by the late Max Holmes and by Colin Legum to the launching of this project and to setting its standards remains invaluable and much appreciated.

A.A. & H.S.

Table of Contents

INTRAREGIONAL AND ISLAMIC AFFAIRS

PALESTINIAN ISSUES

MIDDLE EAST ECONOMIC ISSUES

PART TWO: COUNTRY-BY-COUNTRY SURVEY

List of Maps

Transliteration

The **Arabic** language has been transliterated as follows:

b	for	ب	q	for	ق
d	for	ض، د	r	for	ر
dh	for	ذ	s	for	ص، س
f	for	ف	sh	for	ش
gh	for	غ	t	for	ط، ت
h	for	هـ، ح	th	for	ث
j	for	ج	w (or u)	for	و
k	for	ك	y (or i)	for	ي
kh	for	خ	z	for	ظ، ز
l	for	ل	'	for	ا، ء
m	for	م	'	for	ع
n	for	ن			

In addition, the following should be noted:

Long vowels are not marked for distinction from short ones. Thus ناظر = *nazir*, but also نظير = *nazir*.

The *hamza* is used only in the middle of a word.

The *shadda* is rendered by doubling the consonant containing it.

The *ta marbuta* is not shown, except in construct phrases. Thus *madina, madinat Nasr.*

The definite article is always shown as "al-", regardless of the kind of letter following it.

Exceptions to the above are names of Lebanese and North African personalities who have adopted a French spelling for their names.

In transcribing **Persian**, frequent allowance is made for pronunciation; thus Khomeyni (not Khumayni). Names appearing in both Arabic and Persian texts are transcribed according to the language of the relevant text, thus Hizballah (Arabic) or Hizbollah (Persian).

Recommended Method for Citation from *MECS*

In the interest of accuracy, consistency, and simplicity, the editors of *MECS* recommend the following method of citation. Based on the classification of *MECS* as a periodical, published annually, the method conforms to the *Chicago Manual of Style.*

In a footnote: Asher Susser, "Jordan," *Middle East Contemporary Survey*, vol. X (1986), p. 445.

In a bibliography: Susser, Asher, "Jordan." *Middle East Contemporary Survey.* Vol. X (1986), pp. 425–64.

The accepted abbreviation of the periodical's title is *MECS.* The year is that covered by the volume as indicated on the volume binding and title page, not the year of publication. No mention need be made of editors or publishers, who have changed several times since the establishment of *MECS.* Some styles may require mention of place of publication, usually in parentheses following the title of the periodical. For Volumes I through VII, the place of publication was New York; for Volumes VIII and IX, Tel Aviv; since Volume X, Boulder, Colorado.

List of Initials and Acronyms

ACDA	Arms Control and Disarmament Agency (US)
ADFAED	Abu Dhabi Fund for Arab Economic Development
Adm.	Admiral
Adnoc	Abu Dhabi National Oil Company
AI	Amnesty International
ALF	Arab Liberation Front
AOI	Arab Organization for Industrialization
Aramco	Arabian-American Oil Company
Awacs	airborne warning and control system (radar)
b/d	barrels per day
BD	Bahraini dinar(s)
bn.	billion
BP	British Petroleum
BPC(s)	Basic People's Congress(es) (Libya)
Brig.	Brigadier
Brig. Gen.	Brigadier General
c.	about, approximately
CC	Central Council
cf.	*confer* (compare)
Chevron	Standard Oil of California
CIA	Central Intelligence Agency (US)
c.i.f.	cost, insurance, and freight
Contra	counterrevolutionary
CPSU	Communist Party of the Soviet Union
CSR	Czechoslovak Socialist Republic
cu.	cubic
D.C.	District of Columbia
DECA	Defense and Economic Cooperation Agreement (Turkey and US)
DFLP	Democratic Front for the Liberation of Palestine
DLP	Democratic Left Party (*Demokratik Sol Partisi*; Turkey)
$	US dollar
Dr.	Doctor
DUP	Democratic Unionist Party (Sudan)
EC	Executive Committee (PLO)
ECU	European currency unit
ed.	edition, editor
EEC	European Economic Community
e.g.	*exempli gratia* (for example)
Elf	*Essences et Lubrifiants de France*
est.	estimated
Exxon	Standard Oil (formerly Esso)
ff.	folios, following
FFr	French francs
FLN	*Front de la Libération Nationale* (Algeria)
FM	Field Marshal
f.o.b.	free on board
FRC	Fath Revolutionary Council
FRG	Federal Republic of Germany

ft.	foot *or* feet
GCC	Gulf Cooperation Council
GDP	gross domestic product
Gen.	General
GMT	Greenwich Mean Time
GNP	gross national product
GOP	Grand Old Party (Republicans, US)
GPC	General People's Congress (Libya, YAR)
GPCom	General People's Committee (Libya)
Gunt	*Gouvernement d'Union Nationale de Transition* (Chad)
Hamas	*Harakat al-muqawama al-Islamiyya* (Islamic Resistance Movement)
ICJ	International Court of Justice
ICO	Islamic Conference Organization
IDB	Islamic Development Bank
IDF	Israel Defense Forces
i.e.	*id est* (that is)
IEA	International Energy Agency
IMF	International Monetary Fund
incl.	including, inclusive
INLA	Iranian National Liberation Army
int. ed.	international edition
IOU	I owe you
IRGC	Islamic Revolutionary Guard Corps
IUAM	Islamic Unity of the Afghan Mujahidin
JD	Jordanian dinar(s)
Jr.	junior
KD	Kuwaiti dinar(s)
KDP	Kurdish Democratic Party
KIO	Kuwait Investment Office
km.	kilometer
kwh	kilowatt-hours
£E	Egyptian pound(s)
LF	Lebanese Forces
LNG	liquid natural gas
LNRF	Lebanese National Resistance Front
LPG	liquefied petroleum gas
Lt. Col.	Lieutenant Colonel
Lt. Gen.	Lieutenant General
m.	million
Maj. Gen.	Major General
ME	Middle Eastern
MK(s)	Member(s) of Knesset
Mossad	*Mossad Merkazi le-Modiin u-letafkidim Meyuhadim* (Hebrew for Central Institute for Intelligence and Security)
MWL	Muslim World League
Nato	North Atlantic Treaty Organization
NC	National Command (Iraq)
NDF	National Democratic Front (YAR)
NDP	National Democratic Party (Egypt)
NIF	National Islamic Front (Sudan)
NIS	New Israeli shekels
No.	Number

n.p.	no place of publication indicated; no publisher indicated
NRP	National Religious Party (Israel)
OAU	Organization of African Unity
op. cit.	*opere citato* (in the work quoted)
Opec	Organization of Petroleum Exporting Countries
p.a.	*per annum* (yearly)
PCP	Palestine Communist Party
PDPA	People's Democratic Party of Afghanistan
PDRY	People's Democratic Republic of Yemen (South Yemen)
Petromin	General Organization for Petroleum and Minerals (Saudi Arabia)
PFLP	Popular Front for the Liberation of Palestine
PFLP-GC	Popular Front for the Liberation of Palestine-General Command
PKK	*Parti-ye Karkeran-i Kurdistan* (Kurdish Workers' Party; Turkey)
PLF	Palestine Liberation Front
PLO	Palestine Liberation Organization
PNC	Palestine National Council
PNSF	Palestine National Salvation Front
Polisario	Front for the Liberation of Al-Saqiyya al-Hamra and Rio de Oro
POW	prisoner of war
pp.	pages
PPNF	Progressive Patriotic and National Front (Iraq)
PPSF	Palestine Popular Struggle Front
PRC	People's Republic of China
PSP	Progressive Socialist Party (Lebanon)
RC	Regional Command (Iraq)
RCC	Revolutionary Command Council (Iraq)
Rev.	Reverend
RG	Revolutionary Guards (Iran)
RMT	*Ruhaniyyane Mobareze Tehran* (Combatant Clerics of Tehran; Iran)
RPG	rocket-propelled grenade
RPP	Republican People's Party (*Cumhuriyet Halk Partisi*; Turkey)
SADR	Saharan Arab Democratic Republic
SAIRI	Supreme Assembly of the Islamic Revolution in Iraq
Sama	Saudi Arabian Monetary Agency
SDPP	Social Democrat Populist Party (*Sosyaldemokrat Halkçi Parti*; Turkey)
SISC	Supreme Islamic Shi'i Council
SLA	South Lebanese Army
SNP	Sudan National Party
SPLA	Sudanese People's Liberation Army
sq.	square
SR	Saudi riyal
Swapo	South-West African People's Organization
Texaco	The Texas Company
TL	Turkish lira(s)
TPP	True Path Party (*Doğru Yol Partisi*; Turkey)
Tüsiad	*Türk Sanayicileri ve İş Adamları Derneği* (Turkish Industrialists' and Businessmen's Association)
Türk-İş	*Türkiye İşçi Sendikaları Konfederasyonu* (Trade Union Confederation of Turkey)
UAE	United Arab Emirates
UN	United Nations

UNC	United National Command
UNGA	UN General Assembly
Unifil	UN Interim Force in Lebanon
UNIIMOG	UN Iran-Iraq Military Observer Group
Untso	UN Truce Supervision Organization
UP	Umma Party (Sudan)
US	United States
USSR	Union of Soviet Socialist Republics
VAT	value added tax
Vol.	Volume
WICS	World Islamic Call Society
WTI	West Texas Intermediate
YAR	Yemeni Arab Republic (North Yemen)
YSP	Yemeni Socialist Party (South Yemen)

List of Sources

Newspapers, Periodicals, Irregular and Single Publications

Name *(Place, Frequency of Publication)*	*Abbreviation*	*Notes*
Abrar (Tehran, daily)		In Persian
Adelphi Papers (London, 10 per year)		Published by the International Institute for Strategic Studies
Al-Adwa (Khartoum, twice a week)		
Al-Afaq (Cyprus, weekly)		
Africa Confidential (London, fortnightly)	*AC*	
Africa Research Bulletin (Exeter, England, monthly)	*ARB*	
Al-Ahali (Cairo, weekly)		Organ of the National Progressive Unionist Grouping
Al-'Ahd (Doha, weekly)		
Al-Ahram (Cairo, daily)		
Al-Ahram International (London, daily)		
Al-Ahram al-Iqtisadi (Cairo, weekly)		Published by *al-Ahram*; deals mainly with economic issues
Al-Ahrar (Cairo, weekly)		Organ of the Liberal Party
Al-Akhbar (Cairo, daily)		
Akhbar al-'Alam al-Islami (Mecca, weekly)		Published by the Muslim World League
Akhbar al-Usbu' (Amman, weekly)		
Akhbar al-Yawm (Cairo, weekly)		Weekly edition of *al-Akhbar*
Akhir al-Anba (Khartoum, twice a week)		
Akhir Sa'a (Cairo, weekly)		
Al-'Alam (London, weekly)		
Al-'Alam (Rabat, daily)		Organ of the Istiqlal Party
'Al-Hamishmar (Tel Aviv, daily)		Organ of the United Workers' Party (Mapam)
Alwan (Khartoum, daily)		
Amal (Beirut, weekly)		Official publication of the Shi'ite Amal movement in Beirut

Al-'Amal (Cairo, monthly)		Reflects somewhat socialist views, critical of the regime
Amnesty International Report (London, annually)		
Al-Anba (Kuwait, daily)		Pro-establishment but critical of specific government policies and of US attitudes toward the Middle East
Al-Anwar (Beirut, daily)		
Arab Studies Quarterly (Belmont, MA, quarterly)		Published by the Association of Arab-American University Graduates
Arab Times (Kuwait, daily)	*AT*	
Argumenty i Fakty (Moscow, daily)		
Argus (Beirut, monthly)		
Al-Ayyam (Khartoum, daily)		
Baghdad Observer (Baghdad, daily)		
Baltimore Sun (Baltimore, daily)		
Bamahane (Tel Aviv, weekly)		Illustrated weekly of the IDF
Al-Ba'th (Damascus, daily)		Organ of the Syrian Ba'th Party
Al-Bayadir al-Siyasi (East Jerusalem, fortnightly)		Sympathetic to al-Fath
Al-Bayan (Beirut, monthly)		
Al-Bayan (Dubai, daily)		
Al-Bilad (Jidda, daily)		
Boston Globe (Boston, daily)		
Briefing (Ankara, weekly)		
Chicago Tribune (Chicago, Ill, daily)		
Christian Science Monitor (Boston, daily)	*CSM*	
Country Profile (London, annually)		Published by Economist Publications
Country Reports (London, quarterly)	*CR*	Published by Economist Publications. Formerly *Quarterly Economic Review*
Crescent International (Willowdale, Ontario, monthly)		Islamic affairs
Cumhuriyet (Istanbul, daily)		
Current Digest of the Soviet Press (Chicago, weekly)	*CDSP*	Translation from the Soviet Press. Published by the American Association for the Advancement of Slavic Studies, University of Illinois at Chicago Circle, Chicago

Current History (Philadelphia, monthly)		
Dagens Nyheter (Stockholm, daily)		
Daily Telegraph (London, daily)	*DT*	
Dateline Turkey (Istanbul, weekly)		
Davar (Tel Aviv, daily)		Organ of the Israeli Trade Union Federation (Histadrut)
Al-Da'wa (Riyadh, monthly)		Reflects views of conservative *'ulama*
Al-Da'wa al-Islamiyya (Tripoli, Libya, bimonthly)		
Defense and Foreign Affairs (Alexandria, VA, monthly)		
Defense and Foreign Affairs Weekly (Washington, DC, weekly)		
Defense News (Springfield, VA, weekly)		
Democratic Palestine (Cyprus, monthly)		English-language organ of the PFLP
Department of State Bulletin (Washington, DC, weekly)	*DSB*	
Diario (Madrid, daily)		
Al-Diyar (Beirut, daily)		
Al-Dunya (Beirut, weekly)		Supplement of the Lebanese paper, *al-Haqiqa*
Al-Dustur (Amman, daily)		
Al-Dustur (London, weekly)		Pro-Iraqi. Originally a Beirut weekly reflecting the Iraqi Ba'th views. Since 1977 published in London
The Echo of Iran (Tehran, monthly)		
The Economist (London, weekly)		
L'Espresso (Rome, weekly)		
Ettela'at (Tehran, daily)		
Al-Fajr (East Jerusalem, daily)		Sympathetic to the PLO
Al-Fajr (East Jerusalem, weekly)		English- and Hebrew-language editions of *al-Fajr*
Al-Fajr al-Jadid (Tripoli, daily)		
Al-Fikr al-Islami (Beirut, monthly)		
Filastin al-Muslima (Manchester, monthly)		
Filastin al-Thawra (Nicosia, weekly)		Organ of the PLO. Ceased publication during the war in Lebanon. Resumed publication in Nicosia in 1982
The Financial Times (London, daily)	*FT*	

Foreign Affairs (New York, quarterly)		
Foreign Policy (Washington, DC, quarterly)		
Foreign Report (London, weekly)	*FR*	Published by Economist Publications
Fourteenth October (Aden, daily)		Organ of the Yemeni Socialist Party (YSP)
Frontier Post (Peshawar, daily)		
Al-Ghuraba (Leeds, monthly)		
The Guardian (London, daily)		
Guardian Weekly (Manchester, weekly)		
Gulf News (Dubai, daily)		
The Gulf States (West Sussex, biweekly)		
Gulf States Newsletter (Crawley, West Sussex, biweekly)		
Ha'aretz (Tel Aviv, daily)		
Al-Hadaf (Damascus, weekly)		Organ of the PFLP. Transferred from Beirut after the war in Lebanon
Hadashot (Tel Aviv, daily)		
Ha'olam Hazeh (Tel Aviv, weekly)		Independent; illustrated news magazine
Al-Haqiqa (Beirut, daily)		
Al-Hawadith (London, weekly)		A Beirut weekly, reflecting pro-Phalangist tendencies. Published in London since 1978
Al-Hayat (Beirut, daily)		
Al-Hayat (London, daily)		
Al Hilal al-Duwali (London, bimonthly)		
Al-Hilal International (London, biweekly)		Organ of the "Islamic movement"
Hurras al-Watan (Baghdad, monthly)		A military magazine
Al-Hurriyya (Nicosia, weekly)		Organ of the DFLP. Ceased publication during the war in Lebanon. Resumed publication in Nicosia in 1983
Impact International (London, twice monthly)		
The Independent (London, daily)		
International Financial Statistics (Washington, DC, monthly)	*IFS*	Published by the IMF

International Herald Tribune (Paris and Zurich, daily)	*IHT*	
International Journal of Middle East Studies (Cambridge, quarterly)	*IJMES*	
International Security (Cambridge, Mass., quarterly)		
Iqra (Jidda, weekly)		
Iran Focus (Bonn, monthly)		
Iranian Studies (New York, quarterly)		
Al-'Iraq (Baghdad, daily)		
Iraq al-Ghad (London, biweekly)		
Al-I'tisam (Cairo, monthly)		Organ of the Muslim Brothers
Al-Ittihad (Abu Dhabi, daily)		
Al-Ittihad (Haifa, twice a week)		
Al-Ittihad (Khartoum, daily)		
Al-Ittihad al-Usbu'i (Abu Dhabi, weekly)		
Izvestiia (Moscow, daily)		Organ of the Government of the USSR
Al-Jamahiriyya (Tripoli, Libya, weekly)		
Jane's Defence Weekly (London, weekly)		
Al-Jazira (Riyadh, daily)		
The Jerusalem Post (Jerusalem, daily)	*JP*	
The Jerusalem Quarterly (Jerusalem, quarterly)		
Jeune Afrique (Paris, weekly)	*JA*	Reflects views of Tunisian expatriates
Jewish Journal of Sociology (London, twice annually)		
Jewish Week (New York, weekly)		
Al-Jihad (Peshawar, monthly)		
Jordan Times (Amman, daily)	*JT*	
Le Journal du Dimanche (Paris, weekly)		
Journal of Palestine Studies (Washington, DC, quarterly)	*JPS*	Published by the Institute of Palestine Studies and Kuwait University
Judea, Samaria, and Gaza Area Statistics (Jerusalem, quarterly)		Published by the Israel Central Bureau of Statistics

Al-Jumhuriyya (Baghdad, daily)		
Al-Jumhuriyya (Cairo, daily)		
Al-Jumhuriyya (Ta'izz, daily)		
Jumhuriyye Islami (Tehran, daily)	*JI*	Organ of the Islamic Republican Party
Al-Katib (Jerusalem, monthly)		
Kayhan (London, weekly)		
Kayhan (Tehran, daily)		
Kayhan al-'Arabi (Tehran, daily)		
Kayhan International (Tehran, daily)	*KI*	English-language edition of *Kayhan*
Khaleej Times (Dubai, daily)		
Al-Khalij (Abu Dhabi, daily)		
Al-Kifah al-'Arabi (Beirut, weekly)		
Krasnaia Zvezda (Moscow, daily)		
Kull al-'Arab (Paris, weekly)		
Literaturnaya Gazeta (Moscow, weekly)		Organ of the Union of Writers of the USSR
Al-Liwa al-Islami (Cairo, weekly)		Islamic publication of the ruling National Democratic Party
Los Angeles Times (Los Angeles, daily)	*LAT*	
Ma'ariv (Tel Aviv, daily)		
Al-Madina (Jidda, daily)		
Maghreb-Machrek, Monde Arabe (Paris, quarterly)		
Al-Majalis (London, weekly)		
Al-Majalla (London, weekly)		Published by Saudi Research and Marketing (UK)
Majallat al-Azhar (Cairo, monthly)		
Al-Masa (Cairo, weekly)		
Al-Masira (Beirut, weekly)		
Le Matin du Sahara (Rabat, daily)		
Mélanges de l'Institut Dominicain des Études Orientales du Caire (Cairo, annually)		
Al-Mawqif al-'Arabi (Cairo, monthly)		

Memo (Limassol, biweekly)		
The Miami Herald (Miami, FL, daily)		
The Middle East (London, monthly)	*ME*	
Middle East Business Intelligence (Washington, DC, twice monthly)		
Middle East Currency Report (New York, nine per year)		
Middle East Economic Digest (London, weekly)	*MEED*	
Middle East Economic Survey (Nicosia, weekly)	*MEES*	Published by the Middle East Research and Publishing Center, Beirut
Middle East Executive Report (Washington, DC, monthly)		
Middle Eastern Studies (London, quarterly)	*MES*	
Middle East Insight (Washington, DC, bimonthly)		
Middle East International (London, monthly)	*MEI*	
Middle East Journal (Washington, quarterly)	*MEJ*	Published by the Middle East Institute
Middle East Policy Survey (Washington, biweekly)		
Middle East Review (New Brunswick, NJ, quarterly)		
Mideast Markets (London, fortnightly)	*MM*	Published by *FT* Business Information
Milliyet (Istanbul, daily)		
Mir'at al-Umma (Kuwait, weekly)		
Al-Mithaq (East Jerusalem, daily)		
Monday Morning (Beirut, weekly)		
Le Monde (Paris, daily)		
Monthly Statistical Bulletin (Amman, monthly)		Published by the Central Bank of Jordan
Al-Muntalaq (Beirut, bimonthly)		
Al-Muharrir (Paris, weekly)		
Al-Musawwar (Cairo, weekly)		
The Muslim (Islamabad, daily)		
Al-Mustaqbal (Paris, weekly)		Pro-Saudi
Al-Mustaqbal al-'Arabi (Beirut, quarterly)		
Al-Nahar (Beirut, daily)		

Al-Nahar (East Jerusalem, daily)		
Al-Nahar al-'Arabi wal-Duwali (Paris and Zurich, weekly)	*NAD*	Weekly international edition of *al-Nahar*
Al-Nashra (Athens, biweekly)		
Al-Nashra (Nicosia, weekly)		Deals with opposition movements in various Arab countries
Nation (Jerusalem, daily)		
Neue Kronen-Zeitung (Vienna, daily)		
New African (London, monthly)		
New Cyprus (Northern Nicosia, irregular)		Turkish-Cypriot periodical
Newsweek (New York, weekly)		
New Times (Moscow, weekly)		English-language editon of *Novoe Vremia*
The New Yorker (New York, weekly)		
The New York Times (New York, daily)	*NYT*	
Al-Nida (Beirut, daily)		
Nidal al-Sha'b (Beirut, weekly)		
Notes et Études de l'Institut de Criminologie de Paris (Paris, irregular)		
Le Nouvel Observateur (Paris, weekly)		
Al-Nur (Cairo, weekly)		Islamic publication of the Liberal Party
The Observer (London, weekly)		
October (Cairo, weekly)		
Oman Daily Observer (Muscat, daily)		
Opec Bulletin (Vienna, monthly)		
Orbis (Philadelphia, PA, quarterly)		Published by Foreign Policy Research Institute
Orient (Hamburg, quarterly)		
L'Orient le Jour (Beirut, daily)		
El Pais (Madrid, daily)		
Petroleum Economist (London, monthly)	*PE*	
Philadelphia Inquirer (Philadelphia, PA, daily)		
Le Point (Paris, weekly)		

Policy Papers (Washington, irregular)		Occasional papers published by the Washington Institute for Near East Policy
Pravda (Moscow, daily)		Organ of the Central Committee of the CPSU
Al-Qabas (Kuwait, daily)		
Al-Qabas International (London, daily)		
Al-Qadisiyya (Baghdad, daily)		
Al-Qawmi al-'Arabi (Beirut, twice a month)		
Quarterly Economic Review (London, quarterly)	*QER*	Published by Economist Publications Ltd. Now called *Country Reports*
Al-Quds (East Jerusalem, daily)		Known for favorable views toward Jordan
Le Quotidien de Paris (Paris, daily)		
Al-Ra'y (Amman, daily)		
Al-Raya (Khartoum, daily)		Organ of the National Islamic Front
Al-Ra'y al-Akhir (London, monthly)		Reflects critical views of the establishment in Arab states
Al-Ra'y al-'Amm (Kuwait, daily)		Conservative
La Repubblica (Rome, daily)		
La Revue du Liban et de l'Orient Arabe (Beirut, weekly)		
Risalat (Tehran, daily)		
Risalat al-'Iraq (Monthly)		No place of publication indicated — clandestine
Al-Riyad (Riyadh, daily)		
Ruz al-Yusuf (Cairo, weekly)		
Al-Sabah (Tunis, daily)		
Al-Sada (Tunis, weekly)		
Al-Safir (Beirut, daily)		Reflects Libyan views
Al-Sakhra (Kuwait, weekly)		Organ of al-Fath
Saudi Gazette (Jidda, daily)		
Sawt al-'Arab (Cairo, daily)		
Sawt al-Sha'b (Amman, daily)		
Sawt al-Umma (Tehran, fortnightly)		The Arabic publication of the Ministry of Islamic Guidance

Al-Sayyad (Beirut, weekly)		
Al-Sha'b (Cairo, weekly)		Organ of the Socialist Labor Party
Al-Sha'b (East Jerusalem, daily)		Sympathetic to the PLO
Al-Sharq (Beirut, daily)		Pro-Syrian
Al-Sharq al-Awsat (London, Jidda, and Riyadh, daily)		
Al-Sharq al-Jadid (London, monthly)		
Al-Shira' (Beirut, weekly)		
Shu'un Filastiniyya (Nicosia, monthly)		Published by the PLO Research Center
Shu'un al-Sa'a (London, monthly)		
Al-Siyasa (Khartoum, daily)		Organ of the Umma Party
Al-Siyasa (Kuwait, daily)		
Al-Siyasi (Cairo, weekly)		
Der Spiegel (Hamburg, weekly)		
La Stampa (Turin, daily)		
Strategic Studies (Islamabad, quarterly)		Published by the Institute of Strategic Studies
Al-Sudani (Khartoum, daily)		
Sudan Times (Khartoum, daily)		
Süddeutsche Zeitung (Munich, daily)		
Sunday Times (London, weekly)	*ST*	
Al-Tadamun (London, weekly)		
Al-Tadamun al-Islami (Mecca, monthly)		
Tariq al-Intisar (Nicosia, bimonthly)		
Al-Tayyar al-Jadid (London, weekly)		
Tehran Times (Tehran, weekly)	*TT*	
Al-Thawra (Baghdad, daily)		Organ of the Iraqi Ba'th Party
Al-Thawra (Damascus, daily)		
Al-Thawra al-Islamiyya (London and Washington, monthly)		Organ of the Islamic Revolutionary Movement in the Arabian Peninsula
Third World Quarterly (London, quarterly)		
Time (New York, weekly)		

The Times (London, daily)		
The Times of Oman (Muscat, daily)		
Tishrin (Damascus, daily)		
Tribuna Ludo (Warsaw, daily)		
Turkey Briefing (London, bimonthly)		
Al-Ufuq (Nicosia, weekly)		
'Ukaz (Jidda, daily)		
Al-Umma (Cairo, weekly)		Organ of the Umma Party
Al-Usbu' (Khartoum, daily)		
Al-Usbu' al-'Arabi (Beirut, weekly)		
USIS Report (Tel Aviv, irregular)		Published by USIS, US Embassy, Tel Aviv
US News and World Report (Washington, DC, weekly)		
Al-Wafd (Cairo, daily)		Organ of the New Wafd Party
Al-Wahda (Abu Dhabi, daily)		
The Wall Street Journal (New York, daily)	*WSJ*	
The Washingtonian (Washington, DC, monthly)		
The Washington Post (Washington, DC, daily)	*WP*	
The Washington Times (Washington, DC, daily)	*WT*	
Al-Watan (Khartoum, weekly)		
Al-Watan (Kuwait, daily)		Pro-Syrian; sometimes critical of Kuwait's Government
Al-Watan (Muscat, daily)		
Al-Watan al-'Arabi (Paris, weekly)		Pro-Iraqi
World Marxist Review (London, monthly)		
Al-Yamama (Riyadh, weekly)		
Al-Yaqza (Kuwait, weekly)		Reflects pan-Arab tendencies
Al-Yawm (Amman, daily)		
Al-Yawm al-Sabi' (Paris, weekly)		Affiliated to the PLO
Yedi'ot Aharonot (Tel Aviv, daily)		

Al-Zahf al-Akhdar (Tripoli, Libya, weekly)	Ideological weekly of the Revolutionary Committees; appears in both Arabic and English editions

News Agencies

Full Name	*Abbreviation*
Aden News Agency (Aden)	ANA
Agence France Presse (Paris)	AFP
Algérie Presse Service (Algiers)	APS
Associated Press (New York)	AP
Associazione Nazionale Stampa Associata (Rome)	ANSA
Emirates News Agency (Abu Dhabi)	ENA
Gulf News Agency (Manama)	GNA
Iraqi News Agency (Baghdad)	INA
Islamic Revolution News Agency (Tehran)	IRNA
Jamahiriyya Arab News Agency (Tripoli)	JANA
Jordanian News Agency (PETRA; Amman)	JNA
Kuwaiti News Agency (Kuwait)	KUNA
Maghreb Arabe Presse (Rabat)	MAP
Middle East News Agency (Cairo)	MENA
Novinska Agencija Tanjug (Belgrade)	TANJUG
Pan-African News Agency (Dakar)	PANA
Qatari News Agency (Doha)	QNA
Reuters (London)	
Saudi Press Agency (Riyadh)	SPA
Sudanese News Agency (Khartoum)	SUNA
Syrian Arab News Agency (Damascus)	SANA
Telegrafnoe Agentstvo Sovetskovo Soiuza (Moscow)	TASS
Tunis Afrique Presse (Tunis)	TAP
Wakalat al-Anba al-Filastiniyya (Palestinian News Agency; Damascus)	WAFA

Radio and Television Stations, and Monitoring Services

(Radio stations known by the location of their principal transmitter are not listed — their names being self-explanatory.)

Name	*Abbreviation*	*Notes*
American Broadcasting Company	ABC	Headquarters in New York City
British Broadcasting Corporation	BBC	
British Broadcasting Corporation, Summary of World Broadcasting: The ME and Africa	SWB	Monitoring reports published in English translation
Columbia Broadcasting System	CBS	New York
Daily Report: Middle East and Africa	DR	Monitoring reports published in English translation by the US Foreign Broadcasting Information Service
Daily Report: Soviet Union	DR:SU	
Israel Defense Forces Radio	R.IDF	
Joint Publication Research Services: Near East and North Africa Soviet Union	JPRS	English-language translation from foreign press. Occasionally includes monitoring reports as well

Sub-Saharan Africa		
West Europe		
Middle East Television	METV	Cyprus
Nippon Hoso Kyokai (Japan Broadcasting Corporation)	NHK TV	Tokyo
Public Broadcasting Service	PBS	New York
Al-Quds — Palestine Arab Radio	R. al-Quds	PFLP-GC radio, broadcasting from Syria
R. of the Toilers of Iran		Radio station of the Iranian opposition group with leftist tendencies, broadcasting from Iraq
R. Peace and Progress		Official USSR station transmitting from Moscow to the ME
R. SPLA		Voice of the Sudanese People's Liberation Army
United States Information Agency	USIA	Washington
United States Information Service	USIS	Washington
Voice of the Arabs	VoA	Cairo
Voice of Free Lebanon		Military station of the Lebanese Phalanges
Voice of Israel	VoI	Israeli national radio
Voice of Lebanon	VoL	Radio station operated by the Lebanese Phalanges
Voice of the Masses	R. Baghdad, VoM	A series of special programs in Arabic, Kurdish, and Farsi, broadcast over R. Baghdad for a few hours each day
Voice of National Resistance		Radio station connected with *al-Amal*, Lebanon
Voice of Palestine (Algiers)	VoP (Algiers)	PLO daily program over R. Algiers
Voice of Palestine (Baghdad)	VoP (Baghdad)	PLO main radio station, transferred from Beirut after the war in Lebanon. Began transmitting in 1982
Voice of Palestine (Clandestine)	VoP (Clandestine)	PLO clandestine station transmitting from Sidon
Voice of Palestine (San'a)	VoP (San'a)	PLO daily program over R. San'a
Voice of the People		Communist Party clandestine radio station, based in Lebanon
Wireless File	WF	Published by the USIA Library, Washington
Worldnet		USIS global television satellite network

Note: Radio and news agency material not otherwise attributed is available in Hebrew translation at the Moshe Dayan Center archives.

Notes on Contributors

AMI AYALON, PhD (Princeton University, 1980). Senior Research Fellow at the Moshe Dayan Center. Senior Lecturer, Department of Middle Eastern and African History, Tel Aviv University. Author of *Language and Change in the Arab Middle East* (1987) and numerous articles on modern Middle Eastern political and cultural history. Editor of *Regime and Opposition in Egypt under Sadat* (1983, in Hebrew).

OFRA BENGIO, MA (Tel Aviv University, 1986). Junior Research Fellow at the Moshe Dayan Center. Fields of specialization: Contemporary Middle Eastern history, modern and contemporary politics of Iraq and the Arabic language. Author of *The Kurdish Revolt in Iraq* (1989 in Hebrew) and articles.

ROBERT O. FREEDMAN, PhD (Columbia University). Dean of the Peggy Meyerhoff Pearlstone School of Graduate Studies and Professor of Political Science at the Baltimore Hebrew University. Author of *Economic Warfare in the Communist Bloc: A Study of Soviet Economic Pressure against Yugoslavia, Albania and Communist China* (1970) and *Soviet Policy toward the Middle East since 1970* (1975, 1978, 1982). Editor of *World Politics and the Arab-Israeli Conflict* (1979), *Israel in the Begin Era* (1982), *The Middle East since Camp David* (1984), *Soviet Jewry in the Decisive Decade 1971–80* (1984), and *Soviet Jewry in the 1980s: The Politics of Anti-Semitism and Emigration and the Dynamics of Resettlement* (1989).

HILLEL FRISCH, PhD (Hebrew University, 1989). Instructor in the Department of Political Science, The Hebrew University, and Research Fellow at the Truman Institute for the Advancement of Peace. Coauthor of *Israel, the Palestinians and the West Bank* (1984), and published articles on Palestinian politics and economics in the Israeli-administered territories. Title of thesis: "Palestinian Political Institution-building in the Territories 1967–1985."

MORDECHAI GAZIT, MA (Hebrew University). Senior Research Fellow at the Moshe Dayan Center and the Leonard Davis Institute for International Relations, Hebrew University. Formerly Director-General, Office of the Prime Minister of Israel (1973–75); Director-General, Israel Ministry for Foreign Affairs (1972–73); Ambassador to France (1975–79); Minister, Embassy of Israel, Washington, D.C. (1960–65); Fellow, Center for International Affairs, Harvard University (1980–81).

GIDEON GERA, PhD (Tel Aviv University, 1978). Senior Research Fellow at the Moshe Dayan Center. Fields of specialization: current politics of the Arab world; the Iraqi-Iranian War. Author of *Libya under Qadhdhafi* (1983, in Hebrew).

JACOB GOLDBERG, PhD (Harvard University, 1978). Senior Research Fellow at the Moshe Dayan Center. Chairman of the Editorial Board of the Moshe Dayan Center Occasional Papers Series. Fields of specialization: the modern and contemporary history of the Arab world with particular reference to Saudi Arabia. Publications: *The Foreign Policy of Saudi Arabia: The Formative Years, 1902–1918*; coeditor of *The Soviet-American Competition in the Middle East*.

WILLIAM M. HALE, MA (Oxon.), PhD (Australian National University). Senior Lecturer in Politics, School of Oriental and African Studies, England. Author of *The Economic and Political Development of Modern Turkey* (1981, 1983). Coauthor of *Aspects of Modern Turkey* (1976) and *Four Centuries of Turco-British Relations* (1984). Published numerous articles on Turkish politics and economic development.

WILLIAM W. HARRIS, PhD (University of Durham, 1979). Lecturer in Strategic Geography, Australian Defense Force Academy, University of New South Wales. Fields of specialization: political geography of the Middle East and the South Pacific. Frequent visits and periods of residence in Lebanon from 1983 to the present. Published papers on Lebanese political developments, especially on Syrian interventions. Author of *Taking Root: Israeli Settlement in the West Bank, the Golan and Gaza-Sinai 1967–1980*.

ELIYAHU KANOVSKY, PhD (Columbia University, 1961). Professor, Department of Economics at Bar Ilan University; Senior Research Fellow at the Dayan Center, Tel Aviv University. Visiting Ludwig Jesselson Professor of Economics, Yeshiva University, NY, 1989–90. Field of specialization: Middle East economics. Published books and articles on economics of the Middle East.

JOSEPH KOSTINER, PhD (London School of Economics and Political Science, University of London, 1982). Research Fellow at the Moshe Dayan Center; Lecturer in the Department of Middle Eastern and African History at Tel Aviv University. Fields of specialization: history and current affairs of the Arabian Peninsula states. Published several papers on this subject. Author of *The Struggle for South Yemen* (1984).

MARTIN KRAMER, PhD (Princeton University, 1982). Associate Director and Senior Research Fellow at the Moshe Dayan Center. Fields of specialization: Islamic and pan-Islamic activism. Author of *Islam Assembled: The Advent of the Muslim Congresses* (1986), and published articles on the modern history of the Middle East; editor of: *Protest and Revolution in Shi'i Islam* (1985, in Hebrew); *Shi'ism, Resistance and Revolution* (1987).

BRUCE MADDY-WEITZMAN, PhD (Tel Aviv University, 1988). Junior Research Fellow at the Moshe Dayan Center, and Post-Doctoral Fellow, 1988–89 at the Jewish-Arab Center, Haifa University. Fields of specialization: contemporary Middle East history, inter-Arab relations, and the Arab-Israeli conflict. Published articles on Arab politics, and the Iraqi-Iranian conflict. Title of thesis: "The Crystallization of an Arab State System: Inter-Arab Politics, 1945–1954."

DAVID MENASHRI, PhD (Tel Aviv University, 1982). Senior Research Fellow at the Moshe Dayan Center and Senior Lecturer in the Department of Middle Eastern and African History, Tel Aviv University. Field of specialization: the history and politics of Iran. Author of: *Iran: A Decade of War and Revolution* (1990), and *Iran in Revolution* (1988, in Hebrew). Editor of *The Iranian Revolution and the Muslim World* (1990), and published papers on Iranian politics.

YOSEF OLMERT, PhD (London School of Economics and Political Science, University of London, 1984). Research Fellow at the Moshe Dayan Center. Lecturer in the Department of Middle Eastern and African History at Tel Aviv University. Fields of specialization: political and ideological history of Syria and Lebanon. Published papers on various aspects of political development in Syria and Lebanon.

UZI RABI, BA (Tel Aviv University, 1986). Researcher at the Moshe Dayan Center and Instructor in the Department for Middle Eastern and African History and in the Preparatory Program, Tel Aviv University. Fields of specialization: Persian Gulf states and Palestinian armed operations.

ITAMAR RABINOVICH, PhD (University of California, Los Angeles, 1971). Professor, Department of Middle Eastern and African History, Tel Aviv University, and Senior Research Fellow at the Dayan Center. Dean of the Faculty of Humanities, Tel Aviv University. The incumbent of the Yona and Dina Ettinger Chair in Contemporary History of the Middle East. Fields of specialization: the modern and contemporary history of the Arab world with particular reference to Syria, Lebanon, and inter-Arab affairs. Publications: *Syria under the Ba'th 1963–66: the Army-Party Symbiosis*; *The Lebanese Civil War: A Documented History* (in Hebrew); and *The War for Lebanon 1970–83*; coeditor of *From June to October: The Middle East between 1967–73*; *The Middle East and the United States: Perceptions and Policies*; *Israel in the Middle East 1948–82*; and *Ethnicity, Pluralism, and the State in the Middle East*.

YEHUDIT RONEN, BA (Tel Aviv University, 1977). Junior Research Fellow at the Moshe Dayan Center. Fields of specialization: Sudan and Libya. Contributed to previous volumes of *MECS* as well as to a number of edited volumes on the Middle East.

HAIM SHAKED, PhD (School of Oriental and African Studies, University of London, 1969). Professor, Department of Middle Eastern and African History, Tel Aviv University. Head of the Shiloah (now Moshe Dayan) Center (1973–80); Dean of the Faculty of Humanities, Tel Aviv University (1975–80). Fields of specialization: modern and contemporary history of the Middle East. Author of *The Life of the Sudanese Mahdi*, and coeditor of *From June to October: The Middle East between 1967–73* and *The Middle East and the United States: Perceptions and Policies*. Editor in chief of *Mideast File*. Chairman, Editorial Board of the Moshe Dayan Center Monograph Series.

ALI T. SHEIKH, Senior Research Fellow at the Institute of Soviet and East European Studies at the University of Miami and Research Fellow at the Institute of Strategic Studies in Islamabad. Published articles on Southwest Asian Security.

BENJAMIN SHWADRAN, MA, PhD (Clark University, 1945). Taught Middle Eastern Studies in the New York School for Social Research; Professor of Middle Eastern Studies and Director of the Middle East Institute, Dropsie University, Philadelphia; taught in Hofstra University, New York. Professor of Modern Middle

East History at Tel Aviv University since 1973. Formerly editor of *Middle Eastern Affairs* and of the Council for Middle Eastern Affairs Press. Among his publications are *Middle East Oil and the Great Powers* (three editions); *Jordan, a State of Tension; The Power Struggle in Iraq; General Index Middle Eastern Affairs; Neft Hamizrah Hatikhon: Berakha Veiyum; Middle East Oil: Issues and Problems*; and *Middle East Oil Crises since 1973.*

STEVEN L. SPIEGEL, PhD (Harvard University). Professor of Political Science at the University of California, Los Angeles. Author of *The Other Arab-Israeli Conflict: Making America's Middle East Policy, From Truman to Reagan* (1985), numerous articles on American foreign policy and Middle East politics, and coeditor of *The Soviet-American Competition in the Middle East* (1987).

ASHER SUSSER, PhD (Tel Aviv University, 1986). Senior Research Fellow at the Moshe Dayan Center and Head of the Center. Fields of specialization: history and politics of Jordan and the Palestinians. Author of *Between Jordan and Palestine: A Political Biography of Wasfi al-Tall* (1983, in Hebrew); *The PLO after the War in Lebanon* (1985, in Hebrew); monographs and papers on Jordanian and Palestinian history and politics.

JOSHUA TEITELBAUM, MA (Tel Aviv University, 1988). Junior Research Fellow at the Moshe Dayan Center and Instructor in the Overseas Students Program, Tel Aviv University. Fields of specialization: Palestinian history and politics, modern Islamic movements, and the history of the Arabian Peninsula. Researching PhD dissertation on "The Hashimite Kingdom of the Hijaz, 1916–1925."

YAEL YISHAI, PhD (Hebrew University, 1976). Professor of Political Science, University of Haifa. Author of *Israel: The Peaceful Belligerent 1967–1979* (with A. Sella); *Land or Peace: Whither Israel* (1987); and *Interest Groups in Israeli Politics* (1987). Has published numerous articles on Israeli domestic politics.

PART ONE: CURRENT ISSUES

THE MIDDLE EAST IN PERSPECTIVE

1988: A Shift of Accent

ITAMAR RABINOVICH

The year 1987 was defined by Haim Shaked in *MECS* as one in which the stalemate that had characterized the Middle East for some time was broken. The process of movement and change was accelerated in 1988. Furthermore, two sets of developments shifted the focus of regional politics from the Gulf area to the Arab-Israeli part of the region.

One set of developments concerned the war in the Gulf. For nearly eight years the war between Iran and Iraq had been a dominant factor in the international and regional politics of the ME. The superpowers had managed for several years to steer clear of direct involvement in the war, yet they had been interested and active. Then they were drawn into more open intervention, which increased the danger of escalation. The war's repercussions for the oil industry and oil economy of the ME had similarly been very significant. In theory, a war in the Gulf between two major oil producers that included attacks on oil installations and oil tankers could have played havoc with the international oil market and could have driven prices up. In practice it did not; rather, it induced the two combatants and other oil producers to seek an increase in production, thus contributing to a decline in prices and to a decline in the region's oil economy. The loss of oil income and the preoccupation with threats of armies and the Iranian revolutionary message led to a considerable reduction in the Arab world's collective power.

Loss of income, power, and confidence led to a rearrangement of priorities. Iraq, the Arab oil-producing states of the Gulf region and, to a lesser extent, most of the other Arab states were preoccupied during much of the decade with the war and with the menacing prospect of an Iranian victory. In fact, some Arab states were almost as alarmed, particularly during the war's early years, by the prospect of a sweeping Iraqi victory. In this scheme of things the conflict with Israel lost some of its acuteness in Arab eyes. The Egyptian-Israeli peace treaty of 1979, which had been universally condemned in the Arab world at the time, came to be seen in a somewhat different light. It was now viewed as a measure which stabilized the other part of the ME while the Gulf region was aflame; which freed the Egyptian Army to serve — should the need arise — as a protector of the weaker Gulf states; and which contributed to the safety of the Red Sea as an alternative waterway to the Gulf.

Gideon Gera's essays in *MECS* 1987 and 1988 describe how the patterns of the Gulf War changed in these two years. The growing direct involvement of the superpowers, the escalation of the war's level and, finally, Iran's inability to shoulder the burden led in August 1988 to the termination of fighting in circumstances that amounted to a slight Iraqi victory.

This particular turn of events brought about an immediate sense of relief from the threat of an Iranian victory. The specter of victorious revolutionary armies sweeping west and south, and the prospective boost to the fundamentalist challengers of the regimes in power were removed. Iraq's Arab neighbors were also relieved by the modesty of its victory. A sweeping Iraqi victory might have turned Saddam Husayn into an unbearable neighbor.

The immediate sense of relief was accompanied by the realization that the end of fighting did not necessarily signify the end of war, and certainly not the end of the conflict. Well before the cease-fire of 1988, the conflict between Iran and Iraq came to be widely perceived as a long-term dispute, similar in some respects to the Arab-Israeli conflict. From this perspective, the termination of hostilities in August 1988 could be seen as marking the beginning of a transitional period during which the belligerents would rehabilitate their economies and seek to prepare for a potential renewal of fighting at a later date.

A feeling that this, indeed, could be the case seemed to be substantiated by Iraq's conduct in the aftermath of the cease-fire. Saddam Husayn's regime chose to settle two scores — with the Kurdish minority at home and with the rival Ba'th regime in Syria. The Kurds in northern Iraq were dealt with swiftly and brutally with gas. Against Asad's Syria, Iraq acted with some caution, avoiding a direct confrontation and choosing to punish its archrival by encouraging the latter's own rivals in Lebanon. One important consequence of this trend of events was the effective Maronite resistance to Syria's attempt to impose a staunch Syrian supporter as Lebanon's new president in September. The willingness and ability of the Maronites to ward off Syrian pressure and to foil, later on, a joint American-Syrian attempt to impose another pro-Syrian candidate derived apparently also from promises of Iraqi aid and support. An overoptimistic interpretation of these promises may also have prompted Gen. Michel 'Awn, the head of Lebanon's "Christian Government," to challenge Syria with unprecedented audacity.

Iraq also lent support and encouragement to another foe of Syria, Yasir 'Arafat, but this, too, was conducted with a light touch. Saddam Husayn's attention continued, for the most part, to be focused on Iran.

During the first half of 1988, while the Gulf War was coming to an end, the Palestinian uprising in the West Bank and Gaza Strip — the *intifada* — was altering the state of the other major regional dispute — the Arab-Israeli conflict. The *intifada* broke out in December 1987 in the immediate aftermath of the Amman Arab summit of November. That conference, the first full-fledged summit to have met since September 1982, reflected the Arab world's concerns and priorities at that time. It focused on the Gulf War, paying little attention to the Palestinian issue. 'Arafat, furthermore, was slighted by the host, King Husayn, and by other Arab leaders — yet another manifestation of the PLO's declining fortunes at the time.

Against this background, the outbreak of the *intifada* and, as it turned out, its success provided an ironic and telling illustration of the manner in which a perceived political reality in the ME could be transformed swiftly. It was widely assumed in December 1987 and during the early weeks of 1988 that the "events" in the West Bank and Gaza were no more than yet another violent spasm, and that the techniques applied so effectively for 20 years would take their effect shortly. Only in the early spring of 1988 did the novelty and full import of the *intifada* come to be widely understood.

The extent of the change which had taken place since the Amman summit was manifested by the next Arab summit conference, held in Algiers in June 1988. This summit was devoted to the *intifada* and centered on the PLO and its chairman. The change of priorities thus displayed by the Arab world was but one of the *intifada*'s several important consequences. It may be useful to list them under the following headings:

(a) The *intifada* broke the pattern of Israeli-Palestinian relations as it had crystallized and existed for 20 years. Since June 1967, Israel had been able to control the West Bank and Gaza with relative ease. Critics of Israel's official policies pointed to the long-term costs of the occupation and to the dangers it posed to the future of Israeli society and polity, but successive Israeli governments found it expedient to maintain the status quo rather than pay the price and run the risks of seeking a far-reaching solution in the terms available at the time. Successive PLO attempts through a variety of strategies to challenge and undermine Israel's control failed. The dominant element in this configuration was the readiness of the bulk of the Palestinian population to comply with Israel's rule. This changed with and through the *intifada*, as a sizable portion of the population willingly defied the Israeli authorities and participated in acts of semiviolent opposition.

The limited violence exerted by the Palestinians was matched by the limited use of violence by the Israeli Government in its own effort to quash the *intifada*. The public debate in Israel ranged along a broad spectrum, from those advocating a political solution and the concessions it required, to those arguing that a swift suppression was both necessary and feasible. The minister of defense and the Israel Defense Forces opted for a middle-of-the-road formula: the *intifada* was contained but not suppressed. Life in Israel itself was barely affected, but the political ramifications of this state of affairs were far reaching.

(b) As has already been mentioned, the Palestinian national cause and the PLO as a movement and organization, have been the main beneficiaries of the *intifada*. The uprising was not begun by the PLO and initially was not controlled or guided by it. But in the absence of national political leadership in the West Bank and Gaza and with a tradition of the local leadership's deference to the PLO, it took the latter little time to take charge of the *intifada*. As will be argued below, this did not amount to full control; but the degree of control and identification sufficed for the PLO's political purposes. The PLO's gains were made primarily at the expense of its three main adversaries — Israel, Jordan, and Syria.

(c) By spring Jordan felt clearly that its position in the West Bank and Gaza was seriously eroding, that the option of being Israel's negotiating partner over the future of these territories had been, at least temporarily, invalidated and that more ominous dangers lurked in the future, such as a spillover of the *intifada* into the East Bank and the far-reaching implications of either Palestinian statehood or a radicalization of Israeli policies. The loosening of the Jordanian State's ties to the West Bank and Gaza, effected in stages since the summer of 1988, was a response to these developments. King Husayn was seeking to control damages, to clear the way for the PLO to try (and fail) to accomplish what he himself had failed to provide, and to prepare for a potential exacerbation of the challenge to his kingdom.

(d) Syria's response to the success of the *intifada* was ambivalent. The Asad regime savored the blow inflicted on the attempt to bring about an Israeli-Jordanian or Israeli-Jordanian-Palestinian settlement. In a similar vein, it argued that the *intifada* supported the Syrian line that there was no reason to capitulate and that Arab perseverance and resistance were bound to win. At the same time, the leaders of the Syrian Ba'th, like other wielders of power in the Arab world, could not fail to see the potential ramifications of the *intifada* for their own regimes; a civilian population defying a superior military force could become a dangerous precedent. Nor did they relish the gains made by their rival 'Arafat. Most important, they had suspected all along that a success of the uprising could mount the PLO on a track leading to a settlement with Israel. Asad's Syria could cope with the problem of Israel's continued occupation of the Golan Heights; but found it infinitely more difficult to cope with the fact that another Arab state regained the territory it had lost in 1967. Since 1977, much effort had been invested by Asad in trying to prevent and subsequently derail an Egyptian-Israeli agreement and then to prevent a replication of that policy by either Jordan or the PLO. When the threat became a more concrete threat in the spring of 1988, Asad's regime decided to avoid an open confrontation with the PLO and with its own patron, the Soviet Union. But it lost no opportunity of indicating its displeasure with the PLO's policies and of seeking to obstruct them in subtler ways that did not amount to a frontal attack.

(e) Mention has been made above of the change in the relationship between the PLO and the Palestinians residing in the West Bank and Gaza, despite the perpetuation of the PLO's traditional political hegemony. The role of the local population in launching and sustaining the *intifada* gave them a hitherto unfamiliar sense of confidence *vis-à-vis* the PLO. The change was most significantly manifested in the pressure they exerted on the organization to change its political line and to take measures that would facilitate a political settlement with Israel. In their dialogue with the PLO, those speaking in the name of the West Bank and Gaza argued that the population could not carry the burden of the *intifada* indefinitely. It was the PLO alone that could convert the achievements of the *intifada* into concrete political assets, and it was the organization's responsibility to do so. Conversely, by failing to so act, the PLO's leaders would be responsible for missing a unique opportunity.

(f) The pressure from the West Bank and Gaza was, indeed, one of the most important factors which induced the PLO to alter its line in phases during the later part of 1988. Beginning with Bassam Abu Sharif's article in June, going through the declaration of statehood and the other statements made in Algiers in November and culminating in 'Arafat's speech and statements in Geneva, the PLO mainstream leadership crossed a crucial line. Several important issues remained vague and open, but there was no denying the fact that it had formally adopted a policy of seeking a settlement with Israel on the basis of a two-state solution.

(g) On this basis, the departing Reagan Administration discarded the policy maintained by three successive administrations since 1975 and opened an official dialogue with the PLO. This decision ended an awkward period for Washington and more particularly for Secretary of State Shultz. Between 1985 and 1987 the Administration's policy toward the Arab-Israeli conflict had been predicated on the effort to bring about an Israeli-Jordanian agreement. After the illusory success of the London agreement of April 1987, there came a loss of direction. The *intifada* and its effect on public opinion in the US increased the pressure on the Reagan Administration to relinquish its discreet semipassive policy and launch, in March 1988, what came to be known as the Shultz initiative. Like several earlier ventures in the ME, this new attempt evaporated without real results. The Administration's decision, in December, to open a dialogue with the PLO could be interpreted on several levels: as a realistic readjustment to a changing reality, as an attempt to help the orientation it actually favored inside Israel, or as a measure designed to pave the way for a more radical change of policies by the incoming Administration.

The American presidential elections of November 1988 were an important event for the ME as well. George Bush had been Ronald Reagan's vice president for eight years. As such he had played a role in the formulation and execution of the Administration's ME policies. It was generally expected that his election would result in some changes in Washington's ME policies, but not in a radical realignment. A Democratic administration under Michael Dukakis was expected to introduce far greater changes.

The other important elections held in November 1988 were in Israel. Israeli elections are not a single-issue affair, but more than on previous occasions the elections of this year focused on the Palestinian issue. The *intifada* served to intensify the debate on this question within Israeli society. It also contributed, in the short run at least, to strengthening the nationalist right wing. Like the elections of September 1984 those of November 1988 produced a national unity government; unlike them they turned the Likud leader, Yitzhak Shamir, into a single prime minister without the rotation agreement of 1984.

It was up to the prime minister and his senior partners to decide on Israel's response to the dual challenge of the continuing *intifada* and the PLO's new political line. But it took two full months for the new Israeli Government to be formed. Its response did not materialize until well into 1989.

THE MIDDLE EAST AND WORLD AFFAIRS

The United States and the Middle East in 1988[1]

STEVEN L. SPIEGEL

It was a year of contrast in American policy toward the Arab-Israeli dispute: a year of hope and frustration. It was a year when the pressures of external developments for initiative seemed to compete with the dynamics of the domestic election process which demanded quiet and stability. It was a year when the expectations of the experts were constantly confounded by unanticipated developments both in Washington and in the region — in the Arab-Israeli arena as well as the Persian Gulf. The bulk of this chapter will deal with the former, after which we will turn to the latter.

In the international environment, a series of events encouraged Washington's attention to the Arab-Israeli arena: the *intifada*; the August cease-fire in the Iraqi-Iranian War; King Husayn's withdrawal from West Bank affairs; clear signs that the Soviet Union was prepared to play a more moderate role in the area than heretofore; the emerging proliferation of long-range ballistic missiles and chemical weapons in the region; and the growing divisions among American Jews about their proper role *vis-à-vis* Israel.

On the domestic scene, George Bush and Michael Dukakis rapidly emerged as the leading candidates for the Republican and Democratic parties' nominations, respectively. Although a significant minority of the Democratic Party behind the Rev. Jesse Jackson questioned Dukakis's position on the Middle East, there was a high degree of consensus between the two parties. In the end, the ME did not play a major role in the presidential campaign. Although the positions of the two candidates were examined from time to time, neither was prepared to adopt dramatic stances on the issue.

There is a commonly held belief that the US does not take major initiatives toward the Arab-Israeli dispute in an election year, because neither party wishes to risk alienating Israel's supporters. However, in 1988 there were four mitigating factors. First, history suggests that administrations do often respond to concerted criticism on a particular issue as a term ends. For instance, President Johnson took major initiatives toward the Vietnam question in 1968. Henry Kissinger moved strongly on southern African issues in 1976 in the wake of criticism that he had ignored the Black-White problem in that part of the world. President Carter began to assume a tougher posture toward the Soviet Union in 1980, in the wake of the invasion of Afghanistan. Similarly, the Reagan Administration was criticized by its opponents for failing to launch an initiative regarding the ME. These criticisms were accelerated after the beginning of the *intifada*. There was consequently an incentive for George Shultz as secretary of state and as the leading administration figure in the development of ME policy to take a strong stand as a means of justifying his past actions.

The second domestic factor mitigating the usual election year inhibitions was that Shultz, since 1983, had established a position of unusual trust with American Jews and Israelis. He was widely regarded as the most pro-Israeli secretary of state in history. After the *intifada* began, this relationship of faith between Israelis and Shultz provided him with political capital that could be exercised in pursuit of a ME initiative, election year or no. Therefore, if Shultz pursued an initiative he would largely be protected from the conventional criticism an administration might suffer if it adopted policies opposed to Israel in an election year.

The third factor moderating election year pressures was the fundamental division within the Israeli Government between the Labor and Likud parties. Since most policies pursued by Shultz would likely receive support from the Labor Party, the Reagan Administration was protected from domestic protests.

Fourth, the reputation of Ronald Reagan as the strongest president in favor of Israel in American history further emboldened the Administration. There was a widely held belief among Israel's supporters — liberals and conservatives, Democrats and Republicans — that the next president, Bush or Dukakis, would not be as positively disposed toward Israel. Therefore, whatever action Reagan and his associates took would likely be more favorable than that of their successors in the view of many of Israel's supporters, which provided the Administration with additional political capital.

The combination of unusually severe external pressures and weak domestic inhibitions help to explain the origins of the Shultz initiative in early 1988. Three other elements in the Shultz approach to the ME should be cited in explaining the origins of the initiative which became the central focus of American policy toward the area in the first half of the year.

First, the methods demonstrated in this initiative were fundamentally similar to those pursued in the Reagan Plan of 1982 (see *MECS* 1981–82, pp. 30ff.), which was in essence the first Shultz initiative. In both cases, a situation of instability in the area (the Lebanon crisis in 1982, the *intifada* in 1988) was translated into an American plan. It was revealed in Washington as a consequence of the efforts by State Department officials to produce a compromise which they believed was appropriate. An effort to gain the support of both Arabs and Israelis then followed. In both cases, a Likud prime minister (Begin 1982, Shamir 1988) was bitterly opposed to the plan and the US was ultimately disappointed by the behavior of King Husayn. The Shultz approach in both 1982 and 1988 demonstrated the weaknesses of attempting to prepackage a program in Washington instead of negotiating a possible compromise through mediation efforts with both sides, as Henry Kissinger and Jimmy Carter had attempted. In this sense, the Shultz initiative was distinctive of the former secretary of state's particular approach to Arab-Israeli peace negotiations, but one which can be seen as unsatisfactory.

Second, Shultz had come to office determined to address the Palestinian question squarely. Indeed, he had stated at his 1982 confirmation hearing that "...the legitimate needs and problems of the Palestinian people must be addressed and resolved — urgently and in all their dimensions."[2] He never gave up on this goal, but he meanwhile suffered a series of disillusionments: with Jordan and Saudi Arabia, and with the Arab parties generally as a result of their failure to accept the Reagan Plan or the Israeli-Lebanese agreement of May 1983 which he had brokered. He was thereby led toward a closer relationship with Israel and a policy of waiting until developments would allow for a new initiative. In this sense, the situation in early 1988 was consistent with Shultz's conception of the kind of conditions which would allow a return to American activism.

Third, in the "wait and see" period Shultz had fostered contacts and approaches between King Husayn and Shimon Peres, which had continued from 1985 to 1987. These policies had ended in failure. Similarly, Israelis (and their American allies) who had claimed that the status quo in the West Bank and Gaza would continue indefinitely were proven incorrect. This strengthened the position of those in Washington, especially in the State Department's Bureau of Near East and South Asian Affairs, who had argued all along that the status quo was not a viable solution to the Palestinian question.

Thus, in early 1988, there were a variety of pressures acting upon the Administration to take some kind of initiative to break the logjam in the Arab-Israeli peace process. These pressures easily overcame the natural reluctance to take major steps in the last year of an administration. Indeed, the lame-duck status of the Administration served ironically to add the pressure of time on the participants as a further incentive for action. There simply was no room left for delay.

If the Shultz initiative of the early part of the year may seem surprising to some observers, the action in December of initiating a dialogue with the PLO may appear to be an attempt to "ease the way" for the incoming kindred Republican administration. However, despite the reputation of the transition as a period of no policy action, there is something of a tradition in American policy for administrations late in their tenure to take unpopular steps. In the 1970s, this tendency related especially to arms sales. Thus, Kissinger in 1976 had established the basis for the sale of arms to Saudi Arabia, which would later emerge as a major controversy in the Carter Administration in the middle of 1978.[3] Even more starkly, the Carter Administration offered, after its defeat in late 1980, to initiate the sale of Awacs jets to Saudi Arabia despite promises to the contrary in 1978. The Reagan Administration rejected the offer, but it was roughly equivalent in its portent and controversial nature to the decision to open a dialogue with the PLO in 1988.[4]

In addition to domestic permissiveness, external pressures were growing. By late 1988, the combination of Israeli and Jordanian refusal to accept the Shultz initiative, the decision by Husayn to withdraw from involvement in the West Bank, and the continuing upheaval within the Palestinian movement created pressures and opportunities for action. The victory of the right in the Israeli elections and the perceived increasing danger in the area through the proliferation of long-range ballistic missiles and chemical weapons further conspired to create a sense of urgency. Many of the same frustrations and hopes which had operated on the Reagan team to create the Shultz initiative worked similarly late in the Administration to move in the direction of the opening to the PLO. In this case, however, the readiness of PLO chairman Yasir 'Arafat to utter words which appeared to conform to long-standing American criteria was the final trigger in an extended flirtation.

Thus, three events dominated the American approach to the Arab-Israeli dispute in 1988: the Shultz initiative, the election, and the decision to enter into a dialogue with the PLO. An understanding of these three events goes far toward explaining American policy during the year.

THE UNITED STATES AND THE ARAB-ISRAELI CONFLICT

THE SHULTZ INITIATIVE

As the *intifada* continued intensely through January, it first appeared that the US did not have major plans for a policy change. Bogged down in the procedures regarding an international peace conference as the forum for Arab-Israeli negotiations throughout most of the mid-1980s, the Administration appeared focused on this issue. (For further discussion of the positions of ME governments toward the initiative, see chapter on the Middle East peace process.)

In retrospect, the public turning point was the visit by Egypt's President Mubarak at the end of the month (for details, see chapter on Egypt). Upon greeting him, President Reagan declared, "The danger of allowing the Palestinian problem to fester is evident and reinforces the urgency of moving toward negotiations...."[5] On the surface, Mubarak's visit appeared to have failed. He pressed both the Administration and Congress to support a UN-sponsored international conference as an umbrella for direct Arab-Israeli negotiations. Shultz, however, continued to support "direct face-to-face negotiations" as the "way to achieve results." Yet, in a luncheon toast to Mubarak he also hinted where his thinking might be leading. "I believe we have come to the point where illusions about the past and old approaches to resolve the problems need to be tested against the new realities."[6]

While Mubarak was still in the US, a secret visit by Philip Habib to meet with Husayn in Amman was leaked. It also became clear that Shultz had met in recent days with representatives of both the Likud and Labor in the Israeli governing coalition and with two West Bank Palestinian leaders, Hana Siniora and Fa'iz Abu Rahma. In case anyone had any doubts, Shultz told the House Foreign Affairs Committee on 2 February that "the recent turmoil in the West Bank and Gaza Strip demonstrates that the status quo in the Middle East peace process is not an option."[7]

The press was filled with reports of a new American initiative aimed at shortening the Camp David timetable for a Palestinian autonomy and for discussions on a final disposition of the territories along with some form of imminent West Bank and Gaza self-rule. Initial optimism within the Administration was fueled by Prime Minister Shamir's apparent willingness to participate in the initiative being formulated and by hopes that Husayn's failure to reject the proposals was an indication of his possible interest in the plan.[8] Shultz had also been briefed on Camp David and the autonomy negotiations of 1979–82, and had been astonished at the range of agreement reached between the Egyptians and Israelis on the contours of an autonomy regime.[9]

Despite widespread skepticism that lame-duck Israeli and American administrations could produce a successful peace process in an election year in both countries, pressures by Arab heads of state, the Israeli Foreign Ministry, and by American groups and individuals sympathetic to both Israel and the Palestinians encouraged Shultz to embark on a new negotiating process emphasizing "substance" rather than "the procedures" of how to hold an international conference.[10]

Therefore, in late February, Shultz headed for the ME as the president declared in a prepared statement at a news conference on 24 February: "Any process that is undertaken must meet Israel's security needs and satisfy the legitimate rights of the Palestinians."[11] But meeting the president's provisos proved to be as difficult as the skeptics had anticipated. On this first of three major trips to the area in the first half of

1988, Shultz presented what he called a "package" of proposals. Supported by Israeli Foreign Minister Peres, he sought to begin talks on a comprehensive "peace settlement" promptly.

The Shultz initiative was breathtaking in its attempt to square the circle of differing Israeli and Arab conceptions of how the peace process should be conducted. As revealed in the press and in several statements by Shultz himself and his aides upon his return to the US, the plan envisioned an accelerated timetable of the original Camp David conception. As accepted at Camp David, a Palestinian autonomy would be implemented for a five-year period when the parties agreed on the framework for electing a Palestinian Council and the authority which that council would have. No later than the end of the third year of the five-year period, negotiations would begin on the final status of the West Bank and Gaza Strip. In 1979–82, since Jordan and the Palestinians refused to participate in the negotiations and Israel, Egypt, and the US were not able to agree on the rubric for the Palestinian Council, the whole process never began. Israel was thereby left in control of the territories, confirming to many Arabs their criticism of the Camp David process.

Attempting to address these concerns, Shultz's plan envisioned a significantly different process. This program was to begin with an international conference, to be held hopefully in mid-April. The secretary-general of the UN would invite the "parties involved in the Arab-Israeli conflict" to attend as well as the five permanent members of the UN Security Council — the US, France, Great Britain, China, and the Soviet Union. If the conference was a recognition of the Arab insistence on an international framework, its responsibilities were consistent with the Israeli conception, because it would not have the right to impose solutions or veto agreements reached between the parties. According to several reports, it would be similar to the kind of international conference envisioned in the Husayn-Peres London agreement of April 1987 (see *MECS* 1987, chapter on the Middle East peace process), at least the Peres understanding of those agreements. In a position which clearly rejected a PLO role at the conference, Shultz maintained that all participants would have to accept UN Resolutions 242 and 338 and renounce violence and terrorism.

Two weeks after the convening of the international conference (Shultz hoped by 1 May), negotiations would begin between Israel and each of its willing neighbors. Although he was attempting to entice Syria into joining the peace process, the primary focus remained on the Palestinian question. Shultz and his team envisioned that an Israeli and Jordanian-Palestinian delegation, with American involvement, would begin work on the arrangements for a transitional period on the West Bank and Gaza in which there would be limited self-rule for the Palestinians. The US would open the talks by submitting a draft agreement and the objective would be to complete the talks within six months (that would be by 1 November if the Shultz timetable were followed). The transitional period would begin three months after the conclusion of these talks and would last for three years. Thus, the Camp David process had been accelerated with what had once been called autonomy negotiations to be completed in a relatively short time (six months) and the transition period that they arranged would last three instead of five years. The Shultz program would have led to a busy year:

15 April, convocation of the international conference;

1 May, beginning of bilateral negotiations between Israeli and Jordanian/Palestinian delegations with American mediation;

1 November, completion of these negotiations;

1 February 1989, beginning of a three-year transition period in the West Bank and Gaza.

But there was more. The Arabs feared that the talks on the final status of the territories would be delayed, leaving them in permanent "autonomy." Therefore Shultz proposed that seven months after transitional negotiations began (he hoped that it would be at least a month after the negotiations on the transitional period had ended and two months before the "autonomy" was to be implemented), the final-status talks would be initiated. According to the Shultz timetable, these talks would begin on 1 December 1988. They would enable the Arabs to see that the final status of the territories was being discussed even before the transitional period had begun. It would also mean that the representatives elected under the transitional agreements would be able to take part as members of a joint Jordanian-Palestinian delegation during the final-status negotiations.

Although the transition period was to last for three years, Shultz proposed that the objective of the final-status negotiations would be completed within one year and, therefore, two years before the end of the interim regime. However, in an appearance before the Senate Budget Committee on 17 March, he attempted to clarify his thinking by arguing that while the final-status talks might begin before the transition arrangements had been implemented "decisions about final status would take place only *well after* the transition arrangements had been in place and people had had an opportunity to see how they worked."[12]

How did the parties react to these sweeping proposals? President Mubarak of Egypt gave qualified support. In Israel, on his trip in February, Shultz found that despite the backing of Foreign Minister Peres, Prime Minister Shamir continued to resist the three basic elements of the approach, namely, the concept of accelerating the transition period in the occupied territories envisioned in the Camp David Accords, the idea of an international conference of any kind, however ceremonial, and the notion of placing "preconditions" on the final status of the territories without first obtaining Palestinian guarantees of peace and security.[13] The prime minister's fear that Israel would be expected to relinquish all or most of the West Bank and Gaza Strip was evident. In a side trip to London to meet with Husayn, which interrupted his stay in the area, Shultz also found serious resistance to his proposals from the Jordanian monarch.

The most dramatic point in the trip, however, occurred on 26 February. The secretary had hoped to meet with a group of Palestinians from the West Bank. Indeed, Hana Siniora, editor of the Jerusalem newspaper *al-Fajr*, had traveled to Rome to talk with PLO representatives to investigate whether a ban on meeting Shultz in Jerusalem would be lifted. The PLO had refused. Therefore, in an act unusually theatrical for the typically dour secretary, he stood in the flowering courtyard of the American Colony Hotel in East Jerusalem to deliver a public message to the Palestinians.[14]

Speaking directly to the Palestinians who might have joined him, Shultz made four points. First, Palestinians must actively participate in deciding their own future. He added that the Palestinians must gain political and economic control over their lives and that legitimate Palestinian rights and Israeli security could exist together. Second, these efforts must be part of a "broader effort to reach a comprehensive settlement" which would be based on UN Resolutions 242 and 338 "in their entirety." Thus, Shultz rejected Shamir's argument that Israel had abided by UN Resolutions 242 and 338 by its withdrawal from Sinai. Third, he told the Palestinians that the settlement must be achieved through negotiations and that experience had shown that "you can have an agreement with Israel, and it will be kept by Israel." Fourth, he called for imminent, rapid negotiations.[15]

Thus, Shultz demonstrated both the US Administration's frustration at its inability to talk to the Palestinians and its insistence that Palestinians should be prepared to negotiate. This concern would be more evident later in the year. He also recognized that he was running out of time for his plan to be operative. "We have a workable plan," he concluded, "and we are ready to commit our efforts to it."[16] Indeed, the abbreviated timetable had clearly been prepared with the 20 January 1989 deadline for the end of the Administration clearly in mind.

Despite the resistance of all parties except Mubarak and Peres, Shultz presented his plans to the Arabs and the Israelis on a "take it or leave it" basis. It was an "integral whole," as assistant secretary of state Richard Murphy put it to a House Foreign Affairs subcommittee on 15 March. "It will not work if the parties accept some portions and reject others."[17]

Shultz and Murphy were both prepared to accept Soviet participation in an international conference without it being conditional on increased immigration of Soviet Jewry or renewed diplomatic relations between Israel and the Soviet Union. However, they reiterated that in no way would the US allow the international conference to become an authoritative or a plenipotentiary body. Murphy made clear that the Palestinians who would be part of a joint Jordanian-Palestinian delegation would have to be "credible with their own people" and also "people whose very presence is not going to drive Israel away from the negotiating table."[18] In other words, the US was seeking moderate Palestinians resident in the territories as members of the delegation, consistent with its position for the last several years.

In March, Reagan and Shultz made much of the fact that no party had actually said "yes" but no one had said "no" either to the American plan. Reagan was explicit in a meeting with Shamir at the White House on 16 March in pointing out publicly that Shamir had not yet rejected the plan.[19]

Shultz returned to the ME in early April with the objective of inducing the positive responses which had thus far eluded him. On the eve of his departure, the secretary held a highly publicized meeting with two Palestinian Americans who are members of the Palestine National Council (PNC). The US had long claimed that the PNC, the PLO's parliament-in-exile, was not an integral part of the PLO and that there were council members who were not members of the PLO. Nevertheless, his meeting with Professors Edward Said and Ibrahim Abu Lughod elicited howls of protest from Israelis as well as from many of Israel's American supporters (see chapter on the Palestine Liberation Organization). It was another symbolic gesture intended to remind all parties of the importance the US attached to Palestinian participation in the peace process.

Upon arriving in Israel, the secretary attempted to prod the prime minister into accepting his plan by taking a more vocal position than on his earlier trip. With the apparent intent of taking his case directly to the Israeli public over the head of the prime minister, Shultz accepted a series of interviews with Israeli television and newspaper editors. In these public statements, he made clear that the US plan was based on a "land for peace" formula and an interpretation of UN Security Council Resolution 242, which assumes that its call on Israel to give up occupied territories in exchange for peace, applied to all fronts.[20] This position was tantamount to informing Israel that the US would expect it to withdraw from a substantial part of the West Bank and the Gaza Strip as part of any settlement. On the other hand, he also indicated his opposition to a return to the pre-1967 borders and to an independent Palestinian state.[21] The secretary of state made similar public appearances in Amman to try to elicit support for his initiative, but by the time he had completed his trip he was still faced with the reality that only Egypt had provided a qualified endorsement.

On his final visit to the ME as secretary of state in June, Shultz was similarly unsuccessful. Husayn continued to indicate his reluctance to enter peace talks with Israel, unless he had assurances beforehand that the Israelis would give up territory on the West Bank. He expressed doubt about the divided Israeli Government's ability to accept the process that Shultz had envisioned. Thus Husayn offered support, but not an endorsement. Prime Minister Shamir's opposition to the initiative also remained unchanged. On this trip, however, Shultz was more explicit than previously on the dangers for Israel of not accepting his proposals. He stated on his arrival that "the continued occupation of the West Bank and Gaza, and the frustration of Palestinian rights, is [*sic*] a dead-end street. The belief that this can continue is an illusion."[22] Despite the secretary's increased criticism and tougher line, Shamir was unmoved.

The Shultz initiative was over, but it left a peculiar anomaly in its wake. If the US sought to be active in ME diplomacy and if the conventional route to activism was blocked by the participants, then perhaps it would be necessary to encourage a different kind of process. Thus, the failure of the Shultz initiative would eventually redirect US attention from Jerusalem, Cairo, and Amman to Tunis.

THE ARAB-ISRAELI ISSUE IN THE 1988 PRESIDENTIAL CAMPAIGN

Because of the *intifada*, the Arab-Israeli issue was constantly in the news throughout the year. Nevertheless, candidates were generally wary of criticizing Israel or offering controversial proposals for fear of negative political repercussions. In particular, the Arab-Israeli problem did not play a major role in the Republican primaries. All candidates assumed a conservative geopolitical stance, with varying degrees of support for Israel as a strategic asset to the US. On the Democratic side, there was also strong support for Israel, but it was defined in different terms. Senator Joseph Biden of Delaware had major Jewish support for his longtime backing of Israel, but by 1988 he was out of the race due to accusations of plagiarism. Bruce Babbitt of Iowa provided rare criticism of Israel in the early days of the *intifada*, but he fared poorly in his home state and dropped out of the race.

By the New York primary in April, there were three major candidates remaining in the Democratic contest. Senator Albert Gore of Tennessee took a decidedly pro-Israeli stance. The Rev. Jesse Jackson had long been critical of Israeli diplomatic and military policies and sympathetic to a dialogue between the US and the PLO, and an independent Palestinian state on the West Bank and Gaza Strip. In New York, he was fresh from a victory in the Michigan caucuses where a coalition of Blacks, Arab Americans, and the far left of the party had been able to defeat all rivals. The combination of a caucus arrangement in Michigan and the strength of Arab

Americans, especially in the auto industry and the Detroit area, were critical, but largely unnoticed, factors in this achievement by Jackson. Therefore, in New York, Jackson appeared to be deceptively strong. With the help of vociferous comments by Mayor Edward Koch of New York, Jewish voters were encouraged to take a strong position in opposition to Jackson and defeat his chances for the Democratic nomination. Since Jewish voters represent 25% of a typical New York primary, this was not an inconsiderable injunction.

The third candidate and leading contender, Governor Michael Dukakis of Massachusetts, had a long record of support for Israel and Jewish causes. Not only was his wife Jewish, but as governor he had taken important stands against the boycott of Israel, in favor of strong American positions regarding Soviet Jewish emigration and in support of a Holocaust Museum in Washington. He was also the first governor to sign a joint economic development project with Israel.

Yet during the campaign, Dukakis assumed a posture of reserved sympathy. Either out of inexperience or the anticipation of the nomination and election to the presidency, he adopted positions that outsiders often call "presidential' — vague suggestions of differences with specifics of Israeli policy within a context of strong support. For example, on 3 March, 30 senators signed a letter to Secretary Shultz endorsing his initiative and accepting his interpretation of UN Resolution 242, as including "land for peace" on all fronts.[23] They indicated their disagreement with Prime Minister Shamir if he was opposed to territorial compromise. This letter was much criticized in the Jewish community for fear it might jeopardize Israel's negotiating stance or would be seen as a sign of reduced support for Israel. When Dukakis visited former president Jimmy Carter in Plains, Georgia shortly afterward, a reporter asked if either one of them would have signed the letter. Carter answered positively and Dukakis — not wishing to embarrass the former president — seemingly agreed.

The governor was, therefore, under some pressure when he addressed the Conference of Presidents of Major American Jewish Organizations on 11 April. Although his speech strongly backed Israel, in answer to a question he declined to oppose the creation of a separate Palestinian state on the ground that the parties themselves would have to negotiate a settlement. Dukakis spent several weeks explaining that since any solution would have to be acceptable to both sides and since Israel would undoubtedly oppose such a state, he would too. A possible political asset — criticism of the idea of an imposed peace by the US — had been turned into a negative for Dukakis.

Nevertheless, the issue did not hurt him in New York, because even though many Jewish voters might have preferred Gore's position on Israel, most voted for Dukakis because they thought he would be more likely to defeat Jesse Jackson and because his positions were more conventionally northeastern liberal. During the California primary, Dukakis made an unusually vehement statement in favor of Israel in a lengthy *Los Angeles Times* interview.[24] Yet he was still reluctant to meet with groups of American Jews after the unsuccessful session before the Conference of Presidents.

By then, Vice President Bush was actively pointing out to influential friends of Israel that, unlike Dukakis, he opposed the creation of a Palestinian state. In a further distinction to Dukakis, Bush organized a prestigious group of experts, most close to the pro-Israeli community, who produced a position paper (released in mid-July) in the candidate's name. It promised to intensify significantly US-Israeli strategic cooperation in important ways.

By summer, Dukakis was a victim of Jewish fears that the Rev. Jesse Jackson would exercise influence on his ME policy. The campaign's mishandling of the issue at the Democratic convention served to confirm these anxieties. The Jackson and Dukakis forces split over the ME platform. The majority plank, in keeping with the vague nature of the 1988 Democratic platform, promised to maintain the special relationship with Israel and "to provide new leadership to deliver the promise of peace and security through negotiations."[25] The minority plank, presented by the Jackson forces, went much further, advocating a peace "based on mutual recognition, territorial compromise, and self-determination for Israelis and Palestinians...."[26] Of the three minority planks presented to the convention as a whole, only the ME resolution was not actually voted on, but was withdrawn by the Jackson forces. This decision made it appear that the Democratic convention might actually have endorsed the proposal if it had come to a vote. In addition, during the debate over the two planks, the pro-Israeli forces were completely outgunned by a pro-Arab demonstration. It had never occurred to Israel's backers or the Dukakis campaign to prepare a demonstration in favor of Israel. Fortunately for the Dukakis candidacy, the debate over the ME plank occurred at a time when national television was not covering the convention.

In contrast, the Republican platform presented a detailed plank sympathetic to Israel and was lauded by many pro-Israeli activists as unprecedented, perhaps even the most pro-Israeli in history. Tom Dine, executive director of Aipac (the America-Israel Public Affairs Committee, the pro-Israeli lobby in Washington), called it "the best statement of American interests in that part of the world that has been produced by either party in history."[27]

If the Bush forces had won the early sparring on the ME for pro-Israeli and especially Jewish attention and backing, Dukakis was later able to recoup. Secret Bush polls showed that American Jews were the only identifiable group whose support for the vice president actually declined after the convention. The nomination of the young and controversial Republican Senator Dan Quayle for the vice presidency appears to be the reason.[28] The Dukakis trend in the Jewish community continued when both candidates addressed the B'nai B'rith international convention in Baltimore on 7 September. Bush delivered a somewhat leaden speech, touting the accomplishments of the Administration, especially in the area of strategic cooperation. In perhaps the most memorable passage, he stated, "...some people still have trouble saying the words, 'Israel, strategic ally.' Well, I don't. Israel, strategic ally. It's got a nice ring to it. The ring of hard, enduring reality."[29] However, he also added that "the Palestinians must be involved in every step of the negotiations. There will be no peace without them." He went on to suggest that "the creation of a Palestinian state will not lead to peace. But we must be clear on another matter, too. Neither will annexation of the territories by Israel or their permanent control by military occupation."[30]

Dukakis, on the other hand, gave a strong speech, enthusiastically setting out his understanding of the shared values between the US and Israel and touching a variety of bases such as arms sales to the Arab states, strategic cooperation, the peace process, and aid to Israel and to Soviet Jews. He pointed out that unlike Bush he was prepared to acknowledge Israel's sovereignty over an undivided Jerusalem as the capital of the country. The vice president supported maintaining the unified, undivided nature of the city. Dukakis promised never to recognize a "unilateral declaration of a Palestinian state or government in exile."[31] In perhaps his most quotable section he declared:

> From the day of Israel's rebirth four decades ago, we Americans have understood that Israel's fate is our fate. That when Israel is threatened, all those who cherish freedom are threatened. Israel — like the United States — is a special place. Born in conflict. Dedicated to freedom and democracy. Committed to peace. Resolute in defense of its people and *our* shared values.[32]

In the end, then, these were two candidates strongly supportive of Israel and of increased steps toward strategic cooperation with that country. They both favored American financial support for Israeli development of an anti-tactical ballistic missile system designed to counter the impact of long-range ballistic missiles, were opposed to dealing with the PLO unless it met American conditions, and favored direct Arab-Israeli negotiations and a genuine peace between the parties. Both, likewise, favored an exploration of Moscow's intentions toward the ME, but expected changes on the part of the Soviets on such issues as diplomatic relations with Israel and the treatment of Soviet Jews.

In essence, despite the slight differences between them on a Palestinian state and the future status of Jerusalem, the primary distinction remained that Dukakis, as a governor, had limited foreign policy experience, a long record of pro-Israel statements, and was running on a Democratic platform vague on details. Bush, on the other hand, had many years of government service, a long period of interest in the ME, and was running on a platform unusual in its details devoted to the region, especially in its emphasis on strong US-Israeli ties. He had also been part of an administration which had been noted widely for its strong support of Israel.

Bush suffered from certain deficits. Two prominent former Reagan Administration officials, Alexander Haig and Jeane Kirkpatrick, had claimed that he had not been a supporter of Israel during two 1981 controversies: selling Awacs jets to Saudi Arabia and the Israeli destruction of the Iraqi nuclear reactor (for details see *MECS* 1980–81, pp. 52–54, 182 ff.). Others argued he was likely to be overly deferential to bureaucrats. As his opponents soon discovered, these were the types of criticisms which were not translated into campaign issues in 1988.

Both leaders supported the Shultz initiative. Dukakis appeared somewhat more interested than his opponent in comprehensive arrangements with Soviet leader, Mikhail Gorbachev, and with human rights questions, but Bush seemed more concerned about relations with Arab states. Yet these were only inferences from campaign statements and past records. The campaign did not reflect major variations in Arab-Israeli matters, except on isolated details.

Since both candidates were strongly supportive of Israel and the peace process, no outspoken supporters of the Palestinians or the Arab states were to be found among their major foreign policy advisers. As the campaign continued, the Arab-Israeli question in particular was not a major issue in a political battle distinctive for its absence of serious discussion of issues. In the Jewish community, where many had expressed concern about the possible role of the Rev. Jesse Jackson in a Dukakis administration, the issue seemed to fade, particularly with the nomination of Senator Dan Quayle, the beginning of discussion of the impact of a Bush presidency on the future of the Supreme Court, and accusations of anti-Semitism by particular Bush operatives (even though they were promptly denounced and removed by the campaign).[33]

Thus, the similarity between the candidates on the Arab-Israeli issue allowed that question to play a smaller role in the voters' decision. Bush continued to have strong backing from many stalwarts in the pro-Israeli community who were impressed with his firm stands, especially on strategic cooperation, during the campaign, and who feared the return to a type of "Carterism" should Dukakis emerge victorious. The governor's failure to announce a foreign policy task force further deepened this sense of concern among pro-Israeli "insiders." Not only had Bush done so, but this device had been used with considerable success by the Reagan camp in 1980 to deflect criticism of the candidate as inexperienced and inadequately prepared to deal with foreign policy.

In the end, however, Jews voted heavily for Dukakis. According to *The New York Times/CBS* news poll, Dukakis received 64% of the Jewish vote while Bush received 35%. By contrast, according to the same poll, Mondale had received 67% to 31% for Reagan in 1984, and in 1980 the split had been 45% for Carter, 39% for Reagan and 15% for Representative John Anderson's independent third party effort.[34] Except for the 1968 election, when Democrat Hubert Humphrey received 81% in a losing cause, no Democrat, since 1932, has won the presidency without receiving at least 70% of the Jewish vote.[35] It is also worth noting that *The New York Times* poll gave Bush a slightly higher Jewish vote than other comparable analyses.

In any case, the 1988 campaign left both major candidates as enigmas. Neither provided indications of how he would propose to deal with the problems raised by the *intifada*; no serious analysis or careful plans were provided. The closest either Bush or Dukakis came to specifics was the endorsement of a report by a prestigious group of analysts working under the auspices of the Washington Institute for Near East Policy.[36] This group, chaired by former vice president Mondale and Lawrence Eagleburger (who was appointed deputy secretary of state after the election), opposed the international conference idea and advocated an emphasis on preparing the ground for negotiations over an extended period of time before undertaking a particular initiative. The study group also stressed the importance of engaging "Palestinian representatives" and Jordan in negotiations and the significance of a transition period in which Palestinian capacity to live with Jordan and Israel would be tested. Beyond these hints of future direction, all parties were reduced to awaiting the emergence of a new policy under a new president.

AGREEMENT TO A DIALOGUE WITH THE PLO

No one knows whether the acceptance of the Shultz initiative by Prime Minister Shamir would have resulted in Jordanian acquiescence and the beginning of negotiations under the plan. We do know, however, that the Shamir rejection was followed by Husayn's withdrawal from active engagement in the West Bank (see chapter on Jordan). The US was then confronted with a situation in which the Jordanian option appeared to be, at least temporarily, moribund. Therefore, to many American analysts the only route left was some kind of dialogue with the Palestinians.

A further disturbing development during the summer pressing policy-makers to address the Arab-Israeli conflict was the growing signs of regional proliferation of both long-range ballistic missiles and chemical weapons. Indeed, a variety of developments throughout the year added to growing American nervousness about the state of the ME arms race and the role of the US therein:

(1) In March, word leaked out that the Saudis had purchased Chinese CSS2 missiles with a range of 1,900 miles, capable of hitting targets in both Iran and Israel.[37]

(2) By midyear, there were rumors that the Syrians and Libyans might also purchase ballistic missiles from China, in particular the M-9, a 375-mile-range missile then still under development.[38]

(3) In July, the Saudis signed a $29bn. arms deal with the British to purchase 40–50 *Tornado* fighter jets to replace the US F-15 as the workhorse of the Saudi Air Force. The Saudis made it clear that they preferred American arms, but were not prepared to undertake another wrenching conflict with Israel's friends in Congress.[39]

(4) In August, a compromise was reached between Israel's Congressional supporters and the Administration on the sale of 40 F-18 fighter bombers to Kuwait. In particular, the planes would be equipped with *Maverick G* antiship missiles instead of *Maverick D* antitank missiles.[40]

(5) The same month, Iran and Iraq agreed to a cease-fire in their nearly eight-year-old war.[41] The use of chemical weapons by Baghdad was a critical factor in persuading Iran to agree to an end to hostilities. The Iraqis then proceeded to use these weapons against defenseless Kurdish rebel villages within their own country (see chapter on Iraq).[42]

In this light and in the wake of the stalled peace process and the continuing *intifada*, Shultz delivered a major address on the ME to the Washington Institute for Near East Policy on 16 September. He reminded his audience that "comprehensive peace requires peace between Israelis and Palestinians" and that "the status quo serves the interest of no party."[43] Shultz reviewed much familiar ground as in his support of direct negotiations in the context of a carefully limited international conference, of the exchange of territory for peace, and of a transitional period "to help the parties adjust to working with each other to implement an agreement."[44] He emphasized the "strategic reality of Jordanian-Palestinian interdependence."[45] He cautioned against the creation of an independent Palestinian state or permanent control or annexation of the West Bank and Gaza. He urged the constant enhancement of the Egyptian-Israeli peace treaty and he also stressed the need to address the Palestinian refugee problem. While acknowledging that Israel must withdraw from territories, he added that Israel would never "return to the lines of partition or to the 1967 borders."[46]

However, the most important part of his speech was contained in two different paragraphs. Seemingly addressing 'Arafat directly, he stated at one point that:

> No participant in the peace process can wave the flag of justice in one hand and brandish the weapons of terrorism in the other. All participants must renounce violence and terrorism. Each must agree to negotiate on the accepted international basis of UN Security Council Resolutions 242 and 338.[47]

Later, he stated:

> Palestinians must renounce terrorism and violence, they must accept the right of Israel to exist in peace and present themselves as a viable negotiating partner. They cannot murder or threaten other Palestinians who maintain contact with Israeli authorities.[48]

Shultz was thus making clear, as he had done repeatedly in the past, that the US would adhere strictly to its demands that the PLO recognize 242 and 338, renounce terrorism and accept Israel's right to exist before the US would enter a dialogue with it. By stating that the US would also not accept either a unilateral PLO declaration of independent Palestinian statehood or a government-in-exile, he also seemed to be trying to influence the coming PNC meeting, which was widely expected to take stands that might be acceptable to the US.

The meeting held in Algiers in mid-November, however, was disappointing from an American perspective. 'Arafat dramatically declared independence for a Palestinian state with Jerusalem as its capital, but he did not define its borders. Although the PNC document which was accepted did refer to UN Security Council Resolutions 242 and 338, it called for the convening of an international conference, based on both resolutions, and an independent Palestinian state. Not only was Israel's right to exist not explicitly recognized, but the PLO reaffirmed its commitment to terrorism against the Jewish state by again invoking the Cairo Declaration issued by 'Arafat in 1985 (see *MECS* 1984–85, p. 369). In that statement, the PLO reserved the right to conduct "military" acts within territories controlled by Israel. Although American officials in both the State Department and in the Bush transition team admitted that there had been steps forward in the Algiers document, they still regarded it as insufficient. America's conditions had not been met.[49]

The next step in the unfolding drama was a request by 'Arafat for a visa to address the UN General Assembly in light of the Palestinian declaration of independence. In a stunning announcement on 26 November, Shultz denied the visa application. "The US Government has convincing evidence that PLO elements have engaged in terrorism against Americans and others....Mr. 'Arafat, as chairman of the PLO, knows of, condones, and lends support to such acts; he therefore is an accessory to such terrorism."[50]

In making this decision, Shultz was apparently affected by four factors. First, his opposition to terrorism remained a central tenet of his global belief system. As he told one interviewer, "if the thing I'm remembered for is most of all a strong and great resolve to resist and combat terrorism...I'll feel that it is a proud accomplishment."[51]

Second, he was apparently deeply affected by two recent incidents. Abu al-'Abbas, the mastermind of the 1985 *Achille Lauro* hijacking, in which an American passenger was murdered (see *MECS* 1984–85, pp. 91–93) received a special place of honor at the PNC meeting in Algiers. During the conference, he made insulting remarks to the American media suggesting that the incident was of no consequence. Similarly, Col. Hawari, a close associate of 'Arafat, had recently been convicted *in absentia* of terrorist activity by a French court.[52]

Third, Shultz may have hoped by his rejection of the visa request to press the PLO toward more explicit statements than had been made in Algiers.

Finally, he was obviously attempting to influence positively the coalition discussions then occurring among Israeli parties in an effort to block the establishment of a narrow right-wing coalition.

Thus, despite the opposition of America's allies and many in the US foreign policy community, Shultz took a forthright position which precipitated the transfer of the UN General Assembly meeting to Geneva so that 'Arafat could deliver his address. This meeting was set for 13 December. The vote itself to change the locus of the UN session was a clear rebuff to the US.

A peripheral series of negotiations now emerged center stage. Swedish Foreign Minister Sten Andersson had months earlier set in motion a basis for contacts between the PLO leadership and several American Jews. Through the happenstance of personal contacts, the center of this activity was the US section of the Tel Aviv-based International Center for Peace in the Middle East. However the individuals involved acted on their own. On 21 and 22 November, days after the Algiers meeting but before Shultz's rejection of 'Arafat's visa, some of the Jews involved met secretly in Stockholm with a PLO delegation, headed by Khalid al-Hasan, chairman of the PLO's foreign affairs committee. Together they produced a possible statement for joint release. After the Shultz denial, 'Arafat agreed to meet with them in Stockholm to announce the declaration publicly. Although the five American Jews present declared that there was "no further impediment to a direct dialogue between the United States Government and the PLO,"[53] many US officials still remained skeptical. In fact, Shultz had seen the proposed document before he rejected 'Arafat's visa application.[54]

The Stockholm Declaration, released on 7 December, represented a purported explanation of the Algiers Declaration and took the same position on linking UN Resolutions 242 and 338 with Palestinian self-determination, thereby in essence redefining the famous UN statements as if they accepted a Palestinian state. It proceeded to claim that the PNC had "established the independent State of Palestine and accepted the existence of Israel as a state in the region."[55] It also claimed that the PNC had "declared its rejection and condemnation of terrorism in all its forms, including state terrorism,"[56] which presumably referred as well to Israel.

Although the Jewish representatives did not officially represent anyone but themselves, the fact that the meetings occurred certainly affected the political environment in Washington. Morris Abram, chairman of the Conference of Presidents of Major American Jewish Organizations, charged that "these American Jews naively permitted themselves to be used by the PLO chairman" as "willing dupes prepared to broadcast his latest deceptions."[57] Shultz declared that 'Arafat had still not met American conditions for the opening of a dialogue.

Nonetheless, history suggests that when a significant body of American Jews appears to differ with Israeli policy, US officials can, if they choose, use the apparent rift as an opening for an initiative. More important, "third parties" (in particular, Andersson) had led Shultz to believe that the speech by 'Arafat in Geneva on 13 December (six days after the release of the Stockholm declaration) would meet American conditions.[58] Indeed, Shultz had called the Israeli ambassador to the US and told him that the US would begin a dialogue if 'Arafat, as expected, uttered the key phrases Washington demanded.

When the speech was delivered, the Administration was disappointed when 'Arafat continued to rely on a comprehensive settlement within the framework of UN Resolutions 242 and 338, which he still tied to Palestinian self-determination. State Department spokesman Charles Redman indicated that the US would enter a "substantive dialogue with the PLO" if it addressed American requirements "clearly, squarely, without ambiguity." He concluded, "that didn't happen, and as a consequence, the speech did not meet our conditions."[59]

Yet a process had begun. The Egyptian president and foreign minister intervened to gain 'Arafat's enunciation of the "magic words" as they had come to be known in

Washington. In addition, Sweden and several Arab states had reportedly continued to pressure the PLO leader.[60] Thus, in a news conference on 14 December, 'Arafat made a statement in which he claimed that "self-determination means survival for the Palestinians and our survival does not destroy the survival of the Israelis as their rulers claim."[61] He also accepted UN Resolutions 242 and 338 "as the basis for negotiations with Israel within the framework of the international conference."[62] He went on to suggest that not only was he accepting the UN's 1947 partition plan (Resolution 181), but that according to it "the right of all parties concerned in the Middle East conflict to exist in peace and security"[63] was reaffirmed. He added that this right applied to "the state of Palestine, Israel, and other neighbors according to the Resolutions 242 and 338."[64] Finally, perhaps the statement that had the greatest effect on Shultz was his apparent renunciation of terrorism. "I repeat for the record that we totally and absolutely renounce all forms of terrorism, including individual, group, and state terrorism."[65]

This statement was not completely unequivocal. It was not what President-elect Bush had demanded when he said, "I want it clear. I want it unambiguous. I want it so that nobody can argue with what has been said."[66] It was not a renunciation of the PLO covenant, which both Bush and Dukakis had called for during the campaign as an additional condition for engaging in a dialogue with the PLO. Yet 'Arafat's statement was sufficient for American officials who had come to believe that failure to talk to the PLO was a growing limitation on their ability to conduct serious negotiations and who had sweated through weeks of sometimes tumultuous, sometimes tortuous signaling.

Therefore, in a news conference held several hours after 'Arafat's statement, Shultz announced that he was designating Robert Pelletreau, the US ambassador in Tunis, as the only authorized channel for a dialogue with PLO representatives. He stated that the 'Arafat statement was an unambiguous acceptance of American conditions. Shultz added that the initiation of a dialogue did not "imply an acceptance or recognition by the United States of an independent Palestinian state." He made it clear that "it is also important to emphasize that the United States' commitment to the security of Israel remains unflinching."[67]

Although Shultz continued to maintain in his news conference that the US had accepted a dialogue with the PLO only in response to a change in 'Arafat's statements, it is clear that a number of events had contributed to a sense in Washington that an adjustment was necessary, and 'Arafat had provided the minimum excuse. First, the *intifada*, the failure of the Shultz initiative, and Husayn's withdrawal from the West Bank had led to a sense that the Palestinians, including the PLO, were the only avenue left for new directions. Second, the position of Israel had steadily declined in recent months within the US as a consequence of its handling of the *intifada*, the uncertain election results, and the continuing wrangling over a new coalition. In particular, the "Who Is a Jew" controversy had led to growing reexaminations among many American Jews of their relationship to Israel. Perhaps one of the reasons this controversy was so virulent was that many American Jews, reluctant to criticize Israel on security questions, expended their pent-up frustration in a more acceptable form of criticism. Additionally, the "Who Is a Jew" controversy, by its very nature, led to a perception among many Jews in the US that Israelis were questioning their identity as Jews. Instead of Israel maintaining what had become a form of Jewish pride and identification, the Israeli Government, during coalition negotiations, seemed about to become a repository for challenging Jews' self-perception. If a right-wing government were to be formed, Israel might well become an embarrassment as well. The Jewish-American delegations continually visiting Israel in the latter weeks of 1988, in protest against potential impending Israeli actions, added to the atmosphere facilitating a major Washington move which might be criticized by Israel.

For Shultz, however, the possibility of expanding American horizons seemed to be the most important factor, once he had become convinced that 'Arafat had indeed made an acceptable statement. It would be inaccurate, however, to suggest that American policy toward the major issues in dispute in the Arab-Israeli conflict had changed. The US still favored a Jordanian-Palestinian federation, in which the Palestinians gained a role in the rule over most, but not all, of the territories occupied by Israel. As Shultz had made clear repeatedly, he did not favor a return to the 1967 frontiers. The tenuous nature of the American move was revealed by the controversy over whether 'Arafat had threatened Bethlehem Mayor Elias Freij on 1 January 1989, for proposing a truce in the territories.

As 1988 ended then, the US confronted new opportunities, but these were strongly circumscribed. Washington still disagreed totally with the PLO conception of a Palestinian state imposed on Israel by an international conference. The organized American-Jewish community had decided that it was fruitless to oppose a decision already made by Shultz, whose prestige and respect in the community continued. It was also clear, however, that this community would hold American negotiators to high standards in their discussions with the PLO. By the end of the year, community leaders had already begun to take positions demanding that the US convey to the PLO leadership Washington's opposition to any form of terrorism and to an imposed peace, either by the superpowers or by an international conference; its support for a Jordanian-Palestinian solution; and its opposition to a return to the 1967 borders. The testing of the PLO was a theme already being sounded, by which the US would challenge 'Arafat to encourage Palestinians on the West Bank and Gaza Strip to deal directly with the Israelis, to support an end to the *intifada*, and to adopt a Sadat-like practical policy of reconciliation and normalization with Israel. If 'Arafat was perceived as adopting such a position and there was no movement in Jerusalem, tensions would arise with both Washington and American Jewry. Meanwhile, another popular argument often heard at the end of 1988 was that peace negotiations would constitute a lengthy process before a settlement would be reached. There would necessarily be phases of implementation that would be undertaken during the course of an unfolding reconciliation between Arab and Jew.

By the end of the year, some of Israel's supporters were even beginning to suggest that if the PLO had truly undergone a transformation and if 'Arafat's statement in Geneva on 14 December was authentic, then other Arab countries like Saudi Arabia and Jordan ought to be able to recognize Israel and deal directly with it. According to this argument, if the PLO had indeed now accepted Israel's right to exist, no further political impediment should stand in their way.

While the State Department might not be expected to sympathize with all of these positions, they were widely accepted by most in the pro-Israeli community as well as by many Congressmen favorable to Israel. Although the US was entering a period of ferment in its ME policy, consistent with the advent of a new administration, its fundamental positions remained, at the end of 1988, distinctly different from the PLO's. In the absence of a crisis or an unexpected opportunity such as an initiative by the Arab or Israeli side, official Washington at the end of the year was in a mood to explore the implications of its new avenue with the PLO, while allowing events to unfold in the area and encouraging those on both sides who would move in the direction of a favorable peace process.

In the end, then, American policy had not altered as radically as both the Arabs and Israelis might have assumed. The year of 1988 had been a confusing one filled with cautious activism on the part of the US. How memorable the most important development of the year — the initiation of a dialogue with the PLO — would prove to be would be determined by later events.

IMPLICATIONS FOR US RELATIONS WITH THE SOVIET UNION

Both the Shultz initiative and the opening of a dialogue with the PLO broke dramatic new ground in terms of American policy toward the Soviet Union. Traditionally, the US, and especially the Reagan Administration, had been opposed to any kind of Kremlin role in the Arab-Israeli peace process. The initiative provided for a Soviet presence at a ceremonial international conference which would serve as an umbrella for peace negotiations. Although the Soviet position was still only procedural and symbolic, the initiative had crossed an important line: in the future the US might be prepared to accept a substantive Soviet role in the peace process.

The new relationship with the PLO was predicated on a moderated PLO position, for which the Kremlin was given a modicum of credit, especially in terms of the pressure Soviet representatives had exerted on their clients to gain a degree of Palestinian compromise at the November PNC meeting in Algiers.[68] To official Washington, Soviet influence was seen as moving in a more positive direction than in the past. Moscow had indirectly helped to provide conditions which made the dialogue with the PLO possible. When combined with the improving dialogue between Jerusalem and Moscow, the basis for new superpower contacts had been established.

During the year, American policy-makers continued a sporadic dialogue with Soviet representatives in terms of the Third World, including the ME, a further signpost of improving superpower relations.[69] The consequence of the Shultz initiative, a moderated PLO position, improved Soviet-Israeli relations, and the increasing Soviet-American dialogue suggests that 1988 was a year when the possibility of Soviet-American cooperation regarding the Arab-Israeli peace process became at least conceivable. In the future, the US will judge Moscow on the basis of whether its policies continue to move in a positive direction toward Israel and Soviet Jews, toward a demonstrated willingness to exert pressures on its clients, and toward restraint in the shipment of arms to radical Arab states. If Soviet-American relations continue to improve and if Moscow appears to assume a more moderate position in the ME, the willingness of the US to engage in practical steps involving the Soviet Union in the Arab-Israeli peace process will be likely to intensify.

THE UNITED STATES AND THE PERSIAN GULF

Unlike the Arab-Israeli arena, American policy toward the Persian Gulf in 1988 confronted decisive developments. The year dawned with the US heavily embroiled in the protection of neutral shipping in the Gulf. This activity, begun in July 1987 (see

MECS 1987, chapter on the United States and the Middle East), had led to frequent clashes with Iran and a clear tilt in American policy toward Iraq. Although it initially originated in response to Kuwaiti requests for protection and in order to preclude Soviet involvement, the origins of escalated American activity can be found in a desire to assuage Arab fury over the Iran-Contra affair.

By early 1988, an "Iranian spring offensive" was anticipated. Instead, by early March, Iran and Iraq were engaged in an almost daily exchange of missiles which became known as "the war of the cities" (see also chapter on the Iraqi-Iranian War). This dramatic and lethal interchange represented an escalation of the war and an engagement of both nations' civilians. The attacks appeared to increase the danger of escalated American combat in the area, a peril which was enhanced when the frigate *Samuel B. Roberts* struck a mine in the Persian Gulf near Bahrain on 14 April. The next day, the US Navy was able to locate and destroy two mines which were similar to the type known to have been used previously by Iran near the site of the incident. The Administration might have retaliated directly against Iranian territory, but instead, on 18 April, six American warships shelled two Iranian oil-drilling platforms, which the Reagan Administration claimed were being used as radar stations. Later that day, US naval forces sank or disabled six Iranian ships which had attacked American vessels in a series of clashes in the southern Gulf.[70] This incident was a further indication that the US had become engaged on the Iraqi side, even while claiming neutrality.

As if to confirm the greater flexibility allowed the Iraqis by American involvement, at the same time (18 April) Iraqi forces recaptured the Faw peninsula in southern Iraq from Iranian occupiers after a surprise attack the previous day.[71] This was a major departure from the static and defensive posture of Iraqi forces for several years. Now it was Iraq rather than Iran which was proceeding on the offensive. This move was followed on 25 May by another successful surprise attack by the Iraqis in the Shalamcha area east of Basra.[72] As if to underscore the seeming moderation of Iran which suddenly found itself on the defensive, Tehran resumed diplomatic relations with Paris in mid-June.[73]

On 3 July, however, one of the most dramatic incidents of the war — certainly the major event involving the US — occurred. The US cruiser *Vincennes* shot down an Iranian commercial jet minutes after becoming engaged in a skirmish in the Persian Gulf with several Iranian gunboats. All 290 persons aboard the jet were killed. Despite the sophisticated *Aegis* radar system aboard the ship, it was not able to distinguish between a civilian and a military aircraft. A later naval report, on 19 August, attributed the mistake to the nervousness and inexperience of the ship's crew, resulting in the plane being mistaken for an F-14 fighter aircraft. By contrast, Secretary of Defense Frank Carlucci claimed that "crew errors were not crucial" and that Iran itself was chiefly responsible for the incident. At the time of the shooting, Reagan called it "an understandable accident."[74]

The response of the international community to the American error was muted. For example, a UN Security Council resolution unanimously adopted on 20 July expressed "deep distress" over the shooting down of the airliner. The US was not condemned.[75] Perhaps no clearer evidence could be presented of Iran's isolation. The shooting down of the Iranian airliner seemed to symbolize both the military and diplomatic depths into which Iranian policy had fallen. Thus, on 18 July, Iranian

President 'Ali Khameneh'i in a letter to UN Secretary-General Javier Pérez de Cuellar accepted UN Security Council Resolution 598 which had been passed on 20 July 1987. The resolution called for an immediate cease-fire in the Iraqi-Iranian War and the withdrawal by the troops of both sides to internationally recognized borders. Iran's failure to accept the resolution, which had been approved by Iraq, had been a major source of American opposition to Iran's posture in the Gulf during the previous several months. The stalemate over the resolution had further impeded efforts to end the war. The day after Iran accepted Resolution 598, Iran's leader, Ayatollah Khomeyni, said in an official statement that the decision to end the war "was more deadly than taking poison"[76] (see also chapter on Iran).

The UN secretary-general held separate talks with the foreign ministers of both countries a week later in New York. Finally, he was able to announce on 8 August that Iran and Iraq had accepted UN peace terms calling for a cease-fire to take effect on 20 August, when the cease-fire did begin. Although the peace talks later stalled, the cease-fire was instituted and at least temporarily the Iraqi-Iranian War was ended.[77]

The US was thus faced with a new and intriguing opportunity for the exercise of its diplomacy and influence. Its actions in the Gulf had clearly helped the war to come to an end and had benefited the Iraqis who unexpectedly had emerged with a measure of victory. Despite considerable self-congratulation by American officials and specialists, and a general attitude that the American intervention had been a success, Washington did not gain the full fruits of its engagement. In particular, American relations with Iraq deteriorated because of widespread reports of Baghdad's use of chemical weapons. As early as mid-March there had been indications that the Iraqis had used chemical weapons against the border town of Halabja after it was captured by the Iranian Army. However, as the war ended, a UN report seemed to corroborate Iranian charges of widespread use of chemical weapons by Iraq. Although the report also suggested Iranian use, a far stronger censure was accorded Iraq.[78] Clearly, the Iraqi use of chemical weapons had contributed to the Iranian decision to end the war (see chapter on the Iraqi-Iranian War).

At this time, there were also widespread reports of Iraqi use of chemical weapons against both Iranians and its own rebellious Kurdish population (see chapter on Iraq). This led to rising Congressional criticism both of Iraqi actions and the muted State Department response. A general souring of Washington's relationship with Baghdad ensued as growing reports yielded to increasing American horror.

On the other side, the Iranians — although appearing deceptively moderate for several months — continued to harbor resentment against the American role and in particular the downing of the Iranian airliner in July. The results of this bitterness could be seen by early 1989 in the increasing tension of Iranian politics, the growing ascendency of fundamentalist factions, the Ayatollah's attacks on author Salman Rushdie, and possible Iranian complicity in the downing of Pan-American flight 103 in January.

Thus, however the US may have contributed to the end of the war by its presence, it was left with hostile attitudes toward the American role by both sides. Dramatically, in early 1989, Soviet Foreign Minister Eduard Shevardnadze traveled to the area and visited both Baghdad and Tehran. It would have been inconceivable for an American secretary of state to make a similar trip.

By the end of 1988, as Americans looked back on the year, there was a deep sense of relief that the war had ended and that the American pressure could be gradually diminished. The fear of American involvement in hostilities had obviously been reduced to near zero. Whatever the vagaries of the future American role with either Baghdad or Tehran, the end of the war was cause for Washington's celebration. However, the US remained unable to improve relations with Tehran and the new opening to Iraq remained diffident at best. Certainly, Washington had not succeeded in using its substantive aid to Iraq in the war as a means either of preventing the use by Iraq of chemical weapons or of gaining Baghdad's support for its Arab-Israeli peace initiatives. The cease-fire was a major achievement, but as in the Arab-Israeli arena, the Reagan era ended amidst uncertainty accompanied by a mixture of disappointment and anticipation.

NOTES

For the place and frequency of publications cited here, and for the full name of the publication, news agency, radio station, or monitoring service where an abbreviation is used, please see "List of Sources." Only in the case of more than one publication bearing the same name is the place of publication noted here.

1. The author would like to thank Jay Footlik, Dana Hyde, William Kuluva, Stacy Perman and Barbara Seeley for their assistance in the preparation of this manuscript.
2. *NYT*, 14 July 1982, p. A12.
3. Jimmy Carter, *Public Papers of the President*, Vol. 1 (1978), (Washington, DC: The Government Printing Office, 1979), p. 490. (Excerpts from President Carter's 9 March news conference).
4. Confidential interviews.
5. *DSB*, 2,133, April 1988, p. 72.
6. *WP*, 30 January 1988, p. A14.
7. *NYT*, 3 February, p. A8; *WSJ*, 2 February 1988.
8. *WP*, 3 February; *WSJ*, 2 February 1988.
9. *WP*, 24 February 1988, p. A20.
10. Ibid.
11. *DSB*, 2,134, May 1989, p. 9 (news conference: 24 February 1988).
12. Testimony by Secretary of State George Shultz before the Senate Budget Committee, 17 March 1988.
13. *WP*, 26 February, p. Al; *NYT*, 25 February 1988, p. A3.
14. *NYT*, 4 March 1988.
15. *DSB*, 2,134, May 1989, p. 56 (news conference: 26 February 1988).
16. Ibid.
17. Testimony by assistant secretary of state Richard Murphy before the Subcommittee on Europe and the Middle East of the House Foreign Affairs Committee, 15 March 1988.
18. Ibid.
19. White House background briefing — readout on the meeting of Israeli Prime Minister Yitzhak Shamir with President Reagan; 16 March 1988.
20. *WP*, 4 April 1988, p. A1.
21. *DSB*, 2,135, June, p. 6 (interview with Secretary of State Shultz, 3 April 1988).
22. *WT*, 6 June 1988, p. A10.
23. Letter submitted by 30 US senators to Secretary of State Shultz, 3 March 1988.
24. *LAT*, 26 May 1988.
25. 1988 Democratic platform, as approved by Democratic Party platform committee in Denver, 24–25 June 1988.
26. Minority plank, as submitted to Democratic Party platform committee in Denver, 24–25 June 1988.
27. Stewart Ain, "GOP's Platform Plank on Israel Seen as Push for Jewish Vote," *Jewish Week*, 19 August 1988.

28. Confidential interviews.
29. Bush's speech, B'nai B'rith convention, Baltimore, 7 September 1988.
30. Ibid.
31. Dukakis's speech, B'nai B'rith convention, Baltimore, 7 September 1988.
32. Ibid.
33. *WP*, 11 September 1988, p. A7.
34. *NYT*, 10 November 1988, p. B6.
35. Stephen D. Isaacs, *Jews and American Politics* (Garden City, NY: Doubleday & Co., 1974), pp. 151–53.
36. *Building for Peace: An American Strategy for the Middle East*, The Washington Institute's Presidential Study Group, The Washington Institute for Near East Policy, 1988.
37. *WP*, 18 March 1988, p. A1.
38. *LAT*, 14 July 1988, p. 1.
39. *NYT*, 9 July 1988, p. 4.
40. *NYT*, 31 July 1988, p. 1.
41. *NYT*, 21 August 1988, p. 6.
42. *WP*, 9 September 1988, p. A1.
43. Speech delivered by Secretary of State Shultz before the Washington Institute for Near East Policy, 16 September 1988.
44. Ibid.
45. Ibid.
46. Ibid.
47. Ibid.
48. Ibid.
49. *NYT*, 17 November 1988, p. A5.
50. *NYT*, 27 November 1988, p. A5.
51. Worldnet's "Dialogue," USIA Press Release No. 246, 30 November 1988, p. 9.
52. *WP*, 1 November 1988.
53. *NYT*, 8 December 1988, p. A12.
54. *WP*, 18 December 1988, p. C1.
55. *NYT*, 8 December 1988, p. A12.
56. Ibid.
57. *WP*, 7 December 1988, p. A37.
58. *NYT*, 14 December, p. A10, 15 December 1988, p. A6.
59. *NYT*, 14 December 1988, p. A10.
60. *NYT*, 15 December 1988, p. A6.
61. *NYT*, 15 December 1988, p. A7.
62. Ibid.
63. Ibid.
64. Ibid.
65. Ibid.
66. *NYT*, 15 December 1988, p. A6.
67. Ibid.
68. *NYT*, 26 February 1989, p. E3.
69. Leonard Binder, "The Changing American Role in the Middle East," *Current History*, Vol. 88, No. 535 (February 1989), p. 97.
70. *WP*, 19 July 1988.
71. *WP*, 18 April 1988, p. A17.
72. Chronology 1988, *Foreign Affairs*, Vol. 68, No. 1 (1989), p. 235.
73. *NYT*, 16 June 1988, p. A14.
74. Chronology 1988, *Foreign Affairs*, Vol. 68, No. 1 (1989), p. 236.
75. *WP*, 19 July 1988.
76. *WSJ*, 22 July 1988, p. 18.
77. *NYT*, 8 August 1988, p. A1.
78. *NYT*, 2 August 1988, p. A1.

The Soviet Union and the Middle East in 1988

ROBERT O. FREEDMAN

Despite being a year of ethnic unrest and major domestic political change in the USSR, 1988 was also an active one for Soviet diplomacy in the Middle East. At the beginning of the year, Moscow was faced with the dual challenges of reacting to the *intifada* and the intensification of the Iraqi-Iranian War. While the war ended in a cease-fire during the summer — a development warmly welcomed by Moscow — the *intifada* continued and, in part, contributed to the decision by the Palestine National Council (PNC), in November, to declare the creation of a Palestinian state. The Soviet Union's rather ambiguous reaction to this development reflected Moscow's desire to support the mainstream PLO while also continuing the slow, but steady, improvement of its relations with Israel. The improving relations between Moscow and Jerusalem were marked, at the end of 1988, by Israel's prompt return of four criminals who hijacked a Soviet plane to Israel in December, and by Israeli aid to the Soviet Union following the Armenian earthquake, a week later.

THE SOVIET UNION AND THE GULF

MOSCOW, IRAN, AND IRAQ

The most pressing problem for Moscow at the beginning of 1988 was the escalation of the war between Iran and Iraq (see chapter on the Iraqi-Iranian War), which had enabled the US to strengthen its position among the Gulf Arabs by amassing a large fleet to escort Kuwaiti tankers. At this time Moscow was still tilting toward the Iranian position while at the same time trying to maintain its position in Iraq and among the Arab states supporting Iraq — a very difficult balancing act to perform.

Thus, on 24 December 1987, Moscow agreed to a unanimous Security Council decision to consider sanctions to compel Iran to comply with a cease-fire,[1] but an angered Iran then permitted a group of Afghan demonstrators to attack the Soviet consulate in Isfahan.[2] Moscow lodged a "strong protest" with Iran, claiming that the attack had been carried out by a "group of fanatical elements from the Afghan counterrevolutionaries who are based in Iran."[3] One week later, a commentator on Iranian television took a highly caustic view of the change in Soviet strategy and warned Moscow not to continue its new policy:

> ...The Soviet Union feels that because of the possible threat to them posed by the continuation of the war, the reactionary Arab leaders are daily inclining more and more toward the United States and the West. The culmination of this inclination could be seen in the Amman conference and the Gulf Co-operation Council [GCC] summit. The Russians feel that if they continue their previous

> line, they may lose the astronomic loans from the Arabs and their future economic-political presence in Arab countries. They also feel that if they do not react more strongly toward Iran, the Americans will become the only defender among the Arab reactionaries, and this will pave the grounds for the United States to take strategic steps where the future of the Middle East is concerned. At this juncture, the Soviet Union has altered its stand; it is gradually moving away from its previous position toward a more overt stand on the war. At the same time it is trying, as much as possible, to postpone the moment of decision.
>
> Moscow's request to the United Nations secretary-general to pay another visit to the region stems precisely from this. But is this a logical policy at a time when the Americans are still prepared at the slightest smile from Tehran to sell out all the Arabs for the sake of establishing a small relationship with Iran? What will the Russians gain from this stand? The United States understands very well Iran's sensitive role in the region and if, under such conditions, the Russians join in the arms embargo, they will destroy all the bridges that have been built so far. Moreover, because of their intrinsic fear of communism and the natural compatibility between their systems and capitalism, the Arabs will certainly not turn toward the Soviet Union. The only outcome of the Russians' act can be that the Americans will benefit and their position will be strengthened.
>
> The strength that Iran has shown in the past year in the Persian Gulf proves the seriousness of the remarks by our officials that if such a plan is implemented, all Persian Gulf ports will become obsolete. If the Russians go along with the Americans in this, they will be repeating the same mistake they once made when they leased their tankers to Kuwait. The difference, though, is that it is easy to make up for some mistakes, but difficult or impossible to do so for others.[4]

In February 1988, Moscow made a major move to improve its position in the ME and throughout the Islamic world by announcing its decision to pull out of Afghanistan. The Soviet withdrawal could be expected to improve relations both with the Arab world and Iran. President Mikhail Gorbachev sent special envoys to virtually every Arab state as well as to Iran, to inform them of the withdrawal and seek their aid in assisting it, by using their influence to get Pakistan and the US to agree to Soviet conditions for the withdrawal at the Geneva talks.[5] The Iranian regime, while welcoming the Soviet move and calling it a "positive development," nonetheless expressed reservations that it might be a ploy to keep the Najibullah regime in power and prevent the "Afghan Muslim people and revolutionaries" from controlling their own country.[6] Soviet Deputy Foreign Minister Vladimir Petrovsky flew to Iran on 11 February to explain the withdrawal to the Iranian leadership, but was told by Iranian Foreign Minister 'Ali Akbar Velayati that Iran expected the Mujahidin to have a "fundamental and decisive" role in the future of Afghanistan, which should be "independent and nonaligned."[7] Majlis Speaker 'Ali Akbar Hashemi Rafsanjani went so far as to offer Petrovsky a deal on this point, noting that "if you are determined to pull out of Afghanistan, we are prepared to assist you, so that after your departure there will be no US domination in Afghanistan."[8]

While Velayati was to give an overall positive evaluation of the Petrovsky visit,[9] differences on the role of the Mujahidin remained. On 23 February, the Afghan Muslim Council issued a strongly worded anti-Soviet statement in Tehran rejecting the idea of any compromise with "Soviet-inspired groups who are responsible for the social calamities in Afghanistan."[10] Meanwhile, Soviet-Iranian relations continued to be irritated by what Tehran saw as Soviet acquiescence in the continued US attempts to achieve an arms embargo against Iran.[11] Despite extensive US and Arab pressure, the USSR continued to delay action on the sanctions. Neither the Moscow visits of Saudi Foreign Minister Prince Sa'ud al-Faysal and Iraqi Foreign Minister Tariq 'Aziz,[12] the repeated urgings by the US Administration and Congressional leaders,[13] nor the Riyadh visit of the Soviet Foreign Ministry's Middle East department head, Vladimir Polyakov, seemed to move Moscow to do anything more than give oral support to the idea of sanctions.[14]

If the Soviet Union's balancing act on the sanctions issue appeared to be costing it diplomatic support both in Iran and in the Arab world, and to raise questions in Washington regarding the real effect of Moscow's "new thinking" on Soviet foreign policy, Moscow's relationship with Iran was to suffer another severe blow at the end of February when Iraq launched a missile attack against Iran.[15] The Iranian leadership denounced the USSR for supplying Iraq with the missiles, and Iranian protesters marched on the Soviet Embassy in Tehran and the Soviet Consulate in Isfahan, shouting "death to Russia."[16] Moscow denied supplying the missiles, but the Iranian leadership rejected the Soviet denials. Rafsanjani asserted that the Iranian people would "never forget the Soviet Union's impudence" in supplying Iraq with missiles; "this will definitely affect our future relations" with the USSR, he stated.[17] Rafsanjani also asserted at a news conference that the Soviet Union was "currently pursuing a policy of hypocrisy and duplicity" by putting the missiles at Iraq's disposal, and providing parts to modify the missiles and increase their range.[18] Meanwhile, Iran's Deputy Foreign Minister Muhammad Javad Larijani, speaking at a press conference in Tehran, noted that on his recent trip to Moscow he "clearly told the Soviet president and prime minister that any missile or bomb given to the tottering regime of Iraq by the Soviet Union will first hit Tehran-Moscow relations before hitting Iranian soil."[19]

The Soviet Union, clearly troubled by the Iranian response to the Iraqi missile barrage, sought to assuage Iranian anger by leading an effort in the UN Security Council to achieve an end to the "war of the cities."[20] The Soviet effort was to prove ineffective. One month later, Tehran denounced the US-Soviet agreement on Afghanistan that was signed in mid-April in Geneva, because it did not include the Mujahidin.[21] Moscow was then to use another ploy to try to improve ties with iran; on 20 April it sought to exploit politically the US attack on Iranian offshore oil platforms which followed the mining of a US warship. The US attack coincided with a major Iraqi offensive in the Faw peninsula;[22] and Radio Tehran, claiming that the US attack was aimed at giving "direct support" to Iraq, denounced the "Eastern and Western superpowers" for aiding Iraq.[23] Soviet commentators criticized the American action, which quickly escalated into a battle between the US and Iranian navies, with TASS commentators calling the attack "an act of aggression" and "a gangster-like act."[24] A Soviet Foreign Ministry spokesman, Vadim Perfilyev, labeled it a "gross violation of international law" taken in "total disregard for world public opinion."[25]

The ploy, however, did not appear to meet with much success. TASS news analyst

Valery Vavilov somewhat ruefully acknowledged this when he deplored Rafsanjani's claim that the US attack was part of a "coordinated campaign of the United States, the Soviet Union,and Kuwait."[26] A Radio Peace and Progress broadcast in Persian to Iran, on 25 April, made this point more clearly, denouncing Iranian claims that the USSR was "hand in hand" with the US in a coordinated effort to destroy the Islamic Republic, and that Iran was now a target of hostile actions agreed to by the Soviet Union and the US.[27] Moscow also deplored Iran's role in splitting Muslim unity through its refusal to end the war (diplomatic relations between Iran and Saudi Arabia had just been broken by Riyadh — see chapter on Saudi Arabia), with another Moscow Radio Peace and Progress broadcast in Persian going so far as to assert:

> Those who support a protraction of the Iran-Iraq conflict hide their spiteful programs under the shield of religious slogans. They regard war as a decisive means in the struggle for leadership in the Islamic world. Such a policy can yield the most dangerous results under current international conditions.[28]

By June, Soviet-Iranian relations had sharply deteriorated. This development was spelled out in detail by an Iranian newspaper in an editorial on 27 June:

> The Iranian nation and leadership have been alarmed at the rate Iraq's arsenals have been stockpiled after Gorbachev took the helms of power. Long-range Soviet missiles have rained on innocent Iranian civilians. Soviet MiGs are responsible for a very large number of Iranian nonmilitary casualties. And these inhumane events have unfolded parallel to Mr. Gorbachev's image-building efforts at home and abroad....As things appear to be, the Soviets have failed to win substantial influence in Tehran. Nearly 10 years of diplomatic, political, and economic relations with the Islamic Republic has surely not placed the Kremlin in a better position than the White House in the eyes of 50 million Iranians.[29]

Moscow tried again to exploit a US-Iranian clash in early July, when a US cruiser, after a battle with Iranian gunboats, accidentally shot down an Iranian civilian airliner. Soviet commentators, strongly endorsing the Iranian version of the incident, condemned the action, with one hinting that it was "premeditated aggression"[30] and others, including *Pravda,* calling it "cold-blooded murder" and an attempt to intimidate Iran.[31] Moscow also sought to use the airbus affair to mobilize diplomatic pressure on the US to pull its naval forces out of the Gulf — a goal shared by Iran.[32]

In any case, less than three weeks after its airliner was shot down, Iran agreed to accept UN Resolution 598. Suffering major losses on the battlefield in the April-July 1988 period, including the loss of the Faw peninsula, and in the face of both missile and poison gas attacks by Iraq, Iran changed its previous position and reluctantly accepted the UN resolution without conditions, in an action which Khomeyni himself called "more lethal for me than poison."[33] (For further discussion of the background to the Iranian decision, see chapter on Iran.) As might be expected, the USSR warmly welcomed an end to the war that had caused it so many problems in the ME for the past eight years.[34] Yuli Vorontsov immediately flew to Tehran to consult with Iranian leaders. Reportedly he took the opportunity to condemn, once again, the shooting down of the Iranian airliner as an "act of barbarity," hoping to undermine the US position in Iran and turn over a new leaf in Soviet-Iranian relations.[35] According to the Soviet account of the visit, Vorontsov also urged the Iranian leadership to help to "normalize the situation in Afghanistan."[36] Rafsanjani, however, in a speech on 11 August claimed that the Soviets had offered to cut their arms shipments to Iraq if Iran agreed to support "the subservient government in Afghanistan" — an action which Iran rejected "on principle."[37]

Meanwhile, Iran's acceptance of UN Security Council Resolution 598 did not end the war, as both Iran and Iraq continued their military efforts to gain political advantage, while UN Secretary-General Javier Pérez de Cuellar sought to work out a cease-fire. In the midst of the fighting, another Arab delegation came to Moscow on 10 August, seeking Soviet support to end the war. Moscow sought to use the visit to gain support for the ouster of the US fleet from the Gulf; the Arab delegation, composed of Kuwaiti Foreign Minister Shaykh Sabah al-Ahmad al-Jabir and Iraqi Minister of State for Foreign Affairs Sa'dun Hammadi, clearly wanted the USSR to pressure Iran. Shaykh Sabah stated that the role of the superpowers should be "to back the direct negotiations between the two parties and pressure, in the event those negotiations fail, the party that is not prepared to achieve peace and that exploited the 598 Resolution to realize a truce."[38]

On 20 August, a month after Iran formally accepted UN Resolution 598, a cease-fire finally came into effect. The Iran-Iraq conflict, however, appeared to move simply from the battlefield to the bargaining table. The two sides continued to dispute such issues as the validity of the 1975 Algiers Treaty, which set their boundary along the midpoint of the Shatt al-'Arab shipping channel, the return of prisoners of war, and the clearing of the Shatt al-'Arab of mines and sunken ships.[39] But despite the wrangling, the fighting had stopped. In an official government statement welcoming the cease-fire, Moscow sought to capitalize on the situation by offering, once again, to withdraw its small force of warships from the Gulf if the US and its Nato allies also removed their fleets. The USSR also suggested that the security of the sea lanes in the Gulf could be ensured by a system of guarantees by the permanent members of the Security Council — a proposal reminiscent of Foreign Minister Eduard Shevardnadze's call for a UN Gulf fleet in September 1987. So as not to alienate Iran by its proposal, however, Moscow promised to "carefully take into account the considerations of the Persian Gulf states which, needless to say, have the principal and greatest stake in turning the Persian Gulf into a zone of security, good-neighborliness and cooperation."[40]

In evaluating their position in the ME once the cease-fire had gone into effect, the Soviet leadership evidently saw it as much improved. On the one hand, the bulk of the Arab states, while angered, had not been totally alienated by Moscow's tilt to Iran; with the *intifada* raging, they could be expected to shift their attention back to the Israeli-Palestinian conflict, an arena where there was a great deal of room for cooperation with Soviet diplomacy, particularly in the effort to bring about an international conference. On the other hand, while Iran had clearly been angered by the extensive Soviet arms shipments to Iraq (Rafsanjani's speech on 11 August had noted this point clearly as had a number of statements by other Iranian officials), the Iranian Government had also benefited from the Soviet delaying tactics that prevented the imposition of an arms embargo. Moscow now hoped it could begin to build a more positive postwar relationship with Tehran. A senior Soviet diplomat, Alexander Zotov, writing in *New Times* after Iran had formally accepted UN Resolution 598, sought to justify this aspect of Soviet diplomacy during the war:

> It goes to its [Soviet diplomacy's] credit that it showed restraint over the demands of a number of Western and other countries that Iran be 'punished' for procrastination over the acceptance of Resolution 598 and a blockade be imposed on it under an appropriate Security Council resolution. Such a resolution would hardly have worked — it is enough to recall the Irangate affair — and, worse still, it could only have encouraged Iran's belligerent rejection of outside pressure.[41]

Nonetheless, the Soviet Union had a number of obstacles to overcome before there could be any significant improvement in Soviet-Iranian relations. Besides Iran's continuing unhappiness over Soviet arms supplies to Iraq, Moscow had to be concerned that as Iran began its postwar reconstruction it would become economically dependent on the Western states and Japan and this would cause Iran to move toward the West politically. Indeed, when the war ended, a major debate broke out in Tehran as to the proper course to take in reconstruction (see chapter on Iran), with Khomeyni himself, in a major speech on 4 September urging Iran not to become dependent on the US or USSR:

> God willing, the warrior Iranian people will maintain their revolutionary and sacred rancor and anger in their hearts and use their oppressor-burning flames against the criminal Soviet Union and the world-devouring United States and their surrogates.[42]

While the debate raged in Tehran over whether or not to incur foreign debts in reconstruction,[43] Moscow Radio sought to influence the debate by noting:

> Some in Tehran fear that Western companies may exploit Iran's weakened economy and may possibly impose unsuitable conditions on Iran when concluding agreements with it...There are several ways to resist the pressure by Western companies. *As was justly and timely noted in Tehran,* one of these measures is the balanced expansion of economic relations with the West and the East, namely with the Soviet Union....[44] (Author's emphasis.)

The Iranian leadership was to choose to balance its economic ties between East and West, but Moscow was not to be the sole major Communist economic partner. China, which had supplied Iran with *Silkworm* missiles during the war, was actively courted as a postwar economic partner. When the Chinese Deputy Foreign Minister for Political Affairs, Qi Huaiyaun, visited Iran in mid-August he was told by Hamid Mirzadeh, the Iranian deputy prime minister for executive affairs who was also the Iranian head of the Tehran-Beijing economic commission, that the good wartime relations between China and Iran could improve further in postwar times.[45] Mirzadeh told a visiting Chinese economic delegation one week later that he hoped China would play a major role in Iran's economic relations with foreign countries.[46] Agreements between the two countries were not long in coming. On 3 September an agreement was signed on cooperation in dam construction and energy;[47] and on 27 September Mirzadeh announced on his return from a trip to Beijing for the fourth session of the Iran-Beijing economic commission that an agreement had been reached to boost Sino-Iranian trade from $500m. in 1988 to $600m. in 1989, that discussions were held on building two Iranian power stations, and that an Iranian Consulate would be opened in Shanghai.[48]

Moscow, whose total trade with Iran in 1987 was only $250m.[49] — half the Sino-Iranian 1988 figure — also sought to capitalize on Iran's desire to develop economic cooperation. For its part, as in the past, Iran appeared to be exploiting Moscow's policy of seeking improved political relations by first strengthening economic ties. Thus, when Soviet Deputy Minister of Foreign Economic Relations Benjamin Korolev came to Iran for the 14th Tehran International Trade Fair in September, and declared Moscow's eagerness "to upgrade mutual economic, technical,and cultural ties with Iran,"[50] he was told that Iran's policy *vis-à-vis* the USSR had always been based on mutual interest, understanding, and noninterference; Tehran wished the forthcoming session of the joint Iranian-Soviet economic commission to be a "turning point" in mutual relations.[51]

The economic commission, which met in Moscow in early December, did reach a number of agreements including the resumption of Iranian natural gas shipments to the USSR and the building of two dams across the Aras River which serves as a border between Iran and the USSR. A protocol on other types of economic cooperation was also signed, including the development and upgrading of transport links between the two countries.[52] Heading the Iranian delegation to Moscow was Muhammad Irvani, Iran's minister of economy and finance, and he was invited to meet with Soviet Prime Minister Nikolai Ryzhkov on 6 December. The talks took place in what was described as a "businesslike and friendly atmosphere" where a "thorough exchange of views" took place — Soviet parlance for disagreement.[53] Among the areas of probable disagreement was Iran's aid to the Afghan rebels, which had led to increasingly critical treatment of Iran by the Soviet media. For example, Igor Belyayev, in a *Literaturnaya Gazeta* article on 2 November, stated that Iran, having failed in its efforts to export the Islamic Revolution to Iraq, was now trying to reroute the "Islamic march" to Afghanistan, and was making use of the 2m. Afghan refugees on Iranian soil to accomplish this task.[54] Belyayev's *Literaturnaya Gazeta* colleague, Konstantin Kapitonov, took a similarly dim view of Iran, noting that there were many more prisons there under Khomeyni than in the Shah's day and that the Government of Iran had been trying to turn "most of the population into robots who, on orders from above, mindlessly apply pressure on any dissidence or the slightest expression of opposition."[55] But it was not only the increasingly free Soviet press that was unhappy with Iran's policy, domestic and foreign. On 2 November *Pravda,* reflecting Soviet government policy, reported a "resolute protest" by Afghanistan to Iran because of Iranian Foreign Minister Velayati's meeting with Afghan rebel leaders, whom he urged to continue the war.

In addition to Iranian aid to the Afghan rebels, Moscow was concerned about Iran in the period following the cease-fire for two reasons. One was the possibility that in the postwar period Iran and the US might be reconciled, because many of Iran's factories had been built by US firms, and Iran was now planning its reconstruction. Once Iran had accepted Resolution 598, the US sent a message to Iran proposing normalization of relations.[56] Although Iran's initial reply did not satisfy the US,[57] the strong US position condemning Iraq's use of poison gas against its Kurdish minority (both the Senate and House called for sanctions) held out the possibility of improved ties. Continuing to play the zero-sum game in political competition with the US over

Iran, Moscow deprecated the US reaction. A Radio Peace and Progress broadcast in Persian to Iran claimed it was only a tactical move by the US, designed to motivate Iranian "extremist circles" to impede the Geneva talks (between Iran and Iraq) and "drag Iran into the orbit" of US policy.[58] Moscow also sought to play down the Iraqi action as based on "vague reports,"[59] in part because of fear that the issue might cause the still tenuous peace talks to break off, a concern Moscow displayed throughout the rest of the year. Rafsanjani criticized the US condemnation of the Iraqi use of poison gas, claiming the US should have shown this concern earlier when Iraq had used chemical weapons against Iran; but he was also highly critical of the USSR for not openly protesting against the Iraqi use of poison gas.[60] The end result of the poison gas episode was that it did not lead to an improvement in US-Iranian relations, and for this Moscow may well have been grateful; yet Soviet behavior on the poison gas issue could only have raised questions in Tehran about how much Moscow could be trusted in the postwar period.

A final problem Moscow had with Iran in the latter part of 1988 was the Iranian treatment of the Tudeh, the Iranian Communist Party. Once Iran accepted UN Resolution 598, the Iranian regime cracked down hard on opposition groups, and executed a number of political prisoners, including members of the Tudeh Party (see chapter on Iran). Moscow's initial complaints were limited to the clandestine Radio of the Toilers of Iran in Persian.[61] But it escalated its criticism in November, with a Radio Peace and Progress broadcast to Iran discussing the UN Human Rights Commission report which denounced Iran for mistreatment of political prisoners.[62] On 7 December, Moscow took another step when *Pravda* published a Tudeh Party statement condemning the executions and appealing to the UN to save the political prisoners still alive in Iranian jails. Coming at the time when the Iranian economic delegation was visiting Moscow, the *Pravda* report was clearly meant to signal Soviet displeasure at the Iranian executions. The Soviet leadership, despite its *perestroika, glasnost,* and "new thinking" (which minimized the role of ideology in world affairs), evidently felt it could not sit idly by while communists who looked to Moscow were killed, without at least noting Soviet unhappiness with the development. On balance, however, as in the past, the Soviet leadership felt that state-to-state relations took precedence over the fate of any foreign Communist party, and Moscow quickly resumed its efforts to improve ties with Iran. In a Moscow Radio broadcast on 10 December — only three days after the *Pravda* article — the Soviet commentator hailed the success of the joint economic commission's meeting which "elevated Soviet-Iranian relations to a new stage" and appealed for Iranian help in securing a settlement in Afghanistan.[63]

While Moscow throughout 1988 worked to improve relations with Iran, it was also mindful of its ties with Iraq which emerged as a major Arab power with its military victories over Iran at the end of the war. Moscow's supply of modern weapons to Iraq had assuaged the Iraqis during the USSR's tilt to Iran; but in the postwar situation, with military supplies less politically useful and with Moscow's continuing efforts to woo Iran, problems in Soviet-Iraqi relations loomed on the horizon. The meetings between Soviet and Iraqi diplomats once Iran had accepted UN Resolution 598 were described by the Soviet media as taking place in an atmosphere "of frankness and friendliness" and as being "constructive and businesslike."[64] Nonetheless, Moscow could take solace from the fact that the dispute over poison gas led to a deterioration in US-Iraqi relations,[65] as did US efforts to prevent Argentina from developing the medium-range *Condor II* missile that was being developed with Iraqi financial assistance.[66] Reflecting the deteriorating US-Iraqi relations, Iraqi Foreign Minister Tariq 'Aziz declared on 19 September that he would not agree to New York as the site of Iran-Iraq peace talks for security reasons and because "I cannot go to a town where there is a campaign against the Arabs."[67] In addition, a projected plan for Iraq to buy an idled US steel plant in Texas fell through.[68] Although the anti-Iraqi economic sanctions were never enacted by Congress, US-Iraqi relations deteriorated further in mid-November when a senior US diplomat was expelled from Iraq and the US, in turn, expelled an Iraqi diplomat.[69]

MOSCOW AND THE OTHER GULF STATES

While Moscow was able, at least in the short run, to profit diplomatically from the deterioration in US-Iraqi relations, it had to take actions of its own to improve its position elsewhere in the Gulf. On 1 August, the Soviet Union and Qatar announced the establishment of diplomatic relations, Qatar being the fourth GCC state (after Kuwait, the United Arab Emirates, and Oman) to have done so.[70] As in the case of Oman's establishment of diplomatic ties with the USSR in 1985 (see *MECS* 1984–85, pp. 50, 414–15), Qatar's move appeared, at least in part, to stem from a dispute with the US. In March 1988, the US had protested against Qatar's illegal acquisition of US *Stinger* missiles and asked for their return. When Qatar, involved in a territorial dispute with neighboring Bahrain, wanted the US to get Bahrain to relinquish its claim to the settlement of Zubara on Qatar's western coast in return for giving back the *Stingers* (or at least telling the US their serial numbers, so the US could trace the illegal diversion), Washington refused, reportedly because such US action would infringe on Bahrain's sovereignty.[71] Subsequently Qatar moved to establish diplomatic relations with the USSR, and Moscow, in turn, used the Qatari action to try to strengthen its position in the Gulf. In early November, Qatari Foreign Secretary Shaykh Hamad Ibn Sulaym al-Thani went to Moscow and met with a number of Soviet officials, including Foreign Minister Shevardnadze. The joint communiqué, issued at the end of his visit, supported the Soviet proposal for a UN regional security system to ensure the safety of shipping in the Gulf.[72] Moscow also used the opportunity provided by the visit to appeal for the establishment of diplomatic relations with Bahrain and Saudi Arabia, the only two remaining GCC countries not to have diplomatic relations with the Soviet Union.[73]

Moscow's relations with Kuwait, long the friendliest GCC state to Moscow, also showed improvement in 1988 although, as in the past, Kuwait cleverly moved to improve its relations with both superpowers to maximize its security. In what was in some ways a repetition of the 1984 events (see *MECS* 1983–84, pp. 39–41), Kuwait appealed to the US for weapons, ran into Congressional opposition, was courted by Moscow which signed an arms deal with it, and then went on to sign a major arms deal with the US. In 1988, however, US-Kuwaiti relations were much closer than in 1984, both because of the tanker reflagging and because of Kuwait's tough stand against terrorism (a Kuwaiti airliner had been hijacked in March 1988, but Kuwait refused the demands of the hijackers; see chapter on Kuwait). Consequently, the Reagan Administration actively fought Congressional opposition and ultimately secured

Congressional support for an arms sale worth almost $2bn., which included 40 F-18 fighter planes and antiship *Maverick* missiles. The fact that Saudi Arabia, which had also been seeking a major arms deal with the US, turned instead to Britain as a result of Congressional opposition was another factor influencing the Congressional decision to approve the sale. But Kuwait also compromised by agreeing not to have refueling capability for the F-18s and to forgo the air-to-ground version of the *Maverick* missiles, thus satisfying Congressional critics who feared that otherwise the weapons could be used against Israel by Kuwait or another Arab state to which the weapons could be transferred.[74]

While Congress debated the arms sale, Kuwait signed a deal with the Soviet Union on 9 July, reportedly for an estimated $300m., with Kuwait Defense Minister Shaykh Nawaf al-Ahmad stating that the agreement included 245 Soviet BMD-2 armored personnel carriers.[75] Following the arms agreement, Kuwaiti Chief of Staff Maj. Gen. Muzayyid 'Abd al-Rahman al-Sani' journeyed to Moscow where he met with the Soviet Chief of Staff Marshal Sergei Akhromeyev. The latter was quoted by the Kuwaiti news service as saying that Moscow would "consider" any specific arms request by Kuwait and indicated that the response would be "positive."[76]

In sum, therefore, Moscow's position in the Gulf may be considered to have been strengthened in 1988. The end of the war led to an improvement in Soviet-Iranian relations while Moscow did not lose any significant diplomatic ground in Iraq, in part because of the sharp deterioration of US-Iraqi relations. In addition, Soviet-Kuwaiti relations remained good, while Moscow scored a gain to its position by establishing diplomatic relations with Qatar. Saudi Arabia and Bahrain, on the other hand, continued to resist Soviet offers to establish diplomatic ties.

MOSCOW, ISRAEL, AND THE PEACE PROCESS

Moscow was to face a more difficult set of problems in dealing with the Arab-Israeli conflict in 1988. On the one hand, it wanted to cultivate good relations with Israel (or at least the appearance of good relations), so as to positively impress the US and also create the conditions for convening an international conference on the ME. On the other hand, however, it also sought to cultivate the PLO again, now that the 'Arafat-Husayn agreement had been declared null and void by the 1987 PNC meeting in Algiers. In addition, the *intifada,* which broke out in December 1987, caught the Soviet Union — as well as Israel — by surprise, and it was to take almost six weeks for Moscow to react to it officially.

To be sure, the USSR moved quickly, from a propaganda point of view, to try to exploit the *intifada.* Thus, already in December 1987 a Soviet government report linked the Israeli "repression" of the protestors with a newly signed US-Israeli military cooperation agreement;[77] nor was Moscow silent with regard to the US abstention on a UN Security Council resolution condemning Israel.[78] Yet, aside from condemning Israeli policy and constantly linking the US to Israeli actions, Moscow took no substantive action in regard to the uprising until mid-January, despite Arab urgings.[79] There were, of course, the usual Palestinian solidarity meetings, a World Federation of Trade Unions declaration, a statement by Soviet Muslims, an Afro-Asian People's Solidarity Organization condemnation, and even a message from Gorbachev to 'Arafat noting that the "violent measures Israelis were using against the

Palestinians aroused anger and indignation in the Soviet people."[80] Interestingly, the Gorbachev message also noted that "one must not ensure one's own rights and security by flouting the rights of others" — a statement which foreshadowed Gorbachev's later remarks to 'Arafat in Moscow, that the PLO had to take into consideration Israel's security needs. In addition, perhaps concerned that its consular delegation in Israel might be terminated by Israel for lack of a reciprocal Israeli mission in Moscow — at a time when having accurate information on developments in Israel was highly important — Moscow agreed in principle in mid-January to receive an Israeli consular delegation, although no date was set for the visit.[81] The Foreign Ministry press spokesman, Gennady Gerasimov, stated in a press briefing that the resumption of Soviet-Israeli relations would be possible "within the process of a Middle East settlement."[82]

The major Soviet response to the uprising came on 20 January when Soviet Foreign Minister Shevardnadze wrote a letter to the UN secretary-general, in which he called for the Security Council to begin consultations at the foreign minister level, to both establish and start up a mechanism for an international conference on the ME.[83] This was an effective propaganda ploy for Moscow, given that both Israel and the US rejected the Shevardnadze proposal while the Arab states generally supported it.[84] Nonetheless, the US was galvanized into action by the Palestinian uprising to the point that Secretary of State George Shultz, after first dispatching Philip Habib and Richard Murphy to the ME, set out himself on what was to be the first of four trips in the winter and spring to bring about a peace agreement (see chapter on the United States and the Middle East). Moscow's negative public reaction to the peace efforts of the American envoys generally emphasized two points. First, that the US efforts were just another attempt to make a "separate deal," like the Camp David agreement, while in the process diverting attention from the Palestinian uprising.[85] Second, that the US portrayal of the uprising as "spontaneous" was merely an effort to undermine and discredit the PLO.[86] Popular Front for the Liberation of Palestine (PFLP) leader Na'if Hawatima, who was invited to Moscow in early February by the Afro-Asian People's Solidarity Organization, noted in an interview with *Izvestiia*:

> The aim of all these allegations is clear — to discredit the PLO as allegedly not enjoying authority and influence among the population of the occupied territories and instill mistrust of this organization. To our deep regret, some Arabs have fallen into this propaganda trap.[87]

In addition, Soviet propaganda, which all along had been linking Israel's repression of the Palestinians on the West Bank and Gaza to US support of Israel, cited the US plan to close the PLO mission to the UN as yet another anti-Palestinian and anti-Arab action.[88]

Gorbachev's announcement in early February that he was pulling Soviet troops out of Afghanistan strengthened the Soviet position in the Arab world. In his messages to Arab heads of state about the withdrawal, Gorbachev reportedly warned them against accepting the Shultz ME peace plan, while stating that the withdrawal from Afghanistan "would help the USSR devote more time to other Middle East problems like the Gulf War and the Palestinians."[89]

Meanwhile, Shultz was having a difficult time during his journeys to the ME. While no side, including Syria, gave an out-and-out "no" to his plan, there was little support for it beyond then Israeli Foreign Minister Shimon Peres and Egyptian President Husni Mubarak (see chapter on the Middle East peace process). As it became clear that the Palestinian uprising was continuing and that Shultz's efforts had proved unsuccessful, and with another US-Soviet summit again on the horizon, Moscow took a less negative role in ME diplomacy, seeking to win Israeli and American support for an international conference. In its description of the meeting between Shevardnadze and the seven-man Arab committee which came to Moscow in mid-March to discuss ME problems, TASS, while emphasizing that Israel had to withdraw from *all* occupied territory, nonetheless also stated that the participants in the talks agreed on the need to ensure the right of *all* states and peoples of the region to a safe existence. It also expressed the view that in evaluating the US peace proposals, the main criterion should be the extent to which "they accord with the task of achieving a comprehensive and lasting Middle East settlement with due regard for *the balance of interests of all the parties* involved in the conflict."[90] The TASS report also noted that the sides agreed that the international conference "should be a permanently functioning forum within the framework of which talks would be held and *mutually acceptable decisions taken*" (author's emphasis). Then Gorbachev himself, meeting in early April with the general secretary of the Italian Communist Party, Alessandro Natta, appeared to further soften the Soviet position on renewing diplomatic relations with Israel when he stated that "within the framework of preparing to hold the [international] conference, a way will be found also toward renewing normal relations between the USSR and Israel." In an obvious effort to demonstrate that the conference would not be coercive, Gorbachev also reportedly noted that "the most varied multilateral and bilateral talks could take place within it," and, instead of calling for PLO representation at the conference, referred only to representatives of the Palestinian people.[91]

The main Soviet signal to Israel was to come during 'Arafat's visit to Moscow in early April. During talks with Shevardnadze and Gorbachev, the PLO leader was told that Israel's interests, including its security interests, had to be taken into consideration in any peace settlement along with those of the Palestinians. Specifically, Gorbachev noted:

> The Palestinian people has extensive international support and this is the earnest of the solution of the main question for the Palestinian people — the question of self-determination. Just as *recognition of the State of Israel and account for its security interests,* the solution of this question is a necessary element of the establishment of peace...in the region on the basis of the principles of international law.
>
> The Soviet Union persistently works for a just and all-embracing settlement *with due account for the interests of all — both Arabs, including Palestinians, and Israel.* It is prepared to interact constructively with all the participants in the peace process.
>
> The Soviet view of the essence of the settlement is the following:
>
> The withdrawal of Israeli troops from territories occupied in 1967 — the West Bank of the Jordan, the Gaza Strip, and the Syrian Golan Heights — is the key precondition of a settlement.
>
> The Palestinian people *has the right to self-determination in the same*

> *measure as it is ensured for the people of Israel.* How will the Palestinians [*sic*!] exercise this right is exclusively their own business.
>
> An international conference under the aegis of the UN organization is the most effective mechanism of a settlement. *Recognition by all its participants of Resolutions 242 and 338 of the UN Security Council and the lawful rights of the Palestinian people, including the right to self-determination, should become the legal basis of the conference.* The conference should be attended by representatives of all sides drawn into the conflict, including the Arab people of Palestine, and also the permanent members of the UN Security Council.
>
> The conference presupposes most diverse forms of interaction of its participants. As to the role of the permanent members of the UN Security Council, it will be to create a constructive atmosphere for the conduct of talks at the conference. For this purpose, in particular, they can collectively or individually table proposals and recommendations.
>
> The invitations to all participants in the conference are to be sent by the UN secretary-general.

Gorbachev also showed an understanding attitude to the idea of a single Arab delegation at the international conference, TASS said.[92]

While Gorbachev's comments may have been aimed at convincing Israel it had nothing to fear from an international conference, it would appear that 'Arafat, despite his assertion that this was "the most successful of all his visits" and that there was "complete unity of views," did not like all that he heard.[93] Not only did the TASS statement note that there was a "businesslike atmosphere" (the usual Soviet term for very low-level agreement), but 'Arafat, after leaving the USSR, said that Gorbachev did not ask him to recognize Israel, an assertion that would appear to be inconsistent with both the tone and content of Gorbachev's public statement.[94] Two of the issues that may have irked 'Arafat were Gorbachev's unwillingness to state that the PLO was the sole legitimate representative of the Palestinian people and his refusal to use the term "Palestinian state"; the Soviet leader limited himself to the more ambiguous term "self-determination." These may well have been further tactical gestures to the Israeli leadership which was united on its opposition to the PLO and to a Palestinian state, if on little else, as well as to the US, which also opposed the PLO and a Palestinian state. In an interview with a Kuwaiti newspaper, a Soviet Foreign Ministry official, Alexander Ivanov Galitsyn, in response to a question about a Palestinian state, noted that "it was the first time the Soviet leadership did not discuss a Palestinian state. This is not a rescindment [*sic*!] of the Soviet stand, but we believe some flexibility should exist."[95] He then went on to state in response to a question about Palestinians who were dispossessed in 1948:

> We as realistic politicians can only discuss the establishment of a state in the West Bank and Gaza. Palestinians living abroad can return to this state. Israel is a *fait accompli.* Talking about the repatriation of the 1948 Palestinians is something extreme.

Gorbachev's gesture to Israel during 'Arafat's visit was accompanied by a further low-level improvement in state-to-state relations between the USSR and Israel. Komsomol, the youth organization of the Soviet Communist Party (CPSU), invited a group of Mapam (a left-of-center, but non-Communist party) youth to visit the USSR;[96] Soviet ham radio operators were permitted to talk to their counterparts in Israel;[97] a famous Soviet singer, Alla Pugachova, gave concerts in Israel,[98] and the Soviet Union even began to allow Soviet Jews to visit Israel as tourists.[99] There appeared to be a brief cooling of ties in April after the assassination of Abu Jihad, which the Soviet media blamed on Israel and linked to the signing of a memorandum on security cooperation between the US and Israel; this appeared to be yet another example of Soviet disinformation aimed at weakening the US position in the Arab world.[100] Still, Moscow also welcomed the apparent reconciliation between Syrian President Hafiz al-Asad and 'Arafat that was precipitated by the assassination, with Moscow Radio, in Arabic, hailing it as "a very important event."[101] It was also possible that Soviet negotiators took a hard line on the ME during Shultz's visit to Moscow in late April because Moscow felt it had to demonstrate a tougher ME stance in the aftermath of the Abu Jihad assassination (Abu Jihad was after all, a close comrade of 'Arafat, who had just visited Moscow). Whatever the reason, Assistant Secretary of State Richard Murphy reportedly told Israel's UN ambassador, Moshe Arad, that the talks were "not productive" and that the Soviets were "rigid" in their attitudes.[102]

By the beginning of May, however, with a US-Soviet summit less than a month away, Moscow again began to send signals to Israel. Peres made a surprise visit to Hungary — the first such visit by a major Israeli leader to a Soviet bloc state (other than Romania) since the 1967 war. Peres, who had been interviewed by the Hungarian government newspaper in April (a month after the formal establishment of the diplomatic interest sections agreed upon in 1987),[103] met with a number of top Hungarian officials, including Prime Minister Karoly Grosz.[104] Given the very close ties between the USSR and Hungary, it is difficult to believe that the Soviet Union had not approved the visit, despite Shevardnadze's assertion at a news conference in mid-May that "the visit by the Israeli foreign minister to Hungary has no bearing on Soviet-Israeli relations. This was an independent step, taken within the framework of bilateral relations."[105]

From Hungary, Peres went on to Madrid, to a meeting of the Socialist International where, as in 1987, he had meetings with Soviet officials. This time he was reportedly assured by Soviet Middle East specialist Alexander Zotov that the proposed international conference would not have the authority to impose a settlement.[106] Interestingly, lest Prime Minister Shamir assumed that Peres was using the meeting for partisan political purposes on the eve of the Israeli Knesset elections, World Jewish Congress President Edgar Bronfman, who was visiting the USSR, was given a message to carry to Shamir that emphasized the same point.[107] Meanwhile, to improve the atmosphere further, there was another marked increase in the exodus of Soviet Jews, with 1,086 leaving in April and 1,145 in May — both monthly figures higher than any month since 1981.[108]

As the date of the summit neared, Moscow stepped up its diplomatic activity. On 18 May, Peres met with the Soviet ambassador to the US, Yuri Dubinin, in Washington and was read a Soviet position paper on the ME.[109] Once again Peres was told that in Moscow's view, an international conference could not impose a settlement, and also that any negotiations had to be based on UN Resolution 242.[110] While Dubinin again pressed the issue of Palestinian self-determination, he also promised to look into the delay in the Soviet issuing of visas for Israel's consular delegation that was due to go to Moscow. A week later, Peres's adviser Nimrod Novick was told by Vladimir Tarasov, deputy director of the Soviet Foreign Ministry's Middle East Department, that Moscow would issue visas for the Israeli consular delegation after the superpower summit.[111] Peres, predictably, sought to get the maximum political benefit from the Tarasov statement, stating that the USSR had come a long way in its relations with Israel, while Shamir's supporters, also predictably, sought to minimize the move. Yossi Ben-Aharon, director-general of Shamir's office, accused Peres of "constant theatrics" in depicting the USSR as moving toward a more favorable attitude toward Israel.[112] It should be noted that Shamir and his Likud backers were not the only ones skeptical about the amount of genuine movement in the Soviet position. A number of US officials, including Secretary of State Shultz, expressed similar skepticism, with one American close to the ME negotiations remarking that Peres was engaged in "wishful thinking."[113]

It was perhaps to quiet such skeptics that Gorbachev, in his press conference following the summit, went further than ever in seeking to reassure Israel that Moscow would take Israeli interests into account at an international conference:

> We stand for a political settlement of all issues, with due account for the interests of all sides concerned and, of course, for the principled provisions of the relevant UN resolutions. We are talking about the fact that all the Israeli-occupied lands be returned and the Palestinian people's rights be restored. We said to President Reagan how we view the role of the US, but we cannot decide for the Arabs in what form the Palestinians will take part in the international conference. Let the Arabs themselves decide, while the Americans and we should display respect for their choice.
>
> Furthermore, we ought to recognize the right of Israel to security and the right of the Palestinian people to self-determination. In what form — let the Palestinians together with their Arab friends decide that. This opens up prospects for active exchanges, for a real process. Anyway, it seems to me that such an opportunity is emerging.
>
> I will disclose one more thing: we said that following the start of a conference — a normal, effective conference, rather than a front for separate talks — a forum which would be interrelated with bilateral, tripartite, and other forms of activity, we will be ready to handle the issue of settling diplomatic relations with Israel.
>
> We are thus introducing one more new element. This shows that we firmly stand on the ground of reality, on the ground of recognition of the balance of interests. Naturally, there are principal issues — the return of the lands, the right of the Palestinian people to self-determination. I should reiterate: we proceed from the premise that the Israeli people and the State of Israel have the right to their security because there can be no security of one at the expense of the other. A solution that would untie this very tight knot should be found.[114]

When one analyzes the Soviet leader's statement, it appears to be a Soviet version of an "evenhanded" position on the Arab-Israeli conflict. While Gorbachev called for the return of all lands occupied by Israel and the Palestinian people's rights of self-determination, he did not stipulate a specific role for the PLO at the conference, leaving that for the Palestinians and the Arabs to decide. In addition, he stated that Soviet-Israeli diplomatic relations could be restored following the start of the conference, and that the USSR recognized Israel's right to security. Much of what Gorbachev said was vague; nonetheless, the tone toward Israel was positive, something recognized even by Shamir who noted in New York that Gorbachev was a "great man and a great leader,"[115] and that the tone of Soviet statements had changed.[116] Shamir, however, questioned whether the substance of the Soviet position had changed, and indicated that, having been invited to meet with Shevardnadze in New York, he would, as in the past, press for increased emigration of Soviet Jews to Israel and the restoration of diplomatic relations.

The Soviet leadership, in deciding to arrange the Shevardnadze-Shamir meeting, seems to have been motivated by one major consideration. With Shamir's Likud Party gaining in the polls against Labor, there was a good chance that Shamir would form Israel's next government, and Moscow may well have wished to signal its willingness to deal with him. The Soviets sent Shamir a further signal during the talks — which both sides publicly characterized as "useful and constructive" — by announcing the time of the forthcoming Israeli consular visit to Moscow (mid-July).[117] This enabled Shamir to demonstrate to the Israeli public that he, too, could obtain benefits from Moscow, not just Peres. Several days later Israel agreed to renew, for an additional three months, the visas of the Soviet consular delegation in Israel, thus enabling Moscow to keep a diplomatic presence in Israel.[118] On 18 July, the Israeli diplomatic delegation arrived in Moscow.[119]

RELATIONS WITH OTHER ARAB STATES AND THE PLO

While Moscow was moving to improve its ties with Israel, it was not neglecting the Arab world. On the eve of the Arab summit in Algiers in early June, the Soviet leadership could probably draw satisfaction from a number of developments that seemed to improve Moscow's position among the Arabs — despite the warming of Soviet-Israeli relations. First and foremost, its decision to leave Afghanistan had removed a great deal of the perception of a Soviet "threat" to the Arab world. On 14 May, three weeks before the Arab summit, the Soviet commander in Afghanistan, Lt. Gen. Boris Gromov, promised that 25% of the Soviet forces would be out of Afghanistan by the end of May.[120] Second, a number of the inter-Arab and regional disputes that had plagued Soviet policy in the past seemed on their way to resolution. On 4 April, Ethiopia and Somalia agreed to normalize relations,[121] and on 16 May Algeria and Morocco announced their decision to restore diplomatic relations after a break of 12 years because of the conflict over the former Spanish Sahara[122] (see chapter on inter-Arab relations). Next, Libya, on 26 May, declared an end to its war with Chad, and Qadhdhafi stated he would recognize the Habré Government of Chad with which he had long been in conflict.[123] Diplomatic relations were restored between the two countries at the beginning of October (see chapter on Libya). In addition, Qadhdhafi moved to improve ties with Tunisia, another country with which he had been in conflict. The move toward greater cooperation in the Maghrib was seen as a positive development by Moscow, not only because it reduced conflict in the region and laid the foundation for greater inter-Arab cooperation, but also because the Soviet leadership may have felt that, acting together, such major North African states as Algeria and Morocco could curb Qadhdhafi's often erratic behavior.[124] It should be noted, however, that serious problems continued to exist in the Maghrib. In September, a major battle took place between Polisario forces and the Moroccan Army, and in October large-scale rioting erupted in Algeria, which threatened the regime of Chedli Benjedid, a development which greatly concerned Moscow since Algeria was one of its closest Arab friends.[125]

A third development improving the Soviet position in the Arab world was Moscow's *rapprochement* with Egypt, which reached its culmination with the visit of Egyptian Foreign Minister 'Ismat 'Abd al-Majid to Moscow on 19 May (see chapter on Egypt). 'Abd al-Majid, the highest-ranking Egyptian to make an official visit to the Soviet Union since 1977, met both with Shevardnadze and Gorbachev (according to an Egyptian source, Moscow made a change in 'Abd al-Majid's itinerary so that Gorbachev could personally meet with him, to symbolize the improvement in Soviet-Egyptian relations).[126] During the visit, the two states signed an agreement whereby the USSR would expand the annual production capacity of the steel mill at Hilwan from 850,000 tons to 1.5m. tons and would complete the aluminum plant at Naj' Hammadi.[127] In addition, Egypt and the USSR signed an agreement to establish an intergovernmental commission on trade and economic cooperation.[128]

In seeking to explain the rapid warming of Soviet-Egyptian relations, it would appear that a decision had been made in Moscow to reject the old policy of trying to isolate Egypt because of the Camp David agreements, if only because Egypt had successfully reintegrated into the Arab world by the beginning of 1988 despite Camp David. Instead, given the fact that Egypt had become an active supporter of an international conference to solve the Arab-Israeli conflict, Moscow evidently decided to work with Egypt and capitalize on its increased influence in the Arab world to help arrange for the conference or, at the minimum, to isolate politically and bring diplomatic pressure on Israel and the US who continued to oppose the conference. The decision of Moscow's close Arab ally, South Yemen, to restore diplomatic relations with Egypt in early February may be seen as a major signal of the change in Soviet policy.[129] As a sign of the new *rapprochement,* Moscow Radio broadcast an Arabic language interview with 'Abd al-Majid in which he praised the improvement in Soviet-Egyptian relations, and the Egyptian foreign minister invited Shevardnadze to visit Egypt, a trip he was to make in early 1989.[130]

The improvement in Soviet-Egyptian relations, like the improvement in Soviet-Israeli relations, was not greeted warmly by the two Arab states most strongly opposed to both Egypt and Israel — Libya and Syria. While Libya made its opposition known in editorials and radio broadcasts which raised questions about Soviet policy,[131] it continued its close military relationship with the Soviet Union as visits by the Soviet air defense commander at the end of December 1987[132] and the commander in chief of the Soviet Navy in mid-March 1988 indicated.[133] Nonetheless, Qadhdhafi's decision to moderate his foreign policy and improve his ties with neighboring states may have been due, in part, to his having received nothing but oral support from Moscow during his confrontations with the US in 1986, and to his feeling that he would be better protected by becoming part of a Maghrib alignment.

Syrian opposition to the Soviet policy was a more serious problem for Moscow. While Syria was the primary Soviet ally in the Arab world, its quarrels with Iraq, Egypt, and the PLO continued to hamper Soviet efforts to achieve Arab unity, and

Syria's continued confrontational approach to Israel raised the prospect of an Israeli-Syrian war at a time not desired by Moscow. Throughout 1988, the USSR continued to repeat the message Gorbachev had given Asad in 1987 — that in the nuclear age, political solutions had to be found for regional conflicts.[134] For their part, the Syrians noted publicly that there had been no change in Israeli policy and that Syria had to receive more weapons to keep up with the weapons supplied to Israel by the US or developed by Israel itself, such as the new Israeli satellite.[135] There were a number of reports of major arms deals between the Soviet Union and Syria in 1988 which, if true, would indicate that Moscow had decided to continue to arm Syria with modern weaponry so as to maintain its influence in that country even as Moscow was improving ties with Egypt and Israel.[136] The Soviet Union did deny, however, a *New York Times* charge that it was supplying poison gas equipment to Syria;[137] and Soviet commentators minimized the agreement reached with Syria in May 1988 that gave the USSR quasi-base rights for its fleet to use the Syrian port of Tartus. *Krasnaia Zvezda* called it a "material and technical supply point" which included "two tenders and two storehouses on dry land" that was to be used by the Soviet fleet for preventive maintenance and for rest and relaxation for Soviet sailors.[138] Possibly because it was not getting all the weaponry it wanted from the Soviet Union, Syria was rumored to be trying to acquire M-9 missiles from China.[139]

In any case, by the eve of the Arab summit in June the Soviet position in the Arab world had been strengthened despite the inter-Arab conflicts that had remained, and the lack of Syrian and Libyan support for the Soviet policy of *rapprochement* with Egypt and Israel. Gorbachev's message to the Arab summit called for Arab unity on a "constructive and realistic basis" (a change in the previous Soviet call for Arab unity on an "anti-imperialist basis"), for Palestinian self-determination, and for free development and safe existence for all states and peoples in the region.[140]

As far as the summit itself was concerned, Soviet ME commentators hailed what they perceived as the unity in the Arab world displayed by the conference, unity highlighted by the fact that Qadhdhafi attended an Arab summit for the first time in 15 years.[141] The summit also met the Soviet policy goals of calling for an international conference on the ME, with the PLO represented on an equal footing; supporting Palestinian self-determination and national independence; calling for the complete withdrawal of all Israeli troops from the occupied territories; and criticizing US support of Israel.[142] Nonetheless, the summit did not reject the Shultz plan and, while giving the PLO oral support, did not provide it with the funding it requested to support the *intifada.* In addition, the degree of Arab unity was something less than the Soviet commentators had indicated as 'Arafat somewhat caustically noted in a *New Times* interview.[143] With the rise of *glasnost,* such journals as *New Times* felt free to break with the *Pravda* and TASS lines on the summit, and Leonid Medvenko asserted:

> ...My impression was that effective unity as regards the Palestinian uprising was patently lacking. Not just cooperation, but even mutual understanding between the Arab patriotic organizations is only just beginning to take effect....[144]

So matters stood until King Husayn changed the diplomatic equation in the ME by publicly severing Jordan's connection with the West Bank at the end of July. Whatever the king's motivations (see chapter on Jordan), his action, together with pressure from the leaders of the *intifada* on the West Bank and in Gaza, led the PLO in less than four months to call for an independent Palestinian state at the PNC meeting in Algiers in mid-November. In the interim, Moscow took a cautious stand. Unwilling to alienate Jordan, with which relations had been slowly improving, and concerned about the continuing divisions within the PLO, the Soviet leadership issued no formal Soviet government statement on the king's action, and Soviet commentators were circumspect in their analysis of it. A newspaper interview in late August with Karen Brutents, deputy director of the CPSU Central Committee's International Department, appeared to reflect Moscow's hopes as to the most desirable outcome:

> ...It is difficult now to discuss this action...its results are unclear and...the Palestinian stand on it is not specified...however, if the Jordanian move consolidates the Palestinian stand, leads to an active and effective Palestinian participation in the international peace conference, and secures further Jordanian support for this direction, then the results of this move will be positive.[145]

During the three-and-a-half months between the king's severing of ties with the West Bank and the PNC meeting in Algiers in November, Moscow played host to a number of different Palestinian groupings, from the mainstream Fath to the Marxist Democratic Front for the Liberation of Palestine (DFLP), as strategy was being worked out for the PNC. That Moscow was in favor of the PLO declaring publicly its support for a two-state solution for the Arab-Israeli conflict was in little doubt, because precisely this solution had been part of the Soviet ME peace plan since 1976. Writing in *Izvestiia* in mid-September, as Palestinian thinking moved toward a two-state solution, the paper's commentator, Konstantin Geivandov, made this point clear:

> The Palestinian uprising on the Israeli-occupied West Bank of the Jordan River and in the Gaza Strip, now in its 10th month, could not better illustrate the new realities that have arisen in recent decades in this region of the Middle East. And against that backdrop, the step taken by the Jordanian leadership in announcing an end to its administrative and legal ties to the West Bank of the Jordan was a logical one — logical in so far as it is intended to help some people rid themselves of persistent illusions and remind others of their historical responsibility.
>
> First, King Husayn's decision dashed the hopes of those who were counting on the "Jordanian scenario" to settle the Palestinian problem and identified the real people who must be dealt with in negotiations on this problem, i.e., the Palestinians. Second, it offered the Palestine Liberation Organization the status of sole legitimate representative of the Palestinian people, a fact that was confirmed at the recent Arab summit meeting in Algiers, and it made possible a whole series of political and diplomatic initiatives aimed at securing the Palestinians' right of self-determination.
>
> One would like to believe that the Palestine Liberation Organization will use the existing situation for the good of its people. Specifically, an extraordinary session of the Palestine National Council is planned for October, at the Palestine Liberation Organization's initiative, for the proposed purpose of

discussing ways and means of restoring the Palestinian Arabs' national rights. The possibility of declaring an independent Palestinian state and creating a government-in-exile is one such means that is under discussion. In the given case, what is intended?

First of all, let us return to the 1947 UN Resolution No. 181 on the partition of Palestine, which became the legal foundation for the appearance of the State of Israel. But this resolution stipulated the creation of two states from the partition of Palestine: Jewish and Arab. And each was assigned territory of appropriate dimensions. The second part of this United Nations' resolution has yet to be fulfilled, and it must be acknowledged that the leaders of certain Arab states are by no means the least to blame for this. Therefore, it is proposed that if the PLO, in acting to gain the Palestinians' right to self-determination, now declares the creation of an independent Arab state on the grounds of Resolution 181, it will rectify an injustice permitted more than 40 years ago. Moreover, the Palestine Liberation Organization's recognition of Resolution 181 would lay the groundwork for the observance of international law in the Arab-Israel conflict.[146]

The PNC that was held in mid-November (possibly a tactical mistake, because holding it after, rather than before, the 1 November Israeli elections cost the PLO a chance to influence Israeli public opinion),[147] decided to establish a Palestinian state, renounce terrorism, and accept UN Resolution 242 (implicitly recognizing Israel's right to exist) with the proviso that an international peace conference was held. The vote in favor was 253–46 with the DFLP and PFLP opposing the acceptance of 242, but agreeing to go along with the consensus[148] — reportedly, in part, because of intensive lobbying by the Soviet Union[149] (for more details, see chapter on the Palestine Liberation Organization).

In any case, the PLO action did not go far enough to meet US conditions for talks with the PLO, which included the unambiguous acceptance of UN Resolution 242, explicit renunciation of terrorism (the PLO document obfuscated this somewhat), and explicit recognition of Israel's right to exist. Moscow itself exercised some ambiguity in reacting to the PNC declaration, perhaps in an effort not to alienate either Israel or the US, both of whom continued to oppose a Palestinian state, and also to mollify the Israelis who were angered by the USSR's vote in October to exclude Israel from the UN. The official Soviet government statement noted only that the USSR "recognized the proclamation of a Palestinian state," not the state itself:

> Resolutions adopted by the extraordinary session of the Palestine National Council held in Algiers have met with interest and approval in the Soviet Union. Taken together, these resolutions, which are infused with the lofty sense of realism and responsibility demonstrated by the leadership of the Palestine Liberation Organization, are a great contribution to the process of a just political settlement in the Middle East.
>
> As a result, a situation has developed in which all parties directly involved in the conflict proceed from a recognition of the fact that the path to peace and peaceful coexistence among Arabs and Israel lies through negotiations based on Security Council Resolutions Nos. 242 and 338, and of the equal rights of Jewish and Arab states to exist in Palestine. It is important that the highest

> representative body of the Palestinian people proclaimed its adherence to generally accepted principles of international intercourse.
>
> The Soviet Union has unfailingly supported the Palestinian people in its efforts to secure its inalienable national rights, including the right to create an independent state of its own. Our people understand the feelings of political uplift and enthusiasm in connection with the decisions taken by the Algiers session of the Palestine National Council. The Soviet Union, true to the fundamental principle of freedom of choice, recognizes the proclamation of a Palestinian state, guided by the understanding that the achievement of a comprehensive settlement will also result, in practice, in the culmination of the historically important process of that state's creation.[150]

Moscow also hailed Egypt's decision to formally recognize the Palestinian state, claiming the decision was a serious blow against Camp David and a contribution to the strengthening of pan-Arab unity.[151]

Meanwhile, the US, still considering 'Arafat a terrorist, denied him a visa to visit the US to address the UN — an action severely criticized in the Arab world, and by Moscow.[152] In a major address to the UN in December, Gorbachev took the opportunity to lash out at the US for its action and expressed Moscow's "solidarity" with the PLO, which had taken a "constructive step facilitating the search for an untangling of the Middle East knot." In another part of his speech, however, Gorbachev made his most extensive statement to date on the "deideologization" of international relations. Given the importance of this section of his speech — and the negative effect it was to have on Moscow's relations with the radical states of the Arab world (and elsewhere) — Gorbachev's words are worth noting in detail:

> The deideologization of interstate relations has become a requirement of the new stage. We are not renouncing our convictions, our philosophy, or traditions. Neither are we calling on anyone else to give up theirs. Yet we are not going to shut ourselves up within the range of our values. That will lead to spiritual impoverishment, for it would mean renouncing so powerful a source of development as sharing all the original things created independently by each nation. In the course of such sharing, each should prove the advantages of his own system, his own way of life and values, but not through words or propaganda alone but through real deeds as well.
>
> That is indeed an honest struggle of ideology, but it must not be carried over into mutual relations between states. Otherwise we will simply not be able to solve a single world problem; arrange broad, mutually advantageous, and equitable cooperation between peoples; manage rationally the achievement of the scientific and technical revolutions; transform world economic relations; protect the environment; overcome underdevelopment; or put an end to hunger, disease, illiteracy, and other mass ills. Finally, in that case, we will not manage to eliminate the nuclear threat and militarism.[153]

Meanwhile, 'Arafat was continuing to gather support for his Palestinian state, and the US became increasingly isolated because of its denial of a visa to the PLO leader. The UN overwhelmingly (154–2) voted to move to Geneva for a special session where 'Arafat could freely address the organization.[154] In a speech and statement to a press conference there, 'Arafat finally met the American conditions for a US-PLO dialogue;[155] the dialogue was begun in mid-December with a meeting between American Ambassador to Tunisia Robert Pelletreau and PLO leader Yasir 'Abd Rabbuh.[156] Moscow's reaction to this event was ostensibly positive, but the Soviet leadership may well have been concerned that just as the US had successfully mediated peace between Egypt and Israel in the 1973–79 period, and in the process moved Egypt from the Soviet to the American orbit, it would have a similar effect on the PLO by mediating peace between the Palestinians and the Israelis. It was possibly for this reason that the official Soviet statement on the US decision to begin a dialogue with the PLO followed its praise of the American action as an "important positive step" with a call for convening the international conference.[157]

Just as US-PLO relations had begun to improve, so too did Soviet-Israeli relations. This was due, however, less to Soviet actions — the Israeli consular mission in Moscow was severely circumscribed in its activities[158] — than to Israeli policies. At the beginning of December, Israel promptly returned a group of four hijackers who had flown to Israel after seizing a busload of children as hostages and releasing them in return for an aircraft. Moscow warmly praised Israel for its role in the affair and Israel, for the first time since the 1967 war, got a positive treatment in the Soviet press.[159] Gorbachev himself, during his UN visit which took place after the hijacking, was photographed by the Agence France Press shaking hands with Israel's UN ambassador, Yohannan Bein.[160] Gorbachev reportedly told Bein: "I want to thank the Israeli people for the efficient cooperation we received with regard to the hijacked airplane...there is a lot of goodwill and friendship in the Soviet Union toward Israel."[161] Gorbachev had to cut short his stay in the US because of a massive earthquake in Armenia, and here again Israel proved helpful to the USSR. Israel sent medical teams and four tons of medical supplies, and set up a field hospital in the city of Kirovakan. The Israeli team, which was praised in the Soviet press, found and saved three women who had been buried alive in the rubble.[162]

Nonetheless, despite Israel's assistance in these two episodes, there was little letup in Soviet criticism of Israeli actions in the ME. A *Pravda* article on 30 December, for example, took a dim view of the policies of Israel's newly formed coalition government. On the same day, however, *Izvestiia* published an article critical not only of Israeli "terror in the occupied territories," but also of a meeting of Islamic fundamentalists who were planning to wage a *jihad* (holy war) against Israel, and of Damascus-based PLO factions which were trying to undermine 'Arafat's leadership in the PLO.

In sum, 1988 was a very active year for Moscow in the ME, with events in the latter part of the year posing significant challenges for future Soviet diplomacy.

NOTES

For the place and frequency of publications cited here, and for the full name of the publication, news agency, radio station, or monitoring service where an abbreviation is used, please see "List of Sources." Only in the case of more than one publication bearing the same name is the place of publication noted here.

1. E. A. Wayne in *CSM,* 4 January 1989.
2. Celestine Bohlen in *WP,* 28 December 1987.

3. *Pravda,* 28 December 1987.
4. Tehran TV (in Persian), 8 January — DR, 12 January 1988.
5. TASS, International Service, 19 February — DR:SU, 22 February 1988.
6. R. Tehran (in English), 10 February — DR, 11 February 1988.
7. R. Tehran (in Persian), 14 February — DR, 16 February 1988.
8. Tehran TV (in Persian), 12 February — DR, 18 February 1988.
9. R. Tehran (in Persian), 18 February — DR, 19 February 1988.
10. IRNA, 23 February — DR, 23 February 1988.
11. R. Tehran (in Persian), 22 February — DR, 23 February 1988.
12. Don Oberdorfer in *WP,* 10 February; Patrick Tyler, ibid., 8 February 1988.
13. Warren Richey in *CSM,* 14 January 1988.
14. *WP,* 22 February 1988.
15. *NYT,* 1 March 1988.
16. For Iranian descriptions of the demonstrations, IRNA, 4, 6 March — DR, 4, 7 March; Bill Keller in *NYT,* 7 March; David Remnick in *WP,* 7 March 1988.
17. DR, 21 March 1988.
18. Tehran TV, 24 March — DR, 25 March 1988.
19. IRNA (in English), 6 March — DR, 7 March 1988.
20. IRNA, 9 March — DR, 9 March 1988.
21. IRNA (in English), 14 April — DR, 15 April 1988.
22. On the Faw offensive, Patrick Tyler in *WP,* 18 April, 3 May 1988.
23. R. Tehran (in Persian), 19 March — DR, 20 April 1988.
24. TASS, 20 April — DR:SU, 20 April 1988.
25. TASS (in English), 20 April — DR:SU, 21 April; for more balanced descriptions of the battle, John Eishman, Jr. in *NYT,* 19 April; George C. Wilson and Molly Moore, in *WP,* 19 April 1988.
26. TASS (in English), 19 April — DR:SU, 20 April 1988.
27. R. Peace and Progress, 25 April — DR:SU, 26 April 1988.
28. R. Peace and Progress, 12 May — DR:SU, 13 May 1988.
29. *KI,* 27 June — DR, 13 July 1988.
30. R. Moscow (in English), 7 July — DR:SU, 8 July 1988.
31. *Pravda,* 15 July; *Krasnaia Zvezda,* 10 July — DR:SU, 14 July 1988.
32. Fox Butterfield in *NYT,* 16 July 1988.
33. Khomeyni's statement, R. Tehran, 20 July — DR, 21 July; Khomeyni, in his speech, was bitterly critical of both the US and the USSR; see James Bill, "Why Tehran Finally Wants a Gulf Peace," *WP,* 28 August 1988.
34. R. Moscow (in Persian), 18 July — DR:SU, 20 July 1988.
35. IRNA, 21 July — DR, 22 July 1988.
36. *Pravda,* 23 July 1988.
37. IRNA (in English), 11 August — DR, 11 August 1988.
38. KUNA, 10 August — DR:SU, 11 August 1988.
39. For a Soviet view of the historical origins of the Shatt al-'Arab dispute, see Yakov Borovoi and Dmitry Zgersky, "Shatt al-'Arab: The Price of Those 192 Kilometers," *New Times,* No. 37, 1988.
40. *Pravda,* 22 August — *CDSP,* Vol. XL, No. 34, 1988.
41. Alexander Zotov, "A Burden for Pérez de Cuellar," *New Times,* No. 31, 1988.
42. Elaine Sciolino in *NYT,* 5 October 1988.
43. On the debate see *Kayhan,* 18 August — DR, 19 September, and on the Friday Prayer Sermon by Iran's President Ali Khameneh'i, R. Tehran (in Persian), 16 September — DR, 19 September 1988.
44. R. Moscow (in Persian), 12 October — DR:SU, 19 October 1988.
45. IRNA (in English), 18 August — DR, 18 August 1988.
46. IRNA (in English), 25 August — DR, 25 August 1988.
47. IRNA, 3 September — DR, 9 September 1988.
48. IRNA, 27 September — DR, 27 September 1988.
49. IRNA, 17 September — DR, 19 September 1988. Trade was up, however, from the $100m. level of 1986.

50. IRNA, 18 September — DR, 20 September 1988.
51. IRNA (in English), 19 September — DR, 20 September 1988.
52. TASS, 8 December — DR:SU, 9 December 1988.
53. TASS, 6 December — DR:SU, 7 December 1988.
54. Translated in DR:SU, 8 November 1988.
55. *Literaturnaya Gazeta,* 30 November — DR:SU, 1 December 1988.
56. David Ottaway in *WP,* 25 July 1988.
57. Mark Mathews in *Baltimore Sun,* 1 August 1988.
58. R. Peace and Progress (in Persian), 12 September — DR:SU, 15 September 1988.
59. *Pravda,* 11 September 1988.
60. Friday Prayer Sermon by Rafsanjani, R. Tehran, 23 September — DR, 26 September 1988.
61. R. of the Toilers of Iran, 31 July, 12, 16 September — DR, 2 August, 21 September 1988.
62. R. Peace and Progress (in Persian), 5 November — DR:SU, 30 November; Paul Lewin in *NYT,* 3 November 1988.
63. R. Moscow (in Persian), 10 December — DR:SU, 13 December 1988.
64. TASS, 30 July — DR, 1 August; INA, 14 September — DR:SU, 15 September 1988.
65. E. A. Wayne in *CSM,* 12 September 1988, for an analysis of the effect of the poison gas issue on US-Iraqi relations.
66. Don Oberdorfer in *WP,* 14 September 1988.
67. Patrick Tyler in *WP,* 20 September 1988.
68. *NYT,* 23 September 1988.
69. David Ottaway in *WP,* 17 November; Elaine Sciolino in *NYT,* 18 November 1988. Allegedly, the US official had been visiting Kurdish areas of Iraq without the requisite Iraqi government permission.
70. *Pravda,* 1 August 1988.
71. On the US-Qatar dispute, see the reports by John H. Cushman, Jr. in *NYT,* 1 April, and Patrick Tyler in *WP,* 6 October 1988.
72. *Pravda,* 6 November 1988.
73. R. Moscow (in Arabic), 4 November — DR:SU, 7 November 1988.
74. For reports about the progress of the US-Kuwaiti arms deal, see David Ottaway in *WP,* 10 July; E.A. Wayne in *CSM,* 5 August and the AP report in *JP,* 28 August 1988.
75. Cited in *AT* — DR, 18 July 1988.
76. KUNA, 31 August — DR:SU, 1 September 1988.
77. *Pravda,* 20 December 1987.
78. *Pravda,* 24 December 1987.
79. TASS, 28 December — DR:SU, 29 December 1987, reported a meeting between Voronstov and a group of Arab diplomats on 26 December 1987 to discuss "the dangerous situation in the Israeli-occupied Palestinian territories."
80. R. Moscow, 16 January — DR:SU, 19 January 1988.
81. TASS, 26 January — DR:SU, 27 January; R. Jerusalem, 20 January — DR:SU, 20 January 1988. Perhaps as a signal to Moscow, the Israeli Foreign Ministry in December had granted only a one-month extension to the visas of the Soviet consular delegation in December 1987 (interviews with Israeli Foreign Ministry, July 1988, and US Embassy, Moscow, January 1988).
82. TASS, 19 January — DR:SU, 20 January 1988.
83. *Izvestiia,* 22 January — DR:SU, 22 January 1988.
84. Pavel Demchenko in *Pravda,* 2 February 1988.
85. *Pravda,* 26 February 1988.
86. *Pravda,* 9 February 1988.
87. *Izvestiia,* 6 February 1988 — DR:SU, 12 February 1988.
88. TASS, 11 February — DR:SU, 18 February 1988.
89. KUNA, 23 February — DR:SU, 24 February 1988.
90. TASS, 18 March — DR:SU, 21 March 1988. A TASS report on 4 April — DR:SU, 5 April 1988, noted that the USSR had no "fundamental objections" to the intermediate steps preferred by the US, but "such steps can yield a positive result only in the context of a comprehensive settlement."

91. R. Moscow, 3 April — DR:SU, 4 April; Reuters report, *JP*, 31 March 1988.
92. TASS, 9 April — DR:SU, 11 April 1988. (Author's emphasis.)
93. R. Moscow, 9 April — DR:SU, 11 April 1988.
94. AP report, *JP*, 13 April 1988.
95. *Al-Siyasa*, Kuwait, 26 April — DR:SU, 2 May 1988.
96. Michal Yudelman, *JP*, 8 March 1988. Three days later, *JP* reported a meeting between an Israeli and a Soviet diplomat at the UN, in which the Soviet diplomat reportedly stated that the PLO terrorist attack on an Israeli bus in early March was a tremendous mistake, and openly wondered if the PLO had any coherent policy.
97. Jonathan Karp in *JP*, 15 April 1988.
98. For a wry comment on the Pugachova tour, see the article by a former refusenik, Yosef Begun, in *JP*, 14 April 1988. Begun called for more Israeli artists to tour the USSR.
99. Gorbachev's purpose in allowing such tourism may have been to lessen the pressure from Soviet Jews to leave the country permanently. An estimated 10,000 Soviet Jews were to visit Israel in 1988.
100. TASS, 22 April — DR:SU, 25 April; for the text of the memorandum of agreement, see *JP*, 22 April 1988.
101. R. Moscow (in Arabic), 25 April — DR:SU, 26 April 1988.
102. Menachem Shalev and Wolf Blitzer in *JP*, 29 April 1988.
103. For a description of the interview see AP report, *JP*, 15 April 1988.
104. For a description of the Peres visit, which Hungary played down, see Menachem Shalev and Lisa Billig in *JP*, 10 May; and Henry Kamm in *NYT*, 10 May 1988.
105. TASS, 12 May — DR:SU, 13 May 1988.
106. *JP*, 11 May 1988.
107. Bernard Josephs in *JP*, 16 May 1988.
108. David Remnick in *WP*, 9 June; also Philip Taubman in *NYT*, 18 May 1988. For an analysis of developments dealing with Soviet Jewry, see Robert O. Freedman (ed.), *Soviet Jewry in the 1980s* (Durham: Duke University Press, 1989).
109. For the reported text of this document see *JP*, 10 June 1988.
110. Wolf Blitzer in *JP*, 19 May 1988.
111. *JP*, 25 May 1988.
112. Glenn Frankel in *WP*, 25 May 1988.
113. Wolf Blitzer in *JP*, 20 May 1988.
114. *Pravda*, 3 June — DR:SU, 3 June 1988.
115. Elaine Sciolino in *NYT*, 7 June 1988.
116. Wolf Blitzer in *JP*, 9 June 1988.
117. For reports on the Shamir-Shevardnadze talks, Don Oberdorfer in *WP*, 10 June; Elaine Scionlino in NYT, 10 June; and Menachem Shalev in *JP*, 12 June 1988. According to Israeli Foreign Ministry sources, however, Shevardnadze was "disappointed" by his talks with Shamir.
118. Menachem Shalev and Asher Wallfish in *JP*, 13 June 1988.
119. *Izvestiia*, 1 August 1988 carried a description of the role of the Israeli delegation by V.P. Perfilyev, deputy press spokesman. See also AP report in *NYT*, 29 July; and Gary Lee in *WP*, 29 July 1988. It should also be noted that the chief rabbi of the city of Rehovot in Israel, Rabbi Simha Kook, was given a visa to visit the Soviet Union in late June 1988 despite the fact that he put on his visa application that the purpose of his visit was to "teach Jewish Law and visit synagogues"; *JP*, 24 June 1988.
120. Steven R. Weiseman in *JP*, 15 May 1988. Gronov's comments, of course, may also have been intended to influence the atmosphere of the US-Soviet summit at the end of May 1988.
121. TASS, 26 April — DR:SU, 27 April 1988.
122. Reuters report, *NYT*, 17 May 1988.
123. Steven Greenhouse in *NYT*, 27 May. Moscow's positive response to this event — which averted the possibility of a Soviet-American or Soviet-French clash over Chad, may be seen in the TASS report, 30 May — DR:SU, 31 May 1988.
124. R. Moscow (in Arabic), 15 July — DR:SU, 20 July 1988.
125. The concern was reflected in an article in *Pravda*, 7 October 1988.

126. *Al-Musawwar,* 27 May — DR:SU, 3 June. For Gorbachev's speech welcoming 'Abd al-Majid, see *Pravda,* 21 May 1988.
127. AFP, 19 May — DR:SU, 20 May 1988.
128. *Pravda,* 22 May 1988.
129. *WP,* 10 February 1988.
130. R. Moscow (in Arabic), 21 May — DR:SU, 24 May 1988.
131. JANA (in Arabic), 16 September — DR, 20 September 1988.
132. *Krasnaia Zvezda,* 23 December — DR:SU, 24 December 1987.
133. TASS, 14 March — DR:SU, 15 March 1988.
134. Gorbachev's message to Asad on the 25th anniversary of the 8 March 1963 Ba'thist Revolution in Syria, TASS, 7 March — DR:SU, 7 March and Deputy Foreign Minister Yuli Voronstov's talk with Asad in Damascus in July,*Pravda,* 21 July 1988.
135. The clearest exposition of the Syrian position is found in a TASS interview with the outspoken Syrian Defense Minister Mustafa Talas, DR:SU, 6 October 1988.
136. *Davar,* 11 July reported that Moscow was sending *Sukhoi*-24 ground-attack bombers to Syria — DR, 11 July; on 6 July the *JP,* citing Israeli Defense Ministry sources, said Moscow was sending more SS-21 ground-to-ground missiles to Syria. The SU-24 deal was also reported by *al-Ittihad,* Abu Dhabi, on 29 August, along with a sale of MiG-29 aircraft — DR:SU, 29 August. Israeli Defense Minister Yitzhak Rabin, in an interview on Israeli TV on 30 August, discussed a sale "at the beginning of 1988" of tanks and SS-21 missiles and possibly other aircraft — DR, 31 August 1988.
137. *Argumenty i Fakty,* 3–9 September — DR:SU, 2 September 1988. The story originated in the visit to Damascus of the Soviet chief of chemical warfare. It is possible, given Iraq's use of poison gas and its enmity toward Syria, that the Syrian Government wanted countermeasures against Iraq. It is also possible, however, that Syria was actively engaged in the development of chemical weapons itself as a countermeasure against Israel's nuclear capability.
138. *Krasnaia Zvezda,* 15 September — DR:SU, 16 September; for another view of the Tartus "facility," see Robert Pear in *NYT,* 28 August 1988.
139. Ya'acov Lamdan in *JP,* 12 December who cited the Lebanese weekly *al-Muharrir,* and David Ottaway in *WP,* 23 June 1988. Reportedly, Syria's debt to the USSR for military purchases totaled $16.5 bn. by the end of 1988.
140. DR, 7 June 1978.
141. R. Moscow, 10 June — DR:SU, 13 June; TASS, 9 June — DR:SU, 10 June; *Pravda,* 12 June 1988.
142. For the summit communiqué read by Arab League Secretary-General Chedli Klibi on Algerian TV — DR, 10 June; for reports describing the atmosphere of the summit, Youssef Ibrahim in *NYT,* 10 June; and George D. Moffett in *CSM,* 10 June 1988.
143. 'Arafat was interviewed by Leonid Medvenko, "A Time to Throw Stones and a Time to Collect Them," *New Times*, No. 36, 1988.
144. Ibid.
145. *Al-Ittihad,* Abu Dhabi, 23 August — DR:SU, 25 August 1988.
146. *Izvestiia,* 18 September 1988 (translated in *CDSP,* Vol. XL, No. 38, 1988).
147. A terrorist attack on the eve of the election in which several Israelis were killed when their bus was firebombed hardened Israeli attitudes against the PLO. Soviet press spokesman Gennady Gerasimov condemned the attack although he also condemned "state terrorism." However, in a clear rebuke of the perpetrators of the attack, he stated: "With respect to this specific act, one also has to ask: who gains from this, particularly on the eve of the parliamentary elections in Israel?" *Pravda,* 1 November 1988 (translated in *CDSP,* Vol. XL, No. 44, 1988).
148. The text of the political program of the PNC was printed in the *NYT,* 17 November. See also Youssef Ibrahim, ibid., 15 November 1988.
149. George D. Moffett in *CSM,* 15 November 1988.
150. *Pravda,* 19 November (translated in *CDSP,* Vol. XL, No. 46, 1988). Gerasimov gave a legalistic argument for the Soviet Union's limited recognition: "Our practice knows no precedents when a state would be recognized while its territory was under foreign occupation and which had no government at the moment of recognition." TASS (in English), 24 November — DR:SU, 25 November 1988.

151. R. Moscow, 21 November — DR:SU, 22 November 1988.
152. *Izvestiia,* 29 November 1988.
153. *Pravda,* 8 December — DR:SU, 12 December 1988.
154. *WP,* 3 December 1988.
155. 'Arafat's press conference statement was published in *NYT,* 15 December. See also Robert Pear, ibid., 15 December; and David Ottaway and John Goshko in *WP,* 15 December 1988.
156. Patrick Tyler in *WP,* 17 December 1988.
157. *Pravda,* 18 December 1988.
158. Interview with Arye Levin, head of the Israeli consular mission in Moscow, Jerusalem, 4 January 1988.
159. For a Soviet account of the hijacking see Vitaly Bordunov, "A Drama Brought to an Early Finale," *New Times,* No. 50, 1988. Arye Levin himself was interviewed by *New Times* and his photograph appeared in the story.
160. Walter Ruby in *JP,* 9 December 1988.
161. Ibid.
162. David Remnick in *WP,* 22 December 1988.

The Afghanistan Conflict: The Soviet Withdrawal

ALI T. SHEIKH

For Afghanistan, 1988 was a year of decisions and compromise. After nine years of bloody war in Afghanistan, the arduous negotiations in Geneva eventually promised the return of over 100,000 Soviet soldiers from Afghanistan and some 5m. Afghan refugees from neighboring Pakistan and Iran. Except for the Soviet withdrawal, which neared completion at the end of 1988, the future composition of the government in Kabul, the return of refugees, and the reconstruction of Afghanistan all seemed distant goals at year's end.

The war had raged in Afghanistan since April 1978, when the People's Democratic Party of Afghanistan (PDPA) seized power in Kabul, causing a spontaneous reaction and resulting in a mass exodus of the Afghan population to the neighboring countries. The direct Soviet intervention in the last weeks of 1979 rapidly transformed the character and scope of the Afghan resistance. What previously had been a significant yet limited localized tribal warfare, coupled with religious opposition against a reformist and centralized rule, soon became a broader national resistance against a foreign occupation force.

The Soviet intervention was viewed as a move in the direction of the Indian Ocean and the Persian Gulf. Within days of its occurrence, Islamabad called a special session of the Islamic countries' foreign ministers in Islamabad. The conference expelled Afghanistan from its ranks and issued appeals for Islamic solidarity and collective defense of the Muslim world. President Carter offered Islamabad a $400m. aid package and declared the Persian Gulf an area of vital US interests to be defended by all means, including military ones.[1] Pakistan rejected Washington's offer as "peanuts" see (*MECS* 1979–80, pp. 51–52), but later accepted the Reagan Administration's six-year, $3.2bn. package of economic and military aid in 1981.

As the fighting in Afghanistan intensified, American and other regional and international support expanded. Initially, the US provided the Afghan resistance with only Soviet-type equipment that was either replicated in specially adapted factories in Egypt, purchased from former recipients of Soviet military aid, or reportedly purchased from Israel, which had captured Soviet-made weapons in Lebanon. In July 1981, a major press leak claimed that the US was providing the Mujahidin with financial assistance and had arranged the purchase of weapons in the international market; Saudi Arabia had undertaken to provide aid "equal to or greater than that of the US"; and the Egyptians were providing training for the guerrillas and served as the major source of arms — supplying weapons obtained from the Soviet Union during the years of Egyptian-Soviet friendship.[2]

During the period from 1980–87, the US was reported to have orchestrated an expanding multilateral program of some $2bn. in weapons aid to the resistance.[3] The government aid was supplemented by a significant separate pipeline from Saudi

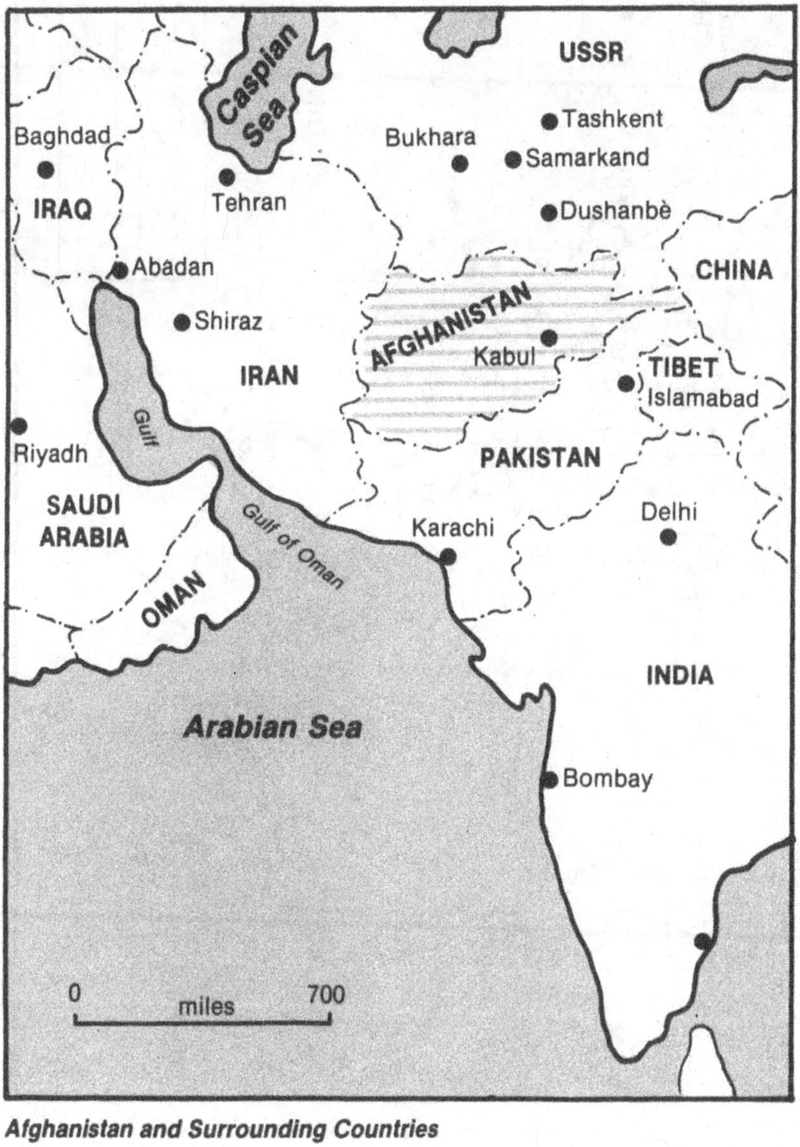

Afghanistan and Surrounding Countries

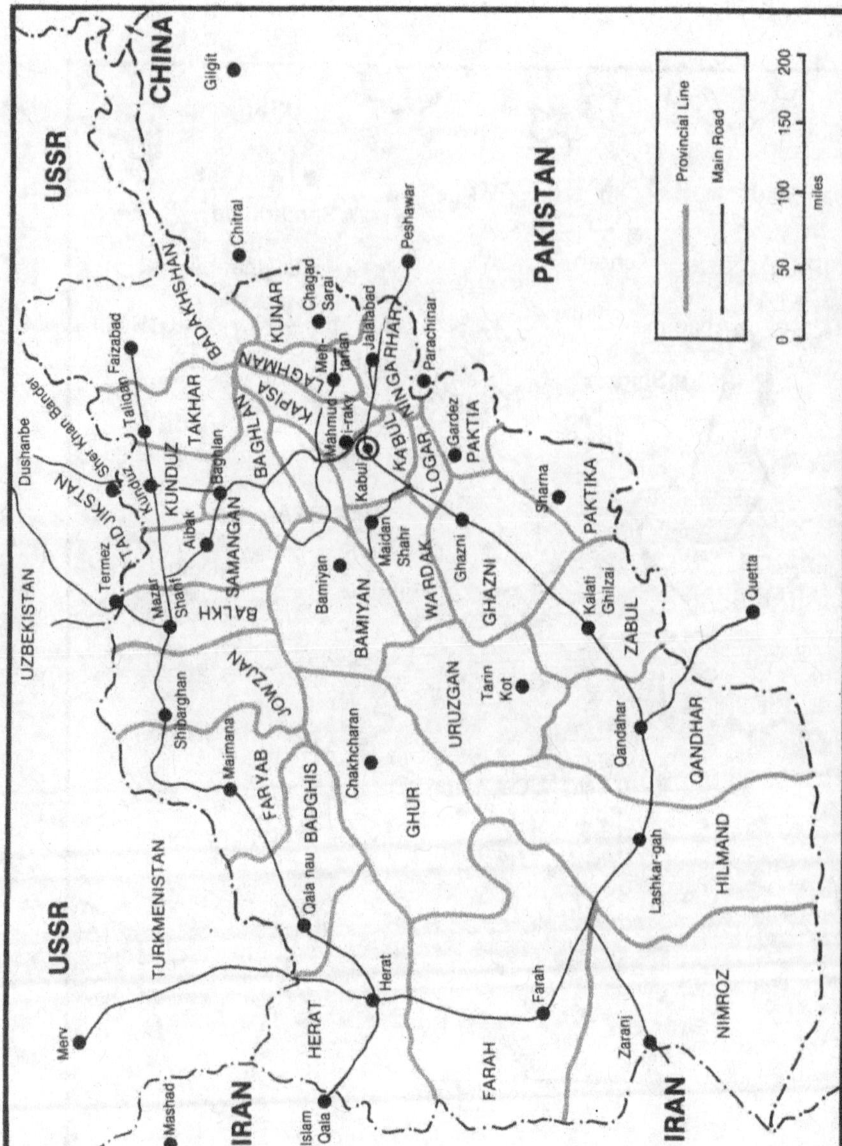

Afghanistan

Arabia and other countries in the Persian Gulf and the Middle East. In April 1985, President Reagan signed a National Security Decision Directive (NSDD No. 166) that called for efforts to drive Soviet forces from Afghanistan "by all means available."[4] By March 1986, the Reagan Administration decided to provide heat-seeking, anti-aircraft *Stinger* missiles to the guerrillas. Although the first *Stingers* were used in Afghanistan in September 1986, it was not until early 1987 that *Stingers* were being deployed in significant numbers. Since then, according to American officials, the Mujahidin had shot down at least 270 Soviet aircraft. About one aircraft per week was believed to be a good estimate of Soviet losses in 1988.[5]

While demonstrating continuity in the Soviet policy of involvement in Afghanistan along the ideological and strategic lines inherited from various predecessors, Soviet leader Mikhail Gorbachev in 1985 nonetheless initiated a reassessment of the conflict in Afghanistan. He called Afghanistan a "bleeding wound," and initiated a series of efforts to disengage and withdraw Soviet forces from that country, including a flexible negotiating position in the stalemated Geneva talks. At the conclusion of the Washington summit in December 1987, Gorbachev said, "...We want to achieve a settlement of the [Afghan] situation, put an end to the bloody internal conflict and prevent relapses.... We do not want the establishment of a pro-Soviet regime in Afghanistan."[6]

NEGOTIATIONS AND THE ACCORDS

The year began with a growing optimism that Moscow was now finally willing to withdraw its forces from Afghanistan. In an increased effort to find a way out, Soviet Foreign Minister Eduard Shevardnadze visited Kabul in the first week of January and declared that "1988 will be the last year of the Soviet military presence in Afghanistan."[7] Yuri Alekseyev, chief of the division of the Soviet Foreign Ministry that deals with Afghanistan, Iran, and Turkey, declared that the pullout would be completed even if it left the possibility of continued civil war in the country. Alekseyev said that the Afghan ruling party "did not claim any monopoly on power."[8] For the first time actually giving a date for possible withdrawal, *Pravda* announced that the starting date for the pullout could be 1 May if the Geneva accords were signed by 1 March.[9]

As events unfolded, it became clear that Moscow's decision to extricate its forces from Afghanistan would require intense negotiations and hard bargaining processes in which all the parties would virtually reverse their previous negotiating positions in order to extract more concessions. Moscow's growing eagerness to withdraw was, therefore, tempered by competing demands not only from within, but also by the Mujahidin, Islamabad, Washington, and Kabul.

The Reagan Administration raised issues that were not covered in the Geneva negotiations. Instead of the previously negotiated "Day One" formula, which had envisioned the suspension of supplies to the Mujahidin beginning with the Soviet withdrawal, US Secretary of State George Shultz emphasized that if the schedule of Soviet withdrawal was "front-loaded" (i.e., the majority of Soviet soldiers would leave in the first half of the withdrawal), the US would gradually phase out supplies to the Mujahidin as the withdrawal became irrevocable. Also, for the first time, Shultz linked the question of supplies to Afghan guerrillas with the continuation of Soviet supplies to the Afghan Army.[10]

Gen. Zia, taking up a demand that was Moscow's till the previous December, added that some members of the PDPA must be allowed to take part in a successor government and that this must be worked out before the agreements were signed in Geneva. Islamabad later demanded that Moscow should also stop arms assistance to the Kabul regime.[11] Responding to such demands, a Soviet commentator conceded that the PDPA would have to surrender a substantial portion of its power to its opponents and that the "radicals on both sides" — the PDPA and the guerrillas — should be excluded from power.[12] Shevardnadze accepted the American condition of front-loaded withdrawal, but asserted that the issue would be decided by the Soviets and Afghans. Moscow's willingness to face the fall of Kabul at this time was highlighted when Shevardnadze said that the PDPA cadres' relatives in the Soviet Central Asian Republics would provide them refuge if the Mujahidin captured the city.[13]

Momentum was finally provided by Mikhail Gorbachev in early February when he declared that, if a settlement could be reached in Geneva by 15 March, the Soviets would start front-loaded withdrawal within two months and would complete the process in 10 months. Even if the proposed period was two months longer than the one Islamabad had demanded, Gorbachev's initiative put pressure on Pakistan to accept the deal. Gorbachev further said that Moscow would be happy to have "an independent, nonaligned, and neutral state" on its southern borders and hoped that the resolution of the Afghan conflict would set an example for the resolution of other regional conflicts such as the Iraqi-Iranian War and the ME conflict.[14]

Many technicalities remained to be worked out, however. Washington, insisting on "reciprocal obligations," announced continued military support for the Mujahidin until the US was "satisfied with the agreement" and there was a "symmetrical cessation" of military supplies to the Afghan combatants.[15] Washington did not support Islamabad's position on a transitional government, preferring instead a "parallel track" outside the framework of the Geneva talks.

The Islamic Unity of the Afghan Mujahidin (IUAM, also known as the Unity), the alliance of seven Afghan guerrilla groups in Peshawar, ruled out any possibility of sharing power with the PDPA, opposed the idea of a peacekeeping force, and refused to give any guarantees not to attack the withdrawing Soviet troops unless the Soviet Union began direct talks with them.[16] As Islamabad pressed the IUAM to set up an interim government, the differences between the Unity's four fundamentalist and three moderate parties deepened, to the extent that two parties in the alliance resigned from the IUAM.[17] The latter were later brought back in the Unity as Pakistan temporarily shelved its efforts.

Moscow rejected the US demand for a Soviet halt of military supplies to the Afghan Government. The Soviet Foreign Ministry's adviser on Afghan affairs, Nikolai Kozyrev, who was also heading the Soviet monitoring team for the Geneva talks, insisted that Soviet military supplies to Kabul were an aspect of Moscow's historical relationship with Afghanistan dating back to the treaty of 1921, and contended that "It would be like Moscow asking the US to end its military aid for Pakistan."[18] He urged that since both subjects fell outside the framework of Geneva agreements, such new issues should not be linked to these talks.[19] He thus indicated that a window of opportunity existed for resolving the two issues outside the scope of the Geneva settlement.

In a move that was intended to apply pressure on the US and Pakistan, Shevardnadze threatened that continued US aid to the Afghan resistance would preclude Washington from being a guarantor of the peace settlement.[20] In Washington in search of a compromise, he also suggested that the "the Afghan question can be resolved without US guarantees."[21] Subsequently, Moscow was reportedly exploring a strategy under which Pakistan — not the US — would become the major guarantor for an end to the conflict.[22]

On the other hand, both Washington and Islamabad preferred a negotiated deal, in order to give them leverage over the withdrawal timetable and the flow of Soviet arms into Afghanistan afterward. To break this diplomatic impasse that was threatening a negotiated settlement, Washington proposed two major variations: first, a moratorium on military aid by either superpower to its local ally for a period of one year; second, an agreement under which the superpowers could continue to supply their clients on a balanced basis.[23] By refusing to cancel its military supply agreements with Kabul, Moscow thus left the "positive symmetry" that would allow military aid to Afghan combatants as the basis for a compromise.[24]

The symmetry formula was initially meant to allow Washington to continue supplying weapons to guerrillas during the troop pullout "at an equal and balanced level," an understanding that was not to become a formal part of the accord, and that reportedly assumed that both sides would heavily supply their clients before a troop withdrawal began.[25] In fact, both sides did step up supplies to their respective clients in the following months. There still remained some other obstacles, however: the two superpowers had to convince their respective clients in Kabul and Islamabad. Under domestic, Soviet, and American pressures, Islamabad formally abandoned the prior formation of an interim government as a precondition for the signing of a peace agreement in the final session of the Geneva talks.[26] The understanding envisioned a "private negotiating role" for Diego Cordovez, the UN mediator, to continue seeking an interim government even after the signing of the formal agreements. Further, eager to sign an agreement under mounting domestic pressure that had aggravated the rift between Gen. Zia and the then civilian prime minister, Mohammed Khan Junejo, Islamabad assured Washington assistance would be allowed to continue to the Afghan resistance through its territory.[27]

Afghan Foreign Minister Abdul Wakil agreed on talks for a new government with the guerrilla groups once the peace settlement was signed, and reduced another month from the proposed 10-month withdrawal schedule. In a move that threatened to jeopardize the agreement, Kabul raised an old colonial border dispute with Pakistan as a condition for signing the agreement.[28] Furthermore, Shevardnadze, in Kabul, encountered resistance from Najibullah, who did not agree with the symmetry proposals.[29]

Moscow therefore summoned Najibullah to a meeting with Gorbachev in Tashkent where their joint statement, apparently referring to the continued supplies to the guerrillas, claimed that "the last obstacles to concluding the agreements have now been removed." Instead of mentioning previously described "fraternal relations" and Afghanistan's "national democratic revolution," the joint statement said that Afghanistan's internal structure in the future "will rest on a multiparty system in the political field and on a multisectoral basis in the economic sphere."[30]

Thus, the way was cleared for a formal agreement by the US and the Soviet Union to permit continued military assistance to the Afghan parties, and the accords were signed in Geneva on 14 April 1988. They consisted of four instruments: the first, between Pakistan and Afghanistan, dealt with noninterference and nonintervention in each other's affairs; the second, between the US and the Soviet Union, contained declarations of international guarantees; the third, between Pakistan and Afghanistan, sought the voluntary return of Afghan refugees; the fourth dealt with the interrelationship among the concerned parties regarding the withdrawal of Soviet troops. A separate memorandum covered arrangements with the UN for implementation of the accords.[31] Not part of the accords, but filed simultaneously, was the US "Letter of Intent" that pledged American supplies to the Mujahidin as long as the Soviets continued supplies to the Afghan Army.

The accords failed to satisfy all concerned parties. First of all, perceiving the Geneva accords as a sellout, the Mujahidin leaders refused to be a party to them. A guerrilla leader, Gulbuddin Hikmatyar, even threatened that Pakistan's signing of the Geneva documents would lead to "disgruntlement and disturbances" among the 3m. Afghan refugees and threatened to move his offices to Iran.[32] Moreover, Islamabad's understanding with Washington on continued supplies to the Afghan combatants was inherently contradictory with the accord that prohibited Pakistan from supplying the insurgents.[33]

THE TWO PHASES OF WITHDRAWAL

Instead of the initially agreed two-month "cooling-off" period between the signing of the accords and withdrawal, Moscow began its withdrawal in May, a month ahead of time. Starting with Jalalabad, the Soviets withdrew first from more vulnerable provinces near the Pakistani border. As the pullout progressed, the guerrillas stepped up their military campaigns. Many of the evacuated garrisons and some of the provincial headquarters quickly changed hands. With heavy fighting reported in at least six Afghan provinces, up to nine districts reportedly fell to the Mujahidin.[34] Subsequently, Moscow provided air support from bases inside its territory to the Afghan forces to help recapture the provincial capital of Kunduz, in northern Afghanistan, and asserted that these were not a violation of the accords.[35] Soviet planes and troops subsequently carried out a number of offensive operations in places where Soviet troops had earlier withdrawn.[36]

Nevertheless, the first phase of withdrawal was carried out with relative smoothness, and by July the Soviet troops had withdrawn from 19 of Afghanistan's 31 provinces.[37] By mid-August, they had handed over to the Afghan Army 10 of 18 main bases and garrisons: Baraki Barak, Daulatabad, Faizabad, Gardez, Ghazni, Jalalabad, Kandahar, Kunduz, Lashkargah, and Ruhabad. The eight remaining Soviet bases were said to be in the provinces of Baghlan, Herat, Kabul, Parwan, Samangan, and at Hayratan in Balkh province, which was used as a crossing point for the returning troops.[38]

However, the Geneva accords encountered serious difficulties soon after they were signed. Kabul accused Pakistan of violating the agreement by sending armed men into Afghanistan, firing across the border, running guerrilla training camps, and restricting the return of refugees. Acknowledging intensified pressure, the Soviet commander in Afghanistan, Lt. Gen. Boris Gromov, conceded that from 15 May, when the Soviet pullout began, to 15 July, the guerrillas had carried out almost 3,000 armed attacks and 96 ambushes.[39] Perhaps exaggerated to put pressure on Pakistan, there were in fact fewer reports of direct attacks on Soviet troops. Moscow charged Washington and Islamabad with continuing supplies to the guerrillas and indicated that, as a result, it might slow its troop withdrawal.[40]

Within two weeks of the completion of the first phase of withdrawal in mid-August, the rebel sieges around cities like Jalalabad, Kandahar, Herat, and Kunduz were effectively loosened and the guerrillas stepped up their rocket attacks on Kabul.[41] Moscow acknowledged increased rocket attacks in a number of provincial capitals (Ghazni, Laghman, Nangarhar, Balkh, Paktia, Parwan, and Baghlan) and strategically important areas (Khost and Gardez).[42] With such attacks, the Mujahidin apparently intended to bring about the collapse of the Kabul regime by shaking the morale of the Afghan Army and undermining the confidence in the regime.

In a manifestation of increased frustration, Moscow criticized UN observers in Afghanistan for failing to enforce the accords.[43] In October, Moscow introduced into Afghanistan MiG-27 jet fighters and SS-1 *Scud* missiles and, from its territory, undertook bombing operations with its long-range *Backfire* bombers in order to break the siege around cities like Kandahar.[44] Given the inaccuracy of the supplied missiles, they were believed to be intended to bolster the morale of the regime in Kabul and to frighten Pakistan and the Mujahidin. Contrary to its assurances at the signing of the accords, Moscow undertook extensive air raids during the second phase of withdrawal; they were said to be continuing at a rate of more than 100 sorties a day.[45] This hardening stance culminated in Moscow's decision in November to suspend the withdrawal of its remaining forces with the comment that "What is important is not when it will be continued, but when will it be completed."[46] Despite a declared freeze on withdrawal, both Islamabad and Washington showed confidence that the Soviets would complete the withdrawal.[47]

SOVIET WITHDRAWAL STRATEGIES

For Pakistan and the US, the general presumption behind the insistence upon a front-loaded withdrawal with a short timetable was that Kabul would not be able to survive for very long without Soviet forces. A view, shared by the Mujahidin and the Reagan Administration, held that the Kabul Government could, in the words of Deputy Assistant Secretary Robert Peck, "splinter and fall of its own weight even before the final Soviet pullout."[48] In Moscow, as some Soviet military commanders in Afghanistan conceded, there were several opinions on the prospects of Kabul's survivability. Gen. Zia, however, believed that the Kabul regime would survive up to eight months after the Soviet pullout.[49] It was precisely because of these presumptions that the parties concerned adopted various strategies to meet their objectives.

Moscow's withdrawal strategies were primarily influenced by three objectives: first, to withdraw with as much safety and face-saving as possible. Second, in the absence of any workable mechanism that would ensure an orderly transition, to avoid Kabul's fall for as long as possible. Third, to prevent the withdrawal strategies from hampering its improving relations with Washington.

The first objective was secured by creating deliberate ambiguities, first, on the actual schedule of withdrawal, and then, on the very future of the Geneva accords. Moscow thus tried to secure breathing space by negotiating cease-fires at local levels in various regions. It created a deliberate uncertainty on the completion of withdrawal, on the future role of Soviet advisers, military supplies to the Kabul regime, air strikes from its bases in Central Asia, and Kabul's political future.

The second objective was secured by adopting extremely flexible political and military strategies. Moscow simultaneously initiated extensive military operations, local truces with field commanders, and direct negotiations with the guerrilla leaders based in Iran and Pakistan. This was also determined, at least in part, by the Mujahidin's unpredictable and often disunified military campaigns, and by Moscow's growing friction with the regime in Kabul. The Soviet military commander in Afghanistan announced that the Soviets would leave behind equipment and facilities worth about $1bn.[50] Further, Moscow also supplied new weapons systems to Kabul before initiating direct negotiations with the IUAM.

The third objective was secured by focusing all of Moscow's criticisms of alleged violations of the accords on Pakistan and virtually ignoring the role of the US — which was, after all, the principal supplier of weaponry to the Mujahidin.

On the role of advisers, it appears, there were differences not only between Moscow and Kabul, but within the Soviet Union itself. It seems that in contrast to the political leadership, which had remained silent on the issue, the Soviet military, or at least some Soviet commanders in Afghanistan, wanted Moscow to leave military advisers at the corps or possibly brigade level.[51] Gen. Aleksei Lizichev, head of a Defense Ministry department that oversees Communist Party interests in the Army and Navy, announced that Moscow "would consider this request" if the Afghans appealed for advisers after the withdrawal was completed.[52] Najibullah's claim that Soviet military advisers would remain behind after the troop withdrawal did not invoke any Soviet reactions, but was disputed by Washington.[53]

Regarding local cease-fires, Moscow entered into a set of negotiations with the local field commanders, particularly in the areas around Kabul and along the withdrawing routes. In the Panjsher Valley, for example, there existed a virtual cease-fire with the Panjsher's guerrilla commander, Ahmad Shah Masoud.[54] Subsequently, Soviet media coverage of Masoud became extremely favorable and he was reportedly also offered the post of defense minister in the Kabul Government.[55]

During 1988, the Kabul regime redrew Afghanistan's political and administrative map giving rise to the prospects of the country's partition. In March, a new province, Sar-i-Pol, was carved out of the southern portions of Jouzjan and Balkh provinces. Presented as a new homeland of the Hazara people, a "Hazara National Central Council" was formed in the new province. Later, a separate office to oversee economic development was established in the north, the only area to have such a position.[56] By isolating Balkh and Jouzjan provinces, Kabul was believed to be preparing to make a stronghold which in the future could provide a base for the PDPA Government in case Kabul fell, or to launch a guerrilla war of its own.

By carving out areas from Laghman and Kunar provinces, Kabul created in July another province called Nuristan, with administrative authority of the Nuristani tribes over the internal affairs of the province. In August, declaring Bamyan as a neutral area, Kabul withdrew its forces from the province. In October, Kapisa, Paktika, and Kunar provinces were merged, respectively, into Parwan, Paktia and Nangarhar provinces.[57] Insignificant in itself, this reorganization was perhaps an attempt to diminish the importance of possible Mujahidin conquests of provincial capitals.

During the withdrawal, Kabul-Moscow friction grew and the Soviet media became increasingly critical of the Afghan Party and Government. For the first time, it disclosed Soviet casualties in Afghanistan: 13,310 killed, 35,478 wounded, and 311 missing.[58]

The Kunduz incident perhaps best illustrated the growing friction between Kabul and Moscow. When Kunduz temporarily changed hands upon the Soviet troop pullout, Gen. Gromov publicly refused to help the Afghan Army recapture the town despite Afghan government requests to the Soviet ground forces in the area for help.[59] While Gen. Gromov announced that the city was in the hands of the rebels, Afghan Foreign Minister Abdul Wakil said in Moscow that the fall of Kunduz was "fabrication and misinformation." Abdul Wakil said that the general's statement was not "authentic," because "What is authentic and reliable is the statements made by the Government of Afghanistan."[60]

Feeling abandoned, Najibullah contradicted Moscow's policy by raising the issue of symmetry and urging that, if "there must be a cutoff of aid for the Afghan Government, there must be a cutoff of all American aid to the Pakistani Government."[61] In a statement that did not elicit any Soviet reaction, Najibullah said that he might ask the Soviet Union to delay the withdrawal of troops if Pakistan continued to allow the shipment of weapons to the guerrillas.[62]

Such differences continued to grow during the second half of the year. The nonparty minister for rural rehabilitation and development, Mohammed Asif Zahir, said that the civilian war dead numbered 1.35m., and that 500 people were still being killed each day on both sides. He also said that while the "extremists" were a minority on both sides, "the reins were given in the[ir] hands... while the moderates were sitting in the middle, waiting for the pendulum to let up." In an unprecedented degree of *glasnost,* he even gave credit to the guerrillas for "their sacrifice of 10 years."[63] Echoing criticisms that had begun to appear in the Soviet press, Prime Minister Hassan Sharq added that the "Afghan people do not have much confidence" in the ruling party or in the Mujahidin.[64]

Soviet charges of Pakistani violations gradually became more strident. In a meeting with his Pakistani counterpart in Moscow, Shevardnadze said that Pakistani aid to the guerrillas "cannot go on indefinitely"[65] and that Moscow reserved "the right to take such measures that are necessitated by the situation."[66] In August, on his fifth visit to Afghanistan in 18 months, Shevardnadze criticized Pakistan for "systematically and seriously violating its pledges to prevent interference."[67]

In line with its desire not to let the complicated situations in Afghanistan hamper its relations with the US, Moscow vehemently criticized Pakistan for violating the accords and hardly mentioned the US in that regard. Compared to the previous emphasis on "imperialist" interferences with the help of "local reactionary circles," Shevardnadze said that "When we criticize Pakistan for nonobservance [of the Geneva accords] we also, of course, have in mind the US," because it "also bears a portion of responsibility."[68] Later, a State Department official disclosed that an understanding existed between the two superpowers that the Soviet Union would not accuse the US of violating the accord.[69]

Kabul also placed the accent of its criticism on Pakistan, saying that "Pakistan [and] not the US, had violated the accords."[70] In almost all of Kabul's protest notes lodged with the UN on reported violations, it hardly mentioned US supplies.

Moreover, praising the US as "great, civilized," Kabul sought US assistance in the revitalization of the Afghan economy.[71]

Moscow and Kabul thus continued to criticize Pakistan throughout the year except for a brief interval when Gen. Zia was killed in an air crash in August, two days after the completion of the first phase of Soviet withdrawal. Moscow showed a renewed hope for the improvement of bilateral relations with Pakistan.[72] However, as Benazir Bhutto, the new prime minister, pledged to continue Pakistan's policy on Afghanistan,[73] Moscow's hopes that post-Zia Pakistan would abruptly change its policy on Afghanistan gradually faded away. In fact, air and ground violations of Pakistan's territory increased and Pakistan, showing less patience, shot down five Afghan aircraft violating its airspace between August and November.[74] In November, Islamabad charged Kabul with having carried out 104 air violations, 328 ground violations, and 96 incidents of sabotage since the signing of the Geneva accords.[75]

Despite this ever-growing tension, Islamabad and Moscow agreed on the text of the UN General Assembly resolution on Afghanistan that called for "scrupulous respect for and faithful implementation" of the Geneva accords. For the first time since Soviet intervention in 1979, the resolutions in the General Assembly had not criticized the Soviet Union.

MUJAHIDIN STRATEGIES

As the withdrawal progressed, the IUAM began to put into action a multifaceted, loosely coordinated strategy that stepped up attacks on remaining Soviet bases. Initial strategies included exploring the possibility of a military coup in Kabul and infiltrating small mobile hit teams trained in urban guerrilla warfare.[76] In Kabul, a "night letter war," warning people to stay indoors, was followed by a brief phase of bomb blasts in the city and by waves of long-range rocket attacks of varying degrees of intensity. The primary purposes of these operations were, however, to remind the regime of the formidable threat that the Mujahidin posed and to demoralize the pro-regime forces.

However, two issues emerged as sources of friction between the field commanders and their political leaders in Peshawar, on the one hand, and between them and Islamabad and Washington, on the other: attacking the withdrawing Soviet troops, and laying sieges and launching frontal attacks on cities like Kabul.

1. *Attacking the Withdrawing Soviet Troops:* Under American and Pakistani counsel, the IUAM offered Moscow a safe passage for its withdrawing units.[77] Concurrently, some field commanders continued attacking departing troops. The resistance forces on the whole refrained from attacking the withdrawing Soviets. In fact, by not blocking the withdrawal routes, they indirectly also encouraged the pullout.

2. *Attacking Cities:* Fearing that the Mujahidin might lose their momentum, Islamabad encouraged frontal attacks on evacuated cities and garrisons. Thus, during the initial months of withdrawal, the guerrillas were planning a major push to capture the cities of Ghazni, Gardez, Kandahar, Jalalabad, and even Kabul.[78] The purpose of the Mujahidin's strategy of concentrating their attacks only on major targets was to capture a major city, preferably near the Pakistani border, where the IUAM could establish a parallel government.[79]

Predicting a breakthrough within days, some commanders announced that the Mujahidin would be in Jalalabad by 1 June,[80] giving rise to speculation about the fall of cities like Kandahar, Ghazni, Herat, and Jalalabad. The optimism of quick victories was so high that the designated head of the interim government and then-head of Unity declared their intention to move their offices to Afghanistan.[81]

Both the US and Pakistan supported enhanced military coordination, and hoped that political change in Kabul would come quickly, especially if the guerrillas scored early military victories. However, both reportedly advised the IUAM to forgo frontal attacks against positions that it could not sustain and to abstain from hindering the Soviet withdrawal by attacking convoys or shooting at Soviet officers who were about to leave the country.[82] Seeking to restrain the IUAM from attacking Kabul while the Soviets were still there, Pakistani and American specialists encouraged the IUAM to strangle Kabul slowly by cutting off the few highways that allowed the capital food and fuel supplies, thereby making the besieged city solely dependent upon relief supplied by air planes that could be threatened by *Stinger* missiles.[83]

Many of the commanders refused to support the effort, arguing that an all-out attack against cities would have meant heavy casualties and alienation of the local population.[84] On the other hand, some commanders believed that such victories were important both to maintain morale and to seize more weapons.[85] Further, because of air attacks and government force resistance, the guerrillas were obliged to lift their sieges of various cities, like Kandahar and Herat and garrisons like Spin Boldak and Midan Shehr. After the guerrilla retreats, Soviet-Afghan forces bombed those areas specifically to make the point that any area falling to the Mujahidin would invite reprisal raids.[86] Finally, conceding that "We have learned the lesson of Kunduz," some Mujahidin groups did not want to suffer heavy casualties for conquests that they could not sustain. The lack of an agreement between the moderate and fundamentalist groups became more evident with their reported mêlée over the future of Kandahar city.[87] As a result of increasing differences between the resistance leaders in Pakistan and their commanders, the plans to attack and occupy cities gradually fizzled out.

The rocket attacks on the city also subsided,[88] but were resumed later with less intensity. The guerrillas opened new offensives, decided to close the Salang tunnel and declared their intention to attack the Soviet forces,[89] but were held back at Washington's urging.[90] Yet, the Unity publicly warned that it would fight at Jalalabad despite the American call for restraint.[91]

Concurrently, while avoiding direct interference that would create the impression that the US was trying to "micro-manage" its Afghanistan policy, the Reagan Administration took various steps to assure the IUAM of its continued support and to promote unity among them. The Administration's goal during the period of withdrawal was said to be to keep the commanders focused on fighting rather than on the squabbling among their political leadership in Peshawar.[92] However, the contradictions inherent in trying to be involved and uninvolved confronted Washington in many ways.

In response to guerrilla pressure to recognize them as a provisional government, Washington assured them of recognition if their provisional government "control[led] territory and establishe[d] a civil administration, possesse[d] the capacity to assume the international obligations of Afghanistan, enjoy[ed] broad support and possesse[d] the attributes of effective government." Additionally, it was also added that they would earn recognition from the US provided "they stuck together and worked with the commanders."[93] Thus encouraged, the guerrilla leaders sent teams to three provinces of Afghanistan — Paktia, Loghar and Kunar — to evaluate possible sites for a provisional government. Their leaders envisioned the imminent establishment of a provisional government across the border, possibly at Zazi in Paktia province.[94]

Washington's major purpose in encouraging an interim government was to reserve the right to provide whatever forms of support it considered appropriate. This latitude would reduce pressures on Islamabad for violating the Geneva accords, and also would establish a direct pipeline of support to the Afghan resistance. Not satisfied with Pakistan's handling of the guerrillas, and seeking to encourage Kabul's speedy fall, in August Washington appointed a special envoy to coordinate US policy directly with the Mujahidin.[95]

EFFORTS TO ESTABLISH AN INTERIM GOVERNMENT

LOYA JIRGA

Under the Geneva accords, Diego Cordovez was empowered to pursue the issue of an interim government. Cordovez increased his efforts to convene a *Loya Jirga* (traditionally an assembly of tribal chiefs), to oversee the formation of a transitional government that should be representative of all the elements of the country. With Soviet encouragement, he called for a cease-fire and creation of a "temporary" new government to replace the government in Kabul by 1 September. Because of vehement opposition from the Afghan resistance, Cordovez revised his earlier optimism of an early session of *Loya Jirga,* and suggested that it should be called not later than 1 March 1989, two weeks after the Soviets were expected to have completed their withdrawal. Led by Afghans of "recognized independence and impartiality," who would pledge not to serve in any future government, the proposed interim government would replace the PDPA regime, and plan for the gathering of a vast council of tribal elders that would set up a permanent government acceptable to all sides in the Afghan conflict.[96]

The Mujahidin saw in Cordovez's endeavors an attempt to keep the members of the Kabul Government in power and refused to even meet him. The US reportedly opposed these UN efforts and, later, Kabul criticized the idea and Moscow also withdrew its support.[97] Responding to the Unity's complaints, UN Secretary-General Javier Pérez de Cuellar relieved Cordovez of his negotiating position and personally took charge of the Afghan talks. The UN secretary-general, however, declined to initiate new efforts unless other such efforts then under way with Pakistan and the Soviet Union were exhausted.[98]

SHURA

On Pakistani encouragement, the Unity leaders announced nationwide parliamentary elections to be held later in the year and signed an agreement for the creation of a provisional government to be based inside Afghanistan.[99] The previously named president of the IUAM's interim government, Ahmad Shah, in November named a "transitional" government to replace the Kabul regime.[100] Later, the Unity extended the date for a national election to choose the 400-member national assembly to January 1989.[101] Compared to the Soviet efforts of a broad-based government of national reconciliation, and the UN efforts of a neutral interim government to be formed by holding a national *Jirga*, Pakistan moved with its proposal of organizing a *Shura* (a term used in traditional Islamic vocabulary for a consultative council). Islamabad also moved to get Iranian support on the issue.[102] These efforts were also stalled, primarily because of Pakistan's desire to promote certain groups within the IUAM and because the issues of the proportionate representation of various IUAM parties and the participation of the local field commanders, former King Zahir Shah and the Iran-based Shi'i parties, remained unsettled.

GOVERNMENT OF NATIONAL RECONCILIATION

After the Geneva talks on an interim government were stalled, Moscow moved to get support for the control of leading positions in the future broad-based government by moderate elements of the PDPA. In October, as new ambassador to Kabul, Yuli Vorontsov (also the first deputy foreign minister) embarked on a policy of party streamlining. In the party meeting, between 17 and 50 Central Committee members were arrested for "dogmatism and factionalism."[103] Soon thereafter, Moscow reportedly suggested that Afghan Prime Minister Hassan Sharq should be named as Najibullah's replacement, a move rejected by both Washington and the IUAM.[104] Subsequently, Moscow initiated a new two-track policy that sought an international conference, on the one hand, and direct negotiations with the Mujahidin on the other.

Reviving Kabul's proposal of new talks on Afghanistan between the two superpowers, Afghanistan, Pakistan, and the UN secretary-general,[105] Gorbachev called for an international conference on Afghanistan under UN auspices during his visit to India in November.[106] Almost simultaneously, Kabul sought demilitarization of Afghanistan under international supervision.[107] This was followed by Najibullah's call to Saudi Arabia, to mediate among rival parties, and his later effort to secure the Jordanian king's mediation to convince Saudi Arabia to host such talks in Mecca.[108] On the second track, that of direct negotiations with the Mujahidin, Islamabad hosted, under Soviet pressures, the first direct negotiations between Moscow and the IUAM. Compared to the initial Soviet interest to restrict dialogue to discussion on the return of Soviet troops missing in action, the guerrillas tried to convince Moscow that they would not be a threat to Moscow if they ruled from Kabul.[109] This action cleared the way for high-ranking, wide-ranging discussions in Ta'if.[110]

Even if Moscow emphasized that the talks were being held with the agreement of Kabul, the Kabul regime was not only excluded from the negotiations owing to the IUAM's refusal to talk to the PDPA regime, but also was not informed about the agenda of the talks by Moscow.[111] On the other hand, various parties in the IUAM opposed holding talks with Moscow and there was no unified position on various issues in the negotiations.[112] Nevertheless, the Mujahidin rejected both a Soviet cease-fire offer and suggestions of power sharing with the Kabul regime. In negotiations, the Unity leaders presented four conditions: withdrawal from Afghanistan, transfer of power to the Mujahidin, payment of reparations to Afghanistan for damages caused by the war, and an end of Soviet interference in Afghanistan's internal affairs.[113] Pakistan, reversing its previous policy, also opposed inclusion of the PDPA in the proposed broad-based government.[114]

In his first direct contacts, Vorontsov also met the former King Zahir Shah in an effort "to bring the Afghans together at one table." The Mujahidin, however, saw it as a Soviet effort to divide them and said that Moscow should talk to the Mujahidin alone.[115] The biggest stumbling block, however, was the future of the PDPA regime on which the parties remained uncompromising. Direct negotiations having virtually stalemated, Gorbachev called in the UN General Assembly for a complete cease-fire in Afghanistan and a complete cessation of any supplies of arms to the Afghan belligerents from 1 January 1989, deployment of an international peacekeeping force in the country, and the convening of an internationl conference on the neutrality and demilitarization of Afghanistan.[116] Rejecting the Gorbachev proposals, President Reagan asked the Kabul regime to step down, Pakistan called them both "unrealistic and unacceptable," and Mujahidin leaders dismissed them.[117]

With political breakthrough virtually out of sight, Moscow reaffirmed its commitment to withdraw by saying that it might complete withdrawal by leaving ahead of time.[118] Thus, the year ended with reports that the Soviets were preparing to resume their withdrawal and had begun dismantling the last of their bases at places like Farah and Shindad.

Throughout the year, both Gorbachev and Shevardnaze had stressed in their public statements that, after the end of war in Afghanistan, a similar Soviet-American cooperation could produce results in the ME.[119] But the initial hopes that the agreement of Afghanistan had set a precedent with potential application far beyond that problem alone were dashed by the end of the year as the conflict continued to rage in most of Afghanistan.

Soviet withdrawal strategies had only partial success. While Moscow was successful in proceeding with withdrawal without major casualties, it failed to secure an agreement on the orderly transition of power in Kabul; while the concluding of alliances with the field commanders released some pressure on Kabul and reduced attacks on the withdrawing Soviet troops, it strengthened the local field commanders' positions in their respective areas, almost always at the cost of Kabul's authority. While direct dialogue with the Mujahidin put Moscow in the positive light of compromise and flexibility, the negotiations failed to bring over even the "good Muslims," as the IUAM had previously agreed, in the Mujahidin's proposed coalition government. And while Moscow was able to promote some moderates within the Kabul regime, it failed to get any acceptance for them from Washington, Islamabad, or the Mujahidin. In all, therefore, Moscow's failures in Afghanistan in 1988 outnumbered its successes.

NOTES

For the place and frequency of publications cited here, and for the full name of the publication, news agency, radio station, or monitoring service where an abbreviation is used, please see "List of Sources." Only in the case of more than one publication bearing the same name is the place of publication noted here.

1. *State of the Union Address,* 23 January 1980.
2. *NYT,* 10 March 1981.
3. Robert Pear, "Arming Afghan Guerrillas: A Huge Effort Led by US," *NYT,* 18 April 1988.
4. *WSJ,* 9 October 1985.
5. David Evans, "A Deadly Weapon: Afghan Tribesmen Carrying a *Stinger,*" *Chicago Tribune,* 8 April 1988. For a discussion of Soviet-Afghan strategies, Craig Karp, "Eight Years of Soviet Occupation," *DSB,* March 1988, No. 2,132, pp. 1–24.

6. *The Muslim,* 12 December 1987.
7. TASS, 4, 6 January 1988.
8. Bill Keller, "Charting the Road Out," *NYT,* 8 January 1988.
9. *Pravda,* 11 January 1988.
10. David K. Shipler, "Shultz Urges End of Soviet Arms Aid in Afghan Pullout," *NYT,* 8 January 1988.
11. Mushadid Hussain, "Pakistan's Position on Afghanistan: An Appraisal," *Frontier Post,* Peshawar, 21 February. For Gen. Zia's interview outlining other Pakistani demands, *WP,* 23 January 1988.
12. Paul Quinn-Judge, "Reasons Abound for Soviet Pessimism on Afghan War," *CSM,* 22 January 1988.
13. Carlos J. Williams, "Soviet Official Sees No Postwar Role in Afghan Regime," *The Miami Herald,* 22 January 1988; Antero Pietila, "Soviet Official Predicts End of Afghan War," *Baltimore Sun*, 7 January 1988.
14. *Pravda,* 9 February 1988. For text of Gorbachev statement, "Setting Forth Soviet Position on Afghan War," *NYT,* 9 February 1988.
15. Neil Lewis, "US Insists Soviets Stop Sending Arms to Afghan Regime," *NYT,* 5 March 1988.
16. Abbas Rashid, "Afghanistan: Uncertain Prospects," *The Muslim,* 11 January 1988.
17. Henry Kamm, "Afghan Rebels' Discord Rises as Soviet Withdrawal Nears," *NYT,* 9 March; "Afghan Opposition Leader Resigns from Alliance," *CSM,* 14 March 1988.
18. Paul Lewis, "Soviets Won't End Afghan Arms Aid," *NYT,* 11 March 1988.
19. Edward Cody, "Soviet Says US, Pakistan Imperil Afghan Pact," *WP,* 11 March 1988.
20. *Izvestiia,* 30 March, 1988. See also, Don Oberdorfer, "US Pakistan Demand 'Balance' in Afghan Military Aid Cutoffs," *WP,* 1 April 1988.
21. Andrew Borowiec, "Moscow Warns of Its Own Afghan Solution," *WT,* 6 April 1988.
22. Elaine Sciolino, "Soviet Hints It Might Compromise on Arms Aid to Afghan Guerrillas," *NYT,* 31 March 1988.
23. E. A. Wayne, "US is Adamant on Cutoff of Soviet Arms to Kabul," *CSM,* 28 March 1988.
24. Paul Lewis, "Arms Aid Reported Fading as Block to Afghan Peace," *NYT,* 6 April 1988.
25. Paul Lewis, "US and Soviets Would Suspend Arms Shipments after an Accord," *NYT,* 8 April 1988.
26. Paul Lewis, "Pakistan Sees a Superpower Role in Ending Afghanistan Stalemate," *NYT,* 17 March 1988.
27. David Ottaway, Don Oberdorfer, "Soviets Indicate Assent to US Plan," *WP,* 8 April 1988.
28. Paul Lewis, "Officials Assert Border Dispute is Obstacle in Afghan Talks," *NYT,* 23 March 1988.
29. Antero Pietila, "Gorbachev Confers with Afghan Leader," *Baltimore Sun,* 7 April 1988.
30. For text of the Soviet-Afghan statement, "Last Obstacles Have Been Removed," *NYT,* 9 April. For an Afghan party view, "The Day that Brought Us Hope," *World Marxist Review,* Vol. 31, No. 6, June 1988, pp. 128–30.
31. For text of the accords, "Documentation," *Strategic Studies,* Vol. XI, No. 3 (Spring 1988), pp. 107–18.
32. Henry Kamm, "Afghan Hard-Liners Dominate Rally against Accords," *NYT,* 17 April 1988.
33. For a clause-by-clause analysis of the accords, Rossane Klass, "Afghanistan: The Accords," *Foreign Affairs,* Vol. 66, No. 5 (Summer 1988), pp. 922–45.
34. Edward Giradet, "As Soviet Troops Head Home...," *CSM,* 13 May 1988.
35. Michael Parks, "Soviets Admit Planes Aided Kabul, Deny Breaking Pact," *LAT,* 1 September 1988.
36. E. A. Wayne, "Troops May Go, but Soviet Afghan Legacy Remains," *CSM,* 12 August 1988.
37. "Afghan: Half of Soviets Gone," *The Miami Herald,* 29 July 1988.
38. Paul Lewis, "UN Reports Soviet Pullout from 10 Afghan Bases," *NYT,* 17 August 1988.
39. "Rebels hold Afghan City After Pullout," *The Miami Herald,* 15 August 1988.
40. "Soviets Hint at Slowing Afghan Pullout," *WP,* 29 May 1988.
41. "Afghan Guerrillas Attack Kabul Airport with Rockets," *LAT,* 29 August 1988.

42. "Kabul Rocket Attack Kills 35, TASS Reports," *NYT,* 29 September 1988.
43. Elaine Sciolino, "Soviets Say UN Group Ignores Pakistani Acts," *NYT,* 30 September 1988.
44. Norman Kempster, "US Sees Soviet Breach in Afghanistan Buildup," *LAT,* 1 November 1988.
45. "Soviets' Afghan Raids Are Criticized by US," *NYT,* 17 December 1988.
46. Michael Parks, "Soviets Suspend Afghan Pullout," *LAT,* 5 November 1988.
47. William Coughlin, "Shultz Dismisses Fears Soviets Might Overstay in Afghanistan," *WT,* 9 November 1988.
48. Michael Wines and Jimm Mann, "Afghan Rebels' Arms Loss Put at $80 Million," *LAT,* 3 May 1988.
49. Steven Weisman, "A First Soviet Unit Quits Afghanistan," *NYT,* 19 May 1988.
50. Richard M. Weintraub, "Soviets Begin Withdrawing Troops from Afghanistan," *WP,* 16 May 1988.
51. Richard M. Weintraub, "Afghan War Moves into Crucial Turn," *WP,* 19 May 1988.
52. "Soviet Losses Number 13,310 in Afghanistan," *The Miami Herald,* 26 May 1988.
53. David K. Shipler, "Afghan Ruler Says Soviet Advisers Will Remain after Troop Pullout," *NYT,* 29 April 1988. Ironically, reflecting on a sense of betrayal that prevailed in Kabul at the time, an Afghan official reportedly said, "If advisers did not leave, they will be shot — by us, not the *dushmans* [guerrillas]"; Paul Quinn-Judge, "Soviet General Downbeat on Afghan Government Prospects," *CSM,* 25 July 1988.
54. "Soviets Reported to be Setting Truces with Rebels," *CSM,* 13 April 1988.
55. Bernard Weinraub, "Rebel Target; Kabul Morale," *NYT,* 29 August 1988.
56. Paul Lewis, "New Afghan Area: A Soviet Toehold?" *NYT,* 1 April; Bernard Weinraub, "Russians Leaving an Afghan Legacy," *NYT,* 31 August 1988.
57. "Najibullah Government Redrawing Afghanistan Map," *Dawn,* 26 November 1988.
58. Philip Taubman, "Toll in the Afghan War: Soviet Lists 13,310 Dead," *NYT,* 26 May 1988.
59. "Rebels Hold Afghan City after Pullout," *The Miami Herald,* 15 August 1988.
60. "Vital Town is Retaken, Afghan Says," *NYT,* 16 August 1988.
61. "Afghan Asks Improved US Ties," *NYT,* 25 April 1988.
62. Elaine Sciolino, "Afghan Chief Rattles Saber at Pakistan," *NYT,* 8 June 1988.
63. Henry Kamm, "Kabul Government Aide Says Rebuilding Will be Daunting," *NYT,* 27 November 1988.
64. Richard Beeston, "Soviets Out to Purge Afghan Hard-liners," *WT,* 26 October 1988.
65. "Shevardnadze Deplores Pakistan's Afghan Role," *NYT,* 1 August 1988.
66. "Vital Town is Retaken, Afghan Says," *NYT,* 16 August 1988.
67. "Soviets: Troops Out of South Afghanistan," *The Miami Herald,* 6 August 1988.
68. Elaine Sciolino, "Gandhi Faults Islamic Rule for Kabul," *NYT,* 11 June 1988.
69. Ibid.
70. Steven Weisman, "Kabul Says Pakistanis Will Help Arm Guerrillas," *NYT,* 22 May 1988.
71. "Afghan Asks Improved US Ties," *NYT,* 25 April 1988.
72. Bill Keller, "Moscow Sends Condolences and Hints of Better Relations," *NYT,* 19 August. For Kabul's reactions, Bernard Weinraub, "In Kabul, Relief over Zia's Death," *NYT,* 17 August 1988.
73. "No Change in Afghan Policy, Says Bhutto," *Dawn,* 4 December 1988.
74. "Afghanistan Report 30 Dead on Plane," *NYT,* 22 November 1988.
75. "Afghan Plane Shot Down," *Dawn,* 21 November 1988.
76. Edward Girardet, "Afghan Coalition Seems Remote," *CSM,* 19 April 1988.
77. Henry Kamm, "Afghan Rebel Alliance Leader Outlines His Cause," *NYT,* 20 April 1988.
78. Steven Weisman, "Afghan Guerrilla Campaign Sputters," *NYT,* 13 July 1988.
79. Henry Kamm, "Afghan Rebel Alliance Leader Outlines His Cause," *NYT,* 20 April 1988.
80. Jonathan Landau, "Soviet Troops Reported Besieged in Afghanistan's 2nd-largest City," *Philadelphia Inquirer,* 13 May 1988.
81. "Afghanistan Peace Accord Won't End War, Rebels Vow," *The Miami Herald,* 17 April; "For Rebels, a Green Light," *NYT,* 16 May 1988.
82. Edward Girardet, "Mujahideen Find Kabul Can Put up a Tough Fight," *CSM,* 28 June 1988.

83. Richard Erlich, "As Soviets Depart, Three Wars Rage in Afghanistan," *WT*, 17 May 1988.
84. For views of Abdul Haq, a major commander around Kabul, Paul Lewis, "Afghan Rebel Sees Peril in UN Aid," *NYT*, 23 June 1988.
85. For view of Amin Wardak, a prominent commander in the province of Wardak, Donatella Lorch, "Afghan Guerrillas Map the Post-Soviet Future," *NYT*, 15 August 1988.
86. "Rebels Hold Afghan City After Pullout," *The Miami Herald*, 15 August 1988.
87. Donatella Lorch, "Afghan Gridlock: Factions Vie for Ancient Crossroad and for Nation's Future," *NYT*, 12 September 1988.
88. Barbara Crossette, "Afghan Leadership Reported at Odds," *NYT*, 19 October 1988.
89. Barbara Crossette, "Push Is Reported by Afghan Rebels," *NYT*, 9 November,and her "Afghan Rebels Reported Blocking Highway and Killing 20 Russians," ibid., 13 November 1988.
90. E. A. Wayne, "Washington Urges Restraint by Both Sides in Afghan Conflict," *CSM*, 9 November 1988.
91. William Coughlin, "Shultz Dismisses Fears Soviets Might Overstay in Afghanistan," *WT*, 9 November 1988.
92. E. A. Wayne, "Afghan Rebels Making Gains," *CSM*, 13 June 1988.
93. Robert Pear, "Afghan Rebels Get Support from US for a Government," *NYT*, 6 May 1988.
94. Edward Girardet, "Afghan Power Struggle," *CSM*, 9 May 1988.
95. Robert Pear, "US and Afghan Guerrillas Debate New Raids," *NYT*, 25 September 1988.
96. Paul Lewis, "Stricter Observance of Afghanistan Pact Pledged," *NYT*, 2 August 1988.
97. Selig Harrison, "Inside the Afghan Talks," *Foreign Policy*, No. 72 (Fall 1988), pp. 31–60.
98. "New Move for Afghan Issue Settlement," *Dawn*, 24 November 1988.
99. Edward Girardet, "Afghan Coalition Seems Remote," *CSM*, 19 April 1988.
100. "Afghan Guerrillas Name Transitional Government," *CSM*, 20 June 1988.
101. "Afghan Guerrillas Plan Elections, New Government," *LAT*, 1 November 1988.
102. "Pakistan, Iran's Views Identical," *Dawn*, 16 November 1988.
103. Barbara Crossette, "National Unity Eluding Afghan Chief," *NYT*, 26 October 1988.
104. Elaine Sciolino, "Soviets Said to Offer Afghan Premier as a Conciliator," *NYT*, 30 October 1988.
105. TASS, 31 August 1988.
106. Umashankar Phadnis, "Gorbachev Attacks US, Pakistan," and his "USSR, India for Reconciliation," *Dawn*, 20 November 1988.
107. Paul Lewis, "Afghan Premier Seeks UN Peace Plan," *NYT*, 10 November 1988.
108. Michael Parks, "Soviets Seek New Afghan Negotiations," *LAT*, 6 November 1988.
109. "Mujahideen Assurances to USSR," *Dawn*, 30 November 1988.
110. "Mujahideen, Moscow Talks Open in Ta'if," *Dawn*, 5 December 1988.
111. Henry Kamm, "Soviets and Afghan Rebels Meet in Saudi Arabia," *NYT*, 4 December, and his "Afghan Official Calls Lasting Cease-fire a Top Goal in Talks," *NYT*, 8 December 1988.
112. "Mujahideen Call for Soviet Pullout," *Dawn*, 6 December 1988.
113. "Soviet Pullout on Schedule," *Dawn*, 7 December 1988.
114. "Pakistan Welcomes Ta'if Talks," *Dawn*, 13 December 1988.
115. Clyde Haberman, "Soviets Urge Afghan King to Join Talks on Nation,"*NYT*, 25 December 1988.
116. For the text of Gorbachev speech, "In Gorbachev's Words: To Preserve the Vitality of Civilization," *NYT*, 8 December 1988.
117. "President's News Conference on Foreign and Domestic Issues," *NYT*, 9 December. Foi Pakistan's reaction, "Gorbachev Proposals Termed Unrealistic," *Dawn*, 9 December; and for the Mujahidin's "Gorbachev's Pleas Criticized," *Dawn*, 10 December; and "Gorbachev's Proposal Rejected," *Dawn*, 12 December 1988.
118. Paul Quinn-Judge, "Soviets Hint Early Afghan Exit," *CSM*, 20 December 1988.
119. Philip Taubman, "Moscow's New Slant on the Mideast," *NYT*, 12 April 1988.

ARAB-ISRAELI RELATIONS

The Middle East Peace Process

MORDECHAI GAZIT

The peace process was unusually eventful in the year under review. The Palestinian uprising in the West Bank and the Gaza Strip (with a total of almost 300 dead in the course of the year) forced the PLO leadership to take the political decision that made possible the start of a dialogue with the US in December.

In Israel, the uprising convinced even Likud supporters that the status quo in the territories could not continue much longer. However, the two major political blocs, the Likud and the Alignment, remained divided over the solution best for Israel.

The basic positions of Israel and the Palestinians remained unchanged. The PLO continued to insist on an international conference as the only setting for a settlement, believing that it would not achieve Palestinian self-determination and independence through direct negotiations with Israel. The PLO was convinced that Israel had to be pressured to make concessions, the mechanism for such pressure being the international conference which the PLO and Jordan had conceived in 1985. The PLO would represent the Palestinians at such a conference.

The Palestinian objectives received strong UN support again in the year under review when the UN General Assembly on 15 December adopted overwhelmingly (138 for, 2 against, 2 abstentions) a resolution calling for the convening of an international conference with the participation of the Security Council's five permanent members. For the Arab countries and their supporters, this was a very significant achievement. However, since the resolution supported all PLO demands it unified Israel in its opposition to such an international framework. An international conference was no longer only an important procedural device, it had become the means of imposing clearly defined terms on Israel. The Israelis reasoned that should they accept the harsh terms laid down by the UN, they could dispense with the conference altogether and make the concessions to the Palestinians directly.

The PLO/Arab objectives were precisely those which Israel had been opposing since 1967: withdrawal from all the territories, including East Jerusalem, the establishment of a Palestinian state in the West Bank and the Gaza Strip, the right of the Palestinian refugees to choose between return to Israel and compensation, and the dismantling of the Israeli settlements in the territories. These demands reappeared in the UN resolution. Even moderates in Israel found them difficult, those who were ready to recognize the PLO and negotiate with it, affirmed their opposition to most, if not all, of these demands. They could reconcile themselves to a Palestinian state alongside Israel on condition that it gave up some territory which Israel deemed vital to its defense, agreed to be demilitarized, and left East Jerusalem under Israeli sovereignty. Other Israelis opposed negotiations with the PLO because they preferred to negotiate with King Husayn, but this position lost some of its ground after Husayn announced his disengagement from the West Bank in the summer of 1988 and his recognition of the declaration of a Palestinian state by the 19th Palestine National Council (PNC) in November. By the end of the year under review, the likelihood that Jordan would, nevertheless, play a decisive role in any future settlement remained considerably reduced. Statements in the US and in Israel to the contrary were probably based on the assumption that confederative links between Jordan and the Palestinian entity on the West Bank could be taken for granted, thus leaving Jordan in the picture.

The *intifada* (uprising) in the occupied territories spurred the US to renew its diplomatic efforts. Three shuttle missions by US Secretary of State George Shultz gave birth to US proposals (see chapter on the US and the Middle East) which, with the exception of Syria, the other countries directly concerned — Egypt, Jordan,and Israel — did not reject but neither did they accept them. With a new administration in office in the US and with the PLO more acceptable than before to the US, the fate of these proposals still remained to be determined.

Some American and Israeli critics maintained that Shultz's effort came a year too late. They argued that Shultz should not have hesitated to act after Husayn and Shimon Peres, the Israeli vice premier, formulated the London document in April 1987 (see *MECS* 1987, chapter on the ME peace process). The weakness of this criticism, however, was that at that time, the issue of Palestinian participation in negotiations in a joint Jordanian-Palestinian delegation could not be resolved. Relations between the PLO and Jordan were then at their nadir. It was highly unlikely that Jordan would have moved without Palestinians designated by the PLO, but the PLO would certainly have withheld its cooperation. Furthermore, for Husayn, an effective Soviet role in the international conference had always been a precondition for his participation. But, even at the end of 1988, after two more Reagan-Gorbachev summit meetings since April 1987, US-Soviet agreement on cooperation in ME peace efforts was far from certain. Another obstacle was Husayn's commitment to Syria's President Hafiz al-Asad not to negotiate a separate agreement with Israel.

The difficulties ahead remained forbidding. Inside the PLO were hard-line groups unwilling to make concessions beyond having accepted Israel's right to exist. However, the PLO also knew that the *intifada* could not continue indefinitely and that the Palestinian population was exposed to much suffering.

In Israel, the 75,000 settlers in the occupied territories and their supporters had become an important political force. The Israelis felt increasingly frustrated. International public opinion was highly critical; domestically, they were far from united on questions of policy. They were also much concerned that they might become a minority in their own country if they held on to the territories and their Palestinian population. The demographic data were most disconcerting. In 1988, there were already over 600,000 Arab children aged eight or less in Israel and the territories; only somewhat less than the number of Jewish children in the same age group. All these were compelling reasons that convinced most Israelis that the status quo was no longer a viable option.

In what follows, the positions of the various ME states *vis-à-vis* the peace process and the roles they played in it in 1988 are examined and analyzed. For a discussion of the American and Soviet roles, see chapters on the US and the ME and the USSR and the ME, respectively.

JORDAN

The year under review was unusually significant for Jordan in general and for its role as an important participant in the peace process in particular. Husayn's decision to sever the kingdom's administrative and legal ties with the West Bank (31 July)[1] forced the PLO to adopt decisions it had been avoiding. The PLO could no longer shun those decisions after Husayn clearly stated publicly that Jordan would let the Palestinians secede from the East Bank and set up an independent Palestinian state. True, for many years Husayn had been saying that in negotiations with Israel he would not act without the Palestinians, namely, the PLO, and that Jordan's role in the peace process would not be a substitute for that of the Palestinians themselves. However, Husayn's actions and declared policies had been predicated on the assumption that Jordan would be a senior partner in negotiations with Israel. In the Amman accord of 1985, Jordan and the PLO had spelt this out: a joint Jordanian-Palestinian delegation would be formed to negotiate with Israel within the framework of an international conference (cf. *MECS* 1984–85, p. 523). The outcome of the negotiations would enable the two states — Jordan and Palestine — to unite in a confederation. It was generally taken for granted that Jordan would lead and the Palestinians would follow.

Husayn's 31 July statement contained a commitment to continue Jordan's participation in the peace process, but this commitment was not meant to nullify the original purpose of the king's announcement. Jordan would no longer pursue policies which could be perceived to hamper PLO objectives.

In assessing the king's announcement, two questions needed to be clarified. The first was: were the American and Israeli assessments that Jordan was the key to the settlement of the Palestinian issue well founded? It can be argued that the vain Jordanian efforts to reach agreement with the PLO in the six months following the publication of the Reagan proposals (1 September 1982) proved that the Palestinians had the power to veto Jordan's policy in matters concerning them. The events that led to Husayn's decision in February 1986 to suspend the Amman accord proved the same point. A year later, the 18th PNC (April 1987) abrogated the Amman accord and in effect rejected the very idea of a joint Jordanian-Palestinian delegation. The result was that the US peace efforts in 1987 and 1988 had no real chance of success even when energetically pursued. Claims to the contrary were often made by the Alignment leader Shimon Peres in Israel and occasionally also in Jordan, but they were not substantiated.

The second question concerned the role that Jordan could realistically be expected to play in any peace process in light of both its disengagement from the West Bank and the PLO's growing assertiveness which was fed by the *intifada*. At the end of the year under review it seemed clear that Jordan's role was considerably reduced.

Jordan's attitude toward the Shultz mission which occupied the diplomatic scene for most of the first half of 1988 sheds more light on these two questions.

Signs heralding the change in Jordan's policy appeared several months before it occurred. In 1988 Husayn replied in the affirmative when asked if he expected to be joined by the PLO in negotiations with Israel, but he added prudently that such at least had been the understanding in 1985.[2] There was no hint that the king would first accept, and soon thereafter almost insist on, an independent Palestinian delegation to talks. Even concerning the most crucial issue of the conflict — the territorial question

— Jordan did not seem to object to a degree of ambiguity. It was reported in January that Jordan was ready to make substantial border concessions to Israel. This surprising report emanated from a prominent member of the British Labor Party who had visited Jordan, where he had met with Prime Minister Zayd al-Rifa'i and Foreign Minister Tahir al-Masri. According to this visitor, no one in Jordan really believed that Israel would go back to the June 1967 lines.[3]

Assuming that this report was not to be taken literally, it showed that Jordanian officials still found it useful, in talking to visiting dignitaries, to de-emphasize their insistence on Israeli withdrawal from all territories.[4] On this issue, too, Jordan would soon revert to the traditional unambiguous language.

Toward the end of January, two senior US diplomats, Philip Habib and Richard Murphy, came to Amman to prepare Shultz's visit. The White House spokesman noted on 1 February that no breakthrough had been made in the talks,[5] which was hardly a surprise. The king's positions were well known, and he reiterated them in a long interview just before Shultz arrived. The gap between the Jordanian and US positions remained as wide as ever. In the interview, Husayn hinted that Jordan was ready to disengage from the West Bank. He said that like all Arabs he felt morally responsible for the Palestinians on the West Bank, but "did not have the same sense of responsibility for them" that he had for his own subjects on the East Bank.[6] Prime Minister Rifa'i, talking several days later, found it necessary to warn that if the new American plan proposed self-rule rather than self-determination for the Palestinians on the West Bank, Jordan would consider the plan a "gimmick." He made a significant new point when he said that Jordan laid down no preconditions concerning how the PLO was to be represented at the international conference. This was one of the first indications that Jordan would not, or could not, do very much to form a joint Jordanian-Palestinian delegation. Rifa'i also insisted on an "ongoing role" for the international conference and said that a one-time meeting would not do.[7]

The statements by Husayn and Rifa'i did not augur well for the Shultz mission, but there was a tendency to believe that they were bargaining counters. After all, so the reasoning went, Rifa'i had also expressed satisfaction that the US had become actively engaged again in the peace process and that the American plan provided for the talks about a final settlement to start even before the talks on a transitional period had been completed.[8]

At the end of February, Shultz came to the area on what was to be his first trip. Husayn was not in Amman, he was undergoing medical treatment in London. However, even before Husayn met with Shultz there on 1 March, the secretary of state was told in Amman by Crown Prince Hasan that Jordan would no longer press for a joint Jordanian-Palestinian delegation at the ME talks; instead, it would support a separate PLO seat at the conference table.[9] Shultz's meeting with Husayn in London lasted for three hours. A Jordanian statement described the meeting as quite negative. The reiteration of Jordan's policy included an expression of the hope that the US could consult with the Soviet Union and other Security Council members. This was hardly meant to express confidence in US peace efforts. Still, the king did not want to appear to have rejected Shultz's proposal, which was why the statement added that the king felt that the US ideas "needed to be developed" further to bring them into harmony with Arab requirements.[10] Although the Soviet Union had no real reason to fear that Husayn would accept the US proposal, General Secretary Gorbachev deemed it necessary to send Husayn a message which reached the king soon after Shultz had left.[11]

Shultz did not give up. After consulting with President Reagan in Brussels he returned to London for a second meeting with Husayn. Explaining this, the White House spokesman said there were "some reasons for optimism."[12] At the second meeting, Shultz presented Husayn with the outline of the US proposals, which he soon thereafter also presented to the Egyptian and Israeli leaders. (For text, see Appendix I.) Shultz had conceded a vital point: he had agreed to holding an international conference two weeks before the negotiations on transitional arrangements began.[13]

Notwithstanding this new element in the US proposals, Husayn decided to consult first with other Arab leaders before replying.[14] In addition, a meeting between Rifa'i and Soviet Foreign Minister Eduard Shevardnadze also took place. In a joint statement, Rifa'i and Shevardnadze noted "the expediency of continuing substantive talks with the US Administration," i.e., they did not oppose such talks but cautioned against the "danger of partial, separate understanding."[15] A second trip by US envoy Habib to Amman (20 March) did not elicit a clear Jordanian reply. But his report contained nothing to dissuade Shultz from continuing the diplomatic effort. Moreover, his meeting with two prominent Palestinian-Americans (26 March) encouraged Shultz to believe that the chances for direct discussions between the US and the Palestinians during his next trip were much improved. If such a meeting came about, it would also help his mission in Jordan.

Shultz arrived in Amman (5 April) after talks in Israel. In a press conference in Jerusalem (3 April) he made a statement which was bound to have a strong effect on his chances of success in Jordan. He told the Israeli press that he was opposed to the PLO, that he would not support an independent Palestinian state, and that he would not expect Israel to return to the 1967 lines.[16] He then reiterated this statement in an interview with six Jordanian newspaper editors in Amman (5 April). On borders, he said that it did not seem to him to be in the cards that Israel "would just go back to the 1967 borders"; a "territorial compromise" was one of the possibilities that Security Council Resolution 242 did not exclude. On the PLO, he noted that its covenant stated that Israel had no right to exist, advocated terrorism, and refused to accept UN Resolution 242 as the basis for negotiations. The US, he said, would not talk to the PLO until it changed its stand. On the demand for an independent Palestinian state, he said that to establish it on the West Bank and in Gaza "made no sense." Shultz disappointed the Jordanian editors when he told them that the US understood Israel's concerns with its security and would continue to assist Israel. The US would not exert pressure on Israel.[17]

The immediate Jordanian reaction was to instruct its media not to publish the complete interview. The editorial comments were, as expected, highly critical. In the talks in Amman, before this incident occurred, Husayn took care again not to close the door on further efforts by Shultz. He did this by posing many questions about the US proposal. One question was whether the US included the Palestinians living outside the occupied territories in its definition of a Palestinian. Shultz preferred to understand this question as indicating Husayn's serious interest in peace efforts.[18] But the reality was less encouraging. Jordan expressed willingness to continue the dialogue with the US even indefinitely, but only on the basis of a six-point document which contained the principles that would guide Jordan in any effort to settle the Arab-Israeli conflict and the Palestinian problem. (For text, see Appendix II.) Husayn said that Jordan's attitude toward the US proposals would be "determined by the extent to which they correspond to these principles." This was precisely what the king had told Shultz in London a month earlier. If anything, the Jordanian position had stiffened. Once again, Jordan insisted on Israeli withdrawal from all the occupied territories and reiterated that it would neither represent the Palestinians at the conference nor negotiate the settlement on behalf of the PLO. Jordan did not exclude the possibility of a joint Jordanian-Palestinian delegation if the PLO and the other parties agreed, but even under such an arrangement there would be two separate delegations. Rifa'i noted that the Palestinians should have the right to return to their former homes in Israel and the settlement ought to include Syria. The international conference envisaged by Jordan had to be "effective in its scope and mechanism" and not a merely ceremonial affair, even if it lacked the power to impose a settlement. Rifa'i said the Jordanian position was "nonnegotiable." This blunt statement was truthful even if Rifa'i did say that Jordan did not reject the US initiative.[19] Husayn and Rifa'i saw no reason not to cooperate with the US at a time when they felt that the US was "inching closer to the kingdom's perceptions."

It was important to Jordan that the Soviet Union's views on all issues concerning a settlement were almost identical with its own. This had been the case for some time; Husayn and his collaborators had on several occasions expressed satisfaction with the Soviet position.[20]

Jordan also made several points which were not really new. Their very reiteration, however, indicated some tactical flexibility. The US was urged to declare that the Palestinians were entitled to self-determination even if in doing so it stressed its opposition to a PLO-led Palestinian state. Jordan knew that the PLO strongly disagreed with this approach. However, in 1985 in talks with the PLO, Jordan had taken the line that self-determination meant elections *after* which the question of leadership would be determined. Concerning what Rifa'i termed Israel's security requirements, there could be "some border modifications" when the 1949 armistice line would be converted into a permanent boundary. It was perhaps significant that Rifa'i did not, on this occasion, talk about reciprocal modifications.

The differences with the US continued to prove unbridgeable. In May, Jordan published Shultz's answers to the queries Husayn raised in April. Four stumbling blocks remained. (1) The US continued not to recognize Palestinian rights to self-determination; it was only ready to support Palestinian civil and political rights. (2) The US remained opposed to an independent Palestinian state and favored instead, a Jordanian-Palestinian confederation. (3) The US adhered to its view that an international conference must be a framework for direct negotiations without coercive or veto powers. (4) The phases and timetable set out in the US proposals indicated no change in the US position; Jordan insisted that both phases, the transitional and the final, should be simultaneous. The only reply that Jordan considered satisfactory concerned the question about the Palestinians outside the occupied territories, "the Palestinian diaspora." The US stated that its proposal applied to them as well.[21]

Shultz came to the region, and to Jordan, on his third trip immediately after the Reagan-Gorbachev summit in Moscow. During his brief stay in Amman (3 June) he made a serious effort to present the US position in a more conciliatory manner. In declaring that "implementation of Resolution 242, and addressing the political rights of the Palestinian peoples and Israel's security concerns remained the key elements of the peace settlement advocated by the US," he seemed to accept that the question of "political rights" was an important adjunct to Resolution 242. He also stated that the concept of "exchange of territory for peace" applied to all fronts. However, he qualified this somewhat when he added that the question of withdrawal had to be "discussed among the parties themselves."[22]

The likelihood that Shultz's refurbished formulations would impress the Jordanians was immediately decreased by Soviet statements that no "material" change in the American stand had emerged during the Moscow summit. The Soviet ambassador to Jordan said "they [the Americans] are talking about something and we are talking about something else again."[23]

From a whole string of Jordanian pronouncements in May it was possible to conclude that Jordan was reappraising its policies.[24] Then, at the Arab emergency summit (7–9 June) which met in Algiers to discuss the *intifada,* Husayn gave full expression to his views. He left no one in doubt that his patience was running out. The US had given Jordan and Egypt a commitment that Resolution 242 would be implemented in six months. Twenty-one years had gone by and although Jordan, so the king said, had always been ready to reach a settlement and had cooperated with UN and US peace efforts, no progress had been made through no fault of his. US policy continued to be one of support for Israel. US peace initiatives were in reality no more than efforts at crisis management. The king was equally critical of the PLO's ingratitude. Everything Jordan did was perceived by it as motivated by desires for gain and hegemony over the West Bank and its inhabitants. The PLO insisted on considering Jordan as a competitor, overlooking the fact that Jordan was acting in "compliance with the call of Arab leaders at the 1974 Rabat summit." However, not only the PLO, but Israel too was misperceiving Jordan's role in the West Bank. Israel's policies were based on the assumption that it could achieve its "expansionist" goals either in or through Jordan. The gist of the king's address was his renewed affirmation that Jordan would accept anything the PLO decided concerning its participation in the international conference. Furthermore, Jordan would abide by all unanimous Arab summit resolutions.[25]

The *intifada,* the unending strife with the PLO, Israel's adamant positions, and the futile American peace efforts led Husayn in the summer of 1988 to conclude that his chances of retrieving the West Bank were quickly receding. He was painfully aware that his influence over the West Bank Palestinians, never too great, was doomed to disappear altogether. It was time to consider what effect this would have on the East Bank Palestinians. A week before the king's 31 July announcement, sources close to the Jordanian Government said that the impending changes were the result of the seven-month *intifada* and followed Jordan's ascertainment of a decline in West Bank Palestinian support for it.[26] The feelings of deep disappointment notwithstanding, in having to announce Jordan's disengagement from the West Bank, Husayn promised to continue to support the Palestinians.[27] The king's commitment to continue Jordan's participation in the peace process was explained as stemming from the fact that Jordan's border with Israel was longer than the borders of the West Bank and the Gaza Strip put together. But Jordan's participation would be subject to the six-point document. "Political observers" in Amman noted that the king's step would leave the

US and Israel no choice but to negotiate directly with the PLO.[28] The message that the king wanted to convey to the US and Israel was that without PLO backing Jordan would no longer be an active partner in the peace process.

There was reluctance in Israel and the US to accept this message at face value. Shultz expressed his conviction that Husayn would remain engaged in the peace process, and said that "if there is going to be peace between Israel and its neighbors, then Jordan is involved." Murphy came to Jordan a week after the king's disengagement announcement. After talking to the king, Murphy noted that Husayn had stressed Jordan's commitment to comprehensive peace in the region.[29] This somewhat encouraged the US and Israel, for whom Husayn remained the negotiating partner.

Until the close of the year under review, Husayn adhered to his declared position, namely that the Palestinians, not Jordan, must be the major party to any solution. Being a "confrontation state," Jordan would continue to be vitally interested in a comprehensive peace settlement, not separate and partial ones. Jordan, according to the king, had a "case and a cause" which was to support the Palestinians.[30] Husayn was proud of Jordan's many efforts toward making the international conference an almost universally accepted vehicle for a settlement. This important achievement for the Arabs would be jeopardized if Jordan ceased promoting the conference.

According to Rifa'i, Jordan would attend an international conference along with other Arab countries. Its contribution there would be a "pan-Arab" one. What Israel called the "Jordanian option" was no more. Jordan had made it very clear that the West Bank was not part of Jordan; it was Palestinian.[31]

Even in what was known to have been a prenegotiated exchange of statements between Husayn and Peres in separate television interviews on an American network (20 October), Husayn took great care to explain that he could not say that "Jordan was ready to alter its position." Jordan was prepared to go to an international conference in a joint delegation with the Palestinians only if they asked it "categorically" to do so. Significantly, the king specified that a joint delegation really meant two delegations — a Jordanian and a Palestinian — each having equal status.[32] Thus, although Husayn knew how much a different kind of statement could have helped Peres 10 days before the Israeli elections (1 November), he refused to make it; he felt obliged to disappoint Peres even on the question of the joint delegation.

The problem of PLO representation was not Jordan's sole problem. Husayn could not ignore Syria. He admitted that his position was not different from that of Syria's both concerning the international conference and the "circumstances that should prevail in order to achieve a settlement."[33] In proclaiming that Jordan and Syria held the same views, Husayn was in effect saying that he agreed with Syria's maximalist views. Yet, it was most unlikely that Husayn, for so long a key figure in peace efforts, had joined rejectionist Syria.

THE PALESTINIANS AND THE PLO

The year 1988 was very eventful for the Palestinians and the PLO. The *intifada* was only three weeks old when the year began and there was no certainty that it would endure for many months; but as the year wound down, the end was not in sight. At the beginning of the year, it was generally believed that the unrest might end as suddenly as it had started. If this happened, the *intifada* would have been in vain and the Palestinians would not have been brought any closer to their goal of self-determination as expressed in an independent state.

The Palestinians watched the American diplomatic efforts in the region, soon to be known as the "Shultz proposals," with much concern. PLO Chairman Yasir 'Arafat found them at odds with PLO policy on five counts: they opposed Palestinian self-determination, an independent Palestinian delegation to the international conference, an international conference with coercive authority, an independent Palestinian state and, finally, the PLO itself.[34]

The PLO ordered a total ban on meetings with Shultz in the region. One explanation for this order was that there could be no meetings with a country which refused to recognize the PLO and its representatives. Moreover, US efforts were bound to fail since no solution was possible without the PLO.[35]

In actual fact, the US attitude toward Palestinian demands was not altogether negative. Shultz met twice early in the year with well-known Palestinian figures. The first encounter (27 January) was with two Palestinians from the territories, both of them persons who had never denied their pro-PLO sympathies.[36] Two months later, he met with two well-known American-Palestinian academics, who were respected members of the PNC.[37] Both professors had obtained permission from 'Arafat to attend the meeting. A PLO commentator noted that in their capacity as PNC members they were part of the Palestinian decision-making process.[38]

Shultz also indicated his goodwill toward the Palestinians in a more significant manner, by making a declaration concerning them as early as February during his first shuttle mission to the region. That statement, made in East Jerusalem, added new elements to the existing US position. It acknowledged for the first time the Palestinian right to control "political and economic decisions that affect their lives." No less significantly, it acknowledged that "Palestinians living outside the territories have concerns which need to be resolved." This meant that the Palestinian diaspora was included in the US peace efforts.[39]

As regards the decisions adopted by the 19th PNC in Algiers in November (see below) it is noteworthy that most of their elements had been part of the PLO policy for some time. On the basis of resolutions adopted at previous PNC meetings and in particular the 18th (April 1987), 'Arafat recapitulated the PLO positions early in 1988, as follows:

(a) Acceptance of all UN resolutions, including 242 and 338. All UN resolutions constituted one "organic whole." The PLO would not discard some and retain others. It accepted UN Resolution 181 of 1947 which provided in its first clause for the establishment of a Palestinian state and in its second clause, of a Jewish state. Israel, however, so he noted, rejected the first clause.

(b) The PLO was ready to negotiate with the "Israeli enemy" at a UN-sponsored international conference. The PLO would attend the conference on equal footing with other parties.

(c) The PLO challenged Israel and the US to declare their acceptance of the international conference. The purpose of the conference would be the resolution of the Palestinian question.

(d) The PLO was seeking to protect the Palestinians in the occupied territories by means of UN forces to be sent there.
(e) The PLO rejected the offer to establish autonomy in the West Bank and the Gaza Strip.[40]
(f) It was equally opposed to the Shultz proposals no matter how packaged. In effect, the US was offering a Jordanian-Israeli condominium over the territories instead of an independent Palestinian state.[41]
(g) The Palestinians would agree to be part of a joint Arab delegation to an international conference, although they preferred a delegation of their own. They rejected the idea of a joint delegation with Jordan.[42]

'Arafat had reason to be pleased with his meeting with Mikhail Gorbachev in Moscow in April. Gorbachev affirmed his support for the *intifada,* his adherence to an "effective," as opposed to a ceremonial, international conference, and he assured 'Arafat that the Soviets recognized the PLO's right to participate in the international conference in an independent or unified Arab delegation on an equal footing with the other parties. The Soviets viewed all UN resolutions as pertinent to a settlement. Resolutions 242 and 338 were concerned with resolving the territorial issue, i.e., Israeli withdrawal. The other UN resolutions were important, because they provided for the Palestinian people's national rights. By this, the Soviets meant self-determination and an independent state.

'Arafat, in repeating in several interviews that he had assured Gorbachev that the PLO accepted all UN resolutions including 242 and 338, stressed the right to existence for all states in the region, including Israel. It was interesting that 'Arafat said this to Gorbachev who had told him that Israel, like all countries in the region, should enjoy security (see section on the Soviet Union in this chapter).[43]

On the eve of the emergency Arab summit conference in Algiers (7–9 June) a statement written by Bassam Abu Sharif, a close adviser to 'Arafat, was circulated. It drew considerable attention when it reached Washington, not because it contained points not made before by 'Arafat and his supporters in the mainstream, pragmatic PLO groups, but because it was clearly articulated. The statement was written with the purpose of making the best possible impression on American and Israeli public opinion. On direct talks, for example, it stated: "...the means by which the Israelis want to achieve lasting peace and security is direct talks, with no attempt by any outside party to impose or veto a settlement. The Palestinians agree.... We feel that any settlement that has to be imposed by an outside power...will not stand the test of time."[44]

The author did not explain how this statement squared with the PLO's insistence on an "effective" international conference to which Israel was opposed. A week later, he said that the PLO needed an "effective" conference in order to obtain an international guarantee from the two superpowers and the permanent members of the Security Council. The angry outcry of some of the more extreme elements in the PLO that the statement was guilty of "deviationism" did not dampen the enthusiasm it had aroused in the American media.[45] 'Arafat did not disavow his close adviser's statement, but did say that it was not an official PLO document.[46]

'Arafat declared himself satisfied with the resolutions of the Arab summit conference.[47] The conference decided to extend all necessary assistance to the *intifada.*

Financial aid was promised although the exact sum remained secret; the secretary-general of the Arab League, Chedli Klibi, called the amount "most satisfactory."[48]

In contacts between the PLO and Jordan at the conference, the Jordanians objected to several formulations which the PLO was about to recommend; when agreement was reached, it appeared that harmony was restored.[49] However, it was not unlikely that these differences contributed to Husayn's decision, six weeks later, to announce Jordan's disengagement from the West Bank. The king acted without informing the PLO in advance and 'Arafat complained about this, pointing out that Husayn had been in contact with a number of Arab states on the matter.

The PLO Central Council reacted immediately, but with extreme caution. It decided to study the implications of the Jordanian steps through contacts with "fraternal Jordan," and to convene the PNC.[50] Soon after, however, the PLO concluded that the Jordanian decision was one of the most important achievements of the *intifada.* 'Arafat announced that the PLO would assume the responsibilities resulting from the Jordanian move.[51] Other PLO spokesmen welcomed the decision, because it constituted Jordanian recognition of the PLO's responsibility for the Palestinians and for the future of the occupied territories.[52]

The 19th PNC met in Algiers on 12-15 November. In preparing the meeting the PLO leadership discussed various options. It was obvious that one of them was the proclamation of an independent Palestinian state. Another was the establishment of a provisional government. The PLO knew that a dramatic decision was called for to fill the void created by Jordan. The "popular committees" in the occupied territories — according to 'Arafat, there were about 200 of them[53] — were pressing not to let the opportunity pass. The uprising needed a boost in morale and expected it to come from the PLO. Salah Khalaf put it succinctly: "We are facing a stage where an announcement of an initiative is inevitable to match the uprising and Jordan's decision to cut links with the West Bank."[54]

'Arafat's chances of getting the more extreme faction inside the PLO, in particular George Habash (Popular Front for the Liberation of Palestine; PFLP) and Na'if Hawatima (Democratic Front for the Liberation of Palestine; DFLP) to back him this time improved when it became clear that the Soviets promised support for a solution based not only on Resolution 242, i.e., Israeli withdrawal, but also on other Palestinian demands, including the "right to return and [Palestinian] independence on the basis of international legitimacy."[55] "International legitimacy" referred to the UN Resolution 181 of 1947 calling for partition, which the Arabs had rejected. Moreover, the Palestinian Covenant of 1968 (Article 19) stated clearly that the partition of Palestine and the establishment of Israel were "entirely illegal." To accept the partition resolution as the basis of "international legitimacy" meant that Palestinian leaders, such as Hawatima and Habash, were now reconciled to a Palestinian state in part of what had been the British Mandate (1922–48). Whether this also meant reconciliation with Israel's existence was a different matter. 'Arafat himself, and most of his mainstream supporters, had already accepted Resolution 181 some time ago. He could now say that the resolution was the international Palestinian state's "birth certificate," just as it had been Israel's.[56]

Two problems, however, remained. The first was that the US and Israel would suspect that the reference to Resolution 181 indicated that the PLO demanded that Israel accept the 1947 borders. Such a demand was totally unrealistic and unacceptable even to the Soviet Union which supported the Palestinians on all other matters. The second problem was that the internationally accepted basis for a settlement of the Arab-Israeli conflict since 1967 had been Security Council Resolution 242 which 'Arafat and the PLO had yet to accept unambiguously. In an attempt to get over this hurdle the PNC did not mention this resolution in its Declaration of Independence,[57] referring only to Resolution 181. A reference to Resolution 242 appeared in the PNC's final statement, which was adopted by an overwhelming majority (265 to 46). The reference to the resolution appeared in the paragraph dealing with the "necessity of holding an effective international conference." The conference would be held on the basis of Resolutions 242 and 338, that much was admitted in the document. But it added the phrase: "and the assurance of the legitimate rights of the Palestinian people...in accordance with the resolutions of the UN regarding the Palestinian cause".[58] By adding this phrase the document created ambiguity as to whether Resolution 242 had been accepted unconditionally. The US thought that it had not and that the PLO had not fulfilled the conditions the US had laid down for recognizing the PLO. *The New York Times* wrote about a "letdown in Algiers" and said that the PLO "knows the words needed to trigger US action — and hasn't said them yet."[59] This US reaction was a serious setback for the PLO.

A month later a group of private American Jews met with 'Arafat in Stockholm, at the initiative of Sweden's foreign minister, Sten Anderson. A joint statement issued after the meeting did not differ enough from the PNC final statement to change the US position.[60] A week later, 'Arafat addressed the UN General Assembly specially convened in Geneva to enable him to address it, after the US had denied him a visa to address the assembly in New York. Once again, his statements on terrorism, Resolution 242, and acceptance of Israel were found lacking in precision.[61] After some behind-the-scenes diplomacy, including Egyptian urging, 'Arafat held a press conference in which he made the statement the US wanted him to make. On Resolution 242, he said that he "accepted it as a basis for negotiations with Israel within the framework of the international conference." This time, there was no linkage between Resolution 242 and other UN resolutions. On acceptance of Israel, he said that he acknowledged the "rights of all parties concerned with the Middle East conflict to exist in peace and security, including the state of Palestine, Israel, and other neighbors in accordance with Resolutions 242 and 338."[62] Within four hours of 'Arafat's statement, President Reagan authorized the start of a "substantive dialogue with the PLO." Within a week, the first US-PLO meeting took place.[63]

EGYPT

Egypt's position in the Arab world improved dramatically in 1988 after all Arab countries with the exception of Syria, Libya, and Lebanon restored diplomatic relations with it. However, Egypt continued to believe that it would not regain its status of *primus inter pares* among the Arab states as long as it remained the only Arab country to have a peace agreement with Israel. To change this, the difficult Palestinian question would have to be settled. A decade had passed since Camp David and not only had there been no progress toward resolving this problem, but the situation of the Palestinians had seriously deteriorated. The *intifada* provided painful proof of that. It also lent considerable urgency to the vital Egyptian national interest not to remain alone in their peace with Israel. It was no longer sufficient to maintain that peace at almost freezing point. Feeling compelled to move the peace process off dead center, Egypt acted energetically to do so during the year under review.

Egyptian leaders were not ashamed to admit their discomfort.[64] At the same time, they were not discouraged. Egypt's equally good relations with Jordan and the PLO and its excellent relations with the US uniquely qualified it to play a role in the peace process. It may have been sheer coincidence that a day before US President Reagan welcomed President Mubarak to the White House (28 January) and encouraged Egypt to join the US "in taking a leadership role" in the diplomatic efforts, a Palestinian leader said in an article that Mubarak was probably the most qualified mediator available, one "of the few influential figures in the world who was on speaking terms with both the PLO and Israel."[65]

As the peace process unfolded in 1988, Egypt certainly played a meaningful role but for most of the year it was the US, through the Shultz mission, that carried the ball. It cannot be excluded, however, that Mubarak's initiative in late January which took the form of a five-point proposal and his visit to the US served as a catalyst at a crucial moment when the US Administration was weighing whether to renew its efforts. Mubarak based his move on the assumption, which proved correct, that the Reagan Administration, its preoccupation with the presidential campaign in the US notwithstanding, could be persuaded to act.[66] There was reason to believe that preliminary contacts with Israelis had taken place just before Mubarak left for the US. An Israeli minister, Ezer Weizmann, who is on particularly good terms with Mubarak, published a series of proposals[67] (see section on Israel in this chapter) and his closest collaborator met with Mubarak's political adviser, Usama al-Baz. The five-point plan put forward by Mubarak in one package never had a chance of being accepted by Israel or even by the US. Israel was bound to reject its suggestions to place an international force in the occupied territories to protect the Palestinians, to convene an international conference that would provide for Palestinian self-determination, and to end all Israeli settlement operations. Mubarak probably never believed that his proposals would be accepted, but if he presented them in order to prod the US into action he was fully rewarded. In a matter of days after leaving Washington, US diplomacy was reengaged in the ME.

A month later, Shultz visited Cairo and was gratified with his meeting there. Egypt signaled its support for the US initiative and Shultz announced that both he and Mubarak agreed that the American ideas were sound. Mubarak did not have any particular problem with any of its components.[68] Significantly, on the eve of Shultz's arrival, Mubarak declared that the autonomy provisions of the 1978 Camp David accords were no longer acceptable to Egypt. Similar statements were also made by Foreign Minister 'Abd al-Majid and 'Usama al-Baz.[69] Clearly, Mubarak viewed the new Shultz proposals as a step away from the Camp David autonomy framework.

Egypt's backing was especially important to the US when Shultz tried to meet with a Palestinian delegation. Egypt pleaded with 'Arafat to agree to a delegation comprising Palestinians who were not formally identified as PLO members. The Egyptians warned that the Palestinians might "miss an historic opportunity." 'Arafat, however, was adamant.

Egypt believed that "positive" changes had occurred in the US position. The *intifada* made it impossible for the Americans to continue viewing the Palestinian issue as quiescent. They had finally come around to seeing it as urgent, to accept the need for holding an international conference and even for setting a tentative date for its convocation. Although Egypt did have some reservations about Washington's proposals, it felt that it was wise to encourage the US in the hope that its policy would eventually come closer to Egypt's.[70]

As for Mubarak, he was convinced that the Americans had already covered a considerable distance since, thanks to his good offices, the US secretary of state was willing to talk to the Palestinians and the question that remained unsettled was the venue. Therefore, he believed that "the ball was in the Arab court" and said so in March.[71]

The Egyptians blamed Israeli Prime Minister Yitzhak Shamir for being the sole obstacle to the international conference idea. The question of Palestinian representation was merely "procedural" and it could be easily resolved if the UN secretary-general sent an invitation to the PLO. Such an invitation did not imply, however, that the PLO would give up its demand for independent Palestinian representation and would be satisfied with being represented at the conference in a unified Arab delegation. Mubarak attempted to explain what Egypt meant by saying that the Palestinians must be part of a Jordanian-Palestinian delegation.[72] This position, however, it soon emerged, was much less firm and consistent. With regard to the Israeli argument that the conference would impose solutions and, therefore, put Israel at a disadvantage, Egyptian spokesmen pointed out that Egypt had never stated that the conference would have coercive authority. However, this did not mean that the Arabs would "submit to the Israeli stand."[73]

The Egyptian stand was well known: Israel must agree to barter land for peace.[74] Only after the land was recovered would the Arabs decide what to do with it. The question of whether there would be a Palestinian state was an exclusively Arab affair and there was no point to premature talk about the final objective, because it would frighten other parties to the international conference.[75] Thus phrased, it was clear that Egypt was anxious not to foreclose anything. Its continuing efforts to bring about agreement between Jordan and the PLO imposed prudence on Egyptian public statements concerning Palestinian statehood, even though Egyptian support for it had been made known in the past and would occasionally be reiterated in 1988.[76]

Egypt's close ties with the PLO and with 'Arafat led it to several frequently articulated conclusions: (1) that 'Arafat was a well-intentioned, flexible, and indeed, the most moderate Palestinian leader; (2) that the divisions among the Palestinians were so deep that all progress was impeded; the Palestinians must close ranks and agree on policy if there was to be progress; (3) that an understanding between the PLO and Jordan was absolutely crucial to the success of the efforts to convene an international conference. Egyptian prodding no doubt played a role in the events inside the PLO which enabled that organization to achieve an unprecedented show of unity in the PNC in November 1988.[77]

Even though Shultz's two later visits to the area (April and June) proved fruitless, Mubarak continued to encourage the US secretary not to give up, declaring that every trip brought something new and narrowed the differences.[78] But Minister of State for Foreign Affairs Butrus Butrus-Ghali was less considerate. He said that the US initiative would fail unless the US made it "compatible with the realities confirmed by the Palestinian uprising...and adopted a more decisive stand toward Shamir's opposition."[79]

On the face of it, the positions of the Soviet Union were in harmony with those of Egypt. A joint communiqué published in May summing up 'Abd al-Majid's talks in Moscow attested to it. 'Abd al-Majid and Shevardnadze expressed support for a conference which would include the PLO and praised the *intifada*.[80] These clear statements notwithstanding, the Egyptians realized that at the Reagan-Gorbachev summit, the Soviets rather than insisting that the PLO should attend the conference had agreed to leave the matter to the Arabs and said that they would respect their decision.[81]

Egypt perceived the Soviet role as essential, particularly as East-West tensions subsided. Egypt favored an active Soviet role in the peace process, an "active Soviet presence on the Middle East stage and a positive role in an international peace conference." Moreover, it believed that a settlement achieved with Soviet participation would be better for the Arabs than one achieved with US assistance alone.[82] In making this judgment the Egyptians echoed what the Jordanians and the PLO had often said before them.

Husayn's announcement that Jordan would sever its legal and administrative ties with the West Bank (31 July) caused Egypt to intensify its diplomatic efforts but did not require a basic policy reassessment. If until then Egypt had exerted itself to improve Jordanian-PLO relations and coordination, it was now even more urgent to persist in such efforts. On the morrow of the king's decision, 'Abd al-Majid said that the peace process now needed a "united Arab front, mainly based on effective Jordanian-Palestinian coordination." Mubarak made the same point a week later.[83] Egypt was encouraged by Husayn's statement that Jordan would not abandon its role in the peace process. In the following weeks, the Egyptians did their utmost to influence the resolutions the PLO would adopt at the forthcoming PNC meeting. When a high-level Palestinian delegation came to Cairo, Egypt reaffirmed its fullest support for Palestinian aspirations and promised it would be the first state to recognize the PNC resolutions,[84] but it also called upon the PLO to adopt "realistic" policies and to coordinate "every step" with Jordan. To increase their leverage over the PLO, Mubarak instructed the Egyptian foreign minister to put his political and legal counsel at the PLO's disposal.

Generally stated, Egypt recommended that the PLO adopt an "internationally acceptable" program as a prelude to any announcement about the form the Palestinian entity or state would take.[85] 'Arafat's address before the Socialist Group of the European Parliament in Strasbourg (13 September) provided proof that Egyptian efforts were producing results; soon after that speech 'Arafat met with Mubarak in Cairo.[86]

On the basis of several frank and extended interviews given by Mubarak and 'Abd al-Majid to Arab papers during this period (August to December), while they and other senior Egyptians steered the PLO and 'Arafat toward making the policy declarations upon which the opening of a dialogue with the US depended, it seemed possible to summarize Egyptian thinking as follows:

(a) The American position was in the process of changing. Reagan, in a joint meeting with 'Abd al-Majid and Peres (26 September), referred to the "political rights" of the Palestinians. The use of these words indicated that the US no longer considered Palestinian rights narrowly. Furthermore, according to 'Abd al-Majid, Reagan had urged Israel to deal with the Palestinian issue "politically." These were significant statements and were to be considered as commitments made by the highest level in the US Administration. Further changes in the US position could be expected if the PLO acted wisely.

(b) Egypt was making great efforts to find a formula that would enable the PLO to participate in the international conference. One preferred solution would be a joint Jordanian-Palestinian delegation. This, however, was esentially an issue that could only be resolved through the PLO, and at the 'Aqaba meeting among Mubarak, Husayn, and 'Arafat (22 October), Husayn and 'Arafat accepted this solution.[87]

(c) Egypt did not envisage the solution within an exclusively Jordanian framework, as did the US and Israel, but rather within confederal ties between the Palestinian state and Jordan. This arrangement was discussed at 'Aqaba, and Husayn and 'Arafat appeared to favor it.[88]

(d) The PLO must accept Security Council Resolutions 242 and 338, renounce terrorism, and recognize Israel. Even after Jordan's severance of links with the West Bank, these US requirements had to be met.

(e) PLO demands that the occupied territories be administered provisionally by the UN were unrealistic. Instead, Egypt favored a PNC decision to set up an interim government. Egypt would support such a decision only if the PNC first formulated a reasonable political program.

(f) UN Resolution 181 ("partition"), although 41 years old and rejected by the Arabs in 1947, should be invoked to legitimize the Palestinian demand for a state. Exactly as Israel considered that resolution its "birth certificate," so must the Palestinians. The importance of Resolution 181 was that it established the principle of a Palestinian state. The Egyptians were certainly aware that the PNC's acknowledgment of Resolution 181 was tantamount to formal acceptance of the two-state solution to the conflict. Thereafter it would be possible to argue that the Palestinian Covenant, which laid claim to the whole of Palestine, had lost all, or at least most, of its validity. Also, Resolution 181 gave the Palestinians the element that was missing in Security Council Resolution 242, namely a reference to Palestinian self-determination. Egypt argued that in accepting Resolution 242 so as to accommodate the US, the PLO did not compromise anything since Resolution 181 provided for a Palestinian state.

(g) In urging the PLO to accept Resolution 181, Egypt made it clear that the borders defined in that resolution were no longer relevant. The borders that Egypt would support for the Palestinian state would be those of 1967.[89]

(h) For these steps to succeed, 'Arafat must exert his leadership inside the PLO, overcome opposition, and forge a united stand.

Throughout 1988, Egypt pursued its diplomatic effort relentlessly but had only modest expectations about what could be accomplished during an election year in both Israel and the US. As for the future, it was far from certain that the international conference would meet in 1988, because the Arab countries had first to agree on a joint position. In effect, what was needed was for the Arabs to accept the Palestinian positions as agreed between Mubarak and 'Arafat, and stand united behind them.[90]

The declarations adopted by the 19th PNC (12–15 November) were by and large a victory for Egypt's policy. It was, therefore, natural for Egypt to issue immediately a statement of support for the "declaration of the Palestinan state" whose establishment it saw as "an important step toward achieving a peaceful settlement."[91] However, although this language appeared satisfactory for the most part, it contained an element of reserve. It distinguished between support in principle for a Palestinian state and immediate recognition of that state. The reason for this caution was not altogether clear. One explanation was that Egypt did not want to expose itself to the accusation that in granting recognition to the state it violated the Camp David accords (1978), which left the final status of the territories in abeyance until settled by negotiations.[92] The Egyptians argued that "supporting the declaration" was stronger than "conventional recognition."[93] Finally, five days after the publication of the first statement, an official Egyptian spokesman put an end to the confusion by stating that although expressing support was "stronger and more advanced" than recognition, Egypt affirmed that it recognized the Palestinian state effective as of 15 November.

The formal clarification cleared the way for one more visit by 'Arafat to Cairo (21, 22 November). Mubarak availed himself of a joint press conference with 'Arafat to mention Egypt's support for the PNC resolutions which, in that order, "recognized Resolution 242, proclaimed the establishment of the Palestinian state, defined its borders as those which existed in 1967, announced the establishment of a confederal union with Jordan, and renounced terrorism." Mubarak added that this was also Husayn's stand.[94]

The accelerated pace of Egypt's diplomacy was kept up during the last weeks of the year. There were more visits to Cairo by Husayn (30 November-1 December) and 'Arafat (3–5 December). In the meetings between Mubarak and Husayn, the Palestine question was not the only one on the agenda. It had become likely that Egypt would be invited to the next Arab summit, i.e., would be asked to return to the Arab League after an absence of a decade. This would happen, however, only if all Arab League countries agreed; this meant, in effect, that Syria had to consent. To achieve this, Husayn met with President Hafiz al-Asad. Egypt preferred not to describe Husayn as a mediator between Egypt and Syria, but to view him as a man of goodwill who, concerned about Arab divisiveness, had become a force for reconciliation.[95]

In Mubarak's meeting with 'Arafat, the main topic was the PLO chairman's forthcoming speech at the UN General Assembly in Geneva. Mubarak again promised 'Arafat to give him Egypt's unlimited support, and, in fact, Mubarak did not disappoint 'Arafat. 'Abd al-Majid's speech in Geneva clarified the often vaguer pronouncements of 'Arafat. Egypt's prestige and credibility were thus committed to convince the UN of the PLO's intent.[96]

Mubarak, for his part, was even more generous in vouching for the PLO's intentions. He not only praised 'Arafat's Geneva speech, but said that he was convinced of 'Arafat's sincerity in denouncing terrorism. Moreover, he gave his own interpretation of a crucial sentence in 'Arafat's speech when he affirmed that 'Arafat had noted that Israel must exist within secure borders, the pre-1967 borders. 'Arafat had not really been that explicit.[97]

To persuade the US Administration to accept 'Arafat's pronouncement as meeting the requirements it had laid down in 1975, Mubarak sent three messages to Reagan and held a long telephone coversation with Shultz. On 15 December, as Egypt welcomed the US decision to open direct talks with the PLO, it could look back with satisfaction at the difficult diplomatic task it had accomplished in 1988. (For further discussion, see chapter on Egypt.)

SYRIA

In the year under review, the Syrian Ba'th regime remained as deeply convinced as ever that its mission was to be in the vanguard as the Arab nation moved toward the attainment of its national goals. First and foremost was the "liberation of Palestine from the Zionist occupier." This objective, although difficult and not immediately attainable, was to be relentlessly pursued. Because of its ideological convictions, the Syrian regime neither could nor wished to cooperate with peace efforts led by the US, which the Syrians perceived as "Israel's benefactor and strategic ally." The Syrian regime, however, could not ignore pragmatic considerations in the daily conduct of its policies. One of them was the Syrian economy.

Syria's economic problems in 1987 did not disappear in the year under review (for details, see chapter on Syria). Nevertheless, Syria continued to spend half of the state budget on defense.[98] The attainment of strategic parity with Israel remained its avowed national goal. President Asad reaffirmed that parity was the basis of Syria's struggle to "achieve comprehensive peace." Claims of major progress toward closing the military gap with Israel were made from time to time.[99] There was no reason to question Syrian determination to pursue this policy, but it was also obvious that the grave difficulties that confronted Syria would force it to modify some of its policies or, at least, some of its tactics. This explains, in part, its readiness to receive Shultz and Assistant Secretary Murphy whenever they were in the area. Another reason was the desire to keep tabs on US moves, so as to be better placed to influence Arab policies toward the US initiative. Syria preferred not to disqualify itself by completely boycotting the Shultz mission.

Just before Shultz came to Damascus (27 February) on what would be his first visit in 1988, there was a flurry of diplomatic activity in the Syrian capital which involved Vladimir Polyakov, director of the Soviet Foreign Ministry's Middle East and African Department, and Jordan's prime minister, Zayd al-Rifa'i.[100] The Syrian media quickly rejected the US ideas as "worse than the Camp David accords" and called Shultz's efforts a "waste of time."[101] Still Syria could not completely ignore the fact that the visit marked an improvement in relations with the US, since it took place despite Syria's being on the State Department list of states supporting terrorism. This may explain why Asad acted with circumspection. On the one hand, he criticized the US proposals, "because he found nothing new in them," even predicting their failure, but he also said that Syria would "not want to block roads which others wanted to pursue" on condition that they do not "lead to relinquishment and surrender." Arabs must beware of haste in searching for a solution.[102]

Six weeks later, Shultz visited Damascus again (5 April). Asad's attitude was, if anything, even more uncompromising. He enumerated four conditions for peace: the international conference must be effective and wield full powers; Israel must withdraw completely from all the occupied Arab territory; Palestinian national rights, including self-determination and statehood, must be recognized; and the Arab side must participate in the international conference through a united Arab delegation.[103] These four conditions were a reiteration of often-articulated traditional Syrian positions and they came as no surprise. They did not mention Security Council Resolutions 242 and 338, but Syrian Foreign Minister Faruq al-Shar' explained that not mentioning them did not imply that real differences existed between Syrian and Soviet positions. The Soviets, he said, had always recognized Israel and had supported these two Security Council resolutions. More significant, he said, was the fact that the Soviets were also referring to other UN resolutions concerning the Arab-Israeli conflict and the Palestine question to which the Syrians attached great importance. The Soviets supported, in essence, all Arab demands. Shar' also made it clear that in demanding a unified Arab delegation to the international conference Syria envisaged PLO participation in it.[104]

For a brief moment in the spring of 1988, it looked as if Asad and 'Arafat would reach an understanding about their future relations. They met in Damascus (25 April) in a meeting described as "cordial, warm, and positive." Those who thought that an agreement between Syria and the PLO would eventually be hammered out argued that Asad found himself isolated in his attempts to reduce 'Arafat's influence, since most Arab countries and the Soviet Union continued to support the PLO.[105] Asad's predicament motivated him to seek reconciliation with 'Arafat. This theory, however, proved wrong. Asad's suspicion that 'Arafat was looking for a way to take part in the US-led peace process proved justified toward the end of the year when the PLO leader made the statements which were a US precondition for opening a dialogue between them. Syria refused to recognize the Palestinian state proclaimed by 'Arafat in November. All it did was to remind everyone that it had always supported the establishment of an independent Palestinian state, support for the principle of Palestinian statehood but not for the Algiers proclamation. One official explanation of Syria's attitude was that it tended to divide the Palestinians and the *intifada*. 'Arafat and other PLO leaders were accused of "deviation" and of "selfishness."[106] The Syrian-backed Palestinian organizations went much further by attacking the PNC decisions as "surrender" and "treason."

It was obvious that Asad, to quote one informed observer,

> never stopped considering the PLO and the Palestinian national movement an instrument for the promotion of his strategic aims in the region; at the core of these aims was the establishment of a defensive-offensive buildup against Israel by a 'Greater Syria' which would include Jordan, Lebanon, and a Palestinian state. All these countries would be under Syrian tutelage or influence.[107]

Shultz's third visit to Damascus (6 June) was as fruitless as the previous two. The Syrian media stressed with a great deal of satisfaction that the Moscow summit, whence Shultz had come, had not produced an American-Soviet meeting of minds. The Syrians appeared absolutely certain that the Americans had been unable to weaken the Soviet pro-Arab stance. The Shultz initiative was again described as "capitulatory" and doomed to failure.[108]

ISRAEL

From the Israeli point of view, there was little in the year 1988 that would cause satisfaction or generate optimism. The Palestinian issue became more pressing as the uprising in the territories showed no sign of abating. Statements throughout the year by Israeli leaders that the *intifada* would soon end or, at least, be brought down to a manageable level, remained unfulfilled. The disagreement between the two major political blocs in Israel, the Likud and the Alignment, remained as sharp as ever. Both, however, saw eye to eye on the need to pacify the territories and to seek a political solution. The elections in Israel and the US, scheduled for the end of the year, seemed far enough away in January not to paralyze the start of the diplomatic process.

At the end of January, Peres and Shamir each sent senior officials to Washington. Mubarak's announcement that he was about to put forward new ideas to resolve the Palestinian issue (see section on Egypt in this chapter) contributed, no doubt, to the resolve of the two Israeli leaders, suspicious of each other, to promote their policies in Washington. Peres's envoy was the first to visit Washington and his mission was of a general nature, to plead for increased US activity in the peace process. He proposed a revival of the conference idea as first propounded by Shultz in October 1987: a one-time meeting with only the US and the Soviet Union participating.[109]

A day after Peres's envoy returned to Jerusalem, Shamir's took off (25 January), having been invited by Shultz to come to Washington.[110] The Americans wanted to convey to the Israelis the outlines of the proposals they were preparing. The US was fully aware that Shamir's cooperation was crucial. Shamir had been throughout in close touch with Shultz and informed him about a recent proposal that he had made to Mubarak: the renewal of the Egyptian-Israeli autonomy talks suspended since 1982.

The immediate reason for Shamir's thinking that Mubarak might be amenable to the proposal, was Mubarak's interview with the Kuwaiti daily *al-Anba* (6 January). In what appeared to be a complete change of mind, Mubarak said that if only Egypt had continued the autonomy talks "we would have been in a better shape." He complained that if the Arab countries had not attacked Egypt for holding those talks "we would now have been in an advanced stage of the autonomy solution."[111] In the wake of this interview, Shamir asked Mubarak and the US to resume the talks. He argued that the time that had passed since the talks were suspended had shown that autonomy was the only solution that could bring the sides closer to peace.[112] Shamir had never ceased saying that autonomy was the only way out. He knew that autonomy was not a controversial issue in Israel. Peres, though never its ardent supporter, was not altogether opposed; when he expressed his doubts it was to point out that no one among the Arabs was willing to accept it.

Shamir sent a long message to Shultz (17 January) explaining his thinking. He complained that Husayn kept misinterpreting his position when he said that for Israel the territorial issue was nonnegotiable. He reaffirmed Israel's commitment to the Camp David accords, which stated explicitly that negotiations on the West Bank's permanent status would begin as soon as possible after three years of autonomy there. Although this Israeli position was well known, its repetition at a time when Shultz was discussing whether to renew American diplomatic efforts carried some weight.[113]

Unexpected support for the autonomy idea came from Ezer Weizmann, a member of the Labor Alignment, a cabinet minister, and a man with good connections in Cairo. Weizmann published an article in which he made several points, some of which were in line with Shamir's thinking: (1) that peace efforts needed "to be the policy of the two big parties, not one party alone"; (2) that the Camp David accords (i.e., autonomy) were the only accepted basis for negotiations; (3) that after a transition period of autonomy governed by a joint Jordanian-Palestinian authority, a plebiscite of the residents would indicate the permanent solution they preferred; among the options offered in the plebiscite Weizmann did not mention an independent Palestinian state.[114] The Weizmann proposals contained several points, mostly procedural, to which Shamir was bound to take exception, but significantly, he could accept Weizmann's substantive points without much difficulty. But realtions between Shamir and Peres had by then deteriorated so much that even if Weizmann's ideas reflected Peres's thinking, they could not have become the basis of a Likud-Labor policy. Missing altogether from Weizmann's proposals was the international conference, without which, according to Peres, there could be no negotiations.[115] Shamir continued to be absolutely opposed to the international conference. Weizmann proposed holding a meeting among representatives of Egypt, Jordan, the US, and Israel to start the process going, which was precisely what Shamir also proposed. Mubarak, however, rejected the proposal and reiterated the demand for a conference with the participation of the five permanent members of the Security Council.[116]

On 27 January, Shultz met with two Palestinians, Hana Siniora and Fa'iz Abu Rahma, from the occupied territories (see section on the Palestinians and the PLO in this chapter). Shultz had appealed personally to Shamir to allow them to leave Israel for Washington.[117] The meeting, no doubt, had symbolic value, but as on similar occasions when Palestinians from the territories met with foreign leaders, Siniora and Abu Rahma, too, told Shultz that they were not qualified to speak for the Palestinians. This was the PLO's prerogative.

The US renewed its efforts in the region immediately thereafter. Ambassador Philip Habib arrived in Amman on 29 January and a week later Assistant Secretary of State Richard Murphy came to Jerusalem. Shamir was certain, on the basis of reports from his special envoy, that the American proposals would closely follow his own and that the international conference idea had been discarded. He thought that the US effort would focus primarily on the substantive issues that divided the parties; the procedural questions would be dealt with later.[118] However, Shamir soon realized that he was wrong: the US proposals were described as a blend of procedure and substance, with procedure being given priority. The proposals envisaged progress in stages of short duration and in keeping with a timetable. Six months were considered sufficient to reach agreement over transitional arrangements (the term autonomy was avoided). Once achieved, the agreement would be put in place by means of elections. It was deemed equally important to set from the outset the date on which the final-status negotiations would begin. The date would precede the beginning of the transitional stage. This short timetable,Shultz explained, was based on the assumption that "no one would be satisfied until we had come to grips with the final-status type issues."[119] This approach ran counter to Shamir's which was based on phases, each of which would determine what would happen next; the success of one phase would form the basis for the next. Under the Camp David accords Israel would be ready to discuss the territories' final status, but would refuse to do so at the outset of the process as the US now seemed to envisage it.[120]

This difference notwithstanding, the talks between Shamir and Shultz, who was on the first leg of his mission (25–26 February), were completely relaxed. Shultz told Shamir that during his talks in Moscow, before coming to the region, he had rejected the Soviet demand for a conference with PLO participation and with authority to intervene in the negotiations. Equally reassuring to Shamir was Shultz's not asking him to give a commitment to trade land for peace. However, after talking to the Jordanians in Amman and with Husayn in London, Shultz proposed convening an international conference as early as 15 April in order to launch the two-stage negotiations, with the first stage beginning on 1 May. The conference would not be altogether ceremonial; Shultz described it as a "point of reference." A letter to Shamir, to Peres, and other regional leaders, dated 4 March, stated that "the parties to each bilateral negotiation may refer reports on the status of their negotiations to the conference, in a manner agreed." The letter also said that the conference would "not be able to impose solutions or veto agreements reached," but it was an open question as to what would happen when a party referred controversial issues to the conference plenary.

Furthermore, Shultz also said in his talks with Shamir, as in his letter, that the US would submit a draft agreement at the outset of the negotiations on transitional arrangements.[121] Shamir found this particularly disconcerting, because as he saw it, once the Americans had produced their draft Israel would have to assume that the US considered it as fair and would not support Israeli demands for changes. Shamir assumed that Shultz was making these concessions to persuade Jordan to accept the American proposals, but he was also certain that Shultz would fail. Jordan would never give its unqualified consent; it would want Syria, the PLO, the Soviet Union, and the Security Council's other permanent members at the conference. Shamir thought that because of the *intifada* Husayn had lost interest in regaining the West Bank; he would not want it even as part of a confederation with Jordan, because it would mean a Palestinian state in part of the Jordanian kingdom.

Shamir developed his arguments against the Shultz proposals in several interviews:

(a) Shultz had not explained why he had come to accept a conference of the kind to which he had been opposed for so long. All he had said was that it was because Jordan insisted.

(b) Shamir was convinced that the proposals in their latest form left the door wide open to PLO participation in the conference. One condition, namely that the PLO would have to recognize Israel's right to exist before being admitted to the conference, was missing from the document.

(c) The proposals nowhere mentioned direct negotiations, only "bilateral" ones. There was a distinct difference between the two.

(d) There was no reference at all to a peace treaty, only to "comprehensive peace."

(e) In not providing for a sufficiently long transition period, the US proposals endangered the prospects of peaceful coexistence developing during the first and most critical period.[122]

Peres and the Alignment exerted strong pressure on Shamir to accept the proposals. But Shamir could afford to ignore the pressure, because Shultz had told him that the details of the proposals could still be changed, even though they constituted an integral whole. Shamir knew that the Alignment did not control enough Knesset votes to call for early elections, and the Inner Cabinet, the government's policy-making body, was equally divided between the Likud and the Alignment. Therefore, the Alignment preferred not to put the matter to the vote because of the certain tie. Shamir felt free to go to Washington for talks with Reagan and Shultz as arranged, unencumbered by any cabinet decision and able to present a case for changes in Israel's favor without announcing acception or rejection of the proposals themselves.

On 3 March, 10 days before Shamir left for the US, 30 US senators, including many with long records of support for Israel, sent a letter to Shultz. They said that they did not expect Israel to give up all the territory occupied in the Six Day War, but expressed their dismay at Shamir's resistance to the concept of Israel's ceding territories in exchange for peace.[123]

To counter the effect of this letter Shamir sent his own to two US senators, in which he stated, among others: "...the Government of Israel is committed to negotiate the ultimate disposition of Judea, Samaria [the West Bank], and Gaza in the context of the implementation of the Camp David accords." He pointed out that unlike Sinai, which was uncontested Egyptian territory and was returned to Egyptian sovereignty, the West Bank and Gaza having been occupied militarily by Jordan and Egypt, they lacked agreed sovereignty. Therefore "their status must be determined in the peace negotiations."[124] In making this statement he reiterated what was agreed at Camp David (1978), but it was not insignificant that he said that in the peace negotiations, i.e., the negotiations that would follow the transitional stage, the final status of the territory would be an open question. This was as far as Shamir was prepared to go to meet the "land for peace" formula.

Shamir's visit to Washington turned out much better than expected. In his talks with Shultz and Reagan, Shamir repeated his reservations about the American proposals and about the international conference in particular.[125] His interlocutors were clearly disappointed. Reagan's statement after conferring with Shamir (16 March), while friendly as usual, also contained two remarks which were perceived as expressions of displeasure with Shamir's stance. The president said that the US would neither abandon its initiative nor would it "slice it apart." He noted also that "those who will say no to the US plan, and the [Israeli] prime minister has not used this word, need not answer to us, they will need to answer to themselves and their people as to why they turned down a realistic and sensible plan to achieve negotiations."[126]

The key phrase in Reagan's statement, about those rejecting the proposal who "need not answer" to the US, was most reassuring to Shamir. It implied that the US would not use pressure to attempt to change Israel's position. In concrete terms, it meant that the memorandum of agreement institutionalizing the existing strategic cooperation between Israel and the US would be signed as planned; it was signed on 21 April.[127] Shamir was also relieved that he had been right in assuming that the US would not insist on an early response to Shultz's letter of 4 March (for text see Appendix I).

Shamir believed that since Jordan had not accepted the American proposal and was not about to change its attitude, Israel need not be overly concerned with having disappointed the Americans by not having given them an unequivocal reply. Furthermore, Shultz was not about to back away from his proposals; on the contrary, he intended pursuing his efforts by means of a second tour early in April. Shamir, therefore, could safely continue his wait-and-see tactics. After all, the Americans were aware of the division in Israel's Inner Cabinet and knew that a draw would in effect amount to an official rejection of the Shultz proposals.[128]

Peres continued to demand an early decision, arguing that Israel should be in the forefront of all peace efforts and not wait for Jordan to sabotage the Shultz initiative. However, when the Inner Cabinet adopted no decision (23 March), the Alignment went along with the Likud. The gap between the Alignment's declared intentions and its actual behavior when encountering the Likud's stonewalling caused even some of its sympathizers to wonder what motivated it.[129]

Shamir and Peres were united in their criticism of Shultz's meeting with the two American-Palestinian professors at the end of March[130] (see section on the Palestinians and the PLO in this chapter). Shamir told the Knesset that he took "a very grave view" of the meeting. Israel was concerned on two counts. First, because both academics were known PNC members and the US was committed to Israel not to "recognize or negotiate" with the PLO. Second, because reports had reached Jerusalem that the US had agreed with Egypt and Jordan to let the UN secretary-general invite the PLO to the conference. Shamir had been hostile to the conference even when he assumed that the PLO would not be invited; this latest development, if true, did not augur well for the second Shultz mission (1–8 April).

The exact purpose of the mission was unclear to the Israelis, perhaps because Shultz was not particularly aiming at Israel this time. He could hardly expect a real change in Shamir's position so soon after the talks in Washington. Still, Shultz felt the trip would be more than justified if he heard something new from Husayn. Also, he planned to use his stay in Israel and Jordan to explain his policy to the public in both countries.

In his public media appearances in Israel Shultz emphasized several points:

(a) The kind of conference Israel feared was not at all the kind he was proposing.

(b) The US was opposed to the PLO.

(c) The US was opposed to an independent Palestinian state. (It was impossible, he said, to "make out of the space of the West Bank and Gaza something that made sense as a national entity."

(d) He did not expect Israel to withdraw to the 1967 lines.

(e) The US would not exert pressure on Israel.[131] (It is noteworthy that he made the same points in Amman; see section on Jordan in this chapter.)

The official part of his visit was devoted to separate talks with Shamir and Peres. Since it was pointless to discuss the international conference again, the talks centered on the Israeli views of the transition period. Shultz doubted whether they would interest the Jordanians at all; they wanted to know whether Israel accepted the land-for-peace proposition. Even before Jordan officially released the text of the six-point document which it handed to Shultz during his visit to Amman (5 and 7 April; see section on Jordan in this chapter), Shamir was utterly convinced that the PLO and the Syrians would not let Husayn move.[132] Peres, too, was aware of the constraints under which the king was operating. However, unlike Shamir, he was ready to accommodate the king to the maximum compatible with the Israeli interest as he perceived it. According to one report, Peres gave Shultz a letter for Husayn expressing hope that agreement would be reached, because without it the region would face catastrophe.[133]

Shultz's shuttle mission in April did not achieve much, but it convinced him that all concerned were most careful not to reject the proposals presented in the document of 4 March. However, Shamir's objection to some of the key elements in the American package constituted a real obstacle. On the Arab side, there was yet no indication of willingness to have Husayn, rather than the PLO, represent the Palestinians in negotiations or to accept for the territories a status other than independent Palestinian statehood.

A month later (9 May), the US announced that Shultz would resume peace efforts in the area in early June. In the two months between Shultz's second and third ME tour, diplomatic activity had not come to a halt; its focus had shifted temporarily from the US to the Soviet Union. Peres held talks with Soviet representatives in Europe (10–11 May) and soon thereafter with the Soviet ambassador in Washington, Yuri Dubinin (17 May; see section on the Soviet Union in this chapter). Peres was encouraged by these meetings and he said that they pointed to a steady improvement in the Soviet attitude toward the Arab-Israeli peace process. Shamir disagreed with this evaluation, as did the State Department which maintained that the Soviets were still far from the US position; the two countries had "starkly different positions."[134] Peres, however, was not convinced. He maintained that the Soviets were no longer setting preconditions for settling the conflict and no longer insisting on a coercive conference, even if they continued to reject a conference that would be a mere "umbrella."[135]

The reason for this difference of views was not far to seek. Peres had become convinced that Husayn would not participate in an international conference if the Soviets were not coequal parties with the Americans. This conviction led him to comment favorably on changes, even hardly perceptible ones, in Soviet positions concerning the peace process. By doing so, he not only hoped to encourage the Soviets to go a little further, but also to improve bilateral relations. Because of his complete opposition to the international conference, Shamir was suspicious of all efforts, be they American or Israeli, to reach agreement over holding a conference, since such agreement would surely be based on a compromise and give a meaningful role to the nonregional participants, including the Soviet Union.

Peres met with Reagan and Shultz on 17 May and, as on similar occasions, stated his readiness to cooperate fully with the Administration's peace efforts. This time the US, in an unusual White House gesture, praised Peres publicly. A long statement described Peres as a man with a "vision for the future" who recognized the "increasing danger of the status quo" and the "negative consequences of passivity and delay in the search for a settlement." The statement repeated a point made in March during the Shamir visit about leaders who, failing to exploit realistic opportunities, "will have to answer to their own people." The statement was taken as a signal of US support for Peres in the coming Israeli election and implied criticism of Shamir.[136]

Shamir reacted cautiously to this rebuke. He noted that US policy had been careful not to intervene in political disputes in Israel, and he expressed hope that the US would remain faithful to this precept.[137] To defend his position, he often used the argument that Shultz himself had publicly used, namely, that none of the others involved (Jordan and the Palestinians) had given him a positive answer. There was much truth in this argument.

If Shultz had hoped to meet with a Palestinian delegation during his six-day tour

(3–8 June) of the capitals in the area, he was bound to be disappointed. Efforts made by Egypt to this end failed. Even if the US and the Soviet Union had perhaps made "a little bit" of progress at the Moscow summit (end of May) toward narrowing their differences on the Arab-Israeli conflict, it was plainly not enough.[138] The Shultz mission was really an attempt to persuade all involved that the US effort was still alive. This attempt was particularly important on the eve of the Arab summit meeting; it would be considerably more difficult for the assembled leaders to reject an initiative which had just been given momentum. Moreover, Shultz sincerely believed that the US proposals were the only ones with a reasonable chance of being accepted. He considered it his duty to carry them forward as much as possible and then bequeath them to the next US administration.[139]

During this mission, Shultz spent only 10 hours in Israel. The main message that he conveyed to Shamir and Peres, again in separate meetings, was that the Jordanian king had not abdicated his role in the negotiations; like all the other parties, he was anxious to pursue the peace process.[140] At best, this message meant that at the conclusion of the secretary's third and final tour, prospects of progress were as they had been, not promising.

The resolutions adopted at the Arab summit in Algiers were considered in Israel as a mere reiteration of the traditional Arab positions. Some Israelis, Peres included, believed that Husayn had, all in all, done rather well in Algiers; he had "remained loyal to his principles" and shown "constancy."[141] The Israeli assessment that little, if anything, was about to change in Arab thinking and tactics explained why the Abu Sharif document (see section on the Palestinians and the PLO in this chapter) was not recognized as heralding a shift in PLO policy.[142]

The Alignment, too, remained indifferent to this document, because it espoused the PLO idea of an independent Palestinian state which the Alignment continued to oppose. Labor, the Alignment's major component, was ready, in accordance with its policy since 1967, to give back to Jordan, and to Jordan only, a considerable part of the West Bank. When this happened Jordan would, in effect, become a Jordanian-Palestinian state and the danger of a separate Palestinian state would be averted. Defense Minister Rabin stated that he was ready to give up 60% of the occupied territories in return for peace.[143]

Other Israelis, including a group of retired generals, known for their somewhat dovish views, declared their readiness to concede even more territory than Rabin was. However, warning that total withdrawal would put Israel in jeopardy, they recommended keeping land vital for Israel's defense and making arrangements such as demilitarization of vacated territory, maintenance of early warning stations, and deployment of the Israel Defense Forces along the Jordan River.[144] Their ideas were, on the whole, remarkably similar to those of the Alignment platform, that insisted on defensible borders for Israel, by which it meant territorial changes in Israel's favor in several defined locations (the Jordan Valley, the area northwest of the Dead Sea, the Etzion bloc north of Hebron, and the environs of Jerusalem). The rest of the West Bank would be demilitarized and other security measures considered vital to Israel would be adopted. The Jordan River would be Israel's security border.

Husayn's decision to sever Jordan's ties with the West Bank took Israel by surprise. According to one report, the king conveyed a message to Peres through a third party sometime in July, warning him against going too far in his election campaign with statements about the "Jordanian option"; at some stage, Jordan would be forced to repudiate such statements.[145] Peres, however, kept on repeating that the Jordanian option was a geopolitical fact; that the king knew only too well that if the problems of the West Bank were not solved, his own regime would be endangered and that therefore, sooner or later, he would negotiate with Israel.[146] After the king announced his disengagement, Peres explained that it was aimed at the Palestinians and did not change the essential fact that Jordan's longest border was with Israel. As long as the West Bank residents held Jordanian passports and the bridges over the Jordan were open, the king's announcement was only a declaration of intent devoid of practical implications. Peres issued a statement saying that Israel remained ready to negotiate a peace treaty with Jordan and with the Palestinians, a solution to their problem.[147] What he meant was that the Alignment was ready to negotiate interim agreements with the Palestinians, but not with the PLO. Jordan would be more than welcome to join such negotiations, but its participation was not essential. However, a peace settlement and the border questions would be discussed with Jordan.

Peres could not resist the temptation to recall that only 16 months earlier there had been a good chance for negotiations with Jordan on the basis of the London document (see chapter on the Middle East peace process, in *MECS* 1987). "But someone here," he said, referring to Shamir, "prevented it." Since then, conditions had become much less favorable, but Israel ought, nevertheless, to take the lead in the peace process, undeterred by Husayn's decision.[148]

For many Israeli doves who had been pressing inside the Alignment for negotiating with the PLO, Husayn's decision was a welcome development. For the hawks, who supported the Jordanian option and insisted on keeping a sizable part of the West Bank, this was a setback. Both groups were disappointed that the king had not delayed his decision until after the Israeli elections.[149]

Closer to the elections, the Alignment came out with a detailed statement (17 October). Most of it was a reaffirmation of old positions. Some of the newer points deserve mentioning:

(a) After a three-to-six-month period of calm in the territories, free elections would be held.

(b) Israel would negotiate with the elected Palestinian leadership on interim measures.

(c) Should Israel reach agreement with a Jordanian-Palestinian delegation on a final settlement, the Alignment would call for a referendum in Israel to decide the issue.

The Alignment positions were on the whole flexible on procedure (i.e., the international conference and negotiations with a Palestinian delegation) but less so on substance (no return to the 1967 lines, Jerusalem and its vicinity would remain under Israeli sovereignty).[150]

Unlike Peres, Shamir accepted the king's announcement at face value. The king meant what he said, namely that he definitely rejected the notion of a territorial compromise. Shamir thought that since the king wished to obtain total Israeli withdrawal, his own withdrawal ought not to sadden Israel. Israel desired peace with Jordan and was prepared to reach agreement with it. As for the West Bank, Israel was committed to the Camp David accords and would be ready to negotiate an autonomy arrangement for the Palestinian inhabitants.[151] The Likud election platform, drafted after Husayn's announcement, defined that party's position as follows:

> The State of Israel has a right and a claim to sovereignty over Judea, Samaria, and the Gaza Strip. Israel will assert this claim and act to implement it. The autonomy arrangements agreed at Camp David are a guarantee that in the western part of the Land of Israel [Eretz Israel] there will be no more territorial partitioning and that under no circumstances will a Palestinian state be set up there. The autonomy agreed upon is not a state, it is not a sovereign entity, and does not constitute self-determination.

In its operational part, the Likud platform promised that the party would make efforts to renew the negotiations on "full autonomy for the Arab inhabitants" of the West Bank.

Shamir's own statements were less forbidding than these formulations. What he said during the election campaign brought these formulations closer to what he had said in his letter to the two US senators (see above). In a debate with Peres a week before the elections he stated that the fate of the West Bank would be decided in negotiations, i.e., not unilaterally by Israel. On one occasion, he denied Alignment charges that the Likud policies would turn Israel into a binational state in which the Arabs would in a matter of years outnumber the Jews. He said that his party would not annex the territories or its 1.5m. Arab inhabitants.[152] Shamir was opposed also to the imposition of autonomy on the territories since doing so would mean forcing upon the inhabitants something they did not want, and which was arrived at without negotiation. The aim of autonomy as envisaged at Camp David was to build trust between the Palestinians and Israelis, and this could not be done by fiat.[153]

Peres needed to convince the Israeli voter that if he won the elections there would be an Arab leader ready to negotiate with him. The only possible one was clearly Husayn. However, since Husayn had disengaged himself from the West Bank, real proof was needed to convince the Israelis that the king remained interested. Peres, therefore, encouraged a well-known US television personality to arrange two separate interviews, one with the king and one with him. He assumed that the king would make the right statements, but things turned out quite differently. The American broadcaster revealed that Peres had initiated the interviews and made it look as if Peres had involved non-Israelis, the Jordanian king, and American television, in his election campaign. In any case, the king did not really make the kind of statement that Peres expected of him (see section on Jordan in this chapter). Peres made the best of a bad job and claimed that the king had said, "Yes, I am ready [to negotiate]," but this was stretching a point somewhat.[154]

The outcome of the general election in Israel again forced the Likud and the Alignment to form a national unity government, with Shamir heading it for the whole four-year term. The new coalition's policy guidelines contained few new points: there was emphasis on the Camp David accords and a stated readiness to resume negotiations "to give full autonomy to the Arab residents in Judea, Samaria, and the Gaza District." Both were unmistakably in line with Likud's thinking. There was no reference to an international framework as a means to facilitate direct negotiations. Even the idea which Shamir had accepted in October 1987 about limited two-superpower auspices was not mentioned. All that was left of the Alignment's "Jordanian option" was a promise that Israel would "call on Jordan to begin peace negotiations and would consider proposals for negotiations."[155] This notwithstanding, one Labor leader, Rabin, thought that the Alignment should give "Likud a chance to implement their peace plan."[156] As the year came to a close, reports were circulating that Shamir was examining new ideas, such as not excluding limited superpower auspices. It was much too early to assess the seriousness of these rumors, because no detailed plans were published.

The resolutions of the 19th PNC (see section on the Palestinians and the PLO in this chapter) were immediately rejected by both Shamir and Peres as insincere. Peres discounted interpretations that the PLO had recognized Israel.[157] A month later, the US announced its readiness to open a dialogue with the PLO. Once again, the Likud and the Alignment saw eye to eye. In a note to Shultz, Peres criticized the American step as "premature."[158] No matter how much the Likud and the Alignment disagreed about the risks Israel should take for peace with the Arabs, both were equally opposed to negotiating with the PLO. The reason for their opposition was occasionally frankly spelt out. Israel would not talk to the PLO not only because the PLO considered Israel's very existence as illegal, but also because the PLO hoped to establish an independent Palestinian state and, therefore, was bound to reject any proposal Israel could make within the limits set by its national policy.

THE SOVIET UNION

On the conclusion of the Soviet-American summit meeting in Moscow (1 June) General Secretary Mikhail Gorbachev told a press conference that the Soviet Union had watched the US deal by itself with the Arab-Israeli conflict for several years. The US, however, had failed and only when the US realized its failure could a Soviet-US dialogue on the Arab-Israeli conflict develop. According to Gorbachev, the US had come to understand that the Soviet Union ought to participate in the peace process. The Soviets for their part were ready, he added, "to cooperate with the US in a constructive manner."[159]

The Soviet-US dialogue had begun in 1985. Since then over half a dozen meetings at the experts' and summit levels had taken place.[160] Arab insistence on a substantive Soviet role in the peace process and in the international peace conference, first evidenced in the Amman accord between King Husayn and Yasir 'Arafat in 1985, coincided with Gorbachev's assumption of power. The new Soviet leader did not take long to develop an active diplomacy directed at all countries in the ME. It resulted in markedly improved relations with the moderate Arab countries (Oman, the United Arab Emirates, Bahrain, Kuwait, North Yemen, Jordan, Egypt, and Saudi Arabia), displaying unconcern that this policy conflicted with its ties to Syria.[161] Concerning Israel, the Soviets continued to maintain in 1988 a posture of openness. Contacts at various levels took place and an Israeli consular delegation was permitted to come to Moscow, the latter in reciprocation for Israel's acceptance of a similar Soviet mission in July 1987. Cultural exchanges, almost totally absent for 20 years, made a modest appearance. Yet Moscow was still not ready to restore diplomatic relations with Israel. Such relations would have to wait until a significant change in the Arab-Israeli peace process took place, specifically until Israel agreed to participate in a Soviet-endorsed international peace conference. In the years immediately preceding 1988, it was still doubtful whether Gorbachev would liberalize significantly the Soviet Union's emigration policy; the 20,000 Jews who left the country during the year under review dissipated such doubts.

All these steps served one purpose: terminating the American monopoly of the Arab-Israeli peace process. The Soviet objective was to enable their diplomacy to play in that process the role of which they had been deprived since 1973.

The success of *perestroika* in the Soviet Union depended, however, so much on Western goodwill and aid that Gorbachev was careful to pursue his ME diplomacy in a manner designed not to arouse undue concern in Washington. He knew that the Americans were clearly not about to change their basic assessment that the US and the Soviet Union did not have identical interests in the region. Yet he also reasoned that the Americans, like the Soviets, were certainly opposed to another major Arab-Israeli war which could lead to Great Power confrontation. The conclusion was that the Soviet Union must follow a policy of conflict avoidance, if conflict resolution still proved unattainable.[162]

Gorbachev's book *Perestroika* contained a significant passage: that the Soviets realized that it was at present difficult to reconcile the differences between the parties (i.e., the Arabs and Israel) and more time was needed, "but they did not want at all that the waiting process toward a settlement or that the very objectives of this process damage in any way the interests of the US and the West." At the same time, he realized that the collaborative spirit he and Foreign Minister Eduard Shevardnadze were radiating would not by itself win the Americans over completely. The Americans would not yet let their guard down. Israel, too, would remain wary of Soviet attempts to play an increasing role in the peace process. The Soviets were still Syria's and the PLO's closest ally and continued to support maximalist Arab positions in the UN.

This notwithstanding, even the Israelis had to acknowledge that it was no longer true that the Soviet Union was interested in regional instability or that tension between Israel and the Arabs served its overall interests.[163] Soviet views had, indeed, undergone real change in this respect. However, this could not be said about the specifics of how to settle the conflict, because regarding these, Soviet positions remained essentially unmodified. The Soviets continued to insist on an international conference to settle the Arab-Israeli conflict. Gorbachev himself made it clear that the conference must be a "normal effective" one, "not just an umbrella for separate talks, but a forum that would be tied in with bilateral, trilateral, and other forums of work."[164] A hint of flexibility concerning the structure of the conference and its *modus operandi* could be discerned when Gorbachev remarked that some questions pertaining to the conference might require "more work and effort."[165]

He was, however, unbending with regard to the territorial issue: Israel would have to return "all Israeli occupied lands and restore the rights of the Palestinian people." The Palestinians had a right to self-determination and it was up to them and "their Arab friends" to decide how to express that right. The Soviets took it for granted that the PLO represented the Palestinians.[166] In an attempt to reassure Israel, Gorbachev said that the Soviet Union recognized its right to security and promised to take up the question of "regularizing diplomatic relations when the international conference opened."[167]

The gap between the Soviet and US positions proved too wide to bridge in the year under review, but not for want of trying. The diplomatic contacts between the two countries were frequent. The Americans were careful to brief the Soviets about their moves before launching them. Thus, for example, Shultz visited Moscow in February prior to his tour of ME capitals. In his meeting with Gorbachev, Shultz explained his proposals on the ME. The Soviet leaders' reaction, as reported by the TASS news agency, was that the American ideas failed to take into account the interest of all the parties in the area and were short-term, interim steps. This unfavorable comment was somewhat mitigated by the observation that the Soviet Union was not opposed to these steps as such, but believed that only an international conference and a comprehensive approach could produce real results.[168] The Soviet Union, while strongly skeptical, would not obstruct the Shultz mission. This did not, however, prevent Moscow from increasing its diplomatic activity in ME capitals on the eve of Shultz's arrival in the area.[169]

Throughout the year, Soviet diplomatic moves served to remind the US and Israel that only the Soviet Union could provide the peace process with its missing elements. A striking illustration of this was given in April. At the very moment when Shultz was touring the region for the second time in his effort to promote his peace proposals and was preparing to go to Moscow, Gorbachev met with PLO chairman Yasir 'Arafat, using the occasion to tell him that just as Palestinian self-determination was a necessary element of peace, so too were the recognition of Israel and its security interests.[170] The message Moscow wanted to convey to Washington was that in a Soviet-US agreement, the Soviet Union would claim a role equal to that of the US. Its relations with the PLO justified such a claim. At the same time, the statement Gorbachev made in 'Arafat's presence was meant to refute US criticism that Moscow was not playing a constructive part in the ME. Soviet efforts to impress the US of its indispensability were also aided by Jordanian statements to the effect that Jordan and the Soviet Union held identical views on the peace process. Crown Prince Hasan said that Jordan wanted the USSR to have the power of "decision making and arbitration" at the international conference.[171]

The contacts between the Soviets and Palestinians greatly intensified in the weeks preceding the PNC in Algiers in November. The Soviets were in touch with all groups in the PLO and urged the PLO to adopt "realistic and flexible resolutions."[172] They certainly recommended to the PLO that it should accept Security Council Resolution 242 and recognize Israel. On other outstanding issues, such as the proclamation of an independent Palestinian state and the formation of a provisional government, they counseled prudence, but added that they would respect any Palestinian decisions.[173]

It was, therefore, a foregone conclusion that the Soviet Union would recognize the PNC declaration of the independent Palestinian state. The Soviet Foreign Ministry spokesman clarified this recognition saying that since the Palestinian state was occupied at present and had no permanent government, the Soviet Union considered its recognition as "a political rather than a legal international step." At the same time, the spokesman also said that Soviet recognition was meant to help "the setting up of an independent Palestinian state on the basis of UN resolutions."[174]

APPENDIX I: THE SHULTZ PROPOSALS

Letters Presented by United States Secretary of State to Egypt, Jordan, and Israel during his Second Trip to the Region, February-March 1988

THE SECRETARY OF STATE
WASHINGTON

March 4, 1988

Dear Mr. Prime Minister,

I set forth below the statement of understanding which I am convinced is necessary to achieve the prompt opening of negotiations on a comprehensive peace. This statement of understanding emerges from discussions held with you and other regional leaders. I look forward to the letter of reply of the Government of Israel in confirmation of this statement.

The agreed objective is a comprehensive peace providing for the security of all the states in the region and for the legitimate rights of the Palestinian people.

Negotiations will start on an early date certain between Israel and each of its neighbors which is willing to do so. These negotiations could begin in May 1, 1988. Each of these negotiations will be based on United Nations Security Council Resolutions 242 and 338, in all their parts. The parties to each bilateral negotiation will determine the procedure and agenda of their negotiation. All participants in the negotiations must state their willingness to negotiate with one another.

As concerns negotiations between the Israeli delegation and the Jordanian-Palestinian delegation, negotiations will begin on arrangements for a transitional period, with the objective of completing them within six months. Seven months after transitional negotiations begin, final status negotiations will begin, with the objective of completing them within one year. These negotiations will be based on all the provisions and principles of United Nations Security Council Resolution 242. Final status talks will start before the transitional period begins. The transitional period will begin three months after the conclusion of the transitional agreement and will last for three years. The United States will participate in both negotiations and will promote their rapid conclusion. In particular, the United States will submit a draft agreement for the parties' consideration at the outset of the negotiations on transitional arrangements.

Two weeks before the opening of negotiations, an international conference will be held. The Secretary-General of the United Nations will be asked to issue invitations to the parties involved in the Arab-Israeli conflict and the five permanent members of the United Nations Security Council. All participants in the conference must accept United Nations Security Council Resolutions 242 and 338, and renounce violence and terrorism. The parties to each bilateral negotiation may refer reports on the status of their negotiations to the conference, in a manner to be agreed. The conference will not be able to impose solutions or veto agreements reached.

Palestinian representation will be within the Jordanian-Palestinian delegation. The Palestinian issue will be addressed in the negotiations between the Jordanian-Palestinian and Israeli delegations. Negotiations between the Israeli delegation and the Jordanian-Palestinian delegation will proceed independently of any other negotiations.

This statement of understandings is an integral whole. The United States understands that your acceptance is dependent on the implementation of each element in good faith.

Sincerely yours,
George P. Shultz

SOURCE: *Yedi'ot Aharonot*, 6 March 1988.

APPENDIX II: JORDAN'S SIX-POINT DOCUMENT

The following document was handed by King Husayn to US Secretary of State George Shultz during the secretary's second trip to the area in April 1988:

(1) Inadmissibility of the acquisition of territory by war. Israeli withdrawal from the occupied territories is the basis for the settlement of the Arab-Israeli conflict, and the establishment of a just and durable peace.

(2) Settlement of the Arab-Israeli conflict requires settlement of the Palestinian problem in all its aspects, including the right of the Palestinian people to self-determination.

(3) Settlement of the Arab-Israeli conflict and the Palestinian problem must be comprehensive. Negotiations to arrive at a comprehensive settlement can only take place within the international conference.

(4) The international conference will not be merely a ceremonial international gathering structured for the sole purpose of launching direct negotiations. It should reflect the moral and constant weight of the five permanent members of the Security Council in assisting all the parties to arrive at a comprehensive, just, and lasting peace.

(5) The principles of Security Council Resolution 242 apply to all the occupied Arab territories and are the basis for negotiations in the bilateral committees.

(6) In exercising its sovereign right, Jordan is prepared to attend the international conference with the other interested parties. Jordan will not represent the Palestinian people at the conference nor will it negotiate the settlement of the Palestinian problem on behalf of the PLO. Jordan is also prepared to attend the conference in a joint Jordanian-Palestinian delegation if the concerned parties accept this arrangement.

SOURCE: *JT*, 9 April — DR, 11 April 1988.

NOTES

For the place and frequency of publications cited here, and for the full name of the publication, news agency, radio station, or monitoring service where an abbreviation is used, please see "List of Sources." Only in the case of more than one publication bearing the same name is the place of publication noted here.

1. R. Amman, 31 July — DR, 1 August 1988.
2. Husayn's interview with Jordan TV, 14 January — DR, 15 January 1988.
3. *Ha'aretz,* 12 January 1988. The British politician was Gerald Kaufman, the Labor Party's foreign policy spokesman.
4. Jordan's position concerning total Israeli withdrawal had never varied since 1967. Since the 1967 lines were identical with the 1949 armistice lines, Jordan did not exclude the possibility of minor changes on a reciprocal basis (see, e.g., Rifa'i's press conference, R. Amman, 8 April — DR, 11 April 1988).
5. White House spokesman Marlin Fitzwater, 1 February, reported in *Ma'ariv,* 2 February 1988.
6. Husayn's interview with *Der Spiegel,* 1 February — DR, 3 February 1988.
7. Rifa'i's interview with *JT,* 6 February — DR, 12 February 1988.
8. Rifa'i's interview with Jordan TV, 11 February — DR, 12 February 1988.
9. *IHT,* 1 March; *Ma'ariv,* 4 March 1988.
10. Jordan TV, 1 March — DR, 2 March; *JP,* 3 March 1988.
11. R. Amman, 1 March — DR, 2 March; *JP,* 3 March 1988.
12. Ibid.
13. For the text of Shultz's complete proposal in English see *Yedi'ot Aharonot,* 6 March 1988.
14. Reuters report from Amman as reported in *JP,* 15 March 1988.
15. *JP,* 21 March 1988.
16. *Ma'ariv,* 4 April 1988.
17. USIS text, 7 April; Shultz also made a similar statement on Israeli TV, 5 April, USIS official text, 12 April 1988.
18. *JP,* 7 April 1988.
19. Rifa'i's interview with *JT,* 9 April — DR, 11 April 1988.
20. Deputy Chairman of the Russian Soviet Federated Socialist Republic Council of Ministers, Nikolay Trubilin, in a press conference, *al-Dustur,* Amman, 13 April — DR, 14 April; Husayn's interview with AFP, 10 May — DR, 10 May 1988.
21. Ibid., also in *al-Mustaqbal,* 16 April — DR, 21 April 1988.
22. R. Amman and Jordan TV, 4 June — DR, 6 June 1988.
23. Ambassador Alexander Zinchuk as reported by *JT,* 5 June — DR, 6 June 1988.
24. Husayn's speech, 3 May — DR, 6 May and his interview with *al- Qabas,* 11 May — DR, 13 May; Information Minister Hani al-Khasawna's interview with *al-Dustur,* Amman, 21 May — DR, 29 May 1988.
25. Husayn's summit address, 8 June — DR, 9 June 1988.
26. R. Monte Carlo, 25 July — DR, 26 July 1988.
27. See Note 1 above.
28. R. Monte Carlo, 30 July — DR, 1 August 1988.
29. Shultz, on CBS "Face the Nation" Program, 31 July; Murphy's press statement, R. Amman, 9 August — DR, 10 August 1988.
30. Husayn's news conference, Jordan TV, 7 August — DR, 8 August; address to the Royal War College, 27 August — DR, 29 August; interview with *al-Anba,* Kuwait, 6 September — DR, 8 September 1988.
31. Rifa'i's interview with *al-Anba,* Kuwait, 10 September — DR, 13 September 1988.
32. Husayn's interview with ABC's "Nightline" TV program, 20 October 1988.
33. Husayn's interview with BBC, 25 November — DR, 25 November 1988.
34. *Süddeutsche Zeitung,* 18 March, as reported by *JP,* 20 March; 'Arafat to *L'Espresso,* 3 July — DR, 11 July 1988.
35. Yasir 'Abd Rabbu, head of PLO Information Department, R. Monte Carlo, 31 March — DR, 1 April; 'Arafat's interview, R. Monte Carlo, 3 June — DR, 6 June 1988.

36. Hana Siniora, editor of *al-Fajr* (East Jerusalem) and Fa'iz Abu Rahma, former head of the Gaza Strip Bar Association.
37. Professors Edward W. Said and Ibrahim Abu Lughod, of Columbia and Northwestern Universities, respectively.
38. VoP (Baghdad), 1 April — DR, 4 April 1988.
39. Shultz's statement at the American Colony Hotel (East Jerusalem), 26 February, *JP,* 28 February 1988.
40. 'Arafat's news conference, 15 January — SWB, 18 January; also CBS interview, 17 January; *JP,* 18 January; interview with *al-Hawadith,* 29 January — DR, 29 January 1988.
41. *IHT,* 'Arafat's interview, 12–13 March 1988.
42. *IHT,* 12–13 March; Faruq Qaddumi, VoP (San'a), 3 June — DR, 6 June; 'Arafat's interview with *al-Sharq al-Awsat,* 9 August — DR, 12 August 1988.
43. 'Arafat's Kuwait press conference, 13 April — DR, 20 April; interview VoP (Baghdad), 10 May — DR, 18 May; interview, R. Monte Carlo, 3 June — DR, 6 June 1988.
44. *NYT,* 22 June 1988.
45. For condemnations of the document see R. al-Quds, 20 June — DR, 21 June 1988.
46. 'Arafat's interview with *L'Espresso,* 3 July — DR, 11 July 1988.
47. *Davar,* 13 June; Salah Khalaf's interview with *al-Qabas,* 15 June — DR, 17 June 1988.
48. Klibi's interview with *al-Sharq al-Awsat,* 21 June — DR, 24 June 1988.
49. *Al-Qabas,* 16 June — DR, 20 June, and ibid., 23 June — DR, 29 June 1988.
50. PLO Central Council statement, VoP (Baghdad), 3 August — DR, 4 August; 'Arafat's interview with *al-Sharq al-Awsat,* 9 August — DR, 12 August 1988.
51. KUNA report, 8 August — DR, 9 August 1988.
52. 'Abd Rabbu's interview with *al-Bayan,* Dubai, 7 August — DR, 9 August 1988.
53. 'Arafat's interview with *al-Ittihad,* Abu Dhabi, 8 September — DR, 13 September 1988.
54. Khalaf to *al-Bayan,* Dubai, 7 September — DR, 8 September 1988.
55. Hawatima's interview with *al-Anba,* Kuwait, 19 October — DR, 21 October 1988.
56. 'Arafat's Strasbourg speech, 14 September — DR, 15 September 1988.
57. *Al-Fajr,* 21 November; Algiers TV, 15 November — DR, 15 November 1988.
58. *Al-Fajr,* ibid. The text of the statement in DR, 16 November 1988.
59. *NYT,* 20 November 1988.
60. *JP,* 8 December; R. Stockholm, 7 December — DR, 8 December 1988.
61. R. Cairo, 13 December — DR, 14 December 1988.
62. VoP (Baghdad), 15 December — DR, 16 December; *NYT,* 18 December 1988.
63. 'Abd Rabbu's interview with *al-Anba,* Kuwait, 18 December — DR, 20 December 1988.
64. Muhammad Basyuni, Egypt's ambassador in Israel, interview with *Ma'ariv,* 8 February — DR, 10 February 1988.
65. Hana Siniora, editor of *al-Fajr,* in a *WP* article, 28 January 1988.
66. MENA, 22 January — DR, 25 January 1988.
67. *Yedi'ot Aharonot,* 12, 22 January; *JP,* 21 January 1988.
68. *IHT, WSJ,* 29 February 1988.
69. Mubarak address to students, *al-Akhbar,* Cairo, 24 February — DR, 29 February; 'Abd al-Majid, MENA, 15 February, and al-Baz, R. Monte Carlo, 12 February — DR, 19 February 1988.
70. Usama al-Baz's interview with *al-Sabah,* 22 March — DR, 23 March; Butrus Butrus-Ghali's interview with R. Monte Carlo, 1 April — DR, 4 April 1988.
71. Mubarak's interview with *al-Ra'y al-'Amm,* as reported by *JP,* 16 March 1988.
72. Mubarak's press conference, 12 April — DR, 13 April, and interview with *al-Musawwar,* 27 July — DR, 28 July 1988.
73. Usama al-Baz's press conference, 22 March — DR, 23 March 1988.
74. 'Abd al-Majid's interview with Egyptian TV, 8 April — DR, 11 April 1988.
75. Mubarak; see Note 9 above.
76. See chapter on ME peace process, *MECS* 1987, where Mubarak was quoted as having said that Egypt was the only country in favor of a Palestinian state (interview with *al-Tadamun,* 4 June — DR, 17 June 1987). Butrus-Ghali in an interview with *al-Anba,* Kuwait, 22 June — DR, 29 June 1988, said that a Palestinian state would coexist with the State of Israel. He did not, however, exclude the possibility of a state confederated with Jordan.

77. Mubarak's speech, R. Cairo, 21 July — DR, 21 July and interview with *al-Siyasa,* Kuwait, 14 May — DR, 17 May 1988.
78. MENA, 7 June — DR, 7 June 1988.
79. Interview with *al-Anba,* Kuwait, 22 June — DR, 29 June 1988.
80. MENA, 21 May — DR, 24 May 1988.
81. Mubarak's interview with *al-Hurriyya,* Tunis, 17 June — DR, 21 June 1988.
82. Butrus-Ghali; see Note 16 above.
83. 'Abd al-Majid's statement, R. Cairo, 2 August — DR, 2 August; Mubarak's press statement, MENA, 9 August — DR, 9 August 1988.
84. MENA, 18 August — DR, 18 August; Butrus-Ghali's interview, R. Cairo, 8 September — DR, 9 September 1988.
85. 'Abd al-Majid's interview with *al-Musawwar,* 21 September — DR, 16 September 1988.
86. MENA, 21 September — DR, 21 September 1988. This was not to be their last meeting before the PNC session in November.
87. Mubarak's interview with *Yedi'ot Aharonot,* 21 October — DR, 24 October; 'Abd al-Majid, MENA, 25 October — DR, 26 October; *al-Ra'y al-'Amm,* 24 October — DR, 26 October 1988.
88. Mubarak's interview with German TV, 25 October — DR, 26 October 1988. Mubarak said: "They [Husayn and 'Arafat] are in agreement about confederation...there are no differences...."
89. This summary is based on the following interviews: 'Abd al-Majid in *al-Sharq al-Awsat,* 10 October — DR, 12 October; *al-Hawadith,* 17 October — DR, 12 October; R. Monte Carlo, 29 October — DR, 31 October; and Mubarak's interview with *al-Ra'y al-'Amm,* 18 October — DR, 19 October 1988.
90. Mubarak's interview with *al Ra'y al-'Amm,* 18 October 1988.
91. 'Abd al-Majid's speech, 2 November — DR, 3 November; his statement, 15 November — DR, 15 November 1988.
92. *Davar,* 20–21 November 1988.
93. 'Abd al-Majid, 19 November — DR, 21 November 1988.
94. Joint Mubarak-'Arafat press conference, 21 November — DR, 22 November 1988. Mubarak listed these items in several interviews (e.g., with *al-Sharq al-Awsat,* 6 December — DR, 7 December 1988).
95. Al-Baz's interview with *Sawt al-Sha'b,* 2 December — DR, 2 December 1988.
96. 'Abd al-Majid's UN General Assembly speech, 13 December — DR, 14 December 1988.
97. MENA, 14 December — DR, 15 December 1988.
98. *Ha'aretz,* 12 July 1988, articles by Yossi Olmert and Ariel Levitte.
99. Asad's address to the General Federation of the Workers Union, 12 November — DR, 14 November; Syrian Minister of Information Muhammad Salman's interview by *al-Thawra,* Damascus, 3 November — DR, 13 November; Gen. Hikmat al-Shihabi, chief of staff, 31 July — DR, 2 August 1988.
100. *Al-Sharq al-Awsat,* 7 February — DR, 18 February 1988.
101. *Tishrin,* as reported by *JP,* 4 April 1988.
102. Asad's address to the Ba'th rally marking the 25th anniversary of its rise to power, R. Damascus, 8 March — DR, 10 March 1988.
103. R. Damascus, 5 April — DR, 6 April 1988.
104. Shar'’s interview with R. Monte Carlo, 15 April — DR, 20 April 1988.
105. *WP,* 27 April 1988.
106. Shar'’s interviews with *Le Monde,* as reported by R. Damascus, 13 September — DR, 14 September; with *al-Hawadith,* 7 October — DR, 7 October; and with *al-Sharq al-Awsat,* 11 October — DR, 13 October 1988.
107. Moshe Maoz, *Ha'aretz,* 23 November 1988.
108. R. Damascus quoting *al-Thawra,* Damascus, 9 June — DR, 17 June 1988.
109. *NYT,* 22 January; *Ma'ariv,* 29 January 1988.
110. Shamir's interview, Israeli Educational TV, 26 January — DR, 27 January 1988.
111. Quoted by Yossi Ben Aharon, director-general of the Prime Minister's Office, *Ha'aretz,* 17 January 1988.
112. Shamir's interview with *Ha'aretz,* 2 February 1988.

113. *Ma'ariv*, 11 March; director-general of the Prime Minister's Office interview with VoI, 7 April — DR, 7 April 1988.
114. *Yedi'ot Aharonot*, 12 January 1988.
115. For example, Peres's interview on VoI, 25 February — DR, 25 February 1988.
116. *Ha'aretz*, 27 January 1988.
117. *Ma'ariv*, 29 January 1988.
118. Shamir's interview on VoI, 30 January — DR, 1 February 1988.
119. Shultz's address to Council of Foreign Relations in Washington, D.C., 9 February; *JP*, 15 February 1988.
120. Director-general of Israel's Prime Minister's Office, interviewed on VoI, 11 February — DR, 12 February 1988.
121. For complete text, see Appendix I. *Ma'ariv*, 4 March 1988, carried a detailed description of talks between Shamir and Shultz.
122. Shamir's interviews, *Ha'aretz*, 11 March; *Ma'ariv*, 11 March; R. IDF, 11 March — DR, 11 March 1988.
123. *NYT*, 6 March 1988.
124. *NYT*, 10 March 1988.
125. Shamir was supported on this by no less a figure than former secretary of state Henry Kissinger who said (20 March) that "an international conference presupposes an agreement on substances between the US and Israel...it would be a mistake to go to a conference without a substantive undertanding between the US and Israel" (*JP*, 23 March 1988).
126. *JP*, 17 March 1988.
127. *NYT*, 18 March 1988.
128. *JP*, 20 March 1988.
129. *JP*, 20, 25 March; *Ha'aretz*, 13 March 1988.
130. *NYT*, 26 March 1988.
131. Shultz's interview with Israeli journalists and editors, *Ma'ariv*, 4 April; interview on Israeli TV, 4 April; USIS Official Text, 21 April 1988.
132. Director-general of the Prime Minister's Office, VoI, 7 April — DR, 11 April 1988; Dan Meridor, a Knesset member close to Shamir, interviewed on VoI, 7 April — DR, 11 April 1988.
133. *Yedi'ot Aharonot*, 10 April — DR, 13 April 1988.
134. *Yedi'ot Aharonot*, 12 May — DR, 13 May; *JP*, 19 May 1988.
135. Separate interviews with Shamir and Peres on Israel TV, 3 June — DR, 6 June; Peres's interview, VoI, 8 June — DR, 9 June 1988.
136. *JP*, 20 May; *NYT*, 17 May 1988.
137. Interview on Israeli TV, 19 May — DR, 20 May 1988.
138. Shultz's interview on PBS, as reported in *JP*, 3 June 1988.
139. *NYT*, 5 June 1988.
140. Director-general of the Prime Minister's Office, interviewed on R. IDF, 5 June — DR, 6 June 1988.
141. *JP*, 9 June 1988.
142. Peres's Knesset statement, 13 July — DR, 14 July 1988.
143. Rabin's interview with *JP*, 11 March; interview on VoI, 2 May — DR, 2 May 1988.
144. See, e.g., *Ma'ariv*, 3 June; *Ha'aretz*, 12 June 1988.
145. *'Al-Hamishmar*, 24 July — DR, 28 July 1988.
146. Peres's Knesset statement, 20 July — DR, 27 July; *JP*, 13 July — DR, 23 July 1988.
147. Interview on R. IDF, 29 July — DR, 29 July; *Ma'ariv*, 1 August 1988.
148. Peres's interview on R. IDF, 29 July — DR, 29 July; ibid., 12 August — DR, 12 August 1988.
149. Peres's interview on VoI, 22 August — DR, 23 August 1988.
150. VoI, 17 October — DR, 18 October; Rabin's interview on Israeli TV, 17 October — DR, 18 October; *Ma'ariv*, 21 October 1988.
151. Shamir, as reported by Israeli TV, 31 July — DR, 1 August 1988.
152. Shamir's interview on VoI, 24 October — DR, 24 October; report in *Nation*, 26 October — DR, 26 October 1988.
153. Shamir's interview on VoI, 12 September — 13 September 1988.

154. Peres-Shamir joint interview, Israeli TV, 22 October — DR, 24 October 1988.
155. *JP*, 27 December 1988.
156. *JP*, 25 November 1988.
157. *JP*, 18 November 1988.
158. *JP*, 19 December 1988.
159. *Ma'ariv*, 1 June; *Ha'aretz*, 2 June 1988.
160. Richard Murphy, press conference, 25 June 1988; USIS Official Text, 30 June 1988.
161. Galia Golan, "Gorbachev's Middle East Strategy," *Foreign Affairs*, Vol. 66, No. 1, 1987.
162. Ibid.; *Ma'ariv*, 15 April 1988.
163. Interview with the director-general of the Israel Ministry for Foreign Affairs, *Ha'aretz*, 16 September 1988.
164. Gorbachev's press conference, 1 June; *CDSP*, XL, No. 22, 29 June 1988.
165. *Ma'ariv*, 1 June 1988.
166. See, e.g.,the statement read by Soviet Ambassador to Washington Yuri Dubinin to Israeli Foreign Minister Shimon Peres at their meeting in May, *JP*, 10 June 1988.
167. See Note 6 above.
168. *Ma'ariv*, 23 February 1988.
169. Vladimir Polyakov, the director of the ME Department of the Soviet Ministry for Foreign Affairs, visited Cairo and the Soviet ambassador met with Yasir 'Arafat in Tunis.
170. AP reporting from Moscow, 10 April; *Ma'ariv*, 10 April; *JP*, 10 April 1988.
171. Prime Minister Rifa'i to Reuters, as published in *Ma'ariv*, 14 April and DR, 21 March 1988.
172. Polyakov's interview with *Le Quotidien de Paris*, 14 October 1988.
173. R. Moscow in Arabic, 12 October; MENA report about a PLO delegation's visit to Moscow, 15 October; Deputy Foreign Minister Vladimir Petrovsky's interview with *al-Hawadith*, 20 October 1988.
174. *JP*, 25 November 1988.

Armed Operations

UZI RABI and JOSHUA TEITELBAUM

The Palestinian uprising which erupted on 9 December 1987 and continued throughout 1988 produced a new context that shaped most of the year's armed activity in all arenas — Israel proper, the West Bank and Gaza, Lebanon, and internationally. Similarly, the intensified political activity in the region, which to a large extent was prompted by the uprising, also had a bearing on the level and nature of operations, as Palestinian organizations, both mainstream and other, sought to preserve the process or foil it. The result was a period of intense violence that was most costly in terms of casualties. The violence also spilled out of the region. Two major incidents took place in the international arena: the sabotaging of the *Ship of Return* in February and the assassination of PLO leader Khalil al-Wazir (Abu Jihad) in April, both widely assumed to be the doing of Israel.

In southern Lebanon, Israel's routine military activity continued. In 1988, it was marked by a rise in the number of special operations designed to secure Israeli control over that restive area.

Major operations are discussed below. Statistical data on the armed operations are presented in the Appendix.

THE WEST BANK, GAZA STRIP, AND ISRAEL

The number of operations against Israeli targets in the West Bank and Gaza Strip grew bolder and more numerous in 1988. About 2,800 armed operations were recorded, compared to 670 in 1987.[1] Operations were mostly carried out by locally organized squads and individuals, but also by squads affiliated with Palestinian organizations. The majority used readily accessible weapons, such as incendiary bombs, stones, and knives that were typically employed in a spontaneous manner. During 1988, 49 stabbing attempts were recorded compared to 19 in 1987. Still more common was the use of incendiary bombs and stones. This type of activity, familiar in recent years, became a daily matter. As many as 1,390 firebombings were recorded in comparison to 140 in 1987. In October and November, for instance, 89 squads engaged mostly in firebombings were uncovered by the Israeli security forces.[2] About 1,260 buses as well as other vehicles were damaged in the West Bank and Gaza during the period under review, in assaults in which many Israelis were injured. At times, this type of activity caused fatalities, as was the case in the 30 October firebombing of a bus near Jericho, which resulted in the death of five Israelis, among them a mother and her three children (see below).

Stone-throwing and firebombing became a serious problem for the Israel Defense Forces (IDF), and various measures were introduced to check them. In the summer the rules of opening fire were changed and IDF soldiers were permitted to shoot firebombers. The IDF also initiated preemptive as well as punitive operations; for example, in September about 200 men, organizers, and suspected perpetrators were arrested in Qalqiliyya.[3] Other deterrent measures included the sealing and demolishing of houses and deportation to Lebanon. Local Palestinians, some of them village headmen, who were suspected of collaborating with the Israeli authorities, also became targets for assaults. In September, for example, no less than six such suspects were murdered. This posed the IDF with yet another problem that consumed much energy and manpower.

The attackers of IDF soldiers and Israeli settlers rarely used gunfire. The Palestinian organizations apparently feared that this sort of activity would draw a severe IDF reaction which might seriously restrict their ability to carry on with the uprising. One exception to this rule was the killing by pistol of an IDF soldier in Bethlehem. Toward the end of the year, however, a certain increase in the use of light weapons was recorded. It was apparently carried out by squads affiliated with hard-line Palestinian organizations as a countermeasure to 'Arafat's diplomatic initiatives in the wake of the Algiers Palestinian National Council (PNC; see chapter on the PLO).

One direct result of the escalating activity was a sharpening of the already existing friction between Jewish settlers and Arab inhabitants. The settlers bore the brunt of stoning and firebombing activity and at times initiated their own retaliatory acts. In November, for instance, following the stoning of a settler's vehicle near Qalqiliyya in which one person was injured, a group of settlers entered Qalqiliyya and sabotaged about 20 vehicles belonging to Palestinians.[4] The tense atmosphere between settlers and Palestinians sometimes caused incidents to turn fatal. In April, a group of young settlers hiking in the vicinity of Bayta village (near Nablus), who got scared when local Arabs began to throw stones at them, opened fire on the crowd. The incident resulted in the death of two Palestinians and an Israeli girl and the injury of several others.[5] In another incident, in May, an Israeli settler fired at two of his Arab neighbors whom he erroneously thought to be attackers, killing one of them and injuring the other.[6] The evolving feeling of insecurity led the settlers to consider the formation of their own armed patrols. The IDF allocated a considerable number of its troops to keep the two rival populations apart and prevent acts of retaliation.

The Palestinian uprising spilled over into Israel proper. Armed activity similar to that in the West Bank and Gaza was carried out, albeit on a much smaller scale. As many as 423 incidents were recorded in 1988, compared to 158 in 1987.[7] Stone-throwing and firebombing of Israeli vehicles were common mainly in mixed cities such as Jerusalem. Moreover, the number of explosive charges planted in various locations in Israel increased, and attacks on IDF soldiers in order to steal their weapons occurred frequently.

Another important result of the uprising was the radicalization of Israeli Arabs. Demonstrations of solidarity with the uprising were held and leaflets of the United Leadership of the Uprising meant for distribution in the territories were printed in Israeli Arab villages. This sympathy was also reflected in the growing readiness of Israeli Arabs to be involved in armed activity. In December, a PLO-affiliated squad comprising Israeli Bedouins, two of them IDF soldiers, was uncovered (see below). Another squad, consisting mainly of Israeli Druzes and affiliated with the Popular Front for the Liberation of Palestine- General Command (PFLP-GC) was exposed in the same month; its members sought to establish a solid infrastructure for armed activity within the Druze community in northern Israel.[8] Another kind of activity was attacks on suspected collaborators. In October, a West Bank resident was killed on these grounds by two Israeli Arabs while on a visit in the Israeli Arab village of Umm al-Fahm.[9]

The free access of Israeli Arabs to all sites in Israel proper allowed them to sabotage private and state-owned property with relative ease. A typical instance of a group benefiting from this advantage was that of a squad comprising mainly Israeli Arabs, which was affiliated with the Democratic Front for the Liberation of Palestine (DFLP). Operating in Tel Aviv, they disconnected thousands of telephone lines and set many vehicles ablaze. They carried on with such activities for several weeks, until exposed in December.[10] More threatening and difficult to control was the wave of arson, carried out mainly at the peak of summer. The deliberate setting of fires had been seen in previous years, but on a much smaller scale. According to a spokesman of the Jewish National Fund (the body responsible for forestry matters), fires set in May-June caused five times more than the average damage of an entire summer season. In June alone, 60 cases of arson were recorded. Most arson incidents took place in areas adjacent to Israeli Arab villages.[11] At times, arson operations were carried out to pass a "test of admittance" to a Palestinian organization. A Fath-affiliated group of arsonists, led by a resident of Umm al-Fahm, was uncovered at the beginning of 1989 by the Israeli security forces.[12]

The uprising and its ramifications resulted in growing tension between Jews and Arabs, mostly in mixed cities such as Acre and Nazareth. But it affected Jewish cities as well. Thus in August, several incendiary bombs were thrown on the street in the town of Or-Yehuda — where many West Bank and Gaza Arabs were working and temporarily residing — by Jews who sought to have the Arabs accused of the act, so that they would be driven out of town.[13]

THE DIMONA BUS HIJACKING — AN ATTEMPT TO RESTORE AN ERODED POSITION

The Israeli-Egyptian border, where IDF presence was relatively meager, was a scene of occasional crossing attempts by fida'i squads. These efforts came to fruition in March, when a three-man fida'i unit hijacked an Israeli commuter bus carrying workers from Beer Sheba to the Dimona Nuclear Research Facility. The incident resulted in the death of three Israelis and the injury of eight others. The attackers were also killed.

Having infiltrated into Israel from Egypt the day before, the group stayed overnight near the Nafha Jail south of Beer Sheba. In the morning they first encountered a military vehicle driven by four IDF officers and attacked it with hand grenades and light weapons. The officers managed to flee unharmed while the attackers took over the car and headed north. Upon reaching the 'Aro'er Junction, they opened fire at passing vehicles, among them the commuter bus which was thus brought to a halt. The driver and all but 11 passengers managed to escape before the squad commandeered the bus. In the course of bargaining with the Israeli security forces over the release of Palestinian prisoners jailed in Israel the attackers began to kill passengers. An Israeli antiterror unit stormed the bus and killed the three armed men.[14]

Responsibility for the attack was claimed by the PLO. In an announcement over the PLO radio from Baghdad, it was stated that the attack was carried out in retaliation for the February killing of three PLO officers in Limasol, Cyprus (see below).[15] It was quite clear that the organization felt a need to reaffirm its military relevance in light of the fact that the uprising had been locally initiated, with the PLO becoming involved only at a later stage. Another possible motive for the operation was the desire to respond to the Shultz initiative which tried to circumvent the PLO.

It was not the first time in 1988 that such groups attempted to infiltrate across the Egyptian border. A similar attempt had been made in February, but was aborted by the IDF.[16] The effective sealing off of the Lebanese border, combined with political constraints imposed on operations through Jordan, left the Egyptian border — the one least frequented by IDF patrols — the most attractive for potential infiltrators. Ironically, then, the "peaceful border" became more menacing than other borders. The Israeli concern was expressed in the course of negotiations held between Egypt and Israel in March, when demands were made that Egypt increase the policing of its side of the border. The Egyptians responded favorably. Security measures on the Israeli side of the border were tightened as well.

THE FIREBOMBING NEAR JERICHO — A LETHAL EXAMPLE OF A TYPICAL EVENT

The operational patterns in recent years and particularly in 1988 were best exemplified by the 30 October firebombing of an Israeli bus near Jericho.

The attack resulted in the death of five Israeli citizens — among them a mother and three children — and the wounding of four others. It was the highest death toll in a single attack since the beginning of the uprising.[17] Several hours later, three Arab inhabitants were apprehended by the Israeli security forces. It became clear that the three constituted a locally organized fida'i squad whose members — like most active squads in the West Bank and Gaza — were not affiliated with any Palestinian organization. Rather, they acted hastily and abruptly without forethought or preparation. The group was apparently responsible for other firebombings in the area as well.[18]

According to Israeli experts, the attack, which coincided with the Israeli general elections, most likely increased the number of votes for the right-wing parties.[19] The PLO, attempting to counter such a development or perhaps promote a moderate image for itself, denounced the attack, calling on the Israelis "to vote for peace."[20]

THE BEDOUIN SQUAD — AN INSTANCE OF ISRAELI-ARAB RADICALIZATION

Illustrative of the radicalization in the Israeli Arab community was the fida'i squad comprising 13 Israeli Arabs, two of them IDF soldiers, which was affiliated with the PLO and uncovered in December. Most members were from the Bedouin village of Ibtin, near Haifa. They were motivated primarily by nationalistic fervor, which was boosted by the Palestinian uprising in the West Bank and Gaza and supplemented by the prospect of financial rewards.[21]

The squad's leader, Samir Sarsawi, contacted the PLO during a visit to Egypt in September 1987, where he met his operators and underwent a short paramilitary training course. He was ordered to recruit additional members and carry out spectacular attacks in crowded places. Sarsawi maintained contact with his operators through coded phone calls as well as several rendezvous in various countries, such as Hungary and Greece, where he was given money and instructions.[22]

Several unsuccessful attacks, such as the October 1987 hurling of a dud grenade in Haifa and a number of attempts to kidnap IDF soldiers, were attributed to the squad. It also engaged in firebombing and vehicular arson.[23] But the most spectacular of the squad's activities was the 20 August grenade attack on a crowded pedestrian mall in Haifa, which resulted in the injury of 25 Israelis, among them a family of seven.[24]

The squad's activity was denounced by Bedouin as well as Jewish leaders who asserted that they would not permit the incident to mar peaceful coexistence between the communities. Two arson attempts, however, one at the mosque in Ibtin and the other at a Haifa synagogue, seemed to shed a rather pessimistic light on these assertions.

LEBANON

Armed operations in South Lebanon against IDF and South Lebanese Army (SLA) targets continued in 1988. As in previous years, attacks were carried out by forces organized within the Lebanese National Resistance Front (LNRF; *Jabhat al-Muqawama al-Wataniyya al-Lubnaniyya*), an umbrella framework including Shi'i, Palestinian, and left-wing elements, mostly pro-Syrian. Operations within the security zone included launching Katyusha rockets, light arms attacks, and roadside charges.

A considerable increase in cross-border infiltration attempts shifted the focus of activity southward to the Lebanese-Israeli border. During 1988 there were 25 infiltration attempts compared to five in 1987. This increase was probably yet another result of the Palestinian uprising, since most attempts were made by the various moderate as well as hard-line Palestinian organizations who tried to outdo each other in expressing solidarity with the uprising. PLO affiliates, which at the beginning of the year stood out as the most active infiltrators across the border, curtailed their level of operation almost to a minimum at the year's end in keeping with PLO moves aimed at displaying moderation, as announced at the November PNC and subsequently. Still, crossing attempts persisted and were even intensified, mostly by PLO hard-liners seeking to derail the political process. This was exemplified by the 26 December abortive attempt by a three-man Fath Revolutionary Council (FRC) squad to reach Israel; they were killed by the IDF.[25] On the whole, infiltration attempts were designed either for demonstrative purposes or to capture Israeli hostages who could be exchanged for Palestinian prisoners in Israeli jails. Several squads managed to reach the border and encounter IDF units on Israeli territory. Others were intercepted by IDF and SLA troops while still in the security zone. In this regard, the security zone seemed to be fulfilling IDF expectations.

The access of those seeking to cross the Lebanese-Israeli border became easier in 1988 than in previous years. They were often guided by residents of the security zone. Also, Israel Air Force (IAF) air raids — the core of IDF retaliatory activity in South Lebanon — were gradually losing their effectiveness. The IDF was compelled to reassess its policy in South Lebanon and upgrade its once-effective deterrence in the region. "Air raids are safer, but also can be adjusted to and are thus less effective. Our *modus operandi* should be diversified in both timing and method," explained the IDF chief of staff, Lt. Gen. Dan Shomron.[26] On 2 May, the IDF launched "Operation Law and Order" into and beyond the security zone (see below). The raid marked a change in Israel's military policy in South Lebanon. Ever since the 1985 retreat to the security zone, IDF preemptive operations were carried out on a smaller scale. Furthermore, this was the first time that the IDF initiated a large-scale confrontation with the radical Shi'i organization Hizballah outside of the security zone. The operation in May was the first in a series of preemptive, large-scale operations that were intermittently launched thereafter. They were mostly aimed at Hizballah, but also at Palestinian forces, as in the case of the December raid on a PFLP-GC stronghold in al-Nai'ma (see below). Added to the inter-Shi'i strife between Amal and Hizballah (see chapter on Lebanon), such IDF operations contributed to reducing the latter's operational capability. Hizballah, however, was not altogether paralyzed; it still proved capable of initiating a spectacular operation like the October car bombing near the Metulla border-crossing point in which eight IDF soldiers were killed and seven others were wounded (see below).

The SLA took part, at times crucially, in IDF activities. Patiently nurtured by Israel, the SLA became a reliable partner in operations against their mutual rivals. It proved able to police the zone effectively. Military harassment within the zone was answered with SLA bombardments of villages outside of it; Hizballah attacks on SLA posts were repulsed; and, perhaps most important for Israel, several squads attempting to infiltrate Israel were intercepted by the SLA. These SLA successes might well have been the cause for the two attempts made on the life of its commander, Gen. Antoine Lahad. The second of these, in November, was carried out by the Lebanese Communist Party (working within the framework of the LNRF), and severely injured him.[27] So effective was the SLA that at a certain point Israel was reported to have begun reducing its military presence in South Lebanon.[28]

The effective sealing off of the Lebanese border led to an expansion of fida'i activity into the naval arena. On several occasions, Palestinian squads, mostly using lightweight rubber boats, were intercepted by the Israel Navy. Such was the case in September when three fida'i men, on their way to carry out an attack in Israel proper, were intercepted and killed off the Lebanese coast.[29]

IDF LARGE-SCALE PREEMPTIVE OPERATIONS

"OPERATION LAW AND ORDER"

On 2 May, the IDF embarked on a large-scale operation — "Law and Order" (see above) — into and beyond the security zone's eastern sector, lasting 72 hours. At the background was a recent intensification of cross-border infiltration attempts into Israel. It culminated in April, when four squads reached the border area, out of the seven which attempted that during the same month. Some of them came very close to reaching Israeli settlements. The interception of these squads took a relatively high toll in IDF casualties. The most serious was an attempt by a DFLP group on 26 April, which resulted in the death of two IDF soldiers, one of them a lieutenant colonel.[30] Moreover, the squads were often given shelter and guidance by South Lebanese residents, who thus facilitated their approach to Israeli territory. The operation was designed to regain the once-effective Israeli deterrence in South Lebanon and, more specifically, to eliminate the infrastructure of Palestinian armed activity in the area by apprehending those behind the recent upsurge of crossing attempts and their local accomplices.

The task force, comprising several hundred IDF troops, cut off four small villages north of the zone which were suspected havens for Palestinian squads and Lebanese collaborators. Concurrently, SLA troops conducted house-to-house searches. Arms caches were confiscated and the population was warned not to collaborate with fida'i organizations. However, no arrests were reported, seemingly because all members of the Palestinian and left-wing groups had already fled north.[31]

Later in the day, the task force attacked Maydun village. Recently deserted by its inhabitants, Maydun served as a forward position for Hizballah armed action against IDF and SLA targets in the security zone and the border area. Hizballah was known to cooperate with Palestinian organizations in cross-border infiltration attempts. Moreover, the Hizballah influence in the Maydun area threatened to drive a wedge between the Christian enclave in Jizzin and the security zone, which if it succeeded could have ominous consequences for the SLA.[32]

Hitherto, IDF activity against Hizballah consisted mostly of air raids; at times, IDF patrols clashed with Hizballah men inside the security zone. Never before had Israel initiated such a large-scale confrontation with the organization outside the zone. The attack on Maydun was thus a turning point in IDF military activity against Hizballah. The fact that Maydun was not inhabited by a civilian population defined it as a purely military target and enabled the IDF to unleash a massive conventional attack.[33]

Heavy artillery shelling of Maydun and surrounding targets was followed by the fall of the village. Several hundred IDF paratroopers, backed by tanks and helicopter gunships, raided the village. They were met with fierce resistance from Hizballah men, well entrenched and using mortars, RPG, and artillery from within the village and the surrounding hills. IDF helicopter gunships attacked and destroyed positions around the village. Ten hours later the village was taken. IDF casualties were three dead and 17 wounded, while Hizballah casualties amounted to over 40.[34]

The attack on Maydun had yet another aspect. Many of the infiltration attempts carried out in April came from the Syrian-controlled eastern sector of the border. A week before the raid, Israel's defense minister had singled out Syria as responsible for the recent upsurge of infiltration attempts. By raiding Maydun, the IDF stopped short of a direct confrontation with the nearby Syrian forces. Israel, it seems, carefully calibrated its response in order not to break its tacit agreement with Damascus regarding the freedom of maneuver in Lebanon, but succeeded in warning Syria against further involvement in armed operations against Israeli targets.[35]

Later in the month, another large-scale operation was carried out by a combined IDF-SLA force against al-Luwayza village, a Hizballah stronghold outside of the security zone. Hizballah casualties reportedly amounted to 20 dead and 25 wounded.[36] Both attacks inflicted heavy blows on Hizballah, partially accounting for the letup in its activity. The Israeli chief of staff best defined the new policy: "If we do not meet them north of the security zone, they will meet us inside it and near the border."[37]

THE RAID ON AL-NA'IMA

On 9 December, combined IDF naval, land, and air forces raided and severely damaged PFLP-GC installations in the al-Na'ima area, about 15 km south of Beirut. The attack resulted in the death of more than 20 PFLP-GC men, among them Abu Jamil, the organization's commanding officer of the South Lebanese arena and the man responsible for armed activity in Israel proper. One high-ranking IDF officer was killed in the attack and three soldiers were wounded.[38]

Ferried ashore by IDF gunboats, the troops quietly approached and then attacked Ahmad Jibril's PFLP-GC headquarters, which was well entrenched in underground bunkers. According to Lebanese sources, the IDF used trained police dogs carrying explosives and gas to drive Jibril's men out into the open.[39] Throughout the operation, the troops were assisted by constant bombing by IDF helicopter gunships and gunboats. While making preparations for evacuation, it was discovered that a four-man team was missing, but it was, nevertheless, decided to proceed with the withdrawal. The missing soldiers were later evacuated in an airborne rescue operation.[40]

The raid was the IDF's deepest ground attack into Lebanon since its 1985 withdrawal. It necessitated a particularly high level of coordination as well as accurate operational intelligence. This raid, like the one on Maydun, testified to the IDF's changing policy toward Lebanon, i.e., the initiation of ground attacks against less accessible targets. "Should the IDF limit itself to protecting the border area and to acting within the security zone without attacking the terrorist organizations' rear, the price of terrorism would become heavier,"[41] explained the IDF chief of staff.

The PFLP-GC, a Syrian-based Palestinian organization, had planned and carried out numerous operations against Israeli targets by air, land, and sea. The most spectacular of these was the November 1987 hang glider attack (for details, see *MECS*, 1987, pp. 107–8). Many of these operations originated at the PFLP-GC headquarters in al-Na'ima. The goal of the raid was to disrupt the organization's ability to plan and execute armed activity by pushing it into a more defensive posture. One strategic by-product was to drive home to the organization that it was not immune to a direct attack by the IDF.

The IDF deemed the raid an operational success. Still, the decision to leave IDF soldiers behind enemy lines — rarely taken in the past — became a topic of debate in Israel. Referring to the partial evacuation, the IDF chief of staff said he feared Israel would be thrust into a military as well as a political imbroglio with Syria, Jibril's sponsor, since its troops were stationed nearby. No wonder then that Defense Minister Rabin stressed that had he known the raid on the PFLP-GC stronghold would have developed the way it did, he would not have given it the go-ahead.[42]

HIZBALLAH CAR BOMBING — REPLENISHING OPERATIONAL CREDIT

On 19 October, a suicide driver detonated a car bomb packed with some 150 kg of explosives next to an IDF convoy. The attack took place about 300 meters north of the Israeli-Lebanese border-crossing point at Metulla. The convoy was gathering to pass through the gates when the driver drew up alongside and detonated the device, killing himself in the process. The attack resulted in the death of eight IDF soldiers and the injury of seven others.[43] Responsibility for the attack was claimed by the "Islamic Resistance," a cover name for Hizballah. According to a statement issued on behalf of the organization to the Lebanese media, the attack was carried out to mark the anniversary of the Prophet Muhammad's birthday and as a gesture to the Palestinian uprising.[44]

The spectacular attack was meant to demonstrate the organization's ability to act despite the erosion in its position caused both by IDF attacks on its bases and the ongoing inter-Shi'i strife between Hizballah and the more moderate group of Amal (for details, see chapter on Lebanon). Also, its activity against Western targets in Lebanon, i.e., the abduction of US and West European citizens, became less effective due to differences with Iran, Hizballah's sponsor, following the winding-down of the Gulf War.

The attack was the most severe blow dealt to the IDF in South Lebanon since March 1985, when a similar incident carried out by the Syrian Social Nationalist Party resulted in the death of 12 IDF soldiers. Ever since, car bombing became a widespread, though rarely efficient, weapon adopted by Hizballah and other groups operating against the IDF and the SLA in South Lebanon. Most of the 16 attempts made in 1985 had failed due to the effective IDF and SLA sealing off of all northern entrances into the zone. Consequently, car bombing within the security zone had declined almost to nil.[45] For this reason, the undetected approach of a car bomb so close to the Israeli border was in itself a surprise to the IDF. An extensive inquiry launched by the IDF and the SLA revealed that the car bomb had been assembled within the security zone, while explosives had been smuggled into the zone with the aid of local residents.[46] Following the event, hundreds of Shi'i residents of the zone were reportedly interrogated by the SLA, five of them being arrested on suspicion of complicity in the attack.[47]

Senior Israeli officials vowed to retaliate. Hizballah, for its part, asserted that any Israeli action would be detrimental to IDF and SLA soldiers held captive by the organization.[48] All the same, the IAF carried out several waves of intensive bombings on Shi'i as well as Palestinian bases, leaving behind a high toll in casualties. "The main purpose of the air raids was deterrence, to ensure that everyone in Lebanon gets the message since a successful attack like the car bomb is likely to become a model for imitation," explained a senior Israeli official.[49]

THE INTERNATIONAL ARENA

The level of armed operations carried out against Jewish and Israeli targets in the international arena remained low in 1988. They consisted mainly of planting bombs near Israeli and Jewish sites and resulted in relatively meager damage. Such, for instance, was the case with the explosions in front of the Israeli embassies in Manila and Tokyo in February and March, respectively.

In keeping with the PLO's 1985 Cairo declaration, according to which the organization would not engage in acts of terror except within Israel, the PLO continued in 1988 to refrain from such operations outside of Israel. The policy of reaping the political fruits of the uprising in the territories was crowned with success in December when the US agreed to begin a dialogue with the PLO. Attacks on targets outside of Israel would have been totally counterproductive at this stage. The PLO denounced some of the operations carried out by other organizations against Western targets, such as the December sabotage of a Pan-Am airliner (see below). The organization adhered to this policy in spite of two blows dealt to it, both of which were attributed to Israel: the February sabotaging of the *Ship of Return* and the April assassination of Khalil al-Wazir (see below).

However, attacks apparently carried out by hard-line Palestinian organizations against Western targets caused Jewish and Israeli casualties. One was the July attack on a Greek ferry, the *City of Porus*, during an interisland cruise, in which several masked gunmen fired automatic weapons and hurled grenades onto the crowded deck, then set the ship ablaze. The attack resulted in the death of nine passengers — one of them reportedly a French Jewish woman — and the injury of about 90 others.[50] The attack was generally believed to be the doing of the Libyan-based FRC, led by Abu Nidal, since the methods used were compatible with those employed by Abu Nidal's group in attacks in Rome and Vienna airports in December 1985 (see *MECS* 1984–85, pp. 93–94) and in an Istanbul synagogue in September 1986 (see *MECS* 1986, pp. 79–80).

Far more lethal was the blowing up of a civilian airliner on 21 December. A Pan-Am jumbo jet *en route* from London to the US, with 259 passengers and crew — among them two Israelis — exploded over the town of Lockerbie in Scotland, killing all passengers. Eleven local residents were also killed by falling debris.[51] Following the incident, the US and Britain launched a wide-scale investigation and concluded that the plane's destruction was a result of sabotage. The bomb was believed to have been made of high explosives, probably Czech-made Semtex that was easy to acquire and hard to detect. It was set off by a small blasting cap connected to a timer or to an altimeter.[52] Another theory suggested that the bomb was designed to explode over the ocean — where evidence would be almost impossible to recover — and was prematurely detonated due to a faulty mechanism. The investigators assumed the bomb was in an item of luggage, unknowingly carried aboard by one of the passengers on a connecting flight from Frankfurt.[53]

Responsibility for the attack was claimed by the "Guardians of the Islamic Revolution," a pro-Iranian organization. The announcement claimed that attack was in revenge for the shooting-down of an Iranian airliner in the Persian Gulf by a US warship in July[54] (see chapter on the Iraqi-Iranian War). Past experience, however, pointed to three Palestinian organizations as equally likely perpetrators, since this kind of activity had already been attributed to them: the Libyan-based FRC, led by Abu Nidal; the Syrian-based PFLP-GC; and the Iraqi-based "15 May faction," led by Abu Ibrahim, who is considered to be an expert on altimeter bombs. The possibility that one of the three groups mentioned above served as a proxy for the Iranian Government should not be overlooked. Of the three, Jibril's PFLP-GC became the prime suspect. Two months prior to the attack, 14 PFLP-GC operatives, equipped with an altimeter and large quantities of plastic explosives, were detained in West Germany. Among them was Qasim al-Dalqamuni, Jibril's chief operations officer for overseas activity. According to the German authorities, the group was planning to bomb an El Al airliner on the eve of the November PNC. Being a consistent advocate of the armed struggle against Israel, Jibril openly opposed what he considered the PLO's new path of moderation. It was not unlikely, then, for Jibril to blow up a US airliner, particularly since the PLO had achieved a political breakthrough by convincing the US to negotiate with it directly. A PFLP-GC spokesman, however, denied any involvement in the attack. As for the PLO, the organization denounced the attack and offered assistance in uncovering the perpetrators.

THE *SHIP OF RETURN* – THE FOILING OF A PUBLIC RELATIONS MANEUVER

On 15 February, underwater sabotage crippled the *Ship of Return*, a PLO ferry berthed at Limasol, which was due to carry Palestinian deportees on a symbolic voyage to Israel. Less than 24 hours earlier, three PLO military officers, who had purchased the 6,151-ton vessel for the PLO, were killed in Limasol by an explosive charge planted in their vehicle. Both incidents were evidently linked.[55]

The *Ship of Return* was intended to duplicate the 1947 journey to Palestine of several thousands Jewish refugees on board the *Exodus*. In the latter case, the British Mandatory authorities boarded the ship when it approached Haifa and prevented the passengers from disembarking. Clearly, the *Ship of Return* was a public relations maneuver, designed to embarrass Israel by suggesting a similarity between the Jews of 1947 and the Palestinians of 1988, and thus underscoring the Palestinians' right to a homeland. It was yet another means of attracting international public attention, which had already been focused on the Palestinian issue since the outbreak of the uprising.

The pretext for the journey was the deportation to Lebanon of four Palestinians from the West Bank and Gaza. The ship was due to depart with about 100 deportees accompanied by journalists and various celebrities.[56] The journey was postponed several times owing to the refusal of the Greek shipowners to charter the vessel, apparently out of concern for their future business relationship with Israel. There was very likely also Israeli pressure. The PLO was consequently forced to buy a vessel rather than hire one. The *Sol-Phryne*, one of the vessels used to evacuate PLO members from Beirut in 1982, was purchased several days before the sabotage by an unknown company, apparently acting for the PLO.

The operation was regarded by Israel as a hostile act. Accordingly, Defense Minister Rabin stated shortly before the sabotage that Israel would stop the vessel in "ways it deems suitable."[57] Following the incident, there were conflicting claims of responsibility by both Jewish and Arab radical groups. The PLO, however, pointed to Israel, claiming it was the only party interested in stopping the ship and vowed to retaliate. A PLO spokesman declared in Tunis that the organization was no longer committed to the 1985 Cairo declaration, which called on both sides of the conflict not to engage in armed operations in the international arena.[58] Retaliation followed, but it was in Israel proper, when a bus was hijacked in Dimona in March (see above). The PLO announced that the *Ship of Return* would leave on its journey at a later unspecified date.[59]

THE ASSASSINATION OF ABU JIHAD

On 16 April, the PLO military commander, Khalil al-Wazir, alias Abu Jihad, was assassinated by a crack commando team at his house in Sidi-Bu Sa'id, an elegant suburb of Tunis. His driver and two of his bodyguards were also killed in the attack. His wife, daughter, and son, who were also in the house during the attack, were left unharmed.

According to eyewitnesses and Tunisian security sources, the squad comprised about 30 men, seven or eight of whom carried out the actual killing, while the others were backup. The assailants wore military outfits and masks and carried guns with silencers with which they killed the bodyguards and driver. The assailants broke into the house and killed Abu Jihad and then escaped in three rented vehicles, which were later found abandoned at the seashore. There were no clues to the attackers' identity.[60] Clearly, the operation was carefully planned and professionally executed.

Abu Jihad was one of the shrewdest and most resourceful leaders of the PLO. He was regarded as the number-two man within the organization and, in recent years, as 'Arafat's most likely successor. An enthusiastic proponent of the armed struggle against Israel, he used to argue that guerrilla warfare was vital; that it could provoke Israeli reprisal and thus draw Arab states into armed confrontation with Israel over the Palestinian issue. In 1973, Abu Jihad became the man in charge of the "Western Sector," the PLO's apparatus for armed activity in Israel proper and in the West Bank and Gaza.[61] Ever since then he was regarded as the architect of armed activity against Israel. He personally briefed and often bade farewell to the perpetrators of some of the most spectacular attacks, such as the one on the Israeli coastal town of Nahariyya in June 1974, which left four dead and six wounded; the taking of hostages at the Savoy Hotel in Tel Aviv in March 1975, which resulted in the death of 11 and the wounding of 11; and the hijacking of an Israeli bus in March 1978, which resulted in the death of 35 Israelis and the wounding of 80 others.

Abu Jihad's position within the West Bank and Gaza was a unique one. Besides heading the prestigious "Western Sector," he was a senior member of the Joint Palestinian Jordanian Committee for the distribution of financial resources to the West Bank. As such, he further strengthened his power base in the area. With the outbreak of the Palestinian uprising in the West Bank and Gaza, he soon reportedly began funneling money and instructions to local operatives in order to sustain the level of activity. In fact, Abu Jihad himself was quoted as saying that he was commanding the uprising.[62]

Abu Jihad's death caused profound grief in the Arab countries, which in many places was expressed by mock funerals. An especially stormy wave of riots in the West Bank and Gaza followed. Several Arab states and the PLO blamed Israel for the assassination. Israel, however, refrained from any formal comment on the killing. The combination of Israel making no special effort to deny such accusations and a series of unofficial disclosures mostly to the foreign media added to suspicions that Israel was responsible.

From press reports it emerged that the operation was carried out by a combined team of Israel's intelligence agency (Mossad) and a special hand-picked IDF commando unit known as *Sayeret Matkal* (reconnaissance unit of the General Staff) assisted by the Israeli Navy and Air Force. The raid was monitored and coordinated by some of the IDF's leading officers from a Boeing 707 flying over the Mediterranean outside of Tunisian airspace. Some time before the attack, several Arabic-speaking Mossad agents carrying false Lebanese passports had arrived in Tunisia to provide the team with operational intelligence and logistical support. On the night of the mission the Mosad agents awaited the commando unit, which arrived by rubber dinghies launched from an IDF missile boat, and drove the unit to its destination in three rented vehicles.[63]

Killing Abu Jihad was frequently discussed by Israel, but was ruled out, despite the long bill of particulars against him, probably because of an Israel-PLO tacit agreement not to harm each other's leaders. However, the slaying of Abu Jihad was reconsidered after the March hijacking of a bus near Dimona (see above), credit for which was claimed by the PLO and which was probably planned by Abu Jihad. Equally important, Israel assumed that Abu Jihad was orchestrating the uprising. Israel's desire to demonstrate a firm hand against terrorism and to deflate the uprising made the assassination worthwhile despite the possible repercussions. The decision was taken in the course of two meetings of Israel's 10-member Inner Cabinet, the first immediately after the bus hijacking and the second shortly before the operation itself.[64]

The killing of the PLO's most senior military figure was a severe blow to the organization and the Palestinians at large, since Abu Jihad was first and foremost a symbol of the armed struggle. PLO officials vowed to avenge the killing. A spokesman for the organization again declared in Tunis that the organization was no longer committed to the Cairo declaration. Nevertheless, the PLO's main problem following Abu Jihad's death did not seem to be retaliation for the attack; rather it was finding an equally skilled person to fill Abu Jihad's shoes.

APPENDIX: STATISTICAL DATA

The following statistical data of armed operations are based on IDF sources.

TABLE 1: THE WEST BANK AND GAZA: INCIDENTS

Date	Type of Event				
	Disturbances including stone-throwing	*Incendiary bombs*	*Knife assaults*	*Planting of charges*	*Gunfire*
9 Dec. 87–9 Jan. 88	1,359	109	5	6	1
10 Jan.–10 Feb. 88	1,769	98	5	1	—
11 Feb.–11 Mar. 88	2,084	164	6	5	—
12 Mar.–12 Apr. 88	1,782	152	2	8	4
13 Apr.–10 May. 88	1,319	119	3	6	—
11 May.–10 Jun. 88	1,529	163	1	14	1
11 Jun.–8 Jul. 88	1,572	121	5	10	1
9 Jul.–9 Aug. 88	1,410	108	3	7	—
10 Aug.–9 Sept. 88	1,852	113	3	7	—
10 Sept.–10 Oct. 88	2,328	83	7	7	—
11 Oct.–9 Nov. 88	1,703	58	4	2	—
10 Nov.–8 Dec. 88	1,595	58	1	7	3
9 Dec.88–12 Jan. 89	2,790	44	4	5	5
Total	**23,092**	**1,390**	**49**	**85**	**15**

TABLE 2: THE WEST BANK AND GAZA: CASUALTIES

Date	Local Residents		Israelis	
	Killed	*Wounded*	*Killed*	*Wounded*
9 Dec.87–9 Jan. 88	26	214	—	30
9 Jan.–8 Feb. 88	19	225	—	42
9 Feb.–8 Mar. 88	25	285	—	37
9 Mar.–8 Apr. 88	39	385	—	55
9 Apr.–8 May 88	35	332	—	22
9 May.–8 Jun. 88	11	243	—	42
9 Jun.–8 Jul. 88	10	283	—	32
9 Jul.–8 Aug. 88	20	208	—	33
9 Aug.–8 Sept. 88	16	327	1	28
9 Sept.–8 Oct. 88	18	537	—	32
9 Oct.–8 Nov. 88	17	350	4	35
9 Nov.–8 Dec. 88	10	281	—	23
9 Dec. 88–9 Jan. 89	26	441	2	33
Total	**272**	**4,150**	**7**	**444**

TABLE 3: LEBANON: INCIDENTS 1988

Date	Type of Incident			
	Infiltration attempts	*Clashes*	*Roadside charges*	*Katyusha rockets*
January	1	1	13	2
February	2	1	14	4
March	2	1	21	2
April	7	1	14	1
May	—	3	16	1
June	1	3	14	1
July	—	2	17	—
August	2	1	24	—
September	2	—	18	6
October	2	2	11	—
November	3	5	10	—
December	3	3	6	1
Total	**25**	**23**	**178**	**18**

TABLE 4: LEBANON: CASUALTIES 1988

	IDF		SLA		Others*	
Date	*Killed*	*Wounded*	*Killed*	*Wounded*	*Killed*	*Wounded*
January	1	4	—	6	10–16	31
February	4	3	1	10	9	12
March	—	2	1	10	29–45	36–40
April	2	13	3	38	23	12
May	3	17	3	23	50–70	25–30
June	—	2	1	—	12	7
July	1	1	—	6	6	1
August	—	9	2	2	12	2
September	—	—	—	5	9	14–15
October	8	10	1	6	50–55	85
November	1	—	12	3	14	18
December	1	—	2	5	9	—
Total	**21**	**61**	**26**	**108**		

* Including Shi'i, Palestinian, and left-wing elements.

NOTES

For the place and frequency of publications cited here, and for the full name of the publication, news agency, radio station or monitoring service where an abbreviation is used, please see "List of Sources." Only in the case of more than one publication bearing the same name is the place of publication noted here.

1. *Yedi'ot Aharonot*, 24 January 1989.
2. *JP*, 8 December 1988.
3. *Ha'aretz*, 14, 23 September 1988.
4. *Yedi'ot Aharonot*, 27 November 1988.
5. *IHT, Ma'ariv*, 7 April; *Ha'aretz*, 28 April 1988.
6. *Ma'ariv*, 8 May; *JP*, 9 May 1988.
7. *Yedi'ot Aharonot*, 24 January 1989.
8. VoI, 27 September — DR, 28 September 1988.
9. *JP*, 18 October 1988.
10. *Ha'aretz*, 16 December; *Ma'ariv*, *Hadashot*, 30 December 1988.
11. *JP*, 12, 16 June 1988.
12. VoI, 1 February 1988.
13. *Ha'aretz*, 26 August 1988.
14. *The Guardian, Ma'ariv*, 8 March 1988.
15. VoP (Baghdad), 7 March — DR, 8 March 1988.
16. *JP*, 12 February 1988.
17. *Ma'ariv, Hadashot*, 1 November; *Ha'aretz*, 23 December 1988.
18. *Ha'aretz*, 1 November 1988.
19. *JP*, 1 November 1988.
20. *Ha'aretz*, 1 November 1988.
21. *Ha'aretz*, 4 December; *Yedi'ot Aharonot*, *JP*, 7 December 1988.
22. *Yedi'ot Aharonot*, 25 December 1988, 7 January 1989.
23. *Ma'ariv*, 7 December 1988.
24. *Ha'aretz*, 21 August; *Ma'ariv*, 22 August 1988.
25. *Ma'ariv, Yedi'ot Aharonot*, 27 December 1988.
26. *Ha'aretz*, 11 December 1988.
27. R. IDF, 8 November — DR, 9 November 1988.
28. *Ma'ariv*, 2 September 1988.
29. *Ha'aretz*, 25 September 1988.

30. *Ma'ariv*, 27 April; *JP*, 28 April 1988.
31. *Ma'ariv*, 4 May 1988.
32. *Ma'ariv*, 5 May; *FT*, 6 May 1988.
33. *JP*, 5 May 1988.
34. *JP*, 3, 5 May 1988.
35. *Ha'aretz, JP*, 6 May 1988.
36. *IHT, JP*, 26 May 1988.
37. VoI, 14 July — DR, 14 July 1988.
38. *Ma'ariv*, 11 December 1988.
39. R. al-Quds, 9 December — DR, 9 December 1988.
40. *Ha'aretz, Yedi'ot Aharonot*, 11 December 1988.
41. *Ha'aretz*, 12 December 1988.
42. *Ma'ariv*, 18 December 1988.
43. *JP, Ha'aretz*, 20 October 1988.
44. *Yedi'ot Aharonot*, 20 October 1988.
45. *Ha'aretz*, 20 October 1988.
46. *JP*, 21 October; *Ha'aretz*, 23 October 1988.
47. VoI, 20 October — DR, 20 October 1988.
48. R. Beirut, 20 October — DR, 21 October 1988.
49. USIS, 27 October 1988.
50. *Ha'aretz*, 12 July; *Ma'ariv*, 13 July; *JP*, 21 July; *NYT*, 27 July 1988.
51. *FT*, 23 December 1988.
52. *Newsweek*, 9 January 1988.
53. *FT*, 29 December 1988.
54. *FT*, 23 December 1988.
55. *Ha'aretz, Ma'ariv*, 16 February; *IHT*, 17 February 1988.
56. *NYT*, 15 February; *Ha'aretz*, 16 February 1988.
57. *JP*, 16 February 1988.
58. *Ha'aretz*, 16 February 1988.
59. R. Monte Carlo, 15 February — DR, 16 February 1988.
60. *NYT, JP, Ma'ariv*, 17 April 1988.
61. *Hadashot, Ma'ariv*, 17 April; *NYT*, 18 April; "The Killing of Abu Jihad," *The Washingtonian*, June 1988.
62. *NYT*, 18 April 1988; *Bamahane*, 28 May 1986.
63. *The Guardian*, 19 April; *NYT*, 23 April 1988.
64. *Ma'ariv, The Guardian*, 20 April; *IHT*, 22 April 1988.

INTRAREGIONAL AND ISLAMIC AFFAIRS

Inter-Arab Relations

BRUCE MADDY-WEITZMAN

The broad lines of divisions into two Arab camps laid down in the late 1970s and early 1980s had weakened considerably during the previous 12 months, despite the absence of a fundamental shift in orientation by any of the Arab states (see *MECS* 1987, chapter on inter-Arab relations). This continued to be the case in 1988: developments in both the Gulf War and the Palestinian *intifada* (uprising) in the West Bank and Gaza, and in the aftermath of the 1987 Amman summit conference which formally opened the door to Egypt's full reentry into Arab affairs, all reinforced the trends of the previous year. One important consequence was that Syria, the leader of the oppositionist bloc, stood increasingly alone: its Arab fellow-travelers (Algeria, Libya, and the People's Democratic Republic of Yemen [PDRY]) frequently parted company with it, at least tactically, at various various junctures (all three on Syria's positions toward the Iraqi-Iranian War and the Palestinians, Algeria, and the PDRY regarding Egypt's place in the system). Syria's alliance with non-Arab Iran thus provided it with even fewer benefits while exposing it to Arab criticism. At the same time, the widely trumpeted breakthrough in Syrian-Iraqi relations at the November 1987 Amman summit proved to be without substance, and the atmosphere between Baghdad and Damascus returned to its former mutually hostile and belligerent state. This became more disturbing for Syria in the fall of 1988, when Iraq, having compelled Iran to adhere to a cease-fire, adopted a more active anti-Syrian posture in Lebanon, complicating Syrian efforts to engineer the election of a new president there. Its failure to do so and the resulting constitutional crisis in Lebanon led to numerous Arab calls for a special summit on Lebanon, much to Syria's distaste. One immediate Syrian response to its growing isolation was to employ more conciliatory language toward Egypt, hinting at a possible shift in Syria's fundamental opposition to Cairo and its peace with Israel. Another, probably planned earlier, but motivated by the same desire to ease its isolation, was to begin the process of restoring diplomatic relations with Morocco (broken off two years earlier following King Hasan's meeting with Israel's Prime Minister Shimon Peres; see *MECS* 1986, p. 102).

Syria's minority status and the resultant softening of its language toward Egypt were also the product of another development — the Palestinian uprising. Initially, the Syrians had wholeheartedly welcomed the outbreak of the *intifada*, as it served to bring the Arab-Israeli conflict back to center stage only a month after the November 1987 Amman summit had focused on the Gulf War (thus highlighting Syria's problematic stance). For Damascus, the *intifada* would hopefully weaken Israel's deterrent posture, engender a renewed Arab consensus behind the confontation states, with Syria in the lead, and deflect Arab criticism from Syria's alliance with Iran. From the June Algiers summit onward, however, the PLO began translating the *intifada* into political gains at both Syria's and Jordan's expense. Jordan quickly fell into line behind the broad Arab consensus supporting the PLO; Syria was much more reluctant, although its opposition to Yasir 'Arafat seemed increasingly illegitimate in Arab terms. Not yet on the horizon by year's end, but surely of concern, was Syria's fundamental dilemma: what to do in the event of a renewed Middle East peace process enjoying wide Arab and international support, a process which would most probably focus on the Israeli-Palestinian nexus, and not on Israeli-Syrian issues.

For Egypt, the year was one of consolidating the benefits reaped at the 1987 Amman summit. President Husni Mubarak personally visited 11 Arab capitals, some of them more than once, as Egypt sought to project an image of strength and leadership in the cause of the entire Arab nation. Thanks to Iraq's successes on the battlefield and the resulting cease-fire with Iran, Egypt's loudly proclaimed commitment to Arab national security did not have to be put to the test, to Cairo's satisfaction. Three more Arab states renewed full diplomatic relations with Cairo, leaving only three — Syria, Libya, and Lebanon — without full ties. In addition, Cairo was readmitted to a number of Arab League-affiliated organizations from which it had been suspended. By year's end, it was almost inconceivable to envisage Egypt's absence from the next Arab summit meeting, whenever it were to convene. Ten years after the Baghdad conferences which imposed a boycott on Egypt following its peace with Israel, the resolutions enacted there were practically a dead letter.

Subregional conflicts and issues continued to figure importantly in the calculations of many of the Arab states, albeit in ways somewhat different than previously. Sudan was less of a focus of rival attention from Egypt and Libya partly because of Libya's decreased capacity for regional mischief-making, but even more so because Sudan's massive internal problems rendered it unfertile territory for Libyan aspirations. In the southern part of the Arabian Peninsula, relations between the two Yemens and between the PDRY and Oman continued to remain on an even keel. The Gulf Cooperation Council (GCC) states continued to maintain their special relations with one another (albeit not totally tension-free) within the collective framework established in 1981. Iraq's turning back of the Iranian threat and the resulting cease-fire allowed GCC leaders to breathe more easily than at any time since Iran first took the offensive against Iraq in 1982; although, inevitably, apprehensions increased regarding the future regional role of Iraq's vastly strengthened armed forces. Finally, in the Maghrib, the signs of a regionwide thaw in 1987 bore dramatic fruit in 1988: Algeria and Morocco restored full diplomatic relations with each other in May after a break of 12 years, and reached considerable agreement on ways of ending the war in the Western Sahara. The following months witnessed significant progress toward a diplomatic resolution of the war under UN auspices. Thanks to this breakthrough in Algerian-Moroccan relations, the first summit of the heads of the five Maghrib states convened in Tunis, and was followed up by much preliminary work toward the establishment of an all-Maghrib political framework modeled on the GCC. Much of their motivation to proceed derived from the awareness in Algeria, Morocco, and Tunisia of their countries' acute domestic problems caused by massive population growth, economic stagnation, and growing Islamic fundamentalism. Their sense of urgency was confirmed by the massive internal unrest that shook Algeria during October, which was followed with profound concern throughout the Maghrib and the rest of the Arab world.

Broadly speaking, the inter-Arab year can be divided into two, roughly equal, phases marked off by the June Algiers summit, King Husayn's decision in late July to disengage from the West Bank, and Iran's decision on 17 July to accept a cease-fire with Iraq. Consequently, the texture and content of inter-Arab relations during the latter half of 1988 was significantly different from that in the first half.

THE *INTIFADA* AS AN ALL-ARAB ISSUE

THE ROAD TO ALGIERS

The outbreak of unrest in the West Bank and Gaza Strip in December 1987 was immediately given pride of place in the Arab media, which hailed the "heroes of the stones" in their struggle against Israeli rule. The responses of Arab governments, by contrast, were much slower in coming.[1] This was so for a number of reasons: an initial underestimation of the likely duration of the *intifada*, an awareness of their limited ability to influence the situation, and the fact that their collective attention was still directed in large part toward the Gulf. On the other hand, the genuine and widespread resonance of the *intifada* within Arab societies, as well as its potential for exploitation by opposition movements *within* many of the Arab states, dictated involvement.

The first collective Arab effort to address the new situation came on 23–24 January, with a meeting of Arab foreign ministers in Tunis. The level of participation was high: 16 of 21 Arab League members were represented at the foreign ministerial level; the PLO delegation was reinforced by Executive Committee Chairman 'Arafat, indicating the importance he attached to the meeting.

Both Libya, which along with the PLO had been the first to call for the special session, and Syria sought to capitalize on the *intifada* to improve their respective positions in the inter-Arab matrix. To this end, each submitted a working paper to the session; together with one submitted by the PLO, they formed the basis for discussion.

Their common thrust was the need to mobilize broad financial and political support behind the uprising. Nonetheless, they differed on a number of significant points. Libya's working paper proposed channeling $150m in Arab aid to the Palestinians in the territories through the Red Cross, with an additional $200m to be donated annually through unspecified avenues.[2] Presumably, Libya did not object to the PLO having a hand in the distribution of the funds, as indicated by Mu'ammar Qadhdhafi's meeting with 'Arafat on his way to Tunis on 23 January. The meeting was the most clear-cut sign of the thaw in Libyan-PLO relations which had begun during the previous year. 'Arafat and Qadhdhafi would meet four more times during 1988. However, Libyan support for the uprising and its renewed dialogue with the PLO did not involve any shift in its fundamental position regarding the Arab-Israeli conflict: the Libyan delegate voiced strong opposition during the conference to the broad Arab consensus behind seeking a political solution through the convening of an international conference.[3]

Syria's foreign minister, Faruq al-Shar', for his part, came to the meeting (following consultations with the Saudi leadership) with a general plan to establish a ministerial committee to monitor Israeli actions against the Palestinians in the territories and to press the Arab case before the members of the Security Council.[4] Financial aid to the Palestinians, Shar' stated, should be channeled through the Arab League (so as to avoid giving the PLO exclusive control over the funds); moreover, Arab residents of the Golan Heights should also receive financial assistance.[5] Although Syrian-PLO relations continued to be tense, Shar' did remain in the hall during 'Arafat's speech. While pressing the ministers for political and financial backing, 'Arafat, too, sought to ease Syrian-PLO tension; he specifically thanked Syria for its part in the lifting of the siege of Palestinian refugee camps in Lebanon by the Amal militia.[6] (See *MECS* 1987, chapter on Lebanon.)

The conference was not without its moments of friction. Still smarting from the wholesale rush by Arab countries to restore full rélations with Egypt in the aftermath of the Amman summit, Faruq al-Shar' called on those who had done so to demand that Cairo break off its ties with Israel. After all, he declared, the goal of allowing the restoration of Arab-Egyptian relations had been to pry Egypt away from Israel's embrace. Shar''s proposal was voted down by a majority of 14.[7] The Jordanians, for their part, expressed opposition to a PLO-suggested formulation which seemed to include those Palestinians residing in Jordan as being represented by the PLO.[8]

The conference made two operative decisions. Financial pledges were made, reportedly amounting to $100m.–$200m. However, the ministers preferred not to fix a specific sum, declaring only that everything that was necessary would be provided. The money's distribution, obviously bound to face Israeli opposition, was to be made through unspecified multiple channels; presumably these channels included the special "uprising fund," which was essentially PLO-controlled; international welfare organizations; and the joint Jordanian-PLO "Committee for Occupied Homeland Affairs".[9] On the political side, Syria's proposal for a ministerial committee was amended; the conference established a committee of seven members (Tunisia, Saudi Arabia, Algeria, Iraq, Syria, Jordan, and the PLO, joined by Arab League Secretary-General Chedli Klibi), and charged it with drawing up a joint plan to implement Arab summit resolutions on the Arab-Israeli conflict, establishing a joint Arab position at the UN, making contacts with representatives of the Security Council's five permanent members and other important countries, and lobbying for a comprehensive settlement to the conflict by means of an international conference.[10] 'Arafat expressed satisfaction with the committee's establishment: Syria's unrealized intention, he said, had been to create a committee which would keep watch over the uprising (and thus place a limit on Palestinian independence of decision-making).[11] Faruq al-Shar', for his part, likewise pronounced himself content with the outcome of the conference, stating that it reflected 80% of the Syrian viewpoint.[12] Still, it was clear to all that the measures adopted would have only limited impact by themselves.

The first meeting of the newly established ministerial committee was held in Tunis on 20 February. Delegations to lobby Security Council members were subsequently formed, and their visits began in mid-March.[13] However, almost no new Arab financial assistance was tendered. a fact bitterly noted by 'Arafat;[14] one consequence was an increase in tension between the PLO and Saudi Arabia, the PLO's chief financial benefactor (see chapter on Saudi Arabia).[15]

Concurrently, Algeria took the lead, with 'Arafat's blessing, in calling for the convening of an emergency Arab summit conference to deal with the *intifada*. The idea to convene a summit had already been gestating in various quarters: Morocco's King Hasan, for example, had suggested in mid-February that a summit be held within four to six weeks.[16] On 8 March, the wheels of inter-Arab diplomacy moved into higher gear, as Algeria's Foreign Minister Ahmad Talib Ibrahimi formally addressed a letter to Arab League Secretary-General Klibi calling for a summit. The summit's attraction for the PLO was obvious: it would offer an ideal opportunity to reinforce the centrality of the Arab commitment to the Palestinian cause, the PLO's leading role, and 'Arafat's own personal prestige, only months after the Amman summit had given the Palestinian question lower priority. For Algeria, the summit call was consistent with both its patronage of the PLO and its increasingly active profile in wider Arab affairs during the previous two years. There was also an emotional component to Algeria's promotion of a summit; according to a senior PLO official, President Chedli Benjedid was openly bitter about the Arab world's "wavering" and "negative" response to the *intifada*.[17] Both the PLO and Algeria desired that the summit be held at the beginning of April in order to establish a common Arab response to US Secretary of State George Shultz's diplomatic initiative which they both rejected.[18] (For details on the Shultz initiative see chapter on the US and the Middle East; for the Arab response, see chapter on the Middle East peace process.)

The call for a summit drew a less than enthusiastic response. The president of the United Arab Emirates (UAE), Shaykh Zayid Ibn Sultan Al Nuhayyan, stated that there was "no need" for a summit, since the Arab states already supported the Palestinians.[19] Even those who favored it disagreed on both its timing and content. The first problem was the Shultz initiative; most Arab leaders preferred not to place more obstacles in the secretary's way, but to let his initiative first run its course. Jordan, which of all Arab states stood to benefit the most from the Shultz initiative, was reportedly holding back its formal agreement to a summit while trying to win PLO approval for a joint Jordanian-Palestinian delegation to an international peace conference (as had been stipulated — according to Jordan — by the 1985 Husayn-'Arafat agreement and annulled by the PLO in 1987).[20] On this, the Jordanians came up empty-handed. On 10 April, Arab League foreign ministers, meeting in Tunis in an extension of the Arab League Council's ordinary session of 30 March, agreed that the summit would meet sometime after 17 May, the end of the Muslim holy month of Ramadan. On 8 May, Algeria officially announced that it would host the summit on 6 June and Algerian diplomats began touring Arab capitals armed with formal invitations.

A number of matters reflecting the basic lines of division in the Arab world still needed to be addressed during the month-long run-up to the summit. Many of the Arab states strongly desired that Egypt be invited to attend; Jordan took the lead in officially asking Algeria to issue Egypt an invitation.[21] With his eye on the Gulf War and on Egypt's contribution (both potential and actual) to "Arab national security," King Husayn also proposed the creation of a pan-Arab force of at least 30,000 men.[22] Presumably, this could be approved only at the summit level. The Gulf War and Iran's perceived threat to Saudi Arabia was on the minds of others too. This fact was noted by the PLO: assured that the summit would focus mainly on the Palestinian question, the PLO moved to satisfy Iraq by asking that the war be placed on the summit agenda.[23]

Both Syria and Libya were opposed to these suggested alterations to the summit's agenda. Syrian President Hafiz al-Asad made it clear to Chedli Benejedid (who was personally amenable to the idea of Egypt's participation) that Syria would not attend the summit if Egypt were present.[24] Syria was also opposed to renewed discussion of the Gulf War, for it promised to invite criticism for Syria's failure to distance itself further from Iran and consummate its promised *rapprochement* with Iraq. Qadhdhafi, too, was adamant in insisting on a single-issue (the *intifada*) summit; the introduction of any other topic, he argued, would be an act of "high treason."[25] He warned that if Egypt were accepted back into the Arab League, then Libya, along with two or three other countries, would leave.[26]

Both Qadhdhafi and Saudi Arabia's King Fahd tried their hand at mediating between Asad and 'Arafat in the aftermath of the assassination of 'Arafat's deputy, Khalil al-Wazir (Abu Jihad), in Tunis on 16 April (see chapter on armed operations). Abu Jihad's funeral in Damascus provided the occasion for a Syrian-PLO dialogue. A meeting between Syrian Vice President 'Abd al-Halim Khaddam and the head of the PLO Political Department, Faruq Qaddumi, paved the way for 'Arafat's arrival in Damascus, accompanied by a Libyan envoy, on 24 April for a meeting with Asad. It was 'Arafat's first trip to Damascus since being bundled out of there in June 1984. According to the PLO's number-two man, Salah Khalaf (Abu Iyad), the PLO and Syria were in general agreement regarding the *intifada*, the Shultz initiative, the substance of the proposed international conference, and the agenda for the forthcoming Arab summit. However, they disagreed on the PLO-Egyptian relationship, on PLO contacts with Israeli groups and individuals, on the tactics to settle the Arab-Israeli conflict, on the Palestinian presence in Lebanon, and on the possible readmission of anti-'Arafat Palestinian factions into the PLO.[27] The last two points were of greatest immediacy: bitter fighting for control of Palestinian camps in the Beirut area between 'Arafat's loyalists and Syrian-backed Palestinian dissidents resumed on the eve of the summit. For this, 'Arafat placed the blame squarely on Asad.[28] The fighting continued after the summit, despite Libyan efforts to oversee a cease-fire,and brought the Syrian-PLO dialogue to a halt. (For details, see chapters on the PLO, Lebanon, and Syria.)

THE ALGIERS SUMMIT

Three months elapsed between Algeria's call for an emergency summit to find ways to bolster the Palestinian uprising and its actual convocation. The response to the call had been less than overwhelming; moreover, important inter-Arab differences, such as between Syria and Iraq, and Syria and the PLO, remained unresolved. Nonetheless, Algerian and PLO persistence in working for a summit paid off: on 6 June Arab leaders convened in Algiers, a meeting which was quickly dubbed "the *intifada* summit."

The level of attendance was high, indicating the desire of Arab leaders to display their solidarity with the Palestinian cause. King Fahd and King Hasan were both present, after having been absent from the Amman summit seven months earlier. Moreover, Hasan's participation both formally sealed the recent restoration of diplomatic relations between Morocco and Algeria and also set the stage for an all-Maghrib summit (see further below). Also noteworthy was the presence of Qadhdhafi — he had last attended a full-fledged Arab summit conference in 1969. Overall, 17 Arab heads of state and PLO Chairman 'Arafat were present. The only countries not represented by their heads of state were Somalia, which sent its minister of state for foreign affairs; Oman, which sent a special envoy of Sultan Qabus; and Iraq, whose president, stated Iraqi delegation head, First Deputy Premier Taha Yasin Ramadan, was "needed in the confrontation theater."[29]

Despite the widespread Arab desire for Egyptian participation, Cairo remained excluded, to Syria's and Libya's satisfaction. Egyptian anger with the Algerians increased as Algiers failed to honor Egypt's request that its diplomatic representative in the Algerian capital be invited to observe the summit's festive opening session. Adding insult to injury, the Iranian ambassador was invited (he walked out during Klibi's opening speech attacking Iran).[30] In an attempt to remind the summit-goers where real power lay in the Arab world, Husni Mubarak met with Saddam Husayn in Baghdad on 6 June.

For those present in Algiers, the discussions were lacking in the tension and drama which usually characterize Arab summit conferences. "What a quiet summit," a Moroccan diplomat noted. "Everyone agrees with everyone."[31] This was a bit of an overstatement: PLO differences with Syria and Jordan, Syria's differences with Iraq, and Qadhdhafi's mercurial views provided the summit with some room for debate. So did the suggestion by Saudi Arabian Foreign Minister Sa'ud al-Faysal that Egypt be permitted to attend the summit without reinstating its membership in the Arab League, a proposal rejected by Syria.[32] However, open confrontations were generally avoided.

At the same time, the contrast between the respective statuses of 'Arafat and Husayn, in comparison to seven months earlier at the Amman summit, was striking. There, 'Arafat had been initially snubbed by Husayn and the Palestinian issue discussed only in passing (although resolutions satisfactory to the PLO were adopted). In Algiers, the tables were turned. 'Arafat was a central figure, confidently putting forth his demands: collective Arab political support designed to bring international pressure on Israel; reiteration of previous summit resolutions recognizing the PLO as the sole, legitimate representative of the Palestinians, and the right of independent Palestinian decision-making; the convening of an authoritative international peace conference in which the PLO would participate on an equal footing, either as an independent delegation or as part of a joint Arab delegation; material support, amounting to $400m. annually and safeguarding the security of Palestinian camps in Lebanon while ensuring the right of Palestinians there to armed struggle against Israel.[33]

By contrast, Husayn and his accompanying entourage felt on the defensive throughout the conclave. Repeatedly, they deemed it necessary to reiterate Jordan's support for the uprising and for the PLO.[34] Husayn and 'Arafat met twice during the gathering to coordinate their stands and iron out disagreements; just as in January at the foreign ministers' meeting, these included the question of control over funds to be channeled to the territories, and a clause in the PLO's "working paper" submitted to the summit proclaiming that it represented the Palestinian people both inside and outside the territories.[35] According to one Arab newspaper, the Soviets had asked Algeria's President Benjedid on the eve of the summit to help prevent a PLO-Jordanian confrontation which would result in an outright rejection of the Shultz initiative and thus damage the prospects of an upcoming American-Soviet foreign ministers' meeting.[36]

In a lengthy speech to the summit's first working session, on the morning of 8 June, Husayn spelled out Jordan's position. The purpose of the Amman summit, he reminded his audience, had been to achieve Arab reconciliation:

> an essential requisite for [effectively] facing external challenges.... The Algiers summit convenes in order to deal with these challenges directly. Foremost among them is the Zionist challenge to the Arab nation in general and to the Palestinian Arabs in particular.

To understand the current situation, he continued, one must know what came before. Husayn then proceeded to give an account of his family's and Jordan's 70-year association and interaction with the Palestinian issue, wrapping Jordan's policies in the mantle of pan-Arabism. The Jordanian-Palestinian link, he said, was strengthened by the April 1950 union between Jordan and the West Bank, an act falsely characterized by both Israelis and some Arab writers as "annexation."[37] The period of union, from 1950–67, was "a living model" of Arab unity aspirations. However, if it was now "the wish of the Palestinian people's representatives to separate from Jordan at present," he declared, then Jordan would "bless and respect" their will, just as it had done in 1950.

The king then moved to the post-1967 era, summarizing Jordan's two-pronged policy of supporting "steadfastness [of the Palestinians in the territories] and political action in order to recover the occupied territories."[38] Its most recent expression, he said, was Jordan's efforts, made in coordination "with the Arab brethren concerned, particularly Syria," to alter the Shultz initiative proposals so as to bring them into conformity "with the bases of the Arab position." Nonetheless, he acknowledged, Jordan's actions created certain "sensitivities" and "suspicions" among PLO leaders. "We came to be seen as competing rather than cooperating... strengthen[ing] their emphasis on moving toward a separation from us." Aware of these sensitivities "at quite an early stage [1972]," Husayn personally put forward his plan to establish "a federal order," the United Arab Kingdom, composed of two states, Jordan and Palestine. "At the time it seemed...the most acceptable in that it affirmed the Palestinian identity, preserved the complementarity between the two states, and reflected the distinctive relationship between the two peoples."

Having spoken "frankly and in a comprehensive manner," Husayn turned to the issue at hand, the formulation of a "unified Arab stand" to support the uprising and advance the Palestinian cause. Politically, he preferred adhering to the principle of an "effective" international conference with participation by the PLO "on an equal footing," but "without tying [Arab] hands with regard to details on the manner of PLO participation," thus leaving room for modified aspects of the Shultz initiative. Jordan, he said, would welcome any arrangement: an independent delegation, a joint Arab delegation, or any other (e.g., a Jordanian-Palestinian one) in order to facilitate the convening of the conference. However, he continued, if PLO and Arab leaders chose to create an independent Palestinian state and then insist on PLO participation as a separate delegation to an international conference:

> even if this does not lead to the convening of the conference, we shall not differ with them on that. In all circumstances, we stand ready to agree to whatever the brother Arab leaders unanimously adopt.

Regarding financial aid to the Palestinians in the territories, the main point was that the aid should reach its destination by whatever means possible. Jordan did not have to be "the sole conduit for support." He then elaborated on the economic assistance Jordan had rendered to the territories since 1967, all done, he insisted, without any selfish motive on its part.

Finally, he reiterated that whatever decisions the summit would take, Jordan would continue to fulfill its "national responsibility of supporting the uprising and its resistance to occupation." However, to do so, Jordan needed help. The Baghdad summit's financial commitments to the confrontation states and the PLO were in their final year, he reminded Arab leaders. Only half of the commitments had been met, and Jordan and Syria were now in need of "sustained support" in order "to be able to withstand the aggressive and expansionist Zionist designs as long as the Arab-Israeli conflict continues."[39]

One thing was clear from Husayn's speech. While he believed that his policies had, and continued to offer, the best chance of making progress in the Arab-Israeli peace process, he would not directly challenge the PLO or buck the emerging Arab consensus behind it. More than ever before, it was paramount for Jordan that it should not appear to be placing any obstacles in the Palestinians' path.

Syria, too, avoided any overt disagreements with the PLO, although according to one report, the Syrian delegation stated that the PLO working paper was insufficient, because it did not specify the material support needed to fuel the uprising.[40] 'Arafat, for his part, made special mention in his speech of "the opening of a new page in Palestinian-Syrian relations," calling it "a good omen."[41] On the final day of the summit, 'Arafat and Asad met in Asad's hotel suite, with accompanying officials, to "coordinate support for the uprising."[42]

As is usually the case at Arab summits, issues not on the formal agenda, most notably the Gulf War, were nevertheless discussed, this time at the third closed session, on 9 June. Unlike at Amman seven months earlier, this time there was no sense of urgency, thanks to Iraqi successes at the front. Still, for the Iraqis, it was important to win maximum backing. First Deputy Prime Minister Ramadan had already served notice the previous evening that Iraq was not satisfied with Syria's position. "We want those who have not yet understood," he declared, "to understand that the Iranian aggression is parallel to the Zionist aggression, is similar to it, and is its partner."[43] According to a Gulf newspaper, a joint Iraq-Gulf states' working paper sharply condemning Iran formed the basis of the discussion and the resulting sections of the conference's final statement dealing with the Gulf.[44]

Algeria, Libya, and Syria tried, each in its own way, to prevent another harsh condemnation of Iran. Concerned with maintaining an appearance of balance between Iran and Iraq, the Algerian press dropped the section of Secretary-General Klibi's opening speech which attacked Iran, and the Algerian delegation initially offered a more mildly worded resolution than the one tendered by Iraq.[45] Qadhdhafi's position was more convoluted, befitting Libya's tilt in 1987 toward a more even-handed, less pro-Iranian stance. His strong anti-American position, however, made him repeat the warning Libya's representative voiced at the Amman summit: Iran must be rescued from America's embrace, a danger which had manifested itself through US arms sales to Iran and the willingness of certain Iranian leaders to restore Tehran's links with Washington. He also proposed that a resolution condemning Iran also include a similar condemnation of American aggression in the Gulf of Sidra. On the other hand, he gave out signals indicating displeasure with Iran's behavior in Lebanon (to Syria's safisfaction, no doubt).[46] The most pronounced indication of the change in

Libya's position came in Qadhdhafi's meeting with Ramadan. According to the latter, Qadhdhafi blessed Iraq's recent victories on the battlefield and expressed a desire to develop bilateral ties. Unlike Algeria and Libya, Syria displayed no softening of its opposition to the anti-Iranian language of the proposed resolution. Asad's reservations on this, said Ramadan after the summit, were "impudently expressed" during the closed session.[47]

The summit's final statement and two supplementary resolutions contained few surprises. The section on the Palestinian uprising stressed the participants' "commitment to providing all necessary aid, in all forms and by all means to the Palestinian people to ensure the continuation of their resistance and uprising behind the PLO's leadership." No exact sums of financial support were mentioned, to the bewilderment and disappointment of some.[48] Klibi explained, in response, that the Arab League had no authority to supervise the disbursement of material support; this was up to the PLO and supporting states.[49] However, the sums cited by the PLO both in the media and in official statements were both consistent and in line with previous PLO demands: the PLO was to receive $128m. immediately, plus $43m. per month for the remainder of the year.[50] The summit also adopted the PLO's call to place the West Bank and Gaza "under temporary UN supervision" in order to protect Palestinian civilians from Israel's "oppressive and inhuman practices," as an interim measure preceding the establishment of a Palestinian state.

Similarly, the final statement reiterated the summit participants' commitment to support the frontline states (i.e., Jordan and Syria) without mentioning specific sums or any commitment to renew the pledges of the Baghdad summit. One Arab newspaper did state that aid levels were fixed for Jordan ($150m.) and Syria ($250m.);[51] another report stated that the specifics would be left to Syria's and Jordan's bilateral contacts with the oil states.[52] More generally, the Amman resolutions pertaining to the Arab-Israeli conflict were reiterated in full: adherence to the 1982 "Fez principles" as a basis for solving the conflict; support for the convening of an international peace conference under UN auspices, to be "based on the UN resolutions [i.e., not only UN Security Council Resolutions 242 and 338] calling for the 'Zionist entity' [a term used frequently throughout the statement] to withdraw fully from all Arab and Palestinian-occupied territories and to secure the national and well-established rights fo the Palestinian people"; (the description of the proposed conference as "authoritative" was dropped from the final communiqué in an effort to demonstrate flexibility towards the US; 'Arafat stated that he had successfully insisted that the word "effective" be used to describe the conference, although it did not in fact appear);[53] and insistence on the PLO's participation in the conference on an equal footing, given its status as the "sole, legitimate representative of the Palestinian people."

With regard to the Gulf, the statement reflected the will of Iraq and the GCC states. Iran's "intransigence" was declared to be the cause of the war's continuation, a statement whose inclusion Syria had opposed. The Amman resolutions condemning Iran's "aggression... threats against the Arabian Gulf states... interference in their internal affairs... continued occupation of Arab territories in Iraq...and its refusal to comply with Security Council Resolution 598" (which called for a cease-fire) were reiterated. So was the call on the international community "according to the sequence of its active articles." (Syria had unsuccessfully opposed this at Amman.) In addition, the summiteers reiterated their "full solidarity" with Iraq in all of its efforts and praised its recent military victories, a position which stemmed from their "adherence to pan-Arab responsibility" and "determination to defend pan-Arab security and protect Arab land." (The Iraqis had strongly pushed for this emphasis on the pan-Arab aspects of the conflict.)[54] Finally, they expressed their determination "to stand by the Arab Gulf states in facing up to any foreign aggression," condemned all forms of Iranian "terrorism... violence and subversion" against the Gulf states, particularly Saudi Arabia and Kuwait, and endorsed Saudi Arabia's efforts to avoid a repeat of the previous year's violent confrontation with Iranian pilgrims during the *hajj* (for details, see chapter on Saudi Arabia).

Reports conflicted as to the precise nature of Syria's reservations over this section of the final statement. In addition to Asad's statements during the sessions, Radio Damascus tersely announced that Syria had expressed reservations over statements concerning Iran.[55] According to Iraq's Ramadan, all the paragraphs in the final statement were unanimously approved; Syria had not expressed a formal reservation, and supported Resolution 598, but opposed the denunciation of Iranian aggression. In this, and in the absence of any Libyan objection, Ramadan professed to find improvement since the Amman summit.[56] Similarly, Klibi declared "clearly and finally" that "there was no reservation from any side on the fundamental issues."[57]

On other matters, the final statement proclaimed the indivisibility of Arab national security: "Any aggression against the sovereignty of any member state, or any act of terrorism against such a state constitutes aggression against the whole Arab nation." The examples cited were all acts committed by or ascribed to Israel (the 1981 attack on Iraq's nuclear reactor, the attack on PLO headquarters in 1985, the assassination of Abu Jihad in Tunis, and Israeli actions in Lebanon). Qadhdhafi would have certainly preferred that the US bombing of Libya in 1986 be included as well; just as certainly, the drafters of the statement chose not to do so. Instead, they made it a separate, if immediately proximate, item. The very next paragraph reaffirmed Arab support for Libya against American aggression and the "continuous threats against its security", and endorsed Libya's stand on the dispute over the Gulf of Sidra. On Lebanon, the final statement had little to offer beyond reiterating well-worn expressions of support, this despite Lebanese President Amin Jumayyil's impassioned plea for Arab support for "the legitimate authority" in Lebanon.[58] Finally, the statement expressed satisfaction with the "positive developments" both in inter-Arab relations and in the international arena. In the inter-Arab sphere, the conferees vowed to work harder to consolidate relations and "strengthen joint Arab action." Internationally, they hoped that the budding "international *détente*" would (a) help the nations of the world achieve their aspirations of "freedom and self-determination" and guarantee their "sovereignty and independence," and (b) contribute to both solving the pressing social and economic problems in the developing world and removing the "imbalance" in the international economic system. (For the full text of the final statement, see Appendix I.)

Postmortems of the summit were generally favorable. 'Arafat contrasted the Amman summit, where "there was an attempt [to] write off the Palestinian question" to the just-concluded proceedings: Algiers, he declared, had been the scene of a "new era," in which a "new Arab will" had been born.[59] Radio Damascus proclaimed Syria's satisfaction with the summit's having given priority to the Arab-Israeli conflict over other problems; in doing so, and in sticking to previous Arab summit resolutions on the conflict, the "credibility" of Syrian policies was confirmed.[60] Algerian Foreign Minister Ahmad Talib Ibrahimi rejected criticism that Arab leaders had moved too slowly; the "detailed preparation" over three months was one of the factors which ensured the summit's success. Algeria, he continued, intended to build on the summit's successes to try and further "clear the Arab atmosphere" (referring to differences between Syria and the PLO, Syria and Lebanon, the PLO and Jordan, the PLO and Lebanon, and the two Yemens).[61] Even Qadhdhafi praised the summit's results. Earlier, he had caused a stir by wearing white gloves, apparently in order to avoid shaking hands with any Arab leader who had touched the hand of Shimon Peres, the Israeli leader, e.g., King Husayn and King Hasan.[62] In the end, however, he proclaimed the summit to be the "most successful of all," even if he had been "surprised by some of the sentences" in the final statement. He especially praised King Husayn, for his "unexpected" condemnation of American policy.

Overall, the summit was not one of the more memorable inter-Arab gatherings. Still, its importance was not negligible. In comparing the Algiers summit with that in Amman seven months before, a number of points stood out. Arab leaders at Amman had heralded "a new era" in inter-Arab affairs based on a major improvement in Syrian-Iraqi relations and on Syria's willingness to share in the Arab consensus against Iran. By the time of the Algiers summit, these had proved to have been exaggerated expectations, although Iraq's victories against Iran rendered a shift in Syria's position less pressing. Syria remained in the minority, and a shrinking one at that. On the positive side, Syria could point to the renewed Arab interest in the Arab-Israeli conflict. The main beneficiary, however, was not Asad but the man he so detested, 'Arafat. While Arab financial pledges remained suspect, the reassertion of political support for the PLO under his leadership left his primary rivals (Husayn and Asad) with little room for maneuver. 'Arafat even managed to strengthen his ties with Qadhdhafi (flying to Tripoli for further meetings immediately after the summit) without altering his positions. 'Arafat even used the presence of international media representatives at the summit to float an important trial balloon, the "Bassam Abu Sharif document," whose formulations on the components of an Arab-Israeli peace were more conciliatory than existing official PLO policies (for details, see chapter on the Palestine Liberation Organization).

FROM THE ALGIERS SUMMIT TO THE ALGIERS PNC MEETING

Developments in the immediate aftermath of the Algiers summit highlighted the PLO's contrasting fortunes: in Lebanon, the position of 'Arafat's loyalists became even more precarious; in the wider Arab arena, its standing was significantly enhanced.

In Lebanon, the increased pressure applied by Syria, this time via its anti-'Arafat Palestinian clients, resulted in the defeat of 'Arafat's loyalists and their withdrawal from Palestinian camps in Beirut (for details, see chapter on the Palestine Liberation Organization). 'Arafat repeatedly sought to mobilize Arab pressure on Syria to ease its grip. At the end of June, he pressed both Libya and Algeria to intervene with Syria on his behalf. In July and August, he repeatedly called for an emergency Arab League Council meeting to put Syria in the dock, but was unsuccessful. In October, he added his voice to Iraq's denunciations of Syria and calls for an emergency summit in Baghdad (see below).[63]

In the wider Arab arena, however, the picture was far more favorable. True, Arab pledges of financial support made at Algiers were unredeemed in the following months. More importantly, however, were the political implications of the Algiers summit: these became clear on 31 July, when Husayn announced his decision to sever all "legal and administrative ties" with the West Bank, in line with the spirit of the Algiers resolutions confirming the PLO's primacy. At Algiers Husayn had forthrightly stated his own views and preferences, but to no avail. Now, he moved to carry out his pledge to abide by the Arab consensus and not stand in the PLO's way. His motivations were complex: a desire to avoid the appearance of obstructing the Palestinians, to insulate his kingdom from the currents of the *intifada* across the river, and to challenge the PLO to do better (for a fuller analysis, see chapter on Jordan). The PLO was caught by surprise. But after some initial confusion, it realized the nature of both the challenge and the opportunity posed by Husayn's declaration and responded accordingly (see chapter on the Palestine Liberation Organization).

Initial Arab reaction to Husayn's decision was generally favorable, if somewhat hesitant. Most governments adopted a wait-and-see attitude, until the implications of Husayn's move became clearer. Algeria and, more importantly, Egypt took the lead in seeking renewed coordination between the PLO and Jordan, in order to avoid a rupture that would damage Arab efforts to present a united front *vis-à-vis* the peace process. Egypt's actions were consistent with its long-standing strategy: "any rational Palestinian policy," declared Mubarak, "must acknowledge the special nature of the Palestinian-Jordanian relationship, and the fact that Jordan has a basic role to play in attaining peace." Jordan's role, he explained, did not diminish the Palestinian role; rather, it strengthened it.[64]

Egypt's efforts climaxed on 22–23 October at a tripartite summit between Mubarak, Husayn, and 'Arafat held in Jordan's port city, 'Aqaba. Four sessions were held, during which Mubarak encouraged 'Arafat to both (a) formulate a joint stand with Husayn in light of American opposition to separate PLO representation in the negotiating process;[65] and (b) adopt, at the forthcoming Palestine National Council (PNC) meeting, what Egyptian Foreign Minister 'Ismat 'Abd al-Majid termed "realistic and practical formulas, as the coming phase requires."[66] No joint communiqué was issued at the minisummit's conclusion. However, both the Egyptians and King Husayn pronounced themselves generally satisfied. The meetings, Mubarak stated, witnessed "no conficts of interest."[67] As a result, declared 'Abd al-Majid, Jordan and the PLO now:

> feel more and more that both are inevitable partners for ending the Israeli occupation of the Arab territories and that any Palestinian future without a strong and firm relationship with Jordan is difficult to imagine.[68]

For Husayn, the meetings had symbolically confirmed his importance to both the Palestinians and to future Arab-Israeli diplomacy. Husayn denied that either the matter of a joint Jordanian-Palestinian delegation to a peace conference or the principle of a Jordanian-Palestinian confederation had been addressed at 'Aqaba, as it was "premature" to discuss them. What was important, he said, was the change in the PLO since his 31 July speech: now that they have "direct responsibility," they "tackle issues more seriously and precisely."[69]

The PNC's declaration of independence and its political program, adopted at

Algiers on 15 November, marked the peak of the PLO's year-long effort to translate the *intifada* into political gains. In terms of relations with the Arab world, it undoubtedly strengthened its status. The Algiers declarations won near-unanimous praise apart from Syria's ostensibly favorable, but in fact ambivalent, statement of support (see chapter on Syria). Most Arab governments formally recognized the "State of Palestine" and upgraded PLO offices to embassy status (see chapter on the Palestine Liberation Organization). Arab governments, led by Egypt, Saudi Arabia, and Kuwait acted in concert during the following weeks on the PLO's behalf, pressing the US to grant 'Arafat a visa so he could address the UN General Assembly in New York, condemning US failure to do so, spearheading the transfer of the Assembly session to Geneva, and pressing George Shultz, this time successfully, to acknowledge that 'Arafat had met Washington's long-standing conditions for a dialogue with the PLO (see also chapter on Egypt). In inter-Arab terms, this flurry of diplomatic activity, raising as it did the prospects for renewed momentum in the peace process, contributed to Syria's increased willingness to countenance a dialogue with Egypt and its return to the Arab League, so as to avoid being left without influence in the coming stages (see below).

THE CONFLICT IN THE GULF

FROM THREAT TO CEASE-FIRE

The Amman summit had raised Arab expectations that the perpetually poisoned relations between Syria and Iraq would soon become a thing of the past.[70] However, consummating the initial steps taken at Amman to repair Syrian-Iraqi ties proved to be more difficult than expected.

A preliminary bilateral dialogue was initiated during the following weeks, but its pace was deemed unsatisfactory by King Husayn and Saudi officials (see *MECS* 1987, p. 134). Contacts apparently continued into 1988. According to a Syrian official, aviation officials met in Baghdad in mid-January to discuss the resumption of air links; other subjects being discussed were said to include the refurbishment of their respective embassies (relations had been broken off by Iraq in October 1980), a renewal of telephone links, and further exchanges of delegations.[71]

Syria, at this juncture, was interested in at least the appearance of progress in order to satisfy its benefactors in the Gulf and Husayn. At the same time, Damascus sought once again to reconcile its proclaimed adherence to Arab solidarity with its relationship with Iran. Thus, at the end of December 1987, Syria launched a diplomatic initiative designed to bring about a dialogue between the GCC states and Iran. Syria was reportedly also suggesting a postponement of Iran's scheduled offensive against Basra, in return for a halt to Iraqi raids on Iranian shipping.[72] Success would significantly bolster Syria's inter-Arab standing by providing evidence for its long-held claim that its leverage on Iran served to prevent the expansion of the war.

This was exactly what the Iraqis feared;[73] they sharply criticized Syria's diplomatic forays, but their annoyance with the GCC states for being amenable to such a dialogue and to Syrian mediation was kept under wraps. Syrian mediation in the Gulf, said Iraq's information minister, was "contrary to the spirit and resolutions of [the Amman] summit."[74] Foreign Minister Tariq 'Aziz depicted Syria's role as "upside-down." Damascus should abide by the common Arab stand and act like an Arab country, not like the UN secretary-general or a European country, he argued.[75] Not content with verbal condemnations, Iraq moved to demonstrate more forcefully the worthlessness of Syria's efforts: on 10 January, it resumed its attacks on Iranian shipping in the Gulf, after a 10-day halt. Shortly afterward, Syrian efforts to promote a GCC-Iran dialogue petered out, Syria's claim of progress notwithstanding.[76]

On 27 January, Iraq renewed its full-scale propaganda attacks against Syria, which had been halted following the Amman summit. Soon thereafter, Iraqi President Saddam Husayn reportedly asked King Husayn to cease his mediation efforts between Iraq and Syria,[77] and Syrian-Iraqi relations reverted to their "normal," i.e., mutually hostile and vituperative state. For Baghdad, the improvement of bilateral ties with Syria could not be separated from Syria's stance on the war and its relationship with Iran. As for Iraq's allies, particularly Jordan and the GCC states, the hopes which had been raised during the previous nine months for a real Syrian-Iraqi *rapprochement* had proven unfounded. There was some consolation, however. The need to put pressure on Iran by effecting a Syrian-Iraqi *rapprochement* and concomitant weening away of Syria from Iran became progressively less urgent in the following months, thanks to a string of Iraqi victories at the front and the failure of Iran's long-heralded offensive against Basra to materialize. (For details, see chapter on the Iraqi-Iranian War). One indication of the increasing sense of confidence among Arab Gulf states was Saudi Arabia's decision on 26 April to sever diplomatic ties with Iran in the wake of continuing recriminations over the deaths of the hundreds of Iranian pilgrims during the previous year's *hajj* and disputes over Saudi efforts to limit the number of Iranian pilgrims for the coming one (see chapter on Saudi Arabia). (The Saudis had refrained from cutting ties the previous year, notwithstanding their strong efforts to bring about a collective Arab decision to break off relations.)

The climax came on 17 July, with Iran's official acceptance of a cease-fire with Iraq on the basis of UN Security Council Resolution 598, even though it was, for Khomeyni, a decision "more lethal... than poison."[78] It took one more month for the fighting actually to cease, during which time Iraq penetrated anew into Iranian territory (c. 100 km. in depth, in some sections). Iraq also adopted a tough diplomatic posture, insisting initially that Iran agree to the principle of direct negotiations before the cease-fire could take effect. On this, the Saudis joined the permanent members of the UN Security Council in pressuring the Iraqis to be more flexible; they also advised them to cease their military advances. The Iraqis strongly denied the existence of any pressure from the Arab world.[79] Nonetheless, they did soften their diplomatic position and wind down their offensive. The cease-fire officially took effect on 20 August; for the time being, the modern ME's most destructive war — one which had come to be *the* single most important concern of the Arab system during the 1980s — had come to an end.

AFTER THE CEASE-FIRE

The advent of the Iranian revolution and the course of the Iraqi-Iranian War had been decisive in causing Iraq to discard its traditionally radical, odd-man-out position in the Arab spectrum and to forge close ties with the conservative, pro-Western Arab regimes instead. The cease-fire induced speculation both in the region and beyond as to whether or not Iraq, having emerged from the war battered but far stronger militarily than it had been in 1980, would maintain both its existing position on the inter-Arab continuum and its low profile in Arab-Israeli matters. The most immediate, if largely unvoiced, apprehensions were in the Gulf: after all, Iraq had laid claim to Kuwait in 1961 and had supported for many years afterward radical opposition groups in the region. Saddam Husayn sought to allay these concerns: historically, he told a gathering of Arab information ministers in Baghdad:

> the Arab nation's trend has always been peace, love, and enlightenment, not hegemony... This generation cannot logically part with its history and become hostile the moment it possesses a financial, military, scientific, or other capability.

Technological and scientific advances in the Arab world, he declared, should be shared among countries without fear: "the Arab who is afraid of his Arab brother will be exploited by the foreigner." Interference in one another's internal affairs must be forbidden. In this respect, he stated, Iraqi-Saudi relations were a model for others to emulate.[80] Even before the cease-fire, a sympathetic interviewer sought to verify the meaning of Saddam's promotion of Arab unity thus:

> You seem to want to reassure the Arabs, especially those who think a strong Iraq would want to control and wield influence through its unity slogan... to dissolve a certain entity or erase a certain character.

Saddam responded that:

> There must be complete reassurance in Arab relations. Mutual trust among Arabs is the firm foundation on which Arab unity should be built...increasing faith in ... the principles... of [Saddam's 1980] pan-Arab declaration [see *MECS* 1979–80, pp. 195–96] because it lays down the foundations of a bright and revitalized future for the Arab nation. I am confident that many of our Arab brothers now understand us better than they did 10 years ago.... The top task at present is promoting inter-Arab trust...[which will create the] solid foundations of the desired Arab unity in the long run.[81]

As it happened, Iraq's relations with the GCC states remained amicable for the time being, even as both Kuwait and Saudi Arabia moved with dispatch to repair their damaged relations with Iran (for details, see chapters on Iran, Saudi Arabia, and the Gulf states). Still, the gradual resumption of the Gulf states' traditional position of balancing themselves between their two more powerful neighbors was a possible source of future tension with Iraq;[82] so was the question of the repayment of Iraq's war debt, estimated at $60bn.

Iraq's relations with other Arab states also remained basically unaltered in the months after the cease-fire. If there was some change, it was in the direction of reinforcement. Iraqi-Egyptian relations had been transformed during the 1980s from unbridled hostility and competition to close cooperation, thanks to Iraq's need for Egyptian assistance as a counterweight to Iran. By the middle of the decade, Cairo-Baghdad relations had become closer than at any time since the emergence of the Arab League in 1945. Thus, it was not surprising that Mubarak sought both to reinforce Saddam's attempt to soothe jittery Arab nerves and to shield Iraq from Western criticism in the wake of its employment of chemical weapons against the Iraqi Kurds (see chapter on Iraq). Following his meeting with Saddam on 7 October, Mubarak declared that he was:

> fully convinced that Iraq wants peace and that it most sincerely seeks to establish it... [and that it] does not seek to take anything which does not belong to it. It also does not want to violate the rights of Iran or anybody else... [it] does not seek to commit aggression, but rather it defends its rights and sanctities... [Iraq's] sincere desire [was] to embark on... the battle of reconstruction and...the resumption of the development process... [In addition,] Iraq...[was] subject to an unjust campaign in recent months... [in which] feeble charges [had been] made against it.[83]

Iraq's appreciation for Jordan's unswerving support throughout the war was manifested on 16 August by its presentation to Jordan of captured Iranian weapons and equipment, including 90 *Chieftain* tanks, 60 M-47 tanks, 19 British-made *Scorpion* light tanks and 35 M-113 personnel carriers.[84] Jordan, for its part, joined with Egypt in both proclaiming Iraq's benevolent intentions and denouncing the "suspect" campaign against Iraq in the West over Iraq's use of chemical weapons against its Kurdish population.[85] The support of the Arab majority bloc for Iraq on this issue was formally expressed in an Arab League Council resolution charging that "American media lies of alleged Iraqi employment of chemical weapons against Kurdish rebels [were] designed to influence the course of the Iraqi-Iranian peace talks in Geneva."[86]

As in the previous two years, King Husayn sought throughout 1988 to lessen tensions between Syria and Iraq. As it happened, however, the two countries became even more embittered in the months after the cease-fire. On the morrow of Iran's acceptance of the cease-fire, a Syrian newspaper commentary lambasted the Iraqis: "In whose interest was it," the paper asked, "to start this... most tragic of wars?" Future Arab generations had been bequeathed a "chronic problem more dangerous than the Zionist occupation: namely, hostility between the Arabs and Iran."[87] The Iraqis answered in kind: "The most dangerous plague [to strike] the Arab nation throughout the past 20 years," declared Ramadan, was "the treasonous phenomenon of Hafiz al-Asad." Consequently, he declared, Syria should be expelled from the Arab League, diplomatically shunned, and have its financial assistance cut off.[88]

More importantly, Iraq moved forcefully to penalize Syria for its alliance with Iran where it was most vulnerable: Lebanon. Iraq quickly extended military aid to the anti-Syrian Christian forces. According to a Western news agency, the aid, valued at tens of millions of dollars, began to flow in March. It included 18 Soviet-made rocket launchers, 64 T-55 tanks, 20 armored troop carriers, three artillery batteries, 30 heavy caliber machine guns, and approximately 100,000 shells and rockets.[89] On the political plane, Iraq sought to help block Syria's efforts to engineer the election of a new Lebanese president in September. Iraq's allies apparently approved of Baghdad's anti-Syrian activism. One Arab weekly, quoting sources close to Syria, stated that the intelligence services of Iraq, Egypt, and the PLO were acting together against Syria's position in Lebanon, particularly in West Beirut, and that some GCC states were channeling funds to anti-Syrian groups there.[90]

Syria's failure on 23 September to get a new Lebanese president chosen plunged Lebanon into its worst constitutional crisis ever, one which threatened to institutionalize the existing *de facto* partition. Iraq, for its part, was emboldened even further, quickly recognizing the anti-Syrian emergency government proclaimed by Gen. Michel 'Awn (it was the only Arab state to do so). In the following months, Baghdad attempted to promote trade and economic links both with the 'Awn

Government and private Lebanese investors.[91] Moreover, the Iraqis, taking advantage of Arab concern with the events in Lebanon, launched a diplomatic effort to convene an emergency Arab summit in Baghdad to discuss the new crisis. Ideally, the summit would formulate a new Arab position on Syria's role (which had been legitimized by the 1976 Cairo and Riyadh summits; see *MECS* 1976–77, pp. 147–50), since Syria was deemed responsible for the current dangerous situation.[92] One pro-Iraqi Arab weekly called for the creation of a new Arab deterrent force from countries not previously involved in Lebanon to oversee the holding of new elections in Lebanon and the withdrawal of Israeli and Syrian forces, and for the cessation of Arab aid to Syria if it blocked Arab League efforts.[93]

Parallel to Iraq's efforts, the UAE President Shaykh Zayid and King Husayn also publicly supported the idea of a special summit, although they framed their calls in ways designed to avoid antagonizing Asad. Both Mubarak and 'Arafat quickly followed, as did the foreign ministers of the GCC, at a meeting in Riyadh on 1–2 November. In response, Arab League Secretary-General Klibi initiated a round of contacts in order both to determine the possibility of convening a summit and to put forward concrete suggestions to solve the crisis.[94] Asad made it clear to Klibi that he was willing to attend, but only on condition that the summit would not serve as a platform for anti-Syrian attacks, and that other Arab states would agree to aid Syria to support its role in Lebanon.[95] The Syrians also activated their own diplomatic efforts: on 25 October, Vice President Khaddam flew to Jordan to meet King Husayn,[96] while Foreign Minister Faruq al-Shar' concurrently visited all of the GCC states apart from Saudi Arabia to explain the Syrian position.

In the propaganda battle, Syria responded to Iraq's attacks in kind. Ostensibly, declared a Radio Damascus commentary, Iraq had ceased its cynical policy of "outbidding" on Arab-Israeli issues in 1978. In fact, however, it premeditatedly made use of the unanimity achieved at the Baghdad summit to divert the Arab world from the original objective of confronting Israel and Anwar al-Sadat's policies, employing it in a non-Arab, treacherous, and marginal conflict.[97] Asad also sought to remind Saddam that he was capable of responding in kind to Iraqi meddling in Syria's domain, playing host on 18 October to Muhammad Baqir al-Hakim, the chairman of the Tehran-based Supreme Assembly of the Islamic Revolution in Iraq.

The Saudis, Soviets, and Jordanians were all concerned over the renewed tensions between Syria and Iraq. King Husayn was particularly active in seeking to bridge the gap between Damascus and Baghdad. He also suggested a widening of the proposed summit agenda, to include the issues of the *intifada* and the Arab-Israeli peace process, particularly in the wake of the Israeli and American elections, and that its venue be Riyadh, the place designated for the next "ordinary" Arab summit.[98] A preparatory foreign ministers' conference would pave the summit's way and would renew the activities of the Arab League's Follow-up Committee, first established in 1976 to assist with the resolution of the Lebanese crisis (for its establishment and activities, see *MECS* 1976–77, p. 507, and 1980–81, pp. 245–46).[99]

The idea of a special summit on Lebanon quickly receded into the background due to Syrian-Iraqi differences. Baghdad, while continuing to favor the idea, also declared its readiness to confine a meeting on Lebanon to the ministerial level, if that was what the others preferred.[100] A meeting scheduled for the end of December was postponed until the beginning of 1989.

At the same time, hopes for the early convening of the Riyadh summit with a broader agenda had been raised by year's end, thanks to a new development: a spate of statements by Asad and other Syrian officials indicating their willingness to countenance the restoration of links with Egypt and the lifting of Egypt's suspension from the Arab League. These statements were accompanied by others recognizing Egypt's importance in the Arab arena, paying tribute to the "sacrifices of the Egyptian people" on behalf of the Arab struggle against the "Israeli enemy," absolving Mubarak from responsibility for the acts of Sadat and praising Egypt's recognition, despite Israeli pressures not to do so, of the PNC's declaration of independence.[101]

Both the Saudis and the Jordanians were involved in encouraging Syria in this direction. During his visit to Riyadh from 13–15 December, Asad discussed with King Fahd both the possibility of holding the Riyadh summit with Egypt present, and also the Lebanese problem and Syrian-PLO relations.[102] Asad undoubtedly pressed the Saudis for a renewed aid commitment if he accepted Egypt back into the Arab fold, although the Saudis denied reports to that effect.[103] Thanks to Husayn's efforts, the Syrians halted their propaganda attacks against Egypt.[104]

Overall, Syria's behavior provided a classic illustration of inter-Arab dynamics, with one state (Syria) responding to a negative change in the balance of power (growing Iraqi strength on both Syria's western and eastern flanks, its own weakening in Lebanon and *vis-à-vis* the Palestinians, fears of further diplomatic isolation in the Arab-Israeli arena, and uncertainties as to the intentions of its Soviet patron; on the latter, see chapters on Syria, and the Soviet Union and the Middle East) by sending friendly signals to the other significant Arab power (Egypt). If consummated in an Arab summit with Egypt present, this move would surely be rewarded by renewed Arab financial aid commitments, at a time when the annual grants proffered at the Baghdad summit were expiring. Ideally, this move would also reinforce Syria's position in Lebanon and insure that any effort to activate the Arab-Israeli peace process would take Syria's interest into account.

EGYPT AND THE ARAB WORLD

The following is a brief survey of Egypt's place in the Arab system in 1988. For a more detailed examination, see chapter on Egypt.

By the end of 1988, Egypt's 10-year struggle against the Baghdad resolutions was nearly complete. Three more countries had renewed full diplomatic relations with Cairo: Tunisia, on 23 January; the PDRY, on 9 February; and Algeria, on 24 November. Only Syria, Libya, and Lebanon (under Syria's influence) remained recalcitrant. Egypt had been readmitted to a number of Arab League-affiliated organizations, such as the Arab Economic Unity Council, the Arab Educational, Cultural, and Scientific Organization, the Arab Labor Organization, the Arab Fund for Economic and Social Development, and the Arab Organization for Investment and Agricultural Development; it also resumed its membership in various nonofficial Arab professional, vocational, and sports federations. The final act, readmittance to the Arab League itself, seemed imminent. In the meantime, according to the League Secretary-General Klibi, Egypt had "contributed significantly" in the preparation of the much-discussed, long-delayed amendment to the Arab League charter (for earlier efforts, see *MECS* 1980–81, pp. 250–51).[105] Mubarak, for his part, emphasized that

Egypt's readmittance to the league would not be accompanied by its insisting on the return of Arab League headquarters to Cairo from Tunis.[106]

One concrete sign in 1988 of Egypt's renewed centrality was Mubarak's travel itinerary: he made official visits to 11 Arab countries — the six GCC states, Morocco, the Yemeni Arab Republic (YAR) (the first visit by an Egyptian president in 25 years, i.e., since the Yemeni civil war),[107] Sudan, Iraq (three times), and Jordan. (Mubarak and Husayn met on eight occasions during the year; they have visited each other a total of 34 times since relations were renewed in October 1984.) Another was the existence of "joint higher committees" between Egypt and nearly every Arab state with which it had diplomatic relations, designed to deepen and expand bilateral cooperation in various spheres. A third was, as in previous years, Egypt's persistent efforts to achieve a Jordanian-PLO understanding in order to advance the Arab-Israeli peace process.

Egypt's overall foreign policy course was confidently spelled out by Foreign Minister 'Abd al-Majid in a speech to the ruling National Democratic Party's Committee on Arab Affairs. Egypt's general objectives, he explained, were five-fold:

1. to "expand the scope of Arab support for finding a peaceful and just settlement of the Arab-Israeli conflict";
2. to "find suitable formulas for cooperation between Egypt and the Arab countries and for the reciprocal and consolidated application of Egyptian and Arab resources and capabilities for the benefit of all parties" (he cited the various joint higher committees as a concrete application of this objective);
3. to "find practical concepts for Arab bilateral and collective security arrangements" against external threats;
4. to "avoid futile political and military adventures and not to slip into the trap of costly regional conflicts" (a lesson, presumably, of both the Gulf War and Egypt's involvement in Arab-Israeli wars and in the Yemen), while playing "a positive role in finding suitable solutions for these differences far from the policies of blocs, which scatter Arab efforts and invite foreign intervention" in the region; and
5. to have Egypt's "democratic atmosphere... respect for human rights... policy of tolerance and reconciliation and... dislike or extremism... emulated throughout the Arab world" (a new, more benign expression of Egypt's self-styled leading role in the Arab world).[108]

EGYPT AND THE GULF

Mubarak's triumphant January tour of the GCC states was designed to both celebrate the renewal of diplomatic relations following the Amman summit (of the GCC states, only Oman had refused to break off ties in 1979) and to emphasize Egypt's commitment to Gulf security in the face of the still-menacing Iranian challenge. In an interview given to a Kuwaiti newspapper, Mubarak's adviser on political affairs, Usama al-Baz, reiterated that Egypt would "stand beside Kuwait and other Arab countries to repulse any aggression." Its motives were not purely altruistic; rather, explained al-Baz, it stemmed from Egypt's understanding that its own, particular national security was inextricably linked to Arab national security as a whole. "We cannot protect our security," he said, "if the Arab countries, particularly those surrounding us, are threatened." For now, he explained, the Kuwaitis were not in need of outside Arab forces; nor were the Kuwaitis asking for the dispatch of an Egyptian-Jordanian "rapid deployment force" to the area. While not confirming the rumored existence of such a force, al-Baz did emphasize that Egypt and Jordan were expanding coordination in the military sphere, and that Egypt would be pleased to include other Arab states as well. Not only would defense capabilities be enhanced and the need for foreign expertise diminished, but "the forces of each country [would] be capable of moving in various areas."[109]

Cooperation with the Gulf states expanded further in the following months. Militarily, this reportedly involved Egyptian arms sales, such as the *Amoun* air-defense system for Kuwait and *Fahd* armored personnel carriers to a number of countries ($235m.-worth between May and October, according to one source), training, the dispatch of Egyptian advisers and instructors to all of the GCC states and further Gulf investment in the Egyptian-controlled arms production plants — the Arab Organization for Industrialization.[110] Economically, Egypt sought to obtain increased Gulf investment in it, from both private and public sources. Politically, Egypt reiterated its commitments to Kuwaiti security following an alleged Iranian attack in late March against Kuwait's Bubiyan Island (which, according to Iran, was being used by Iraq for military purposes).[111] Thereafter, the Iranian threat diminished. Overall, Egypt had reaped considerable benefit over the previous two years by appearing as the much-needed balancing, stabilizing force against Iran's ambitions and without having to actually commit troops.

EGYPT AND THE MAGHRIB STATES

Relations with both Morocco and Tunisia expanded considerably; the final normalization of ties with Algeria, after innumerable vicissitudes, was of special satisfaction to Cairo, given Algeria's "progressive" credentials.

Mubarak's visit to Morocco on 2–4 February was followed by many high-level exchanges. The first session of the newly-established joint higher committee, headed by their respective prime ministers, met in Cairo on 28–31 May during which they concluded a number of cooperation agreements in various fields, among them energy, agriculture, transportation, tourism, information, and health. They also committed themselves to increasing the volume of trade exchange to $100m. by the end of 1989 (which would amount to a tenfold increase over a period of two years), to encouraging joint projects in small and medium-sized industries, and establishing a permanent subcommittee for industrial coordination to meet at least once annually.[112] Cooperation also extended to the military sphere, with their respective defense ministers exchanging visits during the latter part of 1988, and a military protocol being signed on 1 December.[113]

Similarly, the first session of the Tunisian-Egyptian joint higher committee, chaired by their prime ministers, was held on 16–19 April in Cairo. Here, too, decisions were made to bolster cooperation in numerous fields, such as trade, tourism, education, culture, and the media. The liberalization in Tunisia's political life following the ouster of Habib Bourguiba in November 1987 further contributed to a sense of shared outlooks: the closing statement at the end of the sessions referred to Tunisia's "interest in the leading democratic experience" of Egypt, "particularly the multiple-party system, which also characterizes the Tunisian experience."[114]

By contrast, the road to restoring Egyptian-Algerian relations was full of pitfalls. The gradual warming in relations since 1985 had previously raised Egyptian expectations on a number of occasions, only to leave them unfulfilled and Egyptian sensitivities bruised. This scenario repeated itself in even sharper form at the Algiers summit in June. Not only was Egypt not invited to attend the summit; its chargé d'affaires in Algiers was not even invited to observe the opening session. The result was a bitter exchange between the Egyptian and Algerian media which lasted for a few weeks and Egypt's recall of its representative in Algiers for consultations.[115] According to one Egyptian commentator, Egypt's dignity had been slighted by Algeria's insistence that an announcement of the resumption of full ties be made while an Egyptian envoy was in Algiers, instead of a joint announcement being issued in the two capitals.[116] The latter method was, in fact, the one used to proclaim the restoration of full ties in November.

THE EGYPTIAN-SUDANESE-LIBYAN TRIANGLE

As in recent years, Egypt's relations with its closest Arab neighbors in 1988 were often uncomfortable. Libya's efforts to strengthen its links with Sudan, highlighted by a proposed "unity charter" in the fall of 1988 (see chapters on Libya and Sudan), continued to be closely and apprehensively watched by Cairo. Its own relations with Khartoum remained delicate. Important strands in Sudanese political life favored a more neutral and less cozy relationship with Egypt than in the past, and Egypt's refusal to extradite Sudan's former president Ja'far al-Numayri was a continued irritant. More positively, there were fewer arguments over the contractual nature of Sudanese-Egyptian relations, with the 1987 "Brotherhood Charter" (see *MECS* 1987, p. 138) having effectively superseded their previous joint defense and integration pacts. In addition, Cairo continued to maintain links with important elements in Sudanese political life. Regionally, Egypt continuously sought to mediate between Sudan and Ethiopia in order to end Ethiopia's support for the rebellion in southern Sudan. Sudanese leaders, for their part, tried to mediate between Egypt and Libya, to demonstrate Sudan's own neutrality, and to hopefully distance Sudan from the Egyptian-Libyan rivalry. Given Sudan's fragile state, compounded in 1988 by natural disasters, the maintenance of the existing equilibrium both within Sudan and in the region could be viewed with some satisfaction by Egypt.

Egyptian-Libyan relations remained volatile. Libya's vehement opposition to Egypt's return to the Arab League, the restoration by other Arab states of diplomatic relations with Cairo, and periodic harsh attacks by both the Libyan media and Qadhdhafi himself rankled the Egyptians. So did such acts as Qadhdhafi's demonstrative announcement on 28 March that Libya was unilaterally lifting all border controls between the two countries and withdrawing Libyan troop concentrations from the area (Mubarak responded scornfully that there were no troop concentrations there in the first place).[117] Nonetheless, there were a number of positive developments. In talks held under the auspices of the International Labor Organization during the last quarter of the year, significant progress was made regarding compensation for the thousands of Egyptian workers expelled from Libya during the summer of 1985.[118] Concurrently, the two countries ceased their mutual propaganda attacks. The result was a spate of speculation in the Arab press about the possible renewal of Libyan-Egyptian relations. The Libyans hastened to deny the possibility, "so long as the Zionist flag flies [in Cairo]."[119] By the year's end, their relations remained as uneasy as ever, marred by mutual mistrust and harsh accusations.

MAGHRIB AFFAIRS

Dramatic breakthroughs fundamentally altered the substance of intra-Maghrib politics in 1988. Diplomatic relations between Morocco and Algeria were renewed and important progress was made on ending the 13-yar-old war for the Western Sahara. The Algerian-Moroccan *rapprochement* enabled an all-Maghrib summit to be convened on 10 June, which was followed by substantive steps toward the creation of a formal institutional structure for the "Greater Arab Maghrib," with the GCC framework serving as a model. Libyan cooperation in the process, its concurrent strengthening of its bilateral ties with both Algeria and Tunisia (see chapter on Libya), and the stabilization and liberalization of Tunisian political life during the first year of the post-Bourguiba era, also contributed to the optimistic, even heady atmosphere. Sobriety, however, was quickly restored, thanks to the widespread civil unrest in Algeria during October, in which over 500 persons died; the disturbances in Algeria were followed with much concern both in the Maghrib and throughout the Arab world. For Algeria and its neighbors, it drove home the very real social, economic, and political challenges facing them. Moreover, the events in Algeria reinforced the felt need among Maghrib elites to establish a wider political and economic framework in order to cope better with these challenges.

ALGERIA, MOROCCO, AND THE ROAD TO AN ALL-MAGHRIB SUMMIT

In 1987, Algeria had indicated a possible willingness to decouple its insistence on obtaining a solution for the Western Sahara issue based on self-determination from the normalization of relations with Morocco (see *MECS* 1987, pp. 140–41). In mid-December 1987, a preparatory committee of experts from the foreign ministries of the two countries met in Rabat, where they discussed matters such as reopening their common frontiers, border demarcation, and bilateral trade and transit.[120] Concurrently, a UN-Organization of African Unity (OAU) "technical team" visited the region to make preliminary recommendations on holding the long-delayed referendum among the Western Saharans to determine the region's future. However, the budding Algerian-Moroccan dialogue was frozen during the following months: Morocco continued to reject Algeria's "mechanical linking" of strengthening bilateral and regional ties with progress toward a solution for the Western Sahara,[121] while Algeria remained committed to just that.[122] Consequently, the media in the two countries engaged in a new round of mutual accusations and condemnations.[123]

Meanwhile, Algeria turned its attention elsewhere, moving to deepen its bilateral relations with Libya and Tunisia. It sought to generate regional diplomatic momentum by including Libya in wider Maghrib affairs, suggesting Libya's accession to the 1983 tripartite Treaty of Friendship and Concord, involving Algeria, Tunisia, and Mauritania (for its origins, see *MECS* 1982–83, p. 215). President Benjedid was quite frank in explaining his motives for pursuing closer ties with Libya: a policy of accommodation and political restraints, he told a Western interviewer, would "neutralize" Libya, "freezing" its efforts to destabilize its neighbors and engage in terrorism. By signing the treaty, Qadhdhafi would be promising, in effect, "not to interfere, not to export one's experience to any other country, [and] to respect the existing regimes" and frontiers.[124] The Libyans seemed amenable: Qadhdhafi accompanied Benjedid to his festive meeting with Tunisia's President Zayn al-'Abidin Ben 'Ali at the Tunisian border town of Sakiet Sidi Youssef on 8 February (the anniversary of France's bombing of the town 30 years earlier during the Algerian Revolution). On 19 March, Libya's number-two man 'Abd al-Salam Jallud visited Algeria on the fifth anniversary of the signing of the tripartite agreement. His statement that Libya supported Benjedid's "initiative of developing unity action between Libya and Algeria into four-sided action, to include Tunisia and Mauritania"[125] seemed to indicate Libya's willingness to acede to the agreement, but in fact it did not. The agreement did not contain the unity elements essential to Qadhdhafi; he continued to promote his own plans for closer ties with Algeria and Tunisia, and for a more meaningful all-Maghrib framework as steps towards comprehensive Arab unity (see chapter on Libya).

Benjedid steadfastly denied that his diplomatic efforts were intended to isolate Morocco in the Maghrib,[126] but it is doubtful whether Morocco viewed matters so benignly. However, Rabat could be sanguine about the results: not only did Libya have its own agenda, but Tunisia, which had traditionally sought to maintain good relations with all of its Maghrib neighbors, was committed to Morocco's inclusion "in all development phases of Maghrib unity," a position noted appreciatively by King Hasan.[127] Consequently, the focus returned to the Moroccan-Algerian sphere.

Progress was made during March with an unannounced meeting in Marrakesh, Morocco, between two senior Algerian officials, Muhammad Cherif Messaadia (the head of the Permanent Secretariat of Algeria's ruling *Front de la Libération Nationale* [FLN]) and Gen. Larbi Belkhayr (Benjedid's Cabinet director), and King Hasan, Interior Minister Driss Basri and the king's senior political adviser, Ahmad Reda Gudeira.[128] The two Algerians returned to Rabat on 10 May, bearing an official invitation to the upcoming Arab summit conference in Algiers.[129] The Algerians agreed, desiring a successful summit and being satisfied, for the moment, with Hasan's cooperation with the UN-sponsored initiative on the Western Sahara, and eager to move the Greater Arab Maghrib process forward. Gudeira and Driss journeyed to Algiers to finalize matters, and on 16 May the two governments issued a joint statement proclaiming the restoration of diplomatic relations after a 12-year hiatus. The statement's clause pertaining to the Western Sahara indicated that common ground had been found: it expressed support for international efforts "to find a just and lasting solution" to the conflict, to be achieved by "a free referendum of self-determination [which would] be conducted in an atmosphere of complete sincerity and free from all pressures."[130]

The two governments moved rapidly to expand their ties. Both appointed senior diplomats to serve as ambassadors in each other's capitals. On 31 May, Algeria's interior minister visited his Moroccan counterpart. Upon completion of the visit, it was announced that the movement of people and goods between the two countries would be permitted gradually, starting on 5 June; visa requirements would be abolished; and air routes would be reopened. Larger transportation and communication matters were left to be studied further by a joint committee.[131] The border opening, in particular, was highly popular on both sides.[132] Two meetings of the joint committeee were held in June, one on 5–11 in Algiers, and one on 20–24 in Rabat. On 6 July, the two interior ministers signed the minutes of the joint committee, which dealt with matters such as the entry and residence of each other's nationals, air, land, and sea transport, posts and telecommunications, cooperation between border municipalities, tourism, and the combating of locusts. The next day, the energy ministers of the two countries presided over the ceremonial linking of electricity grids at the Moroccan border town of Oujda; they also examined the possibility of building a liquid natural gas line from Algeria across Moroccan territory to the sea.[133]

The ceremonial highlight of the Algerian-Moroccan *rapprochement* was Hasan's arrival in Algiers for the Arab summit conference aboard his royal yacht. A minor incident involving the presence of a Polisario representative at an official banquet was quickly dealt with.[134] In his speech at the summit's closing session, Hasan repeatedly referred to the "special feelings" between the two countries, and expressed his own gratitude for the assistance extended by the Algerian people to Hasan and his father, King Muhammad V, during their exile in Algeria in 1954.[135] Qadhdhafi and Ben 'Ali also addressed the closing session, thus giving it a distinct Maghribi flavor. Ben 'Ali, in particular, referred to the "new atmosphere prevailing over the western wing of the Arab homeland"; in language more reminiscent of Qadhdhafi than is usually the case among Tunisians, he expressed confidence in the developing process of building "a great Arab Maghrib free from borders, which might serve as the solid basic structure for a comprehensive Arab unity."[136] While this was undoubtedly a rhetorical flourish, Ben 'Ali could draw much satisfaction from what followed: on 10 June, one day after the conclusion of the Arab summit, the five heads of the Maghrib states (Hasan, Benjedid, Qadhdhafi, Ben 'Ali and Mauritania's Maaouya Ould Sid Ahmad) met together in the first all-Maghrib summit.

"BUILDING THE EDIFICE OF THE GREATER ARAB MAGHRIB"

The 10 June gathering and the subsequent steps taken during the remainder of 1988 to develop a regional institutional framework reflected a broad degree of like-mindedness regarding both the challenges facing the Maghrib countries (rising population, large foreign debt, economic stagnation, potential problems posed by Muslim fundamentalism, the decision of the European Economic Community [EEC] to tighten European economic integration by 1992) and the steps required to meet them. Maghrib unity, in Benjedid's words, was to be implemented according to three principles:

> 1. a political will to respond clearly to all questions related to fulfillment of common strategic political objectives of all the region's countries;
> 2. a practical and solid program to enhance trade exchanges, employ all integration capabilities, and carry out joint projects in the interest of the Maghrib market;
> 3. a definition of the conditions in the region's countries and of the similarities in their consumption and production needs, to allow all countries of the region, whenever possible, to take major and steady steps toward economic integration.

With these principles in mind, the summit decided to create a "Grand Political Commission" to "prepare the ground for joint work."[137] Senior cabinet members from all five states conducted its first meeting on 13–14 July, in Algiers. The commission established, in turn, five specialized subcommissions, also made up of senior officials, which met during the following months. One, dealing with organization and structure, met in Tripoli on 17–18 September and adopted a draft plan for an all-Maghrib political structure. Another, focusing on economic affairs, met in Algiers on 18 September. Proposals for financial and customs integration were drawn up by a third, meeting in Rabat, also in mid-September. The following week, on 21 September, an information and education commission met in Mauritania's capital, Nouakchott. And on 24 September, the social and human affairs commission, meeting in Tunis, agreed on the principle of abolishing visa requirements for travel by their nationals between member states; adopted measures pertaining to pest control and natural disasters (the region was at that moment trying to cope with a massive invasion of locusts); and formulated a plan for the protection of Maghrib minorities abroad.[138]

On 27–28 October, the grand commission (consisting of Tunisian Prime Minister Hedi Baccouche, Moroccan Foreign Minister 'Abd al-Latif al-Filali, Algeria's FLN leader Messaadia, Libya's Maj. al-Khuwaylidi al-Humaydi, and Mauritania's Foreign Minister Col. Muhammad Sidina Ould Sidya) reconvened to assess the reports of the subcommissions. Jurists were reportedly studying EEC regulations to help formulate the projected unity accord (rankling the Libyans, who preferred to find Arab and Islamic precedents). In addition, agreement was reportedly reached on the creation of a Maghrib court of justice and a joint customs regime. Throughout the process, Qadhdhafi continued to insist that the creation of the Greater Arab Maghrib be a step toward comprehensive unity; as long as this was the case, he stated, he did not care what kind of regime the union had.[139]

Nonetheless, there was some disagreement over the pace of future steps. Tunisia pressed for the holding of an early summit conference where an all-Maghrib structure (with a common market and a permanent secretariat) would be brought into being; Algeria, on the other hand, opposed quick action, apparently preferring that further progress be made on the Western Saharan issue (see below).[140] The meeting ended with a general commitment to hold another summit which would finalize the creation of an all-Maghrib political framework, but without setting a date. Presumably, the 19 December meeting between the foreign ministers of Algeria, Tunisia, and Mauritania (the first such meeting in four years) was designed to further coordinate policies regarding the next phase of Maghrib diplomacy. Clearly, by the end of 1988, the process of "building the edifice" had gone well beyond the purely declaratory stage.

THE WESTERN SAHARAN PEACE PROCESS

Numerous mediators, acting alone or on behalf of various international organizations, had tried their hand over the previous 13 years to settle the Western Sahara dispute, but to no avail. By 1988, however, a number of elements had converged to increase the chances of a diplomatic solution. Morocco had succeeded, at great cost, in establishing a system of "defensive walls" which severely limited Polisario's freedom of action in much of the "useful Sahara." At the same time, the war's drain on Morocco's treasury, the continued military stalemate, and the possibility of improving relations with Algeria all necessitated greater Moroccan diplomatic flexibility. The Algerian leadership viewed matters similarly and, while seeking an equitable settlement for Polisario, was less inclined to hold out for its former, maximalist demands. For

Polisario, the gradual shift in Algeria's position; Libya's continued reluctance to renew its military support (suspended in 1983–84), despite Qadhdhafi's meeting with Saharan Arab Democratic Republic (SADR; Polisario's government-in-exile) President Muhammad 'Abd al-'Aziz in February (for Qadhdhafi's ideological opposition to the creation of an independent state in the Western Sahara, see *MECS* 1984–85, p. 132, and Note 163, p. 144); and the general atmosphere of all-Maghrib *rapprochement* — all compelled serious reassessment. Thus, the UN-OAU mediation effort, spearheaded by UN Secretary-General Javier Pérez de Cuellar, found fruitful ground for its work.

As far back as 1981, Hasan had agreed to a referendum among the inhabitants of the area to determine its future. Major questions remained, however. One was the question of determining eligibility among what was once a seminomadic population, a problem compounded by an exodus to Morocco in the 1950s and 1960s to escape Spanish rule, and a much larger one to camps in Algeria in 1976, where they were joined over the years by drought-fleeing refugees from a number of other African countries (a census of the area taken by the Spanish in the fall of 1974 counted a total of 73,497 Sahrawis; Polisario officials argue that the figure was too low).[141] Another was formulating the exact wording of the referendum (offering independence?, incorporation into Morocco? autonomy?). A third question was the status of Moroccan troops and administration during an internationally supervised referendum. Finally, there was Polisario's demand, backed by OAU and UN resolutions, for direct negotiations with Morocco on these issues.

Hasan reiterated Morocco's position on these issues on a number of occasions. To assuage Algerian concerns that Morocco would try to rig the voting, Hasan declared that he had "no interest ... in having a false vote."[142] However, he said, Morocco would not agree to withdrawing from the area in advance of the referendum: French troops in Algeria, he pointed out, had been confined to barracks during the 1962 referendum on independence, but had not been withdrawn. Nor could Morocco be expected to enter a Greater Arab Maghrib framework if it was not first "in control of all of its national soil." As for direct negotiations with Polisario, he declared, Morocco could not lower its prestige by meeting with a nonstate actor on the basis of equality.[143] What Hasan did envisage was some kind of autonomy for the area within the Moroccan Kingdom, referring to Germany's *Länder* system as a model for the regionalization of Morocco.[144]

The diplomatic process shifted into higher gear beginning in April. The OAU chairman, Zambian President Kenneth Kaunda, visited the region (his views were not to Morocco's liking). One month later, Pérez de Cuellar (whom the Moroccans did like) paid a brief visit, and pursued further contacts at the OAU summit in Addis Abada on 26–28 May. Shortly after Pérez de Cuellar's visit came the renewal of Moroccan-Algerian relations. The move caught Polisario leaders off guard (although they tried to cast it in a positive light),[145] and apparently helped to force a reassessment. By the fall, two leadership reshuffles had taken place, with more pragmatic elements gaining the upper hand.[146]

As the UN mediating team formulated its proposals during June and July, high-level Polisario and Moroccan representatives met under Saudi auspices in Jidda for two weeks following earlier contacts that were reportedly held in Algeria. No agreement was reached on the outstanding issues, but progress was made; for the first time,

Polisario apparently indicated that it would settle for less than complete independence. According to an Arab newspaper, three formulas for referendum suggesting some kind of association with Morocco were discussed: (1) a "Soviet" model, which would preserve SADR's membership in the OAU, and presumably in the UN, along the lines of the Soviet Ukrainian and Byelorussian republics; (2) political autonomy and economic freedom for the proposed entity, with defense and foreign affairs remaining the provenance of the central government in Rabat; and (3) autonomy for the residents, with the territory being made an integral part of the Moroccan Kingdom (the latter was said to be Hasan's preferred option).[147]

On 11 August, the UN's plan was presented to the Moroccan foreign minister and a Polisario representative in New York. According to news reports, the plan included the following elements: a cease-fire, an exchange of prisoners of war (PoWs), a 2,000-man international peacekeeping force to monitor the cease-fire, and an accompanying administrative apparatus to organize a referendum to determine the area's future (with eligibility to be determined by the 1974 Spanish census, which found 73,000 residents; this would therefore exclude the large number of Moroccans, c. 100,000, who had settled in the territory since then), a reduction of Moroccan forces in the territory from 100,000 to 25,000 troops, and the retirement of Polisario's 8,000-man force to its bases. Not yet settled was the exact wording of the referendum question. By the end of August, both Polisario and Morocco gave their general assent to the plan.[148]

However, Polisario continued to demand direct negotiations with Morocco in the light of day in order to fix the dates of the cease-fire and referendum, as well as the complete withdrawal of Moroccan troops and administration from the area before holding the referendum. Its acceptance of the UN initiative, it explained, was made after the UN secretary-general and the acting OAU president had promised improvements on Morocco's proposals.[149] Diplomatically, they received strong backing from Algeria at a nonaligned foreign ministers' conference in Nicosia. After a sharp exchange between the Algerian and Moroccan foreign ministers, the conference supported Algeria's demand that a previous resolution calling for direct Polisario-Moroccan negotiations be reaffirmed. To further drive home their demand, Polisario launched a large-scale military operation, involving 2,500 men, against Moroccan forces on 16 September. The battle, one of the fiercest in years, claimed hundreds of casualties on both sides, with Morocco losing an important field commander.[150] On 20 September the UN Security Council unanimously approved the secretary-general's proposed peace plan and authorized him to appoint a special representative to continue diplomatic efforts.

By the end of 1988, further progress had been made. The head of Polisario's negotiating team revealed that his side had now agreed that not all Moroccan troops would be withdrawn before the referendum (he spoke of a maximum of 10,000 while the UN plan spoke of 25,000). In addition, Polisario was demanding the removal of 10,000 Moroccan citizens during the balloting and the release of all political prisoners and PoWs. The referendum, he said, should be held only a year after an agreement was signed to permit the return of the Saharan population.[151] Even more important was the change in Hasan's position on direct negotiations. On 12 December, he told a French interviewer that the doors to his palace were open to hear the views of anyone from the other side of the Sahara (i.e., Polisario), and on 31 December Polisario announced a unilateral cessation of hostilities, pending talks with Hasan.[152] Thus, as the year closed, the possibility of a negotiated solution to the long-running conflict in the Western Sahara was brighter than it had ever been.

CONCLUSION

Both in the region and beyond, a number of important developments had occurred during 1988: the cessation of hostilities in the Gulf, the Palestinian uprising, the constitutional crisis in Lebanon, the dramatic changes in Soviet foreign policy and American-Soviet relations (and the resulting winding down of various regional conflicts, e.g., Afghanistan), and the concrete strides among the EEC countries toward economic integration. Their myriad implications for the Arab system could not yet be fully assessed, but their impact was already being felt. In particular, all of the above developments posed significant challenges, in one way or another, for Syria, whose oppositionist stance on nearly every issue of substance had been one of the hallmarks of inter-Arab politics during the 1980s. Syria's responses to these challenges would undoubtedly contribute heavily to the substance of inter-Arab relations in what seemed to be a newly emerging period in Arab and regional politics. As for its main Arab rivals, Egypt could feel far more comfortable with the way developments were unfolding; in fact, the area of foreign policy has been the most unmitigated success story of the Mubarak years. Iraq's future course, on the other hand, was less clear; although it clearly possessed the potential to initiate a major change in inter-Arab alignments, there were no indications that it was about to do so.

Apart from the cut and thrust which has always characterized inter-Arab politics, two other, related, matters of substance gained further prominence in 1988: the heightened awareness within the Arab world, five years after the end of the "oil decade,"[153] of the Arab world's economic and developmental plight, and the continued interest in creating larger economic and poltitical groupings in order to cope with the very real social, economic, and ultimately political challenges facing Arab governments.

Despite the massive transfer of funds from the West to the Arab world between 1973–81, no fundamental restructuring in Arab-Western relations had taken place. Nor had the inequalities and disparities *within* the Arab world been substantially altered, despite the creation of a "new Arab social order,"[154] characterized by a functional division of labor between the oil-producing countries and the manpower-rich/resource-poor countries. As one scholar trenchantly put it, the 1970s, were "likely to go down in history as the decade in which the Arabs missed the boat"; instead of establishing unity on the basis of fruitful economic cooperation, the Arab states developed new patterns of wastefulness and political rivalry.[155] Moreover, what had been created was a "rentier economy", with important negative political and developmental consequences.[156] Collective Arab failures were illustrated in two areas. The first was the gap between the much-trumpted plan in 1980 to promote a "decade of Arab development" (see *MECS* 1980–81, p. 234) and the meager results. As of the middle of the decade, the percentage of inter-Arab trade stood at less than 10%.[157] According to a report by the Abu Dhabi-based Arab Monetary Fund, the obstacles facing inter-Arab trade included:

> a weak production base, poor services accompanying trade such as transport, finance insurance, and information exchange, [and] drawbacks caused by trade, financial, and monetary problems.

Other economic indicators were just as gloomy. The Arab world's food needs, stated the report, were growing twice as fast as production, which could lead to a food import bill of $45bn. a year by the year 2000. Total Arab exports had declined to a third of their 1980 level. The foreign debts of 12 selected Arab countries was estimated at $66bn., one-third accounted for by Egypt, one-fifth by Algeria, and one-sixth by Morocco (Iraq was apparently not included in the list of debtors). All this was in the light of continued demographic pressures: the total population of the 21 Arab states reaching nearly 200m. in 1986, with 60% concentrated in Algeria, Sudan, Egypt, and Morocco.[158] The second, more purely political indicator of the limitations to Arab solidarity was the expiration and nonrenewal of the 10-year financial commitments to Arab confrontation states at Baghdad in 1978 — commitments more than 50% of which had not been honored and had failed to fundamentally alter the Arab-Israeli balance of power.

Qadhdhafi's solution was familiar, grandiose, and largely discredited: an all-Arab federation in which existing entities would preserve their particular character, whose initial charter could be signed on 1 September 1989 (at the 20th anniversary celebrations of his coming to power), with the project to include economic and cultural dimensions such as Arab water and cereal authorities, an Arab natural gas pipeline with a unified network, and an Arab Academy of Sciences.[159] A more modest and agreed-on way of coping with the challenges facing the Arab world was to seek to expand on bilateral and multilateral cooperation projects through the establishment of more formal frameworks. As noted above, substantial progress was measured in the Maghrib; King Husayn indicated toward the end of the year that his stepped-up efforts to bring about Egyptian-Syrian and Iraqi-Syrian reconciliation also included similar lines of thinking.[160] These developments would bear watching. At the same time, it was clear that larger political and economic frameworks would provide no panacea for the ills of the collective Arab body. Nor could they be divorced from the mutual suspicions, rivalries, and competitiveness which have characterized inter-Arab politics for over four decades.

APPENDIX I: FINAL STATEMENT ISSUED AT THE CONCLUSION OF THE ALGIERS SUMMIT CONFERENCE OF 7–9 JUNE 1988

At the initiative and invitation of His Excellency President Chedli Bendjedid of the Algerian Democratic and Popular Republic, their majesties, highnesses, excellencies, kings, presidents, and princes of the Arab states held an emergency summit conference in the Algerian capital from 7–9 June 1988.

Stemming from its commitment to the historic pan-Arab responsibility, the summit discussed current and future challenges facing the Arab nation, and the dangers directed against its existence in this crucial and difficult period. The summit emphasized the will to protect pan-Arab security and to safeguard Arab lands. The summit saluted the uprising by the Palestinian Arab people, which represents a step in its struggle that has been continuing for more than half a century in its capacity as an integrated part of the Palestinian revolution. This has contributed to the consolidation of Arab solidarity. The summit also proudly saluted the heroism shown by the Palestinian people in their fight against Israeli occupation, and their fight against Israeli occupation, and their excellent determination to liberate their occupied territories and exercise their right to return to their land, to self-determination, and to establish an independent state on their national soil under the leadership of the PLO, their sole legitimate representative.

The summit also saluted the struggle by the Syrian citizens on the Golan and the struggle by the Lebanese patriotic resistance in South Lebanon against the Israeli occupation of the Arab territories.

The summit studied the measures necessary to support the uprising, for consolidating its effectiveness, and ensuring its continuation and escalation. The summit stressed its commitment to providing all necessary aid, in all forms and by all means, to the Palestinian people to ensure the continuation of their resistance and uprising behind the PLO's leadership until the fulfillment of their rightful national aims.

The summit reiterated its commitment to support the states at the frontline with the Israeli enemy in a way that enables them to consolidate their defensive abilities and reinforce their ability to liberate the occupied Arab territories and restore usurped Arab rights.

The summit stressed that the continued Israeli occupation of Arab land and denial of the proven national rights of the Palestinian people, and their oppressive measures, which have taken the form and substance of war crimes against unarmed Palestinians, clearly confirm the racist aggressive character and expansionist ambitions of the Israelis.

The summit calls on the UN Security Council to shoulder its responsibility to force Israel to implement UN resolutions and international agreements and to end its oppressive and inhuman practices; to work to establish immediate and complete Israeli withdrawal from all occupied Arab territories; and to place Palestinian territories under temporary UN supervision that will secure protection of the citizens and secure the proven national rights sof the Palestinian people.

The summit reviewed developments aimed at establishing peace in the Middle East. The summit realized that these efforts are still characterized by slowness, ineffectiveness, and inability to confront the Israeli position, which insists on rejecting peace.

The summit stressed again that the principles adopted by the Arab summits, especially those included in Fez summit resolutions in 1982, constitute a basis for solving the Arab-Israeli conflict, and its central issue — the Palestinian question. It reiterated its support for convening an international peace conference on the Middle East under UN auspices, with international legitimacy, and based on the UN resolutions calling for the Zionist entity to withdraw fully from all Arab and Palestinian occupied territories and to secure the national and well-established rights of the Palestinian people. The conference should be held with the five permanent Security Council members and all parties concerned in the conflict in the region, including the PLO — the sole legitimate representative of the Palestinian people — being on equal footing, with the same rights as other parties.

The conference considers legislation issued by some foreign states against the Arab boycott of the Zionist entity to be hostile to Arab rights, intended to end the isolation of the Israeli entity, and to improve its economic capacity while it continues to occupy Arab territories.

The conference reiterates the commitment of the member countries to continue implementing the regulations of the boycott, viewing it as a legitimate means that has been and is being, practiced by other states and international groups.

The conference noted US perseverance in a policy favoring Israel and hostile to the firm national rights of the Palestinian people. It condemned this policy, which encourages Israel to continue its hostilities and violations of human rights, hinders efforts to establish peace, and contradicts US responsibilities, in its capacity as a permanent Security Council member, to maintain international peace and security.

The conference expressed its great appreciation for the stands of the Nonaligned Movement, the OAU, the Islamic Conference Organization, the socialist bloc, the European states, the people with parliamentarian systems, and the peace- and freedom-loving forces that have supported the Palestinian people in their just struggle. The conference condemned the racist and repressive practices of the Israeli occupation authorities in the Arab and Palestinian occupied territories.

The conference examined the conditions of crisis faced by Lebanon, and expressed its support for it in ending the Israeli occupation in southern Lebanon. The conference stressed its stand in support of Lebanon in defending its sovereignty, security, and unity of its territories, and emphasized its assistance toward ending the state of war it is witnessing spreading the sovereignty of the state over all Lebanese soil, and saving its economy. It vehemently called for unity of efforts to achieve national concord.

The conference saluted the Lebanese national resistance, affirming the continuity of its comprehensive support and the reinforcement of the Lebanese people's steadfastness in the face of the Israeli occupation.

The conference studied with great interest the Iraqi-Iranian War and the perils resulting from its continuation due to Iran's intransigence and insistence on continuing the war, which has greatly influenced the utilization of Arab energy and potential to face up to Zionist aggression. The conference affirmed the resolutions adopted at the extraordinary Amman summit that expressed the Arab stand on the Gulf War, on Iranian aggression and threats against the Arabian Gulf states, and on Iranian interference in their internal affairs. The conference renewed its full solidarity with Iraq, supporting it in the legitimate defense of its sovereignty, independence, and territorial integrity, and lauded its response to the peace initiative and acceptance of UN Security Council Resolution 598 which calls for an honorable, comprehensive, just, and lasting settlement to the conflict.

The conference reiterated its rejection and condemnation of Iran's continued occupation of Arab territories in Iraq, its continuation of the war, and its lack of response to Arab and international peace initiatives and UN resolutions, and for its refusal to comply with Security Council Resolution 598.

The conference calls on the international community to shoulder its responsibility in implementing this resolution, in word and spirit and according to the sequence of its active articles. The conference calls on the Security Council urgently to take the necessary steps to ensure Iran's compliance with that resolution under the rules of the UN charter.

The conference saluted with pride and admiration Arab Iraq's liberation of al-Faw and Shalamcheh and renewed its full solidarity with Iraq in liberating the rest of its territories occupied by Iran, proceeding from an adherence to pan-Arab responsibility and affirming the determination to defend pan-Arab security and protect Arab land.

The conference reviewed the threats resulting from the continuation of the Iraqi-Iranian War, which has become a threat to the security and stability of some states in the region, particularly Kuwait, and reaffirmed its resoltuion adopted at the extraordinary Amman summit, expressing the determination of the members states to stand by the Arab Gulf states in facing up to any foreign aggression. The conference also condemned all forms of terrorism being practiced by Iran against the Gulf Arab states, represented by its interference in the internal affairs of those states and its use of violence and subversion endangering the internal security of some Arab Gulf states, particularly of Kuwait and the Kingdom of Saudi Arabia.

The conference expressed its solidarity with, and support for, the steps taken by the Kingdom of Saudi Arabia to organize pilgrimages to the holy house of God, and for the facilities and assistance it gives to pilgrims. The conference affirms the need to respect the holy places, the rites of pilgrimage, the security and safety of pilgrims, and the sovereignty of the Kingdom of Saudi Arabia.

The conference affirmed its conviction that Arab national security is indivisible and that any aggression against the sovereignty of any member state, or any act of terrorism against such a state constitutes aggression against the whole Arab nation. In this context, the conference reiterated its condemnation of Israeli aggression against Iraq in hitting its nuclear reactor; its repeated aggression against Tunisia by hitting the PLO headquarters and assassinating martyr Khalil al-Wazir; and the continuous Israeli aggression against Lebanon, against innocent civilians.

The conference reaffirms its condemnation of the US aggression against the Libyan Arab Jamahiriyya and its support for the latter in the face of the continuous threats against its security. The conference expressed its backing and support for Libyan sovereignty in the Gulf of Sidra in accordance with international conventions.

After studying the challenges and dangers facing the Arab nation, with a view to guaranteeing the preservation of the national interest and its future generations, and protecting its security, the conference expressed satisfaction with the positive developments in inter-Arab relations. It stressed its determination to work more to improve relations among all Arab states in a way that would consolidate their relations and strengthen joint Arab action, boosting its institutions.

The conference reaffirmed its condemnation of international terrorism in all forms and with all sources, particularly the organized state terrorism practiced by the Zionist entity against the Palestinian people and in the Arab region. The conference considers international terrorism to be a violation of ethical and humanitarian principles and a violation of international standards and conventions. It rejects attempts to equate terrorism with the legitimate national struggle by people for liberation and independence.

The conference affirms its condemnation of racism in all its forms in South Africa, and the racist alliance between the Zionist entity and the Pretoria regime.

The conference also affirms its full solidarity with the people of South Africa and its support for the liberation movements in South Africa; for the African confrontation states in their struggle against the Pretoria regime to put an end to apartheid and to enable the people of South Africa to retrieve their freedom, sovereignty, and independence.

While saluting the OAU on its 25th anniversary, the conference expresses deep appreciation to the African states and people for their continuing support and backing for the just Arab causes, primarily on the Palestinian question. The conference also affirms its conviction of the need to strengthen and promote Arab-African cooperation, and to reinvigorate its organs and institutions to attain common objectives.

The conference expressed interest in the positive developments in the international scene, in the signs of *détente* and relaxation of tension, and in the resolving of regional conflicts, particularly the beginning of gradual nuclear disarmament. The conference also expressed hope that this international *détente* would help boost the objectives and principles to which all people in the world aspire — goals that have been affirmed by the nonaligned states in their various congresses — in a way that would meet people's aspirations for freedom and self-determination and guarantee the sovereignty and independence of these people; in a way that would contribute to international efforts to help developing countries resolve their social and economic problems; in a way that would remove the imbalance in the international economic system, the dangerous negative aspects of which have an impact on Third World states.

In this respect, the conference affirmed the need for the policy of international *détente* to cover the resolution of regional problems in a just manner, the elimination of war in other areas, and the declaration of regional areas like the Mediterranean basin, the Indian Ocean, and others as areas free of nuclear weapons.

The conference expressed its great appreciation for His Excellency President Chedi Bendjedid, president of the Democratic People's Republic of Algeria, for his initiative in convening this conference and for his good efforts to provide the conditions for its success. The conference also praises the wisdom with which His Excellency has managed the conference sessions, which greatly contributed to the conference's success and the reaching of important results likely to strengthen the Palestinian people's uprising and hasten the march toward common Arab action.

The conference expressed its deep thanks to the Algerian Government for having kindly hosted this conference, and for the good organization and preparation for it. The conference also addresses to the struggling Algerian people its sincerest appreciation for their heroic struggle for freedom and independence, and its gratitude for the warm care and hospitality given to the participants.

SOURCE: Algiers TV, 9 June — DR, 10 JUNE 1988.

APPENDIX II: ADDITIONAL RESOLUTIONS OF THE ALGIERS SUMMIT CONFERENCE OF 7–9 JUNE 1988

The extraordinary Arab summit in Algiers adopted two resolutions on the Palestine question, in addition to the final communiqué. The first resolution comes under the subhead "Supporting the poplar Palestinian uprising,"while the second comes under the subhead "The international Middle East peace conference."

The first resolution regarding the support to be provided for the uprising calls for:

(1) Displaying commitment to providing all types of support and backing to ensure the continuation of the uprising and the

Palestinian people's resistance to the Zionist occupation through the PLO, considering that it is the sole legitimate representative of the Palestinian people, and also through the available international channels until their objectives of regaining their inalienable national rights, including their rights to repatriation, to self-determination, and to establish their independent state on their national soil with Jerusalem as its capital, are achieved.

(2) Rejecting all partial and separate solutions regarding the Arab-Israeli conflict and considering any plans that do not guarantee the exercise of these rights as plans that hinder the efforts being exerted to achieve a just peace in the region and also as plans that encourage the continuation of the occupation and Israeli intransigence.

(3) Calling upon the UN Security Council to shoulder fully its responsibilities toward Israel's violation of the Geneva conventions, to force Israel to allow the return of the deportees in accordance with UN Security Council Resolutions 605, 607, and 608, and to work toward ending the occupation immediately, dismantling the settlements and placing the occupied territories under transitional UN supervision to provide their residents with protection.

(4) Calling upon the international community to confront the official state terrorism being perpetrated by Israel with the support of some international forces against the Palestinian Arab people and its violations of the sovereignty of some Arab states.

(5) Calling upon the US Government to change its stand, which is hostile to the Arab nation and to the inalienable national rights of the Palestinian people, as it refuses to recognize the PLO, the sole legitimate representative of the Palestinian people, as a basic party to the Arab-Israeli conflict; calling upon it to end its unlimited support for Israel — support which encourages Israel to go to extremes in its pursuit of the policy of aggression and expansion.

(6) Entrusting the Arab ministerial committee for supporting the uprising with continuing its contacts with the permanent member states of the UN Security Council, and also with international groups.

(7) Approving the information plan drawn up by the standing information committee regarding the uprising.

(8) Continuing the provision of facilities to the PLO and to the Palestinians in Arab states.

The last three paragraphs called for the continuation of efforts with the Islamic states and with the Nonaligned Movement member states, the enhancement of cooperation with the socialist bloc states and the strengthening of Arab-African cooperation.

On the international Middle East peace conference, the summit reiterated the following principles:

(1) Israel's withdrawal from all the Palestinian and Arab territories occupied in 1967, including Arab Jerusalem.

(2) Canceling all annexation measures and dismantling the settlements established by Israel in the Palestinian and Arab territories since 1967.

(3) Placing the West Bank and Gaza Strip under UN supervision for a transitional period that does not exceed several months.

(4) Enabling the Palestinian people to exercise their inalienable national rights, including their rights to repatriation, self-determination and establishment of their independent national state, with Jerusalem as its capital, on their national soil, under the PLO, their sole legitimate representative, in accordance with the relevant UN resolutions.

(5) Guaranteeing the freedom of worship and exercise of religious rituals for those affiliated to all religions in the holy places in Palestine.

(6) The UN Security Council must draw up peace guarantees for all states concerned, including the independent Palestinian state.

Second [as heard], the Arab states call for the convening of a UN-sponsored international Middle East peace conference on the basis of international legitimacy and the UN resolutions, which affirm the complete Israeli withdrawal from all occupied Palestinian and Arab territories and also guarantee the Palestinian people's inalienable national rights to repatriation, to self-determination, and to national independence with the participation of the five permanent members of the UN Security Council and all parties to the conflict, including the PLO, which must attend on an equal footing enjoying the same rights given to the other parties participating in this conference.

SOURCE: VOP (San'a), 10 June — SWB, 13 June 1988.

NOTES

For the place and frequency of publications cited here, and for the full name of the publication, news agency, radio station, or monitoring service where an abbreviation is used, please see "List of Sources." Only in the case of more than one publication bearing the same name is the place of publication noted here.

1. The lack of prompt action was lambasted by both the PLO and Libya. For example, a VoP commentary decried the "lazy" Arab response to the uprising, referring to "the blood of lazy cells which flows slowly and calmly through the veins of Arab foreign ministers." (VoP [Algiers], 14 January — DR, 15 January 1988.) Qadhdhafi, for his part, was especially sarcastic: "The Arabs, who number 150m., what did they do for the Palestinians who they see everyday on television? They cross their legs, smoke, and get drunk and watch the television because there are films about persecuting the Palestinians." (Tripoli TV, 21 January — DR, 25 January 1988.)
2. R. Monte Carlo, 23 January 1988.

3. AFP, 24 January; *al-Tadamun*, 30 January — 5 February 1988.
4. R. Monte Carlo, 23 January 1988.
5. R. Monte Carlo, 24 January — DR, 25 January 1988.
6. *Al-Tadamun*, 30 January — 5 February 1988.
7. R. Monte Carlo, 24 January — DR, 25 January 1988. An exact breakdown of the vote, including abstentions, was not available.
8. AFP, 24 January 1988.
9. R. Monte Carlo, 24 January — DR 25 January; *al-Mustaqbal*, 20 January; JNA, 25 January — DR, 26 January 1988. According to one Arab commentator, Syria wanted to prevent the PLO from establishing a permanent Arab-supported fund, and thus insisted that the "uprising fund" be used only to assist Palestinians in the West Bank and Gaza, and only so long as the uprising continued. (Lamis Adoni, in *MEI*, 6 February 1988).
10. *Al-Sharq al-Awsat*, 27 January 1988.
11. *Al-Mustaqbal*, 20 January 1988.
12. R. Monte Carlo, 23 January 1988.
13. *Al-Qabas*, 5 March 1988.
14. According to him, Iraq and Kuwait had proffered financial assistance ($3m. and $5m., respectively), via UN agencies, for the families of those killed in the uprising. (*Al-Qabas*, 22 February, cited by KUNA, 22 February — DR, 22 February 1988.)
15. *Al-Mustaqbal*, 12 March; *al-Muharrir*, 26 March 1988.
16. Interview in *al-Jumhuriyya*, Cairo, 18 February — DR, 24 February 1988.
17. R. Monte Carlo, 11 March — DR, 15 March 1988.
18. *Al-Qabas*, 10 March; 'Arafat interview with VoP (Algiers), 13 March — DR, 16 March 1988.
19. Mubarak interview in *al-Ra'y al-'Amm*, 12 March, cited by MENA, 11 March — DR, 15 March 1988.
20. *Al-Sharq al-Awsat*, 27 March 1988.
21. *Al-Qabas*, 18 March, 3 April; *JT*, 24 May — DR, 24 May 1988.
22. AFP, 10 May — DR, 10 May 1988.
23. *Kull al-'Arab*, 23 May; INA, 26 May 1988.
24. R. Damascus, 23 May — DR, 24 May; *al-Ittihad*, Abu Dhabi, 31 May; *Ma'ariv*, 3 June 1988.
25. TANJUG, 3 June — DR, 3 June 1988.
26. Tripoli TV, 28 March — DR, 29 March 1988.
27. R. Monte Carlo, 28 April — DR, 28 April 1988.
28. *NYT*, 1 June 1988.
29. R.Baghdad, 5 June — DR, 6 June 1988.
30. *Al-Wafd*, 11 June 1988.
31. Amnon Kapuliek in *Yedi'ot Aharonot*, 10 June 1988.
32. R. Monte Carlo, 9 June — DR, 10 June 1988.
33. *Al-Ra'y*, APS, 8 June — DR, 8, 9 June; *al-Tadamun*, 11 June 1988.
34. *Al-Ittihad*, Abu Dhabi, 7 June; interviews with Chief of the Royal Court Marwan al-Qasim, and Minister of Court 'Adnan Abu 'Awda, R. Amman, 8 June — DR, 9 June 1988.
35. *Al-Qabas*, 7 June 1988.
36. *Al-Siyasa*, Kuwait, 2 July 1988.
37. "How many in the young generation of Palestinians or Arabs," he asked, "...realize that the Jordanian Arab Legion managed to rescue the greater portion of what remained of Palestine, including Arab Jerusalem in the 1948 war?... How many are aware that it was the representatives of the Palestinian people who initiated the demand for union?... How many ...realize that national identity and not state identity was the prevalent notion in the forties and fifties... [and] that the decision... was a victory for the idea of Arab unity prevalent at that time?" (R. Amman, 8 June — DR, 9 June 1988.)
38. The acceptance by Jordan and Egypt of Resolution 242, Husayn stated, was based on "an American commitment to its implementation in no more than six months." (Ibid.)
39. Ibid.
40. R. Monte Carlo, 9 June — DR, 10 June 1988.
41. VoP, San'a, 9 June — DR, 10 June 1988.

42. R. Monte Carlo, 9 June — DR, 10 June 1988.
43. *Al-Thawra*, Baghdad, 9 June — DR, 14 June 1988.
44. *Al Ra'y al-'Amm*, 10 June 1988.
45. *Al-Majalla*, 15–21 June; *al-Tadamun*, 4 July 1988.
46. *Al-Ra'y al-'Amm*, 10 June; *al-Tadamun*, 4 July 1988.
47. INA, 10 June — DR, 13 June 1988.
48. R. Monte Carlo, 9 June — DR, 10 June; *Mir'at al-Umma*, 15 June 1988.
49. Klibi's postsummit press conference, Algiers TV, 9 June — DR, 10 June 1988.
50. *Al-Bayadir al-Siyasi*, 18 June; *al-Siyasa*, Kuwait, 4 July (which stated that the sums had already been decided upon at the April foreign ministers' meeting); 'Arafat's interview in *al-Sharq al-Awsat*, 9 August 1988.
51. *Al-Siyasa*, Kuwait, 4 July 1988.
52. R. Monte Carlo, 17 June — DR, 20 June 1988.
53. In doing so, said Klibi, "we have departed from the oratorical method and adopted the practical method," in order to improve the chances of convening the conference. The conference should be, he continued, "effective" and "significant," intervening "whenever matters become critical to make proposals and guide the participants toward respecting international law. This is what we want, but no Arab has said that this conference should impose." (Klibi's postsummit press conference, Algiers TV, 9 June — DR, 10 June; 'Arafat's press conference, Algiers TV, 10 June — DR, 13 June 1988.)
54. *Al-Siyasa*, Kuwait, 4 July 1988.
55. R. Damascus, 9 June — DR, 10 June 1988.
56. *Al-Siyasa*, Kuwait, 14 June — DR, 14 June 1988.
57. Klibi's postsummit press conference, Algiers TV, 9 June — DR, 10 June 1988.
58. The "salvation of Lebanon," Jumayyil declared, "is the responsibility of its Arab family." (VoL, 9 June — DR, 10 June 1988.)

    Discussions on the Lebanese issue may have been a bit livelier than indicated by the final statement. Qadhdhafi reportedly declared his intention to bring home the token Libyan contingents attached to the Arab Deterrence Forces (in reality, Syrian troops) in Lebanon. The UAE's Shaykh Zayid was said to have challenged Syria to do the same, instead of appointing itself Lebanon's guardian. Asad's alleged response was that the Syrian forces in Lebanon were internal security forces maintaining law and order. Lebanon, geographically, was a part of Greater Syria, just as the Arabian Peninsula was one geographic unit. Syria had no intention, he assured Shaykh Zayid, of remaining in Lebanon in order to fulfill its natural rights. Still, the day was not far off when the division of "natural Syria" by the 1915 Sykes-Picot agreement would be erased. In fact, the "uprising of stones" in Israeli-occupied territories was the first stage in the process. *Al-Sharq al-Jadid*, 11 July 1988.
59. Tripoli TV, 11 June — DR, 13 June 1988.
60. R. Damascus, 11 June — DR, 14 June 1988.
61. R. Algiers, 16 June — DR, 17 June 1988.
62. An alternative explanation was that he was afraid of somehow being poisoned by Israeli intelligence, as he alleged had happened to Jamal 'Abd al-Nasir. (*Al-Ra'y al-'Amm*, 10 June 1988.)
63. VoP (Baghdad), 27 October — DR, 28 October 1988.
64. Interview in *al-Ahram*, 20 October — DR, 25 October 1988.
65. *Al-Ra'y al-'Amm*, 24 October — DR, 26 October 1988.
66. Speech to Egypt's ruling NDP Arab Affairs Committee, MENA, 2 November — DR, 3 November 1988.
67. R. Cairo, 23 October — DR, 27 October 1988.
68. See Note 66.
69. Interview in *al-Hayat*, 27 October — text published by JNA, 27 October — DR, 28 October 1988.
70. According to one Gulf newspaper, both sides had ceased almost completely hostile actions against each other during the past year. (*Al-Qabas International*, 19 December 1987.)
71. The renewal of Syrian-Iraqi relations, said Syria's ambassador to Jordan, was "natural," and thus only a matter of time. (*Al-Jazira*, 16 January; *al-Qabas*, 25 January 1988.)
72. *The Times*, 12 January 1988.

73. According to an Iraqi source, Saddam Husayn had warned Asad at the Amman summit in the presence of other Arab leaders against this course, saying: "Take note, as you play the role of the intermediary, I will say that you have started to conspire and renounce your commitments. (*Al-'Iraq*, 4 April — JPRS, 10 June 1988.)
74. INA, 21 January — DR, 21 January 1988.
75. R. Monte Carlo, 26 January — SWB, 28 January 1988.
76. *FT*, 13 January 1988.
77. *Al-Qabas*, 13 February 1988.
78. R. Tehran, 20 July — DR, 21 July 1988.
79. *Al-Anba*, Kuwait, 16 August — DR, 18 August 1988.
80. R. Baghdad, 6 September — DR, 7 September 1988.
81. Interview in *al-Tadamun*, 6 February — DR, 12 February 1988.
82. *Al-Muharrir*, 10 December 1988. The same report stated that a majority of the GCC states had opposed the idea of Iraq's becoming a member of the GCC.
83. Interview in *al-Ahram*, 20 October — DR, 20 October 1988.
84. R. Amman, 16 August, Amman TV, 17 August — DR, 17 August 1988.
85. R. Amman, 11 September — DR, 12 September; King Husayn's interview in *al-Siyasa*, Kuwait, 8 December, text broadcast by R. Amman, 8 December — DR, 9 December 1988.
86. KUNA, 13 September — DR, 13 September 1988.
87. *Al-Thawra*, Damascus, 19 July 1988.
88. *Al-Thawra*, Baghdad, 13 August — DR, 14 August 1988.
89. Reuters, cited by R. Beirut, 18 October — DR, 19 October 1988.
90. *NAD*, 26 September 1988.
91. *Al-Nahar*, 7 November; *NAD*, 14, 21 November 1988.
92. Syria, declared Tariq 'Aziz, had placed only two options before Lebanon — "submission or partition." (INA, 20 October — DR, 21 October 1988.)
93. *Al-Watan al-'Arabi*, 30 September 1988.
94. These suggestions were said to include reaching a consensus around a new president and implementing political reforms. (*Al-Nahar*, 28 October 1988.)
95. *Al-Qabas International*, 26 October 1988.
96. Khaddam was reported by a pro-PLO publication to have expressed his anger at Husayn's support for a meeting to discuss the Lebanese crisis. (*Al-Bayadir al-Siyasi*, 19 November 1988.)
97. R. Damascus commentary, 13 October — DR, 19 October 1988.
98. Interview with *al-Hayat*, London, 27 October, text issued by JNA, 27 October — DR, 28 October 1988.
99. *Al-Shira'*, 7 November 1988.
100. R. Baghdad, 26 October — DR, 27 October 1988.
101. *Ma'ariv*, 23 December; *Le Monde*, 28 December 1988.
102. R. Monte Carlo, 15 December 1988.
103. According to the French magazine *Le Point* (2 January 1989) Asad had asked for $800m. For the citation, and the Saudi denial, see SPA, 9 January — SWB, 12 January 1989.
104. R. Monte Carlo, 15 December 1988. (On 6 December, Jordan's Crown Prince Hasan flew to Baghdad to try and achieve a similar cessation between Syria and Iraq. *Al-Ittihad*, Abu Dhabi, 7 December 1988.)
105. Interview in *al-Sharq al-Awsat*, 21 June — DR, 24 June 1988. On 27 June, Egypt's Consultative Council endorsed a committee report calling for an amendment of the Arab League charter. Suggested changes included making resolutions passed by a majority vote binding on all members (obviating the need for unanimity); properly defining the relationship between the league and its specialized organizations; making the 1950 joint defense pact more effective; and creating an Arab Court of Justice, to which judges would be appointed in advance and which would have binding authority over member states. (R. Cairo, 27 June — DR, 30 June 1988.)
106 Interview in *al-Hurriyya*, Tunis, 17 June, quoted by TAP, 17 June — DR, 21 June; and *al-Ra'y al-'Amm*, 19 October 1988.
107. Taking note of Egypt's involvement in Yemen (disastrous by Egyptian standards), YAR President 'Ali 'Abdallah Salih welcomed Mubarak by telling his audience that Egyptian-

Yemeni relations had been "baptized by blood." (R. San'a, 23 May — DR, 23 May 1988.
108. See Note 66.
109. Interview in *al-Siyasa*, Kuwait, 4 January — DR, 12 January 1988.
110. *FR*, 31 March; *Jane's Defence Weekly*, 16 April; *AT*, 27 June — DR, 29 June; *al-Qabas*, 25 October — DR, 27 October 1988. For a review of the armed forces and weapons systems of the Gulf countries, see Ze'ev Eytan and Shlomo Gazit (eds)., *Middle East Military Balance, 1988*–89 (Tel Aviv, 1989).
111. *Al-Sharq al-Awsat*, 2 April 1988.
112. MENA, 31 May — DR, 1 June 1988.
113. The agreement reportedly included provisions for Moroccan units to participate in Egyptian military maneuvers and joint training programs. (*Al-Majalla*, 30 November 1988).
114. MENA, 19 April — DR, 20 April 1988.
115. AFP, 25 June — DR, 27 June 1988.
116. Ibrahim Sa'da, in *Akhbar al-Yawm*, 11 June 1988.
117. Tripoli TV, 28 March, R. Cairo, 30 March — DR, 29, 30 March 1988.
118. KUNA, 7 October — DR, 11 October; *al-Sharq al-Awsat*, 27 October 1988.
119. Statement issued by the People's Committee of the People's Bureau for Foreign Liaison, Tripoli TV, 24 November — DR, 25 November 1988.
120. *Al-Ittihad*, Abu Dhabi, 3 January 1988.
121. Interview with the ex-Moroccan prime minister, Maati Bouabid, *al-Majalla*, 17 February — DR, 1 March 1988.
122. AFP, 4 February 1988.
123. For Algerian and Moroccan press reviews, see APS, 24 January — DR, 27 January; MAP, 25 January — DR, 28 January 1988.
124. *IHT*, 8 February 1988.
125. R. Algiers, 19 March — DR, 24 March 1988.
126. See Note 121.
127. Statement by Prime Minister Hedi Baccouche, *Le Matin du Sahara*, 1 February — DR, 11 February; King Hasan interview in *al-Jumhuriyya*, Cairo, 18 February 1988.
128. *Al-Muharrir*, 9 July 1988.
129. *JA*, 25 May 1988.
130. R. Algiers, 16 May — DR, 17 May 1988.
131. R. Algiers, 1 June — DR, 2 June 1988.
132. *FT*, 6 June 1988.
133. APS, 7 July — DR, 8 July; *Le Monde*, 7, 10–11 July 1988.
134. The presence of the SADR diplomat, engineered apparently by Algerian officials not enamored of the *rapprochement*, and fearful of a sellout of the Polisario, occasioned Hasan's leaving the dinner forthwith and returning to his yacht. Algerian authorities subsequently asked the SADR representative to leave, enabling Moroccan diplomats to take part. Following the dinner, Benjedid paid a courtesy call on Hasan aboard his yacht. (MAP, 9 June — DR, 10 June; *al-Dustur*, London, 11 July 1988.)
135. Algiers TV, 9 June — DR, 10 June 1988.
136. Ibid.
137. Benjedid's interview in *al-Hawadith*, 24 June — DR, 28 June 1988.
138. R. Tunis, 24 September — DR, 26 September 1988.
139. Tripoli TV, 6 September — DR, 7 September 1988.
140. *Al-Sharq al-Awsat*, 29 October; *al-Mustaqbal*, 5 November; *al-Muharrir*, 12 November 1988.
141. John Damis, *Conflict in Northwest Africa* (Stanford, Cal.: Hoover Institute, Stanford University Press, 1983), p. 8.
142. MAP, 15 February — DR, 18 February 1988.
143. Interview in *al-Jumhuriyya*, Cairo, 18 February — DR, 24 February 1988.
144. Interview in *Le Monde*, 3 August 1988.
145. *ME*, July 1988.
146. *FT*, 13 October 1988.
147. *Al-Qabas*, 6 August; *FT*, 12 August, 13 October 1988.

148. *NYT*, 31 August; *FT*, 31 August; R. Algiers, 1 September — DR, 2 September; *MEI*, 9 September 1988.
149. AFP, 8 September — DR, 12 September 1988.
150. *FT*, 21 September 1988.
151. *Al-Muharrir*, 26 November 1988.
152. Interview in *Le Point*, 12 December, cited by *FT*, 31 December and *al-Mustaqbal*, 31 December 1988.
153. Gad Gilbar, "The Middle East 'Oil Decade' in Perspective," in *MECS* 1986, pp. 246–57.
154. Sa'ad Eddin Ibrahim, *The New Arab Social Order* (Boulder, Col.: Westview Press, 1982).
155. Malcolm Kerr, "Rich and Poor in the New Arab Order," in Tawfiq E. Farah (ed.), *Political Behavior in the Arab States* (Boulder, Col.:Westview Press, 1983), p. 147.
156. Hazem Beblawi, "The Rentier State in the Arab World," in Beblawi, and Giacomo Luciani (eds.), *The Rentier State* (London: Croom Helm, 1987).
157. Samir Makdisi, "Al-'Itimad al-Iqtisadi al-Mutabadal wal-Siyada al-Qawmiyya," *al-Mustaqbal al-'Arabi*, April 1987, p. 94. His figures cover the period through 1983, but he states that they reflect the situation in subsequent years as well.
158. AFP, reported by *Gulf News*, 11 April — JPRS, 31 May 1988.
159. Algiers TV, 9, 10 June — DR, 10, 13 June 1988.
160. Interview in *al-Siyasa*, Kuwait, 8 December, text broadcast by R. Amman, 8 December — DR, 9 December 1988.

An Uneasy Truce in Islam

MARTIN KRAMER

For eight years, the Muslim world had been consumed by warfare on the frontier between Iran and Iraq, a conflict that had expanded into a contest between two rival visions of Islam. The war had poisoned the relations between the two great schools of Islam, Sunni and Shi'i, and had even violated the sacred space of Mecca. It had underlined the differences between Arab and Persian cultures, the two historical pillars of Islamic civilization. And the bloodshed had make a mockery of the supposed solidarity of Islam against the real and imagined injustices done by the West in Muslim lands. The Muslim world thus breathed a long sigh of relief in July, when Iran finally accepted a cease-fire and the shooting and missile-firing stopped. Internal reconciliation remained distant, but the Muslim world had stepped back from the abyss.

The advance of Iranian-style Islamic revolution was halted, perhaps even reversed. Now it was the turn of Sunni fundamentalism to boast of its power, drawing encouragement from successes in Afghanistan and Palestine. The failure of Islam to propel Iran to victory did not dampen their enthusiasm: Sunni fundamentalists had concluded several years earlier that no good could come to Islam from the Gulf War, and they had made no emotional investment in Iran's cause. Their growing influence along the rim of the Mediterranean pointed to a shift in the fulcrum of the struggle for Muslim primacy, away from the Gulf with its heavy Shi'i overtones, and into the traditional heartland of Islam.

THE PILGRIMAGE CONTROVERSY

For the first half of 1988, until the unexpected cease-fire, much of the world of Muslim activism remained preoccupied with the lingering effects of the Mecca incident of 31 July 1987. The deaths of several hundred Iranian pilgrims, most of them apparently shot by Saudi security authorities during a demonstration, had torn open sectarian scars that even the Iraqi-Iranian War had not touched. Holy places still retained their centrality in the psychological geography of believers, both Sunni and Shi'i, and the events in Mecca — birthplace and cradle of the Islamic faith and polity — reached into Islam's very core. Even the Palestinian *intifada* did not displace the pilgrimage controversy from its place of primacy in the internal discourse of Islam. From the blood-stained ground of Mecca's streets, the pilgrimage controversy passed to printing presses, airwaves, and above all to conference halls throughout the Muslim world. (For the development of the pilgrimage controversy since Iran's revolution, see *MECS* 1981–82, pp. 284–88, 301–3; 1982–83, pp. 238, 249–51; 1983–84, pp. 175–77; 1984–85, pp. 161–64; 1986, pp. 149–51; 1987, pp. 172–74.)[1]

CONFERENCE AND COUNTERCONFERENCE

As 1987 drew to a close, both Saudi Arabia and Iran had hosted rival Islamic conferences, in Mecca and Tehran, that brought the sectarian tension within Islam to a breaking point (see *MECS* 1987, pp. 174–76). The two antagonistic states — and much of Sunni and Shi'i Islam — had ended the year denouncing one another in high-pitched monologues, first over the pilgrimage, later over the very admissibility of the other's Islam.

From the midst of this venomous debate there emerged the idea of bringing Sunnis and Shi'is, Saudis and Iranians, together at a conference table to promote a cooling of sectarian tempers. The initiative belonged to the London-based World Islamic Council, under the directorship of Salim 'Azzam. A certain ambiguity surrounded the political orientation of 'Azzam. A naturalized Saudi and former Saudi diplomat, he had nonetheless attempted to build a reputation as an independent figure concerned with reconciling Islam from within. In recent years, his organization had sponsored widely international gatherings of Muslim activists on neutral ground in Europe, Asia, and Africa. (For past conferences, see *MECS* 1983–84, p. 174; 1986, p. 146; 1987, pp. 160–61.) The council was associated with Ahmad Ben Bella, former Algerian president, now Islamic activist, whose Lausanne apartment had become a meeting ground for Shi'is and Sunnis. 'Azzam now tried his mediating hand once again, sponsoring an "Islamic Unity Conference" that met in Islamabad from 16–17 February.[2]

Saudi King Fahd sent 'Abdallah 'Abd al-Muhsin al-Turki, director of the Imam Muhammad Ibn Sa'ud Islamic University in Riyadh, as his personal representative, along with a message that made a plea for sectarian reconciliation and "rational behavior" on the part of Iran.[3] Iran sent a delegation led by Ayatollah Ahmad Jannati, head of the Islamic Propagation Organization in Tehran. Also in attendance was Iran's foremost Sunni client, Shaykh Sa'id Sha'ban from Tripoli, Lebanon. Sha'ban himself had played the role of a go-between after the Mecca incident, trying to mediate between Saudis and Iranians (see *MECS* 1987, p. 170). Other participants included Muhammad Hamid Abu al-Nasr, the general guide of the Egyptian Muslim Brethren; 'Umar 'Abd al- Rahman, a leader of the Egyptian Jihad organization; 'Abd al-Rahman Khalifa, general supervisor of the Muslim Brethren in Jordan and the Gulf; Hasan al-Turabi, leader of Sudan's National Islamic Front; Qazi Ahmad Husayn, head of the Pakistani *Jama'ate Islami*; Necmettin Erbakan, leader of Turkey's National Salvation Party; 'Abd al-Fattah Muru, secretary-general of Tunisia's Islamic Tendency Movement; and Afghan resistance leaders Gulbuddin Hikmatyar and Yunis Khalis. (Ben Bella was prevented from attending by unspecified political circumstances, but sent a lengthy message to the conference.) This constituted an impressive array of Sunni Muslim activists, mostly identified with the Muslim Brethren, who now tried their hand at reconciliation.

But the conference itself did not move Islam closer to inner peace. Sha'ban, a Sunni speaking in eloquent Arabic, took up his appointed role of arguing for Iran, and clashed with Turabi in a heated exchange over the Iraqi-Iranian War. This dialogue of the deaf produced a final statement that held Iraq responsible for starting the war, Iran for continuing it. The Saudis and a delegation of Iraqi-based Syrian Muslim Brethren lobbied against the first half of this resolution; Sha'ban, against the second. One pro-Iranian critic did not hesitate to declare the conference "part of the current

Saudi campaign against Iran."[4] Other pro-Iranian sources saw the conference as a victory for Iran, since Saudi Arabia had participated in a conference that clearly labeled Iraq the aggressor.[5] But like the war itself, the conference had no victor or vanquished. It represented but one more rhetorical skirmish in the battle between two contradictory visions of Islam.

In this battle, Iran was decidedly on the defensive. This became evident again during the sixth Conference on Islamic Thought, which met from 1–4 February in Tehran. The gathering, always held around the anniversary of the revolution, brought together more than 450 persons from 18 countries. But this year the event received less attention in Iran, because the Mecca incident had worked to confine the gathering to Iran's Shi'i clientele. The conference, devoted to the theme of human rights in Islam, was addressed by Iran's speaker of the Majlis, Hujjat al-Islam 'Ali Akbar Hashemi-Rafsanjani, and by Iranian President 'Ali Khameneh'i. As might be expected, the conferees denounced the West for applying a double standard of human rights, condemned the US and Iraq, blamed the Saudis for the Mecca killings, and called for the internationalization of Mecca and Medina.[6] The same resolutions were adopted in a score of pilgrimage conferences convened by Iran's supporters around the world.[7]

Saudi Arabia responded in kind. In Saudi eyes, the Mecca incident of 1987 had the effect of lining up much of Sunni Islam behind Saudi interpretations of the pilgrimage, if not of Islam itself. Saudi Arabia continued its efforts to build popular support among its many foreign friends and clients in the world of Muslim activism. As in the past, the burden fell largely upon the Mecca-based Muslim World League (MWL; *rabitat al-'alam al-Islami*; on the MWL, see *MECS* 1981–82, pp. 295–97; 1982–83, pp. 246–47; 1983–84, pp. 165–66; 1984–85, p. 149; 1986, pp. 132–33; 1987, p. 158).[8] The MWL had organized a large conference in Mecca in October 1987, gathering MWL-supported Muslim activists who issued an unequivocal condemnation of Iran for its supposed responsibility for the Mecca tragedy (see *MECS* 1987, pp. 174–75). It had also supported numerous local pilgrimage conferences held in the Muslim world and beyond. Now the MWL worked to organize yet another world conference that would reach the same conclusion, but do so under other authoritative Islamic auspices, on ostensibly neutral soil.

This idea evoked a positive response in Cairo from the Shaykh al-Azhar, Jadd al-Haqq 'Ali Jadd al-Haqq. In Egypt, too, adherents of revolutionary Islam refused to recognize the established authority of the state-directed institutions of Islam. As the sectarian divide opened wider, Egyptian security authorities increasingly sought to identify this Islamic opposition as "Khomeyniite," and so burden it with foreign, non-Arab, and Shi'i associations. Further arrests of members of a "Khomeyniite" group first broken up by security authorities during the previous year, kept alive the allegation that Iran was behind Islamic unrest in Egypt.[9] The leading Saudi and Egyptian authorities in Islam had long shared a common interest in countering Iran's vision of Islam. This shared interest blossomed into actual cooperation, with the convening in Cairo of the eleventh conference of al-Azhar's Academy of Islamic Research (*majma' al-buhuth al-Islamiyya*).[10] The conference, gathering 215 participants from 88 countries, met from 4–8 March.

The Cairo conference, formally devoted to questions of Islamic missionary activity (*da'wa*), actually served as yet another Sunni forum for the condemnation of Iran. It represented, above all, the shared concerns of al-Azhar and the MWL, but also involved individual activists or official representatives from Morocco, Iraq, Kuwait, Qatar, Sudan, the United Arab Emirates, and Jordan, and like-minded Islamic organizations, such as the Baghdad-based Popular Islamic Conference (on which, see *MECS* 1982–83, pp. 243–45; 1984–85, p. 151). In his opening address to the conference, Egyptian President Husni Mubarak set the tone of the gathering by asking rhetorically whether Iran's "aggression is an Islamic tide and its bloody action is a struggle for the sake of Islam."[11] The conference passed a resolution condemning the Iranian pilgrims and the Iranian regime for their alleged desecration of Mecca in 1987, and ruled that demonstrations and marches during the pilgrimage violated the sanctity of the holy cities. The resolutions called the Iranian-backed idea of the internationalization of Mecca "foreign to Islam," and offered full support for Saudi measures to preserve Mecca and Medina against any recurrence of the previous year's events.[12] These resolutions drew upon the learned lecture of Jadd al-Haqq, who buttressed his discussion of the pilgrimage with references to classical Islamic sources.[13]

In addition to these and other resolutions, the conference decided to establish a World Islamic Council for *Da'wa* and Aid (*al-majlis al-Islami al-'alami li'l-da'wa wa'-iqhatha*), which would coordinate the international activities of the Azhar, the MWL, the Popular Islamic Conference, and other Islamic missionary and aid societies. A September meeting set down a constitution for the new organization, chose Cairo as its permanent seat, and selected Kamil al-Sharif as secretary-general.[14] Although originally Egyptian, Sharif had spent many years in Jordan, where he had served as minister of religious endowments. A prominent supporter of the Muslim Brethren, he was known for his long-standing ties to Saudi Arabia and the MWL. Funds for the new organization were to come from donations from governments and the participating institutions. Twenty-five years earlier, the MWL and the Azhar had been bitter rivals: they had served as Islamic instruments wielded by their respective governments to discredit one another. A shared interest in discrediting Iran now brought them together in a close alliance. But it remained to be seen whether the new council would achieve coordination between two great centers of Sunni Islam that had a long history of rivalry, and still jealously guarded their independence.

THE CONSENSUS OF REGIMES

The Jidda-based Islamic Conference Organization (ICO), consisting of 45 states and the PLO, had functioned for two decades as a subtle instrument of Saudi influence in the Muslim world. (On the ICO, see *MECS* 1981–82, pp. 283–84, 298–301; 1982–83, pp. 235–37; 1983–84, pp. 158–65; 1984–85, pp. 146–48; 1986, pp. 127–30; 1987, pp. 153–58).[15] Saudi Arabia did not overtly manipulate this organization of Muslim states. But it exercised tremendous influence behind the scenes, through the financing and staffing of the ICO. Although the annual conferences of foreign ministers and the triennial summits were open forums for debate, the deck of the ICO was stacked heavily in favor of Saudi Arabia. For this reason, Khomeyni's Iran had often absented itself from ICO conferences, most recently from the Islamic summit held in Kuwait in January 1987. The ICO had been paralyzed for close to a decade by the Gulf War, becoming a comfortable forum for Saudi Arabia and Iraq, but utterly useless as an instrument of Muslim mediation.

Few surprises were anticipated from the 17th annual ICO conference of foreign ministers, convened in Amman from 21–25 March. By this time, no one expected a breakthrough in the Gulf War as a result of ICO diplomacy. "To be realistic," said the conference chairman, Jordanian Foreign Minister Tahir al-Masri, "we have to acknowledge that continued Arab, Islamic, and international mediation efforts with Iran have failed and the war is spreading and increasing in intensity. To achieve reconciliation during this conference and at this level is doubtful."[16] Nor would the conference be able to do much more than reiterate past support of the Palestinian cause, and its manifestation in the form of the *intifada* taking place but a few kilometers from the conference setting. Although the ICO secretariat issued many appeals for Muslim solidarity with the Palestinians, member states had rejected the idea of an emergency ICO summit only the month before.[17]

The truly new issue on the agenda was the pilgrimage. Saudi Arabia had two principal aims at the conference. The first was to secure further condemnation of Iranian conduct during the pilgrimage, so as to allow the Saudi authorities to ban all demonstrations during the pilgrimage. The second was to win the conference's assent to a cutback in the number of pilgrims — a cutback so formulated as to bring about a drastic reduction in the number of Iranian pilgrims. Saudi Arabia had received support for its pilgrimage policy from Sunni Muslim activists and religious authorities; now it sought the seal of approval of Muslim governments.

But would Iran, a lapsed ICO member, put up a fight? Iran had no doubt that the ICO foreign ministers would reiterate their established position on the Gulf, calling upon Iran to accept a cease-fire in accord with UN Resolution 598. Had this been the only item affecting Iran on the agenda, Iran might have followed its usual custom of boycotting the proceedings. But Iran apparently did see some point in trying to influence the outcome of the first pilgrimage debate under ICO auspices. Iranian Foreign Minister 'Ali Akbar Velayati made his decision at the last possible moment, deciding only a few days before the conference that Iran would be represented — but by a foreign ministry official rather than himself.

At Amman, Saudi Arabia sought to give its policy the character of the express will of the world of Islam. The Saudi delegation did so by having Jordan submit a draft resolution on the sanctity of Mecca and Medina, which condemned Iran and supported Saudi pilgrimage measures.[18] In his speech, Jordanian Foreign Minister al-Masri attacked "the perverse, aggressive regime" of Iran for intervening in the affairs of other states, committing aggression against Iraq, dealing with Israel, allowing Iranian Jews to emigrate to Israel, and subverting the pilgrimage.[19] This relieved the Saudi delegate, Sa'ud al-Faysal, of the need to engage in similar polemics. When he did mount the podium, he cited the expressions of support by "states, bodies, organizations, and Islamic centers.... The list truly represents an Islamic unanimity which is beyond any doubt."[20] The Saudi delegation then put forward a memorandum regarding the pilgrimage, stating that in order to improve services to pilgrims, Saudi Arabia wished to limit their number, by instituting annual national quotas of 1,000 pilgrims per million population for a period of three years. Although this proposal made no explicit mention of Iran, its intent was transparent: Iranian pilgrims constituted the largest foreign delegation, and imposition of the proposed quota would mean the reduction of their annual numbers from 150,000 to 45,000. Iran sought to counter this move by presenting the findings of its own committee of inquiry into the Mecca incident, and demanded the establishment of an ICO committee to investigate the tragedy.[21]

But the political committee overwhelmingly approved the Saudi-inspired resolutions, dealing a decisive defeat to Iran. The head of the Iranian delegation then announced his country's withdrawal from the conference, charging that "Saudi Arabian money spent at the conference has prompted the resolutions," and that the conference was "a great puppet show."[22] Iran's half-hearted participation in the conference had been to no avail. The final resolutions denounced "the riots and destruction perpetrated by the Iranian pilgrims," reiterated the Saudi "right to take any measures necessary to prevent a repetition of riots and anarchy," and supported the Saudi plan to reduce the number of of pilgrims.[23] At Amman, Saudi Arabia could rightly claim to have won yet another round in its continuing campaign against Iran.

This preoccupation with the pilgrimage stood in striking contrast to the neglect of other issues that fell within the ICO's purview. There were 87 items on the agenda of the conference, 34 on the agenda of the political committee. Most of these items had long figured in ICO agendas, and a consensus had been reached long ago about support for the PLO and a Palestinian state, support for the Afghan resistance, and the need for Iran to accept a cease-fire in the Gulf War. Once again, there were small skirmishes over these resolutions, but no change in their substance. Despite the *intifada*, ambiguities over the Palestine question abounded, as they always had. As in the past, the conference called upon all Muslim states having relations with Israel to sever them; yet it determined that the 19th foreign ministers' conference would be held in Cairo, thus placing the final seal on Egypt's rehabilitation within the ICO. (On Egypt's return to the ICO, see *MECS* 1983–84, pp. 160–62; 1984–85, 146–47; 1987, p. 155.) Syria protested this move, demanding to know how an ICO foreign ministers' conference could meet in a country where Israel's flag flew freely.[24] But Syria could do nothing to brake the continuing process of Egypt's reintegration — a process supported by the great majority of ICO member states, and driven to its ultimate conclusion by the choice of Cairo as a future conference site.

The ICO itself remained caught in a web of internal contradictions. Its great success story, the Islamic Development Bank (IDB), showed signs of fatigue in its fight against the Muslim world's deepening dependence on the West. Trade among ICO member states hovered at a mere 10% of their total imports and exports, and the prevailing trend was one of decline. The recession had led to a drop in IDB financing activities; the latest reported figure for 1986–87 showed $740m., down from $849m. the previous year. In some instances, subscriptions by member states to the IDB's working capital were far overdue.[25] Yet the IDB remained the most significant achievement of the ICO. Even Iran, which had not joined in the IDB in the Shah's days, and remained estranged from the ICO in the age of Khomeyni, finally applied for IDB membership in 1988.[26]

The ICO secretariat had become almost a parody of an international organization, consumed with its self-preservation, open to political manipulation, deep in deficit because of wasteful spending. Even the ICO's biggest Saudi backer, Foreign Minister Sa'ud al-Faysal, complained of the "inflation of administrative and financial spending" in the ICO, and declared that there was need for "rationalizing expenditures." He urged member states to meet their commitments to the ICO, and especially "to pay in full their decided quota."[27] The secretariat's budget for 1987–88 came to $7.6m., down from $8m. the previous year; total unpaid debts of member states to the secretariat stood at $18.75m., as of June 1987.[28]

The Amman conference elected Niger Prime Minister Hamid Algabid as the ICO's new secretary-general, to replace the Pakistani Sharifuddin Pirzada. Algabid had been schooled in law and public administration in Abidjan and Paris, and had trained at the International Monetary Fund in Washington. He had served in numerous ministerial positions — commerce, transport, finance — and for four years had been Niger's prime minister, a position from which he resigned in order to take over Pirzada's post.[29] "When Pirzada took over from Habib Chatti [of Tunisia] four years ago, we thought that as an Asian he would be a better organizer," said an anonymous ICO official. "But unfortunately we were wrong. Very little has been achieved over the last four years."[30] Now the task fell to an African, in accord with the ICO practice of rotating the position among Arabs, Asians, and Africans.

But it was not the personality or geo-ethnic origins of the secretary-general that had crippled the ICO. The domination of Saudi Arabia and its Gulf allies had cost the ICO its neutrality. "It is true rich Muslim countries have influence," said the Jordanian chairman of the Amman conference, "but they do not dominate."[31] But during the conference, Saudi Arabia had assured that influence by announcing donations to the Islamic Solidarity Fund ($6m.), the Jerusalem Fund ($2m.), and other ICO activities ($2m.).[32] Without Saudi support, the ICO would have collapsed long ago. Yet Saudi Arabia had exacted a political price for opening its purse, one so steep that it had cost the ICO much of its credibility. The ICO had failed to accomplish a reconciliation between two member states whose war had torn Islam apart, and later in the year, when both sides wished for neutral auspices to police their cease-fire, they turned to the UN. Only the healing of Islam's self-inflicted wounds could restore the ICO to the halcyon days it had known in the 1970s — and that healing was bound to be a slow one.

THE PILGRIMAGE OF 1988

Fortified by major Islamic conferences in Mecca and Cairo, and the resolutions of the ICO foreign ministers in Amman, the Saudis shifted their attention to the next pilgrimage. In Mecca and Cairo, the Saudis had been urged by the self-appointed authorities of Sunni Islam to ban all demonstrations and marches during the pilgrimage. In Amman, a majority of Muslim governments gave their consent to a cut in the number of pilgrims that would reduce the Iranian contingent by two thirds. The Saudi authorities now sought to translate these resolutions into a far-reaching revision of the informal understanding that had come apart in 1987, and which had become a thorn in the Saudi side. The Saudi Government sought to diminish the quantity and quality of the Iranian pilgrimage, by admitting only 45,000 Iranian pilgrims, and by banning the marches allowed in Mecca and Medina during previous years. Iran took the position that both these measures constituted Saudi neglect of its obligations toward Islam: the Saudis, claimed Iran, wished to prevent the great majority of Iranian Muslim pilgrims from arriving, and proposed to keep those who did arrive from fulfilling a fundamental part of the pilgrimage ritual.

The Saudis claimed that it was not their intention to exclude the Iranians;[33] even Khomeyni himself would be welcome.[34] But they were reasonably certain (and probably hopeful) that the new terms would provoke Iranian self-exclusion. Khomeyni performed as expected by declaring it impossible for Iran's pilgrims to go on pilgrimage and not demonstrate against "world arrogance."[35] Although Syrian mediation made possible the dispatch of an Iranian delegation to Saudi Arabia in April to discuss the matter, the talks changed nothing. The Iranians insisted on the sending of a full contingent of 150,000 pilgrims, as well as the right to demonstrate in Mecca and Medina as in past years. If these demands were not met, the delegation warned, Iran would boycott the pilgrimage. But the Saudi authorities stood firm, citing what they called "the consensus of the Islamic nation." The three-year limitation on the number of pilgrims would remain in force, and if Iranians dared to demonstrate, Saudi Interior Minister Prince Na'if warned, they would be "quelled by force."[36] Khomeyni's pilgrimage supervisor, Hujjat al-Islam Mehdi Emami-Jamarani, was probably right in declaring that had Iran's pilgrims "acted like those who wish to be servile to the Saudi regime and performed an American-style *hajj,* they definitely would have agreed to receive 300,000 of our pilgrims."[37]

On the delegation's return to Iran, a new round of accusations began, yet Khomeyni did not issue an unequivocal announcement of a pilgrimage boycott. Saudi Arabia therefore took a decisive step by severing relations with Iran on 26 April. The timing of the move suggested a Saudi desire to eliminate the prospect of attendance in Mecca by any Iranian pilgrims, although the severing of relations was the subject of a lengthy internal Saudi debate that involved wider political considerations (see chapter on Saudi Arabia).[38] In Iran itself, arrangements for the sending of 150,000 pilgrims proceeded into June, but no preparations for accommodation and guides could be made in Mecca. Only when time ran out did Tehran decide to translate its stand into a formal boycott. Iran then claimed to have been excluded; Saudi Arabia claimed that Iran excluded itself.

The subsequent polemics reiterated the old charges of religious deviation. The Saudi Council of Ministers declared that the Iranians, by "causing havoc" during the pilgrimage, had "moved outside the Islamic consensus."[39] The Iranians accused the Saudis of preventing Muslims from fulfilling the fundamental obligation of pilgrimage. Any Muslim with the means to perform the pilgrimage was entitled to do so; the Saudi implementation of a quota system demonstrated their incompetence.[40] In Khomeyni's message marking the first anniversary of the "massacre," he accused the "centers of Wahhabism" of "sedition and espionage." At Mecca in 1987, "the sword of blasphemy and division, which had been hidden in the hypocritical cloak of Yazid's followers and descendants of the Umayyad dynasty, God's curse be upon them, had to come out again from the same cloak of Abu Sufyan's heirs to destroy and kill."[41] Whatever his intention, Khomeyni's resort to this historical analogy constituted a sectarian allusion — despite his claim, in the very same message, that it was the US and the Saudis who tried to portray the Mecca events as a sectarian clash.

Once it became clear that Iranian pilgrims would not arrive, rumors began to fly that Iran would insinuate its supporters among pilgrims from other countries, and particularly among the Shi'i pilgrims.[42] Counterrumors then charged that Saudi security forces had been beefed up by reinforcements from Egypt, Morocco, and Turkey.[43] During the pilgrimage, Iran claimed that demonstrations had indeed taken place in Mecca,[44] a claim denied by the Saudi authorities.[45] In fact, a number of Pakistani Shi'is launched a small demonstration in Mecca; they were arrested at the airport before leaving, and were only released following the intervention of the

Pakistani Government.[46] It would appear that the pilgrimage passed without serious incident, amidst the most stringent security measures ever implemented by the Saudi regime. On arrival, pilgrims from certain countries were subjected to rigorous searches and interrogation. "Are we nonbelievers that Saudi agents treat us like animals at the airport?" complained a Libyan pilgrim.[47] As a preventive measure, younger pilgrims were banned under some of the new quotas. For example, Lebanese pilgrims under the age of 40 were not issued visas. Combined with a sharp drop in the number of Lebanese visas (in line with the new quota system), Saudi Arabia succeeded in blocking the participation of large numbers of Iran's Lebanese Shi'i clients.[48]

The absence of Iranian pilgrims in 1988 brought an enforced truce to the pilgrimage, not a peace. But the surprise announcement by Iran of its willingness to accept a cease-fire in the Gulf — an announcement made in the very midst of the pilgrimage — held out the prospect of a reconciliation. Only a few days after the announcement, Saudi King Fahd told the heads of of pilgrimage delegations that he "regretted" the absence of Iranian pilgrims.[49] It was the first sign of a possible diminution in the sectarian tension generated by Islam's fratricidal war. With the cease-fire, the Muslim world took a first first tentative step toward internal reconciliation.

IRAN: REVOLUTION IN ONE COUNTRY?

On 18 July, Iran announced its unconditional acceptance of a cease-fire in its war with Iraq, in accord with UN Resolution 598. The impending end of the war had profound implications for the the region as a whole. For Iran, the war had represented a crusade of truth and a vindication of the revolution's message of Islam; but with Iran's growing military frustration, the war had become a bottomless pit of regrets. With the cease-fire, Iran admitted that it could not remake the Arab world in its own image. Yet over the years, Iran had built certain political assets in the Arab and wider Muslim world, under the rubric of "exporting the revolution." These were Muslim movements, mostly Shi'i, that owed a high degree of fealty to the Imam Khomeyni. Some of these assets had directly served the war effort, others provided Iran with a more general influence in the Muslim world. Now that Iran had conceded defeat in war, the wider Muslim world awaited with anticipation Iran's decision on whether to keep these foreign assets of the revolution, or trade them away for a normalization of relations with existing regimes. (This chapter discusses the implications of the cease-fire for Iran's relations with Muslim movements. For the development of these relations, see previous volumes of *MECS*. For the causes and wider repercussions of the cease-fire decision, see the chapters on the Iraqi-Iranian War, and inter-Arab affairs.)

This question remained tied up with the struggle over the control of foreign policy. Despite their differences, a concerted effort had been made by speaker of the Majlis 'Ali Akbar Hashemi Rafsanjani and President 'Ali Khameneh'i to centralize foreign policy and entrust its execution to Foreign Minister 'Ali Akbar Velayati. Yet many other Iranian figures sought a hand in foreign affairs, and their disagreements surfaced again in 1988. Some of these figures thought that Rafsanjani and Khameneh'i had adopted too soft a line. This view was championed by Interior Minister 'Ali Akbar Mohtashemipur, former Iranian ambassador to Syria, who had a reputation for his fervent support of Muslim movements elsewhere. According to some sources, he even controlled many of the funds sent to Hizballah in Lebanon.[50] In June he gave an interview in which he rejected a cease-fire in the the Gulf and called for more support of Lebanon's Hizballah.[51] This earned him a reprimand from Khomeyni, for venturing outside the jurisdiction of his own ministry. But Mohtashemipur's view had the sanction of Khomeyni's heir designate, Ayatollah Husayn 'Ali Montazeri, known for his devotion to the cause of Shi'ism beyond beyond Iran's frontiers.

Others thought Rafsanjani and Khameneh'i were too indulgent of the extremists. In September, Prime Minister Mir Husayn Musavi offered his resignation to Iranian President Khameneh'i, claiming that the government had lost much of its authority in foreign affairs. "Today, the affairs of Afghanistan, Iraq, and Lebanon are in your hands," he reportedly complained, lamenting that "external operations" had taken place without his knowledge:

> Only after an airplane is hijacked are we informed. Only when a machine gun opens fire in one of the streets of Lebanon and the sound of it echoes everywhere do we find out about the incident. Only after explosives are discovered in the possession of our pilgrims in Jidda [in 1986] do I find out about it. Unfortunately, and in spite of the damages and harm caused by these actions to the country, such operations can take place at any time, at any hour in the name of the government.[52]

The reference to hijacking evoked the April hijacking of a Kuwaiti airliner to Mashhad, in which two passengers were murdered (see chapter on Kuwait). No incident better demonstrated the continuing debate over whether Iran should approach other Muslim movements as a revolution or as a state. The hijackers, apparently Lebanese Shi'is, demanded the release of 17 Shi'i terrorists held by Kuwait, in a virtual replay of the hijacking of a Kuwaiti airliner to Tehran in December 1984 (see *MECS* 1984–85, pp. 154, 403–4). As in that earlier instance, there was considerable evidence for on-the-ground collaboration with the hijackers.[53] The Kuwaiti press went so far as to link the hijacking with Mohtashemipur and the Iraqi Shi'i exile group, the Islamic Action Organization.[54] Velayati, on the other hand, was deeply embarrassed and actually offered his sympathies to his Kuwaiti counterpart. A struggle went on behind the scenes in Iran over the extent of support to be offered to the hijackers — a struggle ultimately resolved by allowing the hijacked airliner to refuel and leave. The event served as a reminder that although many of the most powerful men in Iran sought to put terrorism behind them, the regime had raised up cadres of revolutionary zealots who still had influential friends in important Iranian ministries.

The cease-fire seemed to signal that the day of the undiscriminating zealot had passed. A month after the cease-fire announcement, Rafsanjani told the world that "if you believed that we wished to export the revolution by force, you were mistaken. Do not repeat this mistake in the future. We never thought that the revolution could be exported through force."[55] As one astute observer wrote, "after a decade of exhortations and passionate proselytism, and a war they could not conclude on their own terms, the governors of [Iran] must fully understand that their pan-Islamic revolution did not catch hold."[56] But there was no reason for Iran to throw away those gains that it had made during the turbulent decade of Shi'ism, especially in arenas away from the Gulf. What the cease-fire did mean was the beginning of a serious taking of Iran's stock in the Muslim world, and a reassessment of the tone of its message. Shaykh Sha'ban, Iran's Sunni client from Lebanon, summarized the emerging approach. There were Muslim movements that found themselves in a situation like that faced by the Prophet Muhammad in Medina; but most faced a climate reminiscent of Mecca before its conquest. To such movements, Iran had to preach patience and guile, not revolution. "We do not say to a new Islamic movement that does not have the power to change the regime: 'Commit suicide by engaging the regime in battle.' Rather we say: 'Come in contact with other Islamic movements until the appointed day.'"[57] For those in Iran who wished to see other Muslims emulate their revolution, and for Iran's admirers in other lands, the cease-fire in the Gulf meant the distancing of the appointed day, even as they affirmed its inevitability. In one sense, the new position represented a return to the old ways of Shi'ism, of awaiting some distant redemption while enduring the oppression of the present.

THE SAUDI-IRANIAN VERBAL TRUCE

Following the cease-fire, Islam's sectarian war of words died down, amidst some sporadic verbal firing. A last shot was fired at the first ICO conference of ministers of information, which met in Jidda from 11–12 October. The Muslim world, so the ministers believed, had to preserve its foundations against "the subversive ideological invasion" that threatened to "belittle and cast doubt" on Islam. The Muslim media had to counter this threat, and the ministers agreed to establish a standing committee and meet in conference every two years. Iran did not attend the conference; Saudi King Fahd expressed his regret at Iran's absence, since the conference was "a conference of all Muslims, not a Saudi conference."[58] The conference also hailed the cease-fire in the Gulf. But the resolutions also opposed the "extremism and violence" that so damaged the image of Islam, determining that "the climax of this deviant course led to bloody aggression against God's holy mosque in Mecca" in 1987. The resolutions also called for a Gulf peace that would guarantee Iraq's sovereignty "over its territories and waters," a stand in clear accord with Iraq's position in peace negotiations.[59] Perhaps the highlight of the conference was King Fahd's repudiation that the Saudis were adherents of Wahhabism, a charge made by the Iranian media in order to evoke memories of the distant days when Wahhabism was regarded by Sunni Muslims as a deviation. "Wahhabism," said King Fahd, "does not exist."[60]

The resolutions provoked a heated Iranian denunciation of the conference, "which is backed by the Wahhabi regime of the Hijaz — a regime which is outside the bounds of Islam."[61] This response had special significance in light of King Fahd's denial of the distinct existence of Wahhabism.[62] Clearly Saudi Arabia, which had emerged victorious in the verbal war for Islam, would have to go farther if it were to reconcile Iran. King Fahd did so shortly after the information ministers' conference. Asked about the pilgrimage, Fahd declared that Iran

> is a Muslim state and its people are a Muslim people...difference in points of view does not mean that differences are permanent....As far as Iran is concerned, the problems will certainly end and they will be replaced by concord, friendship, and harmony. If we simply look at the problems between the Kingdom and Iran, we will find that they are minuscule.

Fahd then announced a suspension of the media war with Iran: "Let us start behaving in this way and we hope that we will be treated in the same way."[63] Iranian

Foreign Minister Velayati immediately expressed Iran's desire to end the "problems" between the two countries.[64]

The verbal cease-fire between Saudi Arabia and Iran found expression almost immediately, in the second Conference on Islamic Unity held at Tehran University from 25–26 October 1988. This forum had last met in January 1981, when it was convened during the week of the Prophet's birthday in order to refute the ruling by a leading Saudi cleric that the observance of the Prophet's birthday was incompatible with Islam. Since Shi'is and most Sunnis observe the birthday, the original aim was to cast Saudi "Wahhabism" as a deviation from ecumenical Islam. (For the first conference, see *MECS* 1981–82, pp. 290–91.) This time, however, the organizers sought to use the conference to tone down the sectarian debate, now that a truce had been implemented in the polemical war.

Ayatollah Ahmad Jannati presided over the conference, which reportedly gathered 700 *'ulama* and thinkers. In an opening speech, Rafsanjani called for the establishment of an international academy of Muslim *'ulama* to solve problems internal to Islam, especially between Sunnis and Shi'is. Rafsanjani admitted it would be difficult to create such an academy in the present circumstances, "since most Islamic countries are ruled by the forces of arrogance," but he called for an effort to find *'ulama* who were not committed politically. Finally, he proposed that the new academy be located as near as possible to Mecca.[65] This constituted a conciliatory speech, since Rafsanjani omitted the usual demand for the internationalization of the holy cities. Khameneh'i sounded a similar note in the Friday sermon immediately following the conference. "A group of mercenary pencil-pushers from Arab and non-Arab countries are sitting around waiting for certain people to say something, so that they can start a fight between Shi'is and Sunnis." Khameneh'i urged his listeners to avoid providing a pretext to those who would sow discord: "First, bear no grudges against your brother Muslims...Second, do not needle others about their sensitivities." If a sect sees that another is sensitive about something, it should not provoke them about this sensitivity." Khameneh'i then echoed Rafsanjani, asking that *'ulama* "from both sides and from various Islamic sects sit together and jointly review Islamic issues."[66]

The Gulf War cease-fire had produced a lull in the sectarian polemic that had so afflicted the Muslim world. Yet the truce was as fragile as the cease-fire itself; its continuation depended on the translation of the cease-fire into peace along the age-old frontier of Sunni-Shi'i confrontation. In the meantime, both sides kept their polemical powder dry, making no fundamental doctrinal concessions that they might later regret.

THE CHANGING FORTUNES OF SHI'I OPPOSITION

Iran's apparent defeat took the wind out of several Muslim movements supported by Iran, although they did not all pay the same price for the cease-fire. The Iraqi Shi'i opposition, which had been based largely in Tehran, was most affected by the end of hostilities. (On this opposition, see *MECS* 1983–84, pp. 170–71, 483; 1986, pp. 144–46; 1987, pp. 169–70.) The various Iraqi Shi'i opposition movements could no longer pursue their aims from Iranian soil. Rafsanjani explained that those Iraqi Shi'is who had fled to Iran:

> must consider Iran their homeland, like Iraq....If there is peace, we should first

> try to ensure the safety, according to international law, of those wishing to return to Iraq. If they are not safe in Iraq, this is their home. Our nation should receive the Iraqi brothers and sisters who are among us, as Iranians.[67]

There was a certain nobility in this plea, with its recognition that Iran owed an obligation to those Iraqi Shi'is whom Iran had led to a dead end.

But the Iraqi Shi'i opposition would not forget the cause for which it had made great sacrifices, nor lose itself in Iranian anonymity. On the contrary, its leaders remained determined to carry the struggle into the postwar phase. The Tehran-based Supreme Assembly of the Islamic Revolution in Iraq (SAIRI) announced that it respected Iran's decision, but would continue the "armed struggle" within Iraq, as it had done before Iran's revolution.[68] Sayyid Muhammad Taqi al-Mudarrisi, the leader of the Islamic Action Organization, also affirmed that his organization would carry on the armed struggle: "It is true that the war has ended, but our *jihad* against Saddam's regime will not end."[69] The spokesman of the Islamic Action Organization, Shaykh Muhsin al-Husayni, pointed out that the Islamic opposition to the Iraqi regime long predated the Iranian revolution. The cease-fire meant that the Iraqi people themselves would have to bear the burden of toppling the Iraqi regime, from within Iraq itself.[70]

But these groups could no longer plan or conduct the armed struggle from Iranian soil, and some began to issue their military communiqués from Beirut. The head of SAIRI, Hujjat al-Islam Muhammad Baqir al-Hakim, paid a visit to Damascus, met with Syrian President Hafiz al-Asad, and announced that his organization had drawn "closer" to the Syrian regime, in the hope of continuing the struggle. Asked whether he had discussed transferring SAIRI's operations to Syria, Baqir al-Hakim answered that Syria occupied an important geographic and strategic position *vis-à-vis* Iraq, and that Syria had been "firm" in its strategic support of the cause of Iraq's opposition.[71] During the visit, Baqir al-Hakim explored the possibility of creating a united front with other Iraqi opposition groups that were not Shi'i or Islamic in outlook.[72] Baqir al-Hakim claimed that Iran had placed no limits on SAIRI's activities following the cease-fire, and that SAIRI wished only to expand some of its activities in Syria. But neither did he rule out the possible transfer of the center of the Shi'i opposition to Syria or Lebanon.[73]

This was the extent of SAIRI's options, for the wider world was not a safe place for members of the Iraqi Shi'i opposition, given the long arm of the Iraqi regime. On 17 January, one of Muhammad Baqir al-Hakim's brothers, Sayyid Mahdi al-Hakim, was assassinated in the Khartoum Hilton, during a visit to Sudan at the invitation of Hasan al-Turabi's National Islamic Front. Mahdi al-Hakim had a long record of opposition to the Iraqi regime, but had preferred to operate free from Iranian control, and so based himself in London.[74] His fate — and the fact that even in London three attempts had been made on his life — were a solemn warning to Iraqi Shi'is who considered moving their base of operations outside the orbit of the Iranian-Syrian alliance. (For more on the Iraqi Shi'i opposition's dilemma, see chapter on Iraq.)

The Saudi Shi'i opposition, represented above all by the Organization of the Islamic Revolution in the Arabian Peninsula, also regarded the cease-fire with apprehension. An anonymous spokesman of the Shi'i opposition said that the movement was aware of certain moves towards improvement of Saudi-Iranian relations in the wake of the cease-fire, but this would not affect the activities of the

Shi'i opposition. Unlike certain other Islamic "revolutionary movements," the indigenous opposition to the Saudi regime existed before the Iranian revolution. It had deep roots in the people, it had preserved its "freedom of decision," and would continue its struggle regardless of Iran's policy. While it was not yet clear what Iran's relationship to Islamic liberation movements would be,

> we expect that the Government of the Islamic Republic will never entirely abandon the Islamic movements...it would not be wise of the leadership of the revolution to abandon its allies, who stood by it in the most difficult circumstances, just as we assume that the relationship between the leadership of the revolution and the Islamic movements has been a fundamentally strategic relationship.[75]

There could be no doubt that the truce in the war of words did not apply to the Shi'i opposition, which continued to operate clandestinely in the predominantly Shi'i eastern province of Saudi Arabia. The Saudi crackdown on the Shi'i opposition in the second half of the year culminated in 17 executions and 300 arrests. The opposition's response was to launch a campaign of assassinations against Saudi diplomats abroad: one was killed in Ankara in October, an attempt was made against another in Karachi in December, and a third was assassinated in Bangkok in January 1989.[76] (For more on the opposition activities, see chapter on Saudi Arabia.)

Iran's grip on the Saudi Shi'i opposition had always been tenuous, since Iran had wavered between confrontation and *rapprochement* in its relationship with Saudi Arabia before the Mecca incident. To make its threats against Saudi Arabia more credible it gave much attention to the statements of two new opposition groups. The Hijazi Hizballah and Islamic Jihad issued numerous statements and threats against Saudi Arabia, while professing their absolute fealty to the Imams Khomeyni and Montazeri.[77] Whether they actually existed as anything but creations of Iran was another question. Certainly the statements issued under both these names sought to capitalize on the fearsome reputations of the Lebanese Hizballah and Islamic Jihad.

In recent years, Iran had made considerable inroads among the Shi'is of Pakistan, who numbered nearly 14m. and constituted the largest Shi'i population outside Iran. There the blow of the cease-fire was compounded by the assassination on 5 August of Sayyid 'Arif Husayn al-Husayni, on his return from morning prayer in Peshawar.[78] Husayni, leader of the Movement for the Introduction of Ja'fari (Shi'i) Jurisprudence (*tehrike nifaze fiqhe Ja'fariyya*), had led the protest of Pakistan's Shi'is against subjugation to Sunni law within the framework of Pakistan's Islamization program.[79] A fervent supporter of Iran, he also had been the point man of the anti-Saudi campaign in Pakistan. The Mecca incident, in his words, was an "American intrigue": "The present war is between Islamic Iran and the United States, in which the latter exploits the Saudis."[80] On the day of his assassination he was to have addressed a conference in Lahore on the need to liberate Mecca and Medina from US-Saudi domination.[81] But Iran remained cautious in the support it extended to the Shi'i minority in Pakistan, which constituted a sectarian powder keg.

Iran also went to some pains to assure that it would not be blamed for fanning another Shi'i fire: the Shi'i Azeris of the Soviet Union. The outbreak of Azeri violence against Armenians during the year, over the future of the disputed region of Nagorno-Karabakh, highlighted the survival of Azeri identity. *Glasnost* had made it possible for Azeri Shi'is to observe the rituals of *'Ashura*, which had long been banned. Now portraits of Khomeyni occasionally appeared in Azeri demonstrations in Baku. Iran was careful not to inflame this conflict, although it did seek a measure of influence among coreligionists across the border, through very subtle radio propaganda and the cultural activities of the Iranian consulate in Baku.[82] But Iranian support of Shi'is struggling against the Soviet Union remained confined to Afghanistan (see below).

IRAN'S THREATENED FOOTHOLD IN LEBANON

Nowhere had Iran succeeded in inculcating its message among non-Iranian Shi'is as in Lebanon. The Lebanese Shi'i Hizballah constituted the only mass movement inspired by Iran outside that country's frontiers. Hizballah had reached the dimensions of a serious rival to the long-established Amal movement — a rivalry that spilled over in 1988 into inter-Shi'i bloodshed that had no precedent in the history of Lebanon. The cease-fire in the Gulf, combined with the outbreak of violence and assassinations between Hizballah and the Syrian-backed Amal movement, raised new questions regarding the future of Hizballah in an Arab world no longer under the shadow of Iran's revolution. (What follows is a discussion of developments in Iran's relationship with Hizballah. For Hizballah's role in Lebanese affairs, and especially its confrontation with Amal, see chapter on Lebanon. For Iran's past role in the creation of Lebanon's Hizballah and the movement's growth, see *MECS* 1983–84, pp. 171–73; 1984–85, pp. 155–59; 1986, pp. 139–44; 1987, pp. 165–69.)

There remained a consensus in Iran that Hizballah represented a worthwhile investment. Hizballah had served Iran very well in time of war, and could do so through an uneasy peace. Its capacity for intimidation had no small deterrent value; it was arguably worth a few good divisions. Unlike the other Arab Shi'i movements sponsored by Iran, Hizballah had a territorial foothold, from which Iran could conduct a wide range of activities. Finally, Hizballah gave Iran a say in the Arab-Israeli arena that added to its international and regional weight and partly compensated for Iran's diminished stature in the Gulf. The closer Hizballah operated to the frontier of Israel, the more convincing was Iran's claim to the status of a confrontation state.

Hizballah also needed Iran. The movement's growing penetration of the south led in 1988 to a series of pitched battles with Amal, first in the south, then in the southern suburbs of Beirut. In this contest, Hizballah lost ground in the south, gained ground in Beirut, but faced the prospect of growing Syrian control over its main strongholds. Throughout the trying year of Shi'i civil war, Iran acted firmly in support of Hizballah, intervening with both Syria and Amal at crucial points. Had Iran abandoned Hizballah, the movement might well have been destroyed by its Shi'i adversary, acting in concert with Syria. But Iran sent mission after mission to Damascus and Beirut to assure that Hizballah escaped the full price of its defeats and gained the maximum benefit from its victories.

The cease-fire in the Gulf placed new strains on the relationship. Hizballah lost some of its value to Iran, and Iran suddenly seemed much more remote from Lebanon than when Iranian forces battled Iraq on Iraqi soil. The cease-fire was bound to create a morale problem in Hizballah. Unlike its Shi'i parallels in the Gulf, Hizballah had been created by Iran, and owed its continued existence to Iranian support in everything from finances to mediation with Syria. Few in the movement believed that the movement could establish an Islamic state against the will of neighboring states and other Lebanese communities, unless Iran exercised a wide influence in the region. Hizballah's prospects were therefore tied inextricably to the regional standing of Iran. In July 1986, Husayn al-Musawi, a leading Hizballah ideologue, explained the prerequisites for Islamic government in Lebanon:

> A prerequisite for establishing Islamic government in Beirut is victory over the Zionist regime, and this victory will be achieved through reliance on God. On the other hand, as long as the banners of Islam do not wave over Baghdad and an Islamic government is not established in that land, the establishment of Islamic rule in Lebanon is not likely.[83]

This analysis remained just as sound two years later, when the cease-fire was announced. Hizballah, schooled in obedience to the Imam Khomeyni, endorsed the cease-fire between Iran and Iraq.[84] Yet the Iranian decision still had to be explained to those in Hizballah who sensed a decline in Iran's standing. An article in *al-Muntalaq*, the mouthpiece of the Hizballah-backed Union of Lebanese Muslim Students, put forward two contradictory arguments. The article suggested that even though the cease-fire spelled the end of the war, martyrdom in the path of God constituted a spiritual victory greater than the military setbacks. Had not the Imam Husayn in the seventh century achieved spiritual victory in the midst of defeat and martyrdom? This line of argument asked Hizballah to see victory not as an accumulation of military successes but as an accumulation of suffering, in the old Shi'i tradition. But Hizballah's message had always combined a demand for sacrifice with a promise of victory — in this world, not the next. And so the article's other argument suggested that the cease-fire was really an attempt to buy time and regroup, in accord with the precedents set by the Prophet Muhammad in the first wars of Islam.[85] Despite their professed desire to sacrifice themselves like the Imam Husayn, most in Hizballah really wanted the temporal triumph of the Prophet Muhammad.

There were those in Hizballah who had been indoctrinated over several years with visions of that victory, who still saw the movement's mission in eschatological terms, and who would not lower their expectations. In Hizballah, this faction was led by a number of firebrand *'ulama* of the second rank, including Ibrahim al-Amin and Hasan Nasrallah, and by Hizballah's operational commanders, al-Hajj Husayn al-Khalil, 'Abd al-Hadi Hamada, and 'Imad Mughniyya. These men sought to keep Hizballah in a state of perpetual *jihad* against all those who opposed their vision of an Islamic Lebanon. Their most powerful allies in Iran were Montazeri and Mohtashemipur, and they worked in close cooperation with the Iranian Revolutionary Guards Corps detachment in the Biqa' valley. It was this faction that brought Hizballah into direct conflict with Amal, and that undermined the intensive mediation efforts conducted by the Iranian Foreign Ministry, Ayatollah Ahmad Jannati, and others. They also maintained a firm grip on their foreign hostages by making impossible demands for their release. For this faction, the cease-fire was a crushing blow, and they were appalled by the rumors that followed, to the effect that Iran would order all the hostages released, cut Hizballah's finances, or even drop the movement in return for normalization of relations with the West and Western investment in Iran's own reconstruction.[86]

Yet there were those in Hizballah who were emotionally prepared for the cease-fire. They had concluded some time ago that an Iranian victory was not in the cards, and so favored the insinuation of the movement into the mainstream of Lebanese politics. To them, it was pointless for Hizballah to tilt at windmills by waging a *jihad* against the West when Iran itself had called a truce. They favored releasing the hostages, strengthening ties with Rafsanjani and Khameneh'i, and getting down to the business of building Islam in their own country. Ayatollah Sayyid Muhammad Husayn Fadlallah stood at the forefront of this school, and he was reported to be at the center of a major debate on the "Lebanonization" of Hizballah. Since its inception, Hizballah had rejected the very idea of Lebanon, calling instead for the integration of Lebanon into a greater Islamic state. But as victory evaporated in the Gulf, Fadlallah reportedly urged the movement to seek a foothold in the Lebanese political system, and reach out to political leaders outside the fundamentalist camp.[87] This strategy entailed a new relationship with Iran, one based on an equal partnership rather than Lebanese subservience to Iranian dictates. "We agree with Iran," Fadlallah reiterated during the year, but

> we are not agents of Iran, as the media try to depict us. We do not owe allegiance to Iran in the full sense of the word....We are part of the world Islamic movement, whose solid base is represented by Iran. We have the freedom to have our own views on special Lebanese affairs when speaking to Iranian brothers and others.[88]

On the Iranian side, Rafsanjani was said to favor the idea of partnership, and Fadlallah reportedly enjoyed his confidence.

Fadlallah also supported Rafsanjani's desire to shut down the aggressive "exporters" of revolution in Iran: "The export of the Islamic revolution has been deformed as a result of a number of acts of violence such as kidnapping and explosions, which, it is claimed, have been provoked by Iran." In contrast, Fadlallah believed that "a gentle approach is best."[89] But by the end of the year, Rafsanjani and Fadlallah had not yet had their way, and the future course of the movement remained entangled in Iranian and Lebanese Shi'i rivalries.

Mindful that he could never command the allegiance of the zealots of Hizballah, Rafsanjani encouraged efforts by the Iranian Foreign Ministry to keep channels open to Amal. Iran's past policy had been to build its influence in Amal behind the back of Amal leader Nabih Barri. But following the first Hizballah-Amal battles in February, Barri purged his movement, most importantly by expelling a leading Amal security official, Mustafa al-Dirani, for his Iranian allegiances. On that occasion, Barri denounced Iranian "interference," and informed Iran that all its contacts with his movement had to go through him.[90] To maintain any influence in Amal, the Iranian Foreign Ministry was forced to go directly to Barri. During their mediation missions, Rafsanjani's emissaries met regularly with Barri, and sought a new understanding with the movement's leadership, offering financial support for the movement. Late in the year, the Iranian Foreign Ministry even invited him to visit Iran. Barri postponed the visit, but did not refuse the invitation.[91] Rafsanjani also continued to cultivate the head of the Supreme Islamic Shi'i Council (SISC), Shaykh Muhammad Mahdi Shams al-Din, who visited Tehran for talks on several occasions. Shams al-Din praised what he called the "new stage" in Iranian foreign policy, which had become "objective and realistic," unlike past policies which had "damaged the Islamic trend in Lebanon."[92] All this was met with consternation by the zealots of Hizballah, who saw

Barri as an American agent and completely rejected the authority of Shams al-Din and the SISC. When Shams al-Din visited Montazeri in Qom, he was reportedly accosted by militant Lebanese students studying in religious seminaries there, who beat his bodyguards and called out "Death to Shams al-Din!" Shams al-Din was extricated by some Revolutionary Guards.[93]

According to some reports, Iran reduced the level of its financial support for Hizballah following the Gulf cease-fire. It was impossible to know whether this was indeed the case. The truth seemed to be that Iran had decided to support existing initiatives but avoid new commitments. Iran provided Hizballah's wages and salaries; food and medical aid; pensions for families of martyrs; aid to education; the costs of armed escorts for Hizballah's leaders; support for scouting, charitable associations, and civil defense work; money for military operations; and support for Sunni groups affiliated with Hizballah (such as Shaykh Sa'id Sha'ban's Islamic Unification Movement).[94] The most important project completed during the year was a new hospital near the Beirut airport. The project had been funded by the Beirut branch of Iran's Martyrs' Foundation. In the past, the Martyrs' Foundation had reimbursed government and private hospitals for the medical expenses of Hizballah's fighters and their families, but the cost of these services was so high that it made sense to build a Hizballah-affiliated hospital.[95] The Lebanese branch of the Iranian Reconstruction Jihad was active mostly in the Biqa' valley, where it organized agricultural cooperatives, renovated houses, and built shelters, schools, and water reservoirs.[96]

By the close of the year, Hizballah was a threatened remnant of the decade of zealotry in Iranian foreign policy. In the short term, Iran remained committed to sustaining Hizballah. But the movement's long-term prospects depended upon the imponderables of the internal struggle within Iran and the goodwill of a mistrustful Syria. No longer the vanguard of Islam's strike force against the West and Israel, Hizballah seemed poised to become yet another Lebanese militia, its hands stained more with Shi'i blood than any other.

QADHDHAFI'S ISLAMIC CALL

On the sidelines of the struggle between Iranian and Saudi interpretations of the faith, Mu'ammar al-Qadhdhafi continued to promote his eclectic vision of Islam. That Islam was militantly anti-Western. Yet it differed from the Saudi interpretation in its antinomian bias, and was distinguished from the Iranian interpretation by its anti-clericalism. Qadhdhafi's Islam struck a responsive chord in parts of Black Africa and Southeast Asia, where Libya's missionary enterprise invested its greatest resources. Responsibility for projecting Libyan Islam beyond the country's borders was borne by the Tripoli-based World Islamic Call Society (WICS, *jam'iyyat al-da'wa al-Islamiyya al-'alamiyya*; on the past activities of the WICS, see *MECS* 1981–82, pp. 293–94; 1982–83, p. 245; 1984–85, p. 161; 1986, pp. 146–48; 1987, pp. 161–62).

The WICS achieved its aims first of all through the training and sponsorship of Muslim missionaries. In the 1987–88 academic year, the WICS's missionary college in Tripoli enrolled 142 students; a reunion of graduates in August gathered 228 missionaries from 29 countries.[97] A Damascus branch of the college enrolled 700 students,[98] and operated under the auspices of the mufti of Syria, Shaykh Ahmad Kiftaru, who visited Libya under WICS auspices in August.[99] The WICS also maintained offices in various cities around the world, which identified worthy grantees and administered Libyan funds to Islamic centers and individuals. These offices not only spread the message of Libyan Islam, but also held annual commemorations of the April 1986 US bombing of Libya.[100] The office in Harari, Zimbabwe, was especially active in the affairs of the local Muslim community, and represented perhaps the most important outpost of the WICS in Black Africa.[101] Something of its role could be learned from a testimonial written by a 28-year-old convert to Islam from Zimbabwe. The WICS not only invited him to an Islamic conference in Libya, but also sent him on the pilgrimage to Mecca.[102] Another technique of influence was the traveling medical "caravan," drawing on the precedent established by Christian missionaries in Black Africa. According to the description of one such caravan, doctors worked alongside professional Muslim missionaries, who established contact with local Islamic societies in host countries. At the end of their visits, the caravans donated their equipment and supplies to local hospitals.[103]

Finally, there were the WICS's own conferences. In this year of sectarian tension, the WICS convened a conference on the subject from 11-13 May in Tripoli; its resolutions called on all Muslims to set aside differences of sect and school.[104] The event went unnoticed in the wider Muslim world. The seventh session of the WICS's International Council met in San'a from 29 October-2 November.[105] A WICS-sponsored conference of Libyan-backed Muslim activists met in Malta from 15–20 November to discuss the cultural defense of Islam against the intellectual attacks of Christian missionaries, Orientalists, and Zionists. The gathering resolved to establish a new Center for Study of the Islamic World (*markaz dirasat al-'alam al-Islami*) in Tripoli, which would constitute the academic arm of the WICS.[106] These and the other activities of the WICS enjoyed the continuing financial support of the Libyan regime. Qadhdhafi called for opening up new branches of the WICS, declaring that Libya "will contribute from its state budget to the building and setting up of these branches in the Islamic world."[107] During the year the WICS became an endowed institution, when the profits of a new five-tower office and conference complex in Tripoli were consecrated to its use.[108]

The cooperation between the WICS and Syria indicated that the WICS was meant to do more than spread Islam to Africans or compete with missionary organizations sponsored by other states. Just as the MWL worked to combat alleged Shi'i distortions of Islam, the WICS battled the ideas of the Muslim Brethren, who constituted a domestic threat to Libya and Syria.[109] Qadhdhafi, in his August address to the alumni of the WICS missionary college, declared that the Muslim Brethren and similar movements had "harmed Islam as much as Western Christian colonialism," and were "a discredit to Islam." The Brethren conspired with the US, which financed the Brethren to fight other Muslims; it was a "satanic and Zionist group." Had the Muslim Brethren in Syria turned their "crimes" into a *jihad* against Israel, "the Golan would probably be free. But they did not fire a single bullet in the direction of the Golan or Palestine. They blew up houses, bridges, and factories; they killed [Syrian] military cadets [in Aleppo in 1979]; they killed military commanders."[110] In another tirade against the Muslim Brethren (and the Islamic Liberation Party), Qadhdhafi declared that the name of the Muslim Brethren was synonymous with "agents of America....An American officer in the American intelligence was the leader of the Libyan Muslim Brethren. What was their outcome? We slaughter them like sheep and goats without regret."[111] Islam as propagated by the WICS on behalf of Libya and Syria represented the militant Arab nationalist response to the challenge of the Muslim Brethren, continuing (yet distorting) the tradition of Nasir's Egypt that Qadhdhafi held so dear. The offensive of the WICS served as a reminder that while the threat of transnational Shi'ism receded, the challenge of transnational Sunni militancy remained.

THE TRANSNATIONAL MUSLIM BRETHREN

Despite the long-standing presence of the Muslim Brethren in most countries of the Middle East, little was known about the network that linked them together. In some countries, the Muslim Brethren operated openly; in others, they functioned clandestinely. To protect those who did operate secretly, the visible Muslim Brethren rarely spoke about the support they offered to their covert colleagues, and the subject became one of much speculation.

Certainly the Muslim Brethren had a sense that they belonged to a worldwide movement. When the Palestinian Muslim Brethren in Gaza published their "covenant" in August, its second article declared it "a branch of the branches of the Muslim Brethren in Palestine. The Muslim Brethren movement is an international organization [*tanzim 'alami*], and is the largest of the Islamic movements of modern times."[112] There clearly existed a network of informal ties between the leaders of these branches, maintained at conferences held around the Muslim world (see *MECS* 1983–84, p. 174; 1986, p. 146; 1987, pp. 160–61). The February conference on Islamic unity that met in Islamabad (see above) served just this purpose. But the question remained: Were the Muslim Brethren organized on a more formal basis?

New evidence that such a framework might exist appeared in a rare interview given by 'Adnan Sa'd al-Din, who had been the leader of the Syrian Muslim Brethren at the time of the uprising against the Syrian regime in Hamah in 1982 (see *MECS* 1981–82, pp. 847–55). In the interview, Sa'd al-Din revealed that the Muslim Brethren were governed loosely by a higher "command" (*qiyada*) or "council" (*shura*) of the "international organization" (*tanzim 'alami*), whose members "would not want me to mention their names." Asked why so much secrecy surrounded the higher command, Sa'd al-Din replied that "the Brethren movement has always been persecuted in Arab lands....The Brethren do not believe in secret action, which they completely reject, but the movement unfortunately is sometimes forced to resort to secret action, not by choice."[113]

Sa'd al-Din, long a leading figure in the world of Muslim Brethren activism, made this claim because of his differences with the higher command, which no longer recognized him as leader of the Syrian Brethren.[114] But the Egyptian general guide of the Muslim Brethren, Muhammad Hamid Abu al-Nasr, continued to maintain that "there is no official organization, but rather a harmony of feelings and agreement on serving the Islamic idea. It is simply a spiritual bond that links the activities in the Arab and Islamic states in the service of Islam and of the Arabs."[115] Yet it seemed probable that the informal relationships between the parts of the movement were undergoing a process of institutionalization.

ISLAM FOR AFGHANISTAN AND PALESTINE

While the war within Islam came to a merciful halt during the year, the *jihad* against non-Muslim occupiers made significant gains on two fronts and excited the imagination of Muslim activists. In Afghanistan, a Muslim resistance registered a victory in compelling the Soviet Union to cut losses and withdraw its forces from what had become a deadly adventure. The victory of the Afghan *mujahidun* against a world power revalidated fundamentalist conviction in the wider Muslim world, especially among Sunnis. In the West Bank and Gaza, the uprising against Israel partially employed the rhetoric of a Muslim struggle against a non-Muslim oppressor. Muslim observers who were inclined to do so tagged the uprising an Islamic *intifada*, and cited the resort to an Islamic interpretation of the conflict by young activists in Muslim movements outside the control of the PLO. While the debate in Iran raised questions about the value of Islam as the foundation of the state, there could be no doubt about the continuing power of Islam to mobilize masses against non-Muslims perceived as occupiers and oppressors.

THE AFGHAN *JIHAD* AND THE MUSLIM WORLD

Saudi Arabia made the heaviest material and political investment of all the Middle Eastern parties interested in the Afghan war. The Saudis hoped to mold the Islam of the Afghan resistance in their own image, through education and financial support. The MWL had an office in Peshawar, Pakistan, the logistical base of the Sunni Afghan resistance. This office opened 150 Qur'an study centers in Afghan refugee camps, and 85 Islamic schools inside Afghanistan itself.[116] This complemented the humanitarian aid offered by Saudi Arabia to the Pakistan-based Afghan resistance, which totaled SR445m. at the start of 1988.[117] Relief aid and education constituted the overt dimension of Saudi involvement in the war waged by the Sunni *mujahidun* against the Soviet-backed regime in Kabul, but many other Saudi agencies were involved in the Afghan arena. There were also several hundred Arab volunteers in the ranks of the Afghan *mujahidun*. Most of these were Egyptians, Sudanese, and Saudis, sent by branches of the Muslim Brethren. In Afghanistan they tended to join the *Ittihade Islami* of the Saudi-backed 'Abd Rabb Rasul Sayyaf, or the *Hizbe Islami* of Gulbuddin Hikmatyar.[118] Saudi Arabia's presence in the refugee camps and its financial support for the armed struggle were intended to win the Saudis influence over a new Afghan regime whenever it emerged.

In the field of diplomacy, the Saudis also employed Muslim clients to mediate between the Soviet Union and the *mujahidun*. At one point this role was played by Ma'ruf al-Duwalibi, Saudi protégé and international Muslim activist, who met with leading Soviet officials. In Moscow, he proposed solutions undoubtedly coordinated with Saudi Arabia, and declared himself "satisfied with the way [the Soviets] both listened and talked to us."[119]

This was all the more important given Iran's support of the Shi'i component of the Afghan resistance. Iran's setback in the Gulf did not diminish its interest in the creation of a friendly successor regime in Afghanistan, and in a solution for the 1.5m. Afghan refugees in Iran. Iran invested much in the support and training of the eight Afghan factions based in Iran, most of which were Shi'i in composition. One of the most important of these groups, *Nasr,* best expressed the antagonistic position of the

Iran-based resistance toward the US-Soviet Geneva accords for Soviet withdrawal: "Despite commotion over peace, reconciliation, and coalition rule, the armed struggle will continue."[120] A spokesman for *Nasr* warned the Soviet Union that "the heroic people of Afghanistan will never compromise and are determined to establish an Islamic republic in Afghanistan."[121]

But unlike the Shi'is of Lebanon or Iraq, the Afghan Shi'is were in a clear minority, and Iran therefore sought a dialogue with the Peshawar-based Sunni resistance. This had been impossible so long as the rival coalitions were mobilized in the Mecca controversy. At the height of the controversy, the Peshawar-based groups supported by Saudi Arabia conducted a campaign to discredit the Iran-based coalition, declaring that its leader, Sayyid Husayn 'Alemi, was born not in Afghanistan but in Iranian Khorasan.[122] But as memories of Mecca receded, Iran opened a dialogue with the Peshawar-based Burhanuddin Rabbani, the leader of the *Jami'ate Islami*, which had large numbers of resistance fighters in Herat and the north. During a visit to Iran, he allegedly promised Iran that Afghan Shi'is would receive a fair share in the distribution of power in a new coalition, in return for Iranian assistance to the Peshawar-based groups.[123] Saudi Arabia may not have been pleased by the opening of the dialogue, and pro-Saudi sources claimed that Rabbani returned empty-handed.[124] Later (in 1989) it would become clear that the initiative failed, when the provisional government elected by the *shura* of the Peshawar-based groups did not include the Iran-based resistance. (For other aspects of these issues, see chapter on the Soviet withdrawal from Afghanistan).

CLAIMING THE ISLAMIC *INTIFADA*

Nothing so electrified the world of Islamic activism as the role played by Islam in the Palestinian *intifada.* The hegemony within Palestinian nationalism of the PLO and the left had created the impression that the resurgence of Islam passed over Palestine. Yet the events of the *intifada* revealed the depth of an Islamic current that ran beneath Palestinian nationalism, sometimes complementing and sometimes contradicting the strategies of the PLO. (For the role of Islam in the *intifada*, see chapter on the West Bank and Gaza Strip.)[125]

As the role of Islam received more attention, the various outside contestants to Islamic primacy sought to exercise influence over this emerging Islamic movement, and claim it as their own. The strongest claim belonged to the Muslim Brethren, who had a long history of activism in the West Bank and Gaza.[126] There the movement sometimes went under the name of the Islamic Resistance Movement (*harakat al-muqawama al-Islamiyya*; widely known by its acronym, Hamas). PLO chairman Yasir 'Arafat recognized the importance of the Muslim Brethren when he visited the general guide of the Egyptian Muslim Brethren, Muhammad Hamid Abu al-Nasr, in November. He was rewarded with a statement by Abu al-Nasr that endorsed the declaration of Palestinian independence made at the Algiers Palestine National Council (PNC). But the statement also affirmed the Palestinian right to establish its state and government over all the land of Palestine. While endorsing the PLO's readiness to enter an international conference on the basis of UN Resolutions 181, 242, and 338, Abu al-Nasr declared that the UN never had the right to alienate so much as a grain of Palestinian soil to the "Zionist entity."[127] In this respect, the Muslim Brethren movement generally adopted the line followed by Hamas: limited endorsement of the PLO's diplomatic tactics, combined with a principled rejection of a two-state solution. (In its own communication to the Algiers PNC, Hamas had reiterated the religious obligation to liberate all Palestine, while agreeing to the establishment of a Palestinian state on any part of Palestine that might be liberated.)[128]

Saudi Arabia also exercised some indirect influence through the Muslim Brethren, but it preferred to open its own channels to the Palestinian Islamic establishment. It did so through the MWL, which had forged ties with the Islamic establishment in Jerusalem even before the *intifada*. The mufti of Jerusalem and head of the Supreme Muslim Council, Shaykh Sa'd al-Din al-'Alami, was a member of the MWL's Supreme World Council of Mosques, and met with MWL secretary-general 'Abdallah 'Umar Nasif during a visit to Mecca in April.[129] Israeli sources noted the influx of considerable sums of MWL money, not only to the West Bank and East Jerusalem, but to Muslim religious institutions in Israel itself. A Saudi opposition source even claimed that Nasif planned to visit the West Bank,[130] but the visit did not take place. The Islamic aspect of the *intifada* also prompted persons in the Saudi religious establishment to call for the Islamization of the Palestinian struggle against Israel. According to Nasif and Shaykh 'Abd al-'Aziz Ibn Baz, mufti of the kingdom, the Palestinian shift from an ideology of liberation to one of *jihad* constituted the secret of the *intifada*'s success. Islam, not Arabism, offered the firm base upon which to build the struggle for Palestine.[131] By these declarations, the Saudi religious establishment clearly wished to gain some influence over the emerging Palestinian Islamic movement. But by its ties with the established 'Alami, the MWL indicated the usual Saudi preference for a conservative and institutionalized brand of Islam. 'Alami, however, had no intention of limiting his contacts to Saudi Arabia. In June, he paid his first visit to Tripoli, Libya, where he thanked Libya's WICS for its "generous support."[132]

Iran also claimed a corner of the *intifada*, for having inspired the Palestinian Islamic Jihad. This small group, which thrived principally in Gaza, viewed Khomeyni as the harbinger of the *jihad* for the liberation of Palestine. Its spiritual leader, Shaykh 'Abd al-'Aziz 'Uda, was deported in April to Lebanon. He then gave a news conference at the Iranian embassy in Beirut, where he declared that "the Islamic victory in Iran restored trust and faith to the souls of Muslims, and played a role in driving the Islamic revival forward...the *intifada* is an echo of the victories of the Muslims in Lebanon and Iran."[133] Once the leaders of the movement arrived in Lebanon, they came under the wing of Hizballah. When Hizballah convened the First World Conference in Support of the Islamic *Intifada* in Occupied Palestine, from 20–21 December in Beirut, the event was attended by another expelled leader of the Palestinian Islamic Jihad, Shaykh Ahmad Muhanna. Also in attendance were Abu Musa and Ahmad Jibril, the ubiquitous Shaykh Sa'id Sha'ban, Hizballah spokesman Sayyid Ibrahim al-Amin, Montazeri's Beirut representative Shaykh Muhammad Isma'il Khaliq, and Hizballah clerics Shaykh Na'im Qasim and Shaykh Hasan Tarad.[134] Iran and Hizballah made much of the Islamic aspect of the *intifada*, claiming that the West had sought to conceal this face of the uprising. But Iran had hardly any contact with the Islamic forces inside Palestine, and spokesmen of the Muslim Brethren-affiliated Hamas were at pains to distance themselves from Iran.

The Gulf cease-fire, the "Islamic *intifada*," and the Soviet withdrawal from Afghanistan were interpreted in many fundamentalist publications as evidence for the end of internal strife and the impending triumph of Islam over its perceived enemies.

But by the end of the year, Muslims had become preoccupied not by invading armies or foreign armadas, but by a book: Salman Rushdie's novel, *The Satanic Verses*. The first Muslim condemnations of the book appeared in the latter half of 1988,[135] although the storm did not break until 1989. (The causes and effects of the Rushdie affair will be assessed in *MECS* 1989.) Like the perceived desecration of Mecca in 1987, the perceived defamation of the Prophet Muhammad in Rushdie's book did even more than Afghanistan or Palestine to stir the Muslim world — and divide it once again.

NOTES

For the place and frequency of publications cited here, and for the full names of the publication, news agency, radio station, or monitoring service where an abbreviation is used, please see "List of Sources." Only in the case of more than one publication bearing the same name is the place of publication noted here. The publication *al-'Alam* cited here is the London weekly.

1. See also Martin Kramer, "Tragedy in Mecca," *Orbis: A Journal of World Affairs*, Vol. 32, No. 2 (Spring 1988), pp. 231–47; *idem*, "La Mecque: la controverse du pèlerinage," *Maghreb-Machrek*, No. 122 (October-November-December 1988), pp. 38–52; and the (pro-Saudi) summary of the events of each pilgrimage in *al-Siyasa*, Kuwait, 26 May 1988.
2. This account relies on *al-'Alam*, 27 February; IRNA, 19 February — DR, 19 February; *KI*, 20 February 1988.
3. Text of Fahd's message, *al-Sharq al-Awsat*, 17 February 1988.
4. Criticisms of the conference by Kalim Siddiqui, *Crescent International*, 16-31 May 1988.
5. E.g., *al-Thawra al-Islamiyya*, April 1988.
6. Khameneh'i's speech, *Kayhan al-'Arabi*, 2 February; IRNA, 1 February — DR, 2 February; Rafsanjani's speech, IRNA, 4 February — DR, 5 February; report of conference, *Kayhan al-'Arabi*, 4, 6 February; *KI*, 6 February; interviews with some conference participants, *Kayhan al-'Arabi*, 27 February 1988.
7. Some of these are described in *Kayhan al-'Arabi*, 16 July 1988. For an exhaustive catalogue of participants in various Islamic conferences sponsored by Iran during 1988, see Xavier Raufer (ed.), "Iran Islamique: L'Appareil mondial," *Notes et Etudes de l'Institut de Criminologie de Paris*, No. 9, March 1989.
8. Two books have recently appeared on the MWL. See Reinhard Schulze, *Islamischer Internationalismus im 20. Jahrhundert. Untersuchungen zur Geschichte der Islamischen Weltliga (Mekka)* (Leiden: Brill, 1988); and R. M. Sharipova, *Panislamizm syegodnya. Idyeologiya i praktika Ligi Islamskogo Mira* (Moscow: Nauka Press, 1986).
9. See chapters on Egypt in *MECS* 1987 and this volume; new details from MENA, 15 June — DR, 16 June; interview with "official spokesman" of the group, *al-Thawra al-Islamiyya*, August 1988.
10. For the first eight conferences of the Academy, see J. Jomier, "Les congrès de l'Académie des Recherches Islamiques dépendant de l'Azhar," *Mélanges de l'Institut Dominicain des Études Orientales du Caire*, Vol. 14 (1980), pp. 95–148. The ninth conference is described in *MECS* 1982–83, p. 248. I omitted an account in *MECS* of the tenth conference, which met in Cairo from 1–7 November 1985.
11. Mubarak's speech, R. Cairo, 5 March — DR, 8 March 1988.
12. Text of resolutions, *Majallat al-Azhar*, April; *Akhbar al-'Alam al-Islami*, 14 March 1988; special annex to *al-Tadamun al-Islami*, Ramadan 1408.
13. Text of his paper, *al-Fikr al-Islami*, April 1988.
14. Text of constitution, *Majallat al-Azhar*, October-November 1988.
15. A brief account of the ICO's structure, organization, and subsidiary bodies is provided by *al-Dustur*, Amman, 9 March 1988.
16. *JT*, 22 March 1988.
17. Reports on summit initiative, *al-Jumhuriyya*, Cairo, 2 February (citing *al-Ra'y al-'Amm*); *Iqra*, 11 February 1988.

18. R. Amman, 22 March — DR, 23 March 1988.
19. Amman TV, 21 March — DR, 23 March 1988.
20. Sa'ud al-Faysal's speech, SPA, 23 March — DR, 25 March 1988.
21. Text of speech by Iranian representative, *Kayhan al-'Arabi,* 9 April 1988.
22. AFP, 24 March — DR, 24 March 1988.
23. Final resolutions, *al-Dustur,* Amman, 26 March 1988.
24. Syrian Foreign Minister Faruq al-Shar', quoted by R. Damascus, 25 March — DR, 29 March 1988.
25. *ME,* August 1988.
26. *Al-Da'wa al-Islamiyya,* 8 June 1988.
27. Sa'ud al-Faysal's speech, SPA, 23 March — DR, 25 March 1988.
28. *Al-Da'wa al-Islamiyya,* 20 January 1988.
29. Biographical details provided by Hanspeter Mattes, "Hamid Algabid," *Orient,* Vol. 29, No. 3 (September 1988), pp. 337–39.
30. *ME,* December 1988.
31. *JT,* 22 March 1988.
32. Donations acknowledged in conference resolutions, *al-Dustur,* Amman, 26 March 1988.
33. "Responsible source" in Saudi Ministry of Pilgrimage Affairs and Religious Endowments, R. Riyadh, 29 February — DR, 1 March 1988.
34. Comment by Na'if, SPA, 12 April — DR, 13 April 1988.
35. R. Tehran, 11 April — DR, 12 April; *FT, IHT,* 12 April 1988.
36. Interview with Na'if, *al-Siyasa,* Kuwait, 2 May; accounts of the meetings in interview with head of Iranian delegation, R. Tehran, 19 April — DR, 20 April; in round table devoted to subject, Tehran TV, 16 June — DR, 21 June; Saudi version in SPA, 19 April — DR, 20 April; interview with Na'if, *al-Siyasa,* Kuwait, 2 May 1988.
37. Tehran TV, 16 June — DR, 21 June 1988.
38. Severing of relations analyzed in *Kayhan al-'Arabi,* 30 April; *al-Thawra al-Islamiyya,* June 1988.
39. Saudi Council of Ministers' statement, SPA, 28 June — DR, 30 June 1988.
40. Mehdi Karrubi, Tehran TV, 16 June — DR, 21 June 1988.
41. Message of Khomeyni on occasion of the Mecca "massacre" and Iran's acceptance of UN Resolution 598, R. Tehran, 20 July — DR, 21 July; *Kayhan al-'Arabi,* 23 July (special issue); *al-Hilal al-Duwali,* 16–31 August 1988. Abu Sufyan was a member of the Prophet Muhammad's tribe who had originally opposed Muhammad; his son, Yazid, was responsible for the killing of the Imam Husayn; and another son, Mu'awiya, founded the Umayyad dynasty. The family and the dynasty are deemed usurpers in the Shi'i reading of early Islamic history.
42. *Al-Siyasa,* Kuwait, 18 June; *ST,* 17 July 1988.
43. R. Tehran in Turkish, 5 May — DR, 11 May 1988.
44. R. Tehran in Arabic, 23 July — DR, 26 July 1988.
45. *Al-Yawm,* 22 July 1988.
46. IRNA, 29 August — DR, 31 August 1988.
47. IRNA, 22 May — DR, 25 May; Saudi security measures detailed in *al-'Alam,* 6 August 1988.
48. On the drop in Lebanese visas, see *Kayhan al-'Arabi,* 14 July; IRNA, 29 June — DR, 30 June; demonstrations by Lebanese Shi'is against the cut, *Kayhan al-'Arabi,* 16 July 1988.
49. SPA, 25 July — DR, 25 July 1988.
50. *FR,* 26 January 1989.
51. *Kayhan,* Tehran, *Ettela'at,* 7 June 1988.
52. Text of letter, *Kayhan,* London, 6 October; discussed in *Le Monde,* 8 October 1988. The authenticity of the letter cannot be guaranteed.
53. For this evidence, see *ST,* 17 April; *ME,* May 1988.
54. *Al-Qabas,* 12 April 1988.
55. Rafsanjani's sermon, R. Tehran, 19 August — DR, 22 August 1988.
56. Fouad Ajami, "Iran: The Impossible Revolution," *Foreign Affairs,* Vol. 67, No. 2 (Winter 1988–89), p. 136.

57. Interview with Sha'ban, *Kayhan al-'Arabi*, 30 July 1988. The specific instance he refers to is that of the Tunisian Islamic movement.
58. Text of Fahd speech, *al-Fikr al-Islami*, November 1988.
59. Text of final statement, SPA, 12 October — DR, 19 October; *al-Fikr al-Islami*, November 1988.
60. King Fahd's speech, *al-Fikr al-Islami*, November 1988.
61. R. Tehran, 13 October — DR, 14 October 1988.
62. Saudi Shi'i opposition sources also took issue with Fahd; see *al-Thawra al-Islamiyya*, November 1988.
63. SPA, 20 October — DR, 24 October 1988.
64. IRNA, 23 October — DR, 24 October 1988.
65. IRNA, 25 October — DR, 26 October; *Kayhan al-'Arabi*, 26 October 1988.
66. Khameneh'i's sermon, R. Tehran, 28 October — DR, 31 October 1988.
67. Rafsanjani's prayer sermon, R. Tehran, 19 August — DR, 22 August 1988.
68. Text of SAIRI statement, *Kayhan al-'Arabi*, 23 July 1988.
69. *Al-Thawra al-Islamiyya*, October 1988.
70. Interview in *al-Thawra al-Islamiyya*, August 1988.
71. *KI*, 19 November; text of Baqir al-Hakim's interview, *Kayhan al-'Arabi*, 24 November 1988.
72. Report on negotiations for a "covenant of joint action," *al-Thawra al-Islamiyya*, December 1988.
73. Interview with Baqir al-Hakim, *Kayhan al-'Arabi*, 26 November1988.
74. Obituary of Mahdi al-Hakim, *KI*, 6 February; comments by various opposition figures on his work, *Kayhan al-'Arabi*, 12 March 1988.
75. *Al-Thawra al-Islamiyya*, September 1988.
76. *FR*, 12 January 1989.
77. Texts of statements by Hizballah of Hijaz, 23 June — DR, 24 June; 5 September — DR, 7 September; AFP, 5 October — DR, 6 October; statement by Islamic Jihad of the Hijaz, *Kayhan al-'Arabi*, 18 July 1988.
78. Obituary, *KI*, 13 August; various Shi'i statements on assassination, *Kayhan al-'Arabi*, 13 August 1988.
79. See Munir Ahmed, "The Shi'is of Pakistan," in Martin Kramer (ed.), *Shi'ism, Resistance, and Revolution* (Boulder: Westview Press, 1987), pp. 282–84.
80. Maleeha Lodhi, "Pakistan's Shia movement: an interview with Arif Hussaini," *Third World Quarterly*, Vol. 10, No. 2 (April 1988), pp. 806–17.
81. R. Tehran, 21 July — DR, 22 July; *KI*, 13 August 1988.
82. *FR*, 19 January 1989.
83. Interview with Husayn al-Musawi, *Kayhan*, Tehran, 27 July 1986.
84. Text of Hizballah statement on Iran's acceptance of UN Resolution 598, *al-Nahar*, Beirut, 22 July 1988.
85. *Al-Muntalaq*, September 1988.
86. See, for example, the report on the supposed disbanding of Islamic Jihad, *al-Shira'*, 8 August; the reported cut in funds to Hizballah from $11m. to $1m. a month, *al-Shira'*, 19 September 1988.
87. *Al-Shira'*, 19 September 1988.
88. Interview with Fadlallah, R. Monte Carlo, 13 May — DR, 20 May 1988.
89. Interview with Fadlallah, *Cumhuriyet*, 19 August — DR, 25 August 1988.
90. AFP, 18 March — DR, 21 March; discussion of Dirani's defection, *JP*, 2 March 1988.
91. *Al-Shira'*, 5 December; see also Voice of Free Lebanon, 31 August — DR, 31 August 1988.
92. Interview with Shams al-Din, *Amal*, 2 December 1988.
93. *Al-Shira'*, 26 December 1988.
94. These categories, which appear to be accurate, are listed by *al-Tadamun*, 19 March — DR, 25 March 1988. The figures given for each category total about $16m. a month (not including emergency reserve funds). Israeli officials placed Iran's investment in Hizballah at about $100m. a year, and noted that Western diplomatic sources estimated the support at even higher levels; see interview with Uri Lubrani, *Ha'aretz*, 3 June 1988.

95. Inauguration of hospital, *al-Nahar*, Beirut, 31 October; hospital described, *al-'Alam*, 19 November 1988.
96. Description of activities, *al-'Ahd*, 18 November 1988.
97. *Al-Da'wa al-Islamiyya*, 17 August 1988.
98. *Al-Da'wa al-Islamiyya*, 8 June 1988.
99. *Al-Da'wa al-Islamiyya*, 31 August 1988.
100. *Al-Da'wa al-Islamiyya*, 27 April 1988.
101. On the assistance to Muslim institutions in Zimbabwe, see *al-Da'wa al-Islamiyya*, 11 May 1988.
102. *Al-Da'wa al-Islamiyya*, 6 January 1988.
103. Description of a caravan in Botswana, *al-Da'wa al-Islamiyya*, 6 January 1988.
104. Resolutions of conference, *al-Da'wa al-Islamiyya*, 25 May 1988.
105. Details on meeting, *al-Fikr al-Islami*, December; *al-Da'wa al-Islamiyya*, 9 November 1988.
106. Report on conference, *al-'Alam*, 10 December 1988.
107. Qadhdhafi's speech, Tripoli TV, 21 August — DR, 23 August 1988.
108. Description of complex, *al-Da'wa al-Islamiyya*, 14 September1988.
109. On this opposition, see George Joffee, "Islamic Opposition in Libya," *Third World Quarterly*, Vol. 10, No. 2 (April 1988), pp. 615–31.
110. Text of Qadhdhafi's speech, Tripoli TV, 21 August — DR, 23 August; *al-Da'wa al-Islamiyya*, 31 August 1988.
111. Qadhdhafi speech to teachers, Tripoli TV, 28 January — DR, 30 January 1988.
112. *Mithaq Harakat al-Muqawama al-Islamiyya — Filastin*, pamphlet dated 18 August 1988.
113. *Al-Watan al-'Arabi*, 3 June 1988. On Sa'd al-Din, see Thomas Mayer, "The Islamic Opposition in Syria, 1961–1982," *Orient*, Vol. 24, No. 4 (December 1983), pp. 589–609.
114. The revelations came in the context of an internal struggle among the Syrian Muslim Brethren. Since Hamah, the Syrian Brethren had split into several factions, and their leadership had become a hotly contested issue. Sa'd al-Din led a faction based in Iraq, which called for the continuation of armed struggle against the Syrian regime. Shaykh 'Abd al-Fattah Abu Ghudda led another faction based in Saudi Arabia, whose representatives had met with agents of the Syrian regime to seek some compromise. Both leaders claimed the title of general supervisor (*muraqib 'amm*) of the Syrian Brethren. Sa'd al-Din complained that the higher command, seeing the division in the ranks of the Syrian Brethren, had intervened in the affairs of the Syrian branch to declare Abu Ghudda the general supervisor. This intervention, said Sa'd al-Din, was illegal according to the constitution of the Syrian Brethren, and he continued to claim the title of general supervisor. For a summary of the divisions among the Syrian Brethren, see *ME*, April; on Abu Ghudda's latest negotiations with the regime, see *al-Muharrir*, 16 January 1988.
115. Hamid Abu al-Nasr's interview, *al-Sharq al-Awsat*, 11 January — DR, 15 January 1988.
116. *Akhbar al-'Alam al-Islami*, 21 March 1988.
117. *Akhbar al-'Alam al-Islami*, 18 January; discussion of the various Islamic aid agencies working among Afghan refugees, *al-Da'wa*, 4 January 1988.
118. Discussion of the Arabs in the resistance, AFP, 21 February — DR, 23 February; *al-Jihad*, Peshawar, May 1988.
119. Interview with Ma'ruf al-Duwalibi, *al-Sharq al-Awsat*, 5 January — DR, 13 January 1988.
120. Declaration by *Nasr*, R. Tehran, 24 June — DR, 24 June 1988.
121. Quoted by IRNA, 30 January — DR, 2 February 1988.
122. *Al-Dustur*, London, 25 January 1988.
123. *FR*, 5 January 1989.
124. *Al-Majalla*, 14 June 1988.
125. See also Jean-François Legrain, "Les islamistes palestiniens à l'épreuve du soulèvement," *Maghreb-Machrek*, No. 121 (July-August-September 1988), pp. 5–42.
126. On this movement, see Mohammed K. Shadid, "The Muslim Brotherhood Movement in the West Bank and Gaza," *Third World Quarterly*, Vol. 10, No. 2 (April 1988), pp. 658–82.
127. Text of statement, *al-Ghuraba*, Leeds, December 1988.
128. Text in *al-Ghuraba*, December 1988.
129. Reported in *Akhbar al-'Alam al-Islami*, 18 April 1988.
130. *Al-Thawra al-Islamiyya*, January 1988.

131. *Akhbar al-'Alam al-Islami*, 5 January 1989.
132. *Al-Da'wa al-Islamiyya*, 6 July 1988.
133. *Kayhan al-'Arabi*, 16 April; *al-Thawra al-Islamiyya*, May 1988.
134. Account of conference, *al-'Alam*, 7 January 1989.
135. See *Impact International*, 28 October-10 November (cover story); *al-Ghuraba*, November 1988.

The Iraqi-Iranian War

GIDEON GERA

After almost eight years of fighting, a cease-fire between Iran and Iraq went into effect at midnight, 20 August 1988. By the end of the year it had still held, although the settlement of the conflict seemed distant. A month earlier, facing possible military collapse, Iran suddenly accepted UN Security Council Resolution 598 (which stipulated an initial cease-fire) after having practically rejected it for a year (see *MECS* 1987, pp. 190–91). Earlier in the year, Iraq embarked on an offensive strategy, aggressively employing all available means to compel the Iranians to desist: striking massively at Iranian cities, using chemical weapons on a large scale, and engaging its elite formations in a series of attacks that dislodged the Iranians from its territory. Western involvement in safeguarding shipping in the Gulf continued until after the cease-fire.

THE LAST STAGES OF THE WAR

THE IRANIAN OFFENSIVE IN KURDISTAN

The much-promised Iranian grand offensive in the southern sector did not materialize in early 1988, probably because the Iranians assessed their chances of achieving a breakthrough there as very slim (see *MECS* 1987, pp. 181, 193).[1] Instead, the offensive, codenamed "*Val Fajr* (Spring) 10," was carried out unexpectedly in Sulaymaniyya province, northeastern Kurdistan. This option had been gradually prepared by the occupation of Mawat, which secured a foothold on the road to Sulaymaniyya from the north. Early in 1988, the Iraqis were pushed westward from Khormal on the border by stepped-up irregular actions by Islamic Revolutionary Guard Corps (IRGC) and Kurds.[2]

The main Iranian operation began with a combined arms assault[3] on 15 March 1988, which carried the attackers across mountains and winter torrents into the plain of Halabja, a regional town which they occupied on 16 March, and southward toward the Darbandikhan reservoir and dam. The Iranians failed to reach the dam on the southern shore of the lake (they claimed to have advanced up to 8 km. from it); their efforts on the road north to it petered out, as did irregular operations connected with the offensive (incuding one against Panjwin, 40 km. north of Halabja).[4] The Iranians were stopped not least by repeated Iraqi use of poison gas. The first and and most notorious of these chemical attacks was against Halabja, in which c. 5,000 Kurdish civilians perished and 7,000 were injured (see chapter on Iraq).[5] The Iraqis, for their part, accused Iran of having used cyanic gas at Halabja, an accusation which the Iranians vehemently rejected, but which US sources took up, at least once (see below).[6] Later, smaller scale Iranian attacks from the direction of Mawat (northeast of Sulaymaniyya) had no effect.[7] However, the Iranians held on to the region of Halabja until their general retreat in July 1988.

The proclaimed objective of *Val Fajr* 10 was "to destroy the enemy's war machine and to *liberate* another Kurdish inhabited area of Sulaymaniyya province."[8] Indeed, as Speaker of the Majlis Rafsanjani noted, for the first time tens of thousands of Iraqis, mainly Kurds, had come under Iranian control and 1,000 sq. km. were occupied.[9] A further aim, according to Rafsanjani, was to disprove that Iran could no longer muster manpower for an attack.[10] But a more tangible objective of strategic importance was the Darbandikhan dam, which was supplying c. 250 megawatts to Baghdad and much of the electricity used in northeastern Iraq.[11] But again the Iranian offensive, the last in the war, was a failure. As in previous instances, the Iranians succeeded in the initial phases only; they did not attain their strategic objective, neither were they able to turn their gains into strategic achievements (cf. *MECS* 1987, p. 181).[12] Furthermore, they caused great suffering to their Kurdish allies.

The Iraqi objective was to contain the Iranians near the border in order to deny them any strategic gain, such as control of the dam or the approaches to Sulaymaniyya. The Iraqis considered the Halabja region by itself as devoid of strategic importance.[13] After initial confusion, during which some of their units were routed, they devised their tactics probably on the basis of two main considerations: reluctance to reinforce the defense with elite formations (habitually kept as general reserves), which were in the midst of preparations for their imminent offensive (see below),[14] and implacability in face of Kurdish "shameful services for Iran," which facilitated the occupation of Halabja. This may explain their brazen and repeated use of poison gas.[15] Indeed Iraqi Minister of Defense ʻAdnan Khayrallah declared during a visit to battle headquarters at the height of fighting that "Iran's insistence on destruction compels us to reply to war with war, using *all* available means to defend our country and people."[16]

The Iraqi summing up of the battle reflected these tactics: "A successful defensive battle by the standard of a protracted war...[it] absorbed the momentum of [the attackers'] thrust and destroyed...the agents who acquiesced to disgrace."[17]

THE WAR OF CITIES — ROUND FOUR

The fourth round of "the war of cities" began with a 27 February raid on a refinery near Tehran. It was to be different from previous rounds: for the first time Iraq was able to retaliate in kind for Iranian missile strikes against Baghdad, as they had accumulated a stock of their recently developed al-Husayn missile (probably an improved-range and reduced payload *Scud*-B missile, with a claimed range of 650 km.) with which they had already threatened Iran in November 1987 (cf. *MECS* 1987, p. 184). When the Iranians, disregarding or disbelieving another warning, launched two or three missiles on Baghdad on 29 February, the Iraqis responded by launching twice that number on Tehran the same day. The exchange of missiles continued with a few lulls until 20 April, when Iraq stopped after the Iranians had acquiesced to certain conditions posed by Baghdad such as firing the last round. The Iranians aimed their missiles mainly at Baghdad, the Iraqis at Tehran as the prime target, but also at Qom ("the center of Khomeyniite falsehood and charlatanism")[18] and at Isfahan. Altogether, the Iraqis had launched 189 missiles, according to their announcements; the Iranians published no numbers, but probably launched no more than 60.[19]

No reliable assessment of the effect on Baghdad, which suffered many casualties, has been available. However, that city was more accustomed to missile attacks than the at least 7m. inhabitants of Tehran, on whom the impact of almost daily hits was probably severe, as it was on their fellows in other Iranian cities that were struck. For the first time in eight years, the war was brought home to Iranian city dwellers (a few earlier air raids excepted). Many (estimates varied between tens of thousands to more than 1m.) fled the capital. More than a thousand civilians were killed and thousands injured.[20] The Iranian leaders rushed to improve civil defense and tried to rally the morale of the population in two ways. First, they depicted Iran (not for the first time) as facing an international conspiracy, in which the US, Israel, and the USSR cooperated. The latter was directly accused of taking part in the missile assault, by supplying Iraq with recently produced missiles (allegedly manufactured in 1985–86) and equipment necessary to increase their range. The Soviets officially denied having supplied Iraq with missiles capable of such strikes.[21] Second, they announced advances in Iran's own missile program, which although being still in the testing and development phase, showed promise of producing missiles for retaliation.[22]

THE IRAQI RECONQUEST OF THE FAW PENINSULA

At dawn on the first day of Ramadan (17 April), the Iraqis launched an all-out assault on the IRGC garrison entrenched across the Faw peninsula ("A few IRGC and Mobilization Corps battalions," according to President Khameneh'i).[23] The attack, codenamed *Ramadan al-mubarak* (Blessed Ramadan) was carried out by the elite Presidential Guard Forces and the Seventh Army Corps, with massive artillery and air support and probably some use of poison gas. The Iraqi objective — reoccupation of the peninsula — was attained by noon 18 April 1988. The Iranians were completely surprised; those who could, escaped over one remaining bridge.[24]

According to President Saddam Husayn the attack had been planned since the loss of Faw in May 1986. The Presidential Guards, a central reserve force, had been earmarked for the operation, reinforced, and specifically trained on similar terrain and in winter and summer conditions. The battle of Halabja almost interrupted the preparations, as had some earlier emergencies along the front, which required urgent reinforcements.[25]

The Iraqis, possibly surprised by their swift victory, were jubilant. In their press the achievement was called "a qualitative change in the war."[26] Possibilities hitherto considered almost unattainable opened up to them. First Deputy Prime Minister Taha Yasin Ramadan revealed the profound relief of the Iraqi leadership when stating that "the liberation [of Faw]...had revived self-confidence among the Iraqis ... [It] was a deep-rooted shake of the Iraqi spirit."[27]

For the Iranians the loss of Faw underscored that they could no longer outflank Basra, which they were unable to overrun.[28] At first the Iranians tried to minimize the reverse they had suffered; only later did Rafsanjani admit publicly that Faw was a great loss.[29] The Iranians attributed their misfortune to poison gas and foreign help. They alleged that Kuwait had helped Iraq by permitting the use of Bubiyan island; Kuwait denied this but rejoiced publicly at the Iraqi gain. The Iranians vented their anger by launching at Kuwait on 20 April a *Scud* missile, which caused no damage.[30] They also accused the US of aiding the Iraqis directly by helicopter attacks on Iranian positions and indirectly by their raid against two Iranian oil platforms on 18 April (see below).[31]

THE NEW IRAQI STRATEGY

The surprise attack at Faw signified a change in Iraqi strategy which had been maturing since the end of 1987, a change from explicit defensive to offensive. An Iraqi evaluation of the situation in early 1988 might have included the following:

(1) The Iraqi diplomatic initiative of 1987, which had resulted in Security Council Resolution 598, was petering out. Iran was not responsive and further international pressure on it to comply — in the form of an arms embargo imposed by the council — was blocked by the Soviets. The failure of efforts by the US, while presiding over the Security Council in February, to get the resolution passed and the US-Soviet agreement on Afghanistan reached by the two foreign ministers in Moscow on 23–25 February (four days before the fourth round of the "war of cities"), probably convinced the Iraqis that they could no longer expect an international arms embargo on Iran.[32]

(2) The strong support they had received at the Arab summit conference in Amman in November 1987 had no practical import. The rupture of diplomatic relations with Iran was not made mandatory. Syria tried to mediate between some Gulf states and Iran (see chapter on Syria); indeed the United Arab Emirates (UAE) and Oman were putting out peace feelers toward Iran.[33] Furthermore, the developing Palestinian *intifada* attracted most Arab attention.

(3) Domestically, the economic situation had improved in 1987 and the country was calm.

(4) Militarily, the Iraqi arsenal was full, a stock of long-range missiles was accumulating, and the Iranians seemed unable to mount another grand offensive. Moreover, it appeared that Iraqi intelligence on Iran was improving; it may have pointed to exacerbating power struggles and war-weariness.[34]

The overall picture then, was that despite its improved situation, Iraq was no closer to its aim of ending the war, that Iran could still afford to continue with it, that international and even Arab indifference toward Iraq was growing, and that a political ambiance of "demoralization" among the Iraqi population and troops had to be guarded against.[35] This picture may have been at the background of Saddam Husayn's decision, for the first time since 1982 (the brief Mehran episode of 1986 excepted), to embark on an offensive strategy, whose main risk was heavy casualties including among the elite Presidential Guards as well.[36] As a defensive measure of last resort against Iranian surprises, the Iraqis relied on their chemical weapons. Thus, the massive missile bombardment of Iranian cities was intended not only to increase the costs of war to Iran, but also to broadcast Iraqi frustration to the world.[37] The renewed tanker war (see below) could also be seen as a signal to vacillating Gulf states and possibly to the US. The Faw offensive was the greatest risk; when it paid off, the new strategy became public and was to guide Iraqi operations until the cease-fire.

> Iran's...refusal of the peace option as outlined in Resolution 598 will lead to determined battle to regain occupied land...by adopting an offensive approach....We must now be prepared for action [similar to] the Blessed Ramadan operation, so that we can fly our banners over enemy occupied positions in our...land *and the territory affecting our units' security and from where attacks originate against our international border*.[38]

FURTHER IRAQI OFFENSIVES

On 25 May, five weeks after reoccupying Faw, the Iraqis resumed their offensive in the southern sector. In "a lightning attack" they ousted the Iranians from their dearly acquired (in January 1987) foothold east of Basra (Shalamja), then drove c. 25 km. toward the international border. The operation, codenamed *Tawakkalan 'ala Allah* (We rely on God) was again spearheaded by the Presidential Guard Forces and had been well planned.[39] Thus the threat to Basra was completely removed.

Saddam Husayn exploited this additional success of his new strategy to underline to both his public at home and to the Iranians that this was not fortuitous:

> Time favors us rather than the Iranians....We are guided by...standards of modern times...they are guided by charlatanism and humbug....We are not saying the IRG[C] are not good fighters. But they are unguided. They are not fighting the way they did say two years ago. Some might say that the liberation of Faw is connected with certain circumstances, [was] caused by an Iranian oversight, an Iraqi deception, or by Iran's engagement in certain places...[that] this is due to the presence of military capabilities in this or that place....However, the Shalamja lesson entrenched al-Faw's great lesson that this capability is present in all Iraqi Army Corps.[40]

The Iranians quickly admitted their withdrawal.[41] Their reverse accelerated the decision to reorganize their high command, which put Rafsanjani in charge (see below). But this could not turn the tide. An Iranian counterattack to dislodge the Iraqis failed three weeks later, causing Rafsanjani to describe it as a practice attack and withdrawal operation.[42]

The last phase of regaining Iraqi territory in the southern sector took place a month later. On 25 June, the Presidential Guard Forces reoccupied the Majnun "islands" in the Hawr al-Huwayza marshes, held by Iran since 1984. Their assault was facilitated by massive diversionary attacks on both flanks. The "islands" were defended, according to the Iranians, by irregulars of the Supreme Assembly of the Islamic Revolution in Iraq (SAIRI; see *MECS* 1986, p. 160), whose retreat was attributed to the Iraqi use of poison gas (which the latter denied).[43]

While lauding his troops for their latest success, Saddam Husayn accused the US of informing Iran in advance of the impending offensive and of the Iraqi preparations for it, adding that the accurate operational details had been published in *The Washington Post*.[44] The US denied this.[45]

Both belligerents continued irregular warfare between them. The Iranians employed their Kurdish organizations in northern Iraq as in previous years. To increase coordination among themselves and to step up their fight after the Halabja atrocity, six Kurdish groups formed a coalition in May, but no real increase in their operations followed.[46] On the Iraqi side, the main irregular organization was the Iranian National Liberation Army (INLA), formed by the *Mujahidine Khalq* movement (cf. *MECS* 1987, p. 183). Their first major effort, obviously with strong Iraqi support and for maximum publicity, led to the temporary occupation of the Iranian town of Mehran in the central sector (19–22 June).[47]

Meanwhile, the Iraqis had also taken the offensive in Sulaymaniyya province. Slowly advancing in that mountainous terrain, they occupied Mawat and reached the border on 30 June.[48] The Iranians then shortened their front lines by withdrawing from their remaining foothold at Halabja on 12 July 1988.[49]

The last Iraqi offensive before Iran accepted a cease-fire was carried out northeast of ʻAmara. Again spearheaded by the Presidential Guard Forces, the Iraqis reoccupied Zubaydat on the frontier and advanced into Iran, capturing the town of Dehloran on 13 July, and reportedly overrunning an Iranian regional headquarters. It seemed that the Iraqi attack was aimed at two regular Iranian divisions, which were allegedly destroyed and 7,000 of their troops captured. Having achieved their objective, the Iraqis withdrew into their border in three days, on 16 July.[50]

CHEMICAL WARFARE

During 1988, Iraq increased its use of chemical weapons. Its chemical weapon capability had become well established and it reportedly produced several thousand tons of chemical agents (including mustard, tabun, and sarin gases) and different kinds of ammunition. First employed as a weapon of last resort in 1983 and 1984, poison gas turned into a terrifying component of the Iraqi offensive strategy. Iran began to produce chemical weapons in the mid-1980s and reportedly used them against Iraqi troops.[51]

The best-known instance of the use of poison gas against the Iranian advance in Kurdistan in March was the attack on the Kurdish town of Halabja. Apparently defenseless on the battlefield, Iran successfully enlisted international sympathy. Foreign journalists were taken to the scene and the UN were asked to investigate.[52] Furthermore Rafsanjani publicized the Iranian effort to build a countercapability; it seemed that with foreign help Iran quickly set up production of mustard, blood, and nerve gases.[53] Some details of this Iranian effort appeared in the press in early 1989.[54]

Following previous investigations (cf. *MECS* 1987, p. 183) the UN secretary-general dispatched an investigation team to the area, which found evidence of the use of poison gas in both Iraq and Iran, but did not visit Halabja. In its report it refrained from blaming either side.[55] Neither did Resolution 612 adopted by the Security Council on 9 May, which called on both sides not to use chemical weapons. Iran considered the resolution "pointless and ineffective."[56]

For its part, Iraq accused Iran of first use at Halabja and contended that "in their legitimate...self-defense our people are determined to use all available means against...the invader." The Iranians vehemently denied the Iraqi charge.[57] Furthermore an Iraqi spokesman threatened Iran (following Rafsanjani's above-mentioned statement) that "a number of major Iranian towns" might be targeted for chemical warfare attacks as a "deterrent and retaliatory measure."[58] At a press conference in Bonn in early July, the Iraqi foreign minister publicly admitted his country's use of poison gas, but blamed Iran for first use ("at the start of the conflict") and for invading Iraq: "You should not forget...that there was a barbarian wave after wave from the Iranian side to invade our country."[59]

The Iraqis seemingly employed poison gas during their offensives, including the final one in the central sector in late July. A UN report of 1 August clearly confirmed this.[60] At the Paris conference on chemical warfare in January 1989, the Iranian foreign minister put at 50,000 the number of Iranians injured by Iraqi chemical weapons, 10% of whom had died.[61]

When Iraq employed chemical weapons to subdue its Kurdish population after the cease-fire, a major outcry in the West resulted in another resolution by the Security Council (No. 620 of 20 August 1988), which firmly condemned the use of chemical weapons, but again without naming Iraq or Iran. The US Senate and Administration and the European Parliament condemned Iraq, but this did not stop Iraq from expanding its chemical weapons capabilities. Seen from Baghdad this capability had paid off handsomely, first keeping it from losing the war and later helping it to rout its enemy.[62]

AIR AND SEA OPERATIONS

There was no substantial change in the pattern of air and sea operations during 1988. The Iranian Air Force somewhat increased the volume of its sorties, which were intended mainly to support ground operations.[63] The Iraqis continued intermittent attacks on Iranian economic targets and sporadic raids on key oil installations in the Gulf, such as Kharg, Lavan (raided at least five times) and the Larak transshipment center which was raided spectacularly on 14 May, when five tankers and some other ships were hit and 54 seamen killed.[64] Following its long-standing policy not to permit any country to export oil through the Gulf if it itself was unable to do so,[65] Iran responded by attacks on unescorted ships headed for or coming from Kuwait and Saudi Arabia, which it considered allies of Iraq.[66] These attacks coincided with larger operations, such as the offensive at Faw and air attacks in the Gulf. On 31 July, Iran officially announced that no more ships would be attacked; the last one took place on 4 August.[67]

Altogether c. 90 ships were attacked in the Gulf from 1 January-20 July 1988. Since the beginning of the "tanker war" in May 1981 there had been c. 540 attacks on ships by both sides.[68]

The foreign navies present in the Gulf continued their routine operations, the main one being the US Navy's convoying of reflagged Kuwaiti tankers (cf. *MECS* 1987, pp. 186–87). Apparently no mines were laid by the Iranians until early April (up to 14 April at least 17 old mines were destroyed).[69] But on 14 April a US frigate hit a mine off Qatar after sighting some more, and 10 of its crew were injured. During the following week US, French, Italian, and Dutch minesweepers neutralized 12 mines, at least some of which had been laid recently.[70] On 18 April the US Navy retaliated by destroying two Iranian oil platforms on Sassan and Sirri islands, each said to produce 150,000 barrels per day (b/d) and alleged to have also served military purposes. In an ensuing sea battle, two Iranian frigates and some missile boats were hit (one of each was sunk) by US ships and aircraft, with a US helicopter being lost. The Iranians then attacked a UAE oil rig.[71] The American action coincided with the Iraqi reconquest of Faw, leading the Iranians to accuse the US of helping the Iraqis (see above). Following the Iraqi raid on Larak the Iranians again accused the US of collaborating with Iraq, by communicating with its attacking aircraft, jamming Iranian radar systems, and supplying Baghdad with postoperational air photos.[72] A fortnight earlier, President Reagan had decided to extend US naval protection to neutral, non-Communist shipping.[73] Evidently tension in the Gulf was increasing, but this did not change Iranian policy: "[The US] knows that every time Iraq attacks a ship, another ship will be attacked in retaliation," Rafsanjani said.[74] Meanwhile, to deter and counter the possible operational deployment of *Silkworm* shore-to-ship missiles in the Strait of Hormuz, the US cruiser *Vincennes*, equipped with a most powerful radar system, was sent into the Gulf at the end of May.[75] On 2 May, the *Vincennes* and some other ships had sunk an Iranian gunboat trying to attack a tanker. On 3 May, the same ship had been involved in the worst incident of the year when two of its missiles downed an Iranian passenger aircraft (the regularly scheduled Iran Air flight 655), killing all 290 people on board. Apparently, the plane had been mistaken for an Iranian F-14 fighter. Obviously the memory of the May 1987 sinking of the *Stark* (in which 37 US seamen were killed) because of its captain's hesitations (see *MECS* 1987, p. 186) was still strong. The report of the official US commission of inquiry revealed that crew error led to the *Vincennes* captain's error, that "machines did not fail man; the men failed the machines."[76]

Iran considered that the aircraft was deliberately downed. For months it had seen itself "really at war with the US. In Faw they officially entered into war with us."[77] But vehement calls for revenge, for fighting the US "on the political, economic, cultural, and military fronts" were soothed by Khomeyni, who asked for Rafsanjani to be supported. Rafsanjani reacted soberly, saying that revenge should be taken when convenient to Iran, and he warned about the possibility of a US provocation.[78] The sympathy and shock expressed worldwide, and even by its Arab neighbors, led Iran to exploit the incident in its very first appeal to the Security Council to condemn the US. The council refused to do so and adopted instead a lukewarm resolution on 21 July that the Iranians described as of "little content and little effect."[79]

RAFSANJANI APPOINTED AS ACTING COMMANDER IN CHIEF

The defeat at Faw and the subsequent eviction from the foothold east of Basra were serious warnings to the Iranian leadership that the balance of war was tilting against them. Obviously Iranian forces were outnumbered at the critical points, were inefficiently organized, supported, and commanded, and possibly were also losing their nerve in face of the Iraqi arsenal, especially chemical weapons.[80] Changes in Iran's conduct of the war became urgent.

On 7 May, the chief of staff of the Iranian Armed Forces Joint Staff was replaced by a younger general, 'Ali Shahbazi.[81] The connection with the Faw defeat was not clear.[82] On 2 June, Khomeyni issued a decree announcing a major reorganization of the supreme command. The decree appointed the just-reelected Speaker of the Majlis, 'Ali Hashemi Rafsanjani as acting commander in chief of all Armed Forces and detailed the tasks assigned to him.[83] These tasks and comments thereupon by Rafsanjani and others provided an unusually frank glimpse of the dismal state of the Iranian war effort in its eighth year. Some of these were:

(1) Establishment of a central command headquarters. This was given first priority in order to improve the direction of the war. By 1 July this headquarters, in which the government, IRGC, and the Armed Forces were represented, had been formed.[84]

(2) Full coordination of the armed forces, IRGC, the Mobilization Corps (Basij), and the security forces, the "acceptable" merger of relevant departments and organizations, including logistics, and the elimination of duplicate and nonessential organizations. This task underscored some of the major Iranian weaknesses: the term "acceptable" referred to the political obstacle in the way of streamlining the war effort, as the leadership had decided not to merge the IRGC with the regular military.[85] An immediate problem was the lack of trained combat forces at the front, which was corrected by concentrating scattered Gendarmerie units, by mobilizing

trained volunteers, and by reducing the considerable manpower assigned to support roles. Furthermore, repeated logistical failures (e.g., the offensives against Basra 1987 and Halabja 1988) on the battlefield required urgent reforms.[86]

(3) Concentration of military industries, the provision of defense requirements, the consolidation of logistical, technical, engineering, and combat training, and of research resources. As both the military and the IRGC owned industries and training establishments, the duplication and waste had become notorious.[87]

(4) Improved utilization of available resources. This again seemed to allude to the lack of combat-ready manpower. The reliance upon volunteers was proving ineffective in the protracted war. Rafsanjani was planning to rely basically on regular and organized forces, which meant more efficient conscription, for a longer period of service, and an improved call-up system of reservists.[88]

Khomeyni's decree was the outcome of a long debate among Iranian leaders (for the internal repercussions, see chapter on Iran), who had come to realize that the way they were conducting war led them to defeat. In Rafsanjani's words: "Recurrent procrastinations are no longer possible." He added later that "so far, our policy has been that normal life should continue...[but] present circumstances dictate a change."[89] According to Montazeri, then Khomeyni's heir designate, full coordination of the Armed Forces should have been achieved years earlier. "Nowhere else...does a country have five armed forces" with huge organizations, he said. He added acerbically: "Do you know why the war has lasted for so long?...We had no planning, [no] coordination, or a unified command."[90] Demands voiced in the Majlis to inquire into recent setbacks and to punish those guilty were denounced by Khameneh'i as not being "our Islamic way."[91]

In retrospect, these measures could be seen as a belated attempt to revitalize Iranian defenses, but also as leading toward the cessation of hostilities.

THE CEASE-FIRE AND AFTER

THE ESTABLISHMENT OF THE CEASE-FIRE

On 18 July, Khameneh'i informed the UN secretary-general that Iran officially and unconditionally accepted Security Council Resolution 598, thus waiving its former condition that the formation of a committee to determine who was the aggressor should precede the establishment of a cease-fire. The secretary-general took immediate steps to implement a cease-fire.[92] An advance UN team arrived in Tehran on 26 July and came to Baghdad three days later.

This dramatic step, which surprised the world and stunned the Iranian people, was depicted by Iran's leaders as "no improvised decision but the outcome of long and thorough reflection"[93] (a reflection which possibly began at latest on Rafsanjani's appointment as acting commander in chief).[94] Agreeing to the assessment of the leadership, Khomeyni "drank the poisoned chalice of accepting the resolution," because he considered it "to be in the interest of the revolution and the system."[95] But he and others refused to detail their reasons, as these were said to involve military and political secrets.[96] However, as in their presentations of the deteriorating military situation during the preceding weeks, Iranian leaders emphasized the determination of "global arrogance," that is, of the US, USSR and their allies, and of "Arab reactionaries to the region," to prevent an Iranian victory by supporting Iraq militarily, politically,and financially.[97] According to Rafsanjani, the "turning point" was the destruction of the Iranian passenger plane, which had to be considered as a warning by the US that "it may commit immense crimes" which "could lead to extraordinary losses for our people" if Iran continued the war.[98] In addition to increasing external pressure and international isolation, other factors played a role in the Iranian decision: (1) internal debates and tension (see chapter on Iran), and growing war-weariness (cf. *MECS* 1987, p. 193);[99] (2) the increasing inability of the Iranian economy to sustain the war effort in face of external pressure, lower oil prices, and the growing population;[100] (3) military factors, which may have been even more decisive: the setbacks of 1988, which nullified most of the Iranian gains of previous years; the psychological effect of Iraqi chemical weapons and air and missile power; the lack of major weapons systems and spare parts for them and the dwindling number of volunteers, on whom Iranian operations depended.[101] In brief, Iran had reached the limits of its capabilities.

The initial Iraqi verbal reaction was extreme skepticism and suspicion. It was argued that Iranian statements were ambiguous and contradictory, as they included denunciations of Iraq and called for further mobilization. Therefore, the war would, and in fact did, continue until Iranian intentions became clear.[102] But it seemed that the Iraqi leaders quickly understood that a real change had occurred in Tehran and that a cease-fire could be imminent. They decided not only to preempt Iranian diplomatic maneuvers to reach a "partial" solution, but also to press for last-minute gains on the ground. Iraq proposed five steps to the UN secretary-general "to distinguish between what is tactical and serious" in the Iranian position: (1) a meeting as soon as possible between representatives of the two countries at UN headquarters for "direct talks" on the sequential implementation of Resolution 598; (2) immediate beginning of clearing by the UN of the Shatt al-'Arab for navigation; (3) unimpeded navigation for Iraq in the Gulf; (4) no further Iranian attacks or interception of third party ships; and (5) active involvement by the secretary-general and the Security Council.[103]

At the same time Iraq launched an offensive, codenamed *Tawakkalna 'ala Alla* 4, whose objectives were officially defined as regaining national territory, capturing as many prisoners as possible to ensure the safe return of Iraqi prisoners of war, and destroying enemy forces. Any penetration into Iranian territory would be temporary.[104] In the southern sector, the Iraqis withdrew after two days,[105] their main thrust being in the central sector. There, spearheaded by the Presidential Guards, the Iraqis attacked on a 170 km.-broad front, occupying a number of border towns and advancing toward Bakhtaran (Kermanshah). Included in the attacking force was the INLA, which took the lead when Iraqi forces withdrew.[106]

It appeared however that Iraq miscalculated, despite the many prisoners it had captured. A Saudi official commented that in their attempt to humiliate the Iranians, the Iraqis "may again be going a bit too far."[107] The Iraqi offensive, and especially the employ of the INLA, gave the Iranian leaders an opportunity to rally the people around them for the defense of the country, in a way reminiscent of the early phase of the war. Thousands went to the front, responding to urgent appeals for Iranian volunteers and were joined by President Khameneh'i himself.[108] Later Rafsanjani observed that "there are people at the front now that...had never gone there before."[109] The stubborn Iranian defense (in which tribal forces, the IRGC, and Army paratroops and helicopters participated) stopped the INLA column 35 km. west of Bakhtaran. Counterattacking, the Iranians drove the invader back to the frontier before the end of the month, mopping up and executing collaborators.[110]

On the diplomatic front, Iran immediately rejected the Iraqi demand for direct talks as an excuse to delay the cease-fire.[111] This demand also reportedly irritated the members of the Security Council.[112] Having failed to change the positions of the two foreign ministers, who had met separately with him, the secretary-general decided to declare a cease-fire on his own authority.[113] Following that, and probably after some Arab urging, Saddam Husayn gave in by demanding that direct talks be held immediately *after* the cease-fire was established. He further demanded that the Shatt al-'Arab waterway be opened for Iraqi use and that UN forces remained deployed until a comprehensive peace was reached.[114] On 8 August, the secretary-general announced that a cease-fire would be effective beginning 0400 hours GMT on 20 August and that direct talks would begin in Geneva on 25 August.[115] Iran immediately responded it would cease initiating any military operations. However, Mas'ud Rajavi, the leader of the Iranian opposition movement *Mujahidine Khalq*, announced that his INLA would continue its war against the Khomeyni regime.[116]

A new UN force, the United Nations Iran-Iraq Military Observer Group (UNIIMOG) was promptly set up and its advance teams were in place before the cease-fire. Commanded by a Yugoslav general, Slavko Jovic, the group consisted of 350 observers and an air unit (a small naval unit would be added once the parties agreed on UNIIMOG patrolling the Shatt al-'Arab and adjacent waters in the Gulf) and another 160 military and civilian support personnel. The observers and military personnel were drawn from 26 countries. Headquarters were set up in Baghdad and Tehran, the commander spending alternate weeks in each capital; an assistant chief observer with the rank of brigadier general resided in each. The observers were deployed in four sectors on the Iranian (Saqqez, Bakhtaran, Dezful,and Ahwaz) and three on the Iraqi side (Sulaymaniyya, Ba'quba, and Basra), each sector controlling a number of team sites, located as far forward as possible. The length of cease-fire line, monitored by a team, varied from 70 km. in the south to 250 km. in the mountainous north.[117]

Up to the last days of fighting, Iran seriously expected further Iraqi attacks. Its forces were continuously exhorted to be alert and prepared even after the cease-fire.[118]

The cease-fire held despite many recurrent mutual accusations of violations,[119] despite the continuing deadlock of negotiations (see below), and a propaganda war.[120] On 8 February 1989, the Security Council prolonged the UNIIMOG mandate for another six months.

At sea, both sides concurred that the cease-fire lines included the Gulf down to the Strait of Hormuz. The first Iraqi ship sailed through the Strait on 20 August, and the Iranian port of Bandar Khomeyni was opened to shipping a day later.[121] The main threat at sea continued to be mines. The US Navy estimated in mid-October that c. 150 mines had still to be destroyed.[122] From the end of September, the Iranian Navy swept parts of the Gulf, especially clearing a large area around Kharg island.[123] Kuwait, which was very worried, and other Arab Gulf states requested Western minesweeping to continue.[124]

After the cease-fire, Western naval presence in the Gulf was reduced. At year's end, the US Middle East Task Force counted 25 ships, compared with 34 in January.

Italian, Belgian, and Dutch vessels left the area, while at year's end Britain and France still had nine and seven ships there respectively. The US Navy changed its operations in the Gulf at the end of September from "escorting" (i.e., convoying) to "accompanying" ships, and in December to "monitoring," (i.e., keeping track of ships and being ready to respond).[125] By the end of 1988, Kuwait was considering terminating the reflagging arrangement it had with the US because of cost (it had constantly presented reflagging as a purely commercial deal).[126]

A political-military problem both belligerents had to face with the cease-fire and ensuing negotiations was the fate of their "proxies" — the organizations which had carried out irregular warfare for them. It would appear that both sides kept open a future option of reactivating these organizations. These included:

(1) *Kurdish organizations* which had fought with Iran: with the end of hostilities Iraq undertook large operations to "remake the face of Kurdistan," in which poison gas was used and some Kurdish regions were depopulated. According to Saddam Husayn, Iraq acted against "a group of collaborators with Iran," which collapsed after the Iranian withdrawal. In early September, Iraq extended an amnesty to all Kurds but one, Jalal Talabani, who "did not consider himself an Iraqi."[127] For their part, Iran granted refuge to the Kurds who had fought with it. "The Kurds are now alone. Iran cannot do anything important deep in Iraqi territory apart from...[opening] the borders of our country."[128]

(2) *SAIRI*: Refugees from Iraq who had fought for Iran, were to be treated like Iranians after the war and would be free to go anywhere. On a visit to Damascus, the head of SAIRI, Muhammad Baqir Hakim, reiterated the continuation of its struggle against the Iraqi regime, despite Iran's acceptance of Resolution 598[129] (see chapter "An Uneasy Truce in Islam").

(3) *Mujahidine Khalq* (INLA): When their active participation in some Iraqi offensives became official, the Iranian official attitude toward them was clearly articulated. "They call themselves Islamic, but they are worse than the communists and the Tudehites."[130] After the INLA offensive toward Bakhtaran was repulsed at the end of July, Khomeyni decided to consider all *Mujahidine Khalq* members as warriors against Allah and to execute not only those who had participated in the war but also those imprisoned in Iran. About 2,500 of them were executed accordingly from the cease-fire until the 10th anniversary of the revolution in February 1989.[131] As mentioned above, the *Mujahidine Khalq* had earlier decided to continue their war against the Iranian regime.[132]

THE NEGOTIATIONS

On 25 August direct negotiations between the belligerents began in Geneva, chaired by the UN secretary-general. They continued sporadically into 1989. On 1 September, the secretary-general appointed Jan K. Eliasson, Sweden's permanent representative to the UN, as his special representative to the Iran-Iraq peace talks.[133] Until the end of 1988 four rounds of talks were held: (1) from 25–26 August in Geneva; (2) from 10–13 September in Geneva; (3) from 1–2 October, in New York; and (4) 1–11 November, in Geneva.

It took only one day for the two sides' divergent views of the negotiations to emerge. Although both insisted on the implementation of Resolution 598, the emphases were different, reflecting their conflicting interests and deep mutual distrust.

Iraq, posing as victor, pressed for rapid and tangible gains; Iran, continuing the war by diplomatic means, determined not to cede any leverage or advantage it had, even if that meant delay in setting up the committee which was to determine responsibility for the war.[134]

On the second day (26 August 1988) the talks stumbled on paragraph 1 of the resolution: "Withdrawal of all forces to the internationally recognized boundaries without delay." While Iran had withdrawn from Iraqi territory, Iraq still occupied 1,000–2,000 sq. km. of Iranian land.[135] Iraq refused to agree to a timetable unless Iran agreed to the clearing of the Shatt al-'Arab for navigation. When Iran indicated agreement, proposing that each party dredge its side of the waterway, Iraq demanded that after reopening the waterway, the cease-fire lines would follow the eastern shore of the Shatt. This reflected the Iraqi claim to full sovereignty over the waterway, a claim Iran totally rejected. Iran based its rejection on the 1975 Algiers agreement, which fixed the boundary along the deepest point (*Thalweg*) of the waterway (see *MECS* 1979–80, p. 14). Iran considered that agreement and the pacts and protocols pertaining to it — which had all been officially documented at the UN — as valid, permanent, and unchangeable. In any case, it saw the issue of the Shatt as irrelevant to the cease-fire.[136] The Iraqi position was that the treaty no longer existed, having been violated by Iran eight years before when it "interfered in Iraq's internal affairs." Furthermore, argued the Iraqi foreign minister, both sides must benefit equally from the first steps taken after the cease-fire: as Iran had begun to use its ports, the UN should clear Iraq's only outlet to the sea. According to Iraq, the Shatt issue was part of the paragraph on cease-fire, and not of Paragraph 4 as Iran argued, because freedom of navigation included clearing the waterway.[137] It should be remembered that the text of Resolution 598 includes no reference to the 1975 Algiers agreement (for text see *MECS* 1987, pp. 193–94). Unsurprisingly, the secretary-general reported to the Security Council after the first round that the talks were deadlocked. Until an agreement on withdrawal to internationally recognized boundaries was reached, it would be impossible to make progress.[138]

In the third round of talks, the secretary-general proposed a four-point plan to advance implementation:[139]

(a) Consolidation of arrangements governing the cease-fire, including freedom of navigation through the Strait of Hormuz (Iran would exercise "self-restraint" in searching ships, as Iraq considered searches a restriction on free navigation);

(b) Withdrawal of forces to the internationally recognized boundaries within about two weeks;

(c) Release and repatriation of prisoners of war;

(d) The urgent clearing of the Shatt al-'Arab.

It was obvious to the secretary-general that any agreement between the parties on these issues was no more than a convergence of views in principle. While Iran was ready to accept the plan, provided the 1975 agreement was observed concerning withdrawal and dredging, for Iraq any linkage between dredging and the 1975 agreement was unacceptable.[140]

The continuing impasse in the negotiations and the belligerents' mutual distrust cruelly affected the fate of the prisoners of war. According to the most recent estimates, 35,000 Iranians were held by Iraq, of whom 19,284 were registered by the International Committee of the Red Cross. Iran claimed that the real number was c.

53,000 prisoners. Iran held 70,000 Iraqis, 50,182 of whom were registered, among them Arabs from other countries (the number of Egyptians being variously estimated at 100–3,000).[141] Both sides had released disabled and sick prisoners since October 1985, on humanitarian grounds. In September 1988, 72 Iraqis were exchanged for 25 Iranians. Altogether 775 Iraqis and 645 Iranians were exchanged under these terms.[142]

Although discussed from the very first round of talks, the prisoners' issue had become entangled in the overall problem of implementation. An Iraqi proposal to speed up the exchange on humanitarian grounds was seen by Iran as a further obstruction of the implementation of Resolution 598 and especially of Iraqi withdrawal. Iran insisted that an exchange should take place only in the context of the resolution (Paragraph 3) and the secretary-general's four-point plan, because withdrawal was considered more important than repatriation.[143] However, as the fourth round of direct ministerial talks proceeded in Geneva, both countries agreed on 8 November to release 1,526 sick and disabled prisoners (411 Iranian and 1,115 Iraqi) in a 12-day shuttle. But when the operation began on 24 November, Iran released only 52 out of a daily quota of 115, arguing that the rest were either no longer sick or disabled, or had demanded asylum in the presence of Red Cross representatives. Iraq angrily reciprocated, releasing only 19 out of the previously agreed quota of 41. After two more days of reduced exchanges, Iran suspended the operation until Iraq had released all the held-back Iranian prisoners.[144] In February 1989, Iran again announced its readiness to release some prisoners, but no exchange took place.[145]

At the beginning of 1989, both sides were in agreement that no substantive progress toward a "comprehensive, just, and honorable settlement" as envisaged in Resolution 598 had been achieved. While Iraq accused Iran of blockading its ports by its refusal to let the UN clear the Shatt and of obduracy on the prisoners' issue, Iran continued to complain about Iraqi occupation of some of its territory.[146] The repeated Iraqi attempts to accelerate the repatriation of its prisoners (some having already spent eight years in captivity) raised the possibility that this had become a political problem in Iraq. In any case, the obvious Iraqi anxiety made the less-pressed Iranians feel stronger in the negotiations, and more obstinate.

During the months of negotiations, it became clear that Iran was gaining by its strict insistence on the sequential implementation of Resolution 598 (a position previously held by Iraq). This was a different kind of war, in which, as Rafsanjani unrepentantly pointed out, Iran had not yet achieved the downfall and trial of Saddam Husayn or attained "its rights," but through "the present way" might achieve its objectives "if the resolution [598] was correctly interpreted."[147] Iraq, by its actions — including the posing of preconditions for negotiations and unwillingness to accept the secretary-general's proposals — possibly alienated its supporters and contributed to Iran's improved international image. As put by a competent observer: "Iraq might find itself winning the war, but losing the peace as Iran skillfully adopts a new policy of reasonableness and cooperates fully with the UN."[148]

PRELIMINARY BALANCE AND OUTLOOK

By the spring of 1989, as the cease-fire continued, one could assume that the eight-year-long war between Iran and Iraq had come to an end, at least for the time being. Both war-weary countries did not exclude the possibility of another outbreak of hostilities, but neither seemed keen on initiating it. Meanwhile, both continued the diplomatic struggle between them and were busily rearming, rebuilding, and reorganizing.[149] For Iran especially the strengthening of its worn-down military capabilities had first priority, which its leaders emphasized repeatedly.[150]

The end of hostilities offered an opportunity for drawing lessons and dressing the balance of achievements and failures, of the losses and damage incurred by both belligerents.[151]

Iran officially announced that 123,240 of its military had been killed. The breakdown given was: 79,664 of the IRGC and Basij, 35,170 of the Armed Forces, 5,061 of the Gendarmerie, 2,075 of the Construction Jihad, 1,006 of the Revolutionary Committees, and 264 policemen. In addition, 60,711 were missing in action, some of whom might have been taken prisoner. The number of wounded or disabled was not given. The estimate of the US Department of State was higher: 300,000 killed and 450,000 wounded, out of a population of 50m.[152]

No official statement on *Iraq*'s casualties had been made.[153] The State Department estimated that Iraq suffered more than 120,000 killed and 300,000 wounded. Another estimate was close to 150,000 killed and 250,000 injured. This meant almost 0.8% killed out of a population of 16m.[154]

It may be too early to assess the cost of the war. Table 1 shows one early estimate

TABLE 1: ESTIMATED MAXIMUM COST OF THE GULF WAR* 1980–88

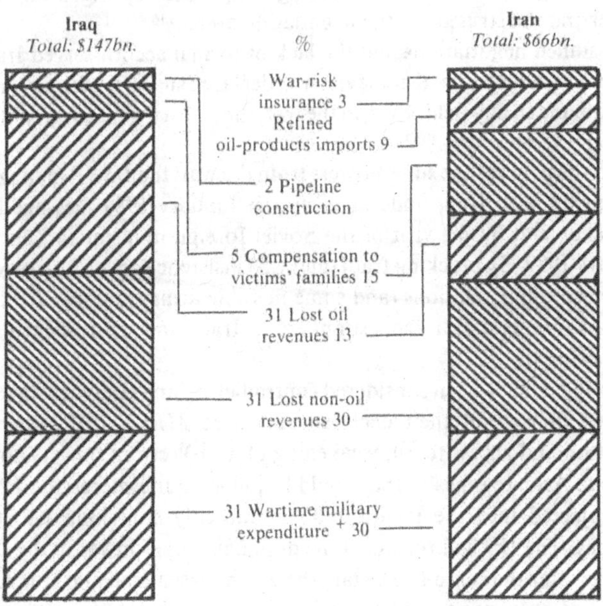

* Excludes damage to infrastructure.

\+ Arms purchases and personnel costs.

SOURCE: *The Economist*, 20 August 1988.

Before addressing the unavoidable question "Who won?" it seems useful to recall some principal elements of the strategic balance between the two countries after the cease-fire:

— Iran has three times the land mass of Iraq. Compared with Iran, Iraq is practically landlocked and has no strategic depth. In compensation, Iraq has developed pipelines for the export of its oil and a medium-missile capability to offset the vulnerability of its capital and to deter aggressors.[155]

— Iran has three times the population of Iraq. On a per capita basis, Iraq's casualty rate has been higher than Iran's. Iran's society has proven to be more resilient than Iraq's. This made for greater Iranian tolerance of a war of attrition and for Saddam's prudence about casualties.

— Although Iran accumulated almost no foreign debt (Iraq would probably shrug off hers), its economy was in a shambles (to which the peripeties of the regime contributed heavily). It could not call on Arab help or for expanded European credits, as Iraq had done. Its military expenditures will not decrease, as in addition to maintaining constant preparedness, it has to rearm urgently.

— Iraq has superior military capabilities, at least for the foreseeable future, especially in modern weapon systems such as attack aircraft, missiles, and chemical warfare.

So who won? A sober assessment is that there has been no clear winner or loser. Iraq clearly had the upper hand on the battlefield, but could not have "won" the war, while Iran did not "lose" it. Iran, ever more skillful in diplomacy, stopped a deteriorating military situation from getting worse by accepting the cease-fire and transferring the struggle to the negotiating arena.[156]

The stalled negotiations and the lack of formal accord served Iranian claims that the war was continuing. Khomeyni even declared success: "We have not been defeated or conquered in any field. Even in the war, the victory went to our nation. The enemies have achieved nothing."[157]

As to the gains of the superpowers from the war: the *USSR* managed to improve its relationship with Iran, underlined by the January 1989 message by Khomeyni to Gorbachev and by the visit of the Soviet foreign minister to Tehran at the end of February 1989. By blocking Iraqi (and US) insistence on a UN arms embargo on Iran and by economic relations (and some possible arms supplies), the Soviets balanced their position as major arms suppliers to Iraq (and their alleged role in the Iraqi missile effort).

US policies have been considered contradictory and equivocal in recent analyses.[158] But seen in view of their declared aims (see *MECS* 1987, pp. 191–92) — free navigation and access to oil, weakening of anti-Western powers, and strengthening moderate Arab regimes — they could be judged quite successful. US military power was projected into the region and undoubtedly contributed to the cessation of hostilities. The US had remained the dominant superpower in the Gulf.

A year after the cease-fire began, the war between Iran and Iraq had not yet really ended. Not only was a sudden conflagration possible, because the two armies were facing each other and at some places very closely, but more importantly, because the conflict was continuing stubbornly. As it seemed, a settlement, a peace agreement as envisaged in Resolution 598, might take years to achieve and meanwhile both sides gave high priority to enhancing their military posture. The question arose whether a stable peace could be attained at all in such an unstable region. If so, it might be accompanied by a regional and domestic realignment of political forces. Possibly the most one could hope for at that stage was the minimum goal of maintaining the cease-fire.

NOTES

For the place and frequency of publications cited here, and for the full name of the publication, news agency, radio station, or monitoring service where an abbreviation is used, please see "List of Sources." Only in the case of more than one publication bearing the same name is the place of publication noted here.

1. E.g., Rafsanjani: "Normally we carry out operations under favorable conditions, as we do not wish to embark on mere military adventurism," Tehran TV, 19 March — DR, 22 March 1988.
2. R. Tehran, 17, 18, 19 January — SWB, 21 January; R. Tehran, 13, 14, 15 March — DR, 14, 15 March 1988.
3. Khomeyni congratulated the IRGC, Basij, Kurds, army paratroops and aviation, and the Air Force. Naval teams also participated. R. Tehran, 17 March — DR, 17 March; *The Times*, 22 March 1988.
4. R. Tehran, 16, 17, 24, 27 March, 12 April; Tehran TV, 18, 19 March; IRNA, 16, 24 March, 13 April — DR, 16, 18, 24, 28 March, 13 April 1988.
5. There seems to be some confusion on the date of the Halabja atrocity: it was first reported to have occurred on 16 March — R. Tehran and IRNA, 17 March — DR, 18 March 1988. Later the date of 17 and 18 March appeared in Iranian reports. Cf. Foreign Minister Velayati, IRNA, 6 April--DR, 7 April; *idem*, IRNA, 2 June — DR, 3 June 1988; IRNA, 5 January — DR, 6 January 1989. In another gas attack against IRGC units on 25 March, the sons of Rafsanjani and Prosecutor-General Kho'iniha were reportedly injured; IRNA, 29 March — DR, 29 March 1988.
6. *Al-Ra'y*, 29 March — DR, 29 March; Foreign Minister Tariq 'Aziz to UN secretary-general, INA, 29 March — DR, 30 March; WF, 30 March; Iranian denials, e.g. R. Tehran, 31 March; IRNA, 6 April — DR, 7 April 1988.
7. IRNA, 19, 22 May — DR, 20, 24 May 1988.
8. R. Tehran, 16 March — DR, 16 March 1988. Emphasis added.
9. R. Tehran, 16 March, IRNA, 20 March — DR, 17, 22 March 1988.
10. Tehran TV, 19 March — DR, 22 March 1988.
11. *The Economist*, 2 April; *MM*, 4 April 1988. If blown up, the dam could have at least partially flooded the capital. The Iranians later had a captured Iraqi division commander explain the strategic importance of Halabja region; IRNA, 31 May — DR, 1 June 1988.
12. *Al-Majalla*, 17 May 1988.
13. Foreign Minister Tariq 'Aziz, *Sawt al-Sha'b*, 25 March — DR, 25 March; INA, 12 April — DR, 13 April; Saddam Husayn, R. Baghdad, 2 July — DR, 5 July 1988.
14. Saddam Husayn, R. Baghdad, VoM, 24 May — DR, 25 May; R. Baghdad, 2 July — DR, 5 July 1988.
15. R. Baghdad, VoM, 19 March — DR, 21 March 1988. Rafsanjani described the gas attack on Halabja as revenge on people who had welcomed the Iranians; R. Tehran, 5 April — DR, 7 April 1988.
16. INA, 18 March — DR, 18 March (emphasis added); cf. *al-Thawra*, Baghdad, 28 March 1988, stating that "Iraq is determined to defend [itself]...by using all kinds of weapons"; INA, 28 March — DR, 28 March 1988.
17. R. Baghdad, VoM, 17 April — DR, 18 April 1988.
18. R. Baghdad, VoM, 2 March — DR, 3 March 1988.
19. The missile exchange is amply documented in the communiqués of both sides. For the beginning, see IRNA, 27, 28, 29 February, R. Baghdad, VoM, 28, 29 February — DR, 29 February, 1 March. For the end see, R. Baghdad, VoM, 20, 26 April, R. Tehran, 21 April,

IRNA, 28 April — DR, 21, 22, 27, 29 April. For the number of missiles launched, see also R. Baghdad, VoM, 14 March — DR, 15 March; *FT*, 27 April 1988.

20. *NYT*, 21 April; *FT*, 27 April; *The Guardian*, 19 March 1988. By 11 March 1988, Iran had suffered more than 300 killed. *NYT*, 14 March 1988.
21. Ayatollah Musavi-Ardebili, R. Tehran, 4 March — DR, 7 April; Rafsanjani, R. Tehran, 24 March — DR, 24 March 1988. Rafsanjani's accusations sustain the general view that the *al-Husayn* missile is a reduced warhead and extended fuselage version of the Soviet *Scud*-B missile. E.g. *Defense and Foreign Affairs*, June 1988, p. 11; Soviet Foreign Ministry spokesman — DR, 4 March 1988.
22. IRNA, 28, 29 March, Tehran TV, 7 April — DR, 29, 30 March, 13 April 1988. Later in the year, Revolutionary Guards Minister Rafiqdust said that Iran was producing five types of ground-to-ground missiles, to be employed if the war of cities resumed. Tehran TV, 3 June — DR, 6 June 1988.
23. R. Tehran, 1 July — DR, 6 July 1988.
24. On the assault. R. Baghdad, VoM, 17, 18 April — DR, 18 April; INA, 19 April — DR, 19 April; R. Baghdad, VoM, 24 April — DR, 25 April 1988; *al-Tadamun*, 30 April; *The Economist*, 23 April 1988. On the use of poison gas (allegedly mustard gas) that at some point was said to have "contaminated Abadan," IRNA, 17, 18 April — DR, 18, 19 April 1988.
25. Saddam Husayn, R. Baghdad, VoM, 24 April — DR, 25 April; *al-Tadamun*, 30 April 1988. Cf. the admission by Rafsanjani that Iraq did not employ its "principal forces" in its defense. R. Tehran, 3 June — DR, 6 June 1988.
26. *Al-Thawra*, Baghdad, 19 April — DR, 20 April 1988.
27. INA, 14 May — DR, 16 May 1988; cf. the problems in the relationship between the political and military leaders of Iraq caused by the loss of Faw; *MECS* 1986, pp. 364–66.
28. *The Economist*, 23 April 1988.
29. R. Tehran, 20 May — DR, 23 May 1988.
30. R. Tehran, 18, 20 April, R. Kuwait, 18 April; Tehran TV, 22 April — DR, 18, 21, 25 April 1988. The Iranians did also broadcast an appeal by Kuwaiti Hizballah to "inflict crushing blows on the subservient Persian Gulf governments....The Kuwaiti ruling family has played a consistently disgraceful role [in the war]." R. Tehran, 4 May — DR, 5 May.
31. R. Tehran, 18 April, Tehran TV, 21 April — DR, 18, 22 April 1988. Rafsanjani was more subtle, stating that helicopters were unidentified, but were positively non-Iraqi, and that more evidence was required; Tehran TV, 18 April — DR, 19 April 1988.
32. Cf. Interview with Foreign Minister 'Aziz, *al-Watan al-'Arabi*, 6 May — DR, 10 May 1988. I wish to thank Dr. Gary Sick for his comments on this point.
33. *Le Monde*, 2 February; *al-Wafd*, 4 February; cf. *The Economist*, 26 February, 5 March 1988.
34. Cf. *al-Majalla*, 17 May 1988, p. 27.
35. *Le Monde*, 23 March 1988.
36. "We should not sacrifice human lives unless there is a dire national need to do so...[The] president...and leadership do not want to relinquish Iraqi blood unless it is absolutely necessary to liberate the land." Foreign Minister 'Aziz, *al-Watan al-'Arabi*, ibid. An offensive strategy had been urged on Saddam by some of his high command since 1986; *MECS* 1986, p. 366; cf. *IHT*, 26 May 1988.
37. Significantly, the war of cities was ended by Iraq after the reconquest of Faw.
38. Defense Minister 'Adnan Khayrallah, INA, 23 May — DR, 23 May (author's emphasis.) Cf. *IHT*, 12 May; *NYT*, 19 June 1988.
39. INA, R. Baghdad, VoM, 25 May — DR, 25, 26 May; *IHT*, 26, 31 May; *Le Monde*, 27, 29–30 May 1988. On Iraqi planning, cf. *The Economist*, 4 June 1988.
40. R. Baghdad, 28 May — DR, 31 May 1988.
41. R. Tehran, 25, 26 May — DR, 26, 27 May 1988.
42. R. Tehran, 13, 14 June, IRNA, 14 June — DR, 14, 15 June 1988. Iraqi commanders were praised for repulsing Iranians; R. Baghdad, 13 June — DR, 14 June; *NYT*, 14 June 1988.
43. R. Baghdad, VoM, 25, 26 June; INA, 26 June; R. Tehran, IRNA, 25 June — DR, 27 June 1988.

44. INA, 28 June — DR, 29 June 1988. (Actually it had been published in *WT*.) Cf. *NYT*, 19 June 1988.
45. *Le Monde*, 3–4 June 1988.
46. IRNA, 9 May — DR, 10 May 1988. Cf. Summary by the commander of Ramadan headquarters, R. Tehran, 13 June — DR, 16 June 1988.
47. INA, 19, 22 June — DR, 20, 23 June; *Le Monde*, 30 June reported that the actual attack was by Iraqi troops and INLA used it for media exposure.
48. R. Baghdad, VoM, 14, 17, 22, 30 June — DR, 15, 19, 23, 30 June 1988.
49. IRNA, 14 July 1988; Rafsanjani attributed the withdrawal to the "new conditions created by the war." Tehran TV, 13 July — DR, 15 July 1988.
50. INA, R. Baghdad, 13, 15 July, R. Tehran, 13 July, R. Baghdad, VoM, 16 July — DR, 14, 15, 18 July 1988.
51. Testimony of CIA Director William M. Webster at Senate Foreign Relations Committee, 1 March 1989, USIS Official Text, 4 April 1989.
52. *IHT*, 24 March 1988. For detailed Iranian complaint to UN, see R. Tehran, 2 March — DR, 22 March 1988.
53. Webster, ibid., R. Tehran, 24 March, 30 April — DR, 25 March, 26 April 1988.
54. *IHT*, 30 January 1989.
55. R. Tehran, 27, 30 April — DR, 28 April, 3 May; Tehran TV, 5 May — DR, 6 May 1988.
56. IRNA, R. Tehran, 10 May — DR, 11 May; IRNA, 11 June — DR, 14 June 1988.
57. Letter of Iraqi foreign minister to UN secretary-general, INA, 29 March — DR, 30 March 1988. For a US report confirming Iranian use of chemical weapons, see WF, 30 March 1988.
58. *Al-Ra'y*, 29 March — DR, 29 March 1988.
59. *IHT*, 2–3 July; editorial report — DR, 1 July 1988; cf. the argument of the Iraqi minister of defense quoted above, p. 96.
60. IRNA, 23 July — DR, 26 July; *NYT*, 2 August; *IHT*, 11 August; *The Economist*, 8 August 1988.
61. IRNA quoted in editorial report — DR, 9 January 1989. On the Iraqi reaction, cf. INA, 7 January — DR, 9 January 1989.
62. Webster, ibid. (see Note 51 above); *IHT*, 9, 10–11, 14 September 1988, 14–15 January 1989; *Le Monde*, 4–5 September 1988; *The Economist*, 3, 10, 17 September 1988, 14 January 1989.
63. Tehran TV, 7 April— DR, 13 April; *IHT*, 2–3 July 1988.
64. *IHT*, 16, 18 May; *Le Monde*, 18 May; *The Economist*, 21 May 1988.
65. Again stated by Khameneh'i, R. Tehran, 17 May — DR, 18 May 1988.
66. Rafsanjani, R. Tehran, 3 May — DR, 3 May 1988.
67. VoL, 31 July — DR, *IHT*, 1 August 1988.
68. *FT*, 19 July, 10 August 1988. The data on attacks vary, the most reliable being those of Lloyds, London. For slightly different numbers, see Gary Sick, "Slouching toward Settlement: The Internationalization of the Iran-Iraq War, 1987–88," (manuscript).
69. *NYT*, 14 January, 15 April 1988.
70. Ibid., 15, 16 April; *The Economist*, 23 April; ANSA, 19 April, R. Paris, 20 April, R. Hilversum, 20 April — DR, 20, 21, 22 April 1988. The reason for the sudden Iranian spate of mining is unknown. It may have been in response to the "war of cities" or to an air raid on Lavan on 6 April or for some obscure internal Iranian reason; *NYT*, 21 April 1988.
71. *NYT*, 19 April; IRNA, AFP, 18 April, R. Tehran, GNA, 19 April — DR, 18, 19 April; IRNA, 10 May — DR, 11 May 1988.
72. R. Tehran, 20 May — DR, 23 May 1988.
73. *NYT*, 30 April 1988.
74. R. Tehran, 20 May — DR, 23 May 1988.
75. *NYT*, 29 May; *IHT*, 2–3 July 1988.
76. *The Economist*, 27 August 1988; cf. Les Aspin, *IHT*, 19 October 1988.
77. Rafsanjani, IRNA, 20 May — DR, 20 May 1988.
78. R. Tehran, 4, 5 July — DR, 5, 6 July 1988.
79. R. Tehran, 22 July — DR, 22 July 1988.
80. E.g. the appeal of President Khameneh'i to volunteers at the front: "Remain present on the

scene, do not leave the war zone, be ready to be called up by officials in charge of the war"; R. Tehran, 17 May — DR, 18 May 1988.

81. R. Tehran, IRNA, 7 May — DR, 9 May 1988; Shahbazi, born in 1946, was described as "the youngest commander." Previously he had served four years as deputy chief of staff for coordination and,before that, saw combat while serving at the Ahwaz guerrilla warfare headquarters.
82. R. Peace and Progress (in Persian), 16 May — DR, 19 May 1988.
83. R. Tehran, IRNA, 2 June — DR, 3 June 1988. One of Rafsanjani's previous "military" appointments was as commander of the "joint command post" of the IRGC and the Armed Forces (*Khatem al-Anbiya* headquarters), R. Tehran, Tehran TV, 18 March — DR, 21 March 1988.
84. Rafsanjani, R. Tehran, 3 June, 2 July — DR, 6 June, 6 July 1988.
85. Even while engaging the US Navy in the Gulf, the Iranian Navy and the IRGC naval forces operated independently. Adm. Malekzadegan, Tehran TV, 21 April — DR, 22 April; R. Tehran, 4, 10 June — DR, 7, 10 June 1988.
86. Rafsanjani, R.Tehran, 3, 4 June, 2 July — DR, 6, 7 June, 6 July 1988; Rafiqdust, Tehran TV, 3 June — DR, 6 June 1988. According to Rafsanjani, some 80% of the Iranian fighting forces were conscripts or short-term volunteers; R. Tehran, 15 April — DR, 18 April 1988. The usual Iranian reaction to battlefield crisis or defeat was to appeal for volunteers, who were urgently dispatched to the front.
87. Rafsanjani, R. Tehran, 3 June — DR, 6 June; Ayatollah Montazeri, R. Tehran, 6, 29 June — DR, 7, 30 June 1988.
88. R. Tehran, 2 July — DR, 6 July; Tehran TV, 13 July — DR, 14 July 1988. The duration of compulsory service in Iran was 28 months since fall 1987, and 24 months previously.
89. R. Tehran, 3 June — DR, 6 June; Tehran TV, 2 July — DR, 6 July 1988.
90. R. Tehran, 6 June — DR, 7 June 1988.
91. *Le Monde*, 8 June; R. Tehran, 1 July — DR, 6 July 1988.
92. Text of letter: KUNA, 18 July, IRNA, 21 July — DR, 18, 22 July; *NYT*, 19, 20 July 1988.
93. Deputy Foreign Minister Larijani, *La Repubblica*, 27 July — DR, 29 July; cf. Rafsanjani, Tehran TV, 18 July — DR, 19 July; *NYT*, 19 June 1988; an Iraqi version: INA, 30 July — DR, 4 August 1988. On reaction of Iranians, cf. *IHT*, 8 February 1989.
94. *The Economist*, 25 June; cf. *Le Monde*, 20 July; *al-Majalla*, 30 August 1988.
95. R. Tehran, 20 July — DR, 2 July 1988.
96. Ibid.; Rafsanjani, Tehran TV, 18 July — DR, 19 July 1988.
97. Khameneh'i, R. Tehran. 1 July — DR, 6 July 1988.
98. Tehran TV, 18 July — DR, 19 July 1988.
99. Cf. *CSM*, 17 February; *The Times*, 24 March; *Le Monde*, 17 May, 3 June; *The Economist*, 2 April, 4 June 1988.
100. *NYT*, 6 June 1988.
101. Khameneh'i, R. Tehran, 1 July — DR, 6 July 1988; General Command Headquarters statement, R. Tehran, 18 July — DR, 18 July; *ME*, September 1988.
102. Statements by Iraqi foreign and information minsters, INA, 18, 19 July — DR, 18, 20 July 1988. Iranian statements cited above did emphasize that the war was continuing.
103. INA, 20 July — DR, 21 July 1988.
104. R. Baghdad, 22 July — DR, 25 July 1988.
105. R. Baghdad, VoM, IRNA, 24 July — DR, 25 July 1988.
106. INA, 26 July — DR, 26 July; *IHT*, 25 August 1988.
107. *NYT*, 27 July 1988.
108. R. Tehran, 23, 24, 25 July, IRNA, 24 July — DR, 25, 26 July; cf. *MM*, 8 August 1988.
109. R. Tehran, 29 July — DR, 1 August. He later said that 130,000 men went to the front; R. Tehran, 19 August — DR, 19 August 1988.
110. Ibid.; IRNA, 28, 29 July — DR, 28 July, 1 August; INA, 29, 30 July — DR, 29 July, 1 August 1988. In a handwritten note Khomeyni praised the paratroopers of Kermanshah. This was said to be the first time he had sent a note to encourage army forces. *Kayhan*, London, 11 August — JPRS, 8 September 1988. According to Tehran, INLA suffered 1,734 killed; *IHT*, 25 August; cf. *The Economist*, 30 July 1988.
111. R. Monte Carlo, 20 July, R. Tehran, 22 July — DR, 20, 25 July 1988.

112. *NYT*, 22 July 1988.
113. Ibid., 4 August 1988.
114. R. Baghdad, 6 August — DR, 8 August 1988.
115. *NYT*, 9 August 1988.
116. TANJUG, 10 August — DR, 12 August; *IHT*, 25 August 1988.
117. The countries participating in the group were: Australia, Austria (also contributed a medical section), Bangladesh, Canada (also provided a 525-strong signals unit to ensure communcations for the first months of the operation before it was replaced by UN civilians), Denmark, Finland, Ghana, Hungary, India, Indonesia, Ireland (also provided a military police unit), Italy, Kenya, Malaysia, New Zealand (also provided the air unit), Nigeria, Norway, Peru, Poland, Senegal, Sweden, Turkey, Uruguay, Yugoslavia, and Zambia. *Report of the Secretary-General on the United Nations Iran-Iraq Military Observer Group* (for the period 9 August 1988 to 2 February 1988). Security Council Document S/20442, 2 February 1988. See *NYT*, 9, 11 August; *Le Monde*, 12, 14 August 1988.
118. E.g., IRNA, 18 October, 2 November — DR, 19 October, 2 November 1988.
119. 1,960 of them had been registered up to 20 January 1989 with UNIIMOG, which confirmed only a quarter of them; the most serious concerned Iranian flooding of no-man's land for a length of 60 km. north of the Shatt in September, to create a water obstacle between the belligerents. A later serious incident occurred in February 1989 when an Iraqi ambush reportedly killed five Iranian soldiers.
120. *Report of the Secretary-General* (see Note 117 above); *IHT*, 9 March; for typical complaints, cf. R. Tehran, 31 August, INA, 2 September — DR, 31 August, 6 September 1988.
121. IRNA, 20, 22 August — DR, 22, 23 August 1988.
122. *NYT*, 23 October 1988.
123. R. Tehran, 3, 24 October — DR, 3, 25 October 1988; IRNA, 2 January — DR, 3 January 1989.
124. *NYT*, 23 October; *IHT*, 8 December 1988.
125. *NYT*, 17 September; *IHT*, 26 September, 8 December 1988.
126. *IHT*, 8 December 1988.
127. *IHT*, 25 August; *The Economist*, 3, 17 September; INA, 7 September — DR, 8 September 1988. Talabani was received at the State Department in Washington in June to the outrage of the Iraqis.
128. Rafsanjani, Tehran TV, 1 September — DR, 2 September 1988.
129. Ibid.; IRNA, 16 August, 21 October — DR, 17 August, 25 October 1988.
130. Rafsanjani, R. Tehran, 8 June — DR, 9 June 1988.
131. *Le Monde*, 2 March 1989; cf. *The Economist*, 3 December 1988.
132. *IHT*, 25 August 1988.
133. *NYT*, 2 September 1988.
134. In an interview before the cease-fire, Foreign Minister Velayati asked rhetorically: "Can Iran use existing elements...in the UN to the benefit of Iran?" Tehran TV, 11 August — DR, 12 August 1988.
135. IRNA, 7 November — DR, 8 November 1988; Deputy Foreign Minister Besharati, R. Tehran, 1 January — DR, 4 January 1989.
136. Velayati, Tehran TV, 11 August — DR, 12 August; KUNA, 26 August, IRNA, 27, 28 August, R. Tehran, 29 August — DR, 29, 30 August; *NYT*, 27 August 1988. Iran insisted it had not abrogated the 1975 accord after the revolution. IRNA, 8 September — DR, 9 September 1988.
137. *NYT*, 29 August; INA, 29 August, GNA, 28 October, R. Baghdad, 30 October — DR, 30 August, 31 October 1988. Quite a different line of argument was used by First Deputy Prime Minister Taha Yasin Ramadan: (1) The 1975 agreement did not supersede the 1913 agreement signed between the two countries (this alludes to the Constantinople protocol of 4 November 1913 between the Ottoman Empire and Persia, according to which most of the waterway was under Ottoman sovereignty), on the basis of which a political settlement should be reached (IRNA, 3 September — DR, 5 September 1988); (2) Baghdad would not compromise any of its legitimate rights under any circumstances. A new peace agreement

should annul all previous accords, particularly that of 1975, which was imposed on Iraq (KUNA, 1 December — DR, 1 December 1988).

138. KUNA, 29 August — DR, 29 August; *NYT*, 30 August 1988.
139. *IHT*, 12 September; *NYT*, 9 October; IRNA, 17, 18 October — DR, 18 October 1988.
140. *Report of the Secretary-General* (see Note 117 above), p. 9; R. Tehran, 8 October, INA, 2 November — DR, 11 October, 2 November; *IHT*, 10 October; Tariq 'Aziz, R. Baghdad, 9 November — DR, 9 November 1988. The hard line over the waterway may possibly be a tactical Iraqi position, but,as the negotiations continue to drag on, this seems less probable. See Laurie Mylroie, "Iraq's Changing Role in the Persian Gulf," *Current History*, Vol. 88 (February 1989), p. 98.
141. *Al-Siyasa*, Kuwait, 24 August, IRNA, 16 November — DR, 30 August, 17 November; *NYT*, 9 November; *The Economist*, 5 November 1988.
142. IRNA, 12 September, 24, 28 October, INA, 30 October — DR, 15 September, 25, 28, 31 October 1988.
143. INA, IRNA, 20 October — DR, 20, 21 October; *IHT*, 4 November 1988; IRNA, 2 January — DR, 3 January 1989.
144. INA, IRNA, 10, 24 November, IRNA, 5 December — DR, 25 November, 6 December; *NYT*, 25, 28 November 1988.
145. *IHT*, 10 February 1989.
146. IRNA, 2 January, Saddam Husayn, R. Baghdad, VoM, 6 January, INA, 6 January — DR, 6, 9 January 1989.
147. R. Tehran, 21 September — DR, 22 September 1988.
148. Graham E. Fuller, *IHT*, 11 October 1988.
149. Internal repercussions in Iran and Iraq are beyond the scope of this chapter.
150. E.g., Khameneh'i, IRNA, 17 October — DR, 18 October; Rafsanjani, IRNA, 2 November — DR, 2 November 1988. Iran has been making a major effort to lift arms embargoes in various countries.
151. These questions will probably be amply discussed in the growing literature on the war. I have found the following of great help: Graham Fuller, "War and Revolution in Iran" and Laurie Mylroie, "Iraq's Changing Role in the Persian Gulf," both in *Current History*, Vol. 88 (February 1989), pp. 81ff. and pp. 89ff. respectively.
152. IRNA, 18 September — DR, 19 September 1988. According to Khomeyni 2,500 "seminary students" were among the killed; R. Tehran, 22 February — DR, 23 February 1989; Mylroie, ibid., p. 91.
153. On the relative openness of Iranian society in comparison with Iraq, which had been often noted during the war, see Fuller, ibid., p. 82.
154. Mylroie, ibid., p. 91; Amazia Baram, "After the Iran-Iraq War — What?" *The Jerusalem Quarterly*, No. 49 (Winter 1989), p. 85. A later estimate reckoned almost double that number. *The Economist*, 20 December 1989.
155. Cf. Tariq 'Aziz, *al-Musawwar*, Cairo, 10 June — DR, 15 June 1988.
156. Fuller, ibid., p. 82. Cf. *IHT*, 23 August 1988; *Le Monde*, 4 January 1989.
157. R. Tehran, 22 February — DR, 23 February 1989.
158. E.g., Gary Sick, "Trial by Error: Reflections on the Iran-Iraq War," *MEJ*, Spring 1989, pp. 230–45, and "Slouching toward Settlement: The Internationalization of the Iran-Iraq War" (manuscript); Janice Gross Stein, "The Wrong Strategy in the Right Place: the US in the Gulf," *International Security*, Vol. 13, No. 3 (Winter 1988–89), pp. 142–67.

PALESTINIAN ISSUES

The Palestine Liberation Organization

JOSHUA TEITELBAUM

Nineteen-eighty-eight was a momentous year for the PLO. The uprising (*intifada*) in the West Bank and Gaza Strip catapulted the Palestinian issue to the top of the international agenda and rescued the organization from the political ignominy which was its lot following the Amman summit of November 1987. It was the catalyst for bringing the PLO to declared positions that put the organization closer than ever before to the acceptance of a two-state solution to the conflict. The organization's diplomatic efforts were crowned with success when in December the US opened an official dialogue with the PLO. While the PLO was not directly responsible for sparking the uprising, it viewed the event as the inevitable result of the long years it had spent trying to sustain the Palestinian identity and maintain the struggle.

The political opportunities afforded by the uprising were not without accompanying threats. First, the uprising elevated the political weight of the Palestinians in the territories (*filastiniyun al-dakhil*), threatening to transform the conflict into one solely over the future of the West Bank and the Gaza Strip and thus undercut the PLO's goal of reaching a solution that would also deal with the Palestinians outside of Palestine (*filastiniyun al-kharij*). A dilemma was thus created for the PLO. On the one hand, in order to achieve progress in the international arena on the Palestinian issue and maintain its political relevance, the organization had to show moderation and give the impression that its ultimate and final goal was solely a Palestinian state in the territories. On the other hand, there was always the danger that should the residents of the West Bank and Gaza feel unable to continue the uprising or sense their newfound strength, they might push for a separate solution to their own problem. The organization's leadership thus did its best to achieve concrete political gains without undermining its "phased program" approved in 1974, which set a program for the liberation of all of Palestine. That this remained the strategy of all PLO factions was clear from the common denominator in all statements: the constant demand for an independent state, as well as self-determination and the right of return. The PLO's constituent groups differed only in the degree to which they were willing to concede tactical concessions: much of Fath and the Palestine Communist Party (PCP) were willing to concede more while the Democratic Front for the Liberation of Palestine (DFLP) and the Popular Front for the Liberation of Palestine (PFLP) feared that tactical concessions might lead to strategic ones. A common language was reached at the 19th session of the Palestine National Council (PNC) in Algiers in November which declared the independent State of Palestine, but even there the PFLP expressed certain reservations about the political statement of the PNC that accompanied the declaration. Both organizations also noted that statements made by PLO Executive Committee (EC) chairman Yasir 'Arafat at a press conference in December following his speech to the UN General Assembly were not binding on them.

THE PLO AND THE *INTIFADA*: PERCEPTIONS AND DILEMMAS

The uprising in the administered territories was a windfall for the PLO, reversing its political fortunes. As such, the *intifada* provided the organization with a newfound confidence and a feeling of strength, and became its main political asset. At the same time, it was a political challenge to the PLO since the initiative was not the organization's. The uprising forced the PLO to prove to the residents of the territories that it could achieve concrete political gains that would bring the Israeli presence to an end. This factor alone brought about the most significant changes in PLO political thinking since 1974. While residents of the West Bank and Gaza were overwhelmingly supportive of the PLO, the organization was jealous of its representative status and was at pains to show that it was running the *intifada*. This trend was strengthened in reaction to US and Israeli efforts to find local Palestinian interlocutors instead of the PLO. The organization thus had to take over the *intifada*, direct its energies as much as possible, and make sure that the interests of the uprising's leadership remained those of the PLO, namely, a solution to the Palestinian problem as a whole which went beyond the mere future of the West Bank and Gaza. That the *intifada* and the PLO be identified as one and the same thing was thus an existential question for the latter. Proving this was a complicated task since the initiative for sparking the uprising was taken by Islamic organizations, particularly in the Gaza Strip, which did not join the PLO-affiliated Unified National Command of the Uprising.

THE INITIAL CHALLENGE: ASSERTING PLO PRIMACY AND THWARTING LOCAL INITIATIVES

It had become axiomatic that in general terms the PLO enjoyed the overwhelming support of the Palestinians in the West Bank and the Gaza Strip. Yet when it became apparent in about mid-January, and particularly around the time of the initiative of US Secretary of State George Shultz in February, that the uprising was developing into a permanent feature, the PLO set about trying to co-opt the uprising, both on the ground in the West Bank and Gaza and in the international arena. The PLO was aware that the uprising's success and the ensuing political benefit to the organization was predicated on letting the local leadership dictate the pace and nature of the *intifada*. But where the organization's representative status was threatened, the PLO moved quickly to prevent local initiatives from getting beyond its control. This was the red line beyond which the PLO could not let local Palestinians go. To do so would, in PLO eyes, turn the Palestinian problem into one of the West Bank and Gaza alone.

Although 'Arafat had authorized the meeting of *al-Fajr* editor Hana Siniora and Gaza attorney Fa'iz Abu Rahma with US Secretary of State George Shultz in Washington in late January, he made it clear that this was solely to emphasize to the US "the crimes being committed against our people."[1] But when it became apparent in early February that Shultz was planning a full-scale peace initiative and intended coming to the region (see chapter on the Middle East peace process), the PLO moved to assert its primacy over the West Bankers.

Leading West Bank and Gaza personalities, however, wanted to meet with Shultz. A Nazareth-based newspaper published an article by Da'ud Kuttab, a journalist close to Hana Siniora, in which he wrote that 'Arafat had authorized six of his leading backers, including Siniora, to meet with the secretary of state.[2] It was reported that the authorization had even been recorded in 'Arafat's own voice and had reached US diplomats in Israel. Several of those on the list met with US envoy Walter Cluverius in Jerusalem on 20 February and were very hopeful that the PLO would authorize the meeting with Shultz, even though on the previous day the organization had officially declared that it would not.[3] When West Bank and Gaza leaders persisted in pressing for the meeting, the PLO issued a strongly worded warning: "The masses of our people have decided to boycott...Shultz's visit. Woe unto him who meets with the Zionist Shultz. Our people will have no mercy on anyone who deviates from the will of our giant people."[4] The meeting never materialized, and while trumpeting its success in preventing it, the PLO "reiterate[d] its readiness to meet with the US Administration on any level and in any Arab or foreign capital through a delegation composed of Palestinians from inside as well as outside our occupied homeland...."[5]

When the PLO felt it had succeeded in aborting US attempts to dictate meetings with Palestinian representatives from the territories only and thus asserted the priority of its representative status, 'Arafat announced that the organization had begun forming a delegation from within and without the territories for a meeting with Shultz in Cairo. It was reported from Jerusalem that the delegation would include Palestinian-American professors Ibrahim Abu Lughod and Edward Said, and the deported editor of the East Jerusalem daily *al-Sha'b*, Akram Haniyya. All three were PNC members.[6] This meeting also did not materialize.

What did materialize was a meeting authorized by 'Arafat between Said and Abu Lughod and Shultz in Washington on 26 March. As US officials put it, these were US citizens who were PNC members, but not members of the PLO.[7] The PLO praised the meeting, but disputed (as did Israel, for that matter) this artificial US distinction:

> In their capacity as PNC members, Brothers Abu Lughod and Said decide the work of the executive authority. In other words, they are part of Palestinian decision-making. Consequently, the meeting with them is a meeting with the Palestinian decision-makers, that is, the PLO Executive Committee. How can they separate the PNC, as a legislative authority, from the PLO, or its Executive Committee, as an executive authority, particularly since Brothers Abu Lughod and Said went to meet Shultz charged and authorized not only by the PNC but also by the executive authority represented by the PLO Executive Committee, in fact, by Committee Chairman Brother Yasir 'Arafat.[8]

Remarks by Abu Lughod himself soon after the meeting reflected the fundamental PLO perception of the unity of the Palestinian people and its representatives, as well as the small victory the meeting constituted.

> On other occasions the US has recognized the existence of the Palestinian people in the occupied land, as it has the rights of that people. And now, with this meeting, it has recognized the other part of the Palestinian people, that part which lives in dispersion, clinging to its homeland and its legitimate rights, just as the part living in the occupied land clings to its homeland and legitimate rights.[9]

When Shultz returned to the region in early April, local Palestinians, anxious to meet with the secretary of state, claimed that the PLO had authorized a meeting.

However, Sa'id Kan'an, a Nablus businessman, stated that unless 'Arafat came out publicly in favor of the meeting, it would not take place. "Otherwise we fear for our lives," he stressed.[10] In the event, the PLO boycott of the Shultz visit was maintained.

For the PLO, the question was one of guarding the principle of the unity of the Palestinian people and of its status as its sole representative. If the uprising brought the West Bank and Gaza Strip part of the Palestinian issue to the center of world attention, then this was good. But the PLO felt it necessary to remind the world that the problem was more complex and involved than that. Fath Central Committee member Salah Khalaf (Abu Iyad) expressed it thus: the Shultz plan "helps the Palestinians within [the territories]...There are 1.725m. Palestinians living in the occupied territories and 3.5m. outside. What is the solution for the Palestinians living outside the territories? The Shultz plan gives them no hope. The problem remains."[11] Khalid al-Hasan, also a member of the Fath Central Committee and an adviser to 'Arafat, said that the PLO enforced a boycott of the meeting not because it does not trust the Palestinians living in the territories, but because "our battle is to prevent the separation of the Palestinians living in the territories from the rest."[12]

In ideological terms, the Shultz initiative was just too little, for in the PLO perception the *intifada* had achieved something much bigger. The Palestinian issue was at the top of the international agenda and now it was up to the PLO to stake its true claim. The *intifada* was "the militant march and the massive sacrifices offered in [the refugee camps of] Sabra, Shatila, al-Burj [in Lebanon], the West Bank, the Gaza Strip, the Galilee, and the Negev....There can be no solution...unless the Palestinian people's national inalienable rights are attained, headed by their right to repatriation, self-determination, and establishment of an independent national state whose capital is Jerusalem."[13] This was the essence of the PLO's phased strategy. (For a detailed discussion of this trilateral formula, see below.)

Since the uprising had focused world attention on the West Bank and Gaza, the PLO felt a need to assert that the *intifada* was its doing and was essentially not spontaneous. At the beginning, when the uprising was perceived in the media as having been initiated by Muslim activists in the Gaza Strip, the PLO denied this interpretation and contended that the Islamic trends were part of the PLO. As the uprising progressed and became more widely based, the organization portrayed it as the end result of years of work and as being inexorably linked to PLO efforts in several arenas. Khalil Quqa, a deported leader of Hamas (the Muslim Brotherhood branch in the territories — see chapter on the West Bank and Gaza Strip) from Gaza, made just the kind of statements the PLO feared: "The Islamic movement is proud that it started the uprising on the night of 8 December [1987] and early the next day. I mean to be specific in saying this." When asked bluntly if he accepted the PLO's leadership, Quqa replied, "We recognize the PLO as a leader of the organizations represented in it."[14] Since Hamas was not in the PLO, the meaning of Quqa's answer was clear. Along with its refusal to become a part of the PLO, Hamas refused to become a part of the Unified National Command of the uprising in the territories (on the Unified Command, see chapter on West Bank and Gaza Strip). In August, Hamas succeeded in enforcing a strike on a different day than that called for by the Unified Command.[15]

The Islamic movement, then, offered a real challenge. Already in 1987, the PLO had sensed the growing strength of the Islamic movement in the West Bank and Gaza and consequently had given some Muslim figures (probably, but not necessarily, from

Islamic Jihad) representation in the Central Council (CC). The organization also made other efforts to strenghthen ties with Muslim fundamentalists (see *MECS* 1987, pp. 216–17). In an interview published in the Fath journal *al-Sakhra*, Salah Khalaf had discussed the problematics of Fath's relationship with Hamas. The Muslim Brotherhood had rejected several overtures by Fath for greater representation in the PNC, arguing that the PLO was a narrow, regionally based organization and non-Islamic. Khalaf issued an appeal to the Brotherhood to join the PLO so the PLO could be the sole legitimate representative of the Palestinian people.[16] Then, when the uprising broke out, 'Arafat was at pains on several occasions to convince his audience that the uprising had nothing to do with initiatives by Islamic movements.[17] PLO EC member Faruq Qaddumi contended that media reports portraying the uprising as the work of "Muslim fanatics" were orchestrated by Israel in order to gain European sympathy and to cover up its brutal handling of the demonstrations.[18]

In a more practical vein, during his visits to Cairo, 'Arafat met with the Muslim Brotherhood leader, General Guide (*murshid al-'amm*) Muhammad Hamid Abu al-Nasr, apparently in an effort to convince the latter to persuade Hamas leaders to join the Unified Command.[19] The PLO weekly *Filastin al-Thawra* also published a statement issued by Abu al-Nasr following the 19th PNC in November (see below). The statement expressed the Muslim Brotherhood's support for the Palestinian declaration of independence, but also its reservations concerning the PLO's acceptance of UN Resolutions 181, 242, and 338, as they implied recognition of Israel and concession of part of Palestine. If a "ministate" was established, then this must be only a step on the way to the complete liberation of Palestine. Nevertheless, Abu al-Nasr explained, the Palestinians must maintain unity of ranks and continue the *intifada* at all costs.[20] It was due to the latter appeal to unity that the statement was printed in the PLO organ.

To assert its prominence in the organization of the uprising, the PLO emphasized the unity of the Palestinian struggle outside as well as inside the territories. 'Arafat often stressed that the *intifada* had begun on 26 October 1986, when West Bank and Gaza Palestinians protested the fate of Palestinians in Lebanon who were under attack in the war of the camps (see *MECS* 1986, pp. 194–96). "Since then," added 'Arafat, "the waves of the uprising have not receded."[21] In this manner, he sought to reduce the *intifada* and place it in a string of events in which other concentrations of Palestinians were involved. When asked if he considered the uprising the PLO's greatest achievement, he replied: "It is one of the PLO's greatest achievements."[22] Likewise, 'Arafat often referred to "the generals of the stones [the young people leading the *intifada*]," and "the generals of the rocket-propelled grenades [the 'RPG kids' who fought Israel in Lebanon in 1982]" as being a part of the same movement.[23]

Similarly, contentions in the press that the uprising was of spontaneous generation tended to distract from the role of the PLO. Such claims, stated DFLP Secretary-General Na'if Hawatima, were intended to isolate Palestinians inside the occupied territories from their conationals outside.[24] Fath Central Committee member Khalil al-Wazir (Abu Jihad) rejected such claims vehemently, stating that the *intifada* was the fruit of a "long struggle...inside and outside Palestine."[25] Salah Khalaf put it this way: "The *intifada* is our child. I am very proud of this child because it is better than its parents."[26] For the PLO, the nature of the relationship with those in the territories was clear, regardless of its complexities: "At the top of the pyramid is the PLO leadership, then comes the Unified National Command of the uprising in the occupied territories which acts as a field command, and then come the popular committees."[27] In reality, the relationship was much more intricate than this (see chapter on West Bank and Gaza Strip).

In addition to the controversy over meetings with Shultz, other incidents during the year illustrated the tension between the leadership inside and the PLO outside the territories. Initiatives that emanated from the territories were received by the PLO with demonstrated ambivalence. A document conciliatory toward Israel written by 'Arafat's press adviser, Bassam Abu Sharif, which gained publicity in mid-June (see below), was well received by several leaders in the territories but condemned by many PLO leaders, such as Salah Khalaf and Faruq Qaddumi. Faysal al-Husayni, considered to be the leading supporter of Fath in the territories, was very positive about the Abu Sharif document. "Most of the Palestinians in the occupied territories," said al-Husayni, "do not understand the criticism leveled against Sharif from outside the occupied territories."[28] Sari Nusayba, a professor at Bir Zayt University and, along with Fa'iz Abu Rahma and Hana Siniora, a supporter of the most pragmatic trend within Fath, completely endorsed the Abu Sharif document in an interview with Siniora's *al-Fajr*. Nusayba praised its forthrightness and clarity. In order to complement it, he added, the Palestinian leadership "must also provide a daring, imaginative and revolutionary peace initiative.... We must be clear about the fact that it is not part of our intention to destroy the State of Israel."[29]

In early August, a "plan for unveiling the independence document" (*mashru' i'lan 'an wathiqat al-istiqlal*) found in Faysal al-Husayni's office served to further illustrate the growing self-assertiveness of the leadership in the territories toward the PLO leadership outside. The plan proposed to institutionalize and thereby assert the representative status of the leaders of the territories by creating a legislative body for an independent state to be made up of 152 people who were mentioned by name; they would then automatically be made members of the PNC. Such a step would increase the voting power of West Bank and Gaza residents far beyond their proportion in the Palestinian population as a whole. This kind of representation, whether in an interim government or in a Palestinian delegation for negotiations with Israel, raised alarms in the PLO. The plan noted that this technique — creating a state that was occupied — "will have a stronger influence on diplomatic activity than any other political initiative that could be presented by the Palestinian side."[30] The document did not mention an international conference, a cornerstone of PLO policy, and, most importantly, while referring to the need to negotiate the right of return or compensation of refugees, it left out the issue of self-determination. Such a formulation could be understood to mean that a Palestinian state in the West Bank and Gaza would in itself constitute Palestinian self-determination, a position consistently denied by the PLO (see below).

It was no surpise then that the PLO was decidedly nonsanguine about the document. While noting only that al-Husayni's document included "good ideas," Khalid al-Hasan chose to downplay its significance, suggesting that the document constituted discussion points and that it was not a full-blown unilateral initiative.[31] Following the publicity over the document, it was reported that 'Arafat had rebuked West Bank leaders and was not prepared to let them take any further steps; he even accused them of trying to form an alternative leadership.[32]

As the convening of the PNC came closer more stringent calls were heard in the

West Bank and Gaza for the PLO to adopt a realistic program which would cash in on the results of months of struggle. These calls reflected even more the shift in the balance of power, giving leaders in the territories a greater say in PLO policy. They came not only from moderates like Siniora who were often at odds with 'Arafat, but also from the Unified Command, which included leftist elements. The PLO had no choice but to take their views strongly into consideration. Siniora's *al-Fajr* wrote, "Palestinians...in the occupied territories...patiently bearing all of [the uprising's] consequences, are looking to the 19th PNC and the Palestinian leadership in the diaspora to give them concrete and real answers to what will come next....There is no room left for rhetoric."[33] Beginning with "Call No. 24" issued in late August, the Unified Command called on the PLO leadership to take brave and realistic action in order to turn the *intifada* into political achievements in the international sphere.[34] Moreover, residents began to organize petitions to be sent to the leadership, advocating similar positions. It was this kind of pressure from within the territories that eventually proved crucial in moving the PLO toward unprecedented political positions. Statements of this kind had the effect of convincing 'Arafat of the need for a diplomatic initiative, and, when the decision had been taken, of supporting his efforts within the Palestinian camp.

In late December, however, Faysal al-Husayni and the mayor of Bethlehem, Elias Freij, crossed a red line. In remarks communicated by MK Yair Tzaban (Mapam) following a meeting with al-Husayni while in administrative detention, al-Husayni said that he would support elections in the territories, strongly implying that they could be held before an Israeli withdrawal. The PLO's EC, meeting in Baghdad, issued a statement condemning the idea out of hand, and al-Husayni soon retracted.[35] At the end of the year, Freij told the press that he had proposed a UN-sponsored truce in the territories. He too was widely condemned by the PLO, and 'Arafat himself threatened him with death, saying that anyone who tried to stop the uprising "exposes himself to the bullets of our people." Freij withdrew his proposal.[36]

WHAT THE *INTIFADA* WROUGHT: THE VIEW FROM TUNIS

The PLO viewed the *intifada* as a massive achievement. Although only time will finally tell whether this was so, it is already clear that the uprising served as the main catalyst in a process that had begun after the 1967 war and had gradually changed the international perception of the conflict, from one of Arab refusal to recognize and live in peace with Israel to one of Palestinian rights. The PLO leadership often analyzed the changes brought about by the uprising. Foremost among them were: (1) the wave of sympathy generated for the Palestinian cause in the West, as reflected in media coverage, which resulted in shifting the focus of international debate on Palestine and the revealing of the "real nature" of Israel; (2) the involvement of Israeli Arabs in support of the *intifada*, a process which served to strengthen the PLO's claim to represent and demand self-determination for all Palestinians; (3) the polarization of Israeli society (see chapter on Israel), which furthered short-term tactical aims as well as long-term PLO goals; (4) the rise in PLO relevance and standing in the Arab arena; and (5) political compensation for the loss of the Lebanese territorial stronghold.

One of the goals of PNC member Edward Said, ever since he published his *Orientalism* in 1978, has been to bring about a "new discourse for and of the Arabs."[37] By mid-1988 it had become clear to Said that thanks to the *intifada* much had been accomplished toward that goal since "there is little sympathy for Israel now." Said felt vindicated: "Slowly the great disparity diminishes between Western praise and admiration for Israel as a democracy and pioneering state, on the one hand, and, on the other the ignorant opprobrium Palestinians have had heaped on them since their world was shattered in 1948."[38]

PLO leaders echoed similar sentiments. 'Arafat said that the Palestinians had forced "the rewriting of history with a Palestinian dialect, based on Palestinian facts...."[39] "David now is the Palestinian David," he said on another occasion.[40] In an article devoted to an assessment of the *intifada* the PLO journal *Shu'un Filastiniyya* stated:

> The uprising has succeeded in shattering...the traditional stereotype which connected the Palestinian people with terrorism....All the gallons of ink spilled and the slogans raised since...1948 never succeeded in revealing [Israel's real nature] and condemning it as the uprising has done. The uprising has returned the conflict between Israel and the Palestinians to its natural roots....[41]

All this had been possible, said 'Arafat, because Israel's real nature had been exposed: "Where is the democracy of the Jewish State of which Zionists all over the world had bragged? That state has been exposed to the world as a racist fascist state ruled by a gang of fanatics even worse than South Africa."[42]

The PLO was also gratified by the role the uprising played in increasing political mobilization of Israeli Arabs, termed by the PLO "the Arabs of 1948" (see chapter on Israel). For the PLO, this gave added credence to their claim for self-determination for all Palestinians (on the concept of self-determination and Israeli Arabs, see below). In a report presented to the CC, Khalil al-Wazir emphasized the importance of the uprising's influence on "the masses in the areas occupied in 1948."[43] The Voice of Palestine often made a point of addressing itself to all Palestinians, including those living in Israel:

> Hail to you, our fighters in...Nablus, Gaza, Hebron, Ramallah, Bethlehem, Rafah, Jericho, Tulkarm, Salfit, Qalqilya, Jibalya, Balata, al-Shat, Jalazun, [all in the West Bank and Gaza], Nazareth, Shafa 'Amr, Umm al- Fahm, and Kafr Qasim [all in Israel]; hail to our revolutionary brothers in all the cities, villages, and refugee camps in Palestine. This is your great uprising which will not stop until our people's rights are attained.[44]

For 'Arafat, too, the involvement of Israeli Arabs was to be praised, and he often included the Galilee, the Triangle, and the Negev when describing the pervasiveness of the uprising.[45] EC member and director of the Palestine National Fund, Jawid al-Ghusayn, reiterated this train of thought, commenting, "The [Unified National] Command...also has members inside Israel....Those in Israel are working under the PLO banner, in total harmony with the people, in order to remove the usurping enemy...."[46]

The lack of a serious military option over the years had led the PLO to put great stock in enhancing social and political tensions in Israel in order to defeat the state through disintegration from within (see *MECS* 1987, pp. 220–21). Thus, in the past, the organization had sought to emphasize the social gap between Israelis of European origin and those from Asia and Africa. Therefore, the intense political controversy in

Israel generated by the *intifada* was the cause for much hope in the PLO. Some Palestinian leaders saw this tension as a threat to Israel's existence and, therefore, of long-term strategic importance for the PLO, while others thought it most important for shorter term, tactical political gains. Thus 'Arafat said, "the Zionist theory of a Jewish homeland has been shaken," and "Israel is in the midst of a profound crisis of conscience and I do not believe its existence is in very good health."[47] *Shu'un Filastiniyya* wrote, "The goal at the top of the uprising's list is to sow confusion in the ranks of the enemy in order to pave the way for the destabilizing of its rule in the West Bank and Gaza." The *intifada* had succeeded in this because it was able, according to the PLO, to touch the issues to which Israeli society was sensitive due to its "democratic nature" (quotation marks in text).[48] Israeli society, noted Khalaf, had indeed been polarized by the uprising.[49]

The uprising also performed a useful function for the PLO with respect to the Arab governments. It received great popular support from the people of the Arab countries, and generated significant private donations. Remarks by Mahmud 'Abbas (Abu Ma'zin), a Fath representative on the EC, sought to turn the growing importance of the Palestinian question on the Arab agenda into a new leverage for increasing funding of the organization:

> The uprising has...created a new atmosphere among the Arabs....Arabs everywhere are now dealing with the Palestinian question in a way that is more positive and more effective....It is hoped that the support of the Arab countries...will...become compatible with their people's feelings....What the Arab countries have offered until now is less than what is needed.[50]

'Abbas's complaint was not without reason: the Arab governments were less than forthcoming in paying directly into the PLO treasury. According to 'Arafat, at the Algiers summit in June (see chapter on inter-Arab relations), an immediate grant of $128m. was approved along with a commitment to a monthly donation of $43m.; however, during the summit Arab officials disputed 'Arafat's assertions, stressing that they had agreed only to negotiate periodically the needs of the PLO for the uprising.[51] In August, 'Arafat said that the PLO had not received any of the money,[52] and in early 1989 Khalaf noted dryly that "we hope to receive even 10% of the assistance extended to the *Mujahidin* in Afghanistan."[53]

In a political sense, the *intifada* served also as compensation for the loss of the PLO's position of eminence in Lebanon in 1982. 'Arafat and other leaders blamed Syria for the PLO defeat there and for the ensuing dissent it fostered within the organization (see *MECS* 1983–84, pp. 303–7). But despite Syrian efforts, the uprising had once again restored the Palestinian issue to what the PLO believed to be its rightful place.[54] Faruq Qaddumi gave expression — albeit perhaps exaggerated — to this perception of being compensated when he noted that the uprising had created a new situation and that it would no longer be necessary for the Palestinians to carry out armed operations from Lebanon.[55]

There were other victories brought about by the *intifada*, namely, Jordan's disengagement from the West Bank and the opening of a dialogue with the US. These are discussed separately below under their own headings.

REAPING THE PROFITS: THE INTERNAL POLITICAL DEBATE AND PALESTINIAN DIPLOMACY PRIOR TO THE PALESTINE NATIONAL COUNCIL

As noted above, the uprising was a catalyst which prompted all trends within the PLO to take more realistic positions that would have a chance of moving the political process forward while achieving major political gains. Some kind of US recognition, or at least a dialogue with Washington was at the top of the PLO's list. Jordan's late July decision to renounce its claim to the West Bank (see chapter on Jordan) greatly accelerated this process. 'Arafat had held this view for several years, at least since the end of the Beirut episode in 1982. As the uprising progressed, other leaders began to fall in line. Most notable in this regard was Salah Khalaf. The DFLP and the PCP also supported a serious political initiative, as did, in his own way, the PFLP secretary-general, George Habash. All camps agreed on the phased program for the total liberation of Palestine, founded on the principles of self-determination, an independent state, and the right of return (on the phased strategy, see below). The debate within the PLO thus focused on means and tactics and the price to be paid. The PFLP and part of the DFLP were mostly concerned lest tactical concessions lead to strategic ones. They were worried that 'Arafat would go too far without consulting them, and therefore often raised the need to implement the various organizational reforms agreed upon at the 18th PNC in 1987 (see *MECS* 1987, pp. 204–6). It followed, then, that in the internal debate 'Arafat and his supporters endeavored to present their new declared positions as variously a refinement of, or an improvement on, earlier positions that were a part of the wider Palestinian consensus. They denied that they constituted concessions. As such, the discussion resembled the previous debate over the adoption of the phased strategy, held as a result of the movement toward a settlement which began in late 1973.[56]

The debate focused on practical steps to be taken, such as declaring independence and forming a provisional government or a government-in-exile. But if the PLO was to become a part of the process and, in particular, open a dialogue with the US, it had to concede on three specific points: accept Resolutions 242 and 338, recognize Israel, and renounce terrorism. As these conditions were apparent to all, the discussions centered on how to do this at the least possible cost to internal unity and to the strategic goals embodied in the phased strategy.

The idea of a government-in-exile had been raised from time to time in PLO history, mostly as an effort by one Arab government or another to control the organization. The PLO had realized this and always rejected the option. There was also the haunting memory of the "Government of All Palestine" formed in the Gaza Strip following the end of the 1948 War, which was a painful fiasco. It was believed that such a step would be extremely controversial in the organization and hence it was not worth discussing, at least until the PLO was closer to attaining some of its goals. The idea was first mooted again immediately after the outbreak of the *intifada* in December 1987, with 'Arafat being a vocal supporter of it since he believed that it was the best way to assure PLO representation (see *MECS* 1987, pp. 232–33).[57] Wazir, Khalaf, Habash, Hawatima, and the PCP, all believed that the idea was premature, and would detract from other efforts to capitalize on the uprising.[58] Most leaders did not oppose the idea in principle, and a committee headed by jurist Anis al-Qasim was formed to investigate the option. Meanwhile, the CC, meeting in Baghdad in January 1988, could agree on little more than a call for UN forces to protect the Palestinians in the territories.[59]

A TRIAL BALLOON: THE DOCUMENT OF BASSAM ABU SHARIF

Soon after the beginning of the *intifada*, the PLO made several efforts to consolidate gains and capitalize on the international attention generated by the uprising for the Palestinian cause. There were reports in mid-January that the PLO had contacted Israel and offered a cease-fire in exchange for Israeli consent to a PLO presence at an international conference. The PLO publicly denied the rumors.[60] In the public relations realm, the most significant event was the ill-fated "Ship of Return" operation. Following deportations of Palestinian activists in December, the PLO vowed to return them and others on a ship to be named *al-'Awda* (The Return). The plan's aim was twofold: to focus world attention and to bolster the organization's prestige in the territories. Following about a month of preparation which served to whip up the international media, on 15 February a blast ripped a hole in the ship, which was moored in Limassol, Cyprus. The mine, widely assumed to have been planted by the Israelis, effectively scuttled the operation (for more details, see chapter on armed operations).[61] In addition to publicizing the Palestinian cause, the episode publicized the man behind the event, Bassam Abu Sharif, a vocal adviser to 'Arafat and, until recently, a member of the PFLP. (On the circumstances surrounding his leaving the PFLP, see *MECS* 1987, p. 217.)

At the Arab summit in Algiers in June, the Palestinian delegation distributed a "Palestinian Dossier" to foreign journalists which included various articles and extracts. Included among them was an unsigned essay entitled "PLO View: Prospects of a Palestinian-Israeli Settlement." It soon became known that it had been written by Bassam Abu Sharif. The article marked a turning point in PLO political language. While in part it reiterated statements made by 'Arafat since about 1986 (i.e., acceptance of UN Resolutions 242 and 338 in conjunction with self-determination or with other UN resolutions), it was remarkable for its conciliatory tone. The essay expressed sympathy for Israeli concerns as well as those of the Palestinians. Although pointedly underscoring the Palestinian right to self-determination while according Jews no equal right, a position wholly consistent with the strategy of phases, the document did stress that Jews and Palestinians "have the right to run their own affairs." It mentioned a "lasting peace" between Palestinians and Israelis "because no one can build his own future on the ruins of another's." While noting the need for an international conference, the document addressed Israeli fears on this score by speaking out against an imposed solution, stating, "We see no way for any dispute to be settled without direct talks between the parties to that dispute."[62] In interviews in which he explained the essay, Abu Sharif reemphasized that the direct Israeli-Palestinian talks would be within an international conference.[63] It was thus apparent that despite its conciliatory tone, in content the document fell short of representing a departure from PLO policy.

While certainly also designed to put forth an image of PLO moderation, the document constituted a trial balloon both toward the US and *vis-à-vis* internal PLO politics. Abu Sharif would not have floated such a balloon without prior consultation with 'Arafat, but the tactic allowed the PLO chairman to check which way the wind was blowing. For 'Arafat, the document was deniable. The US recognized this and, while it was reported that the US had been informed through the Saudis that it represented official policy,[64] a State Department spokesman stated, "If the PLO is serious about moderating its positions so as to make a practical contribution to the peace process, it can do so in an authoritative way." Nevertheless, the spokesman said that the document contained "positive points" and had a "constructive tone."[65] 'Arafat, for his part, never openly admitted that he had had anything to do with it. When asked directly if it represented his position, he replied, "I will not tell this to you, but to a US representative."[66] This, of course, was one of the main purposes behind the document — to test the waters in Washington.

In the Palestinian arena the Bassam Abu Sharif document was widely criticized. George Habash said that it was an example of the right-wing leadership's [Fath's] "policy to quickly exploit the uprising and make free concessions to the enemy."[67] The EC member from the PFLP, Mustafa al-Zibri (Abu 'Ali Mustafa), demanded that 'Arafat publicly distance himself from the document.[68] The DFLP's Hawatima also rejected the document, insisting that no one had the right to operate outside the PLO leadership or "release trial balloons."[69] In Fath, Qaddumi and Khalaf came out strongly against the document. Khalaf, while noting that he did not object to the purpose of the document (i.e., to project a moderate image), stressed that he objected to the introduction of "new language in the Palestinian arena at a time when the Palestinian people are continuing their heroic uprising against Israeli occupation."[70] It was reported that they had demanded Abu Sharif's suspension from the PNC, and Mustafa al-Zibri even asserted that the EC had set up a committee to "investigate" the appearance of the document.[71] Nothing further was ever heard of these initiatives. In any event, 'Arafat received an inkling of which way the wind was blowing, and soon the official PLO radio broadcast a strident attack on Abu Sharif.[72]

JORDAN'S DISENGAGEMENT: THE IMMEDIATE CATALYST FOR THE PALESTINE NATIONAL COUNCIL

The Abu Sharif document might have been the last shot in a PLO political initiative if not for King Husayn's announcement at the end of July (see chapter on Jordan). Husayn's move was both a blessing and a challenge to the PLO. It removed the king, at least for the time being, as a serious interlocutor along with or on behalf of the Palestinians, dashing any potential pressure that might be brought to bear on 'Arafat by the Americans to work through Jordan and removing the "Jordanian option" from the political agenda. At the same time, the move was of such importance that it forced an internal PLO dialogue concerning a political initiative which would fill the vacuum left by Husayn. It also laid a heavy financial burden on the PLO.

The king's announcement threw the Palestinian leadership into a frenzy of internal consultations and external diplomacy. It revived the government-in-exile option and prompted the leadership to think seriously about a workable political initiative. Since 1973 the organization had done its utmost to maintain its representative status in the diplomatic arena and its relevance to the settlement process. Following the weakening of the PLO's position in the aftermath of the 1982 war in Lebanon, 'Arafat had been forced to work through Husayn (see *MECS* 1983–84, pp. 211–14; 1984–85, pp. 195–209; 1986, pp. 165–72), an effort that had caused much internal strife. But when 'Arafat failed to make the necessary concessions, Husayn suspended coordination with the PLO in 1986 (see *MECS* 1986, pp. 442–49), and the PLO leader consequently embarked on an effort at internal consolidation, culminating in the 18th PNC in 1987 (see *MECS* 1987, chapter on PLO).

The outbreak of the uprising and the Shultz initiative had brought about a series of meetings between Jordanian and Palestinian delegations in Amman during the first three months of the year. Moreover, there were still decisions to be made as to the disbursement of about $20m. in Saudi funds donated to the joint PLO-Jordanian committee.[73] But the *intifada* was strengthening the PLO's hand, and whatever thoughts the organization or Jordan might have entertained about reopening political talks quickly became irrelevant.[74] "My people will not [support King Husayn]" 'Arafat said as early as February.[75] The subject of a joint Jordanian-Palestinian delegation to an international conference was totally ruled out by the PLO, and Jordan now held the position that this would come into being only if the PLO wanted it.[76] Internal solidarity and the *intifada* were now the name of the game for the PLO.

When the Arab summit convened in June solely for the purpose of extending support to the PLO and the uprising, it was clear that Husayn had lost any ground *vis-à-vis* the PLO he may have gained at the November 1987 summit in Amman. The decision of the Arab summit in June to grant funds for the uprising to the PLO (see above), independent of Jordan, was the final signal to Jordan that it had lost the battle.

Husayn's speech came on the heels of an announcement terminating Jordan's ambitious and moribund development plan for the West Bank initiated in 1986 (see *MECS* 1986, pp. 451–57, and chapter on Jordan in this volume). The announcement was warmly received by the PLO as a "positive step in the right direction" which needed to be enhanced by authentic and sincere "joint cooperation."[77] All indications were that the PLO did not anticipate the magnitude of the next step in that direction.

Husayn's speech announcing the dismantling of legal and administrative links with the West Bank was hailed by the PLO leadership as a victory for the *intifada*, but there was much anger over the lack of prior consultation and the financial burden the PLO now had to bear. The CC rejected the king's contention in his speech that the disengagement steps had been taken in response to the wishes of the PLO. "Jordan adopted [the measures] without any consultations with or the knowledge of the PLO," it stressed in a statement.[78] A later broadcast on the Voice of Palestine was very harsh: "Our enemies have mobilized all their forces, their alliances, and all the means of exhaustion and pressure, not to mention their attempts to cripple us by making us assume all the burdens."[79] Palestinians, who often called threateningly for the "democratization of Jordan,"[80] well understood the basic motivation underlying the king's move. "The Jordanian ruler has understood lately that the only way left for him to protect his regime on the East Bank is not necessarily linked to controlling the West Bank, but rather to permanently disengaging the one from the other."[81]

Against its will, it then fell to the PLO to shoulder various financial responsibilities in the West Bank, yet the Arab countries were not coming through with the funds 'Arafat said were promised to the organization. There were several meetings during the rest of the year between Jordanian and Palestinian officials, most notably the tripartite 'Aqaba summit with Egypt in October (see chapter on Egypt). Jordan, of course, was not interested in burning its bridges with the West Bankers and, hence, did not put serious obstacles in the way of PLO efforts to compensate them financially.[82] The PLO announced that it would assume full responsibility for the workers affected by the Jordanian decision in early August to terminate the salaries of several thousand civil servants. On 1 October, the Voice of Palestine broadcasted instructions to West Bank civil servants on how to pick up their salaries which had been deposited by the PLO in the Arab Bank in Amman.[83]

ON THE ROAD TO ALGIERS: POSITIONS AND DEBATE ON THE NEW PALESTINIAN INITIATIVE

The realization that the leadership had to embark on a political initiative gathered increased momentum and urgency after the Jordanian move. In the Fath mainstream, including even Salah Khalaf, this policy was reflected in statements that were moderate in tone and reminiscent of the Abu Sharif document which had been condemned previously. The content of what the PLO was proposing also represented movement in the direction of what was needed for recognition by the US.

This realization bore striking similarities to the situation in 1973 and 1974 when the PLO was confronted with movement toward a settlement of the conflict in the Middle East, which threatened to make the organization irrelevant to the political process. At that time Khalaf had said:

> We must read history so as to extract lessons for ourselves. What were the mistakes of our previous leaders?...Their mistake was adhering to our people's historical rights without adopting stage-by-stage programs of struggle under the obtaining conditions."[84]

The 10-point program entitled "The Phased Political Program" (*al-barnamaj al-siyasi al-marhali*), adopted at the 12th session of the PNC in 1974, embodied the notion that the total liberation of Palestine had to come in stages, the first of which was establishing an "independent, combatant national authority for the people over every part of Palestinian territory that is liberated."[85] The basis of the phased strategy was to be the right of return and the right to self-determination on the whole of the soil of the homeland. The program also included an important deviation from the Palestinian National Covenant in that it advocated the use of "all means" of struggle, "first and foremost armed struggle"; the covenant had stressed armed struggle as the "only" means to liberate Palestine. In 1977, at the 13th PNC, the PLO approved a change in the phased program, this time basing it on the right of return, self-determination, and establishing an independent *state* on Palestinian national soil (author's emphasis; see *MECS* 1976–77, pp. 203–7).[86] Now, to quote Khalaf, the "obtaining conditions" had changed once again.

While continuing, as it had done in past years, to opt for a calculated ambiguity in its pronouncements, political reality forced the Fath mainstream to moderate them particularly, but not only, in the Western media. Fath was still committed to the phased strategy and often made veiled and not-so-veiled references to it, as it did not want to bring about a conflict with the other factions.

Salah Khalaf was the key figure who brought on the change in the tactical position of the Fath mainstream, which eventually drew with it the other factions. Less than two weeks after the Jordanian move, Khalaf stressed in an interview, as he had done similarly in 1974, that it was now "incumbent on the PLO to take steps which would facilitate international recognition, particularly American. This...can be achieved through presenting an internationally acceptable political program...."[87] To add to the moderate tone, he noted in another interview that when the PLO established a provisional government it would adopt a political program "which would be entirely different from the PLO's existing national charter." When Khalaf was asked if the fact that the PLO now supported General Assembly Resolution 181 (the 1947 partition resolution) meant that the organization recognized Israel, he replied: "Of course, because Resolution 181 refers to an Israeli state." On another occasion, he added that he could not imagine that Israel would reject the resolution, since in doing so it would call its own existence into question.[88] In an interview with *Der Spiegel* he argued disingenuously, "When we refuse to recognize...Israel it is not because of reasons of principle, but because we do not know which Israel we would actually recognize, since until now Israel has not defined its borders."[89] Yet Khalaf was aware that such statements would arouse the ire of the other organizations (they did, and were widely condemned by the DFLP and PFLP),[90] and was quick to point out in interviews to the Arab press that the PLO's new program would be "a mechanism for carrying out the phased plan of action [adopted by the PNC in 1974]."[91] Nabil Sha'th, a leading Fath member and the chairman of the PNC's political committee (who gained fame in the US as a leading moderate in 1989) told the Egyptian weekly *al-Ahali* that "the borders of the independent Palestinian State are the borders of all of Palestine." PNC Speaker 'Abd al-Hamid al-Sa'ih stated that the PLO would establish a state on any part of Palestine, but that did not mean conceding the rest of Palestine. In fact, he added, "we will continue to demand it. This is the essence of our phased policy."[92]

As part of the diplomatic offensive, 'Arafat took the lead in making moderate statements. The French Jewish writer Marek Halter reported that the PLO chairman told him that the covenant had been annulled by subsequent PLO decisions and that the PLO wanted a state alongside Israel. When Halter published this, a PLO spokesman in Tunis issued a statement commenting that the declarations attributed to 'Arafat by Halter were "without foundation [and] aimed only at distorting the positions of the PLO."[93] 'Arafat used a similar tactic in his press conference on the occasion of his speech before the European Parliament in Strasbourg in September: he stunned journalists by bizarrely welcoming them with the traditional Jewish greeting for the Jewish New Year, *Shana Tova* (a good year).[94]

All the factions agreed that the Palestinian leadership was called upon to take political action that would change the status quo. This was done by defining more clearly the immediate goal — a Palestinian state in the West Bank and Gaza — and by taking as moderate a stand, defined by some of the more radical factions as concessionary but by others as realism, as was deemed possible and necessary to achieve that goal. Salah Khalaf was frank about this:

> In order to return [to us] some of the land we must fulfill the conditions imposed by the international community concerning a settlement and by doing so put the US and Israel under pressure....At this stage, and considering the balance of power, it is impossible to talk about more than a state in the [West] Bank and the [Gaza] Strip with its capital in Jerusalem.[95]

Filastin al-Thawra wrote: "Our historical rights and aspirations should not be an obstacle to us, since we are on the threshold of a partial, albeit historical, victory in the West Bank and Gaza."[96]

Habash's approach to the conflict also underwent a change due to the uprising. In an 18-page article in the PFLP's weekly, *al-Hadaf*,[97] he engaged in a comprehensive stocktaking of the Palestinian movement's confrontation with Zionists. Following a long analysis of the successes of Israel despite the "unnaturalness" of its existence, he stressed that one of the main reasons behind its success was the ability of the Zionist movement to use international forces to its advantage. The Zionist State was founded, noted Habash, on the basis of the international legitimacy (*al-shar'iyya al-duwaliyya*) embodied in the partition resolution of 1947. But now, with the uprising, international opinion had turned against Israel. Coming into line (*iltiqa*) with the positions held by the international community was thus a necessity. But how, asked Habash rhetorically, can this be accomplished "while guarding the essence of our demands and goals...?" He suggested that it could be done by maintaining the strategy of a phased solution. The Palestinians must maintain the program of return, self-determination, and the founding of an independent state. Habash stressed the propaganda value of this program, which had brought about international support. It was counterproductive to raise the Palestinians' slogans which reflected their final goals, since these would have the effect of preventing the mobilization of the international community. In any event, emphasized Habash, the gaining of the "right of return and setting up an independent state would bring the Palestinians more than half the way to liquidating the Zionist-imperialist plan in our country and to realizing the ultimate goals of our people...." Since world opinion favored an international conference, the Palestinians should take advantage of this and turn the conference, as Khalaf also said about the new Palestinian tactics, into the mechanism for executing the phased program. By remaining committed to a phased program, the Palestinians would not have to give up their final strategic goals, since time was working in their favor. Israel's real nature as a "destructive cancerous beast" (*al-wahsh al-sartani al-kasir*) had already begun to be recognized by the international community and it was only a matter of time before the world would act against it. In this respect Habash shared the same concept of time working in the Palestinians' favor as did Fath, which also put much faith in the notion that demographics would, in time, accomplish all (see below). Habash's argument amounted to an endorsement of one particular political step that in itself was radical for the PLO: the declaration of a Palestinian state founded on the international legitimacy guaranteed by UN Resolution 181 (see below).

The general political perception and approach of the DFLP (and that of its ally, the PCP) to the new situation was similar to that of Fath. The DFLP emphasized the need for a new Palestinian political initiative, which should continue to be based on the phased national program of the right of return, self-determination, and an independent state.[98] The PLO should not "lose an opportunity to make a breakthrough in the direction of a just solution" and should thus support and strengthen the uprising.[99]

SPECIFIC PROPOSALS: DECLARING A STATE, A GOVERNMENT-IN-EXILE, RESOLUTIONS 242 AND 338

The move eventually agreed upon by all factions was to declare an independent state of Palestine, without defining its borders. It was reasoned that this would present an international conference with a *fait accompli*, namely, a state that was under occupation. Thus a Palestinian state would be the starting point for negotiations and not a topic to be negotiated.[100] It was a particularly logical move since conditions were ripe for a consensus on declaring the state on the basis of the 1947 partition resolution, even though that resolution had been specifically rejected in the covenant. The understanding of all the factions was that this resolution constituted international sanction for the Palestinian State, even if it had been rejected by the Arab countries and the Palestinians at the time. The fact that the resolution also called for a Jewish state was an unpleasant reality that could not but be acknowledged, yet the resolution's primary importance was that it sanctioned a Palestinian state. The principle of declaring independence and a draft declaration announcing it were approved in mid-October at a meeting of the Palestinian leadership, which also included a leader from the Palestine Popular Struggle Front (PPSF), a small Syrian-oriented organization that had been part of the Palestine National Salvation Front (PNSF) and had not participated in the 18th PNC.[101] There was reported Soviet pressure not to make the announcement at a PNC before the Israeli elections, and it appears that this advice was taken seriously.[102]

The issue of declaring an independent state based on UN Resolution 181 had won unanimous approval. Yet there remained the issue of a government-in-exile; and, as will be remembered, the main goal of the new PLO initiative was to give support to the *intifada* by achieving a dialogue with the US and thus maintaining the organization's relevancy to the settlement process. For this, there remained the stumbling blocks of recognizing Israel's right to exist, accepting Security Council Resolutions 242 and 338, and the renunciation of terrorism (see chapters on the US and the Middle East and on the Middle East peace process). There were also diplomatic pressures on the PLO leadership in this regard and considerations regarding the possible effect the decisions might have on the US and Israeli elections in November.

The issue of forming a government-in-exile or a provisional government was decidedly more controversial than the idea of declaring a state. The general concept was supported by the main factions following Husayn's speech,[103] but soon international pressure, the lack of a commitment by Western states to recognize the government,[104] and disagreement over the composition of the proposed government moved the leadership to decide on postponing its creation. The move was not supported by the USSR and, more importantly, it would force the PLO to deal with difficult questions with respect to its representative status and the participation of representatives from the territories. Hawatima, for instance, initially supported the immediate formation of a government-in-exile comprised only of the factions of the Palestinian resistance and controlled by the EC. This step, he argued, would head off Western attempts to form a government from "outside the PLO" [i.e., comprised of residents of the territories].[105] He clarified on another occasion that he was referring to people such as Hana Siniora and Fa'iz Abu Rahma.[106] Sulayman al-Najjab, EC member and head of the PCP, summed up the primary concerns: "If we form a [provisional] government now, what will be the relations between this government and the PLO Executive Committee? We oppose and warn of the danger of forming two power centers within the Palestinian leadership."[107] Instead, it was decided to recommend to the PNC to approve a provisional government in principle, but to leave it to the EC to set it up when that body saw fit to do so. A provisional government was eventually chosen as opposed to a government-in-exile, since the former was by definition temporary and would not force the PLO to answer, even at a later stage, the difficult questions noted above.[108]

Security Council Resolutions 242 and 338 presented the thorniest of the problems confronting a new PLO initiative, but this time it was clear that the issue had to be tackled seriously. Since 1985, 'Arafat and others in Fath had been willing to adopt a formula accepting 242 and 338 along with the right to self-determination or combined with all UN Resolutions on the Palestinian question (see *MECS* 1984–85, pp. 201–4), but neither of these formulations had ever been adopted by the PNC, which had specifically rejected Resolution 242 as a matter of course. Fath's goal was now to convince the other factions to accept 242 with the above reservations and make this PNC policy. Fath officials argued that a realistic program had to be based on international legitimacy, and this included 242. The organization should, therefore, take the "brave step" of accepting the resolution along with the right to self-determination.[109] This would mean accepting the resolution not as is, but as it "should be."[110] *Filastin al-Thawra* wrote that 242 could be accepted — with self-determination as a rider — as the basis for an Israeli withdrawal from the territories captured in 1967.[111] Khalaf brought in the Soviets on his side, maintaining that a special Soviet emissary had been despatched in early November in order to convince the Palestinian factions to accept that formula.[112]

The DFLP was considerably less enthusiastic about a specific mention of Resolution 242 in the political declaration of the coming meeting of the PNC. For Hawatima, even if coupled with self-determination, this was not enough since there was no mention of a Palestinian state. Instead he favored a catchall clause mentioning UN resolutions that recognized Palestinian rights and a strong emphasis on the phased program of return, self-determination, and an independent state.[113] Hawatima in particular was singled out by Khalaf as opposing political flexibility.[114] The EC representative from the DFLP, Yasir 'Abd Rabbuh, who was often at odds with Hawatima and sometimes seemed more in tune with 'Arafat's thinking, supported 242 with self-determination and other relevant UN resolutions. He argued, as did Fath, that the resolution contained "useful elements since it affirms the principle of withdrawal and the non-acquisition of territory by force."[115]

The PFLP vehemently opposed the mention of 242 or other UN resolutions and wanted to base the PNC's political declaration solely on a demand for the UN to perform a trusteeship role in the occupied State of Palestine.[116] Beyond that, the PNC should specifically endorse the principles upon which the PLO was founded [i.e., the Palestine National Covenant] as well as the phased program of 1974.[117]

On the issues of recognizing Israel, Fath limited itself prior to the PNC to various statements to the Western press (see above) that implied recognition. The other factions did not make such statements. With respect to renouncing terrorism, there was no discussion since the organization did not consider what it was doing to be terrorism and it had no intention of renouncing something in which it did not believe it engaged.

THE 19th SESSION OF THE PALESTINE NATIONAL COUNCIL

The "extraordinary" 19th session of the Palestine National Council convened on 12–15 November at the al-Sanawbar palace about 15 km. west of Algiers, under the slogans "the session of the *intifada* and national independence" and "the session of the martyr Abu Jihad" (for the assassination of Khalil al-Wazir on 16 April, see chapter on armed operations). The guerrilla organizations attending were Fath, the PFLP, the DFLP, the Palestine Liberation Front (PLF), the PCP, the Arab Liberation Front (ALF), and the PPSF.[118] Out of a total of 447 PNC members, 338 attended. Many of those absent were prevented from attending by Syria, Jordan,and Israel.[119]

PNC Speaker Shaykh 'Abd al-Hamid al-Sa'ih opened his address to the session with words of praise for the Algerian hosts, noting that Algeria was an example to the Palestinians. While stressing that the Palestinians "must not forget those in the occupied homeland whether in the part occupied in 1948 or the part occupied in 1967," he begged the members to "take account of all the world and international circumstances in their debates."[120] This combination of phrases reflected the general PLO consensus that maximum demands would be retained (i.e., self-determination for the Arabs in Israel, "the Arabs of 1948" in PLO parlance), even though it was necessary to consider international demands for a more moderate PLO position. 'Arafat's opening speech concentrated on one of the main themes noted above, the unity of the Palestinians outside and inside Palestine. "The generals of [the] stones are in creative revolutionary harmony with the RPG heroes," he declared. He also called upon US President-elect George Bush to take an unbiased position on the Palestinian issue.[121]

Since it had been decided earlier to declare a state and to accept in principle but postpone the actual formation of a government-in-exile, the disagreement over Resolution 242 remained the main bone of contention during the session. In general, Fath, the DFLP, and the PCP supported the specific mention of Resolution 242, coupled with all relevant UN resolutions and the right to self-determination, or, according to some in Fath, coupled with self-determination only. The PFLP appeared to have become more flexible than before (see above), and during the PNC took the position that all relevant UN resolutions should be noted, with no specific mention of Resolution 242.[122]

An examination of the arguments marshaled by those supporting the Fath and the DFLP position is instructive, for they illustrate the reasoning and strategy behind the language finally adopted. Both underlined the understanding that the final political statement was founded on the phased plan. Khalaf — in a speech during a closed session from which, according to *al-Anba*, the delegates left "dazzled...by [his] wisdom...and decisiveness" — said that the Palestinian State "is for the following generations; in its youth it will be small, and, God willing, it will become bigger and spread east, west, north, and south." Khalaf noted that he had always opposed UN General Assembly Resolution 181 on the partition of Palestine, but since the *intifada* he was asking himself if he had not been foolish. "I desire the liberation of Palestine, but how [should we go about it]? Step by step. We have to devise a proper method of liberation."[123] Similarly, a DFLP official told the Political Committee that the political statement stemmed from the phased program; although it mentioned Resolution 242, it carefully bound it up with other UN resolutions which guaranteed Palestinian rights.[124]

Both Fath and the DFLP argued that the specific mention of 242 and 338 was an unfortunate necessity dictated by international pressure. Khalaf stated that he had no illusions: the US would not accept the political statement as a basis for opening talks with the organization; the proposed formula was designed primarily to satisfy the Soviets and enable them to work more effectively on behalf of the Palestinians. He emphasized that the statement, with 242 in it, would present a flexible PLO position and help it to garner support in the international arena. And in any case, 242 would be "surrounded" by other resolutions that protected and guaranteed Palestinian rights. Moreover, Khalaf argued, "how can we abandon the children and the youth of the *intifada*, leaving it to them to liberate the land and [perhaps] bring about other international resolutions [more favorable to the Palestinian cause], while we wait here and are satisfied with issuing reports on their acts of valor?" The continuation of the armed struggle would protect the political statement and prevent it from being used against the Palestinians. Hawatima stated that the PLO, in order to reach a settlement, had to integrate Palestinian rights with what the international community required. In any case, the PLO maintained the right to reject 242 if, in the future, it was presented as the only basis for a political settlement. Qaddumi contended that the PLO could accept 242 with the reservations proposed and then work to change the UN decision.[125]

The argument of the PFLP against specific mention of Resolution 242 was that the *intifada* had not yet reached its maximum political effectiveness and thus it was counterproductive to make the concession that mentioning 242 entailed.[126] The PFLP had always harbored suspicions that Fath was interested in settling for a Palestinian state in the West Bank and Gaza only, and that 242, even with self-determination, opened the way for such a settlement. Concerns of this sort lay behind the demand by the PFLP, and the DFLP for that matter, for a greater degree of "collective leadership" in the PLO (see below). But in 1987, the PFLP had returned to the PLO umbrella after several years out in the rain (see *MECS* 1987, chapter on the PLO), and it was not about to remove itself from the organization so quickly. Moreover, it was concerned lest a lack of unity affect the *intifada*. Therefore, when it came down to a final decision, the 46 supporters of the PFLP voted against the political statement, but remained in the PLO. "Unity is the foundation for everyone," Mustafa al-Zibri stressed. "We want to preserve the right to register our reservations, but we want to remain allies and friends."[127] Allowing a vote was unprecedented in the PNC, where resolutions had always been adopted by acclamation only. But the PFLP had been allowed to register officially its reservations, and 'Arafat and his supporters had won the day.

THE DECLARATION OF INDEPENDENCE, POLITICAL STATEMENT, AND OTHER RESOLUTIONS: MAIN POINTS

The Declaration of Independence (*i'lan al-istiqlal*; for text, see Appendix I) — which bore a striking resemblance to the Israeli declaration of 1948 — was penned by the Palestinian poet and EC member Mahmud Darwish. It emphasized the birth of the Palestinian Arab people on the land of Palestine, and asserted that despite the various invasions of Palestine throughout history, which had deprived the people of national independence, the "undying connection between Palestine and its people secured for the land its character and for the people its national genius." The Palestinian people were thus characterized by a total identity between the land and man. But at the time when the modern world was forming a new value system, the document continued, the Palestinian people were left aside.

The international sanction (or legitimacy, *al-shar'iyya al-duwaliyya*) on the basis of which the State of Palestine was declared and which guaranteed the right of the Palestinian people to sovereignty and national independence was UN General

Assembly Resolution 181 of 1947, "which partitioned Palestine into two states, one Jewish, one Arab...." This was the case, even though, stressed the document, that resolution was an historical injustice (*al-zulm al-ta'rikhi*) that had deprived the Palestinian people of its right to self-determination. The acceptance of Resolution 181, even with these reservations, represented a significant departure from the *letter* of the Palestine National Covenant, which termed the partition resolution and the establishment of Israel as fundamentally invalid (*batil min asasihi*); it did not represent a departure from the *spirit* of the Covenant (see below).

Without reference to or differentiating between the West Bank and Gaza on the one hand and the borders of the State of Israel on the other, the declaration noted that the Israeli forces had occupied Palestinian land, a step which was a violation of the Palestinians' rights of return, self-determination, independence, and sovereignty on the land of their homeland.

The declaration gave recognition to the *intifada* for bringing the Palestinian saga to "*one* [author's emphasis] of its most decisive junctures"; however, it gave the PLO full credit for leading the struggle on behalf of the Palestinians.

Palestine, noted the declaration, is an Arab state and an indivisible part of the Arab nation. It belongs to Palestinians wherever they may be. It is a democracy which guarantees the right to form parties and which does not discriminate on the basis of race, religion, color, or sex. Moreover, Palestine is a peace-loving state which believes in settling disputes by peaceful means and rejects the use of force, violence, or terrorism against its territorial integrity or that of any other state.

The state of Palestine, with its capital in Jerusalem, was proclaimed by Yasir 'Arafat on 15 November at 1:38 a.m.[128]

The "program of the political statement" (*mashru' al-bayan al-siyasi*; for text, see Appendix II) represented a victory for the pragmatic group in Fath and, once again, was testimony to the leadership of 'Arafat and his policy of making maximum tactical concessions in order to achieve a Palestinian state in the West Bank and Gaza.

Unlike the resolutions of the 18th PNC (1987), the statement did not open with the traditional clause, "emanating from the Palestine National Covenant" (*intilaqan min al-mithaq al-watani al-Filastini*). In fact, the covenant was not mentioned at all, as the PNC deemed that such mention would be counterproductive to the PLO's efforts to achieve Western, particularly US recognition. The document opened with a long preamble highlighting the unity of the Palestinian people and the uprising, emphasizing that the PLO was the sole legitimate representative of the Palestininian people, "all our people" (*kull sha'buna*), everywhere. The uprising, the statement noted, had garnered overwhelming international support, and had isolated Israel. Israel's "beastly [and] inhuman" (*al-wahshiyya al-la insaniyya*) behavior had "exposed the Zionist lie about the democracy of the Zionist entity that has managed to deceive the world for forty years." Israel, continued the document, had been revealed in all its ugliness, exposing its true self, that of "a fascist, racist, colonialist state built on the usurpation of the Palestinian land and the extermination of the Palestinian people." The long preamble to the statement also mentioned the PLO's "national program" (another name for the strategy of phases), and referred several times to the rights of return, self-determination, and to establish an independent Palestinian state.

The statement then moved on to the details of the PLO's new political position, emphasizing that these details were based on all that had preceded in the text (*wa-intilaqan min kull ma taqaddama*). The principles of the PLO's position were to be carried out "within the framework of...the resolutions of the United Nations...in such a manner that safeguards the Palestinian Arab people's rights to return, to self-determination, and the establishment of their independent national state on their national soil, and that institutes arrangements for the security and peace of all states in the region." With respect to the operative clause concerning the specific basis for the convening of the "effective" international conference, the statement declared that the conference should:

> be convened on the basis of United Nations Security Council Resolutions 242 and 338 and the attainment of the legitimate national rights of the Palestinian people, foremost among which is the right to self-determination, and in accordance with the principles and provisions of the United Nations Charter concerning the right of peoples to self-determination, and by the inadmissibility of the acquisition of the territory of others by force or military conquest, and in accordance with the relevant United Nations resolutions on the question of Palestine.

Among the other detailed points in the PLO's position as expressed in the political statement was a solution to the refugee problem " in accordance with the relevant United Nations resolutions." Here the PNC was referring to the right of return or compensation embodied in General Assembly Resolution 194 of 1948, although the specific phrasing might have been designed to lead the untrained observer into thinking that the organization was referring to Resolution 242, which also deals with the refugee problem.

A reference to Israel's security was to be found in the sentence asking the Security Council to "formulate and guarantee arrangements for security and peace between all the states concerned in the region, including the Palestinian State."

On the issue of terrorism, while the PNC emphasized its adherence to UN resolutions which assert the right of peoples to resist foreign occupation, it stated its "rejection of terrorism (*rafduhu lil-irhab*) in all its forms, including state terrorism," and noted its commitment to previous PNC resolutions on the subjects, as well as the Cairo Declaration of 7 November 1985 (see *MECS* 1984–85, pp. 208, 369).

The PNC also issued a "proclamation forming the Provisional Government of the State of Palestine" (*i'lan tashkil al-hukuma al-mu'waqqata li-dawlat Filastin*). According to the document, the government would be set up at the soonest appropriate time to be decided by the CC. The government would be comprised of reliable people from inside and outside the occupied territories, in a way which would guarantee national unity. The policy of the government would be based on the independence document, the PLO's political program, and the resolutions of the sessions of the PNC. Until the government was formed, the document concluded, the EC would have the responsibilities and authority of a provisional government.[129]

The recommendation of the "*intifada* committee" (*tawsiyat lajnat al-intifada*) included an outline of various means for strengthening the uprising. Of particular interest was a greeting to "the sons of our people in the areas of 1948 [i.e, Israel]," which emphasized "the important role they play in strengthening the uprising, keeping their national identity despite all the attempts at obliteration and assimilation."[130]

THE SIGNIFICANCE OF THE RESOLUTIONS OF THE 19th PALESTINE NATIONAL COUNCIL

As noted above, the language of the decisions of the 19th PNC (in addition to later declarations, for which see below) brought the PLO closer than ever before to the acceptance of a permanent solution to the conflict, based on two states in Palestine. This was evident in the references to a Jewish state, the partition plan of 1947, the specific mention of Resolution 242 which implies the acknowledgment or acceptance of Israel's existence, and the fact that the covenant was not mentioned. Nevertheless, there was much ambiguity and the option was clearly left open for the phased strategy which perceives a West Bank and Gaza state as the first step toward the total liberation of Palestine. Moreover, an abolition of the covenant or significant revisions to it, which would have represented a major change, even an about-face, did not take place. It was, therefore, evident that the change in PLO thought evinced in the documents represented movement toward the recognition of Israel, rather than some kind of existential change or quantum leap.

More than anything, the decisions of the 19th PNC were aimed at diplomatic gains. "The ball," said 'Arafat in a press conference at the end of the PNC session, "is now in the American court."[131] During the PNC, it was clear that the PLO was engaging in a deliberate policy of disinformation with respect to the official text of the political statement. Several spokesmen told Western journalists that the organization would accept 242 and 338 unequivocably. For several days, the PLO refused to provide an official English or French translation of the document. Even the Arabic text was embargoed until after the Declaration of Independence was read.[132] The result of this deft handling of the media was that Western newspapers initially published "excerpts" from the political statement which were much more moderate than the final, official text. Thus *The New York Times* reported on 15 November that the PNC had approved a platform "making Security Council Resolution 242 the main basis for an international peace conference."[133] The disinformation campaign was still apparent two days later when the same paper published an "unofficial US government translation" of the document, in which the concluding sentence of the operative paragraph on the international conference was "in accordance with the resolutions of the United Nations regarding the Palestinian and Arab territories that [Israel] has occupied since 1967, including Arab Jerusalem."[134] This was considerably more moderate than the official language of "in accordance with the relevant United Nations resolutions on the question of Palestine," because *The New York Times*' version focused on a solution for the Palestinian issue in reference to the West Bank and Gaza only. Khalid al-Hasan told *The Jerusalem Post*, "The statement says, 'The international conference will be held on the basis of 242 and 338 - full stop'."[135]

In the direction of the Arab world, the PLO broadcasted three different versions of the critical passage on 242 and 338. The earliest of these omitted entirely any reference to Resolutions 242 and 338.[136]

In essence, the PNC political statement was exactly what Salah Khalaf only a week before the session said it would be: "Sophisticated in rhetoric, but not in content" (*mutatawwaran bil-lugha wa-laysa bil-madmun*). "The content," continued Khalaf, "had been decided upon at our PNC session in 1974, when we put together our phased program."[137] An examination of the essential components of the phased program which are interwoven throughout the documents — the right of return, the right to self-determination,and the right to national independence, particularly the former two — reveals the truth of Khalaf's formulation.[138]

Self-determination is understood by all PLO factions to mean that the Palestinians themselves should determine their own destiny. Palestinians, as defined in article 5 of the covenant, are all those Arabs who in 1947 lived in Palestine, and after the State of Israel was established either remained in the area of Mandatory Palestine or became refugees, including the descendants of all the above. In the Declaration of Independence, the PNC acknowledged that the 1947 partition resolution formed two states, one Jewish and one Arab. But in the PLO view, the partition resolution could be considered an international sanction for the Palestinian State only, since it had committed "an historical injustice" in denying the Palestinians their right to self-determination. The Declaration of Independence represented a departure from the language of the covenant, which considered the partition resolution "fundamentally invalid." But the spirit and intent of the covenant remained. Since in the PLO view the establishment of Israel usurped the Palestinians' right to self-determination, to continue to insist on that right invalidated Israel's claim for a similar right. For the PLO, Jewish self-determination — Zionism — and Palestinian self-determination were diametrically opposed and hence mutually exclusive. That is what 'Arafat meant when he disingenuously argued in an interview in *Time* magazine that "[n]owhere [in the Covenant] is there mention of the elimination of Israel. We are opposed to a Zionist state.... We don't want a racist state in this area."[139]

PLO spokesman and *Filastin al-Thawra* editor, Ahmad 'Abd al-Rahman, writing a week after the PNC, hinted broadly that the PLO had not really accepted the idea of two states: "Palestine, which is shaped like a dagger, does not recognize the concept of partition. What is now happening with the declaration of our independence is not the partition of the dagger, but rather the entry into the homeland."[140]

That formulation of the trilateral demand, in which the right of return, the right to self-determination, and the right to an independent state were mentioned separately indicated that the PLO viewed them as three distinct items. Without specifically recognizing that Palestinian self-determination would be fulfilled once a state in the West Bank and the Gaza Gaza Strip was founded, the PLO continued to opt for an open-ended solution, whereby full Palestinian self-determination will be achieved, perhaps, although not exclusively, through peaceful means. Fath EC member Mahmud 'Abbas stated, "We have not given up the idea of [Arabs and Jews] coexisting within a democratic secular state. We remain committed to it and will not abandon it even after we have established our state. But we will wage a peaceful stuggle to realize it."[141] In the Declaration of Independence the partition resolution was referred to as the basis for Palestinian sovereignty and independence, but not for self-determination. This implied that once a state was established on any part of Palestine — in this case the West Bank and Gaza — full self-determination would still remain a goal.

PLO leaders often justified their refusal to identify the borders of the Palestinian State by stressing that Israel had not defined its own borders. But another explanation was offered by Jawad al-Bashiti in an article entitled "Rights not Borders" in *Filastin al-Thawra* a week before the PNC session:

> The PLO is being asked to define the West Bank and the Gaza Strip as the

> borders of the state. Defining the borders of the Palestinian State means that the PLO has, officially, conceded its historical rights to all of Palestine. Moreover, it means that the PLO has officially decided that these rights were absolute lies. The inescapable implication of such a decision would be that the PLO sanctions the notion that the Jewish people have national rights in...the land of Palestine.[142]

What was noted above concerning the Declaration of Independence holds true for the important clause in the political statement which specifically mentioned Resolution 242. As indicated above, the language of the political document "enclosed" 242 within several safeguards, notably the right to self-determination and other UN resolutions pertaining to the Palestinian issue. But self-determination, as seen by the PLO, applied to all Palestinians, everywhere (including Israel, and, for that matter, Jordan), and therefore seemed to subvert effectively the whole concept of living in peace as embodied in the resolution. Moreover, UN resolutions on the Palestinian issue include General Assembly Resolution 3236 (1974) — which made no reference to Israel or the right of states to secure and recognized boundaries, but stressed the Palestinians' right to self-determination several times as well and the right of the refugees to return — and General Assembly Resolution 3379 (1975) which equates Zionism with racism. The PLO acceptance of the "Zionism is racism" resolution, and its policy of "not want[ing] a racist state in this area," appeared to undermine the notion put forth by the PLO in the Western media that the organization had fully accepted a two-state solution at the 19th PNC.

The insistence on the right of return in the political statement was collective, not individual.[143] As such, the right of return, combined with the PLO conviction that the *intifada* was spreading to Israel proper and that demography would eventually bring about a Palestinian majority in Israel, represented a vision of the Middle East without a Jewish state. All the same, in 1988 and 1989 various Fath members and sympathizers exhibited flexibility on the issue of the right of return, implying that the modalities for its implementation as an individual and not a collective right could be negotiated at an international conference.[144]

Any true acceptance of a two-state solution at the 19th PNC (and, for that matter, even in 'Arafat's Geneva speech and press conference, on which, see below) seemed to have been further belied by the lack of a reference to such a solution as being final and definitive. The absence of such a reference was conspicuous in view of a statement by Walid Khalidi, a Palestinian scholar and a former member of the PNC. Writing in *Foreign Affairs*, Khalidi outlined what he believed were the "building blocks" of a "just settlement," "without equivocation." Khalidi's outline, which was based on a two-state solution, stressed that the settlement would receive the guarantees of the Arab and Islamic summits as "*point final*" (Khalidi's emphasis).[145] Khalidi left out "self-determination," since for him this concept was implicit in the establishment of a West Bank and Gaza state as the permanent solution to the Palestinian problem, and he saw no need to discuss it.

The uprising strengthened the PLO perception that time was in its favor; that processes were at work which would inevitably bring about Israel's end. The Jews were not a people and the Zionist entity was artificial wrote Khalid al-Hasan in 1986.[146] Israeli society would inevitably disintegrate due to its ills and growing emigration. In 1988, al-Hasan told an interviewer that the PLO had commissioned a poll that had shown that 52% of Israelis wished to emigrate. Those wanting to emigrate were mostly in the 20–50-year-old age group while those who did not were either under 20 or above 50. He added that the organization had offered several Israeli families the opportunity to emigrate, whereupon 300 families comprising about 3,000 persons approached the PLO which in turn settled them in France.[147] "We are *with* the tide of history," 'Arafat told *Playboy*, "while Israel is *against* it" (italics in text).[148] It was the PLO's perception of time which allowed many in the leadership to feel comfortable with tactics that represented no real concessions of magnitude or historical importance. Time would take care of the strategic goals. Hasan al-Batal, a commentator for *Filastin al-Thawra*, wrote a few months before the PNC session:

> The Palestinian people in Israel [the Galilee, the Triangle, and the Negev] are the strategic guarantee [*al-ihtiyati al-istratiji*] of the inevitable attainment of a democratic state in all the land of Palestine..., and as for the Palestinian people in Jordan, they constitute the second strategic guarantee of the completion of the Arab part of the Palestinian mission...the democratization of the Arab East [*al-Mashriq*]."[149]

Faruq Qaddumi gave further expression to the role of Israeli Arabs in his report to the PNC. The uprising, he stressed, had "caused new flames to burst forth from the glowing embers [of Palestinian nationalism] in the Galilee, the Triangle, and the Negev, turning the Green Line into something as ephemeral as the strands of a spider's web (*kal-wahm al-'ankabuti*)."[150] The Green Line, meant Qaddumi, was vanishing as the Palestinian consciousness of Israel's Arabs grew.

The 19th PNC, with all of its ambiguities and efforts to keep the PLO's options open, put the crowning touch on a series of developments in PLO positions. In 1974, the PNC had announced a strategy of phases for the total liberation of Palestine, which would begin with a "fighting national authority" on any part of liberated territory; in 1977, that it would set up a state. In 1988, the state was proclaimed. The 19th PNC, noted Salah Khalaf, had taken the phased program and had "breathed life into it in order to construct an apparatus (*aliyya*) that would set it in motion."[151]

FROM ALGIERS TO GENEVA VIA STOCKHOLM: THE DRIVE FOR A DIALOGUE WITH THE UNITED STATES

The Algiers decisions were important for 'Arafat particularly since he had been able to put 242 into an official PNC document. As was often the case after a PNC (see, for instance *MECS* 1987, pp. 224–25), he then proceeded to go far beyond his official mandate, to the chagrin of the PFLP and part of the DFLP, and began to work toward his goal of opening a dialogue with the US. Although 'Arafat occasionally expressed surprise that the US had not been convinced by the Algiers documents, he knew full well that there was a long way to go to fulfill the US conditions. On the issue of recognizing Israel, no high-level PLO official seriously contended that the PNC had done so. Salah Khalaf stressed that "acceptance of 242 and 338 does not mean recognizing Israel."[152] The process that led to 'Arafat's fulfilling these conditions to the satisfaction of the US took him through several secret contacts via third parties and two public attempts by him to get around meeting the conditions until he finally did so at a press conference in Geneva. Immediately, the US opened its first official talks with the PLO, thereby putting the finishing touch on 'Arafat's diplomatic efforts.

'Arafat first tested the waters when on 24 November he requested a visa to the US in order to address the UN General Assembly.[153] Two days later, the US rejected the request because he "knows of, condones and lends support to" acts of terrorism (see chapter on the US and the Middle East). It cited particularly the operations of the Hawari group and Force 17 since the 1985 Cairo Declaration,[154] which the PLO upheld as amounting to its abandoning terrorism, although it did not believe that it engaged in activity covered by that term.

The PLO turned Washington's snub into a political triumph. Since many at the UN thought that the US had exceeded its authority as the UN host country, the General Assembly on 2 December voted by a massive majority to move the whole session to Geneva so 'Arafat could make his speech.

Meanwhile, the Swedish Goverment had been active in arranging talks between several politically active American Jews and PLO officials, including Khalid al-Hasan, in Stockholm. The first meeting was held secretly on 20 November, and the US was kept informed by the Swedes.[155] Shultz was shown the text of an agreement negotiated by the two parties (this early text was never published), and pronounced it interesting, but said that it meant nothing unless 'Arafat went public with it. 'Arafat eventually informed the Swedish Government that he would, and a larger delegation of American Jews flew to Stockholm to meet with him, Yasir 'Abd Rabbuh, and others on 6 and 7 December.

On 7 December, 'Arafat and the Americans appeared at a press conference where the agreement on which they had agreed was read. The Stockholm document (see Appendix III), presented as an "explanation" of the Algiers resolutions, was more 'Arafat's interpretation and in fact represented a significant departure from them. It explicitly mentioned that the Algiers documents called for a two-state solution, Israel and Palestine. Resolutions 242 and 338 were qualified by self-determination only, and the formula "all relevant UN resolutions" was confined to the Palestinian refugee problem. The document said that the PNC had declared its "rejection and condemnation of terrorism in all its forms, including state terrorism." Most significantly, the document stated that the PNC had established "the independent state of Palestine and accepted the existence of Israel as a state in the region."

The Stockholm statement represented substantial progress over the PNC decisions, but the document was only an "explanation" of them, and so many of the problems of the PNC resolutions themselves remained. Moreover, while the press was reporting that 'Arafat had signed the document,[156] 'Arafat was telling Radio Monte Carlo that he never had, maintaining that "I only sign documents with officials and members of government....I want to remove any misunderstanding after I have seen that certain papers attributed the document [to me]."[157] On the other hand, 'Arafat appeared to endorse the document by taking part in the press conference and confirming that it represented a "correct summary of what was said in Algiers."[158] The clause on the acceptance of Israel's existence, while short of the *de jure* recognition of Israel's right to exist, as the US sought, and while being conditional on the establishment of an independent state of Palestine, brought the PLO closer to a true acceptance of a two-state solution. The sentence on terrorism was likewise insufficient for the US, which insisted that the PLO "renounce" terrorism, not just "reject" and "condemn" it. The US said that 'Arafat would have make the correct statements directly and clearly.[159]

On 13 December, 'Arafat addressed the UN General Assembly in Geneva in front of a massive press corp and Cable News Network cameras which transmitted the speech to the US (for text, see Appendix IV). The Swedish Government had continued to be active and was trying to get 'Arafat to meet the US conditions. But the Geneva speech, although close, was not what the US expected.

The speech contained much that was reminiscent of the strategy of phases, such as a reference to the self-determination of 6m. (*sic*) Palestinians.[160] But its tone was overwhelmingly positive, like that of the Bassam Abu Sharif document, and 'Arafat turned directly to the Israeli people. The Palestinians, said 'Arafat, do not strive for a destiny at the expense of another people. (This statement appeared on the cover of *Filastin al-Thawra* on 18 December, and was evidence of the seriousness of 'Arafat's new initiative.) In the body of the speech, 'Arafat presented the decisions of the PNC fairly accurately, although he did not mention that the partition resolution was a "historical injustice." The terrorism clause was again inadequate for the US, as it was solely a "rejection" of terrorism.

The substantial progress, as far as the US was concerned, was when 'Arafat outlined the operative parts of the Palestinian peace initiative. Here, the 242 and 338 clause was explicit, without being surrounded by "self-determination" or "all UN resolutions." But the clause concerning the recognition of Israel was not explicit enough for the US. 'Arafat stated that the PLO sought a comprehensive peace for "the State of Palestine, Israel, and other neighbors," but then used a catchall phrase noting only "respect" (*ihtiram*) for "the right to exist in peace and security for all."

Since the speech was still unsatisfactory for Washington, the Swedish and Egyptian governments continued to put pressure on 'Arafat to do the bidding of the US. On 14 December, the PLO chairman convened a press conference, and finally said the "magic words" (for text, see Appendix V).[161] He was even more explicit on 242 and 338, said that peace was a strategy and not an interim tactic,and that "in my speech...it was clear that we mean our people's rights to freedom and national independence...and the right of all parties concerned...to exist in peace and security...including the State of Palestine, Israel, and other neighbors...." With respect to the terrorism clause, 'Arafat said that he "announced it yesterday in no uncertain terms, and yet, I repeat for the record that we totally and absolutely renounce all forms of terrorism, including individual, group, and state terrorism."

On the same day, the US announced that it would enter a dialogue with the PLO. Formal and official talks were held on 16 December between members of the PLO EC and the US Ambassador to Tunisia Robert Pelletreau in which both sides presented their positions. The talks were described as constructive, and 'Arafat, who did not participate, said they represented an important step in the right direction.[162]

'Arafat had accomplished what he had set out to do. What the US had insisted on was not pure semantics, but a sincere PLO commitment to live in peace with Israel. 'Arafat seemed to have done just that. But he had acted, as was his habit, as an individual. Statements made at a press conference were hardly binding, and the tortuous route traveled in order to get to the press conference formulations illustrated both the constraints 'Arafat felt on his own views as well as those of his partners in

Fath and the PLO. The official Arabic translation of 'Arafat's press conference statement quoted him as saying that the PLO "rejects" terrorism (*narfuduhu*), not "renounces."[163] A few days after the press conference, he told Vienna Television: "I did not mean to renounce. Our [PNC] resolutions condemned all forms of terrorism — individual terrorism and state terrorism. Actually, I only repeated what our Palestine National Council had accepted."[164]

Yet he was serious about a dialogue with the US, and he knew what had to be done. He received the endorsement of the EC for what he said in his speech and at the press conference.[165] The EC member from the DFLP, 'Abd Rabbuh, participated in this decision, but the PFLP representative, Mustafa al-Zibri, absented himself. In Damascus, Habash and Hawatima issued a joint statement stressing that 'Arafat's remarks at the press conference contradicted PNC resolutions. Moreover, the organizations added, they "do not commit the PLO to anything and they do not represent official policy."[166]

THE DEFEAT IN LEBANON AND RELATIONS WITH SYRIA

Early in 1988 there was some hope for an increased presence of pro-'Arafat Palestinians in Lebanon. In January, Amal announced that it was making a "gesture to the *intifada*" and lifting the siege it had held around the Palestinian camps in Beirut and in the south for more than three years (see *MECS* 1984–85, pp. 218–22; 1986, pp. 194–96; 1987, pp. 230–31). The PLO greeted the move as "the first result of the uprising."[167] It was thought in several circles that the way might be open for a reconciliation with Syria, particularly following the assassination of Khalil al-Wazir (Syria agreed to bury him there) and 'Arafat's visit to Damascus in April after the funeral. But Syria eventually put on the pressure again, this time using another proxy, the Fath rebels of Sa'id Musa Muragha (Abu Musa). In July, 'Arafat's supporters suffered severe defeat at the hands of the Fath rebels, with full Syrian backing. The *intifada* and any political victories that might be associated with it thus became all the more important.

The Fath rebels began their attack in early May on 'Arafat strongholds in the Beirut refugee camps. The attack was aided by massive shelling from Syrian-held areas, particularly on the Shatila camp. The PLO left no doubt as to whom they believed was behind the onslaught. It referred to the "demented and rancorous stand the traitors of the Syrian regime have adopted."[168] Khalaf, referring to Mustafa Talas, said, "In Syria there is a defense minister who is more concerned about growing roses and good cooking than about liberating Palestine."[169] On 27 June, Shatila was overrun by the Fath dissidents, and most of the fighting then concentrated on the Burj al-Barajina camp. 'Arafat's appeals to the Arab world[170] fell on deaf ears. Burj al-Barajina was captured in early July and the 'Arafat loyalists were evacuated to Sidon.

The move to Sidon, however, threatened to renew the fighting between 'Arafat's supporters and Amal. There were occasional clashes, the most severe being in November, and were probably not unconnected with Syrian opposition to the upcoming PNC.[171] In late December, a truce was announced (see also chapter on Syria.)[172]

ORGANIZATIONAL DEVELOPMENTS

Although in 1988 the organizational ramifications of the assassination of Khalil al-Wazir in April (see chapter on armed operations) were difficult to assess, there were reports of maneuvering within Fath for the several positions that al-Wazir had held in the organization (head of the Department of Occupied Territories Affairs[173] and the "Western Sector" apparatus, which handles military operations) and in the PLO (Palestinian cochairman of the joint Jordanian-Palestinian committee and Deputy Commander of the Forces of the Palestinian Resistance).[174]

Mahmud 'Abbas took al-Wazir's place on the Jordanian-Palestinian committee, but, most likely in order to avoid infighting, 'Arafat apparently appointed a temporary six-man committee comprised of senior Fath members to head the Western Sector.[175] There were also reports of tension between al-Wazir's widow, Intisar (Umm Jihad), who wanted to assume some of her husband's tasks, and 'Arafat,[176] but there was no confirmation by the end of the year of a permanent successor to al-Wazir in any of the aforementioned positions, except the one filled by Mahmud 'Abbas.

Relations between the organizations under the PLO umbrella tended to be strengthened by the unity desired by everyone in order to promote the *intifada*. This was evident from Habash's not bolting the PLO after the PNC explicitly mentioned 242 and 338. Yet both the DFLP (particularly Hawatima) and the PFLP continued to be wary of 'Arafat and the concessions he might make. They persisted throughout the year in calling for the PLO to adopt the "collective leadership" and the organizational reforms agreed upon at the 18th PNC in 1987, as well as to take 'Arafat to task for his various visits to Egypt (see chapter on Egypt), which too were, in their view, a violation of the resolutions of the 1987 PNC (see *MECS* 1987, p. 224).[177] Yet even after Hawatima's and Ḥabash's rejection of 'Arafat's press conference statements (see above), it was clear that their organizations saw no purpose in, or chance of, mounting a more forceful challenge to his leadership.

In April, 'Arafat visited Libya for the first time since 1982 and during the rest of the year he made several additional visits to Tripoli (see chapter on Libya). 'Arafat's visits were connected with raising funds for the uprising and ameliorating his situation in Lebanon, but Libyan involvement with the Palestinian issue also centered during the year on reconciliation efforts between the PLO and the organizations in the PNSF. Two meetings of the various factions were held in Tripoli in April and September, but they led to nothing.[178]

Ahmad Jibril's Popular Front for the Liberation of Palestine-General Command and Syria mounted a serious propaganda effort against 'Arafat when in early January Jibril opened a radio station — "*al-Quds, al-idha'a al-'arabiyya al-filistiniyya 'ala tahrir al-ard wal-insan*" (Jerusalem, the Palestinian Arab Radio for the Liberation of the Land and Mankind) — which broadcasted to the West Bank and Gaza from Damascus.[179] In the beginning, the station could be monitored easily in the territories and was quite popular, but in midyear the Israelis apparently began to jam it. The station broadcasted the contents of the leaflets of the Unified Command of the Uprising with significant omissions, such as references to the PLO. In the broadcasts, the leaflets were signed by the popular committees, and not the PLO-affiliated Unified Command. It also broadcasted the announcements and leaflets of the anti-PLO Hamas. The station broadcasted instructions in guerrilla warfare and the names of "collaborators," many of whom were 'Arafat supporters. The Voice of Palestine appealed to the residents of the territories to ignore the "suspect radio [station]."[180]

The PLF lost one of its leaders, Tal'at Ya'qub, who reportedly died of a heart attack in Algiers just a few days after attending the PNC session.[181] Ya'qub's presence at the session was evidence of the closing of the rift between his and Muhammad 'Abbas's factions of the PLF, a process which had begun in the previous year. According to 'Abbas, the two were on the verge of formalizing the union of their two factions at a general conference.[182] Yet there were indications during the year that full elimination of the rift was still in the future. It was reported that 'Abbas had ordered a postmortem on Ya'qub's body, probably to allay any suspicions of his culpability for Ya'qub's death.[183] Ya'qub's supporters, now led by Abu Nidal al-Ashkar,[184] were responsible for an attempted infiltration into Israel in late December,[185] and a few other attempts in early 1989. That these attempts were carried out by PLF members who went out of their way to identify themselves as supporters of Tal'at Ya'qub indicated that there was still a way to go in order to remove the remnants of the enmity between the factions.

THE PLO AND THE ARMED STRUGGLE

'Arafat's renunciation of terrorism, a diplomatic imperative, was not perceived by the PLO as having anything to do with the armed struggle. For the organization, it remained a legitimate form of resistance, guaranteed by the UN. The 19th PNC endorsed the armed struggle and PLO leaders were frank about their desire to see it continue.

On the eve of the 1987 PNC session, Fath had successfully infiltrated the Lebanese border near Kibbutz Manara. The attack had the desired effect on those meeting in Algiers, as it showed 'Arafat's commitment to armed struggle. In 1988, two separate unsuccessful Fath infiltration attempts, one in late October (by Force 17), and the other during the 1988 PNC session, seemed to point to similar considerations of timing being in effect. The DFLP was also particularly active on the eve of the PNC (see chapter on armed operations).[186]

From the end of the PNC session to the end of 1988, there were no reports of attempted or successful Fath incursions into Israel, but there were several unsuccessful attempts by other factions that were in Algiers. These were the PPSF and the Tal'at Ya'qub faction of the PLF. In early 1989, the DFLF and the PFLP carried out several attempts. Those attempts by the radical organizations were aimed at showing their independence from Fath and at distancing themselves from the Geneva press conference statements; Fath apparently preferred not to carry out attacks while it was engaged in a diplomatic offensive. 'Arafat did not oppose such attacks in principle — his organization in fact supported them — but he may or may not have approved of the timing.

Fath differentiated between the armed struggle and the *intifada*. The leaders of the uprising were instructed not to use firearms as a matter of policy, for two reasons. One was that such use might give the Israelis a pretense for cracking down even harder than ever, and the effectiveness of the uprising was predicated on its continuation. The other reason was that the *intifada* had brought media attention because it was — except for rocks, sharp instruments, and firebombs — essentially unarmed popular resistance. But these rules did not hold true for Israel proper. As Salah Khalaf told a Saudi weekly:

> The uprising will not use firearms, but our armed struggle will not rest, and every area in our homeland where there is no uprising will be open to our fighters...to carry out military operations. We divide our activities between the popular uprising, which has won the support of world opinion by employing peaceful means, and the armed and legitimate struggle which will not cease until our enemy feels that there is no hope in doing what he does and will then come to the negotiating table.[187]

For the PLO, the diplomatic struggle went hand in hand with the armed struggle. Again, Salah Khalaf:

> We consider political activity to be one of the methods in [our] struggle; but our other methods remain and we will not renounce them....The armed struggle continues. We have not ceased and we will not cease [the use of] our other methods.[188]

APPENDIX I: DECLARATION OF INDEPENDENCE, 15 NOVEMBER 1988[189]

In the name of God, the Compassionate, the Merciful.

Palestine, the land of the three monotheistic faiths, is where the Palestinian Arab people was born, on which it grew, developed, and excelled. The Palestinian people was never separated from or diminished in its integral bonds with Palestine. Thus the Palestinian Arab people ensured for itself an everlasting union between itself, its land, and its history.

Resolute throughout that history, the Palestinian Arab people forged its national identity, rising even to unimagined levels in its defense as invasion, the design of others, and the appeal special to Palestine's ancient and luminous place on that eminence where powers and civilizations are joined...All this intervened thereby to deprive the people of its political independence. Yet the undying connection between Palestine and its people secured for the land its character and for the people its national genius.

Nourished by an unfolding series of civilizations and cultures, inspired by a heritage rich in variety and kind, the Palestinian Arab people added to its stature by consolidating a union between itself and its patrimonial land. The call went out from temple [Arabic uses the general term *ma'bad*, more properly translated as "place of worship"], church, and mosque to praise the Creator, to celebrate compassion, and peace was indeed the message of Palestine. And in generation after generation, the Palestinian Arab people gave of itself unsparingly in the valiant battle for liberation and homeland. For what has been the unbroken chain of our people's rebellions but the heroic embodiment of our will for national independence? And so the people were sustained in the struggle to stay and to prevail.

When in the course of modern times a new order of values was declared with norms and values fair for all, it was the Palestinian Arab people that had been excluded from the destiny of all other peoples by a hostile array of local and foreign powers. Yet again had unaided justice been revealed as insufficient to drive the world's history along its preferred course.

And it was the Palestinian people, already wounded in its body, that was submitted to yet another type of occupation over which floated the falsehood that "Palestine was a land without people." This notion was foisted upon some in the world, whereas in Article 22 of the Covenant of the League of Nations (1919) and in the Treaty of Lausanne (1923), the community of nations had recognized that all the Arab territories, including Palestine [the Arabic refers to Palestinian and Arab peoples, not territories], of the formerly Ottoman provinces were to have granted to them their freedom as provisionally independent nations.

Despite the historical injustice inflicted on the Palestinian Arab people resulting in their dispersion and depriving them of their right to self-determination, following upon UN General Assembly Resolution 181 (1947), which partitioned Palestine into two states, one Arab, one Jewish, yet it is this resolution that still provides those conditions of international legitimacy [or sanction — *al-shar'iyya al-duwaliyya*] that ensure the right of the Palestinian Arab people to sovereignty and national independence.

By stages, the occupation of Palestine and parts of other Arab territories by Israeli forces, the willed dispossession and expulsion from their ancestral homes of the majority of Palestine's civilian inhabitants was achieved by organized terror; those Palestinians who remained, as a vestige subjugated in its homeland, were persecuted and forced to endure the destruction of their national life.

Thus were principles of international legitimacy violated. Thus were the Charter of the United Nations and its resolutions disfigured, for they had recognized the Palestinian Arab people's national rights, including the Right of Return, the Right to Independence, the Right to Sovereignty over territory and homeland.

In Palestine and on its perimeters, in exile distant and near, the Palestinian Arab people never faltered and never abandoned its conviction in its rights of return and independence. Occupation, massacres, and dispersion achieved no gain in the unabated Palestinian consciousness of self and political identity, as Palestinians went forward with their destiny, undeterred and unbowed.

And from out of the long years of trial in ever mounting struggle, the Palestinian political identity emerged further consolidated and confirmed. And the collective Palestinian national will forged itself in a political embodiment, the Palestine Liberation Organization, its sole, legitimate representative, recognized by the world community as a whole, as well as by [the UN and] related regional and international institutions. Standing on the very rock of conviction in the Palestinian people's inalienable rights, and on the ground of Arab national consensus, and of international legitimacy, the PLO led the campaigns of its great people, molded into unity and powerful resolve, one and indivisible in the triumphs, even as it suffered massacres and confinement within and without its home. And so Palestinian resistance was clarified and raised into the forefront of Arab and world awareness, as the struggle of the Palestinian Arab people achieved unique prominence among the world's liberation movements in the modern era.

The massive national uprising, the *intifada*, now intensifying in cumulative scope and power on occupied Palestinian territories, as well as the unflinching resistance of the refugee camps outside the homeland, have elevated consciousness of the Palestinian truth and right into still higher realms of comprehension and actuality. Now at last the curtain has been dropped around a whole epoch of prevarication and negation. The *intifada* has set siege to the mind of official Israel, which has for too long relied exclusively upon myth and terror to deny Palestinian existence altogether. Because of the *intifada* and its revolutionary irreversible impulse, the history of Palestine has therefore arrived at a decisive juncture [Arabic: one of its most decisive junctures].

Whereas the Palestinian people reaffirms most definitely its inalienable rights in the land of its patrimony:

Now by virtue of natural, historical, and legal rights and the sacrifices of successive generations who gave of themselves in defense of the freedom and independence of their homeland;

In pursuance of resolutions adopted by Arab summit conferences and relying on the authority bestowed by international legitimacy as embodied in the resolutions of the United Nations Organization since 1947;

And in exercise by the Palestinian Arab people of its rights to self-determination, political independence, and sovereignty over its territory;

The Palestine National Council, in the name of God, and in the name of the Palestinian Arab people, hereby proclaims the establishment of the State of Palestine on our Palestinian territory with its capital Jerusalem (Al-Quds Ash-Sharif).

The state of Palestine is the state of Palestinians wherever they may be. The state is for them to enjoy in it their collective national and cultural identity, theirs to pursue in it a complete equality of rights. In it will be safeguarded their political and religious convictions and their human dignity by means of a parliamentary democratic system of governance, itself based on freedom of expression and the freedom to form parties. The rights of minorities will duly be respected by the majority, as minorities must abide by decisions of the majority. Governance will be based on principles of social justice, equality, and nondiscrimination in public rights on grounds of race, religion, color, or sex under the aegis of a constitution which ensures the role of law and an independent judiciary. Thus shall these principles allow no departure from Palestine's age-old spiritual and civilizational heritage of tolerance and religious coexistence.

The State of Palestine is an Arab state, an integral and indivisible part of the Arab nation, at one with that nation in heritage and civilization, with it also in its aspiration for liberation, progress, democracy,and unity. The State of Palestine affirms its obligation to abide by the Charter of the League of Arab States, whereby the coordination of the Arab states with each other shall be strengthened. It calls upon Arab compatriots to consolidate and enhance the emergence in reality of our state, to mobilize potential, and to intensify efforts whose goal is to end Israeli occupation.

The State of Palestine proclaims its commitment to the principles and purposes of the United Nations, and to the Universal Declaration of Human Rights. It proclaims its commitment as well to the principles and policies of the Non-Aligned Movement.

It further announces itself to be a peace-loving state, in adherence to the principles of peaceful coexistence. It will join with all states and peoples in order to assure a permanent peace based upon justice and the respect of rights so that humanity's potential for well-being may be assured, an earnest competition for excellence be maintained, and in which confidence in the future will eliminate fear for those who are just and for whom justice is the only recourse.

In the context of its struggle for peace in the land of love and peace, the State of Palestine calls upon the United Nations to bear special responsibility for the Palestinian Arab people and its homeland. It calls upon all peace- and freedom-loving peoples and states to assist it in the attainment of its objectives, to provide it with security, to alleviate the tragedy of its people, and to help to terminate Israel's occupation of the Palestinian territories.

The State of Palestine herewith declares that it believes in the settlement of regional and international disputes by peaceful means, in accordance with the UN Charter and resolutions. Without prejudice to its natural right to defend its territorial integrity and independence, it therefore rejects the threat or use of force, violence, and terrorism against its territorial integrity, or political independence, as it also rejects their use against the territorial integrity of other states.

Therefore, on this day unlike all others, 15 November 1988, as we stand at the threshold of a new dawn, in all honor and modesty we humbly bow to the sacred spirits of our fallen ones, Palestinian and Arab, by the purity of whose sacrifice for the homeland our sky has been illuminated and our land given life. Our hearts are lifted up and irradiated by the light emanating from the much blessed *intifada*, from those who have endured and have fought the fight of the camps, of dispersion, of exile, from those who have borne the standard of freedom, our children, our aged, our youth, our prisoners, detainees, and wounded, all those whose ties to our sacred soil are confirmed in camp, village, and town. We render special tribute to that brave Palestinian woman, guardian of sustenance and life, keeper of our people's perennial flame. To the souls of our sainted martyrs, to the whole of our Palestinian Arab people, to all free and honorable peoples everywhere, we pledge that our struggle shall be continued until the occupation ends, and the foundation of our sovereignty and independence shall be fortified accordingly.

Therefore, we call upon our great people to rally to the banner of Palestine, to cherish and defend it, so that it may forever be the symbol of our freedom and dignity in that homeland, which is a homeland for the free, now and always.

In the name of God, the Compassionate, the Merciful.

Say: 'O God, Master of the Kingdom, Thou givest the Kingdom to whom Thou wilt, and seizest the Kingdom from whom Thou wilt. Thou exaltest whom Thou wilt, and Thou abasest whom Thou wilt; in Thy hand is the good; Thou art powerful over everything.'

Sadaqa Allahu al-'Azim.

APPENDIX II: POLITICAL STATEMENT OF THE 19TH SESSION OF THE PALESTINE NATIONAL COUNCIL, ALGIERS, 12–15 NOVEMBER 1988[190]

In the name of God, the Compassionate, the Merciful.

In the valiant land of Algeria, hosted by its people and its President Chedli Benjedid, the Palestine National Council held its nineteenth extraordinary session — the session of the *intifada* and independence, the session of the martyred hero Abu Jihad — in the period between 12 and 15 November 1988.

This session culminated in the announcement of the rise of the Palestinian State in our Palestinian land, the natural climax of a daring and tenacious popular struggle that started more than 70 years ago and was baptized in the immense sacrifices offered by our people in our homeland, along its borders, and in the camps and other sites of our diaspora.

The session was also distinguished by its focus on the great national Palestinian *intifada* as one of the major milestones in the contemporary history of the Palestinian people's revolution, on a par with the legendary steadfastness of our people in their camps in our occupied land and outside it.

The primary features of our great people's *intifada* were obvious from its inception and have become clearer in the 12 months since then during which it has continued unabated: it is a total popular revolution that embodies the consensus of an entire nation — women and men, old and young, in the camps, in the villages, and the cities — on the rejection of the occupation and on the determination to struggle until the occupation is defeated and terminated.

This glorious *intifada* has demonstrated our people's deeply rooted national unity and their full adherence to the Palestine Liberation Organization, the sole, legitimate representative of our people, all our people, wherever they congregate — in our homeland or outside it. This was manifested by the participation of the Palestinian masses — their unions, their vocational organizations, their students, their workers, their farmers, their women, their merchants, their landlords, their artisans, their academics — in the *intifada* through its Unified National Command and the popular committees that were formed in the urban neighborhoods, the villages, and the camps.

This, our people's revolutionary furnace and their blessed *intifada*, along with the cumulative impact of our innovative and continuous revolution inside and outside of our homeland, have destroyed the illusion our people's enemies have harbored that they can turn the occupation of Palestinian land into a permanent *fait accompli* and consign the Palestinian issue to oblivion. For our generations have been weaned on the goals and principles of the Palestinian revolution and have lived all its battles since its birth in 1965 — including the heroic resistance against the Zionist invasion of 1982 and the steadfastness of the revolution's camps as they endured the siege and starvation in Lebanon. Those generations — the children of the revolution and of the Palestine Liberation Organization — rose to demonstrate the dynamism and continuity of the revolution, detonating the land under the feet of its occupiers and proving that our people's reserves of resistance are inexhaustible and their faith is too deep to uproot.

Thus did the struggle of the children of the RPGs outside our homeland and the struggle of the children of the sacred stones inside it blend into a single revolutionary melody.

Our people have stood fast against all the attempts of our enemy's authorities to end our revolution, and those authorities have tried everything at their disposal: they have used terrorism, they have imprisoned us, they have sent us into exile, they have desecrated our holy places and restricted our religious freedoms, they have demolished our homes, they have killed us indiscriminately, and premeditatedly, they have sent bands of armed settlers into our villages and camps, they have burned our crops, they have cut off our water and power supplies, they have beaten our women and children, they have used toxic gases that have caused many deaths and abortions, and they have waged an ignorance war [*sic*] against us by closing our schools and universities.

Our people's heroic steadfastness has cost them hundreds of martyrs and tens of thousands of casualties, prisoners, and exiles. But our people's genius was always at hand, ready in their darkest hours to innovate the means and formulas of struggle that stiffened their resistance, bolstered their steadfastness, and enabled them to confront the crimes and measures of the enemy and carry on with their heroic, tenacious struggle.

By standing firm, continuing their revolution, and escalating their *intifada*, our people have proved their determination to press ahead regardless of the sacrifices, armed with the great heritage of struggle, an indomitable revolutionary will, a deeply entrenched national unity that has been rendered even stronger by the *intifada* and its attendant struggles inside and outside our homeland, and total adherence to the nationalistic principles of the Palestine Liberation Organization and its goals of ending the Israeli occupation and achieving the Palestinian people's inalienable right to repatriation, self-determination, and the establishment of the independent Palestinian State.

In all this, our people relied on the sustenance of the masses and forces of our Arab nation, which have stood by us and backed us, as demonstrated by the wide popular support for the *intifada* and by the consensus and resolutions that emerged at the Arab summit in Algiers — all of which goes to confirm that our people do not stand alone as they face the fascist, racist assault, and this precludes any possibility of the Israeli aggressors' isolating our people and cutting them off from the support of their Arab nation.

In addition to this Arab solidarity, our people's revolution and their blessed *intifada* have attracted widespread worldwide solidarity, as seen in the increased understanding of the Palestinian people's issue, the growing support of our just struggle by the peoples and states of the world, and the corresponding condemnation of Israeli occupation and the crimes it is committing, which has helped to expose Israel and increase its isolation and the isolation of its supporters.

Security Council Resolutions 605, 607, and 608 and the resolutions of the General Assembly against the expulsion of the Palestinians from their land and against the repression and terrorism with which Israel is lashing the Palestinian people in the occupied Palestinian territories — these are strong manifestations of the growing support of international opinion, public and official, for our people and their representative, the Palestine Liberation Organization, and of the mounting international rejection of Israeli occupation with all the fascist, racist practices it entails.

The UN General Assembly Resolution 21L/43/1 of 4/11/1988, which was adopted in the session dedicated to the *intifada*, is another sign of the stand the peoples and states of the world in their majority are taking against the occupation and with the just struggle of the Palestinian people and their firm right to liberation and independence. The crimes of the occupation and its savage [or beastly], inhuman practices have exposed the Zionist lie about the democracy of the Zionist entity that has managed to deceive the world for 40 years, revealing Israel in its true light — a fascist, racist, colonialist state built on the usurpation of the Palestinian land and the annihilation of the Palestinian people, a state that threatens and undertakes attacks and expansion into neighboring Arab lands.

It has thus been demonstrated that the occupation cannot continue to reap the fruits of its actions at the expense of the Palestinian people's rights without paying a price — either on the ground or in terms of international public opinion.

In addition to the rejection of the occupation and the condemnation of its repressive measures by the democratic and progressive Israeli forces, Jewish groups all over the world are no longer able to continue their defense of Israel or maintain their silence about its crimes against the Palestinian people. Many voices have risen among those groups to demand an end to these crimes and call for Israel's withdrawal from the occupied territories in order to allow the Palestinian people to exercise their right to self-determination.

The fruits that our people's revolution and their blessed *intifada* have borne on the local, Arab, and international levels have established the soundness and realism of the Palestine Liberation Organization's national program, a program aimed at the termination of the occupation and the achievement of our people's right to return, self-determination, and statehood. Those results have also confirmed that the struggle of our people is the decisive factor in the effort to snatch our national rights from the jaws of the occupation. It is the authority of our people, as represented in the Popular Committees, that controls the situation as we challenge the authority of the occupation's crumbling agencies.

The international community is now more prepared than ever before to strive for a political settlement of the Middle East crisis and its root cause, the question of Palestine. The Israeli occupation authorities, and the American Administration that stands behind them, cannot continue to ignore the national will, which is now unanimous on the necessity of holding an international peace conference on the Middle East and enabling the Palestinian people to gain their national rights, foremost among which is their right to self-determination and national independence on their own national soil.

In the light of this, and toward the reinforcement of the steadfastness and blessed *intifada* of our people, and in accordance with the will of our masses in and outside of our homeland, and in fidelity to those of our people that have been martyred, wounded, or taken captive, the Palestine National Council resolves:

First: On The Escalation and Continuity of the Intifada

A. To provide all the means and capabilities needed to escalate our people's *intifada* in various ways and on various levels to guarantee its continuation and intensification.

B. To support the popular institutions and organizations in the occupied Palestinian territories.

C. To bolster and develop the popular committees and other specialized popular and trade union bodies, including the attack groups and the popular army, with a view to expanding their role and increasing their effectiveness.

D. To consolidate the national unity that emerged and developed during the *intifada*.

E. To intensify efforts on the international level for the release of detainees, the return of those expelled, and the termination of the organized, official acts of repression and terrorism against our children, our women, our men, and our institutions.

F. To call on the United Nations to place the occupied Palestinian land under international supervision for the protection of our people and the termination of the Israeli occupation.

G. To call on the Palestinian people outside our homeland to intensify and increase their support, and to expand the family-assistance program.

H. To call on the Arab nation, its people, forces, institutions, and governments, to increase their political, material, and informational support for the *intifada*.

I. To call on all free and honorable people worldwide to stand by our people, our revolution, our *intifada* against the Israeli occupation, the repression, and the organized, fascist official terrorism to which the occupation forces and the armed fanatic settlers are subjecting our people, our universities, our institutions, our national economy, and our Islamic and Christian holy places.

Second: In the Political Arena

Proceeding from the above, the Palestine National Council, being responsible to the Palestinian people, their national rights and their desire for peace as expressed in the Declaration of Independence issued on 15 November 1988; and in response to the humanitarian quest for international *entente*, nuclear disarmament,and the settlement of regional conflict by peaceful means, affirms the determination of the Palestine Liberation Organization to arrive at a comprehensive settlement of the Arab-Israeli conflict and its core, which is the question of Palestine within the framework of the United Nations Charter, the principles and provisions of international legality, the norms of international law, and the resolutions of the United Nations, the latest of which are Security Council Resolutions 605, 607, and 608, and the resolutions of the Arab summits, in such a manner that safeguards the Palestinian Arab people's rights to return, to self-determination, and the establishment of their independent national state on their national soil, and that institutes arrangements for the security and peace of all states in the region.

Toward the achievement of this, the Palestine National Council affirms:

1. The necessity of convening the effective international conference on the issue of the Middle East and its core, the question of Palestine, under the auspices of the United Nations and with the participation of the permanent members of the Security Council and all parties to the conflict in the region including the Palestine Liberation Organization, the sole, legitimate representative of the Palestinian people, on an equal footing, and by considering that the international peace conference be convened on the basis of United Nations Security Council Resolutions 242 and 338 and the attainment of the legitimate national rights of the Palestinian people, foremost among which is the right to self-determination and in accordance with the principles and provisions of the United Nations Charter concerning the right of peoples to self-determination, and by the inadmissibility of the acquisition of the territory of others by force or military conquest, and in accordance with the relevant United Nations resolutions on the question of Palestine.

2. The withdrawal of Israel from all the Palestinian and Arab territories it occupied in 1967, including Arab Jerusalem.

3. The annulment of all measures of annexation and appropriation and the removal of settlements established by Israel in the Palestinian and Arab territories since 1967.

4. Endeavoring to place the occupied Palestinian territories, including Arab Jerusalem, under the auspices of the United Nations for a limited period in order to protect our people and afford the appropriate atmosphere for the success of the proceedings of the international conference toward the attainment of a comprehensive political settlement and the attainment of peace and security for all on the basis of mutual acquiescence and consent, and to enable the Palestinian State to exercise its effective authority in these territories.

5. The settlement of the question of the Palestinian refugees in accordance with the relevant United Nations resolutions.

6. Guaranteeing the freedom of worship and religious practice for all faiths in the holy places in Palestine.

7. The Security Council is to formulate and guarantee arrangements for security and peace between all the states concerned in the region, including the Palestinian State.

The Palestine National Council affirms its previous resolutions concerning the distinctive relationship between the Jordanian and Palestinian peoples, and affirms that the future relationship between the two states of Palestine and Jordan should be on a confederal basis as a result of the free and voluntary choice of the two fraternal peoples in order to strengthen the historical bonds and the vital interests they hold in common.

The National Council also renews its commitment to the United Nations resolutions that affirm the right of peoples to resist foreign occupation, colonialism, and racial discrimination, and their right to struggle for their independence, and reiterates its rejection of terrorism in all it forms, including state terrorism, affirming its commitment to previous resolutions in this respect and the resolution of the Arab summit in Algiers in 1988, and to UN resolutions 42/95 of 1987, and 40/61 of 1985, and that contained in the Cairo Declaration of 1985 in this respect.

Third: In the Arab and International Arenas

The Palestine National Council emphasizes the importance of the unity of Lebanon in its territory, its people, and its institutions, and stands firmly against the attempts to partition the land and disintegrate the fraternal people of Lebanon. It further emphasizes the importance of the joint Arab effort to participate in a settlement of the Lebanese crisis that helps crystallize and implement solutions that preserve Lebanese unity. The Council also stresses the importance of consecrating the right of the Palestinians in Lebanon to engage in political and informational activity and to enjoy security and protection; and of working against all the forms of conspiracy and aggression that target them and their right to work and live; and of the need to secure the conditions that assure them the ability to defend themselves and provide them with security and protection.

The Palestine National Council affirms its solidarity with the Lebanese nationalist Islamic forces in their struggle against the Israeli occupation and its agents in the Lebanese south; expresses its pride in the allied struggle of the Lebanese and Palestinian peoples against the aggression and toward the termination of the Israeli occupation of parts of the south; and underscores the importance of bolstering this kinship between our peoples and the fraternal, resistant people of Lebanon.

And on this occasion, the Council addresses a reverent salute to the long-suffering people in our camps in Lebanon and its south, who are enduring the aggression, murder, starvation, destruction, air raids, bombardments, and sieges perpetrated against the Palestinian camps and Lebanese villages by the Israeli army, air force, and navy, aided and abetted by hireling forces in the region; and it rejects the resettlement conspiracy, for the Palestinian's homeland is Palestine.

The Council emphasizes the importance of the Iraq-Iran cease-fire resolution toward the establishment of a permanent peace between the two countries and in the Gulf region, and calls for an intensification of the efforts being exerted to ensure the success of the negotiations toward the establishment of peace on stable and firm foundations; affirming, on this occasion, the price of the Palestinian Arab people and the Arab nation as a whole in the steadfastness and triumphs of fraternal Iraq as it defends the eastern gate of the Arab nation.

The National Council also expresses its deep pride in the stand taken by the peoples of our Arab nation in support of our Palestinian Arab people and of the Palestine Liberation Organization and of our people's *intifada* in the occupied homeland; and emphasizes the importance of fortifying the bonds of resistance among forces, parties, and organizations in the Arab national liberation movement, in defense of the right of the Arab nation and its peoples to liberation, democracy, and unity. The Council calls for the adoption of all measures needed to reinforce the unity of struggle among all members of the Arab national liberation movement.

The Palestine National Council, as it hails the Arab states and thanks them for their support of our people's struggle, calls on them to honor the commitments they approved at the summit conference in Algiers in support of the Palestinian people and their blessed *intifada.* The Council, in issuing this appeal, expresses its great confidence that the leaders of the Arab nation will remain, as we have known them, a bulwark of support for Palestine and its people.

The Palestinian National Council reiterates the desire of the Palestine Liberation Organization for Arab solidarity as the framework within which the Arab nation and its states organize themselves to confront Israel's aggression and within which Arab prestige can be enhanced and the Arab role strengthened to the point of influencing international policies to the benefit of Arab rights and causes.

The Palestine National Council expresses its deep gratitude to all the states and international forces and organizations that support the national rights of the Palestinians, and affirms its desire to strengthen the bonds of friendship and cooperation with the Soviet Union, the People's Republic of China, the other socialist countries, the non-aligned states, the Latin American states, and the other friendly states, and notes with satisfaction the signs of positive evolution in the position of some West European states and Japan in the direction of support for the rights of the Palestinian people, applauds this development, and urges intensified efforts to increase it.

The National Council affirms the fraternal solidarity of the Palestinian people and the Palestine Liberation Organization with the struggle of the peoples of Asia, Africa, and Latin America for their liberation and reinforcement of their independence; and condemns all American attempts that threaten the independence of the states of Central America and interfere in their affairs.

The Palestine National Council expresses the support of the Palestine Liberation Organization for the national liberation movements in South Africa and Namibia under the leadership of Swapo with a special salute to our brother combatant, Nelson Mandela — against the racist regime of Pretoria; demands that the people of the two countries be enabled to attain their liberty and independence; and also expresses its support for the African confrontation states and its condemnation of the racist South African regime's aggression against them.

The Council notes with considerable concern the growth of the Israeli forces of fascism and extremism and the escalation of their open calls for the implementation of their policy of annihilation and individual and mass expulsion of our people from their homeland, and calls for intensified efforts in all arenas to confront this fascist peril. The Council at the same time expresses its appreciation of the role and courage of the Israeli peace forces as they resist and expose the forces of fascism, racism, and aggression; support our people's struggle and their valiant *intifada*; and back our people's right to self-determination and establishment of an independent state. The Council confirms its past resolutions regarding the reinforcement and development of relations with these democratic forces.

The Palestine National Council also addressed itself to the American people, calling on them all to strive to put an end to the American policy that denies the Palestinian people's national rights, including their sacred right to self-determination, and urging them to work toward the adoption of policies that conform with the human rights charter and the international conventions and resolutions and serve the quest for peace in the Middle East and security for all its peoples, including the Palestinian people.

The Council charges the Executive Committee with the task of completing the formation of the Committee for the Perpetuation of the Memory of the Martyr Abu Jihad, which shall initiate its work immediately upon the adjournment of the Council.

The Council sends it greetings to the United Nations Committee on the Exercise of the Inalienable Rights of the Palestinian People, and to the fraternal and friendly international and nongovernmental institutions and organizations, and to the journalists and media that have stood and still stand by our people's struggle and *intifada.*

The National Council expresses deep pain at the continued detention of hundreds of combatants from amongst our people in a number of Arab countries, strongly condemns their continued detention, and calls upon these countries to put an end to these abnormal conditions and release those fighters to play their role in the struggle.

In conclusion, the Palestine National Council affirms its complete confidence that the justice of the Palestinian cause and of the demands for which the Palestinian people are struggling will continue to draw increasing support from honorable and free people around the world; and also affirms its complete confidence in victory on the road to Jerusalem, the capital of our independent Palestinian State.

APPENDIX III: JOINT DECLARATION OF PLO DELEGATION, LED BY YASIR 'ARAFAT, AND A GROUP OF AMERICAN JEWS, STOCKHOLM, 7 DECEMBER 1988[191]

The Palestine National Council met in Algiers from 12–15 November 1988, and announced the Declaration of Independence, which proclaimed the State of Palestine, and issued a political statement.

The following explanation was given by the representatives of the PLO of certain important points in the Palestinian Declaration of Independence and the political statement adopted by the PNC in Algiers.

Affirming the principle incorporated in those UN resolutions, which call for a two-state solution of Israel and Palestine, the PNC:

1. Agreed to enter into peace negotiations at an international conference under the auspices of the UN with the participation of the permanent member of the Security Council and the PLO as the sole legitimate representative of the Palestinian people, on an equal footing with the other parties to the conflict; such an international conference to be held on the basis of UN Resolutions 242 and 338 and the right of the Palestinian people to self-determination, without external interference, as provided in the UN

Charter, including the right to an independent state, which conference should resolve the Palestinian problem in all its aspects.

2. Established the independent State of Palestine and accepted the existence of Israel as a state in the region.

3. Declared its rejection and condemnation of terrorism in all its forms, including state terrorism.

4. Called for a solution to the Palestinian refugee problem in accordance with international law and practices and relevant UN resolutions (including right of return or compensation).

The American personalities strongly supported and applauded the Palestinian Declaration of Independence and the Political Statement adopted in Algiers and felt there was no further impediment to a direct dialogue between the United States Government and the PLO.

APPENDIX IV: YASIR 'ARAFAT, SPEECH BEFORE THE 43RD SESSION OF THE UNITED NATIONS GENERAL ASSEMBLY ON THE PALESTINE QUESTION, GENEVA, 13 DECEMBER 1988[192]

Mr. President, Honorable Members:

It never occurred to me that my second meeting with this honorable assembly since 1974 would take place in the hospitable city of Geneva. I had thought that the new political positions and postures evolved by our Palestinian people in the course of the Algiers meeting of the Palestine National Council (PNC), all of which have been made public and extremely well received internationally, would have necessitated my travel to the United Nations headquarters in New York to brief you on our resolutions and projections on the issue of peace in our homeland as formulated by our PNC, the highest legislative authority in the Palestinian body politic.

I am both proud and happy to meet with you today, here in Geneva, after an arbitrary American decision barred me from going to you there. I am proud because I am in your midst and you are the highest rostrum for the problems of justice and peace in the world. I am happy because I am in Geneva, where justice and neutrality are a guidepost and a constitution in a world where the arrogance of power drives some to lose their sense of neutrality and justice. The resolution passed by your esteemed assembly, with 154 member nations voting to move the session here, was not a victory over the American decision but an unprecedented landslide for the international consensus in favor of justice and peace. It is proof that our people's just cause has become embedded in tha fabric of the human consciousness.

Our Palestinian people will never forget the position taken by this honorable assembly and these friendly states in support of right and justice and in defense of the values and principles for which the United Nations organization was established. This position will be a source of confidence and security to all peoples subjected to injustice, oppression, and occupation and struggling, like the Palestinian people, for freedom, dignity, and survival.

I extend deep gratitude to all nations, forces, and international organizations and personalities who backed our people and supported its national rights — particularly our friends in the Soviet Union, the People's Republic of China, the socialist countries, the nonaligned states, the Islamic states, the African states, the Asian states, the Latin American states, and other friendly states. I also thank the Western European nations and Japan for their latest stands toward our people and I invite them to take further steps positively to evolve their resolutions in order to open the ways for peace and a just settlement in our region, the Middle East.

I reiterate our solidarity with and support for the liberation movements in Namibia and South Africa in their struggle, and our support for the African frontline states against the aggression of the racist South African regime. I seize this opportunity to express my gratitude to those friendly states which took the initiative in supporting us, in endorsing our PNC resolutions, and in recognizing the State of Palestine.

And I will not miss this opportunity to thank warmly His Excellency the secretary-general of the United Nations, Mr. Javier Pérez de Cuellar, and his assistants for their relentless efforts to achieve humanity's aspirations for international *détente* and the settlement of its problems particularly those related to the Palestine question. I also extend my thanks and appreciation to the chairman and members of the United Nations Committee on the Exercise of the Inalienable Rights of the Palestinian People on their endeavors for our people's cause, and I salute the nonaligned nations' "Committee of Nine on the Palestine Question" for all its constructive contributions to our people's cause.

And to you, Mr. President, my warm congratulations on the occasion of your election as president of this assembly. I have full confidence in your wisdom and insight. I also congratulate your predecessor on his skillful handling of the proceedings of the previous session. Lastly, I extend warm greetings and thanks to the Swiss Government and people for making this meeting possible.

Mr. President, Honorable Members:

Fourteen years ago on 13 November 1974, I received a gracious invitation from you to expound the problem of our Palestinian people before this dignified assembly. Here I am returning to you after all these eventful years to see new peoples taking their places in your midst, crowning thereby their victories in the battles for freedom and independence. To the representatives of these peoples, I extend the warm congratulations of our own. Let it be known that I return to you with a stronger voice, a firmer determination, and a greater confidence to reiterate my conviction that our struggle will bear fruit and that the State of Palestine, which we proclaimed at our Palestine National Council, will take its place among you to join [hands with] you in consolidating the charter of this organization and the Universal Declaration of Human Rights, in putting an end to the tragedies afflicting humanity, and in upholding the principles of right, justice, peace, and freedom for all.

Fourteen years ago, when you told us in the General Assembly hall: "Yes to Palestine and the people of Palestine, yes to the Palestine Liberation Organization, yes to the inalienable national rights of the people of Palestine," a few imagined that your resolutions would carry little weight, failing to realize that these resolutions were among the springs that watered the olive branch I carried that day. Since then, we have watered it with blood, tears, and sweat, and it has turned into a tree with roots entrenched in the ground, and a stem reaching for the sky promising to bear the fruits of victory over coercion, injustice, and occupation. You gave us hope that freedom and justice would triumph and we gave you a generation of our people that has dedicated its life to the realization of that dream. It is the generation of the blessed *intifada,* which today is wielding the homeland's stones to defend the honor of this homeland and be worthy of belonging to people thirsting for freedom and independence.

I bring you greetings from those heroic people, from our men and our women, from the masses of our blessed *intifada,* which now enters its second year with great momentum and painstaking organization, using a civilized, democratic approach to weather and confront occupation, coercion, tyranny, and the barbaric crimes committed daily by the Israeli occupiers. Greetings to you from our young men and women in the occupation forces' prisons and collective detention centers. Greetings from the children of stones who are challenging occupation forces armed with warplanes, tanks, and weapons — an unarmed Palestinian David facing a heavily armed Israeli Goliath.

I said in concluding my address in our first encounter that as chairman of the Palestine Liberation Organization and leader of the Palestine revolution, I reaffirmed that we do not wish to see a drop of Jewish or Arab blood shed, that we do not want the continuation of the fighting for one extra minute. I appealed to you then to spare us all these ordeals and sufferings and to speed up work on the foundations of a just peace based on securing the rights, hopes, and aspirations of our people and the equal rights of all peoples.

I said that I was calling upon you to stand by the struggle of our people to exercise its right to self-determination and to enable our people to return from the exile into which it was driven at gunpoint. I solicited your help to end this injustice to which successive generations of our people have been subjected over several decades so that they can live free and sovereign on their soil and in their homeland, enjoying all their national and human rights. The last thing I said from this rostrum was that war breaks out from Palestine and that peace starts in Palestine.

The dream we entertained at the time was to establish a democratic State of Palestine in which Muslims, Christians, and Jews would live with equal rights and obligations as one unified community, like other peoples in this contemporary world.

We were shocked to hear Israeli officialdom interpret this Palestinian dream — inspired by the spiritual heritage that illuminated Palestine and the civilizational and humanitarian values calling for coexistence in a free democratic society — as a scheme to destroy and obliterate their entity.

Mr. President:

We had to draw the necessary conclusion regarding the gap between this reality and the dream. We set out in the Palestine Liberation Organization to look for realistic and attainable formulas that would settle the issue on the basis of possible, rather than absolute, justice while securing the rights of our people to freedom, sovereignty, and independence; ensuring for everyone peace, security, and stability; and sparing Palestine and the Middle East wars and battles that have been going on for forty years.

Didn't we, Mr. President, take the initiative of relying on the charter and resolutions of the United Nations, the Declaration of Human Rights, and international legitimacy as the basis for the settlement of the Arab-Israeli conflict?

Did we not welcome the Vance-Gromyko communiqué of 1977 as a move that could form the basis of a proposed solution to this conflict? Did we not agree to participate in the Geneva conference on the basis of the American-Egyptian statement of 1977 to push forward the prospects of a settlement and peace in the region? Did we not endorse the Arab peace plan in Fez in 1982 and later the call for an international peace conference under the auspices of the United Nations and in keeping with its resolutions? Did we not underwrite the Brezhnev plan for peace in the Middle East? Did we not welcome and support the Venice declaration by the European Community as the basis for a just peace in the area? Did we not welcome and support the joint initiative of presidents Gorbachev and Mitterrand on a preparatory committee for the international conference? Did we not welcome scores of political statements and initiatives put forward by African, Islamic, nonaligned, socialist, European, and other groups and states for the purpose of finding a peaceful settlement based on the principles of international legitimacy?

What has been the attitude of Israel on all this, even though not a single one of the aforementioned initiatives or plans or communiqués lacks political balance or overlooks the claims and interests of all the parties to the Arab-Israeli conflict?

Israel's response to all this has been the schemes; the fanning of the flames of conflict with more destruction, devastation, and bloodshed; and the expansion of the confrontation fronts to include brotherly Lebanon, which was invaded by the occupation troops in 1982, an invasion punctuated with slaughters and massacres perpetrated against the Lebanese and Palestinian peoples, including the Sabra and Shatila massacres. Until this moment, Israel continued to occupy parts of South Lebanon, and Lebanon faces daily raids as well as air, sea, and land attacks on its cities and villages and our camps in the south.

It is painful and regrettable that the American Government alone should continue to back these aggressive and expansionist schemes as well as Israel's continued occupation of Palestinian and Arab territories, its crimes, and its iron-fist policy against our children and women. It is painful and regrettable, too, that the American Government should continue refusing to recognize the right of six million Palestinians to self-determination, a right which is sacred to the American people and other peoples on this planet.

I remind them of the position of President Wilson, author of the two universal principles of international relations, i.e., the inadmissibility of the acquisition of territory by force and the right of peoples to self-determination. I remind them, too, that when the Palestinian people were consulted by the King-Crane Commission in 1919, they chose the United States as the mandatory power. Circumstances having prevented that, the mandate was given to Britain. My question to the American people is this: Is it fair that the Palestinian people should be deprived of what President Wilson prescribed?

The successive American administrations realize that the only birth certificate for the establishment of the State of Israel is

Resolution 181, approved by the General Assembly on 29 November 1947, and endorsed at the time by the United States and the Soviet Union. It provides for the establishment of two states in Palestine, one Palestinian Arab and one Jewish.

How then does the American Government explain its position which acknowledges and recognizes the half of the resolution that pertains to Israel and rejects the half pertaining to the Palestinian State? How does the United States Government explain its lack of commitment to the execution of a resolution that it has endorsed on more than one occasion in your esteemed assembly, i.e., [UNGA] Resolution 194, which provides for the right of the Palestinians to return to the homes and properties from which they were evicted and for compensation for those wishing not to exercise this right?

The United States Government knows that neither the US nor anyone else has the right to apportion international legitimacy and fragment the provisions of international law.

Mr. President:

The uninterrupted struggle of our people for its rights has been going on for several decades during which it has offered hundreds of thousands of martyrs and wounded and endured all kinds of tragedies. On the contrary, its adherence to its Palestinian homeland and national identity has grown stronger.

The leaders of Israel, in their intoxication, deluded themselves into believing that, after our exodus from Beirut, the Palestine Liberation Organization would be thrown into the sea. Little did they expect our march into exile to turn into a procession of return to the homeland, to the field of battle, to occupied Palestine. The result was the heroic popular *intifada* which is there to stay until the fulfillment of our goals of freedom and national independence.

I take pride, Mr. President, in being one of the sons of these population [*sic*], whose men, women, and children are writing with their blood an outstanding epic of national resistance and who are performing legendary miracles daily to sustain their *intifada* and make it grow until it can impose its will and prove that right can prevail over might. We salute with deep pride our people of the *intifada* as the authors of a unique democratic revolutionary experiment.

Theirs is the faith that could not be crushed by Israel's military machine; that could not be killed by any kind of ammunition; that could not be shaken by the burial of people alive, the breaking of bones, the inducement of miscarriages, or the usurpation of water resources; and that could not be deterred by detention, internment, exile, deportation, collective punishment, the demolition of homes, the closure of universities, schools, trade unions, associations, institutions, and newspapers; or the laying of siege to camps, villages, and towns. Those brutal reprisals have only served to strengthen that faith, spreading it to every household and giving it roots in every inch of our national soil.

A people with such a heritage and such a history is invincible. All the forces of tyranny and terror cannot sway its deep-rooted faith in its right to its homeland and in such values as justice, peace, love, coexistence, and tolerance. The rifle of the revolutionary has protected us from liquidation and the destruction of our national identity in the arenas of hot confrontation. We are fully confident of our ability to protect our green [olive] branch in the arenas of political confrontation.

The worldwide embrace of our just cause, pressing for the realization of peace based on justice, demonstrates clearly that the world has unequivocally identified the predator and the prey, the aggressor and the victim, the struggler for freedom and peace and the terrorist. The day-to-day practices of the occupation army and the gangs of fanatic armed settlers against our people, women and children, have unveiled the ugly face of Israeli occupation and exposed its true aggressive nature.

This growing worldwide awareness has reached Jewish groups within Israel itself and outside. Their eyes have been opened to the reality of the problem and the essence of the conflict, particularly since they have witnessed the inhuman, day-to-day Israeli practices that undermine the tolerant spirit of Judaism itself.

It has become difficult, if not impossible, for a Jew to reject racial persecution and uphold freedom and human rights while remaining silent about Israel's crimes against Palestinian human rights, the Palestinian people, and the Palestinian homeland, particularly the ugly day-to-day practices of the occupiers and gangs of settlers.

We distinguish, Mr. President, between the Jewish citizen whom the Israeli ruling circles have continuously sought to disinform and mislead and the practices of the leaders of Israel. We realize that there are within and outside Israel courageous and honorable Jewish people who do not condone the Israeli Government's policy of repression, massacres, expansion, settlement, and expulsion and who recognize the equal rights of our people to life, freedom, and independence. On behalf of the Palestinian people, I thank them all for their courageous and honorable stance.

Our people does not want a right which is not its own or which has not been vested in it by international legitimacy and international law. It does not seek its freedom at the expense of anyone else's freedom, nor does it want a destiny which negates the destiny of another people. Our people refuses to be better or worse than any other people. Our people wants to be the equal of all other peoples, with the same rights and obligations. I call upon all peoples of the world, especially those which were afflicted by the Nazi occupation and considered it their duty to close the chapter of coercion and oppression by one people against another and to lend a willing hand to all the victims of terrorism, fascism, and Nazism, to see clearly today the responsibilities cast upon them by history toward our downtrodden people, which wants its children to have a place under the sun in their homeland — a place where they can live in freedom, like the rest of the children of the world.

Mr. President:

It is cause for optimism that our struggle should culminate in the ongoing *intifada* when the international atmosphere is marked by a serious and sustained quest for international *détente*, accord, and progress. We are heartened by the successes scored by the United Nations and its secretary-general in contributing effectively to settling many problems and defusing trouble spots around the world in this new environment of international *détente*.

Surely, it is impossible to consolidate this new, positive international climate without addressing problems and trouble spots around the globe. This would enable us to formulate a more accurate and reliable yardstick to assess the endeavors of man and nations and to brace for the next century and the challenges and new responsibilities it will lay before us in terms of averting wars and destruction and promoting more freedom, well-being, peace, and progress for mankind.

No one, Mr. President, would dispute the fact that the Palestine problem is the problem of our contemporary world. It is the oldest on your agenda. It is the most intricate and complex. Of the regional issues, it poses the most serious threat to international peace and security. Hence, its priority among the issues that should command the attention of the two superpowers and all the countries of the world. Hence, the need for an effort to outline a course for its equitable solution — a solution that would spread peace across the Middle East.

We in the Palestine Liberation Organization — as a leadership responsible for the people of Palestine and its destiny, loyal to the struggle of our people, venerating the sacrifices of our martyrs, eager to contribute to the prevailing climate of coexistence and *détente*, and [the] consensus of the need to participate in the peaceful efforts to find a political settlement that would put an end to the tragedies of wars and fighting and would open the way for peaceful coexistence under international law — summoned our Palestine National Council to convene in an extraordinary session in Algiers last 12–15 November, the purpose being to specify and clarify our position as a main party to the Arab-Israeli conflict, which cannot be settled without its participation and approval.

It pleases me to inform you, with great pride, that our Palestine National Council, through a totally free exercise of democracy, has again demonstrated its ability to shoulder its national responsibilities, endorsing serious constructive and responsible resolutions which pave the way for us to reinforce and highlight our desire and contribution to find a peaceful settlement that would secure the national and political rights of our people as well as peace and security for everyone else.

Mr. President:

The first and decisive resolution of our Palestine National Council was the proclamation of the establishment of the State of Palestine, with the Holy City of Jerusalem [al-Quds ash-Sharif] as its capital. The State of Palestine was declared:

* By virtue of the Palestinian Arab people's natural, historic, and legal right to their homeland, Palestine, and of the sacrifices of their successive generations in defense of the liberty and independence of their homeland;
* Pursuant to the resolutions of the Arab summit conference;
* By the authority of international legitimacy, as embodied in the resolutions of the United Nations since 1947;
* In implementation of the Palestinian Arab people's right to self-determination, political independence, and sovereignty on their soil, and in conformity with your successive resolutions.

It is important for me, in repeating this historic proclamation before the international community, now that it has become one of the official United Nations documents, to reaffirm that this decision is irreversible and that we will not relent until it succeeds in casting off the occupation, enabling our Palestinian people wherever they may be to exercise their sovereignty in their state, the State of Palestine. In it they shall develop their national and cultural identity and enjoy full equality in rights. Their religious and political beliefs and their human dignity shall be safeguarded under a democratic parliamentary system of government built on freedom of opinions; the freedom to form parties; the protection of the rights of the minority by the majority and respect for the decision of the majority by the minority; social justice and equal rights, free of ethnic, religious, racial, or sexual discrimination; a constitution that guarantees the rule of law and the independence of the judiciary; and on the basis of total allegiance to the centuries-old spiritual and civilizational Palestinian heritage of religious tolerance and coexistence.

The State of Palestine is an Arab state; its people are an integral part of the Arab nation and of the nation's heritage, its civilization, and its aspiration to attain its goals of social progress, unity, and liberation. [The State of Palestine] is committed to the Charter of the League of Arab States, the United Nations Charter, the Universal Declaration of Human Rights, and the principles of nonalignment.

It is a peace-loving state committed to the principles of peaceful coexistence and it shall strive with all states and peoples to attain a permanent peace built on justice and respect of rights.

It is a state which believes in the settlement of international and regional disputes by peaceful means in accordance with the charter and resolutions of the United Nations. It rejects threats of force, violence, terrorism, or the use of these against its territorial integrity and political independence, or against the territorial integrity of any other state, without prejudice to its natural right to defend its territory and independence.

It is a state which believes that the future can only bring security to those who are just or have come back to justice. This, Mr. President, is the State of Palestine which we proclaimed and which we shall endeavor to embody so that it can take its place among the states of the world and share creatively in shaping a free world where justice and peace prevail. Our state, God willing, shall have its provisional government at the earliest possible opportunity. The PNC has mandated the PLO Executive Committee to assume the functions of the said government in the interim.

To embody the aforementioned decision, our Palestine National Council adopted a series of resolutions. I am keen to spotlight the most salient of these, which underline our serious determination to pursue the path of an equitable peaceful settlement and to exert maximum effort to ensure its success.

Our PNC reaffirmed the necessity of convening an international conference on the issue of the Middle East and its core, the Palestinian issue, under the auspices of the United Nations and with the participation of the permanent members of the Security Council and all parties to the conflict in the region, including, on an equal footing, the Palestine Liberation Organization, the sole, legitimate representative of the Palestinian people, on the understanding that the international conference will be held on the basis of Security Council Resolutions 242 and 338 and the safeguarding of the legitimate national and political rights of the Palestinian people, foremost among which is its right to self-determination.

Our PNC reasserted the need for Israel's withdrawal from all the Palestinian and Arab territories it occupied in 1967, including Arab Jerusalem; the establishment of the Palestinian State; the annulment of all expropriation and annexation measures; and the dismantling of the settlements established by Israel in the Palestinian and Arab territories since 1967, as called for in the Arab summit resolutions of Fez and Algiers.

Our PNC also reaffirmed the necessity of seeking to place the occupied Palestinian territories, including Arab Jerusalem, under the supervision of the United Nations for a limited period, to protect our people, to create an atmosphere conducive to the success of the proceedings of the international conference toward the attainment of a comprehensive political settlement and the achievement of peace and security for all peoples and states in the Middle East, on the basis of mutual consent, and to enable the State of Palestine to exercise its effective authority in these territories, reaffirmed earlier by the resolutions of the Arab summits.

Our PNC called for the settlement of the issue of Palestinian refugees in accordance with the pertinent United Nations resolutions. It guaranteed freedom of worship and the right to engage in religious rites for all faiths in the holy places in Palestine. And it reconfirmed that the relationship between the fraternal Jordanian and Palestinian peoples is a privileged one and that the future relationship between the State of Palestine and the Hashemite Kingdom of Jordan will be built on confederal foundations, on the basis of the two fraternal peoples' free and voluntary choice, in consolidation of the historical ties that bind them and the vital interests they hold in common. The PNC reaffirmed the need for the Security Council to draw up and guarantee arrangements for security and peace between all the states that are parties to the conflict in the region.

It is important for me, Mr. President, to point out that these resolutions, in their content and wording, reflect our firm desire for peace and freedom, and our total awareness of the climate of international *détente* and of the eagerness of the international community to achieve balanced solutions that address the claims and fundamental interests of the parties in conflict. These resolutions attest to the solemnity of the Palestinian people's position on the question of peace; that they are committed to peace and believe that it should be secured and guaranteed by the Security Council under the aegis of the United Nations. These resolutions constitute a firm, unambiguous response to all arguments, prejudices, stands, and pretexts used by some nations to cast doubt on the position and policy of the Palestine Liberation Organization.

At a time when our people were voting for peace through their *intifada* and their representatives in the PNC, thereby confirming their positive response to the prevailing mood of *détente* in international relations and to the growing trend toward the settlement of world conflicts by peaceful means, the Israeli Government was fanning the flames of aggressive, expansionist conflicts, and religious fanaticism, thereby announcing its adherence to the option of belligerence and the dismissal of our people's right.

The Palestine side, for its part, has formulated clear and responsible political positions which conform with the will of the international community, to promote the convening of the international peace conference and the success of its proceedings. The gratifying and courageous international backing as expressed in the recognition of the State of Palestine is further proof of the credibility of our course and resolutions and their compliance with the international will for peace.

While we greatly appreciate the free American voices that have explained and supported our position and resolutions, we note that the US Administration remains uncommitted to evenhandedness in its dealings with the parties to the conflict. It continues to demand from us alone the acceptance of positions which cannot be determined prior to negotiation and dialogue within the framework of the international conference.

I would point out here that the answer to the many questions being posed, regardless of their source, rests solely on the acceptance of the equality of the two parties to the conflict and on the recognition of their equal rights of a reciprocal basis. And if the policies applied on the ground are any reflection of the policymakers' intentions, it is the Palestinian side that has more cause to worry and to demand reassurances about its fate and its future, facing as it does a State of Israel that is bristling with the latest arms, including nuclear weapons.

Mr. President:

Our Palestine National Council has reaffirmed its commitment to the UN resolutions that uphold the right of peoples to resist foreign occupation, colonialism, and racial discrimination, and their right to struggle for independence. It has also reaffirmed its rejection of terrorism in all its forms, including state terrorism, emphasizing its commitment to its past resolutions in this regard, to the resolution of the Arab summit in Algiers in 1988, to UN Resolutions 42/159 of 1987 and 61/40 of 1985, and to what was stated on this subject in the Cairo Declaration of 7 November 1985.

The position, Mr. President, is clear and free of all ambiguity. And yet, I, as chairman of the Palestine Liberation Organization, hereby once more declare that I condemn terrorism in all its forms, and at the same time salute those sitting before me in this hall who, in the days when they fought to free their countries from the yoke of colonialism, were accused of terrorism by their oppressors, and who today are the faithful leaders of their peoples, stalwart champions of justice and freedom. I also offer a reverent salute to the martyrs who have fallen at the hands of terrorism and terrorists, foremost among whom is my lifetime companion and deputy, the martyr-symbol Khalil al-Wazir, and the martyrs who fell in the massacres to which our people have been subjected in the various cities, villages, and camps of the West Bank, the Gaza Strip, and South Lebanon.

Mr. President, Honorable Members:

The situation in our Palestinian homeland can bear no more waiting. Our people and our children, leading our march to liberty, holding aloft the torch of freedom, are being martyred daily for the sake of ending the occupation and laying the foundation of peace in their free, independent homeland and in the region as whole.

For this reason, the Palestine National Council, taking into consideration the circumstances of the Palestinians and the Israelis and the need for a spirit of tolerance between them, built its resolutions on foundations of realism.

The United Nations bears a historic, extraordinary responsibility toward our people and their rights. More than forty years ago, the United Nations, in its Resolution 181, decided on the establishment of two states in Palestine, one Palestinian Arab and the other Jewish. Despite the historic wrong that was done to our people, it is our view today that the said resolution continues to meet the requirements of international legitimacy which guarantee the Palestinian Arab people's right to sovereignty and national independence.

The acceleration of the peace process in the region requires special efforts on the part of the international community, particularly the United States and the Soviet Union, who bear a great responsibility toward the cause of peace in our region.

The United Nations, the permanent members of the Security Council, and all international blocs and bodies have a vital role to play at this stage. In my capacity as chairman of the PLO Executive Committee, presently assuming the functions of the provisional government of the State of Palestine, I therefore present the following Palestinian peace initiative:

First: That a serious effort be made to convene, under the supervision of the secretary-general of the United Nations, the preparatory committee of the international conference for peace in the Middle East — in accordance with the initiative of President Gorbachev and President Mitterrand, which President Mitterrand presented to your assembly toward the end of last September and which was supported by many states — to pave the way for the convening of the international conference, which commands universal support except from the Government of Israel.

Second: In view of our belief in international legitimacy and the vital role of the United Nations, that actions be undertaken to place our occupied Palestinian land under temporary United Nations supervision, and that international forces be deployed there to protect our people and, at the same time, to supervise the withdrawal of the Isaeli forces from our country.

Third: The PLO will seek a comprehensive settlement among the parties concerned in the Arab-Israeli conflict, including the State of Palestine, Israel, and other neighbors, within the framework of the international conference for peace in the Middle East on the basis of Resolutions 242 and 338 and so as to guarantee equality and the balance of interests, especially our people's rights, in freedom, national independence, and respect the right to exist in peace and security for all.

If these principles are endorsed at the international conference, we will have come a long way toward a just settlement, and this will enable us to reach agreement on all security and peace arrangements.

Mr. President:
I hope it is clear to everyone that our Palestinian people, determined though they are to gain their legitimate national rights to self-determination, repatriation, and the ending of the occupation of the Palestinian State's territory, are equally determined to strive for those goals by peaceful means within the framework of the international conference under the sponsorship of the United Nations and in accordance with its charter and resolutions. I assure you that, like all other peoples on earth, we are a people that yearns for peace — and perhaps with greater enthusiasm, considering our long years of suffering and the harsh conditions that plague us and our children, who are deprived of the normalcy of a life free of war, free of tragedy, free of the torment of exile, free of hopelessness and daily anguish.

So let the voices supporting the olive branch, peaceful coexistence, and international *entente* be heard. Let all hands join in defense of a historic, possibly irreplaceable opportunity to put an end to a tragedy that has lingered too long and cost thousands of lives and the destruction of hundreds of villages and cities. We reach for the olive branch because it sprouts in our hearts from the tree of the homeland, the tree of freedom.

Mr. President, Honorable Members:
I come to you in the name of my people, offering my hands that we can make true peace, peace based on justice. I ask the leaders of Israel to come here, under the sponsorship of the United Nations, so that, together, we can forge that peace. I say to them, as I say to you, that our people, who want dignity, freedom, and peace for themselves and security for their state, want the same things for all the states and parties involved in the Arab-Israeli conflict. And here, I would address myself specifically to the Israeli people in all their parties and forces, and especially to the advocates of democracy and peace among them. I say to them: Come, let us make peace. Cast away fear and intimidation. Leave behind the specter of the wars that have raged continuously in the furnace of this conflict for the past forty years. Set aside all threats of wars to come, whose fuel could only be the bodies of our children and yours. Come, let us make peace. Let us make the peace of the bold, far from the arrogance of power and the weapons of destruction; far from occupation, oppression, humiliation, murder, and torture.

Say: 'O Peoples of the Book! Come to common terms,' so that we can build peace in the land of peace, the land of Palestine. 'Glory to God in the highest, and on Earth peace, goodwill toward men.' 'O Lord, Thou art the peace, and the peace is of You, and the peace shall return unto You. Let us live, O Lord, in peace, and enter Heaven Thy house, the house of peace.' Finally, I say to our people: The dawn approaches. Victory is at hand. I see the homeland in your holy stones. I see the flag of our independent Palestine fluttering over the hills of our beloved homeland. Thank you. Peace be upon you, and God's mercy and His blessings.

APPENDIX V: YASIR 'ARAFAT, TEXT OF PRESS CONFERENCE STATEMENT, GENEVA, 14 DECEMBER 1988[193]

Let me highlight my views before you. Our desire for peace is a strategy and not an interim tactic. We are bent on peace come what may, come what may.

Our statehood provides salvation to the Palestinians and peace to both Palestinians and Israelis.

Self-determination means survival for the Palestinians and our survival does not destroy the survival of the Israelis, as their rulers claim. Yesterday in my speech I made reference to United Nations Resolution 181 [on the partition of Palestine] as the basis for Palestinian independence. I also made reference to our acceptance of Resolutions 242 and 338 as the basis of negotiations with Israel within the framework of the international conference. These three resolutions were endorsed by our Palestine National Council session in Algiers.

In my speech also yesterday, it was clear that we mean our people's rights to freedom and national independence, according to Resolution 181, and the right of all parties concerned in the Middle East conflict to exist in peace and security, and, as I have mentioned, including the State of Palestine, Israel, and other neighbors, according to Resolutions 242 and 338.

As for terrorism, I announced it yesterday in no uncertain terms, and yet, I repeat for the record. I repeat for the record that we totally and absolutely renounce all forms of terrorism, including individual, group, and state terrorism.

Between Geneva and Algiers, we have made our position crystal clear. Any more talk such as "The Palestinians should give more' — you remember this slogan? — or 'It is not enough' or 'The Palestinians are engaging in propaganda games and public relations exercises' will be damaging and counterproductive.

Enough is enough. Enough is enough. Enough is enough. All remaining matters should be discussed around the table and within the international conference.

Let it be absolutely clear that neither 'Arafat, nor any [one else] for that matter, can stop the *intifada*, the uprising. The *intifada* will come to an end only when practical and tangible steps have been taken toward the achievement of our national aims and establishment of our independent Palestinian State.

In this context, I expect the EEC [European Economic Community] to play a more effective role in promoting peace in our region. They have a political responsibility, they have a moral responsibility, and they can deal with it.

Finally, I declare before you and I ask you to kindly quote me on that: We want peace. We want peace. We are committed to peace. We are committed to peace. We want to live in our Palestinian State, and let live. Thank you.

NOTES

For the place and frequency of publications cited here, and for the full name of the publication, news agency, radio station, or monitoring service where an abbreviation is used, please see "List of Sources." Only in the case of more than one publication bearing the same name is the place of publication noted here.

1. 'Arafat to R. Monte Carlo, 19 February — DR, 19 February 1988.
2. *JP*, 19 February; VoI, 19 February — DR, 19 February1988.
3. *Ha'aretz*, *Hadashot*, 21 February; VoP (Baghdad), 19 February — DR, 19 February 1988.
4. VoP (Baghdad), 20 February — DR, 20 February 1988.
5. VoP (Baghdad), 27 February — DR, 27 February 1988.
6. 'Arafat to R. Monte Carlo, 27 February — DR, 27 February; *The Guardian, Ma'ariv*, 1 March 1988.
7. *JP*, 25 March 1988.
8. VoP (Baghdad), 1 April — DR, 4 April 1988.
9. Abu Lughod to *al-Majalla*, 6 April, reprinted in*Shu'un Filastiniyya*, No. 181, April 1988, pp. 151–52.
10. *JP*, 30 April 1988.
11. AFP, 15 April 1988.
12. Al-Hasan to *al-Musawwar*, 1 April 1988.
13. Fath statement, VoP (Baghdad), 7 March — DR, 8 March 1988.
14. Quqa to *al-Anba*, 8 October 1988.
15. *Boston Globe*, 28 August; *JP*, 5 September 1988.
16. Khalaf to *al-Sakhra*, 1 December 1987.
17. See, for example, 'Arafat to *Filastin al-Thawra*, 21 January 1988.
18. KUNA, 23 January — DR, 23 January 1989.
19. *Al-Nur*, 19 October 1988.
20. *Filastin al-Thawra*, 27 November 1988. For a detailed analysis of the relationship between Fath and the Islamic trend, see Hala Mustafa, "al-Tayyar al-Islami fi al-Ard al-Muhtalla," *al-Mustaqbal al-'Arabi*, No. 7, 1988, pp. 75–90.
21. 'Arafat to *ME*, March 1988.
22. 'Arafat on VoP (Clandestine), 10 May — DR, 10 May 1988.
23. 'Arafat to VoP (Algiers), 14 March — DR, 19 March 1988.
24. Hawatima to *al-Qabas*, cited in KUNA, 24 January — DR, 25 January 1988.
25. Al-Wazir to *al-Safir*, quoted by AFP, 27 January — DR, 27 January 1988. See also Qaddumi to *al-Watan*, cited in KUNA, 23 January — DR, 23 January 1988.
26. Khalaf to *Der Spiegel*, 29 August — DR, 31 August 1988.
27. VoP (Baghdad), 24 January 1988.
28. Al-Husayni to AFP, 30 July 1988. See also *Ha'aretz*, 7 July 1988.
29. Nusayba and Siniora in *al-Fajr* (English), 17 July 1988.
30. *JP*, 7 August 1988.
31. Al-Hasan to *al-Sharq al-Awsat*, 11 August 1988.
32. Israel TV, 14 August — DR, 17 August 1988.

33. *Al-Fajr* (English), 14 August 1988.
34. *JP*, 24 August 1988.
35. *JP*, 29 December; PLO EC statement, VoP (San'a), 28 December — DR, 29 December 1988.
36. *JP*, 30 December 1988, 8, 9 January 1989; *NYT*, 6 January 1989.
37. Edward W. Said, "Forward," *Arab Studies Quarterly*, Vol. 4, Nos. 1 and 2, 1982, p. xii.
38. *WP*, 26 April 1988.
39. 'Arafat to VoP (Algiers), 14 May — DR, 16 May 1988.
40. 'Arafat to R. Monte Carlo, 5 February — DR, 9 February 1988.
41. *Shu'un Filastiniyya*, June 1988.
42. 'Arafat to *al-Sharq al-Awsat*, 9 August 1988.
43. The report is printed in *al-Yawm al-Sabi'*, 22 February 1988.
44. VoP (Baghdad), 24 February 1988.
45. See, for example, 'Arafat to R. Monte Carlo, 5 February — DR, 9 February; 'Arafat on VoP (Baghdad), 7 May — DR, 9 May 1988.
46. Al-Ghusayn to *al-Tadamun*, 19 March 1988.
47. 'Arafat to *al-Sharq al-Awsat*, 9 August; and to *La Stampa*, 16 February 1988.
48. *Shu'un Filastiniyya*, July 1988.
49. Khalaf to *al-Qabas*, 13 October 1988.
50. 'Abbas to *al-Hawadith*, 15 April 1988.
51. *NYT*, 10 August 1988.
52. AFP, 26 August 1988.
53. MENA, 9 February 1989.
54. 'Arafat to *al-Sharq al-Awsat*, 9 August 1988.
55. See reports on remarks by Qaddumi in *al-Ittihad*, Abu Dhabi, 17 March, and *al-Nahar*, 28 March 1988.
56. See Alain Gresh, *The PLO: The Struggle Within* (London: Zed Books, 1985), pp. 156–71.
57. *IHT*, 25 January 1988.
58. Hawatima to *al-Hurriyya*, 10 January; Khalaf and al-Wazir to *al-Hawadith*, 15 January; Habash to *al-Nida*, 7 February; *Tariq al-Intisar*, 1 February 1988.
59. *IHT*, 10 January 1988.
60. Israel TV, 13 January, R. Monte Carlo, 14 January — DR, 14 January; VoP (Baghdad), 8 February 1988.
61. *ME*, April 1988.
62. Quotations are from full text in *JP*, 24 June. Excerpts were published in *NYT*, 22 June, and *WT*, 15 June 1988.
63. See, for example, Abu Sharif to R. Monte Carlo, 25 June — SWB, 27 June.
64. *WT*, quoted in WF, 21 June 1988.
65. *FT*, 25 June 1988.
66. 'Arafat to TANJUG, 24 June — SWB, 27 June.
67. Habash to Voice of the People, 9 August — DR, 11 August 1988.
68. Statement by al-Zibri, 5 July 1988, quoted in *Democratic Palestine*, No. 30, September 1988.
69. Hawatima to *al-Qabas International*, 19 July 1988.
70. Khalaf to R. Monte Carlo, 3 July — DR, 3 July 1988.
71. *Al-Watan*, 3 July; Abu 'Ali Mustafa to AFP, 23 July 1988.
72. VoP (Baghdad), 29 June 1988.
73. VoP (San'a), 5 March — DR, 5 March; R. Monte Carlo, 8 March — DR, 9 March 1988.
74. For an indication of the positions of the parties during these early talks, see the reported protocol of a discussion between Prime Minister Zayd al-Rifa'i and EC member Mahmud 'Abbas in *al-Qabas*, 1 February 1988.
75. 'Arafat to the foreign affairs editor of the Hearst newspapers, quoted in *JP*, 17 February 1988.
76. 'Arafat to *al-Sharq al-Awsat*, 9 August; King Husayn quoted in *NYT*, 8 May 1988.
77. VoP (Baghdad), 30 July — DR, 30 July 1988.
78. CC statement, VoP (Baghdad), 3 August — DR, 4 August 1988.
79. VoP (Baghdad), 9 August — DR, 11 August 1988.

80. See, for example, *Filastin al-Thawra*, 21 August 1988.
81. *Filastin al-Thawra*, 14 August 1988.
82. See EC member 'Abdallah Hurani's interview with MENA, 15 August — DR, 17 August; *al-Ra'y*, 15 August 1988.
83. VoP (Baghdad), 23 August — DR, 23 August; VoP (Baghdad), 1 October — DR, 3 October 1988.
84. Gresh, op. cit., p. 158.
85. English text of program in Itamar Rabinovich and Jehuda Reinharz (eds.), *Israel and the Middle East* (New York: Oxford University Press, 1984), pp. 312–13.
86. For an instructive analysis of the phased program after the 13th PNC, see Matti Steinberg, "The PLO and the Mini-Settlement," *The Jerusalem Quarterly*, No.21, Fall 1981, pp. 129–44.
87. Remarks by Khalaf cited in MENA, 12 August — DR, 15 August 1988.
88. Khalaf to *Le Journal du Dimanche*, 14 August; and to Vienna TV, 22 August — DR, 25 August 1988.
89. Khalaf to *Der Spiegel*, 29 August — DR, 31 August 1988.
90. R. Monte Carlo, 15 August — DR, 15 August 1988.
91. Khalaf to *al-Anba*, 7 September 1988.
92. Sha'th to *al-Ahali*, 24 August; al-Sa'ih to *al-Madina*, 17 July 1988.
93. *Le Monde*, 31 August; *NYT*, 30 August; PLO response and Halter's subsequent rejoinder, *Le Monde*, 7 September 1988.
94. *IHT*, 15 September 1988.
95. Khalaf to *al-Qabas*, 7 October 1988.
96. *Filastin al-Thawra*, 11 September 1988.
97. *Al-Hadaf*, Damascus, 15 May 1988.
98. See, for example, *al-Huriyya*, 9 October 1988.
99. *Al-Hurriyya*, 23 October 1988.
100. See, for example, Khalid al-Hasan to R. Monte Carlo, 9 September — DR, 9 September 1988.
101. VoP (Baghdad), 11 October — DR, 12 October; GNA; KUNA, R. Monte Carlo, 10 October, MENA, 9 October — DR, 11 October 1988.
102. *JP*, 14 October 1988.
103. 'Arafat in *FT*, 10 September; Habash in *NYT*, 11 August; *al-Hurriyya*, 16 October 1988.
104. See, for instance, *Ha'aretz*, 19 August, 6 September 1988.
105. Hawatima to *al-Anba*, 19 October 1988.
106. Hawatima to *al-Anba*, 6 November 1988.
107. Al-Najjab to R. Algiers, 13 November — DR, 14 November; see also 'Abd al-Rahim Ahmad, EC member from the ALF, to *al-Bayan*, Dubai, quoted in ENA, 22 October — DR, 24 October 1988.
108. For elaboration on the problematics of this issue, see Hani al-Hasan to *al-Anba*, 11 September 1988.
109. Khalaf to *al-Qabas*, 7 October 1988.
110. Khalid al-Hasan to R. Monte Carlo, 9 September — DR, 12 September 1988.
111. *Filastin al-Thawra*, 11 September 1988.
112. Khalaf to *al-Mustaqbal*, 12 November 1988.
113. *Al-Hurriyya*, 9, 16 October; Hawatima to *al-Anba*, 19 October, 6 November 1988.
114. Khalaf to *al-Mustaqbal*, 12 November 1988.
115. 'Abd Rabbuh to *al-Watan*, 29 October 1988.
116. Habash to *IHT*, 24–25 September; and to *FT*, 24 September 1988.
117. Mustafa al-Zibri to *al-Hadaf*, 2 October 1988.
118. VoP (Algiers), 12 November 1988. The PPSF had attended the dialogue preceding the 18th PNC in 1987 but had withdrawn and not participated in the actual session (see *MECS* 1987, p. 207). The organization, a component of the PNSF, had expressed a desire to return to the PLO and the EC at the 19th session. It said that it would be a part of the PLO, while opposing Resolution 242 (see *al-Ittihad* [Abu Dhabi], 29 October, 25 November; *al-Usbu' al-'Arabi*, 28 November 1988).
119. *Filastin al-Thawra*, 20 November; AFP, 12 November 1988.

120. VoP (Algiers), 12 November — DR, 14 November 1988.
121. Ibid.
122. R. Monte Carlo, 13 November — DR, 14 November; R. Algiers, 14 November 1988.
123. *Al-Anba*, 13 December 1988.
124. *Al-Hurriyya*, 20 November 1988.
125. *Al-Anba*, 13, 14 December 1988.
126. *Al-Hadaf*, Damascus, 20 November; Mustafa al-Zibri in *al-Anba*, 14 December; Habash to Algiers TV, 13 November — DR, 15 November 1988.
127. Mustafa al-Zibri in *IHT*, 14 November; see also Habash to AFP, 13 November 1988.
128. *JP*, 16 November 1988.
129. Text in *Filastin al-Thawra*, 20 November 1988.
130. Ibid.
131. *NYT*, 16 November 1988.
132. *JP*, 18 November 1988.
133. *NYT*, 15 November 1988.
134. *NYT*, 17 November 1988.
135. *JP*, 18 November; see also 'Arafat in *JP*, 15 November 1988 for a similar comment.
136. VoP (Baghdad), 15 November — DR, 16 November. See DR editorial report which notes the discrepancies in DR, 1 December 1988.
137. Khalaf to *al-Yawm al-Sabi'*, 7 November 1988.
138. Analyses of the rights of return, self-determination, and establishing an independent state in earlier periods of PLO history are to be found in Matti Steinberg, op. cit., and in Asher Susser, "Double Jeopardy: PLO Strategy toward Israel and Jordan," *Policy Papers*, No. 8, 1987.
139. 'Arafat to *Time*, 7 November; see also similar statement in *JP*, 17 February 1988.
140. *Filastin al-Thawra*, 27 November 1988.
141. 'Abbas to *al-Musawwar*, 26 August 1988.
142. *Filastin al-Thawra*, 6 November 1988.
143. On the right of return, see W. Thomas Mallison and Sally V. Mallison, "The Right of Return," *Journal of Palestine Studies*, Vol. 9, No. 3, Spring 1980, pp. 125–36.
144. See, for example, Ibrahim Abu Lughod to *JP*, 1 April; and Khalaf to *Der Spiegel*, 29 August — DR, 31 August 1988.
145. Walid Khalid, "Towards Peace in the Holy Land," *Foreign Affairs*, Spring 1988, pp. 771–89.
146. These assertions comprise the "auxiliary option" formulated by al-Hasan following the termination of political "coordination with Jordan" in 1986–87. The "auxiliary option" is outlined by al-Hasan in *al-Anba*, 21, 22, 23 October 1986, and is thoroughly analyzed by Susser, op. cit., pp. 32–36.
147. Khalid al-Hasan to *al-Musawwar*, 1 April 1988.
148. 'Arafat to *Playboy*, September; see also 'Arafat to VoP (Algiers), 14 March — DR, 16 March 1988.
149. *Filastin al-Thawra*, 21 August 1988.
150. *Al-Nashra*, Athens, 28 November 1988.
151. Khalaf to *al-Yawm al-Sabi'*, 28 November 1988.
152. Khalaf to *al-Qabas*, 15 November 1988.
153. *NYT*, 26 November 1988.
154. News report and official US statement in *NYT*, 27 November 1988.
155. Details of the Stockholm talks are to be found in the recollections of one of the American Jews, Rita Hauser, as told to the *NYT*, 17 December 1988.
156. See, for example, KUNA, 7 December — DR, 8 December 1988.
157. R. Monte Carlo, 8 December — DR, 9 December 1988.
158. R. Stockholm, 7 December — DR, 8 December 1988.
159. *NYT*, 8 December 1988.
160. In the past, the PLO had always spoken of 5m. Palestinians; see, for example, quotation from a statement by 'Arafat in *NYT*, 4 February 1988. The most recent statistics put the number of Palestinians, including Israeli Arabs, at 4.675m.; see *The West Bank and Gaza: Israel's Options for Peace* (Tel Aviv: Jaffee Center for Strategic Studies, Tel Aviv

University, 1989), p. 206. The use of the number 6m. seems to have been designed to draw sympathy for the plight of the Palestinians by equating it with the fate of the Jews at the hands of the Nazis in World War Two.

161. For more details of the press conference, see *WP*, 16 December and *NYT*, 17 December 1988.
162. R. Tunis, 18 December — DR, 20 December 1988.
163. Arabic translation in *Shu'un Filastiniyya*, January 1989. The verb *rafada* is most commonly understood to mean "reject," although it can also mean "abandon." The Arabic text, when read over VoP (Baghdad), 15 December — DR, 16 December 1988, was translated as "reject." Had the PLO wished to convey the clear meaning of "renounce," it could have used the Arabic term for it.
164. Vienna TV, 19 December — DR, 20 December 1988.
165. EC statement, VoP (San'a), 28 December — DR, 29 December 1988.
166. *JP*, 28 December 1988.
167. VoP (Baghdad), 24 January 1988.
168. VoP (Baghdad), 9 August — DR, 11 August 1988.
169. Khalaf to *Der Spiegel*, 29 August — DR, 31 August 1988.
170. See, for example, VoP (San'a), 5 July — DR, 6 July 1988.
171. R. Beirut, 4 November — DR, 7 November; KUNA, 9 November — DR, 10 November 1988.
172. *IHT*, *JP*, 26 December 1988.
173. See the monthly publication of this department, which includes sections on "the territories occupied in 1967" and "the territories occupied in 1948", *Al-Ard al-Muhtalla: Waqa'i' wa-Ahdath* (n.p.: n.p., but probably Bisan Press, Nicosia).
174. See reports in AFP, 18 April; *al-Siyasa*, Kuwait, 8 May 1988.
175. *Al-Sharq al-Awsat*, 25 May 1988.
176. *Al-Muharrir*, 18 June, *al-Shira'*, 7 November 1988.
177. Hawatima to *al-Hurriyya*, 21 February; *al-Hadaf*, Damascus, 15 May; R. Monte Carlo, 22 September — DR, 23 September; R. Monte Carlo, 22 October — DR, 24 October 1988.
178. TANJUG, 12 April; *al-Ittihad*, 6 September 1988.
179. Editorial report, SWB, 5 January; editorial report, DR, 22 January 1988.
180. VoP (Baghdad), 25 January — DR, 26 January 1988.
181. KUNA, 18 November — DR, 18 November; *JP*, 20 November 1988.
182. Muhammad 'Abbas to *al-Siyasa*, Kuwait, 5 December 1988.
183. *Al-Qawmi al-'Arabi*, 3 December 1988.
184. *Davar*, 17 March 1989.
185. VoL, 28 December — DR, 29 December 1988.
186. *JP*, 25 October; IDF spokesman, Information Branch, "Major Incidents on Israel's Northern Border, 1985–1989," March 1989.
187. Khalaf to *al-Yamama*, 16 November 1988.
188. Khalaf to *al-Madina*, 24 November 1989.
189. Official translation, WAFA, Algiers, 17 November 1988, printed in *JPS*, Vol. 18, No. 2, Winter 1989, pp. 213-16. A comparison with the official Arabic text in *Filastin al-Thawra*, 20 November 1988 has established that the English text is not very accurate. Discrepancies, where significant, are interpolated in the text, as are certain clarifications.
190. Official translation, 22 November 1988, printed in *JPS*, Vol. 18, No. 2, Winter 1989, pp. 216–23. A comparison with the Arabic text, *Filastin al-Thawra*, 20 November 1988, has established that the English translation is accurate. In the paragraph concerning terrorism, the reference should be to UN Resolution 42/159, as correctly noted in the Arabic. This resolution was passed in March 1988 and not in 1987, as in the English, and not in 1967, as in the Arabic.
191. *IHT*, 8 December 1988.
192. Official translation, WAFA, Washington, DC, 15 December 1988, printed in *JPS*, Vol. 18, No. 3, Spring 1989, pp. 161–71. A comparison with the original Arabic text in *Filastin al-Thawra*, 18 December 1988, has established that the translation is accurate.
193. *JPS*, Vol. 18, No. 3, Spring 1989, pp. 180–81. 'Arafat's statement was made in English.

The West Bank and the Gaza Strip: The *Intifada* From Spontaneous Disturbances to Organized Disobedience

HILLEL FRISCH

The events of 1988 in the West Bank and the Gaza Strip mark a watershed in the history of the Palestinians. From the Palestinian perspective, the near monopoly over shaping their political fate, hitherto exercized by the PLO outside the territories, has shifted inward. The inhabitants, for long a rather marginal factor in Palestinian politics, have now come to play an important role alongside the PLO abroad. The Israeli military authorities, confronted by continuous large-scale disturbances, likewise had been required to acknowledge the growing prominence of local Palestinians. Not only has Israel allocated unprecedented resources in quelling the *intifada*, but it has also been forced to discard long-standing policy principles regarding the administration of the territories. On the international agenda, the local inhabitants' role was a major factor in catapulting the issue of Palestinian statehood to prominence. All three aspects will be dealt with in this chapter.

The New Year in the territories began after three weeks of unprecedented violence and demonstrations, principally in Gaza but increasing also in the West Bank. From the Palestinian point of view, success of the *intifada*, or uprising, presented a new challenge to the political forces in the territories, which in the past decade had crystallized into mass movements, but which had clearly not been responsible for the *intifada*. Evidence for this is the fact that it broke out in Gaza where the movements affiliated to the PLO were weaker than in the West Bank. Assuring the continuation of the uprising and increasing its scope and intensity became the principle goals of the Palestinian national movement. For the political movements affiliated to the PLO, not only was the continued success of the *intifada* at stake, but so was the question of who would lead it. The Islamic groups had taken the lead in the first three weeks of the uprising.[1] Now it was up to the national movement to make amends and transform a spontaneous uprising into organized mass disobedience, revolt, and increased Palestinian control of the day-to-day affairs of the inhabitants of the territories at the expense of the civil and military administration. The Islamic groups might be encouraged to cooperate, but the Palestinian national movement had to monopolize leadership. The tasks in the territories were clear: there had to be a leadership to define the tactical goals of the uprising, and there had to be organizational means, however rudimentary, to achieve them. Without these two ingredients, the *intifada* could prove as ephemeral as were past disturbances termed "*intifada*" by the national movement.[2]

IN SEARCH OF LEADERSHIP

Ostensibly, the creation of a leadership should have been easy for a movement which had spawned four broad-based organizations, Fath's Shabiba, the Democratic Front's al-Wahda, the Popular Front's Jabhat al-'Amal, and the Palestine Communist Party (PCP). All of these had youth, student, labor, health,and women's organizations under their umbrella, and possessed considerable influence in the other "national institutions" established over the years in Palestinian society. However, the obstacles were considerable. First, it was clear that the *intifada* involved sectors of Palestinian society far beyond those reached by these organizations or the "national institutions" under their influence. Maintaining the *intifada*'s momentum at the very least required a leadership known beyond the confines of these organizations. But the fate of the leadership of the Supreme Muslim Council in 1967 and the National Steering Committee of 1979–82 argued against the creation of a well-known charismatic leadership. The maiming of Mayors Bassam Shak'a of Nablus and Karim Khalaf of Ramallah, and the deportations of Fahd al-Qawasima, mayor of Hebron (who was later assassinated in Amman) and of Muhammad Milhim of Halhul (see *MECS* 1979–80, pp. 276, 278), were stark reminders of the failure of a recognized, public leadership to challenge a military occupation.

Competition amongst the various factions for control posed a second problem. Essentially, this competition mirrored the struggle "outside" in the PLO ranks: the quest for dominance by Fath and its "independent" supporters versus a sharing of power demanded by the leftist factions, or — as they termed themselves in this context — the "democratic forces within the PLO." Aligning the priorities between those "inside" with those "outside" was a third problem. Though this problem touched on programmatic aspects with which we will deal later, it was again a matter of power and leadership, for it was essential to define who decided what. Though analytically these were three discrete problems, in fact, they clearly overlapped.

New Year's Day of 1988 set the stage for the conflict over leadership. It was on that day, designated to commemorate the establishment of Fath, that the largest and best organized faction in the territories failed to mobilize inhabitants in the territories. The media reported 1 January as one of the quietest days since the outset of the *intifada*. Predictably, only in the Balata refugee camp, a Shabiba stronghold, were there disturbances.[3] According to opposition forces, the failure of Fath, though the organization was never explicitly identified, was due to confusion in defining the *intifada*'s goals, especially in the communiqué signed by the "national forces in the occupied territories" and distributed on 17 December 1987.[4]

This failure prodded the PLO leadership outside to activate its independent and more charismatic supporters inside the territories and have them attempt to establish a leadership of the *intifada*. At a press conference in East Jerusalem, on 5 January, a group of 15 prominent Palestinians mostly identified with the PLO mainstream, headed by Hana Siniora and Mubarak 'Awad, dramatically called for the inauguration of a territories-wide campaign of civil disobedience, including a partial boycott and tax resistance, and mass refusal to carry identity booklets.[5] Siniora, the editor of the pro-Fath *al-Fajr* newspaper, used it to expound his views.[6] Despite endorsement by the PLO mainstream outside, Siniora failed to win broad support, even among pro-Fath supporters in the territories. Hikmat al-Masri (former speaker of the

Jordanian Parliament) said that economic boycott was not practical, "because a factory that refused to pay taxes would be subject to swift retribution by the authorities who could hold up imports of essential commodities."[7] Dr. Sari Nusayba, a professor of philosophy at Bir Zayt University, questioned the ability of Palestinians such as Siniora to lead the struggle. He was quoted as saying:

> My analysis is that, sooner or later, we will have civil disobedience. But when it comes about, it will come from the same people who are in the streets throwing stones and closing their shops and going to jail and suffering the brutal mistreatment by the Israeli soldiers. These are the people who are going to call for a civil disobedience and they will be followed by the rest of us.[8]

The leftist factions adamantly rejected the campaign as being premature. Siniora, particularly, came under bitter attack for trying to establish "a dubious leadership" (*qiyada mashbuha*) in the territories "which was to be allied with the imperialist forces which would abort the *intifada*."[9] They questioned Siniora's intentions, recalling the "defeatist" proposals he had made during 1987, which called for Palestinian political participation in the Jerusalem municipal elections, a move severely censured by most Palestinian factions (see *MECS* 1987, pp. 258–61).[10] "Call number 3" by the United National Command (UNC) of the *intifada* (see below), dated 17 January, adopted the program in part, but rejected its author. It called for partial boycott of Israeli goods and the nonpayment of value added tax (VAT), proving that what was at stake was a struggle for power, not a war over ideas. The Democratic Front for the Liberation of Palestine (DFLP), the Popular Front for the Liberation of Palestine (PFLP), and the PCP, which played a significant role in the creation of the UNC, made sure that pro-Fath independents would not play a leading role in the *intifada*. The postponement of the campaign the following day spelled a further defeat for Fath.[11]

Worrisome, too, for the PLO mainstream and Fath supporters was the expulsion of four activists on 12 January, three of whom were leading Shabiba and Fath members, Jibril al-Rajub (aged 35) of Dura, Hisham 'Uthman Muhammad Hadr (26) of Balata, and Jamal 'Abdallah Shaqr Jabara (28) of Qalqiliyya.[12] The expulsion indicated the intent of the authorities to hit particularly hard at Fath and Shabiba organizations in the territories.

Perhaps this defeat is what compelled the organizational branch of Fath to make common cause with the leftist factions and to set up the UNC at the beginning of the second week of January. The leftist factions took most of the credit for the creation of the UNC and the credibility of their claim was borne out by the silence of Fath sources concerning its origins. Its formation had much to do with "call number 2" issued on 10 January in the West Bank specifying 11–13 January as days of general strike; the call was followed throughout the territories. So was 15 January, a Friday which commemorated the martyrs and *Arab al-Aqsa*. According to a Gazan sociologist and PDFLP activist deported in July,[13] the call drafted by the "democratic forces," a code name for the DFLP and the PCP, was grudgingly accepted by Fath and the PFLP only after its warm reception by the general public. Though it was signed by "the United National Command of the *intifada*" (*al-qiyada al-wataniyya al-muwahhada lil-intifada*), in fact only a coordinating committee of the four factions existed before its issuance.[14] The significance of declaring 15 January "*Arab al-Aqsa* day" must also be pointed out, for by doing so the leftist factions recognized the power of Islamic symbols and were ready to employ them. This overture no doubt facilitated cooperation with the al-Jihad al-Islami group. The cooperation of al-Jihad al-Islami was underscored by the leaders of the three major PLO factions: the deported Fath Shabiba leader, Hisham 'Uthman Muhammad Hadr; Na'if Hawatima of the DFLP, and the deported Popular Front activist, Bashir al-Khayri.[15]

The formation of the UNC did not spell the end of the struggle for leadership within PLO ranks. The problem of defining the relationship between the PLO outside and the UNC remained, in a sense, the thorniest problem facing the *intifada*'s emerging leadership. It was reminiscent of an old problem, faced by the first Palestinian National Front which was formed in 1973 of PLO factions and what was then the Jordanian Communist Party, concerning the relationship between the PLO mainstream, in particular Fath, and the organized political forces inside. Fath had always demanded a strictly hierarchical relationship between the PLO outside and the organized political forces in the territories.[16] The leftist factions, especially the Communists, who until the 18th Palestine National Council (PNC) meeting were not formally a part of the PLO, sought a more equal relationship that would allow the inside to make, at least, the day-to-day tactical decisions concerning the struggle in the territories.

The conflict revolved around three issues. First, calls numbers two, three, and five demanded the dismissal of appointed municipal and village councillors and the holding of free municipal elections without setting prior conditions of UN trusteeship or total Israeli withdrawal. Evidently, the UNC was seeking to confer greater legitimacy and power within the PLO through the vehicle of free municipal elections. After "call number six," this demand was dropped. Second, certain factions, most notably the PDFLP and the PFLP, recasted the UNC as "the kernel of the national front" of the *intifada*.[17] Judging from the long enmity of Fath to the concept (despite its prominence in all PNC resolutions since 1977), one can only surmise that the struggle over the role of the UNC remained. Third, the leftist factions demanded — as they had regarding the Palestinian National Front — that the UNC be the sole channel of funds and the sole link between the PLO and the territories.[18]

A *modus vivendi* developed between the PLO mainstream and the UNC, the emergent secret leadership of the territories, only after a protracted struggle that extended into February. Again it involved Palestinian personalities associated with the PLO mainstream. Having failed to win widespread support through political extremism, the pro-Fath personalities adopted a platform of moderation aimed at securing immediate gains for the *intifada*. On 14 January, a group of prominent pro-Fath personalities, which included the acting president of Bir Zayt University, Dr. Gabi Baramki; the ousted deputy mayor of Ramallah, Fr. Ouda Rantisi; and Dr. Sari Nusayba, issued a document in the name of the "National Palestinian Institutions" calling for (1) allowing people in the territories to contact the PLO, (2) abolishing restrictions on political activity, (3) abolishing the VAT, (4) diverting money collected as taxes to funds for development, and (5) ceasing the [Israeli] exploitation of water resources.[19] Similar, though more explicit, demands were included in a 14-point memorandum presented by Siniora and Fa'iz Abu Rahma a week later to US Secretary of State George Shultz during his first visit to the area since the outbreak of the *intifada*.[20] The leftist factions denounced the meeting with Shultz, pointing out that it contravened past precedents.[21] (Local Palestinians of all political shades, including pro-Jordanian personalities, had boycotted Shultz on his previous visit to the area in October 1987; see *MECS* 1987, pp. 261–62).

Significantly, both documents omitted reference to the possibility of free municipal elections without preconditions which had been emphasized in the calls of the UNC, even though these documents mentioned the need for allowing political activities in the territories. These demands were opposed by the PLO organizations within the territories, including Fath. Thus, Jibril al-Rajub, the deported Fath activist, declared his opposition to bringing the *intifada* to an end in return for the cessation of suppression, "for the *intifada* had clear political objectives including the establishment of the Palestinian State."[22] This declaration was obviously directed at the viewpoint of Palestinian personalities such as Nusayba, Siniora, and Fa'iz Abu Rahma. The UNC's position regarding them was spelled out in "call number 6" of 3 February. It denounced "attempts of the American State Department to make prominent some of the local notables [*wujuh*] in order to produce an alternative leadership to the legitimate leadership," and assured those "who try to represent the *intifada* from outside [the PLO] and create a dubious leadership with the aim of presenting concessions and spreading defeatism. The people will be waiting in ambush and they will be stricken by despair and complete failure."

Shultz's subsequent visit to the area marked the political demise of these personalities. Despite reports that certain Palestinian figures were adamant about meeting with Shultz and that 'Arafat agreed to enable six personalities from the territories to hold discussions with him,[23] the PLO ordered them to boycott Shultz and 15 of those invited to meet with him complied.[24] That the UNC had the support of its constituency in refusing to deal with Shultz is attested by the casualty rate in the territories; nine persons were killed over the weekend of Shultz's visit, the highest casualty rate since the outbreak of the *intifada.*[25]

The PLO's directive to boycott the meeting was part of a deal struck with the UNC. The UNC dropped the demand for free municipal elections in both the West Bank and the Gaza Strip from "call number 7." By "call number 3" the signature affixed to the calls placed the PLO before the "United National Command of the *intifada.*" The sequence reflected the order of precedence insisted upon by the PLO mainstream and Fath, its organized nucleus, regarding the relationship between the outside center and the organized political forces inside the territories. The matter became doubly important to the PLO in light of the success of the inside in perpetuating the *intifada* and the tardiness of the PLO outside to come to its aid. Nevertheless, *al-Hurriyya,* the DFLP official organ, continued to publicize the calls without reference to the PLO up to "call number 7" indicating that differences over the relationship between the local leadership and the PLO mainstream continued into February and later.[26] The PLO in return recognized the UNC as the sole leadership in the territories. Henceforth, not only were Palestinian personalities denied any leadership role, but their role as spokesmen was also significantly reduced. The *modus vivendi* assured political integration between the two components of the Palestinian national movement, one "outside," the other "inside" the territories, on a level that had never been achieved in the past. The UNC, with the support of the PLO abroad, was now able to devote itself to the organization of the *intifada.*

THE UNITED NATIONAL COMMAND

So secretive was the UNC and so successful had it been in perpetuating itself — in utter contrast to past attempts in the territories, in which secret leaderships were quickly exposed by the authorities — that one may justifiably ask whether such a leadership existed at all? If a "leadership" is some form of standing committee which gives orders to subordinates in the distant corners of the territories, the answer is probably no. If a "leadership" is something broader, like a forum of rotating individuals representing the constituent factions which formally belong to the leadership that hammers out general policy and directives, but does not orchestrate events on the ground, the answer is probably yes for a number of reasons.

It is important to recall that the UNC crystallized one month after the *intifada* had begun, that is to say, after the inhabitants had proved their ability to sacrifice, organize at the grass-root level, and keep busy an array of Israel Defense Forces (IDF) which reportedly had doubled in numbers in the West Bank and tripled in Gaza.[27] Similarly, the most important collective undertaking of the *intifada* in its initial stages, the commercial strike, preceded the UNC's establishment.[28]

The UNC's task, then, was not so much to mobilize support (as, for example, the task of the National Steering Committee) or command the *intifada*, but to direct it toward more efficient lines. More important, it was to emphasize the goals which rendered the self-directed sacrifice exhibited by the inhabitants worthwhile for the future, so that ardor should not flag. The UNC's functions then, were to suggest the best organizational modes, to define the stages of conflict at every juncture, and to promote morale. It is no coincidence that the UNC became synonymous with the calls it released, for the "call," not "command," is a reflection of a moral as opposed to organizational leadership.[29] This meant that the UNC was not the apex of a pyramidal structure, but something set apart from the organizational modes created on the district and local levels. In this way, the imprisonment of activists further down the line did not imperil the continuation of the UNC.

The abandonment of the pyramidal, hierarchical structure which prevailed in the previous attempts at creating a territorial leadership, is exemplified in the descriptions of the relationship between the UNC and the popular committees by Palestinian analysts. Khalil Shahin, writing in *al-Hadaf*, the official journal of the PFLP, explicitly states that the call, not some fixed organizational hierarchy, acts as the basic link between popular committees and the UNC on the one hand, and between one popular committee and another. These are spread out "horizontally," we are told by Shahin, "connected with other areas only through the implementation of the directives and programs of the UNC contained in the calls which it issues."[30] The arrest of what the Israeli authorities described as the "writers" of "call number 11" also suggests that we are dealing with a group of representatives who were probably replaced or rotated, rather than with a general command of certain individuals.[31]

Just as the abandonment of the pyramidal structure and the formation of a moral rather than organizational leadership, grew out of events preceding the setting up of the UNC, so was the rotation of representatives made possible by past successes. For nearly a decade, factions within the PLO in the territories had labored to expand their political activities there. From these activities, whose cadres were mainly from student ranks, but augmented appreciably by *muhararun*, freed prisoners as well, there emerged what Palestinian sources describe as "mid-level area leadership."[32] These were the activists of the "organized frameworks" (*al-utur al-tanzimiyya*). The growth of this leadership was indicated, first, by the increasing use of town arrests, initiated in 1979 by the Israeli authorities in which detainees were confined to their areas of residence and then, from 1986 onward, by the use of administrative detention which replaced the previous milder form of punishment.[33] Those arrested were primarily activists in these frameworks.[34] Thus, a large pool of potentially qualified members of the UNC emerged long before the *intifada* broke out. This situation was radically different from that which existed under the National Steering Committee, when the arrest of a member was a heavy blow to the whole committee. The fact was that the Israeli authorities had failed to strike a blow at the UNC despite the administrative arrest of over 2,600 activists by September[35] and despite the purported arrest of four Gazan members of the UNC, Tawfik Abu Husa (aged 27) and Ihad al-Ashhar (22) of Fath, Tawfik Mabhuk (41) reputedly a Communist representative, and Marwan al-Kafarna (32) of the PFLP.[36]

The UNC was a coalition of primarily political forces, with only a minority of "national personalities," composed of Fath, the DFLP, the PFLP, the PCP, and — at least according to Palestinian nationalist sources — al-Jihad al-Islami.[37] Al-Jihad al-Islami, the radical terrorist movement which had previously been supported by Fath, was later denied membership in the UNC. A statement to the Agence France Presse in April 1988 stated that "the Jihad does not participate in the leadership bodies of the *intifada* and does not participate in the drafting of the calls of the Unified Command of the Popular Uprising in the Occupied Territories."[38] Nevertheless, there are indications that al-Jihad al-Islami participated at least in the distribution of UNC communiqués three-through-six for, on 10 April, the Israeli authorities announced the arrest of such distributors including members of unspecified "religious organizations."[39] Making public their arrests might have goaded al-Jihad al-Islami to stress three days later that they did not participate in the drafting of these calls. The Hamas (Arabic abbreviation for *harakat al-muqawama al-Islamiyya* — the Islamic Resistance Movement), formed in January by groups belonging to the Muslim Brotherhood, probably never participated in the UNC.[40]

The moral leadership could count on the existing political structures to assure a modicum of compliance to the calls of the UNC.[41] The UNC never formally identified itself as a coalition of forces, and in none of its communiqués have its constituent members been identified. Rarely had any one political grouping publicly taken the credit for playing a major role. As a moral leadership, it was important to present oneself as an entity that is more than the sum total of its constituent members. Just as participation in the *intifada* transcended the individual political movement, so was there a need for a leadership that transcended party lines. The UNC also included new activists in the national and popular committees.[42]

THE *INTIFADA*: STRATEGY AND TACTICS

THE COMMUNIQUÉS

The primary task of the UNC was drafting what had erroneously been translated "communiqués" but in fact should be translated "calls," or "appeals." A communiqué is a bureaucratic message, a "call" assumes moral assent to its contents. Through the calls, which were refined over the year, the UNC became an invisible government parallel to that of the Israeli Government.

These calls were designed to fulfill several tasks. By "call number 3" they acquired a fixed structure which facilitated quick recognition. On the top line, the word *nida* ("call") was repeated three times. Below it was the slogan. "There is no voice higher than the voice of the *intifada*; there is no voice higher than the voice of the Palestinian people [*al-sha'b*] — the people of the Palestine Liberation Organization." Then came a headline stating the major event or theme covered by the call, a text of approximately 1,000 words, and finally the signature by "the Palestine Liberation Organization, the United National Command of the *intifada*." During Muslim holidays, the masthead usually included the religous invocation *Bismillah al-Rahman al-Rahim* ("In the name of God, the Merciful, the Compassionate"), attesting to the public awareness of the Muslim holiday but without undue rigor, as befitted a primarily secular body.

Devising a fixed pattern for the text was a slower process, but it too reached its mature state by mid-March with "call number 11." As a general rule it included three parts: (1) a statement of policy in which the UNC spelled out what it considered the major issues in the struggle, including an analysis of Israeli moves and the reiteration of the major goals of the *intifada*, usually in reference to regional and international events; (2) a list of directives interspersed with praise for specific places, areas,and segments of the population for their bravery or quick compliance with UNC directives, and threats to those who refused or procrastinated; and (3) a list of days to be marked by specific actions or general strike lasting until the issuance of the next call. Throughout most of the year, almost every day was given a specific purpose. From "call number 25," dated September, this practice was changed, and only half of the days were specified for each period.

The frequency at which the calls were issued was slowed down considerably over the year. The first six calls came out between 8 January and 2 February, at intervals of five days on average. The subsequent 13 calls came out between mid-February and early June, at 10-day intervals. The intervals then increased to two weeks, between late June and September, when calls 20 to 26 appeared. By the year's end, the calls had come to appear only once every three weeks. A total of 31 calls appeared in 1988. Both phenomena may be attributed to the increasing institutionalization of the *intifada*.

ORGANIZATION OF THE *INTIFADA*

Developing the organizational structure of the *intifada* was one of the UNC's major goals.[43] The seemingly grass-root and highly localized commercial strikes in the cities of the West Bank and Gaza provided the initial stimulus. To assure the participation of all merchants required a committee to enforce it. Similarly, the forced openings of shops by the authorities called for committees of locksmiths to repair the damage just as the need to prevent pilfering of these shops stimulated the formation of committees to assure internal security.[44] In general, as the number of tactical goals defined by the calls increased so was there a corresponding broadening of organizational modes to assure that they be met.

Not all the stimuli to organize were generated internally. Israeli policy, too, contributed to the proliferation of organizations to deal with changing situations. Provisions committees to supply food sprang up to cope with the policy of sealing off whole camps, increasingly employed by the authorities during January, just as closing off areas to the press created a need for information committees to provide Palestinian perceptions and statistics of the prevailing situation to the foreign press.[45] Finally, committees were formed to coordinate the activities of the specialized committees.

Three interlocking structures emerged during the *intifada*. The dominant political forces — Fath and its affiliated Shabiba movement, the PCP, the DFLP and its affiliated al-Wahda movement, the PFLP and Jabhat al-'Amal — provided the organizational link between the UNC and the organizations mentioned below.[46] The Israeli authorities directed most of their blows at this level of organizational leadership, either through deportation of activists, such as Fath and Shabiba activist Jibril al-Rajub (a prisoner released during the PFLP-GC-orchestrated prisoner release in 1985 and an aide to Faysal al-Husayni), or through extensive and prolonged administrative arrest, as in the case of 'Adnan Damiri (one of the founders of the Shabiba Movement for Social Work and former president of the al-Najah National University student council). Damiri was one of hundreds of Shabiba activists detained when the Israeli authorities declared the Shabiba movement illegal.[47]

What the Palestinians termed "the organizational frameworks," which are best described as the service wings of the political forces, formed the second, lower-interlocking structure. These were the bodies created over the previous decade by the constituent organizations of the PLO to deepen their hold at the grass roots of Palestinian society by providing needed social services. In this way, the factions won legitimacy amongst segments of the population who balked at illegal political activity or who possessed the traditional mistrust of politics. These bodies included the Shabiba Movement for Social Work; women's organizations, such as the PFLP's Committees of Palestinian Women *Lijan al-Mar'a al- Filastiniyya*), the PDFLP's Women's Action Committees (*Lijan al-'Amal al-Nisa'i)*, and the Communist Committees of the Palestinian Woman (*Lijan al-Mar'a al-'Amila al-Filastiniyya*); the two major labor federations, one belonging to Fath, another to the Communists, and their affiliated unions; and the four health relief committees similarly affiliated to the political forces described above. The activities of this structure were, similarly, curtailed by the Israeli authorities although not to the same extent as the first. One notable case was that of the Shabiba movement, which was outlawed *en masse* on 20 March.[48]

The emergence of the popular committees and their affiliated organizations — an innovation of the *intifada* represented the third and major structure. The popular committees, whose necessity was conceived as far back as the late 1970s during the period of the National Steering Committee,[49] were formed horizontally, at the district level, as in the case of the 37 Fath popular committees in Gaza and uncovered by the authorities in August;[50] at the municipal level, as in the case of Bayt Sahur;[51] or at the village level, as in the case of Batir.[52] The popular committees chose the course of confrontation with the authorities according to the conditions set by the calls and coordinated between the service organizations of the second structure and the specialized committees it either created or enveloped.

Most of the popular committees, except those controlled directly by a single movement, also had links with the first structure, mainly through their personnel. The organized political forces were keen on including their own members in the popular committees as well as in the organizational structures affiliated to them.[53] This was strongly suggested by the distinction made in the UNC communiqués, especially during the first months, between the popular and the national committees. The role of the popular committees, at least in the initial stages, seems to have been to coordinate the committees involved in public services. The national committees, composed of the representatives of the organized political factions, seemed to be involved in violent activity designed to augment the *intifada* and were closely linked with the strike forces variously called *lijan al-dariba, quwa al-dariba, majmu'at al-dariba*, or *furuq al-dariba.* They also watched over the popular committees.[54]

The term "national committees" gradually disappears from the calls, indicating perhaps that as the political forces gained more control of the spontaneously generated popular committees, there was less need for separate "political" committees to oversee their "functional" or "civilian" counterpart. The two became intertwined and both the *furuq al-dariba,* the military arm, and the specialized service committees were brought under their jurisdiction.[55]

The *furuq al-dariba* were charged by the UNC with three major tasks. First of all, they had to augment the *intifada*'s level of violence within the guidelines set by the calls. This meant organizing demonstrations, throwing rocks, and most of all, increasing the use of petrol bombs and other forms of incendiary bombs. Palestinian sources suggest that these groups consisted mainly of students and former prisoners, the most highly mobilized groups in the Palestinian population before the *intifada* and the best organized within frameworks such as the Shabiba.[56] The few reports of arrests in which groups membership was specified also suggest membership prior to the outbreak of the *intifada*.[57] The second task was to punish collaborators or get them to repent publicly (*tawba*). Striking at the collaborators meant reducing the authorities' ability to maintain their information networks amongst the population.[58] Finally, the strike forces were to uphold the authority of the UNC by punishing those who refused to abide by its directives in the calls. The appointed mayors and councillors who remained at their posts despite directives to resign were repeatedly singled out as targets of these forces.[59]

Such was the organizational structure of the *intifada* in its broad contours. It was above all a loose structure, perhaps deliberately so. The purpose of the *intifada* was to increase participation of all segments of society, thus generating ever-expanding circles of organization. Better that such organization be rudimentary and widespread than tight-knit but limited. The inconsistency in the communiqués suggests that the UNC recognized local initiative and, thus, regional differences in organizational modes. If not, why did four terms appear in the calls for the strike forces alone? After all, the organizations set up prior to the *intifada* had achieved a high level of standardization so that in most of the universities and other institutions of higher learning, the same five political groupings competed in student elections under the same names since 1983. If the organizational mode was "wrought in steel," as some Palestinian sources stated,[60] how could popular committees in Gaza be uniparty and engulf a whole region, while in Bayt Sahur they were truly popular — extending beyond political boundaries — yet were confined to the particular town?

A loose organizational structure might have emerged from recognition of local initiative and resourcefulness,[61] but it may also have been due to a certain lack of unity of the political forces and organizations activating sorts of structure. The fact is that the "organized frameworks" — those described as the second structure — did not succeed throughout 1988 in creating overall federations despite initiatives in the labor movement in the West Bank, which itself remained divided in four parts and in two federations.[62] A similar lack of success is seen perhaps more critically in the health services which not only lacked coordination among the various committees, but were also afflicted by antagonism between these committees and the health establishment centered in the Physicians' Union with headquarters in Bayt Hanina.[63]

There were also limits, economic and otherwise, to the ability of Palestinian society to organize. Efforts to create a popular educational system failed after the first wave of enthusiasm.[64] Many calls of the UNC, particularly the later ones, called for the reopening of the established school system in the West Bank.[65] So insistent was the UNC on this point that in "call number 28," issued at the end of October, the call turned into a plea urging the population "to keep the schools open and not to give the occupation authorities more pretexts to close them again." In the West Bank educational institutions were kept closed by military order for most of the year, while in Gaza the situation varied with student conduct in the different schools.[66] Why, then, should the UNC seek reopening of the schools if its avowed goal was to establish parallel institutions and cut ties with the military government, if not for the lack of success in creating an alternative school system? Palestinians both inside and outside the territories voiced disappointment over the pace of institution building in the territories, noting the absence of basic institutional mechanisms such as a territory-wide Committee of General Education and a Health Board which would coordinate the action of the various health organizations and institutions.[67]

THE STRATEGY

It was clear to the *intifada*'s emerging leadership that an intense but short uprising, however massive and violent, would not alone achieve the removal of Israeli occupation. From the very start, the *intifada* was perceived in political rather than physical terms: collective violence alone could not force Israel to withdraw.[68]

The contents of the various communiqués pointed this out clearly. "Communiqué number 2" of 10 January sought immediate and limited gains, such as ending the desecration of holy places, the ouster of Minister Ariel Sharon from the Old City of Jerusalem (where he had resided), withdrawal of the Army from cities, camps, and villages, and, above all, the dissolution of the appointed municipal, village, and camp councils and the holding of local elections. Within one week, the range of demands widened considerably, to include the Palestinians' right of return, self-determination, and an independent state. It soon became obvious that the *intifada* was to continue for a long time and that only by diplomacy in the international arena, where the PLO had a monopoly, could these goals be achieved. The striking change in the scope of the goals reconfirmed the preeminence of the PLO, for it became obvious that the *intifada* could not alone achieve them.

This is perhaps why it was personalities from Fath who first suggested a prescription for protracted struggle. Although Mubarak 'Awad's and Hana Siniora's call for graduated civil disobedience was met with derision, this was not because of the action suggested, but because of those suggesting it. "Call number 3" of 17 January adopted at least the major elements of the proposal: the boycott of Israeli goods and preparation for a wholesale stoppage of payment of the VAT which was introduced into the territories in 1976 (at which time it precipitated large-scale disturbances). On the same day, a communiqué issued by "The PFLP in the Occupied Territories," a vociferous detractor of Siniora — called for "civil disobedience" (*'isyan madani*), the same term employed by Siniora and 'Awad.[69] Since civil disobedience is not a concept usually employed by an avowed revolutionary faction, one can assume that the faction borrowed it from Siniora and 'Awad and legitimized it.

In "call number 8" of 19 February, the public was informed that civil disobedience involved, in addition to organization and economic warfare, attempts to strike at the occupation's monopoly of governance. "It is a long and rocky road. But this is the only sure road. Let the revolutionary wave rise through new steps towards civil disobedience and let us divest the occupation of its monopoly on authority." The conceptual broadening of the term called for a parallel widening of the tactics to achieve it. The call for the first time stressed the need to return to working the land, stating that even a small tract of land in front of the home could provide for many of one's basic needs. The Vietnamese example was cited a successful precedent. At this point, 'Awad's contribution to Palestinian doctrine was reconciled with the more staple revolutionary slogans of Palestinian nationalism.

Divesting the authorities of their monopoly of governance by detaching Palestinian society from its hold and creating an autonomous authority of its own became the primary strategic goals of the UNC from February on. The standing demand that appointed municipal and village councillors resign — first put forth as a prerequisite for holding municipal elections and crystallizing a local leadership — was soon voiced in the context of a struggle to create a countergovernment. In "call number 7" of 14 February, appointed municipal committee members were praised for resigning. A stern warning was addressed to those who did not do so: "The masses of the tremendous *intifada* will know how to deal with anyone who violates the national consensus."

It was now the turn of the employees in the tax department and the police force to resign. The sequence of calls on the matter demonstrates how the UNC increasingly advocated a stage-by-stage approach. In "call number 9" issued on 1 March, the UNC demanded that the over 5,000 employees in the civilian administration, excluding teachers, immediately resign. But "call number 10" issued 10 days later, reduced the scope of that directive by 80%, through calling only for the resignation of the police and the employees of the civil administration's tax and customs bureau. The change was not without reason: when the instruction was directed at so large a group as in the ninth call it went unheeded; when it was directed at a smaller and more specific group the response was positive and almost immediate. Thus, 350 policemen, roughly one third of the force in the territories, resigned within three days of the distribution of the tenth communiqué.[70] By 15 March the number increased to 500, including 95% of the force in Gaza.[71] To demand that men, most of whom had to support large families, give up their livelihood and pension funds, required effective coercion. It was easier for the strike forces to coerce a small group than a large one. The brutal killing of an Arab policeman in the 'Aqabat Jabar refugee camp near Jericho on 8 March, presumably for collaboration with the authorities, also had much to do with the massive resignations which occurred.[72]

Evidently, then, the UNC realized that the pace of disengagement had to be slowed down considerably. It was only in "call number 14" of 20 April that the scope increased once again, and even then only modestly: a demand was made for all directors-general in the offices of the civil administration to resign, accompanied by a notice that the PLO Executive Committee had decided to support all policemen, and tax and customs employees who resigned.

Economic conditions in the territories also required slowing down the pace of disengagement. They were explicitly indicated in the calls. For example, "call number 13" urged the local factories to absorb more workers but, in one and the same breath, emphasized that during strike days employers must refrain from laying off employees or reducing salaries. No wonder the calls for further resignations became considerably less frequent and picked up once again only after the PLO Executive Committee pledged to provide for those who resigned. In early June, "call number 18" called for the resignation of all employees in the civil administration's transport, licensing, organization,and housing departments, and the bureaus issuing identity cards and registering residents.[73] Strategically, the UNC was seeking to advance its struggle toward complete disengagement. Even so, the substance of this directive did not match the severity of "call number 9."

The burden of achieving disengagement was also placed on the population at large. Reducing the people's dependence on legal permits and other bureaucratic papers forms an integral part of any civil disobedience strategy. To recall, so drastic a measure as burning identity cards had been urged by Siniora in early January. The UNC did not go as far in this area for several reasons, not least of which was the necessity to maintain identity cards for the 100,000 workers employed in Israel who were easy targets for surveillance. In fact, the UNC addressed the matter only in response to a challenge by the authorities, when the latter issued new registration cards in Gaza to facilitate surveillance. "Call number 15" of 30 April called for foiling the authorities' attempts to confiscate identity cards. The call went unheeded. The UNC persisted, and in "call number 18" in early June it urged the population to refuse to accept the new cards. The clear-cut language used in "call number 28" (29 October) calling upon the population "to cut off ties with the civil administration as much as one can," is proof that this was easier said than done.

The same gradual approach was taken in three other policy areas, the boycott of Israeli products, the refusal to pay taxes, and the limitations on employment in the Jewish sector. As we have seen, the call to boycott Israeli goods wherever local Arab equivalents existed dates as far back as calls numbers 3 and 6. In "call number 9" of 22 February all "Zionist goods" were mentioned, but then the call was neither obligatory nor absolute as it talked of merely "strengthening" the boycott. In "call number 15" of 30 March the directive was repeated in a matter-of-fact manner. "The boycott of work in the Zionist settlements and the boycott of Zionist goods will lead inevitably to the additional disintegration of the Zionist entity's economic infrastructure." The call specified the products in addition to cigarettes, soft drinks, and papergoods, where this boycott could be made effective and how to achieve it. Home gardening, livestock production, and cottage industries were said to be means of achieving savings in vegetables, poultry, and clothing which would also hurt the Israeli economy. Damage done to the Israeli economy by the *intifada*, estimated at hundreds of millions of dollars, was especially highlighted in the thirteenth call of 10 April. Only in the eighteenth call issued at the end of May was the population specifically commanded to boycott all Israeli goods, both industrial and agricultural. By July, that order, too, was transformed into a threat. "Call number 21" of 6 July called upon the strike forces to deal with wholesale distributors of Israeli goods. In August, the demand moved down to the level of groceries.[74]

The payment of taxes, symbolizing recognition of authority, was another major issue addressed by the UNC calls. It was likewise addressed cautiously. The demand to refrain from paying VAT appeared in "call number 5" of 27 January. There the gradual approach was manifested in the demand itself. The call urged the population merely to prepare itself to burn the tax books, but not to carry out the directive, indicating that for the time being refraining from paying VAT sufficed. "Call number 11" of 19 March left the matter to the local organizations, and extolled shopkeepers and professionals for refraining from paying all taxes. It urged more organization in ensuring "these group decisions." Almost a full three months elapsed before the demand was made in "call number 14" on 20 April, to refrain from paying taxes altogether.

May of the directives in the calls were obeyed, in particular those regarding strike days, the prescribed hours in which shops were to remain open, days of commemoration and, seemingly, the establishment of the organizational structures of the *intifada*. On the other hand, however, there was also much resistance to many demands. The call for the resignation of appointed council members first made in "call number 3," had by "call number 8" turned into direct threats. By the 15th call, dated 30 April, the most prominent recalcitrants, traitors in the eyes of the UNC, were specifically named and warned. They included Dr. 'Abd al-Majid al-Zir, mayor of Hebron, Khalil Musa Khalil, mayor of Ramallah, Hasan al-Tawil, mayor of al-Bira, and Jamil Sabri Khalaf, the pro-Jordanian mayor of Jericho (see *MECS* 1986, p. 209). "The measures that have been taken against them," the call stated, "are merely a warning to them." In fact, only one prominent appointed mayor in the West Bank had by that time resigned, Hafiz Tuqan of Nablus.[75] (The fate of Tuqan's predecessor, Zafir al-Masri, who was assassinated by the PFLP in March 1986 [see *MECS* 1986, p. 208], and a mass demonstration organized by Fath supporters following the assassination of Fath leader Abu Jihad, during which Tuqan was specifically denounced, may explain why he chose to do so in contrast to the mayors of other big towns.)

UNC directives were resisted by other segments of the population as well, including the police and employees in the tax bureaus. To recall, they were especially called upon to resign in early March. As the UNC itself admitted, by the end of May that demand had yet to be obeyed completely by many in the police and among tax employees.[76] The same was true of the directors-general, even though their obstinancy at the time was only three weeks old, having been called to resign for the first time in "call number 15."

An emphasis on civil disobedience rather than violent struggle might have prodded the UNC, with the help of factions such as the DFLP and the PFLP, to add a dimension of violence to an uprising that became known as "the uprising of rocks." The first call to activate "a war of molotovs and rocks" appeared in "call number 6," the same call that introduced the concept of civil disobedience. Obviously, its authors were anxious to allay fears amongst the PLO factions advocating "violent struggle" that a campaign of disobedience should not be interpreted as a campaign of nonviolence, a term which appeared in the name of a "study center" in Jerusalem headed by Mubarak 'Awad. The call to wage war on the settlements which appeared in "call number 7" 10 days later may also have had something to do with the adoption of both a concept and a term that had firm roots in nonviolence.[77] For the first time, the UNC called for offensive action by waging war on the settlements. Up to that point the violent struggle was urged against the soldiers of the occupation situated in the Palestinian towns, camps,and villages. Now the aim was to strike at enemy targets immediately outside their areas of residence. The escalation in the level of violence, however, should be seen in its proper light. No call to adopt armed struggle was ever made in the communiqués of 1988.

At least on one matter of policy the "inside" restrained the PLO and its constituent factions abroad. Publications of the PLO outside the territories enthusiastically urged in early summer a scorched earth policy of setting fire to forests, orchards, and fields in Israel proper, presumably in retaliation for a deliberate policy of uprooting Palestinian orchards in the territories.[78] Arson, indeed, occurred on an unprecedented scale during the course of the summer. By late June, fire had consumed more than double the acreage burnt in all of 1987.[79] Yet, the UNC advocated this policy only once in "call number 19" of 8 June.[80] Forcing open local schools that were closed down by the authorities, for which the UNC called in "call number 11" in March, was another directive issued only once.[81] The latter directive, however, failed while arson continued throughout the summer.

No restraint was exercised toward one section of the population, the collaborators. The campaign was launched first against the pro-Jordanians in the territories. "Call number 5" urged a boycott of *al-Nahar,* the pro-Jordanian Jerusalem newspaper which had replaced *al-Quds* after it had adopted a pro-PLO line during 1986. *Al-Nahar* was charged with distorting the situation in the territories during the Amman conference in November 1987, and creating the impression that the population was loyal to Jordan by publishing a memorandum signed by 700 individuals basically supporting Jordanian policy (see *MECS* 1987, pp. 262–63).

The turn of those collaborating with the Israeli authorities came with the issuance of "call number 8" of 19 February. "What is happening in our homeland," stated the communiqué, "is nothing but the halo of hope in the deepening of our victory and the tightening of the noose on every diseased pit and corrupt snare in purifying our cities, towns, and camps of all those who support that which is not Palestine." The call had almost immediate results. During the month of January before a policy against collaborators was adopted, only one Arab was wounded for being a suspected collaborator. By the end of February, four Arabs were killed on that ground.[82]

The lynching of Muhammad 'A'id 'Abdallah in Qabatiyya in northern Samaria, on 23 February, was by far the most dramatic and best publicized case. His house was attacked by hundreds of inhabitants with rocks and incendiary bombs. 'Abdallah climbed the roof and began shooting with an *'Uzi* submachine gun for which he had a permit, killing two children, aged 4 and 13, and wounding several others. After the children's funeral, the inhabitants once again attacked his house. They removed his wife and children, burnt the house, and caught him fleeing the area. He was hung on a nearby electric pole. A foreign television crew filmed the lynching.[83] The fact that troops stationed nearby did not intervene for lack of knowledge of what was happening had serious repercussions. The immediate impression was that the authorities were not backing their informers, even though the town was soon raided by a 100-man IDF force, 30 were arrested, and two homes were blown up by the authorities.[84]

Presumably, many informers and collaborators, intimidated by the lynching, repented publicly for past conduct promising that in the future they would remain loyal to the Palestinian cause.[85] "Call number 9" of 1 March praised the lynching: "We hail the struggle of the inhabitants of Qabatiyya who taught a lesson to one who betrayed his homeland and his people."

ISRAELI POLICY

Never had Israeli policy crystallized into a coherent strategy regarding the territories as had the Palestinian adoption of civil disobedience. The major moves made by the Israeli Administration came in reaction to Palestinian policy rather than in anticipating it. The worst appeared right at the beginning: the Israeli Administration started the new year on a dismal note. The civil administration seemed to be suffering from a lack of personal contacts with the vast majority of the population. Those with whom it was in contact appeared to have lost control of events. There was also a lack of intelligence regarding mass mobilization, as the organized demonstrations in Jerusalem in December 1987 clearly proved.[86]

The situation was not much brighter on the military side. On 12 January, Chief of Staff Lt. Gen. Dan Shomron noted that the IDF deployed more troops in Gaza to contain violence there than had conquered the area in 1967.[87] The size of the forces in the West Bank was estimated at double the number stationed there before the *intifada*; it was three times bigger in Gaza, which was the focus of disturbances during the first months of unrest.[88] The equipment of the troops was found lacking and their training was inadequate — as one might assume of an army which had always wished to maintain its offensive posture and resisted policing duties as much as possible.[89] It was now forced to prepare and equip itself to contain mass civilian violence.

Ultimately, it was the political leadership within Israel which had to formulate a clear strategy to contain the violence. An account of a cabinet deliberation on the matter on 12 January shows just how difficult that was because of the deep personal and ideological rivalries in the national unity government. At that meeting, held on the third day of a successful strike called by the UNC, Prime Minister Shimon Peres (Labor) and Minister of Agriculture Ariel Sharon (Likud) were reported to have called each other "liar," while Minister of Defense Yitzhak Rabin (Labor) rejected two proposals by Sharon and one by another Likud minister, Yitzhak Moda'i.[90] Such differences and harsh language were to characterize later cabinet debates of the issue.

While no changes were made in the government's decision-making mechanism — a proposal by Sharon, who urged the establishment of a minicabinet to deal with the uprising, was turned down — there was a gradual change in Israeli tactics, beginning as early as January. In December 1987, upon the outbreak of the *intifada*, the reaction to it was almost purely military. Rabin issued "tough" guidelines calling primarily for increased military presence. The only extraordinary move in civilian affairs was the temporary closure of some 900 schools in the territories. Another proposal of an essentially civilian nature, the option of selective deportations, was seriously considered and debated (see *MECS* 1987, pp. 266–68). All this changed by the second week of January. Military measures alone were deemed insufficient. On 9 January, the authorities for the first time departed from prevailing custom and limited press coverage of events by closing off certain areas in the territories to journalists.[91] The next day, the Israeli daily *Ha'aretz* reported that the authorities intended to impose collective curfews on Gaza refugee camps, which would also prevent Arab laborers from going to work in Israel. The measure was considered as a response to what the coordinator of government activities in the territories, Shmuel Goren, termed "the luxury of the *intifada*," namely the state in which inhabitants of the territories worked in Israel during the day and demonstrated at night.[92] This was the first time Israel knowingly interfered with the pattern of labor relationships characterizing the ties between the territories and Israel since 1969, and was ready to pay the economic price of having Arab labor idled not only by strikes but also by imposed curfews.

The policy was immediately applied to Gaza. At first only the Jibaliyya refugee camp was placed under complete and prolonged curfew. The decision, applied on 1 January, was taken for security reasons, as Jibaliyya, the largest camp in the Gaza Strip with an estimated population of 52,000, was the locus of disturbances during the first month of the *intifada*. On 10 January, such a curfew was imposed on the nearby Shati camp. On 11 January, it was extended to include Dir al-Balah in the southern sector of Gaza, and on 12 January it was extended to Nusayrat, al-Burj, and Mu'azzi camps located in the central zone. Khan Yunis camp in the south had been under curfew intermittently since 7 January. Only Rafah was mostly unaffected.[93] Ian Murray of *The Times,* in an article dramatically entitled "Curfew starves Gaza refugees into submission," reported hunger and medical problems in the area due to prolonged curfew. He also noted its pacifying effects.[94]

Area-wide curfew was also employed in the West Bank, and by 4 February as many as 170,000 inhabitants, over one fifth of the population, were placed under it, but to little avail.[95] The month of February in the West Bank, according to all the major indicators, was the most violent of all, despite widespread curfews. Having exhausted the use of military force, it was now up to the civil administration to devise measures which would be sufficiently costly to the population to dissuade it from supporting the *intifada*'s political hard core.

The move toward a formulation of a specifically "civilian" policy of punishment began in the wake of the Qabatiyya lynching (see above). Shmuel Goren believed that sanctions would be an appropriate response.[96] The rural areas were highly dependent on exporting their produce to Jordan and this was denied the inhabitants of Qabatiyya, who had been placed under total curfew since the lynching. Israel had already compromised on the principle of free-flow of Arab labor into its territory by imposing an area-wide curfew; now it compromised on an equally, if not more important, policy of the open bridges with Jordan.[97] The denial of gas supplies to Arab gas stations reflected the implementation of the new "economic" policy against the population at large.[98]

Punishment, however, was insufficient to contain organized civil disobedience which aimed at disengagement from Israeli administration altogether. The authorities soon realized that they were not only facing a war of political violence, but a war over political authority. Once again, the formulation of new policy came in reaction to a particular event, this time the resignation of over half the local police force in the territories in the second week of March. The civil administration was now prepared "to bring out the big guns" at its disposal, in the words of one journalist, in order to demonstrate that authority ultimately rested with the Israeli Government, rather than with the UNC. The new moves included making the granting of import and export licenses contingent upon payment of property and value added taxes, a decision timed to mark the end of the 1987 fiscal year on 31 March; the imposition of similar conditions in issuing car and drivers' licenses; restrictions on money transfers into the territories over the bridges; the prohibition of export of agricultural produce (applied to villages that were especially unruly); and the disconnection of telephone communications between the territories and the outside world.[99] The latter move was taken because leaflets of calls numbered 8, 9, and 10 had not been distributed in large numbers and most of the information was disseminated over the PLO radio broadcasting from Baghdad.[100] It then became altogether clear that their final formulation was made by the PLO. The cutting of telephone lines was designed to hamper the process of formulation.

This policy was officially enunciated in an interview with Maj. Gen. Yitzhak Mordechai, commanding officer of the Southern Command responsible for security in Gaza. He formulated it thus: "First and foremost, there is military pressure. In addition, there is a series of activities which create economic hardship, specific arrests, administrative arrests,and bureaucratic activity, all of which are aimed at showing who is the boss."[101] His remarks contrasted markedly with those made by Maj. Gen. 'Amram Mitzna, commanding officer of the Central Command responsible for security in the West Bank, who stated laconically a few weeks earlier that "policy has not changed" in the territories.[102]

The new policy of intervention in the civilian affairs of the inhabitants to demonstrate Israeli's authority reached its zenith by the end of April, after especially severe disturbances in the wake of Abu Jihad's assassination on 16 April. The authorities reacted with a week-long curfew imposed on 400,000 Palestinians and a month-long closure of gas stations, ending on 23 April.[103] Having exhausted both law enforcement and administrative moves, the authorities decided that now was the time to attack the most hallowed symbol of UNC authority stipulating when shops throughout the territories should be open for business. The authorities did so in the most sensitive place and where it counted most, in East Jerusalem. Twenty-five shopkeepers were summoned to open in the morning and close in the afternoon, exactly the reverse of what the UNC called upon them to do.[104] Internal Israeli political dissension kept this bid from succeeding, and Rabin admitted squarely: "We have failed."[105] The Israelis had to concede grudgingly that the territories were under dual authority; its inhabitants went out on strike and demonstrated in response to the appeals of the UNC; they complied with the authorities under duress in meeting their tax obligations and keeping their documents in order. This Israeli defeat preceded a victory of sorts in Gaza a week later. Thousands of Gazans waited in long lines to pick up their new identity cards in contravention of UNC calls not to do so.[106]

It was this realization of the dual authority, perhaps, which led Rabin to suggest openly the possibility of beginning a dialogue with the emergent leader of the *intifada* in the territories rather than solely trying to defeat them. The first signs of such thoughts were expressed in an interview with *Ha'aretz* on 11 June.

> It is possible that some of the inhabitants of the territories who are presently imprisoned because they were involved in incitement or the organization of violence will be the Palestinian leaders of the territories in the future...I do not believe right now that I can identify this new leadership [that would make

> peace]... Even if this leadership exists, there is no sign that it is ready to solve it by way of talks.[107]

An attempt to speak to pro-Fath academics four days later failed. Dr. Gabi Baramki, acting president of Bir-Zayt University; Dr. Nabil Ja'bari, chairman of the board of trustees of Hebron University (who had been placed under administrative arrest for 68 days for allegedly using the university's administrative offices to transfer PLO funds into the territories); and Dr. Nafiz Nazzal, former lecturer at Bir Zayt University refused to show up for the meeting in keeping with the spirit of "communiqué number 19" which called those participating in such meetings "collaborators." Palestinian sources did claim that a week earlier Rabin had met with supporters of both the PLO and Jordan as well as with Islamic fundamentalists including Dr. Ibrahim Yazuri, the secretary of *al-Mujamma' al-Islami.*[108]

STRIKING AT THE POLITICAL HARD CORE

Israeli administrative and economic measures were primarily aimed at the ordinary inhabitant in the territories. Israel, however, hoped to drive a wedge between the political hard core leading the *intifada* and those most active in setting up the organization which made it effective, on the one hand, and the general population which supported it on the other. The Israelis made strenuous attempts to attack the hard core itself and the organizations with which they were associated.

These moves were aimed at three groups of activists: (1) the *muharrarun,* former prisoners belonging to the various factions of the PLO and the Islamic movement, who had served sentences for terrorist activities and who, upon release, became political and spiritual leaders in the political arms of their organizations; (2) activists and functionaries in the hundreds of "national institutions" and public service arms of the organizational frameworks, such as the Shabiba; and (3) those engaged in violence ranging from stone throwing to the use of incendiary bombs, and occasionally firearms and other weapons. Each group (their memberships occasionally overlapping) was handled differently. The members of the first group were prime candidates for deportation. Because of international pressure against deportation and consequently the limited use of such a penalty, most of those in this category were placed under administrative arrest for six months. Most of the second group were placed under six-month administrative arrest with the option of extending that period indefinitely. Those in the third group were imprisoned for a minimum of 18 days and often longer, were tried and either sentenced to prison or fined, or both.

The relationship between prior imprisonment for terrorist activities and subsequent political activism had become clear in the first wave of deportations at the outset of the *intifada* on 12 January. Three of the four deportees — PFLP leader Bashir al-Khayri (aged 45), Fath leader Jibril al-Rajub (35), and Shabiba leader Jamal 'Abdallah Jabbara (28) — had served extended prison sentences for terrorist activities. Upon their release they became leading political activists. The latter two were released in the 1985 prisoner exchange with Ahmad Jibril's PFLP-GC. The fourth deportee, Hisham 'Uthman Hadr (26), was the only one not to have served time in prison for previous terrorist acts, although he was imprisoned in 1983 for activities in the Shabiba movement, and the authorities stated that he was planning such acts for the future.[109] The deportation of five others was postponed pending appeals before a military review committee. Three of them, one from the Qalandiyya refugee camp and two from Gaza, were Fath or Shabiba activists, while the other two, both of Gaza, were Islamic fundamentalists. Of these last two, one was the chairman of the Islamic Association in Gaza, associated with the Islamic Brotherhood, and the other a member of the Salafiyyun, a religious organization connected with al-Jihad al-Islami. Thus, all the activists without a terrorist past were expelled for advocating violence; for those with such records no explanation was given.[110]

Widespread criticism in Western Europe over the deportation was expressed long before it was actually carried out.[111] The US condemnation came in its aftermath.[112] Nevertheless, Israel continued its policy of deportations. On 11 April, eight more were deported. They included the five who had appealed, mentioned above, in addition to two men from Jenin and one from Gaza; the latter was the spiritual leader of al-Jihad al-Islami.[113] The same number were deported on 19 April. Six of the eight in this last group were from Bayta, a village in which an Israeli girl from a nearby settlement was killed; the other two were Shabiba and Fath activists from Kufr Diq and Nablus.[114]

Israel was especially censured for the deportation of Mubarak 'Awad, the head of the Jerusalem-based "Center for the Study of Nonviolence," following a lengthy appeal process and a landmark High Court of Justice ruling that the deportation was legal.[115] Though the matter discussed in the 16-page ruling was technical — it revolved around the question of whether a resident of East Jerusalem, who was therefore also an Israeli citizen, could legally be deported — 'Awad's deportation was seen to involve a whole array of human rights issues. 'Awad was the only deportee amongst the 33 expelled in 1988 with no affiliation to an illegal organization which advocated violence. The Israeli authorities, who had initiated expulsion procedures concerning 'Awad before the *intifada,* considered him a key actor in the call for mass civil disobedience. Palestinian sources credited him with adapting this doctrine to local needs.[116]

The last two waves of deportation in 1988 conformed to the patterns set in the first two. On 1 August eight people were expelled; they were all leading activists in the major political organization operation in the territories and some had served time for terrorist activities.[117] Finally, on 17 August, four people were expelled from Gaza, specifically for their activities in the popular committees and the strike forces. Three of them had been formerly convicted for terrorism, while the fourth was a spiritual leader of al-Jihad al-Islami, in prison since 1986 after being sentenced for delivering a gun to Fath agents.[118]

According to the State Department Report on Human Rights in the Territories published in January, there had been over 2,600 administrative detainees by September compared to 360 in 1987.[119] The most prominent of those detained was Faysal al-Husayni who had been imprisoned since September 1987. The arrest order was extended in March, for another three months. He was released on 9 June, only to be detained yet again on 31 July for the usual six-month period.[120] Those arrested for committing acts of violence, most of whom were youths, numbered over 7,000.[121]

The Israeli authorities struck at organizations as well. The universities and schools in the West Bank were the first to be closed down. Although none of these schools was formally run by nationalist organizations, the linkage between violence and the presence of such organizations within the schools was common knowledge long before the *intifada*. The universities were closed down in December 1987 for one month. The closure was then extended until further notice on 2 February. By then it had been decided to close down the whole school system.[122] Schools were reopened in early May, only to be closed down once again on 19 June.[123] A different policy was applied in Gaza. There the school system formally remained open but individual schools were closed down whenever the authorities deemed it necessary for security reasons.

Over six months elapsed before the authorities concentrated their blows at the core of the "national institutions." Political motives, Palestinian sources claimed, determined the timing. In August, an array of institutions was closed down, including the Jerusalem Federation of Charitable Societies, composed of over 100 public service associations; the In'ash al-Usra benevolent society in al-Bira (the largest in the West Bank); the Professional Unions' Complex, the roof organization of all professional unions in the West Bank; and the offices of the Fath-dominated Federation of Labor Unions in Nablus. These moves were made after the "declaration of independence document" was discovered (see chapter on the Palestine Liberation Organization). In the Palestinians' view, the Israelis were anxious to close down the very institutions that could play a role in such a state so as to forestall its establishment.[124] The Arab Studies Society headed by Faysal al-Husayni was closed down on 31 July.[125]

THE SPREAD AND INTENSITY OF THE *INTIFADA*

Data on violent incidents, casualties, protests, and demonstrations, as well as troop deployment are the best indicators of the scope and intensity of the *intifada*. Three major trends were noted in 1988. The first was the shift of the locus of the *intifada* from Gaza to the West Bank, commencing in the February and reaching its zenith one month later. This shift was probably the most pronounced development. Henceforth, the intensity of violence was roughly commensurate with proportions of these two areas in the total population of the territories. A second trend was the correlation maintained between various techniques of action: as mass demonstrations decreased, acts of violence by individuals, such as throwing incendiary bombs or burning down forests and crops, increased. The third important development was the institutionalization and stabilization of violence at one level, with only relatively small changes over time.

The shift in the locus of violence from Gaza to the West Bank in February and March was clearly reflected in Israeli troop deployment. According to Israeli sources, at the onset of the year the number of forces deployed in Gaza was three times the number stationed there before the *intifada*, and twice that in the West Bank.[126] By early March the ratio was reversed: troop deployment in the West Bank was four times its pre-*intifada* level, while remaining three times the level in Gaza.[127] Data regarding Palestinian casualties, both dead and wounded, and the number of incidents involving such acts as stone throwing, demonstrations, and tire burning, reflected the *intifada*'s scope and intensity as well. By early March, 49 Palestinians were killed in the West Bank and 418 wounded compared to 28 and 228, respectively, in Gaza.[128] By 31 March, the number of dead in the West Bank had risen to 80, nearly a 6% increase, while in Gaza the death toll stood at 31, an 11% increase. Similarly, the number of wounded increased in the West Bank by 67.5% during that period, from 419 to 700, while in Gaza it increased by 31.6% from 218 to 300.

These increases were correlated with increases in violent incidents. In the West Bank, the number of such incidents rose from 3,750 in early March to 4,831 by its end, a 28.8% increase, compared to a 19% increase in Gaza, from 1,160 to 1,370 (a level of violence which was well below Gaza's proportionate share of the population).[129] Partial data reveal that this trend increased in the course of the *intifada*. By early August, the IDF spokesman revealed that 166 Palestinians had been killed in the territories, of whom only 53 were Gazans.[130] In Gaza, 26 were killed in the first two months of the *intifada* compared to 27 during the next five months.[131]

Other partial data also suggest that the patterns of violence changed. By the end of March, 6,210 incidents of demonstrations and rock throwing had been registered, an average of over 1,540 incidents per month, since the beginning of the *intifada*. By early August, the figure had risen to 12,303, indicating an average of 1,525 incidents per month for the period of April to August — a slight decline of incident intensity.[132] Firebombings, on the other hand, increased in the latter four months, 533 compared to 469 in the first four months, and the use of explosive charges increased from 16 to 57. Cases of arson jumped from 121 to 252 because of the approaching summer.[133] The earlier statistics do not distinguish between stone throwing and demonstrations. They do indicate, however, how persistent the violence became, for the change of trends was only minor. In other words, violence became a permanent feature in both areas (for more details, see chapter on armed operations).

BAYTA: A CASE OF MUTUAL RESTRAINT

Many refugee camps, villages,and towns in the territories became scenes of violent confrontations involving deaths and casualties, but few were as indicative of the poignancy of the *intifada* as Bayta, a village of some 4,000 just south of Nablus. There, strife between Jewish settlers who regarded the West Bank as their birthright and a Palestinian village became intertwined with what Palestinians felt to be a struggle for "freedom and independence," as they so often noted in the UNC's calls. On 6 April, a group of 16 teenage vocationers from nearby Ellon Moreh, a Gush Emunim settlement, was attacked near Bayta. One Israeli girl and one local Palestinian were killed; the group's armed escort was seriously wounded; and some 14 Israeli youngsters were slightly hurt.[134] The Army responded immediately: sensing that the conflict could degenerate into communal warfare, it had to be stopped by decisive action. The village was therefore sealed off; all males 15–60 years of age were rounded up; 14 homes were demolished; and six inciters were ordered to be deported.

The Israeli press was at first alarmed. The daily *Ha'aretz* asked in an editorial: "Is this just one incident, or is it a preliminary step signaling a shift from riots, in which Arabs demonstrate their hostility to Israeli occupation, to a war between the two peoples for whom the land of Israel constitutes a common homeland?"[135] Gradually, however, both the Israeli authorities and the press came to view the incident as tragedy of misunderstanding rather than an attempted communal massacre. The Army offered compensation to one of the men whose homes were destroyed, thus acknowledging his role in trying to protect the youngsters who, so it seemed, erringly strolled into the village. The Israeli press echoed these feelings by demanding a thorough investigation before accusing either side.[136]

The Palestinian reaction was similar. A detailed article by an Israeli Arab in *Filastin al-Thawra,* the official PLO organ, emphasized the role the local inhabitants played in protecting the youngsters and claimed that the Israeli girl was killed by the group's armed escort and that the latter was wounded as a result of an act of self-defense.[137] The reactions on both the Israeli and Palestinian sides answered the question posed by the *Ha'aretz* editorial. Neither side, it seemed, wished the conflict to turn the *intifada* into a full-scale communal war.

FORMULATING THE POLITICAL TARGETS: THE QUEST FOR INDEPENDENCE

Palestinian analysts credit the UNC with giving purpose and direction to the *intifada* by coining the short slogan, "freedom and independence." The slogan first appeared in "call number 3" of 17 January, when the UNC was consolidating its moral authority. One must assume then that the slogan echoed the yearning of the thousands who were prepared to sacrifice for the continuation of the *intifada.* However, the substance of the words which appeared alongside the slogan had to meet the requirements of the various Palestinian factions seeking to lead the *intifada.* "Freedom and independence" meant the right of return to the land (*haqq al-'awda*), the right to self-determination,and the establishment of a Palestinian state. Obviously, such a formula was the common denominator which enabled all the forces to coalesce, within the territories as well as outside them. Yet the reiteration of this formula by itself could hardly realize any immediate political gains or set off any kind of peace process, as the boycott of Shultz suggested (see above).[138] In a sense it was an inauspicious beginning, since the political leadership seemed to be more extreme than the PLO abroad. A modification of the defintion was palpably in order.

The first signs of change appeared in the wake of the Gorbachev-Reagan summit. In a communiqué addressed to these two world leaders, the UNC called for the convening of an international peace conference in which all the parties to the conflict, including the PLO, would participate on an equal footing. It also called for the realization of Palestinian national rights including self-determination and the establishment of an independent state. The communiqué, however, did not mention the right of return.[139] The emphasis thus shifted from advocating a formula satisfactory to a radical faction such as the PFLP to the adoption of a policy line reflecting the thinking of the PLO mainstream.

By summer, the Palestinians within the territories were taking the lead in insisting on the Palestinian state but not necessarily on the fulfillment of the right to self-determination or the right of return. The Abu Sharif document gave the Palestinians inside the legitimacy to stick to the more limited demand without evoking the formula of UNC calls. King Husayn's disengagement decision of 31 July, and the disclosure of the "independence document" found in Faysal al-Husayni's Arab Studies Society proved to be the impetus of what became a major drive — lasting over three months — to bring the PLO to declare Palestinian statehood and implicitly recognize partition of Palestine as a valid solution to the Palestinian problem (for more details, see chapter on the Palestine Liberation Organization).

King Husayn's move — which began with the scuttling of the gradiose five-year development plan and culminated in the decision to dismiss or retire the 21,000 employees of Jordanian institutions in the territories — left a vacuum, which people long known for their desire to establish a Palestinian state in the territories were eager to fill.[140] While the PLO waivered in its response to the Jordanian moves, *al-Fajr* responded with alacrity by publishing three editorials on the need for the chambers of commerce, the professional unions, and the municipalities to sever all links with Jordan and become "complete and independent Palestinian institutions."[141] Thus, for the sake of indigenous state-building, *al-Fajr* urged an even faster pace of severance of ties than that dictated by Jordan. Where all this might have been leading was suggested by a large headline in the newspaper on 6 August, stating: "The PLO is studying the establishment of a government-in-exile [or] the proclamation of the birth of the Palestinian State."[142] PLO representative in Holland, 'Afif Safiyya, hardly a man to justify headlines, was quoted as the source. *Al-Fajr* was clearly trying to apply pressure on the PLO to move toward a declaration of a Palestinian state.

The disclosure of an "independence document" a week later, presumably found and leaked by the Israeli security services,[143] gave the campaign for the independent state another boost. *Al-Fajr* immediately published the text under its main headline and at the bottom of the page published an interview with Mustafa Natsha, Hana Siniora and Sari Nusayba, all of whom indirectly endorsed its contents. The document called for the establishment of a Palestinian state based on the 1947 Partition Plan as part of an overall strategy of elevating the *intifada* from a war of rocks alone "into the orbit of political initiative, by embarking on a diplomatic campaign of Palestinian make and initiative which would add strength to the blessed *intifada*, propelling it to the international conference."[144] Again the newspaper made use of main headlines to drive the point home. "The PLO is studying the establishment of a government-in-exile and the ratification of *the* document of the declaration of the state." This was especially interesting, as the daily felt that the actual document should be accepted. Again the source was nondescript — an unnamed Palestinian official in Kuwait.[145]

The UNC showed greater restraint on the subject, for obvious reasons. The UNC was "the fighting arm" of the PLO in the territories, but it had no mandate to make the fateful decisions which affected the future of the Palestinian people as a whole. It was also a collective leadership and this meant, once again, reaching decisions to which all its constituent organizations would consent. Palestinian newspapers, not so restricted, could show more initiative and independence. But even the calls were gradually drawn into pushing for statehood. "Call number 24" of 22 August assured the public that there was no political vacuum in the wake of Jordan's disengagement. Referring to the PNC scheduled to convene shortly, the UNC stated that "we have confidence that the council in its emergency session will adopt a clear, comprehensive program that will amass the most international support for our people's national rights and that will take practical steps to aid the *intifada* and develop it."[146] It was clear that "practical steps" alone were not sufficient; what was needed was a bold political decision. "Call number 27" of 9 October went even further. Amongst a list of demands addressed to Israel and the international community (in a style reminiscent of the early calls) was a request "to ensure international protection for the masses of our unarmed people for not more than several months to facilitate the establishment of the independent state for our people with Jerusalem as its capital."[147] "Call number 28," issued at the end of October, no longer had to convey the message indirectly; it was entitled "The Call of Independence," in preparation for the declaration of independence that was made in the 19th meeting of the PNC on 15 November[148] (for details, see chapter on the Palestine Liberation Organization).

Israeli policy in anticipation of the declaration perhaps best indicated how much the inhabitants of the territories sought a decision which would help translate their sacrifices into meaningful political gains. The authorities, in addition to declaring a total curfew for three days on all of Gaza and seven communities in the West Bank affecting over half of the entire population in the territories,[149] also cut off all electricity to the territories to make it impossible to view the PNC meeting on television and engage in festivities surrounding the event.[150]

SUMMARY: THE RESILIENCY OF THE *INTIFADA*

Having been prevented from celebrating, local Palestinians responded with violence. Thus, on 16 December, eight Palestinian demonstrators were killed in Nablus, the highest number killed in one day since the beginning of the *intifada*. Such violence amidst growing economic hardship — in the wake of a 35% drop in the value of the Jordanian dinar between July and December — only served to emphasize the resiliency of the *intifada*.[151] So did, in a way, the paltry accomplishments of the UNC's civil disobedience campaign. On the other hand, while it is true that most employees in the tax, customs, police,and driver registration departments resigned, and the boycott of Israeli goods was partially effective, the goal of disengagement was not achieved in 1988.[152] Inhabitants of the territories continued to carry identity cards issued by the Israeli Administration, 80%–90% of the workers continued to work within Israel and in Israeli settlements in the West Bank,[153] and the Jewish population in the territories continued to grow from 67,000 inhabitants in 1987 to 71,000 by November 1988, albeit more slowly than in the past.[154] Even the effectiveness of the popular committees was questioned. Samir Subihat, a deported Bir Zayt University Shabiba student leader, emphasized that while in certain villages these committees had succeeded in attending to the day-to-day problems of their inhabitants "nevertheless we cannot say that the popular committees have been able to create an alternative authority yet, even though the kernel and the will [to do so] exist."[155]

Their sacrifices, over 200 dead according to Israeli sources and 430 according to Palestinian sources,[156] and 9,000 wounded since the outbreak of the *intifada*, were rewarded mostly on the international plane. That the Palestinian problem and the prospects of Palestinian statehood had become major issues on the international agenda was, no doubt, due to the outbreak and persistence of the *intifada*. In the territories themselves there was only one notable political accomplishment scored by the *intifada*, seemingly of minor immediate importance yet rather significant: in October a protocol was signed by an Israeli Interministerial Team with two Arab associations, one in Gaza, the other in the West Bank, allowing the direct export of agricultural produce from the territories under local brand names.[157] The matter had already been negotiated between Israel and the EEC during the previous year (see *MECS* 1987, p. 251). For the first time, an agreement on terms of equality was signed between Israel and inhabitants in the territories.

It was clear, however, that the *intifada* was being waged in order to realize the aspirations of the Palestinians as a whole. On the international plane, the accomplishments seemed to render the sacrifices worthwhile, for at the end of the year the *intifada* showed no signs of abating.

NOTES

For the place and frequency of publications cited here, and for the full name of the publication, news agency, radio station, or monitoring service where an abbreviation is used, please see "List of Sources." Only in the case of more than one publication bearing the same name is the place of publication noted here.

1. *Al-Qabas*, 11, 12 January; *Ma'ariv,* 8 July 1988.
2. *Shu'un Filastiniyya,* No. 62 (1977), p. 228; No. 105, (August 1980), p. 7; No. 126 (May 1982), p. 4.
3. *Ma'ariv,* 1 January; on Balata see Ian Murray in *The Times,* 8 January 1988.
4. According to Jamal Zaqut, a Democratic Front activist deported in August, *al-Hurriyya,* 25 December 1988.
5. *JP,* 6 January 1988.
6. *Al-Fajr,* East Jerusalem, 7, 8 January 1988.
7. *JP,* 6 January 1988.
8. *JP,* 7 January 1988.
9. *Al-Hurriyya,* 17, 24 January 1988.
10. *JP,* 7 January 1988.
11. *JP,* 8 January 1988.
12. *Ma'ariv,* 13 January 1988.
13. *Al-Fajr,* East Jerusalem, 2 August 1988.
14. *Al-Hurriyya,* 25 January 1988.
15. *Al-Safir,* 15 January; *al-Hurriyya,* 7, 21 February 1988.
16. *Al-Hadaf,* Damascus, 6 March; interview with Dr. Shaul Mishal, *Ha'aretz* (weekend supplement), 29 April 1988.
17. Na' if Hawatima in *al-Hurriyya,* 21 February 1988.
18. *Al-Hadaf,* Damascus, 13 March 1988.
19. *Ha'aretz,* 15 January 1988.
20. *Al-Ra'y,* 28 January 1988.
21. *Al-Hadaf,* Damascus, 7 February 1988.
22. *Al-Safir,* 15 January 1989.
23. *Hadashot,* 20 February; *Yedi'ot Aharonot,* 22 February 1988.
24. *Yedi'ot Aharonot,* 26 February 1988.
25. *Yedi'ot Aharonot,* 28 February 1988.
26. See "call number 6" in *al-Hurriyya,* 14 February 1988.
27. *JP,* 1 January 1988.
28. *Al-Hadaf,* Damascus, 13 March; remarks by Ahmad Jabar and Jamal Zaqut in *al-Hurriyya,* 25 December 1988.
29. See Nasir Arruri in *MEI,* 2 December 1988.
30. *Al-Hadaf,* Damascus, 13 March 1988.
31. *JP,* 25 March 1988.
32. *Al-Hadaf,* Damascus, 13 March 1988.
33. *Amnesty International Report 1986,* p. 336.
34. Ibid.
35. The State Department Report on Human Rights in Israel and the Territories, reprinted in *Ha'aretz,* 9 February 1989.
36. *JP,* 9 May 1988.
37. *Al-Hadaf,* Damascus, 21 February, 13 March 1988.
38. AFP, 13 April quoted in *Tariq al-Intisar,* 1 May 1988.
39. *Ha'aretz,* 11 April 1988.
40. I assume this to be the case from an article written by Muhammad Nizal in *Filastin al-Muslima,* 1 March 1988, in which he pejoratively calls the leadership the "so-called Unified National Command" and stresses that even they recognized the importance of Islam and used Islamic slogans in their communiqués. *Filastin al-Muslima* is a Muslim Brotherhood publication published in Great Britain. See also VoP (Baghdad) text of "uprising command," "statement on unity in occupied territories," 22 January 1988.
41. Ahmad Jabir in *al-Hurriyya,* 25 December 1988.

42. *Al-Hadaf,* Damascus, 21 February 1988.
43. *Filastin al-Thawra,* 18 September 1988.
44. *Al-Hadaf,* Damascus, 13 March 1988.
45. Ahmad Jabir in *al-Hurriyya,* 25 December 1988.
46. Ibid.
47. *Al-Ittihad*, Haifa, 11 January 1989.
48. *Ha'aretz,* 21 March 1988.
49. *Al-Mithaq,* 4 April 1982.
50. *Ha'aretz,* 11 November 1988.
51. *Ha'aretz,* 22 July 1988.
52. *Ma'ariv,* 23 September 1988.
53. *Al-Hadaf,* Damascus, 10 July 1988.
54. *Al-Hurriyya,* 24 January; see also "Bayan lijan al-tansiq al-wataniyya," ibid., 1 March 1988, which uses the terms interchangeably.
55. *Ma'ariv,* 18 August 1988.
56. *Al-Ufuq,* 24 April 1988.
57. *Ma'ariv,* 18 August 1988.
58. *Al-Hadaf,* Damascus, 19 April 1988.
59. See, for example, "call number 9" (1 March), "15" (30 April), "16" (22 May 1988).
60. *Al-Hurriyya,* 21 February 1988.
61. *Al-Hadaf,* Damascus, 10 July 1988.
62. *Al-Hadaf,* Damascus, 15 May, 12 June 1988.
63. *Al-Hadaf,* Damascus, 10 April; interview with Dr. Samir Katba, *al-Hadaf,* Damascus, 26 June 1988.
64. Uri Nir in *Ha'aretz,* 3 March 1989.
65. "Call number 27" (9 October), "28" (29 October), "29" (20 November), "30" (5 December 1988).
66. *Ha'aretz,* 3 March 1989.
67. Ahmad Jabir in *al-Hurriyya,* 25 December; Sari Nusayba, "Time for Palestinian Offensive," *MEI,* 2 December 1988, p. 18.
68. *Al-Hadaf,* Damascus, 13 March 1988.
69. *Al-Hurriyya,* 24 January 1988. The communiqué shows how quickly the concept gained currency amongst all the PLO factions; Ahmed Kan'an, *al-Hadaf,* Damascus, 6, 13 March 1988.
70. *Yedi'ot Aharonot,* 13 March 1988.
71. *Yedi'ot Aharonot,* 16 March 1988.
72. *Al-Hadaf,* Damascus, 5 June 1988.
73. "Call number 18," 28 May 1988.
74. "Call number 24," 22 August 1988.
75. *Ma'ariv,* 19 April 1988.
76. "Call number 17," 17 May 1988.
77. *Al-Hadaf,* Damascus, 21 February 1988.
78. *Al-Hadaf,* Damascus, 3 July 1988.
79. *Ma'ariv,* 20 June 1988.
80. *JP,* 14 June 1988.
81. *Ma'ariv,* 25 March 1988.
82. Yochai Sela, *Ha-Hitkomemut ba-Shtahim - Maazan Beynayim* (December 1987-June 1988), Tel Aviv University, pp. 29, 31.
83. *Yedi'ot Aharonot,* 24 February 1988.
84. *Yedi'ot Aharonot,* 26 February 1988.
85. *Al-Hadaf,* Damascus, 20 March 1988.
86. Uri Nir in *Ha'aretz,* 3 January 1988.
87. *JP,* 13 January 1988.
88. *JP,* 1 January 1988.
89. Ibid.
90. *JP,* 13 January 1988.
91. *JP,* 10 January 1988.

92. *Ha'aretz,* 10 January 1988.
93. *Ma'ariv,* 18 January 1988.
94. *The Times,* 19 January 1988.
95. *Ha'aretz,* 5 February 1989.
96. *Yedi'ot Aharonot,* 2 March 1988.
97. *Ma'ariv,* 13 March 1988.
98. *Ha'aretz,* 13 March 1988.
99. Uri Nir in *Ha'aretz,* 18 March 1988.
100. *Ha'aretz,* 17 March 1988.
101. R. IDF, 2 April 1988.
102. R. IDF, 8 April 1988.
103. *NYT,* 25 April 1988.
104. Ibid.
105. *JP,* 24 April 1988.
106. *IHT,* 11 May 1988.
107. *Ha'aretz,* 11 June 1988.
108. *JP,* 15 June 1988.
109. *Ma'ariv, al-Ra'y,* 13 January 1988.
110. *Ma'ariv,* 14 January; *The Times,* 6 January 1988.
111. *The Times,* 5 January 1988.
112. *The Guardian,* 14 January 1988.
113. *JP,* 12 April 1988.
114. *JP,* 20 April 1988.
115. *JP,* 6 June 1988.
116. *Filastin al-Thawra,* 29 May; *Ma'ariv,* 15 April 1988.
117. *Al-Fajr* (English ed.), East Jerusalem, 3 August; *JP,* 2 August 1988.
118. *Ma'ariv,* 18 August 1988.
119. See text in *Ha'aretz,* 9 February 1989. *Amnesty International Report 1988,* p. 239.
120. *Al-Fajr* (English ed.), East Jerusalem, 3 August 1988.
121. *Ha'aretz,* 9 February 1988.
122. *IHT,* 3 February 1988.
123. *IHT,* 26 June 1988.
124. *Al-Fajr* (English ed.), East Jerusalem, 4 September 1988.
125. *JP,* 1 August 1988.
126. *JP,* 1 January 1988.
127. VoI, 8 March 1988.
128. *Yedi'ot Aharonot,* 5 March 1988.
129. *Yedi'ot Aharonot,* 1 April 1988.
130. *Ha'olam Hazeh,* 13 July 1988.
131. *JP,* 8 July 1988.
132. *Yedi'ot Aharonot,* 1 April; *JP,* 7 August 1988.
133. Ibid.
134. Glen Frankel, *IHT, The Guardian,* 8 April; VoI, 6 April 1988.
135. *Ha'aretz,* 7 April 1988.
136. *Ha'aretz,* 11 April 1988.
137. *Filastin al-Thawra,* 7 May 1988.
138. See "special communiqué," 23 February 1988.
139. *Al-Hadaf,* Damascus, 12 June 1988.
140. *JP,* 28, 29 July 1988.
141. *Al-Fajr,* East Jerusalem, 6, 7, 8 August 1988.
142. On the special role of "the inside" in promoting the declaration of independence see *Tariq al-Intisar,* 1 October 1988, pp. 41–42.
143. *JP,* 7 August 1988.
144. *Al-Fajr,* East Jerusalem, 8 August 1988.
145. *Al-Fajr,* East Jerusalem, 9 August 1988.
146. See also call from Junayd Prison Committee supporting "communiqué number 24" in *al-Ittihad,* Abu Dhabi, 5 October 1988.

147. *JP,* 11 October 1988.
148. "Call number 28," 29 October 1988.
149. *JP,* 13 November 1988.
150. Jerusalem Domestic Radio, 16 November 1988.
151. Paul Pasch, *Monetary Dualism in the West Bank* (Jerusalem: The West Bank Data Project, forthcoming).
152. Joel Greenberg in *JP,* 30 December 1988.
153. *JP,* 18 November 1988.
154. *Ha'aretz,* 18 November 1988.
155. *Tariq al-Intisar,* 1 October 1988.
156. *Al-Katib,* January 1989, p. 36.
157. *Al-Nahar*, East Jerusalem, *al-Quds,* 12 October 1988.

MIDDLE EAST ECONOMIC ISSUES

Middle East Oil Developments 1988

BENJAMIN SHWADRAN

INTRODUCTION

To understand the developments in the Middle East oil arena, we should carefully examine developments in the Organization of Petroleum Exporting Countries (Opec), which has dominated the petroleum industry of the ME and, in a sense, the energy question of the Western world since 1960. But first, an introductory remark is in order.

Opec was organized in 1960 with Venezuela's initiative to fight the concessionary oil companies, which exploited the oil-producing countries. From the outset, Opec identified itself as a group interested in, and operating on, economic principles; it was not and would not become involved in political issues. Its primary purpose was to obtain from the concessionary companies the restoration of the two price cuts which the companies had made in 1959 and 1960.

Until 1970, Opec failed in its efforts because of extraneous negative factors. But in 1970 Opec began a march of progress that culminated in 1976 when almost all ME oil-producing countries succeeded in nationalizing their oil industries. In the decade of the 1970s, the organization's achievements reached their peak.

Since the end of 1981, however, Opec has been in constant difficulties and has gone through serious crises. The press and books, and even textbooks, often describe Opec as a cartel. Opec is not and could not function as a cartel. A cartel is a group of manufacturers who produce or supply a common product or service. The members agree not to permit economic factors of free supply and demand to determine the price of the product in free competition. If the group has exclusive control of the manufacture, all members are bound to charge the price set by the cartel. If, however, the producers do not have exclusive control of the supply of the product, the cartel resorts to the two instruments of control: limited production and set price.

The greatest beneficiaries of cartels are the small producers, because with the cartel's protection they obtain the highest price for their product. The large producers limit their outlet and carry the small producers as long as the possibility of expanding the market is very limited. However, as soon as the large producers see opportunities for expanding their market by lowering prices, they throw off the small producers and the cartel is terminated. Discipline is a basic element of a cartel: members are subject to the group's decision until they are dismissed for disobedience and lose all the benefits of membership.

Opec is a unique organization, lacking all the characteristics of a cartel. Members are not companies but sovereign nations and not subject to the group's discipline. The organization as such has no executive power over members. Resolutions must be unanimously adopted by Opec's conference and then must be confirmed by each member government. At the time of its founding, Opec's powers were not clearly defined; at first, Saudi Arabia challenged Opec's power to set the price of oil and claimed that this was each member's sovereign prerogative. Not until 1982 was Opec ready to deal with the power of controlling production.

The efforts to enforce the observance of the set prices and the production quotas make up the story of Opec's trials and tribulations since March 1983. Although all the ME members are oil producers and exporters, they had different orientations and conflicting interests. The producers with tremendous reserves — Saudi Arabia, Kuwait, and the United Arab Emirates (UAE) — are politically conservative and expect their oil resources to last a very long time. Hence their determination to keep prices low so that their supplies to the consuming world continue and no alternatives to oil are developed and enter the market to compete with oil.

The medium and small producers with limited reserves and a radical, anti-Western orientation — Algeria, Libya, and Iran — wanted to raise prices and exhaust their oil resources as fast as high prices could accomplish this. The cuts in production were to be made by the big producers.

Opec's fatal mistake in the 1970s and early 1980s of steadily, rapidly, and enormously raising the price of oil decisively changed the world's oil supply patterns.

From 1982 to 1988 when the demand for Opec oil dropped continually from about 33m. barrels per day (b/d) to about 16m. b/d, the importance of ME oil to world energy supply was severely reduced and Opec could no longer play its role as the major, if not the sole, provider of the Western world. Not being a cartel that could discipline its members both on prices and production levels, almost all Opec members cheated on overproduction and undercharged on pricing. These practices created production gluts and serious deficits in revenue. The various committees set up by conferences on production and price monitoring, which even engaged independent professional auditors, failed to achieve results.

After the Opec crisis of late 1981,which caused a drop in the demand for oil and consequent reduction in prices, Opec leaders found culprits for both. The first were the non-Opec producers. They had increased the supply of oil in the world market which caused the drop in prices, because they had sold their oil much below the prices set by Opec. Moreover, the non-Opec producers refused to join Opec or even to cooperate in stabilizing the oil market. The second culprits were the consumers themselves. Stockpiling was always considered a menace to the organization's power; now that the consequences of the crisis affected all members, the consumers were the villains, because they did not reduce their consumption of oil which would have lowered the price, but their systematic drawdown of their stockpiles cut demand, which brought down the price.

Opec's problems during 1988 revolved around the conflicts between the conservative, big producers and the smaller, radical producers. Charges and countercharges were made of cheating on production and prices. Practically all the members resorted to barter arrangements between producers and purchasers, countertrade deals, netback setups, and distanceless shipments of oil cargoes. Some members gave substantial discounts from the established Opec prices; others charged their contracted customers spot-market prices, which were systematically elaborated by Dubai and Oman. The organization was preoccupied with the non-Opec producers and the efforts of the minor non-Opec producers to work out some measure of cooperation with Opec. Later in the year, Opec had to face the determination of the

Gulf Cooperation Council (GCC), which was pursued by an almost obsessive fear that Opec might lose its position as the major world oil supplier, to greatly increase production. The main force behind this drive was Saudi Arabia. Finally, the November conference was hailed as a turning point in Opec's internal relations and external standing.

PRODUCTION AND PRICES, FIRST QUARTER

Opec faced two basic interrelated issues: production and prices. Overproduction would cause prices to drop, which in turn would produce an increase in output in order for the producers to maintain their levels of revenue. On the other hand, cuts in production would reduce the share of Opec oil in the world market.[1]

Early in January, Saudi Arabia, Indonesia, and Venezuela warned that if other members violated last December's roll-over agreement, they would not consider themselves bound by it.[2]

The internal divisions in Opec inevitably involved the question of production versus prices. On 18 January, Opec President Rilwanu Lukman stated that "quotas are far more important than pricing." He explained that while Opec had not abandoned the $18 a barrel target "it would be ridiculous to expect prices to hold rock solid at $18." Yet he noted that some Opec members were offering discounts in various forms in order to move their oil to market. He insisted that members adhere strictly to Opec agreements on production quotas (15.06m. b/d, not including Iraq) and official prices. Nevertheless, he stressed that the non-Opec restraint was the key to price stability. He concluded by asserting, "We expect to see prices firming over the next few months."[3]

The deep antagonism between Saudi Arabia and Iran (see chapter on Saudi Arabia), and mutual accusations of cheating on production and prices prevailed throughout the year. Early in January 1988, Iranian deputy oil minister Kazem-pur Ardebili accused Saudi Arabia of netbacking. On 14 January, Saudi Arabia described the allegation as totally devoid of truth, and an official of the Saudi Oil Ministry said:

> I am surprised at such a statement from the Iranian deputy oil minister, who is personally responsible for continuously giving discounts on sales of Iranian crude to all customers, since it is Iranian discounts which have reached around $3bn. that are the real cause of the collapse in prices.[4]

In February and March, when Iran, Saudi Arabia, and Nigeria adjusted their prices to market-related pricing, production began to increase far beyond the 15.06m. b/d. On 18 February, Algerian Minister of Energy and Petrochemical Industries Belkacem Nabi complained that the difference between official and spot-market prices for Algerian crudes was more than $2.40 per barrel, and he declared: "We cannot ask our customers to accept this kind of gap." He felt that the level of the 13 Opec members' production had to come down, and he stressed that Opec members have to decide whether they were going to defend the price. He asserted that 16m. b/d might be the right level for Opec output. He charged that members declare for $18 a barrel and at the same time give discounts.[5]

Early in March, as a result of a heavy glut in the oil market, the price of crude was pushed down to below $14 a barrel. This prompted some members to demand the convening of the Price Monitoring Committee; some members even called for an emergency session of the conference. While Algeria asked for a cut in production, Saudi Arabia opposed any cut in output.[6] President Lukman opposed any hasty action.

The convening of the Price Committee became a highly controversial issue among Opec members. In mid-March, Iran, Libya, and Algeria were vigorously agitating for convening the committee (members: Algeria, Saudi Arabia, Venezuela, Nigeria, and Indonesia). On 23 March, Saudi Arabia Oil Minister Hisham Nazir declared that it was not urgent to convene the committee. Thereupon, Algeria charged that Nazir's statement caused the price of Brent Crude (North Sea benchmark crude) to drop to $14 a barrel. The issue of convening the Price Committee brought the basic divisions in Opec to the surface. The Persian Gulf producers (members of the GCC) opposed any measures that would curtail oil production and raise prices, which would result in a repetition of the 1986 fiasco. The radical producers, on the other hand, wanted to cut production — of the big producers — which would raise prices. Meanwhile, practically all members based their price structures on the market-related prices of Dubai and Oman. At the end of March, it was announced that the Price Committee would meet in Vienna on 9 April. The very announcement produced a swift rise in oil prices. Brent Crude, which traded at $14 a barrel, jumped to $15.33.

CONSULTATIVE CONFERENCE IN APRIL

Ever since 1981, when the demand for Opec oil began to drop steadily and the non-Opec producers began to play an ever-growing role in the world petroleum supply market, Opec made repeated efforts to bring them into some sort of an international oil cartel. Opec's efforts failed with the great producers.[7] Opec leaders contacted and even negotiated with the smaller non-Opec producers and obtained promises of cutting production but not full commitments. In 1988, an attempt was made by some non-Opec producers not to join Opec, but to reach some basis of cooperation.

Seven non-Opec producers — Mexico, Oman, Egypt, China, Malaysia, Colombia, and Angola — met in London in the Mexico Embassy during March to discuss measures of cooperation with Opec in view of the constant deterioration of world petroleum prices. Norway, the USSR, and Brunei were also invited, but did not respond; Colombia withdrew. The remaining six were in contact with Opec officials; when it was announced that the Price Committee was to meet in Vienna on 9 April, the six non-Opec representatives were invited. The Price Committee, with the addition of Kuwait, negotiated with the six. The meeting between the two groups was scheduled for 23 April; this was to be followed, two days later, by a consultative conference of all the members to respond to any deal worked out with the non-Opec producers. In the negotiations, the committee members were sharply divided: Iran called for an across-the-board 5%–10% cut; Indonesia, Nigeria, and Venezuela pressed for production cuts, while Saudi Arabia advocated a barrel-for-barrel cut between the two groups.

On 27 April the non-Opec group submitted its proposal: it would cut its exports by 5%, about 183,000 b/d during May and June. In return, Opec members would reduce their output by 5% during the same period. The members of the Price Committee and Kuwait responded with three different proposals: that the non-Opec producers increase their cuts to 300,000 b/d instead of 183,000 b/d, and Opec's cut be limited to 500,000 b/d; that the non-Opec producers' cut be based on barrel-for-barrel by Opec; and that there be no cut in Opec production, but imposed adherence to quota discipline.

On the following day, the Opec consultative conference opened in Vienna to deal with the six non-Opec producers' proposal. After rehashing the established group positions, the proposal was rejected. The conference recommended the appointment of a committee of experts to deal with definitions of crude oil production under Opec rules (issue condensates). In May, Saudi Arabian Oil Minister Hisham Nazir justified his government's rejection of the proposal and indicated that his country's attitude would be the same at the conference in June. Iranian Oil Minister Gholam Reza Agazadeh replied by attacking Saudi Arabia's position that it would not reduce a single barrel from its quota, and urged the other members to force Saudi Arabia to agree to the majority position.[8]

In a press statement on 5 May, Venezuela's minister of energy and mines declared that had Opec accepted the non-Opec producers' proposal of a 5% cut in production "it would have had a tremendous positive psychological impact on the market, apart from meaning that production in the second quarter would be cut by some 500,000 b/d which would have a tangible effect...Prices today would be $1 per barrel higher than they are."[9]

In anticipation of an agreement between Opec and non-Opec producers to cut production, oil prices in early April jumped to the highest level of the year. West Texas Intermediate (WTI) was traded at $17.85 a barrel. After the non-Opec offer was rejected prices began to weaken. Nevertheless, early in May prices began to stabilize in anticipation of the conference early in June. WTI was traded at $17 a barrel.

A most devastating picture of Opec after the failure of the consultative conference was given by the editor of the *Middle East Economic Survey (MEES),* Ian Seymour, reporting from the conference in Vienna:

> At this stage, the way forward for Opec looks less clear than at almost any point in its history. What seems to be happening is that Opec is confronted with a whole slate of first-order problems — relations with the non-Opec producers, quota allocations in the light of widely differing perceptions of supply and demand, a probable renewed effort to overcome the perennial impasse of the Iraqi quota, and a veritable minefield of potential booby traps embedded in the forthcoming efforts to iron out production definitions — at a time when relations within Opec have reached a new low. The Vienna consultative conference must certainly rank as one of the worst tempered Opec gatherings on record in terms of barbed and hostile exchanges between the participants.[10]

THE 11–14 JUNE CONFERENCE IN VIENNA

As the midyear conference in June approached, two committees of experts were to meet in Vienna to prepare studies on some of the issues on the conference agenda. The Economic Commission Board was to review the current and projected state of the oil market, with particular reference to supply/demand forecast for the second half of 1988. It was to meet on 30 May. The special committee set up to deal with definitions of crude oil production under Opec rules was to meet on 2 June. The main concern of the conference, however, was the perennial question of production and prices as affected by the various groupings within Opec and the impact of external events.

After the US attack on Iranian installations in the Gulf in April (see chapter on the Iraqi-Iranian War), prices of crude oil rose. Brent was trading at $18 a barrel. A few days later, however, prices dropped by $1 a barrel, because the markets did not believe that a long-term threat to oil supplies existed.[11]

In the middle of May, the Saudi oil minister declared that overproduction of at least six Opec members was the main cause of weak oil prices.[12] Output of Opec producers in May was above agreed quotas. It averaged 18.6m. b/d, up from the 17.5m. b/d average during the first quarter of 1988. The biggest overproducer was the UAE. The conference was, naturally, to take up the issues of production and prices.

The conference which opened on 11 June[13] had four options before it concerning how to tackle the major issue: (1) reduce the overall output ceiling and individual quotas in concert with reciprocal cutbacks by non-Opec exporters; (2) leave ceiling and quotas as they are; (3) increase the ceiling and quotas for the second half of the year; or (4) leave ceiling and quotas as they are for the third quarter, with a possibility for an increase in the fourth quarter.[14]

The differences among the groups were so sharp that the conference adjourned for a day. The immediate pressing issue was whether to change the production agreement of the 12 members to limit it to 15.06m. b/d. The limit had been extended in December and was to expire on 30 June. The other issue was support for the $18 price. After four days of bitter debate, the conference decided to extend the production agreement to the end of 1988. This decision could be seen either as a rigid position of the differing groupings, or as a compromise. The Gulf member states insisted on production increase, while the radical member states demanded a production decrease. Iraq continued to refuse to sign. The UAE was dissatisfied with its quota. The issue of the non-Opec negotiations was largely ignored. The next meeting was set for 21 November in Vienna.[15]

In the week following the conference, the prices of crude dropped 50 cents a barrel. Buyers in Japan were discussing reduced contract prices with Iran, Kuwait, and Saudi Arabia. One week later, Iran, Libya, Algeria, and Venezuela asked for an emergency meeting to discuss ways of halting the slide in world oil prices. The Gulf Arab states opposed calling an emergency meeting. Prices were $15 a barrel.[16]

The June 1988 conference no doubt marked a low point in Opec's history. The negotiations with the non-Opec producers came to nothing in an atmosphere of near contempt. The divisions within the organization became sharper than ever on the issue of overall production and quotas. All the conference could do was extend the existing agreement. A number of members were dissatisfied with their quotas. Contract customers were determined to lower prices and reduce the quantities to be lifted. The world oil market was unstable.

BETWEEN CONFERENCES

PRODUCTION AND PRICES

Developments after the June conference followed the same pattern of difficulties as before, but with perhaps greater intensity. Early in July, former Indonesian energy minister Dr. Subroto was named Opec secretary-general. On this occasion, Subroto stated that overproduction, high stocks, and failure to bring back Iraq into the Opec quota system were responsible for the weak oil prices. After the conference, spot-market prices for crude oil fell by about $1 a barrel. The situation was aggravated when Abu Dhabi ordered the producing companies operating in the emirate to increase oil production.[17]

Iran thereupon accused Saudi Arabia and the Gulf producers of causing the decline in the oil prices. On 13 July, Tehran Radio declared that the Saudis were undermining Opec interests by pursuing a market share policy and the "developments in the oil market over the past month reveal the political intentions of the Opec minority wing — Kuwait, Saudi Arabia, the UAE, Qatar, and Iraq — to push down oil prices."[18]

On 24 July, Saudi King Fahd said about oil and Opec:

> We reduced our oil production from 10m. b/d to 4.35m. b/d to preserve Opec. Regrettably it is a grave error for any Opec country to sell at a price lower than the official price, but this is reported in the press. You can hide anything except oil. You cannot put it in your pocket. You sell oil to the companies and the companies say they bought it for $16 a barrel when the official price is $18 a barrel. You cannot hide that.

He concluded by asserting that "despite the drop in the state's revenues from oil, both the Kingdom and its citizens are doing well."[19]

A deep split in Opec broke out between the Gulf Arab producers and the other producers. Saudi Arabia was to produce less than its quota at the beginning of 1988, but when the others did not follow suit, Saudi Arabia increased production above its quota. The UAE never abided by its quota. Opec as a whole had been producing more than the demand for its oil. Prices came down.[20]

It has not been clearly established what motivated the Gulf producers to reduce prices. Some analysts believe that it was aimed at hurting Iran in its war with Iraq. Others believe that it was an effort to reach agreement in Opec. But a careful examination of the policies of the big Gulf producers reveals that the motive must have been their determination to retain for Opec the role of the great, if not the exclusive, oil supplier of the world markets, previously called by Saudi Arabia a "fair share" of the market policy, but which ended in a disastrous failure. Whatever the motive, after the end of the June conference, the price of crude oil slid by about $2 a barrel. For a while, because of the Iranian airbus tragedy and the explosion of an oil platform in the North Sea, prices climbed upward, but they soon continued to decline.[21]

END OF THE IRAQI-IRANIAN WAR AND ITS IMPACT

As the UN Security Council was making repeated efforts to establish first a cease-fire and ultimately peace between Iran and Iraq, the question arose as to what the impact of Security Council success would be on Opec and on the oil supply market.

Opinion differed. On 20 July, UAE Oil Minister Mani' Sa'id al-'Utayba said that he believed that a cease-fire in the Gulf War would lead to greater coordination in Opec and thus to higher oil prices. He noted that the market reacted favorably. He asserted: "The end of the Iran-Iraq War will make Opec strong and put it in the leadership once more."

On the same day, US Secretary of Energy John Herrington said that an end to the Gulf War could mean an extra 2m.–3m. b/d of oil in the market within a year or two, causing problems for US energy policy. War debts and reconstruction would increase oil production and as a result "you are going to see excess oil production, in my estimation. It may not happen in the short run, but you are going to see it in the long run. I am talking of one year, two years if the war ends."[22] If this prediction came true prices would be forced down, which would mean that "the US Government in coming years is going to have to deal with the viability of the US oil and gas industry on a very critical level."[23]

The answer to these speculations was given by the parties concerned. UN Security Council Resolution 598 was adopted in July,[24] and both belligerents accepted it on 20 August. Early in September, Iranian Deputy Oil Minister Kazem-pur Ardebili stated that the long-term policy was to raise production capacity to 4.5m. b/d. He maintained that Iran's intention was to stick to its present Opec-set production quota of about 2.4m. b/d and to work within Opec to eliminate excess output in support of an $18 a barrel price. He called on Saudi Arabia and Kuwait to change their three-year-old policy of overproduction that was aimed at reducing prices to put pressure on Iran. As regards Iraq's request for production parity with Iran (about which later), Ardebili said: "By no means can there be parity between Iranian and Iraqi output. We insist that Iraq be brought into the Opec quota." Ardebili believed that the reconstruction of Iran and Iraq would result in overproduction.[25]

While touring the Gulf states early in October, Iraqi Oil Minister 'Isam 'Abd al-Rahim al-Shalabi said in Kuwait:

> Now, after the cease- fire, people are asking us to reduce our production. But, what do we do about reconstruction, about our debts, about the production we lost during the last eight years? In the early days of the war, our output fell from 3.7m. b/d to 650,000 b/d. Other countries took advantage of this and we suffered. Now we want it back. So if it is going to be parity, then we will have to add over and above what we have lost during the war in order to finance reconstruction and pay back our debts. As a result of the war, Iraq is indebted to many countries and banks, and the only source of income with which to pay those debts is crude oil.[26]

The weekly *US News and World Report* noted early in September that the prospects of rising output from Iran and Iraq to rebuild their war-battered economies, came at a time when Opec countries were already pumping about 20m. b/d, some 3.5m. b/d above the official ceiling. The highest quota violators seemed to have been Saudi Arabia, Kuwait, and the UAE.[27]

THE UAE POSITION

During the Iraqi-Iranian War primarily Abu Dhabi's oil reserves rose greatly, and it was classified as potentially the third great ME producer, after Saudi Arabia and Kuwait. It was very dissatisfied with its quota of 948,000 b/d (the other producer in the group was Dubai).

On 14 February, UAE Oil Minister Mani' Sa'id al-'Utayba announced that the UAE had reduced oil production to below its quota in an effort to maintain the $18 a barrel price. The spot market price was $16. Al-'Utayba denied reports that the UAE offered discounts to its oil customers.[28] About two months later, the Abu Dhabi National Oil Company had offered its term-contract customers in Japan in March retroactive financial compensation to help offset the difference between official prices and the market prices during December 1987 and January-February 1988. This entailed 90 cents a barrel for lifting in December, $1.50 a barrel in January, and $2 for lifting in February, in spite of the oil minister's declaration that his country would not deviate from the official prices.[29]

Early in July, after the end of the June conference, two disturbing factors increased tension in Opec: oil price deterioration, and production indiscipline, especially the UAE unilateral repudiation of the Opec quota. Yet the organization opposed any possibility of convening an emergency conference or even a meeting of the Price Committee. The objectors to the meeting were the Gulf producing members under the leadership of Saudi Arabia and Kuwait. The UAE raising its production from 948,000 b/d quota to 1.5 m. b/d evoked strong protests from Indonesia and Ecuador.[30]

About the same time, *MEES* analyzed the situation of the UAE action:

> The UAE has now definitely repudiated the quota of 948,000 b/d allocated to it under the current Opec production agreement which was renewed until the end of 1988 at the Opec conference in Vienna last month. Instead the UAE has unilaterally adopted what it described as an "unofficial" quota of 1.5m. b/d.

This was taken to be final and nonnegotiable, whatever pressures might be forthcoming from Opec members or elsewhere.[31]

PRICE MONITORING COMMITTEE

After grave and long hesitation, the Price Committee decided to meet on 3 August in Lausanne, Switzerland. At the same time it was announced that the secretary-general would attempt to tackle the most pressing issue in Opec — UAE overproduction — by visiting Abu Dhabi to persuade the UAE to abide by its official Opec quota.[32] The very act of convening the Price Committee was hazardous for its possible impact on the market and on prices. Moreover, the committee itself was powerless to act on the issues; it could only call for an extraordinary session of the conference to deal with the issues. The major problem was overproduction of the Gulf producers. Total July production averaged 19m. b/d. Secretary-General Dr. Subroto visited the UAE and spoke with Shaykh Zayid who assured him that his country would abide by the Opec decision.[33]

On 3 August, the price committee met in Lausanne and had before it six items: (1) Prices: Opec members were divided on the question of lower oil prices. The Gulf Arab producers were not disturbed by the drop in prices. While the others were very anxious to raise prices as rapidly and as high as possible, Iran's oil revenue went down 22% during the first half of 1988, to an estimated $3.7bn., compared with the first six months of 1987. (2) Iraq's quota: Iraq demanded that its production quota be equal to that of Iran, but Iran strenuously objected to parity. Other members also objected to parity for Iraq, because they would have to contribute from their shares to Iraq's increase, or increase the overall ceiling. (3) UAE's overproduction by 50% of its quota. (4) The Partitioned Zone: Saudi Arabia and Kuwait, which shared the 200,000–300,000 b/d gave the proceeds from the zone's oil to Iraq, and it was not included in the quotas of the two partners. After the cease-fire, the two owners were pressured to include the oil of the zone in their quotas. (5) Condensates: the various types of condensates were not included in the export quotas. The conference asked the committee to submit recommended definitions. Finally, (6) the committee was to find a solution for the non-Opec producers' efforts to stabilize the market. The committee also received the report of the secretary-general of his visit to the UAE and its outcome.

The price committee failed to arrive at any conclusions and decided to meet again. The result was a drop in oil prices of about $1 a barrel. Brent dropped to about $14.50, some $4.50 below the official Opec target.[34]

THE 21–28 NOVEMBER CONFERENCE IN VIENNA

PRODUCTION AND PRICES

It would seem that as the November conference was approaching, the outstanding difficulties became more intense and more threatening. The basic issues of production and price levels, which caused the divisions, became more acute and endangered the very existence of the organization. The main actors in the drama remained the same. Early in September, it was reported that the UAE production in July averaged 1.45m. b/d; it rose to 1.7m. b/d in August and was programmed to increase to 1.95m. b/d in September.[35] On 12 September, Abu Dhabi's crown prince repeated the UAE demand for an Opec quota that would give his country "its natural weight among the oil-producing countries." He stressed that the UAE's allocated quota (948,000 b/d) was not fair and did not match the large oil potential of the emirate.[36] Four days later, the 28th anniversary of Opec's founding, the crown prince urged Opec to adopt an output and pricing structure which would ensure that members adhere to their quotas. About the UAE policy he declared. "Our oil policy calls for defending the organization, safeguarding its achievements, and working inside and outside Opec so as to reach a wise oil policy which guarantees the rights of all these producing states."

The impact of these developments on the oil price was immediate. On 6 September, oil prices hit a seven-year low on the international spot market. Brent dropped to $13.75 for cargoes to be lifted in October. The glut was caused by Opec members cheating and the ineffective Iran-Iraq cease-fire. Opec production reached 20m. b/d. *The New York Times* reported that oil prices had dropped to the lowest level since late 1986; WTI was sold at $14.16 a barrel.[37]

Warnings that oil prices could drop below $10 a barrel prompted Opec to convene a meeting of the Price Committee. On 12 September, spot market prices dropped to $11.13 a barrel; Brent sold at $12.97. The major cause of the price deterioration was overproduction by Opec members, particularly the Gulf producers. When it was announced that the Price Committee was to meet on 25–26 September in Madrid, oil prices went up by about 50 cents a barrel. Analysts were, however, skeptical about the rise. The main overproducers were the UAE, Kuwait, Iraq, and Saudi Arabia.[38]

Opec's production practices were in conflict with the world statistical economic oil production and consumption. Opec production in the first half of 1988 rose 11% over the same period the previous year. Non-Opec, non-Communist production rose during the same period by 3%. World oil consumption during the same period went up by 2%.[39]

PRICE COMMITTEE MEETING (25–26 SEPTEMBER)

At the conclusion of its two-day meeting in Madrid on 26 September, the Price Committee stated:

> It is essential that Opec must review its operation and strategies in the context of current circumstances, for the short, medium and long terms, especially concerning the price of oil and production mechanisms to support it, in the light of the expressed positions of member countries.

It decided to meet on 20 October in Madrid jointly with the Long-Term Strategy Committee with the addition of Iran, Iraq, and Kuwait.[40]

Assessing the outcome of the two-day meeting of the Price Committee, the editor of *MEES*, Ian Seymour, said: "Of course, none of the problems of production indiscipline, which are threatening to bring about another price crash, have been solved or even alleviated." He noted that the current production agreement was still suffering from *de facto* nonrecognition by three major Opec countries, Iran, Iraq, and the UAE as well as widespread violations of quotas by other members.[41]

The production and prices situation was rapidly deteriorating, and when Saudi Arabia decided to increase its 4.34m. b/d in September to 5.7m. b/d, it precipitated a very serious problem. The abandonment of its quota was a clear challenge to the constant quota violators to restrain output or face the consequences of a flooded market.[42] On 30 September, oil prices fell sharply on signs that Saudi Arabia was increasing production in an already glutted market. Prices tumbled to their lowest levels in more than two years.[43]

LOW EBB IN OCTOBER

October was Opec's most difficult month in 1988. Production discipline was practically nonexistent, prices were fluctuating but mostly downward; the basic differences between the groups intensified, and at times it looked as if the very existence of the organization was at stake. The scheduled conference of 21 November would have to adopt very strong measures to rehabilitate the organization.

On 3 October, Brent was traded at $12 a barrel for December delivery. The Iranian oil minister accused four Opec members — Saudi Arabia, Iraq, Kuwait, and the UAE — of flooding the market. On the next day, Brent fell to $11.35 in Tokyo. On 7 October, Dubai oil sold in London at $9.20 a barrel. Opec members were selling oil at prices linked to spot market levels, which were about $8 below Opec's reference price of $18.

Saudi Arabia's aims were explained as keeping prices low until financial hardship would force Opec members to quota discipline. Rumors were circulating that Saudi Arabia was about to leave Opec. Saudi Arabian Oil Minister Hisham Nazir promptly denied the rumors, but King Fahd declared that his country would not accept other producers' overproduction at its expense. Saudi Arabia would reduce its production level only after the other members abided by their quota assignments.[44]

On the other hand, *The New York Times* reported that Iran and Iraq had pledged for reconstruction — estimated at $30bn. — increasing oil production, a move that prompted Saudi Arabia to threaten the members to raise its own output to guarantee a further drop in oil prices.[45]

By mid-October, the International Energy Agency (IEA) estimated that non-Opec producers were averaging an output of 29.1m. b/d in the third quarter of 1988. Average Opec production in the same period was 20m. b/d — the highest quarterly output since 1980. Demand for Opec crude was only 17.5m. b/d.[46]

As the meeting of the Opec committee approached, the GCC met in Riyadh on 16 October and issued a statement that envisaged a total output of 19m. b/d with quotas increased on proportional lines from a base ceiling of 17.429m. b/d, which included an Iran-Iraq parity allocation of 2.369m. b/d for each for 1989. This was the recommendation of the GCC to the joint committee, which was to meet in Madrid on 20 October.[47] Anticipating that the joint committee would recommend reduced Opec output, prices rose, and WTI went up on the New York Mercantile Exchange to $14.92 a barrel.[48]

According to *Time* magazine, instead of causing a cut in oil production, the Iran-Iraq cease-fire unleashed a price war. Three key producers, Saudi Arabia, Kuwait, and the UAE, raised output, pushing Opec daily production to 21m. barrels, 2m. above current demand. The resultant glut brought down the spot price to just above $10 a barrel. Libya called for an emergency conference which was promptly rejected by Iraqi Oil Minister al-Shalabi. Norway and Mexico threatened to increase output unless Opec reimposed production discipline.

After the 1979 second oil crisis, Opec produced 60% of the world's oil output. In October, it had fallen to 40%. Consumers learned to be less dependent on Opec oil. The UAE cut prices in order to dispose of the increased output of over 1.5m. b/d. Saudi Arabia declared on 4 October that it "had done enough for Opec" and would no longer accept unequal production quotas.[49]

The joint committee met for three days (20–23 October) and could not achieve anything tangible except issue a very ambiguous statement. It was to meet again on 17 November, in Vienna, just before the opening of the conference. A plan to reduce the production level by about 3m. b/d was reportedly rejected by Iran. Prices fell to $13 a barrel.[50]

At the end of October, *MEES* reported that the UAE had produced 1.95m. b/d in September, 1.9m. b/d in October, and was programmed for the same level in November.[51]

The latest estimate of supply and demand in the November issue of the IEA's monthly *Oil Market Report* put Opec's crude output in October at 21.1m. b/d, the highest monthly average in more than four years, and some 3.3m. b/d over the present 15.06m. b/d ceiling plus Iraqi production of 2.7m. b/d. Saudi Arabia's crude output rose to an average of 5.5 m. b/d (excluding the neutral zone); Kuwait averaged 1.5m. b/d (also excluding the neutral zone), and the UAE averaged 2m. b/d, well in excess of its self-proclaimed quota of 1.5m. b/d.[52]

Despite the efforts and pledges to restrict production, output in November continued to rise. Early in the month, Opec was reported to have reached a seven-year high in oil output of nearly 23m. b/d. Saudi Arabia was pumping about 7m. b/d, and the UAE production was reaching 2m. b/d.[53] In the middle of November it was reported that Dubai crude was trading at $10.50, $7 below the Opec reference price.[54]

THE CONFERENCE

The conference opened in Vienna on 21 November, and set 23 November as a deadline for its attempt to heal the rift between Iran and Iraq. However, when Iran refused on

23 November to concede to Iraq's demand for quota parity, the conference adjourned for a day for the resumption of formal talks. Meanwhile, oil prices dropped. Four days later it was reported that an accord on production limits had been reached after Iran agreed to grant Iraq production parity with itself. The Iranian delegate left for Tehran to get his government's approval. The total overall production ceiling was to be limited to 18.5m. b/d; Iran and Iraq were each given 2.6m. b/d, the price target was $18 a barrel. Oil prices moved upward.[55]

The following day, the conference talks on a package deal to cut production were stalled by Saudi Arabia's last-minute proposal that the Opec oil prices be pegged at $15–$18 a barrel.[56] Iran rejected the proposal. For a while it looked as if the package deal was not going to be accepted and that the Opec committee and conference had failed. However, under pressure from the majority, Saudi Arabia withdrew its proposal and the conference was able to conclude its labors successfully.[57]

The conference faced the same six issues as the Price Committee (outlined above) plus the committee's reports. After 12 days of intense negotiations, including committee sessions prior to the conference, Opec concluded its conference on 28 November with a new agreement on production, complete with definitions of quotas and condensates. The resolution signed in Vienna provided for an Opec production ceiling of 18.5m. b/d for the first half of 1989. The two main positive achievements were the deblocking of the Iran-Iraq impasse and the final agreement on the definitions of condensates.[58] What remained unresolved was the UAE quota observance. Under the Opec agreement it was granted 988,000 b/d, but the UAE output was 1.5m. b/d. The promises given by the UAE oil minister were very ambiguous.

THE AGREEMENT

(1) Overall production ceiling of 18.5m. b/d for all 13 members.

(2) Target price $18 a barrel to be achieved as soon as possible.[59]

(3) In the event of confirmed violation of allocated production level by any member country, other member countries will consider themselves free of their obligations under the resolution.

(4) Setting up a monitoring committee composed of Algeria, Indonesia, Iran, Iraq, Kuwait, Nigeria, Saudi Arabia, and Venezuela with a mandate to (a) monitor the evolution of market prices with a view to ensuring stability; (b) supervise the strict adherence of member countries to the stipulated production levels; and (c) take the necessary steps to correct any violations; the committee was to meet in March 1989 to review the outcome of the agreement.

(5) The same committee was to be responsible for preparing a long-term strategy, including the allocation of permanent quotas, to be presented to the conference.

(6) Regarding non-Opec producers, Algeria, Indonesia, Kuwait, Nigeria, Saudi Arabia, and Venezuela were mandated to contact non-Opec producing/exporting countries with a view to soliciting their cooperation in support of market stability through production cuts.

(7) The conference also adopted definitions on condensates to distinguish between crude and gas condensates as regards quotas.

(8) As regards quotas, the conference granted parity to Iraq and Iran, but both were given an increase in the percentage of the 18.5m. b/d, 2.64m. b/d instead of 2.515m. b/d, with proportionate reductions for the other 11 members.[60] The quota was based

on the December 1986 agreement, not signed by Iraq. The Riyadh October GCC formula, though not accepted, served as a base for the 28 November agreement. The conference was to convene again on 5 June 1989.[61]

AFTER THE NOVEMBER CONFERENCE

November production, regardless of the determination to restore production beginning 1 January 1989, reached a new peak of nearly 23m. b/d.[62] The nominations for December were as high or even higher than the actual output in November.[63]

In view of the UAE experience with Opec during 1988, the question arose whether the organization could set oil prices. On 12 December, in an interview with the Sharja daily *al-Khalij,* UAE Oil Minister al-'Utayba said:

> Setting prices is no longer Opec's responsibility. At the beginning of 1988 Opec started to price its crude on the basis of the spot market, like any other producer. One thing should be made clear. Determining prices is the province of the oil market, and Opec came to this conclusion after it failed to play the role of price setter on its own. We might have been able to play this role in coordination with all the non-Opec producers, who at present account for more than 60% of world production. We must distinguish between setting prices, and the parties who do so, and deciding on production levels. This leads us to the fact that if Opec produced 23m.–24m. b/d it could stay at this level of production without any increases for the period until the oil market began to reflect better prices and the price reached $18 a barrel, which is the goal we are aiming for, and then increase it gradually, while not forgetting our past experience when we raised the price by astronomical amounts.[64]

After the November Opec production agreement, prices for Brent and Dubai remained steady and practically unchanged, the former at $14.27 and the latter at $11.60. However, when the report of November's increased production became known, downward pressure on prices was being exerted.[65]

In summarizing the developments of 1988, the *Petroleum Economist (PE)* stressed overproduction as the perennial problem of Opec, which was exacerbated by the ending of the Gulf War, resulting in Opec producing far more than the market required.[66] The *PE* also noted editorially that production during the year was well above the nominal quotas. Inevitably the prices declined.

> The oversupply was evidence that the sellers, or most of them, had abandoned the official reference price of $18 and were, by one device or another, selling at a discount. On the spot market the price of Brent blend had sagged from $18 at the beginning of 1988 to below $15 by March. With various ups and downs it reached a low of $12 in October. It recovered to almost $15 after the November agreement, but has since eased off.[67]

Whom did the Opec leaders blame for their almost disastrous difficulties? Except for the UAE oil minister's denial to Opec of the price-setting power, and his open assertion that Opec's astronomical oil prices were responsible for the prolonged oil crisis, a number of Opec leaders blamed outsiders, the non-Opec producers and the Western oil consumers, for the deterioration of and the instability in the oil market.

Addressing the Third International Energy Conference on 6 December 1988, Opec Secretary-General Dr. Subroto discussed the November agreement and its problems. He said: "Foremost among the first set of problems is the attitude of most non-Opec oil producers." They have continually increased their oil production levels by simply undercutting Opec prices and thus aggravating the deterioration in world oil prices and "undermining our organization's ability to continue its price defense policy and market leadership." He attacked Western economic and fiscal policies for reducing oil consumption.[68]

In answer to a question on 5 December as to what the non-Opec producers should be doing to support oil prices, Iraqi Oil Minister al-Shalabi replied:

> The Opec countries cannot bear the whole burden of price support on their own. The non-Opec producers have been taking advantage of Opec and not been acting responsibly in this regard. All of them — including the USSR and the North Sea — should do their share in restraining output and defending prices.[69]

An Opec editorial about the November conference agreement, entitled "A Turning Point," said about the non-Opec producers:

> We must, however reiterate that this agreement did not come about without much sacrifice on the part of Opec member countries. In spite of their dire economic situation, they had to rein in production to well below their capacity, to ensure a stable oil market. Yet, as good as this agreement may be, if it is to provide more than a breathing space, then it urgently requires support from other producers. With this in mind, we call on all major non-Opec producers to take steps to rein in their production — only by so doing will they be seen to be shouldering their responsibility. Theirs is not to reap where they did not sow, but to join Opec in stabilizing the market, from which they all benefit.[70]

Thus by the end of the tempestuous year and the final patching-up of the November agreement, Opec refused to blame itself for its misfortunes and found scapegoats for all its ills.

Before assessing the ME oil developments in 1988 we should deal with the expansion of the oil-producing countries into the downstream operations.

DOWNSTREAM OPERATIONS

The pattern of the struggle of the ME producing countries with the foreign concessionary companies to nationalize their oil industry developed along two lines: financial and physical. The financial line was the level of royalty payments. The original provisions in the concessions called for 16% of company's profits or 4–6 shillings per ton of oil produced. By the early 1950s it was changed to 50% profits, and in the 1970s it reached 85% of profits and 20% royalties. It ended with participation in the foreign companies, first 25%, 60% and, in 1976, total nationalization.

The physical line began when the producing countries forced the companies to utilize the gas that was separated from the oil and flared. First the gas was used for power generation of company plants, then for general industrial use, then for home use and ultimately the gas, both separated from the oil and from gas mines, was liquified as LPG and LNG for export. The next step was the establishment of national oil companies. At first their powers and functions were limited, but slowly they assumed greater and greater powers and functions and were able to operate the industry after nationalization.

Oil industry operations consist of four stages: production, refining, transportation, and marketing. The first is called "upstream;" the other three are called the "downstream" phases. The concessionary companies were integrated, that is, they performed all four operations. The major achievement of nationalization was the upstream, production phase. The activation of the downstream phases was determined by each producer's circumstances. While some countries had refineries built by the foreign companies, which supplied refined oil products for local consumption and for export, others had very limited refining facilities and they launched a refinery-building program. The bulk of oil remained crude. In fact, one of the Opec membership requirements is export of crude; Opec did not and does not deal with refined oil. Some countries began building tanker fleets to enter the transportation field. The most difficult phase was marketing, because it was very complex and very costly, involving marketing networks, wholesale bulk distributing facilities, and thousands of retail stations.

Of the four phases of the industry, upstream production was the most profitable, and it even paid for some of the very costly operations of the downstream operations. After the major integrated companies operating in the ME lost their concessions, they began to dispose of their refining and distribution facilities in Europe, which some ME producers acquired (see *MECS* 1987, pp. 290–91). The latest development is that Opec members have entered some downstream operations in foreign countries to enable them to dispose of great quantities of oil as well as reap profits from these operations.

SAUDI-TEXACO DEAL

After the Aramco companies were nationalized, the companies continued to lift their shares of Saudi oil under a special price agreement. When Texaco was undergoing a bankruptcy restructuring, Saudi Arabia entered into exploratory talks about acquiring some of Texaco's facilities. In the middle of July, it was reported that Saudi Arabia was about to buy a 50% share in three of Texaco's huge refineries and a marketing network in 23 East Coast and Gulf Coast states. A key provision of the deal was the Saudi Arabian commitment to supply up to 600,000 b/d of crude to the three refineries, representing 69.4% of the company's total refining capacity of 886,000 b/d. The deal would be worth an estimated $2bn. to Texaco.[71]

On 10 November, the Saudi Arabian oil minister and the president of Texaco signed in London the definitive agreement, which was to become operative on 31 December and was to last for 20 years. It provided for organizing a new joint venture company, Star Enterprise, with headquarters in Houston, Texas; Saudi Arabia would own 50%, for which it would pay $812m. and supply 600,000 b/d of crude. Included were Texaco's three major refineries: Port Arthur, Texas (250,000 b/d capacity), Convent, Louisiana (225,000 b/d capacity), and Delaware City, Delaware (140,000 b/d capacity). Texaco's marketing facilities included in the deal consisted of 49 terminals, 1,450 owned or leased service stations, and a branded distribution network of more than 10,000 stations. The agreement covered Texaco's refining and marketing facilities in 23 East Coast and Gulf Coast states and the District of Columbia.[72]

The importance of this new and almost revolutionary undertaking was assessed by the parties involved and by outside analysts. Hisham Nazir declared: "The objective is very simple and that is to create a very strong [Saudi Arabian] oil industry which is able to stand on its feet and remain there in a highly competitive market." He stressed that the deal marked a major initial initiative in a campaign designed to secure for Saudi Arabia its "proper share" in the world oil market. To this end, the Texaco agreement would be followed by a series of similar downstream joint ventures in various markets throughout the world. He declared that Saudi Arabia would embark on such ventures "wherever it is economically viable for us to do so, and whenever we feel that it will secure a market for us — whether in the US, in Europe, in the Far East, or everywhere else."

The Texaco spokesman stated that the Saudi participation was to provide the company with benefits worth an estimated $1.8bn. Saudi Arabia was to provide a major stake in oil refining and marketing in the US, the world's biggest fuel consumer. The editor of *MEES* wrote that the agreement was a great step in Saudi Arabia's oil policy — full downstream integration of the Saudi oil industry by means of joint ventures with powerful players in the world market. *MEED* wrote:

> The deal has substantial implications for Opec. It provides for up to about 17% of the Kingdom's exports in the present quota system to be delivered at market rates rather than Opec prices. Analysts say this will give the Kingdom greater flexibility to deliver crude to the final consumer and retain market share when there is an oil glut in world markets.[73]

KUWAIT AND BRITISH PETROLEUM

Kuwait's oil reserves are second only to those of Saudi Arabia. Oil production in Kuwait, however, did not correspond to its immense reserves. It was perhaps the first state in the region to limit production primarily for conservation. Being small in area, having a relatively small population, and receiving huge revenues from the oil, Kuwait was the ME's most outstanding welfare state.[74] Kuwait undertook, first under British "guidance" and later on its own, foreign investments, especially in oil industry undertakings. It established in London the Kuwait Investment Office (KIO) which managed investments abroad.

British Petroleum (BP; formerly Anglo-Iranian Oil Company), one of the "Seven Sisters" greatest world oil companies, was controlled by the British Government, which held a majority ownership. While the British Government sold its shares, BP offered shares to the public. On 16 October 1987, KIO acquired 9.9% of BP's total shares. In February 1988, the KIO's BP shares reached 21.68% of the company shares. This percentage would entitle Kuwait to a seat on the company's Board of Directors and a voice in the company's management and policies. On 20 February, Kuwaiti Oil Minister 'Ali Khalifa al-Sabah said in London that his country had no plans to seek a management role in BP, and its stake of some 20% was seen only as a long-term investment.[75]

This development alarmed the British Government, and in May it launched a Monopolies' and Mergers' Commission investigation into whether the KIO's stake in BP was against the public interest. On 9 August, Kuwait pledged not to raise its 21.68% stake in BP and to limit its activities in the company. But the British

Government maintained that it could not accept the Kuwait undertaking while the inquiry into the holdings was going on.[76] At the end of September, the commission recommended to Trade and Industry Secretary Lord Young that the Kuwait 21.68% holding in BP was against the public interest. Thereupon, Lord Young ordered the KIO to reduce its holding in BP from 21.68% to 9.9% within 12 months.[77] On 9 October, the Kuwait Government expressed "extreme regret and astonishment" at the British Government's decision to force the KIO to divest itself of more than half of its stake in BP. A Kuwaiti cabinet minister said his government had decided "to do what is necessary to protect its economic interests in Britain." In London, the KIO asked the British Government for an extension of the 12-month limit.[78] Late in December, the Kuwait Government expressed satisfaction with Lord Young's decision to extend the deadline from one year to three years, until 4 October 1991.[79] On 3 January 1989, BP announced that it would buy back 11.7% of its shares from the KIO, which would leave the KIO 9.9%. The buy-back was to cost BP £2.4bn. ($4.3bn.) and would result in a profit for Kuwait of £380m. ($684m.).[80]

OTHER DOWNSTREAM MOVES

In July 1988, it was reported that Venezuela had been acquiring downstream interests in the main consuming countries. It owned 450,000 b/d in foreign refining capacity, of which 250,000 b/d were in the US, and was looking for an additional 250,000 b/d capacity.[81]

Nigeria was driving to acquire downstream assets in consuming countries; it was negotiating with Elf Aquitaine for the purchase of a share in its refining and marketing operations in France.[82]

The UAE was concentrating on increasing downstream investment. The International Petroleum Company said it was considering 10 schemes in marketing, refining, and petrochemicals in 1988. Abu Dhabi was reportedly attempting to increase its 10% stake in the Spanish refining *Compañia Española de Petróles.* During the year, its stake in Total rose from 5% to 9%.[83]

Libya's National Oil Corporation established a new company, Foreign Petroleum Investments Corporation, for the purpose of acquiring downstream facilities abroad. The new corporation was also to act as holding company for two investments already made by Libya — a 70% stake in the Cremona refinery in Italy, and a 50% stake in the 80,000 b/d capacity Coastal refinery in Hamburg, West Germany. Later in the year, Libya acquired oil distribution facilities in Italy and Malta.[84]

The entrance of Opec producers into the downstream operations in the oil-consuming countries is first and foremost the next logical stage of their development as outlined above. The first to enter this field were the big producers because they had the necessary resources, both financial and oil. But the others followed and they were invited to do so by the Saudi oil minister; as noted above, they were not only Gulf producers. The motives for the action was straightforwardly and eloquently presented by Saudi Arabia's oil minister at the press conference on 11 November following the signing of the Texaco-Saudi Arabia agreement. Since the ventures were entered into by individual producers, the not-too-tight bonds which held Opec together must now become even looser. This new development had serious implications for Opec and also for the countries in which the investments were made.[85] The reaction of Britain to the Kuwait BP venture is instructive. There has also been speculation that a combination of the big oil producers and the big international companies might form a new international oil cartel. The future holds the answers to these speculations.

ASSESSMENT

Opec's experiences of the hectic developments of 1988, production levels, price levels, Iraqi-Iranian War, negotiations with non-Opec producers, and constant internal friction and clashes reflected the basic differences among members and their positions on the issues that concerned the Opec conferences and committees. The nature of the organization prevented it from forcing members to abide by decisions; this prompted members to act individually or in groups to advance their interests. The Gulf Arab states, dominated by the big producers, were determined to keep prices at "reasonable" levels in order to achieve a double objective: to dissuade consumers from developing alternatives to oil and to prolong the period of pumping the oil reserves. The indispensable means for achieving this end was a production level that would prevent prices from rising.[86]

On the other hand, the radical states with relatively smaller reserves were determined to make the most of their current production. The only way to achieve that was to cut production, which would drive up prices; the cuts should, of course, be made by the big producers. The divisions in Opec were also grounded in political differences. The first group, conservative, was led by Saudi Arabia; the second group, radical, was led by Iran. When Iran was at war with Iraq, Saudi Arabia openly and defiantly supported Iraq financially and transported Iraqi oil. Iran charged repeatedly that Saudi Arabia's motives were political.[87]

The story of ME oil development in 1988 was the struggle of the two groups of sovereign states within Opec. Cheating, in a great variety of ways, was the most characteristic aspect of the actions of members in the production and prices phases of the industry. Charges and countercharges of cheating on both scores were hurled by one group against the other and by one member against another.

The price of oil in the world markets was determined by the position and charges made by the groups. Table 1 indicates clearly the ups and downs of the oil prices in reaction to what was taking place in the Opec conferences and committees. The first major clash between the groups about production and prices, and the offer of the six non-Opec producers to cut production produced the consultative conference late in April. The outcome was a total failure. The midyear meeting of the conference in June witnessed bitter accusations of cheating on production levels. It achieved nothing. The oil overproduction of Opec members resulted in gluts in the market. The term-contract customers, thereupon, pressed the producers to lower the prices even below the spot-market prices of Oman and Dubai.[88] A number of producers have openly adopted the spot prices. The lower the prices the greater the pressure to increase production to obtain the same revenue. The climax was reached in October when Opec production was about 3m. b/d above the official ceiling. The tension between Iran and Saudi Arabia rose to such a point that rumors were spread that Saudi Arabia had decided to leave Opec.

The Iraqi-Iranian War complicated and aggravated the intergroup and intermember relations in Opec. When the year opened, Iraq was not part of the production agreement and without a quota. After the cease-fire was signed, the battle of quota parity between the two former belligerents broke out; Iran steadfastly and determinedly refused to grant Iraq parity. For a while it looked as if the November conference would fail as had the June meeting. In the end, however, under great pressure, Iran conceded parity to Iraq and the road to agreement was cleared. But could both Iran and Iraq abide by their limited quotas? The answer must inevitably be "no," because both have stated that their oil resources were the only source of funds for their reconstruction plans and their repayment of war debts.

The November conference concluded with an agreement signed by all 13 members; it provided for an overall production ceiling of 18.5m. b/d and an $18 a barrel price target. Has this agreement changed the basic interests of the groups in Opec? It is more than doubtful.

The turning of a number of members into the downstream refining and marketing operations in the Western consuming countries — Saudi Arabia, Texaco — and investments in foreign oil enterprises — Kuwait, BP — have no doubt affected Opec deeply and will weaken further its hold on members.

TABLE 1: 1988 CRUDE OIL PRICES – DOLLARS PER BARREL
(Brent Brand, England; Dubai Fateh, Dubai)

Date	*Brent*	*Dubai Fateh*	*Date*	*Brent*	*Dubai Fateh*
6 January	18.00	15.55	6 July	14.50	12.80
13 January	16.30	15.10	13 July	14.06	12.04
20 January	16.75	15.65	20 July	14.95	13.25
27 January	16.38	15.28	27 July	15.40	13.60
3 February	16.05	15.52	3 August	14.97	13.15
10 February	16.10	15.27	10 August	15.02	13.20
17 February	16.00	15.10	17 August	14.77	13.17
24 February	15.40	14.60	24 August	14.93	13.28
2 March	13.70	13.40	31 August	14.55	12.97
9 March	13.95	12.60	7 September	13.20	11.68
16 March	14.53	13.25	14 September	14.21	12.40
23 March	15.35	13.70	20 September	13.43	11.90
29 March	15.70	14.00	27 September	12.66	10.88
6 April	15.45	13.50	4 October	11.80	9.75
12 April	16.69	15.00	11 October	13.40	10.05
20 April	16.78	15.20	18 October	12.88	11.00
27 April	17.37	15.93	25 October	12.10	10.17
4 May	16.13	14.65	1 November	12.10	10.40
11 May	16.53	15.05	8 November	12.55	10.54
18 May	16.63	14.97	15 November	13.00	10.95
25 May	16.34	14.86	22 November	12.15	9.85
1 June	16.40	14.73	30 November	14.20	11.85
8 June	16.30	14.40			
15 June	15.67	14.15	6 December	14.27	11.60
22 June	15.18	13.55	13 December	15.20	12.50
28 June	14.80	13.12	30 December	16.20	13.35

Source: *MEED*, 2 January 1988–13 January 1989.

TABLE 2: PRODUCTION ACCORDS (Volumes in thousands b/d)

	December 1986 Agreement		*Riyadh 16 October Formula*				*October-November 1988 Agreement*	
	Quotas	*%*	*Quotas*	*%*	*Ceiling 18.5m. b/d*	*%*	*Quotas*	*Difference*
Algeria	667	4.02	667	3.83	708	3.76	695	-13
Ecuador	221	1.33	221	1.27	235	1.24	230	-5
Gabon	159	0.96	159	0.91	169	0.90	166	-3
Indonesia	1,190	7.17	1,190	6.83	1,263	6.70	1,240	-23
Iran	2,369	14.27	2,369	13.59	2,515	14.27	2,640	+125
Iraq	1,540	9.23	2,369	13.59	2,515	14.27	2,640	+125
Kuwait	996	6.00	996	5.71	1,057	5.60	1,037	-20
Libya	996	6.00	996	5.71	1,057	5.60	1,037	- 20
Nigeria	1,301	7.84	1,301	7.46	1,381	7.32	1,355	-26
Qatar	299	1.80	299	1.72	317	1.68	312	-5
Saudi Arabia	4,343	26.16	4,343	24.92	4,610	24.45	4,524	-86
UAE	948	5.71	948	5.44	1,006	5.34	988	-18
Venezuela	1,571	9.46	1,571	9.01	1,667	8.85	1,636	-31
Totals	**16,600**	**100.00**	**17,429**	**100.00**	**18,500**	**100.00**	**18,500**	**0**

SOURCE: *MEES* Supplement, 28 November 1988.

NOTES

For the place and frequency of publications cited here, and for the full name of the publication, news agency, radio station, or monitoring service where an abbreviation is used, please see "List of Sources." Only in the case of more than one publication bearing the same name is the place of publication noted here.

1. Buyers were pressing Opec members to adopt market-related prices. Iran, Iraq, Oman, Dubai, and Qatar went over fully to market-related prices, while Saudi Arabia, Kuwait,and Abu Dhabi were sticking to official prices. However, even they were subject to buyers' pressure. *MEES*, 11 January 1988.
2. *MEES*, 4 January 1988.
3. *MEED*, 30 January-5 February 1988. Two factors: Iraq's refusal to accept a quota and Saudi Arabia's determination not to become a swing producer again. Opec production in January averaged 17.9m.–18m. b/d.
4. *MEES*, 18 January 1988.
5. *MEES*, 22 February 1988.
6. The *NYT* reported that Opec officials were studying a plan to reduce oil output by 5%, 850,000 b/d, because oil prices declined 20% in the past two weeks bringing down prices to $13–$14 a barrel. *NYT*, 13 March 1988.
7. For the attempts, see Benjamin Shwadran, *Middle East Oil Crises since 1973* (Boulder and London: Westview Press, 1986), p. 184 and *passim*; *MECS* 1983–84, pp. 268–71; *MECS*, 1984–85, pp. 259 and *passim* ; *MECS* 1986, pp. 228 and *passim*; *MECS* 1987, pp. 277–78 and *passim*.
8. *MEES*, 16 May; *MEED*, 13 May 1988.
9. *MEES*, 23 May 1988.
10. *MEES*, 9 May 1988.
11. *MEED*, 29 April 1988.
12. *MEED*, 20 May 1988.
13. The date was changed from 7 June to avoid a clash with the Arab League summit meeting in Algiers.
14. *MEES*, 30 May 1988.

15. *MEED*, 24 June; *JP*, 16 June 1988.
16. *MEED*, 1 July; *JP*, 10 July 1988.
17. *MEED*, 8 July 1988.
18. *MEES*, 18 July 1988.
19. *MEES*, 1 August 1988.
20. *MEED*, 22 July 1988.
21. Ibid.
22. Both nations would need time to rebuild their production capacity and restore their loading facilities. *NYT*, 29 July; *JP*, 19 July 1988.
23. *MEES*, 25 July 1988.
24. *Time*, 1 August 1988.
25. *MEED*, 2 September 1988.
26. *MEED*, 7 October 1988. The weekly noted: "The declaration of a cease-fire in the Gulf War in August has led to a renewal of old discords rather than the hoped-for reconciliation." Ibid., 21 October 1988.
27. *US News and World Report*, 10 September 1988.
28. *Ma'ariv*, 19 February 1988.
29. *MEES*, 14 March; *MEED*, 19-25 March 1988.
30. *MEES*, 11 July 1988.
31. *MEES*, 4 July 1988.
32. *MEES*, 25 July 1988.
33. *MEES*, 8 August 1988.
34. *MEES*, 8 August; *MEED*, 12 August 1988.
35. *MEES*, 5 September 1988.
36. *MEES*, 19 September 1988.
37. *NYT*, 11 September 1988.
38. *MEED*, 23 September 1988. Estimates of Opec production in August-September were running about 20m.–20.5m. b/d. *MEES*, 26 September 1988.
39. *PE*, p. 287, September 1988.
40. *MEED*, 7 October 1988.
41. *MEES*, 3 October 1988.
42. *MEED*, 21 October 1988. The weekly noted: "The rise in volume had the predictable effect of driving spot prices below $10 a barrel in the first week of October."
43. *NYT*, 2 October 1988.
44. *JP*, 10 October 1988.
45. *NYT*, 9 October 1988.
46. *MEED*, 14 October 1988.
47. *MEES*, 24 October 1988. Seymour said that this solution was the only one that could come out from the joint committee.
48. *WSJ*, 24 October 1988.
49. *Time*, 24 October 1988.
50. *WSJ*, 24 October; *MEES*, 24 October 1988.
51. *MEES*, 31 October 1988.
52. *MEES*, 7 November 1988.
53. *WSJ*, 2 November; *MEED*, 11 November 1988.
54. *JP*, 16 November 1988.
55. *NYT*, 27 November 1988.
56. There has been speculation as to the motive of Saudi Arabia in proposing the change in the target price. *MEED* suggested that it was to assert its influence in Opec, *MEED*, 9 December 1988. Iran saw in Saudi Arabia's surprise intervention less than an hour after Iran's consent, an act of sabotage, *JP*, 28 November 1988.
57. *MEED*, 9 December 1988.
58. For a full technical explanation of condensates and the definitions, see *MEES* Supplement, 28 November 1988.
59. *MEES* editor Seymour said about prices: "All one can say for certain at this stage is that the prospects look very much better with the Vienna Agreement than they would have done without them." Ibid.

60. See column 3 in Table 2.
61. *MEES* Supplement, 28 November 1988.
62.

Algeria	660	
Ecuador	300	
Gabon	170	
Indonesia	1,100	
Iran	2,600	
Iraq	2,700	
Kuwait	2,000	
Libya	1,200	
Nigeria	1,450	
Qatar	300	
Saudi Arabia	6,500	
UAE	2,050	
Venezuela	1,800	
Neutral Zone	150	(war relief)

MEES, 5 December 1988.
63. Ibid.
64. *MEES*, 19 December 1988.
65. *MEED*, 16 December 1988.
66. *PE*, p. 390, December 1988.
67. Ibid., 2 January 1989.
68. *Opec Bulletin*, pp. 7–8, January 1989.
69. *MEES*, 12 December 1988.
70. *Opec Bulletin*, p. 3, November-December 1988.
71. *PE*, p. 236, July; *NYT*, 19 June; *Time*, 27 June 1988.
72. *WSJ*, 11 November; *MEES*, 14 November; *MEED*, 25 November 1988.
73. Ibid.; *PE*, p. 415, December 1988.
74. See Benjamin Shwadran, *The Middle East, Oil and the Great Powers*, 3rd ed. (New York: John Wiley & Sons, 1973), pp. 412–13, 420–23.
75. *MEED*, 27 February-4 March 1988.
76. *MEES*, 15 August; *MEED*, 19 August 1988.
77. *MEES*, 10 October 1988.
78. *MEES*, 17 October; *PE*, p. 358, November 1988.
79. *MEES*, 26 December 1988–2 January 1989.
80. *MEED*, 13 January 1989. For Kuwait's efforts and achievements in downstream refining and marketing operations especially in Europe see *MECS* 1987, pp. 290–91.
81. *PE*, p. 236, July 1988.
82. Ibid., p. 246.
83. *MEED*, 23 December 1988.
84. *PE*, p. 84, March 1988; *MEES*, 18 April, 5 September 1988.
85. In December, a number of US senators addressed a letter to Secretary of the Treasury Nicholas Brady saying that the Texaco-Saudi Arabia deal could "seriously increase US dependence on foreign oil, threaten the US oil industry, and jeopardize the well-being of American consumers." The letter asserted that the deal would give the Saudis unprecedented influence on US downstream refining outlets. It questioned whether the Saudi company would be subject to antitrust laws. *JP*, 11 December 1988.
86. On 5 December 1988, 'Ali Khalifa al-Sabah said: "We will continue to emphasize price moderation, not for the sake of the consumers but because it is the safest way to maximize our revenues over the life of the reserves." *Opec Bulletin*, p. 6, January 1989.
87. In evaluating the 28 November agreement, the Kuwait oil minister declared: "Its most important feature is not the ceiling or the quotas of individual countries *per se*, but the attempt to bury the political divisions that have overshadowed Opec deliberations in the past. This was done by solving the Iran-Iraq quota problem and the definition problems which have bedeviled Opec in the past, and more importantly but less explicitly by the smaller reserve countries recognizing that for the larger reserve countries, especially those

in the Gulf, talk of moderate pricing is not politically motivated but the result of legitimate long-term interests." Ibid.

88. Oman was not an Opec member, but tried to follow Opec prices. However, as production destabilized, Oman followed the spot market prices for term-contract customers. At the end of the month, prices were adjusted retroactively to the average of the spot price. Dubai, although part of the UAE, followed the same independent procedure as Oman.

Jordan's Economy: From Prosperity to Crisis

ELIYAHU KANOVSKY

Following the end of the 1970–71 civil war in Jordan, and the 1972 lifting of the Syrian embargo on trade and transit, Jordan enjoyed a decade of high-level prosperity. Between 1972 and 1982 gross national product (GNP), in real terms (corrected for inflation), rose by an unusually high rate of 9–10% p.a. Despite very rapid population growth (almost 4% p.a.), per capita GNP rose by a respectable average annual rate of 5–6%. Investment in infrastructure, industry, and agriculture, and in other sectors, was far higher than in earlier decades, and in most sectors production expanded rapidly.[1]

Since 1983 there has been a very marked, almost abrupt, change for the worse. The economy has been in serious recession. Gross domestic product (GDP) rose by a paltry 2% p.a. between 1982 and 1987, implying a per capita *decline* of close to 2% p.a. GNP, a better measure of incomes, showed zero growth, i.e., an average annual *decline* of almost 4% on a per capita basis. Private consumption per capita, a measure of living standards, peaked in 1983. Between 1983 and 1987 it declined by a massive 23%, according to official accounts.[2] At this writing (March 1989) no data were yet available for 1988, but there was every indication of a continued downtrend.

The most visible sign of the gathering crisis was the decline in central bank foreign exchange reserves from about $1.2bn. in 1979-81 to $413m. at the end of 1987. The almost steady erosion since 1982 was followed by a precipitous plunge during the course of 1988 to $68m. in August 1988, equivalent to about *ten days* of commodity imports. In 1979 foreign exchange reserves had been the equivalent of *seven months* of imports. The official exchange rate dropped from one Jordanian dinar (JD) equal to $3.04 at the end of 1987 to $2.64 in September 1988, and then plummeted to less than two dollars by the end of the year. The Central Bank announced various measures to stem the flight of capital, and, in November 1988 the government announced an austerity program including a variety of new taxes, a complete ban on "luxury" imports, and far higher customs duties on many other goods. The projected budget for 1989, announced at the end of 1988, called for a real cutback in spending of as much as one sixth. In presenting the 1989 budget the finance minister reassured the people that the economy "stands on a strong base" but that structural defects must be corrected, including the imbalance between the service sectors and the "productive" sectors, increasing budgetary deficits, and growing unemployment.[3] Possibly the most critical and dangerous problem was the precipitous rise in unemployment, especially among university and community college graduates.

The almost abrupt change from a decade of high-level prosperity to a worsening recession since 1983, and crisis in 1988, requires explanation. The questions to be addressed are: what were the underlying factors accounting for the decade of prosperity

The author wishes to express his sincere gratitude to the Lucius N. Littauer Foundation and to its president, Mr William Frost, for the research grant in support of this study.

followed by six years of economic deterioration, culminating in a severe economic crisis? A related, and more difficult question is: what is the outlook for the future?

THE HISTORICAL BACKGROUND[4]

1948–67

Following the Arab-Israeli war of 1948, the Kingdom of Jordan, with a population of 375,000, annexed the area subsequently referred to as the West Bank, with an indigenous population of 460,000. Another 350,000 Palestinian refugees who left the new State of Israel settled in the expanded Kingdom of Jordan. The kingdom had absorbed about one half of the Palestinian refugees. Almost all the others were in the Gaza Strip (then under Egyptian rule), Syria, and Lebanon. Though the Palestinians (the inhabitants of the West Bank plus the refugees) constituted well over two thirds of the population of the kingdom, political and military power remained in the hands of the Transjordanians. The king was, and remains, an absolute monarch. Nonetheless this major demographic change had important long-term, economic, as well as political and social repercussions. By and large, the Palestinians were far more educated, far more skilled, and more urbanized than the Transjordanians. The fact that Jordan, unlike the other Arab countries, granted the refugees citizenship greatly facilitated their integration and economic absorption.

A World Bank mission which visited Jordan in the mid-1950s arrived at very pessimistic conclusions regarding the country's economic future. The reality proved to be otherwise. Between the mid-1950s and 1966 the average annual rate of growth of (real) GDP was 7–8% p.a. According to some estimates the unemployment rate in 1966 was as low as 4–5%, i.e., close to full employment. By the mid-1960s about two thirds of the Palestinian refugees were fully employed, and most of the others had part-time or seasonal jobs.

The East Ghor canal, completed in the early 1960s, stimulated the growth of modern agriculture, especially fruits and vegetables — some of which were exported to the neighboring Arab countries. But other sectors including phosphates, oil refining for domestic consumption, and various light industries advanced more rapidly. Considerable investments were made in infrastructure — electric power, roads, the port of ‘Aqaba, etc. However, the service industries were dominant. In terms of foreign currency earnings, the export of services was of primary importance including tourism which expanded rapidly in the 1960s, and remittances from a large and growing number of Jordanians working abroad, mainly in the Arab oil states. But, despite the substantial growth in exports of goods and services, there was a large and persistent import surplus. However, this was more than covered by foreign aid — almost all grants — and the Central Bank's gold and foreign exchange reserves rose almost annually.

1967–72

The severance of the West Bank from the Kingdom of Jordan, as a consequence of the Six Day War, had but a temporary effect on the East Bank's economy. Between 1948 and 1967 the kingdom had put far greater emphasis on the development of the East Bank economy. The Palestinians claimed that this policy was politically motivated. But there were also cogent economic considerations favoring East Bank development.

The phosphate mines and the country's only port were located in that part of the kingdom. The location of the oil refinery was determined by the pipeline (Tapline) from Saudi Arabia. The East Bank's agricultural potential was more promising. The East Ghor canal project was located there. The only important sector in which the West Bank was predominant was tourism based on the historic sites of Jerusalem and its environs.

There is considerable evidence that while the West Bank was far more advanced economically when it was annexed to the Kingdom after the 1948 war, by the early 1960s the roles had been reversed. Per capita production in industry and agriculture, and of GDP, as a whole, was significantly higher in the East Bank. Since wage levels were higher and job opportunities more plentiful in the East Bank, there was a very sizable internal migration from west to east in the 1950s and 1960s — prior to the Six Day War. On the eve of the 1967 war, close to 60% of the kingdom's population resided in the East Bank — in marked contrast with the situation in 1949 when it had been less than 40%. In addition there was a steady migration to the Arab oil states. The 1961 census reported that over 60,000 Jordanians — about 9% of the labor force — were working abroad. On the eve of the Six Day War their number had risen to close to 100,000.

The war itself caused no direct damage to the East Bank economy. The main problem was the influx of about 260,000 refugees from the West Bank, including a small number from the Gaza Strip. All the indicators showed that the economy was in a strong upswing in 1969 and the first half of 1970. Grants from the rich Arab states, the US, and some other countries rose from $88m. in 1966 to $129m. in 1969. According to one estimate the strong economic advance reduced unemployment to a level even lower than had prevailed before the war.

However, the economic recovery was aborted by the civil war between the Jordanian Army and the Palestinian armed factions which erupted in full fury in September 1970. The hostilities, the large-scale destruction of property, and the disruption of transportation sharply reduced production. By mid-1971 the Jordanian Army succeeded in eliminating or expelling the Palestinian militias, and hostilities ceased. However, the actions of some Arab states in support of the Palestinians made a bad situation worse. Iraq and Egypt banned trade with Jordan. Libya and Kuwait "suspended" their financial aid, but Saudi Arabia did not, and the US increased its support. But by far the most powerful economic blow was the Syrian closure of its border. The embargo shut off access to Beirut which was the main port of entry for Jordanian imports. Moreover, Syria and Lebanon, unlike Egypt and Iraq, were important trading partners of Jordan. The Syrian embargo caused severe damage. But, during the course of 1972, Syria gradually eased its embargo, and ended it toward the end of that year. The deep recession of 1970–71 was coming to an end and the economic indicators were pointing upward in 1972.

EXTERNAL EVENTS AND THEIR IMPACT ON JORDAN'S ECONOMY SINCE 1972

The Yom Kippur War had very little impact on Jordan's economy. Other than a small contingent sent to Syria, Jordan stayed out of the war. Even during the hostilities in October 1973 the movement of goods and people across the Jordan bridges continued, as it had since 1967.

The oil shock of 1973–74 greatly increased the revenues of the Arab oil-exporting states and their financial support for Jordan rose to far higher levels. No less important, the booming economies in the oil states attracted millions of foreign workers, and the number of Jordanians working in these countries rose very rapidly. The second oil shock of 1979–80 raised both financial aid and workers' remittances to even higher levels. Moreover, Jordan's proximity also gave it an advantage in terms of exports to the booming economies. On the negative side was the higher payment for Jordanian oil imports, but the overall balance was highly favorable.

The civil war in Lebanon began in 1975, about a month before Egypt reopened the Suez Canal. The frequent closure of Beirut — the main port of entry for Jordanian imports — made it all the more urgent to develop 'Aqaba, and the reopening of the canal reduced the shipping costs for imports from the West through 'Aqaba.

The Iraqi-Iranian War, which began in September 1980, closed the Gulf to Iraqi shipping, and 'Aqaba served as an important alternative route for imports. Subsequently, the Iraqis also shipped some crude oil and refined products by truck through Jordan to 'Aqaba, for export to various countries. In addition to earnings from transit trade, exports of Jordanian goods to Iraq rose strongly.

The hostilities in Lebanon brought some indirect benefits to Jordan. Some of the wealthier Lebanese fled to Jordan, and some international firms, which had maintained regional headquarters in Beirut, relocated to Amman. Some of the wealthier Arabs from the oil states who had previously spent their leisure time and money in Beirut went, instead, to Jordan. The construction industry received a strong boost from all of these events, including rising incomes of Jordanians, especially as a consequence of remittances. Homes built by wealthy Arabs from other countries, new tourist facilities, and rising investments in infrastructure by the government, financed mainly by foreign aid, stimulated the boom in construction.

But since 1982 or 1983 the external stimuli to Jordan's economic growth have, for the most part, been weakening. The oil boom which reached its peak in the early 1980s turned into an oil crash. Saudi Arabia and other oil exporters have been incurring growing budgetary and balance of payments (current account) deficits and have cut back sharply on foreign aid, and on various domestic investment projects. As a consequence, they have reduced their employment of foreign labor, and wage rates declined strongly in these countries. Moreover, Saudi Arabia and other countries in the Gulf are developing industry and agriculture, and are reducing their imports. As the Iraqi-Iranian War dragged on, Iraq's financial situation deteriorated, and it, too, cut back on imports. Moreover, Jordanian suppliers to Iraq were threatened with bankruptcy due to the latter's failure to pay for the goods. The Central Bank of Jordan was compelled to lend Iraq hundreds of millions of dollars, which it could ill afford, in order to pay the Jordanian suppliers.

A closer look at the Jordanian economy should give us a better understanding of the factors underlying Jordan's current economic crisis.

AGRICULTURE

Though the irrigated area has increased since the early 1960s, well over 90% of the cultivated area has remained unirrigated. As a consequence, yields are subject to wide annual fluctuations related to the vagaries of the weather. This is especially true of wheat and other grain crops largely confined to the rain-fed areas. Thus, for example, wheat production (the main grain crop) which peaked at 131,000 tons in 1983, fell in the following years to a low of 31,000 tons in 1986, and then rose sharply to 109,000 tons in 1987. On the other hand fruit and vegetable production, largely grown in the irrigated Jordan Valley, was generally in a rising trend.[5] The overall index of agricultural production shows a rapid growth rate of 15% between 1975 and 1981, followed by a sharp slowdown to less than 5% p.a. between 1981 and 1987. But these figures have a strong upward bias. The real growth rate of farm production between 1975 and 1987 was significantly lower.[6] But, though farm production has risen, its share of GDP dropped from 13–14% in 1969–72 to about 7–8% in 1979–82 and remained at about that level until 1987. Agriculture's share of the labor force also dropped from 18–20% in the early 1970s to 7–8% in 1986. According to official estimates there was a strong absolute decline in farm employment. However, these estimates have a downward bias. A large share of the foreign workers in Jordan are employed in the farm sector, and many are believed to be illegal, i.e., unregistered by the authorities.

Food exports were rising until the early 1980s — mainly fruits and vegetables to the neighboring Arab countries. Since then farm exports have been encountering difficulties and, in terms of export earnings, were in a downward trend until 1987. This was due both to stiffer competition from other exporters, mainly Turkey, and to the development of indigenous agriculture in the Gulf states.

Food imports have traditionally been far higher than exports. But the deficit (agricultural exports minus agricultural imports) rose from $35m. p.a. in 1968–70 (about the same as in 1964–66) to about $350m. in 1980–82. Part of the increase in the food deficit was due to higher international prices, but, for the most part, it reflected higher quantities. Since then there has been a decline to about $300m. in 1985–87.[7] But this was mainly due to a substantial decline in world farm prices, rather than lower volumes of food imports. About two thirds, or more, of the country's food consumption is imported. The sharp rise in 1988 in world food prices, especially grain and feed crops, has most probably widened Jordan's trade deficit in agriculture.[8]

The government offered various subsidies to agriculture — including very high procurement prices for wheat and barley, and, more recently, for tomatoes, and provided water for irrigation at highly subsidized rates. By and large,the farm sector was relatively neglected during the boom period of the 1970s and early 1980s. A British economic journal gave the following assessment of the farm sector in 1988: "Agriculture in the kingdom remains poorly managed...the marketing of fruit and vegetables both internally and abroad, has...been chaotic....The absence of effective quality control is...a barrier to [exports]...to Europe" -- which has been, for many years, a goal of the authorities.

The 1986–90 Development Plan calls for much more investment in various agricultural projects, the expansion of the area under irrigation, and a growth rate of production of close to 8% p.a.[9] The current economic crisis may impel the government to put greater emphasis on this sector, but barring very favorable weather conditions, the target is probably overambitious.

INDUSTRY

The government takes an active role in fostering industry through tariff protection, subsidies, favorable tax treatment and low-cost credits, and, in some cases, the grant of monopoly rights and a complete ban on competitive imports. In most of the larger enterprises, as well as in many medium-sized industries (by Jordanian standards) the state is a large or major shareholder. While the economic philosophy of the government favors private enterprise, the state would undertake investment on its own, or in partnership with the private sector, if the latter was unwilling or unable to invest in those enterprises which the government deemed to be important for economic development. There are laws encouraging private investment, foreign as well as domestic, but these have not succeeded in attracting significant foreign investment in industry.

Phosphate mining has long been a major industry and production has been expanding almost steadily, with the bulk exported to various countries, in particular to South and East Asia. Jordan is the world's fourth largest producer, exceeded only by Morocco, the US, and the USSR. Production rose from 1m. tons in 1966 to 1.6m. tons in 1968, then, as a result of the civil war and the Syrian and Indian embargoes, dropped to 0.7m. tons in 1972. Subsequently there was a major expansion to 4.7m. tons in 1982 and 6.8m. tons in 1987.[10]

Two major projects were initiated toward the end of the 1970s: extracting potash from the Dead Sea, and the fertilizer complex at 'Aqaba based on the processing of phosphate rock. The fertilizer complex includes facilities for the production of various derivative chemicals. These, and other major industries including refined oil products (based on imported crude oil), and cement, are joint ventures between the government and the private sector with the government usually the major shareholder. Both the potash and fertilizer complexes, designed largely for export, were beset with technical difficulties and lengthy delays in construction which added significantly to costs. But the main problem was the sharp decline in international price levels. The feasibility studies made in the mid-1970s projected far higher prices — and profitability. Production of potash, fertilizers, and various chemicals began in 1982–83. However, even in 1988, the 'Aqaba plant was producing at only 65% of planned capacity,[11] which adversely affected profitability. By 1986 the fertilizer company had accumulated losses of some $150m. Investment in this complex had been about $500m. The government decided on a takeover by the Jordan Phosphate Company.[12] The potash company recorded its first profit in 1988 — $12m., on sales of 1.3m. tons.[13] The investment in this project had also been close to $500m.

Major investments were also made in expanding cement production in the expectation that the construction boom would continue in Jordan itself as well as in the neighboring Arab oil states. But the "oil crash" sharply reduced construction in the neighboring Arab states, as well as in Jordan. In 1987 a barter agreement with Egypt was instrumental in reversing the sharp decline in cement production which had taken place the previous year.[14]

In addition to the above-mentioned larger industries there is a wide range of more traditional industries including food processing, textiles, construction materials, furniture, pharmaceuticals, and others.

In 1985–87, industry (including mining and manufacturing) accounted for 20–21%

of GDP (agriculture's share was 8–9%) and 10–11% of total employment.[15] In terms of *commodity* exports, industrial and mining products accounted for over three fourths of the total. However, the export of services was predominant (see below).

In the plan period 1981–85, value added in industry was to rise by a most ambitious 17.8% p.a., based mainly on the new industries — fertilizers and potash. In reality the growth rate was 4.9%.[16] In the 1986–90 plan the goal was set far more modestly at 4.9%. But actual performance in the first two years of the plan was disappointing; value added actually declined.[17] The main factor was the recession in the neighboring Arab oil states which reduced demand for many of Jordan's industrial products, and the problems encountered by the fertilizer and potash industries. Moreover, investment in industry declined, and this may well have an adverse impact on production in the next few years.

CONSTRUCTION

The rapid growth in remittances from Jordanians working abroad, the expansion of public expenditures on infrastructure (financed by foreign aid), large-scale investment in industry (by the public and private sectors), and, to a smaller extent, investment by wealthy Arabs from the neighboring countries, stimulated a major construction boom in the 1970s. Construction expanded almost sixfold between 1972 and 1982. Subsequently there was a very sharp contraction of one third by 1987. This sector's share of GDP rose from 5% in 1972 to 10–11% in 1979–83 and then declined to 7% in 1987. Its share of total employment rose from 8% in 1972 to 16% in 1979, and then declined to 11% in 1986.[18] There is every indication that the downtrend continued in 1987 and 1988.

The rapid decline in this sector since the early 1980s was due, directly and indirectly, to the oil crash in the neighboring countries which adversely affected remittances, financial aid to the government of Jordan (and the latter's allocations to infrastructural investment), private investment in real estate by wealthy Arabs from neighboring countries, and, to some extent, the completion of the major fertilizer and potash projects in the early 1980s. The sharp drop in prices of real estate and of rentals, and the emergence of much empty office space and unsold housing since the mid-1980s, have constrained new construction.[19]

The sharp drop in construction activity has had spillover effects on the whole economy. It affected those industries engaged in the production of building materials, furniture, and various household products. The recessionary effects of these developments have been pervasive.

ENERGY

Until recent years Jordan's energy supplies were based entirely on imported oil. After several years of exploration small quantities of oil were discovered in 1984. In 1987 domestic oil production was a minuscule 500–650 barrels per day (b/d) while domestic consumption was about 60,000 b/d. In 1987 a large natural gas field was discovered. The plans call for the utilization of gas for the generation of electric power in order to reduce dependence on imported oil.

Energy consumption rose very rapidly in the 1970s and early 1980s. Subsequently there was a sharp slowdown. Between 1982 and 1987 energy consumption rose by 4.3% p.a. in sharp contrast with the 15.4% growth rate between 1974 and 1982. Electric power consumption rose even more rapidly — by 20.1% p.a. in the earlier period, dropping to a 15.6% growth rate between 1982 and 1987.[20] The slowdown in energy use was due, for the most part, to the economic recession in the latter period, and, in part,to higher prices for refined oil products which were raised a number of times since 1981. In 1984, the government announced plans to reduce the growth rate in energy consumption to zero within two years in order to cut back on its large outlays on imported oil.[21] The price increases and the recession did slow down the rate of growth in oil consumption but the goal of zero growth was not achieved despite the stagnancy in economic growth in 1983–87.

Until 1985 Jordan's refinery received all of its crude oil from Saudi Arabia via Tapline. Since then Jordan has been importing most of its crude and some refined products — not produced domestically — by truck from Iraq.[22] The oil from Iraq is in lieu of cash payment for Jordanian exports to that country.

Electric power generation has risen rapidly — as noted earlier. It was estimated that over 95% of the population, including over 90% of the rural population, enjoyed the benefits of electric power in 1986.[23]

As an oil importer Jordan benefited from the decline in international oil prices since 1982. At its peak in 1982 Jordan's oil import bill was over $650m. By 1987 it had declined to $360m. — for a larger volume of oil.[24] However, as noted earlier, in most respects Jordan was adversely affected by the slump in world oil prices.

TOURISM

In the conventional presentation of the GDP by economic sectors, tourism is not listed separately. The closest approximation is found in the balance of payments under the heading "income from travel."[25] The rise in tourist income during the 1960s was reversed, until 1971, as a consequence of the 1967 war and the civil war. Subsequently there was a sharp recovery. Tourist income in 1975 was $112m. as compared with $32m. in 1966. By 1981 it had risen to $548m., *exceeding commodity exports*. In the following years there was very little growth. In real terms (measured in constant dollars) the $580m. in tourist income in 1987 was less than in 1981.[26] The 1981–85 Development Plan had projected a very rapid growth in tourist income reaching over $900m. in 1985; in reality it was $518m. There was considerable investment in hotel building, including both expansion and modernization, but the projected rise in tourism, especially from the Western countries, failed to materialize. On the contrary; there was a significant decline.[27]

Excluding arrivals from Arab countries and others from the poorer countries in the region — many of whom came to seek jobs in Jordan — the figures show that the number of arrivals in Jordan, mainly Europeans and Americans, rose until 1981 reaching 254,000, and then declined to 163,000 in 1987.[28]

The various development plans recognize the country's tourist potential, in particular its archaeological sites and desert ruins, as well as the attractions of 'Aqaba for tourists from the northern countries. Under the "Open Bridges" policy adopted by Israel and Jordan since the 1967 war, tourists visiting Jordan have ready access to the historic sites in Jerusalem and Bethlehem. The civil war in Lebanon since 1975 diverted some Arab tourism from Beirut to Jordan. Jordan also benefited from tourism from the booming Arab oil countries. But these stimuli waned during the 1980s, while Jordan failed to attract more European and American tourists. In fact, there was a strong absolute decline. This failure has been an important contributory factor to the country's economic stagnation since the early 1980s.

SERVICES

Jordanian officials have frequently noted and deplored the fact that the share of services is disproportionately large and the various development plans have stressed the importance of measures designed to alter the economic structure in favor of the goods-producing sectors (agriculture, mining, manufacturing, construction, and public utilities). As compared with other countries at a similar level of per capita production and income, Jordan's economy is, indeed, strongly oriented toward services including transportation and communications, trade and finance, various personal and business services, as well as government services, both civilian and military.

The share of transport in GDP trended upward from 9.5% in 1972–74 to over 11% in 1986–87. This was due to many factors including the rapid growth in imports and in exports of bulk commodities such as phosphates, fertilizers, potash, and others, as well as the rapid growth in transit trade, especially to Iraq, following the outbreak of the Iraqi-Iranian War in 1980. The share of other nongovernmental services trended downward during the 1980s. This was also true of government services — until 1985. This was apparently due, in large measure, to the relative decline in military outlays, until 1984–85.[29] However, since 1985 the trend has been reversed with the share of government services in total GDP rising from 18% in 1984 to over 21% in 1987. This was due both to a more rapid growth in military expenditures, and to policies designed to cope with rapidly rising unemployment since the mid-1980s through make-work jobs in the public sector.

The share of services, as a whole, was declining quite rapidly from 69–70% of GDP in 1971–73 to 60–61% in 1980–82. The main commodity-producing sectors, in particular construction and industry, were expanding rapidly. Since 1983 the trend has been reversed with the share of services rising to 63–64% in 1986–87.

A similar picture emerges if we examine the share of services in total employment and in exports. In 1972 services accounted for 65% of total employment; in 1979, it was down to 62%. In the 1980s there was a sharp rise, reaching 70% in 1986.[30] The share of services in total exports of goods and services was even more lopsided, with services accounting for 76% in 1972, 84–85% in 1980–83, and then declining to 77% in 1987. The recent drop in remittances (included in the export of services) and the initiation of exports from the new industries, mainly potash and fertilizers, increased the share of commodities in total exports.[31]

The unusually high share of services is attributable to many factors of which the following are most pertinent:

(1) The persistently high import surplus (imports of goods and services minus exports of goods and services) is financed mainly by foreign aid and tends to orient the economy toward services required to transport and maintain the imported goods.

(2) The very high ratio of Jordanians working abroad, and their remittances, also

finances a high level of imported goods associated with the provision of local services.

(3) Jordan has a high level of military and other security expenditures, adding significantly to the share of services in the economy.

(4) The rapid growth in transit trade, especially to and from Iraq, also boosted the share of services.[32]

(5) Moreover, tourist services, noted earlier, are subsumed in the various service sectors. Though tourist income was stagnant in recent years, the $580m. earned was high in relation to the country's GNP of $5.5bn. in 1987.

(6) As compared with other countries at similar levels of per capita income, Jordan puts greater emphasis on high educational and health levels. This is evident from enrollment ratios in school and in higher education, as well as population per physician and other indicators of health standards.[33]

ECONOMIC GROWTH AND THE ALLOCATION OF RESOURCES

As noted earlier, Jordan enjoyed very high rates of economic growth in the decade 1972 to 1982, followed by stagnancy since then. GDP rose by 8% p.a. (in real terms) between 1972 and 1982, while GNP rose even more rapidly (mainly due to the influx of remittances), by almost 10% p.a. Between 1982 and 1987 the growth rate of GDP was 2% p.a., and of GNP, zero, while the population growth rate was close to 4% in both periods. In other words, on a per capita basis, GDP (a measure of production within the country) declined strongly, and GNP (a measure of incomes) declined even more sharply.[34]

In a country like Jordan with a persistently high import surplus in relation to its GDP, financed largely by foreign aid, available resources are better measured by the GDP plus the import surplus. The import surplus was rising almost steadily until 1982.[35]

How were the increased resources allocated? The various development plans aimed at reducing economic dependence by restraining the growth in private and public consumption in order to allocate more resources to investment. In other words, gross national saving should rise more rapidly than GNP and finance a growing share of investment, thereby reducing the need for foreign aid.

The share of gross investment in total available resources did rise rapidly from 13% in 1972–73 to 25% in 1980–82, a very high level by international standards, and far higher than had been achieved in earlier periods. In 1960–66 the ratio was 12–14%. But the growth rate of GDP in 1972–82 was about the same as in 1960–66. In other words, the incremental capital-output ratio was far higher in the latter period. This was apparently due to far greater investment in infrastructure, in irrigation, and in major industrial projects (potash, fertilizers, cement, and others) which are capital-intensive. But the far higher incremental capital-output ratio was also due to the lengthy delays, and serious technical problems which arose in the implementation of the major industrial projects — noted earlier — which raised costs and delayed the start-up in production. The underutilization of capacity in some of the large new industries also raised the effective incremental capital-output ratio.

The 1981–85 Development Plan projected even higher levels of investment than had prevailed in the latter half of the 1970s. In reality, since 1982, there has been a serious decline in both absolute and relative terms. The ratio of gross investment to resources was about 19% in 1984–87 as compared with 25% in 1980–82.[36]

Gross national saving is defined as GNP minus consumption (public plus private). The national accounts indicate that until 1975 (including the pre-1967 period) gross national saving was negative. In other words consumption exceeded GNP, and the import surplus, financed by foreign aid, was the source not only of investment but also of part of consumption. In every year since 1976 (with the exception of 1979) saving has been positive — a very distinct improvement. Between 1980 and 1987, the ratio of gross national saving to GNP ranged between 4% and 12% with no distinct trend. In other words, between 1980 and 1987 gross national saving financed, on average, 25% of investment. The balance was financed by foreign aid. Gross national saving was far less than had been envisaged in the 1981–85 Development Plan which had projected that the ratio of gross national saving to GNP would rise steadily, reaching 38% by 1985. In fact, the ratio was 15% in 1985. Moreover, the plan had projected a continued growth in the absolute level of investment; instead there was a strong decline.[37]

It is important to emphasize that these figures are incomplete, in particular those pertaining to public consumption. There are significiant off-budgetary expenditures, especially military, and there is a strong presumption that these are excluded from the national accounts pertaining to resource allocation as well as from the budgetary accounts.[38] In other words, the reported national accounts understate public consumption, and, by implication, overstate gross national saving.

The goals of the 1986–90 Development Plan are far more modest than those of its predecessors. The plan calls for a growth rate of GDP of 5.1% p.a., an average annual increase of 3.2% in consumption, and a 5.3% growth rate for investment.[39] Figures available at this writing for the first two years of the current Development Plan, 1986 and 1987, indicate that even these modest goals were missed by a wide mark. GDP rose by somewhat over 2% p.a.; and investment (gross fixed capital formation) fell, even when measured in nominal terms. Private consumption also declined.[40]

THE BUDGETARY ACCOUNTS

As noted earlier, the reported budgets of the central government are incomplete since they exclude some military expenditures financed by foreign aid, and also exclude some subsidies to agriculture. Though the government espouses an economic philosophy which favors private enterprise, it plays a major role in the economy due, in no small measure, to the fact that it is the recipient of large-scale foreign aid. It is the sole or majority shareholder of major enterprises, in addition to the usual functions of government in terms of providing and maintaining the infrastructure, health and education, and a wide range of other services.

The ratio of government expenditures to GDP is a good measure of the state's involvement in the economy. In 1968–72 this ratio averaged 48%. Subsequently there was a very strong rise to a peak of 68.5% in 1979. The government's resources, from taxes and other domestic sources, and from foreign grants, rose strongly, but spending rose even more rapidly. All categories of spending expanded, including both current civilian as well as (reported) military expenditures, but capital expenditures, i.e., for investment purposes, rose most rapidly. Rising revenues (from domestic and foreign sources) did not catch up with escalating expenditures and large deficits emerged averaging 16.5% of GDP in 1976–79. The deficits during the 1970s were financed largely by concessional loans from some Arab states, the US, and a number of Western countries. Subsequently there was some restraint on spending and the ratio of government expenditures to GDP declined to 48–50% in 1983–85. The cutbacks were most strongly felt in capital outlays, i.e., investment. However, faced with the deepening recession the government increased its spending sharply in 1986 and 1987 to 60% of GDP in an attempt to stimulate the economy. Current spending (civilian plus reported military outlays) was raised, but the biggest increase was in capital expenditures.[41]

The budgetary deficit — measured as a ratio of GDP — had risen from 9% of GDP in 1972–75 to 17–18% in 1976–79 (annual averages). As noted earlier, government spending, as a ratio of GDP, peaked in 1979, and then declined strongly (in relative terms) until 1985. Moreover, foreign grants rose strongly between 1979 and 1981. The fiscal deficit fell to 10–11% of GDP in 1980–83. This was followed by a small increase to 12% in 1984–85 and then a sharp rise to 19–20% in 1986–87. The continued decline in grants received from the Arab oil states, and the increase in government spending in order to stimulate the economy resulted in large-scale deficit spending. What is worse, while during the 1970s the bulk of the deficits was covered by concessional loans (i.e., long-term low-interest loans, usually with a grace period of five to ten years until payments were to begin), the loans taken during the 1980s to cover the deficits, were, to a far greater extent, commercial loans. Furthermore, the grace period was ending for many of the loans taken in the previous decade. Total debt service (annual payments of principal and interest for both foreign and domestic loans) rose sharply from $120m. in 1980 to $430m. in 1987, of which two thirds was to foreign creditors. But these figures understate the magnitude and the burden of the debt since they exclude payments on external loans related to military purchases abroad. In 1980 debt servicing (excluding military loans) absorbed 16% of domestic revenues (i.e., excluding foreign grants and all loans); by 1987 the ratio had risen to 27%. (For a discussion of Jordan's foreign debt, see below.)

The government's domestic revenues are from two broad sources, taxes and nontax revenues. There is a small income tax, but the main taxes are indirect — customs, excise taxes on cigarettes, alcoholic and some other beverages, and the like, taxes on property and on sales of real estate, departure taxes, stamp duties, etc. Nontax revenues include various licenses and fees, operating surpluses of the postal system and telephone services, work permits for foreigners, and charges for various governmental services. Since income tax collections have constituted less than 10% of total domestic revenues in recent years, and there has been no broad-based tax (such as a national sales tax), discretionary increases in fees, customs duties, excise taxes, and various other sources of revenue have been frequent. Despite the buoyancy of the economy, the ratio of domestic revenues to GDP showed little change between 1974 and 1977, ranging between 25% and 27%. The reason was simply the sharp increase in foreign aid, including both grants and concessional loans. These receipts precluded the immediate necessity to become fiscally more independent. By 1980 the ratio had fallen to 23%.

The 1981–85 Development Plan called for a reduction in dependence on foreign aid and, in fact, the ratio of domestic revenues to GDP rose to 27–28% in 1981–85. But, one of the important fiscal goals stipulated in the 1981–85 plan was that domestic revenues should rise far more rapidly so that by 1985 they should cover the government's current expenditures (civilian and military). In other words, foreign aid should be utilized solely for investment. The steady decline in foreign grants which began in 1982 — not foreseen by the planners in 1981 — added to the importance of achieving this goal. There was a distinct improvement — the ratio of domestic revenues to current expenditures rose to 83% in 1981–85, as compared with 66% in the previous five years.[42] But this was far short of the goals, and the government was compelled to have greater recourse to loans to cover the shortfall.

As the economic recession worsened in 1986 and in 1987, and foreign grants continued to fall, the government stepped up its expenditures sharply to 60% of GDP (as compared with about 50% in 1983–85), and also raised various customs duties, and a variety of fees and charges. Domestic revenues rose strongly, from 27–28% of GDP in 1984–85 to 32% in 1986–87, but this was far short of announced goals and only partly made up for the decline in foreign grants. The budgetary deficit, which had risen from 9% of GDP in 1982–83 to 12% in 1984–85, escalated to 19–20% in 1986–87. As a consequence, the public debt rose rapidly while its composition worsened, as a far greater share was financed by commercial, rather than concessional loans. The financial crisis which erupted in 1988 was a direct result of these and other developments.

THE MILITARY BURDEN

It could be assumed that the omission of military expenditures from the budgetary accounts pertains mainly to arms imports. In other words, reported military expenditures apparently reflect local spending and exclude the value of imported weapons. A comparison of reported military expenditures in the Jordanian accounts with estimates published by the US Arms Control and Disarmament Agency (ACDA) both with respect to the magnitude of military expenditures and their ratio with respect to GNP, shows a wide gap, with the latter's estimates higher, or far higher than those reported in the Jordanian fiscal accounts.[43] Moreover, grants received by Jordan as reported in the balance of payments are invariably far higher than those reported in the budgetary accounts.[44] One could assume that that part of grants received not included in the budgetary accounts was allocated to off-budgetary military spending, mainly arms imports. What compounds the difficulties of an analyst is that, at least in recent years, the ACDA estimates of Jordanian military expenditures also appear to exclude arms imports. Thus, for example, for 1981–83, ACDA estimated Jordan's arms imports at $1.1bn. p.a, while it estimated Jordan's military expenditures at only $679m. p.a. The Jordanian accounts reported an even lower figure — $516m. p.a. (annual averages). The official Jordanian budgetary accounts obviously did not report arms imports, and there was a strong presumption that they were also excluded from the published balance of payments.

Given the limitations of the data what can we conclude? Even if the absolute figures are incomplete, the overall trends and changes over time may reflect reality. Both the official Jordanian figures and the ACDA estimates indicated that the ratio of military expenditures to GNP declined strongly. The Jordanian estimates showed a drop from 20% in 1972–74 to 11% in 1983–85 (annual averages). The ACDA estimates showed a decline from 36% to 17–18% for the same period. However, it appears that the downtrend was reversed in 1985 with the ratio of military expenditures to GNP rising from 10.6% in 1984 to 13.5% in 1987, according to the budgetary accounts. (At this writing, ACDA estimates are available only until 1985.)

Clearly one of the major factors accounting for the decline in the military burden until the early 1980s was the rapid growth in the economy. However, since 1985 military expenditures (as reported in the fiscal accounts) have been rising while the economy has been stagnant. Hence, the recent uptrend in the military burden. It also appears that the magnitude of (unreported) Arab aid to finance Jordanian arms imports has diminished — as has been the case with respect to reported Arab grants mainly for civilian purposes. King Husayn stated in 1983 that the failure of Arab states to meet their financial obligations (undertaken at Arab summit conferences) had compelled Jordan to rely on commercial loans to pay for arms imports.[45] According to press reports, an arms deal with France was concluded in September 1985 for $340m., and another with Spain in March 1986 for $90m.[46] In February 1988, an order was placed with France for 20 *Mirage*s and for the modernization of older French aircraft at an estimated cost of $350m. The following month an order was placed with a British firm for *Tornado* bomber aircraft, also at a cost of $350m.[47] The reports indicated that most of these purchases were to be financed by credits from the sellers. In February 1989 it was reported that three West German banks agreed to lend Jordan over $300m. in order to finance the purchase of the *Tornado* aircraft.[48]

No figures are available regarding the servicing of the foreign debt on account of military purchases abroad, or of the size of the debt, but there is little doubt that these debts aggravated the economic crisis in Jordan. The arms imports also necessitated increased local military spending for bases, maintenance, etc. It was reported that in August 1988 — shortly following the cease-fire in the Iraqi-Iranian War — Iraq gave Jordan, as a gift, a substantial quantity of weapons of US and UK origin which Iraq had captured during the war, including tanks and personnel carriers. Iraq's arms were mainly of Soviet origin.[49] It was not clear whether these arms were to replace existing equipment. Otherwise, it implied a further increase in local military spending in order to absorb and maintain the newly acquired weapons.

In addition to local spending on the military forces and arms imports from abroad, there is also an indirect economic burden. Even if the budget fully reported military outlays it would not reflect the foregone civilian production of those employed in the armed forces. This is most relevant when there is full employment. Between the mid-1970s and early 1980s there was full employment in the country and hundreds of thousands were working abroad. Under these circumstances the foregone production of those in the armed forces was significant. However, during the 1980s a severe unemployment problem has arisen, mainly amongst the more educated. At the same time about 150,000 foreign workers were employed in Jordan in agriculture and in other manual occupations shunned by the more educated Jordanians. Whether a reduction in the size of the armed forces and their availability to the civilian economy would also reduce the number of foreign workers in Jordan, or merely add to the ranks of the unemployed, is difficult to know. (On the labor force, see further below.)

Based on official population estimates and the size of the armed forces reported by ACDA, the figures show that the ratio of the armed forces to the adult male population (ages 18–64) declined from 18–19% in 1974–75 to 14–15% in 1984–85.[50] In absolute terms there has been an increase from 65,000 in 1980 to 81,000 in 1985.

The armed forces accounted for one sixth of total employment in the latter year.[51] Moreover, these estimates do not include internal security forces, for which no estimates have been available. All in all, the burden of defense was a substantial one for Jordan and aggravated the crisis.

THE BALANCE OF PAYMENTS

COMMODITY EXPORTS

Following the end of the civil war and of the embargoes imposed by some Arab countries in 1970–71, exports rose rapidly — by about 17% p.a. between 1971 and 1981, measured in real terms. With the completion of the major industries, in particular potash and fertilizers, there was another spurt in exports in 1983–87. However, international price levels for these commodities were unfavorable and the export price index (for Jordan's commodity exports, as a whole) declined sharply between 1984 and 1987.

There were important changes in the composition of exports.[52] In 1964–66, food (mainly fresh fruits and vegetables) accounted for close to one half of total exports, and phosphates for another third, and the balance consisted of various manufactured products. In the immediate post-1967 period, the ratios were about the same. By 1984–87, food exports had declined drastically (in relative terms) to 13% of total commodity exports, and phosphates to somewhat over one fourth. Potash and fertilizers, and a small quantity of cement, also accounted for one fourth of total exports, and a wide variety of manufactured goods for one third. The latter were from various light industries including cigarettes, wood products, soap and detergents, pharmaceuticals, textiles, batteries, ceramics, plastics, furniture and various household items, as well as building materials.

There were also important changes in the direction of trade. With the exception of phosphates which were sold mainly to various Asian and East European countries, the neighboring Arab countries were the main clients of Jordanian goods. The oil boom in the neighboring countries, as well as greatly increased sales to Iraq following the outbreak of the war in 1980, gave a powerful boost to Jordan's exports. There was, however, some movement away from overwhelming reliance on Arab markets. The Arab share of Jordan's total commodity exports declined from 72–73% in 1972–73 to 60% in 1982–83. As the new industries came into production (fertilizers, potash, etc.) the Arab share fell to 50% in 1984–87.[53]

Sales to the neighboring Arab countries between 1984 and 1987 were stagnant. This was a consequence of recessionary conditions prevailing in the oil countries, and Iraq's deteriorating financial situation as the war continued. In fact Jordan was compelled to extend credit to Iraq for its purchases from Jordan. In effect Jordan was paying its exporters for their sales to Iraq; otherwise, they were threatened with bankruptcy. In mid-1988 it was reported that Iraq owed Jordan $600m.[54] To put this figure into perspective it might be noted that Jordan's total commodity exports in 1987 were $735m.

As noted earlier, marketing was a major problem inhibiting agricultural exports. Quality control and packaging were deficient and competition from Turkey as well as from Saudi farmers has been eroding Jordan's market for agricultural produce in the neighboring Arab oil states. With respect to industrial exports, Jordan also faces serious obstacles. According to an evaluation of a British economist, "Most Jordanian exports are basic, low-technology goods such as plastic products, tried and tested medicines, household furniture, and a range of other basic consumer items....Jordan's problem is that Saudi Arabia [and other countries in the region are] developing a similar range of industries on a highly subsidized basis...which Jordan cannot afford. Much of Jordan's trade is conducted on a countertrading [barter] basis... phosphate and fertilizer sales are...often on a barter basis...unwanted goods have to be accepted [from the trading partners]."[55] In mid-1988 Jordan concluded a barter agreement with Brazil, a major importer of potash.[56] In recent years barter agreements were also concluded with Syria, Egypt, and with other countries. What this indicates is that much or most of Jordan's industry is unable to compete in world markets in terms of price and quality — hence, the recourse to bilateral trade agreements with less-developed countries based mainly on barter.

COMMODITY IMPORTS

Between 1971 and 1981 imports, measured in constant prices, rose by 17% p.a., about the same rate as exports. Imports rose more moderately in 1982–83, and remained at about the same level in 1984–87. In dollar terms there was a decline in imports in 1986–87 mainly as a result of the sharp drop in oil prices, as well as of other commodities, especially food. Higher customs duties designed to reduce imports, and a sharp slowdown in investment were also instrumental in reducing imports in recent years.

Within the various categories of imports, the sharpest growth rate since the early 1970s was in consumer durable goods, reflecting rapidly rising living standards, and in capital goods until 1982–83. Subsequently there was a sharp decline in capital goods imports reflecting the drop in investment, as noted earlier.[57] Excluding oil imports from Saudi Arabia, and more recently from Iraq (in partial payment of Iraq's debt), imports from the Arab countries were minor. The Western countries and Japan were the source of most imports of both consumer and capital goods.Some of this trade was in the context of foreign aid extended to Jordan in the form of concessional loans and grants.

THE TRADE DEFICIT

The trade deficit rose precipitously from somewhat over $200m. in 1972 to $2.5bn. in 1982. Subsequently there was a steep drop to $1.8bn. in 1987. The sharp rise between 1972 and 1982 reflected a number of factors: (1) Since commodity imports were initially far greater than commodity exports, the similar rate of growth in both, in terms of volume, widened the trade deficit in absolute terms. (2) There was a strong rise in international prices for both exports and imports, further widening the trade deficit when measured in current dollars. (3) There was a deterioration in Jordan's terms of trade between 1975 and 1982. Oil prices, in particular, rose sharply. Oil imports rose from less than $10m. in 1972 to $655m. in 1982 partly as a result of a greater volume of imports but mainly due to far higher prices. (4) The food deficit (food exports minus food imports) rose strongly from $63m. in 1972 to a peak of $390m. in 1982.

The sharp decline in the trade deficit between 1982 and 1987 was due to a number of factors including the sharp drop in oil and food prices as well as of other imported commodities. The food deficit in 1987 was almost $100m. lower than in 1982 and the oil import bill declined by over $300m. The government imposed greater restrictions and higher duties on a number of so-called luxury imports. And, as noted earlier, there was a sharp drop in capital goods imports as investment waned.

TRADE BETWEEN JORDAN AND THE WEST BANK (JUDEA AND SAMARIA)

Jordanian data do not provide estimates of trade with the West Bank. (It is possible that as a consequence of King Husayn's disengagement announcement in the summer of 1988 [see chapter on Jordan], Amman would begin to publish statistics on its economic relations with the West Bank.) This section is therefore based on data published by Israel's Central Bureau of Statistics.[58]

Measured in current dollars, Jordan's exports to the West Bank ranged between $4m. and $5m. p.a. in 1972–80. Subsequently, there was an uptrend to about $10m. in 1986–87 (annual averages). Israeli statistics provide two categories of trade: agricultural and industrial products. Jordan's agricultural exports to the West Bank were insignificant. In relation to Jordan's total commodity exports, its sales to the West Bank were declining rapidly during the 1970s, from 11% in 1972–73 to 1.4% in 1980–81, and then remained at that level until 1987.

The factors underlying these developments included the following: the agricultural surpluses in both the West Bank and in Jordan consisted largely of fruits and vegetables; in other words, there was little complementarity in this sector. Jordan has an overall agricultural deficit which has widened in the past two decades. Jordan's exports of phosphates, fertilizers, and potash are overwhelmingly to a number of Asian and Eastern European countries. As for various manufactured goods, Israel's industry is far more advanced than Jordan's, and, as noted earlier, the latter has difficulty competing in world markets in terms of price and quality.

Jordan's imports from the West Bank are far greater than its exports, rising from $23m. in 1972–74 to $72m. in 1985–87 (annual averages). In relation to Jordan's total commodity imports, the share of the West Bank declined during the 1970s, from 7% in 1972–74 to 3% in 1980–82 and remained at about that level until 1987. While Jordan's sales of agricultural produce to the West Bank are insignificant, between one third and one half of the West Bank's sales to Jordan consist of farm produce. Apparently a large part of these sales is destined for further shipment to other Arab countries through Jordanian middlemen.

Thus, while geographic proximity, family and other personal ties, and the use of Jordanian currency in the West Bank (recognized by Israel along with its own currency as legal tender there), facilitate trade between Jordan and the West Bank, limited complementarity, the small size of the market, and competition with Israeli industry tend to restrict its scope.

THE EXPORT AND IMPORT OF SERVICES (INVISIBLES)

That Jordan's economy is dominated by services is clearly evident from an examination of the balance of payments as well as of the composition of GNP and the labor force.

Remittances of Jordanians working abroad formed the main service export. According to the official accounts, remittances rose from $21m. in 1972 to a peak of

$1,237m. in 1984, and then declined to $938m. in 1987.[59] Actually remittances are believed to have been far higher. The official accounts reported only transfers through the banks. One unofficial estimate suggested that remittances were actually 50–100% higher than reported in the official accounts.[60] Another writer suggested that if one added imports in kind brought into the country by Jordanians working abroad, and the foreign currency converted through money changers, one should add about 60% to the figure for remittances reported in the official accounts. Using the latter estimate would suggest that remittances in 1984 — the peak year — were about $2bn. To put this figure into perspective, one might note that foreign grants received by Jordan in that year were $688m. and that domestic exports (excluding transit trade) were about the same. Viewed differently, remittances were equivalent to one half of GDP in 1984 — a massive infusion into the economy. The sharp decline in remittances between 1984 and 1987 was a major blow to the economy.

Another important service export is tourism (see above). Income from that source in 1985–87 was $544m. (annual average), not far below commodity exports which averaged $575m. p.a. in the same period. As already noted, transit trade also assumed major importance since the beginning of the Iraqi-Iranian War when Jordan became a major alternative route for Iraqi exports and imports.

Investment income, mainly interest from foreign exchange reserves held abroad, peaked at $205m. in 1982, and then dropped sharply to $58m. in 1987. This was due both to the steep decline in foreign exchange reserves from $1,049m. at the end of 1981 to $413m. five years later, and the far lower interest rates prevailing in recent years.[61]

On an overall basis, the export of services (including reexports) accounted for 80% of total exports in 1972–73, rising to 84% in 1981–82 and then declining to 78% in 1988–87. The rise and subsequent fall in remittances were responsible for most of the fluctuations.

With respect to imports, commodities are dominant, accounting for close to 80% of total imports in 1972–73, then declining (in relative terms) to about 70% in the 1980s. The more rapid growth in the import of services in recent years was due to a number of factors. As labor shortages emerged in the latter half of the 1970s (due both to increasing prosperity at home and more Jordanians leaving for lucrative jobs in the Gulf countries), Jordan began to import labor on a large scale. The remittances sent home by these workers constitute payment for imported services. However, even at their peak, in 1984, they were $254m., while remittances of Jordanians were officially estimated at $1,237m.

Expenditures of Jordanians on travel abroad had also risen strongly, reflecting higher incomes, and the growing number of Jordanians studying and visiting abroad. Another factor which adversely affected the balance of payments was the rapid growth in interest payments to creditors abroad (see below). Interest payments had risen sharply, from $79m. in 1980 to $279m. in 1987. This reflects both the rapid growth of the foreign debt and the worsening of its composition, with commercial, rather than concessional loans constituting a growing share of the foreign debt.

THE IMPORT SURPLUS, AID, AND EXTERNAL DEBT

Jordan has traditionally had an import surplus, i.e., imports of goods and services have exceeded exports of goods and services. The positive balance in the service accounts was insufficient to offset the trade deficit. So long as grants received by the government (plus much smaller unilateral transfers from abroad received by individuals and organizations in Jordan) approximated the import surplus, the balance of payments was in good shape. There was very little foreign private investment. The balance on current account (exports of goods and services plus unilateral transfers received, minus imports of goods and services) was positive for the 1972–80 period as a whole. The government also received relatively large concessional loans from various Arab and Western governments as well as from international agencies. As a consequence of both positive current account balances and the receipt of concessional loans, central bank foreign exchange reserves rose from $211m. at the end of 1971 to $1,107m. at the end of 1980, while gold reserves also rose from 797,000 to 1,021,000 ounces during the same period.[62]

The deterioration in the balance of payments began in the early 1980s. Grants from the Arab oil states were dropping, as well as concessional loans. Total grants received dropped almost steadily from a peak of $1.3bn. in 1980 to $600m. in 1987. Remittances leveled off and then began to drop in 1985. Commodity imports declined after 1982, mainly as a consequence of lower oil and food prices, but service imports continued to trend upward. Iraq's deteriorating financial situation affected transit trade as well as Jordan's commodity exports. As noted earlier, Jordan began to extend credits to Iraq in 1983.

Beginning with 1982, the balance on current account took a sharp turn for the worse. There were four consecutive years of massive deficits, averaging $312m. p.a. in 1982–85. What is worse, a large part of these deficits was covered by reducing foreign exchange reserves from $1,049m. in 1981 to $400m. in 1985. Import restrictions were tightened in 1985–86 (higher import license fees, some increases in tariffs, and a ban on some imports), but these measures were insufficient. The US agreed to provide $250m. in additional aid, over a three-year period.[63] In 1986 the current account deficit dropped sharply to $40m., reflecting, in large measure, a decline of close to $300m. in payments for oil imports as oil prices plummeted. In 1987, there was again a sharp deterioration and the current account deficit rose to $352m.

Two important items have been omitted: (1) Arms imports are excluded from the official accounts (as noted earlier, there are reports that in recent years Jordan had concluded a number of agreements for arms imports based on credits). (2) The current account in the balance of payments includes interest payments paid to abroad (as well as receipts from abroad) but does not include payments on account of principal. In other words, the authorities faced the problem of financing very large current account deficits and, in addition, payments on account of principal. The external public debt rose from $171m. in 1972 to $1,240m. in 1980 and $3,835m. in 1987. But the servicing of the debt rose far more steeply, from $7m. in 1972 to $136m. in 1980, and $555m. in 1987. One way of measuring the size of the debt is to relate it to GNP. By this measure there was an increase from 28% in 1972 to 34% in 1980, followed by a steep rise to 70% in 1987. A better measure of the foreign debt burden is to relate the annual servicing of the debt, payments on account of principal and interest, to the country's foreign currency earnings in that year, i.e., exports of goods and services (including remittances). This ratio rose from 4.5% in 1972 to 5.4% in 1980 and then escalated to 17.2% in 1987. If one adds grants to foreign currency earnings, the ratios were: 2.1%, 3.6%, and 14.5%, respectively.[64] It should be emphasized again that these figures exclude the servicing of the debt related to military purchases, which, according to unofficial accounts, also escalated during the 1980s. It was reported, in 1988, that Jordan was 11 months in arrears in payments on a $250m. debt to the US for arms purchases.[65]

One of the more difficult questions to answer is why, in the face of a deteriorating balance of payments since 1982–83, the Jordanian authorities maintained an artificially high exchange rate. In fact, there was even a slight *revaluation,* from $2.75 per JD1 in 1983 to $2.95 in 1987.[66] A gradual devaluation might have stimulated exports of some goods and services, such as tourism, and restricted imports of goods and services, without strong inflationary effects. Instead, there was a sudden and sharp collapse of the dinar beginning in mid-1988. The crisis which erupted in 1988 will be the subject of the concluding sections of this study.

THE LABOR FORCE, EMPLOYMENT, AND UNEMPLOYMENT

The authors of the 1981–85 Development Plan noted the "dearth of information, statistical data, and studies, related to manpower planning, supply and demand [for labor] and [its] distribution by sector, occupation, sex, educational attainment, and wages."[67] There has been little change since then. Data on the labor force force are scarce, and often of dubious quality. Figures given by Ministry of Labor officials have often differed widely from those given by the Ministry of Planning and the Department of Statistics. Hopefully, despite the limitations, we can delineate overall trends and some broad orders of magnitude.

POPULATION AND MIGRATION

According to the census of November 1979 (the first taken since 1961) the population was 2.1m., including over 100,000 foreigners, but excluding Jordanians abroad. The Department of Statistics estimated that by 1985 the population had grown to 2.7m., suggesting a growth rate of 3.8% p.a. between 1979 and 1985, of which 3.4% was the rate of natural increase and the balance net migration.[68] Jordan's rate of natural increase is unusually high, even for less developed countries. By way of comparison, the population growth rate in Egypt during the same period was significantly lower — 2.8%.[69] Extrapolating these growth rates suggests that Jordan's population was about 3m. in 1988.

The large-scale migration of Jordanians seeking higher-paying jobs in the Arab oil states was already apparent in the 1961 population census which found that 61,000 Jordanians were employed abroad (aside from accompanying family dependents), or about 9% of Jordan's labor force. This migration continued during the 1960s, and accelerated during the 1970s and early 1980s in response to the oil boom. The under secretary of labor estimated in 1981 that there were about 300,000 Jordanians working abroad, of whom about one fourth were in Saudi Arabia; another fourth in Kuwait; and 15% in other Arab countries in the Gulf. The remaining 100,000 were in various Western countries, mainly in West Germany and the US. Presumably, the latter were permanent emigrants.[70] With rare exceptions, the Arab oil states in the Gulf do not grant citizenship to foreigners. They must periodically renew their work and residence permits and can be expelled at any time.

As the oil boom waned, and the governments in the oil countries curtailed spending, their need for foreign workers diminished. Construction was the sector most affected by the cutbacks. But most Jordanians working in the oil states are professionals — teachers, doctors, accountants, and in various other white-collar jobs, of whom relatively few were fired. Nonetheless there have been some dismissals of Jordanians since 1984.[71] The Ministry of Labor estimated that there were 339,300 Jordanians working abroad in 1985.[72] Its estimate for 1987 was 325,000. It was also estimated that, including family dependents, the number of Jordanian expatriates was between 800,000 and 1m. in 1985.[73] However, while relatively few Jordanians had lost their jobs in the Gulf countries, the oil states had ceased to be the "safety valve" for the rapidly growing Jordanian labor force. Moreover, the salaries of those remaining in the Gulf states had been "cut drastically."[74] Given the rising unemployment situation at home, Jordanians preferred to take wage cuts rather than return, so long as they had the option.[75] The decline in remittances since 1984, noted earlier, reflected these developments.

The booming economy in Jordan in the 1970s combined with growing emigration, created labor shortages. Beginning with the mid-1970s a growing number of workers from the poorer Arab countries migrated to Jordan. The 1979 census found that 102,000 foreigners were residing in Jordan, of whom 45,000 were employed, the others being accompanying family members. Subsequently, their numbers increased rapidly, possibly reaching a peak in 1984 or 1985. According to official estimates the number of foreign workers in Jordan reached 143,000 in 1985 and then fell to 130,000 in 1986.[76] But apparently there is a large number of foreigners working illegally, not included in the official estimates. One source suggested that, in 1987, the number of foreigners working legally was 98,000 plus another 80,000 working illegally. The report suggested that around 75,000, mainly Egyptians, were employed in agriculture and construction doing the sort of jobs which "Jordanians regard as demeaning." A much smaller number of foreigners consisted of highly skilled workers from the Western countries, while others were domestic workers from the Far East and Indian subcontinent, as well as in other occupations.[77] One report states that about 10,000 Sri Lankan women were working as domestic servants in Jordan.[78] Apparently having a Sri Lankan maid is a status symbol in Jordan.

In response to growing unemployment in Jordan the authorities have been increasing the fees of foreign workers for their work permits, and have intensified their search for illegals. The Ministry of Labor announced that between 22 July and 10 October 1987, over 4,000 foreigners working illegally were deported, and their employers were fined. The ministry stated that it was continuing to search for an estimated 70,000 Egyptians and 10,000 Syrians working illegally.[79]

What these reports seem to suggest is that, in 1987, the number of foreign workers in Jordan was about 150,000, accounting for possibly 30% of total employment.[80] The number of Jordanians working abroad was about double that number. However, the gap between the remittances sent home by Jordanians and those transferred by the foreign workers in Jordan was much wider, \$938m. as against \$184m. (leaving aside remittances through unofficial channels). The Jordanians abroad were, by and large, more educated and more skilled, while the foreigners in Jordan were, for the most part, low-paid unskilled or semi-skilled manual workers. Furthermore, wage rates were generally far higher in the Arab oil states.

THE DISTRIBUTION OF THE LABOR FORCE BY SECTORS

Every few years official estimates are published of the total number employed with a breakdown by economic sectors. No estimates are offered with respect to nationals and foreigners, their occupations, educational levels, etc.

It is obvious that the published estimates with respect to agriculture are far too low. They show that the number employed in agriculture declined from 54,000 in 1972 (17% of total employment) to 42,000 in 1979 (10% of total employment) and then dropped further to 37,000 in 1986 (7.5% of total employment). While the downtrend probably reflects reality, there is little doubt that there were many more working in agriculture than indicated in the official estimates.[81] Crown Prince Hasan asserted in 1988 that there were 150,000 foreign workers "largely in agriculture."[82] The official estimates show 37,000 engaged in agriculture in 1986, including both Jordanians and foreigners.

The share of total employment in industry (including mining, manufacturing, electricity, and water) shows a small upward trend from less than 10% in the early 1970s to 11–12% in the 1980s. Construction was booming in the 1970s, and then slackened in the 1980s. This sector accounted for 8% of total employment in 1972, rising sharply to 16% in 1979, and then dropped to 11% in 1986. Transportation shows a rising trend, especially in the 1980s, as transit trade, especially to and from Iraq, expanded. Employment in this sector rose from 6–7% of total employment in 1972–75 to over 9% in 1986. But aside from transportation, trade, and finance, the largest sector by far is what is defined as "public administration, defense, and other services" which includes the civil service, the armed and internal security forces, educational, health, and other public services. This category rose from one third of total employment in 1972 to 47% in 1986. As noted earlier, the number in the armed forces rose moderately. However, the number engaged in health, education, and other services increased rapidly. No figures are available for the size and growth of the internal security forces. An American scholar wrote in 1987 that the "secret police [were] everywhere."[83] The rapid growth in employment in "public administration and defense" explains, in part, the difficulty faced by the Ministry of Finance in its drive to curb government expenditures and the budgetary deficit.

EDUCATIONAL LEVELS

In terms of educational levels Jordan is probably the most advanced of the Arab states, replacing Lebanon which has been racked and wrecked by a vicious civil war since 1975. The data show that the enrollment ratio in primary schools has reached 99% and on the secondary level rose from one third in 1970 to almost 80% in 1985. The greatest expansion was in higher education. The number studying in universities in Jordan rose from 5,500 in 1972 to over 26,400 in 1985. Since the later 1970s there has also been a very strong growth in the number of students at community colleges, teachers' colleges, and other post-secondary schools. In 1985 the number of students in these schools equalled those in Jordanian universities. In addition, there were an estimated 50,000 studying in universities abroad.[84] About one fourth of the 18–23 age group was enrolled in higher education.[85] Few less-developed countries have such a large number in higher education in relation to the size of the population.

The problem is that the educational system is hardly geared to the absorptive capacity and requirements of the Jordanian economy. Until recently the students believed that, upon graduation, well-paying jobs awaited them in the Gulf states. In the 1981–85 Development Plan it was projected that, assuming only one half of those studying in universities abroad return, 27% of the new entrants into the labor force would be university graduates and another 26% graduates of the various other post-secondary schools in Jordan. They also projected a continued rise in the labor force participation rate, especially of females.[86] Clearly, neither the planners nor the students anticipated that the demand for more foreign labor in the Gulf states would end so abruptly. What is worse, the recession in Jordan since 1983 also reduced domestic demand for educated manpower.

While the educational system is top-heavy with students in higher education, the economy is short of some middle-level practical skills. Jordan has about three times as many physicians as practical nurses, and over 40% of the nurses are expatriates, often of low quality. The physicians are, almost invariably, Jordanian.[87]

UNEMPLOYMENT

As noted above, since 1983 or 1984 unemployment had become an acute problem due to the recession in the Gulf states and in Jordan. In 1980 the National Planning Council found that there were shortages of some categories of skilled labor in industry, construction, and tourism; in the professions, there were shortages of qualified teachers and nurses. At the same time there were some surpluses, expressed in underemployment of other professionals, mainly physicians and engineers. It also noted that there was a major increase in the number of women, graduates of secondary and higher education, seeking work.[88] In 1981 the under secretary of labor stated that the overall unemployment rate was 2% and that "nearly all are workers between jobs or new job seekers."[89] A 2% rate of unemployment implies serious labor shortages.

In its estimates of labor requirements during the 1981–85 period, the National Planning Council projected that there would be an overall shortage of "about 70,000. It is expected that this shortage will be met by a further inflow of workers from abroad as well as by the return of Jordanians working abroad and a further increase in female participation in the labor force."[90] The reality, however, proved to be entirely different. Instead of shortages there soon emerged growing labor surpluses, i.e., unemployment. According to the Labor Ministry, the unemployment rate had risen to 4.5% in 1983.[91] By 1986 unemployment had risen to 8%, according to Labor Ministry estimates, but the World Bank mission suggested that it was really 13% and *could reach 30% by 1990.*[92]

No less important is the occupational composition of the unemployed. The Civil Service Commission reported that in 1987 it had received 33,000 applications for 8,000 available positions. Ten thousand of the applicants were university graduates, including 780 physicians and 1,800 engineers, another 16,000 were graduates of community colleges, and the other 7,000 were high school graduates.[93] Unemployment in some professional categories was estimated to have reached 20–30%.[94] In 1987, the under secretary of labor stated that 90% of the unemployed in Jordan were graduates of secondary or higher education.[95] Unofficial estimates for 1988 suggest that the overall unemployment rate had reached 14–16%.[96]

The extreme distortions in the labor market are readily apparent. According to the higher unofficial estimates, there were about 80,000 job seekers in 1987. At the same time there were about 150,000 foreigners working in the country. In a press interview in August 1988, the crown prince referred to this anomaly, stating that "with 150,000 workers from abroad, largely in agriculture, I feel that something is tragically wrong."[97] In other words, there was no justification for such a high rate of unemployment amongst Jordanians while foreigners, in even larger numbers, very few of whom were skilled, could so readily be replaced by unemployed citizens. As noted earlier, the government had been taking various measures to curtail the employment of foreigners and to expel those working illegally. In 1988 it banned the employment of foreign accountants, clerical and sales workers, and teachers.[98] In 1986, the Ministry of Labor imposed a fee of JD30 on foreign Arab workers (except in agriculture, where the fee was JD10) and JD50–150 on non-Arab foreign workers, depending on occupation. (In 1986 the Jordanian dinar was equal to $2.86). The goal was to replace all foreign workers. New work permits were being issued only for agriculture and domestic service, apparently since Jordanians shunned these jobs.[99] But the more educated classes considered it socially demeaning to work in those jobs performed by the large majority of foreigners, even excluding agriculture and domestic service.

The authorities were aware of the fact that the measures taken to replace foreigners had limited efficacy. In 1987, the prime minister issued orders to the various ministries, public sector institutions, and local governments, to employ an additional 750 engineers. Orders were also issued to all community colleges and private schools to employ a full-time doctor and two medical assistants. Major industrial establishments were also expected to follow suit. But this make-work policy carries a high economic price and would invite pressure for more make-work white-collar jobs.[100] Its effect would be to increase the budgetary deficit and indirectly aggravate the balance of payments problems.

In the absence of social welfare schemes, such as unemployment insurance as is common in the Western countries, how do the unemployed manage financially? It appears that "families prefer to support their unemployed educated members rather than jeopardize their social status by undertaking manual work."[101] The reference here is to extended families and to what are called tribal networks.[102] The government continued to exert political pressure on the Arab oil states not to dismiss Jordanians working there. Furthermore, the government announced in 1988 that it was willing to subsidize salaries of professionals who would take jobs in the poor Arab countries, where wage levels are far lower than in Jordan.[103] But a mission from North Yemen that came in early 1989, seeking to employ 400 Jordanian physicians, elicited little response.[104]

The problem of unemployment assumed critical dimensions, especially since it was concentrated so heavily amongst the more educated classes. It may well have the potential of posing serious dangers for the future stability of the regime.

A BRIEF SUMMATION[105]

Following the Arab-Israeli war of 1948, the Kingdom of Jordan, with a population of 375,000, annexed the area which came to be known as the West Bank, with an indigenous population of 460,000. In addition, about 350,000 Palestinians who left the newly founded State of Israel went to Jordan. From the point of view of economic development the demographic changes had far-reaching ramifications. At that time the Palestinians were far more advanced than the Transjordanians in terms of skills, educational levels, and so on.

Between the mid-1950s and 1967 the economy advanced rapidly with GDP rising by an average annual rate of 7–8%. Living standards rose, and unemployment was reduced to 5–6% of the labor force. The focus of development was the East Bank (the original Emirate of Transjordan), including phosphate mining, the East Ghor Canal which stimulated a rapid growth in irrigated agriculture, in particular fruits and vegetables, and a number of modern new industries. 'Aqaba, the kingdom's only port, was developed, and there was considerable investment in infrastructure — roads, electricity, water supplies, communications, and so on. Education and health services were given particular emphasis. There was a large migration mainly to the rich Arab states, but internal migration from west to east was much larger. Wage rates were far higher and economic opportunities more abundant in the east. By 1966 Jordan's per capita GNP was estimated to have exceeded that of all the other Arab countries except for the wealthiest oil states and Lebanon. Back in the late 1940s or early 1950s Jordan's economy was amongst the least developed.

The Six Day War of 1967 was short-lived, and inflicted very little damage on Jordan's economy. The immediate problem was the influx of 260,000 refugees who migrated to the East Bank. But about a year after the war the economic indicators were pointing upward and, by 1969, unemployment had declined to prewar levels, or possibly even lower. However, the recovery was aborted by clashes between Palestinian armed groups based in Jordan and the Israeli Army, which culminated in devastating battles between these armed groups and the Jordanian Army. The civil war ended in mid-1971 with the expulsion of the Palestinian militias, but Jordan's economic problems were aggravated by the actions of some Arab countries in support of the Palestinian factions. The most serious damage was inflicted by the Syrian embargo on transit and trade. With the lifting of the embargo in 1972, Jordan resumed its path of rapid economic advance.

The economy grew very rapidly in the decade 1972-82, with GNP rising by almost 10% p.a. in real terms, an even higher rate of growth than in the decade preceding the Six Day War. But the rapid pace of economic growth was far more intricately tied to external stimuli than had been true in the past.

Jordan's participation in the Yom Kippur War of 1973 was peripheral. But the oil shock of 1973–74 and the second oil shock of 1979–80 had powerful indirect effects. Financial aid from the Arab oil states assumed much larger dimensions. But, even more important, the booming economies in these countries attracted millions of foreign workers, including hundreds of thousands of Jordanians. The remittances of the Jordanian workers to their families back home were of much greater magnitude than foreign aid. The rapidly growing economies in the neighboring oil states also opened up markets for Jordanian exports. Tourism, transit trade, and investment by some wealthy Arabs, especially in real estate, added to the external stimuli. There were also minuses. The exodus of so many skilled and professional Jordanians to more lucrative jobs in the Arab oil states created shortages of some skills and raised general wage rates in Jordan. The higher wage rates adversely affected Jordan's ability to compete in external markets. Moreover, since Jordan is wholly dependent on imported oil for virtually all its energy requirements, the escalation in oil prices aggravated the country's trade deficit. However, an assessment of the financial balance, as a whole, would show that with regard to the impact of the oil shocks on Jordan, the pluses greatly outweighed the minuses.

The civil war in Lebanon, which erupted in 1975, also aided Jordan. Some of the wealthier Lebanese fled to Jordan and added to the boom in real estate. The reopening of the Suez Canal, also in 1975, gave an additional boost to the development of the port of ʻAqaba. The Iraqi-Iranian War, which began in September 1980, also benefited Jordan. Since the Gulf was closed to Iraq, Jordan became one of the alternative routes for transit to Iraq. Oil shipments by truck from Iraq via ʻAqaba added to Jordan's earnings from transit trade. Jordanian businessmen also increased their sales of Jordanian goods to Iraq. In short, a host of external stimuli gave a powerful boost to Jordan's economy — until the early 1980s.

The turning point came in 1982 or 1983. The change from a decade of high-level economic growth and prosperity to stagnation and growing economic problems was almost abrupt. The macroeconomic indicators put into sharp focus the direction and magnitude of the change. The following figures compare the average annual rates of growth — or decline — in real terms (i.e., corrected for inflation), in two periods: 1972–82, the period of high-level growth, and the more recent period of economic stagnancy, 1982–87:[106]

	1972–82	*1982–87*
Gross domestic product	7.9%	2.1%
Gross domestic product per capita	2.7%	-1.7%
Gross national product	9.7%	0
Gross national product per capita	5.5%	-3.8%
Gross fixed investment	18.6%	-7.8%
Private consumption per capita	4.5%	-5.0%

GDP is a measure of production within the country, while GNP is a better measure of incomes. In the case of Jordan, the difference between the two measures is attributable mainly to workers' remittances. Remittances climbed sharply in the 1970s and early 1980s and then began to decline.[107] Private consumption per capita is a measure of living standards. The sharp decline in investment since 1983 has negative implications for the future growth of the economy.

In 1981, world oil prices reached their peak, and in the following years the oil revenues of Saudi Arabia and of other oil-exporting countries began their steep descent. Saudi Arabia's oil export revenues fell from a peak of $111bn. in 1981 to $18bn.–$20bn. p.a. in 1986–88. Foreign aid was one of the first items to be curtailed. Grants received by the Government of Jordan which had risen from $185m. in 1972 to $1.3bn. in 1980 and again in 1981, subsequently dropped almost annually, to reach $600m. in 1987. As the revenues received by Saudi Arabia and the other Middle East oil exporters continued to decline, they began to curtail internal expenditures on various investment projects, and their need for foreign workers diminished. Many were dismissed, and the wage rates of those retained dropped sharply. Remittances of Jordanian workers — through official channels — which had risen from a mere $21m. in 1972 to $1.2bn. in 1984, dropped to less than $1bn. in 1987. Remittances through unofficial channels were estimated at another 50–100% and, presumably, also declined in recent years. As Saudi Arabia and other countries in the Gulf were encountering balance of payments (current account) deficits they began to curtail imports —

adversely affecting Jordanian exporters, amongst others. Furthermore, the Gulf states were developing industries and agriculture, often displacing Jordanian products. As the Iraqi-Iranian War dragged on, Iraq's financial situation worsened and it, too, curtailed imports. Many Jordanian businessmen who had exported to Iraq were encountering inordinate delays in payment. In order to bail out its businessmen, the Central Bank of Jordan paid its nationals, in return for IOUs from the Central Bank of Iraq. In mid-1988 it was announced that Iraq owed Jordan a total of $600m. To put this figure into perspective, one might note that Jordan's total commodity exports were $650m.-$700m. p.a. in 1984–87.

But while external developments had a major impact on Jordan's economic growth and subsequent decline, there were also internal factors which aggravated the recessionary forces of recent years.

All the economic sectors advanced in the 1972–82 period, including agriculture, but this sector suffered from relative neglect. Jordan's dependence on imported food rose to the point where an estimated two thirds of food consumption consisted of imports. The food deficit (food exports minus food imports) rose very sharply from $35m. p.a. in 1968–70 to about $350m. p.a. in 1980–82. The increase was due, in part, to higher international prices, but was mainly a consequence of a much greater volume of food imports. Subsequently, the food deficit declined to $300m. p.a. in 1985–87, mainly as a result of lower international prices. No figures were available for 1988, but the far higher international food prices prevailing in that year probably exacerbated the deficit.

The authorities gave high priority to fostering industry. Two major projects were initiated in the later 1970s, designed largely for export, each at a cost of close to $500m. One was the extraction of potash from the Dead Sea and the other production of fertilizers and various derivative chemicals based on the processing of phosphate rock. Both complexes were dogged with technical problems, and lengthy costly delays. What was worse, the prices of these products fell quite sharply in international markets.

A wide range of other industries was developed and expanded, but during the 1980s, industrial exports were encountering obstacles as competition from similar industries in the Gulf, and elsewhere, was intensifying. By and large Jordan's industries are not sophisticated and wage levels are often higher than those of their competitors in less-developed countries. The government's policy of maintaining a high exchange rate compounded the difficulties faced by Jordan's industrial exporters. Bilateral trade agreements, including barter, which almost invariably breeds inefficiencies, became more and more the norm.

Construction enjoyed a boom in the 1970s and early 1980s, based on the expanding inflow of remittances — much of which was utilized for housing — and on large-scale investment by the state in infrastructure and industry. However, in the mid-1980s the boom in real estate prices turned into a crash. The sharp contraction in construction had pervasive effects throughout the economy, in particular in those industries producing building materials, furniture, and so on.

Income from tourism expanded rapidly in the 1970s, based on visitors from the Arab oil states and a growing number of Westerners. In 1981 income from tourism exceeded commodity exports. Subsequently there was a serious decline in visitors from the West and income from tourism stagnated. Jordanian planners had projected a strong continued upswing. The downturn in tourism added to the recessionary forces.

As compared with other countries at similar levels of per capita GDP, the share of services in the economy is inordinately large. This is true of the share of services in GDP, in total exports (goods and services), and in the labor force. Jordan's various development plans had long recognized the importance of restructuring the economy in favor of the commodities-producing sectors, in particular, industry and agriculture. During the 1970s there was some movement in that direction, but the recession since the early 1980s reversed the trend. The large share of services is due to many factors including the size of the armed and internal security forces, and a strong emphasis on educational and health services. Enrollment ratios on all educational levels are far higher than in other less-developed countries. Overall, the share of "public administration, defense, and other public services" in total employment climbed from 34% in 1972 to 35% in 1979 and 46% in 1986. The massive expansion in employment by the government, civilian plus military, puts strong upward pressure on government spending and aggravates the budgetary deficits.

The government's income from domestic sources and from foreign grants rose very rapidly until the early 1980s, but spending rose even more rapidly. In 1976–79 deficits were huge, averaging 16.5% of GDP. These were covered largely by concessional loans from various Arab and Western countries and international agencies. Subsequently there was some relative restraint in government spending and, concurrently, grants from the Arab states rose sharply in 1979–81 (the second oil shock). As a consequence, fiscal deficits fell to 10–11% of GDP in 1980–83. Subsequently, the uptrend in deficits was resumed as grants were diminishing, and in 1986–87 they reached 19–20% of GDP. But while during the 1970s the government was able to cover its deficits largely by concessional loans, the deficits in the 1980s were covered more and more by far more onerous commercial loans mainly from external sources.

In addition to the published budgets there are off-budgetary expenditures, largely payments for military purchases abroad. The *published* budgets show that the ratio of military expenditures to GNP declined from 20% in 1972–74 to 11% in 1983–85. The estimates of the US ACDA show a similar trend but at far higher levels, with the ratio dropping from 35% to 17–18% for the same periods. However, the downtrend appears to have been reversed in 1985. Since GNP has been declining in recent years the same level of military spending necessarily raised the ratio. It also appears that in recent years Jordan concluded various agreements for arms imports based on credits. Unofficial sources reported that in earlier years much or most of Jordanian arms imports were financed by its richer Arab friends.

Jordan's trade deficit grew inordinately from $200m. in 1972 to $2.5bn. in 1982, and then dropped to $1.8bn. in 1987. The recent drop was due to a number of factors, mainly lower oil prices, lower food prices, and some restrictions on imports in recent years. A large part of the trade deficit is offset by a favorable balance in the export and import of services (invisibles). The most important service exports are the remittances of Jordanians abroad, followed by income from tourism. Transit trade, especially to and from Iraq, also grew in importance in recent years.

The import surplus (the export of goods and services minus the import of goods and services) rose very rapidly, from $200m. in 1972–74 (annual average) to a peak of

$1.4bn. in 1982. But until 1981 this hardly posed a problem since it was more than covered by grants. In addition, Jordan received generous concessional loans. As a consequence, Central Bank foreign exchange reserves rose from $227m. in 1972 to a peak of $1,138m. in 1979 and then declined somewhat to $1,049m. in 1981. Moreover, the Central Bank increased its gold reserves. In subsequent years there was an almost steady deterioration. There were four consecutive years, 1982 through 1985, of massive deficits in the current account (exports of goods and services plus grants, minus imports of goods and services) averaging $312m. p.a. This was in sharp contrast with the decade 1972–81, as a whole, when there was a favorable balance in the current account. What is worse, a large part of the deficits in the 1980s was financed by external commercial loans, and most of the balance by running down foreign exchange reserves from $1,049m. in 1981 to $400m. at the end of 1985. Restrictions on imports were tightened in 1985–86, and the US increased its aid. There was a marked improvement in 1986 with the current account deficit declining to $40m., as compared with $260m. in the previous year. But the decline was almost wholly due to lower oil prices. In 1987, there was again a sharp deterioration, with the deficit rising to $352m. Central Bank reserves were maintained by more borrowing.

As one might expect, the consequence of these developments was a sharp rise in the foreign debt, from $171m. in 1972 to $1,240m. in 1980, and $3,835m. at the end of 1987. The servicing of the debt, i.e., annual payments on account of principal and interest, rose from $7m. in 1972 to $136m. in 1980, and $555m. in 1987. One way of measuring the burden of the debt is to relate annual servicing of the debt to earnings from exports of goods and services. This ratio rose slightly, from 4.5% in 1972 to 5.4% in 1980, and then very steeply to 17.2% in 1987. Moreover, the above figures ignore debts arising from arms imports. No official data are available, but press reports indicated that these debts had also risen strongly in the 1980s.

In the face of mounting balance of payments problems it is difficult to understand why the Central Bank maintained and even revalued the currency *vis-à-vis* the dollar. A gradual devaluation of the Jordanian dinar might have stimulated exports and, even more so, restricted imports, without strong inflationary effects. Instead, there was a sharp collapse of the dinar beginning in mid-1988.

Beginning with the mid-1970s, labor shortages began to emerge both because of the rapid growth of the economy and the continued exodus of Jordanians to well-paying jobs in the rich Arab oil states. A growing number of workers from the poorer Arab countries, in particular from Egypt and Syria, as well as from the poor Asian countries, migrated to Jordan. Precise figures are unavailable, but a rough estimate indicated that in 1987 there were some 150,000 foreign workers in Jordan, mainly in agriculture, construction, and in other manual occupations which Jordanians regard as demeaning. The large majority was unskilled or semi-skilled. They accounted for possibly 30% of total employment in Jordan. At the same time, there were an estimated 300,000 Jordanians working abroad, mainly in the Arab oil states. Apparently there was a small decline since 1983 or 1984 when spending cutbacks in the Arab oil states began to reduce demand for foreign labor. The large majority of these Jordanians were professionals and skilled workers, including teachers, accountants, doctors, engineers, and other white-collar workers.

Since 1983 or 1984 unemployment has become an increasingly severe problem. According to official sources, the unemployment rate was 8% in1986, but a World

Bank mission estimated that it had reached 13% and *forecast that it could reach a calamitous 30% by 1990. Unofficial estimates for 1988 suggested that unemployment had reached 14–16%.*

The extreme distortions in the labor market are apparent from the fact that, in 1987, there were some 80,000 unemployed Jordanians (according to the higher estimates, fewer according to official estimates) while, at the same time, there were close to twice as many foreigners working in Jordan. The government has taken various measures to curtail foreign employment by an outright ban on engaging foreigners in certain occupations, by searching for and expelling many foreigners working illegally, and by higher fees for work permits. New work permits were being issued only for agriculture and domestic service, jobs which are apparently the least palatable to Jordanians.

The problem is not only the level of unemployment but its composition. In 1987 an estimated 90% of the unemployed were graduates of universities, other institutions of higher education, and secondary schools. The prime minister issued orders to various ministries, local governments, and public sector institutions to employ doctors and engineers, where the unemployment rate is particularly high. But make-work policies are a poor solution and, at best, very partial. They exacerbate the budgetary deficits at a time when they should be curtailed. The Civil Service Commission reported that in 1987 it had received 33,000 applications for 8,000 positions. Of the applicants, about 10,000 were graduates of universities, 16,000 from community colleges, and 7,000 had completed high school.

The educational system, as it developed in Jordan at least since the 1970s, was geared more to jobs in the Arab oil states than to the needs of the domestic economy. The students flocked to higher education in the belief that well-paying jobs awaited them in the Arab oil states. An estimated one fourth of the 18–23 age group was enrolled in higher education, an unusually high ratio for a less-developed country. Even if few of the Jordanians working in the Arab oil states had hitherto been dismissed, new job openings were hardly available for the many thousands of new graduates of higher education in Jordan. At the same time the ongoing recession in Jordan restricts local demand. The regime is faced with an acute and dangerous problem, which shows every sign of worsening.

1988 – THE DAM BURSTS

Five consecutive years of recession, large balance of payments deficits (in the current account), a rapidly growing burden of external debt, a steady erosion in central bank foreign exchange reserves, and mounting unemployment combined to undermine confidence. Capital flight took on far more serious dimensions and Jordanians abroad became even more wary of exchanging their hard currency for Jordanian dinars. There are no official estimates regarding the magnitude of capital held abroad by Jordanians. One unofficial estimate, published in mid-1988, suggested that it was as much as \$20bn.–\$30bn.[108] Even the lower estimate would imply that private Jordanian holdings abroad were equivalent to about *four times the GNP* or about *seven times Jordan's exports of goods and services (including remittances)* in 1987.

In the face of large balance of payments deficits, a rapid growth in the servicing of the foreign debt, and capital flight, the Central Bank was encountering difficulties in its attempt to maintain an acceptable level of foreign exchange reserves. These had fallen from $1,050m. in 1981 to $413m. at the end of 1987. But maintaining even this lower level required large-scale borrowing from commercial banks. The dam burst during the course of 1988. By mid-1988 foreign exchange reserves were down to a paltry $19m., the equivalent of *two or three days of commodity imports*.

Instead of devaluing the currency since 1982, when balance of payments deficits widened to major dimensions, the Central Bank actually revalued the Jordanian dinar from the equivalent of $2.47 at the end of 1984 to $3.04 at the end of 1987. In effect, this penalized exporters and rewarded importers, further exacerbating the balance of payments deficits. It appears that the Central Bank authorities felt that any devaluation would engender expectations for further devaluations and Jordanians abroad would delay or refrain from transferring their remittances to Jordan.

During the first half of 1988, the gap between the official and free market exchange rates widened. Beginning with June 1988, and especially since October 1988, the dinar went through a steep devaluation. During the first weeks of October the dinar fell very strongly in the free market, and in mid-October the Central Bank announced that it would reduce its intervention in the foreign exchange markets and allow the dinar to float to rates close to those prevailing in the free markets.[109] By the end of the month the dinar was down to $2.26, and even lower in the free market. All in all, during the first ten months of 1988 the dinar was devalued by over one fourth *vis-à-vis* the dollar.[110]

During the latter months of 1988 the government announced a series of "draconian" measures aimed at "arresting the serious and rapid deterioration in the kingdom's economy." These included an outright ban on the importation of vehicles and of other so-called luxury goods, until the end of 1989, and far higher duties on others; a steep rise in annual fees for work permits paid by foreigners; and various other fees and taxes. The prime minister announced that in order to curb the budgetary deficit no new infrastructural projects would be initiated. On the other hand, he also assured the citizenry that despite the devaluation, which raised the dinar cost of imported foods, the prices of basic consumer goods would be fixed.[111] In other words, subsidies would be increased.

The projected budget for 1989 included some additional taxes (on restaurant meals, airline tickets, etc.), and a sharp cut of 23% in capital outlays (investment), even when measured in nominal dinars, and much higher in real terms. On the other hand, the projected budget includes a 10% rise in current spending. Cutting back on current expenditures could only aggravate the severe problem of unemployment amongst university graduates. As noted earlier, the government had given orders to various public institutions to increase their employment of professionals and had announced higher food subsidies. Domestic revenues are expected to decline, both because of the ban on imports of luxury goods, which are heavily taxed, and the overall recession. Barring a large increase in grants received, the budgetary deficit will probably be even higher than projected.[112] The most likely outcome of the sharp devaluation of the currency, plus budgetary deficits, is an increase in inflationary pressures.

In the presentation of the budget for 1989, the prime minister reassured his countrymen that the economy "stands on a strong base," but that there were structural defects including the growth of the service sectors, rising budgetary deficits, overspending of foreign currency, and growing unemployment.[113] Such words were about as reassuring as those of a physician telling his patient that he is in perfect health except for a serious heart condition. In any case, events in early 1989 undermined confidence even more. Jordan failed to make a payment due in January 1989 on a 1984 loan from a consortium of European banks. At around the same time, the government was compelled to withdraw its request for a new $150m. loan it sought from European banks. The response of the banks was poor. Moreover, the ten-year pledge undertaken by the Arab oil states to grant Jordan $1,250m. p.a. expired in 1988. As noted earlier, grants actually received had been diminishing steadily after 1981. In January 1989 the king went to Riyadh to ask for a continuation of Saudi aid.[114] No official statement was made regarding the Saudi response or of other former Arab donors to the urgent requests of Jordan's king.

These developments further eroded confidence in the economy and the dinar continued to float downward. On 8 February 1989, the government announced that it was closing 72 money changers' offices in an effort to stem further speculation against the dinar. A few days later it also closed the offices of some brokerage houses which had been providing services to Jordanians working abroad. By 16 February the official exchange rate was down to $1.85.[115] Between 1 June 1988 and mid-February 1989 the Jordanian dinar had dropped steeply from $2.91 to $1.85 — by over 36%.

But the foreign exchange crisis is, in many ways, a symptom of economic ills, not their underlying cause, although it aggravated developments in the real economy, i.e., production, incomes, employment, and so on. At this writing, official estimates for 1988 are sparse. Unofficial estimates for 1988 indicate a deepening recession. One source suggested that growth in real GDP was only 1.5%, or about one half of that of 1987. This implied a decline of over 2% per capita. In other words, a sixth consecutive year of declining GDP per capita.[116] Unemployment most probably rose to even more critical levels. The end of the Iraqi-Iranian War in mid-1988 was an additional blow to Jordan's economy. Iraq announced that it was stopping crude oil shipments by tanker truck to 'Aqaba. Jordan had invested heavily in many hundreds of trucks and in port facilities, in the expectation that this would be a long-term arrangement.[117]

During the course of 1988 the public foreign debt had climbed by an additional $820m. and the burden of debt payments to almost 20%.[118] According to World Bank estimates, Jordan's debt servicing was over $1bn. in 1988 and was scheduled to rise to $1.2bn. in 1990, even if no new debts were undertaken.[119] These figures did not include debts related to military purchases abroad, or short-term commercial obligations. It was widely expected that Jordan would have little choice but to request a "rescheduling" of the foreign debt, the equivalent of filing for bankruptcy by a private firm.

FUTURE PROSPECTS

The current economic crisis is attributable *both* to external developments which had a powerful negative impact on Jordan, as well as to serious errors of omission and commission by the Government of Jordan. In a previous study of Jordan's economy, completed in December 1983 (see *MECS* 1982–83, pp. 371–408), this author projected, correctly, the decline in oil revenues in the neighboring countries, and their impact on aid, employment and remittances, trade, etc. In reality, the decline in oil revenues in Saudi Arabia and in other Arab oil states was even more rapid than had been assumed. It was also projected, incorrectly, that Jordan's authorities would adopt appropriate and timely economic policies to cope with changing external developments. Based on these assumptions, it was concluded that Jordan's decade of prosperity — 1972 to 1982 — would not persist, that the ambitious goals of the planners as outlined in the 1981–85 Development Plan would most likely not be realized, but that there was a sound economic base for further advancement. In other words, there would probably be a period of difficult adjustment to the external shocks, but that Jordan would subsequently resume the path of economic growth, albeit at significantly lower rates of growth than had been realized in the 1970s.

Various errors in economic policies have been noted, including persistently high budgetary and balance of payments deficits, increasingly covered by onerous commercial loans. In the 1970s and in earlier years, the government had usually exercised fiscal prudence. Between 1972 and 1980 the current account in the balance of payments was positive, and, in addition, Jordan received concessional loans on a large scale and, as a consequence, central bank reserves were rising. In the 1980s the current account was strongly negative, and was financed, in large measure, by expensive loans, and by drawing down central bank reserves. The burden of the foreign debt grew almost exponentially in the 1980s. Instead of a tight fiscal policy, devaluation of the currency, and other appropriate measures, the authorities continued with large budgetary deficits and even raised them in 1986 and 1987, and did very little to curb imports. The revaluation of the currency between 1983 and the end of 1987 could only make a bad situation worse. Barring miracles, the very sharp decline of the Jordanian dinar in 1988 and early 1989 was almost inevitable — and, in many ways, traumatic.

Nor is this a case of Monday morning quarterbacking. Since 1983 or 1984, many Jordanian economists had been calling for strong austerity measures but their advice was not heeded.[120] A Jordanian banker phrased the situation rather cogently in 1983: "The high income of the past led Jordan to behave like an oil country, though we have no oil."[121] Or, in the words of a Jordanian official, in 1988, "We have developed champagne tastes on a beer pocketbook."[122] In other words, the authorities failed to adopt appropriate and timely policies to curb private consumption and government spending. Moreover, Jordan appears to have increased its military expenditures since 1985, and placed large orders in Europe for expensive military equipment to be financed by bank and other commercial loans. Apparently, during the 1970s and early 1980s arms imports were paid for, largely or wholly, by Jordan's richer Arab friends.

Though the planners spoke about diversifying the economy in terms of its external economic relations, away from its narrow regional base, little was done in that direction. As a consequence, the shocks inflicted on Jordan by the oil crash in the neighboring countries, and by the economic problems faced by Iraq as the war intensified, were harsh. Possibly the most severe problem arose from the fact that, as time went on, Jordan's schools of higher education expanded rapidly, and were more and more based on the premise that their graduates would obtain jobs in the oil countries, and less and less on the needs of Jordan's economy. The current very high rate of unemployment amongst university and community college graduates is the direct result of these policies.

The future, at least for the next few years, does not look bright. The sharp devaluation of the currency should be accompanied by much tighter fiscal policy in order to contain inflationary pressures. But, under the circumstances, sharp cutbacks in subsidies and a large-scale cutback in government employment might very well be politically dangerous. As noted earlier the government had adopted make-work policies for professionals and announced higher food subsidies. Hence budgetary deficits may well increase. The danger posed by many unemployed university graduates is real. As one (unnamed) Western diplomat was reported to have observed in 1988: the unemployed "are not...illiterate peasants. They are skilled people and could get organized. It's a recipe for social unrest."[123]

The short-term projections are pessimistic. One analyst projected a decline of 3% in GDP in 1989, in real terms, and that inflation will rise to far higher levels despite the recession — mainly because of the sharp devaluation of the currency.[124] These estimates may well turn out to be conservative.

The present writer would project that, barring some unusually good fortune such as major oil finds, the Western countries will take the lead in increasing aid to Jordan, in addition to a rescheduling of the foreign debt. This may possibly give the necessary time needed by the Jordanian authorities to implement appropriate economic policies which would not be overly dangerous socially and politically. But even under those circumstances, it is hard to see how the problem of large-scale unemployment, which is likely to rise especially among the more educated, is going to be solved. The government is advocating emigration of surplus professionals. The failure to cope with this problem may be the greatest danger facing the regime.

NOTES

For the place and frequency of publications cited here, and for the full name of the publication, news agency, radio station, or monitoring service where an abbreviation is used, please see "List of Sources." Only in the case of more than one publication bearing the same name is the place of publication noted here.

1. See Tables 4, 12.
2. See Tables 6, 12.
3. *IFS*, various issues; *MEED*, 13 January 1989, pp. 24–25.
4. For the sources and references in the section the reader is referred to my previous study of Jordan's economy in *MECS* 1982–83, pp. 371–408.
5. *Monthly Statistical Bulletin*, various issues.
6. See Table 4. Since annual fluctuations are wide, the choice of terminal years is critical. The index of agricultural production has been calculated since 1975 with that year used as a base. But this gives a highly distorted picture, since 1975 was a year of serious drought. If 1974, a year of bumper crops, was taken as the base year, the indicated growth rate would be far smaller. The same bias applies to 1981-87 since 1981 was a year of poor rainfall and 1987 enjoyed far better rainfall.
7. See Tables 2A, 9, 11.
8. *IFS*, November 1988, pp. 82–85.
9. *Country Profile — Jordan 1988–89*, p. 18.
10. See Table 4.
11. *MEED*, 19 August 1988, p. 10.
12. *ME*, October 1988, p. 42.
13. *MEED*, 20 January 1989, p. 12.
14. See Table 4.
15. See Tables 2B and 11.
16. *Country Profile — Jordan, 1988–89*, p. 12.

17. See Table 2A. Even when measured in current prices there was a decline. Constant price data are unavailable.
18. See Tables 2B, 4, 11.
19. *ME,* October 1986, p. 16.
20. *MEES*, 25 July 1988, Table 19.
21. R. B. Satloff, "Troubles on the East Bank: Challenges to the Domestic Stability of Jordan," *The Washington Papers,* (Washington D.C.: The Center for Strategic and International Studies, 1986), p. 23.
22. Table 10. Imports from Iraq and Saudi Arabia listed in the table consist overwhelmingly of oil.
23. *Country Profile — Jordan, 1988–89,* pp. 20–21.
24. See Table 9.
25. In the Development Plan this is the figure used for income from tourism. See Hashemite Kingdom of Jordan, *The Five-Year Plan for Economic and Social Development 1981–1985,* pp. 136–37.
26. *Monthly Statistical Bulletin,* various issues.
27. *MEED,* 24 August 1985, p. 19.
28. *Monthly Statistical Bulletin,* various issues.
29. See Tables 2B and 5.
30. See Table 11.
31. See Table 7. In these estimates I related domestic commodity exports to total exports of goods and services including remittances and transit trade.
32. See Table 4.
33. See Table 12.
34. See Table 12.
35. See Table 7.
36. See Tables 1, 12.
37. See Table 1.
38. See Table 5.
39. *Country Profile — Jordan, 1988–89,* pp. 11–13.
40. See Table 6.
41. See Table 3.
42. See Table 3.
43. See Table 5.
44. See Table 3, note 2.
45. Satloff, op. cit., p. 20.
46. *MEED,* 22 March 1986, p. 18.
47. *CR:* Jordan, No. 2, 1988, p. 8.
48. *MEED,* 3 February 1989, p. 14.
49. *CR:* Jordan, No. 4, 1988, p. 8.
50. Population figures were taken from the Kingdom of Jordan's *Statistical Yearbook,* various issues, and the size of the armed forces from ACDA. See Table 5.
51. The employment figure refers to 1986, and includes foreign workers in Jordan, but excludes Jordanians working abroad. See Table 2.
52. See Table 9.
53. See Table 10.
54. *MEED,* 19 August 1988, p. 2.
55. R. A. Wilson, "Jordan's Trade: Past Performance and Future Prospects," *IJMES,* August 1988, pp. 338–39.
56. *MEED,* 6 August 1988, pp. 14–15.
57. See Table 9.
58. See Table 13.
59. See Table 7.
60. *FT Survey — Jordan,* 26 September 1983, pp. 25–26.
61. See Tables 7 and 8.
62. See Tables 7 and 8.
63. *CR:* Jordan, No. 4, 1985, p. 16.

64. See Table 8.
65. *MM*, 28 November 1988, pp. 4–5.
66. See Table 8.
67. The Hashemite Kingdom of Jordan, The National Planning Council, *Five Year Plan for Economic and Social Development 1981–85*, p. 297.
68. The Hashemite Kingdom of Jordan, Department of Statistics, *Statistical Yearbook*, various issues.
69. *IFS Yearbook 1987*, p. 321.
70. *MEED*, 8 May 1981, p. 22.
71. *CR:* Syria-Jordan, No. 3, 1984, p. 23; *WSJ*, 19 December 1985.
72. *MEED*, 30 August 1986, p. 46.
73. *Country Profile — Jordan 1988–89*, p. 15.
74. Ibid.
75. *MEED*, 19 September 1987, p. 35.
76. *MEED*, 1 August 1987, p. 16.
77. *Country Profile — Jordan 1988–89*, p. 15.
78. *MEED*, 18 November 1988, p. 5.
79. *CR:* Jordan, No. 1, 1988, p. 12.
80. See Table 11.
81. See Table 11.
82. *MEED*, 19 August 1988, p. 7.
83. *Current History*, February 1987, p. 74.
84. See Table 12.
85. *MEED*, 30 January 1988, p. 4.
86. *Development Plan for 1981–82*, p. 294.
87. Hashemite Kingdom of Jordan, Department of Statistics, *Statistical Yearbook 1985; Country Profile — Jordan 1988–89*, p. 9.
88. *Development Plan for 1981–85*, pp. 293–99; *FT Survey — Jordan*, 26 September 1983, p. 27.
89. *MEED*, 8 May 1981, p. 22.
90. *Development Plan for 1981–85*, pp. 294–95.
91. *QER:* Jordan, No. 4, 1985, p. 12.
92. *MEED*, 1 August 1987, p. 16.
93. *MEED*, 30 January 1988, p. 4.
94. *ME*, February 1988, pp. 28–29.
95. *CR:* Jordan, No. 4, 1987, p. 11.
96. *CR:* Jordan, No. 4, 1988, p. 11.
97. *MEED*, 19 August 1988, p. 2.
98. *MEED*, 30 January 1988, p. 4.
99. *ME*, February 1988, pp. 28–29.
100. *CR:* Jordan, No. 1, 1988, p. 12.
101. *MEED*, 30 January 1988, p. 4.
102. *MEED*, 24 February 1989, pp. 2–3.
103. *MEED*, 30 January 1988, p. 4.
104. *MEED*, 24 February 1989, pp. 2–3.
105. The reader interested in the sources is referred to the previous sections of this study.
106. See Table 12.
107. See Table 7. The figures in the table refer to those remittances coming into Jordan through official channels.
108. *MM*, 8 August 1988, pp. 11–12.
109. *MEED*, 28 October 1988, pp. 16–17.
110. *IFS*, December 1988, pp. 316–17.
111. *MM*, 28 November 1988, pp. 4–5.
112. *CR:* Jordan, No.1, 1989, pp. 89–91; *MEED*, 13 January 1989, pp. 24–25.
113. *MEED*, 13 January 1989, pp. 24–25.
114. *MEED*, 17 February 1989, pp. 19–20.
115. *MEED*, 24 February 1989, pp. 2–3.

116. *CR:* Jordan, No. 1, 1989, p. 3.
117. Ibid., p. 15.
118. Ibid., p. 2. The reference here is to the public debt plus the government-guaranteed debt.
119. *ME,* March 1989, pp. 33–34.
120. *MEED,* 18 November 1988, pp. 4–5.
121. *FT Survey — Jordan,* 26 September 1983, p. 26.
122. *ME,* March 1989, p. 34.
123. *ME,* February 1988, pp. 28–29.
124. *CR:* Jordan, No. 1, 1989, p. 3.

TABLE 1: JORDAN — NATIONAL ACCOUNTS (Millions of Jordanian Dinars — Current Prices)

	1972	1973	1974	1975	1976	1977	1978	1979	1980	1981	1982	1983	1984	1985	1986	1987
Government Consumption	68.3	80.0	97.7	110.1	155.9	156.6	190.0	235.3	243.8	285.9	326.1	348.3	376.9	405.2	449.9	459.8
Private Consumption	177.4	183.1	199.8	295.4	362.6	470.5	560.4	722.6	829.3	1,053.2	1,219.5	1,348.1	1,373.9	1,401.7	1,238.4	1,281.7
Gross Fixed Capital Formation	36.3	47.2	63.2	87.9	138.0	197.0	229.1	294.5	397.8	564.8	597.3	502.8	485.6	473.1	459.7	446.0
Change in Stocks	6.0	-8.0	2.4	0.9	12.2	5.5	-6.1	-14.5	6.3	23.1	22.0	7.3	—	16.8	25.3	—
Exports (Goods and Services)	37.0	52.4	80.3	118.9	182.9	228.0	264.6	339.6	468.8	629.8	667.9	637.2	743.2	778.1	630.3	753.6
Imports (Goods and Services)	117.8	136.4	196.1	301.1	430.0	543.4	605.8	824.5	961.7	1,392.6	1,511.6	1,421.0	1,481.2	1,469.0	1,163.7	1,254.8
GDP (Market Prices)	207.2	218.3	247.3	312.1	421.6	514.2	632.2	753.0	984.3	1,164.2	1,321.2	1,422.7	1,498.4	1,605.9	1,639.9	1,686.3
GNP (Market Prices)	221.0	241.5	279.3	376.0	562.4	660.1	781.0	921.3	1,190.1	1,482.7	1,673.4	1,770.3	1,853.6	1,881.8	1,919.4	1,867.9
Gross National Saving	-24.7	-21.6	-18.2	-29.5	43.9	33.0	30.6	-36.6	117.0	143.6	127.8	73.9	102.8	74.9	231.1	126.4
Ratios in Percentages																
Gross National Saving: Gross National Product	-11.2	-8.9	-6.5	-7.8	7.8	5.0	3.9	-4.0	9.8	9.7	7.6	4.2	5.5	4.0	12.0	6.8
Gross National Saving: Gross Investment	—	—	—	—	29.2	16.3	13.7	—	29.0	24.4	20.6	14.5	21.2	15.3	47.6	28.3
Gross Investment: Resources	14.0	12.0	16.6	15.9	18.6	20.8	19.9	19.9	24.0	26.2	24.6	22.6	18.7	19.0	19.8	18.8

SOURCES: *IFS*, various issues; *Monthly Statistical Bulletin*, various issues.

NOTES:

1. It appears that some military expenditures are excluded from the official estimates of government consumption.
2. GDP plus net factor income from abroad equals GNP. In the case of Jordan, most of net factor from abroad is accounted for by remittances of Jordanians working abroad.
3. Gross National Saving equals GNP minus consumption, public plus private.
4. Resources are defined here as GNP plus the import surplus (exports of goods and services minus imports of goods and services).
5. 1987 figures, in this and the other tables, are preliminary estimates.

TABLE 2A: JORDAN — ECONOMIC SECTORS (Millions of Jordanian Dinars — Current Prices)

	1972	*1973*	*1974*	*1975*	*1976*	*1977*	*1978*	*1979*	*1980*	*1981*	*1982*	*1983*	*1984*	*1985*	*1986*	*1987*
Agriculture	26.6	17.6	30.3	26.0	37.3	41.7	58.6	43.6	69.4	75.1	81.8	110.0	98.6	118.7	111.1	127.2
Mining and Quarrying	3.3	4.0	10.8	16.3	17.8	19.9	22.9	27.5	39.9	43.2	45.4	37.9	50.8	62.6	64.4	65.5
Manufacturing	15.2	17.2	29.7	39.7	50.0	58.2	71.4	94.1	127.2	165.1	184.9	176.6	200.0	190.3	177.7	186.9
Electricity and Water	2.5	2.8	3.0	3.1	3.9	5.5	7.2	10.1	17.1	21.0	25.3	28.3	33.5	35.2	42.0	45.4
Construction	9.2	15.2	16.8	19.2	26.6	36.8	51.0	70.5	97.5	110.6	121.9	126.9	127.0	114.1	113.0	101.3
Transport	17.3	17.9	22.8	24.9	32.5	35.9	59.3	62.9	79.7	102.7	123.5	138.4	143.5	146.7	157.2	160.5
Government Services	45.9	46.7	54.3	65.2	81.7	84.4	95.0	129.1	170.2	191.2	218.5	232.0	238.4	264.0	295.9	308.8
Other Services	62.8	67.5	74.7	108.7	128.6	157.5	185.8	230.8	292.2	332.2	368.3	392.3	423.2	459.1	439.8	451.7
GDP (Factor Cost)	182.8	188.9	242.4	303.1	378.4	439.9	551.2	668.6	893.2	1,041.1	1,169.6	1,242.3	1,315.0	1,390.6	1,401.1	1,447.3
GDP (Market Prices)	207.2	218.3	247.3	312.1	421.6	514.2	632.2	753.0	984.3	1,164.2	1,321.2	1,422.7	1,498.4	1,605.9	1,639.9	1,686.3
Plus Workers' Remittances (net)	7.4	14.7	24.1	53.3	131.3	139.8	139.4	156.4	190.7	288.9	319.5	330.1	377.5	310.0	328.1	255.3
Plus Investment Income (net)	6.4	8.5	7.9	10.6	9.5	6.1	9.4	11.9	15.1	29.6	32.7	17.5	-22.3	-34.1	-48.6	-73.7
GNP (Market Prices)	221.0	241.5	279.3	376.0	562.4	660.1	781.0	921.3	1,190.1	1,482.7	1,673.4	1,770.3	1,853.6	1,881.8	1,919.4	1,867.9

SOURCES: *Monthly Statistical Bulletin,* various issues; *Country Profile — Jordan 1988–89* and earlier issues.

NOTES:

1. GDP at factor cost also takes into account imputed bank service charges not shown in the table.
2. GDP at factor cost plus net indirect taxes (not shown in the table) equals GDP at market prices.
3. GDP at market prices plus net factor income from abroad equals GNP at market prices. In the table, net factor income from abroad is broken down into two components: workers' remittances, net (i.e., remittances of Jordanian workers abroad to Jordan minus remittances of foreign workers in Jordan to their home countries) and net investment income, i.e., interest and dividends from abroad minus interest and dividend payments to abroad.
4. The figures for government services apparently understate military services.

TABLE 2B: ECONOMIC SECTORS — SHARES OF GROSS DOMESTIC PRODUCT (At Factor Cost, In Percentages)

	1972	*1973*	*1974*	*1975*	*1976*	*1977*	*1978*	*1979*	*1980*	*1981*	*1982*	*1983*	*1984*	*1985*	*1986*	*1987*
Agriculture	14.6	9.3	12.5	8.6	9.9	9.5	10.6	6.5	7.8	7.2	7.0	8.9	7.5	8.5	7.9	8.8
Industry	11.5	12.7	17.9	19.5	18.9	19.0	18.4	19.7	20.6	22.0	21.9	19.5	21.6	20.7	20.3	20.6
Construction	5.0	8.0	6.9	6.3	7.0	8.4	9.3	10.5	10.9	10.6	10.4	10.2	8.7	8.2	8.1	7.0
Goods-Producing Sectors	**31.1**	**30.0**	**37.3**	**34.4**	**35.8**	**36.9**	**38.3**	**36.7**	**39.3**	**39.8**	**39.3**	**38.6**	**38.8**	**37.4**	**36.3**	**36.4**
Transport	9.5	9.5	9.4	8.2	8.6	8.2	10.8	9.4	8.9	9.9	10.6	11.1	10.9	10.5	11.2	11.1
Government Services	25.1	24.7	22.4	21.5	21.6	19.2	17.2	19.3	19.1	18.4	18.7	18.7	18.1	19.0	21.1	21.3
Other Services	34.3	35.8	30.9	35.9	34.0	35.7	33.7	34.6	32.7	31.9	31.4	31.6	32.2	33.1	31.4	31.2
Services-Producing Sectors	**68.9**	**70.0**	**62.7**	**65.6**	**64.2**	**63.1**	**61.7**	**63.3**	**60.7**	**60.2**	**60.9**	**61.4**	**61.2**	**62.6**	**63.7**	**63.6**

SOURCES: See Table 2A.

NOTES:

1. In this table, industry includes manufacturing, mining, electricity, and water.
2. "Other services" include a wide range of services, business and personal, as well as nonprofit institutions.
3. It is not clear from the national accounts whether the category designated as government services includes the military and internal security forces. They are probably understated.

TABLE 3: JORDAN — THE FISCAL ACCOUNTS (Millions of Jordanian Dinars)

	1972	*1973*	*1974*	*1975*	*1976*	*1977*	*1978*	*1979*	*1980*	*1981*	*1982*	*1983*	*1984*	*1985*	*1986*	*1987*	*Budget 1988*
Total Revenues	**87.1**	**89.8**	**123.4**	**183.2**	**173.8**	**264.4**	**240.2**	**398.2**	**435.4**	**515.5**	**561.8**	**597.6**	**521.1**	**628.6**	**658.1**	**683.7**	**835.9**
Of which:																	
Domestic Revenues	42.6	46.2	65.7	82.6	107.6	142.2	158.5	187.9	226.1	309.2	362.2	400.6	415.0	440.8	514.4	549.7	610.9
	[66.0]	[61.1]	[84.4]	[138.0]	[122.8]	[166.9]	[102.6]	[318.0]	[390.8]	[415.3]	[363.7]	[289.6]	[261.7]	[291.2]	[221.3]	[202.9]	
Foreign Grants	44.5	43.6	57.7	100.6	66.2	122.2	81.7	210.3	209.3	206.3	199.6	197.0	106.1	187.8	143.7	134.0	225.0
Total Expenditures	**101.5**	**119.5**	**146.6**	**204.9**	**262.5**	**337.8**	**361.5**	**515.7**	**563.1**	**647.1**	**693.5**	**705.3**	**720.8**	**805.7**	**981.3**	**1,008.7**	**1,075.4**
Of which:																	
Capital Expenditures	31.0	40.9	43.0	79.2	76.6	142.3	148.6	194.3	227.1	225.6	250.6	251.6	232.7	263.2	410.8	404.2	451.6
Military Expenditures	45.2	48.4	52.5	58.3	104.8	97.0	102.3	132.3	137.0	161.5	182.5	196.0	196.8	224.0	249.6	252.8	256.0
Civilian Current Expenditures	25.3	30.2	51.1	67.4	81.1	98.5	110.6	189.1	199.0	230.0	260.4	257.7	291.3	318.5	320.9	351.7	368.0
Deficit	14.4	29.7	23.2	21.7	88.7	73.4	121.3	117.5	127.7	131.6	131.7	107.7	199.7	177.1	323.2	325.0	239.5
Foreign Loans	7.4	11.4	15.2	16.2	19.9	58.5	90.7	37.6	71.6	76.4	65.3	76.8	122.2	162.4	159.8	89.9	
Memorandum Items:																	
Domestic Revenues: GDP (%)	20.6	21.2	26.6	26.4	25.5	27.7	25.1	25.0	23.0	26.6	27.4	28.2	27.7	27.4	31.4	32.6	
Deficit: GDP (%)	6.9	13.6	9.4	7.0	21.0	14.3	19.2	15.6	13.0	11.3	10.0	7.6	13.3	11.0	19.7	19.3	
Deficit: GNP (%)	6.5	12.3	8.3	5.8	15.8	11.1	15.5	12.8	10.7	8.9	7.9	6.1	10.8	9.4	16.8	17.4	

SOURCES: *Monthly Statistical Bulletin*, various issues.

NOTES:

1. Domestic revenues of the government consist of tax and nontax revenues, the latter including fees, licenses, profits transferred to the treasury from state-owned corporations, etc.
2. The figures for foreign grants received by the government are reported in the fiscal accounts and in the balance of payments (as official transfers). In the latter, the figures are almost consistently higher or far higher. The figures in parentheses are those reported in the balance of payments. It is believed that all or most of the difference represents off-budgetary military expenditures.
3. The estimates for capital expenditures are overstated since they include lending to business firms and other categories of spending which should be more strictly defined as current expenditures.

TABLE 4: JORDAN — INDICATORS OF PRODUCTION

	1972	1973	1974	1975	1976	1977	1978	1979	1980	1981	1982	1983	1984	1985	1986	1987
Index of Agricultural Production (1975 = 100)				100	131	130	212	147	261	236	240	227	250	275	318	314
Index of Industrial Production (1979 = 100)	42	47	50	53	67	69	85	100	120	139	144	151	181	185	188	205
Producion of:																
Phosphates (Thousands of Tons)	709	1,081	1,675	1,353	1,702	1,769	2,320	2,828	3,911	4,243	4,391	4,745	6,213	6,067	6,249	6,845
Potash (Thousands of Tons)											15	283	486	908	1,102	1,203
Chemical Acids (Thousands of Tons)												633	1,195	1,008	1,025	1,203
Fertilizers (Thousands of Tons)											116	302	541	511	551	604
Cement (Thousands of Tons)	661	617	615	598	582	538	553	623	913	965	788	1,269	2,026	2,023	1,795	2,372
Petroleum Products (Thousands of Tons)	605	675	748	828	1,145	1,145	1,397	1,612	1,760	2,126	2,464	2,499	2,511	2,424	2,257	2,405
Textiles (Thousands of Yards)	744	703	722	953	915	870	1,141	1,417	1,646	1,308	1,124	1,131	1,315	2,249	2,249	1,958
Electricity (Millions of kwh)	158	181	213	257	386	551	649	842	1,051	1,175	1,387	1,700	1,967	2,154	2,647	3,124
Construction (Thousands of Sq. Meters)	531	649	517	687	1,069	1,138	1,206	1,734	1,989	2,473	3,122	3,010	2,945	2,210	2,267	2,067
Exports plus Imports Through ‘Aqaba (Millions of Tons)	1.2	1.2	1.5	1.6	3.0	3.1	3.7	5.0	6.6	9.4	11.7	11.2	13.6	14.5	16.8	20.0
Of which: Goods in Transit (Millions of Tons)							0.1	0.2	0.9	3.1	4.4	3.7	4.7	6.1	7.2	9.1

SOURCES: *Monthly Statistical Bulletin*, various issues.

NOTES:

1. The production of potash and fertilizers began in the early 1980s with the completion of the Dead Sea project and the fertilizer complex in ‘Aqaba.
2. The index of industrial production includes both manufacturing and mining.
3. The figures for construction refer to permits and are therefore indicators of future construction rather than actual construction in a given year.
4. The major rise in the transit of goods through ‘Aqaba since 1980 is a result of the Iraqi-Iranian War. As a result of the closure of the Persian Gulf to Iraq, the latter used alternative routes for international trade including transit through ‘Aqaba.

TABLE 5: JORDAN — THE MILITARY BURDEN

	1972	*1973*	*1974*	*1975*	*1976*	*1977*	*1978*	*1979*	*1980*	*1981*	*1982*	*1983*	*1984*	*1985*	*1986*	*1987*	*1988*
Military Expenditures (Millions of Dollars; Jordanian Accounts)	127	147	163	183	316	295	345	441	460	489	518	540	512	568	713	746	751
Military Expenditures (Millions of Dollars; ACDA estimates)	349	304	297	269	507	445	481	631	667	733	718	586	703	719			
Arms Imports (Millions of Dollars; ACDA estimates)	30	50	80	80	140	110	170	100	260	1,100	1,100	1,100	230	625	330		
Grants Received (Millions of Dollars; Jordanian Accounts)	185	186	263	433	370	507	336	1,059	1,311	1,258	1,032	798	681	739	633	596	
Military Expenditures: GNP (%; Jordanian Accounts)	20.5	20.0	18.6	15.5	18.7	14.7	13.5	14.3	12.8	11.6	10.9	11.1	10.6	11.9	13.0	13.5	
Military Expenditures: GNP (%; ACDA estimates)	35.8	36.5	35.1	29.5	42.6	31.8	28.0	31.7	27.7	25.5	21.8	16.3	19.1	17.4			
Armed Forces (Thousands; ACDA estimates)	70	70	70	60	65	70	70	67	65	66	68	72	78	81			

SOURCES: ***Monthly Statistical Bulletin***, various issues; *CR*, various issues; *Country Profile*, various issues; US Arms Control and Disarmament Agency, ***World Military Expenditures and Arms Transfers (ACDA) 1987***, Washington D.C. 1988, and earlier issues.

NOTES:

1. The figures for military expenditures — Jordanian accounts — include internal security. The estimates of the US ACDA appear to exclude them. Hence, the gap between the latter and former estimates is wider than shown in the table.
2. The 1988 figure is the one projected in the 1988 budgetary announcement translated into dollars in accordance with the exchange rate prevailing in the first half of 1988.
3. The estimates for arms imports are from ACDA. The Jordanian accounts provide no estimates. Presumably the official balance of payments estimates exclude arms imports, in whole or in part. Foreign unofficial reports indicate that these were paid for, in whole or in part, by Saudi Arabia and other Arab oil-exporting countries, over and above foreign aid as reported in the balance of payments.
4. The ACDA estimates of Jordan's military expenditures also appear to exclude arms imports, at least in part. In 1981–83 their estimates of Jordan's arms imports greatly exceed their own estimates of Jordan's military expenditures, let alone those published in the Jordanian fiscal accounts.
5. The estimates of the size of the armed forces are from ACDA, and exclude internal security forces. Jordanian official accounts provide no estimates.

TABLE 6: JORDAN — ECONOMIC GROWTH, PRICE LEVELS, AND PRIVATE CONSUMPTION

	1972	*1973*	*1974*	*1975*	*1976*	*1977*	*1978*	*1979*	*1980*	*1981*	*1982*	*1983*	*1984*	*1985*	*1986*	*1987*
GDP 1980 Prices (Millions of Jordanian Dinars)	535	507	480	541	656	698	801	837	984	1,081	1,142	1,171	1,188	1,210	1,241	1,266
Annual Changes in Above (%)	3.8	-5.4	-5.2	12.6	21.2	6.4	14.8	4.4	17.6	9.8	5.6	2.5	1.5	1.9	2.6	2.0
GNP 1980 Prices (Millions of Jordanian Dinars)	571	560	542	652	875	896	990	1,024	1,190	1,377	1,446	1,456	1,470	1,423	1,475	1,443
Annual Changes in Above (%)	3.3	-1.9	-3.2	20.2	34.2	2.4	10.5	3.4	16.3	15.7	5.1	0.7	0.9	-3.2	3.7	-2.1
Private Consumption — 1980 Prices (Millions of Jordanian Dinars)	457	425	388	512	564	638	710	803	829	978	1,054	1,110	1,089	1,078	953	989
Annual Changes in Above (%)	1.9	-7.1	-8.7	32.0	10.1	13.2	11.3	13.0	3.3	17.9	7.8	5.3	-1.9	-1.0	-11.6	3.8
Private Consumption per Capita — 1980 Prices (Jordanian Dinars)	283	254	224	283	298	324	345	376	374	424	439	445	420	400	340	341
Annual Changes in Above (%)	-1.6	-10.3	-11.8	26.5	5.5	8.4	6.6	9.1	-0.7	13.4	3.6	1.2	-5.7	-5.6	-15.0	0.2
Consumer Price Index 1980 = 100	38.8	43.1	51.5	57.7	64.3	73.7	78.9	90.0	100	107.7	115.7	121.5	126.2	130.0	130.0	129.6
Annual Changes in Above — (%)	7.7	11.1	19.4	12.0	11.5	14.6	6.9	14.2	11.1	7.7	7.4	5.3	3.8	3.0	0	-0.3
Wholesale Price Index 1980 = 100				63.5	72.5	77.5	81.7	87.0	100	109.1	112.6	117.1	119.0	120.8	120.3	121.1
Annual Changes in Above (%)					14.1	6.8	5.4	6.5	14.9	9.1	3.2	4.0	1.6	1.5	-0.4	0.7

SOURCES: *Monthly Statistical Bulletin,* various issues; *IFS,* various issues.

NOTES:

1. The Consumer Price Index published by the International Monetary Fund (IMF), *IFS,* had been used as the deflator both for the GDP and GNP (Market Prices). This is the deflator used by the IMF for its estimates of GDP in 1980 prices. These estimates should be viewed as no more than indicators of trends and orders of magnitude, not as accurate measures of annual changes.
2. The estimates for private consumption in 1980 prices were based on the current price estimates for private consumption given in the national accounts deflated by the consumer price index.
3. The estimates for private consumption per capita in 1980 prices, were based on the population estimates in the *Statistical Yearbook* issued by the Hashemite Kingdom of Jordan, Department of Statistics.
4. The Wholesale Price Index is for Amman, and is available only since 1975. The source is the *Monthly Statistical Bulletin.* The IMF does not publish this series, apparently in the belief that it is not very reliable.
5. The percentage changes in each of the series of estimates is based on the original unrounded figures, and may differ very slightly from those given in the table.

TABLE 7: JORDAN — BALANCE OF PAYMENTS — SELECTED DATA (Millions of Dollars)

	1972	*1973*	*1974*	*1975*	*1976*	*1977*	*1978*	*1979*	*1980*	*1981*	*1982*	*1983*	*1984*	*1985*	*1986*	*1987*
Commodity Exports (f.o.b.)	48	74	154	153	207	249	297	402	575	733	752	580	752	789	732	933
Of which:																
Domestic Exports	35	43	123	126	149	183	210	275	403	512	527	441	680	648	643	735
Total Exports of Services	98	161	201	430	794	954	1,145	1,418	1,921	2,409	2,434	2,461	2,519	2,311	2,357	2,305
Of which:																
Remittances of Jordanian Workers Abroad	21	45	75	167	390	470	522	601	794	1,033	1,084	1,110	1,237	1,023	1,185	955
Travel and Transportation (Receipts)	33	51	78	159	272	365	458	616	776	855	854	804	810	914	793	925
Investment Income (Receipts)	12	19	27	35	39	40	51	86	126	201	205	173	101	101	100	58
Commodity Imports (c.i.f.)	266	328	484	731	1,020	1,376	1,502	1,959	2,398	3,170	3,239	3,036	2,784	2,722	2,423	2,694
Of which:																
Reexports	13	31	31	27	58	66	87	127	172	221	225	139	72	141	89	197
Total Imports of Services	67	91	132	224	310	338	570	915	1,062	1,326	1,347	1,213	1,498	1,438	1,399	1,485
Of which:																
Remittances of Foreign Workers in Jordan	—	—	—	—	—	46	66	80	155	158	177	201	254	236	247	184
Travel and Transportation (Payments)	42	50	77	151	167	183	284	402	504	560	550	589	685	731	643	700
Investment Income (Payments)	3	4	7	10	14	18	24	49	79	114	119	128	162	189	241	279
Balance of Goods and Services	-188	-186	-261	-371	-329	-511	-630	-1,054	-963	-1,347	-1,395	-1,202	-997	-1,053	-726	-940
Grants Received by Government	185	186	251	409	353	500	337	1,057	1,313	1,260	1,034	795	688	740	634	599
Balance on Current Account	6	12	3	45	36	-16	-288	-7	374	-39	-333	-391	-265	-260	-40	-352

SOURCES: *Monthly Statistical Bulletin*, various issues; *IFS*, various issues.

NOTES:

1. Reexports are the differences between total exports of goods and the exportation of domestically produced goods. Reexports have increased rapidly in recent years, mainly to Iraq.
2. The figures for remittances refer to those transferred through official channels. Estimates of remittances through unofficial channels would possibly add from 50% to 100% to the sum total of remittances transferred to Jordan.
3. Investment income (receipts), mainly interest from abroad, has declined strongly in recent years, mainly because reserves have dwindled and interest rates abroad have declined. On the other hand, interest payments on the foreign debt have risen sharply as the debt increased, and a greater share of loans from abroad were at market rates of interests, i.e., not concessional.
4. The difference between the balance on goods and services and the balance on current account is unilateral transfers — both grants received by the government and private transfers. The latter are minor and are not shown explicitly in the table.
5. It appears that the importation of arms is excluded, at least in part, from the reported balance of payments, as in the case with the published budgetary accounts.

TABLE 8: JORDAN — RESERVES AND EXTERNAL DEBT

	1972	1973	1974	1975	1976	1977	1978	1979	1980	1981	1982	1983	1984	1985	1986	1987
Foreign Exchange Reserves (Millions of Dollars; End-of-Year)	227	255	297	444	456	627	869	1,138	1,107	1,049	848	798	500	399	413	413
Gold Reserves (Thousands of Ounces; End-of-Year)	797	797	797	797	797	806	816	1,021	1,067	1,080	1,090	1,060	1,061	1,061	1,064	1,002
External Public Debt (Millions of Dollars)	171	208	253	327	400	613	834	1,038	1,240	1,575	1,939	2,346	2,534	3,081	3,483	3,835
Servicing of External Debt (Millions of Dollars)	7	23	23	33	76	49	83	94	136	193	231	226	250	326	424	555
Exports of Goods and Services (incl. Remittances) (Millions of Dollars)	146	235	355	583	1,001	1,203	1,442	1,820	2,496	3,142	3,186	3,041	3,271	3,100	3,089	3,221
Exports of Goods and Services plus Grants Received (Millions of Dollars)	331	421	606	992	1,354	1,703	1,779	2,877	3,809	4,402	4,220	3,836	3,959	3,840	3,723	3,820
Gross National Product (Millions of Dollars)	619	736	869	1,180	1,694	2,005	2,556	3,090	3,605	4,209	4,750	4,877	4,826	4,776	5,486	5,514
Servicing of Foreign Debt: GNP (%)	1.1	3.1	2.6	2.8	4.5	2.4	3.2	3.0	3.8	4.6	4.9	4.6	5.2	6.8	7.7	10.1
External Public Debt: GNP (%)	27.6	28.3	29.1	27.7	23.6	30.6	32.6	33.6	34.4	37.4	40.8	48.1	52.5	64.5	63.5	69.6
Servicing of Foreign Debt: Exports of Goods and Services (%)	4.5	9.8	6.5	5.7	7.6	4.1	5.8	5.2	5.4	6.1	7.3	7.4	7.6	10.5	13.7	17.2
Servicing of Foreign Debt Exports plus Grants Received (%)	2.1	5.5	3.8	3.3	5.6	2.9	4.7	3.3	3.6	4.4	5.5	5.9	6.3	8.5	11.4	14.5
Exchange Rate — Annual Average (US Dollars per Jordanian Dinar)	2.8000	3.0462	3.1113	3.1393	3.0122	3.0375	3.2733	3.3299	3.3543	3.0293	2.8384	2.7550	2.6036	2.5379	2.8583	2.9522

SOURCES: *Monthly Statistical Bulletin*, various issues; *CR*, various issues; *Country Profile*, various issues.

NOTES:

1. The figures for the external public debt include publicly guaranteed debt. In 1987 the government's foreign debt was $3bn., and the government-guaranteed debt another $830m. What is undisclosed is the external public debt arising from arms imports.
2. The rise in the burden of foreign debt — as shown by the various indicators — is due to increasing recourse to loans, rather than grants, and commercial rather than concessional loans, especially in recent years.

TABLE 9: JORDAN — COMPOSITION OF FOREIGN TRADE (Millions of Jordanian Dinars, unless otherwise stated)

	1972	*1973*	*1974*	*1975*	*1976*	*1977*	*1978*	*1979*	*1980*	*1981*	*1982*	*1983*	*1984*	*1985*	*1986*	*1987*
Domestic Exports-Total	12.6	14.0	39.4	40.1	49.6	60.3	64.1	82.6	120.1	169.0	185.6	160.1	261.1	255.3	225.6	248.8
Of which:																
Food	5.0	4.7	10.1	10.7	16.4	20.6	16.9	21.6	24.3	34.0	40.1	36.1	35.0	36.8	29.4	31.8
Phosphates	3.5	4.0	19.5	19.6	19.2	17.3	19.5	26.3	47.2	54.8	57.1	51.6	69.6	66.1	64.8	61.0
Potash											0.2	0.1	14.9	30.9	31.4	28.0
Fertilizers											5.2	20.7	44.0	30.6	29.1	30.1
Cement													2.9	7.1	4.0	10.5
Other Exports-Mainly Manufactures	4.1	5.3	9.8	9.8	14.0	22.4	27.7	34.7	48.6	80.2	83.0	51.6	94.7	83.8	66.9	87.4
Index of Volume of Exports (1985=100)		18.7	26.5	22.8	28.8	34.9	37.5	46.3	57.8	67.4	69.0	68.4	96.0	100	102.6	121.9
Export Price Index (1985=100)		34.5	70.3	79.7	71.7	71.7	69.0	69.5	82.6	94.7	103.6	94.6	103.1	100	86.1	79.9
Imports-Total	95.3	108.2	156.5	234.0	339.5	454.4	458.8	589.5	716.0	1,047.5	1,142.5	1,103.3	1,071.3	1,074.4	850.2	915.6
Of which:																
Food	27.6	30.8	42.4	49.3	81.5	72.2	85.6	100.6	112.6	156.5	177.3	157.1	161.1	152.6	134.4	132.1
Non-Durable Consumer Goods	12.8	13.4	18.0	26.9	28.8	42.5	47.0	62.7	69.5	91.7	117.3	117.6	127.6	138.3	115.1	116.2
Durable Consumer Goods	5.9	6.4	9.2	14.3	23.0	32.4	43.1	51.9	58.0	77.1	73.7	90.3	94.4	78.4	79.7	85.2
Capital Goods	18.6	20.2	40.9	82.9	114.6	184.1	161.2	193.6	246.7	415.0	391.4	310.6	239.0	261.1	195.9	221.6
Crude Oil	3.3	3.3	3.6	22.8	34.4	37.0	43.4	69.0	113.9	174.7	230.7	205.5	204.0	192.6	92.8	118.6
Index of Volume of Imports (1985=100)		23.3	26.1	33.1	49.5	57.8	66.0	77.4	79.3	94.1	103.3	104.2	97.7	100	105.1	109.0
Import Price Index (1985=100)		42.2	53.7	73.7	65.6	67.0	65.1	69.6	86.5	105.3	107.0	97.8	102.7	100	75.3	78.2

SOURCES: *Monthly Statistical Bulletin*, various issues.

NOTES:

1. The production and export of potash and fertilizers began in the early 1980s with the completion of major projects.
2. With the recent completion of new cement plants and the decline in construction, surplus capacity has emerged and Jordan has been exporting cement.
3. Capital goods refer mainly to imported machinery and equipment. Raw materials, other than crude oil, and other imports are not explicitly listed in the table.

TABLE 10: JORDAN — GEOGRAPHICAL DISTRIBUTION OF FOREIGN TRADE (Millions of Jordanian Dinars)

	1972	*1973*	*1974*	*1975*	*1976*	*1977*	*1978*	*1979*	*1980*	*1981*	*1982*	*1983*	*1984*	*1985*	*1986*	*1987*
Domestic Exports — Total	**12.6**	**14.0**	**39.4**	**40.1**	**49.6**	**60.3**	**64.1**	**82.6**	**120.1**	**169.0**	**185.6**	**160.1**	**261.1**	**255.3**	**225.6**	**248.8**
Of which:																
To Arab Countries	9.2	10.1	18.4	16.9	23.9	36.1	42.6	55.7	72.9	114.5	123.3	87.1	132.6	131.6	102.1	129.8
Of which:																
To Iraq	1.5	1.0	1.6	2.4	2.3	4.3	3.4	12.7	28.3	63.5	66.6	26.0	67.8	65.8	42.3	59.9
To Saudi Arabia	2.1	2.5	5.5	4.8	7.5	15.1	17.7	19.4	19.7	20.9	27.6	35.2	38.7	39.1	27.8	26.2
To Communinst Countries	0.4	0.3	2.0	6.4	7.3	4.2	6.4	5.3	15.2	19.5	25.4	21.2	32.8	21.5	28.4	31.3
To India	1.4	1.2	6.6	2.0	1.7	3.9	3.5	6.1	8.0	10.3	16.6	13.7	34.1	45.3	34.1	22.0
To Rest of World	1.6	2.4	12.4	14.8	16.7	16.1	11.6	15.5	24.0	24.7	20.3	37.9	61.6	56.9	61.0	65.7
Imports — Total	**95.3**	**108.2**	**156.5**	**234.0**	**339.5**	**454.7**	**458.8**	**589.5**	**716.0**	**1,047.5**	**1,142.5**	**1,103.3**	**1,071.3**	**1,074.4**	**850.2**	**915.5**
of Which:																
From Arab Countries	16.4	21.7	26.5	46.3	60.9	72.5	86.6	110.6	149.2	213.1	269.8	250.6	245.7	263.6	172.2	233.8
Of which:																
From Iraq	0.7	0.9	0.9	0.6	0.8	0.8	1.1	1.9	2.2	0.8	1.0	4.8	6.0	73.0	80.3	99.4
From Saudi Arabia	3.4	3.4	3.7	22.9	34.5	37.1	43.4	69.5	114.1	175.8	233.5	211.0	208.8	159.1	49.7	76.8
From Western Europe	30.3	34.6	52.5	93.6	146.6	183.9	196.2	261.8	309.3	398.3	398.7	382.8	407.1	403.5	331.0	321.5
From US	16.9	11.3	17.6	24.2	31.0	67.4	33.6	44.3	61.6	166.7	144.3	131.0	119.3	128.0	75.5	93.4
From Japan	4.6	5.3	7.4	17.1	21.5	28.7	30.8	37.3	51.3	71.5	87.4	102.9	79.1	67.8	66.6	53.7
From Communist Countries	8.2	7.7	14.7	18.7	25.1	41.9	50.2	51.4	49.8	81.2	94.8	77.8	64.8	74.4	59.8	70.5
From Rest of World	18.9	27.6	37.8	34.1	54.4	60.3	61.4	84.1	94.8	116.7	147.5	158.2	155.3	137.1	145.1	142.6

SOURCES: *Monthly Statistical Bulletin*, various issues.

NOTES:

1. The major increase in exports to Iraq in the 1980s is a result of the Iraqi-Iranian War.
2. India and a number of East European countries are major buyers of Jordanian phosphates, and, in more recent years, of potash and fertilizers.
3. Saudi exports to Jordan are largely crude oil. In more recent years Iraq has been the main supplier of oil, in partial payment for Jordanian exports to that country.
4. Aside from oil, Jordanian imports are largely from Western Europe, the US, and Japan. Much of this is within the context of aid programs.
5. Most of the trade with Arab, East European, and other less-developed countries is within the context of trade agreements.

TABLE 11: JORDAN — POPULATION AND EMPLOYMENT (In Thousands)

	1972	*1973*	*1974*	*1975*	*1976*	*1977*	*1978*	*1979*	*1980*	*1981*	*1982*	*1983*	*1984*	*1985*	*(Est.) 1986*	*(Est.) 1987*
Population	1,618	1,675	1,735	1,810	1,889	1,972	2,058	2,133	2,218	2,307	2,399	2,495	2,595	2,694	2,800	2,900
Total Employed	314		362	355				421			455				493	
Of which in:																
Agriculture	54		55	49				42			45				37	
Industry	31		34	39				51			51				58	
Construction	25		33	30				67			60				54	
Transportation	21		18	28				32			32				46	
Trade and Finance	77		86	87				78			55				66	
Public Administration, Defense, and Other Services	106		136	122				151			212				231	

SOURCES: The Hashemite Kingdom of Jordan, Department of Statistics, *Statistical Yearbook*, various issues; National Planning Council, *Five Year Plan for Economic and Social Development 1981–1985* and earlier plans; *Country Profile — Jordan 1988–89* and earlier issues.

NOTES:

1. Industry is defined here to include manufacturing, mining, electricity, and water.
2. Labor force estimates are generally considered to be less than reliable. This is especially true for agriculture, and non-governmental services.
3. The population and employment estimates refer to resident population and employment in Jordan. In other words, they do not include Jordanians residing or working abroad, whether temporarily or on a permanent basis. The estimates do include foreigners working in Jordan and their accompanying family members.

TABLE 12: VARIOUS SOCIAL AND ECONOMIC INDICATORS

Average Annual Rates of Growth — %	*1972–82*	*1982–87*	
GDP	7.9%	2.1%	
GDP per Capita	3.7%	-1.7%	
GNP	9.7%	0	
GNP per Capita	5.5%	-3.8%	
Industrial Production	13.2%	7.3%	
Electric Power	24%	18%	
Shipping at 'Aqaba	25%	11%	
Construction	19.4%	-7.4%	
Gross Fixed Investment	18.6%	-7.8%	
Private Consumption	8.7%	-1.7%	
Private Consumption per Capita	4.5%	-5.0%	
Consumer Price Index	11.5%	2.3%	
Population Growth Rate	4.0%	3.9%	
	1970	*1980*	*1985*
Life Expectancy at Birth (Years)	54	61	69
Infant Mortality (per Thousand)	97	69	49
Population per Physician	2,476	1,293	1,046
Enrollment Ratios — Primary School	72%	89%	99%
Enrollment Ratios — Secondary School	33%	69%	79%
Students in Higher Education			
In Jordan (Thousands)	4	34	54
Abroad (Thousands)	21	67	50

SOURCES and NOTES:

1. For the underlying data with respect to the indicators of production, consumption, the consumer price index, and population estimates, and their sources, see Tables 1, 4, 6, and 11. The official estimates for GDP, GNP, private consumption, and gross fixed investment are given in current prices. The consumer price index has been used as the deflator. The estimated real rates of growth should, therefore, be viewed as no more than broad orders of magnitude and indicators of the direction of change.
2. The other figures in this table are derived from the Hashemite Kingdom of Jordan, Department of Statistics — *Statistical Yearbook*, various issues.
3. The figures for the number of students in higher education in Jordan include, for recent years, those enrolled in community colleges. In 1985 about one half of those in higher education were in these colleges. Though the number of students in institutions of higher education in Jordan is high, few are in Master's or Ph.D. programs. In 1984–85, 27,205 were studying in community colleges, 25,929 in Jordanian universities, of whom 1,266 were pursuing the Master's degree and only 11 students a Ph.D. degree. See *Statistical Yearbook 1985*, pp. 69–72.
4. The estimates for Jordanians in universities abroad are, in all likelihood, not very accurate. They show a sharp decline in recent years. The figure given in the table is for 1984, not 1985. The estimate given for 1980 is from the *Statistical Abstract* of that year. The estimate also includes residents of the so-called West Bank. Satloff quotes unofficial estimates of possibly 80,000. See R. B. Satloff, "Troubles on the East Bank: Challenges to the Domestic Stability of Jordan," *The Washington Papers* (Washington, D.C.: The Center for Strategic and International Studies, 1986), p. 120.

TABLE 13: TRADE BETWEEN JORDAN AND JUDEA-SAMARIA (WEST BANK) (Millions of Dollars)

	1972	*1973*	*1974*	*1975*	*1976*	*1977*	*1978*	*1979*	*1980*	*1981*	*1982*	*1983*	*1984*	*1985*	*1986*	*1987*
Jordan's Exports to the West Bank	4.5	3.9	4.5	4.9	3.7	4.7	5.0	5.0	5.4	7.3	8.9	6.8	8.2	8.6	10.9	9.4
Jordan's Imports from the West Bank	25.5	15.8	26.6	34.5	43.0	44.2	62.1	58.1	79.2	74.7	90.5	65.0	83.5	69.3	81.8	63.4
Jordan's Trade Deficit	21.0	11.8	22.0	29.6	39.2	39.6	57.1	53.1	73.7	67.4	81.6	58.2	75.3	60.7	70.9	54.0
Ratios in Percentages																
Exports to West Bank: Total Exports	12.7	9.2	3.7	3.9	2.5	2.5	2.4	1.8	1.4	1.4	1.7	1.5	1.2	1.3	1.7	1.3
Imports from West Bank: Total Imports	9.5	4.8	5.4	4.7	4.2	3.2	4.1	3.0	3.3	2.4	2.8	2.1	3.0	2.5	3.4	2.3

SOURCES: *Judea, Samaria, and Gaza Area Statistics*, various issues; *Monthly Statistical Bulletin*, various issues.

NOTES:

1. Jordanian data provide no figures for trade with the West Bank. The Israeli figures were used, converting them to dollars at the official exchange rate.
2. The Israeli figures indicate that Jordan's exports to the West Bank are almost all industrial. Agricultural exports are minuscule. However, over one third of Jordan's imports from the West Bank consisted of agricultural produce, in recent years. Some of these products, industrial as well as agricultural, are reexported by Jordanian merchants to the neighboring Arab countries.

PART TWO: COUNTRY-BY-COUNTRY SURVEY

Middle East Countries

Basic Data

Country	*Capital*	*Most Important Natural Resources*	*Area 1,000 sq. km.*	*Population in millions (mid-1987)*	*GNP per capita ($US 1987)*
Bahrain	Manama	Crude Oil	1	0.445	NA
Egypt	Cairo	Cotton, Crude Oil, Fruits, Vegetables, Iron	1,001	50.1	680
Iran	Tehran	Crude Oil, Natural Gas	1,648	47.0	NA
Iraq	Baghdad	Crude Oil, Dates, Cement	435	17.1	NA
Israel	Jerusalem	Fruits, Vegetables, Potash	21	4.4	6,800
Jordan	Amman	Phosphates, Vegetables, Fruits	98	3.8	1,560
Kuwait	Kuwait	Crude Oil	18	1.9	14,610
Lebanon	Beirut	Fruits, Citrus Fruits, Vegetables, Forests	10	NA	NA
Libya	Tripoli	Crude Oil, Vegetables, Fruits	1,760	4.1	5,460
Oman	Muscat	Crude Oil	212	1.3	5,810
Qatar	Doha	Crude Oil	11	0.332	12,430
Saudi Arabia	Riyadh	Crude Oil	2,150	12.6	6,200
Sudan	Khartoum	Cotton, Gum, Cereals	2,506	23.1	330
Syria	Damascus	Cotton, Crude Oil, Vegetables, Fruits, Livestock, Phosphates	185	11.2	1,640
Turkey	Ankara	Cotton, Wool, Tobacco, Chrome, Copper	781	52.6	1,210
United Arab Emirates	Abu Dhabi	Crude Oil	84	1.5	15,830
Yemen (North)	San'a	Coffee, Cotton, Sorghum, Fish	195	8.5	590
Yemen (South)	Aden	Cotton, Fruits, Vegetables, Tobacco, Fish	333	2.3	420

SOURCE: *World Development Report 1989* (New York: Oxford University Press for the World Bank, 1989).
NA = not available.

Currencies

Country	Currency Unit	*Approximate Equivalent in Other Currencies** US Dollar	Pound Sterling	Deutsche Mark	Swiss Franc	French Franc
Bahrain	Bahraini Dinar (BD) = 1,000 Fils	2.67	1.39	4.42	3.66	15.02
Egypt	Egyptian Pound (£E) = 1,000 Milliemes	0.45	0.23	0.75	0.61	2.53
Iran	Iranian Riyal (IR) = 100 Dinars	0.015	0.008	0.025	0.021	0.084
Iraq	Iraqi Dinar (ID) = 1,000 Fils	3.24	1.68	5.37	4.44	18.23
Israel	New Israeli Shekel (NIS) = 100 Agorot	0.64	0.33	1.06	0.88	3.60
Jordan	Jordanian Dinar (JD) = 1,000 Fils	2.97	1.54	4.92	4.07	16.71
Kuwait	Kuwaiti Dinar (KD) = 1,000 Fils	3.69	1.92	6.11	5.06	20.76
Lebanon	Lebanese Pound (£L) = 100 Piastres	0.0027	0.0014	0.0045	0.0037	0.015
Libya	Libyan Dinar (LD) = 1,000 Dirhams	3.62	1.88	5.99	4.96	20.37
Oman	Omani Riyal (OR) = 1,000 Baiza	2.61	1.36	4.32	3.58	14.69
Qatar	Qatari Riyal (QR) = 100 Dirhams	0.28	0.15	0.46	0.38	1.58
Saudi Arabia	Saudi Riyal (SR) = 100 Halalas	0.27	0.14	0.45	0.37	1.52
Sudan	Sudanese Pound (£S) = 1,000 Milliemes	0.22	0.11	0.36	0.30	1.24
Syria	Syrian Pound (£SY) = 100 Piastres	0.037	0.019	0.061	0.051	0.208
Turkey	Turkish Lira (TL) = 100 Kurus	0.001	0.00052	0.0017	0.0014	0.0056
United Arab Emirates	UAE Dirham (UAEDh) = 100 Fils	0.27	0.14	0.45	0.37	1.52
Yemen (North)	Yemeni Riyal (YR) = 100 Fils	0.10	0.052	0.17	0.14	0.56
Yemen (South)	South Yemeni Dinar (SYD) = 1,000 Fils	2.95	1.53	4.89	4.04	16.60
$US rate $1		—	0.52	1.6561	1.3700	5.6272

* As quoted by the *Financial Times* in London on 18 April 1988.

The Arab Republic of Egypt
(Jumhuriyyat Misr al-'Arabiyya)

AMI AYALON

Addressing the People's Assembly and Consultative Council toward the end of 1988, President Husni Mubarak mentioned three "auspicious events which constitute landmarks on our path": the return of Taba to Egyptian sovereignty; the rise in the water level of the Nile; and Egyptian writer Najib Mahfuz's winning the Nobel prize for literature. These, Mubarak stated, "kindle hope in our hearts [and] inspire faith in ourselves and our future."[1] Auspicious events, as well as hope and faith in the future, may have played a role on the Egyptian scene in 1988. Yet in that year, as in much of the recent past, the scene was dominated above all by somberness. The country's economy was in deep trouble — so deep, indeed, that the government found itself engrossed in seeking palliatives for the immediate crisis rather than focusing on long-term solutions. The sociopolitical climate was consequently uneasy and often tense; and public frustration continued to be reflected in the expansion of opposition circles, notably the Islamic movement. As no single major event took place in the domestic arena in 1988, it was basically a year of "more of the same." More, that is, of slowly deteriorating material conditions and growing distress. While this was, happily, yet another year that had gone by without a serious outburst, it was also one in which the potentially dangerous public sense of resentment increased under the surface.

If Egyptians had few reasons for satisfaction at home, the foreign front provided them with some. This was especially so with the inter-Arab arena, in which Egypt had celebrated a prolonged "honeymoon" with members of the regional system. Through its often dramatized diplomatic initiatives on issues that topped the Arab agenda, Egypt recovered its long-sought central position in the system. Cairo involved itself in the defense of the Gulf until the summer cease-fire there and, more intensively, in efforts to score political gains for the Palestinians within the framework of the Middle East peace process. Egypt fully identified with the Palestinians in revolt in the occupied territories, an attitude which no doubt helped alleviate the country's identity problems. This sense of solidarity with the Palestinians, on the other hand, inevitably caused further erosion of Israel's standing in Egypt, a standing that was already quite low before the uprising. Egyptian-Israeli relations in 1988 were consequently marked by a low ebb of disillusionment and mistrust.

In the international arena, too, this was a year of much action and satisfaction. Cairo continued to foster its friendship with its chief allies — the US, the countries of Western Europe, and Japan — to improve its relations with the Soviet Union and the Eastern bloc, and to consolidate its ties in Africa and Asia. The convenient international standing which Egypt had acquired showed up brilliantly during the "diplomatic week" in Cairo in February 1989, when the Egyptian capital became a

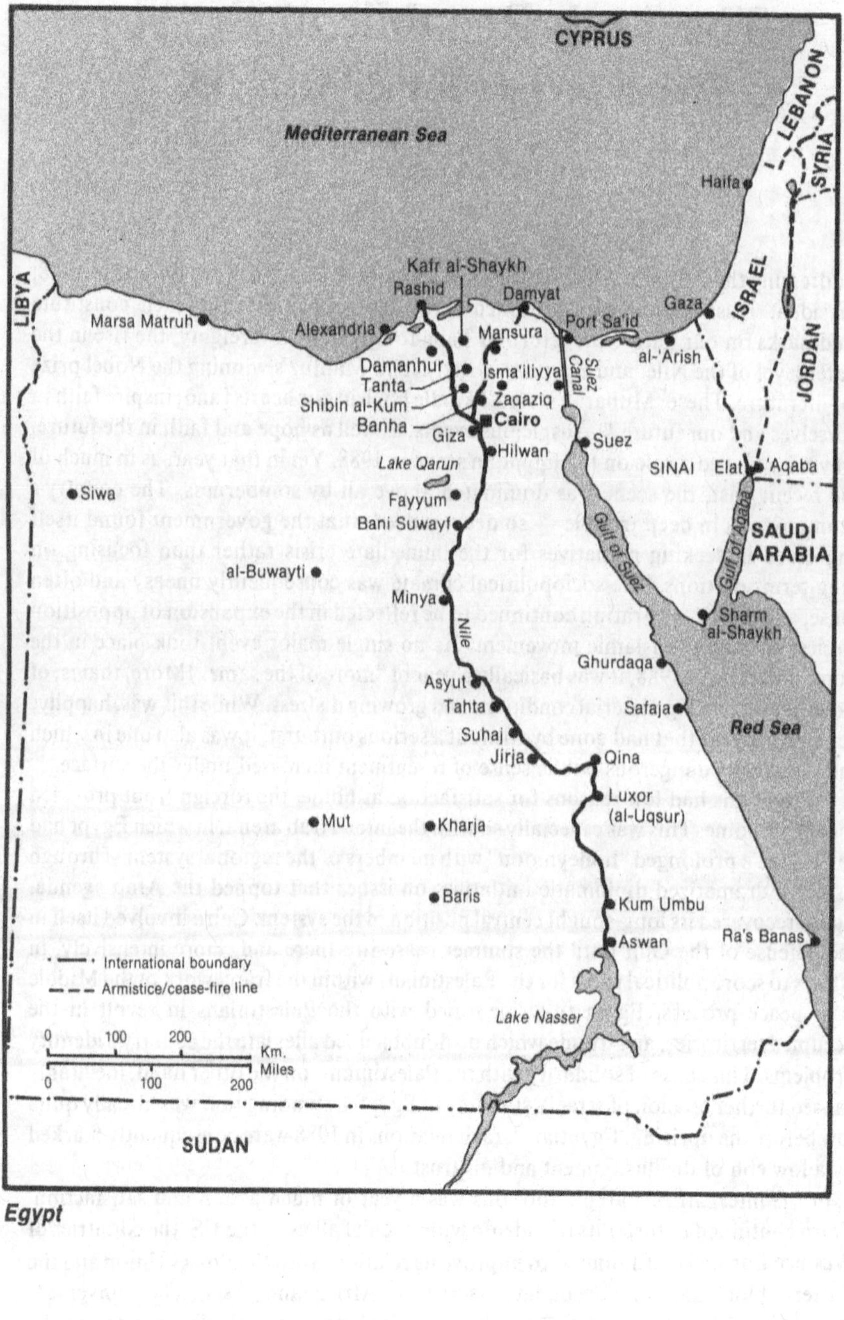
CYPRUS
LEBANON
SYRIA
Mediterranean Sea
Haifa
ISRAEL
LIBYA
Kafr al-Shaykh
Rashid
Damyat
Gaza
Marsa Matruh
Alexandria
Mansura
Port Sa'id
al-'Arish
JORDAN
Damanhur
Isma'iliyya
Suez Canal
Tanta
Shibin al-Kum
Zaqaziq
Banha
Cairo
Giza
Suez
Hilwan
Lake Qarun
SINAI
Elat
'Aqaba
Siwa
Fayyum
Bani Suwayf
Gulf of Suez
Gulf of Aqaba
SAUDI ARABIA
al-Buwayti
Minya
Nile
Sharm al-Shaykh
Ghurdaqa
Asyut
Tahta
Safaja
Suhaj
Red Sea
Jirja
Qina
Luxor (al-Uqsur)
Mut
Kharja
Baris
Kum Umbu
Ra's Banas
Aswan
International boundary
Armistice/cease-fire line
Lake Nasser
0
100
200
Km.
Miles
0
100
200
SUDAN
Egypt

venue for meetings involving Soviet Foreign Minister Shevardnadze, Israeli Foreign Minister Arens and PLO chairman 'Arafat. Years of diplomatic efforts seemed to have yielded a unique status, the like of which Egypt had rarely enjoyed, and Third World countries had seldom attained.

DOMESTIC AFFAIRS

THE ECONOMY: A DEEPENING CRISIS

"I am faced with economic problems which have been accumulating for the past 50, 60, or 70 years. I have embarked on solving the problems, but solution requires a long time."[2] The long-term economic ailments hinted at in these words of Mubarak remained a conspicuous feature of the Egyptian scene in 1988. Yet more upsetting were short-term troubles, amounting to an acute crisis that haunted the country and its leaders throughout the year under review.

The Egyptian population — some 52m. around mid-year — continued to grow, in Mubarak's desperate words, "faster than the speed of sound."[3] But there was no parallel growth in the country's resources. While revenues from several economic sectors (expatriate remittances, tourism, and Suez canal tolls) increased modestly in 1987–88,[4] such added income was easily offset by increased consumption and, more ominously, by a growing debt service. Sinking deeper into debt inevitably resulted from the country's consuming more than it was producing, "like an employee who earns £100 a month and spends £122," according to one Egyptian economist.[5] With a monstrous foreign debt of some $44bn. in 1988, serviced at some $5–$6bn. annually,[6] Egypt was falling behind in repayments, thus dangerously compromising its good standing with old and potential creditors.

Focusing, as a first priority, on the immediate currency crisis, the country's economic leadership feverishly sought an arrangement of debt rescheduling. A deal with the International Monetary Fund (IMF), which had paved the way for rescheduling pacts with several of Egypt's chief Western creditors, had already been concluded in May 1987 (see *MECS* 1987, p. 333). But by early 1988 the deal had collapsed, because Egypt had been unable to meet performance targets imposed by the IMF, notably in reducing budget deficit and cutting state subsidies for basic goods.[7] The IMF now demanded that Egypt hasten economic reforms as a precondition for a new agreement that would allow rescheduling of further debts. Cairo, however, argued that its ability to comply was limited by grave social and political constraints. Mubarak complained that the IMF was "like a quack doctor" who prescribed "a huge dose of medicine in one go instead of a daily pill...If we do as they say," he stated angrily, "we shall sink."[8] Mubarak traveled to Europe twice, in January and September, seeking to enlist the backing of Egypt's allies in the IMF negotiations; Egypt, he argued, was too important an anchor of Western strategy to risk the social upheaval that complying with the fund's demands could prompt (see further below). The European governments expressed sympathy and readiness to assist, but that in itself was insufficient. Desultory talks between Egyptians and IMF officials throughout the year produced little result. By the end of 1988 there was still no arrangement with the fund.

If measures toward reforming the economy and balancing the budget failed to satisfy the IMF, their painful effect was unmistakably felt by the public. Monetary changes accounted, at least in part, for a marked rise in the prices of many basic commodities and other consumer goods.[9] Inflation, which in 1986 was estimated at 20%–25%, had by early 1988 risen to 30% or more.[10] Likewise, efforts to curb imports produced periodic shortages in various staples. Frequent protests in the press clearly reflected the popular frustration with these developments and prompted some heated debates in the People's Assembly.[11] Problems not directly related to the government's recent economic measures also weighed on the public. A steep rise in unemployment in 1986–87 had brought the number of jobless people to c. 2.8m. or more by early 1988.[12] A dangerous decline in the water level in Lake Nasser, Egypt's vital reservoir behind the Aswan Dam, threatened to cut off some 25% of the country's electrical power and compelled the government to introduce rationing measures to conserve electricity during winter and spring. The decline, a result of several years of drought in Ethiopia and Sudan, brought about an unprecedented crisis in the Land of the Nile, where water had always been one of the few things in abundance, as people were called upon to economize on water consumption.[13] This combined with the other grievances to create a pessimistic atmosphere.

In a particularly gloomy speech on May Day, Mubarak spoke frankly and in detail about the afflictions of the present and those still lying ahead for Egypt. The country, he stated, was "at the most difficult stages of a hard road." It was forced to "make its way amid rocks" in facing challenges posed by its own poverty, by international circumstances and "by Mother Nature." The problems, complex in themselves, were further exacerbated by the people's attitude: rather than showing a sense of responsibility, Egyptians were displaying "closed minds, shaky hands and weak spirits." Worst of all were "the mindless increase of consumption and the senseless growth of our population," as well as the low level of production. The people had got used to wasting without regard for the country's dire needs, Mubarak charged: they fed their goats with bread and "put eight or ten cubes of sugar in their tea, to be in a good mood." The population was "multiplying so fast that we are even beating marathon contestants." And, instead of cooperating with their leaders and exerting more efforts, Egyptians were relying on God and on the government to bail them out of their misery. However, Mubarak asserted, "faith alone is not enough. We have to work. To say that God is there and sit cross-legged doing nothing is not a solution. God will not offer anything on a silver platter." Nor will the government, as "there are obstacles that cannot be eliminated by decrees or laws." The solution, therefore, was as much in the hands of the people as it was in those of the government.[14]

This last theme was repeatedly voiced by the president and other high officials, who sought to generate more public awareness of the formidable nature of the problems. In the same vein, Mubarak asked the broadcasting authority to announce the number of new births daily in the two main radio and television news bulletins, along with a weekly analysis of their grave significance, so as to alarm the people.[15] But these and similar educational methods could hardly have more than a negligible effect. They could be of little avail in curbing population growth and consumption and in boosting production, unless accompanied by radical measures, perhaps more radical than those which the government felt it could afford to impose. The name of the game was introducing cuts without crossing the dangerous line beyond which lay the minefield of social unrest. A reminder of the line's existence was offered in September, when Mubarak announced that the government was unable to pay the customary back-to-school bonuses to the public sector. Workers in state-owned plants and offices throughout the country took to the streets to demonstrate their protest, and in one place, al-Mahalla al-Kubra, they clashed with the police, who made many arrests.[16] Nor was the approach of introducing gradual reform without risk; for, as one observer noted, there was "a real danger that in the absence of stronger medicine...Egypt will fall into a cycle of 'stagflation' which will be just as damaging to its long-term stability as a short, sharp shock."[17]

The threat of acute water and electricity shortages was removed by midsummer, as torrential rains in Sudan and Ethiopia replenished the Nile with above-average quantities of water. This, of course, was a source of much joy in Egypt. But it was not paralleled by similar causes for relief in other parts of the generally bleak scene. The bleakness was given a graphic expression in a cartoon entitled "The rope is the solution," showing a man hanging himself because of rising prices and shortage of basic foodstuffs.[18] Given the proverbial optimism and resilience of the Egyptians, the artist may have taken his point to an undue extreme. But surely this optimism and resilience were faced with a harsh predicament in 1988, with harsher tests still to come. Their results were by no means predictable.

DOMESTIC SECURITY AND SOCIOPOLITICAL RELATIONS: ANOTHER YEAR OF PRECARIOUS STABILITY

That the domestic political atmosphere in Egypt should be somewhat unsettled in 1988 was only to be expected, given the country's material realities. That tension should lead to occasional violence was equally normal, the legendary Egyptian tolerance notwithstanding. The year 1988 was relatively calm, compared with 1977, 1981, and 1986 with their dramatic outbreaks. Yet disquiet was unmistakably there, mostly beneath the surface but sometimes above it. Much steam was let off through the ever-more aggressive verbal assaults on the government by its various critics, both organized and unorganized. Otherwise the frustration was reflected in the ongoing expansion of Islamic fundamentalism, in periodic confrontations between security forces and exponents of more radical Islamic views, and in occasional clashes on university campuses.

The exposure, in late 1987, of the Nasserite "Egyptian Revolution" terrorist organization, and the involvement of 'Abd al-Nasir's son in its attacks on Israeli and US diplomats (see *MECS* 1987, pp. 335–36) was a major event that continued to occupy public attention during much of 1988. On 18 February, 20 members of the organization were indicted. The prosecutor demanded the death penalty for 11 of them, including Khalid 'Abd al-Nasir, who was taking refuge in Yugoslavia.[19] In a second hearing of the case, on 1 November, the group's leader Mahmud Nur al-Din reaffirmed the group's opposition to the government policy of peace with Israel.[20] The court's next session was postponed to January 1989.

While the leadership and structure of the Egyptian Revolution seemed to have been dismantled, the cause the group stood for was evidently very much alive. The opposition press expressed open support for the organization's principles and strategy if not its methods. "I sympathize with the Egyptian Revolution," stated a prominent Muslim Brothers' spokesman, "and I am sure that many countrymen share my sympathy [for]... that organization [which] was striking terror into the hearts of the Zionists and filling the hearts of ordinary people with pride."[21] More than 120 lawyers undertook to defend the group's members in court, among them Ahmad al-Khawaja, the doyen of the Egyptian bar. "These men are heroes. They are the sons of Egypt. They have raised guns against Israeli agents, against those who attack the Arabs, in order to defend our dignity and honor", al-Khawaja said.[22] Many others expressed similar sentiments with equal clarity.

There were more signs indicating that the feelings which produced the Egyptian Revolution were still present. Sometime after the arrest of the group's leadership, a statement on its behalf — signed by one "Colonel Rayhan" — announced that the group was "suspending" its operations for six months in order to "reorganize its ranks," thus letting it be known that it would return.[23] Around the same time, another group, calling itself "the Crescent Revolutionary Organization" (*Munazzamat al-hilal al-thawriyya*) made public its existence and pledged to "destroy the US and Israeli embassies in Cairo" and to "kill all Israelis in Egypt."[24] In January, an explosion took place behind the US consulate in Alexandria; a group calling itself "the National Front for the Liberation of Egypt" (*al-Jabha al-wataniyya li-tahrir Misr*) claimed responsibility, vowing to "persist in its armed struggle."[25] And in February yet another group, the "Egyptian Revolutionary Patriotic Commitment" (*al-Iltizam al-watani al-thawri al-Misri*) announced its intention to bring down the regime and replace it with a "national and democratic" one.[26] Such announcements, real or fake, were apparently in line with widespread aspirations and convictions. They seemed to show that the danger of leftist-Nasserite terrorism was still a fact of life in Egypt.

Still more popular, and in the long run more dangerous, was the Islamic opposition, which in 1988 remained as aggresive and vociferous as ever. Its exponents continued to assail the government for its "un-Islamic ways" which, they claimed, accounted for all the troubles besetting the country. A major issue in their criticism this year was the regime's "continued tolerance" of Israel while the latter was "oppressing" the Palestinians and "suppressing their rightful uprising" (see below). Protest demonstrations, typically after Friday noon prayers, often turned into riots in which Muslim radicals clashed with security forces. Such events were most common in the Cairo urban area and the cities of Upper Egypt — Asyut, Minya, Aswan, and elsewhere. Demonstrators sometimes became so excited that they boldly called Mubarak "the enemy of God."[27] The police, for their part, confronted them firmly, regularly used much force and tear gas, and arrested many.

A major clash between members of the fundamentalist al-Jihad group and security forces took place in the Cairo suburb of 'Ayn Shams on 12 and 13 August. Violence broke out as the police were trying to serve arrest warrants on a number of radicals during Friday prayers. The fundamentalists hurled stones and Molotov cocktails, setting police cars and other vehicles ablaze. Riot squads opened fire and launched tear gas grenades to disperse the attackers, then arrested some 180 people including 20 al-Jihad members. At least two people were killed and some 50 injured in the riots, among them several passersby.[28] Interviewed after the incident, Maj. Gen. Mamduh Bura'i, assistant interior minister and public security chief, gave expression to the government's uncompromising approach to the challenge: "The security organs have recently used violence in confronting riots," he warned, and in so doing they were exercising "their legitimate rights, to guard against any attempt to disrupt security."[29]

Serious disturbances broke out again in 'Ayn Shams in December, as units of the security forces launched a search "to clear the area of extremist elements known for instigating troubles and demonstrations."[30] Muslim activists clashed with the police, killing an officer, and many of them were arrested — some 100, according to one source; some 250 according to another, including "the first two ranks of al-Jihad leadership in the area".[31] The riots evoked a spate of excited reactions in the press, which discussed the turning of 'Ayn Shams, hitherto a quiet suburb, into an arena of radical action and violence. "'Ayn Shams has joined Minya and Asyut to form a triangle of terror," one paper noted in dismay; the causes for this development were overcrowdedness (over 800,000 neighborhood residents), extreme poverty, and a high proportion of unemployed, including professionals who previously worked abroad[32] — standard reasons in the background of the phenomenon nationwide. "If it is true that the young [radical] Muslims find support among the poor classes," one author advised the government, "then you will never defeat them with soldiers and armored trucks."[33]

The police continued to monitor the activities of the radical groups and periodically arrested their members. On one occasion, in late May, a clandestine organization with ties to Iran was exposed and 19 of its members were detained. Reportedly engaged in "exporting the Khomeyniite revolution" and preparing for violent action, the group tried to recruit members of other fundamentalist organizations, but failed because the latter "did not believe in the Shi'i call."[34]

The universities, long since a fundamentalist stronghold, likewise remained restive. The Islamic groups (*jama'at*) continued to dominate the political scene and much of the social activities on the campuses. Frequent demonstrations by students to voice their grievances and protest against government policies — notably, again, the regime's relations with Israel — resulted at times in clashes with the police. A series of particularly grave incidents took place in January on the 'Ayn Shams campus, as students who staged a pro-Palestinian demonstration were confronted by security forces. Hundreds of students and security men were reportedly involved, and dozens of students were arrested.[35] In another incident in November at al-Azhar, "scores of students" were badly hit by security men who broke into the campus in order to disperse their demonstration over academic issues.[36]

In November, student union elections took place, following a stormy campaign that was marked by numerous incidents. Students with different political complexions clashed among themselves and with the police, in what some observers described as "the most violent student elections in recent years."[37] Having retained their control over the unions on most campuses as could have been expected, the Islamic groups celebrated the victory by launching parades, in which they chanted that "the university is becoming Islamic again."[38] The government intended it to be otherwise; despite vehement student protests, the ever-effective "campus guards" and police units remained close to the scene of potential troubles, ready to intervene and control any situation that might develop on the sensitive campuses.

On 20 March, the People's Assembly approved a three-year extension of the Emergency Law. The law became effective following President Sadat's assassination in 1981, and was since extended periodically. It was a convenient tool in the government's hands in fighting its more dangerous opponents. The continuous extension of the law had become a major bone of contention between the regime and its critics, who had repeatedly denounced the law as a sign of dictatorship. When the government moved to revalidate the law in 1988, it again came under heavy opposition fire (see below). Mubarak rejected the criticism; the law, he argued, was necessary "in order to confront terrorism [and]... protect democracy and stability in this country." Mubarak sought to remove all doubts: "I am in charge and I have the authority to adopt measures so long as the majority approves. I am in charge of the country's stability."[39]

Whether because of, or regardless of the Emergency Law, the home front in 1988 was as orderly as the government could realistically have hoped, given the precarious socioeconomic circumstances. While Maj. Gen. Bura'i's depiction of the home front as "totally calm and stable" was somewhat too optimistic, the situation could conceivably have been far worse. By the end of the year, it was quite clear that the potential for serious agitation had remained an inseparable part of the Egyptian social and political scene.

THE MULTIPARTY ARENA

There was little novelty in the multiparty scene in 1988, a year with no major power tests between the regime and its legally organized opponents. Nor was there much change in the substance and style of their dialogue. No new parties joined the six already in existence (for details, see *MECS* 1987, p. 325), although efforts by various groups to secure official party status continued throughout the year. One person whose attempt to enter this arena attracted some public attention was the president's brother, Sami Mubarak. As his application for a license (see *MECS* 1987, p. 326) was turned down by the Consultative Council's parties' committee, he gave up his initiative and decided not to take the case to court, because, in his words, he "preferred to give Husni Mubarak a hand in solving Egypt's problems."[40]

In May, a Cairo court rescinded the law requiring acceptance of the peace with Israel as a condition for setting up a party.[41] This resulted in a spate of announcements by groups and individuals of their intention of applying for a party license.[42] By the end of the year some of them were still striving to overcome the necessary bureaucratic and legal obstacles; others were conclusively turned down.

As in the past, the opposition continued to take the government to task for its domestic and foreign policies. The regime was subject to accusations — by now all too familiar — about its "poor economic performance," "totalitarian ways," "false pro-American orientation" and "the shameful peace with Israel." Its critics continued to enjoy extensive freedom of expression unparalleled in the Arab world. The government used the broadcasting media and semiofficial press to respond to these attacks, regularly amplifying statements by the president and other officials. If there was a change in the opposition criticism, it was in the bolder tone its spokesmen used to attack the president in person. In principle, the opposition acknowledged — and was appreciative of — President Mubarak's being "a man who allows his country a measure of freedom and democracy that enable us to differ with him, criticize his decisions, and sometimes be sharp with him."[43] And sharp indeed it was. "We do not want a president whose [personal] opinion prevails in all matters, as was the case in the days of Jamal 'Abd al-Nasir," asserted an editorial in *al-Wafd*;

> We want a president... who does not seek to have the exclusive say and to make exclusive decisions, a soloist surrounded by a chorus echoing his songs, while the hypocritical media applaud and cheer. This is loathsome dictatorship which we shall never accept. We do not want a despotic and tyrannical president.[44]

"President Mubarak's rule," the leftist *al-Ahali* concurred, "is individualistic and characterized by police methods"; it is typified by "conspiracy" and "disregard for the judiciary"; his policies are "a series of hellish measures."[45]

Mubarak responded in kind. He derided "the dozens of vociferous [opposition] newspaper articles that contain nothing but cries and defamations":

> Sometimes I ask myself, in view of all this behavior: when will we have real parties which have clear programs, uncompromising ideology, firm commitment to the higher national interest which should be above all party differences, and cadres who are not ready to change their positions from one election season to another? The answer is that we might need a long time.[46]

Two issues were prominent in the government-opposition verbal exchanges in 1988: the extension of the Emergency Law in March (see above) and the local council elections in November. The opposition parties viewed the regime's continued reliance on emergency regulations as particularly grave, since it was incompatible with the democratic principles that permitted their own existence and of which the president was so proud. As soon as they learned of the government's intention of extending the law, they launched a furious offensive against it. A joint opposition statement depicted the measure as "conclusive proof that the government feels it is isolated from the nation, despite its fake parliamentary majority." Extending the Emergency Law, the statement charged, "was a sign that the government will further undermine freedoms," for "emergency laws protect the worst forms of corruption and looting."[47] One party leader accused the regime of having "become incurably addicted" to the law; "it is addicted to ruling with whip, with prisons and dungeons, and with the stick."[48] The opposition also protested by having its representatives withdraw from several sessions of the People's Assembly and Consultative Council.[49] Government officials reiterated in response that Egypt, as a society building its democratic future, had meanwhile to defend itself against enemies and could not afford to dispense with such an effective device. "Our democracy," Mubarak stated, "has to protect itself...from the recklessness of saboteurs and evildoers."[50]

The other issue which became a matter of sharp controversy was the elections for local councils, scheduled for November. On 5 June the People's Assembly adopted several amendments in the Local Administration Law.[51] The amended law prohibited the formation of coalitions or alliances among parties during local elections — a clear blow to the opposition parties that were considering running on a joint ticket to improve their chances. Outraged, opposition leaders attacked the government for having "a preplanned scheme to abort the democratic process" and for which "the rigging of elections has become normal procedure."[52] On 18 June, leaders of all opposition parties decided unanimously to boycott the elections (for a similar boycott of the 1983 local elections, see *MECS* 1983–84, p. 358), and pledged to contest the constitutionality of the amended law in court.[53] The small People's (Umma) Party, however, later backed down on its support of the boycott and decided to participate.[54]

In the elections, held on 5 November, the ruling National Democratic Party was the only party to have won council seats (403 altogether in the different localities), alongside 40 independent candidates. All People's Party candidates were defeated.[55]

FOREIGN AFFAIRS

EGYPT AND THE ARAB WORLD

THE CONSOLIDATION OF EGYPT'S INTER-ARAB STANDING

If 1987 was the year of Egypt's triumphant return to the Arab fold, 1988 witnessed the normalization and consolidation of its standing in the regional system. Ties restored in November 1987 were now broadly expanded; and more states joined the Arab countries already having embassies in Cairo: Tunisia, which since November 1987 was represented in Egypt by an official with the rank of ambassador, announced the formal resumption of full diplomatic relations in January;[56] the People's Democratic Republic of Yemen followed suit the next month;[57] as did Algeria in November.[58] By the end of the year there remained only three Arab League member states without official relations with Cairo: Syria, Libya, and Lebanon (the latter's foreign policy was effectively formulated in Damascus, not in Beirut, hence in Egypt's eyes it could be "excused").[59] The normalization of relations was not limited to the state level. Egypt was invited to rejoin inter-Arab bodies and forums which had earlier suspended or revoked its membership in them, such as the Arab Council for Scientific Research,[60] the Arab Engineers' Association,[61] the Arab League Education, Science, and Culture Organization,[62] the Arab Economic Unity Council,[63] and the Union of Arab Agricultural Engineers.[64]

Egypt came to resume its centrality in the fragmented Arab system, although it may not have recovered the "cornerstone" status it had once enjoyed. The Arab states, haunted by active confrontation on two fronts — in the Gulf and Palestinian arenas — were prone in 1988 to overlook some of their chronic differences, thus also helping to minimize the significance of Cairo's already-emasculated peace with Israel. Egypt surely displayed a proud "Arab" and "nationalist" stance. With a mighty military potential that had sufficiently impressed the Arabs to open their arms for it (cf. *MECS* 1987, pp. 341, 342), Cairo continued to extend aid to Iraq, and voiced its readiness to support the Gulf states in their struggle. In January, Mubarak went on a tour of the six Gulf Cooperation Council (GCC) states to promote military cooperation and demonstrate "Egyptian understanding of national and pan-Arab security" needs: "We have repeatedly made it known," he stated, "that we would consider a breach of the Gulf countries' security as a breach of Egyptian security and of that of the Arab world as a whole."[65] The message was reiterated on later occasions: "Egypt's commitment to its Arab sisters outweighs any other commitment to any other side," Mubarak's close aide Usama al-Baz reconfirmed in November, during a visit to Abu Dhabi.[66] Cairo showed equal devotion to the Palestinian cause, backing the population in revolt in the occupied territories in word as well as deed and exerting ceaseless diplomatic efforts on its behalf (see further below). For this Egypt won "the highest esteem and appreciation" of Arab states: "Events have proved that the absence of Egypt from the Arab fold was not natural," asserted the president of the United Arab Emirates (UAE), Zayid Ibn Sultan Al Nuhayyan, reflecting the sentiments and views of many Arab governments; "the seriousness of the present stage" no longer allowed the Arab world to retain "the vacuum which was created by Egypt's absence."[67]

Egypt's return to the fold was most noticeable — and least problematic — on the bilateral level of relations with individual Arab states. This was only to be expected, given the manner in which Egypt was reaccepted, through a decision allowing Arab states to resume ties with it separately without abolishing the formal consensual boycott. Cairo embarked with much zeal on expanding the circle of its regional allies, reviving ties with states that had hitherto been too cautious to openly associate themselves with it — such as Saudi Arabia, the Gulf states, and the Yemeni Arab Republic (YAR). At the same time, Egypt continued to invest in improving its relations with its older Arab allies, primarily Jordan, Iraq, and Sudan. The new diplomatic momentum was reflected in Mubarak's many trips to Arab countries in 1988, which took him to the capitals of all GCC states (among them Saudi Arabia), as well as 'Aqaba, Baghdad, and Rabat, in January; to Khartoum in March; to Amman in April; to San'a in May; to Baghdad, again, in June; and once more to the Jordanian and Iraqi capitals in October.

There were still, however, obstacles on the road to full integration in the Arab system. Egypt had yet to be formally readmitted to the Arab League, something that was effectively prevented by its Arab rivals, Syria and Libya. Since Cairo's ties with most league members had been restored, membership of the league itself now carried primarily a symbolic significance. Yet it was not unimportant: Egypt's being outside the league was an irritating anomaly that upset the Egyptians, notwithstanding occasional denials of this by Egyptian spokesmen. Cairo's allies in the system, notably Jordan, Iraq, and the Gulf states, repeatedly called for its readmission and invested diplomatic efforts in securing it, but to no avail. That Egypt was not fully reintegrated was clearly demonstrated in June, when it was left out of the emergency Arab summit that convened in Algiers. Cairo was embittered: the Arab leaders, said Mahfuz al-Ansari, editor-in-chief of *al-Jumhuriyya*, "should know that their message to the Egyptian people has been received and studied carefully; namely, that Egypt should remain outside the Arab camp and Arab League, and that the [November 1987] Amman summit decision [to renew diplomatic ties with Egypt] should remain [no more than] 'a palliative' to alleviate the Arab rage" about Egypt's ostracism.[68] Much of the anger was directed against the host state, Algeria, whose "flagrant and strange hostility" blocked the invitation of Egypt.[69] (See also chapter on inter-Arab relations.)

Later in the year, however, the climate gradually improved. Fences with Algeria were mended, and by November relations with Egypt had been fully restored; and the voices calling for, and predicting, Cairo's imminent return to the league were again loudly heard.[70] There were indications that Syrian and Libyan opposition to readmission was abating and could be overcome. The next Arab summit in which Egypt could participate, however, was postponed until after the end of 1988.

BILATERAL RELATIONS WITH ARAB STATES

While Egyptian diplomacy was joyously busy renewing old Arab ties, Jordan, which had already restored its relations with Egypt in 1984, remained Cairo's closest Arab ally. The heads of the two states continued to contact each other regularly to coordinate policies and frequently traversed the short distance between their countries in mutual visits. Mubarak went to Jordan in January, April, and October. King Husayn reciprocated in March, July, September, November, and December. Both were often accompanied by other high officials. Expressions of friendship abounded: Mubarak referred to "my brother His Majesty King Husayn, whom I am proud to consider a friend and comrade in the procession of liberation and peace."[71] The king likewise said their relations were "characterized by friendship and sincere brotherhood," and affirmed that they shared "one stand and one view... on all issues."[72]

By far the most central item on the Egyptian-Jordanian agenda throughout the year was the Palestinian problem. Both states had a keen interest in pushing the peace process forward, preferably in a manner that would translate the apparent achievements of the Palestinian uprising into political gains for the Arabs. Cairo, which also maintained close ties with the PLO (see below), sought to bring Amman and the organization closer together and make them coordinate their policy and actions. During the first half of the year, there was little political change, and the contacts amounted to no more than exchanges of views. Then came the king's decision in late July to abrogate his country's legal and administrative links with the West Bank (see chapter on Jordan). Seemingly taken by surprise like everybody else, Cairo was instinctively inclined to interpret the step favourably, as beneficial to the Arab cause. "King Husayn is committed to peace and to the peace process... [hence] this decision... [could not] mean that Jordan will abandon the peace efforts," Mubarak suggested, somewhat puzzled.[73] A Radio Cairo commentator spoke of the "courageous decision [that represented] a continuation of Jordan's pioneer role in supporting the Palestinian cause."[74] Such a "well-studied move," an *al-Ahram* editorial similarly observed, "is one of the most important and serious Arab resolutions regarding the Palestinian cause since 1948"; it "asserts a number of principles undisputed by anyone in the Arab world."[75]

Contacts between the two sides were intensified during the last third of the year, with the approaching of the Palestine National Council (PNC) meeting in Algiers that was meant to be an historic event (see chapter on the PLO). In October, on the eve of the PNC, PLO chairman 'Arafat came to see Mubarak in Cairo and the two went to 'Aqaba for a tripartite meeting with King Husayn, where they had "a direct and candid exchange of views to strengthen the future steps and...attain full coordination."[76] The intensive Egyptian-Jordanian dialogue continued, following the dramatic developments in the Palestinian question. These developments prompted Husayn to visit Egypt twice between the PNC and the year's end. (The Egyptian reaction to the PNC resolutions and subsequent moves are discussed below; for the Jordanian reaction, see chapter on Jordan.)

There were other topics in the Egyptian-Jordanian exchanges. The Iraqi-Iranian War, which had caused much concern in both Cairo and Amman until the summer cease-fire, was constantly on the agenda of their talks. Once the fighting stopped, the two leaders expressed "happiness" at the "reassuring" situation in the Gulf. "Our happiness will be much greater," Mubarak stated at a joint press conference with Husayn, "when a final peace agreement takes place between the two countries and when life returns to normal in that region, because this war threatens all of us, just as it threatens the whole region."[77] Jordan was most active in the efforts to readmit Egypt to the Arab League and reportedly played a leading role in generating the momentum, late in the year, to invite Egypt to attend the next Arab summit once it convened.[78] King Husayn was also instrumental in mediating between Egypt and Syria, which improved the climate of their relations (see below).[79]

On the bilateral level, too, the extensive cooperation persisted. The volume of trade between the two states was estimated at c. $250m.[80] In July, a large Egyptian ministerial delegation headed by Prime Minister 'Atif Sidqi came to Amman for a session of the joint Egyptian-Jordanian Higher Committee (see *MECS* 1984–85, p. 367). The committee agreed upon a series of joint projects in the areas of trade, agriculture, industry, infrastructure, tourism, education, and culture. It was decided that the volume of trade would be increased to c. $350m.[81]

"A warm friendship, which developed over the years as a result of common experience," continued to characterize Egypt's relations with Iraq. This friendship, President Mubarak noted, "ties me to my brother, President Saddam Husayn...who is distinguished for his bravery, sincerity, and penetrating vision."[82] Beyond the warmth of such personal sentiments, Cairo continued to be tied to Baghdad by important interests in three major areas: military assistance, economic cooperation, and the large Egyptian emigrant community in Iraq, estimated at some 2m. people.[83] Long a major supporter of Iraq in its war efforts, Egypt's declared readiness to back pro-Iraqi states in the Gulf drew Cairo and Baghdad still closer together. Egypt continued to provide Iraq with military aid until the summer cease-fire — which brought Mubarak to Baghdad in January and again in June, and Defense Minister Abu Ghazala in July — then congratulated Baghdad on the termination of hostilities. There was also close diplomatic cooperation: Mubarak eagerly echoed Baghdad's message to the world that "Iraq wants peace and most sincerely seeks to establish it," and that it "does not seek to take anything which does not belong to it."[84] In the same vein, Cairo denounced the "unjust campaign" and "feeble charges" leveled against Iraq in September, when it was accused of using chemical weapons against the Kurds (see chapter on Iraq), and criticized the US decision to impose economic sanctions on it, as "a peculiar stance, involving incomprehensible hostile sentiments."[85] On the eve of the PNC, as Mubarak engaged in feverish diplomatic action to strengthen Arab backing of the PLO (see below), he went to Baghdad again in October, taking 'Arafat along for tripartite coordination talks with Saddam Husayn, thus showing his appreciation for Iraq's "Arab role."[86] Iraq, for its part, undertook to advance Egypt's cause in the Arab system, and was a vocal supporter of its return to the Arab League.[87] Senior Iraqi officials visited Cairo on several occasions: Deputy Prime Minister Taha Yasin Ramadan in August; Deputy Prime Minister and Foreign Minister Tariq 'Aziz in September; Vice President Muhyi al-Din Ma'ruf in October; and, eventually, President Saddam Husayn himself in November for a surprise visit, his first since becoming president. Husayn's coming to Cairo offered yet another opportunity for mutual expressions of "love, appreciation, and...profound brotherhood."[88]

In May it was announced that the two countries had decided to set up a joint higher committee cochaired by their prime ministers, in order to promote bilateral relations in various fields.[89] Two months later, Egyptian Prime Minister Sidqi came to Baghdad for the committee's first session, heading a delegation comprised of 10 ministers. The committee discussed joint projects in trade, industry, agriculture, information, culture, science, health, and education, including a plan to build a railway line between Cairo and Baghdad via Jordan. Little was reported of the results, but the talks were described as "a success."[90] The two sides signed an agreement regulating the legal status, rights, and working conditions of Egyptians employed in Iraq.[91]

Egyptian-Sudanese relations witnessed a marked improvement in 1988. It was primarily an improvement in atmosphere, which had been somewhat uneasy ever since the 1985 change of regime in Khartoum. The political asylum Egypt gave the deposed president Numayri, Sudan's close ties with Libya which caused concern in

Cairo, and Egypt's friendship with Ethiopia, which upset the Sudanese, all weighed down on Egyptian-Sudanese relations in the post-Numayri era (see *MECS* 1987, pp. 344–45). In 1988, these obstacles were minimized, due both to changes in regional relations involving Libya and Ethiopia, and also because other determinants came to the fore. Natural disasters in Sudan — drought in winter, floods in the summer — and the growing pressures of the southern problem drove the government in Khartoum to increase its cooperation with Egypt and lean on its support. Cairo was generous, and this was appreciated by Sudan.

On 1 March, Mubarak went to Khartoum along with Defense Minister Abu Ghazala, Foreign Minister 'Abd al-Majid, and several other senior officials. The visit, Mubarak's first since 1985, marked a new stage in Egyptian-Sudanese relations. The delegation discussed with its hosts issues concerning regional relations as well as Egypt's assistance to the Sudanese Government in dealing with the southern problem.[92] Having previously extended military aid to Khartoum to help it fight the southern rebels (see chapter on Sudan), Mubarak now moved to reactivate his mediation in the conflict through direct contacts with John Garang, the rebels' leader.[93] Expressing satisfaction with the Egyptian mediation efforts, Sudanese officials noted, however, that "unless there is progress in Sudanese-Ethiopian relations the rebel movement will not respond to any mediation," since the rebels had "become hostage" to Ethiopia.[94] Mubarak was prepared to assist on this front too: during the Organization of African Unity (OAU) summit in Addis Ababa, in May (see below), he met with Sudanese Prime Minister al-Mahdi and Ethiopian President Mengistu in an effort to bridge the gap between the two.[95] Sudanese-Ethiopian relations, indeed, improved during the second half of 1988, although by the end of the year the effect of this improvement on the state of the southern problem had yet to be felt (for details see chapter on Sudan).

Khartoum, for its part, undertook to mediate between Cairo and Tripoli. By midyear, a Sudanese-initiated formula for an Egyptian-Libyan *rapprochement* — based on separating their discordant pan-Arab policies from their common interests as neighbors — was being studied in the three capitals.[96] The initiative produced little result: Egypt, Prime Minister Sidqi told the Sudanese Council of Ministers, accepted "all mediation efforts aimed at normalizing its relations with Libya, but these always fail because of the position of the Libyan side"[97] (see further below).

Egypt and Sudan, likewise, continued their extensive cooperation on bilateral issues. In January, they signed a trade protocol for 1988 totalling $225m.[98] In April, Prime Minister Sidqi went to Khartoum with a ministerial delegation and signed with his counterpart a series of agreements on joint projects in various fields.[99] In July it became known that the Sudanese Government had set up a new "fraternity department" at its Foreign Ministry to coordinate Egyptian-Sudanese relations, "as an acknowledgment... of the special nature" of these ties.[100] In the same month, Sudanese Defense Minister Gen. 'Abd al-Majid Hamid Khalil arrived in Egypt, and the two countries signed a military cooperation protocol providing for an increased exchange of expertise and assistance between them. Another protocol, dealing with the dispatch of Egyptian instructors and technicians to Sudan, was signed a few days later when the Sudanese Chief of Staff Lt. Gen. Faysal Shawir visited Cairo.[101] Finally, Sidqi traveled to Khartoum again in October for talks.[102] Egypt sent relief supplies to Sudan during the winter drought, when it transported foodstuffs worth $250,000;[103] and during the summer floods, when several airlifts of tents, medicine, clothing, and food were organized.[104] These contributions met with Sudanese appreciation and thanks for Egypt's "fraternal stand and painstaking efforts."[105]

The Sudanese-Libyan *rapprochement* toward the end of the year and reports on their unity plan (see chapters on Sudan and Libya) seemed to have caused some nervousness in Cairo once again. One symptom was the statement of the Sudan State Council's vice chairman, Idris al-Banna, designed to appease his Egyptian audience, that the Sudanese-Libyan talks were merely aimed at "clearing the Arab air and closing Arab ranks."[106] Nonetheless, the news remained a potential source of disagreement between Cairo and Khartoum.

Egypt's friendly relations with the Arab countries of the Gulf, which in 1987 were given new impetus by the exigencies of the war, continued to make strides in 1988. Mubarak's trip to these countries in January and his solemn pledge to assist in their defense helped enhance the spirit of amity. "Relations between Egypt and the Gulf states have not ceased at any time," he declared, "these relations will not stop and nothing can stop them, not even the head of a state here in Egypt," because "Egypt's security lies in Gulf security and vice versa."[107] The fact that the Gulf states needed Egypt's military backing and that Egypt sought economic assistance from them gave ground to reports early in the year that Egypt promised to send 10,000 troops to the GCC states in return for a payment of $4.5bn. to cover Egypt's military debts.[108] Mubarak categorically denied these "fabricated" reports, emphasizing that the Egyptians "are not mercenaries."[109] But he announced that his country would never hesitate to offer defense assistance to the Gulf states "should there be any threat."[110] Such declarations of friendship and mutual commitment were made during his visits to each of the states in the region and were repeated in subsequent months. Among the officials who returned Mubarak's visit in 1988 were Bahrain's heir apparent, Shaykh Hamad Ibn 'Isa Al Khalifa, who came to Cairo in February, and UAE President, Shaykh Zayid Ibn Sultan Al Nuhayyan, in the following month. Another mark of the improving relations was the revitalization of the Authority for Military Production, through which Egypt had cooperated in arms production with three Gulf states — Saudi Arabia, Qatar, and the UAE. Suspended since 1979, the authority was revived in May when the partners started negotiating new projects.[111]

Relations with Saudi Arabia, where Mubarak made his first stop on his Gulf tour in January, similarly gained momentum following the resumption of formal ties. Asked about these ties, Mubarak typically depicted them as having always been "ideal, as between two dear brothers"; they "may have suffered when the ties on the ambassadorial level were frozen," yet "the firmness of these historical relations do not subject them to a test or to a shake-up under transitional conditions."[112] Beyond such historical connections there were more immediate common interests. Egypt's military potential and experience in fighting terrorism were assets from which the Saudis could also benefit. In May, Egyptian Deputy Prime Minister and Foreign Minister 'Ismat 'Abd al-Majid traveled to Riyadh, and Saudi Interior Minister Na'if Ibn 'Abd al-'Aziz came to Cairo; both discussed with their respective hosts "issues related to the security of the two countries," beside other matters.[113] These, and other contacts, were at the background to rumors about a secret, three-year Egyptian-Saudi accord on security cooperation, by which Egypt would assist the Saudis in protecting the holy places and other installations during the pilgrimage season. (The reports were denied by both parties.)[114] There was also cooperation on the diplomatic level. Cairo commended the Saudi decision to sever diplomatic relations with Iran in May, as being "in line with the principled policy of the Egyptian Foreign Ministry."[115] The Saudis, for their part, were in favor of Egypt's return to the Arab League and, in the words of their ambassador to Cairo, would "be very happy" if Egypt was invited to attend the regular Arab summit which was due to be held in their own country.[116] Their usual caution, however, prevented the Saudis from backing the Egyptian cause more aggressively.

After the resumption of Egyptian-Saudi relations, there was speculation about a Saudi royal visit to Egypt "shortly." Early in August, the Saudis announced that King Fahd "will visit Egypt very soon."[117] Later that month, however, it became known that the king had decided to postpone his trip indefinitely. The reason apparently was a report in an Egyptian opposition paper, accusing the Saudis of knowingly overlooking Israeli intelligence activities on their soil and charging the royal house with corruption. Outraged at the paper's attempt to "seriously undermine the country's vital interests" by "abusing a fraternal Arab Islamic country which has backed and stood by Egypt," the Egyptian Government suspended the paper's license, a measure quite unusual in recent years.[118] The visit, in any case, was put off until after the end of the year.

Another state with which Egyptian relations were revived in 1988 was the YAR. Mubarak's trip to San'a in May was the first Egyptian presidential visit there in 25 years. In his meeting with his Yemeni counterpart 'Ali 'Abdallah Salih, the two leaders discussed regional and bilateral relations and decided to set up a higher joint committee that would work to bolster relations between them.[119] In October, Yemeni Prime Minister 'Abd al-'Aziz 'Abd al-Ghani came to Cairo at the head of a large delegation for the committee's first meeting. The two sides signed agreements on economic, technical, scientific, and technological cooperation and protocols for cooperation in education, agriculture, and health.[120]

Syria and Libya remained, as they had long been, Egypt's foes in the region. Attempts at mediation failed to alter this basic fact although, in the case of the former, a beginning of a change was noticed toward the end of the year. The Syrian Government felt that there was no room for renewing its relations with the "traitor regime" in Cairo, which had not ceased to be "on the bandwagon of Imperialism and Zionism."[121] This view, to which the Syrian media gave ample expression, was also reflected in acts such as the setting up of a Syrian "national committee for the defense of Egypt's Revolution Organization and Khalid 'Abd al-Nasir," under Ba'th Party patronage.[122] In contrast with this Egyptian officials adopted a restrained line in their references to Syria. Mubarak explained that, because of the common interests of the two countries and the special personal "rapport" he had with Syria's President Asad, Cairo was "eager...to have a working relationship with Syria" and to maintain "a certain minimum of decorum." But this, he insisted, "could only be achieved by efforts on the part of both sides, not just one."[123] The Egyptian media, less reticent, used harsh language in denouncing Syrian behavior, in particular its battle against the Palestinians in Lebanon. "What shame has the Syrian regime brought upon itself by its action against the Palestinian people and their legitimate leadership, while the uprising [in the occupied territories] is attracting the attention, sympathy, and appreciation of the entire world", said an editorial in *al-Ahram*.[124] A Radio Cairo commentator was more blatant:

> For over 10 years they [the Syrians] have not ceased their attempts to impose their control on the Lebanese and Palestinian people. Their instinct for hegemony still controls them in their relationship with all the Arab states. They are hostile to fraternal Iraq for no reason other than that they want their party doctrine to prevail in Baghdad. In their quest for leadership and showmanship they have encouraged Iranian aggression against Iraqi territory.[125]

Toward the end of the year, with the growing spirit of all-Arab solidarity following developments in the Palestinian issue (see chapter on inter-Arab relations), there were reports on efforts by the two governments to mend their fences. In late November, a visit by Usama al-Baz to Damascus, who reportedly came to discuss the "normalization" of their diplomatic ties, gave rise to speculations that formal relations "might be resumed soon."[126] Al-Baz was followed by Jordan's King Husayn, whose attempts at mediating apparently scored some success.[127] As a result of these contacts, the two countries stopped their media campaign against each other. Egyptian Foreign Minister 'Abd al-Majid welcomed the efforts and stated that "Egypt does not object to the turning over of a new leaf, on condition that the intentions of both sides are sincere."[128] According to some reports, Asad reciprocated by notifying King Fahd that Syria was no longer "against readmitting Egypt to the Arab League."[129] The resumption of Egyptian-Syrian relations, however, had not taken place by the end of the period under review.

Repeated attempts were carried out throughout the year to bridge the gulf between Egypt and Libya, involving a number of mediators. None was really successful and all of them together left a sense of frustration in Cairo. In a speech on 28 March, Libyan President Qadhdhafi announced his intention to withdraw all Libyan forces from along the borders with Egypt, abolish the Libyan Eastern Military Zone, and open the hitherto closed borders to free civilian movement.[130] Egypt was prepared, in principle, to welcome such goodwill gestures, and Minister of State for Foreign Affairs Butrus Butrus-Ghali responded by confirming that "the ties between the Egyptian and Libyan peoples are brotherly, good, and strong."[131] Mubarak, however, felt that a measure of skepticism was in order. Qadhdhafi's speech, he said, "will have no impact on Egyptian-Libyan relations, as it is aimed at deceiving the Libyan people. He [Qadhdhafi] said: 'we decided to withdraw forces.' What forces? He has no troops along our borders and neither do we...He says he wants to open the borders. Will he open the borders to [send] bombs or what?"[132] Yet Mubarak was ready to cooperate in attempts to bring him and the Libyan leader closer together. In April, when Qadhdhafi proposed to meet him "somewhere on the Egyptian-Libyan border or in Yugoslavia," he accepted.[133] The meeting never took place, nor did mediation efforts in April and May by the UAE and YAR rulers bear much fruit due to "the colonel's attempts to mar and harm this relationship,"[134] according to Egyptian sources. One such obstructive move was made in a statement by the Libyan news agency, JANA, late in May, claiming that "talk on reconciliation between great Jamahiriyya and Egypt...constitutes a contempt of the scores of martyrs and pure blood spilt on Arab land."[135] Sudan, Tunisia and, again, the UAE were involved in more mediation initiatives during the summer and fall, but these, too, were unsuccessful.[136] Yet another typical instance of *rapprochement* that failed occurred in October-November: Qadhdhafi's instruction to the media to stop responding to the Egyptian "information campaign" against Libya prompted a similar Egyptian decision to cease its media attacks on its western neighbor. But then came a renewed Libyan assault on Egypt, with "the same expressions that had been voiced in the past, which are capable of blowing up any Arab mediation."[137]

In an interview in October, Mubarak reviewed in detail the frustrating vicissitudes of Egyptian-Libyan relations in 1988, relations in which Egypt had been prepared to invest much effort to improve "despite years of bitter experience" with Qadhdhafi. The results, he said, were "absolutely discouraging." No sooner would an agreement be reached between Cairo and Tripoli than it would be foiled by the Libyan leader, who would revert to "shouting over a microphone in the most repugnant voice" and insulting Egypt. Qadhdhafi should have known that "such offenses and absurdities, which the ambitious and rancorous have uttered at various times, have not harmed Egypt but have backfired...I hope," Mubarak said, "the colonel is aware that there is a certain limit beyond which he cannot go in offending Egypt, because Egypt grants a respite, but it does not forget."[138]

EGYPT AND THE PLO

A rather natural result of the dramatic developments that marked the Palestinian scene in 1988 was the greatly improved relations between Egypt and the PLO. These relations grew closer and more intimate as the year unfolded. For the Egyptians, to whom domestic realities provided little but gloom in 1988, a strong sense of solidarity with the Palestinians in revolt and satisfaction with their achievements offered comfort. Egypt felt profound sympathy for the *intifadà* (uprising), which it viewed as a struggle for a just cause through sophisticated and highly moral means. It was an "all-Arab cause" with which Cairo, now back in the Arab fold, fully identified. The Palestinian youngsters throwing stones, the angry Palestinian mothers, striking merchants in the occupied territories, all figured as national heroes in the Egyptian public's eye. This kind of solidarity was at once a popular sentiment and a principle which underlay the government's policy toward the PLO.

The Egyptian media gave ample and colorful expression to this sense of popular involvement. A survey of Egyptian newspaper coverage of the uprising during its first six months (December 1987-May 1988) showed that as many as 2,648 items on the subject were published in the national and opposition press. *Al-Ahram*, for example, published 323 news items, 194 articles, 113 pictures, 3 cartoons, and 173 "other items"; 92% of all news items appeared on the paper's front pages.[139] There were numerous other expressions. A "National Committee for Support of the Palestinian Uprising" was set up early in the year, with Lutfi al-Khuli as its secretary and many public figures as members. It organized frequent support rallies and arranged for foodstuffs, medicines, and other supplies to be sent to the West Bank and Gaza.[140] Expressions of solidarity as well as material contributions came from the unions of workers, lawyers, doctors, and pharmacists, from professors, artists, and from women's groups.[141] Students frequently demonstrated in sympathy with the Palestinians. Shaykh al-Azhar, Imam Jadd al-Haqq added his voice to the supporters, stating that "Muslims and Arabs ought to assist all those [Palestinian] heroes who defend the holy places with their bodies."[142]

Support for the Palestinians was regularly coupled with condemnation of their foes, Israel and the US. Israeli and American flags were burnt in pro-Palestinian demonstrations as a matter of routine. The Egyptian press furiously attacked Israel for its "brutal suppression" of the uprising (see below). When the Palestinian leader Abu Jihad was assassinated in April (see chapter on armed operations), Israel was vehemently denounced for this "dirty operation."[143] Washington was assailed for its decision to close down the PLO's New York office in March, which was condemned as "a frivolous step backward" on the road to a ME settlement;[144] and later, for refusing to grant PLO chairman 'Arafat a visa that would enable him to address the UN General Assembly in New York (see below).

The Egyptian Government's official position reflected a similar attitude, although it was formulated in a more restrained tone. Mubarak, who in principle viewed the uprising as a sound and legitimate line of Palestinian action, sought ways to help the Palestinians translate their achievements on the ground into political gains. During his tour in Europe and the US in January, a major issue was his plan to enhance the momentum of the ME political process (for details, see chapter on the Middle East peace process). In February, and again in March, he played host to 'Arafat who came for consultations. Such efforts were reinforced after midyear, and became increasingly intensive as the PNC drew nearer. In August, Mubarak received a high-level PLO delegation that came to discuss the implications of King Husayn's disengagement from the West Bank; Mubarak pledged to "place Egypt's resources and experience at the PLO's disposal."[145] In September, Egypt allowed the Fath office in Cairo to be reopened,[146] and 'Arafat again came over for coordination talks. The next month, 'Arafat traveled to Cairo twice. At the end of the second visit, he flew with Mubarak to 'Aqaba where they conferred with King Husayn, then to Baghdad for a meeting with Saddam Husayn. In all these diplomatic efforts to enlist broad Arab backing for the PLO on the eve of the PNC, Cairo positioned itself as a key actor. For this it won PLO gratitude and spokesmen for the organization never failed to express their appreciation for the "sincere devotion" of "the big brother Egypt."[147]

The climate of Egyptian-PLO relations in the weeks preceding and immediately following the PNC differed markedly from that which had prevailed during the previous meeting of that forum a year and a half earlier. The PNC of April 1987 produced an anti-Egyptian resolution that had been broadly anticipated, which provoked much anger in Cairo and badly marred their relations (see *MECS* 1987, p. 347, and cf. also *MECS* 1982–83, p. 434). In 1988, by contrast, Egypt felt as "almost a coauthor" of the upcoming "historic Palestinian decision", and fully shared the excited expectation of "the birth of the new Palestinian state." "The Palestinian countdown has begun," an editorial in *al-Akhbar* solemnly declared in mid-October, and "there is no doubt that this important Palestinian step will have a resounding effect in the various capitals of the world."[148] Between then and the PNC a month later this was the major issue of the day in the Egyptian press, to the great neglect of other subjects. Egyptian officials, while more restrained than the press in their statements, were equally expectant.

The PNC's proclamation of an independent Palestinian state on 15 November met with an enthusiastic reaction in the Egyptian media. The PNC was hailed as "a pinnacle of flexible democratic practice," and the declaration of independence as "a masterpiece of distinguished political literature." The resolution, one paper noted, was "characterized by complete objectivity, moderation, commitment to international legality, and a desire for peace and peaceful coexistence to prevail between this new state and other countries, including Israel." It was "the epitome of wisdom when it recognized at this stage the existence of Israel," something which attested to the PLO's self-confidence and which "strips the Tel Aviv leaders of all their excuses for rejecting peace efforts." This decision would strengthen the Palestinians in their struggle; would "block the way of any objection or argument of [Israeli Prime Minister] Yitzhak Shamir"; and would "undoubtedly give an impetus to peace efforts."[149]

As against this, the official Egyptian reaction was at first far more cautious. Cairo procrastinated for five days before joining the many countries that had officially recognized the "independent Palestinian state." On 15 November, the Egyptian Government announced its "support" for the "PNC declaration" (but not its recognition of "the Palestinian state" itself).[150] "Such support," Mubarak explained two days later, "is stronger than recognition."[151] When this somewhat ambiguous formula generated speculations on Egypt's real position and possible motives, Mubarak on 19 November stated — as reported by the Egyptian Middle East News Agency (MENA) — that Egypt "supported all the [Palestinian] Council's resolutions, and this includes recognition of the Palestinian state." But on the same day, MENA issued a correction to the statement, replacing the word "recognition" by "establishment."[152] Foreign Minister 'Abd al-Majid tried to dispel the mist by reiterating that a "support" such as Egypt's was more valuable than "conventional recognition,"[153] but some unclarity still remained. Eventually, to remove all doubts, the Foreign Ministry affirmed on 20 November "that it recognizes the independent Palestinian state" effective as of 15 November.[154] The prolonged Egyptian hesitation was attributed to the various constraints the government had to take into account, among them the arguable incompatiblity of such recognition with the Camp David accords and, on the other hand, Egypt's commitment to the Arab cause. Mubarak may have preferred to chose, more conveniently, his own timing for making the formal move. But the rapidly growing number of states that hastened to offer recognition and the resounding zeal of the media at home, made further postponement inadvisable. Once the formal announcement was made, 'Arafat could again come to Cairo on a triumphant visit (21 November) and be received royally, this time as the "head of a new state."

For the rest of the year Egypt's support of the PLO remained unreserved. Enraged by the US decision not to permit 'Arafat's entry into the country (and thus prevent him from addressing the UN General Assembly in New York), Egypt, along with Jordan, took the lead in the eventually successful efforts to transfer the UN General Assembly session on the ME to Geneva. As these diplomatic efforts were under way, 'Arafat again traveled to Cairo to "listen to the president's wise and sound views" on how he should formulate his forthcoming speech.[155] The PLO reciprocated Cairo's assistance by becoming a vocal supporter of Egypt's return to the Arab League. Thus, by the end of the year Egypt and the PLO were enjoying a honeymoon in their relations, the like of which they had not experienced since the signing of the Camp David accords. (For a further discussion of these relations see chapter on the Middle East peace process).

EGYPT AND ISRAEL

In a year in which Egypt's pan-Arab sentiments gained strength, its solidarity with the Palestinians intensified, and the domestic opposition hostile to Israel grew more vociferous, Cairo's ties with Israel could not but remain "cold" and uneasy. The formal framework of peace was kept intact, nor did the Egyptian Government seriously consider abolishing it. But the general climate of their dialogue was markedly unpleasant, often even tense.

Egyptian public opinion on Israel, shaped above all by the Palestinian uprising, was profoundly negative. If the Palestinian in revolt was a national hero, Israel was his antithesis. The Egyptian media depicted the Israeli as cruel, "barbarian," and vicious. In hundreds of cartoons whose theme was the uprising, Israelis wore large boots that roughly trampled upon Palestinian-held olive branches, strangled peace doves with their ugly hairy hands, or shot Arab children boldly throwing stones at them. Passionate expressions of solidarity with the Palestinians that came from different quarters in Egypt (see above) also served to demonstrate strong anti-Israeli feelings. They reflected deep disappointment with the conduct of Egypt's partner to peace and with the peace itself.

For an Egyptian Government committed to the Camp David principles, this acrid atmosphere created constraints that could potentially jeopardize its peace strategy. "The tragic situation in the West Bank and Gaza cannot be allowed to continue if we are to protect the peace process," Mubarak warned Shamir early in the year.[156] Mubarak did not intend to let events in the territories compromise the fundamentals of his regional policy. "Would it solve the Palestinian problem if I broke off relations with Israel?" he angrily responded to an interviewer's question. He did, however, consider it his duty to exert every effort in the diplomatic arena to change the circumstances that produced the uprising. Israel's rejection of a five-point plan for a settlement, which he put forward in January (for details, see chapter on the Middle East peace process), did not make him give up these efforts, with which he carried on diligently throughout the year.

The gulf between the Egyptian and Israeli positions on the Palestinian issue and the peace process in general remained as wide as it had been in recent years. While Cairo favored the formula of an international conference with PLO participation, Shamir firmly objected to it. Instead, he advocated direct negotiations between Israel and Arab states, and would not hear of talking to the PLO. (The international conference idea had supporters within Israel, above all Deputy Prime Minister and Foreign Minister Shimon Peres and other Labor Party leaders, but it was Shamir who, as premier, determined the government's line; see chapter on Israel, and *MECS* 1987, pp. 349–50). Frequent contacts, direct as well as mediated, failed to bridge this gap. The result was a stalemate behind a facade of intensive diplomatic momentum. Under the circumstances, Mubarak refused to meet Shamir and rejected Israeli proposals for such a summit on several occasions. "It must be clear," he told a journalist who asked him about a possible visit to Israel, "that I do not travel anywhere unless I am sure that there are advantages to, or results from, my travel."[157] Perhaps nothing could better illustrate the gulf between the two states than the Israeli reaction to Cairo's recognition of the PNC-declared "Palestinian state" in November: while for Egypt the recognition reflected the essence of its views and sentiments about the Palestinian issue, Israel felt "regret" and "concern" about the Egyptian move, and notified Cairo that it was "incompatible with the spirit of [the] Camp David [accords]."[158] (For further discussion of Egyptian-Israeli contacts over the year, see chapter on the Middle East peace process.)

Because 1988 was an election year in Israel, where elections to the Knesset were held on 1 November, and because the results could potentially have a profound impact on Israel's foreign policy, Cairo followed the election campaign with much interest. The Egyptians would have preferred to see a Labor victory and a return of Peres to the premiership, so that Israel would be more forthcoming with regard to the international conference plan. Beyond hoping, Mubarak felt he could perhaps influence the Israeli voter's decision, through diplomatic moves that would make the conference idea look more attractive and thus strengthen the camp supporting it within Israel. The much-dramatized, tripartite summit in 'Aqaba, with King Husayn and 'Arafat which he initiated a week before the elections, no doubt aimed at that end alongside its other purposes. An *al-Ahram* editorial immediately after the meeting seemed to confirm this, when it called upon the Israelis to "restructure" their society in the elections, so as to make it receptive to "peace formulas and tune itself for them, not as 'a danger that threatens the future of Israel,' as some of its current leaders claim, who adhere to their old, rotten methods, but as the best way to guarantee its security." The logic of "these rulers," the paper stated, could "easily be defeated through...a search in one's conscience."[159]

The voting results, which reflected a strengthening of the rightist and religious elements yet retained the right-left equilibrium basically unchanged (see chapter on Israel), caused discomfiture in Egypt. "The disappointment is total," stated one leading intellectual.[160] Another writer predicted that "following the victory of the radical racist right," Israel would become more belligerent and violent; "this Israeli Government will lead the peace process to a dead end through its rejection of an international conference and its famous 'Noes'."[161] Such pessimism characterized the great majority of reactions in Egypt. Some, who argued that it did not really matter who won since "neither of the two Israeli camps truly wants peace,"[162] in fact gave expression to similar frustration. The Egyptian Government, however, stated it would readily "cooperate with any government that would be set up in Israel."[163]

One issue which in 1988 became, once again, a central item on the Egyptian-Israeli agenda was Taba. In September 1986, the two states had signed an agreement entrusting the issue to an international arbitration tribunal (see *MECS* 1986, p. 284), thus temporarily removing an annoying obstacle from the road. After a prolonged preliminary phase during which the two sides submitted their claims and documents, and the arbitrators inspected the disputed area, the tribunal in March 1988 moved to weigh the evidence and make a ruling. By April, there was speculation in both Egypt and Israel that the tribunal was about to rule in Egypt's favor. Israel, "greatly concerned" over the "very slim chance" for a ruling on its behalf,[164] now sought to reach a compromise with Egypt outside arbitration; and Cairo, fearing that the arbitration award might be phrased in general terms that would allow Israel to drag out its implementation, declared itself ready to negotiate.[165] Following some two months of bickering over the venue of the talks, negotiations opened in Cairo in early August. They produced no compromise. On 29 September the tribunal announced its verdict, accepting the Egyptian claims and ruling in its favor. Taba, 1.2 sq. km. of sand and beach, was to go back to Egyptian sovereignty.

Throughout the year, Cairo displayed much confidence that the tribunal would return Taba to Egyptian control. "We have participated in arbitration from a position of strength," said the head of Egypt's Foreign Ministry legal department, noting that the arguments heard during the proceedings made Egypt even more sure of a favorable outcome.[166] Once made, the tribunal's decision was received in Egypt with extreme joy that was reflected in a spate of newspaper articles about "the last grain of Egyptian soil" being eventually returned to Egyptian sovereignty, in numerous congratulatory announcements by various private and public bodies that were published in the press, and in the issuing of a special postage stamp to commemorate the event. "God has helped the truth appear and justice prevail," Mubarak said. "With our rights established over this precious part of our soil, we have established our agelong commitment to the noble traditions of our forefathers in safeguarding the great homeland."[167]

What remained now was to agree on the arrangements for implementing the decision. In Egypt, where Israel's image was that of an untrustworthy and sly partner, there was concern that Israel might not cooperate when it came to implementation. Mubarak, however, chose to display more faith: "It is not in the interest of Israel to raise doubts about its willingness to fulfill its obligations. Israel knows very well that the effective way of establishing and spreading peace is by honoring pledges and accords," he said.[168] With this attitude, Cairo readily granted Jerusalem's request that the talks about implementation be postponed until after the 1 November elections and the formation of a new government in Israel.[169] The issues that remained — primarily ownership of the Israeli-built tourist facilities in Taba, and entry arrangements for Israelis once the area became Egyptian — were then settled in several weeks of bargaining carried out in the same uneasy spirit that had marked the Taba negotiations all along. They were concluded in late February 1989 and on 15 March Taba formally became Egyptian again.

EGYPT AND THE SUPERPOWERS

EGYPT AND THE UNITED STATES

Cairo's relations with the US — Egypt's chief foreign ally and supporter — were characterized by a friendly atmosphere in 1988, more so than in the previous year when they were marred by tension over several issues (see *MECS* 1987, pp. 337–38). As in recent years, Egypt received c. $2.3bn. in US aid that was indispensable for its economy. And the two states continued to cooperate in a variety of bilateral fields and coordinate their international policies.

There was much agreement between Egyptian and US positions regarding political developments in the ME during this period. Mubarak went to Washington in January, where he presented his hosts with an initiative designed to end the violence in the West Bank and the Gaza Strip and to launch a dialogue (for details, see chapter on the Middle East peace process). Mubarak and President Reagan agreed to press for a six-month cooling-off period between Israel and the Palestinians, so as to facilitate a renewed momentum of negotiations; and Washington promised to study Mubarak's other proposals, with a view to maintaining the drive of the peace process.[170] The US, by now no longer as firmly opposed to the international conference idea as in 1987 (cf. *MECS* 1987, p. 338), came up with its own diplomatic initiative during the first half of the year, which met with Egypt's blessing and support (see chapters on the US and the Middle East and on the Middle East peace process).

These efforts, however, turned out to be futile and Egyptian papers directed some of their frustration toward Washington, pointing out, so it seemed, the limits of

Egyptian trust in the US. "While Washington always emphasizes that it is a partner to the peace process," the daily *al-Ahram* complained, it embraces "the principle of...absolute alliance with Israel"; this "conflicting and contradictory US stand casts doubt on Washington's real intentions."[171] The theme was repeatedly voiced by the Egyptian press, which often accused the US of offering "flimsy excuses" regarding its "inability to exert pressure on Israel," excuses "which hide a permanent US policy that protects Tel Aviv and defends its crimes."[172]

As if to give substance to the Egyptian complaints, the Administration in November decided to deny PLO leader 'Arafat an entry visa to the US, thereby preventing him from addressing the UN General Assembly in New York (see chapter on the US and the Middle East). Egypt was disappointed. While the official reaction was rather restrained — Mubarak and other high officials expressed "profound regret" and Mubarak contacted Reagan and Secretary of State George Shultz asking them to "reconsider the decision"[173] — the Egyptian press expressed extreme anger. Calling Washington's step "a stupid decision condemned by all," one paper wrote indignantly of the American "unjustifiable and incomprehensible measures, which indicate nothing but the desire to abort the spirit of peace."[174] Another paper suggested that "the decision confirms the United States' 100% partiality to Israel, which undoubtedly exerted desperate efforts" to persuade the US Government to make the move; such a decision, the paper warned, "destroys the US Government's credibility."[175]

The disappointment expressed in these statements soon gave way, again, to more friendly exchanges when Washington announced in December its decision to start a dialogue with the PLO (see chapter on the US and the Middle East). Having long sought to convince the US to take such a step, Cairo reacted with enthusiasm. Usama al-Baz, Mubarak's close political adviser, hailed the decision as "a significant step in the right direction," by which the US had "corrected part of its Mideast policy, especially where the Palestinian cause is concerned";[176] and the Egyptian press ascribed the shift in the American policy to efforts by Mubarak, who succeeded in "convincing the US Administration to forsake its [former] rigid position."[177]

On the bilateral level, the two states continued their extensive cooperation, notably in the economic and military spheres. Economic matters were high on Mubarak's agenda during his January trip to Washington. Among other requests, he asked that Egypt be allowed greater flexibilty in utilizing aid money, that the limitations on Egyptian exports to the US be removed, and that a convenient settlement of Cairo's military debt to the US be worked out. Washington was forthcoming and immediately allocated $500m. for these purposes — in Reagan's words in an *al-Ahram* interview, "out of special concern for Egypt's requests and needs" and out of "appreciation of the Egyptian efforts to build a strong and dynamic economy."[178]

One issue that nonetheless remained unresolved in 1988 was Egypt's military debt of c. $4.5bn. to the US. Having been the subject of extensive and often uneasy negotiations since 1986, the problem had seriously compromised the good climate of their relations (cf. *MECS* 1986, pp. 276–77; *MECS* 1987, pp. 337–38). The original interest rate on these debts was particularly heavy — it was markedly higher than commercial rates current in the late 1980s — and Cairo found it extremely difficult to abide by its repayment commitments. One possible solution considered early in the year called for turning over, with a US government guarantee, all or some of the debts to American commercial banks, who would charge less interest. Egypt was unenthusiastic about the idea, as it felt that even under such improved conditions the burden would remain an unbearable constraint on its economy. Mubarak, therefore, asked Washington to write off completely some of the debt.[179] Reluctant to grant such a demand, yet willing to assist Egypt, the Administration came up with a proposal calling for a 7.5%–14% reduction of the interest, but with the balance to be settled within 20, rather than 26, years.[180] By the end of the year, the proposal was still under consideration.

In military cooperation, the two countries made significant strides in 1988. Deputy Prime Minister and Defense Minister Abu Ghazala traveled to Washington in March, where he and Defense Secretary Frank Carlucci initialed a memorandum of understanding on military cooperation. The US agreed to give Egypt a special status as a non-Nato ally, allowing Cairo access to more sophisticated defense equipment as well as special rights to bid on US defense contracts.[181] Carlucci returned the visit in October-November, when a technical protocol was signed on the joint manufacture of 555 M-1A1 tanks, missiles, missile boats, minesweepers, and nonnuclear submarines.[182]

A temporary shadow was cast on Egyptian-US relations following a diplomatic incident in June. Two officials in the Egyptian military mission to Washington, an admiral and a lieutenant colonel, were suspected of conspiring to smuggle to Egypt high-technology chemicals that could be used to manufacture a sophisticated missile system. The lieutenant colonel was arrested, but released upon claiming diplomatic immunity; he and his colleague were quickly recalled to Cairo. Another Egyptian officer, a colonel based in Salzburg, Austria, who was also involved, was officially indicted on 29 June, along with two US citizens.[183] Embarrassed, the two governments sought to play down the incident. "It is a very important relationship between the US and Egypt," said Frank Wisner, the US ambassador in Cairo, "and problems can be managed."[184] *Al-Ahram* likewise depicted the matter as "much ado about nothing," the "nothing" being a possible error made in good faith.[185] Two months later, the *Washington Post* reported that Abu Ghazala was suspected of being implicated in the plot.[186] Abu Ghazala dismissed the charge as "nothing more than air bubbles made to magnify the issue."[187] Washington seemingly chose to overlook this allegation, preferring to let the incident die away.

EGYPT AND THE SOVIET UNION

The friendly spirit that had marked Cairo's relations with Moscow in the previous year remained very much in evidence in 1988. That these ties were on a level different from that of the Egyptian-American alliance was fully clear to both parties; the Soviet Union as a substitute ally was not considered a serious option in 1988. Within these terms of reference their relations continued to develop nicely.

Official delegates and missions of the two states exchanged frequent visits. Among the many Soviet visitors to Egypt were Karen Brutents, deputy chief of the CPSU Central Committee's international department,[188] Vladimir Polyakov, director of the Soviet foreign ministry's Near East and North Africa Department,[189] and Yuli Vorontsov, first deputy foreign minister,[190] who arrived in January, June, and December, respectively, as special envoys of Soviet leader Gorbachev. Cairo, for its part, sent Deputy Prime Minister and Foreign Minister 'Ismat 'Abd al-Majid to Moscow in May — the most senior Egyptian official to visit the USSR since 1977;

Minister of State for Foreign Affairs, Butrus Butrus-Ghali, in July;[191] and a parliamentary delegation, headed by People's Assembly Speaker Rif'at al-Mahjub, in the same month.[192] In March, the Soviet culture center in Cairo, closed since 1977, was reopened with much ceremony.[193] Later that month, an Egyptian information center was opened in Moscow for the first time.[194]

During 'Abd al-Majid's visit to Moscow, he signed an agreement on economic, trade, technical, and scientific cooperation, thereby giving substance to the trade protocol the two states concluded in December 1987, which provided for a 50% increase in the volume of their trade over a period of three years (cf. *MECS* 1987, p. 339). The two sides also decided to establish a joint intergovernmental committee to handle different aspects of their economic cooperation.[195] The Soviet Union agreed to take part in financing industrial projects included in Egypt's five-year plan. It was estimated that its share in the plan would reach some $5bn.[196]

Another purpose of 'Abd al-Majid's visit was "to discuss proposals and listen to views" on international matters. The two states held similar positions concerning the central issues in the ME: both favored an international peace conference, shared the concern about the ongoing Gulf War (and the relief when it was halted), justified the Palestinian uprising in the occupied territories, and were critical of the Israeli policy toward it. This unity of views was expressed in a joint communiqué upon the completion of 'Abd al-Majid's visit, which also confirmed their agreement on various other issues.[197] It was reflected, likewise, in numerous other statements by Egyptian and Soviet statesmen. A new area of accord in 1988 was the Afghanistan problem: Egypt, which, as an Islamic country, had condemned the Soviet occupation of Afghanistan ever since its invasion in 1979, was most pleased by Moscow's decision to evacuate its forces from there. Egyptian officials welcomed the Geneva agreement on this issue in April (see chapter on the Soviet withdrawal from Afghanistan), and expressed their "hope that the settlement of the Afghanistan problem will be an example for settling other regional conflicts."[198]

'Abd al-Majid's visit in May and the signing of the cooperation agreement were hailed by the Egyptian press as "a new start in Cairo-Moscow relations, in affirming the eagerness of both sides to establish permanent, normal, and balanced relations in an age of international *détente*."[199] One mark of such a new start was the modified tone with which the Egyptian press now treated the USSR. Whereas previously the media often alluded to Egypt's "bad experience in the past" with the Soviets, papers now chose to emphasize "the bright aspects of ties": Egypt, an *al-Ahram* editorial read,

> cannot forget the Soviet Union's great contributions to three of the biggest projects of the age, namely, the [Aswan] High Dam, the [Naj' Hammadi] aluminum complex, and the [Hilwan] iron and steel factories. We hope that the new relations...will follow in the steps of the early era of close cooperation, putting behind us the obstacles encountered in the recent past...[200]

RELATIONS WITH EUROPE

The acute economic crisis, which clearly revealed Egypt's dependence on foreign aid, was responsible for Cairo's intensive contacts with West European governments far more than broad international issues during the period under review. Egypt had particularly close ties with four states: France, West Germany, Italy, and Britain. By

1988 its trade with them totaled c. $3.5bn, or some 80% of Egypt's trade with all EEC states.[201] Mubarak visited the four of them in January, then the first three again in September; both trips were prompted primarily by economic considerations. Frequent contacts were maintained throughout the year regarding Cairo's requests for more aid, the rescheduling of Egyptian debts, and Egypt's demand that the European governments intercede with the IMF on its behalf. The European allies were forthcoming in meeting the Egyptian requests. France and West Germany had reached a quick agreement with Cairo on a debt rescheduling program in 1987 and Italy followed suit early in 1988. West Germany, the leading European investor in Egypt,[202] showed particular flexibility and was prepared to write off "a substantial portion" of Egypt's debt, so as to "inject more vitality into the Egyptian economy." It also offered Cairo a new loan.[203] Egyptian officials often acknowledged with gratitude this cordial European attitude: "Friendly European nations have not wasted any opportunity to build bridges of cooperation with us," Mubarak noted. "We have found substantial understanding among the countries with which our ties are particularly strong."[204]

Cairo also coordinated its international policies, especially on ME issues, with its European allies. EEC states would support any initiative that would regenerate the momentum in the peace process and were in favor of an international conference. When Mubarak visited Europe in January, his political plan for the region (see chapter on the Middle East peace process) won the approval of his various hosts, something that was prominently reflected in their joint statements. France was particularly active in the search for a ME peace formula in cooperation with Egypt, and its interest in regional issues brought President Mitterrand to Isma'iliyya in October.[205] European states, however, played only a secondary role on the ME stage; hence this aspect of their ties with Egypt was markedly less important than their economic relations with it, which were indeed crucial.

Egypt's relations with Eastern Europe — whose ME role was more limited — similarly focused, as in the past, on economic cooperation, although international and regional issues were also often discussed. In 1988 there were especially intensive exchanges with Czechoslovakia. CSR Deputy Foreign Minister Roman Narozny traveled to Cairo in February, to be followed by Foreign Minister Bohuslav Chnoupek, who came in April. The two states held "identical viewpoints...regarding the settlement of regional disputes, foremost being the Middle East crisis," and both supported the withdrawal of Israel from the occupied territories, Palestinian self-determination, and the convocation of an international peace conference.[206] In a somewhat more practical vein, the two sides discussed economic affairs and agreed to increase trade between them — estimated at $154m. in 1987 — and to implement a number of joint production projects.[207] Further negotiations on these issues took place two months later, when a Czechoslovak economic delegation came to Cairo, headed by the minister of trade. Another important East European ally was Romania. Having played a mediating role in ME affairs before, Romanian President Nikolae Ceauşescu came to Cairo in September, reportedly armed with his own initiative designed to facilitate an indirect dialogue between Israel and the PLO with Egyptian and Romanian mediation.[208] This plan, like so many other diplomatic initiatives, failed to produce any significant results.

RELATIONS WITH THE THIRD WORLD

Cairo continued to attach much importance to its ties with Africa, an arena where Egypt appeared as a leader and a supporting, rather than supported, country. Thus a major value of these ties seems to have been in their contribution to Egypt's own national image and pride. It must have given Mubarak much satisfaction to state that "the Egyptian people, here at the entrance to the continent, are still performing their historical duty toward the rest of the continent's peoples with awareness and determination."[209] Egypt had a chance to offer its "contribution to peace and stability in Africa" in June when it became a venue for the peace talks between South Africa, Angola, Cuba, and the US aimed at settling the Angola conflict and securing independence for Namibia (talks which, however, produced little result).[210] In November, Cairo played host to the second congress of the Association of African Socialist and Democratic Parties, inaugurated by the Egyptian president. Mubarak went to Addis Ababa in May to attend the celebrations marking the OAU's 25th anniversary and participate in the African summit, and numerous African leaders and senior officials visited Cairo, among them the Mauritian prime minister (in February), and the presidents of Kenya (April), the Central African Republic (June), and Djibouti (August).

One African region of particular importance to Egypt was the Nile basin countries. First grouped in 1981 (cf. *MECS* 1980–81, p.444; 1983–84, p. 374), the organization of states sharing the Nile waters (entitled "Undugo", Swahili for "cooperation") consisted of Egypt, Sudan, Zaire, Uganda, Burundi, and Rwanda (and excluding, rather conspicuously, Ethiopia). The organization held periodical conferences to discuss matters of common concern. The fifth Undugo meeting, which took place in Cairo in November, provided Egypt, among other things, with a gratifying chance to display its infrastructural, technological, and organizational capabilities.[211]

Cairo continued to develop its relations in Asia. In June, Japan's Minister of Foreign Affairs Sosuke Uno came for a visit. Having extended c. $1bn. in development aid to Egypt between 1960 and 1986,[212] Japan now committed itself to providing more assistance. It also undertook to "increase its efforts to push the peace process in the region."[213] In August, Indonesian Foreign Minister Ali Alatas arrived for a visit, in which he received Cairo's promise to support his country's candidacy as the venue of the next non-aligned movement summit and his own bid for president of the movement for the next three years.[214]

Special attention was given in 1988 to relations with Turkey. The two countries, Turkish President Evren stated, had "decided to put an end to the 'non-active period' in their relations."[215] Mubarak went to Ankara in January at the end of his European tour, and Turkish Prime Minister Turgut Özal returned the visit the following month. The two states agreed to expand and diversify their economic cooperation, and Özal expressed his government's appreciation for Mubarak's ME initiative. Egypt and Turkey, he stated, had "identical views on foreign policy issues," owing to the "similarity of their strategic and geographic positions."[216] There were also other visits to Cairo, by the Turkish chief of staff (in February), the minister of industry and commerce (October), and the deputy foreign minister (November). The Egyptian minister of religious endowments (*awqaf*) traveled to Turkey in October.

NOTES

For the place and frequency of publications cited here, and for the full name of the publication, news agency, radio station, or monitoring service where an abbreviation is used, please see "List of Sources." Only in the case of more than one publication bearing the same name is the place of publication noted here.

1. Mubarak's address, R. Cairo, 10 November — DR, 16 November 1988.
2. Mubarak's interview in R. Cairo, 20 September — DR, 21 September 1988.
3. Mubarak's May Day address, R. Cairo, 1 May — DR, 3 May 1988.
4. For some estimates see the special survey on Egypt's economy in *FT*, 27 June. According to Prime Minister Sidqi, Egypt's earnings in hard currency in 1987–88 rose by $1.6bn. over the previous year's revenues, from $9.7bn. to $11.3bn.; *al-Ahram*, 27 November 1988.
5. Dr. Shakur Sha'lan, the Egyptian-born director of the IMF Middle East bureau, quoted in *FT*, 24 November 1988.
6. *IHT*, 11 March; *FT*, 27 June, 25 October 1988.
7. *IHT*, 11, 26–27 March; *FT*, 9 September 1988.
8. *Al-Ahram*, 9 September 1988.
9. *Akhir Sa'a*, 9 March; *al-Musawwar*, 11 March 1987.
10. *IHT*, 26–27 March; *FT*, 27 June 1988.
11. E.g., *Akhir Sa'a*, 9 March; *al-Musawwar*, 11 March; *Sawt al-'Arab*, 13 March; *al'Ahram*, 1 May 1988.
12. *Ruz al-Yusuf*, 14 March; cf. also *al-Ahram*, 25 March, 1 April 1988. A study quoted by *al-Wafd*, 27 December 1988, indicated that the number of unemployed was "more than 3.5m.," accounting for 22% of the country's labor force.
13. E.g., Mubarak's May Day address, R. Cairo, 1 May — DR, 3 May; *a-Wafd*, 31 May; *al-Jumhuriyya*, Cairo, 13, 15, 17 June; *Sawt al-'Arab*, 24 July 1988.
14. Mubarak's May Day address, R. Cairo, 1 May — DR, 3 May 1988.
15. Mubarak's interview in *al-Musawwar*, 29 July 1988.
16. *Al-Wafd*, 25 September; *JP* (quoting AP), 2 October 1988.
17. Andrew Gowers in *FT*, 27 June 1988.
18. *Al-Wafd*, 20 March 1988.
19. R. Cairo, MENA, 18 February — DR, 18, 19 February. For details see *al-Ahram*, 19, 20, 21 February; *Sawt al-'Arab*, 21 February 1988.
20. *NYT*, 2 November 1988.
21. Muhammad 'Abd al-Quddus in *al-Sha'b*, Cairo, 23 February 1988.
22. *JP* (quoting Reuters), 17 July; *al-Wafd*, 26 December 1988.
23. Quoted in *al-Nashra*, Nicosia, 11 January 1988.
24. *Al-Nahar*, Beirut, 3 October 1987.
25. *Al-Ahali*, 13 January 1988.
26. *Al-Qabas International*, 11 February 1988.
27. E.g., *Ma'ariv*, quoting AP, Reuters, 16 October 1988.
28. R. Cairo, MENA, 14 August, AFP 15 August — DR, 15 August; *IHT*, 15 August 1988. *IHT* reported that five people were killed.
29. *Al-Majalla*, 24–30 August 1988.
30. *Al-Jumhuriyya*, Cairo, 8 December 1988.
31. R. Cairo, MENA, 7, 9 December — DR, 8, 12 December; *FT*, 12 December; IRNA, R. Beirut, Voice of National Resistance, 12 December — DR, 12 December; *al-Musawwar*, 15 December (quoting the number of 250 arrested); *al-Akhbar, al-Ahram, al-Jumhuriyya*, Cairo, *al-Wafd*, 21 December 1988.
32. *Al-Siyasi*, 1 January; *al-Sha'b*, Cairo, 3 January 1989. For other, rather instructive references see *al-Jumhuriyya*, Cairo, 22 December; *Akhbar al-Yawm*, 31 December 1988.
33. *Al-Sha'b*, ibid.
34. R. Cairo, MENA, 14, 15 June — DR, 15, 16 June; *al-Sharq al-Awsat*, 17 June 1988.
35. R. Cairo, MENA, AFP, 12 January — DR, 13 January 1988.
36. *Al-Wafd*, 7 November 1988.
37. *Al-Wafd*, 28 November; *al-Ahali*, 30 November 1988.

38. *Al-Haqiqa*, 26 November. For details on the election results see *al-Akhbar*, 25 November; *al-Jumhuriyya*, Cairo, *al-Wafd*, 28 Novermber; *al-Nur, al-Ahali*, 30 November, *al-Sha'b*, Cairo, 6 December 1988. There were many discrepancies between accounts of the different sources, although the dominance of the Islamic trend was reflected in all of them.
39. Mubarak's May Day address, R. Cairo, 1 May — DR, 3 May 1988.
40. *Al-Jumhuriyya*, Cairo, 2 February, and cf. *al-Majalla*, 16 February 1988.
41. AFP, 8 May — DR, 10 May 1988.
42. SEe e.g., in *al-Ahram International*, 12 May; *al-Wafd*, 14 May; *al-Majalla*, 22–28 June, 4–10 August; *al-Dustur*, London, 8 August; *al-Ahram*, 20 October 1988.
43. Mustafa Sharadi in *al-Wafd*, 4 September 1988.
44. *Al-Wafd*, 28 July 1988.
45. *Al-Ahali*, 25 May 1988.
46. Mubarak's interview in *al-Musawwar*, 29 July 1988.
47. *Al-Wafd*, 31 March 1988.
48. *Al-Sha'b*, Cairo, 22 March 1988.
49. *Al-Wafd*, 31 March; *al-Ahram*, 3 April 1988.
50. Mubarak's May Day address, R. Cairo, 1 May — DR, 3 May 1988.
51. *Al-Ahram*, 5 June 1988.
52. *Al-Wafd*, 5 July 1988.
53. *Al-Sha'b*, Cairo, 21 June; *al-Wafd*, 5 July 1988.
54. *Al-Ahram*, 16 September 1988.
55. *Al-Siyasi*, 6 November; *al-Umma*, 13 November 1988.
56. R. Tunis, 23 January — DR, 25 January 1988.
57. R. Cairo, MENA, AFP, 9 February — DR, 10 February 1988.
58. R. Cairo, MENA, 24 November — DR, 25 November 1988.
59. Mubarak, quoted by R. Cairo, MENA, 24 May — DR, 25 May 1988.
60. *Al-Ahram*, 11 January; *October*, 17 January 1988.
61. MENA, 30 March 1988.
62. R. Cairo, MENA, 5 July — DR, 8 July 1988.
63. *Al-Ahram, al-Jumhuriyya*, Cairo, 8 December 1988.
64. R. Cairo, 1 January 1989.
65. Mubarak's interview, *al-Riyad*, 9 January; *al-Sharq al-Awsat*, 3 May 1988.
66. R. Cairo, MENA, 13 November — DR, 15 November 1988.
67. R. Cairo, MENA, 13 March — DR, 16 March 1988.
68. *Al-Jumhuriyya*, Cairo, 13 June 1988.
69. Ibrahim Sa'da in *Akhbar al-Yawm*, 11 June 1988.
70. *Al-Watan*, 30 November; *FT*, 2 December; *al-Yawm al-Sabi'*, 12 December 1988.
71. Mubarak's May Day address, R. Cairo, 1 May — DR, 3 May 1988.
72. Quoted by R. Cairo, MENA, 3, 25 September — DR, 6, 26 September 1988.
73. R. Cairo, MENA, 9 August — DR, 9 August 1988.
74. R. Cairo, VoA, 3 August 1988.
75. *Al-Ahram*, 5 August 1988.
76. *Al-Akhbar*, Cairo, 23 October 1988.
77. R. Cairo, MENA, 4 September — DR, 6 September 1988.
78. *FT*, 2 December; *Ha'aretz* (quoting AFP), 19 December 1988.
79. R. Monte Carlo, 26 November 1988, quoting "a senior Jordanian source."
80. R. Amman, 18 October — DR, 22 October 1988.
81. For details see *al-Ra'y*, 1 August 1988.
82. Mubarak's interview, *al-Ahram*, 20 October 1988.
83. *Ruz al-Yusuf*, 4 July 1988.
84. Mubarak's interview, *al-Ahram*, 20 October 1988.
85. *Al-Ahram*, 13 September; also *al-Akhbar*, 13 September; Mubarak's interview, *al-Ahram*, 20 October 1988.
86. *Al-Ahram International*, 28 October 1988.
87. *FT*, 2 December 1988.
88. R. Cairo, MENA, 28 November — DR, 29 November 1988.
89. R. Cairo, MENA, 3 May — DR, 5 May 1988.

90. *Ruz al-Yusuf*, 4 July; INA, 5 July — DR, 6 July; *al-Akhbar*, Cairo, 6 July; R. Cairo, 8 July — DR, 8 July 1988.
91. For details see *al-Anba*, Kuwait, 29 August 1988.
92. MENA, SUNA, 1 March — DR, 1, 2 March 1988.
93. *Al-Majalla*, 16 March; Garang reportedly agreed to cooperate — *al-Sharq al-Awsat*, 8 July 1988.
94. Sudanese Minister of Economy and Foreign Trade Mubarak al-Fadil, quoted by MENA, 12 July — DR, 13 July 1988.
95. *Al-Siyasa*, Khartoum, 30 May 1988.
96. MENA, 12 July — DR, 13 July 1988, quoting Sudanese Minister of Economy and Foreign Trade Mubarak Fadil.
97. Prime Minister Sidqi, quoted by R. Omdurman, 10 October — DR, 14 October 1988.
98. MENA, 16 January — SWB, 26 January 1988.
99. R. Cairo, MENA, 10 April — DR, 11 April 1988.
100. *Al-Sharq al-Awsat*, 8 July 1988.
101. R. Cairo, MENA, 14, 16, 17 July — DR, 15, 18 July 1988.
102. R. Omdurman, 10 October 1988.
103. *Al-Akhbar*, 21 March 1988.
104. MENA, 15 September — DR, 16 September; also Mubarak's interview, *al-Ahram*, 20 October 1988.
105. R. Cairo, MENA, 12 October — DR, 13 October 1988.
106. R. Cairo, MENA, 4 October — DR, 5 October; *al-Majalla*, 23 November 1988.
107. Mubarak's interview, *al-Anba*, Kuwait, 6 January 1988.
108. *Al-Siyasa*, Kuwait, 31 December 1987; *al-Musawwar*, 1 January; *The Guardian*, 2 January 1988.
109. Mubarak's interview, *al-Anba*, Kuwait, 6 January 1988.
110. MENA, 11 January — SWB, 12 January 1988.
111. *Al-Khalij*, 7 May 1988.
112. Mubarak's interview, *al-Riyad*, 9 January 1988.
113. *Al-'Alam*, London, 7 May; *al-Siyasa*, Kuwait, 9 May; R. Cairo, MENA, 21 May — DR, 25 May 1988.
114. *Sawt al-'Arab*, 1 May; *al-Safir*, 13 May; R. Cairo, MENA, 2, 21 May — DR, 3, 25 May 1988.
115. *Al-Sharq al-Awsat*, 3 May 1988.
116. Quoted by MENA, 10 August — DR, 11 August 1988.
117. Ibid.
118. The paper was the Nasserite organ *Sawt al-'Arab*. See R. Cairo, MENA, AFP, 24 August — DR, 25 August; *al-Ahali*, 24 August; Musa Sabri's article in *al-Akhbar*, Cairo, 29 August; *Le Monde*, 2 September; *al-Hilal International*, 16 October 1988.
119. R. Cairo, MENA, 24, 25 May; *al-Majalla*, 28 May 1988.
120. R. Cairo, MENA, 17, 19 October — DR, 20 October 1988.
121. R. Damascus, 4 August — DR, 9 August 1988.
122. Ibid.
123. Mubarak's interview, *al-Ahram*, 20 October 1988.
124. *Al-Ahram*, 1 July 1988.
125. R. Cairo, 6 January — DR, 7 January 1988.
126. *Al-Watan*, 30 November; *al-Sharq al-Awsat*, 6 December; *al-Ittihad*, Abu Dhabi, 27 December 1988.
127. R. Monte Carlo, 26 November; *Ma'ariv*, 27 November 1988.
128. MENA, 5 December 1988.
129. *JP*, quoting Reuters, 16 December; *al-Ittihad*, Abu Dhabi, 26 December 1988.
130. JANA, 28 March; *al-Mustaqbal*, 2 April 1988.
131. R. Cairo, MENA, 29 March — DR, 30 March 1988.
132. Mubarak, interviewed by R. Cairo, 30 March — DR, 30 March 1988.
133. R. Cairo, MENA, 12 April — DR, 13 April; *JP*, quoting AP, 14 April 1988.
134. Sa'id Sunbul in *al-Akhbar*, 1 June 1988, where the author reviews the contacts aimed at mediation.

135. R. Tripoli, JANA, 28 May — DR, 31 May 1988.
136. *Al-Wafd*, 11 September; *al-'Alam*, London, 8 October 1988.
137. JANA, 23 October — DR, 24 October; AFP, MENA, 30 October; *al-Jumhuriyya*, Cairo, 21 November 1988.
138. Mubarak's interview, *al-Ahram*, 20 October 1988.
139. *Al-Ahram*, 12, 19, and 26 October 1988.
140. *Al-Yawm al-Sabi'*, 8 February; see also R. Cairo, MENA, 22 May — DR, 24 May 1988.
141. E.g., *Sawt al-'Arab*, 3 January; GNA, 12 January; *al-Wafd*, 2 February; *al-Yawm al-Sabi'*, 8 February; INA, 10 February; *al-Ahram al-Iqtisadi*, 18 April 1988.
142. Jadd al-Haqq's interview in *al-Anba*, Kuwait, 16 February 1988.
143. E.g., R. Cairo, 17 April — DR, 19 April 1988.
144. *Al-Ahram*, 16 March 1988.
145. R. Cairo, MENA, 15, 17, 18 August — DR, 16, 17, 18 August 1988.
146. R. Cairo, MENA, 1 September — DR, 1 September 1988.
147. E.g., 'Abdallah Hurani, quoted by R. Cairo, MENA, 16, 18 August — DR, 17, 18 August; 'Arafat, quoted by R. Cairo, MENA, 17 August — DR, 18 August 1988.
148. *Al-Akhbar*, Cairo, 12 October 1988.
149. *Al-Ahram*, 16 November; *al-Akhbar*, Cairo, 16, 17 November; commentary on R. Cairo, 16, 17 November — DR, 17, 18 November 1988.
150. R. Cairo, MENA, 15 November — DR, 15 November 1988.
151. R. Cairo, MENA, 17 November — DR, 18 November 1988.
152. R. Cairo, MENA, 19 November — DR, 21 November 1988.
153. Ibid.
154. *IHT*, 21 November 1988.
155. R. Cairo, MENA, 4 December — DR, 5 December 1988.
156. *Ha'aretz, JP*, 25 January 1988.
157. *Al-Sha'b*, Cairo, 2 February; GNA, 13 November — DR, 14 November; Mubarak's interview in *al-Anba*, Kuwait, 25 December; *Ha'aretz*, 28 December 1988.
158. *Ha'aretz*, 22 November 1988.
159. *Al-Ahram*, 25 October 1988.
160. Ahmad Baha al-Din in *al-Ahram*, 3 November 1988.
161. Nabil Zaki in *Akhir Sa'a*, 9 November 1988.
162. E.g., Ahmad Baha al-Din in *al-Ahram*, 3 November; Sabri Abu al-Majd in *al-Musawwar*, 4 November; 'Adil Hasani in *al-Masa*, 5 November 1988.
163. Mubarak, quoted in *Ha'aretz*, 6 November 1988.
164. *Ha'aretz*, 23 May 1988.
165. Ibid; *JP*, 31 May 1988.
166. R. Cairo, MENA, 31 July — DR, 1 August 1988.
167. Mubarak's address to the People's Assembly and Consultative Council, R. Cairo, 10 November — DR, 16 November 1988.
168. Mubarak's address, R. Cairo, 10 November — DR, 16 November; similarly Mubarak's interview, *al-Ahram*, 20 October 1988.
169. *Ha'aretz*, 18 October 1988.
170. *NYT*, 29 January; R. Cairo, MENA, 29, 30 January — DR, 1 February; *al-Musawwar*, 5 February 1988.
171. *Al-Ahram*, 27 March, 6 April 1988.
172. *Al-Akhbar*, Cairo, 19 February 1988.
173. R. Cairo, MENA, 27, 28 November, R. Monte Carlo, 28 November — DR, 28, 29 November 1988.
174. *Al-Ahram*, 2 December 1988.
175. *Al-Akhbar*, Cairo, 28 November 1988.
176. Quoted by GNA, 15 December — DR, 16 December 1988.
177. R. Cairo, MENA, 15 December — DR, 16 December; *al-Ahram, al-Akhbar, al-Jumhuriyya*, Cairo, 16 December 1988.
178. *Ruz al-Yusuf*, 25 January; *al-Ahram*, 28 January, 2 February; *al-Musawwar*, 5 February 1988.
179. *Ruz al-Yusuf*, 25 January; *al-Ahram*, 2 February; *al-Musawwar*, 5 February 1988.

180. *Al-Wafd*, 7 August 1988.
181. *FT*, 25 March; R. Cairo, 16 April — DR, 21 April; *al-Sha'b*, Cairo, 3 May 1988.
182. R. Cairo, MENA, 1 November — DR, 2 November; *al-Ahram*, 3 November 1988.
183. *WP*, 25 June; *NYT*, 25, 26, 29 June; *JP*, 29 June, 1, 12 July 1988.
184. *FT*, 27 June 1988.
185. *Al-Ahram*, 26 June 1988.
186. *WP*, 20 August 1988.
187. Abu Ghazala's interview in *al-Sharq al-Awsat*, 31 October 1988.
188. R. Cairo, MENA, 2, 4 January — DR, 5 January 1988.
189. R. Cairo, MENA, 13 June — DR, 17 June 1988.
190. MENA, 6 December — DR, 6 December 1988.
191. R. Cairo, 21 July — DR, 22 July 1988.
192. *Al-Ahram*, 25 July; *Akhir Sa'a*, 27 July 1988.
193. KNA, 15 March; AFP, TASS, 16 March 1988.
194. *Al-Ahram International*, 25 March 1988.
195. R. Cairo, MENA, 20, 21 May — DR, 22 May; *al-Musawwar*, 27 May 1988.
196. AFP, 19 May — DR, 20 May; *al-Ahram al-Iqtisadi*, 6 June 1988.
197. R. Cairo, MENA, 21 May — DR, 24 May 1988.
198. Ibid.
199. *Al-Ahram*, 23 April 1988.
200. Ibid.
201. *Al-Musawwar*, 29 January 1988. Egypt's trade with EEC countries accounted for some 40% of its worldwide trade.
202. *Ruz al-Yusuf*, 25 January 1988. According to this source, aid to Egypt accounted for some 40% of West Germany's foreign aid.
203. *Al-Musawwar*, 8 January; R. Cairo, MENA, 19 March — DR, 21 March 1988.
204. Mubarak's speech, R. Cairo, 10 November — DR, 16 November 1988.
205. R. Cairo, MENA, 25 October — DR, 26 October 1988.
206. R. Cairo, 25, 26, 27, 28 April — DR, 26, 27, 28, 29 April 1988.
207. R. Cairo, MENA, 27 April, 25 June — DR, 28 April, 30 June 1988.
208. *Al-Ittihad*, Abu Dhabi, 11 September 1988.
209. R. Cairo, MENA, 25 January — DR, 26 January 1988.
210. *FT*, 21 June; *Ha'aretz*, quoting AFP, 27 June 1988.
211. R. Cairo, MENA, 2 November — DR, 3 November 1988.
212. R. Cairo, MENA, 25 June — DR, 28 June 1988.
213. Japanese foreign minister, quoted by R. Cairo, 25 June — DR, 28 June 1988.
214. R. Cairo, MENA, 27, 28 August — DR, 29 August 1988. However, the non-aligned conference in Nicosia, Cyprus, in September, approved Yugoslavia for that position; R. Nicosia, 11 September — DR (West Europe), 13 September 1988.
215. *Al-Ahram*, 29 October 1988.
216. R. Cairo, MENA, 13, 14, 15 February — DR, 18 February 1988.

The Gulf States

JACOB GOLDBERG

For the Gulf Cooperation Council (GCC), comprised of Saudi Arabia and the five small Arab states of the Gulf reviewed below, 1988 may prove to have been a turning point. The Iraqi-Iranian War dominated the GCC since its establishment in May 1981, the outbreak of the war in September 1980 having provided the impetus for the formation of the GCC. The eight-year war provided a common agenda for the six GCC states, despite the occasional lack of consensus among them concerning Iran. The aftermath of the war was going to constitute a test in which the ability of the GCC to survive as a meaningful, cohesive organization without the unifying factor of the war would be examined. It was very likely that a fresh impetus of some kind would be needed if the GCC was to progress toward its ultimate declared goal of confederal union.

The Gulf states entered 1989 with a very mixed state of mind. There was an unprecedented buoyant mood caused by the end of the war, the rise in and stabilization of oil prices, and the prospects of an overall economic upturn as an inevitable result of Iraqi and Iranian reconstruction plans. But, on the other hand, eight years of war had also exposed some of the basic weaknesses and limitations of each GCC member state and of the GCC itself. It remained to be seen how the Gulf states would confront the new challenges posed by the postwar period and the new geostrategic conditions in the Gulf.

A CONTINUING IRANIAN CHALLENGE

The Arab summit conference in Amman in November 1987 adopted harsh resolutions against Iran (see *MECS* 1987, pp. 128–34). It was surprising, therefore, that at the GCC Riyadh summit only six weeks later, the countries most affected by the Iranian threat did not condemn Iran and did not call for tough actions against it. Instead, the summit reportedly authorized that an intense dialogue be pursued with Tehran by the United Arab Emirates (UAE), with a central mediating role being given to Syria.[1] The resolutions were a victory for those in the GCC (probably Oman, the UAE, Qatar, and perhaps Bahrain) that strove for accommodation with Iran over Kuwait, which opted for a more belligerent attitude. Even Saudi Foreign Minister Prince Sa'ud said after the summit that "the dialogue with Iran will continue; it has never stopped."[2]

According to various sources, contacts between Tehran and the GCC were under way throughout January in order to prepare a framework for the dialogue. The agenda was to include "commitments by all sides to peaceful coexistence of all the region's states, respect for their sovereignty, noninterference in their domestic affairs, and the full implementation of Security Council Resolution 598." As relayed by Syria, the initial Iranian response was "positive" and called for "optimism."[3] The impression

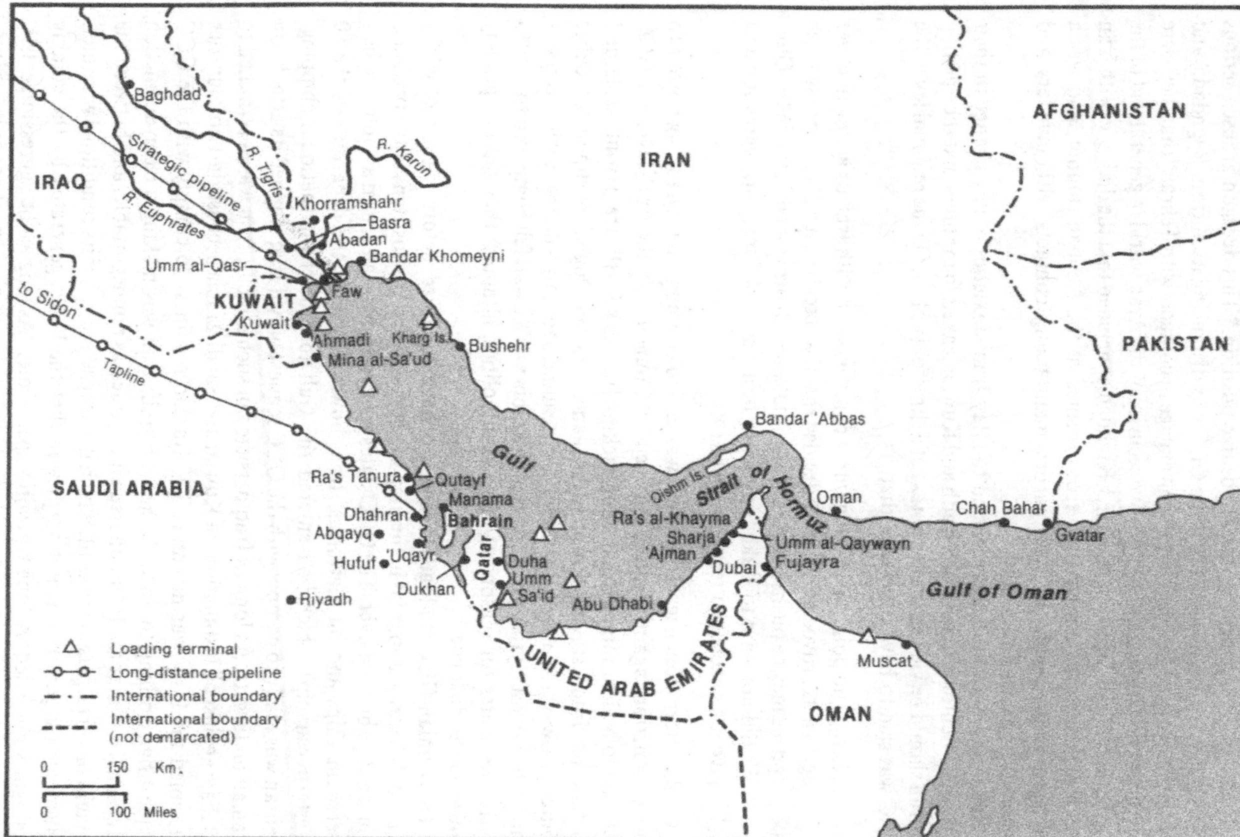

AFGHANISTAN
IRAN
PAKISTAN
IRAQ
KUWAIT
SAUDI ARABIA
Qatar
Bahrain
UNITED ARAB EMIRATES
OMAN
Baghdad
R. Tigris
R. Karun
R. Euphrates
Strategic pipeline
Khorramshahr
Basra
Abadan
Bandar Khomeyni
Umm al-Qasr
Faw
Kuwait
Ahmadi
Kharg Is.
Bushehr
Mina al-Sa'ud
to Sidon
Tapline
Gulf
Ra's Tanura
Qutayf
Manama
Dhahran
Abqayq
Hufuf
'Uqayr
Dukhan
Riyadh
Duha
Umm Sa'id
Abu Dhabi
Qishm Is.
Strait of Hormuz
Bandar 'Abbas
Oman
Ra's al-Khayma
Sharja
'Ajman
Dubai
Umm al-Qaywayn
Fujayra
Chah Bahar
Gvatar
Gulf of Oman
Muscat
Loading terminal
Long-distance pipeline
International boundary
International boundary (not demarcated)
0 150 Km.
0 100 Miles

The Gulf

of an Iranian-GCC *rapprochement* was reinforced by the fact that, unlike the Amman summit which praised Iraq and voiced "profound solidarity" with it, the GCC summit only expressed support for Iraq's "positive position." This decision aroused serious concern among Iraqi leaders that the GCC was distancing itself from Baghdad,[4] and led the Iraqi media to warn those "who engage in contacts with Tehran" that they were helping Syria "endanger the collective security of the Arab world in general and of the Arab states of the Gulf in particular." Baghdad concluded that the dialogue with Iran was a breach in the united Arab front formed at the Amman summit, and was a "dangerous precedent of Arab parties maintaining contacts with invaders and aggressors against Arab rights."[5]

Saudi and Kuwaiti leaders rushed to allay Iraqi anxieties of any change in their position. "Senior officials" in Riyadh and Kuwait leaked to the press that the opening to Iran should be viewed in the context of a threefold policy. On the regional level, the GCC was said to have concluded that:

> There is no point in entering into a confrontation with Iran or acting in anger against its provocations.... We decided that if we escalate, it will be unpredictable and we may be pushed to seek confrontation with the United States in the Gulf. We did not want to make Iran out to be a victim of American aggression and give it an excuse to respond against us.

On the international level, the GCC was said to be going "to push the big powers to pursue sanctions against Iran in the Security Council." On the Arab level, the GCC was said to be determined to continue backing Iraq, to keep the Iraqi front stable, and to "nourish Iraq's staying power with financial aid and logistical support."[6] Other sources, however, claimed that the GCC's readiness to start a dialogue with Iran was caused by intense Syrian pressure; Saudi Arabia and Kuwait felt compelled to bow to Syrian pressures for reasons of inter-Arab politics, although they did not pin any hopes on the dialogue.[7]

The Iranian-GCC dialogue seemed to have collapsed before it even officially started. It became apparent in the preparatory talks that the positions of the two sides could not be bridged over. The GCC states wanted Iran to halt armed assaults on their merchant ships and oil platforms. Iran, however, sought the departure of the 80 Western warships which had entered the Gulf to protect international shipping. Tehran was ready to comply with the GCC request only if Iraq stopped its attacks on Iranian oil targets. As long as Iraq persisted in such attacks, Iran was determined to retaliate against oil installations of Kuwait and Saudi Arabia because the two countries sustained the Iraqi war machine. The Iranian readiness to comply with the GCC request had nothing to do with the war itself; Iran was making a clear distinction between the war at the front, an issue it regarded as nonnegotiable, and between the attacks on oil targets in the Gulf, which it was ready to halt if its conditions were met. Given such a gap, it was not surprising that the hopes generated by the coming dialogue soon faded. As one Kuwaiti paper wrote: "As long as the aggression exists, the call to cooperation or dialogue is nothing but a strategic trap set not only for Iraq, but for the whole Arab world."[8]

Nevertheless, reports about an Iranian-GCC dialogue mediated by Syria persisted. In mid-February, a Kuwaiti paper disclosed the existence of a seven-point Syrian peace plan that had been presented to the GCC leaders.[9] A few days later, Iranian

Deputy Foreign Minister 'Ali Muhammad Besharati said that Iran had agreed to participate in discussions with GCC officials and expressed hope that "the planned talks herald an improvement in our relations."[10] But Saudi officials called such statements "unfounded," stating that "no one had proposed to Iran the holding of a joint meeting with the GCC at any level."[11] The Kuwaitis were blunter. Foreign Minister Sabah Ahmad Al Sabah declared that the GCC states "have placed conditions on a dialogue with Iran," the most important being the "demand that Iran stop meddling in the domestic affairs of GCC countries and pledge not to take hostile action against them."[12] It was obvious that whatever chances there might have been for a dialogue, they evaporated once Saudi Arabia broke off diplomatic relations with Tehran in late April (see chapter on Saudi Arabia).

IN THE AFTERMATH OF THE WAR: PRELIMINARY LESSONS

The cease-fire in the Iraqi-Iranian War in July led immediately to feelings of relief in the GCC countries. They could take pride in the fact that they had emerged relatively unscathed from the eight-year war which had posed serious challenges to their security and very existence. Their immediate goal was to help consolidate the cease-fire, to implement Security Council Resolution 598, and move forward the stalled Iran-Iraq peace process. Opening the GCC's 28th Ministerial Council in early September, Saudi Foreign Minister Prince Sa'ud stated that the GCC's chief interest was "to see the war end in a comprehensive peace agreement and to see security, stability, and peace return to our region."[13] But in order to play a significant role as mediators, the GCC states had to adopt a more balanced policy on Iran and Iraq. Contacts with Tehran were resumed as part of what was described as "an outstretched-hand policy" expressed in frequent visits by GCC and Iranian officials to each others' capitals.[14]

The war, however, led the Gulf states to draw unpleasant conclusions regarding the effectiveness, power, and political influence of the GCC and its future prospects. From the outbreak of the war, the GCC made constant and substantial efforts to halt the conflict, but to no avail. The inescapable conclusion was that the GCC was completely unable to influence either of its two larger neighbors to alter their policies and courses of action. Hence, the GCC's regional power and influence proved to be very limited.

The war also exposed the limited effectiveness of the GCC's combined military power. Neither now nor in the foreseeable future could the GCC match the military capabilities of Iran or Iraq. In the final analysis, the GCC states would have to rely on external forces in order to maintain their independence. The GCC leaders themselves had to be aware of the organization's military limitations and none of the leaders regarded their combined defenses as capable of more than putting up a spirited fight against a major threat. Such external support could come from two sources, Egypt and the US. Thus, despite the end of the war, GCC leaders continued their discussions with Egyptian officials in order to arrive at "strategic, military, and security coordination," aimed at "establishing stability and tranquillity in the Gulf."[15] Likewise, the GCC leaders were aware of the central role of the US if another major crisis evolved in the Gulf. Meeting with President Reagan in late September, GCC leaders expressed appreciation of US cooperation with their countries and said that "this cooperation, and the US presence in the Gulf in general, were instrumental in bringing about the end of the Iran-Iraq War."[16] Thus, the most basic principle in the GCC's national security doctrine — the lofty ideal of "self-reliance" — was tested and found wanting even by the GCC leadership itself.

Therefore, if the GCC could not on its own meet a military challenge, the question arose as to how the GCC could become a significant entity in the region. In the early 1980s, the GCC states' financial clout was perceived as a substitute for more conventional forms of military power and political influence. But with the crisis in the oil market, declining production and revenues, severe cutbacks in all spending programs, and growing budgetary deficits, the strength of the financial muscle largely diminished. Even without the oil crisis, it was also doubtful whether money could really be translated into power and might. The GCC record of financial assistance to other states in the region proved that such generosity did not earn the benefactors any special political benefits from the recipients.

The eight years of war against Iran turned Baghdad into one of the Middle East's strongest military powers. There was growing anxiety in GCC states that in the aftermath of the war, a militarily confident Ba'th regime in Baghdad might turn its attention to its conservative and rich Gulf neighbors.[17] Even before the Iranian revolution and the Gulf War, Iraq — not Iran — was regarded as the regional threat, causing the founders of the GCC in 1981 to exclude Baghdad from the organization (see *MECS* 1980–81, pp. 458–64). The GCC, principally Saudi Arabia and Kuwait, had poured an estimated $30bn. into Iraq during the war to practically enable Baghdad to survive. Likewise, the GCC states might have to stretch themselves in the future to lend a helping financial hand to the reconstruction programs in Iraq. But even the GCC leaders did not believe that such largess gave them immunity from Iraqi political ambitions.[18] How was, then, the GCC to handle the newly perceived Iraqi threat?

RELATIONS WITH THE EEC

After lengthy negotiations, the GCC and the EEC in June signed a preliminary economic cooperation agreement stipulating the gradual liberalization of EEC-GCC trade and the reinforcement of economic and technical cooperation between the two sides. Particular emphasis was laid on facilitating the transfer of technology and the flow of investments from the EEC to GCC states; the promotion of joint ventures; cooperation in the development of their energy sectors; and EEC assistance in developing and diversifying the GCC's agricultural sector by providing new techniques for boosting crop productivity and by establishing agricultural processing industries. The agreement made no change in GCC-EEC trade arrangements; this was to be the subject of the second phase of the agreement, on which negotiations were to start in 1989.[19] Even this second phase was not to infringe on EEC measures protecting the petrochemical industries.

The agreement in essence froze existing EEC-GCC trade relations. The GCC did not achieve its main objective of having the EEC remove the import tariffs on petrochemical products from GCC countries. Nevertheless, the GCC was willing to approve the agreement on the grounds that it was the first step toward total trade liberalization between the two groups. In December, the GCC summit ratified the agreement and authorized the Ministerial Council to enter into talks with the EEC on concluding a full-fledged trade pact.[20]

THE ANNUAL SUMMIT: THE GCC AT THE CROSSROADS

The GCC Supreme Council held its annual meeting in Bahrain in late December. The proceedings and final communiqué reflected the GCC's mixed balance sheet on the eve of the 1990s.[21] There was a long list of positive developments: (1) The Iraqi-Iranian War was over and although a peace agreement remained to be signed, it was unlikely that hostilities would be resumed; (2) tension between the US and the USSR had relaxed; the summit communiqué expressed satisfaction at "the breakthrough in international relations and the trend toward solving regional conflicts through peaceful means"; (3) the Soviet withdrawal from Afghanistan removed an almost decade-old cloud hanging over the Gulf's horizons; it not only relieved the Gulf states of what they regarded as a major security threat, but also paved the way for a significant improvement in relations with Moscow; (4) the declaration of Palestinian independence and the opening of a dialogue between Washington and the PLO were warmly welcomed; (5) GCC attempts to return Egypt to Arab ranks seemed on the verge of realization; Egypt's "pioneering role in Arab affairs" and support for its "participation in any Arab meeting at any level" were frequently cited, to culminate in 1989 in President Mubarak's attending the next Arab summit and in Egypt's readmission to the Arab League; (6) the Opec agreement of late November on production quotas (see chapter on Middle East oil) removed a major controversial issue from the GCC agenda, particularly as the three most conspicuous "cheaters" in Opec were three GCC members — Saudi Arabia, Kuwait, and the UAE. According toBahrain's oil minister, all six GCC oil ministers not only committed themselves to the Opec accord, but also arrived at "a unified oil strategy" for the first time.[22]

But, on the other hand, there were a number of dilemmas and challenges that remained unresolved and were bound to adversely affect the GCC in the future. First, should the GCC cultivate closer ties with Iran as a counterbalance to Baghdad's dangerous ambitions? Could warmer ties with Iran also end its encouragement of militant, subversive groups undermining the security of a number of GCC states? Second, given that peace between Iran and Iraq remained to be concluded and given that Iran did not abandon its radical, export-oriented Islamic message, shouldn't the GCC give priority to closer ties with Iraq as a hedge against a possible resumption of Iranian attempts to inspire subversion? Third, what was to happen to the "Peninsula Shield," the GCC's joint defense forces headquartered at Hafar al-Batin in Saudi Arabia? Should it be permanently sustained by the GCC as a necessary insurance policy, or should it be quietly disbanded now that the Iraqi-Iranian War had come to an end? Fourth, what was to happen to all the plans aimed at the social and economic integration of the six GCC member states — a common market, a unified currency, unified customs tariffs, a common legal system, regional-industrial rationalization, a joint military industry, etc.? It was the postwar period which would tell whether the GCC had reached the peak of its accomplishments or was perhaps still to play a role in Gulf politics in the future.

NOTES

For the place and frequency of publications cited here, and for the full name of the publication, news agency, radio station, or monitoring service where an abbreviation is used, please see "List of Sources." Only in the case of more than one publication bearing the same name is the place of publication noted here.

1. KUNA, 15 January; *al-Mustaqbal,* 16 January 1988.
2. *Le Monde,* 31 December 1987.
3. *FT,* 18 January; *al-Sharq al-Awsat,* 21 January 1988.
4. *Le Monde,* 31 December 1987.
5. INA, 23 January — DR, 25 January 1988.
6. *NYT,* 28 January 1988.
7. *Akhbar al-Usbu',* 31 December 1987; *al-Yawm al-Sabi',* 25 January, 1 February 1988.
8. *Al-Qabas,* 23 January 1988.
9. *Al-Watan,* 11 February 1988.
10. R. Tehran, 16 February — DR, 18 February 1988.
11. SPA, 24 February — DR, 25 February 1988.
12. KUNA, 22 March — DR, 23 March 1988.
13. SPA, 4 September — DR, 7 September 1988.
14. *Al-Usbu' al-'Arabi,* 28 November 1988.
15. *Al-Ra'y al-'Amm,* 7 August 1988.
16. *NYT,* 27 September 1988.
17. *CSM,* 22 December 1988.
18. *FT,* 15 November; *al-Muharrir,* 10 December 1988; *Gulf States Newsletter,* 8 February 1989.
19. *FT,* 26 March; *Memo,* 18 June 1988.
20. SPA, 22 December — DR, 23 December 1988.
21. Ibid.; *Gulf States Newsletter,* 9 January 1989.
22. *IHT,* 21 December 1988.

Bahrain

UZI RABI

Increasing political and socioeconomic difficulties made 1988 a difficult year for Bahrain. It was once again shocked by an Iranian-inspired coup attempt that was foiled at the last minute, but which emphasized the island's political fragility. Once the unchallenged regional banking center, Bahrain was gradually forfeiting this position and was facing a problem of deepening unemployment. Regionally, its dispute with Qatar over the microterritory of Fasht al-Dibal seemed no nearer to resolution, which pushed forward Bahrain's plans to upgrade its armed forces. However, the cease-fire in the Gulf War, and the subsequent clement political environment — especially the thaw in Bahraini-Iranian relations — gave rise to new hopes for a better future.

DOMESTIC AFFAIRS

SUBVERSIVE ACTIVITY

The cell uncovered in Bahrain in December 1987 (for details see *MECS* 1987) proved a far greater threat to the regime than originally portrayed. The three saboteurs, who aimed to destroy Bahraini oil installations, were part of an extensive network bent on toppling the regime. It emerged from Arab press reports that 100 plotters were involved, some of them members of the Bahraini security forces. One group was to assassinate the Bahraini ruler, Shaykh 'Isa Ibn Salman Al Khalifa, while others were to storm vital installations, such as the radio and television station, Manama International Airport, and the US Embassy. Other reports tended to confirm that the coup was to coincide with the meeting of the Eighth GCC Supreme Council in Riyadh on 26 December 1987, but it was aborted three days earlier. The plot was exposed when its masterminds met in Frankfurt where they were detected by the West German security organs, which then warned Manama.[1]

The conspiracy recalled the December 1981 coup attempt (for details see *MECS* 1981–82, pp. 490–92). Both affairs bore the hallmarks of Iranian patronage for its proxy, the Tehran-based Islamic Front for the Liberation of Bahrain, led by Hujjat al-Islam Hadi al-Modarresi. The latter, an Iranian who had fled Iran during the reign of the Shah, had been given Bahraini nationality, but was stripped of it in September 1979, when he attempted to undermine the rule of the Al Khalifa family. Modarresi was later thought to be the leader of the Islamic Republic's clandestine activity against the GCC states and Iraq. According to one report, he would have been nominated president of the would-be Islamic Republic of Bahrain, if the coup had succeeded.[2]

Bahrain ignored the Iranian involvement in the affair by playing down its importance, probably in order not to aggravate its own Shi'i population. Bahrain's decision may also have been related to attempts by GCC states to achieve a cease-fire in the Gulf War (see chapter on the United Arab Emirates), attempts which suggested that it would be better to allay the regional conflict rather than aggravate it. All the same, security was tightened around the Manama International Airport and the King Fahd Causeway and all passengers were checked,[3] apparently to counter the relatively widespread use of fake Bahraini passports for acts of terrorism, the most prominent example being the hijacking of the Kuwaiti airliner in March (for details, see chapter on Kuwait).

Other sources, meanwhile, reported a growing restiveness in Bahrain, chiefly protests against the US presence there. The Tehran Home Service claimed in January that a Bahraini decision to put additional facilities at the disposal of the US aroused a wave of anti-American sentiment. Two Bahraini youths were detained and interrogated for attempting to place bombs in the vicinity of a US Air Force base; as a result, security measures around US installations were tightened. The internal unrest reportedly led to precautions, such as detentions and the imposition of night curfews. But most notable was the decree which reportedly banned the employment of Bahraini Shi'is in the armed forces.[4] One source estimated the number of political prisoners in Bahrain at about 1,500, mostly Shi'is.[5] Yet, given the source of such reports, there is good reason to accept them with caution.

THE ARMED FORCES

The regional tension in general and the Bahraini-Qatari dispute (see chapter on Qatar) in particular pushed Bahrain to markedly upgrade the capability of its armed forces. The Navy — considered to be one of the best among the GCC states — was reinforced with two West German sophisticated combat vessels.[6] The Air Force was strengthened by the first consignments of US F-16 fighter jets and antiaircraft *Stinger* missiles on the basis of deals concluded in 1987.[7] Personnel changes were made in the defense system in April. Staff Maj. Gen. Shaykh Khalifa Ibn Salman Al Khalifa was appointed minister of defense and deputy commander in chief of the Bahraini Defense Force. He was succeeded as chief of staff by Gen. Shaykh 'Abdallah Ibn Salman Ibn Khalid Al Khalifa.[8]

ECONOMIC AFFAIRS — THE ERODING OF A REGIONAL BANKING CENTER

The Bahraini economy continued to be dogged by the regional recession. Bahrain was gradually declining as a regional banking center; about 10 international banks had closed down their offices, while others greatly reduced their staff and activity since the beginning of 1987. The general mood was one of despair. "I've recently been asking myself what on earth are we doing here," lamented a chief executive of one of the foreign banks.[9] This decline was due to a variety of causes, most of them side effects of the recession; most prominent was the issue of non-performing loans, with which most foreign banks were implicated. Many of the borrowers were powerful members of the Bahraini community — large merchant families and even members of the Al Khalifa ruling family — which left the banks with little chance of collecting their loans without making profit-eroding concessions.[10] Considering that the foreign banks' annual contribution to Bahrain's revenues was estimated at 200m. Bahraini dinars (BD), their importance to the economy could hardly be exaggerated.[11] It was premature to anticipate a brighter future for Bahrain's banking system even after the cease-fire in the Gulf War and the subsequent reconstruction of both Iran and Iraq.

Another problem plaguing the economy was the oil sector's continued decreasing contribution to the gross domestic product (GDP). So uncertain were Bahrain's economic prospects for the near future that the government reverted, for the first time since 1978, to a one-year budget. The projected deficit of BD60m. entailed government austerity measures, such as the dismissal of personnel.[12]

Bahrain's quest for alternative sources of revenue was, therefore, all the more intense and concentrated mostly on non-oil industries. The private sector was to provide the momentum in medium- and small-scale industries. Abundant incentives were given to this sector; the National Industry and Petroleum Support Law imposed customs duties on imports of goods manufactured in Bahrain and gave preferential purchasing privileges to companies partly or wholly owned by the government.[13] Another means of diversifying Bahrain's economic base was the attraction of foreign investment and joint-venture partners. The island was promoted as the most suitable location for overseas companies wishing to establish factories in the region. Bahrain's inducements to foreign investment had little competition, because the country was considered a tax haven. Apart from taxes on petroleum-related companies, there were no taxes on corporate profits or individual earnings.[14] Thus, although the Bahraini stock exchange did not open as promised throughout 1988, the island's economy was among the freest in the Arab world.

SOCIAL AFFAIRS

Another problem hanging over Bahraini society was the growing number of unemployed. They were mostly members of the Bahraini working class — estimated at 80,000 people — who were unable to become landlords or businessmen. The possibility that this number would double by the end of the century became all the more alarming in view of the delicate demographic balance in which a Shi'i majority was relatively disadvantaged. Government efforts to create new jobs by creating new industries did not keep up with the annual entry of 4,000 school-leavers into the work force.[15] The solution was sought in stepping up Bahrainization. As a whole, foreigners, mostly non-Arabs, were about 32% of Bahrain's estimated 434,000 population.[16] Their expertise was mostly sought by the private sector, such as downstream industries, computers, and medicine. The government made concerted efforts to reduce their number; stringent measures to monitor the foreign labor force were introduced in 1988. Posts were offered to foreign nationals only when Bahrainis could not fill them. Concurrently, there was a marked increase in training schemes for young Bahrainis.[17] But since the pace of Bahrainization has been slow, dependence on foreign expertise will prevail for some time to come.

On a different level, the government introduced a death penalty for drug trafficking because of the growing number of drug addicts. Other measures, such as education and rehabilitation schemes, were stepped up.[18]

FOREIGN AFFAIRS

REGIONAL POLITICS

Bahrain greeted the cease-fire in the Gulf War with great satisfaction. The war's sociopolitical ramifications were feared more than its economic effects. The demographic fact that about 72% of its population belonged to the Shi'i community plus a renewed Iranian claim to its territory made Bahrain the first likely target among the GCC states of Khomeyni-like agitation. Intense Iranian subversive activity aimed to undermine the Bahraini political strùcture; in 1981 and 1987 attempts were made to topple the Al Khalifa ruling family (for details see *MECS* 1981–82, pp. 490–92). Bahrain could not ignore Iranian hostility; while calling on both sides in the conflict to stop the fighting and support the UN cease-fire resolution, Bahrain let it be understood that it supported Iraq. Together with Saudi Arabia and Kuwait, it formed the pro-Iraqi faction in the GCC. At the risk of further arousing Iranian ire, Bahrain came to rely more heavily on the US naval presence in the Gulf, to the extent of allowing the US Navy to set up headquarters on its territory.

The Bahraini tilt toward Iraq became more evident in 1988, especially as the latter seemed to be gaining the upper hand in the war. The finger was pointed at Iran as the party responsible for the ongoing fighting. "The war will continue," the Bahraini heir apparent, Shaykh Hamad Ibn 'Isa Al Khalifa, said "until the Iranian leadership realizes the cost of the war and is convinced that there is no reason for it to continue."[19] Accordingly, every Iranian hostile act toward a GCC state, such as the hijacking of the Kuwaiti airliner in March and the attack on the UAE's Mubarak offshore oil field in April, drew a Bahraini denunciation. But the most clear-cut expression of Bahraini policy was the June visit of Defense Minister Shaykh Khalifa Ibn Ḥamad Al Khalifa to Shalamchah and Faw, following their occupation by Iraq.[20] Bahraini-Iranian relations deteriorated so much that Prime Minister Shaykh Khalifa Ibn Salman Al Khalifa saw fit to warn Tehran that other states might follow Saudi Arabia's lead in cutting ties with Iran if tension increased.[21]

Not surprisingly then, Bahrain greeted the cease-fire with great relief, since it allayed its fear of Iranian-inspired subversion or even of a military attack. Nevertheless, Bahraini suspicions were on line when demanding an Iranian concession for a comprehensive peace pact, "otherwise the Iranian decision might be interpreted differently, as though its ambition is to achieve a cease-fire, which is exposed to escalations and wars."[22] This demand, which was made by the Bahraini heir apparent, was a prerequisite for a Bahraini-Iranian *rapprochement.* "Now that the war has stopped," Bahrain's prime minister asserted, "it has become necessary to establish other relations with Iran, relations that are far removed from tension."[23] The foreign ministers of both countries met in New York in September to discuss how the cease-fire decision was to be implemented. In November, Iranian Deputy Foreign Minister Muhammad 'Ali Besharati led a delegation to Bahrain and discussed ways of improving relations. An Iranian diplomat was appointed chargé d'affaires in Bahrain, a position hitherto held by a government official.[24]

Bahraini-Iraqi relations remained close in the postwar era; visits were exchanged by senior officials. However, fear of Iraq's growing power pushed Bahrain to remind Iraq of Bahrain's unreserved support during the war: "Iraq triumphed," the Bahraini prime minister stressed, "and we cooperated with it and helped it achieve this victory....Iraq will not forget its brothers' assistance."[25]

Bahraini hopes for a more complete integration within the GCC were expressed, especially on the eve of the ninth GCC summit to be held on the island in December. "The general feeling among us," the Bahraini prime minister asserted, "is that we ought to make ourselves felt as a monolithic force rather than a fragmented entity."[26] Accordingly, efforts were made to clear the atmosphere before the summit. The

Qatari-Bahraini dispute (see chapter on Qatar), for example, was handled prudently and Shaykh 'Isa went as far as to assert that "there are no unresolved disagreements between Bahrain and Qatar. We are one country bound by love and sincerity and have common interests."[27]

BAHRAIN AND INTER-ARAB AFFAIRS

Bahrain continued to advocate Arab solidarity as an "essential basis for all joint Arab action." It repeatedly urged all Arab countries to make efforts to solve problems, such as the Lebanese crisis and the Palestinian issue.

Bahrain praised the Palestinian uprising in the West Bank and Gaza, asserting the Bahraini people's support for it. Financial and moral assistance was given to the Palestinian cause; funds were to be raised through a variety of activities such as savings accounts opened in Bahraini banks; and 12 May was announced as "Palestine Day."[28] But Bahraini support reached its peak at the end of the year with the recognition of the newly announced Palestinian state as a "step toward realizing the Palestinian dream of a state, identity, and flag" and the upgrading of the PLO office in Manama to ambassadorial level.[29]

Bahrain maintained its long-standing relations with the moderate elements in the Arab world, represented by the Maghrib states and Jordan. But most notable were the Bahraini ties with Egypt, which were ostensibly renewed following the 1987 Amman summit, but in reality had never ceased to exist. "Egypt is always in our hearts and we are always with Egypt," Shaykh 'Isa asserted, adding: "Throughout our history, intimate and cordial relations never ceased. We do not forget that the Arab nation, especially Bahrain, is indebted to Egypt. We are educated by Egyptians and our sons were educated at Egyptian universities."[30] The newly formalized links were deepened and confirmed by an exchange of visits by top officials. During his tour of the region in January (see chapter on Egypt), Egyptian President Husni Mubarak met the Bahraini heir apparent in Manama and discussed problems of regional security.[31] Shaykh Hamad paid a reciprocal visit in February, during which he inspected an Egyptian missile plant.[32] Referring to the military aspect of Bahraini-Egyptian relations, Shaykh 'Isa said: "I think we are noticing a concept in cooperation in arms manufacture between Egypt and Arab countries that will result in a joint Arab armament industry."[33] Later in the year, it was reported that Bahraini security teams were to train in Egyptian police schools.[34] Other facets of their relations were cooperation agreements in the fields of economy, information, and culture.

INTERNATIONAL POLITICS

RELATIONS WITH THE UNITED STATES

The Bahraini pro-American stance was conspicuously demonstrated in 1988; Bahrain was the most vocal supporter of the US presence in the Gulf. "We would have liked more, of course," Shaykh 'Isa commented following a US retaliatory attack on Iranian facilities in April (for details, see chapter on Gulf War), "America should stand strong. If they [the Iranians] hit you with one bullet, you should hit them with a hundred," he said.[35] The pro-American policy was stressed all the more following the shooting down of an Iranian civil airliner by a US warship in July (see chapter on Gulf War). "In its capacity as a superpower, the US had enough moral courage to admit that the incident occurred by mistake," the Bahraini daily *Akhbar al-Khalij* commented in an editorial.[36] Bahrain avoided a confrontation with the US on the Israeli-Arab conflict. Bahraini Minister of Information Tariq 'Abd al-Rahman al-Mu'ayyad was of the opinion that "we should not push the Americans to choose between us and the Israelis, because they will choose the Israelis."[37]

As part of its relations with the US, Bahrain provided the US Regional Administration Support Unit with a base, with ship repair and medical facilities. Bahrain, in return, received highly sophisticated weapons, such as F-16 fighter jets. Little wonder then that Bahrain felt offended when its request for *Stinger* missiles was followed by lengthy debates in Congress before approval. "The debate on the *Stingers*," al-Mu'ayyad lamented, "was a great shock to everyone here, especially after all we have done."[38] Nonetheless, Bahrain's position as a valuable US ally was confirmed by several visits of top US officials to the island. Defense Secretary Frank Carlucci came twice in January and in December and conferred with Bahraini officials. Assistant Secretary for Near-Eastern and South-Asian Affairs Richard Murphy visited Bahrain in June.

RELATIONS WITH BRITAIN

Bahraini-British relations were strengthened in 1988 by exchange visits of officials. Prime Minister Margaret Thatcher stopped over in Bahrain on her way to the Far East in July and conferred with the heir apparent and with the defense minister. The major topics discussed concerned Gulf security, such as the implementation of the cease-fire resolution.[39] Shaykh Hamad paid a return visit in September, meeting with Thatcher and top security officials, such as Minister of State for Defense Procurement Lord Trefgarne.

RELATIONS WITH THE SOVIET UNION AND CHINA

Bahrain, hitherto a firm opponent of communism, came closer to establishing ties with the USSR. The shift in its foreign policy was confirmed in June, when in the first official Bahrain-USSR diplomatic contact, Ernest Zverev, Moscow's ambassador to Kuwait, arrived in Bahrain and conferred with Shaykh 'Isa; the Bahraini ruler was briefed about Soviet foreign policy guidelines.[40] Referring to the possibility of establishing relations, the Foreign Minister Muhammad Ibn Mubarak Al Khalifa asserted that the opening of embassies was "only a matter of time."[41] Indications of a Bahrain-USSR economic *rapprochement* were also seen, when Bahrain invited Eastern Bloc states to a trade fair scheduled to take place at the beginning of 1989.[42]

Economic ties with the People's Republic of China (PRC) also seemed to be a prelude to establishing full diplomatic relations. Yang Fuchang, the director of the West Asian and North African Affairs Department of the PRC Ministry of Foreign Affairs, visited Bahrain in April and met the prime minister with whom he reviewed the prospects of cooperation in the economic and trade fields.[43] A Bahraini trade mission was scheduled to be stationed in the PRC in 1989.[44]

NOTES

For the place and frequency of publications cited here, and for the full name of the publication, news agency, radio station, or monitoring service where an abbreviation is used, please see "List of Sources." Only in the case of more than one publication bearing the same name is the place of publication noted here.

1. *Al-Dustur,* London, 11 January; *al-Muharrir,* 27 February; *Ma'ariv,* 29 March 1988.
2. *Al-Dustur,* London, 11 January 1988.
3. *Al-Mustaqbal,* 4 June 1988.
4. R. Tehran, 2, 5 January — SWB, 5, 7 January 1988.
5. AFP, 13 January 1988.
6. *Al-Siyasa,* Kuwait, 4–5 February; *al-Majalla,* 7 June 1988.
7. *Al-Majalla,* 7 June; *al-Bayan,* Dubai, 19 July; *CR,* Bahrain, 1988.
8. GNA, 31 March — DR, 1 April; *al-Siyasa,* Kuwait, 2 April 1988.
9. *FT,* 6 July 1988.
10. *FT,* 27 June, 6 July; *CR,* Bahrain, No. 3, 1988.
11. *FT,* 7 June 1988.
12. *Al-Siyasa,* Kuwait, 30 January; *The Gulf States,* 7 March 1988.
13. *MEER,* 5 April 1988.
14. *MEER,* February 1989.
15. *FT,* 6 July 1988.
16. *CR,* Bahrain, No. 4, 1988.
17. *CR,* Bahrain, Nos. 2, 4, 1988.
18. *CR,* Bahrain, No. 3, 1988.
19. *AT,* 17 April 1988.
20. *CR,* Bahrain, No. 3, 1988.
21. *Khaleej Times,* 2 May 1988.
22. *Al-Siyasa,* Kuwait, 6 August 1988.
23. The Bahraini prime minister to *al-Siyasa,* Kuwait, 14 December 1988.
24. *Kayhan,* 26 October — SWB, 3 November 1988.
25. The Bahraini prime minister to *al-Siyasa,* Kuwait, 14 December 1988.
26. Ibid.
27. Shaykh 'Isa to *Akhbar al-Yawm,* 3 December 1988.
28. *Al-Siyasa,* Kuwait, 6 April, 10 May 1988.
29. GNA, 15 November — DR, 16 November; Shaykh 'Isa to *Akhbar al-Yawm,* 3 December 1988; GNA, 3 January — DR, 4 January 1989.
30. Shaykh 'Isa to *Akhbar al-Yawm,* 3 December 1988.
31. GNA, 13 January — DR, 13 January 1988.
32. *Al-Sharq al-Awsat,* 8 February 1988.
33. Shaykh 'Isa to *Akhbar al-Khalij* as quoted by *AT,* 5 December 1988.
34. *Al-Siyasa,* Kuwait, 3 April 1988.
35. *NYT,* 22 April 1988.
36. GNA, 4 July — DR, 5 July 1988.
37. *NYT,* 24 February 1988.
38. *NYT,* 22 April 1988.
39. GNA, 30 July — DR, 1 August 1988.
40. *Al-Anba,* Kuwait, 2 July; *CR,* Bahrain, No. 3, 1988.
41. *Al-Usbu' al-'Arabi,* 22 August 1988.
42. *Al-Siyasa,* Kuwait, 14 December 1988.
43. GNA, 5 April — DR, 7 April; *al-Bayan,* 24 April 1988.
44. *CR,* Bahrain, No. 4, 1988.

Kuwait

JOSEPH KOSTINER

In 1988, Kuwait continued to concentrate its main efforts on offsetting the effects of the Iraqi-Iranian War on its economy and the welfare of its population. Kuwait had to cope with a variety of threats, ranging from an invasion of Iranian forces, and firing on Kuwaiti tankers in the Gulf to terrorist attacks on Kuwaiti targets. Domestic difficulties compounded the threats emanating from the war: economic recession and a considerable Shi'i minority susceptible to Iranian anti-Kuwaiti propaganda.

Kuwaiti leaders were, therefore, careful to devise policies to meet the different challenges. Internally, the government sought to increase its control over society by censoring the press, overseeing the traffic of foreigners to and from Kuwait, improving public administration, and putting the country's security forces on full alert. Kuwaiti leaders also made particular efforts to improve the economy and while the state budget still showed a deficit, the government focused on tax collection, recruitment of private investors, and on increasing profits from the oil and petrochemical industries.

In foreign affairs, the government continued to rely on the US naval vessels in the Gulf both to protect Kuwaiti tankers through reflagging and to constitute a deterrence against possible Iranian aggression. Kuwait further boosted its security by purchasing sophisticated weapons from several states; it sought to maintain good relations with both superpowers by taking advantage of their sale of arms and military capacity. But it was careful to avoid subservience to and overdependence on the superpowers, particularly the US. Kuwait also used diplomacy to prevent potential opponents, particularly Iran, from taking hostile action against it. Consequently, Kuwait developed complicated relations with Iran involving periods of hostility and *rapprochement*. At the same time Kuwaiti leaders tried to maintain cordial relations with all Arab parties by emphasizing their state's contribution to Arab solidarity. Kuwait's efforts to guarantee its security while maintaining its independence from both foes and supporters characterized its foreign policy in 1988.

INTERNAL AFFAIRS

THE POLITICS OF CONTINUOUS CONTROL

ADMINISTRATIVE REFORMS

Kuwait was preoccupied in 1988, as in earlier years, with economic and security problems resulting from the Iraqi-Iranian War and economic recession. In combination, these problems threatened to upset the state's fragile sociopolitical infrastructure: of the 1,834,756 inhabitants only 763,708 (41.62%) were Kuwaiti citizens, and they constituted only 21.9% of the work force.[1] The many foreign workers and the Shi'i minority, estimated at 20% of the population, were regarded by the Kuwaiti authorities as potential sources of instability. Grave socioeconomic gaps, dissatisfaction of the professional groups and students with the patriarchal rule of the al-Sabah dynasty, and administrative inefficiency[2] added to potential instability. The prolonged war and economic recession provided fertile ground in which these difficulties could generate serious crises. The Iranian-initiated terrorism and anti-Kuwait incitement, combined with redundancy among the unskilled work force and alienation of the business community were viewed as a potential powder keg by the government. It was, therefore, determined to improve the performance of the government bureaucracy and to tighten political control over society.

Changes at the top administrative level were given high priority. The daily newspapers also urged the government to improve its own performance and cut the number of senior, but inefficient, administators in the Departments of Health and Justice.[3] Personnel changes were made in January, when the ministers of interior and defense, of information and social affairs swapped portfolios. The ministers for communications and planning, and the state minister for municipal affairs, were replaced.[4] (See Appendix.) The calls in the newspapers for improved treatment of the "ordinary citizen"[5] prompted the government to establish a new office, "Serving the Citizens Office" in May.[6] In March the Foreign Ministry was restructured to improve efficiency.[7] A governmental decree in October divided Kuwait into five administrative districts (the city of Kuwait, al-Hawwali, al-Farwaniyya, al-Jahra, and al-Ahmadi) for the sake of improved administration.[8]

Fearing mounting criticism from the resourceful and relatively well-informed Kuwaiti press, the government sought to limit newspapers' autonomy and to harness journalists in support of official policy. The minister of information, culture, and higher education, Jabir Mubarak Ahmad Al Sabah explained that the press should reflect "a wide public interest," and "avoid spoiling the atmosphere of stability" or becoming "a cup of poison" in the service of foreign interests.[9] Although no blatant attempts to curb the press were reported, Mubarak did admit that censorship was sometimes imposed.[10] In June, he announced that a new "publicity and printing law" would be enacted to deal with the press.[11] The immediate response of Kuwaiti journalists, as represented by the columnist of *al-Qabas,* Abu Khalid, stressed the obligation of the press to conform to support the state and to be patriotic.[12]

The government continued in its attempts to purge the country of foreigners without harming Kuwaiti development projects, in which most foreigners were employed. In 1987, 10,068 foreigners were expelled.[13] In 1988, the minister of interior decided that the government would evict any foreigner deemed by the security services to be a threat to security, or who had been convicted of three criminal acts, or of one of "dishonor or dishonesty."[14]

THE OPPOSITION

As in 1987, the main opposition activities were carried out by pro-Iranian, Shi'i groups (see *MECS* 1987, p. 371). There were explosions in and around a warehouse at the end of February.[15] A time bomb exploded near a Saudi airline office on 27 April, injuring one Kuwaiti guard.[16] There was another explosion in a Kuwaiti shopping center, on 17 May, with no injuries.[17] Another explosion hit the front of the Kuwait Airlines' offices, killing the two perpetrators, on 19 May.[18] As in 1987, such activities were the work of both Kuwaitis and foreigners. On 22 February, a 31-year old Kuwaiti, Isma'il Sayyid Hasan Sayyid, was sentenced to three years' imprisonment for handing out leaflets calling for the government to be toppled.[19] Others, such as 'Abbas and Sulayman Zaynal (the former was imprisoned with 10 years' hard labor and the latter released on bail) and Muhammad Ibrahim 'Abbas (released on parole), who had been accused of attempting to attack state security officers,[20] were also Kuwaitis. On the other hand, of three men caught and accused of the bombings in late April and early May, one was described as an Iranian and the two others as Arabs, "citizens of states which do not border on Kuwait."[21] Kuwaiti Hizballah broadcast their calls to Kuwaitis to rise against their rulers from Tehran,[22] calls which echoed Iranian propaganda. There were no signs of a deep-rooted, indigenous Shi'i underground movement. The director-general of the Ministry of Awqaf and Islamic Affairs could, therefore, claim that there was no "extremism in the broad sense of the word" but only "extremist individuals" in Kuwait.[23] The assistant to the director-general of the Ministry of Interior stated that Kuwait was not beset by "networks of terrorism" which often plagued the Western world.[24] The government could therefore be satisfied that its policies prevented terrorism on a grand scale. The end of the Iraqi-Iranian War also caused a decline in the Iranian-initiated terrorism against Kuwait.

ECONOMIC CONDITIONS

The government emphasized the need to improve Kuwait's financial situation, which had deteriorated due to declining oil prices. As set by Opec, Kuwait's oil quota for 1988 was 996,000 barrels per day (b/d), which yielded an estimated revenue of 1,788.8bn. Kuwaiti dinars (KD). The revenue from other economic sectors was estimated at KD265.5m.[25] The budgeted expenditures for 1988 were KD3.194bn. and revenue KD2.054bn., leaving a deficit of KD1.4bn (equivalent to $3.6m.).[26] Minister of Finance Jasim al-Khurafi, nevertheless, made a relatively positive forecast, because in 1987 Kuwait had reduced state expenditure by 12%, improved its balance of payments, and developed petrochemical industries. Taxes brought in KD13.5m., 6% more than estimated. The minister and his aides stressed that the deficit would be covered from Kuwait's reserves, which were estimated at $85bn. and growing.[27] The government also started issuing Treasury bills and bonds for purchase by any institution or private person, whether citizen or resident. Bonds were issued to the amount of $4.5bn., which the government was hoping to raise to cover expenditures.[28] The government further intended to close down the unofficial Kuwaiti stock exchange, "the parallel market" (which replaced the Suq al-Manakh) and transfer its operations to the official Kuwait Stock Exchange in order to increase government control over this institution and to get its hands on additional revenue.[29]

Kuwait's foreign aid budget dropped from £11.6bn. in 1981 to £302m. in 1988,[30] another indication of the government's policy of cutting expenditures.

FOREIGN AFFAIRS

OFFSETTING THREATS OF THE GULF WAR

Located only 12 minutes by flight from the battlefields of the Gulf War, Kuwait was exposed to terrorism initiated by pro-Iranian Shi'i groups in Kuwait and abroad; to Iranian attacks on Kuwait or Kuwaiti vessels in the Gulf; and to a constant Iranian campaign of delegitimization. The onus of defense fell on Kuwaiti foreign policy and a variety of military means.[31]

To defend the country and its vessels against a limited or general attack, Kuwaiti spokesmen commented favorably on the military capability of the Gulf states, incorporated within the GCC, and Kuwaiti armed units took part in GCC maneuvers. Kuwaiti leaders often consulted their Saudi Arabian counterparts on security issues. In the words of Minister of Defense Nawaf al-Ahmad al-Jabir, GCC forces were an "acceptable and successful nucleus for a powerful Gulf army"[32] (see also chapter on the Gulf states). It was, nevertheless, clear to Kuwaiti leaders, that while being a good "nucleus," in size and military experience the GCC army was no match for either the Iranian or Iraqi armies and, at best, it could develop into a force of regional magnitude. Kuwait, therefore relied on the American forces for its immediate defense needs. While the official American mandate was only to protect by reflagging Kuwaiti tankers, the US vessels in effect defended the integrity of Gulf states not involved in the war. The US Navy thus constituted both a deterrence against a major Iranian onslaught and against small-scale attacks on Kuwaiti vessels and facilities. Kuwaiti confidence hinged on the success of the American effort.[33]

Kuwait also relied heavily on Iraqi ability to halt Iranian aggression, and its relations with Iraq seemed cordial. Kuwait hailed Iraq's military "steadfastness" and displayed pride in its successful rebuff of an Iranian attack in January, and the recapture of Majnun and Faw in the spring[34] (see chapter on the Iraqi-Iranian War). Favoring the end ofthe war, the Kuwaiti ruler, Jabir al-Ahmad, sent warmest regards to Iraq's leader, Saddam Husayn, for Iraq's acceptance of a cease-fire in August.[35] Ministers of both states exchanged visits to their respective capitals. Kuwait's assistance to Iraq included free passage of logistics through Kuwaiti territory and an unknown amount of financial aid. The overt aid to Iraq focused on a gift of 125,000 b/d of oil from the former neutral zone along the Kuwaiti-Iraqi border, which was in addition to a similar Saudi contribution — together the annual total was $2bn.[36] Western observers expected that upon termination of the war Iraq would renew its claim to Kuwaiti territory, but this issue was of little significance in 1988.

Kuwait also used diplomacy to indicate to Iran that it had not embarked on an anti-Iranian policy. Kuwait was, therefore, determined to underline that it was not a party to the war. "We are playing the role of a mediator between Iraq and Iran and we have never taken sides with one Islamic country against another," the Kuwaiti ambassador in Washington, Sa'ud Nasir Al Sabah, declared.[37] Kuwaiti aid to Iraq, which was criticized by Iran, was described by State Minister for Foreign Affairs Sa'ud Muhammad al-'Usaymi as routine foreign aid. "We are giving aid to sixty-four Third World countries. Why not Iraq?"[38] he asked. Kuwait also rejected as a "cruel lie" Tehran's allegation that the Kuwaiti island of Bubiyan had been given to Iraq for military use.[39] Kuwait was careful to stress that reflagging had not made it subservient to the US. Sa'ud Nasir and 'Usaymi explained that it had been Washington's own decision to establish a presence in the Gulf waters; this presence concerned many states and Kuwait's request had been limited to reregistration of its ships under the American flag.[40] 'Usyami stated that Kuwait was interested in a dialogue with Iran, as part of a "constructive interaction" with Tehran.[41] Kuwait occasionally criticized Iran, notably after an Iranian attack on Kuwaiti or GCC facilities, or to show its identification with Saudi Arabia's decision to cut diplomatic relations with Tehran in May. Kuwaiti papers then stressed that "appeasement" of Iran had proved useless,[42] but Kuwait did not follow in Saudi footsteps, and was careful to maintain its ties with Iran intact.

How effective was Kuwait's combined defense strategy? Iran apparently ceased its attacks on Kuwaiti tankers, which must have persuaded Kuwaiti leaders that reflagging was a major strategic asset.[43] Iran, however, made several small-scale attacks on Kuwaiti facilities. A *Silkworm* missile was launched at, but missed, an onshore Kuwaiti oil field in December 1987.[44] Iranian warships fired on Bubiyan island in late March 1988, injuring two Kuwaiti soldiers.[45] An Iranian *Scud* missile landed near the al-Warfah oil field in late April.[46] Iran was probably involved in the hijacking of the Kuwaiti airliner in May (see below) and in acts of terrorism (see above). Unable to stop Iranian aggression completely, Kuwait succeeded in reducing its scope and damage.

Kuwait judged that the termination of the war would bring Iran to cease its aggression and help increase Kuwait's security. Iran was, therefore, urged over the year to show "restraint" and be "realistic."[47] Tehran's acceptance of UN Resolution 598, calling for a cease-fire, was seen as indicating Iran's decision to stop the war and described by *al-Siyasa*'s editor, Ahmad Jarallah, as a "brave" step which "reflects a high level of political courage."[48] Kuwait continued to criticize Tehran for its evasive conduct during the peace negotiations with Iraq in Geneva,[49] but it was evident that Iran's decision to end the war was welcomed by Kuwaiti leaders and eased their contacts with Tehran.

Kuwait was also interested in maintaining open bilateral relations with Iran. While Iran often criticized Kuwait's "subservience" to Iraq and the US, and attacked Kuwaiti facilities, it was also careful to maintain a dialogue with Kuwait, both via Syria and directly. This led Kuwait to send two officials to Tehran to retrieve its legation building, which had been abandoned after a diplomatic quarrel with Tehran following an Iranian attack on Kuwait in September 1987.[50] In September 1988, after the cease-fire had been declared, Kuwait sent a three-man delegation to Tehran to reestablish its embassy. "We want to forget the past," 'Usaymi declared.[51] Iranian Foreign Minister 'Ali Akbar Velayati visited Kuwait in early October, in what was described as a "courtesy visit."[52]

RESPONDING TO THE KUWAITI AIRLINER HIJACKING

On 5 April, a Kuwaiti airliner *en route* from Thailand to Kuwait was hijacked to Mashhad in Iran. The hijackers, probably pro-Iranian Lebanese Shi'is of Hizballah, demanded the release from a Kuwaiti prison of 17 Shi'i terrorists responsible for bombings in Kuwait in December 1983 in return for freeing the plane and its passengers. The hijackers threatened to blow up the airliner with its passengers if their demands were rejected. The presence of several members of the Kuwaiti royal family on board, distant relatives of the ruler, added to the pressure on Kuwait. The Kuwaiti authorities, through the mediation of third parties, negotiated with the hijackers when they landed in Mashhad and Larnaca (10–14 April) and in Algiers (14–19 April) (see chapter on armed operations). The Kuwaiti response to the hijacking reflected a twofold strategy: it did not compromise Kuwait's national security by meeting the demands of enemies but also showed readiness to use flexible tactics in order to bring the affair to a peaceful end.

Hence, Kuwait's Cabinet declared on the first day of the crisis that it would neither succumb to "blackmail" nor accept the hijackers' demands.[53] In the following days, Kuwait's media kept praising Kuwaiti firmness.[54] But the Kuwaiti negotiating teams, dispatched to where the plane came down, exercised a number of options. In Mashhad, the possibility of Iranian forces storming the plane was considered; but according to the Kuwaiti version, Iran refused.[55] On the other hand, the Cabinet then declared that short of releasing the 17 terrorists, it would be ready to satisfy the hijackers' other demands.[56] When the plane was in Larnaca, Kuwait empowered a PLO team led by the organization's chairman, Yasir 'Arafat, to negotiate the release of some of the passengers. But the assassination of two Kuwaitis on board stiffened the Kuwaiti position on the release of prisoners. Since Cyprus opposed storming the plane, Kuwait was willing to have it leave for Algiers, where the negotiations would be continued.[57] When the hijacked plane reached Algiers, the Algerian negotiating team proposed the release of the crew and remaining passengers in return for the release of the hijackers. The Kuwaiti team at first seemed reluctant to agree but as this appeared to be the only solution, it accepted on 18 April. Passengers were freed, and the hijackers allowed to go off scot-free.[58] Kuwaiti papers hailed the government's success in preventing the release of the 17 terrorists as a great triumph.[59]

OTHER REGIONAL ISSUES

REINFORCEMENT OF ARAB SOLIDARITY: POLICY PRINCIPLES

Kuwait sought to contribute to the trend toward Arab solidarity. In the eyes of the Kuwaiti leadership, only a unified Arab system could cope with the Arab nation's difficulties. Underlying this view were two basic conceptions, one, that for a state as small and vulnerable as Kuwait, the Arab world had to be kept friendly and at peace; and two, that by promoting a position as prestigious in Arab public opinion as Arab solidarity, Kuwait would strengthen its relations with other Arab states by getting them to adopt policies favorable to Kuwait or to issues Kuwait was concerned about.

Four major principles characterized Kuwait's policy toward Arab solidarity: (1) *Objection to parties deviating from the Arab mainstream and thereby obstructing overall stability.* Kuwait favored traditional Arab nationalism and was particularly frustrated by Islamic fundamentalist or ethnic groups with extremist particularist policies. In the words of an editorial in the daily *al-Anba*: "The Kuwaitis are an inextricable part of the Arab world...political sectarianism turns people into wild animals...we refuse to recognize any sectarian or religious privileges. Arabism is the solution. National unity is made up of loyalty to the nation."[60]

(2) *Support of policies accepted by the entire Arab world.* Kuwait supported a political solution to the Arab-Israeli conflict, rather than the rejectionist militant attitude. Ahmad Jarallah noted that the peace strategy articulated by PLO leader Yasir 'Arafat exposed Israel's intransigence and its inability to be absorbed into the Middle East, which would lead to its disappearance from the globe.[61] Other papers reiterated common Arab perceptions, that the Jews distorted the Bible to fabricate a right over Palestine,[62] and that Israeli tourists were dispatched to Egypt to spy and to smuggle drugs and money.[63] Kuwait also strongly supported the effort to return Egypt to the Arab League, which gathered momentum in 1988. "It is necessary to return Egypt to the Arab League," an editorial in *al-Ra'y al-'Amm* said,[64] explaining that the League as symbol of Arab unity, could not perform its duty without Egypt.

(3) *Taking action toward unity.* Kuwait helped convene the Arab summit in Algiers in June, maintained a dialogue with Syria to mediate the Lebanese dispute and the

Iraqi-Iranian War, and hosted the Arab Economists' Union's conference in February.[65] Kuwait also sought to mediate in the Egyptian-Libyan dispute (see chapter on Egypt).

(4) *Using financial aid to prove its commitment to Arab solidarity.* The amounts of foreign aid were considerably curtailed (see above) and *al-Ra'y al-'Amm* declared in March that "the Gulf states are not a milk cow...[they] are now in need of aid, because the ongoing Gulf War has turned them into confrontation states."[66] But Kuwait used government aid, private contributions, and investment in Arab states by Kuwaiti-based firms to advance its policy of cooperation with other Arab parties.

BILATERAL RELATIONS WITH ARAB PARTIES

Following the renewal of its diplomatic relations with Egypt (see *MECS* 1987, pp. 374–75), Kuwait saw the many advantages in this relationship and strove to develop manifold cooperation with Cairo. Egyptian Minister of Defense 'Abd al-Halim Abu Ghazala visited Kuwait in December 1987 "to put a joint venture to support Kuwait's national security."[67] Egyptian President Husni Mubarak visited Kuwait in January 1988 and reiterated Egypt's commitment to the Arab Defense Pact.[68] These two visits might have hinted at Egyptian readiness to help Kuwait against Iranian aggression, but there were no reports of additional strategic cooperation with Egypt (see chapter on Egypt). More specific military collaboration was reported in August, when Kuwait purchased from Egypt 100 armored personnel carriers and an integrated air defense system.[69] Minister of Interior Salih Al Sabah visited Egypt in January to discuss fighting drug smuggling and terrorism.[70] In January, Minister of Finance al-Khurafi alluded to the spectrum of economic contacts with Egypt by announcing that all Kuwaiti investments in Egypt totaled $3,500m.[71] There were reports that the Kuwaiti-based Arab Development Fund planned to invest in an Egyptian defense project based in Rashid and in Egypt's pharmaceutical industry (see also chapter on Egypt).[72]

Kuwait was a staunch supporter of the Palestinians. The ruler, Jabir al-Ahmad, described the uprising in the West Bank and the Gaza Strip as "heroism which renders us speechless." A Palestinian acknowledgment of Kuwait's assistance, he noted, "will do us honor."[73] Kuwait supported the Palestinians mainly in the form of financial aid, which different public organizations and unions provided, and in campaigns promoted by the major newspapers.[74] Kuwait also gave aid to specific institutions such as Al-Maqasid Hospital in East Jerusalem, to individuals such as the widow and sons of the PLO leader, Khalil al-Wazir.[75] (For details about his assassination, see chapter on armed operations.)

In addition to financial assistance, Kuwait also supported the PLO's political initiatives in 1988. Bassam Abu Sharif's document of June, calling for a two-state solution in historic Palestine (see chapter on the Palestine Liberation Organization), received mixed reactions. While *al-Siyasa* and the Islamic-revivalist (Sunni) *al-Mujtama'* criticized the document as a catalyst for precipitating strife within the Palestinian camp and as flirtation with Zionism and the West, *al-Ra'y al-'Amm* considered the document a trial balloon to test Arab and American responses.[76] But in the following weeks, the PLO's advocacy of a political solution gained growing support in Kuwait. An article by the columnist Abu al-Lutuf in *al-Anba* in July criticized the rejectionist PLO faction of Abu Musa as "a snake's head," which sought to undermine 'Arafat's peaceful attitude and disregarded the Palestinian refugees in

Lebanon.[77] The Palestinian National Council's declaration in November of an independent Palestinian state alongside Israel was described by the *Arab Times* as being "in line with the present conditions prevailing in the world arena," which would expose Israel's intransigence.[78] Kuwait also demanded that the US begin a dialogue with the PLO and criticized the American decision to deny 'Arafat a visa to go to New York and address the UN General Assembly in November (see chapter on the United States and the Middle East).[79] PLO leaders acknowledged Kuwait's support and friendship. 'Arafat often visited Kuwait and both he and Salah Khalaf (Abu Iyyad) expressed their gratitude to the Kuwaiti people.[80]

Kuwait also provided humanitarian aid to the Lebanese people; in August it was reported that 375,000 families were enjoying Kuwaiti aid.[81] While Kuwaiti financial help to Syria was reduced to an unknown extent, Kuwait's political ties with Damascus were intensive, focusing on Lebanon, the Gulf War, and the PLO's position. Foreign Minister Sabah al-Ahmad visited Syria in July and Syrian Foreign Minister Faruq al-Shar' visited Kuwait in October.[82] King Husayn of Jordan visited Kuwait in March and November,[83] to discuss Kuwaiti aid to Jordan and other ME questions.

RELATIONS WITH THE SUPERPOWERS AND EUROPEAN STATES

Kuwait's declared policy toward the superpowers was based, in the words of its ambassador to Washington, Sa'ud Nasir, on "equilibrium." He explained that Kuwait approached both superpowers to reflag Kuwaiti tankers, to use their influence to terminate the Gulf War, or to acquire arms.[84] As a small state surrounded by different regional powers and affected by the two superpowers' interests in the Gulf, Kuwait's foreign policy had to consider the interests of both blocs. However, it was evident that Kuwait did not regard its relations with each of the superpowers as cut from the same cloth. It considered the US a supreme strategic defender and a major source of arms, but viewed the Soviet Union as a card to play against the US to coax Washington into a position favorable to Kuwait (that is how it enticed the US into reflagging) and as a superpower whose support was necessary to settle regional problems.

Kuwait's relations with the US in 1988 revolved around the continuation of reflagging, arms sales, and policy differences in the ME.

Continuation of reflagging. Kuwait's spokesmen were firm that the American armada, which supported the reflagging operation, was in the Gulf as a result of an American decision to advance American interests; Kuwait was only interested in "reregistering" 11 of its ships under the American flag and originally favored the presence of an international peacekeeping force in the Gulf.[85] Kuwait reiterated this line to avoid Iran's or the Soviet Union's provocation by displaying too obvious a dependence on the US. Kuwaiti leaders were also careful not to undertake to give the US forces a military base. Nevertheless, Kuwait in fact enjoyed the protection of the US naval umbrella, which, by August 1988, had safely escorted 76 convoys across the Gulf.[86] During Secretary of Defense Frank Carlucci's visit to Kuwait in January, he also made it clear that "his hosts" were satisfied with reflagging. When Kuwaiti Prime Minister Sa'd 'Abdallah Al Sabah visited Washington in July, he repeated his "deep appreciation of the reflagging."[87] *The Washington Post* estimated that the American naval forces were "a bulwark against Iranian aggression," whose benefit exceeded that of safeguarding the Kuwaiti oil flow.[88] Kuwait, therefore, did not hasten to terminate the reflagging. Washington announced its readiness to reduce the size of the

American task force in the Gulf after the announcement of the cease-fire in August;[89] but Kuwait waited until December to declare that "now that the reasons for reflagging are no longer there," there was no further ground for reflagging.[90]

Arms sales. US Under Secretary of State Richard Murphy told Congress in May that the Administration intended selling Kuwait a $1.9bn. package of sophisticated arms that included 40 F-18 aircraft, 300 *Maverick* air-to-ground missiles, 900 laser-guided bombs, 200 cluster bombs, and 660 tactical missiles.[91] Fearing that these weapons might be used against Israel, Congress did not initially endorse the deal. The visit of Sa‘d ‘Abdallah in July sparked off a campaign by Kuwaiti spokesmen and American leaders to legitimize the sale. Secretary of State George Shultz reiterated Kuwait's friendship with the West and its determination to fight terrorism.[92] Sa‘ud Nasir and a number of American officials pointed out the financial benefits to the US of the sale, implying that Kuwait had other purchasing avenues; a small-scale arms deal concluded with the Soviet Union prior to Sa‘d ‘Abdallah's visit to Washington (see below) exemplified the implied threat.[93] A similar predicament with Congress over a US-Saudi deal, which had led Saudi Arabia to purchase *Tornado* aircraft from Britain (see chapter on Saudi Arabia) induced even President Reagan to declare his determination to fight for the successful conclusion of the sale.[94]

Hence, in early August a compromise was reached which facilitated the sale. As both Kuwait and the US objected to excluding some of the weapons contemplated for sale, it was agreed that Kuwait would receive *Maverick* missiles of the G-type rather than the D, which were designed to be used against seaborne targets and bunkers rather than tanks, and F-18 aircraft without an extra refueling capability. The entire package would be delivered in 1994.[95] With the weapons' effectiveness against Israel having been curtailed, Congress endorsed the deal on 5 August and the Kuwaiti Government three days later. Kuwaiti papers insisted that the government had not "compromised" and had only endorsed a "slight modification" to the original deal.[96] Both Kuwait and the US were apparently satisfied.

Different views on Middle East issues. Despite the strategic cooperation between the two countries, differences of opinion concerning a variety of regional issues demonstrated the ideological and conceptual gap between Kuwait and the US. Kuwait frequently criticized US policy toward Israel, calling it too lenient and lopsided in Israel's favor. Kuwait regarded US policy as incapable of stopping Israel's "madness" in the occupied territories and therefore of putting its own relations in the Arab world to the test.[97] The American criticism of Iraq's use of poison gas against the Kurds was regarded as hypocritical and unjust, because the US itself had used nuclear weapons.[98] But these differences did not develop into major political crises.

Kuwait's relations with the Soviet Union reflected its growing appreciation of Moscow's role in the Gulf region and the Kuwaiti leader's traditional fears of Soviet expansionism. Kuwait maintained a continuous dialogue with Moscow over peace and stability in the Gulf, as was evident in the visit of a special envoy, Oleg Grinevsky to Kuwait in February, and in articles and statements in each other's media. Grinevsky emphasized Moscow's support of UN Security Council Resolution 598, and the Soviet government paper, *Izvestiia*, noted Kuwait's vulnerability and interest in a dialogue with Moscow.[99] Kuwait valued Moscow's potential influence with both Iran and Iraq, the Soviet interest in regional stability, Moscow's call for an international peace force in the Gulf, and its readiness to pull out of Afghanistan.[100] But Kuwait also suspected that these positions were aimed at befriending Iran and at "colonizing the region once again." Kuwait was particularly dissatisfied with the Soviet abstention in the vote on imposing an arms embargo on Iran.[101] Kuwait also contravened Soviet interests by maintaining strategic cooperation with the US, by relying on American reflagging, and by assisting the Afghan rebels.[102] Kuwait also criticized Moscow's contacts with Israel.[103]

Kuwait's interest in having the Soviet Union help stabilize the Gulf and its playing the Soviet card to draw Washington to devise policies favorable toward Kuwait enabled it to conclude an arms deal with Moscow in July. Its details are not entirely clear, but, from what is known, it apparently paled in comparison with the deal Kuwait then contemplated with the US. From the Soviets, Kuwait apparently purchased communications equipment, guns,and ground-to-air SAM-8 missiles.[104] No other major military or strategic contacts between the two states were reported.

Kuwait had a tangled relationship with Britain. On the one hand, Kuwait contemplated purchasing military equipment from Britain, reflagged three of its vessels under the British flag,and hosted a visit by British Secretary of Defense George Younger in July.[105] On the other, Kuwait's relations with Britain were overshadowed by the British Government's policy to enforce the antimonopolies law and force Kuwait to sell half of its shares in British Petroleum (BP); Kuwait, which originally held 22% of BP shares, reluctantly accepted the decision.[106]

A Western paper reported that Kuwait would buy 40 *Mirage* 2000, for defensive and offensive use at a cost of FFr.10m.[107] No further details were available. Kuwait's relations with France were cordial; French Minister of Defense Jean-Pierre Chevênement visited Kuwait in September.[108]

APPENDIX: KUWAIT'S CABINET, JANUARY 1988

Prime Minister — Crown Prince Shaykh Sa'd al-'Abdallah al-Sabah.
Deputy Prime Minister and Foreign Minister — Shaykh Sabah al-Ahmad.
Defense Minister — Shaykh Nawwaf al-Ahmad (previously interior minister).
Interior Minister — Shaykh Salim al-Sabah al-Salim (previously defense minister).
Information Minister — Jabir Mubarak al-Ahmad al-Sabah (previously social affairs and labor minister).
Social Affairs and Labor Minister — Shaykh Nasir Muhammad al-Ahmad al-Sabah (previously information minister).
Education Minister and Acting Minister of Higher Education — Anwar 'Abdallah al-Nuri (the higher education is a newly introduced portfolio).
Planning Minister — Dr. 'Abd al-Rahman al-'Awadi.
Public Health Minister — Dr. 'Abdul Razzak Yusuf al-'Abd al-Razzak (new Cabinet member).
Electricity and Water Minister — Dr. Hamud 'Abdallah al-Rughiba (new Cabinet member).
Communications Minister — 'Abdallah 'Abd al-Muhsin al-Sharhan (new Cabinet member).
State Minister for Municipality Affairs — Muhammad 'Abd al-Muhsin al-Rifa'i.
Awqaf and Islamic Affairs Minister — Khalid al-Jasir.
Justice and Legal Affairs Minister — Dari al-'Uthman.
Oil Minister — Shaykh 'Ali al-Khalifa al-Adabi.
Finance Minister — Jasim Muhammad al-Khurafi.
Public Works Minister — 'Abd al-Rahman Ibrahim al-Huti.
Commerce and Industry Minister — Faysal 'Abd al-Razzaq al-Khalid.
Minister of State for Cabinet Affairs — Rashid 'Abd al-'Aziz al- Rashid.
Minister of State for Foreign Affairs — Sa'ud Muhammad al-'Usaymi.
Minister of State for Services Affairs — 'Isa Muhammad al-Mazidi.
Minister of State for Housing Affairs — Nasir al-Rudan.

SOURCE: KUNA, 26 January — DR, 26 January 1988.

NOTES

For the place and frequency of publications cited here, and for the full name of the publication, news agency, radio station, or monitoring service where an abbreviation is used, please see "List of Sources." Only in the case of more than one publication bearing the same name is the place of publication noted here. In this chapter, however, all references to *al-Siyasa* and *al-Anba* are to the Kuwaiti papers of these names.

1. *Al-Siyasa,* 11 September 1988, quotes results of a new census.
2. Milton Viorst, "A Reporter at Large (Kuwait)," *The New Yorker*, 16 May 1988, pp. 43–74.
3. *Al-Ra'y al-'Amm,* 18 February; *al-Siyasa,* 19 February 1988.
4. KUNA, 26 January — DR, 26 January 1988.
5. *Al-Qabas,* 7 March 1988.
6. *Al-Siyasa,* 25 May 1988.
7. *Al-Ittihad,* Abu-Dhabi, 13 March 1988.
8. R. Kuwait, 12 October — DR, 14 October 1988.
9. *AT,* 2 March; *al-Qabas,* 20 May 1988.
10. *Al-Anba,* 4 December 1988.
11. *Kull al-'Arab,* 27 June 1988.
12. *Al-Qabas,* 24 February 1988.
13. *Al-Siyasa,* 9 January 1988.
14. *Al-Qabas,* 10 October 1988.
15. *Al-Siyasa,* 1 March 1988.
16. KUNA, 27 April — DR, 27 April 1988.
17. *Al-Watan,* 10 May 1988.
18. KUNA, 18 May — DR, 19 May 1988.
19. KUNA, 22 February — DR, 22 February 1988.
20. KUNA, 28 June — DR, 29 June 1988.
21. *Al-Watan,* 10 May 1988.
22. R. Tehran, 4 May — DR, 4 May 1988.
23. *Al-Siyasa,* 20 July 1988.
24. *Al-Qabas,* 26 January 1988.
25. *Al-Qabas,* 27 June 1988.
26. *Al-Anba*, 26 April; KUNA, 26 June — DR, 27 June 1988.
27. *Al-Qabas,* 18 September, 2 October; *al-Siyasa,* 25 August 1988.
28. *Al-Ra'y al-'Amm,* 29 February 1988.
29. *MEED,* 3 June 1988.
30. *FT,* 24 October 1988.
31. Cf. KUNA, 27 December — DR, 28 December 1988.
32. Nawaf al-Ahmad interview, *al-Anba,* 20 February 1988.
33. *WP,* 12 January; *FT,* 18 February 1988.
34. KUNA, 14 June — DR, 16 June 1988.
35. *Al-Qabas,* 8 August 1988.
36. *Al-'Alam,* London, 23 January 1988.
37. KUNA, 3 February — DR, 16 February 1988.
38. Quoted by Viorst (see Note 2 above).
39. KUNA, 10 May — DR, 11 May 1988.
40. KUNA, 3 February — DR, 16 February 1988.
41. KUNA, 8 February — DR, 9 February 1988.
42. *Al-Qabas,* 28 April 1988.
43. *FT,* 18 February 1988.
44. KUNA, 9 December — DR, 10 December 1988.
45. KUNA, 30 March — DR, 30 March 1988.
46. KUNA, 20 April — DR, 20 April 1988.
47. Cf. *Al-Ra'y al-'Amm,* 30 April 1988.
48. *AT,* 20 July — DR, 22 July 1988.
49. *Al-Ra'y al-'Amm,* 1 August 1988.
50. *AT,* 23 January — DR, 25 January 1988.

51. *IHT,* 28 September 1988.
52. KUNA, 5 October — DR, 6 October 1988.
53. *Al-Bayan,* Dubai, 7 April — DR, 7 April 1988.
54. Cf. *Al-Ra'y al-'Amm,* 13 April — DR, 14 April 1988.
55. *Al-Siyasa,* 26 April 1988.
56. *Al-Siyasa,* 7 April — DR, 7 April 1988.
57. *IHT,* 13 April; *al-Siyasa,* 16 April 1988.
58. *USIS Report,* 18 April — DR, 19 April 1988.
59. *AT,* 21, 22 April 1988.
60. *Al-Anba,* 24 April 1988.
61. Quoted by *al-Masa,* 10 April 1988.
62. *Al-Watan,* 8 September 1988.
63. *Al-Watan,* 3 November 1988.
64. *Al-Ra'y al-'Amm,* 26 September 1988.
65. KUNA, 6 February — DR, 9 February 1988.
66. *Al-Ra'y al-'Amm,* 25 March 1988.
67. KUNA, 17 December — DR, 17 December 1987.
68. *Al-Qabas,* 12 January 1988.
69. *FT,* 29 June; KUNA, 7 August — DR, 8 August 1988.
70. *Al-Anba,* 22 January 1988.
71. *Al-Qabas,* 8 January 1988.
72. *Al-Ra'y al-'Amm,* 5 October 1988.
73. KUNA, 3 February — DR, 6 February 1988.
74. Cf. *al-Watan,* 5 February; *al-Qabas,* 8 February; *al-Siyasa,* 30 March 1988.
75. *Al-Yaqza,* 19 February; *al-Qabas,* 17 April 1988.
76. *Al-Ra'y al-'Amm,* 19 June; KUNA, 28 June — DR, 28 June 1988.
77. *Al-Anba,* 13 July 1988.
78. *AT,* 16 November 1988.
79. KUNA, 27 June — DR, 28 June; 28 November — DR, 28 November 1988.
80. Cf. KUNA, 1 June — DR, 2 June 1988.
81. *Al-Anwar,* 28 August 1988.
82. KUNA, 5 July, 25 October — DR, 6 July, 26 October 1988.
83. R. Kuwait, 9 March — DR, 10 March; KUNA, 8 November — DR, 14 November 1988.
84. KUNA, 24 March — DR, 25 March 1988.
85. Cf. KUNA, 13 February — DR, 16 February 1988.
86. *NYT,* 10 August 1988.
87. *IHT,* 6 January; *USIS Report,* 12 July 1988.
88. *WP,* 12 January 1988.
89. *NYT,* 10 August 1988.
90. *IHT,* 7 December 1988.
91. *FT,* 11 July; *al-Qabas,* 15 July 1988.
92. *USIS Report,* 12 July 1988.
93. *USIS Report,* 7 July; KUNA, 12 July — DR, 13 July; *NYT,* 14 July 1988.
94. *NYT,* 13 July 1988.
95. *JP, Ha'aretz,* 5 August 1988.
96. DR, 8 August; *al-Watan,* 14 August 1988.
97. Cf. KUNA, 3 February — DR, 4 February 1988.
98. *Al-Anba,* 11 September 1988.
99. *Al-Qabas,* 21 February; *Izvestiia,* 11 May 1988.
100. *Al-Ra'y al-'Amm,* 30 January 1988.
101. Ibid., and 22 October 1988.
102. *Al-Anba,* 27 January 1988.
103. *Al-Ra'y al-'Amm,* 22 October 1988.
104. *JP,* 11 July; *al-Sharq al-Awsat,* 1 August 1988.
105. KUNA, 13 July — DR, 15 July; *FT,* 14 July 1988.
106. *FT,* 10 August; *Al-Ra'y al-'Amm,* 7 October 1988.
107. *Defense News,* 26 July 1988.
108. KUNA, 4 September — DR, 6 September 1988.

Oman

UZI RABI

As 1988 drew to a close the regional environment, after the cease-fire in the Gulf War and in view of expanding Oman-People's Democratic Republic of Yemen (PDRY) relations, seemed much less threatening for Oman. Oman also gained regional and international recognition by virtue of its flexible diplomacy, which enabled it to initiate attempts at mediation between states in confrontation, thus enabling Oman to become more integrated in the Arab and international arenas. Internally, the declaration that 1988 was to be the "Year of Agriculture" again demonstrated Sultan Qabus's gradualist approach to modernization in which development met the Omani people's needs, yet conformed with their traditions.

INTERNAL AFFAIRS

SUBVERSIVE ACTIVITIES

The Omani fear of PDRY-inspired subversion seemed to have dissipated in view of the Omani-PDRY *rapprochement*. However, several Arab magazines reported that the Omani security organs had uncovered a pro-Iranian subversive group — *Haydar al-Ibadiyya* — in February, the first time that an opposition of this sort was known to have acted in the sultanate. The group was led by the head of the Omani Censorship Department, Sabah 'Abd al-Amir, who admitted to having had secret contacts with Iranian officials. Thirty-two other people were arrested, and houses, used as hiding places for ammunition and propaganda pamphlets, were stormed. Efforts were made to apprehend the rest of the group.[1] The fact that most Omani Shi'is were not of Iranian origin and thus less subject to Iranian influence, made the reports more interesting.

ON THE ROAD TO "OMANIZATION"

True to its policy in recent years, the sultanate continued to Omanize its labor force in order to lessen its dependence on foreigners. "The work of a foreigner can never be the same as that of an Omani national," the Omani ruler, Sultan Qabus, explained during his meet-the-people tour. He also advised Omani youth to be less fussy about their place of work.[2] Meanwhile, graduates of secondary schools were being sent to training courses to qualify for employment in ministries and other governmental departments. Plans for Omanization in various fields, which were meant to be fulfilled by 1990, remained: the plan for 90% Omanization in the banking sector;[3] a similar goal was set for the armed forces, where foreigners were still a large number.[4] This was corroborated by Minister of State for Defense Affairs al-Mu'tasim Ibn Hamud Al-Bu Sa'id who stressed the need to Omanize the armed forces, "no matter how high or low the foreigners' positions might be." He stressed, however, that this was not to be done before Omani nationals were properly qualified.[5] The government eased the procedure enabling foreigners' wives to work as part of an attempt to curb the import of labor while at the same time not becoming short of labor.[6] Another social development linked with Omanization, but also significant in itself, was that Omani women were provided with far greater opportunities than women in other GCC states. They were allowed to mix with men in the workplace and even supervised male employees. A prominent example was the reported nomination of the first Omani woman to the post of under secretary; her name and exact title were not stated.[7]

OIL AND ECONOMIC AFFAIRS

The deteriorating oil prices, combined with the relatively high production costs of Omani oil, were particularly alarming for Oman, which found it difficult to cope with a price war. Oman's urging market stability was, therefore, more authentic than that of other oil-producing countries. Not being an Opec member, Oman unilaterally cut back its production by 5%, from 565,000 b/d to 536,750 b/d, in February in an attempt to encourage a similar move by all other producers.[8] The sultanate also participated in the concerted efforts to reduce oil production when serving as Opec/non-Opec go-between. Those efforts failed and when prices slumped further, Oman officially canceled its production cut and joined other producers in giving discounts to lifters. By the end of 1988, Oman reached 600,000 b/d thus surpassing its self-imposed quota.[9] Anticipation of continued low oil revenues cast a shadow over the sultanate's economy. The persisting deficit compelled Oman to maintain budgetary restraint and draw on the international loan market; in August a $100m. loan was concluded with a group of foreign banks.[10] Attempts were made to encourage economic growth, mainly through a stepped-up campaign of exhortation to the private sector. Incentives, such as a five-year income tax exemption, were given to small-scale industrial ventures.[11] The long-awaited establishment in June of the stock exchange, which was scheduled to start functioning in April 1989, was also expected to encourage greater private-sector participation in the economy.[12]

THE "YEAR OF AGRICULTURE"

Sultan Qabus's proclamation that 1988 was the "Year of Agriculture" highlighted the efforts made to reduce dependence on imported foodstuffs, which satisfied about 40% of demand. The reduction was to be achieved mainly through higher productivity in agriculture and fishing, two of Oman's traditional occupations which lost ground when the sultanate switched to an oil-based economy in the 1970s. In 1988, agriculture and fishing accounted for about 3% of Oman's GDP, compared with about 60% in 1965.[13] Increasing local production of foodstuffs also meant reduced dependence on oil revenues, at a time when market fluctuations had negative implications for Oman's economy.

The Fish Company of Oman had been set up at the end of 1987, in order to develop and exploit fisheries with a view to providing employment to nationals and increasing state revenue.[14] Agriculture was added to the school curriculum to encourage young people to seek their livelihoods in this branch of the economy. Fishermen and farmers were given small loans on easy terms for the purchase of equipment. Establishment of fishing villages was also under consideration.[15] This reform necessitated the development and conservation of natural resources, chiefly water. The shortage of water was the most serious problem for Omani agriculture. Desalinated water makes up three quarters of water consumption. The government increased its efforts to modify irrigation systems (*aflaj*) and construct dams to capture and store rainwater runoff.[16] Two leading examples in this area were the water purification projects in Dhofar and the building of the dam at Sohar. The emphasis on agriculture was to be continued through 1989.

FOREIGN AFFAIRS

REGIONAL POLITICS

Throughout the eight-year Gulf War, Oman had to cope with a challenge different from that facing other GCC states. It had not been subject to the same degree of Iranian-sponsored subversive activity as had Kuwait and Bahrain. The Shi'i factor had been less explosive for Oman, since the majority of Omani Shi'is had originated from India, and hence were less subject to Iranian influence. Furthermore, most of Oman's shoreline lies outside the Gulf, which gave Oman an alternative outlet to the sea and afforded its vessels a degree of protection from attack. Its strategic location at the mouth of the Gulf, however, made Oman the only GCC state capable of monitoring the security of the Strait of Hormuz; this countered Iran's threats to blockade the strait. Tension was heightened when Oman joined Western efforts to keep oil flowing freely outside the Gulf. After having overtly supported Iraq in the first phase of the war, Oman now faced Iranian threats of military action and almost clashed with the Iranian Navy. The growing concern for the stability of the Strait of Hormuz, which Oman shares with Iran, and Oman's vulnerability to attack from Iran led Qabus to work out a more even-handed policy.

One of many Omani explanations of this policy was that of Minister of Information 'Abd al-'Aziz al-Rawwas: "It is natural for us to be committed to neutrality. The sultan's view is that the war is destructive and we must use every means of stopping it, regardless of why it erupted or has continued."[17] Within the GCC, Oman (and the UAE) adopted a conciliatory tone toward Iran. It did join the other states in condemning the Iranian raids on Gulf shipping and installations, but objected to practical steps being taken against Iran. In February 1988, for example, Oman objected (within the GCC) to a suggested UN arms embargo as a means of forcing Iran to accept a cease-fire.[18]

With the announcement of the cease-fire in August, Oman was no longer compelled to steer a course between the GCC and Iran; the need to assert neutrality while discreetly assisting the Western efforts to safeguard oil supplies also disappeared. Yet, however relieved Oman was by the prospect of peace, it nevertheless sounded a reservation. Sultan Qabus asserted:

> Officially, the war has ended and we are very pleased with it. However, until a peace agreement is signed...the threat of renewal of war still exists....This caution will never be dissipated unless the forces of the two sides withdraw to international borders, and principles of peace are applied.[19]

Oman regarded the peace process as a bridge to regional stability, which would be achieved only when Iran and Iraq agreed to a peace accord. Accordingly, Oman sought to create a framework in which relations between the two belligerents would become such that they would neither resume the fighting nor attempt to reassert their claims to regional hegemony. Oman reportedly played a leading role in the proposal to create a Gulf security framework embracing GCC states along with Iran and Iraq;[20] the proposal was to be discussed at the December GCC summit in Bahrain, which Oman regarded as crucial to the peace talks between Iran and Iraq. Common economic interests were also considered a basis on which to bring the two belligerents together; Minister of State for Foreign Affairs Yusuf Ibn 'Alawi Ibn 'Abdallah asserted: "These eight GCC states are states with one economic nature. They form an economic region and can constitute an integrated economic axis for the benefit of their people."[21] 'Alawi himself emerged as the leading mediator between the GCC states and Iran; he visited Iran in August and September and held extensive talks with senior Iranian officials. Concurrently, attempts were made to reconcile Saudi Arabia and Iran, which had severed their relations in April 1988. This was apparently the main topic of discussion between King Fahd and Qabus during the latter's visit to the kingdom in December.[22] The Omani ability to remain on good terms with all sides was underlined by Oman acting as a go-between for Iran and the Arabs, as well as between other states. Other subjects that came up during the Omani-Iranian talks were the question of Egyptian prisoners of war held by Iran and the renewal of relations with Western states, such as the US and Britain.[23] The Omani role did not go unnoticed by Iran; on several occasions, Iranian officials praised Oman for having expressed more positive views toward Iran than had other GCC states.[24]

For its part, Oman further cultivated links with Iran. Diplomatic relations, which had been reduced to the level of chargé d'affaires after the outbreak of the Iranian Revolution, were reportedly raised to ambassadorial level. Iran's ambassador to Oman presented his credentials to Qabus in October.[25] Economic ties between the two countries were strengthened as well. Oman's oil minister visited Iran in October for talks on oil policy with his Iranian counterpart. The formation of a joint committee for the expansion of oil and economic cooperation was discussed.[26]

Omani-Iraqi relations also improved after the cease-fire; several high-ranking Iraqi officials visited Oman with messages to Qabus from Saddam Husayn. Among them was Taha Yasin Ramadan, Iraq's first deputy prime minister, who led a delegation to the sultanate in December.[27]

OMAN-PDRY RELATIONS

A final accord on the normalization of Oman-PDRY ties was put in place during the visit of PDRY President Haydar Abu Bakr al-'Attas, who led a high-ranking delegation to the sultanate in October. The visit, the first of its kind, was followed by a joint communiqué, which announced the signing of a comprehensive pact of cooperation in the fields of trade, economic exchange, and communications.[28] But the most significant result was the conclusion of the long-awaited agreement regarding the demarcation of the Omani-PDRY border. Both sides confirmed that only a limited number of issues remained to be solved by negotiation.[29]

OMAN AND INTER-ARAB AFFAIRS

Hitherto, Oman had not been an enthusiastic supporter of the Palestinians or the

PLO. Its attitude toward Israel was less negative than that of most Arab states: long a close and loyal ally of Egypt in the inter-Arab system, Oman had advocated recognition of Israel's right to exist along with recognition of Palestinian political aspirations. It had regarded the PLO with suspicion, especially as some of its left-wing constituent groups, such as the Popular Front for the Liberation of Palestine, had actively supported the Dhofari rebels. Not surprisingly then, the PLO consolidation in the PDRY after its evacuation from Beirut in 1982 had become a matter of concern for Muscat; a PLO representation of any kind was strictly forbidden in Oman.[30]

However, increased Omani involvement in inter-Arab affairs in recent years, and the momentum the Palestinian issue has gained since the outbreak of the uprising in the West Bank and Gaza Strip called for a change in Omani policy. On the whole, Oman showed readiness to support the Palestinian cause. The uprising gained full Omani support as "...an expression of the Palestinian peoples' suffering from oppression" and "the best way to present the Palestinian issue to the world after all political means have failed."[31] But when it came to providing more tangible help in the form of formal links with the PLO, Oman was more reserved. It recognized the newly announced Palestinian State in November (see chapter on the Palestine Liberation Organization), but only in principle. In mid-December, Oman announced its "official and legal recognition of the Palestinian State," after having been persuaded to do so by PLO chairman Yasir 'Arafat's personal envoy, who came to the sultanate to confer with Qabus.[32] Referring to the timing and nature of recognition, Qabus explained:

> The desire to establish the state of Palestine has been declared, but the state itself has not yet been established. Hence, what has actually taken place was the decision to establish this state...The Palestinian brothers have explained to us the nature of recognition which has moral dimensions, so we immediately announced our recognition.[33]

The Omani desire to avoid any formal link with the PLO was all the more evident when the issue of opening a PLO office in Muscat was raised. Omani declarations on the subject were ambiguous. 'Alawi declined either to deny or confirm that the sultanate had agreed to allow a PLO office to operate in Muscat: "The existence or nonexistence of an office in Muscat does not have any effect on Omani support for the Palestinian problem."[34] Later in the year, however, 'Alawi explained more explicitly that Oman preferred to maintain relations with states that conduct their affairs in an orderly manner, rather than with organizations that tend to be irresponsible. While noting that there were Palestinian elements whose interest was incompatible with that of Oman, 'Alawi further emphasized that Oman would establish links with the Palestinian state when it was established.[35] Still, news of an impending 'Arafat visit to the sultanate in January 1989, indicated that this Omani response was not final.

During the year under review, Oman and Syria established relations and exchanged ambassadors.[36] The two countries had never had full-fledged diplomatic ties; the ice was broken when 'Alawi visited Damascus in December 1987 and conferred with his Syrian counterpart, Faruq al-Shar'. Syria reportedly fulfilled an Omani demand, namely the closure of the Popular Front for the Liberation of Oman office and the expulsion of the organization's senior staff from Syria.[37]

The amicable Omani-Egyptian links were best reflected in the enthusiasm with which Oman advocated Egypt's full reinstatement in the Arab fold. "Oman believes

Egypt is an active member within the Arab nation, and its exit from the Arab League damaged the Arab collective activity. This could not be mended without Egypt's reinstatement in the Arab League," Oman's minister of information stated.[38] On a different level, Oman mediated between Egypt and Iran on the release of Egyptian prisoners of war. Oman's minister of state for foreign affairs visited both Cairo and Tehran in September and thereafter stressed that release of the prisoners was merely a procedural question.[39]

OMAN AND THE UNITED STATES

The military nature of Omani-US relations came to the fore in 1988. An Omani request for antiaircraft *Stinger* missiles was turned down by Congress in keeping with an appropriations law declaring that the missiles would not be supplied to any GCC state during fiscal 1988 (for further details, see chapter on Qatar). The Omani request, probably raised during the February visit to the US of the Omani minister of state for defense, was repeated in May when the US ambassador to Oman attempted, in tandem with the State Department, to sway Congress to make "a limited exception" to the law for Oman.[40] But the US reply was not likely to change, particularly since regional tensions seemed to have eased.

Due to its strategic location, Oman was considered a mainstay of US regional policy. In September 1987 Oman signed an agreement permitting the US to establish facilities, presumably on the Musandam peninsula. The US, for its part, was reported to have been involved in improving onshore facilities at Masirah and Sib airports.[41] US recognition of Oman's importance in the region was best reflected in the words of the US Assistant Secretary for Near-Eastern and South-Asian Affairs, Richard Murphy, that US naval operations to protect tankers in the Gulf "would be difficult, if not impossible, without Oman's assistance."[42] Omani opinion was taken into consideration when the US applied its new policy of modified naval protection for shipping in the Gulf following the cease-fire. Omani officials were briefed by US Defense Secretary Frank Carlucci who visited the sultanate in December and they were known to have responded favorably on the issue.[43]

OMAN AND BRITAIN

The sultanate's extensive links with Britain in the field of defense were once again illustrated when, on the basis of a contract signed in 1985, Oman received part of a £25m. shipment of an advanced electronic warfare system.[44] During the year, defense officials exchanged visits: the Omani minister of state for defense visited Britain in February, meeting his British counterpart and other top officials; Britain's naval chief of staff, Adm. Sir John Lighthouse, came to the sultanate in March and conferred with Qabus.

Oman also served as a mediator between Britain and Iran. This may have been one of the topics discussed during Prime Minister Margaret Thatcher's one-day stopover in the sultanate in July.[45]

OMAN AND THE SOVIET UNION

Established in 1985, Omani-USSR relations continued to develop. In March, Soviet Ambassador Victor Posobaluk presented his credentials in Muscat;[46] Oman's ambassador to the USSR had already done so in Moscow in December 1987. A high-ranking delegation led by the Deputy Chairman of the Supreme Soviet Presidium, Georgi Tarazevitch, arrived in the sultanate in April and conferred with Qabus and other Omani officials.[47] In an interview given to the Kuwaiti daily *al-Siyasa,* Qabus explained the changed Omani attitude toward the strongest patron of the PDRY, its onetime enemy: "The Soviet Union is no longer that mysterious state or the Iron Curtain state....We are dealing with a state whose ideology and way of thinking are different from what they were in the past."[48] Nevertheless, Oman hesitated to support a Soviet offer to deploy a multinational naval force in the Gulf. 'Alawi said Oman would examine the details of the proposal and consult other interested nations.[49]

NOTES

For the place and frequency of publications cited here, and for the full name of the publication, news agency, radio station,or monitoring service where an abbreviation is used, please see "List of Sources." Only in the case of more than one publication bearing the same name is the place of publication noted here.

1. *Al-Dustur*, London, 22 February; *al-Watan al-'Arabi,* 26 February; *Kull al-'Arab,* 29 February 1988.
2. *Khaleej Times,* 1 March 1988.
3. *Al-Watan,* Muscat, 5 June — JPRS, 3 August 1988.
4. *Country Profile,* 1988.
5. *Oman Daily Observer,* 19 July — JPRS, 25 July 1988.
6. *Khaleej Times,* 27 February 1988.
7. Ibid.
8. *Al-Siyasa,* Kuwait, 27 February 1988.
9. *CR,* Oman, No. 4, 1988; No. 1, 1989.
10. *MEED,* 9 September 1988.
11. *CR,* Oman, No. 3, 1989.
12. *MEER,* January; *CR,* Oman, No. 2, 1989.
13. *The Gulf States,* 23 January 1989.
14. *CR,* Oman, No. 1, 1988.
15. *Khaleej Times,* 15, 28 February; *The Times of Oman,* 19 May; *al-Mustaqbal,* 26 November 1988; *CR,* Oman, No. 1, 1989.
16. *Al-Watan,* Muscat, 29 May; *Al-Usbu' al-'Arabi,* 28 November; *CR,* Oman, No. 4, 1988; *The Gulf States,* 23 January 1989.
17. *Al-Majalla,* 13–19 July 1988.
18. *FT,* 8 February 1988.
19. *Al-Siyasa,* Kuwait, 17 December 1988.
20. *MM,* 14 November 1988.
21. *Al-Siyasa,* Kuwait, 20 November 1988.
22. *Al-Mustaqbal,* 10 December 1988.
23. *Al-Ittihad,* Abu Dhabi, 8 August 1988.
24. *Al-Muharrir,* 10 November 1988.
25. IRNA, 27 October — DR, 31 October 1988.
26. *Iran Focus,* 10 November, quoting SWB, 3 November 1988.
27. R. Muscat, 11 December — DR, 15 December 1988.
28. R. Muscat, 1 November — DR, 3 November; *CR,* Oman, No. 4, 1988.
29. R. Aden, 1 November — DR, 3 November 1988.
30. *Al-Siyasa,* Kuwait, 19 June 1988.
31. *Al-Mustaqbal,* 9 April 1988.
32. GNA, 12 December — DR, 13 December; GNA, 12 December — DR, 15 December 1988.
33. *Al-Siyasa,* Kuwait, 17 December 1988.
34. *Al-Siyasa,* Kuwait, 20 November 1988.
35. *Al-Hayat,* London, 14–15 January 1989.

36. *Khaleej Times,* 6 April; *al-Ba'th,* 8 July 1988.
37. *Al-Dustur*, London, 18 January 1988.
38. *Al-Majalis,* 6 August 1988.
39. *Al-Siyasa,* Kuwait, 20 November 1988.
40. *NYT,* 12 May; *IHT,* 13 May; *al-Majalla,* 7 June 1988.
41. *MM,* 2 May 1988; *The Gulf States,* 23 January 1989.
42. *NYT,* 12 May 1988.
43. *NYT,* 9 December 1988.
44. *The Gulf States,* 31 October; *CR,* Oman, No. 4, 1988.
45. R. Muscat, 30 July — DR, 1 August 1988.
46. TASS, 24 March 1988.
47. R. Muscat, 5 April — DR, 7 April 1988.
48. *Al-Siyasa,* Kuwait, 17 December 1988.
49. *Khaleej Times,* 15 February 1988.

Qatar

UZI RABI

Despite the effects of the regional recession, Qatar experienced a quiet year throughout 1988. Aiming to prepare itself for a future without oil, Qatar proceeded with the North Field Offshore Gas Project in an environment made far safer by the Gulf War cease-fire. Yet, there remained a cause for concern which outweighed domestic difficulties: the dispute with Bahrain over the tiny island of Fasht al-Dibal had not been resolved despite arbitration attempts by various GCC states. As for the international arena, Qatari-US relations worsened after a clandestine Qatari purchase of US antiair *Stinger* missiles. Meanwhile, or perhaps as a countermeasure, Qatar, hitherto firmly anti-Communist, established diplomatic links with the USSR and the PRC.

DOMESTIC AFFAIRS

THE ARMED FORCES

The Qatari armed forces had c. 8,000 men and an air force with only 14 planes.[1] Because of its limited manpower and relative lack of equipment and aware that it was unable to defend itself against full-scale attacks, Qatar focused on preserving internal order and protecting its borders against minor incursions. The Gulf War and the threats posed by the renewed Qatari-Bahraini dispute (see below) aggravated Qatar's concern with its security, leading it to increase defense allocations. Plans were made to improve land and sea defenses. Qatar reportedly initiated a secret plan known as "Falcon Project," to build either ammunition dumps or to preposition storage facilities for military equipment.[2] Another manifestation of the Qatari resolve to upgrade its military capabilities was the "*Stinger* Missiles Imbroglio" (see below). Military consultants were also changed: Pakistani advisers were reportedly being replaced by Indians and an Indian lieutenant general was nominated as a senior adviser to the Qatari heir apparent and defense minister, Shaykh Hamad Ibn Khalifa al-Thani.[3]

SOCIAL AFFAIRS

Foreign labor and expertise continued to be the backbone of the Qatari economy. Iranians and East Asians, who constituted the majority of the foreign work force, were employed in unskilled, semiskilled and clerical occupations; 80,000 Arabs, mainly Palestinians and Egyptians, and 10,000 other workers of different nationalities, were in variety of managerial and administrative positions.[4] Foreigners were c. 70% of the country's 330,000 population, making Qatari nationals a minority in their own country. Non-Qataris were a similar percentage of the armed forces.[5] No wonder, then, that limiting the number of foreigners and narrowing their scope of activity became a Qatari priority. In the private sector, for example, non-Qataris were barred from owning shares in Qatari companies. In May 1985, it was declared that all foreign participation in private-sector firms, with rare exceptions, was to be liquidated within four years; until then, a 49% foreign participation had been allowed.[6]

At the same time, the government began initiating a job preference system. This policy was best enunciated by Minister of Labor and Social Affairs 'Ali Ibn Ahmad al-Ansari who said that preference in jobs would be given to Qataris, Arabs, and foreigners in that order.[7] The reluctance of Qatari nationals to work in menial occupations and the lack of a technological, educational infrastructure obstructed the road to Qatarization.

ECONOMIC AFFAIRS

Qatari hopes for a recovery in oil revenues were disappointed by the continuing glut on the market. The proposed budget, issued in February, foresaw an increased deficit of 6,1067m. Qatari riyals, which compelled the government to adopt an austerity budget.[8] Meanwhile, the government focused on expanding the non-oil sector in order to diversify sources of revenue and reduce dependence on imported foodstuffs. Private-sector firms were encouraged to invest in light industries and in agriculture.[9]

Qatar proceeded apace with the North Field offshore gas project. One of the largest existing, the field was to be developed in three phases. The first, begun in mid-1987 and expected to last until mid-1992, was to meet domestic demand; an aluminum smelter, expected to become active in 1991, was to use the abundant gas reserves, thereby making aluminum smelting highly profitable.[10] In the second phase, gas would be supplied to several GCC states, and in the third phase, it would be sold internationally. In 1987, contracts had been awarded to the Franco-American consortium of Technip and Bechtel, which was to provide management, consultancy, and engineering designs. In the year under review, contracts were awarded to Qatari firms as well, thus reviving the local market somewhat. The $1.3bn. project, however, placed an additional burden on the Treasury, compelling Qatar to seek a $400m. loan from foreign sources. Considering the fields' extractable deposits of 150 trillion cu. ft., experts estimated that the field would have a crucial effect on the Qatari economy in the coming decades.[11]

FOREIGN AFFAIRS

QATAR AND THE GULF WAR

The cease-fire in the Gulf War occasioned much relief. Qatar had felt constantly imperiled since the outbreak of the "Tanker War" in 1984, in which Qatari-flagged vessels were attacked. It was extremely vulnerable to any disruption of traffic in the Gulf, since all its oil was exported and its food imported by sea. The war, therefore, had been Qatar's main foreign policy concern, although the country was by no means the target of Iranian-sponsored subversive activity that Kuwait or Bahrain had been. On the whole, Qatar remained neutral, being particularly careful not to antagonize Iran. Using pan-Islamic rhetoric, it attributed the war to the Islamic world's failure to unite against Israel. At the same time, Qatar backed the peace efforts, calling on Iran to accept the UN cease-fire resolution, so as not to give foreign powers a pretext for remaining in the Gulf. It also used events, such as the US downing of the Iranian civil airliner in July, to underline the damage caused by the war and the necessity of a peace settlement. The ruler, Shaykh Khalifa Ibn Hamad al-Thani, expressed hopes that the cease-fire would pave the way for a just and lasting peace that would reinforce security and stability in the Gulf.[12] The cease-fire was the beginning of the consolidation of Qatari relations with the former belligerents. Hopes for expansion of Qatari-Iranian relations were expressed by Shaykh Khalifa during a visit to Qatar by Iran's Acting Foreign Minister, 'Ali Muhammad Besharati.[13] A similar declaration was made regarding Qatari-Iraqi relations when Iraqi Deputy Prime Minister Taha Yasin Ramadan visited Qatar in December.[14]

Qatar was an enthusiastic supporter of the GCC as the body most likely to guarantee its well-being, but remained disturbed by the ongoing dispute with neighboring Bahrain over the island of Fasht al-Dibal. At the end of 1987, it had been announced that the matter would be submitted to the International Court of Justice in The Hague for a final ruling, but Bahrain scotched this initiative when it said in February that the dispute would be settled out of court through Saudi mediation.[15] A reported discovery of documents supporting the Qatari position may have been the motive for the Bahraini move.[16] High-level contacts were maintained between officials of both countries throughout the year in an attempt to bridge the gap. The weekly *al-Usbu' al-'Arabi* reported in November that Qatar and Bahrain had discussed sharing the disputed area's oil revenues, and building a causeway over Fasht al-Dibal linking both states.[17] The apparent failure of the talks and the shadow the dispute cast over GCC unity were well reflected in the GCC summit in Bahrain in December when the other member states decided to join the arbitration efforts as a last resort before appealing to The Hague court. The council also hastened to settle the dispute within its ranks in order to keep foreign states from interfering in regional affairs, a policy that most GCC states had strongly supported during the Gulf War.

QATAR AND INTER-ARAB AFFAIRS

Qatar maintained a low profile in the inter-Arab arena, continuing to take no initiatives. It fell in line with the Arab consensus over the situation in Lebanon and the developments in the West Bank and Gaza, two issues which directly affected the large, influential Palestinian community in Qatar.

As regards Lebanon, Qatar repeatedly urged reconciliation among the warring parties in order to overcome the crisis. Qatari officials praised the Palestinian uprising in the West Bank and Gaza, claiming that Palestinians realized that it was the only way to breach Israeli policy. Qatari monetary donations were a more visible sign of solidarity with the uprising; Qatar was among the first to recognize the newly announced Palestinian state in November and to upgrade the PLO mission in Doha to ambassadorial level some time later.[18]

Qatari-Egyptian relations, which had been restored after the 1987 Amman summit, developed further. The Qatari ruler expressed his belief that Egypt, which "has never abandoned its natural role of confronting the enemies of the Arab nation and defending its dignity," would return to the Arab League.[19] Talks were held with Egyptian and UAE officials regarding Qatar's reentry to the Arab Organization for Industrialization (AOI) from which Qatar and other Arab states had pulled out in 1979, following the signing of the Egyptian-Israeli peace accord.[20] Both states concluded an agreement for closer cooperation in the fields of culture and communications.[21] Ways of facilitating Qatari investments in Egypt were discussed during Egyptian President Husni Mubarak's tour of Qatar in January. Nevertheless, three Egyptian companies were blacklisted by the Arab Boycott Office in Doha, an act that underlined the anomaly of Egypt's relations with the Arab world.[22]

QATAR AND THE SUPERPOWERS

Qatari-US relations reached an impasse after Qatar's clandestine acquisition of 12 US shoulder-held *Stinger* missiles was exposed. The missiles were first observed during a military parade in March in Doha. The purchase aroused US fears that use of the missiles — regarded by experts as "the perfect terrorist weapon" — would not be properly monitored.[23] With few exceptions, the US has constantly declined requests for *Stinger* missiles, including those made by GCC states, such as the UAE and Oman. Last December, however, the US agreed, under strict monitoring conditions, to supply the weapon to Bahrain, a loyal US ally, but Qatar's long-standing rival. The Qatari purchase could thus be regarded as an attempt to match the Bahraini buildup. The *Stinger* affair became a major issue in the Qatari-US discussions held during the May visit to Qatar of Vernon Walters, the US president's envoy and US representative at the UN, and the June visit of US Assistant Secretary of State, Richard Murphy. The US request to recover the missiles or have them inspected was turned down on the ground of meddling in Qatari affairs.[24] The US responded by placing a hold on future military and economic cooperation with Qatar.[25]

The most outstanding event in Qatari foreign relations in 1988 was the announcement on 1 August that Qatar and the USSR would establish diplomatic ties. A joint communiqué issued in Paris stated that the decision expressed the desire of both states to boost their friendship and cooperation.[26] In November, Qatari Foreign Ministry Under Secretary Shaykh Hamad Ibn Suhaym al-Thani paid a three-day visit to Moscow, during which he supervised the preparations for the opening of Qatar's Embassy. Hamad also met Soviet Foreign Minister Eduard Shevardnadze and invited him to Qatar.[27] The possibility of a Qatari-USSR *rapprochement* had been hinted at by Qatar in recent years. This was in line with the more favorable general mood on the side of GCC states toward the USSR.

Although denied by Qatar, it seems safe to assume that the proximity of the establishment of Qatar-USSR ties to the Qatari-US imbroglio (see above) was not accidental. Qatar denied reports in the US media that it was to grant USSR naval facilities as a countermeasure to those given to the US by Bahrain.[28] Be that as it may, the way was now open for Qatar to formalize relations with other Eastern Bloc states, most notably East Germany and Hungary, with which Qatar already had established trade links.

Another Communist state with which Qatar established diplomatic ties in 1988 — in July — was the PRC. This move seemed mainly to reflect common economic desires. Chinese officials visited Qatar in August and November to discuss economic and technological cooperation in the area of gas and petroleum.[29]

NOTES

For the place and frequency of publications cited here, and for the full name of the publication, news agency, radio station, or monitoring service where an abbreviation is used, please see "List of Sources." Only in the case of more than one publication bearing the same name is the place of publication noted here.

1. *MECR*, February 1989.
2. *CR*, Qatar, No. 1, 1988.
3. *The Times of Oman,* 15 September 1988.
4. *MEER*, December 1988.
5. *MEER*, February 1989
6. *MEER*, December 1988.
7. *Al-Hawadith,* 4 March 1988.
8. *CR*, Qatar, No. 1, 1988.
9. *MEED*, 30 September; *MEER*, ibid., 1988.
10. *Khaleej Times,* 16 February 1988.
11. *MEER*, ibid.; *The Gulf States,* 25 July; *IHT*, 22 September 1988.
12. GNA, 10 August — DR, 12 August 1988.
13. IRNA, 31 July — DR, 1 August 1988.
14. INA, 7 December — DR, 8 December 1988.
15. *CR*, Qatar, No. 1, 1988.
16. *Al-Mustaqbal,* 9 April; *al-Sha'b,* East Jerusalem, 17 April 1988.
17. *Al-Usbu' al-'Arabi,* 14 November 1988.
18. GNA, 16 November — DR, 17 November 1988; *Yedi'ot Aharonot,* 8 January 1989.
19. *Al-Hawadith,* 19 February 1988.
20. *Al-Ra'y al-'Amm,* 14 April 1988.
21. *Al-Tadamun,* 9 April 1988.
22. GNA, 5 March — DR, 9 March 1988.
23. *IHT*, 1 April, 29 June 1988.
24. *FR*, 11 August 1988.
25. *NYT*, 28 July 1988.
26. GNA, 1 August — DR, 2 August 1988.
27. GNA, 5 November — DR, 7 November 1988.
28. *Al-Ittihad,* Abu Dhabi, 7 October; *CR*, Qatar, No. 4, 1988.
29. *The Times of Oman,* 1 September; GNA, 5 November — DR, 8 November 1988.

The United Arab Emirates

UZI RABI

The most outstanding event in the UAE's internal affairs in 1988 — the reorganization of the oil industry's hierarchy — aimed to make the oil marketing system more efficient but it also symbolized the consolidation of the rule of the Al Nuhayyan in Abu Dhabi. As 1988 unfolded, the fortunes of the UAE became brighter. The cease-fire in the Gulf War, which had inflicted great economic losses on the UAE, was followed by hopes for wider economic horizons by virtue of the country's position as a regional entrepôt. Carrying the banner of Arab solidarity, the UAE further consolidated its position in the regional and inter-Arab arena while also serving as a mediator. Internationally, the UAE continued to develop a wide range of ties with the East and the West.

DOMESTIC AFFAIRS

THE ARMED FORCES

The UAE possessed a relatively advanced army with modern armaments, but it was only a modest force, most of whom were volunteers. Since foreigners made up c. a third of the 43,000 recruits, the UAE made a great effort to increase the local component within the armed forces: it was reported in February that military service would be made compulsory for UAE nationals;[1] attempts were also made to send young men to paramilitary training courses.[2]

The UAE further raised the level of its defenses, chiefly the antiair systems. Toward the end of the year, it announced the conclusion of an accord with France, for the purchase of *Crotale* surface-to-air missiles.[3] Plans for the Tawila naval base, which will be the largest in the GCC, were on the drawing board. The base was to have 60 berths for missile launchers and troop carriers, as well as other facilities, such as ammunition and weapons stores.[4]

THE HIGHER PETROLEUM COUNCIL — AN INSTANCE OF A ROYALIST TAKEOVER

The most outstanding domestic event was the reorganization of the oil industry's decision-making heirarchy. On 5 June the UAE ruler, Shaykh Zayid Ibn Sultan Al Nuhayyan, decreed the establishment of a Supreme Petroleum Council, which was to take over all responsibilities of the Abu Dhabi Petroleum Ministry, and of the Abu Dhabi National Oil Company (Adnoc). The new 11-member autonomous body was to be chaired by the heir apparent, Shaykh Khalifa Ibn Zayid Al Nuhayyan. Four other members were also members of the royal family.[5]

The shake-up in the emirate's oil industry signaled the decline in authority of the

UAE's minister of petroleum and mineral resources, Dr. Mani' Sa'id al-'Utayba, who kept his title, but was appointed to a position in the council well below the other members of the ruling family. After being appointed in 1974, 'Utayba, one of the UAE's highly placed technocrats, was believed to have the greatest influence on the ruling family with regard to oil affairs; he was also a former secretary-general of Opec. During 1988, the UAE's oil strategy, with which 'Utayba was closely associated, failed. Disconcerted by the glut in the oil market and the unprecedented fierce competition for lifters, 'Utayba was determined to follow the Opec reference price of $18 per barrel and refused discounts to term buyers. Liftings of Abu Dhabi's oil soon fell dramatically.

'Utayba's demotion may also have been connected with the acrimonious relations which developed between Adnoc and its foreign associates, who still retained a substantial stake in the emirate's oil industry. This state of affairs was the result of differences regarding oil marketing policy developed by 'Utayba and Dr. Mahmud Hamra Karuha, Adnoc's former general manager. For this reason, Karuha was dismissed in mid-1988, thus leaving the way open for a similar fate to befall 'Utayba.[6]

Another reason for 'Utayba's demotion seemed to have been the different attitudes of Abu Dhabi and Dubai regarding oil exploitation. Not being an Opec member, Dubai rarely heeded the UAE's production ceiling. In view of its very limited oil reserves, Dubai saw little justification for restraining production for the sake of higher oil prices in the long run.[7] Consequently, Abu Dhabi, the leading emirate within the federation and by far the richest in oil reserves, was expected to play the role of swing producer. In practice, this meant that Abu Dhabi was to safeguard the Opec quota set for the entire UAE by cutting back its own. More significantly, the downgrading of 'Utayba — the maker of UAE oil policy and known not to be popular among Dubai's ruling al-Maktum family — was probably expected to ease Abu Dhabi-Dubai coordination on oil affairs. 'Utayba's position further deteriorated when he was deprived of the chairmanship of the Abu Dhabi Gas Liquidation Company in October; he could no longer be considered the important person in the UAE oil sector.

Within a week of reorganizing the emirate's oil administration, the Al Nuhayyan family imposed its authority on the boards of the Abu Dhabi Investment Authority and the Abu Dhabi Fund for Arab Economic Development (ADFAED).[8] The membership of both boards overlapped with that of the Supreme Petroleum Council. These changes reflected the ruling family's monoply of key positions in Abu Dhabi, but it also exposed the limits of authority of persons not members of the Al Nuhayyan family.

The effects of the overproduction of oil were felt immediately. In the middle of June, 'Utayba announced the unilateral raising of the UAE quota from 948,000 to 1.5m. b/d in keeping with the ruling family's policy. Shaykh Kahlifa said: "The UAE share is not a fair one and does not correspond to its huge oil resources. It also does not correspond to the production quotas allocated to other member states in the organization [Opec].... We became victims of all the arrangements on the production quota."[9] The UAE's unilateral step became a matter of immediate concern for Opec, because it encouraged other members of the organization to step up their output without regard to their production quotas. In July, the general secretary of Opec visited the UAE in an attempt to convince Shaykh Zayid to moderate production.[10] During Opec's November meeting, the UAE quota was raised to 988,000 b/d.

Nevertheless, overproduction climbed to 1.7m. b/d in November, even surpassing the UAE's self-declared quota.[11]

OTHER ECONOMIC AND SOCIAL AFFAIRS

Although oil remained the key to the UAE's fortunes, its contribution to its GDP decreased. The continuous slump in oil prices added to the unprecedentedly fierce competition drove the UAE to seek new marketing methods for its crude. In January, it undertook downstream operations when it purchased a 10% stake in the Madrid-based *Compañia Española de Petróles* refinery, to ensure a destination for 6% of its Opec quota. The UAE was also looking for refineries and filling stations in the potentially rich US market.[12] A projected oil swap deal with the USSR was meant to facilitate the sale of crude and gas products in Eastern Europe in exchange for Soviet products.[13] Additional means of lessening dependence on oil were also developed: tourism, which was a relatively new source of revenue for Abu Dhabi, became a prominent means of diversification. Various beautification schemes, such as sporting and recreational facilities were built and new air routes were introduced.[14] Foreign trade was also expected to increase as Iran and Iraq began their postwar reconstruction; Dubai, the Gulf's largest entrepôt and Iran's chief reexporter was particularly expected to benefit. The gradual shift to non-oil sources of revenue was exemplified by the increased activity in the Jabil-'Ali — the Dubai free trade zone, which had a large number of industrial enterprises.[15]

Nevertheless, the projected budget deficit of 1,835bn. UAE dirhams, although reduced by 45%, compelled the UAE to take austerity measures.[16] Privatization of public companies continued — in whole or in part — in order to reduce the government's financial burden. Attempts to attract private investments by issuing bonds or setting up a stock exchange were unsuccessful, because the relevant legislation was still lacking.

Recruitment of skilled nationals for work in the government sector became a priority in 1988. The inability of Abu Dahbi's only university to meet the rising demand led to the formation of an alternative educational system. Accordingly, the government set up a number of national training centers and plans were afoot to build several polytechnics.[17]

The death penalty was introduced for drug trafficking, which has become a serious problem for the GCC states in recent years.[18]

FOREIGN AFFAIRS

THE UAE AND THE GULF WAR

The cease-fire in the Gulf War was greeted with an enormous sense of relief. The eight-year-old war had been a threat to the region and caused the federation economic damage, particularly after 1986 when the increased hostilities in the lower Gulf brought the war closer to the UAE. The first half of 1988 was a dismal period for the UAE: US reflagging of Kuwaiti vessels led Iran to fire on neutral ships, thus increasing the number of vessels, both foreign and local, attacked near UAE shores. In April, Iranian gunboats attacked the Sharja-registered Mubarak offshore oil field in response to a US attack on Iranian targets in the Gulf (see chapter on the Iraqi-Iranian War). The field, one of several that straddles the UAE-Iranian maritime boundary, was attacked even though Iran received half of its revenues, with Sharja, 'Ajman, and Umm al-Qaywayn — three of the seven emirates constituting the UAE — getting the other half. Blaming the US, Iran denied responsibility for the attack, but offered to pay financial compensation.[19] The attack on the Mubarak field recalled the November 1986 attack on the Abu al-Bukush oil field (for details, see *MECS* 1986, p. 320). Once again it was demonstrated that neither distance from the front nor neutrality guaranteed security. The downing of the Iranian airbus by the US in July while *en route* from Iran to Dubai also affected the UAE since some of the 290 victims were its citizens.[20] (For further details on the incident, see chapter on the Iraqi-Iranian War.)

Not surprisingly then, the UAE cheered the Iranian agreement to cease fire. As Minister of State for Foreign Affairs Rashid 'Abdallah put it: "The UAE looks forward to a state of peace and security in the Gulf — a just and acceptable peace whereby inter-Gulf relations are based on neighborliness and noninterference in domestic affairs."[21] The UAE had tried to use diplomacy to stop the war. Within the GCC, it and Oman advocated a more reconciliatory tone toward Iran, with whom it maintained long-standing trade relations, chiefly through Dubai. During the GCC summit in December 1987 it had been entrusted to spearhead a diplomatic offensive to get Iran to agree to the UN cease-fire resolution. A UAE envoy was dispatched to Tehran in January with a message from Rashid 'Abdallah proposing a meeting between the GCC states and Iran. Tehran responded by sending its Foreign Ministry's director-general for Arab and African affairs, Muhammad Husayn Levasani, with a message to 'Abdallah.[22] The meeting, held at the deputy foreign ministerial level, apparently discussed how to get all foreign fleets out of the Gulf, as indicated by the many Iranian and UAE statements to this effect. Other high-ranking Iranian officials, such as Foreign Minister 'Ali Akbar Velayati visited the UAE and brought messages from 'Ali Khameneh'i to Zayid. The UAE was reportedly ready to offer Iran financial compensation, a burden to be shared by all GCC states, in return for Iranian acceptance of the cease-fire.[23] It was not unlikely that the UAE acted as an arbitrator between Saudi Arabia and Iran, who had severed diplomatic relations between them following the August 1987 Mecca incident (see *MECS* 1987, chapter on Islam's enduring feud).

UAE-Iraqi relations improved following the easing of tension in the Gulf. Iraqi officials frequently visited the UAE with messages from President Saddam Husayn to Zayid; in December, Iraq's First Deputy Prime Minister Taha Yasin Ramadan arrived. In July, an agreement was signed strengthening economic and cultural ties.[24]

The easing of regional tension and the increased safety of Gulf shipping helped create a confident mood in the UAE. Yet, like other GCC states, it remained wary of Iran and Iraq, which had tried to achieve hegemony in the Gulf. The UAE, therefore, regarded the expansion of the GCC's range of activities as essential. "Having become an established reality, the GCC is moving steadily and wisely toward achieving closer cooperation among the member states in the political, economic, security, military,and cultural fields," Zayid asserted.[25] Within the GCC, UAE relations were particularly strong with Saudi Arabia, despite the tension created by the issue of oil overproduction. Both states added a physical dimension to their relations in the form of a new road directly linking the two states, which was nearing completion. The existing link, used by traders and pilgrims, passes through Qatar, and Qatari entry and exit visas are required for non-GCC nationals.[26]

THE UAE AND INTER-ARAB AFFAIRS

The UAE actively participated in inter-Arab affairs, seeking to strengthen a pan-Arab consensus with which it could identify. Accordingly, calls were often made for the convocation of inter-Arab forums as the best way to resolve problems, such as the Palestinian issue or the Lebanese crisis. Mediation attempts in regional conflicts and financial help to needy Arab states were other means of promoting the UAE's image as a country carrying the banner of Arab solidarity. Especially amicable links were maintained with the PLO and moderate Arab states, such as Jordan and Morocco, but most notably Egypt.

The Palestinian issue gave the UAE its best opportunity to express its Arab nationalist policy. The UAE enthusiastically supported the Palestinian uprising in the West Bank and Gaza Strip; "The uprising" Shaykh Zayid said, "proved that achieving peace in the region cannot be attained without regard to Palestinian legitimate national rights, the liberation of occupied land, and self-determination."[27] The *al-Ittihad* daily compared the uprising with the 1936 Arab revolt. Support for the uprising was given financial expression too. Zayid personally donated $10m.[28] In March, it was announced that all government and private-sector employees would donate a day's salary to the uprising.[29] Unlike other immigrants, the Palestinian community occupied key positions in education and government service, and constituted a powerful lobby for the Palestinian cause. Not surprisingly, therefore, the UAE was among the first of the Arab countries to recognize the newly declared Palestinian state and to upgrade the PLO office in Abu Dhabi to ambassadorial level.[30]

The UAE, the first Arab country to have restored relations with Egypt following the Arab summit in Amman in November 1987, further strengthened its ties with Cairo in the defense and economic spheres. Egypt was regarded as an Arab source of weapons, which would somewhat reduce UAE dependence on foreign countries. During his visit to Egypt in March, Zayid inspected arms factories.[31] The UAE was also expected to resume participation within the AOI — a joint venture of several GCC states and Egypt for the manufacture of arms — which it had left together with other GCC states after the signing of the Israel-Egypt peace treaty in 1979. In April, the UAE hosted an AOI exhibition of Egyptian armaments.[32] The exchange visits of military delegations further enhanced the military nature of UAE-Egyptian relations.

The UAE financed several projects of Egypt's economic development plan particularly in the fields of agriculture and tourism; for that purpose, ADFAED extended loans amounting up to a $100m. to Egypt.[33] Agreements were signed in the fields of commerce and construction. On the diplomatic level, the UAE supported Egypt's readmission into the Arab League and was expected to act on the latter's behalf at inter-Arab forums, such as the Algiers summit in June. Also, the UAE attempted to bring about a reconciliation between Egypt and Libya, as evidenced by Rashid 'Abdallah's shuttling between Cairo and Tripoli.[34]

UAE-Sudanese relations came into the news when an armed man broke into the UAE Embassy in Khartoum in November and held its staff hostage. The Sudanese security forces stormed the building, apprehended the attacker, and set the hostages free. The attack was apparently not politically motivated; rather it seemed to stem from a UAE refusal to give work permits to a group of Sudanese.[35] The UAE hailed the Sudanese handling of the affair, but when informed a month later that the attacker had been set free, the UAE recalled its ambassador from Sudan "out of concern for his safety."[36] Plagued by other severe political and financial problems, Sudan could not afford to antagonize such a prominent donor to needy Arab countries. A Sudanese clarification two months later that the attacker would soon face trial contained the minor crisis.[37]

THE INTERNATIONAL ARENA

The Arab-Israeli conflict continued to cause the greatest strain in UAE-US relations. UAE officials and media continued their strongly critical tone toward the US. "It is time for the US to realize that its bias toward Israel will cost it its credibility in the Arab region and the world at large," Shaykh Zayid asserted.[38] Editorials in the UAE press treated US initiatives in the conflict with mistrust. *Al-Ittihad* ruled out the Shultz initiative (see chapter on the United States and the Middle East) claiming it aimed at rescuing Israel from the predicament created by the Palestinian uprising.[39] Even the US decision to begin a dialogue with the PLO got a rather lukewarm response, as being positive, but insufficient.[40] The US presence in the Gulf was another cause for friction which was well expressed when the UAE held the US responsible for shooting down an Iranian airbus in July (see chapter on the Iraqi-Iranian War). The cease-fire in the Gulf War allowed the UAE media to make more outspoken statements: "If, through its fleet, the US has played a specific role at a certain period of time in the past, this period has ended.... There is now no justification for the continued US military presence in the Gulf."[41]

Nevertheless, both countries maintained their political, military,and economic relations. Keeping a low profile, the US was reported to have constructed defense installations in the UAE. The weekly *al-Majalla* reported that the UAE had purchased US antiair defense equipment.[42] US officials visited the UAE during their regional tours and discussed regional security problems. Among them was Assistant Secretary of State for Near Eastern and South Asian Affairs Richard Murphy, who arrived in September.

UAE-France relations were military and economic. France has become an additional source for arms procurement as part of the UAE's effort to diversify its sources of supply. The *Mirage* 2000 fighter has become the backbone of the UAE Air Force, and at the end of the year it was reported that France was to supply the UAE with 36 of them. Although concluded in 1984, the implementation of the deal had been delayed due to a dispute over the contract, with the UAE demanding the highest possible specification for the plane.[43] France also served as an outlet for UAE funds: two accords on the facilitation of UAE investment in France were concluded during the January visit of Finance and Economy Minister Edouard Balladur to the federation.[44]

UAE-USSR relations, which were established in 1985, expanded mainly in the economic field. A Soviet delegation arrived in February and both countries agreed to intensify cooperation in the field of technology.[45] In April, an agreement was reached regarding a \$50m. UAE loan to the USSR on favorable terms, the first major financial transaction between the two countries.[46] Several senior Soviet officials visited the UAE in 1988, among them Karen Brutents, head of the Foreign Relations Bureau of the Soviet Communist Party's Central Committee, who arrived in January and conveyed a message from President Mikhail Gorbachev to Zayid.[47] These improved relations affected the UAE's relations with other Eastern Bloc countries. In February, the UAE and Poland signed a protocol aimed at fostering trade and economic cooperation; in the same month, the UAE and Bulgaria signed an air services agreement regulating flights between the two countries. Both agreements were the first of their kind.[48] It was also reported that diplomatic ties with East Germany were under consideration.[49]

East Asia continued to be an area of crucial economic importance for the UAE. Japan was the UAE's largest customer for oil and gas, but also the UAE's principal supplier of advanced civilian technology. No wonder then that their trade relationships had political and cultural aspects. In February, the UAE minister for petroleum and mineral resources visited Japan for coordination of their oil policies. Being a major lifter of Iranian oil, it was not unlikely that attempts were made during the visit to get Japan to exert economic pressure on Iran to push it toward agreeing to the cease-fire;[50] a week after, the Kuwaiti daily *al-Siyasa* quoted Japanese sources as saying that Japan had decreased its crude liftings from Iran.[51] The closer cultural relations were reflected by the holding of a Japanese cultural week in Abu Dhabi in February.[52]

Another Far Eastern country with which economic links were on the increase was the PRC. In December, the opening of a Chinese consulate in Dubai was announced.[53] Talks were held regarding joint ventures in the fields of the economy, technology, and tourism.[54]

NOTES

For the place and frequency of publications cited here, and for the full name of the publication, news agency, radio station, or monitoring service where an abbreviation is used, please see "List of Sources." Only in the case of more than one publication bearing the same name is the place of publication noted here.

1. *Al-Bayan,* Dubai, 24 February 1988.
2. *The Gulf States,* 16 May; *al-Bayan,* Dubai, 27 May 1988.
3. GNA, 22 November — DR, 28 November 1988.
4. *CR,* UAE, No. 1, 1988.
5. *Khaleej Times,* 6 June; *The Gulf States,* 13 June 1988.
6. *CR,* UAE, No. 3; *IHT,* 19–20 November 1988.
7. *FT,* 24 March 1988.
8. *CR,* UAE, Nos. 3, 4, 1988.
9. *Al-Ittihad,* Abu Dhabi, 12 September 1988.
10. *MM,* 22 August 1988.
11. *MEED,* 13 January; *The Gulf States,* 23 January 1989.
12. *The Gulf States,* 25 July 1988.
13. *Khaleej Times,* 27 April 1988.
14. *IHT,* 4 May, 19–20 November 1988.
15. See, for instance, *Khaleej Times,* 1 February 1988.
16. *CR,* UAE, Nos. 3, 4; *Middle East Business Intelligence,* 20 September 1988.
17. *Khaleej Times,* 18 April 1988.
18. *Al-Ra'y al-'Amm,* 4 November 1988.
19. *FT,* 7 May; *MM,* 16 May 1988.
20. *JP,* 5 July; GNA, 10 July — DR, 12 July 1988.
21. *Al-Ittihad,* Abu Dhabi, 5 October 1988.
22. *Al-Hawadith,* 15 Janaury, 11 March; KUNA, 11 January — SWB, 12 January 1988.
23. *Al-Wafd,* 4 February 1988.
24. INA, 6 June — DR, 7 June; *Al-Bayan,* Dubai, 7 June 1988.
25. R. Abu Dhabi, 27 December — DR, 28 December 1988.
26. *Khaleej Times,* 24 February 1988.

27. Ibid., 26 January 1988.
28. Ibid., 6 April 1988.
29. Ibid., 31 March 1988.
30. GNA, 17 November — DR, 18 November; R. Abu Dhabi, 4 January — DR, 4 January 1988.
31. GNA, 13 March — DR, 14 March; *al-Siyasa,* Kuwait, 6 April 1989.
32. *The Gulf States,* 2 May; *al-Hawadith,* 17 June 1988.
33. *MEER,* 20 June 1988.
34. GNA, 8 May — DR, 10 May; *al-'Alam,* London, 8 October 1988.
35. *Ha'aretz,* 10 November 1988.
36. *Al-Ittihad,* Abu Dhabi, 12 December 1988.
37. *Al-Sharq al-Awsat,* 19 January 1988.
38. *Khaleej Times,* 13 February 1988.
39. *Al-Bayan,* Dubai, 7 February 1988.
40. *Al-Ittihad,* Abu Dhabi, 16 December 1988.
41. *Al-Bayan,* Dubai, 12 October 1988.
42. *Al-Majalla,* 7 June 1988.
43. *CR,* UAE, No. 4, 1988; *MEED,* 13 January 1989.
44. GNA, 26 January — DR, 28 January; *al-Siyasa,* Kuwait, 27 January; *Khaleej Times,* 27 February 1988.
45. *Khaleej Times,* 5 February; *al-Sharq al-Awsat,* 9 February 1988.
46. Ibid., 12, 13 April 1988.
47. KUNA, 12 January — DR, 13 January 1988.
48. *Al-Siyasa,* Kuwait, 4–5 February; *Khaleej Times,* 25 February 1988.
49. *CR,* UAE, No. 4, 1988.
50. *Khaleej Times,* 2, 16 February 1988.
51. *Al-Siyasa,* Kuwait, 1 February 1988.
52. *Khaleej Times,* 2 February 1988.
53. *Al-Ra'y al-'Amm,* 25 December 1988.
54. *Al-Ittihad,* Abu Dhabi, 21 January 1988.

Iran
(Jumhuriyye Islamiyye Iran)

DAVID MENASHRI

A DECADE OF REVOLUTION AND WAR

In February 1989, Iran's Islamic Republic celebrated its 10th anniversary. During this decade, the disciples of Ayatollah Ruhollah Khomeyni concentrated on two main targets: the consolidation, institutionalization, and perpetuation of clerical rule and, second, the fulfillment of Khomeyni's ideology. For Iran's new rulers, "Islamic Revolution" was not simply the name of their movement; it reflected their innermost wish to focus on making society conform with Islamic tenets and ideals. In this decade the clerics tightened their grip on power and strengthened their rule,[1] but they were much less successful in solving the problems which had led to the revolution and in realizing their vision of an Islamic Republic. Faced with the harsh realities, they often had to deviate from their initial ideology. The war, which continued for eight years of the first decade, significantly influenced such changes. But the regime's failure to solve the country's basic problems and the accelerated adoptions of a pragmatic policy — or at least what seemed so to the more radical toward the end of 1988 — caused a fierce struggle for power which reached its peak toward the end of the decade.

In its 10th year, Iran was traumatized by the elusive victory in the Gulf War and an enforced cease-fire, something Tehran had rejected all along. It has been the longest war in the modern history of the Middle East.

Revolution and war, then, are the themes of this chapter. Although full assessment of their impact cannot yet be made, it is possible to identify changes in Khomeyni's philosophy during these 10 years, follow the shift in Tehran's policy on the war and outline the major elements of Iranian policy since the cease-fire and, finally, to trace the challenges facing Iran in the aftermath of the cease-fire.

Taking a broad view of the decade, the first part of this chapter evaluates the impact of the revolutionary experience and the war on the ideology of the Islamic Republic. The second part examines the effect of the cease-fire on Iran's reconstruction policy, where trends toward greater pragmatism can be clearly discerned. The chapter will end with a discussion of the background to the new phase of radicalism, which became evident at the time of the anniversary celebrations.

VISION AND REALITY

Iran's Islamic Revolution represented a new kind of power seizure in the ME's modern history. The many coups in this region and in the Third World in the last generation were typically the work of small groups, led mostly by army officers, who endeavored to gain popular support for themselves and their new ideology only after

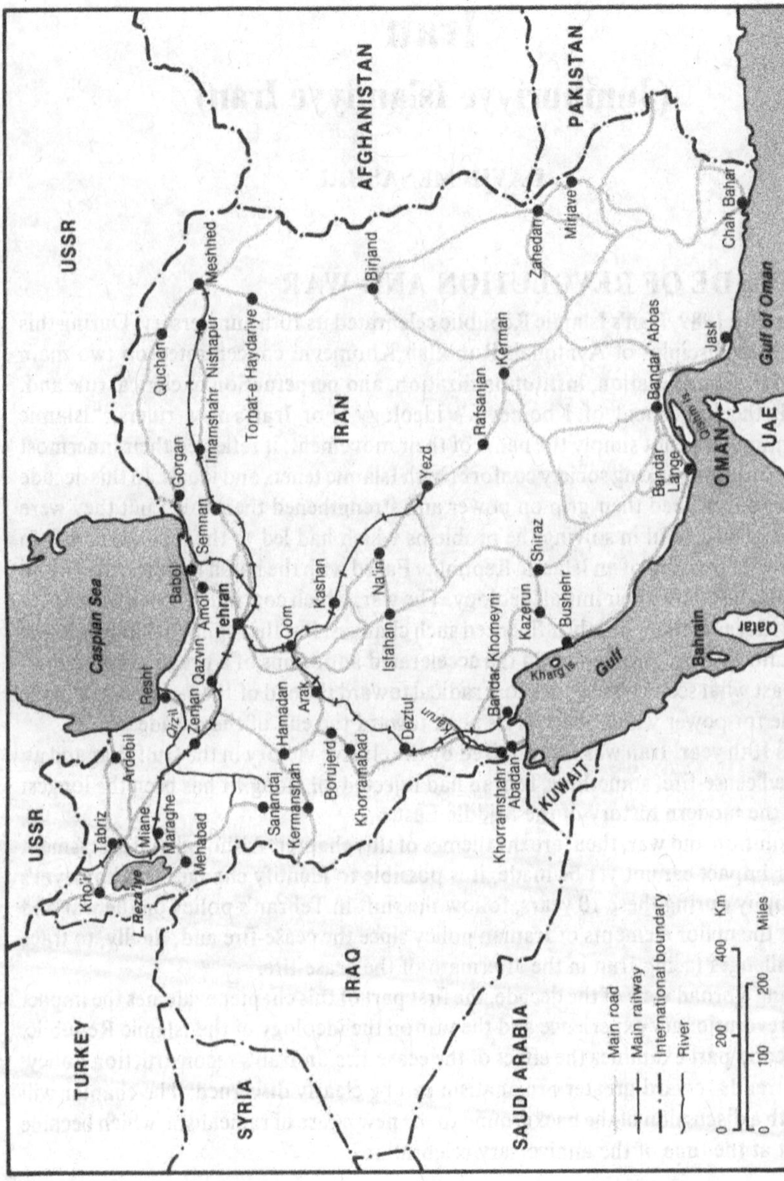
USSR
TURKEY
SYRIA
IRAQ
SAUDI ARABIA
KUWAIT
IRAN
AFGHANISTAN
PAKISTAN
OMAN
UAE
Qatar
Bahrain
Caspian Sea
Gulf
Gulf of Oman
Kharg Is.
L. Reza'iye
Qezil
Karun
Khoi
Tabriz
Miane
Maraghe
Mehabad
Ardebil
Zenjan
Resht
Qazvin
Tehran
Amol
Babol
Semnan
Gorgan
Quchan
Imamshahr
Nishapur
Meshhed
Torbat-e Haydariye
Birjand
Zahedan
Mirjave
Chah Bahar
Jask
Bandar 'Abbas
Bandar Lange
Kerman
Rafsanjan
Yezd
Na'in
Kashan
Qom
Isfahan
Arak
Hamadan
Sanandaj
Kermanshah
Borujerd
Khorramabad
Dezful
Bandar Khomeyni
Khorramshahr
Abadan
Bushehr
Kazerun
Shiraz
Main road
Main railway
International boundary
River
0 200 400 Km
0 100 200 Miles
Iran

their seizure of power. The Iranian Revolution was a striking exception. It was led primarily by men of religion, it enjoyed mass support from its inception, and its "new" ideology was nothing more than a return to the glorious past of early Islam and to the ideology most familiar to Iranians, namely Islam.

Once revolutionary movements have made the transition from opposition to power they often deviate from their radical doctrine. The Islamic Revolution was no exception. As long as Khomeyni headed an opposition movement, he spoke of a "new Iran" modeled on early Islam. Once in power, he knew he could not rule by means of revolutionary slogans, certainly not slogans drawn from seventh-century thought. He and his disciples were called upon to manage, not discuss, affairs of state. They had to compromise with reality, not out of a new-found moderation, but of a pragmatism responsive to the demands of the moment.

Khomeyni's doctrine underwent considerable change after his advent to power.[2] This deviation is evident in the four most important concepts in Khomeyni's creed: the rule of the *velayate faqih* (jurisconsult), "exporting the revolution," "neither East nor West," and improving the lot of the *mostaz'efin* (the dispossessed).[3]

But before discussing these changes, three precautionary remarks seem essential. First, one must guard against equating the fate of Khomeyni's ideology with that of the Islamic regime. The pragmatic interests of the *state* gained supremacy over the radical philosophy of the *revolution* but did not portend the end of clerical rule. The greater the deviations from *revolutionary dogma* (and the concomitant adaptation to new realities) the greater the likelihood that the *Islamic regime* would continue to exist. Second, in some cases the change could only be deduced from analyzing the policy that was carried out, because in their public declarations the leaders of revolutionary Iran often continued to express their loyalty to the old revolutionary dogma. And, finally, there were basic differences among the leaders on these very questions. Since those considered pragmatists have not given up their radical doctrine, and since the more radical may gain more power in future, our discussion is restricted as much as possible to views held in the leadership in the Islamic regime's first decade.

THE CONCEPT OF *VELAYATE FAQIH*

The most significant change wrought by the Islamic Revolution was perhaps the concentration of spiritual and temporal power in the hands of the *vali faqih,* i.e., the Imam Khomeyni. This very concentration, however, faced his disciples with their most crucial challenge, the twofold, yet interrelated, doctrinal and personal problems of the limit of government authority and of the succession.

Since the *vali faqih,* the "leader," is the republic's highest authority, it was crucial for the republic's future stability to guarantee a smooth transfer of power from Khomeyni to his successor. Shi'i tradition and the Iranian constitution of 1979 required that the "leader" be the highest ranking Ayatollah or, if no single theologian is qualified, a group of senior Ayatollahs should be selected to form a Council of Leadership. In 1985, the Council of Experts nominated Ayatollah Husayn 'Ali Montazeri as Khomeyni's designated successor (see *MECS* 1984–85, pp. 433–35), but his authority was never sufficiently recognized, even within the narrow circle of Khomeyni's disciples. Aware of the delicate nature of the question and the importance of resolving it in advance, Khomeyni took two important steps in 1987–88: he revised his will and defined more clearly his vision of the authority of the *velayate faqih* (see *MECS* 1987, pp. 393–97).

Montazeri, it must be remembered, was promoted to the rank of *Ayatollah 'Uzma* (Grand Ayatollah) only during the revolution, mainly because of his loyalty to Khomeyni rather than because of his scholarship. His nomination was, therefore, something of a retreat from Khomeyni's ideology. Moreover, after the nomination, many Iranians had second thoughts about the wisdom of naming him the sole successor. Some arguments were ideological, others political, and still others personal (see *MECS* 1986, pp. 333–34).

Khomeyni apparently revised his will in December 1987 in order to spare Iran a contested succession. Although it is not yet clear what the new will — or, for that matter, the old one — said, it is safe to assume that Khomeyni wished to make his choice more explicit and, even more important, to urge his disciples to unite behind the new leader (or leadership). It could be argued that, in either case, events were leading to a clear deviation from Islamic tradition as well as from Khomeyni's own doctrine and the constitution.

A collective leadership is a problem even at the best of times and certainly so during a period of political-ideological rivalries, as in Iran. Very often in the past, no one was generally accepted as the sole legitimate source of religious authority, and a collective spiritual leadership was established instead. But then, political power was not in the hands of the clerics, but of the Shah. Even if a Council of Leadership were to be formed, tradition and the constitution demanded that it be composed of the most prominent clerics, but in that case, the leadership would not conform with Khomeyni's ideology, because none of the Grand Ayatollahs except for Montazeri followed Khomeyni's line and, late in 1988, even Montazeri was no longer viewed as sufficiently loyal to the imam. None of this distinguished group which, in addition to Khomeyni and Montazeri, included Muhammad Reza Golpaygani, Shihab al-Din Najafi-Mar'ashi, Hasan Tabataba'i Qomi, and Abul-Qasem Kho'i (who lives in Iraq) supported the notion of the *velayate faqih.* Alternatively, the Council of Leadership could include clerics of lower rank. But such choices would be far removed from Khomeyni's vision of the rule of the *velayate faqih.* These questions were of main concern to Khomeyni's disciples. (To solve this problem Khomeyni appointed a 25-member council in April 1989 to review the constitution and prepare an amendment and supplement for approval by a plebiscite. The most significant item on the council's agenda was the issue of the succession.)

In addition, several times during 1987 and 1988, Khomeyni intervened in domestic politics to give more authority to the "politicians" (some of them junior clerics) at the expense of the prominent clerics. In notes exchanged in late December 1987 and early January 1988 between Khomeyni and Hujjat al-Islam 'Ali Khameneh'i and between Khomeyni and the Council of Guardians (*shuraye negahban*), Khomeyni pressured it to approve laws passed by the Majlis, laws it had vetoed on the ground that they were un-Islamic (i.e., the laws on agrarian reform, nationalization of foreign trade, taxation, and labor). This decree of Khomeyni was an important step in stripping the council of its constitutional authority (see *MECS* 1987, pp. 395–97). This council was second to the "leader" in the republic's hierarchy and had been empowered to oversee the conformity of Majlis-made law with Islamic law and the constitution (see *MECS* 1979–80, p. 444).

Early in February 1988, when a group of prominent leaders turned to Khomeyni to help bypass the Council of Guardians in case of disagreement between it and the

Majlis, the Ayatollah's response (6 February) laid down that such an impasse should be resolved by an assembly of the six theologian-members of the council and of six others: President Khameneh'i; Speaker 'Ali Akbar Hashemi Rafsanjani; President of the Supreme Court, Ayatollah 'Abdul-Karim Musavi Ardebili; Prime Minister Mir-Husayn Musavi; Hujjat al-Islam Tavassoli, of Khomeyni's personal office; Prosecutor-General Hujjat al-Islam Muhammad Musavi Kho'iniha — as well as the minister concerned with the proposed legislation.[4] This decree was another clear-cut retreat from Khomeyni's earlier dogma. The authority to "ascertain the interest [of the state]" (a phrase worked into the name of the new assembly: *shuraye tashkhise maslahat*) was entrusted to a mixed (i.e., "political" and theological) assembly, thus stripping the more prominent clerics of the Council of Guardians of their exclusive right to approve legislation. In August 1988, Khomeyni ordered the formation of yet another body, a four-man council consisting of the heads of the three branches of government (Rafsanjani, Khameneh'i, and Ardebili) and Prime Minister Mir-Husayn Musavi, mainly to solve disagreements concerning the reconstruction policy.[5]

In response to a call from a group of Majlis deputies, Khomeyni issued a decree on 31 December 1988 curbing the power of the 13-man assembly. It stated that after the cease-fire "no problem is so urgent that it requires debate in that assembly without [first] being debated in the Majlis and being overseen by the Council of Guardians." But even then, Khomeyni did not strip the new assembly of its power; disagreements between the Majlis and the Council of Guardians would still be brought to the assembly, but it would not be allowed to make laws. Khomeyni said in his decree that "one of the most important issues in the present turbulent world is the role played by time and place,"[6] which was a realization that religious decrees should be adapted to circumstances, a notion he had hitherto totally rejected. In the same vein, Rafsanjani stated that "Islamic scholarship," means "adapting to the requirements of time and place."[7] That Khomeyni himself was aware of the requirements of time and place was again shown when he included the question of the authority of the 13-man council *vis-à-vis* the Majlis and the Council of Guardians among those to be dealt with by the 25-member Council which had been formed in April 1989.

In this way, Khomeyni approved the supremacy of the authority of the state over the philosophy of the revolution. Rafsanjani interpreted Khomeyni's guidelines early in the year, saying: "In our country, the law should follow Islamic doctrine. However, if necessary, priority will be given to government decisions over doctrine."[8] The doctrine has been whittled down in face of the harsh realities. The state has become no less important than the revolution. One could argue therefore, that the authority of the *velayate faqih* as exercised by Khomeyni might not survive him and that the future regime, even if led by Khomeyni's disciples, may not be based on his doctrine. The dismissal of Montazeri (March 1989, see below) made it even less likely that the authority which Khomeyni held would be transferred to one of the senior Islamic scholars; the appointment (April 1989) of a body to amend the constitution's articles concerning the succession was the formal confirmation of the difficulties facing the regime.

THE "EXPORT" OF THE REVOLUTION

Another area of compromise between revolutionary dogma and political reality concerned "exporting" the revolution. The radical Islamic concepts Khomeyni had propounded ever since the late 1960s were meant to apply far beyond the borders of Iran. Closely bound up with pan-Islamic notions, they were aimed at realizing Islamic unity, moral, if not political. The notion of "exporting the revolution" followed naturally.[9]

Even though national considerations were alien to Khomeyni's principles, in particular those concerning relations with the Muslim world, in its relations with the Arab world and at home, Tehran's policy was based on his understanding of Iran's national interest.

Furthermore, "exporting the revolution" meant different things at different times and when addressed to different publics, such as mankind, the Muslim *umma* (community of believers), and the Shi'i community. There were also significant differences of opinion among more pragmatic elements within the revolutionary establishment headed by Rafsanjani, and a more doctrinaire group whose most prominent members were Ayatollah 'Ali Meshkini, Hujjat al-Islam Muhammad Kho'iniha and 'Ali Akbar Mohtashemi. But taken as a whole, the more radical statements regarding the "export" of the revolution, typical of the statements of the regime's early days, were toned down. Leaders no longer spoke of using force to spread the revolution; the emphasis shifted to cultural and ideological themes.

Khomeyni himself, mainly after 1983, consistently refrained from implying any intention of spreading the revolution by force. The course of history, he stressed, made the extension of the revolution inevitable and irreversible. Iran need not "worm its way" into other countries, rather it should walk in "like an invited guest." Until then, Iran's primary duty was to disseminate the Islamic ideology and make the country's "new realities" known, so as to encourage its being "invited" (see *MECS* 1982–83, pp. 542–43). Some of Khomeyni's associates were less restrained and continued to take Khomeyni's earlier views literally; for many of them exporting the revolution was a principal goal to be constantly pursued by the Islamic Republic. But more often than not, they, too, disclaimed any intention of using force to do so.

Though the vision of "exporting the revolution" had not been abandoned, its fulfillment was subordinated to practical determinants. The "export" of the revolution has had to give way to its consolidation in Iran itself, in the hope of making it an attractive model for others. Once again, Iranian national interests took precedence over revolutionary Islamic conceptions. Unsuccessful in exporting their universal ideology, Khomeyni and his disciples came to concentrate on formulating and voicing a Shi'i ideology, but this too did not have top priority. Ten years after, the Hizballahis in Lebanon and the followers of *al-Da'wa* movement in Iraq had come to be more faithful to Khomeyni's initial vision of world order than were the rulers in Tehran.

"NEITHER THE EAST NOR THE WEST"

The notion of "Neither the East nor the West" had similarly undergone considerable change. In the early days of the revolution, Khomeyni declared that all governments, and particularly in Muslim countries, were illegitimate; the Islamic Republic would ignore them and deal directly with peoples. In 1981, Khomeyni still upheld isolation as an ideal for revolutionary Iran (see *MECS* 1980–81, p. 557). In its relations with the superpowers, revolutionary Iran viewed "all infidels" as belonging to "the same camp," as Khomeyni often put it. His concept of nonalignment was "Neither East, nor West." Here, too, the doctrinaire approach was whittled down by realities. In October

1984, Khomeyni had already announced that Tehran wanted "relations with *all countries,*" with the exception of the US, Israel and South Africa. Not to have relations, he said, was "against reason and the Islamic Law" (see *MECS* 1984–85, p. 449).

In July 1988, Iran was compelled to concede that Khomeyni's special version of nonalignment had done the country harm. Rafsanjani said that "by the use of an inappropriate method...we have created enemies for our country." Those who could have remained indifferent, he said, were made to transform their indifference into hostility, and Tehran did not labor to attract the friendship of those "who could have been our friends." He added that the Foreign Ministry had been instructed to "treat the correct path," the path "we should have followed all along."[10] A newspaper editorial said that unlike the past, "the breaking of diplomatic ties should not be considered a principle."[11] The cease-fire was accepted, partly at least, in recognition of the disadvantages of isolation (see below).

THE SOCIOECONOMIC IDEALS

In other fields, when the declared policy did not change, the *de facto* policy did not express the original ideology. This was the case, among others, with the goal of elevating the status of the *mostaz'efin.*

Khomeyni came to power without having enunciated social and economic policies. While his writings stressed the general goals of social justice and economic independence, they contained no specific program of action; but he reiterated in many of his declarations the need to improve the lot of the *mostaz'efin.* After a decade of revolution and war, no material improvement had been achieved. In a Friday sermon on 8 April, Khameneh'i stated: "In our society there are still classes who are living in the gravest deprivation." In an attempt to justify the cease-fire he admitted: "During these 10 years we have not done enough in this field."[12]

After the revolution began, the economy steadily deteriorated. Plans to improve basic services, such as housing, education, and health care were conspicuously unsuccessful. In many areas, there was a change for the worse; soaring prices put many commodities beyond the reach of the *mostaz'efin.* Some of the basic problems that had led to alienation from the previous regime were again evident, sometimes even to a greater degree than a decade before.[13] In every sphere, social and economic strain was increasingly visible; the war was undeniably imposing hardships on the people, but mainly on the *mostaz'efin.* The latter were clearly beginning to feel themselves unjustly treated: having borne the main burden of the revolution and the war, they felt they were not given their right share; on the contrary, the gap between rich and poor persisted under the Islamic regime. Consequently, growing disillusionment among them became evident. This disillusionment frustrated the regime and Khomeyni personally, because of the pledges that had been made to improve the lot of the *mostaz'efin;* it was also becoming a potential threat to the government. No less important was that economic policy had become the main subject of theological-ideological controversy.

It had long been clear that the main disagreements — theological-doctrinal — within the Iranian leadership involved socioeconomic policies; the laws blocked by the Council of Guardians concerned these issues (see above). These disagreements became increasingly evident when different leaders took it upon themselves to explain the importance of Khomeyni's February 1988 guidelines. All made clear that the main disagreements had revolved around social and economic policy and that the reason for the new plan was the desire to take immediate and radical measures to improve the lot of the poor. Thus the prime minister explained that the imam's decree meant giving the government more freedom to solve the problems of the *mostaz'efin.*[14] Khomeyni's assertion that the government should follow the path of "the Islam of the *mostaz'efin*" instead of what he termed "the American version of Islam," similarly revealed the intention of having the government concentrate on social and economic reform.

THE CEASE-FIRE AND ITS AFTERMATH: PRAGMATISM ACCELERATED

IRAN ACCEPTS THE CEASE-FIRE

The decision to accept the cease-fire and the policies adopted in the second half of 1988 for rehabilitating the economy amounted to additional deviations from revolutionary Iran's major principles and policies. Although "war until victory" was not part of Khomeyni's original ideology, it had been a major tenet of the republic related to Khomeyni's basic convictions. Unlike in other issues, Khomeyni was forced to reverse his policy and publicly admit failure,[15] showing that, again, Iran's leaders preferred the state's interest to revolutionary doctrine.

Although there were indications that some leaders, but not Khomeyni, had recognized the need to end the war, such thoughts were not publicly expressed prior to Khomeyni's 18 July announcement. Official policy until then remained unchanged: "War, war until victory." An official government statement in mid-March still held that Iraqi attacks on cities would not weaken Iran's determination "to punish the aggressor." It vowed that Iran would "resist in the battlefields [even] for 20 years," and added that "we are not afraid of lengthening a war on which the fate of future decades and centuries of this oppressed nation depends."[16] On the eve of the Persian New Year, Khomeyni called on the people to go to the fronts and "with the continuation of their efforts, prevent the defeated and desperate 'Aflaqis...[from] reorgani[zing] and [from] tak[ing] a fresh breath."[17] The president then added: "I repeat firmly that our nation...will never accept any [international] pressure...we will continue on our path of chastising the aggressor and toppling the 'Aflaqi regime until the end."[18]

Even though official declarations did not change, there were admissions that problems and pressures did exist. In a press conference broadcast over Tehran television in March, a reporter asked Rafsanjani about the streets of Tehran being "very deserted" and the people looking "very scared."[19] Rafsanjani gave his explanation, but the fact remained that the Iraqi attacks exerted great pressure on Tehran.

Iranian acceptance on 18 July of UN Resolution 598 followed several months of growing signs of Iranian weariness (see below). For some time, the Iranian leaders had been looking for a way out of the war. While the process leading to the decision was clear, what was surprising was that Khomeyni had changed his view so soon and the manner in which Iran declared its acceptance of the cease-fire. What led to the decision? The following seem to have been the most important reasons.

(1) *Developments on the different war fronts threatened Tehran:* The successful Iraqi field offensive from January, the "war of cities," the "tanker war," Iraqi use of

chemical weapons, and attacks on Iranian oil installations put ever-increasing pressure on Iran which came to a head in spring 1988 (for details see the chapter on the Iraqi-Iranian War). The country's leaders came to realize that unless the cease-fire was accepted, Iran would be forced to accept even worse terms later on.

(2) *The domestic situation:* Growing economic pressure forced Iran to reconsider its war policy; the more pragmatic elements, headed by Rafsanjani, who since 2 June had been acting commander in chief, felt sufficiently strong to force acceptance of the cease-fire.

(3) *Iran's conviction that the support of "the world" for Iraq and the American presence in the Gulf would make it impossible for Iran to win the war:* The uncompromising American response to Iranian challenges (see below) were instrumental in changing Iranian policy. On 13 July, five days before the cease-fire was accepted, Rafsanjani said that in the previous two or three months it had been "felt that the enemies of Islam...are very serious about not allowing Iran to vindicate its rights." He made clear that this realization forced the leadership "to make serious changes in the war program and our defense."[20] On 18 July he added that "the enemies of the revolution have decided," at this juncture, "to seriously prevent our rapid victory. Insistence by us at this point could lead to extraordinary losses."[21]

(4) *Rafsanjani's appointment as acting commander in chief on 2 June:* Investigating the military balance, Rafsanjani became more convinced than ever of Iran's need for a cease-fire. For personal, if not ideological reasons, he had to do so, because any future defeats could be blamed on him to his detriment in the contest of power. His presence at the war fronts could also prove harmful to his position in Tehran, as had happened to the former president, Abul-Hasan Bani Sadr, who likewise had been an acting commander in chief in 1981. Furthermore, Rafsanjani was now in a better position to pressure Khomeyni to accept the cease-fire.

(5) *Difficulties in recruiting volunteers and keeping up the troops' revolutionary-religious zeal:* This zeal had been declining and on 2 July, Rafsanjani admitted that "we are in extraordinary need for the extensive presence of volunteer forces, especially trained forces."[22] In a television interview on 13 July, he added that "we cannot rely on a volunteer force, because it is optional and can decline or increase in numbers depending on circumstances." Such an acknowledgment carried much weight in a country that had relied so heavily on the revolutionary spirit of volunteers. However, in his capacity as acting commander in chief, Rafsanjani adopted a new policy. He declared that "in the new strategy our basic reliance is on the regular and organized forces" and "our future goal is to use regular forces";[23] thus he confirmed that Iran had problems recruiting volunteers and that he himself was prepared to rely more on the regular Army at the cost of limiting the authority of the Revolutionary Guards (RG). Faced with fierce opposition by the RG and some radical leaders, he was later forced to give up his intention of amalgamating the RG and the regular Army.

(6) *The absence of coordination and deep disappointments between the Army and the RG,* which seriously hampered the possibility of achieving any significant military success in the near future. This impasse even threatened to influence morale at home. "Some weaknesses," Khameneh'i admitted, "are related to the front line....Then, there are matters related to behind the lines [*sic*!]," but he made clear that the two were interrelated: "When political struggles and differences arise, these struggles cannot distinguish between the front line and behind it; such struggles will leave their mark on the battlefield."[24]

(7) *The shooting down of the Iranian airbus in the Gulf on 3 July may also have accelerated the Iranian decision:* On 8 July, Rafsanjani said the American "decision" to shoot down the plane was intended to save Iraq, by making Iran despair. He warned that "it is possible that more [such] incidents will take place in the future."[25] On 18 July he added: "This was to be considered as a warning rather than anything else."[26] It appears that Iranian leaders used this incident to "convince" Khomeyni to approve the decision (for details on the incident, see chapter on the Iraqi-Iranian War).

Finally, all the leaders, while explaining and justifying the decision, said that "something serious" had happened which forced Iran to retreat from its previous policy, though they did not say what that was. Rafsanjani said on 8 July: "We see the conditions as very critical."[27] He added on 18 July that "the new conditions have led us to turn away" from the previous policy. He added that the decision "depends on many things which I cannot explain for the time being, because most of them concern military and political secrets."[28] Khameneh'i added: "Today, new conditions have been created which call for adoption of new stances."[29] And Khomeyni himself, in his message to the nation on 20 July, said that the decision was taken "due to incidents and factors which...for the time being I will refrain from elaborating on."[30] Iran may have had problems in such areas as arms supply, which forced it to accept the cease-fire, but as of this writing, full details on these and other military problems were yet to be disclosed.

In any case, those favoring acceptance of the cease-fire wished the decision to be made by Khomeyni himself. They were aware that after his death it would be more difficult for his successor(s) to approve such a decision and for the people to accept it. The pragmatists also wished to have the decision approved while they had the upper hand in their conflict with those in the Administration who wanted to continue the war "until victory."

All this notwithstanding, as late as several days before the cease-fire decision was announced, Khomeyni still asked his followers to continue the war effort "until victory." Even when Montazeri, following the shooting-down of the Iranian plane, recommended punitive measures against the Americans, Khomeyni asked him on 4 July, to join hands with Rafsanjani and to "concentrate all their efforts toward the war.... We must all be going toward the fronts for an all-out war against the US and its lackeys.... To ignore the issues of the war is treachery against the prophet of God."[31] Two weeks later, he approved the cease-fire.

It was now essential to stop the war in order to save the revolution. The one reason powerful enough to change Khomeyni's mind was his concern for the revolution. Khomeyni himself linked the two in his message to his followers on 20 July: "God knows," he said, had it not been for this reason, "I would never have agreed." He was ready, he said, to drink "the chalice of poison" only for the sake of the revolution. It is at this time "in the interest of the revolution and the regime (*maslahate enqelab va-nezam*)" to end the war, he declared.[32]

But while the cease-fire may have helped solve some problems, it created others. First and foremost this was the Ayatollah's first major failure. Until then the revolution had been presented (and in many ways was) as a success story. Now Khomeyni had to admit failure. More crucial was the problem of how to explain the failure. Since success had been attributed to God's support for the revolution, did failure mean that

God had abandoned Khomeyni? Had He moved to the side of Iraq, the infidel? Such questions raised problems for the revolution and could weaken the authority of the *velayate faqih*. So could the fact of Khomeyni's disciples being powerful enough to impose their views on him. His dismissal of Montazeri (see below) was an acknowledgment of yet another mistake, because it was he who had approved Montazeri's nomination. Those critical of the government for not ending the war sooner and on better terms, had scored a point. (For such criticism by Iranian officials, see below.) Another quandary was that the Iranian leaders had repeatedly claimed that material improvement must be delayed until the war ended. Expectations were rising (see below), but were unlikely to be satisfied, certainly not soon. All these issues also combined to make reconstruction the country's most crucial problem after the cease-fire.

THE RECONSTRUCTION POLICY

In the postwar, or more cautiously, post-cease-fire period, reconstruction became the order of the day. "Reconstruction has become our nation's slogan," said Khameneh'i.[33] On this, all the actors on the Iranian scene were agreed, but goals, priorities, and methods were under dispute, with each group aware of the ideological, political, and personal implications of the different choices. The debate had crystallized into two distinct, but related, issues: the future of the private sector and the attitude toward foreign aid. But these issues had a bearing on domestic and foreign policy with two entirely different views of revolutionary Iran's future path — one pragmatic and conservative, the other radical and revolutionary — competing with each other.

Late in September, Rafsanjani made it clear that these issues should be seriously discussed and appropriate policies adopted. "We are inevitably faced with new conditions: there is the issue of war...of reconstruction, [of] our relations with non-Islamic countries, with the infidels [i.e., the West], our relations with the Muslims...and our priorities — these are among our chief problems."[34] The president, as he had many times in the past (see *MECS* 1983–84, pp. 431–32) tried to downplay the differences and to create the impression that all groups agreed on the main guidelines of the reconstruction policy. "I categorically announce," he said, "that there are no differences of opinion among the officials... regarding the most essential lines of reconstruction. They are all united." All of them, he said, agreed that Iran's first priority should be reliance on internal financial and human resources in both the public and private sectors; but also that to speed reconstruction, "we need to make use of...foreign resources....There are no differences of opinion regarding this either." He further indicated that the four leaders, gathered to ascertain the interests of the state, are "unanimous in their views regarding this issue." As for himself, he said he was convinced that since "we cannot prolong the issue [of reconstruction] for a hundred years," outside support and encouragement of the private sector were essential. He viewed such foreign support as "a preface for self-sufficiency."[35] He also made clear that "in reconstruction, the public participation is the main element, just as was the case in the... war."[36] Rafsanjani was more mindful of the existing rifts: "We have differences of opinion among ourselves over these issues." But he implied that between the different trends he supported the more pragmatic approach. He reminded the people that the ideal days of early Islam had long passed: "Today...we live under new conditions."[37]

In the autumn of 1988, the more pragmatic faction seemed to have gained the upper hand; but Khomeyni did not unequivocally endorse one faction or the other. In his inmost heart, he probably supported the more radical view, as he had over the war, but the constraints of the situation dictated otherwise. He sent conflicting signals, refusing to add his full weight behind either of the factions and tried as much as possible to maintain a balance between them. In his address to the president and the Cabinet on 30 August, he confirmed that the issue of reconstruction was "extremely important." 'The people should be free in matters of trade," he decreed, but "supervision should be exercised [by the above-mentioned four-man council] to avoid corruption."[38] This meant some support for the more pragmatist reforms, but when Musavi, who advocated more radical economic reforms, was under pressure, Khomeyni came to his rescue. In September, he rejected Musavi's resignation offer (see below) and in November, while appointing Musavi to head the newly founded organization for affairs of the disabled, he said:

> Since, nowadays, there may be some individuals who would want to...harm your rentless and tireless efforts...it is necessary for me to mention this point, that I consider you just as capable [as others] and a person who cares about the Islamic revolution... I endorse and support you."[39]

When the four leaders mentioned in Khomeyni's speech (the President, Speaker, President of the Supreme Court, and the Prime Minister) wrote him inquiring about the extent of their authority to formulate reconstruction policy, the imam reaffirmed on 3 October what he had said a month earlier, but made clear that under no circumstances should Iran abandon its commitment to the "Neither East nor West" principle. Although he implicitly rejected *rapprochement* with the US, by linking reconstruction with foreign policy Khomeyni made clear, perhaps without intending to do so, that public opinion at least considered the two issues interrelated. He also made clear that reconstruction could only be successful through "consultation and cooperation" (i.e., consultation with experts and cooperation between the government and the Majlis, and cooperation between the two with the private sector, and possibly also with foreign firms/governments).[40] Ideologically, Khomeyni thus took another step in transferring authority to a collective group and in deviating from his concept (see above). Politically, he now supported the pragmatists, though he did not totally disapprove of the radicals and their policies. (For a change in his policy early in 1989, see below.)

The issue of the role of foreign countries in postwar reconstruction had a bearing on policy toward the private sector and on foreign policy. Here, too, Rafsanjani led the pragmatists. Early in October, he stated that Iran should "maintain ideals," but also "meet the needs of the people."[41] Iran, he added, "may need experts from abroad" and should encourage the private sector. He went on to blame the radicals as "frozen in their beliefs [i.e., fanatics]...who cannot adjust themselves to the circumstances of the day."[42] Late in November, he said that "we have [already] reached the conclusion that we should make the import of certain vital commodities free, gradually, and place them at the disposal of the private sector."[43] Khameneh'i, too, made clear that since Iran lacked sufficient domestic resources and because time was of the essence, Iran needed external support: "We need both financial resources, technology, and know-how other than our domestic resources and technology. And we shall obtain them from foreigners."[44] He added that since "we cannot prolong the issue [of reconstruction] for a hundred years," outside support and encouragement of the private sector were essential (see above). Khameneh'i reiterated in December that he supported the private sector and that only "some people with inclinations towards a leftist and socialist economy" were attributing a "negative connotation" to the private sector. But he agreed that "differences among some of the clergy" were "a bitter fact."[45] Rafsanjani added that Iran had permitted merchants to buy on credit repayable in one or two years; this was not a good idea, he admitted, "but we have no alternative." He also said Iran had permitted industrialists to sign contracts with their trading partners abroad.[46] Musavi, who had long supported greater government involvement in the economy, held entirely different views from those of Rafsanjani and Khameneh'i.

As long as Khomeyni did not explicitly state his own views, both sides could claim to be faithful to his ideology. Eventually, in November, Hujjat al-Islam Muhammad 'Ali Ansari wrote to Khomeyni, appealing to him to state his views. Ansari's letter said that "two political-ideological schools of thought...have embarked on serious competition." But Khomeyni, unwilling to antagonize either side, gave no clear answer.[47] Yet, the faction led by Rafsanjani now carried much greater weight in shaping reconstruction policy.

THE "NEW" MUSAVI GOVERNMENT

On 6 September, Musavi offered his resignation to the president, saying that he wanted to resign primarily because he suspected that as many as eight of his cabinet ministers would not get the necessary vote of confidence from the newly formed Majlis (see below for the election of the new Majlis). Apparently Khomeyni's declaration on 30 August in favor of the private sector's involvement in foreign trade, in opposition to Musavi's views, had convinced the latter to offer his resignation. Khomeyni, somewhat angered, told him that once he decided to resign, he "should have at least mentioned something to me" (during their meeting a week earlier). This was "no time to complain and resign" he noted, and Musavi should continue to serve as prime minister; any disagreement between him and the Majlis regarding ministerial nominees, should be dealt with by the newly formed Council for Ascertaining the Interests of the State. Musavi thereupon withdrew his resignation.[48] He then submitted 18 nominations for cabinet posts out of the total of 21, and 15 of them were immediately approved by the Majlis. In the vote on the other three, the required threshold was not reached. They were Mohsen Rafiqdust (minister of the RG), Kazem Akrami (education) and 'Abbas 'Ali Zali (agriculture). A week later, Musavi submitted six more nominations: three for these three portfolios and another three for the remaining portfolios. Only one of the six was rejected, that for the Ministry of Commerce. Those Majlis members opposing the nominations criticized mainly the functioning of the ministries of those rejected. Most critical was Hajji Ghaffari, who said that there were thefts in the Ministry of the RG, unlike in the army. The ministry, he said, had a twofold task, producing and purchasing weapons, but it had not produced anything new; it had simply produced the same old weapons and passed them off as innovations. As for arms purchases, the ministry had sent young people abroad with suitcases full of dollars to buy arms, but lacking experience, they had been deceived and paid exaggerated prices for unnecessary equipment (for somewhat similar charges against the ministry in 1985, see *MECS* 1984–85, p. 437).

It is also important to note that many of the ministers approved did not get impressive support. Rughani-Zanjani (minister for planning and budget) was supported by 192 (out of total 270 Majlis members), Dr. Muhammad Farhadi (higher education) by 176, Ayatollahi (mines) 186, Hasan Habibi (justice) 216, and 'Ali Akbar Velayati (foreign affairs) by 225 members, but others did less well: 'Ali Akbar Mohtashami (interior) received only 133 votes, 'Ali Reza Marandi (health) 124, Behzad Nabavi (heavy industries) 128, Shafe'i (industry) 134, and Col. Muhammad Husayn Jallali (defense) only 138.[49]

What are the conclusions? As far as Musavi's personal status was concerned, the picture was by no means clear. The policy guidelines that Khomeyni had just issued (see above) contradicted Musavi's views; he had failed to gain approval for some of his nominees, and he had become more dependent on the president. But in his letter Khomeyni had supported him and even said, "I am fond of you." Furthermore, it had never happened — both to Musavi and other prime ministers of the Islamic Republic — that all their nominations were accepted by the Majlis. Musavi's position in 1985, when he formed his second government following the presidential elections, was even worse (see *MECS* 1984–85, pp. 429–32). Nevertheless, the events of the previous months had weakened Musavi to a degree. Khomeyni's support did not mean support for his policy; it reflected the Ayatollah's policy of keeping top leaders in their positions as long as possible. In the past, Khomeyni had supported even Prime Minister Mehdi Bazargan and President Abul-Hasan Bani Sadr until he could not prevent their dismissal. In 1988, as in 1985, it was Khomeyni who came to Musavi's rescue.

The figures clearly showed the growing power of the pragmatists in the government, even though the new Majlis was relatively radical (see below). Most important in this regard was the limited support that Mohtashemi — the figure-head of the radicals — gained.

The breakdown of the figures reflected a growing dissatisfaction with ministries responsible for public services (education, health, commerce, and agriculture) and ministers of defense and RG.

Although he held on to his portfolio, the prime minister could not advance his policy. Toward the end of the year, pragmatism gained momentum, in domestic affairs as well as in foreign relations.

IMPLICATIONS FOR FOREIGN RELATIONS

As for foreign policy in the narrow sense of the word, here too the pragmatists had greater influence. After the cease-fire, Tehran was more flexible in dealing with its Muslim neighbors despite the initial radical attitude toward them. Rafsanjani was openly critical of past policies toward some Arab states: "If Iran had demonstrated a little more tactfulness" in its relations with Saudi Arabia and Kuwait, he said late in November 1988, "they would have not supported Iraq."[50] A few days later, he added that his country saw "no obstacles" to expanding relations with the Arab countries of the Gulf.[51] Deputy Foreign Minister 'Ali Muhammad Besharati spoke of Iran's desire to "turn over a new leaf" in its relations with the Gulf littoral states. He quoted from the Qur'an to support his view that "bygones are bygones; we should think of the future." Referring to Saudi Arabia, he said: "We are prepared to sit down, talk, and overcome the great misunderstanding between us." Using arguments, which in themselves were a significant retreat from the old revolutionary slogans, he reminded his listeners that "neighborhood is unchangeable" and that "our holy shrines...and our Ka'ba are there. The Prophet is buried in Saudi Arabia. Can we ignore it?"[52] Such statements differed from those made in the early days of the revolution; they reflected a significant change in the tone and contents of Iranian declarations late in the year.

An attempt was also made to improve relations. Many visits were exchanged with Arab countries of the Gulf. Ties with Kuwait were renewed and negotiations with the Saudis were in progress. Radicals expressed opposition to this trend, but the policy approved was again Rafsanjani's. Even early in 1989 when the atmosphere in Iran was much more radical (see below), Tehran continued to deal with the neighboring Arab states from the same pragmatic premises. An exception to this trend was the difficulties that emerged again in Tehran's relations with Syria, its closest ally; Iran was concerned about Syria's policy in Lebanon and, more significantly, with the increasing indications of Damascus's improved relations with Arab countries.[53]

Many pragmatists considered that a change in policy with respect to the superpowers was essential for economic rehabilitation. Here, too, Rafsanjani took the lead in advocating a compromise between the old radical ideology and the new realities. In December, in an attempt to justify the improvement of relations with the outside world, he said that it was "impossible in today's world to be totally independent." Even Japan, he said, was dependent on others, such as the US. In an indirect reference to the need to reconsider the total rejection of the US, he went as far as to claim that "if the flow of oil to the US were to come to a halt...life [everywhere] would become paralyzed." More specifically, he made clear that "there is so much machinery in this country which depends on foreigners to a large degree....There are many projects which cannot be completed with the country's [own] resources."[54] More and more Iranians recognized the need to take such steps, although Tehran was still unwilling to do so.

Early in October, Khameneh'i denied rumors that Tehran was seeking to "compromise with the superpowers, and make concessions on the revolution's principles." He made clear that Iran was determined to "preserve its principles under all conditions," but he also alluded that, in fact, some "writers and orators" had written and said things that could be so interpreted.[55] An article in *Abrar,* an organ reflecting radical views, called on the government not to set aside the revolutionary ideology while it was attempting to expand its foreign relations. The paper emphasized that makers of foreign policy should erase from their minds the idea that Iran should "stretch a begging arm to anyone and any country" in order to end its isolation. The paper reminded them that some foreign countries had only changed the appearance of their policy in an attempt to make their way into Iran like "wolves in sheepskin."[56] Yet, such an article again showed that change was being advocated more than ever.

At this stage, however, public criticism of the US continued. President Reagan's decision in late 1988 to freeze Iranian assets in the US for another year was taken as additional proof of Washington's hostility. Iran's stated policy was forcefully reasserted when former President Carter asked Khomeyni and Rafsanjani to exert their influence for the release of the American hostages in Lebanon. In an oblique reply, Rafsanjani harshly criticized America's hostile attitude toward Iran, and the suppression of human rights in the US and in the Western world in general.[57]

But, more than ever, there were suggestions that Iran should not altogether rule out the possibility of renewing ties with the US. Such voices were heard more loudly after Khomeyni's message to President Mikhail Gorbachev (see below). Referring to President Bush's inaugural address in which he said his Administration would be willing to cooperate to win the release of American hostages in Lebanon, a newspaper suggested that Iran should respond positively. Iran, it said, was at "a very sensitive and vital juncture," and in such a situation "safeguarding national and revolutionary interests...is certainly more important than some slogans."[58] Recalling Khameneh'i's remarks in a Friday sermon that only Tehran could set conditions for reestablishing ties with Washington, one newspaper wrote: "We are certain he [the president], more than anyone else, appreciates that it has been Iran's consistent policy to have friendly relations with any government that shows an equally reciprocal desire for friendship." The paper advised taking up Bush's offer of friendly relations "cautiously and carefully."[59] Rafsanjani said early in February that Iran's foreign policy was not "based on isolation," since it "will get nothing out of isolation."[60] In his address on the 10th anniversary of the revolution, Khameneh'i said that Iran was prepared for "mutual and balanced relations with all countries"; he did not exclude the US.[61] A few days later, the tone became more radical. One example was Khomeyni's message on 22 February in which he once again clarified his policy: "The committed clergy are thirsty for the blood of parasitical capitalists and they have never been in a state of conciliation with them and will never be."[62] But again, taking the entirety of Iranian declarations, the tone in 1988 was unmistakably more pragmatist.

In comparison with some moderate expressions regarding the US, after the cease-fire, an improvement in relations with other countries such as Britain, Canada, France, and the USSR was observable. In the reconstruction era, as previously in the Islamic Republic's short history, Tehran gave preference to Japan and West Germany. Tehran viewed them as ideal partners, ideologically and practically. They had no "imperialist record" and no political aspirations or commitments in the region. Both possessed the advanced technology Iran required and both needed the oil which Iran wished to sell. Japan was particularly welcome in Tehran because it was regarded as a victim of American imperialism in World War II, and it symbolized for Iranians, as well as for other Muslims, the [eastern nations'] potential to modernize and overcome the superpowers. Since the turn of the century, Iranian and other Muslim intellectuals have considered Japan proof that they, too, could advance rapidly; the victory over Russia in 1905 gave hope to many Iranians.[63] While revolutionary Iran viewed almost the entire world as hostile, Japan was an exception. Similarly, the existing restraints notwithstanding, relations with West Germany also improved. Late in November, its Foreign Minister Hans-Dietrich Genscher, who was considered a close friend, visited Iran and expressed views which were welcomed by Tehran as supporting Iranian war policy. While the economic talks seemed promising, Genscher did not appear to achieve much on human rights and the release of the hostages. Similarly, economic relations with France picked up.

On 10 November, Iran and Britain resumed diplomatic relations. Disagreements still remained, but the Iranian authorities overcame their dislike of Britain. Nevertheless, a newspaper wrote a commentary entitled "Britain Is Still Satan's Father."[64] A few days later, a large banner hung on the wall of the British Embassy said: "Death to Britain. We shall not forget British atrocities." (It was soon taken down by security forces.)[65] These were additional evidence of Rafsanjani's disagreements with Musavi and Mohtashemi. Musavi opposed resumption of ties and expressed his views just two days before agreement was reached, but Rafsanjani seemed to have gained the upper hand in shaping foreign policy. (Early in 1989, there was a retreat from the improvement of relations with Western countries; see below.)

Regarding the Soviet Union, there was progress on economic matters, but politically Iran still expected more signs of Soviet goodwill, particularly in exerting influence on Iraq in the peace negotiations before it moved ahead. Later in the year, the cease-fire and the Soviet withdrawal from Afghanistan created a much better environment for improving ties. The better climate was evident in the frequent exchange of visits, mainly of economic delegations. On 10 November, the Soviet deputy foreign affairs minister arrived in Iran to prepare the 11th meeting of the joint economic commission which was held in Moscow in December. During the meeting, TASS and the IRNA signed an agreement on the exchange of news. In mid-November, the Soviet deputy chairman of the state committee for construction came to Iran at the head of a delegation to study cooperation in the construction field. The Iranians were mainly interested in the expansion of the Isfahan steel mill industry, the construction of dams, and the extension of transportation between the two countries. Details were to be discussed in the framework of the permanent commission for economic cooperation between the two countries.[66] A few days later, a Soviet consular delegation arrived in Tehran and signed a memorandum of understanding. The head of the delegation, Vladimir Gudev, said the USSR felt an urgent need to promote its relations with Iran.[67] Also in mid-November, a memorandum of understanding was signed with the deputy director of the Soviet state committee for housing on cooperation in housing, a field in which Iran faced a crucial problem. Later in the same month, Iranian Deputy Foreign Minister Mahmud Va'ezi visited Moscow and reached an agreement on gas exports to the USSR.[68]

But early in 1989, Tehran was willing to go much further. In a message delivered to Gorbachev on 4 January 1989, by a delegation led by Ayatollah Javadi Amoli, Khomeyni criticized communism and Soviet policy. He advised Gorbachev to begin *perestroika* by revising the policy of "your predecessors" regarding the elimination of God and religion. He added that in these days, "communism can be found [only] in the museums" because "Marxism does not provide answers to any of man's real needs." Pointing to the failure of communist economic philosophy, he advised Gorbachev not to seek refuge in Western capitalism, but rather to "turn to truth," to faith. He suggested that Islamic Iran could "easily fill the ideological vacuum in your system." All this was rhetoric. The most important part of the message was its last sentence: "In any case, as in the past, our country believes in good neighborliness and reciprocal relations, and respects them."[69] No less important was the fact that Gorbachev was the first world leader to receive such a message from Khomeyni, which had reportedly been written by Khomeyni himself.[70] Late in February, Soviet Foreign Minister Eduard Shevardnadze visited Tehran and was privileged to meet with the imam. The meeting was the most important part of Shevardnadze's visit. Khomeyni told him he wished "to open a wider horizon in front of you,"[71] and the Iranian media described the visit as a "turning point" in relations between the two countries.

These developments, though not powerful enough to eliminate the basic Iranian apprehension of the USSR, were signs of an attempt to improve relations with

Moscow. The cease-fire in the Gulf and the Soviet withdrawal from Afghanistan had removed major obstacles; *perestroika* has deeply impressed the leaders of Iran. At the same time that new momentum could be observed in relations with the USSR, domestically, too, pragmatism chalked up new successes.

LATE IN 1988 — LIBERALISM AND SELF-CRITICISM

In the last quarter of the year, pragmatism seemed to be riding high. It extended far beyond reconstruction policies, important as they were, and touched upon the wider issues of revolutionary Iran's social and cultural life, much to the annoyance of those loyal to the more radical Islamic-revolutionary tenets of Khomeyni's dogma.

After the cease-fire a more relaxed and more liberal atmosphere could be sensed that was not the result of a new policy but rather of the cease-fire and of what seemed to be the pragmatists' growing power. The trend put in question the wisdom of the regime's past policies. It signaled a retreat — sometimes with the blessing of the revolutionary authorities — from the dogma, beliefs, and Islamic life-style preached and enforced in the early 1980s. Revolutionary zeal seemed to be flagging: more unveiled women could be seen, mainly in Tehran's wealthier neighborhoods, the Komitehs were not seen on the streets as previously, and the pressure for Islamization was reduced. While the war was stopped primarily to save the revolution, the atmosphere after the cease-fire posed another challenge. While no single example is proof of such a trend, a number of examples taken together create the picture that alarmed those still advocating total loyalty to the old ideology. Below are several such examples:

Draft-dodging: The growing number of draft-dodgers indicated that the decline of revolutionary fervor was perhaps one of the main problems facing the regime. The dimensions of the problem were not clear, but its existence could not be ignored before the cease-fire, and certainly not after it. Early in January 1989, Tehran announced a campaign against draft-dodgers. An officer in the armed forces general headquarters said that severe punishments would be meted out to those who evaded their sacred duty.[72] In purely military terms, the problem was still marginal, but it revealed something about the population's morale.

Birth control: Rapid population growth was one of Iran's most crucial problems at the end of the Shah's rule, and it is even more pressing today. But birth control is also one of the most sensitive issues in Islamic society. In the past, clerics criticized the Shah's attempt to curb population growth as anti-Islamic, and since coming to power, if they did not encourage population growth, they did not discourage it either. Recent statistics show that Iran's population has exceeded the 50m. mark and is increasing at the rate of 3.7% yearly, one of the highest in the world. Some 50% of the population are under 17 years of age. How sensitive the issue has been was evident from the Ministry of Health's naming the Persian Year 1368 (beginning 21 March 1989) "Birth Control Year." Minister of Health 'Ali Reza Marandi said that birth-control devices had been ordered from abroad and plans were afoot to educate the people on the hazards of multiple births.[73]

In December, a leading paper came out with a series of articles in support of birth control. Although this and other papers had previously written about this issue, for the first time the *Kayhan* article quoted senior theologians, as well as officials who advocated birth control. Hujjat al-Islam Morteza Moqteda'i, the spokesman of the

Supreme Judicial Council, said that "on the basis of common interest and necessities and [the need] for preserving the regime" a limit could be set to the number of children "in a correct manner and with specific rules." Hujjat al-Islam Muhammad Yazdi asked: "Can we be proud of [a nation of] hungry Muslims who have to beg the infidels of the world for charity?" Aware of the delicate religious implications of the issue, he went on to explain that "before the sperm settles in the womb, any kind of prevention is religiously permissible." Hujjat al-Islam Asadollah Bayat, a member of the Majlis judicial committee, added that since multiplication of the species in Islam is recommended and not obligatory, therefore "if recommended behavior becomes dangerous and has worrying side effects, the Islamic State can prevent it."[74]

Political liberalization: On 31 December 1988, the law on political parties went into effect. Within a few weeks, some 30 groups applied for the Interior Ministry's formal recognition. They included: the Freedom Movement, led by Mehdi Bazargan, which declared its intention of putting up a candidate for president; the Revolutionary Movement of the People of Iran whose leader, Dr. Kazem Sami, was murdered in November; the Association for the Defense of Freedom, led by Muhammad Tavassoli, a former mayor of Tehran; the Islamic Jihad Party, led by Gholam-Reza Jabari; the Islamic Futurist Party, headed by Mustafa Mir-jalili; and the Martyr Navab Safavi Party, led by Muhammad Mehdi 'Abd-Khoda'i.[75] It was not clear how much freedom these movements would be allowed for political activities, and in any case, most of those who applied for recognition were loyal to the regime. But application for recognition itself signaled a change from past practices when political parties were not allowed. The pardoning of many political prisoners on the eve of the republic's 10th anniversary was interpreted as another step in the same direction of liberalization, although prisoners had been pardoned in previous years as well.

Universities: In mid-January, Montazeri called on his personal representatives in the universities to create an atmosphere favorable to the free expression of political views. He said that his representatives, "except for preventing anti-Islamic deeds and inviting others to the truth, should not obstruct free...thought, expression and action, especially in political and social affairs."[76]

Music and chess: On 10 September 1988, Khomeyni decreed that buying and selling musical instruments would be religiously permissible provided that they were not intended for ignoble purposes or to violate religious norms. He also decreed that playing chess would be allowed as long as it was not gambling.[77]

The "ideal woman": Rafsanjani supported a moderate policy even on the sensitive issue of the veil.[78] On 28 January 1989, on the anniversary of the birthday of the Prophet Muhammad's daughter, Fatima, which is celebrated as "Women's Day" in Iran, Tehran Radio broadcast a program that included interviews with women in the streets. Asked who the "ideal woman was," one respondent said a heroine in a Japanese soap opera, very popular in Iran during the war, was the symbol of the ideal woman. She went on to say that Fatima, who has been upheld by the regime as the ideal woman, could not be a model for today's Iranian women, because she belonged to the past. The program was produced by Tehran Radio's "Islamic Ideology Group" and Khomeyni decreed that those responsible for it should be dismissed; if found guilty of intending to insult Islamic feelings, they should be sentenced to death.[79] The broadcast of such a program has clearly demonstrated the degree of liberalism reached at the end of the revolution's first decade.

Penetrating soul-searching and unprecedented self-criticism followed. Criticism of the government's functioning was followed by harsh words against the revolution's most basic principles, with Montazeri taking the lead. Only extracts of what he had said or written became public knowledge.

In a strongly worded letter to Musavi dated 1 October, Montazeri criticized the government for shortages, interference in foreign trade, inflation, intervention by the RG and the Foundation of the Martyrs in commerce, brutal treatment by judiciary and security organizations, failure to encourage private investment in industry and agriculture, lack of coherence among government agencies in domestic and foreign policy, the existence of costly parallel organizations and agencies, unemployment, and mismanagement.[80] A newspaper reflecting the views of conservative circles also came out vigorously against the prime minister. An editorial accused his government of responsibility for "all violations of the nation's goals and the rule of Islamic values." While Musavi claimed that Iran lacked strong laws "to deal with corruption, bribery, and other issues," the paper wrote that "a strong law does exist, but the main problem lies...in its enforcement [by the government]."[81]

Such a tone was unprecedented, but it was only the beginning. Leaders such as Montazeri, Rafsanjani, Khameneh'i, and Ardebili (i.e., the heads of the three branches of government and Khomeyni's designated heir) went much further; they criticized basic policy of the revolution including policy lines supported by the imam.

Early in February, Montazeri said that the anniversary celebrations should be used for reviewing past policies and learning from "past mistakes," since "we had slogans in the past that turned out to be mistakes." Many slogans, he added, "were impossible to carry out." The young Iranian revolutionaries, he added, "are justified" when criticizing us because there was "a big gap between what has been achieved and what they were promised." Admitting that the regime's inexperience had caused "bottlenecks and deficiencies," he went on to point out other problems: unprofessionalism, extremism, selfishness, group [i.e.,factional] inclinations, injustice, ignoring the people and the revolution's genuine values. All these, he said, had caused great damage to the revolution. Hinting that his own views had been censored, he said that the radio and television should not be a monopoly in the hands of the few. There are people in Iran "who are so afraid of persecution they cannot breathe in peace."[82]

Khameneh'i admitted that Iran might not be "even halfway" toward achieving its general revolutionary aims, though "we have started to move in this direction and this is [in itself] very important." If he could start again, he would give "greater centralization to the executive administration," he said.[83]

Some even questioned the wisdom of Iran's war policy, making declarations that had been typical of the opposition. Rafsanjani said that the aim of achieving victory had been "too big a bite." Ardebili said that he was "among those who believe that the war should have been stopped after the liberation of Khorramshahr" in 1982, and that the takeover of the US Embassy in Tehran had lasted too long. Advocating more self-criticism, he said that unfortunately "we are still at the stage of trying to blame others for our sins."[84]

Such criticism from the top leaders was interpreted as a sign that criticism had been permitted. One newspaper, for example, published an editorial lauding Montazeri's criticism. Evaluating the past decade, the paper said that time had been spent on slogans instead of on action. If such a trend continued, the paper warned, the revolution would have to retreat from its objectives.[85] The next day Khomeyni intervened. His decree against Salman Rushdie, the British author of *The Satanic Verses*, stopped the trend toward self-criticism and liberalism (see below).

THE MAJLIS ELECTIONS OF APRIL-MAY 1988: A MARK OF THE SYSTEM'S STABILITY

The Second Majlis having completed its constitutional four-year term, elections for the Third Majlis took place in April (the first round) and May (the second round). The holding of elections on schedule, the formation of competing groups, the relative calm during the campaign, and the election results, all attested to how much clerical rule had become consolidated and stabilized since elections to the First Majlis in 1980.

As in 1984 — and in clear contrast with 1980 — only groups totally loyal to Khomeyni were allowed to participate (see *MECS* 1979–80, pp. 450–54; 1983–84, pp. 433–38). Some movements allowed to run in 1980, such as Mujahidine Khalq and the Tudeh, had long been outlawed; others, like the Freedom Movement (*Nehzate Azadi*), were barred from participation, as they had been in 1984. Thus, in elections to the Third Majlis as in the Second, the campaign was restricted to groups which, however much they may have differed, were all "followers of the imam's line." At this time, conflicts within the purely Islamic groups came to the surface most dramatically among the Association of Tehran's Militant Clerics (see below).

Their rule having become stabilized, the top leadership, who in 1980 had encouraged clerics to run for office or to campaign, now worked to limit their involvement in politics and encouraged other movements to contest the elections, provided they were sufficiently loyal to the revolution. Taking their clue from Khomeyni's earlier declarations, the top leaders now argued against the notion that only clerics had the right to engage in political activity. The leaders advised clerics in senior positions (i.e., *Jum'a Imams*, judges, or functionaries in the revolutionary organs) to refrain "as much as possible" from running for election and from identifying with any of the competing factions or candidates. Presumably recognizing the growing dissatisfaction with the concentration of power in the hands of the clerics, they appealed to groups outside the religious establishment — such as university students, and professors, other professionals, and the bazaar merchants — to run for election. The leaders reminded the public that being religious was not, in itself, a sufficient qualification for a candidate; votes should go to those who were not only loyal to Islam and the revolution, but who were also competent in their field of expertise. The leaders, nevertheless, made it clear that only candidates with proven loyalty to the revolution should be elected and that priority should be given to those who had experienced poverty or, at least, had committed themselves to helping the *mostaz'efin*.

All this was evidence that the clerics felt secure in their power, but were also mindful of growing public dissatisfaction. In many respects, their election campaign reflected that of 1984. But the outcome was different: unlike 1984 when more clerics were elected than in 1980, the results of the 1988 elections showed a clear decline in the number of the professional clergy voted into the Majlis (see figures below).

Another concern of the top leadership was to ensure the largest possible voter turnout. As in the previous two campaigns, they stressed the importance of massive participation for the consolidation of the republic. Above all, they argued, a large turnout would prove to enemies at home and abroad that the people were still "on the scene" (i.e., actually supporting the revolution). The Iraqi attacks on Iranian cities, including on election day itself, made a large turnout an expression of support not only for the regime, but also for its war policy. To encourage participation, the clerics called balloting a "religious duty,"[86] and spread rumors about punishment of those who did not vote.

Polling day was much calmer than in 1980 and gloomier than in 1984. Acts of violence on the part of the opposition groups were few in number and did not disturb the elections. Much more troublesome were Iraqi air attacks. For obvious reasons, the issue of the war was not part of the campaign; all candidates declared their loyalty to Khomeyni's formula of "War, war until victory." But the war could not be ignored; its impact on the country and its effect on the popular mood could not be underestimated. Even the efficient government propaganda machine could not hide the growing public dissatisfaction with the continuation of the war, the "war of cities," the tension in the Gulf, and the recent Iranian losses along the borders.

According to the official count, 17,004,403 voters cast their ballots in the first round, as compared with 15,482,523 in the Second Majlis and 10,874,470 in the First.[87] But clearly the enthusiasm of the earlier years of the revolution had given way to gloom and concern. Many people felt obliged to vote for fear of the consequences of not doing so. Opposition circles claimed that the government had inflated the number of voters and that in many cases it had interfered with the counting of ballots. In Tehran, the Supervision Committee demanded that the ballots in some 30 polling stations be recounted. Pragmatists claimed that the Ministry of the Interior had interfered in favor of the radicals, but Mohtashemi rebuffed such charges and refused to have a recount. Disagreements between the committee and the ministry were so grave that Khomeyni intervened, appointing a two-man committee which approved the results within two days.[88]

Of 270 Majlis members, 179 were elected in the first round, as against 123 in the Second Majlis, and 97 in the First. In the Central Province (Tehran), it was again Rafsanjani who gained the most impressive support (82.2% of the total number of votes). Second was Mehdi Karubi (61.3%), and third Fakhr al-Din Hijazi (44.6%). Rafsanjani and Karubi were also the first and second in 1984, with a strikingly similar measure of public support, 82% and 62.5% respectively. There were many new faces in the Third Majlis, as many as 142 members, or more than half being elected for the first time; and only 35 were elected for the third time.

In the First Majlis there had been 98 "professional clerics" (*mo'amamin*; "those who wear the turban"). In the Second Majlis their number had increased to 122 or almost half of all the members, but it declined to 71, slightly more than a quarter, in the Third Majlis. The number of those "not wearing the turban" increased from 118 in the First Majlis to 147 in the Second and to 189 in the Third.[89] The Third Majlis had more professional-technocrats and fewer professional men of religion, another indication of Khomeyni's determination to limit the political involvement of the clerics and to allow professionalism greater scope to help solve the problems facing the state.

The trend toward greater professionalism could also be seen in the educational background of the Majlis members. We have data about almost all Majlis members.[90] In the First Majlis, 122 members had a traditional-religious education, in the Second they were 153, but in the Third only 68. Those with regular state education numbered

139 in the First Majlis, 122 in the Second, and 204 in the Third. Those with the highest level of religious education (at the level of *ijtihad*) numbered 30 in the First Majlis, 28 in the Second, but only 11 in the Third. As far as "modern" (state) education is concerned, 128 members of the Third Majlis were university graduates, as compared with 74 in the Second and 115 in the First.

The Third Majlis was also much younger than the first two: 71 members of the Third were under 35 years old, as compared with 67 and 37 in First and Second, while 121 were between 35 and 45 (79 and 123 in the First and Second). Only 15 members of the Third Majlis were above 55 (15 and 29 in the First and Second, respectively).[91]

The campaign highlighted sharp differences between conservative and radical clerics. Socioeconomic policy was the main issue on which they differed. Advocating a greater role for the public sector, the radical clerics interpreted statements by Khomeyni (e.g., his decree to the president in January stating that the government could change laws, earlier statements telling the Majlis to pay more attention to the poor, and the formation of the council for ascertaining the interests [of the state] as well as his decree published a week before election day, calling on the people not to vote for candidates who supported what he called "capitalist Islam," "Islam of the property owners" and "American type of Islam," but to vote for the "true Islam of the dispossessed and for those who have tasted the bitter taste of poverty")[92] supporting their policies.

In Tehran, the main contest was between candidates backed by the Tehran Association of Combatant Clerics (*Jame'e Ruhaniyyate Mobarez*) headed by Mahdavi-Kani its secretary-general, and supported by Rafsanjani, Khameneh'i, Ardebili, and Safi and between a hard-line breakaway faction, the Combatant Clerics of Tehran (*Ruhaniyyane Mobareze Tehran*; RMT) in which Kho'iniha, the prosecutor-general, was the driving force. The letter demanded the government take over Iran's prosperous trading sector, put a ceiling on land holdings, and impose higher taxes on the rich. The former pressed for loosening of controls on the private sector and the co-optation of technocrats into the government.

Some 1,600 candidates contested the 270 seats, compared with 1,584 candidates in 1984 and c. 2,000 in 1980. After the Islamic Republican Party was dissolved in 1987, there were no party lists. Among the many competing lists were religious groups active since the inception of the new regime and *ad hoc* lists formed for the elections. Although all of them followed Khomeyni's line, they differed in their approach, mainly to social and economic problems. These differences were not reflected in their public campaign,[93] but were often revealed in the composition of the lists. As in previous contests, some of the candidates were included in most lists, most prominent among them being Rafsanjani and Mehdi Karubi who headed all the lists. But each list had a few distinctive candidates; such variations of the different lists were an important yardstick to examine their success and the relative power of the different groups.

For Tehran's 30 seats, the radical RMT had a few candidates who appeared on all lists (e.g., Rafsanjani and Karubi) and some candidates supported by other groups, but some candidates appeared only on the RMT list. They gained a significant success: only three of the 30 candidates on the RMT list (Anvari, Najafi-'Ilmi, and Muhammad Sadeqi) failed to gain a seat. Moreover, all the 14 representatives elected in the first round (i.e., getting the most votes) were on the RMT list. In its campaign, the RMT said its policy was "to defend the dispossessed and the underprivileged and the implementation of the manifesto of the revolution" (i.e., to help the *mostaz'efin*), "to support the executive branches of government which follow the line of the imam," and to strengthen the Majlis by a free election of representatives.[94] All this showed that the RMT was mainly critical of the republic's social and economic policy and favored more radical steps to help the *mostaz'efin*. The RMT's break with the Tehran Association of Combatant Clerics and its campaign indicated that it was determined to struggle for the advancement of its goals.

Another radical list with similar purposes was "The Coalition of the Dispossessed and the Deprived" *E'telafe Mostaz'efin va-Mahrumin*). As is clear from the name, its main concern was to help the *mostaz'efin*. Other issues raised in their campaign were the need to advance the "line of the imam," to continue the war, and to create the "Islam of the barefoot poor" (*Islame pahberahnegan*). The term *Islame pahberahnegan* crystallized the group's social, economic, and political philosophy, as well as its criticism of the regime's current policy.[95]

The candidates supported by this "coalition" also scored an impressive success. Their 30 candidates for Tehran included some who were common to all other lists, a few who were also on the list of the *Jame'e Ruhaniyyate Mobarez,* many who appeared on the list of the RMT, and a few who were their own candidates. Altogether 23 of the candidates supported by the coalition were elected, most of them new faces who pushed aside some of the better-known contenders on other lists. In other words, only seven candidates who failed to secure the support of this coalition won seats; they were Raja'i Khorasani, Nateq-Nuri, 'Abbas Sheybani, Hasan Ruhani, 'Abbas 'Ali 'Amid Zanjani, 'Isa Vela'i, and Muhammad Reza Bahonar, some of them well known as leading pragmatists. Moreover, of those 14 who were elected in the first round, only one, 'Abbas Sheybani, was not on the coalition list.

On the other hand, out of the 30 candidates of the relatively moderate *Jame'e Ruhaniyyate Mobarez,* only 13 were elected; 10 of them were also supported by the RMT, six of them by the coalition as well. Thus, only three candidates of the *Jame'e Ruhaniyyate Mobarez* who were not supported by either RMT or the coalition were elected: Raja'i Khorasani, Nateq-Nuri, and Bahonar. Some prominent figures on the list of *Jame'e Ruhaniyyate Mobarez,* who in the past had expressed moderate views, were not elected: Muhammad Yazdi, Asghar-Owladi, Dr. Najafabadi, and Muhammad Kermani. These figures indicate the failure of the moderates in the elections.

Classification of Majlis members into one or another group is not an easy task; the fact that most candidates appeared on different lists makes it even more difficult. With this in mind, the election campaign and its results could shed some light on the political mood in the spring of 1988. Below are some conclusions:

* The clerics in power were the real winners. The holding of the election on schedule was in itself an achievement for the regime, which indicated the young republic's relative stability. All Majlis members were, as in the Second Majlis, either professional clerics or their supporters.

* The main issues raised in the campaign — the social and economic problems — were the main challenges facing the regime.

* As between radicals and pragmatists, the former clearly gained the upper hand in this election. But as one could observe in 1988, though the Majlis was more radical, policy was more pragmatic.

A NEW PHASE OF "RADICALISM"

EARLY SIGNS OF "RADICALIZATION": VIOLENT CLASHES

While the struggle for power among leaders came into the open only during the anniversary celebrations in early 1989, it had in fact continued throughout 1988, as it had in earlier years of revolution. Western opinion by and large viewed the struggle as one between "moderates" and "extremists." The situation was much more complex; even identifying individual leaders with one group or another was hard. For one thing, the competing groups were not organized into clear-cut factions, let alone political parties. All proclaimed themselves to be "followers" of the imam's "line," all declared their support for Montazeri (until his dismissal), and Khomeyni took care not to identify himself with any of the factions or disapprove of them.

As usual in Iran, personal rivalries and ideological controversy were often indistinguishable. In his reply to Hujjat al-Islam Ansari, Khomeyni had divided the political-ideological groups into two factions (see above). But it would be wrong to argue that there were no others and that all of them had a coherent ideology; each of the two factions mentioned by Khomeyni consisted of several groups, some pragmatic, some radical. Members had switched loyalties and the alliances had constantly changed. For example, Ahmad Khomeyni, who was identified with the pragmatists in general and with Rafsanjani personally, made an alliance with Mohtashemi, the figurehead of the radicals. Some leaders appeared moderate on one issue and extremely radical on another. For example, Montazeri expressed liberal views on domestic policy, but radical ones on the export of the revolution. To show how complicated the problem is, the following example is instructive. In 1987, when Mehdi Hashemi was executed and Montazeri's supporters were attacked, observers viewed it as a blow to the radicals (see *MECS* 1987, p. 400). In 1989, when Montazeri's supporters, including Mehdi's brother, were attacked, it was generally seen as a blow to the pragmatists. At this stage, therefore, no definite conclusions on the strength of the competing camps could be drawn.

Given these reservations, one can nonetheless make a general distinction between two major trends: pragmatist-conservative and radical-extremist. The first was headed by Rafsanjani; other prominent figures believed to support or identify with it at the end of 1988 were: Khameneh'i (the president), Muhammad Reza Mahdavi-Kani (former minister of interior), Velayati (minister for foreign relations), and Hujjat al-Islam 'Ali Akbar Nateq-Nuri (former minister of the interior). The radicals were headed by Ahmad Khomeyni and Mohtashemi; other prominent members were: Ayatollah 'Ali Meshkini (chairman of the Council of Experts), Mir-Husayn Musavi (prime minister), Ayatollah Muhammad Reyshahri (minister of intelligence), Hujjat al-Islam Muhammad Musavi Kho'iniha (prosecutor-general), Sadeq Khalkhali (chairman of the Majlis's committee on foreign relations), Ardebili (president of the supreme court, who until recently had been more identified with the other group), Mehdi Karubi (head of the foundation of the *Mostaz'efin*) and 'Abdollah Nuri (Khomeyni's representative in the RG).

The struggle between the two camps became violent in late 1988. In November, Reyshahri officially confirmed that some "pseudoclergymen" were executed. He said that since the republic's law applied to all, it was natural that when "pseudoclergymen" committed an offense they, too, would be dealt with according to the law.[96] Early in

December, at a meeting with students, Khameneh'i was asked about "the widespread executions throughout Iran." He denied that there had been large-scale executions, but added that Iran had a death penalty for those "who deserve it."[97] According to most sources, dozens of Montazeri's supporters were then executed. Of greatest impact in political circles was the execution of Hujjat al-Islam Omid Najafabadi, a close aide to Montazeri and former Majlis deputy. Opposition sources reported several attempts to assassinate Rafsanjani and other leading pragmatists: these claims were hard to substantiate.

While public opinion focused on the execution of clerics, the government virtually suppressed the opposition, mainly those with leftist tendencies. Late in 1988, many Tudeh members were put to death and the Mujahidine Khalq were further suppressed. 'Ali Khavari, the first secretary of the Tudeh, said that the number of those killed "exceeds thousands," some of the victims having been high-ranking Central Committee members. He attributed the executions to "the current political crisis of the...regime and its inability to continue its rule."[98] As before, it was not the opposition which posed the main threat to the regime, but rather the struggle for power among the imam's disciples.

TEMPERS INCITED AGAINST SALMAN RUSHDIE

On 14 February 1989, three days after the 10th anniversary of the revolution, and while self-criticism was reaching threatening proportions, Khomeyni published a decree making it a religious duty of Muslims anywhere to kill Rushdie.[99] The decree ushered in a new phase of radicalism. The radicals' outstanding success was the dismissal of Montazeri on 26 March 1989. Other signs of their strength were the dismissal in the same month of prominent officials considered to be pragmatists, such as Larijani, the deputy foreign minister who was the main advocate of improving ties with the West, and Mahalati, the ambassador to the UN, and the appointment of leading radicals to sensitive posts, such as 'Abdollah Nuri, who became Khomeyni's representative in the RG. Additional signs were the attack on Montazeri's supporters in Najafabad, Montazeri's hometown and the eventual house arrest (or jailing) of his son-in-law, Hadi Hashemi, the brother of Mehdi who had been executed in 1987. But the best evidence of the change was that those known for their pragmatist views had adopted rhetoric more radical than that of the radicals. A statement by Rafsanjani in May 1989, in which he suggested that the Palestinians kill five Americans, Frenchmen, or Englishmen for each Palestinian killed in the West Bank and Gaza Strip, was the best example.[100] (For a more detailed discussion of these developments, see chapter on Iran in *MECS* 1989.)

This new wave of radicalism became evident when pragmatism seemed to be riding a wave. The cease-fire, the reconstruction policy, the improved relations with the outside world, and the more relaxed atmosphere in Iran were all evidence of the more pragmatic policy adopted toward the end of the republic's first decade. The shift to radicalism followed the revolution's 10th anniversary celebrations. It should be kept in mind that the power struggle in Iran had not ceased. In the past, Khomeyni had used his authority to strike a balance between the pragmatists and the radicals, often switching his support from one to the other. In mid-1988 he seemed to back the pragmatists by accepting the cease-fire and giving his approval, though unofficial, to their reconstruction policy, but early in 1989, he shifted his weight to the radicals. This change moved the entire political system in a new direction from pragmatism to renewed radicalism.

The pragmatic policies after the war, the somewhat liberal atmosphere late in 1988, and the criticism of the revolution, including some of Khomeyni's basic policies, moved the imam to interfere to save the revolution. In the summer of 1988 he had believed he was serving this aim by following the advice of the pragmatists, in February 1989 he believed he was serving the same aim by supporting the radicals. Following the cease-fire, revolutionary zeal declined and a need was felt to stimulate religious-revolutionary fervor. Toward this end, Rushdie's book served the revolution just as the American hostages had in 1979; it unified the revolutionary forces against the external demonical enemy and stirred up passions around an issue which all believers could, and should, identify with. The focus on an external enemy thus served to divert public attention from the immediate problems at home.

The revolution had raised expectations which, for the most part, remained unfulfilled. The regime, which had used the war to justify the existence of economic problems and had asked for restraint on material improvement, was now called upon to improve the economy. Khomeyni took the lead in trying to lower expectations. He made clear in a number of speeches that "the postwar shortcomings will not be eliminated rapidly and it will take several years until the shortages are removed."[101] An editorial in a daily newspaper even said that the people should be told "to prepare for economic austerity ahead rather than be allowed to flatter themselves with unrealistic hopes for affluence." It made clear that a long time would pass before reconstruction showed significant results.[102]

The pragmatists' failure to solve the country's problems could also explain the return to radicalism; the self-criticism on the eve of the 10th anniversary, mainly by those advocating pragmatism, became a double-edged sword.

The criticism voiced by Montazeri and other leaders (see above) seemed to be the last straw in convincing Khomeyni to move against the pragmatists. Their criticism had led to the radicalism engendered by the need felt to divert popular attention from domestic problems to an outside enemy; and most importantly, Khomeyni felt obliged to intervene and put an end to threats to the revolution. The reorganization of the radicals and Ahmad Khomeyni joining them gave them more power and helped secure Khomeyni's support. The support of Mohtashemi was also instrumental in organizing the radical camp.

The first public expression of the turn to radicalism was the decree concerning Rushdie. His book had offended Khomeyni and most Muslims. It was published some six months before Khomeyni's decree; during this interval much was said against the book in different Muslim communities but Tehran remained silent. The timing of the decree was influenced by the dynamics of the Islamic revolution; Rushdie was not the aim, he was the means for securing revolutionary goals. Early in 1989, the radicals were on the offensive but the outcome of the contest was not clear: on the contrary — the pragmatists led by Rafsanjani seemed as powerful as ever.

THE VICISSITUDES OF PRAGMATISM AND RADICALISM: A RETROSPECT

Those who have closely followed Iranian affairs during the last decade are familiar with the swings in policy from radicalism to pragmatism and back. In the second half of 1988, Tehran seemed to be following a more pragmatic policy, but since the 10th anniversary, policy seemed to return to radicalism. Such changes have been a repeating feature in the Islamic regime, reflecting, as we have seen, the ongoing and deep struggle for power between different groups, each with its distinctive interpretations of Khomeyni's worldview and with its own sectarian and personal interests.

Looking at the first decade as a whole, the general trend was one of gradual pragmatism interrupted by outbursts of radicalism that lasted a few months, or even a year. Although the leading figures, the issues in dispute, and the political alliances changed considerably, there were some repetitive features.

At the time of the seizure of power, the struggle was between the then prime minister, Mehdi Bazargan, who followed a more pragmatic line, and his more radical opponents. When Bazargan's policy seemed to be reaching a peak, the radicals — the students following the imam's line and their patrons, such as Kho'iniha — seized the American hostages and initiated a phase of radicalism that lasted for many months. After a few months in office, President Abul-Hasan Bani Sadr returned to a more pragmatic policy, but in June 1981, he was ousted and a new phase of radicalism began. This phase lasted, again, several months. In late 1983, the clerics themselves, now in control of policy, initiated a more pragmatic phase under the leadership of Rafsanjani. This phase, which lasted longer than previously, peaked with the arms deals with the US in 1985–86. It was followed by another period of radicalism that began with the disclosure of the Iran-Contra affair in November 1986 and went on for about a year. But unlike what had happened in the past when those more radical had the upper hand, this time the more pragmatic among them gained ground. The radicals, too, had their successes: the elections of a relatively radical Majlis, the tension in Iran's relations with France and England in 1987, the events of the Mecca pilgrimage in 1987, and the confrontation with the US in the Gulf. The spring of 1988 saw a new phase of pragmatism, which reached a peak, this time, with Iran's decision to accept the cease-fire and the policy declarations regarding reconstruction. At the beginning of each cycle, the radicals would pick an issue they believed would fan revolutionary zeal and gain Khomeyni's support: the seizure of the American hostages (used against Bazargan), the animosity toward the "liberals" (in the case of Bani Sadr), the American arms sales to Iran (used against Rafsanjani), and Rushdie's book were all such instances. But in the background to all of these cases, the real issue was the struggle for power.

These changes teach us, above all, that the struggle for power is not yet over. Although the nature of the contest, the contenders, and rules of the game have changed, the struggle continues over the nature and for the leadership of post-Khomeyni Iran. In the past, those assuming power following such contests, even those considered radicals, had become more pragmatic; but the more radical the worldview the slower the process of becoming more pragmatic and the less penetrating the pragmatism.

NOTES

For the place and frequency of publications cited here, and for the full name of the publication, news agency, radio station, or monitoring service where an abbreviation is used, please see "List of Sources." Only in the case of more than one publication bearing the same name is the place of publication noted here.

1. One possible yardstick of the relative stability is institutional stability. As against the frequent changes in the first two years or so of the incumbents of senior positions (see *MECS* 1981–82, p. 532), since the spring of 1981 (until summer 1989), there has been no change of president, prime minister, Majlis Speaker, and president of the Supreme Court.
2. Similarly profound changes occurred in his worldview between the 1940s and the 1970s. See my articles: "Shi'ite Leadership: In the Shadow of Conflicting Ideologies," *Iranian Studies,* Vol. 13, Nos. 1–4 (1980), pp. 119–45.
3. For a more elaborate discussion of the points raised here, see my article "Iran: Doctrine and Reality," in Efraim Karsh (ed.), *The Iraq-Iran War: Impact and Implications* (London: Macmillan, 1989), pp. 42–57. I wish to express my thanks to the Jaffee Center for Strategic Studies at Tel Aviv University for their permission to include portions of the above-mentioned article in this chapter. See also the postscript of my book: *Iran: A Decade of War and Revolution* (New York: Holmes & Meier, 1990).
4. *Ettela'at,* 7 February 1988.
5. *Ettela'at,* 31 August 1988.
6. R. Tehran, 31 December — SWB, 3 January 1989.
7. R. Tehran, 1 January — SWB, 3 January 1989.
8. NHK TV, Tokyo, 1 February — SWB, 3 February 1988.
9. For a discussion of Khomeyni's idea of "exporting" the revolution and his actual policy in this regard, see my article: "Khomeyni's Vision: Nationalism or World Order," in David Menashri (ed.), *The Islamic Revolution and the Muslim World* (Boulder: Westview, forthcoming).
10. *Ettela'at,* 3 July 1988.
11. *Kayhan,* 2 July 1988.
12. R. Tehran, 8 April — SWB, 11 April; *Ettela'at,* 23 July 1988, respectively.
13. For a discussion of the social and economic problems on the eve of the revolution, see my book, *Iran: A Decade of War and Revolution,* pp. 1–5. For the economic difficulties during the decade of Islamic rule, see my article "Doctrine and Reality," pp. 47–50.
14. R. Tehran, 9 February — DR, 9 February 1988.
15. See his message to the people of 20 July; *Ettela'at,* 21 July 1988.
16. *Ettela'at,* 15 March; R. Tehran, 14 March — SWB, 16 March 1988. Similarly in the statement released by the War Information Headquarters: R. Tehran, 15 March — SWB, 17 March 1988.
17. R. Tehran, 17 March — SWB, 19 March 1988; "'Aflaqis" is a reference to Michel 'Aflaq, the ideologue of Ba'th teachings vindicated by the War Information Headquarters: R. Tehran, 15 March — SWB, 17 March 1988.
18. R. Tehran, 18 March — SWB, 21 March 1988.
19. Tehran TV, 24 March — SWB, 26 March 1988.
20. *Ettela'at,* 14 July; Tehran TV, 13 July — DR, 14 July 1988. For a similar discussion of the reasons leading Iran to accept the cease-fire, see my book, *Iran: A Decade of War and Revolution,* postscript.
21. *Ettela'at,* 19 July; R. Tehran, 18 July — DR, 19 July 1988.
22. *Ettela'at,* 3 July; R. Tehran, 2 July — DR, 6 July 1988.
23. *Ettela'at,* 14 July; Tehran TV, 13 July — DR, 14 July 1988.
24. *Ettela'at,* 2 July; R. Tehran, 1 July — DR, 6 July 1988.
25. *Ettela'at,* 9 July; R. Tehran, 8 July — DR, 8 July 1988.
26. R. Tehran, 18 July — DR, 19 July 1988.
27. *Ettela'at,* 9 July; R. Tehran, 8 July — DR, 8 July 1988.
28. R. Tehran, 18 July — DR, 19 July 1988.
29. R. Tehran, 18 July — DR, 18 July 1988.
30. *Ettela'at,* 21 July 1988.

31. *Ettela'at*, 5 July; R. Tehran, 4 July — DR, 5 July 1988.
32. *Ettela'at*, 21 July 1988.
33. *Ettela'at*, 8 October; R. Tehran, 7 October — SWB, 10 October 1988. For a similar discussion, touching on the theme of the reconstruction policy, see my book *Iran: A Decade of War and Revolution*, postscript.
34. R. Tehran, 25 September — SWB, 27 September 1988.
35. *Ettela'at*, 8 October; R. Tehran, 7 October — SWB, 10 October 1988.
36. *Ettela'at*, 19 October; IRNA (in English), 19 October — SWB, 20 October 1988.
37. R. Tehran, 25 September — SWB, 27 September 1988.
38. *Ettela'at*, 31 August 1988.
39. *Ettela'at*, 26 November; R. Tehran, 24 November — SWB, 26 November 1988.
40. *Ettela'at*, 4 October; R. Tehran, 3 October — SWB, 5 October 1988.
41. R. Tehran, 9 October — SWB, 11 October 1988.
42. *Ettela'at*, 15 October; R. Tehran, 14 October — SWB, 17 October 1988.
43. *Ettela'at*, 26 November; R. Tehran, 25 November — SWB, 28 November 1988.
44. *Ettela'at*, 17 September 1988.
45. R. Tehran, 6 December — SWB, 9 December 1988.
46. Tehran TV, 17 December — SWB, 20 December 1988.
47. *JI*, 7 November; *Kayhan*, 16 November 1988.
48. *Ettela'at*, 7 September; R. Tehran, 7 September — SWB, 8, 9 September 1988.
49. *Ettela'at*, 13 September; R. Tehran, 12 September — SWB, 9, 14 September 1988.
50. IRNA (in English), 19 November — SWB, 21 November 1988.
51. R. Tehran, 29 November — SWB, 1 December 1988.
52. R. Tehran, 19 November — SWB, 21 November 1988.
53. R. Tehran, 19 November — SWB, 21 November 1988.
54. Tehran TV, 17 December — SWB, 20 December 1988.
55. R. Tehran, 7 October — SWB, 10 October 1988.
56. IRNA (in English), 21 November — SWB, 24 November 1988.
57. See, for example, a Friday sermon by Rafsanjani (R. Tehran, 25 November — SWB, 28 November) and his letter to Jimmy Carter in November (R. Tehran, 28 November — SWB, 30 November). See similarly, Khomeyni's speech, R. Tehran, 7 December — SWB, 9 December 1988.
58. *Ettela'at*, 23 January 1989.
59. *TT*, 29 January 1989.
60. R. Tehran, 1 February — SWB, 2 February 1989.
61. R. Tehran, 14 February — SWB, 14 February 1989.
62. *Ettela'at*, 25 February; R. Tehran, 22 February — SWB, 24 February 1989.
63. A number of obstacles stood in the way of good relations with Japan and West Germany: the fact that Iran's trade with both was unbalanced; the huge petrochemical complex in Bandar Khomeyni; and the anti-Khomeyni activities of Iranian students in Germany.
64. *JI*, 13 November 1988.
65. *Iran Focus*, December 1988, pp. 2–3.
66. *Ettela'at*, 14 November; R. Tehran, 13 November — SWB, 22 November 1988.
67. IRNA (in English), 20 November — SWB, 23 November 1988.
68. *Kayhan*, 30 November — *The Echo of Iran*, 8 December 1988.
69. *Ettela'at*, 9 January; R. Tehran, 8 January — SWB, 10 January 1989.
70. R. Tehran, 13 January — SWB, 16 January 1989.
71. *Ettela'at*, 27 February 1989.
72. R. Tehran, 2 January — SWB, 4 January 1989.
73. *Kayhan*, 19 December 1988.
74. Ibid.
75. IRNA (in English), 9, 12, 14, 24 January — SWB, 12, 13, 17, 25 January 1989.
76. *Kayhan*, 19 January 1989.
77. *Ettela'at*, 10 September; IRNA (in English), 10 September — SWB, 13 September 1988.
78. Tehran TV, 17 December — SWB, 20 December 1988.
79. Investigation proved no malicious intent; those responsible were sentenced to four-five years' imprisonment and 50 lashes, and were later pardoned by Khomeyni. *Kayhan*, 30 January; IRNA, 30, 31 January — DR, 30, 31 January; *Ettela'at*, 31 January 1989.

80. *Iran Focus,* December 1988, pp. 2–3.
81. *Resalat,* 10, 12 November 1988.
82. *Abrar,* 6 February — SWB, 8 February 1989.
83. R. Tehran, 8 February — SWB, 10 February 1989.
84. R. Tehran, 8 February — SWB, 10 February 1989.
85. *TT,* 13 February 1989.
86. See words of Rafsanjani (*Ettela'at,* 6 April) and Khomeyni (ibid., 7 April 1988).
87. It should be noted, however, that between the first elections and the third, the population grew by over 10m.
88. For such disagreements, see an interview with Mohtashemi in *Ettela'at,* 20 April 1988.
89. *Kayhan,* 29 May 1989.
90. The number may exceed the total number of Majlis members, because some members had partly religous and partly state education and because some new members in the First Majlis were elected in by-elections to fill vacant seats in the House.
91. *Kayhan,* 29 May 1988. Data were available for 216 members of the Third Majlis, 260 of the First, and 266 of the Third Majlis.
92. *Ettela'at,* 31 March 1988.
93. See, for example, interviews with Muhammad Khatami and Imam Jamarani in *Ettela'at,* 4 April 1988.
94. See their list in *Ettela'at,* 6 April 1988.
95. *Ettela'at,* 5 April 1988.
96. R. Tehran, 28 November — *The Echo of Iran,* 8 December 1988.
97. R. Tehran, 6 December — SWB, 9 December 1988.
98. R. of the Toilers of Iran, 27 December — SWB, 30 December 1988.
99. *Ettela'at,* 15 February 1989.
100. *Ettela'at,* 6 May 1989.
101. R. Tehran, 10 January — SWB, 12 January 1989.
102. *Abrar,* 11 January — SWB, 11 January 1989.

Iraq
(Al-Jumhuriyya al-'Iraqiyya)

OFRA BENGIO

The most significant development of the year for Iraq was the cease-fire with Iran, which came into force on 20 August, putting an end to the eight-year war, though not necessarily to the conflict between the two belligerents. The cease-fire came at the height of a series of Iraqi military victories which had started on 18 April with the recapture of Faw which marked another turning point in the war. After six years of being on the defensive, the Iraqi Army assumed the initiative, and forced the Iranian Army out of occupied Iraqi territories (at Shalamcheh, Majnun, and areas in the Kurdish north) and forced the Iranian Government to the negotiating table (see chapter on the Iraqi-Iranian War).

Analysts differed on whether to regard the cease-fire an Iraqi victory or not. More important was that Iraq considered it as the most important victory in modern Arab history. The truth of the matter was that Iraq had overcome one of the most serious challenges to its existence in its modern history. The challenge was twofold: along with the war with Iran, Iraq had to cope with the uprising of its Kurds, who acted in concert with Iran. To defeat this uprising and solve the endemic Kurdish problem once and for all, the Iraqi Army used the deadliest weapon a state ever turned against its own citizens: a chemical weapon (in addition to more conventional methods, such as the destruction of entire Kurdish villages and Arabization of the north). Iraq thus managed to maintain its territorial integrity, but did so at a high price; the brutal methods used made the chances of integrating the Kurds into the state even remoter. Thus, while the war may have strengthened national and patriotic bonds among the Arabs — Sunnis and Shi'is alike — it further alienated the Kurds from the body politic.

President Saddam Husayn used the military victories to project himself as a national hero and an omnipotent ruler, but beneath the surface were acute problems, such as pressures for the democratization of the political system. Husayn reacted by announcing steps in this direction, which, as it turned out, were a cover for further eroding the power of the Ba'th Party, the Revolutionary Command Council (RCC), and influential individuals in the ruling circle, while at the same time expanding his own personal rule and that of relatives and supporters. An even acuter problem for Husayn was to contain the ambitions of a victorious army. In various ways, he succeeded in removing this potential danger to himself. Likewise, the regime managed to ease the social and economic crises which are characteristic of a transitional period, and the great uncertainties and dislocations that they entailed.

The military successes and the development of Iraqi-made weaponry catapulted the country to the position of a regional power and a competitor for leadership in the

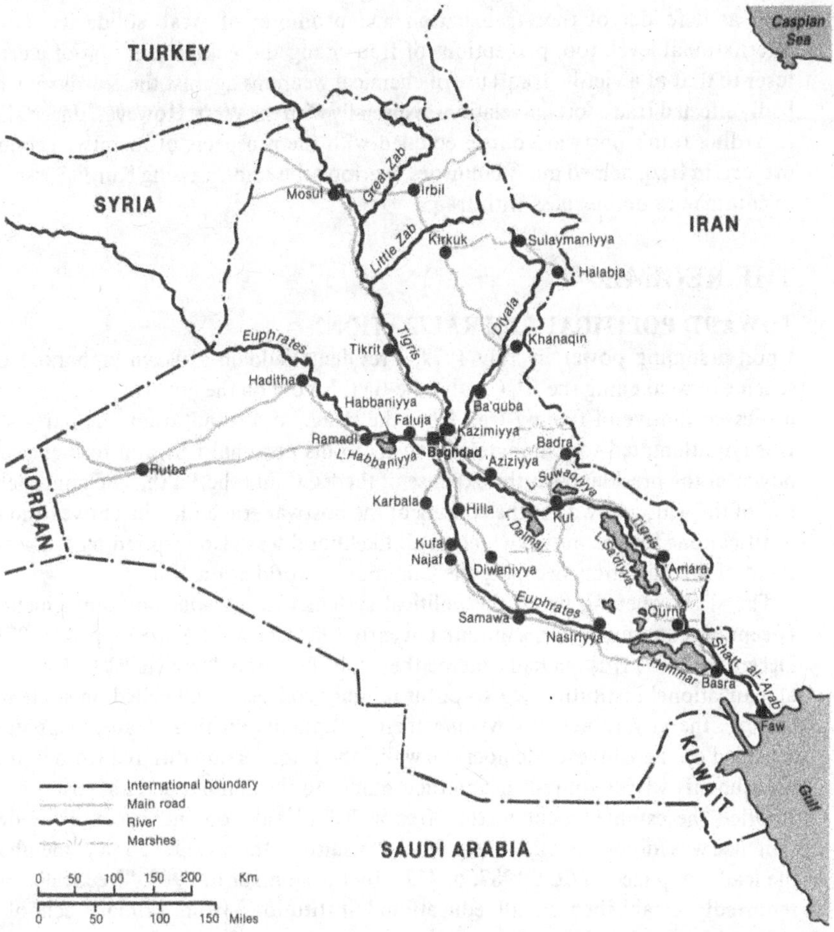
TURKEY
SYRIA
IRAN
JORDAN
KUWAIT
SAUDI ARABIA
Caspian Sea
Gulf
Mosul
Irbil
Great Zab
Little Zab
Kirkuk
Sulaymaniyya
Halabja
Diyala
Khanaqin
Tigris
Tikrit
Euphrates
Haditha
Habbaniyya
Faluja
Ramadi
L. Habbaniyya
Baghdad
Kazimiyya
Ba'quba
Badra
'Aziziyya
L. Suwaqiyya
Kut
Rutba
Karbala
Hilla
L. Dalmaj
L. Sa'diyya
Kufa
Najaf
Diwaniyya
'Amara
Samawa
Nasiriyya
Qurna
L. Hammar
Basra
Shatt al-'Arab
Faw
International boundary
Main road
River
Marshes
0 50 100 150 200 Km
0 50 100 150 Miles

Iraq

Arab world. Iraq made its cautious bid not under the guise of Ba'thi pan-Arab ideology, now regarded as *passé*, but through the development of rhetoric portraying Iraq as defender of the Arab nation and promoter of Arab solidarity. On the international level, too, perceptions of Iraq changed quickly from that of a certain loser to that of a victor. Iraq's use of chemical weapons against the Kurds may have badly effected Iraq's foreign relations, especially with the West. However, uncertainties regarding Iran's postwar course, coupled with the prospects of lucrative economic projects in Iraq, helped many countries overlook the embarrassing Kurdish issue and to continue to do business with Iraq.

THE REGIME

TOWARD POLITICAL LIBERALIZATION?

Upon assuming power in July 1979, President Saddam Husayn embarked on a scheme of weakening the RCC's and the Ba'th's hold on the government. Behind his professed motive of freeing Iraq from the image of a totalitarian one-party state, Husayn attempted to eliminate any rivals to his personal rule and to increase the power of the presidency at the expense of the RCC and the Ba'th. The approaching end of the war, and with it the coming of the postwar era, added incentives and new justifications for the move, which in all likelihood was also inspired by the general trend of liberalization sweeping the Communist world at the time.

The slight opening up of the political system was intended to complement the sweeping economic reforms initiated in early 1987 (see *MECS* 1987, pp. 425–27). In December 1987, Husayn had ordered the establishment of "free walls" (*jidar hurr*) in all educational institutions, "except for military colleges," and called on students to criticize the government by writing their complaints on these walls.[1] Apparently modeled on the Chinese "democratic wall," the Iraqi version differed from it in that the students were required to sign their names to the complaints, a restriction that emptied the establishment of the "free walls" of any content, because the death sentence was imposed on anyone publicly "insulting" the president or any member of the leadership (see *MECS* 1987, p. 437). By the summer of 1988, "free walls" were reportedly established in all educational institutions from primary schools to universities, and at least one complaint was taken up by the National Assembly (*al-majlis al-watani*), the Iraqi Parliament.[2] Explaining the motives for setting up "walls," the head of the Student Union, Anwar Mawlud Dhiban, said that they were designed to inculcate "correct democratic values" and to encourage students to express their "responsible" and "courageous" views on different political, economic, and cultural aspects of life.[3] A slightly different view was expressed by Taha Yasin Ramadan, a member of the RCC, who said that the "free walls" were meant to allow the expression of opinions that did not conflict with "public ethics and the objectives of the revolution."[4]

In early 1988, the RCC decided that hitherto compulsory membership in labor federations, unions, societies, and clubs would become optional.[5] The decree had two aims: to free Iraqis, to a degree, from the embrace of the Ba'thi-led unions which controlled many aspects of their lives and to weaken the Ba'th Party itself by weakening its own organizations, a process which had begun in 1987 with the disbanding of trade unions of the public sector (see *MECS* 1987, pp. 432–34).

Another step toward the opening up of the system was taken in January when, on orders from Husayn, the National Assembly was allowed to inspect ministries and public sector institutions, to question the prime minister and other ministers, and to recommend the punishment of any official found guilty during investigation.[6] On closer analysis, this step would appear less impressive, because the assembly could initiate the questioning only on orders from the president.[7] This step should be seen in the context of Husayn's relentless efforts to weaken the RCC's powers which began with the establishment of the assembly in 1980 as a counterweight to the RCC, had continued in 1982 with the reduction of RCC membership to nine and the inclusion of a Kurdish member, and ended with the convening of joint RCC, Ba'th Regional Command (RC), and cabinet meetings, which reduced significantly the RCC's autonomous powers.[8]

In all likelihood, Husayn regarded the RCC (of which he was the chairman) not only as a rival, but also as an organ which, while indispensable in the formative years, had become redundant after 20 years of Ba'thi rule. At the same time, however, Husayn was reluctant to grant real powers to the assembly. Elections to the assembly, which were scheduled for the end of August, were postponed by six months, because, as the official announcement explained, of "the preoccupation of the people, leadership, and state institutions with circumstances of current battles and consequent results of victory."[9] However, this explanation appeared quite tenuous considering that previous elections — in October 1984 — had been held in the midst of war (see *MECS* 1984–85, p. 464), that preparations for the August elections had started in June, and that by postponing the elections for six months (in reality for more than that) the country would be without an assembly during that period. It was more likely, therefore, that the postponement was a tactic for gaining time and for preparing the ground for the next move.

At the end of November, Husayn announced the decision to move from a one-party to a multiparty system (*ta'addudiyya*), by allowing the formation of new parties with the aim of enlarging the basis of representation in the National Assembly. He emphasized that the decision had been taken two years earlier as a part of the planning for the postwar period, and that all three organs — the RCC, the Ba'th Party RC, and the Cabinet (but, significantly, not the National Assembly) — had taken part in it. On the same occasion, he declared a general amnesty for all political prisoners both inside and outside Iraq except for "those who had acted as agents and spies for Iran and for the hostile Iranian Army."[10]

In attempting to assess the move, one should note that an earlier experience of a national coalition with opposition parties — the Communist and pro-government Kurds (1973–79) — proved a total failure as far as the opposition was concerned. By its very wording, the new decision excluded any genuine opposition parties, as all Kurdish and Shi'i opposition groups had had links with Iran. There were also no signs that Husayn was readier now than previously to relinquish his absolute power; on the contrary, his accumulation of power gathered force. It would appear, therefore, that the promise of democratization was a way of coping with public frustration and criticism in the postwar era, to direct attention into "positive" and well-controlled channels, and to provide a safety valve for wartime pressures. At the same time, the promise was also directed toward the middle and upper classes which Husayn had cultivated through his economic and social reforms. Hoping to turn these classes into an important power base, Husayn could not ignore latent pressures for political liberalization which were an outgrowth, in part, of his previous steps toward privatization of the economy. There was also the need to present a democratic image to the outside world and to counter worldwide criticism of the treatment of the Kurds (see below).

The declaration on the multiparty system could not but have antagonized the Ba'th Party, which had a vested interest in the one-party system and which stood to be the main victim of the change. It was probably to defend the declaration against its critics in the party that Husayn stated outright that the decision had been taken after consultations with it. Yet the question still remained why Husayn risked a clash with his own base of support? It should be remembered that the process of loosening Ba'thi control of the state was gradual (see previous chapters on Iraq in *MECS*) and Husayn probably considered the Ba'th too weak to oppose him on this issue. There were also signs of friction between him and the party. He reminded the public of traitors who had acted against him in 1979;[11] he also occasionally criticized unnamed Ba'thi members, as when he said that there were some Ba'this "who lost themselves and were lost to us,"[12] and on another occasion, he intimated that many times "we became angry" with a Ba'thi member who had lost his principles and "suddenly fell to the earth...from this high ladder."[13] Apparently, Husayn, realizing that the Ba'th was unpopular among the people, sought to draw a line between himself and the party. On one occasion, he warned that he would not allow "even this struggling party to stand between me and Iraqis, because between me and Iraqis...there are direct relations."[14] Throughout, Husayn sought to lower the profile of the Ba'th and downplay its ideological tenets. Thus, for example, speaking on the anniversary of the Ba'th's advent to power on 17 July, he lauded the different sectors in society for their contribution to the revolution and the war, but failed even to refer to the Ba'th by name, let alone to its principles of socialism or pan-Arabism.

What this signified was that Husayn would tolerate the Ba'th as long as it remained an obedient tool in his hands, but would not allow it to conduct any policy that opposed his own or could jeopardize his standing among the people. All told, it was unlikely that Husayn would allow any party to substitute for the Ba'th or take from it its leading role. No known opposition parties, such as the Communists, or new ones have come to the fore, and the whole episode may turn out to be a case of "trying to have one's cake and eat it too."

SADDAM HUSAYN AND FAMILY POLITICS

In sharp contrast to declarations on political liberalization, Husayn at the same time strengthened his personality cult, his own personal rule, and his family's hold on the reins of power. He was greatly assisted in this by the military victories of April-July 1988, which were attributed to his strategic planning, his military skills, and his personal conduct of the most crucial battles.

Even before these victories, the media started referring to Husayn as *al-qa'id al-mansur.*[15] Literally, this appellation means "the victorious leader," but on the symbolic level it evoked memories of Arab-Islamic glory during the reign in the eighth century of the second Abbasid caliph, Abu Ja'far al-Mansur, one of the greatest caliphs of this dynasty, who built Baghdad and who relentlessly fought the Shi'is. Husayn's birthday was the best opportunity for parading his achievements, paying allegiance (*bay'a*) to him and reaching new heights in his cult. The media stressed the symbolism of Husayn's birthday in the month of April, which coincided with the birth of the Ba'th Party, the victory at Faw, and the holy month of Ramadan.[16] The Faw battle, designated also as the "blessed birthday," was described as the dawn of "the era of the new Arabic civilization." Husayn, who was said to have spent two years preparing for the battle, had ushered in a new era for Iraq, "the Iraq of the unique *al-qa'id al-mansur,* Saddam Husayn."[17] *Al-Thawra* described Husayn as "the Ba'th's gift to Iraq and Iraq's gift to the nation."[18] The newspaper also declared that Husayn's birthday should be considered the birthday of the entire Arab nation because he had scored the greatest victories since Salah al-Din al-Ayyubi, 800 years ago.[19] The London pro-Iraqi weekly, *al-Dustur,* declared that "Saddam Husayn has achieved the first military victory in modern Arab history."[20] But Husayn was also the "hero of peace." Hence, in *al-Thawra*'s view, the year 1988 should be considered as "the year of peace, the year of Saddam Husayn."[21] The Kuwaiti *al-Siyasa* went as far as to suggest granting him a Nobel Prize for peace.[22]

The glorification of Husayn called for some practical measures as well. Thus, his birthday was turned into an "Iraqi popular festival"[23] celebrated all over the country by civilians and the Army. Even while the war was still raging and despite the huge Iraqi debts, Husayn initiated a new presidential palace, a new governmental building at a cost of c. $29m.,[24] a new university to be named after him, and a huge city clock with his portrait on all four sides. In July, he created new medals to be called "Saddam's medals," with his portrait. In September, a new district was named after him, "Saddamiyyat al-Basra."

Simultaneously, Husayn intensified his involvement in all walks of Iraqi life. Two examples will illustrate the general trend. Only a fortnight after the National Assembly was granted supervisory powers over the ministries (see above), Husayn was empowered to pension off any minister whom he considered as having failed in his duty.[25] In another measure, he instructed officials to lose weight and, in May, 41 — that is almost all — senior officials were weighed and their "achievements" were published in *al-Thawra.*[26]

In his drive to power, Husayn sought to take with him relatives whom he probably considered more trustworthy, as an old Arab proverb has it: "Me and my cousin against the outsider." With his relatives' help, Husayn hoped to push through his own policies more quickly and effectively, while at the same time keeping power inside the family. It is also possible that Husayn's more influential relatives put pressure on him to have themselves included in the power structure.

The first relatives so favored were his cousins: 'Adnan Khayrallah Talfah, his maternal cousin and brother-in-law (his sister, Sajida, is Husayn's wife); 'Ali Hasan al-Majid, his paternal cousin; and Husayn Kamil (Hasan), another paternal cousin who was also Saddam Husayn's son-in-law, being married to his daughter, Raghd. Together, this trio commanded the most important power centers in the state. Talfah, the oldest and the most experienced of the three, was defense minister (since 1977), deputy commander in chief of the armed forces, and a member of the RCC and of the Ba'th Party RC. Though Talfah was considered a loyal follower of Husayn, his formal powers appeared to be on the decline. Indeed, he was put in the shade by Husayn who endeavored to magnify his own role in the victories.

'Ali Hasan al-Majid was head of security (probably until the end of 1986), a member of the RC (since 1986), and head of the Ba'th Party Northern Bureau (since 1987). In this last office, which gave him party, military, and security powers, al-Majid conducted the most brutal campaigns against the Kurds ever, which probably did not earn him much popularity. This might explain why Husayn distanced himself from al-Majid in 1988. From February, al-Majid ceased accompanying Husayn at his meetings with the military command, a privilege which passed to Husayn Kamil.

The year 1988 witnessed Kamil's meteoric rise to power at the expense of the other two, possibly for three interrelated causes; he was young (34), talented, and energetic; he had succeeded in previous tasks; and he could serve as a counterweight to the other two — Husayn has never had absolute faith in anyone including his relatives. Kamil's rise reached a new peak on 22 March when simultaneously he was made director of the prestigious Military Industries Organization (*hay'at al-tasni' al-'askari*) and acting industry and minerals minister, "besides his other functions" in the Special Security Agency. The Military Industries Organization, which was established on the same day, was to be autonomous and was to combine the functions of the General Institute for Industries and, more interestingly, of the Special Security Agency. Kamil was given the rank of lieutenant general (*fariq*) and all the organization's decisions were to be made by him. It was stressed that the organization's key task would be arms production.[27] Clearly, Husayn was bent on making quick progress in this field and hoped to do so through Kamil, who would be directly responsible to him. Kamil's other appointment was preceded by the amalgamation on 6 March of the Ministries of Industry and of Heavy Industries into one ministry — the Ministry of Industry and Minerals — and the dismissal on 22 March of the two former ministers (see below). In an apparent rebuttal of criticism from the military about the quick elevation of his son-in-law, the president stated that Kamil, in 1982, when he was only a junior officer with the rank of captain (*naqib*), had already started establishing the Republican Guard and brought it to the strength of the "biggest corps in the Army." Moreover, Husayn stressed that he had granted opportunities to others, including academics with greater experience and knowledge than Kamil, but it took them about a year and a half to build only a brigade (*liwa'*). Hence, he was pleased to see a young man capable of achieving anything and everything, Husayn said.[28]

The criticism notwithstanding, Husayn continued promoting Kamil. On 6 May he awarded him and other officials in the Military Organization the *Rafidayn* medal in appreciation for their contribution to the armed forces. On 13 July, he appointed him minister of industry and military industrialization, following an RCC decision to change the name of the ministry (from industry and minerals) and to link to it the Military Industries Organization.[29] At the end of September, the president awarded Kamil five medals of valor (Talfah received only four) and the *Qadisiyyat Saddam* badge for his "outstanding role" in developing the arms industry, for "his supervision of the Republican Guard," and for his participation with the army command in the various battles.[30]

The promotion of Husayn's two sons, 'Uday (24) and Qusay (22), was more cautious, but nonetheless controversial. It was of the greatest importance for Husayn that he form close links between his sons, the military, and the youth. He made a point of taking his sons to the battlefield after the victories at Faw and other places, and according them publicity in the media. The marriage in early 1987 of Qusay to the daughter of Mahir 'Abd al-Rashid, the successful 7th Army Corps commander — had the same purpose, but it failed because Rashid fell into disfavor (see below) and, by the end of 1988, there were reports of Qusay having divorced or separated from his wife. Meanwhile, he became the second deputy of the Olympic Committee which was headed by 'Uday, and in this capacity Qusay awarded 'Uday in January the Olympic medal for his contribution in that field.[31] In October, Qusay made an official visit to Egypt and was received by President Mubarak.[32]

As for 'Uday, Husayn intended grooming him as minister of youth, but without calling it such so as not to antagonize the Ba'thi establishment. It should be remembered that the Youth Ministry was abolished in late 1987 (see *MECS* 1987, pp. 429–30) and probably to mollify the outgoing minister, 'Abd al-Fattah Muhammad Amin al-Yasin, Husayn awarded him in early January the *Rafidayn* medal for "having himself proposed the abolition of his ministry" and for realizing "Ba'thi party values."[33] 'Uday lost no time in filling the vacuum and in January, in his capacity as head of the Olympic Committee (which was the cover name for the Youth Ministry), he started directing Iraqi youth affairs, while also developing relations with ministries of youth in different Arab countries. On 30 January, he participated in a conference of Arab youth and sports ministers in Tunis, and took an important part in its discussions and decisions.[34] In July, he made an important leap forward when he was unanimously elected head of the executive bureau of the Assembly of Arab Youth and Sports Ministers.[35] At the end of August, he was appointed head of the Board of Trustees of the Saddam University for Technology and Sciences. On 15 October, 'Uday was unanimously reelected head of the Olympic Committee for another four years, but on 6 November he announced his resignation.

The mystery surrounding this sudden resignation was gradually dispelled first by a non-Iraqi source[36] and then by Husayn himself. On 22 November, he publicly called on the justice minister to investigate the accusation that 'Uday had killed Kamil Hanna Jajo, Husayn's personal bodyguard, on 18 October. Citing eyewitness accounts by members of the RCC, the high command as well as of relatives of the deceased, Husayn said that the incident had taken place during a party on a tourist island in the Tigris River, near the presidential palace but asserted that the death was unintentional. Husayn then disclosed that 'Uday had made three attempts at suicide and that since 21 October, he had been in prison. Finally, he called on the minister of justice to grant 'Uday a just trial.[37] This public disclosure led Jajo's parents and the heads of some Arab states to put pressure on Husayn to show leniency, but he refused. A week later, the three-man committee investigating the case ordered 'Uday's release from prison.[38] 'Uday later went to Switzerland and then returned to Iraq.

What was one to make of this affair, which at first sight appeared to verge on gossip, but which in reality had a number of political ramifications? The affair was an embarrassment for Husayn who had been trying to create for himself the image of an incorruptible, just, and fair ruler. The fact that he attempted to conceal the affair for more than a month showed the tight corner into which he had been pushed. As for 'Uday, nicknamed "the Prince," and believed to be his father's successor, he had certainly lost momentum in his climb to power and probably his father's goodwill as well. Non-Iraqi sources disclosed that 'Uday was known for his flamboyant and undisciplined behavior, and that he had been accused of at least one other murder in a Baghdad discotheque in 1986.[39] The affair also opened up a rift within the ruling family, because Sajida, Husayn's wife, aroused his wrath by siding with 'Uday. She was reported to have gone into self-imposed exile, either in Iraq or abroad.[40] The political consequence was friction between Husayn and Defense Minister Khayrallah Talfah, Sajida's brother, who took her side in the affair. (It was suggested that this may yet cost him his post.) No less embarrassing was the fact that Jajo, who was also Husayn's food taster, belonged to a family of loyal supporters and to the small Chaldean Christian Sect, whose members were a crucial element in the Republican Guard, which was the regime's ultimate shield. Husayn was said to have gone public on the issue in order, among others, to appease the Guards.[41] Probably the most worrying aspect of the affair was the resentment that it aroused in the ruling elite. 'Uday was reported to have publicly insulted the Kurdish vice president, Taha Muhyi al-Din Ma'ruf, while the latter was attempting to make peace between 'Uday and Jajo during the quarrel. Many members of the ruling elite reportedly criticized Husayn's favoritism and his arbitrariness in releasing two youth ministers, one of them a Ba'thi of long standing, and appointing the inexperienced and controversial 'Uday. However, having made the necessary public confessions and apologies, Husayn moved to bury the affair very quickly, while continuing to strengthen his position.

POLITICIANS AND MINISTERS

For many years now, Husayn had endeavored to control his closest colleagues who formed the inner circle, who had accompanied him on his rise to power and contributed greatly to the longevity of his regime. Husayn's purpose in this policy, which made great headway in 1988, was not to allow anyone to create a rival power center or to unite with others against him. The four personalities to come into consideration under this heading are: 'Izzat Ibrahim al-Duri, Taha Yasin Ramadan, Tariq 'Aziz, and Sa'dun Hammadi (three others — Na'im Haddad, Hasan 'Ali, and Sa'dun Shakir — had been dropped from the leadership or weakened significantly by 1987).

Al-Duri, deputy chairman of the RCC and assistant secretary-general of the Ba'th Party RC, is also constitutionally Husayn's successor. Husayn has had to tread very cautiously in his relations with him; he has had to keep him under close control while granting him all the public, ceremonial powers due to him and to appease him. Despite the tight secrecy surrounding the regime, there were signs that all was not well between the two in the first half of the year. It is true that al-Duri spoke very highly of Husayn, but what he said could have been interpreted as flattery, which has long been the most important weapon of defense in Iraq. More importantly, between March and August, the Iraqi media no longer mentioned him as taking part in meetings of the Cabinet, the RCC, and the RC. We do not know whether al-Duri himself had boycotted the meetings or whether Husayn excluded him from the decision-making process. Nor do we know for sure what caused the strained relations between them. One possibility is that al-Duri had openly opposed the March chemical attack against the Kurds in Halabja (see below). Al-Duri, who was believed to be more sympathetic to the Kurds, had in 1987 criticized the government's harsh measures against them. (See *MECS* 1987, p. 443.) Another possibility is that al-Duri opposed Husayn's high-handed measures and his growing tendency to circumvent his colleagues.[42] The most serious affront to al-Duri was that after having been appointed at the end of June to supervise the elections to the National Assembly and after having made all the preparations for them, he was confronted with the decision to postpone them (see above). Probably feeling the need to mend fences with al-Duri, Husayn encouraged

'Uday to marry al-Duri's daughter. This political marriage could tie al-Duri more closely to Husayn and silence his criticism of the president. It could also enable 'Uday to advance more quickly, eventually succeeding his father. Whether this political marriage is any more successful than the one with the Rashids remains to be seen.

Taha Yasin Ramadan, a member of the RCC, the RC, the first deputy prime minister, and commander in chief of the Popular Army (*al-jaysh al-sha'bi;* the Ba'th Party militia) was for many years considered Iraq's strongman, second only to Saddam Husayn. In 1987, Husayn successfully clipped Ramadan's wings by removing him from all decision making in economic affairs. Ramadan then redoubled his efforts to gain Husayn's goodwill: no other official could compete with him in the glorification of the president in the Iraqi media. In non-Iraqi publications, however, he felt free, not to criticize Husayn, but to express more hard-line views. In 1988, Husayn moved against Ramadan's most important base of power, the Popular Army. The opposition paper *al-Tayyar al-Jadid* reported in March that Ramadan's policy had been so corrupt and his abuse of his powers so gross that the president had granted 'Aziz al-'Ujayli — a high-ranking officer in the Popular Army — wide powers which enabled him to circumvent Ramadan and to purge the Popular Army's headquarters and infuse them with new blood.[43] This has not been verified, but doubtlessly Husayn was wary of the powers Ramadan had accumulated through the Popular Army and years ago Husayn started weakening it. The decision of October (see below) to demobilize the Popular Army could not augur well for Ramadan.

The appointment on 25 July of Sa'dun Hammadi as state minister for foreign affairs was meant to kill two birds with one stone. Tariq 'Aziz, a Christian, had been foreign minister since 1983 and he was believed to be more pro-Western than his colleagues, or at least more able to negotiate with Western officials. 'Aziz was also known as a loyal adherent to Husayn's foreign policy. It is not known whether 'Aziz deviated from Husayn's policy leading to Hammadi's appointment, which could be interpreted as a curtailment of 'Aziz's powers. A more likely explanation is that the appointment — a few days after Iran's acceptance of the cease-fire (see chapter on the Iraqi-Iranian War) — could be interpreted as an attempt to strengthen the Foreign Ministry in preparation for the negotiations with Iran. Moreover, being a Shi'i and having participated in the negotiations on the Algiers Agreement in 1975, Hammadi could be considered as the ideal candidate for the post of state minister for foreign affairs. While not ruling out this possibility, it would appear that internal considerations also came into play. Hammadi was a long-standing Ba'thi, even longer than Husayn himself. He was also the last of the old ideologists, who maintained some of his independence and his radicalism, which cost him the office of foreign minister in 1983. He was made the Speaker of the National Assembly, a post with only ceremonial powers. But Hammadi probably took this post too seriously for Husayn's liking, because he began to demand that the Assembly be given real decision-making powers. It should not be excluded that the decision in January to grant the Assembly supervisory powers was a result of pressures by Hammadi, who may have turned the Assembly into an important power base for himself. Commenting on the decision, Hammadi said that "it was an important step on the way of consolidating the National Assembly's powers" and giving it an important role in society.[44] Such a statement was probably too provocative, and five days before the announcement on the postponement of the Assembly elections (Hammadi had been a great advocate of elections), Husayn named him to the foreign ministry, thus separating him from his political constituency and removing him from an active part in the negotiations with Iran, which 'Aziz undertook. Hammadi was not included in the Assembly which was elected in 1989.

The common denominator in all these three cases was that Husayn sought to dislodge strong men from their entrenched positions and in their place promote new and young people who would feel indebted to him.

The year 1988 witnessed the reshuffling of seven ministries, as the result of either social pressures or Husayn's decisions. The first reshuffle, on 16 January, involved three persons: Justice Minister Mundhir Ibrahim al-Shawi was moved to the Ministry of Higher Education and Scientific Research, replacing Samir 'Abd al-Wahhab al-Shaykhli who remained minister of the interior, while Akram 'Abd al-Qadir 'Ali became minister of justice. As before, the presidential decree did not disclose the reasons for the changes. Only three days before the reshuffle in the Ministry of Justice, Husayn ordered that desertion or evasion of military service and antirevolutionary activity be considered crimes against morality, that "only persons who believe in God" be allowed to enroll in the judicial institute, and that lump-sum payments be made to judges in addition to their salaries, with the president being authorized to increase those payments whenever he saw fit.[45] It seems quite obvious that there was disquiet in the judicial system. A non-Iraqi source said that the manner in which the justice minister appointed judges had been criticized.[46] By changing the minister and increasing the judges' income, Husayn hoped to buy their goodwill and to influence them on crucial issues such as desertion. As to the Ministry of Higher Education and Scientific Research, it is noteworthy that the decree did not mention the name of the outgoing minister, al-Shaykhli, who had initiated the massive military recruitment of students and university teachers, which generated much dissatisfaction among them (see *MECS* 1976, pp. 372–73). An opposition paper noted that al-Shaykhli, who was a leading member in the security apparatus, had been notorious for his high-handed policies against the university staff.[47] The war had badly affected the educational system (see *MECS* 1984–85, p. 466); the appointment of al-Shawi, a man with much experience in the education apparatus (he was education minister in 1972), and the initiation of the "free walls" in the universities (see above) were intended as ways of coping with pressures.

The appointment on 22 March of Husayn Kamil to the Ministry of Industry and Minerals (see above) was at the expense of two ministers, Hatim 'Abd al-Rashid (minister of industry) and 'Abd al-Tawwab 'Abdallah al-Mulla Huwaysh (minister of heavy industries) who had served for less than a year (see *MECS* 1987, chapter on Iraq, Table No. 1). On 9 February, the two had been appointed, together with the minister of oil and the supervisor of military industrialization — Husayn Kamil — as a committee to examine the activities of the Ministries of Industry and Heavy Industries, and within 20 days they recommended their amalgamation. No less significant was *al-Thawra*'s report that both ministers had been the strongest advocates of amalgamation in cabinet discussion. That they would be made to renounce their portfolios was hardly a new phenomenon. What was new, however, was that *al-Thawra* reported the discussion at all and that the paper even cited views of ministers who opposed amalgamation. Those unnamed ministers reportedly believed that the existence of two ministries encouraged beneficial competition in the growing private sector. They also said that a single, combined ministry would put a heavy burden on the minister, who would have 20 departments under him. But these arguments lost out to others in favor of amalgamation, such as the cut in administrative and technical cadres.[48] In any case it was clear that political considerations had been paramount (see above and below).

On 31 March, Muhammad Fadil Husayn was dismissed as housing and reconstruction minister and his under secretary, Tahir Muhammad Hassun al-Marzuk (*sic!*) appointed in his place. The fact that the change was made at the height of "the war of the cities" (see chapter on the Iraqi-Iranian War), which had caused severe destruction in Baghdad and other areas, could indicate that the change was meant to appease the population and perhaps also to offset pressures by the war wounded, who demanded a solution to their housing problems. At the end of July, the new minister reported to Husayn that his ministry had completed in a record time of six months "the housing project for the paralyzed" in Baghdad. Lauding this achievement, Husayn said that the deadline that had been fixed by the specialists was "the deadline of the lazy people."[49]

Most intriguing of all was the dismissal on 11 May of Minister of Health Sadiq Hamid 'Alwash. The decree emphasized that the dismissal had been recommended by the National Assembly, which had come to the conclusion that he had neglected his duties. Of all the ministries, that of health seemed to be the most vulnerable. In 1982, for example, the health minister was executed for negligence (see *MECS* 1982–83, p. 563). The underlying cause for this vulnerability was the great pressure the war had put on the health system, which had to treat both soldiers and civilians.

There had already been signs at the beginning of the year that not all was well in this ministry. On 26 January, the RCC empowered the minister to pension off a physician at the ministry, and to pension off and imprison for six months six senior ministry officials for neglect of duty. On 14 April, four officials in two hospitals, al-Kut and Wasit, were punished. Ten days later, 'Alwash was summoned for questioning by the Assembly as requested by Husayn. Rebutting criticism of neglect and irregularities in his ministry, 'Alwash insisted that shortage of staff or its incompetence was the root cause of the problems, that not only the ministry was responsible for the problems and that, in any case, his ministry had great achievements to its credit.[50] On the day of 'Alwash's dismissal, 22 senior ministry officials, including 13 heads of hospitals, were also dismissed. These developments, which might have been only the tip of the iceberg, made the ministry a far from attractive portfolio. It was only on 1 August that a successor was found to 'Alwash, 'Abd al-Salam Muhammad Sa'id, who became active minister of health. As for 'Alwash, non-Iraqi sources reported that he had died in a mysterious traffic accident.[51]

FROM WAR TO NONBELLIGERENCE

TAMING THE MILITARY

Relations between the military and President Husayn became extremely complex in 1988 due to the Army's sudden shift from the defensive to the offensive and the victories it gained within four months. A victorious and powerful army could be a mixed blessing: it could enhance Husayn's prestige, but it could also be a potential threat. Husayn had, therefore, to maneuver very cautiously between two extremes: on the one hand, building a strong army, encouraging successful commanders, and pushing for victories against Iran and on the other, putting the Army's resources (i.e., the arms industry) under political supervision, checking overly ambitious commanders, and frustrating the drive into Iran.

The war had three important phases, each with its special problems. What follows is an attempt to shed light on these problems. Characteristic of the first phase — January-April — was an anticipated Iranian offensive in the south, which never materialized, and Iraqi setbacks in the north. The most pressing problem in this period was demoralization, as expressed among other things by desertion. During a meeting on 11 January with officers of the 3rd Army Corps, Husayn praised the high morale of these officers, who refused to be transferred to Baghdad, preferring rather to remain at the front. However, the next day he ordered the Ministry of Justice to regard desertion or evasion of military service and working against the revolution as crimes against morality.[52] At the same time, he declared an amnesty for deserters, and for several days police cars patrolled the streets of Baghdad announcing it. On 6 February, 11 high-ranking military doctors, including a major general, were pensioned off or were demoted for issuing diagnoses which transformed "a large number of fighters into nonfighters," or which exempted them from service altogether.[53] According to non-Iraqi sources an estimated 10,000 deserters, split into small groups in the al-Ahwar and 'Amara region, were highwaymen who had threatened law and order, compelling the authorities to use troops to arrest them but without much success.[54]

Nor did the Army's fortunes fare any better in the fighting in the north. On 23 January, R. Baghdad announced the death in a helicopter crash of the commander of the 5th Army Corps, Maj. Gen. 'Abd al-'Aziz al-Hadithi, together with the corps' staff officers and the two pilots. (The corps, whose headquarters were in Irbil, was responsible for fighting the Kurdish insurgents and defending the oil city of Kirkuk.) Iran, however, claimed the helicopter had been hit by its forces. There was also speculation that al-Hadithi's death had been arranged by the regime, which may not have been unlikely considering the conflicts between him and other miltary commanders.[55] Mahir 'Abd al-Rashid, the commander of the 7th Army Corps and probably one of Hadithi's close friends, published a poem in *al-Thawra* in which he called Hadithi's death a sacrifice (*qurban*).[56] Whatever the cause of death, this incident did not raise the morale of the forces in the north. They began to lose ground and in mid-March Halabja fell to the Iranians; and Iraqi soldiers, including senior officers, were captured.[57] At this juncture, Iraqi strategy changed, leading to the recapture of Faw on 18 April.

The victory at Faw was significant not only because it became the turning point of the war, but also because it brought to the surface some of the most intricate problems involving Husayn and the army command. From 18 April onward, Husayn, army officers, government officials, and the media disseminated the line that Husayn was the architect of the victory: it was he who had pushed for the training of the armed forces, especially the Presidential Guard; since May 1986, he had advocated and planned the offensive strategy; had personally conducted the battles; and had raised morale.[58] While Husayn's role in the Faw victory was undoubtedly important, Mahir 'Abd al-Rashid seems to have played the key role in initiating the offensive strategy.[59] In the spring of 1986, following the rout at Faw, 'Abd al-Rashid began to demand such a strategy (see *MECS* 1986, pp. 366–67), an Iraqi initiative, but he was checked by the Iranian offensive in Basra in the winter of 1987. The defeat in the north in March had probably forced Rashid's hand. On 24 March, *al-Thawra* reported an extraordinary meeting between Husayn, Rashid, and the commander of the 3rd Army Corps; it is possible that Husayn finally gave the green light for the operation during this meeting. On the second day of the battle, 'Abd al-Rashid sent a telegram to Husayn, which while paying lip service to Husayn's great contribution, emphasized the key role of the 7th Army Corps and by implication Rashid's, who called himself "an experienced sword."[60] However, 'Abd al-Rashid's success sealed his fate. Sensing a threat, Husayn immediately began to stand in 'Abd al-Rashid's way. In one of his speeches, Husayn confessed that "on the first day of the battle I was happier than on the second...or the third."[61] Attempting on another occasion to lower 'Abd al-Rashid's profile and raise his own, Husayn said that in 1986 he had told him to liberate Faw: "We began to draw up the plan and create its general framework, [but] we entrusted others to draft the details of the plan."[62]

The clipping of 'Abd al-Rashid's wings, which was also intended as a warning to other ambitious commanders, took various forms. Operationally, Husayn prevented the 7th Army Corps from carrying the war into Iranian territory, as advocated by 'Abd al-Rashid (and Talfah) in keeping with the original plan. As a warning to "conceited" officers, Husayn disclosed that following the liberation of Faw some officers, unnamed, "wanted to cross the Shatt al-'Arab because they were able to do so and the land was open without restrictions." However, "I twice kept them from doing so and told them to stop at their land's border."[63] A no less important way of weakening Rashid was the policy of playing off one military arm against the other, in this case the Republican Guard against all the others. It was of the utmost importance to strengthen the Guard and to glorify its role out of all proportion, because it had become Husayn's chief mainstay and shield against other units in the Army. He boasted that within a few years the Guard had become the Army's strongest and largest unit.[64] In an attempt to belittle the role of the 7th Army Corps, the commander of the Guard claimed later that the Guard had shouldered the heaviest burden in the Faw battle.[65] Five days after Faw, the soldiers in the Republican Guard were declared national heroes. Its commander, Iyad Futayyih Khalifa al-Rawi, was promoted to the rank of lieutenant general (*fariq*); he was given 15 medals of valor, the *Rafidayn* and the *Qadisiyya* medals as well as the *Qadisiyya* sword. By the time of the cease-fire, Rawi had been granted 23 more medals. Others in the Guard were accorded similar honors.

In contrast, no honors were conferred on 'Abd al-Rashid, or on any other commander of the 7th Army Corps, which remained in the shadows for the rest of the year. On 10 May, the RCC issued a decree expelling the commander of the 7th division of the corps "for not carrying out his duties in accordance with the liberation plan."[66] Another way of breaking 'Abd al-Rashid was to weaken his family's influence, which Husayn himself had helped to enhance in order to silence him. The first step was taken even before Faw, when one of Rashid's brothers, Hatim 'Abd al-Rashid, was dismissed from the Cabinet (see above). Possibly as a counterweight, another brother, Duham 'Abd al-Rashid, was appointed head of the Audit Bureau in April. A third brother, Brig. Gen. (*'amid*) Tahir 'Abd al-Rashid, commander of the 3rd Armored Division who had excelled in the Shalamcheh battle in May and had even been awarded three medals, died in a helicopter crash in July in strange circumstances. Speculation had it that his death too was arranged by the regime. The separation of Husayn's son Qusay from his wife, Mahir 'Abd al-Rashid's daughter, was another bad omen.[67] As for 'Abd al-Rashid himself, he disappeared in June and there were reports that he was under house arrest. Husayn was probably referring to him when he disclosed the arrest of a commander who had become "conceited."[68]

"Conceit" or "over-confidence" has become a *leitmotif* in Husayn's addresses to the military, reflecting his concern with the army commanders' increasing influence. At the beginning of the year, Husayn lauded commanders who had waged successful battles and "yet did not turn into dictators against the people," as had been the case in Third World countries.[69] After Faw, he warned commanders that victory should not make them ignore shortcomings in their own performance.[70] When decorating Hamid Sha'ban, commander of the Air Force, with the *Qadisiyyat Saddam* medal, Husayn reiterated thc need for commanders to remain "balanced" under all circumstances. While praising Sha'ban for not losing his "balance" even in moments of success, he maintained that "there were officers who did not keep their balance under the pressure of honors heaped on them...hence they lost their souls and we lost them."[71] Later in the year, he disclosed that some people, unnamed, had strayed from the right path "and were executed."[72] On still another occasion, Husayn declared that the good life was basically "a peaceful, civilian life and not one of militarism and war," emphasizing that those who did the most harm were "those soldiers who viewed life as a whole from the angle of their profession and field of specialization."[73]

These rebukes reflected a critical problem that Husayn had to cope with until the cease-fire, namely growing pressures by ambitious commanders to carry the war deep inside Iran, which could be harmful to Husayn because it might unduly strengthen commanders; but no less important, it might jeopardize the prospects for peace with Iran. Husayn repeatedly stressed that the victory "did not lie in the recapture of usurped land,"[74] that it "was not only a military victory" and that Iraq would gain not only by victory in the war, but also by "taking the initiative for peace after winning the war,"[75] that training "was no less important than the land," and that the land could also be regained through negotiations as Egypt had in the Taba case (see chapter on Egypt).[76] It would appear that after Iran's acceptance of the cease-fire on 18 July, the commanders' pressures succeeded and the Army made deep incursions into Iran, although it was emphasized that Husayn himself had commanded the operation, the commander of the 2nd Army Corps in whose sector the operation took place not being mentioned. Another possibility is that Husayn had acquiesced to this thrust in order also to enable other forces to participate in "the new glory."[77] Husayn had to clarify that political considerations had been overriding in deciding the Army's moves. Thus, three days after the incursion into Iran, a military communiqué stated that "in accordance with the principles announced by the political leaders and their policy" it was decided to withdraw Iraqi forces from Iranian land, since Iraq had no "ambitions on any part of Iranian territory."[78] On 8 August, the cease-fire was announced, but it was not known to what extent it was a joint decision of Husayn and the military command. It appears that the military did not accept the cease-fire wholeheartedly, because corps' commanders did not send telegrams of support for four days and when they finally did, the messages were quite lukewarm. Moreover, the commander of the 2nd Army Corps, in whose sector the advance had been checked, did not even send one.[79] The greatest deficiency of the cease-fire from the military command's point of view was that it left Iraq with no bargaining chips for regaining sovereignty over the Shatt al-'Arab. Probably to meet the Army's criticism and to appease it, Husayn decided during a meeting with the military command in September to divert the course of the Shatt al-'Arab (see chapter on the Iraqi-Iranian War).

Behind the conflicts with the military command over operational and policy issues was the potential danger of a military coup by overambitious or frustrated commanders, hence the constant purges. The list is so long that it would not be an exaggeration to say that the war had devoured its commanders, but not necessarily on the battlefield. Among those who lost influence, were purged, or killed in 1988 alone were the commander of the Naval and Coastal Defense Force, commanders of the 1st Special Army Corps, the 1st, 2nd, 3rd, 4th, 5th, and 7th Army Corps (compare table of military command for 1988 with that of 1987). Hamid Sha'ban, commander of the Air Force, retained his office, but he was shunted aside, probably because the Air Force had gained too much power and influence. The other side of the coin was that Husayn showered medals of valor on thousands of officers and soldiers and publicized this in the media.

Discontent among the military came out in the open in December or January, when, according to unverified reports by non-Iraqi sources, there was a coup attempt against Husayn. It is possible that the reported execution of officers — from between 7 and 200 — and the arrest of others, was a preemptive measure taken by Husayn against potential rivals or malcontents.[80] Whatever the case, the president sought to lower the profile of the military, and the cancellation of the celebrations on Army Day (6 January 1989) was interpreted in this way.

SOCIAL DEVELOPMENTS: ACCOMMODATING TO A STATE OF NO WAR

The military victories helped the regime to fight dissent, raise the morale of the population, and gain support for Husayn's Government. The Ba'th lost no opportunity to hold public rallies and celebrations, using them as an outlet for feelings of frustration and weariness brought on by the long war and its hardships. The three-day official holiday on 9-11 August, in celebration of the cease-fire, was a case in point. According to *al-Thawra,* millions of Iraqis took to the streets of cities and villages to celebrate "the day of the days," despite the great heat. They sang and danced from evening till morning, women distributed sweets and refreshments and "anyone with a weapon fired into the air." Overwhelmed by joy, policemen and even members of the air defense joined the carnival of firing into the air, *al-Thawra* reported. Husayn, who participated in the celebrations, was greeted with cheers, "With our souls and our blood, we will redeem you, O Saddam."[81]

The population was no doubt greatly relieved by the cease-fire announcement, but the government had now to deal with a war which had caused 350,000–450,000 casualties,[82] dealt a blow to the economy, and destroyed important parts of the country's infrastructure. Pressing social and economic problems, which had been relegated to secondary importance during the war, demanded a solution to avoid having grave consequences. To the regime's credit, it should be said that it had prepared the ground for their solution, according to Husayn, two years earlier.

In January 1988, the authorities launched an ambitious plan for the construction of

2,040 schools in different parts of the country to be completed within three years.[83] The pressure on the educational system was great: the school population in 1988 was approximately 4.5m., or 28% of the total population.[84] A no less ambitious project was the opening or the construction of five universities, in addition to the existing six. Four of the five were in the provinces — Tikrit, Kufa, Diwaniyya, and Ramadi — and one, for advanced sciences and technology, in Baghdad. The establishment of the universities, particularly in the provinces, was meant to solve the problems of the unequal distribution of educational resources between the periphery and the center, to prevent the influx of youth from the provinces into Baghdad, and to meet the pressure of demobilized soldiers and students whose studies were abruptly interrupted by the war.

Reports in the Iraqi newspapers and measures taken by the authorities indicate that the most pressing problems were in the health system. According to Iraqi statistics in 1987, there were 234 hospitals with 31,713 beds[85] to provide services to civilians and to the Army, where the number of wounded during the entire war was estimated to be in the hundreds of thousands. The health system came under pressures from both civilians and the military, but could cope with neither. We have already mentioned the punishment given to the minister of health and other senior officials with the unenviable task of dealing with this problem (see above). In an attempt to meet these pressures, the authorities encouraged private medicine; the Ministry of Health gave the private sector approval to establish 14 hospitals, each with 450 beds.[86] In July, owners of private clinics were called upon to set aside one day a week for the free treatment of the wounded, as well as relatives of the dead and of prisoners of war. Physicians on pension were also enjoined to volunteer to work at military hospitals. In the provinces, where the problem was apparently most acute, the authorities organized mobile teams to visit villages and remote places. Hospital directors were given enhanced powers to choose staff and encouraged to contact Husayn by phone in order to solve problems and provide better services.

Another problem exacerbated by the war was urbanization. According to Iraqi statistics, the urban population jumped from 39% in 1957 to 72% in 1987.[87] The problem was especially acute in Baghdad, which attracted villagers and people from the provinces and border areas hit by the war, especially Basra. While Baghdad suffered heavily in "the war of the cities" of March-April (see chapter on the Iraqi-Iranian War), with 300–500 deaths,[88] for most of the period life in the capital remained normal, and development projects were implemented despite the war. In the autumn, the authorities launched the building of a satellite town near Baghdad and near Mosul.[89] They also announced the reconstruction of Faw, which has become the symbol of Iraqi victory, and of Basra at a cost of $4.5bn.[90]

The most pressing and most complicated of all the problems was that of demobilization from both the Regular Army and the Popular Army. According to Husayn, the Regular Army at the end of the war had approximately 1,250,000 soldiers,[91] while the number in the Popular Army could be estimated at 1m. (see *MECS* 1983–84, p. 475). Such large numbers put a heavy burden both on the state and the individual, yet any demobilization plan would be a mixed blessing, at least in the short term. At the end of October, the RCC and the Ba'th Party RC decided to stop recruiting soldiers to the Popular Army and to begin studying the problems involved in its demobilization.[92] There were many reasons for demobilizing the

Popular Army and perhaps abolishing it in the long run. It no longer served as a force for protecting Husayn, since the Republican Guard had taken over the responsibility, and Husayn did not want it to become a rival to the Regular Army as had happened in Iran. Neither did he want it to become a channel for enhancing the Ba'th Party's influence at his expense. But most importantly, the Popular Army had become extremely unpopular, especially among students and the youth. Service in the Popular Army having become more or less compulsory, it had adverse effects on the economy and education, while its contribution to the war effort was marginal. Demobilization could also enhance Husayn's popularity among the population. And though the Ba'th Party surely criticized demobilization, it was too weak to oppose it. Ramadan, commander of the Popular Army, was waging a lost battle when he said: "The Popular Army is a magnificent human experiment which has moral and tactical implications, stronger [even] than those of the [Regular] Army."[93]

More complicated was the demobilization of the Regular Army. Besides various military and political considerations, the regime had to take into account the economic and social repercussions of demobilization. It would decrease substantially the burden on the Treasury, but it would also increase the number of those seeking employment, who might create social and economic instability. Accordingly, demobilization which was announced in November, had to be gradual and cautious. Two years earlier (see *MECS* 1987, p. 433) the authorities dismissed foreign workers and women, who had been the main labor force during the war. In the Industry Ministry alone, 24,000 foreigners were dismissed by June.[94] Concerning women, their dismissal was given a moral and patriotic justification, namely, the need to devote themselves to increase the population and to raising their children.

THE ECONOMY: PERILS AND PROSPECTS

The three main economic issues in 1988, were: arms production, privatization, and debt repayment. All three were caused by the war and all had social or political repercussions.

In arms production, by the end of 1988 Iraq had developed three long-range missiles (*al-Husayn, al-'Abbas,* and *al-Faw*) and a short-range missile (*Ababil*); was manufacturing ammunition and artillery, and chemical, and possibly biological, weapons in four centers[95] (about which Iraq remained silent); was cooperating with Egypt and Argentina on developing a new missile, *Condor 2,* with the range of 1,000 km., and a new "super weapon" about which Iraq would only say that two other countries possessed.[96] The arms industry had to provide weapons that would break Iran's morale or act as a deterrent, as was the case with the long-range missiles fired at Tehran or the chemical weapons. The industry was also meant to enhance Iraq's and Husayn's prestige, and to prove to the military that the political leadership had made the Army's interests its first priority. But the regime had also to keep the industry out of the reach of the military establishment if Husayn was to have a lever against it (as shown by the Special Security Agency's involvement in arms development).

The drive for privatization and economic liberalization begun in 1987 (see *MECS* 1987, pp. 430–31) went ahead unabated in 1988. The sweeping measures included: a 22% increase in the funds to finance private-sector imports in the 1988 foreign trade plan;[97] the encouragement of Arab investment as part of the economic restruction program (a law passed in April offered tax exemption and profit repatriation);[98] the announcement in August of the government's plan to privatize 47 state-run factories;[99] the abolition in the same month of the State Tourism Directorate and the privatization of tourist facilities;[100] the leasing of 261 gasoline stations to private interests by October, and the decision to lease 1,000 Iraqi-built tankers to private interests in order to facilitate countrywide door-to-door distribution of kerosene;[101] the establishment in November of a new state bank, al-Rashid, that would compete with the al-Rafidayn bank, which had previously enjoyed a monopoly,[102] and finally the plan for setting up a stock exchange. Minister of Trade Muhammad Mahdi Salih declared in December that agriculture was "fully run by the private sector," while domestic trade was "entirely run by the private sector with the exception of state-run central markets."[103]

For all its blessings, liberalization had its drawbacks, at least in the short term. Iraqis still had reservations about investing large sums, fearing that liberalization would be reversed. War and privatization had negative results, such as the black market, smuggling, commodity shortages, inflation estimated at 40%, and soaring prices, especially of foodstuff.[104] On 13 July, the minister of trade called on the public to cut down on the use of food products, but denied that there was any shortage.[105] On 15 October, the leadership discussed what it called "the steep rise in the price of some basic foodstuffs," claiming that it was due "to exploitation by some exploiting and harmful producers or by those who play a parasitical role in production and marketing."[106] These phenomena were potentially harmful since they could lead to social unrest, which was more difficult to suppress in time of peace, and could jeopardize the economic reforms of which Husayn was the main architect, and hence, Husayn himself. From August onward, the authorities began to announce the release of food products to the markets and also made a special arrangement for families of soldiers, the wounded, and Ba'th Party members to make purchases in the government stores at specially reduced prices. At the end of the year, the authorities acknowledged that the new policy had encountered considerable criticism, especially with regard to sharp price increases caused by the removal of subsidies. However, the government said that the policy would be continued.[107]

Iraq's estimated debt of $50bn.-$60bn.[108] threatened an internal crisis, as well as a crisis of confidence with its creditors, especially Turkey, Italy, Japan, West Germany, and France, a crisis which Iraq overcame. To its Arab creditors, mainly Saudi Arabia and Kuwait, Iraq owed $30bn.-$35bn. and Baghdad had long been suggesting that it would write these debts off, arguing that the war against Iran was waged on behalf of the Arab world as a whole no less than on Iraq's behalf. The Arab creditors were no doubt too weak to oppose Iraq. As for its non-Arab creditors, Iraq had to conduct tough negotiations with each one individually. In these negotiations, a number of elements were in its favor: the military victories, the drive for efficiency and economic liberalization, its ability to overcome the oil crisis, to establish the new pipelines via Turkey and Saudi Arabia (the last to be completed in autumn 1989), and to end the year by producing 2.6m. barrels per day (b/d) with oil revenues amounting to $11bn.[109] Perhaps the strongest cards up its sleeve were its proven oil reserves of 100bn. barrels, next only to Saudi Arabia's, that its oil export capacity after the completion of the Saudi pipeline would be 5m. b/d,[110] and that Iraq was about to enter into an era of huge reconstruction projects.

THE TWO-TRACK POLICY TOWARD RELIGION

Aware of the role of religious zeal in boosting Iranian morale and mindful that religious feelings were deeply ingrained in large sections of the Iraqi population, especially the Shi'is, Husayn doubled his efforts to harness religion to the cause of the war and to manipulate religion for political purposes.

As a gesture to Shi'i sentiments, the new Iraqi missile was named *al-Husayn,* after the Shi'i Imam al-Husayn, but one could not fail to notice that it also alluded to the president's own name. When fixing the date of the attack on Faw, Husayn chose the first day of Ramadan, Islam's holiest month, and gave the operation the code name "Blessed Ramadan" (*Ramadan mubarak*). Immediately after the operation, Husayn and most members of the Iraqi leadership went to Saudi Arabia to perform the *'umra,* the minor pilgrimage. After "Blessed Ramadan," all the other operations were given religious names. Four were named "We relied on Allah" (*tawakkalna 'ala Allah*), another was "Muhammad, The Messenger of Allah" (*rasul Allah*), still another was *al-anfal,* after a *sura* in the Qur'an describing the victory at Badr when a small number of Muslims defeated a large army of non-Muslims. Similarly, in his addresses to military commanders, Husayn made a point of stressing the need to rely on Allah, while also attributing Iraq's victories to Allah's will. Husayn even sought to link himself with religious belief. One newspaper called his family the "family which relies on Allah," while the clergy began calling him a *mujahid* leader, that is a leader who waged a holy war. Attributing divine powers to him, another paper reported that during an Iranian bombardment, walls collapsed but not those on which Husayn's picture had been hung.[111]

There were other authorized manifestations of religiosity: Husayn's order in January that only those believing in Allah could enroll in the judicial institute (see above), strict measures for the observance of the Ramadan fast, a directive in December prohibiting men from cutting women's hair, and official celebrations of religious holidays. Of special interest were the celebrations of Muhammad's birthday in October, when festivals were held all over the country: schools were directed to dedicate the first hour of the lessons to commemorating the birthday. Exhibitions of religious books were held, such books being sold at reduced prices, and popular organizations, as well as the Ba'th Party, participated in the celebration.[112] No less significant was the cooperation between the police and the clergy in harnessing religion in the fight against juvenile delinquency.[113]

These expressions of religiosity should not disguise the ruthless manner in which the regime treated the Shi'i religious opposition. A prominent victim was Mahdi al-Hakim, who was very likely assassinated by a Ba'th Party member[114] on 17 January while on a visit to Sudan. Mahdi belonged to the well-known al-Hakim family from Najaf. His father had been the Grand Ayatollah until his death in 1970. Mahdi al-Hakim, his brothers, and other relatives emerged in the late 1970s and the 1980s as leaders of Shi'i opposition groups. The most famous has been Hujjat al-Islam Muhammad Baqir al-Hakim, chairman of the Supreme Assembly of the Islamic Revolution in Iraq (SAIRI), an umbrella organization based in Tehran. Another brother, 'Abd al-'Aziz al-Hakim, has headed the opposition group *al-Mujahidun.* Family members have paid dearly for their militancy: six were executed in 1983, 10 in 1985, and about 100 were detained in 1983 (see *MECS* 1982–83, p. 579; 1984–85, p.

470). Mahdi al-Hakim himself had been sentenced to death *in absentia* in 1969 for allegedly participating in a coup attempt against the Ba'th. From his self-imposed exile in Dubai and later in London, he had led the opposition against the regime, becoming in time a leading member of al-Da'wa Party (see *MECS* 1986, p. 145). It is not known what provoked his murder but it might have been connected with the preparations being made by Shi'i groups to announce the establishment of a government in exile, patterned after the Islamic Republic of Iran, in Basra, once the city was occupied by Iran,[115] headed by Mahdi al-Hakim.

Baghdad denied any connection with the assassination, but Husayn used the incident to attack "Iranian Shi'ism" and by implication, Iraq's as well. Husayn warned Arabs and Iraqis of Khomeyni's attempts to turn them into "Iranian-style Shi'is," asserting "that the Iranian concept of Shi'i doctrine has always been alien to the Arab mentality." However, he said, "regrettably, many Persian rituals and concepts have found fertile ground among Arab and non-Arab Shi'is," which may undermine pan-Arab security. Husayn said that no one should be offended by his honesty or consider him a "sectarian." On the contrary, it was Khomeyni who was the sectarian. Khomeyni's brand of Shi'ism was deviationist because when "they claim that the transfer of the caliphate to Abu Bakr, 'Umar, and 'Uthman was an act of forgery and that matters should have proceeded in a different chronology...all they want to do is to tarnish the Arabs and their history." Husayn sought in this way to draw a line between Iranian and Arab Shi'ism, disregarding the fact that Iraqi Shi'is held these same beliefs. Attacking Shi'i clerics by implication, he said that when Khomeyni had been in exile in Najaf (1964-78) "he could only come in touch with a bad environment in Iraq and could not see the good Iraq. This led him to believe that all the Shi'is of Iraq sympathized with him and consequently, that he could take over Iraq."[116]

These attacks on Shi'is occurred when Iraq was expecting another Iranian offensive in the south, but Iranian military defeats and the cease-fire changed things overnight, while also delivering a severe blow to the Iraqi Shi'i groups acting under Iranian auspices (for these groups, see chapters on Iraq in previous volumes of *MECS*). These groups had no tangible achievements to their credit in Iraq, neither had they threatened the regime in any substantial manner, but their goals and tactics had been coordinated with Iran. With the cease-fire, however, the opposition's tactics came into conflict with those of Iran, which sought to observe the cease-fire and prevent any anti-Iraqi movement to take shape on its soil. At the end of May, these Shi'i opposition groups held a one-day conference in Tehran, at which they rejected any possibility of peace with the Ba'th and called for the struggle to continue until its downfall. They also demanded that any decision to end the war should accord them the position of "a concerned party."[117] After the cease-fire declaration, concerning which they were not consulted, they declared their determination to continue the struggle against the Ba'th regime. This struggle, however, became increasingly difficult. Iran did not give them much freedom of action and Iraq, notwithstanding the November amnesty, was not inclined to extend it to them or to be lenient regarding their clandestine activity. Confronted with such problems, the Shi'i opposition began to look about for new alliances, and they found a patron in Syria, Iraq's archenemy. The SAIRI chairman, Muhammad Baqir al-Hakim, met in October with Asad; he said he would open an office in Damascus and adopt a new strategy for fighting Husayn's regime both in Iraq and internationally. It remains to be seen whether this new patron will endow the Shi'i opposition with the power it has lacked.

CRUSHING THE KURDISH UPRISING

Relations between the Kurds and the regime reached a new low in 1988. Both went to extremes they had previously been careful to avoid. The regime used chemical weapons against its own Kurdish population, declaring it Iraq's worst enemy. The Patriotic Union of Kurdistan (PUK) departed from the Kurdish movement's declared goal of autonomy and began to demand self-determination for the Kurds thus calling into question the Iraqi State's integrity.

THE HALABJA MASSACRE

On 16 and 17 March, Iraqi airplanes bombed the small Kurdish town of Halabja, situated near the Iranian border, with chemical weapons including mustard gas, cyanide, and tabun. According to different assessments, the attack killed about 5,000 Kurds, injured about 10,000, and caused most of the inhabitants, estimated at 60,000–70,000, to flee.[118] The immediate question was what provoked such harshness by the Ba'th? The answer would appear to be the combination of a feeling of being threatened, of revenge, and tactical calculations. As a result of the Kurdish uprising which has continued for several years, the Ba'thi control over the north deteriorated "dramatically," according to a Senate Foreign Relations Committee report published in February. It said that the uprising "posed a major military threat" to the Ba'th control of the north.[119] At the same time, cooperation between Iran and the Kurdish opposition made significant progress in early 1988, with the Iranian Army shifting its pressure to the northern sector and occupying important Iraqi heights near their common border by March 1988. To add to Iraq's nervousness, the PUK, one of the two largest Kurdish groups, began propagating the idea of an independent Kurdistan, or a federated Iraqi state.[120]

Alarmed by these developments, the regime attempted at the end of February to resume the negotiations with the PUK which had been broken off in 1985 (see *MECS* 1984–85, pp. 470–72). However, the PUK leader, Jalal Talabani, rejected these overtures saying that he would not negotiate with Husayn, but declared himself ready to talk to 'Izzat al-Duri, as he was "firmly convinced" that al-Duri did not agree with what was happening in Iraqi Kurdistan.[121] Simultaneously with the Iranian mini-offensive in the north, the PUK, which had been active in the Sulaymaniyya region, significantly increased its pressure from within. From 27 February, forces of the PUK and 20,000–30,000 Iraqi soldiers fought each other, culminating, according to Talabani, in the capture of Halabja by PUK forces on 14 March.[122] Husayn flew to Sulaymaniyya to discuss with the military command "the means for deterring the invading aggressors."[123] It was probably at this meeting that he gave the green light to use chemical weapons. At the beginning of the year, he had sent a warning to the Kurdish opposition saying: "We will not be lenient with traitors. You know that when we say something we don't just say it."[124] The attack on Halabja was more than an act of reprisal; it was designed to teach the Kurds a lesson and to deter them from cooperating any further with Iran. More important, it was aimed at pressuring Iran to end the war by signaling that Baghdad was capable of bombarding Iranian cities not only with "conventional" bombs as it had done since the beginning of March, but also with chemical weapons which Iraq had no qualms about using even against its own population. After Halabja, Baghdad warned Iran that it "would not receive the invader with flowers" and that it was determined "to defend its land, people, and sanctuaries with all means by using all kinds of weapons in its possession."[125] It would seem that the message was well understood in Tehran; the Iranians mounted no more offensives, and thus the Halabja massacre can be viewed as an important juncture in the war.

The immediate reaction of the Kurds was one of panic, anguish, and a feeling of helplessness. As one survivor put it: "We are not afraid of their guns or planes, we're just afraid of the gas."[126] It would appear that the attack came as a severe shock to the leaders of the uprising, who were completely powerless to protect the civilian population, which had always paid the highest price for the Kurdish resistance. The Halabja massacre produced some second thoughts about the wisdom of cooperating with Iran, but no practical action was taken in this regard, because Iran was the movement's lifeline. At the same time, however, the "Hiroshima of the Kurds" as they called it, drove growing numbers of Kurds into the movement, including apparently also members of the National Defense Regiments (*afwaj al-difa' al-watani*), a special Kurdish auxiliary force which the Ba'th had set up for assisting the Regular Army in fighting their Kurdish brethren as well as the Iranian Army. According to *The Guardian,* Kurds were joining the resistance "like ants," with 4,000 members of the auxiliary forces joining by mid-April.[127] Later evidence for this phenomenon was the amnesty declared in September for Kurdish refugees in Turkey, which specified that members of the armed or security forces, which were included in the amnesty, would not be allowed to rejoin these units.[128]

The massacre also encouraged the Kurdish opposition groups, notorious for their divisiveness, to attempt to close their ranks. In early May, the Kurdistani Iraqi Front (*al-jabha al-Kurdistaniyya al-'Iraqiyya*) was established in Syria as an umbrella organization of opposition groups: the Kurdish Democratic Party (KDP), the PUK, the Socialist Party of Kurdistan, the Popular Democratic Party of Kurdistan, the Kurdish Socialist Party, and the Iraqi Communist Party. The front was significant in several respects: for the first time it united the two main rival groups, the KDP, headed by Mas'ud Barazani (whose power base was along the Turkish border) and the PUK, headed by Talabani (whose power base was in the Sulaymaniyya region). Later in the year, Barazani was made head of the front's political leadership and Talabani of the military. Secondly, the Iraqi Communist Party, which is a binational party including Kurds and Arabs, joined the purely Kurdish front. Thirdly, the front called for the struggle "for...self-determination."[129] It would appear that in the controversy concerning the Kurdish movement's political goals the more radical line advocated by Talabani won out. Barazani, who represented the traditional line of autonomy, began, nonetheless, to advocate "a voluntary union."[130] In the context, however, these calls seemed more removed from reality than ever, for the Kurds were conducting a war of sheer survival.

One of the greatest problems of the Kurdish movement has been its inability to reach out to the outside world and win support for its cause. The Halabja massacre brought the movement short-lived publicity. Talabani was received in various Western countries, including the US and Britain, and though these visits were "purely humanitarian," according to his interlocutors, they aroused the Ba'th to take counteraction. The chemical attack had caused the Ba'th difficult public relations problems. Domestically, it attempted to cover up the case by publishing telegrams of support from individual Kurds and two pro-government Kurdish groups, the Kurdish Revolutionary Party and the Kurdish Democratic Party. In a no less cynical move, it held a ten-day celebration (during which the Halabja affair took place) to commemorate the 11 March 1970 agreement on Kurdish autonomy. In response to the uproar in the world media, Baghdad at first blamed the attack on Iran. Then it totally denied that chemicals had been used but hinted that Iraq had the right to defend its integrity by all possible means. Still later, Baghdad admitted using chemical weapons against the Iranian Army, and then admitted using them in Halabja. Taha Muhyi al-Din Ma'ruf, the Kurdish vice president, made this revelation while on a visit to France, justifying the action by Iraq's right to defend itself against aggression. At the same time, he blamed the plight of the Kurds in Halabja on "Talabanist traitors."[131] In October, the Ba'th announced a plan for building "the new Halabja."

THE SUMMER OFFENSIVE

The cease-fire freed the Iraqi Regular Army to wage an all-out offensive against the Kurds with a view to ending the uprising.

The attack on Kurdistan started on 19 July, one day after Iran announced its acceptance of the cease-fire; according to other sources, the offensive started on 8 August. The Iraqi forces, estimated at 60,000, were supported by tanks, fighter bombers, and helicopters belonging to the 1st and 5th Army Corps stationed in the north, and by units from the Presidential Guard.[132] The offensive, which lasted for six weeks, was described by Western journalists as "stopping short of genocide" or "step-by-step genocide."[133] The European Parliament stated in mid-September that the campaign against the Kurds "led to the death of thousands of innocent civilians and verges on genocide."[134] Turkish Prime Minister Turgut Özal spoke of "the massacre of innocent people."[135] According to various sources, the Iraqis once again used chemical weapons. In early September, an American spokesman stated that the US "was convinced" that Iraq used chemical weapons.[136] Iraq denied these reports vehemently, but even if it had not used such weapons, the memory of Halabja was so terrifying that it sufficed to cause 60,000–100,000 Kurds to seek refuge in Turkey and, in smaller numbers, in Iran.[137] Another source claimed that the KDP had ordered a large-scale evacuation as soon as the chemical attack began.[138] Commenting on this flight, an Iranian Kurdish leader said: "This exodus...is a traditional misfortune, something cyclical and inevitable, like the arrival of the monsoon."[139]

We do not know what resistance the guerrillas put up but apparently they were helpless against this offensive. It was reported that Barazani remained in the area to conduct light guerrilla warfare.[140] On 6 September, by which time the Army had succeeded in asserting its authority in the north, the RCC issued a general amnesty to all Kurds, including those who had fled the country, on condition that they return within 30 days. At the same time, the RCC vehemently attacked the "hirelings" who had been "the meanest and lowest guides of the Khomeyni forces to the cities and villages of the autonomous region" and who "had stabbed the armed forces in the back." Although on the whole Iraqi officials sought to belittle the Kurdish movement and its influence, *al-Thawra*'s commentary expressed authentic fears when it said that those who stood to benefit from the amnesty "dangerously menaced Iraq's independence, its sovereignty, and national (*watani*) unity."[141] Significantly, Talabani was exempted from the amnesty either because the Ba'th considered him too dangerous, or because it hoped to drive a wedge between him and Barazani, or both. According to Iraqi sources, by the end of September more than 40,000 Kurdish refugees had returned to Iraq, but in fact no more than 2,000–3,000 had done so by the end of the year.

REMOVING THE KURDS FROM THE NORTH

As terrible as the chemical attacks on the Kurds were, they should not overshadow the systematic ridding of the north of the Kurdish population. This policy, which has been in effect for many years, but which received greater impetus in 1988, was designed to achieve three main goals: creating a security belt along the Iraqi border in the north, a project initiated in the mid-1970s to prevent help from reaching the Kurdish guerrillas; changing the homogenous Kurdish character of the area by settling Arab inhabitants there, either Iraqis or Arabs from other countries, such as Egypt; and, most important of all, cutting the Kurdish movement's lifeline by destroying the villages which provided the main logistical and human support to the guerrillas. According to various sources, the depopulation campaign involved the destruction of hundreds, and even thousands, of villages and the transfer of their inhabitants, together with residents of Kurdish towns, to special camps inside or outside Kurdistan. About 1m. Kurds were thus moved. US senators described what happened as cultural annihilation and a demographic revolution.[142]

The Iraqi authorities did not attempt to conceal what they had done. The governor of Dhok admitted that in his jurisdiction alone the regime had "evacuated" 200 villages along the Iranian border and that the evacuation policy, which "had been initiated a few years before was already complete in Dhok."[143] Defense Minister Talfah said the government wanted to create a strip along the border without buildings or other facilities and that the policy of forcible migration applied both to Kurds and Arabs. Moving villages to where there was water, electricity, "and the requirements for decent living," he said, was not a policy of annihilation; "annihilation is killing people and demolishing their homes."[144] Admitting that the Kurds were moved to "deep inside Iraqi territory," Foreign Minister Tariq 'Aziz came to the crux of the matter when he said that "many Kurdish rebels used to force the residents of border villages to provide them with shelter and supplies," and that accordingly, "Iraq made a decision to clear the region and eliminate once and for all the places where the rebels used to be."[145]

REPERCUSSIONS OF THE CAMPAIGN AGAINST THE KURDS

The Halabja massacre and the summer offensive triggered different kinds of reactions. The Western media were the most vocal and critical, causing the Iraqi Government a great deal of embarrassment, but until summer, by which time Iraq had emerged as the victor in the war, almost all governments kept silent about the Kurds. Eastern bloc countries remained silent throughout. Expressing his deep frustration over the complete silence of their "natural allies," Talabani contended that it encouraged Baghdad to continue using chemical weapons.[146] Among Western governments, the US took the lead in condemning Iraq for using chemical weapons and for forcibly moving the Kurds; it was also the only government to threaten sanctions against Iraq. These threats, however, came to nothing. All Arab countries except Syria sided with

Iraq in condemning the international media for attempting to besmirch the image of the Arabs and to cast a shadow on Iraq's victory.

The Kurdish issue directly affected Baghdad's relations with Ankara. The flight of the Iraqi Kurds to Turkey faced the Turkish Government with a dilemma; it did not want to grant refuge to the rebellious Kurds, for fear of the influence they might have on the already restive Turkish Kurds, but not granting refuge would further antagonize the Turkish Kurds. The refugees had already created substantial economic and social problems in Turkey and were also likely to hamper relations with Iraq, which was anxious to prevent investigation among the Kurdish refugees into the use of chemical weapons. It was mainly for these reasons that Iraq so promptly extended the amnesty to the refugees. However, as difficult as conditions in Turkey were, the refugees' fear of Iraqi vengeance was too great; the question of the Kurdish refugees, by the end of 1988 was the main point of friction in relations with Turkey (see also chapter on Turkey; for Iraqi debts to Turkey, see below).

Commenting on the analogy which analysts drew between the 1975 Algiers agreement and the 1988 cease-fire — in both cases, the Kurds paid the price for the agreement between Iran and Iraq — Talabani said that in 1988 the guerrillas had not given up fighting; Iran and Iraq had not reached a final agreement, and thus the Kurds continued to to be an indispensable ally to Iran; that the Kurdish groups were acting in concert; and finally that the Kurdish struggle had attracted international attention.[147] Asserting that there were still active guerrilla units in "all provinces of Kurdistan," Talabani nonetheless admitted that they had gone on the defensive, that they had broken into small groups of 5–50 fighters, that they had adopted hit-and-run tactics, and that there remained "only isolated islands of the liberated areas." Nevertheless, he declared, the goal continued to be "an independent Kurdistan within the framework of a democratic Iraq,"[148] which is a contradiction in terms.

Yet, the situation looked quite bleak for the Kurds in 1988. The Kurdish movement and the Kurdish population had suffered one of the greatest blows in their history. The gap between reality and aspirations seemed wider than ever. The Kurds were pushed into a precarious alliance with Syria, after having been temporarily ditched by Iran, at the same time that the new-found Kurdish cooperation had yet to prove itself.

THE IMPACT OF THE END OF THE WAR ON FOREIGN RELATIONS

The cease-fire with Iran faced most of Iraq's allies with a dilemma: should they intensify their relations with Baghdad or should they approach its rival, Iran? The "pro-Iraqi" considerations were weighty: Baghdad appeared the victor in the war, it had huge oil reserves, it had promised to reward its allies with contracts for development and reconstruction projects after the war, and finally most of these allies were already tied to Iraq by the huge debts it owed them. But the anti-Iraq considerations were no less weighty: doubts about Iraq's ability to repay its debts, fear of risking the extension of new credits, and the desire to have a foothold in Iran which was as pressed as Iraq for reconstruction projects, but which was not burdened by heavy debts. The second half of the year was a period of adaptation to new conditions not only for the warring parties, but also for countries which attempted to maneuver between the two.

AMBIVALENT RELATIONS WITH THE UNITED STATES

Relations with the US were extremely ambivalent in 1988. No other country had indirectly contributed to the changing tide of the war and hence to its end as had the US, and yet no other was so furiously vilified by Iraq. Despite the tension on the political-diplomatic levels, economic relations with the US flourished as never before. This ambivalence could be explained by the swift changes in the course of the war to which American policy-makers had to adapt, and by the deep-seated anti-American sentiments which the Iraqi Government sought to manipulate for its own ends.

Until June, the US was virtually Iraq's most important supporter in the conflict with Iran. It was Washington which put pressure, though unsuccessfully, on the other Security Council members, chiefly the USSR, for an embargo on Iran, and it was also Washington which sided with Iraq against the USSR in rejecting a partial cease-fire in April that was meant to end "the war of the cities." The American naval presence in the Gulf was believed to have played a crucial role in breaking Iranian morale and bringing Tehran to the negotiating table. According to an American official, "the perception was growing in Iran that they were at war with the United States as well as Iraq. They felt they were at the endgame in a course toward war with the United States."[149] Military observers believed that Iraq based its attack on Faw on intelligence reports from US satellites.[150] It was also noted that on 18 April, the day that the Iraqi Army attacked Faw, the American naval forces crippled one third of Iran's small Navy.[151] By mid-May, half of the Iranian Navy was reportedly sunk by the US.[152] The American pro-Iraqi stance was strengthened by a Senate Committee report published in February that an Iraqi defeat had become a real possibility that could have "catastrophic" implications for the whole region.[153] At the same time, however, the US was also committed to putting an end to the war, so that no sooner had the parties reached a certain balance after the Iraqi successes in April and May, than Washington began to apply pressure on Baghdad to show greater flexibility in interpreting UN Resolution 598 and accepting a cease-fire (see chapter on the Iraqi-Iranian War). President Reagan's special envoy, Vernon Walters, visited Baghdad in late May reportedly for this purpose.[154] However, it would appear that these pressures were to no avail; accordingly, Washington moved to pressure Iraq on the Kurdish issue. On 9 June, the Ba'th's archenemy, Jalal Talabani, met with Laurence Pope, the director of the State Department's Office of Northern Gulf Affairs. The unprecedented meeting incensed Baghdad, which interpreted it as interference in Iraqi internal affairs and as an attempt to cast a shadow on the Iraqi victory. In evidence, Baghdad said that the meeting took place after the Iraqi military successes. In support for the Iraqi argument one can say that although Washington vehemently criticized the use of chemical weapons in Halabja, it continued its political and diplomatic support for Baghdad for two months more.

Iraq's immediate reaction was to cancel a meeting between Tariq 'Aziz and Secretary of State George Shultz scheduled for 11 June. *Al-Thawra* attacked the US for violating "the principles of noninterference in the internal affairs of others" as well as for maneuvering between Iran and Iraq, warning that Baghdad was capable of retaliating in kind.[155] For his part, Husayn admonished the US for informing Iran about the projected Iraqi attack on the Majnun oil fields at the end of June.[156]

The second round of the war of words took place in September. After the Iraqi offensive against the Kurds, the State Department came out on 8 September with the announcement that it was "convinced" that Iraq had used chemical weapons against the Kurds during the offensive, and that it found it "unjustifiable and abhorrent." Shultz, who discussed this issue with Sa'dun Hammadi during their meeting in Washington on 8 September, warned that although the US attached "great importance" to the further development of relations with Iraq, it did not intend to pursue that course "if illegal Iraqi use of chemical weapons and other human rights abuses continued."[157] Immediately afterward, the Senate voted to impose tough sanctions against Iraq which, if approved by Congress and signed by the president, would have entailed cutting off an estimated $800m. in US credits to Iraq, American opposition to loans to Iraq by international financial institutions, and banning the import of Iraqi oil.[158] The American move triggered a chain of well-orchestrated anti-American reactions. Shortly after the announcement, a demonstration of a quarter of million people took place in Baghdad, with the demonstrators shouting slogans such as: "We strongly denounce the American Knesset's decision to boycott Iraq," "We paid rivers of blood to maintain our independence and we are prepared to pay more."[159] On 12 September, 22 Arab youth organizations held a solidarity rally which condemned "the imperialist US-Israeli conspiracy against Iraq." Iraqi television screened a film called "This is America," showing "the ugly crimes the US committed and continues to commit against mankind."[160] The Iraqi media unleashed an anti-American propaganda campaign. *Al-Thawra* declared that the Iraqis "will not fear the wolves, now that they are armed to the teeth and have experienced combat and methods of fighting."[161] Iraqi officials, while they attacked Washington, seemed careful not to overstep the mark. Husayn denounced the American "uproar" and even claimed that during the war with Iran, Iraq had refused a US offer to supply artillery and shells in return for one of Iraq's Soviet-made T-72 tanks.[162] The most vociferous attack was made by Taha Yasin Ramadan, who is known for his radical tendencies. In a lengthy article, he denounced the Senate which he called "an American Knesset" and a "Zionist Council with an American cover," for its "anti-Arab stands," its continued military supplies to Iran, and its attempts to "extinguish" Iraqi victory. Ramadan asserted that the US benefited from relations with Iraq more than the latter benefited from ties with the US.[163] The harsh Iraqi reaction could be explained as fear of an American boycott which could affect Iraq's international standing, as retaliation against the American "pro-Kurdish" policy, and most important, as the directing of anti-government feelings toward an external target.

It is not known how this sudden outburst of anti-Americanism affected decision making in Washington, but it would appear that the US Administration was not seriously considering severe measures against Iraq, but was only reacting to pressures from the Senate and American public opinion. President Reagan was considering a veto against a Senate and House bill to impose sanctions on Iraq, but the Congress failed in October to take action for what was described as "last-minute technicalities."[164] The Administration reportedly objected to "mandatory sanctions" on the ground that they would complicate peace talks between Iran and Iraq and would not "further the objective...of ending Iraq's unlawful use of chemical weapons."[165] It would appear, however, that the most important considerations were an unwillingness to jeopardize relations with Iraq, especially as relations with Iran remained frozen; expectations of lucrative commercial links after the war; and an unwillingness to drive Iraq into the socialist camp. Thus, by the end of September, the two sides showed signs of reconciliation. On 3 October, shortly after the Congress dropped the Iraqi sanctions, 'Aziz met Shultz in New York and announced afterward: "We affirmed our willingness to have reasonable and good relationships in all fields."[166] As to the chemical weapons issue, the State Department declared its satisfaction with 'Aziz's declaration that Iraq respected all provisions of international law which meant that it forswore the use of chemical weapons in internal as well as international conflicts.[167] And finally, on the Kurdish issue, Baghdad expelled in mid-November an American diplomat who together with a British colleague had visited the Kurdish north and sent cables documenting his suspicion of Iraq's use of chemical weapons in the last offensive.[168] The US retaliated by expelling an Iraqi diplomat. With that, the matter ended.

Despite the friction over the Kurds, diplomatic relations with the US were quite intensive, certainly more so than those with the USSR. Four Iraqi ministers visited the US during the year, including the ministers of finance and of oil. Similarly, senior American officials and four delegations of Congressmen visited Baghdad. The volume of trade was also on the increase. In the first half of 1988, American exports to Iraq totaled $480m., while imports from Iraq came to $493m.[169] In early November, the US agreed to grant Iraq credit facilities for approximately $1bn. to finance its exports to Iraq, which included agricultural commodities, and basic foodstuffs.[170] All in all, in 1988 the US was estimated to have become the major exporter to Iraq.[171]

THE SOVIET UNION'S AMBIVALENT ATTITUDES

The Soviet Union's policy on the Gulf War and its relations with Iraq continued to be ambivalent. This ambivalence reflected the USSR's simultaneous interests in both Iraq and Iran, and its attempts to influence both. The USSR sought to take advantage of Iran's almost complete international isolation to be the first to get a foothold there and to prepare the ground for the postwar era. The USSR and Iran had a common interest in checking the US presence in the Gulf, which increased significantly in 1988. Furthermore, the USSR needed Iran's goodwill for the purpose of discouraging its assistance to the rebels fighting the Soviet forces in Afganistan. For these reasons, the USSR continued to oppose the imposition of sanctions on Iran (see *MECS* 1987, pp. 447–49). When the "war of cities" erupted once again in March, the USSR sided with Iran by initiating a Security Council resolution calling for the halt of the "war of cities" on terms detrimental to Iraq (see chapter on the Iraqi-Iranian War). The USSR later retreated from this initiative because others, notably the US, Britain, and France, opposed it.

Despite these differences, Baghdad continued to tread very cautiously in its relations with Moscow. The USSR remained Iraq's main arms supplier, providing, among other things, the missiles used against Iranian cities. Following a strong Iranian protest, the USSR pleaded that Baghdad had on its own modified the missiles to make them capable of reaching Tehran. According to a British newspaper, East German experts helped Iraq modify the missiles.[172] As relations with Washington became strained in the second part of 1988, Baghdad's ties with Moscow improved. Furthermore, Iraq owed the USSR huge sums (see *MECS* 1987, p. 448) so that it could not afford to antagonize the Soviets. Iraqi officials and the media sought to gloss over the problems, adopting throughout a tone of polite, or implied, criticism. Thus Ramadan said: "We do not think the members of the Security Council are that ignorant and are unaware that Iran has rejected the resolution."[173] For his part, Husayn accused "some [unnamed] external factors" of encouraging Iran, to continue its rejection of Security Council Resolution 598.[174] Moscow, for its part, neither wished Iraq to be victorious nor to be defeated. The way the war ended suited its interests because it left room for maneuver between Iraq and Iran.

On the political and diplomatic level, relations remained cool and except for Tariq 'Aziz's talks in Moscow in early February, there were no exchanges of senior officials. Still both went to pains to emphasize on different occasions their adherence to the treaty of friendship signed in 1972. Trade relations, by contrast, apparently made great headway. It was reported that a 46% rise in the volume of trade with the Soviet Union in 1987 had made Iraq Moscow's most important Arab trading partner.[175] In the first half of 1988, the value of trade increased by 30% compared to the same period in 1987. The USSR was also reported to be involved in building "big projects" (not specified) in Iraq.[176] By the end of the year, Iraq was said to be seeking to buy additional heavy weapons, including the Sukhoi 24 fighter bomber.

IRAQ'S OTHER ALLIES AND THE POSTWAR ERA

West Germany was among the first to attempt to hedge its bets. In 1987, Bonn had already moved to balance its relations between the two belligerents (see *MECS* 1987, p. 447), culminating in what observers described as the important role it played in mediating between the two and getting them to accept the cease-fire.[177] Baghdad was not pleased with this role and Tariq 'Aziz "frankly" told the West German foreign minister during his visit to Bonn in June that Bonn's diplomacy was imbalanced and that it was seeking "to please Iran and support it against Iraq" for economic reaons.[178] But Baghdad was not in a position to oppose these moves because Bonn had economic leverage on both Iraq and Iran. Bonn agreed at the end of 1987 to reschedule Iraqi debts amounting to $2.053 bn.;[179] then, in July, it resumed credit guarantees amounting to $165m.,[180] while also promising both belligerents important economic aid should they cease hostilities and negotiate for peace. Thus, economic diplomacy was said to have won Bonn a privileged position in both countries. Another aspect of Iraqi-West German relations was the reported involvement of West German firms in the development of chemical weapons in Iraq; in January 1989, *Der Spiegel* disclosed that the German Government was aware of the involvement of German firms in the supply of materials conducive to the production of such weapons.[181]

Relations with France, Iraq's main supporter in the West, became tense in the second half of the year. France not only attempted to court Iran (see chapter on Iran), but the French media and public were highly critical of the use of chemical weapons. In October, a French humanitarian association sued three French firms, including Dassault, for providing Iraq with fighter bombers[182] which it used to attack the Kurds with chemical weapons. The association demanded an immediate arms embargo on Iraq. President François Mitterrand called for an international conference in Paris from 7–11 January 1989 to stiffen and extend a 1925 convention banning the use of chemical and biological weapons. Mitterrand also demanded far-reaching trade sanctions against countries using such weapons.[183] Tariq 'Aziz reacted by attacking the Europeans in general: "They sold us these weapons and now they are shedding crocodile tears. The Europeans are hypocrites."[184] In an effort to halt the erosion, Baghdad sent the Kurdish vice president on a special mission to France and other

European countries. Surprisingly enough, during his visit in early November, he admitted the use of chemical weapons in Halabja (see above). But it is not known if this admission was a slip of the tongue, or made on orders from Baghdad. In either case, the disclosure did not contribute to Iraq's public relations in France. The thorniest problem of all was the economic one. During the eight-year war, France had sold Iraq armaments worth $10bn., accounting at times for 40% of French arms manufacture, but when the war ended a drastic decrease was expected.[185] Worse still, by the end of the year Iraqi debts to France amounted to $5.5bn. This huge sum, on which Iraq demanded a three-year moratorium, blocked new French investments in Iraq and France's participation in the postwar reconstruction of Iraq.[186] France felt deprived of the expected benefits of its consistently pro-Iraqi policy, for it could not afford to supply new credits to Iraq. It was to redress this situation that Foreign Minister Roland Dumas, during a visit to Baghdad in mid-December, demanded that Iraq pay off part of the debts so as to enable France to invest in new projects, but by the end of the year no agreement had been reached on the issue.

For all their complexities, relations with Britain seem to have improved in 1988. Britain, together with the US, had pressed for an embargo on Iran. In February, David Mellor, minister of state at the British Foreign and Commonwealth Office, visited Baghdad to discuss with Husayn the development of political and economic ties. Probably as a token of gratitude for Britain's policy during the war and its willingness to extend new credits, Husayn pardoned, during the visit, a British businessman who had served eight years of a life sentence for bribing Iraqi officials. In March, Tariq 'Aziz visited London. In May, a British bank extended to Iraq a $127m. loan in support of the export of UK capital goods,[187] and in November, Britain doubled its credit to Iraq, as compared to the previous year. The $600m. credit[188] was to finance British exports in terms of projects and capital goods. Thus, Britain appeared to be one of the biggest beneficiaries of the postwar construction projects. At the same time, relations also came under pressure because of the chemical weapons issue and the expulsion of three Iraqi diplomats in November for "activities incompatible with their diplomatic status." The speculation was that the expulsions reflected the government's concern with Iraq's surveillance of its exiled opponents in London.[189] Iraq retaliated by expelling three British diplomats, after which relations returned to normal.

Japan, another important source of investments, agreed to extend project credit amounting to $3bn. for a further five years, but it refused to grant Iraq new loans. Turkey refused to grant any fresh credits, because the total Iraqi debt had risen to $2.7bn. and, according to the Turkish prime minister, had done damage to the Turkish economy.[190]

VIGOROUS IRAQI RETURN TO THE ARAB SCENE

The idea of Arab unity, which is the crowning principle of the Ba'thi ideology, has for many years been relegated to a mainly ceremonial status in Iraqi political life. Nonetheless, Arabism and the Arab world have remained Iraq's main terms of reference both in war and in peace. From the onset of the war, Iraq presented it as an Arab-Persian conflict, waged by Iraq on behalf of the whole Arab nation. This argument was again put forward at the beginning of the year, when Iraq's enemy, Syria, made efforts to get the Arab states of the Gulf to compose their differences with

Iran, and thus to isolate Iraq. These Syrian efforts failed, due both to implied Iraqi threats to these countries and the Iraqi Army's subsequent victories.

Iraqi officials and the media trumpeted the victory at Faw as the first Arab victory in modern history, which would have far-reaching implications for the Arab nation as a whole. Commenting on the outcome of the war, Husayn said that "the Arab nation in Iraq has triumphed against the enemies of the nation as well as our enemies," for "if this wave had succeeded there would have been nothing good left in the Arab nation."[191] *Al-Thawra* wrote that this "historical victory" strengthened the nation's self-confidence and was a turning point in the Arab nation's revival; "a new Arab situation has been created after long years of decline."[192] Congratulating the Arab nation from the east to the west, Husayn said that this achievement "will reinforce its opportunity in the world and help in opening the doors wide and making it reassured about its future."[193] Talfah asserted that the great Iraqi victory was "a victory for all the Arabs."[194] The media and officials in certain Arab countries echoed these arguments; thus Jordanian Prime Minister Zayd al-Rifa'i said that "the Iraq of heroism and steadfastness has restored to our Arab nation its glories and self-confidence."[195]

Iraq's eagerness to share its victories with its fellow Arab countries was a covert way of renewing its bid for a leadership role. Iraq's striving for such a role received new impetus from the military victories and the unprecedented strengthening of the Iraqi Army, which made it into the strongest and the most experienced in the whole Arab world. But, far from reassuring fellow Arabs, this newly acquired strength scared not a few of them, especially Syria and the Arab states of the Gulf. Husayn scoffed at them, saying: "One should not count the other's tanks like we count the foreigners'...such a situation should be eliminated in Arab relations." Husayn warned that the enemy was "now capable of making some of us fear the armies, weapons, money, and policy of others among us," but, he said, there was no need for an Arab to fear another Arab, because otherwise he will "bring the foreigner." As to Iraq he said: "It is our duty when we see a frightened Arab to ask him: who is frightening you? We are all your brothers. We are with you."[196] On another occasion, Husayn showed impatience with Arab countries which had become alarmed over Iraq's victories: "We wish they were not alarmed, but if they want to be, that is their problem. Let he who is alarmed go and hit his head against the highest mountain in the north of Iraq."[197]

At the same time, however, Iraq was anxious not to alienate its supporters and allies in the Arab world. As long as the conflict with Iran remained unresolved, Iraq needed the Arab states' political support. Furthermore Iraq owed the Gulf states $30bn.–$35bn., which it probably did not intend to repay, but for which it had to buy their goodwill. Iraq also needed Arab funds for investment in construction projects. One way to allay Arab fears was to emphasize the concept of Arab solidarity and not Arab unity. Husayn declared that: "We no longer believe in the old method of achieving unity with a political declaration between two regimes as a first step toward comprehensive unity...Now, unity in essence and in its realistic revolutionary concept is getting closer."[198] Conferring legitimacy on the existing Arab systems, he said on another occasion that "we Arabs have many systems and inclinations. However, what is required of all of us is not to abolish the present structure and rip up the present fabric, but to place a large tent over all the tents." He admitted that in the past some Arabs, who had been prompted by enthusiasm and a desire to improve the Arab situation, might have thought of "abolishing some tents to build the big tent." However, he contended, experience and reality had proved that this was impractical. Relations among the Arab states should be based on respect for the "peculiarities" of the other countries; solidarity with and interaction between them and noninterference in internal affairs. Husayn reminded the Arabs that he had proposed these principles in February 1980.[199] The stress on these principles reflected the deep erosion in Ba'thi ideology since Husayn's advent to power. These principles were also meant to be a counterweight to Syria's insistence on unity with Iraq, the failure of which Damascus has blamed on Baghdad ever since the unity plan was launched in 1978.

From its newly acquired position of strength, Iraq moved to reward its wartime allies and to punish its opponents. As a chief and consistent ally, Jordan was given shortly after the cease-fire announcement a large consignment of weapons captured as booty, which included 159 tanks. King Husayn was taken on a visit to the tombs of the Hashemite kings of Iraq, a gesture that was not only a mark of homage to the Hashemite rulers, but that also indicated a change in the Ba'th ideology and a readiness to confer legitimacy on the monarchical period in Iraq's history. The problem of Iraq's $650m. debt to Jordan, which affected the Jordanian economy,[200] was solved in August. In December, talks on economic integration culminated in the signing of an agreement for cooperation in various fields. Politically, too, relations were further deepened: President Husayn visited Jordan in May, and King Husayn visited Iraq several times during the year. Still, the king's reported proposal for a confederation between the two countries was rejected by Iraq. Neither was the king successful in his efforts to reconcile Baghdad with Damascus.

Egypt was the principal Arab country which Iraq sought to "reward" after the war. In July, they signed no fewer than eight agreements, the most important being a military agreement to expand cooperation in the areas of training, arms production, and exchange of expertise and information.[201] At the end of July, an Egyptian delegation, headed by the minister of defense, held talks in Baghdad to increase military cooperation between the two countries. Iraq, for its part, in September amnestied all Egyptian convicts.

Political relations were also strengthened with Mubarak making three visits to Baghdad and, most importantly, President Husayn making an impromptu and short visit to Egypt on 28 November. Husayn, who had 10 years earlier orchestrated Egypt's ostracization, now came to Cairo to confer, as it were, his legitimacy on Egypt. Latent problems remained, such as the Iraqi debt of $2bn.,[202] growing Iraqi difficulties in employing Egyptian workers,[203] a different approach as to the Arab-Israeli conflict, and possibly also covert rivalry between them, the strongest countries in the Arab world. Mubarak's denial of rumors that Egypt was concerned with "the emergence of Iraq as a victor"[204] was significant. Nevertheless, their relations were strengthened by the common enmity to Syria (see also chapter on Egypt).

No sooner was the cease-fire announced, than Iraq lashed out at Syria, Iran's ally. Until then, Iraq had confined itself to vitriolic attacks on Syria for its support of Iran and for Syria's efforts to drive a wedge between Iraq and the Arab countries of the Gulf. After the cease-fire, however, Baghdad took more tangible vengeance, particularly in Lebanon. The renewed Iraqi involvement in Lebanese affairs, which went back to 1976, was meant to put pressure on Syria at its most vulnerable point, to weaken Iran's influence in Lebanon and to parade Iraq's capabilities and military might. Iraq ultimately might have wished to bring Syria to its knees and to force it to drop its alliance with Iran by extending political, financial, and military support (including heavy weapons such as tanks) to Syria's enemies in Lebanon, by supporting Syrian opposition against Asad and by pressuring Arab countries to oust Syria from the Arab League, an attempt that failed. These efforts signified a more activist line in the Arab arena. Iraq tried, but to no avail, to get the Arab states of the Gulf to include it in the Gulf Cooperation Council. It also reportedly attempted to establish Ba'thi cells in Egypt, Sudan, Saudi Arabia, and Kuwait.[205] Whatever the facts were, Arab states came to regard Iraq as the strongest among them, and the state with which they should be reconciled, but of which they should beware (see chapters on Jordan, Syria, Egypt, and inter-Arab relations).

IRAQ AND THE ARAB-ISRAELI CONFLICT

Like the other Arab countries, Iraq, too, had to address itself to the sudden turn in the Arab-Israeli conflict brought on by the Palestinian uprising in the West Bank and Gaza Strip. But it was not easy for Iraq to adapt itself to the new situation, torn as it was between presenting the war with Iran as the central pan-Arab issue which merited all-Arab support, and considering the Arab-Israeli conflict as the central pan-Arab issue.

One way of reconciling these conflicting demands was for Iraq to argue that the Palestinian uprising and the war with Iran were two sides of the same coin. Iran and Zionism were long-standing allies whose main aim had always been to weaken the Arab nation and to harm it, as Saddam Husayn put it: "The Zionists and the Tehran rulers [who] are allied against our nation, covet its land and seek to establish false empires."[206] The Zionists, according to Husayn, included not only those in the occupied territories, but also "all the Jews who share with them their aspirations at the expense of the Arabs."[207] Similarly, Iraq's war against Iran was the same war that the Palestinians were waging against Israel, the only difference being the weapons: the Iraqis were using missiles, the Palestinians stones. Iraq believed, one editorial said, "that the road to the liberation of Palestine is through its confrontation of the Iranian aggression."[208] Accordingly, victory in one arena was bound to affect the other. As Ramadan put it, Iraq's victory at Faw would strengthen the Palestinians: "The Palestinian Arab people can forcibly liberate their land from the Zionist aggressions just as the Iraqis did when they liberated, with strong will and arms, the land of al-Faw and al-Shalamcheh."[209] It was further maintained that the Zionists were terrified both by the *intifada* and the Iraqi victories, hence their anti-Iraqi campaign about the use of chemical weapons, which was meant "to divert attention from the Israeli crimes against the Palestinian Arab people and the uprising."[210]

True to its traditional line, Iraq continued to regard Israel as a false, usurper, illegal entity and even as "a cancerous tumor" which should be "uprooted" from Palestine.[211] Husayn declared in February that "when Iraq raises the slogan of the liberation of Palestine, it does not do so for internal consumption, but in order to realize it actually and truly."[212] The founder-leader of the Ba'th, Michel 'Aflaq, declared after the occupation of Faw, that this victory was a commitment "that the victorious Iraqi Army would be in the vanguard in the battle for the liberation of Palestine."[213]

Ramadan added "if the Arabs can overcome the technical problem [namely Israel's technological superiority] this means that Israel is finished."[214]

Iraqi officials and the media kept declaring their support of and solidarity with the uprising, but when it came to deeds, they remained mainly symbolic: monthly payments to the families of the killed in the uprising, the declaration of Baghdad and Jerusalem as twin cities, and the organization of rallies of students and others in support of the uprising. With regard to the controversy over a military versus a political solution to the Palestinian question, Iraq's policy was full of contradictions and ambiguities. *Al-Thawra* asserted that "armed struggle is the only way for realizing the Palestinian people's liberation and the right of return [*'awda*]."[215] However, shortly afterward when addressing an Egyptian audience, Husayn declared: "We must seriously consider any new positive political ideas that appear on the horizon for the attainment of a serious, radical, and comprehensive solution to the Palestinian People's problem [but not a peaceful one that would include Israel]." At the same time he asserted that the *intifada* has aroused great hopes among the Arabs that the liberation [of Palestine] was possible."[216] Sa'dun Hammadi described Iraq's policy as follows: "We support any stand the PLO takes, regardless of our opinion...with regard to the Palestinian cause, we take our stand within the framework of the Arab stand. We do not deviate from what the Arab countries decide."[217] Under the cover of the Arab consensus, Iraq supported the PLO's policy on the international conference and gave its blessing to the declaration of the Palestinian state (see chapter on the Palestine Liberation Organization). 'Arafat himself was a welcome guest in Baghdad. This policy served a number of Iraqi goals at once: it kept Iraq in the mainstream of the Arab world, it acted against the common enemy, Syria, and left the door open to possible future Iraqi participation, or silent acquiescence to, a political solution to the Arab-Israeli conflict.

At the beginning of the year, Tariq 'Aziz declared Iraq's opposition to pressures being applied on Egypt to cut its ties with Israel. In September, Israeli sources leaked a report to the effect that an Iraqi official had initiated a meeting in the US with the Israeli minister of energy, but that the meeting had been canceled at the last moment. Another report, also in September, claimed that President Mubarak had told the Israeli ambassador to Egypt of Iraq's readiness for peaceful negotiations with Israel.[218] These reports were vehemently denied by both Iraq and Egypt, and as they coincided with the approaching Israeli elections, they might have been meant to serve some internal Israeli political purposes. Another possibility was that Israel was sounding out the possibility of an opening toward Baghdad. In July, Israeli officials had sent reconciliatory signals to Iraq, but these were probably interpreted by Baghdad as signs of Israeli apprehensions about the end of the war. Not only Iraqi sources, but Israeli ones as well emphasized the implication of the war's end for Israel: that Iraq would be free within a few years to use armed forces against Israel. Iraq refrained from making such direct threats, but it did cite Israeli sources reflecting apprehensions about Iraq's increasing military power. Baghdad also stressed Israel's deep enmity to Iraq and its intention to harm it.

In summary, Iraq's policy could be described as straddling the fence and leaving all the options open.

TABLE 1: LEADING IRAQI FIGURES (at end of 1988)

Name	*Post*	*Year of Birth*	*Remarks*
Saddam Husayn	President of the republic; chairman of the RCC; secretary-general of the Ba'th Party RC; deputy secretary-general of the Ba'th National Command (NC); chief of the Executive Authority; commander in chief of the armed forces	1937	Sunni. Tikrit
'Izzat Ibrahim al-Duri	Vice-chairman of the RCC; assistant secretary-general of the RC; member of the Ba'th NC	1942 (?)	Sunni
Taha Yasin Ramadan (al-Jazrawi)	Member of the RCC, RC, and NC; commander in chief of the Popular Army; first deputy prime minister	1938	Sunni of Kurdish origin
'Adnan Khayrallah Talfah	Member of the RCC and RC; deputy commander in chief of the armed forces; defense minister	1940	Sunni. Tikrit. Husayn's brother-in-law and cousin
Sa'dun Shakir [Mahmud]	Member of the RCC and RC; secretary-general of the Ba'th Central Vocational Bureau	1939	Shi'i (?)
Tariq 'Aziz	Member of the RCC, RC, and NC; foreign minister; official in charge of the Arab Liberation Movement Bureau of the RCC	1936	Christian
Hasan 'Ali [Nassar al-'Amiri]	Member of the RCC and RC; secretary-general of the Progressive Patriotic and National Front [PPNF]	1938	Shi'i
Sa'dun Hammadi	Member of the RCC and RC; minister of state for foreign affairs; Speaker of the National Assembly	1930	Shi'i
Taha Muhyi al-Din Ma'ruf	Vice president of the republic; member of the RCC; and of the Higher Committee of the PPNF	1924	Sunni Kurd
Muhammad Hamza al-Zubaydi	Member of the RC; minister of transport and communication	1938	Shi'i
'Abd al-Ghani 'Abd al-Ghafur	Member of the RC; adviser to the president with the status of minister; secretary of the Ba'th Party Southern Bureau	1944	
Samir Muhammad 'Abd al-Wahhab al-Shaykhli	Member of the RC; minister of interior; adviser to the president; police chief	1945	Sunni
Sa'di Mahdi Salih	Member of the RC; secretary of the Ba'th Party Baghdad Bureau	1940	Tikrit
'Abd al-Hasan Rahi Fir'awn	Member of the RC; adviser to the president with the status of minister; secretary of the Ba'th Party's al-Furat Bureau	1942	Shi'i
Mazban Khadr Hadi	Member of the RC; adviser to the president with the status of minister; secretary of the Ba'th Party Vocational and Popular Organization	1938	Shi'i (?)
'Ali Hasan al-Majid	Member of the RC; secretary of the Ba'th Party Northern Bureau	1941	Sunni. Tikrit. Husayn's cousin
Kamil Yasin Rashid	Member of the RC; director of the RC Secretarial Office; secretary of the Ba'th Party Central Bureau	1931	

Name	Post	Year of Birth	Remarks
Latif Nusayyif Jasim	Member of the RC; minister of culture and information	1941	Sunni
Fadil Barrak (Husayn)	Reserve member of the RC; head of intelligence	1942	Tikrit. Reportedly dismissed at the end of 1988
'Adnan Dawud Salman	Reserve member of the RC; minister of local government	1940/45	
Radi Hasan Salman	Reserve member of the RC	1938/39	
Husayn Kamil [Hasan]	Minister of industry and military industrialization	1954	Sunni. Tikrit. Husayn's son-in-law and cousin. On 22 March replaced Hatim 'Abd al-Rashid, minister of industry and 'Abd al-Tawwab 'Abdallah al-Mulla Huwaysh, minister of heavy industries
'Isam 'Abd al-Rahim al-Jalabi	Minister of oil	1942	
Karim Hasan Rida	Minister of agriculture and irrigation	1944	Shi'i
Hikmat 'Umar Mukhaylif	Minister of finance	1939	
'Abd al-Qadir 'Izz al-Din	Minister of education	1932	
Mundhir Ibrahim al-Shawi	Minister of higher education and scientific research	1929	Replaced Samir Muhammad 'Abd al-Wahhab al-Shaykhli on 16 January 1988
'Abd al-Salam Muhammad Sa'id	Acting minister of health; director of the Scientific Affairs Department at the Presidential Office		Appointed in August 1988; his predecessor was Sadiq Hamid 'Alwash
'Abdallah Fadil 'Abbas [al-Samarra'i]	Minister of *awqaf* and religious affairs	1941	Sunni
Samal Majid Faraj	Minister of Planning	1936	Kurd
Tahir Muhammad Hassun al-Marzuk	Minister of housing and reconstruction	1946	Replaced Muhammad Fadil Husayn on 31 March 1988
Akram 'Abd al-Qadir 'Ali	Minister of justice	1928	Replaced Mundhir Ibrahim al-Shawi on 16 January 1988
Babakr Rasul Mahmud (al-Pishdari)	Minister of labor and social affairs	1937	Kurd. Reported sacked in mid-1988
Muhammad Mahdi Salih	Minister of trade	1947	
'Abd al-Jabbar Shanshal	Minister of state for military affairs		Sunni
Hashim Hasan 'Aqrawi	Minister of state	1926	Kurd

Name	Post	Year of Birth	Remarks
'Abdallah Isma'il Ahmad	Minister of state	1927	Kurd
Arshad Muhammad Ahmad al-Zibari	Minister of state	1942	Kurd
Ahmad Husayn (al-Samarra'i)	Director of the Presidential Office	1942	
Ahmad 'Abd al-Qadir al-Naqshbandi	Chairman of the Legislative Council of the Kurdish Autonomous Region	1929	Kurd
Sirwan 'Abdallah Husayn al-Jaff	Head of the Executive Council of the Kurdish Autonomous Region	1938	Kurd

SOURCE: Except for the remarks, the list is mainly based on *al-Thawra,* 17 May 1988.

TABLE 2: THE MILITARY HIGH COMMAND

Post	Name
Commander in chief of the armed forces	Field Marshal Saddam Husayn
Defense minister and deputy commander in chief of the armed forces	Gen. 'Adnan Khayrallah Talfah*
Minister of state for military affairs	Gen. 'Abd al-Jabbar Shanshal*
Chief of staff	Lt. Gen. Nizar 'Abd al-Karim [Faysal] al-Khazraji*
Armed forces assistant chief of staff for training	(unknown)
Armed forces assistant chief of staff for operations	Lt. Gen. Husayn Rashid Muhammad [al-Windawi al-Tikriti]*+
Armed forces assistant chief of staff for administration and supplies	Lt. Gen. 'Abd al-Sattar (Ahmad) al-Ma'ini
Commander of the presidential guard forces	Maj. Gen. Iyad Futayyih Khalifa al-Rawi*
Head of political guidance in the Defense Ministry	Maj. Gen. 'Abd al-Jabbar Muhsin*
Head of military intelligence	Maj. Gen. Sabir 'Abd al-'Aziz Husayn al-Duri*
Head of the president's bodyguard unit	Lt. Gen. Sabah Mirza
Air force and air defense commander	Lt. Gen. Hamid Sha'ban Khudayr [al-Tikriti]*
Commander of the naval and coastal defense forces	Brig. Gen. Gha'ib Hassun Gha'ib*+
Commander of the Ist Special Army Corps ("Allah Akbar Forces")	Lt. Gen. Sa'di Tu'ma 'Abbas al-Jaburi*+
Commander of the 1st Army Corps	Maj. Gen. Sultan [Qasim] Hashim Ahmad*+
Commander of the 2nd Army Corps	Maj. Gen. Kamil Sajit 'Aziz*+
Commander of the 3rd Army Corps	Maj. Gen. Salah 'Abbud Mahmud*+
Commander of the 4th Army Corps	Maj. Gen. Iyad Khalil Zaki*+
Commander of the 5th Army Corps	Maj. Gen. Yunis Muhammad al-Dhirib+
Commander of the 6th Army Corps	Maj. Gen. Yaljin 'Umar 'Adil*+
Commander of the 7th Corps	Lt. Gen. Mahir 'Abd al-Rashid (until mid-1988)

* Was given a medal or medals of valor.

\+ Assumed office after a reshuffle during 1988 (for comparison: see Table 2, *MECS* 1987).

NOTES

For the place and frequency of publications cited here, and for the full name of the publication, news agency, radio station, or monitoring service where an abbreviation is used, please see "List of Sources." Only in the case of more than one publication bearing the same name is the place of publication noted here. In the present chapter, however, all references to *al-Thawra* and *al-Jumhuriyya* are to the Baghdad papers of these names.

1. *Al-Thawra,* 10 December 1987.
2. *Al-Thawra,* 19 January; *MM,* 30 May; *MEI,* 24 June 1988.
3. *Al-Thawra,* 19 January 1988.
4. *Al-Watan al-'Arabi,* 5 February — DR, 12 February 1988.
5. *Al-Thawra,* 7 January 1988.
6. *Al-Jumhuriyya,* 4 February 1988.
7. Ibid.
8. In another development, the RCC itself issued a resolution abolishing three of its offices, responsible for Gulf, African, and Arab affairs. *CR:* Iraq, No. 2, 1988.
9. INA, 1 August — DR, 3 August 1988.
10. *Al-Thawra,* 28 November 1988.
11. *Al-Thawra,* 28 February 1988.
12. *Al-Thawra,* 6 May 1988.
13. *Al-Thawra,* 28 September 1988.
14. *Al-Thawra,* 28 February 1988.
15. E.g., *al-Thawra,* 9, 29 March, 3 April 1988.
16. *Al-Thawra,* 24 April 1988.
17. *Hurras al-Watan,* May 1988.
18. *Al-Thawra,* 26 April 1988.
19. *Al-Thawra,* 3 May 1988.
20. *Al-Dustur,* London, 9 May 1988.
21. *Al-Thawra,* 13 August 1988.
22. *Al-Siyasa,* Kuwait, 26 December 1988.
23. *Al-Thawra,* 28 April 1988.
24. *Gulf States Newsletter,* 27 June 1988.
25. *Al-Thawra,* 16 February 1988.
26. *Al-Thawra,* 17 May 1988.
27. *Al-Thawra,* 23 March 1988.
28. *Al-Thawra* (int. ed.), 23 April 1988.
29. The Military Organization, which grouped 11 state enterprises, has been praised by senior government figures for meeting 70%–80% of the Army's needs. *MEED,* 28 July, as quoted by JPRS, 30 September 1988.
30. *Al-Thawra,* 28 September 1988.
31. *Al-Thawra,* 20 January 1988.
32. *Al-Thawra,* 11 October 1988.
33. *Al-Thawra,* 3 January 1988.
34. *Al-Thawra,* 2 February 1988.
35. *Al-Thawra,* 4 July 1988.
36. *MM,* 14 November 1988.
37. *Al-Thawra* (int. ed.), 22 November 1988.
38. It was reported that both Justice Minister Akram 'Abd al-Qadir 'Ali and the presiding judge in 'Uday's case were cousins of 'Izzat Ibrahim al-Duri, 'Uday's father-in-law. *MEI,* 2 December 1988.
39. *FT, IHT,* 22 November; *MM,* 12 December 1988.
40. *MM,* 14, 28 November, 12 December 1988.
41. *MEI,* 2 December 1988.
42. Husayn himself echoed such murmurings in some of his speeches, e.g., *al-Thawra,* 3 January 1988.
43. *Al-Tayyar al-Jadid,* 14 March 1988.
44. *Al-Thawra,* 5 February 1988.

45. R. Baghdad, 6 January — DR, 20 January 1988.
46. *CR:* Iraq, No. 1, 1988.
47. *Al-Tayyar al-Jadid,* 29 February 1988.
48. *Al-Thawra,* 23 March 1988.
49. *Al-Thawra,* 31 July 1988.
50. *Al-Thawra,* 26 April 1988.
51. *FT,* 5 December; *al-Tayyar al-Jadid,* 20 December 1988.
52. R. Baghdad, 13 January — DR, 14 January 1988.
53. *Al-Thawra,* 10 February 1988.
54. *The Guardian,* 2 February; *CR:* Iraq, No. 1, 1988.
55. *'Iraq al-Ghad,* 5 March 1988, quoting *Risalat al-'Iraq,* 13 December 1987, No. 80–81, on these conflicts.
56. *Al-Thawra,* 26 January 1988.
57. 5, 000 acording to *JA,* 6 April 1988.
58. E.g., R. Baghdad, 19, 24, 25 April — DR, 19, 25, 26 April 1988.
59. *CR:* Iraq, No. 4, 1988.
60. For a comparison, see INA, 18 April — DR, 19 April; *al-Thawra,* 19 April 1988.
61. *Al-Thawra* (int. ed.), 23 April 1988.
62. R. Baghdad, 23, 25 April — DR, 26 April 1988.
63. *Al-Thawra,* 29 May; Rawi disclosed this fact earlier; KUNA, 14 May — DR, 16 May 1988.
64. *Al-Thawra* (int. ed.), 23 April 1988.
65. KUNA, 14 May — DR, 16 May 1988.
66. *Al-Thawra,* 18 May 1988.
67. *CR:* Iraq, No. 4, 1988.
68. *Al-Thawra,* 1 June 1988.
69. *Al-Thawra,* 3 January 1988.
70. R. Baghdad, VoM, 24 April — DR, 25 April 1988.
71. *Al-Thawra* (int. ed.), 23 April 1988.
72. *Al-Thawra,* 28 September 1988.
73. *Al-Thawra,* 30 May 1988.
74. INA, 25 June — DR, 27 June 1988.
75. INA, 13, 14 August — DR, 15 August 1988.
76. INA, 25 June, 13 August — DR, 27 June, 15 August; *al-Thawra,* 2 October 1988.
77. *Al-Thawra,* 23 July 1988.
78. R. Baghdad, VoM, 25 July — DR, 25 July 1988.
79. *Al-Thawra,* 12 August 1988.
80. WF, 8, 9 February; *IHT,* 9, 10 February; *The Economist,* 11 February 1989.
81. *Al-Thawra,* 10 August 1988. According to a Western diplomat, the casualties from the falling bullets may have run into hundreds; *NYT,* 25 August 1988.
82. *CR:* Iraq, No. 4, 1988.
83. *Al-Jumhuriyya,* 2 January 1988.
84. *Al-Jumhuriyya,* 22 September 1988.
85. *Al-Jumhuriyya,* 4 December 1988.
86. *Argus,* No. 4, April 1988.
87. *Al-Thawra,* 4 May 1988.
88. *Le Monde,* 27 July 1988.
89. *Memo,* 7 October 1988.
90. *MEED,* 25 November 1988.
91. *Al-Jumhuriyya,* 1 December 1988.
92. R. Baghdad, 30 October — DR, 31 October 1988.
93. *Al-Watan,* Kuwait, 1 December 1988.
94. *Gulf States Newsletter,* 27 June 1988.
95. *CR:* Iraq, No. 1, 1989.
96. *Al-Tadamun,* 30 April 1988; *CR*: Iraq, No. 4, 1988; No. 1, 1989.
97. *Argus,* No. 3, March 1988.
98. *CR:* Iraq, No. 3, 1988.
99. *Baghdad Observer,* 6 August — JPRS, 30 September 1988.

100. *FT,* 16 August 1988.
101. *Memo,* 28 October 1988.
102. *CR:* Iraq, Nos. 3, 4, 1988.
103. *Al-Dustur,* Amman, 13 December — DR, 16 December 1988.
104. *CR:* Iraq, No. 4, 1988.
105. *Al-Jumhuriyya,* 13 July 1988.
106. R. Baghdad, 15 October — DR, 17 October 1988.
107. *CR:* Iraq, No. 1, 1989.
108. *Gulf States Newsletter,* 27 June; *MM,* 22 August; *FT,* 5 December 1988.
109. *CR:* Iraq, No. 4, 1988.
110. *CR:* Iraq, No. 3, 1988.
111. *Al-Dustur,* London, 9 May 1988.
112. On the same occasion, it was disclosed that in addition to the existing 4,350 mosques, the authorities had initiated the building of another 13 and the reconstruction of others at the cost of ID1m.; *al-Thawra,* 22 October 1988.
113. *Al-Thawra,* 23 November 1988.
114. The Sudanese investigation report published in July claimed that according to eyewitnesses the assassin was Iraqi as was his car. SUNA, 22 July — DR, 25 July 1988.
115. *NYT,* 24 January 1988.
116. *Al-Jumhuriyya,* 28 January — DR, 5 February 1988.
117. IRNA, 28 May — DR, 31 May 1988.
118. *The Guardian,* 22 April; *IHT,* 3 August; *Le Monde,* 5 September; *FT,* 7 September 1988.
119. *IHT,* 24 February 1988. According to Kurdish sources, the area controlled by the guerrillas was as large as Lebanon; *FT,* 23 March 1988.
120. *Kayhan al-'Arabi,* 5 November 1987 — JPRS, 20 January 1988. For later declarations, see *al-Tayyar al-Jadid,* 14 March; *Le Monde,* 19 March; *'Iraq al-Ghad,* 13 August 1988.
121. *Le Monde,* 19 March 1988.
122. *The Guardian,* 24 March; *'Iraq al-Ghad,* 13 August 1988. In his interview with *'Iraq al-Ghad,* Talabani rejected Iran's claims that its Army had occupied Halabja, saying that Iranian troops came in after the PUK.
123. *Al-Thawra,* 14 March 1988.
124. *Al-Thawra,* 3 January 1988.
125. *Al-Thawra,* 27 March; INA, 28 March — DR, 28 March 1988.
126. *NYT,* 13 September 1988.
127. *The Guardian,* 22 April 1988.
128. *Al-Thawra,* 26 September 1988.
129. *'Iraq al-Ghad,* 31 May 1988.
130. *'Iraq al-Ghad,* 2 May 1988.
131. *Le Monde,* 10 November 1988.
132. *IHT,* 1, 3-4 September; *NYT,* 1 September 1988.
133. *FT,* 7 September; *IHT,* 8 September 1988.
134. *FT,* 16 September 1988.
135. *IHT,* 8 September 1988.
136. *NYT,* 9 September 1988.
137. *FT,* 1, 3, 9 September; *The Economist,* 10 September; *NYT,* 10 September; WF, 8 September; *MEI,* 9 September; *Le Monde,* 20 September; WF, 21 September; *Diario,* 6 October — DR, 13 October 1988.
138. *The Observer,* as quoted by *JP,* 18 September 1988.
139. *Diario,* 5 October — DR, 14 October 1988.
140. *The Observer,* as quoted by *JP,* 18 September 1988.
141. *Al-Thawra,* 7 September 1988.
142. *FT,* 17 August, 7 September; *IHT,* 25 August, 7 October; *NYT,* 28 August, 16, 19 September; *MEI,* 9 September; *Le Monde,* 20 September; WF, 21 September; *Diario,* 6 October — DR, 13 October 1988.
143. *Al-Dustur,* London, 10 October 1988.
144. *Al-Thawra,* 18 September 1988.
145. *Al-Qabas,* 31 October — DR, 2 November 1988.

146. *'Iraq al-Ghad,* 13 August 1988. Later reports claimed that the Ba'th continued to use this weapon well into October.
147. *Dagens Nyheter,* 17 October — DR, 1 November 1988.
148. *Dagens Nyheter,* 17 October — DR, 1 November; *Diario,* 6 October — DR, 13 October; *Le Monde,* 23 October 1988.
149. *WP,* 20 July 1988.
150. *The Times,* 23 April 1988.
151. *NYT,* 19 July; *NYT Magazine,* 25 September 1988.
152. *NYT,* 8 May 1988.
153. *Le Monde,* 25 February 1988.
154. *MEI,* 4 June; *CR:* Iraq, No. 3, 1988.
155. *Al-Thawra,* 16 June 1988.
156. *Al-Thawra,* 29 June 1988.
157. WF, 8 September 1988.
158. *IHT,* 10-11 September 1988.
159. INA, 11 September — DR, 13 September 1988.
160. INA, 12 September — DR, 15 September 1988.
161. *Al-Thawra,* 11 September 1988.
162. INA, 11 September — DR, 12 September 1988.
163. *Al-Thawra,* 15 September 1988.
164. *JP,* 2 October; *NYT,* 18 November 1988.
165. WF, 12 October; *IHT,* 13 October 1988.
166. INA, 3 October — DR, 4 October 1988.
167. WF, 12 October 1988.
168. *NYT,* 18 November 1988.
169. *NYT,* 28 September 1988.
170. INA, 3 November — DR, 4 November 1988.
171. *CR:* Iraq, No. 4, 1988.
172. *The Independent,* 22 March — DR, 23 March 1988.
173. *Al-Thawra,* 31 January 1988.
174. *Al-Qabas,* 24 February 1988.
175. *Argus*, No. 4, April 1988.
176. INA, 3 November — DR, 4 November 1988.
177. *Le Monde,* 22 July; *ME,* December 1988.
178. *Al-Qabas,* 31 October — DR, 2 November 1988.
179. *ME,* December 1988.
180. *CR:* Iraq, No. 3, 1988.
181. *Der Spiegel,* 30 January 1989.
182. In the meantime, it was disclosed that French pilots flew missions for Iraq in 1983-84, *NYT,* 21 October 1988.
183. *Le Monde,* 5 October; *NYT,* 21 October 1988.
184. *Al-Qabas,* 31 October — DR, 2 November 1988.
185. *Le Monde*, as quoted by *Ma'ariv,* 26 July 1988.
186. *Le Monde,* 13 December 1988.
187. *CR:* Iraq, No. 3, 1988.
188. *MM,* 28 November 1988.
189. *FT,* 19 November 1988.
190. *CR:* Iraq, Nos. 2, 3, 1988.
191. R. Baghdad, 17 November — DR, 18 November 1988.
192. *Al-Thawra,* 15 September 1988.
193. R. Baghdad, 17 July — DR, 18 July 1988.
194. R. Baghdad, 13 September — DR, 15 September 1988.
195. INA, 17 December — DR, 19 December 1988.
196. *Al-Thawra,* 7 September 1988.
197. *Al-Thawra,* 28 September 1988.
198. *Al-Tadamun,* 6 February — DR, 12 February 1988.
199. *Al-Thawra,* 7 September 1988.

200. *CR:* Iraq, No. 3, 1988.
201. INA, 6 July — DR, 8 July 1988.
202. *MM,* 31 October 1988.
203. Ramadan revealed that the number of Egyptian workers was reduced from 2m. in 1985 to 0.5m. in 1988.
204. INA, 7 September — DR, 9 September 1988.
205. *CR:* Iraq, No. 4, 1988.
206. R. Baghdad, VoM, 6 January — DR, 7 January 1988.
207. *Al-Jumhuriyya,* 28 January — DR, 5 February 1988.
208. INA, 17 April — DR, 19 April 1988.
209. R. Baghdad, 6 June — DR, 7 June 1988.
210. R. Baghdad, 19 September — DR, 20 September 1988.
211. INA, 11 September — DR, 13 September 1988.
212. *Al-Thawra,* 18 February 1988.
213. *Al-Thawra,* 7 April 1988.
214. *Al-Musawwar,* 20 May 1988.
215. *Al-Thawra,* 25 January 1988.
216. *Al-Ahram*, 18 March 1988.
217. *Al-Sharq al-Awsat,* 11 September 1988.
218. VoI, 1 September — DR, 1 September; *Ha'aretz,* 23 September 1988.

Israel
(Medinat Yisrael)

YAEL YISHAI

In its 40th year of statehood, Israel (with 4.464m. citizens) approached maturity, but also retained some of its adolescent characteristics. Major problems remained unresolved. The crisis in the welfare services continued, the public health system almost collapsed, there was an outbreak of polio, and the statistics on traffic accidents released by the Central Bureau of Statistics were the highest in the decade.[1] At the same time, there were substantial achievements: Israel entered the space age with the successful launching (on 19 September) of its first satellite, *Ofek 1*; it expanded its international relations despite persistent Arab efforts to limit support for Israel in the world community; and it also passed the democratic test when its citizens participated in elections to the Twelfth Knesset.

Despite these achievements, there was a widespread feeling among Israelis of a dire need for change. Before the elections, Foreign Minister Shimon Peres claimed that "1 November [election day] will be a watershed for the Jewish nation."[2] The statement may have been election rhetoric; but Prime Minister Yitzhak Shamir seemed to concur. "It is impossible to continue for long with the existing system,"[3] he declared several times. The two leaders thus shared the dissatisfaction with the glaring difficulties facing the Israeli polity.

However, the movement toward change was rather slow. Even the Palestinian uprising, the *intifada,* did not substantially change matters. If anything, the uprising in the territories resulted in a net increase in pessimism regarding the likelihood of change.[4] Was Israel, then, on the threshold of a watershed, or was it demonstrating "more of the same"?

POLITICAL AFFAIRS: DOMESTIC ISSUES

THE KNESSET: OLD WINE IN A NEW BOTTLE?

The 1988 elections changed the composition of the Knesset, to which 36 of its 120 members were elected for the first time. Some well-known public figures, such as former foreign minister Abba Eban (Alignment), were absent from the new House. Despite this turnover, the new Knesset did not mirror the Israeli population. More than half of the members were more than 50 years old; three quarters lived in the big cities or the established towns and townships. The new Knesset also had only seven women members, less than any previous Knesset, except for the Seventh (1969–73).[5] While the number of Sephardim (i.e., persons of Asian- African origin) rose to 39, the Ashkenazim (of European-American origin) still constituted the majority, with 75 Members of Knesset (MKs). Like other parliaments of Western nations, the Knesset

Israel, the West Bank, and the Gaza Strip

tends to represent the higher strata of society. Worthy of note is the growing number of MKs with higher education: there were now five PhDs and eight with the academic rank of professor.

As in the past, the Knesset struggled to maintain its autonomy of the government and to improve its public image. In 1988, on a few occasions, the Knesset did not show its most dignified face; harsh and sometimes insulting language was used by MKs when speaking from the podium. One of the Knesset's worst verbal explosions occurred when the Speaker adjourned the session after right- and left-wing MKs exchanged violent recriminations.[6] The persistent emptiness of the chamber also contributed to the diminishing public esteem of the legislature. Much important legislation, such as bills concerning human rights, had remained unfinished. The government often showed disrespect for the Knesset; on one occasion, Transport Minister Haim Corfu served as "minister for all seasons" when he replied to motions for the agenda on behalf of the ministers of health, finance, and defense.[7] The legislature also served as a stage for crass party politics when it increased by 50% the allocation to political parties to help them pay election campaign expenses.[8]

Especially embarrassing was the opening session of the Twelfth Knesset on 23 November, which President Chaim Herzog described as a "shameful spectacle."[9] What was to have been a festive inauguration of the newly elected House was marred by a speech by Acting Speaker Yair Sprinzak (Moledet), who took the opportunity to expound his controversial political philosophy supporting the "voluntary transfer" of the Arab population to Arab countries. The left-wing parties staged a token walk-out by withdrawing to the sides of the chamber. Instead of pledging allegiance, some MKs took the opportunity to protest against Sprinzak's views and vowed to combat racism. Since the High Court of Justice had ruled that there was only one valid text of the pledge, the protesting MKs could not vote for a Speaker until they had taken a valid pledge of allegiance. Therefore, the pledging ceremony had to be repeated much to the new Knesset's disgrace. The incident was so shocking that it prompted Eban, a former acting speaker among his other positions, to comment that "Israeli democracy is in deep trouble and there is no procedural cure."[10] President Herzog also castigated the Knesset for "shaming the state and the nation."[11]

The Knesset took pains to improve its image by enacting laws that would increase its popularity; these, however, reflected the individual MKs' battle for survival as much as the impending party struggle. Until the elections, many MKs were uncertain of being placed in an electoral slot and chose a course to impress their party's central committee, which was charged with approving the list. Thus the Knesset approved laws forbidding MKs from holding salaried positions outside the legislature. In future, only writers, composers, and artists will be able to pursue their professions parallel to their Knesset duties, although a special exemption committee has been empowered to grant similar privileges to others.[12] The Knesset's attempt to gain popularity was especially noticeable with regard to social legislation. The Development Towns Law was passed[13] providing large financial benefits to residents there. Not one of the 44 MKs in the plenum opposed the bill, thus yielding to massive pressures from development towns, 200 of whose leaders were in the chamber during the deliberations. The hasty legislation was criticized by the press as an instance of "ceaseless irresponsibility."[14] But the trend persisted. The Knesset also passed a bill granting demobilized soldiers NIS900 for each year of army service. Although early estimates put its cost at NIS375m. a year, the Knesset went on to approve the bill tabled by MK Amir (Labor) a resident of a Negev development town.[15] The two laws were not implemented; they were shelved after the Treasury warned that if this sum were expended, the budget would have to be cut by 2.6% across the board. Furthermore, a provision was added to the Budget Basic Law, stating that any legislative initiative involving state expenditure must indicate the mode of financing.[16]

Other important legislation resulted from political parties' interest in buttressing their election prospects. Two major issues were at stake: the timing of the local elections and the perennial question of electoral reform. Local elections are held once every five years, apart from the national elections. Under this arrangement, local and national elections coincide every 20 years and this should have happened in 1988. For Labor, that foretold a severe erosion of its municipal strength. Voters, unaccustomed to ballot-splitting, were likely to move rightward as on the national electoral front. Anticipating losses, the Alignment proposed delaying the local elections. Other left-wing factions and the National Religious Party (NRP), much of whose strength lay in municipalities and local councils, were also eager to postpone the local elections.

Both the Likud and the Alignment presented their pro and con arguments in terms of principles rather than expedience. The Likud argued that it was in the national interest that both elections be held at the same time; it was unconscionable to extend the terms of office of locally elected representatives and it was improper to waste scarce resources on an additional election campaign. Labor claimed that simultaneous elections would undo the reform introduced into local government by which local leaders were elected by a direct vote. It further argued that local issues would be swept aside as the voters became embroiled in the discussion of national issues. The principles invoked were fig leaves for a fierce interparty struggle. An amendment delaying local elections for six months passed the Knesset in a preliminary hearing by 59–45.[17] That in itself did not ensure final approval, since all the Knesset committees that handle electoral legislation were headed by Likud MKs, who were hostile to the separation of local and national elections.

The law was buried for six weeks in the House Committee headed by Micha Reiser (Likud) who did his utmost to thwart the bill's processing, and finally assigned the bill to the Law Committee, chaired by Likud MK Elie Kulas. This move triggered strong public criticism; "Israel's representative democracy is under a threat of committee chairmen turned little dictators, who make a travesty out of it," one newspaper said editorially.[18] Although the chairman may not under the law refuse to put the bill on the committee's agenda, he can try to prevent the committee from being called into session which, in this case, he did. The incident clearly exposed the ambiguity surrounding a Knesset committee chairman's prerogatives and the extent to which the plenum can interfere in what chairmen do. The plenum vote to deprive Reiser of his chairmanship was followed by a Likud appeal to the High Court. The court criticized the chairman's dismissal because of the damage it might do to the smooth functioning of Knesset committees, but it declined to overrule the Knesset decision, since the plenum had acted within its lawful authority.[19] Reiser's successor, Rafi Edri (Labor) hastily prepared the bill for approval which took place on the Knesset's last day in session. By 54–0, the Knesset separated local and national elections,[20] the Likud opponents absenting themselves from the vote.

Electoral reform had also been on the Knesset's agenda. Few issues enjoyed as much popular support as it did. Some support came from the disappointment with the Knesset as a barren debating club and the manifest deficiencies of proportional representation, carried over from pre-state political structures. Two possible changes in the system by which the Knesset is elected were proposed. The first, initiated by Gad Ya'acobi (Labor) divided the country into 20 electoral districts, each returning four MKs, for a total of 80, the remaining 40 to be chosen from a national list. The second proposal, initiated by Tel Aviv University professors headed by Uriel Reichman of the Law Faculty, divided the country into 60 electoral districts, each returning one MK, the remaining 60 to be chosen from a national list.

There were reasonable arguments for and against electoral reform. The proponents argued that it would strengthen the links between voters and MKs, would reduce the party machinery's say in the selection of candidates, and would permit the formation of a strong, stable government. The opponents claimed, among others, that small parties would be denied representation, that extremist action might evolve outside parliament, and that MKs elected by a constituency would become partisans of narrow, local interests.

The majority of MKs ostensibly favored reform in one form or another. It was important for the proponents of a change that the initial reading of a reform proposal be held in the Eleventh Knesset, so that the bill could be taken up from that point by the Twelfth Knesset, if the government so desired. The long-mooted reform (endorsing Reichman's proposal) passed the first reading with the support of 67 MKs, eight more than the required minimum.[21] But the substantial majority was partly due to a tactical retaliatory move by the Likud against the religious parties, adamant opponents of the reform, for aligning themselves with Labor in the campaign to separate the local and national elections. On the very same day the religious parties' attempt to amend the Law of Return so that automatic citizenship would be granted only to Jews converted according to Halacha was rejected by Labor, the parties of the left, and one lone Liberal, Sara Doron.

The pro-reform mood did not dissipate after the elections. A rally attended by tens of thousands demanded that electoral reform be a top priority of the future government. The demonstration, said to be the largest since the one protesting against the Lebanon war[22] (see *MECS* 1981–82, p. 648), clearly demonstrated a desire for change. It was attended by MKs from the left (Labor), the center (Shinui-Merkaz), and the right (Likud, Tzomet) thus representing all shades of the political spectrum. Whether or not public pressure was effective remained questionable. But the general feeling was that the one clear message of the elections was that a change in the electoral system was a national imperative.

Another reform bill was tabled toward the end of the year as a private initiative by two Likud MKs, providing for the direct election of the prime minister. The initiative was joined by a few more MKs who gave it their moral support. A public opinion poll taken at the time of the Knesset debate indicated that 81% of respondents of a national sample favored the direct election of the prime minister.[23] The proposed bill gave the premier the authority to appoint his cabinet at his own discretion, while the Knesset could bring down the government and call for new elections by a vote of 73 out of the 120 MKs.[24] This proposal was markedly different from previous attempts to reform the system through the electoral process. Worthwhile noting is the fact that the issue was pushed to the top of the national agenda without previous debate. Nor was it included in any election platform. If the proposal were also endorsed by Labor (which is not totally out of the question) a revolution in Israel's entire system of government could well be under way.

The Knesset in 1988 was also notable for the proposals it rejected. These included a motion to annex the Jordan Valley and to reiterate Israel's claim to the two banks of the Jordan River;[25] a private member's bill to curb parliamentary immunity aimed at extreme left-wing Arab lists;[26] and a bill shortening the prison terms of the members of the Jewish underground.[27] These rejections indicate that the Knesset was not swept up by its die-hard members, but served as a guardian of widely accepted social norms.

The Knesset was also preoccupied with less dramatic matters. It reelected President Herzog to a second term by more than two thirds (82) of the House. Knesset Speaker Shlomo Hillel noted that this near unanimity was a "ray of light" of which Israel could be proud.[28] The results of national unity were vividly reflected as the Knesset's fourth year came to an end. Only a handful of MKs was needed to reject seven motions of no confidence submitted by the small opposition parties.[29] Despite recurring disagreements, the coalition members reportedly departed in a good mood. All factions agreed to form a special panel that would recommend changes in the rules of the House to which they were unsure of returning.

PARTIES AND ELECTION: THE FORMATION OF THE TWELFTH KNESSET

The elections to the Twelfth Knesset were the outstanding political event of 1988. The parties were caught on the horns of a dilemma. On the one hand, it was deemed necessary to display acceptance of democratic procedures and to demonstrate internal cohesion. On the other hand, the elections exacerbated factional strife and generated intra-party tensions. Who were the major contestants, what was their message, how was the contest carried out and what was its outcome?

THE CONTESTANTS

The Religious Bloc

The religious bloc, with 14 mandates in 1984, comprised no less than six parties in 1988, divided by ethnic origin, political ideologies and last, but not least, by personal loyalties. It was assumed prior to the elections that "the multiplicity of parties might result in a net loss for the religious camp in November."[30] Actually, however, the victory of the religious parties was the most dramatic outcome of the elections. An overview of the religious camp reveals a wide variety of opinions, ethnic origins, and life-styles.

Starting from the left there was Meimad (Dimension), a new party led by Rabbi Yehuda Amital, which was organized in reaction to a rightward swing in the NRP. While stressing its devotion to the Land of Israel, the new party neither ruled out territorial concessions, nor did it advocate additional religious legislation. It was supported mainly by a more affluent Ashkenazi religious constituency.[31]

The NRP adopted a more hawkish posture. First on its slate of candidates was Prof. Avner Shaki, an avowed hawk, who was supported mainly by the party's Sephardi members. Among the party's first five candidates were two Matzad (right-wing faction) leaders associated with Gush Emunim. It was noted that the party leadership represented more strictly observant elements than in the past.[32] Only after the elections did the NRP regain its previous balance and choose Zevulun Hammer, a moderate, for the post of religious affairs minister.

Under the banner of Agudat Israel appeared a coalition of the remnants of what had once been the only Orthodox non-Zionist party. In 1988, the list included a representative of Poalei Agudat Israel and of the party's establishment. But the major source of support was the Rabbi of Lubavich, who lives in Brooklyn, and his Habad movement, which played an active role in the election campaign. The party's prime interest was amending the Law of Return. It was also against abortions and against military service for yeshiva students. It demanded special funds for yeshivot.

One hour before the deadline for submitting election lists, a faction seceded from the Aguda and formed Degel Hatora (The Flag of the Tora) which identified with Rabbi Eliezer Schach, the bitter opponent of the Rabbi of Lubavich. The party was supported by an Ashkenazi constituency and followed its leaders' moderate views on security affairs.[33]

The Shas list, representing a Sephardi breakaway from Aguda in 1984, continued to be headed by Rabbi Yitzhak Peretz, despite a widely publicized rift between him and other party leaders. The party had no clear stand on the territorial issue, but tended rightward. A small faction, headed by Shimon Ben-Shlomo, withdrew from Shas to form its own Yemenite list.

All the ultra-Orthodox parties (that is, excluding Meimad and the NRP), could be potential partners in any coalition. Their major interest was in supporting their educational institutions and in advancing religious legislation.

Right-Wing Parties

Three parties were situated at the right end of the political spectrum: Moledet (Homeland), Tehiya (Revival) and Tzomet (Junction). Moledet's main plank was the "voluntary transfer" of the Arab population. It was headed by Rehav'am Ze'evi, a former general of the Israel Defense Forces (IDF), whose platform was arch-hawkish. Tehiya, headed by Prof. Yuval Ne'eman, reiterated its support for a Greater Israel and demanded the immediate annexation of the territories; Tzomet, headed by Raphael ("Raful") Eitan, a former IDF chief of staff, combined both demands. Its platform called for annexation to be followed by a population exchange with Arab countries.[34]

The major event in the right-wing camp was the Central Election Committee's decision on 5 October not to approve Meir Kahane's Kach list. The ruling was based on the Basic Law: the Knesset can ban a list if it rejects the democratic character of the state, or incites to racism. The Supreme Court, to whom Kahane appealed, upheld the committee's decision and disqualified Kach from taking part in the elections. The court stated that the dignity of man and the equality of all Israeli citizens, regardless of race and creed, is a fundamental social tenet. When threatened, this tenet must take precedence, even at the risk of curbing the important democratic right to vote for a particular political party.[35]

The court's ruling not only removed Kahane from the electoral scene, but had far-reaching implications for Israeli law, the most important of which related to the definition of democracy. The court stressed the centrality of equality in a democratic regime; the principle of Israel as a Jewish state may not, according to this ruling, be used to justify discrimination between its Jewish and non-Jewish citizens.

Left-Wing Jewish Parties

"Left" in this context refers only to dovish orientations in foreign policy, since the parties differ on economic policy and on social issues. The parties occupying the left in this sense were Mapam, Ratz (Citizens' Rights Movement), and Shinui-Merkaz. These parties advocated negotiations with the PLO on condition that it recognized Israel and renounced terror. They endorsed the principle of territorial compromise, i.e., the return of land in exchange for peace. Mapam and Ratz were willing to accept a Palestinian state while Shinui supported a Palestinian-Jordanian confederation.

Mapam made its appearance as an independent party in 1988, after 23 years during which it cooperated with the Labor Party in what was called the "Alignment." It was mainly a kibbutz-based party which advocated a centralized, controlled economy. Ratz appealed to the more affluent in the urban population and favored a mixed economy and privatization of state enterprises. Shinui advocated a free market economy based on private initiative and competition.[36] The common denominator of foreign policy was thus insufficient for party unity.

Arab Lists

Three Arab lists competed in 1988. The first, Hadash, an established Communist party maintained its two-state solution. The party is a coalition of various forces, including a splinter group of the defunct Black Panthers, led by Charlie Biton.[37] The second, the Progressive List for Peace, was also an avowed supporter of a Palestinian state. The Likud and Tehiya parties unsuccessfully asked the Central Election Committee to ban it.[38] The third party was a one-man list of 'Abd al-Wahhab Darawsha who demonstratively broke away (on 24 January) from the Labor Party which he represented as an MK, in protest against Defense Minister Rabin's policy in the territories. Darawsha appealed mainly to the Israeli Arabs who voted Labor in the 1984 elections. The new party also advocated setting up a Palestinian state, but focused its attention mainly on domestic issues such as improving conditions of Israeli Arabs.

The Major Parties: Likud

The major event in the Likud was the long-delayed merger between Herut and the Liberal Party on 25 August. Taking the name "The Likud, National Liberal Movement" its two constituents coalesced in the Knesset, government, the Histadrut, and the World Zionist Organization. The distribution of Knesset seats between the two was determined by a team of senior ministers.[39]

The Likud was once again led by Premier Shamir. Its 1988 platform did not markedly differ from the previous one. Its major principles reiterated the Likud's commitment to the Camp David Accords, but the extension of autonomy to the Arabs in the territories was not accepted by all party members. Ariel Sharon, a major opponent, demanded immediate annexation of the West Bank to fill the vacuum created by King Husayn's disengagement from the area[40] (see chapter on Jordan). In social and economic affairs, the Likud advocated populist policies based mainly on the principles of a liberal economy.

The Major Parties: Labor

The Labor Party was also led by its previous leader Shimon Peres who, before the elections, had been an uncontested leader. After the elections, party unity was almost shattered when persons in the senior echelons called for the party's leaders to step down. Ya'acov Tzur (Immigration Minister) said that "the party will have to undergo a radical reform as the result of a failed election strategy."[41] The party's ranks were reunited after the national unity government was formed. Formulation of the party platform was an arduous task, because there was no agreement on the fate of the territories and holding talks with the PLO.[42] A compromise was reached which united the party around the formula of "territories for peace." As Peres put it: "No Labor hawk was opposed to territorial compromise for the sake of peace; no dove would compromise on the unity of Jerusalem nor allow a foreign army to cross the Jordan."[43] Labor's religious plank was also ambiguous; the party remained committed to oppose any amendment to the Law of Return and pleaded for unity among Judaism's different trends, but it did not call for military service for yeshiva students or overturning coercive religious legislation. The Labor Party clearly hoped to get rid of its alleged antireligious stigma and become an attractive prospective partner in a coalition with religious parties.[44]

THE PROCESS OF NOMINATION

The Likud

Herut's internal problems were exposed for all to see during the selection of candidates. At the end of May, Shamir was renominated as party chairman and candidate for premier. While the nomination for the premiership was not contested, there was much brawling over who would follow Shamir as party leader. David Levy, for example, ignored Shamir's instructions[45] and sharply criticized the men nominated to the party's election committee. His chief rival among party leaders was Moshe Arens.

The major battle for selecting candidates for the party's Knesset list occurred in the central committee with its 2,093 Herut members. Elections to the list were held in two stages. In the first round, a 35-member panel was chosen (out of 104 candidates) who were ranked a week later in the course of three rounds of elections into five, seven-member groups. Party officials forbade "taking orders from anyone on how to vote" and insisted that central committee members should not be party to any deals in support of particular candidates, but much wheeling and dealing resulted nevertheless.

The elections within Herut were aimed at achieving full democratization of choosing its Knesset list. The elections took place on 29 June amidst mounting tension among the cliques led by Arens, Levy, and Sharon. The most prominent successful candidates in the first round of elections were Welfare and Labor Minister Moshe Katzav and former UN ambassador Binyamin Netanyahu, both associated with Shamir. The results were a painful blow to Levy, who received sixth place on the list,[46] owing mainly to the fact that he was boycotted by the Arens bloc. Levy then threatened a rift unless he was elected in the second round to the first place in the list after Shamir.[47]

Tension mounted before the second round. The first five positions on the Herut list were reserved for the incumbent leadership.[48] Competition for other positions was bitter. Anyone failing to get elected to the slot of his choice was considered for the next slot, with the advantage of accumulating the votes already won. This advantage did not accrue if one failed to get into his chosen septet; one could try again, but previous votes were lost. The 14 candidates who failed to make the first 21 positions were graded in slots 22–35, according to the number of votes received in the first election round.

The most prominent feature of the list finally chosen was the absence of women and non-Jews. Surprisingly, there were also only a few Sephardi candidates, although 65% of the central committee are of Afro-Asian origin. There were only six new faces in realistic positions. The results also showed that Shamir had no control over the cliques in his party; the combined forces of Sharon and Levy could obstruct any decision made by the premier. Sharon won a personal victory in achieving the second position against Arens, who was elected to third position (despite an early agreement, granting Arens the first place on the list). In addition, only two of Aren's five supporters won a place in the septets. The Shamir-Arens camp increased its strength by one; Levy was the main winner, getting six of his eight supporters into the septets. Herut emerged as a party of factions which reflected personal animosities or loyalties. The Knesset list temporarily concealed this contentious state of affairs.

The Labor Party

Internal rifts were no less conspicuous in the Labor Party. In January, party secretary-general Uzi Baram threatened to resign because of his differences with party leaders over the democratization of party electoral procedures.[49] Initially, Baram demanded the setting up of a 15-member steering committee empowered to make final decisions. The problem was not only organizational, but also ideological. The hawks-doves division left its imprint on all walks of party life. Baram, an ardent dove, was accused of steering the party into a middle-of-the-road direction. The party central committee accepted Baram's demands, but also backed Rabin's hard-line policy on the territories,[50] thereby attempting to eat the cake and yet have it.

Like its rival Herut, Labor also democratized its process of choosing Knesset candidates. For the first time in the party's history, the candidates were elected by secret ballot by the large central committee. The selection was made in two stages. In the first, on 24 April, 23 candidates were chosen from among 50 at 16 Labor branches throughout the country. On 26 May, an additional 29 were chosen by the central committee. The 1,267 central committee members were to choose "the best possible team," but in fact they were also bound by pre-election deals. Six candidates were assured of places at the top of the list.[51] Ezer Weizman's faction, Yahad — which in 1984 was an independent party — was promised three realistic places. Reportedly the largest deals were made by the party's three big branches (Tel Aviv, Jerusalem, and Haifa), the United Kibbutz Movement, the Rabin faction, the Shiluv ("joint action") group, and the "middle generations." At the last moment, smaller factions joined the deal by agreeing to support their mutual candidates. It is estimated that this deal controlled 800 members of the central committee, sufficient to get its candidates onto the Knesset list.[52]

The real battle, however, took place on 15 June when the central committee assigned positions on the list. The outcome was declared a "revolution."[53] The list chosen included younger candidates; there was also greater representation for Sephardi activists and for residents of development towns. Some veteran leaders failed to enlist support, the big surprise being the failure of Abba Eban to get elected. Nevertheless, the list reflected the necessary careful balancing of interests. The self-correcting device of a two-stage selection process proved to be effective by giving the party an image of being "younger, fresher, brighter, and more all-round Israeli than it ever had been before."[54] Only the women did not secure adequate representation. They had not organized a caucus, but instead divided their support among the rival factions. Their loss was even more conspicuous when the party's slate of cabinet ministers was presented to the central committee. The only woman who had been a cabinet minister in the previous government was dropped and no other woman was named to the Cabinet. The small number of women on Labor's Knesset list revived the demand to guarantee them safe places in future.

ELECTION RESULTS AND IMPLICATIONS

Twenty-eight parties competed in the elections to the Twelfth Knesset. Of these, only 16 were veteran parties. The others were newly put together, hoping to take advantage of the proportional representation system. The number of eligible voters was 2,894,000, of whom 12% were non-Jewish. The share of the Sephardim among the Jewish voters grew from 45% in 1984 to 47% in 1988. The Ashkenazi constituency declined from 48% to 46%.[55] The elections were dominated by the issue of the future of the territories. As the campaign got under way, voters gave far more weight to problems of security and peace than to domestic issues. A comparison of the 1988 and 1984 electoral results, by blocs (see Table 1), indicates that voting patterns remained quite stable although some changes were noticeable. The following conclusions emerged:

(1) Three months before the elections, one in five Jewish voters was still "undecided," but the wavering was within blocs.[56] The biggest surprise, and increase in votes, was the rise of the religious bloc from 14 to 18 seats. The religiously observant Jews were estimated at 20%–25% of the population. In 1988 there was a change in the makeup of their Knesset representation. In the past, the NRP, a pragmatic Zionist party, accounted for three quarters of the religious bloc; in 1988, the anti-Zionist Orthodox parties accounted for over two thirds. It thus seemed as if Israel were turning into a right-wing theocracy.[57] Widespread reactions included both disbelief and dismay. A *Ma'ariv* editorial noted that the election results "will mark the end of the Zionist era in Israel," adding that they would cause a complete change in the country's character.[58] But, in actuality, this attainment by the Orthodox had little impact on the post-election government (see below). The rise of the religious bloc was attributed to the massive mobilization effort made by the religious leadership, partly owing to rivalry within the bloc itself.

(2) There was almost a deadlock between the two major parties, Labor and the Likud, which gained 39 and 40 mandates, respectively. In the 1988 elections, the Israeli voters apparently "decided not to decide" on the most crucial issues presented to them. They did not explicitly endorse the Likud's Greater Israel program, nor did they support Labor's initiative for peace entailing territorial concessions. The population split almost evenly on issues such as whether to continue Jewish settlement in the territories and whether to return at least some of the West Bank in exchange for peace.[59]

(3) The two major parties lost strength compared to 1984. Labor's loss was attributed to the prominence of the peace process in the election campaign which it opened with the proposal for an international conference. Dovish voters were unconvinced that such a conference would lead to peace; others considered the international conference an anathema. Furthermore, the "rejuvenation" of the party

list did not seem to produce a new leadership able to tackle the country's problems. The ailing Histadrut enterprises also contributed to the party's dwindling support.

As for the Likud, it lost some of its attractiveness as an anti-establishment party which had won it the support of the unprivileged. It no longer stood up against authority; rather, it now represented authority. The Likud was charged with responsibility for the economic blunders of the mid-1980s. Some of its voters turned away in protest, either because of its "moderation" in security affairs or because of reawakening ethnic grievances. Apparently, Shamir did not attract some sections of the Sephardi constituency as had his charismatic predecessor, Menachem Begin.

(4) The small parties increased their strength at both ends of the political spectrum. The small right-wing parties in 1988 (Tehiya, Tzomet, and Moledet) had a total of seven mandates, as compared to six of the small, right-wing parties in 1984. The left-wing parties (Mapam, Ratz, Shinui) won 10 mandates, as compared to six won by the small left-wing parties in the previous elections. The Israeli voter showed some preference for parties whose message was unambiguous.

(5) The deadlock is less clear-cut if the election results are examined by blocs. Table 1 shows that the electorate is leaning rightward. The left declined while the right retained its electoral strength. This tendency is more visible when at least part of the religious bloc is included in the right-wing bloc. The upshot is that the total in 1988 of those opposing territorial concessions outnumbered those favoring it. A terrorist attack on a bus in which a woman and her three children were killed just before the elections is said to have strengthened the hawkish mood. (For details on the incident, see chapter on armed operations.)

(6) Surprisingly, the Arab bloc did not change, gaining six mandates in both 1984 and 1988. Apparently, the split in the Arab constituency and the massive vote given by non-Jews to Jewish parties explain this lack of change. Many Arab citizens did not vote; the number of eligible non-Jewish voters grew by 27% compared to 1984, but the number of those actually voting increased by only 2%. The Arab leadership failed to mobilize popular support among Arabs, who in 1988 comprised more than 18% of the total population.

(7) Finally, none of the small ephemeral parties entered the Knesset. A few received as much as 0.7% of the total vote; the biggest among them turned out to be the Pensioners' Party. But none received the minimum 1% of the valid votes needed to send one member to the Knesset. Having attracted public attention and added color to the electoral contest, these smaller lists thus failed to serve as an effective channel for entry into the heart of the political arena.

To sum up, the only clear-cut outcome of the 1988 elections was the rise in electoral strength of the religious bloc. Other consequences were more equivocal: a stalemate between Labor and the Likud and a slight tilt toward the right.

THE GOVERNMENT: UNBROKEN CONTINUITY

When the government was formed in 1984, it was predicted that it would be short-lived. But it confounded this prediction and lived out its full four-year term.

The months preceding the elections were characterized by paralysis and feud. The government continued to speak with two voices. The Likud rejected outright US Secretary of State George Shultz's peace plan which was presented in January (see chapter on the Middle East peace process). Prime Minister Shamir held fast to the

Likud line not to relinquish territory under any circumstances, including pressure exerted from the outside, i.e., by the US. The Likud's major objective was to maintain the status quo. Shamir told a cabinet meeting that "unrest [in the territories] won't push the government into political decision." He also rejected any policy change "because of visits."[60] Peres's reaction that "you are speaking on behalf of only a part of the government" reflected the political stalemate. The prime minister, however, could and did block any policy modification. Peres's remark in February, that "Shamir has brought the peace process to a standstill," infuriated the Likud, which demanded that the foreign minister be dismissed.[61] The storm subsided, but indecision prevailed. Shamir believed that the status quo was to Israel's advantage while Labor was staunchly committed to an international conference to break the ME deadlock.

Internal differences did not terminate the coalition's existence. Peres's call, in January, for early elections[62] was dismissed by the Likud, which hoped to gain electoral benefits from the *intifada.* Labor was also reluctant to withdraw from the government, officially because "the havoc that the Likud, governing at will, could wreak on the country during the intervening nine months could be horrendous."[63] There were other good reasons for Labor's remaining in the government. The chances of securing a Knesset majority for early elections were remote and the electorate was conspicuously leaning toward the right, which made exit from the government an undesirable option.

On his second visit in April, Shultz again found a divided Israeli government, but one that did not show any signs of an early death. On the contrary, in what was noted as "a rare show of unanimity" two more ministers — Mordechai Gur (Labor), and Moshe Katzav (Likud) — joined its ranks. Unanimity disappeared shortly afterward when US President Reagan stated, in May, that intractable leaders impede progress toward peace in the ME. The statement followed Peres's meeting with the president and it was believed that Peres had suggested it to Reagan. A demand to dismantle the government followed promptly,[64] but the incident proved to be a storm in a teacup and the two partners remained, perforce, locked in each other's arms.

Another major dispute erupted in the government over the Taba affair. Shamir accused Peres of "working in the interests of the Egyptians." Peres, for his part, reminded the premier that the Likud had voted in favor of the arbitration process when the matter had been brought to the government in September 1986.[65] The mutual accusations reflected the unbridgeable gap between the two partners which had its origins in different world views.

THE NEW GOVERNMENT

The new government, formed on 22 December, was based on the inconclusive results of the 1 November elections. It reflected the wish of the Israelis to pull together as well as their leaning to the right. The government was unprecedentedly large — 26 ministers — with the Likud as the leading party, the Labor as a major partner, and three religious parties, Shas, the NRP, and Agudat Israel as junior partners.[66] Not all the ministers were content with the portfolios given them, among them Health Minister Ya'acov Tzur and Yitzhak Moda'i.[67] The government was formed after 52 days of tough and volatile negotiations.

At its inception, the unity government enjoyed the support of 84 MKs, with 19 opposing and three abstaining.[68] It was formed despite earlier statements by the two major partners pledging not to work together again, unless the other changed its political program. In a televised debate during the election campaign, Shamir had announced his intention not to repeat "the experience of a national unity government." Peres said he would welcome such a government only if it "promoted peace," i.e., endorsed the idea of an international conference.[69] Neither of the two leaders eventually adhered to his commitments.

The government's basic policy guidelines stated that the Camp David Accords were the basis of the peace process. This included a reference to renewing negotiations for full autonomy for the Arab inhabitants of the territories. The international conference was not mentioned. The only leeway, inserted at Peres's demand, was in the clause referring to the government discussing "proposals for negotiations" with Jordan. The guidelines also reflected common ground. Both parties rejected a Palestinian state or talks with the PLO. There was a commitment ruling out any change in sovereignty over Judea, Samaria, and Gaza during the government's term. It was agreed to set up between five to eight settlements in the territories within a year, and to seriously reconsider reform in electoral legislation. The agreement also provided for retention of the status quo on religious matters. Shamir and Peres were authorized to decide when private members' bills on religious matters could be tabled in the Knesset and how coalition MKs should vote on them. The MKs' freedom to abstain on votes regarding religious affairs was highly restricted.[70]

There was little novelty in these principles. Once again the government was split down the middle: cabinet portfolios were equally divided between Likud and Labor; the Inner Cabinet had six members from each party; even deputy ministerial posts were equally divided. However, it was explicitly stated that "the agenda of the cabinet meeting will be determined by the prime minister, who was to remain in office for the entire four years rather than rotate with Peres [as in the 1984 government]".[71] But despite the edge given to the Likud, the guidelines contained clauses which enabled Peres to exert his influence. Both Shamir and Peres had complete freedom to appoint ministers to the Cabinet and no Labor minister could be dismissed by the premier without the vice premier's consent. A secret annex stated that Shamir and Peres would together prepare the agenda of the Inner Cabinet. It also provided that Peres "from time to time" would be briefed on sensitive issues on which Shamir had been informed orally. The main purpose of the annex was to eliminate barriers which had previously hindered the government's functioning: the heart of this effort was a clause providing that if either of the parties decided to leave the government neither would try to set up a narrowly based government, and that both would join together in making a bid for immediate elections.[72]

The formation of the coalition was preceded at the last minute by opposition in the central committees of both parties. In the Likud, the vote was 769 to 642 (55% to 44.5%) in favor,[73] with the rejectionists being led by Ariel Sharon who sharply criticized Labor. The Labor central committee rescinded its opposition to joining a Likud-led coalition and by more than two thirds voted to join the government.[74] The opponents, led by Haim Ramon who was supported by the party's secretary-general, accused the leadership of reneging on the party platform which called for negotiations with Palestinians who recognized Israel and renounced terror. Despite these objections, the party leadership mustered support for a unity government.

THE MAKING OF THE COALITION

As the elections drew to their close, political discord was almost complete. Although the returns favored the Likud only marginally, it was clear from the outset that, with the expected support of the religious and ultranationalist parties, Shamir would have a working, albeit narrow majority in the Knesset. Thus a prompt presidential invitation to form a government coalition was expected. Tentative deals were quickly struck with the smaller parties and a Shamir-headed government seemed to be imminent. But then the coalition negotiations began to seesaw.

The virtual electoral deadlock between the Likud and Labor created what seemed to be almost insurmountable obstacles on the path leading to the formation of a coalition. A proposal to form a short-lived unity government whose sole purpose would be to reform the electoral system was dismissed by both parties. Each had its supporters: parties representing 55 MKs (Labor, left-wing parties,and Arab parties) backed Peres for the premiership, while 52 (Likud, right-wing parties, and the NRP) backed Shamir. The choice between the two was to be determined by the ultra-Orthodox parties. The Likud had a much better chance of forming a narrow coalition, since the religious parties were leaning toward the right. Shamir immediately initiated coalition negotiations with the religious parties, who demanded cabinet portfolios and financial allotments as their price for support. Progress was reported, but it soon became clear that the process would be long and arduous. Following the instructions of their rabbinical mentors, the very same parties that had negotiated with the Likud were now examining a possible agreement with Labor. The religious bloc was thus courted by both parties with each attempting to outbid the other; it was only natural that the religious parties would take advantage of the situation and drive a hard bargain.

Another complication in the negotiations was the competition within the religious bloc. Agudat Israel was pitted against Shas and Degel Hatora. Initially, each of them declared it would not join a coalition with the other.[75] This rivalry prompted Peres to mobilize religious support for his premiership. Bargaining was hard and uncertain. On 9 November, the press reported "a slight tilt toward Labor"; the next day, a headline stated, "Shas now seen tilting to Likud." One of the major reasons for the oscillation was the decision-making process within the religious parties. With the exception of the NRP, they found it hard to decide whether they preferred the Likud or Labor. What caused the prolonged indecision was the fact that the choice was not made by the parties themselves, but by councils of Tora sages. It was for the sages to decide on whom the premiership would be bestowed and the sages pondered halachic issues slowly and were in no haste to make up their minds. For some two weeks they decided not to decide, leaving the country anxiously awaiting the formation of their next government.

When the religious parties finally decided to ally themselves with the Likud, President Herzog called upon Shamir to form the government.[76] Besides the Likud, the new coalition was to include the ultranationalist parties (Tehiya, Tzomet, and Moledet) and the four religious parties. Shamir did not form the government within the allotted 21 days, the major reason being the extreme demands of the Orthodox parties for particular legislation, cabinet portfolios, and financial resources.[77] The Aguda's demand to amend the Law of Return, which would bar Conservative and Reform converts from receiving citizenship under its provisions, was a major bone of contention. Shas was satisfied with a commitment to the passage of a Conversion Law giving rabbinical courts the authority to affirm conversions. The other demands of the religious parties were easier to handle: the directorship of government companies, greater budget allocations to yeshivot (reportedly an annual sum of NIS500m.), and senior cabinet portfolios. Undertakings were also given to the NRP and the nationalist parties for 40 new settlements in the territories.

The shift occurred toward the end of November when Shamir issued a dramatic televised call to the Labor Party not to shut the door on a unity government. In a last-minute development, the Aguda withdrew its support from the Likud, thus enabling Labor to block the formation of a Likud-led government in a confidence vote in the Knesset. Shas followed suit and met Peres for "a friendly private meeting" but Likud-Labor negotiations were already under way. A major hurdle was cleared when Peres accepted the Treasury portfolio instead of the Foreign Ministry. When the ban imposed by Labor's central committee was lifted (see above), progress was quick. On 12 December, Labor and Likud teams began their official talks and the road leading toward a new government was wide open.

The formation of the national unity government was a thorn in the side of the religious and nationalist parties. The Shas leader, Yitzhak Peretz, termed the Likud's behavior "worse than that of the mafia." He warned that Shas would neither forget nor forgive the Likud's "act of treason." The sense of outrage was shared by all the offended parties, which were pushed aside once the broad coalition was formed. But within hours of its formation these offended parties joined the coalition, with Shas leading the way.[78]

Bearing in mind the friction between the Likud and Labor during the final months of the 1988 government, the question is why these strange bedfellows agreed to form another national unity government? The answer seems to be fivefold.

(1) Addressing the Knesset, the prime minister said that "it was the grave problems facing the country that dictated the establishment of a national unity government."[79] Undoubtedly, events in the international arena helped minimize party differences. On 16 December, the first US-PLO meeting took place after PLO chairman 'Arafat indirectly acknowledged Israel's existence and pledged not to engage in terrorism (see chapters on the Palestine Liberation Organization, and the US and the Middle East). Although both Reagan and Shultz had reassured Israel that US support remained intact, the US-PLO dialogue convinced the two parties that a broad government was a national imperative and that only a united front could withstand international pressure on Israel to negotiate with the PLO.

(2) Labor had much to gain from sharing the responsibility of government, especially with regard to the Histadrut enterprises, such as the Koor conglomerate, and the settlement movements. Financial aid for these Histadrut enterprises was essential if these bases of Labor power were to remain viable. The kibbutzim were among the major proponents of national unity, urging the Labor Party to join a broad government.

(3) A narrowly based government built on alliance between either party (most likely the Likud) and minor and/or religious parties was unattractive to both Labor and Likud. Labor could ally itself with the left-wing Jewish parties and with at least one of the religious parties, and could enjoy the tacit support of the non-Jewish parties. The price for such a partnership would have been unbearably high for many Laborites.

The Likud was also situated between its own Scylla and Charybdis. The ultranationalist parties (including Moledet, the "transfer" party which was anathema to most Israelis) pressed the Likud to adopt annexationist policies. In August, following Jordan's cutting of ties, Shamir had already rejected demands from two of his ministers (Sharon and Moda'i) that Israeli sovereignty be extended to the territories,[80] and additional demands to this effect were very likely to be made. The religious parties' insistence on religious legislation and financial allotments was also extremely difficult to satisfy.

(4) Forming a national unity government fitted the public mood. A poll taken during the coalition negotiations revealed that a large majority (63%) favored a wide national government.[81] A public campaign headed by former senior IDF officers (including supporters of both major parties) appealed to Shamir not to set up a government in which a fifth of the participating partners "aid and abet the evasion of army duty by young men and yeshiva students."[82] A huge rally representing all shades of political opinion was held in Tel Aviv on 29 November to protest against the mounting religious influence on public life. President Herzog stepped beyond established norms when, after granting Shamir his request for a second period of 21 days to try to form a government, he appealed to the two major parties for "national unity in the face of adversity." In his appeal, the president referred to the "avalanche" of appeals on the subject he had received from the public.[83]

(5) There were also strong external pressures for the formation of a national unity government. World Jewry exerted strong pressure to impede the establishment of a Likud-religious bloc that would formally establish the religious monopoly of Orthodoxy. The prospects of amending the Law of Return prompted widescale objections from overseas.

In conclusion, the government of January 1988 closely resembled that of January 1987. Both major parties coalesced in what apparently had become a new feature of Israeli politics, a wide unity government. It remained to be seen whether the new government is again an instrument of paralysis, or whether its overwhelming national power will enable it to escape the pitfalls that beset its predecessor and to forge agreement on solutions to Israel's problems.

THE IMPACT OF THE *INTIFADA* ON THE DOMESTIC ARENA

The Palestinian uprising in the territories had a divisive effect on the Israeli polity and society. While many advocated harsher measures to put an end to the violence, others called for negotiations with the insurgents and with those claiming to represent them outside of Israel, namely the PLO. The lack of consensus split leadership and public alike, and was evident in the dialogue both between parties and within them.

After it became evident that the *intifada* was not a short-lived nor a local outburst, two major attitudes emerged. The hard-line attitude was first articulated by Defense Minister Yitzhak Rabin, who stated on 20 January that violent demonstrations would be met with "force, power, and blows." In a Knesset plenum, responding to a no-confidence motion which was defeated, he reiterated that quiet would be restored "by force."[84] Other members of his party, however, were not content with such hard-line policy. For example, Foreign and Defense Committee chairman Abba Eban strongly criticized Rabin's riot-control strategy and denounced his public statement expounding it.[85] Criticism of a different kind was voiced by Likud members.

Agriculture Minister Ariel Sharon, a leading critic, argued that it was precisely the inability, or unwillingness, of the government to use its iron fist that was responsible for the uprising. According to him the blame was on the "divided, stuttering government which was projecting an image of a weak, debilitated Israel."[86] Sharon was echoed by archhawkish Tehiya leaders who appealed to the government to order soldiers facing rioters in the territories to shoot or wound, without waiting until their lives were in danger.[87] Rabin's order of the use of plastic bullets as a means of deterring rioters by increasing their injuries[88] did not quell the hard-liners, who continued to demand that yet more forceful measures be taken in order to put an end to the *intifada.*

Disagreement regarding the handling of the uprising was not limited to the political leadership. It was evident also in the IDF. While there were very few cases of refusal to serve in the territories and army discipline was generally maintained, many soldiers were torn between the Jewish-Israeli values they had been brought up to cherish and the task they were ordered to carry out. On 4 July, a group of reservists met with President Herzog to tell him of their concern that Israel's occupation was damaging the IDF's moral fiber and pushing the soldiers to the limits of their consciences. They chose to speak to the president in order to emphasize what they saw as the nonpolitical essence of the threat to the IDF.

No systematic data were available on the effects of the *intifada* on different segments of society at large. Social scientists[89] assessed that the events in the territories had divided the population into three groups unequal in size. First there were those who, deeply upset by what was happening, were strongly critical of what they considered the government hard line. They demonstrated, published their views in the press, and repeatedly presented to the country's leadership petitions designed to show that they were representing a majority view. Among them were authors, poets, artists, singers, painters, and actors who incorporated themes on the *intifada* into their art. One ballad by a popular singer lamented Israel's handling of the uprising in the following words: "When did we learn how to bury people alive? When did we forget that our children have also been killed?" The song was banned from IDF radio, but was broadcast on the civil radio station. An exhibition of portraits of a hundred Palestinians killed in the uprising gave expression to similar sentiments and caused a public uproar. The strategies employed by the IDF were condemned on moral grounds. But there was also a fear that people encouraged to use violence would become unable to restrict it to specific situations and would turn it into a habit.

A second category consisted of those advocating a typically hawkish approach. For them the government's line was far too mild, even cowardly. They called for tougher measures, including demolition of houses and expulsion of the *intifada* leaders — measures which they believed would put an end to the uprising. On 10 March a group of some thousand women signed a petition in Jerusalem calling on the chief of staff to clear soldiers who, having been filmed by a foreign television crew while beating Arabs, were detained in military jail. Others, like those in the former group, signed petitions, staged public rallies, and engaged intensively in the heated public debate.

But the vast majority of Israelis had learned how to live with the *intifada* and declined to join either of the two groups. They were somewhat concerned, yet they had developed a kind of defense mechanism that allowed them to remain largely indifferent to events in the territories. Many were convinced that the nation was engaged in a war of survival, and there was some sense of disappointment that the IDF had not been able to prevent the *intifada* from running for as long as it had. But a dramatic change of opinion did not follow. Random public opinion polls reflected this trend: on the one hand, there was a gradual increase in the readiness to relinquish some part of the West Bank in return for peace (from 54% in March 1987 to 62% in June 1988); on the other, there was also an expressed desire to continue the policy of Jewish control over the territories.[90] No massive public pressure was exerted in either way. The Israelis displayed that, except for a few intermittent protests, they were prepared to concur with official policy. The *intifada* did not cause a major legitimacy crisis in Israeli society.

POLITICAL AFFAIRS: FOREIGN RELATIONS

Henry Kissinger was once quoted as saying that Israel had no foreign policy, only domestic policy.[91] This assertion proved to be rather accurate in 1988. A decade after the signing of the Camp David Accords Israel spoke with two voices regarding its external affairs. It had no "foreign policy," but two foreign policies, since both Labor and the Likud systematically impeded each other's efforts, the peace process not excluded. Labor persistently advocated an international conference, an idea abhorrent to the Likud. Yet, despite this friction, Israel's foreign relations in 1988 markedly advanced.

At the end of 1988, Israel faced an uncertain world climate. On the one hand, the Palestine National Council decision in Algiers to form a Palestinian state attracted wide attention and sympathy. The US-PLO dialogue breathed new life into the phrase "the whole world is against us." On the other hand, Israel realized that it was not "alone." In December, Kenya decided to renew its diplomatic relations[92] and other African countries were expected to follow suit. Israel could also take comfort in the fact that the UN, not known as a bastion of support for Israel, overwhelmingly rejected by 95–41 with seven abstentions the perennial Arab effort to expel Israel from the UN.[93] The vote indicated that some previous advocates of Israel's expulsion either abstained or voted against. The marked improvement — as compared with 80–89 and 10 abstentions in 1987 — indicated that Israel's diplomacy had taken a great leap forward in 1988.

ISRAEL AND THE UNITED STATES

Secretary Shultz's visit to Israel in February highlighted the rift within the government. The Likud and Labor had constantly been at odds regarding the solution of the Arab-Israeli conflict. As long as external circumstances did not force the government to take a stand on controversial matters, the right remained largely latent. But Shultz's visit forced it into the open. While Labor reportedly pushed for a bipartisan cabinet effort to formulate a common stand, opinions remained irreconcilable,[94] and the differences could not be patched over by a compromise. The failure of Shultz's mission did not mar Israel-US relations. On 21 April, a memorandum of agreement was signed between Shamir and Reagan formally consolidating the already existing cooperation between the two countries. The ceremony, which took place on Israel's Independence Day, put into binding documentary form Israel's status as an ally and committed the US to aid Israel not only during the present Administration, but in future as well.

The US also supported Israel by vetoing a Security Council resolution condemning Israel for one of its incursions into Lebanon.[95] In addition, the US played an active role in the Taba dispute by aiming at a compromise. The visit to Washington of Defense Minister Rabin, in June, provided another opportunity to reaffirm the cordial relationship. Military relations between the two countries were described by the American defense secretary as "very substantial."[96]

Differences between the two states surfaced over the question of trade barriers. Israel was the first country with which the US had signed a Free Trade Area agreement, in 1985. In 1988, it became evident that the barriers imposed by Israel discriminated against US products.[97] The breaches of the agreement were explicable in terms of Israel's anti-inflationary policy (see below).

ISRAEL AND WESTERN EUROPE

A year after the eruption of the *intifada,* Israel's relations with Western Europe turned out to be rather equivocal. Initially, the European Parliament postponed the ratification of trade agreements with Israel on technical grounds, i.e., documents not having been translated in time. Shamir regarded the postponement as "blackmail," a violation of agreement owing to political differences. The main force behind the move was a bloc of socialist parties in the parliament, which, in the Socialist International, condemned violence committed by the IDF in the territories. Europe was so unfriendly that a newspaper editorial in Israel urged the government to reappraise relations with the continent.[98] The enormous and growing trade deficit with the European Economic Community (EEC) — $3.6bn. in 1987 — also seemed to be directly linked to the political differences.

The European reluctance to ratify trade agreements was based on two grounds: one, Israel's failure to implement an agreement permitting Arab farmers in the territories to export their produce directly to the EEC rather than through Israeli intermediaries; two, the allegedly discriminatory Israeli surcharges on European industrial products which the EEC demanded be abolished. After intensive diplomatic efforts, the European Parliament finally ratified the agreements in October, by 31–25 with 19 abstentions,[99] thus assuring the gradual reduction of trade tariffs, the opening of credit lines, and access to the EEC for Israeli products.

RELATIONS WITH EASTERN EUROPE

In an important breakthrough, Israel reestablished links with countries of Eastern Europe which had broken their diplomatic ties with Israel following the Six Day War.

A window to the East was opened when Foreign Minister Peres met in Madrid, in May, with two senior Soviet officials who informed him of their country's willingness to consider Israel's views on the ME. Peres was reported to be "heartened by the talks with the Soviets,"[100] finding in them support for an international conference. A few days after the announcement, it was made known that Moscow would be prepared to issue visas to a five-man Israeli consular delegation, with Israel's agreement to have its mandate limited to technical matters.[101] Meanwhile, arrangements were made for a meeting between Shamir and Soviet Foreign Minister Eduard Shevardnadze in New York. It was noted that Shamir went out of his way to praise General Secretary Mikhail Gorbachev as a dynamic and courageous leader. The Soviet agreement on the Israeli mission was a direct consequence of the Shamir-Shevardnadze meeting in

June.[102] On 26 July, for the first time in 20 years, Israeli representatives left for Moscow. Their task was restricted to examining the empty building in Moscow which had formerly housed the Israeli Embassy. But Israel was, nevertheless, delighted because it was hoped that this small step would produce at least a modicum of understanding between the two countries.

Toward the end of the year, Israel had two unexpected opportunities to improve its relations with the Soviet Union. Firstly, it promptly and efficiently dealt with a hijacked Soviet airliner which landed on 5 December at Ben-Gurion Airport. Secondly, it lost no time in offering its help in the Armenian earthquake disaster in December. In both cases, the motives were humanitarian, but it was hoped that the manifestations of goodwill and friendship would be translated into diplomatic benefits.

Relations with other East European countries improved at a more rapid pace. In May, Peres visited Hungary and learned of that country's wish to increase its trade with Israel. The visit was reciprocated when a Hungarian minister visited Israel for the first time in 20 years.[103] In September, the Israeli premier himself visited Hungary. Although the Hungarian hosts had asked that the visit be downplayed and that Shamir not be accompanied by journalists, the trip was nevertheless a landmark in Israel's foreign relations.[104] "National interest offices" were set up simultaneously in Budapest and Tel Aviv and relations were said to have greatly improved.

Following the improvement with Hungary, relations with Poland were also upgraded when the interests sections of the two countries were elevated to an independent status, no longer being attached to the Dutch Embassy in Warsaw and the Polish National Bank in Tel Aviv, respectively.[105]

RELATIONS WITH EAST ASIA

The real drama of diplomacy was seen in Israel's relations with the People's Republic of China. Rumors concerning the existing ties between the two countries spread in April when Defense Minister Rabin denied a *Sunday Times* report that Israel had signed an agreement to sell China advanced missile technology.[106] It was reported that 100 joint ventures, in fields ranging from electronics to tourism, were under negotiation between Israeli and Chinese firms. Despite Rabin's denial, rumors persisted and in May *The Washington Post* reported that a secret contract had been signed whereby Israel would sell advanced missile warheads to China.[107] That relationships between the two countries were improving could not be denied. In July, it was announced that China would allow organized groups of Israeli tourists to visit the country.[108] In September, the foreign ministers of the two states met in New York in what was described as an "excellent atmosphere."[109] Following the meeting, China reportedly agreed to allow Israel to open a liaison office in Peking. It was also agreed to establish government-linked enterprises in both Israel and China and to coordinate economic projects.[110] Relations advanced to such an extent that in October Israeli sources stated that full diplomatic relations between the two countries would be shortly established.[111] While China denied that such a step was in the offing, the *rapprochement* continued. Chinese delegations arrived in Israel for commercial talks aimed at expanding trade with Israel.

Relations with Japan also improved. Israel had been the first Western country to exchange ambassadors with Japan (1952) after World War II. Relations, however, remained quite modest. No Japanese cabinet minister had visited Israel, the major reason being Japan's dependence on Arab oil. On 26 June, a change occurred with the visit of Foreign Minister Sosuke Uno. There were two reasons for the change: the worldwide glut of oil, which had sharply reduced Japan's dependence on Arab oil; and, more important, the Japanese search for an improvement in their steadily deteriorating image in the US, where the Administration and the Congress were considering setting up barriers against Japanese imports because of Japanese restrictive trade practices. The influential Jewish lobby in the US could prove helpful in this regard.

The Japanese foreign minister's visit had no immediate political consequences. During his 12-hour stay, Uno spent four hours with Palestinians, touring the Dahaysha refugee camp and Jerusalem's Old City. But the significance of the visit was, as the Israeli Foreign Ministry put it, "in the very fact that it was taking place."[112] Israel's commercial ties with Japan were also expected to benefit from the visit. Japan was already Israel's third largest trading partner, with an Israeli surplus of $94m.,[113] but the political opening held promise of massive investments in the Israeli economy.

SOCIAL RELATIONS: TENSIONS AS USUAL

The approaching elections exacerbated social tensions; some problems were perennial, others were linked directly to the competition for votes.

LABOR RELATIONS

Official data regarding strikes in 1988 were not yet available, as of the preparation of this survey, but labor disputes were apparently numerous. Once again, there were more strikes in the public sector than in the private. A relatively new phenomenon was the unrest in Histadrut enterprises, reflecting their economic plight. In May, angry workers at the Alliance tire factory in Hadera occupied management offices to protest against the decision to put the company into the hands of a receiver.[114] Since over 85% of Alliance's shares were held by Koor, a Histadrut conglomerate, the rage was directed at the Histadrut; frustrated workers burning tires were well televised. A month later, the workers of another large factory — Beth Shemesh Engines — staged a violent demonstration in the Treasury building, injuring 14 ministry employees and policemen, and destroying property.[115] They were protesting against government plans to fire 260 of them. In August, the scene repeated itself in Beit She'an, a development town in the north, when workers broke through police barricades at the Kitan textile plant.[116] There were also more conventional attempts to take advantage of the coming elections to get wage increases. Some 50,000 of the country's civil servants went on a 24-hour strike on 14 June, hoping to capitalize on the interparty competition.

In the weeks immediately preceding the elections, labor disputes became widespread. The gas distributors, the schoolteachers (who staged a one-day strike), and bank employees made a last-minute attempt to gain benefits. The general assumption was that the government would be more likely to agree to wage increases in the period before polling day.

Worst hit in 1988 were the health services. It is hard to determine exactly when a strike started or ended because of the chronic work stoppages. The crisis in the health services was not unique to Israel; it was a worldwide phenomenon. The soaring cost of medical services puts a heavy load on the welfare state which, as a rule, dispenses health services on an egalitarian basis. The deterioration of health services had an immediate effect on patients, an estimated 40,000 of whom waited their turn for elective, i.e., nonemergency, surgery.[117]

One of the major reasons for the protracted crisis was the relatively low wages in this sector. However, in 1988 efforts were made to equalize salaries received by workers in the Histadrut's health fund, the Kupat Holim Clalit, and in the state's medical institutions. Kupat Holim Clalit is Israel's largest health fund, insuring over 80% of the population. The fund is an inseparable part of the Histadrut: membership in the former is conditional on membership in the latter. Kupat Holim Clalit is a dual organization: it is a voluntary association representing its members' interests, but owing to its size and the scope of activities, it is a leading actor in the national health system. It is, in a sense, a tail (a voluntary association) that wags the dog (the state). As a voluntary association, it is in the fund's interests to raise the level of its services in order to attract membership and compete with other health funds. It is worth noting that the Histadrut's budget for administrative expenses (excluding medical) is derived from the fees paid to the health fund. Expanding membership is therefore an organizational imperative. At the same time, the fund is heavily dependent on various forms of state financial assistance and, like other Histadrut enterprises, is in grave economic trouble. One of the direct consequences of the fund's dual nature was that its employees' wages were generally higher than those paid by equivalent state institutions. As a voluntary organization, the fund could determine the wages it paid but as a state-dependent institution it was subordinate to the state wage scale. In 1988, these wage differentials gave rise to labor disputes in the health services.

In February, clerks and maintenance workers in the state hospitals staged a strike demanding absolute equality with their Kupat Holim Clalit counterparts. The hospital workers were joined by nurses, who were fighting not for more money but for an improved patient-nurse ratio and a precise job definition for hospital nurses. In July, the nurses staged a 15-day hunger strike outside the Prime Minister's Office, which ended only after the Treasury agreed to increase the number of nursing positions in the public hospitals by 29%.[118]

The longest and most bitter strikes were staged by doctors. In February, the 2,800 doctors of the 32 government hospitals initiated work stoppages which evolved into full-scale strikes. The physicians demanded the same overtime payments as those promised to Kupat Holim Clalit hospital doctors for working a second shift. The increase was to come into effect on 15 February, following an agreement between the health fund and its doctors. The government hospital doctors denounced "the establishment of a two-class public health system," but their protest was premature, since the health fund failed to honor its agreement, because the Treasury refused to finance an arrangement to which it was not a party. The doctors in the Kupat Holim Clalit hospitals then staged their own strike, which reduced the health system to chaos. Finance Minister Moshe Nissim refused to budge, on the grounds that concessions to the doctors would be demanded by other workers, which, in turn, would mean the end of economic stability, for which the minister had labored. In order to thwart any under the table payments to Kupat Holim Clalit doctors, an amendment was tacked onto the Budget Law requiring all non-state bodies subsidized to any degree by the government (including Kupat Holim Clalit) to obtain Treasury approval for their wage agreements.[119] The immediate effect of the amendment was to cause the suspension, if not cancellation, of the second-shift agreement between Kupat Holim Clalit and its doctors.

Once the crisis deepened, senior officials attempted to solve it. Following repeated urging by the health minister, the Cabinet put the health issue on its agenda in mid-May.[120] However, no decision was reached. The government was dragging its feet, being unable to break the deadlock or to convince the doctors to give up their demands or convince the Treasury to yield to them. After three cabinet meetings, a stopgap was devised: a ministerial committee was set up to work out short-term solutions. Simultaneously, a five-member judicial committee was set up to suggest structural changes in the health system. Both committees failed in their purpose and the health system continued to deteriorate, leaving the ill unable to obtain adequate medical care.

A turnabout took place when 10 opposition MKs staged an unprecedented hunger strike outside the Prime Minister's Office on 10 July in an attempt to rouse the government from its torpor.[121] Three days later, the above-mentioned ministerial committee came up with a nine-month program for performing delayed elective surgery, but the doctors rejected the plan. Full work was resumed in hospitals only at the end of August, after an informal agreement had been reached within Kupat Holim Clalit. State doctors were still waiting for equalization of working conditions.

The crisis in the health system vividly exposed weak spots in the Israeli polity. Pressure groups were not strong enough to induce action. At the same time, the government failed to impose its authority and lacked the power to end a lingering stalemate. The victims were the citizens who needed medical care.

INTERCOMMUNAL RELATIONS

The Israeli Arabs were caught, in 1988, in a vise: on the one hand, they supported the Arabs in the West Bank and Gaza engaged in the *intifada*; on the other, they wished to remain loyal to the state. On 20 January, thousands of Israeli Arabs staged a demonstration in Nazareth to protest against the government's handling of the uprising, in what was described as the city's biggest demonstration ever.[122] One editorial claimed that the Green Line (i.e., the pre-1967 cease-fire line) is growing fainter for Israeli Arabs.[123] On 23 February, tension between Jews and Arabs mounted when a bus was stoned on the Nahal 'Iron (Wadi 'Ara) highway (connecting the coastal plain with the Yizreel Valley) and Palestinian flags were hoisted on the roof of a local school. On the whole, however, violence was very rare. Even Land Day (a day of demonstrations and partial strike in the Arab sector, effected every year on 30 March since 1976 to protest the government's land policy in that sector) passed peacefully this year, in striking contrast to the violence in the territories; a strike was staged in some 60 Arab towns and villages, but no confrontations with the police took place. Muhammad Watted (a Mapam activist), told the radio that "Israeli Arabs will be seen as much more complete citizens than they were yesterday."[124] There were even signs of further integration into Jewish society: one example was the admission of Arab farming cooperatives into the Histadrut's Agricultural Center.[125]

Alongside such encouraging signs of accommodation there was also evidence of radicalization. Emotional solidarity with the Palestinians of the West Bank and Gaza was unmistakably visible; by the end of the year it had grown into practical solidarity and support. Israeli Arabs collected thousands of shekels-worth of food, medicine, and other essentials to aid the Palestinians in revolt in the territories. On 9 December, they staged a series of parades and rallies to mark the first anniversary of the *intifada.* A general strike on 10 November, staged in protest against the demolition of illegally built houses in the Arab community, was perhaps another sign of deterioration in Jewish-Arab relations.[126] (Demolition was one of the measures the state used in combating illegal house building in both the Jewish and Arab sectors. In this case, as in so many others, construction without license was officially quoted as the reason for demolition.) It might well be that "Palestinization" of the Israeli Arabs had become inevitable. In 1988, however, they remained full-fledged citizens, loyal to the state and its legal normative order.

The secular religious gap also widened significantly. The most contentious issues were the Mormon-sponsored university, whose right to a land lease on Mount Scopus was finally approved, and the perennial issue of registration of converts which came before the High Court.[127] The right of women to serve on local religious councils[128] and on rabbinical electoral colleges[129] was affirmed. A major breakthrough was the successful first reading of the Enabling Law,[130] which empowers local authorities to pass bylaws banning Sabbath entertainment. The law was drafted after a Jerusalem court ruled that a local authority had no power to impose religious observance on residents, but must leave the problem to a nationwide solution. The solution, said the judge, lay not in legislation, but in tolerance and mutual respect by both the religious and secular elements of the community. But the mounting tension made such a solution unfeasible. The secular-religious gap widened ominously after the elections when the possibility of Israel becoming a theocracy seemed threateningly close. Simultaneously, however, the Orthodox community was legitimized owing to its extensive media exposure and its integration into the political establishment. The November elections brought the hitherto fringe and largely obscure *haredi* (extreme Orthodox) groups right into the living rooms of secular Israelis. The direct confrontation with the Orthodox public triggered much resentment, but it also eroded stereotypes.

According to unofficial reports, the economic gap also widened in 1988. A committee of tax experts — the Sheshinski committee — recommended that the tax burden be shifted from low- and middle-income groups to the top-income groups. The committee proposed levying 25% on capital gains and abolishing all special exemptions. The committee's report was shelved owing to the opposition of powerful interest groups whose profits were jeopardized by the recommendations.[131]

THE ECONOMY: PRECIPITATION DOWN THE SLOPE

The year 1988 was not a good one for the economy. Whereas 1987 was described by the Bank of Israel as a "mixture of lights and shadows,"[132] 1988 was darker. Contrary to expectations and forecasts, economic indicators showed a retreat from economic recovery. This was surprising especially in view of the fact that 1988 was an election year. In the past, the government used to increase spending considerably during election years, thereby causing a temporary sense of affluence; normally this was followed by high inflation and economic instability after the elections. This, however, was not the case in 1988.

The aim of the 1988 economic policy was the maintenance of stability, i.e., budgetary constraints, especially in welfare services (health and education). Although it was an election year, subsidies were cut twice, in May and October. The Treasury was not deterred from taking this measure rather than bribing the citizens and wasting money in order to win votes. Stability was achieved: the monthly consumer price index did not rise sharply as in the past. Annual inflation remained stable at 16.4%, only slightly above the 16.1% increase in 1987. Stabilization, however, also had some adverse consequences and the price paid for its continuation was high.

BASIC INDICATORS

Israel registered its lowest economic growth since 1982, with only a 1% increase in the gross domestic product (GDP). The business sector, generally considered a better yardstick for measuring economic growth, did not grow at all. On the contrary, industrial output fell by 3%; agriculture declined by 8% and the building sector by 3%. Tourism, a major component of Israel's revenue, dropped by 12%.[133] The marked economic slowdown was due to a combination of the following five factors:

(1) The scrapping of the *Lavi* jet fighter (see *MECS* 1987, chapter on Israel) was a hard blow to the economy. In 1987, the *Lavi* accounted for $300m. in domestic industrial sales; in 1988, these fell to nothing. The first to suffer from this decline were the aviation, electronics, and metal industries linked to the defense establishment.

(2) A heat wave with extraordinarily high temperatures in May contributed to the 8% decline in agricultural output. Certain crops, such as avocado, were especially affected. An increase was evident only in the livestock production which grew by 3%.

(3) The *intifada* was responsible for a decrease of some 2.5% in the production of the business sector. Exports to the territories fell by about one third. The number of workers from the territories also declined from 100,000 in 1987 to 80,000 in 1988. Purchases of Israeli industrial goods in the territories dropped from $850m. in 1987 to $250m. in 1988. The textile industry was the biggest victim in one of the industry's worst years, because of its relatively heavy dependence on the markets of the territories; some 3,000 workers were cut from its payroll, and dozens of small plants were closed in 1988. The rise in the number of Israelis called up for reserve service in the territories also contributed to the slowing of the economy.[134]

(4) The major cause of the economic slump was the extremely high interest rates maintained by the Bank of Israel with the Treasury's consent. Firms and individuals realized that they could no longer cover their huge expenditures, created by the high cost of borrowing, by greater profits. The interest-rate policy, one of the pillars of the economic stabilization program, had originally been conceived as a tool to bring down hyperinflation and to keep the foreign currency reserves from being depleted. This policy, however, exacted a toll on the firms and organizations, factories and farm settlements that had counted on inflation and did not keep a tight rein over their own budgets.

(5) Government civilian expenditure, which increased by 3% in 1988, more than the increase in GDP, also hindered economic growth. This increase was the highest of the decade. To the 403,700 government employees, 15,100 were added between January and September 1988, i.e, a rise of 3.7%.[135] At the same time, labor productivity in the business sector rose by only 0.4% in 1988 compared with 2.8% in 1987.[136] The number of working hours in the business sector declined because of the unrest in the territories, but rose by 4% in the public sector.

The consequences of the economic slowdown were:

(1) The slow rise in private consumption, which increased by only 3%–4%, in comparison to 6.4% in 1987. After taking into account the growth in population, this increase means that the standard of living rose by 1%–2%. The picture is less gloomy if one considers the cumulative 9.9% increase in living standards since 1983. Furthermore, wages for an hour's work grew by 7% (in comparison to 8% in 1987). In Israel, private consumption is almost always on the rise, but the problem lies in the fluctuations of wages which generate a sense of insecurity and a tendency to enjoy the present without much thought to the future. Public savings, in fact, remained at only 2% of private incomes, which meant a significant decline in total savings from the previous year.

(2) The slowdown in the economy was also evident in the trade balance. Exports of goods and services dropped 3% in real terms, after an 11% rise in 1987.[137] Civilian imports of goods remained stable after an 11% increase the year before. Toward the end of the year (in October and November) monthly average imports of consumer goods were 17% higher than the previous two months. Apparently, the Israelis were celebrating on the ruins of their crumbling economy.

The conspicuous decline in exports was a direct response to the manufacturers' difficulties caused by the high interest rate and the foreign currency exchange rate. The depreciation of the shekel against the dollar made it extremely difficult to cope with the increased production costs, which included the cost-of-living allowance. The cost of labor per unit output was 7.5% more in the last quarter of 1988 than in the previous quarter. The frozen shekel triggered a vicious circle: responding to the money shortage created by the expectation of a devaluation, the business sector changed dollar-dominated debts in favor of shekel loans. As a result, commercial banks experienced a shekel liquidity problem and had to buy expensive money and to increase the interest rate.

(3) The number of firms facing financial difficulties increased to 3,680, 42% more than in 1987. In 1988, these firms included some of the country's largest concerns, as well as small and newly established companies. Serious financial problems were no longer the exclusive preserve of the private sector, but of the public one as well. The economy was particularly shaken by the crisis facing the large Histadrut concerns, which accounted for 15% of industrial turnover. In July, it became clear that major Histadrut enterprises were bound to collapse unless they were helped. The reasons for the threatened disaster were undue expansion and the excessive compensation paid to workers dismissed from companies in trouble. There were also management blunders: some of the crises could have been averted had there been a better flow of information between the individual companies and the Histadrut central executive committee.[138]

The crises in the Histadrut enterprises reflected not only the economic constraints of 1988, but also the maturation of Israeli society. In the early years of statehood, market forces were not predominant in economic activity; rather the pioneering spirit made it possible to structure economic forces.[139] This, however, created an inbuilt reliance on a subsidy-dispensing bureaucracy. To date, the Histadrut has been conspicuously divorced from marketplace realities, seeking help when necessary from the Treasury which, in 1988, refused to be forthcoming. Radical reorganizations that included changes in a company's management were insufficient to stave off negative developments. Koor, a major Histadrut enterprise, faced liquidation at the request of one of its creditors.[140] Being one of Israel's largest firms (with 27,000 employees), Koor's collapse could have triggered a major national economic crisis. The government promptly responded and agreed to rescue Koor, the proximity to election day which was three weeks off being a decisive factor. The recovery plan adopted called for $20m. in government aid.[141]

(4) Unemployment reached 7.6% of the civilian labor force. More than 100,000 people were seeking jobs in the stagnating economy and thousands more were threatened with the loss of their jobs. The high rate of unemployment was a two-edged sword: a large number of unemployed, concentrated mainly in development towns, together with demobilized soldiers, could be a time bomb with mass emigration one of its results; but the dismissal of workers mirrored a healthy reconstruction of the economy, which will eventually lead to greater efficiency and growth.

One positive economic development in 1988 was the $1bn. decrease in the foreign debt burden. Two thirds of this decrease was the result of the depreciation of the dollar in the international markets. The other third reflected government efforts to cut medium-term debts.[142] The frozen shekel also enabled Israel to get cheaper loans.

Two other events indicated undercurrents in the economy: the energy reform and "Leumigate." In June, a two-year struggle ended when Energy Minister Moshe Shahal (Labor) finally presented his plan to end the long-established government-backed cost-plus system of oil and oil products distribution. The plan was aimed at opening the field to competition in the interests of greater efficiency and saving scarce national resources. The reform proposed releasing roughly one third of the oil companies' business from the cost-plus arrangements, with the other two thirds remaining fully cartelized and tightly regulated. The companies opposed the reform mainly because the government-owned oil refineries were allowed to sell their products independently, at least to large institutional consumers. Shahal had to fight hard for the reform: the workers sided with their employers against the minister; the Histadrut also had a stake in two of the oil companies. Only after Shahal made major concessions was the reform agreement signed.[143] The barriers in the way of this reform plan indicated that the road to privatization, even when accepted in principle by both major parties, was long and arduous.

The biggest winners of 1988 were the five big commercial banks, whose profits soared to give a net yield of 105% of their equity.[144] However, Bank Leumi, one of the major banks, was entangled in a national scandal. For many years the bank was neglected by its owners, Otzar Hityashvut Hayehudim, which was supposed to take care of World Jewry's interests. The results of this neglect were extravagant salaries paid to the bank's senior executives. Although the government spent $2bn. to rescue the bank during the share crisis of 1983 (see *MECS* 1982–83, p. 605), it did not interfere with its financial affairs. However, a member of the Board of Directors, Prof. Shimon Shitrit, charged the bank with financial blunders, bordering on corruption. It was revealed that the board did not thoroughly check the retirement perquisites and benefits included in the employment contracts of 25 senior executives. After much haggling, a new board was appointed.[145] This "Leumigate" scandal demonstrated that Israel was gradually emerging from its formative era and was adopting the norms of a rule-oriented society.

On the eve of 1989, "economic stabilization," the root of many evils, had been declared dead. The new leadership attempted to return the economy to the path of growth and productivity. One of the first measures, taken on 28 December, was a 5% devaluation of the shekel advised by the governor of the Bank of Israel. The immediate reason for the devaluation was the panic buying of foreign currency, which posed a serious threat to Israel's foreign reserves. The new economic plan, which followed in January 1989, added measures complementary to the initial devaluation — notably a cut of interest rates — which were aimed at providing immediate cures for the ailing economy.

To sum up, what was supposed to be a year of celebrations of Israel's 40th anniversary, with an anticipated record number of foreign visitors, turned out to be a year of tension. The economy failed to fulfill the expectations of the recovery plan, social divisions were not healed, and rifts were exacerbated by the election campaign. Before the elections, the government was a coalition of diametrically opposed partners. The November elections were expected to be a watershed for the nation's fate, but this was not the case. The results did not give a clear majority to either of the two major parties, who preferred to establish another unity government rather than pay an exorbitantly high price to small parties. At the same time, the respite which the elections provided made way for a new concerted effort to solve Israel's difficult problems in a spirit of unity, which had not been typical of 1988.

TABLE 1: KNESSET ELECTION RESULTS (IN MANDATES), BY BLOCS, 1984, 1988

		1984	*1988*
Right-wing bloc	Likud	41	40
	Tehiya	5	3
	Tzomet		2
	Moledet	—	2
	Ometz	1	**
	Total	**47**	**47**
Left-wing bloc	Alignment/Labor	44	39
	Mapam		3
	Ratz	3	5
	Shinui-Merkaz	3	2
	Yahad	3	*
	Total	**53**	**49**
Religious bloc	NRP	4	5
	Agudat Israel	2	5
	Shas	4	6
	Degel Hatora	—	2
	Morasha	2	—
	Kach	1	—
	Tami	1	**
	Total	**14**	**18**
Arab bloc	Hadash	4	4
	Progressive Peace List	2	1
	Darawsha	*	1
	Total	**6**	**6**

SOURCE: *Ha'aretz,* 6 November 1988.

* Incorporated in Labor.

** Incorporated in the Likud.

TABLE 2: ECONOMIC INDICATORS 1987–88
(Percentage of change in comparison to previous year)

	1987	*1988*
Gross national product	4.6	1.0
Exports	11.0	-3.0
Imports	10.0	0.0
Wages per hour	6.4	3.5
Production per hour	2.8	0.4
Unemployment (% of labor force)	6.0	7.6
Inflation	16.1	16.4
Savings	—	2.0

SOURCES: *JP,* 22, 30 December 1988, 16 January 1989; *Ha'aretz,* 30 December 1988.

NOTES

For the place and frequency of publications cited here, and for the full name of the publication, news agency, radio station, or monitoring service where an abbreviation is used, please see "List of Sources." Only in the case of more than one publication bearing the same name is the place of publication noted here.

1. A rise of 1%–4% over the previous year in the number of accidents, fatalities, and injuries; *JP,* 17 January 1989.
2. *Ha'aretz,* 12 July 1988.
3. *JP,* 25 December 1988.
4. Ibid., 19 August 1988.
5. Ibid., 20 November 1988.
6. Ibid., 12 May 1988.
7. The House rules clearly lay down that the government may name any minister it wishes to represent it in the Knesset.
8. *JP,* 17 November 1988.
9. Ibid., 24 November 1988.
10. Ibid., 23 November 1988.
11. Ibid., 24 November 1988.
12. Ibid., 26 July 1988.
13. Ibid., 2 March 1988.
14. A. Tal, *Ha'aretz,* 3 April 1988.
15. Ibid., 24 March 1988.
16. Ibid., 29 March 1988.
17. *JP,* 26 May 1988.
18. Ibid., 30 June 1988.
19. For the full version of the High Court's ruling, see *JP,* 3 August 1988.
20. Ibid., 27 July 1988.
21. Ibid., 16 June 1988.
22. Ibid., 13 November 1988.
23. Two thirds of the respondents also favored reform of the electoral system, ibid., 29 December 1988.
24. According to MK Amnon Rubinstein, the Knesset could decide by a simple majority to disperse itself. The proposed amendment allowed the president under certain conditions to disperse the Knesset. Ibid., 29 December 1988.
25. *Ha'aretz,* 19 May 1988.
26. Ibid., 11 May 1988.
27. Ibid., 15 June 1988.
28. *JP,* 24 February 1988.
29. *Hadashot,* 28 July 1988.
30. *Ha'aretz,* 5 May 1988.

31. For more details, see *Ha'aretz,* 29 April 1988.
32. *JP,* 19 April 1988.
33. Ibid., 27 September 1988.
34. Ibid., 10 April 1988.
35. Ibid., 19 October 1988.
36. Shinui-Merkaz was called "the only capitalist party in Israel," ibid., 28 October 1988.
37. Eric Cohen, "The Black Panthers," *Jewish Journal of Sociology,* 14 (1972), pp. 93–109.
38. *JP,* 7 October. The committee's ruling was upheld by the Supreme Court, ibid., 19 October 1988.
39. The Liberals were promised three candidates for every 10 of Herut's, *Hadashot,* 25 August 1988.
40. *JP,* 23 August 1988.
41. Ibid., 3 November 1988.
42. Ibid., 10, 19 August 1988.
43. Ibid., 17 July 1988.
44. Ibid., 24 August 1988.
45. Shamir instructed Likud ministers not to comment on Reagan's statement regarding his negative contribution to the peace process. Levy did precisely so on an Israeli TV news program; quoted ibid., 20 May 1988.
46. Ibid., 1 July 1988.
47. Ibid., 4 July 1988.
48. The five were Yitzhak Shamir, David Levy, Moshe Arens, Ariel Sharon, and Moshe Katzav, ibid., 6 July 1988.
49. Ibid., 8 January 1988.
50. Ibid., 5 March 1988.
51. The candidates were Shimon Peres, Yitzhak Rabin, Yitzhak Navon, Shlomo Hillel, Yisrael Kessar, and Uzi Baram. *Ha'aretz,* 27 May 1988.
52. *JP,* 26 May 1988.
53. Ibid., 16 June 1988.
54. Ibid., 17 July 1988.
55. Ibid., 1 November 1988.
56. Smith Poll, ibid., 22 July 1988.
57. *NYT,* 6 November 1988.
58. *Ma'ariv,* 3 November 1988.
59. *JP,* 5 August 1988.
60. Ibid., 23 February 1988.
61. Ibid., 16 February 1988.
62. Ibid., 19 January 1988.
63. Ibid., 13 January 1988.
64. *Ha'aretz,* 19 May 1988.
65. *JP,* 26 July 1988.
66. The breakdown of portfolios and ministers by party was: Likud — 8 portfolios, 11 ministers; Labor — 8 portfolios, 11 ministers; Shas — 2 portfolios, 2 ministers; NRP — 1 portfolio, 2 ministers; Agudat Israel — 1 deputy minister. *JP,* 26 December 1988.
67. *Ha'aretz,* 26 December 1988.
68. *JP,* 23 December 1988.
69. Ibid., 24 October 1988.
70. For the full text of the guidelines, see ibid., 23 December 1988.
71. For the full text of the coalition agreement, see *Ha'aretz,* 21 December 1988.
72. *JP,* 22 December 1988.
73. *Ha'aretz,* 22 December 1988.
74. Ibid., 19 December 1988.
75. *JP,* 7 November 1988.
76. Ibid., 14 November 1988.
77. For the full list of the religious parties' demands, see *Hadashot,* 25 November 1988.
78. *JP,* 22 November 1988.
79. Ibid., 21 December 1988.

80. Ibid., 5 August 1988.
81. *Yedi'ot Aharonot,* 11 November. Worthwhile noting is that in a September poll, 59% of the respondents said: "Please, not a national unity government again," *JP,* 23 September 1988.
82. *JP,* 24 November 1988.
83. Ibid., 6 December 1988.
84. Ibid., 21 January 1988.
85. Ibid., 24 January 1988.
86. *JP,* 12 February 1988.
87. Ibid., 17 February 1988.
88. Ibid., 30 September 1988.
89. Ibid., 9 December 1988.
90. Ibid., 19 August 1988.
91. Ibid., 14 September 1988.
92. Ibid., 25 December 1988.
93. Ibid., 19 October 1988.
94. Ibid., 19 February 1988.
95. The US was the only one of the 15 Security Council members to support the Israeli position; ibid., 11 May 1988.
96. Ibid., 28 June 1988.
97. Ibid., 7, 8 June 1988.
98. Ibid., 8 May 1988.
99. Ibid., 13 October 1988.
100. Ibid., 19 May 1988.
101. The visas had been held up for more than a half year because of Israel's insistence that the mission be given wide-ranging powers, ibid., 25 May 1988.
102. Ibid., 10 June 1988.
103. Ibid., 5 September 1988.
104. Ibid., 14 September 1988.
105. Ibid., 2 October 1988.
106. Ibid., 4 April 1988.
107. Ibid., 30 May 1988.
108. Ibid., 17 July 1988.
109. *Davar,* 28 September 1988.
110. China also agreed to have an unofficial Israeli representative in the capital who would serve as an academic liaison officer for visiting Israeli scholars, *JP,* 12 October 1988.
111. Ibid., 14 October 1988.
112. Ibid., 27 June 1988.
113. Ibid., 24 June 1988.
114. Ibid., 5 May 1988.
115. Ibid., 2 June 1988.
116. Ibid., 8 August 1988.
117. State Comptroller's Annual Report 1988, (38), p. 193.
118. *JP,* 28 July 1988.
119. Ibid., 4 April 1988.
120. Ibid., 15 May 1988.
121. Ibid., 11 July 1988.
122. Ibid., 24 January 1988.
123. Ibid., 13 April 1988.
124. Ibid., 31 January 1988.
125. Ibid., 10 May 1988.
126. Ibid., 11 November 1988.
127. Ibid., 31 January 1988.
128. Ibid., 20 May 1988.
129. Ibid., 2 June 1988.
130. Ibid., 10 March 1988.
131. The Manufacturers' Association was the major opponent, ibid., 17 February 1988.
132. Ibid., 1 June 1988.

133. Ibid., 21 December 1988.
134. Ibid., *Ha'aretz,* 1 January 1989.
135. Ibid.
136. *JP,* 20 December 1988.
137. Industrial exports, excluding diamonds, dropped 5% in real terms, *JP,* 30 December 1988.
138. Ibid., 31 July 1988.
139. Baruch Kimmerling, *Zionism and Economy* (Cambridge, Mass; Schenkman, 1982).
140. *JP,* 12 October 1988.
141. For details, see ibid., 14 November 1988.
142. Ibid., 30 December 1988.
143. Ibid., 7 June 1988.
144. Ibid., 7 June 1988.
145. Ibid., 8 November 1988.

Jordan
(Al-Mamlaka al-Urdunniyya al-Hashimiyya)

ASHER SUSSER

In the annals of Jordanian history, the year 1988 will surely be remembered as a watershed comparable to 1948, 1967, and 1970. The uprising in the West Bank and Gaza had a most damaging effect on Jordan, as it severely reduced King Husayn's room for maneuver on the Palestinian question and posed a potential threat to domestic stability. Jordan had been fighting a rearguard battle against the Palestinian national revival for 30 years. The *intifada* was as clear an indication as any that Jordan's cause had been lost. It was now a question of damage control in circumstances more adverse than ever.

Husayn's decision, in July, to disengage from the West Bank set the stage for what could become an irreversible renunciation of Jordanian sovereignty over the West Bank and it finally dispelled any illusion that Jordan would substitute for the PLO in any future negotiations. Husayn thus intended to compel the US and Israel to come to terms with direct PLO involvement in the peace process. But perhaps even more important, he sought to challenge the PLO to prove its diplomatic mettle and really shoulder the full responsibility of its representative status by paving the way for progress toward a peaceful settlement.

The disengagement was not a final Jordanian abdication from involvement in the question of Palestine, and the Jordanian position remained strewn with internal contradictions and inconsistencies. Jordan still had a vital interest in a central role in the ultimate settlement of the Palestinian problem. For demographic and geopolitical reasons Jordan could not simply dissociate itself from Palestine. Jordan had, however, changed its *modus operandi* in the peace process. Instead of actively seeking to subordinate the PLO to Jordan's peace-making strategy and thereby secure a settlement that would ensure Jordanian supremacy in the relationship with Palestine, Jordan shifted the onus of containing Palestinian militancy onto Israel and the US.

Israeli desiderata and PLO interest in an association with the East Bank could dictate the formation of some form of special relationship between Jordan and a future Palestinian entity or state. Jordan, however, no longer subscribed automatically to the concept of confederation. Whether or not Jordan would accept confederation in the future depended on the balance of forces between Jordan and the Palestinians. Jordan would prefer to enter such an association from a position of strength, but to do so required the reinforcement of the East Bank state. As Jordan's economy plunged into its worst crisis since 1967, the prospects of transforming Jordan into a bastion of Hashemite power did not seem to be particularly promising, at least not in the short term.

The *intifada* and its domestic and regional ramifications coupled with an economy

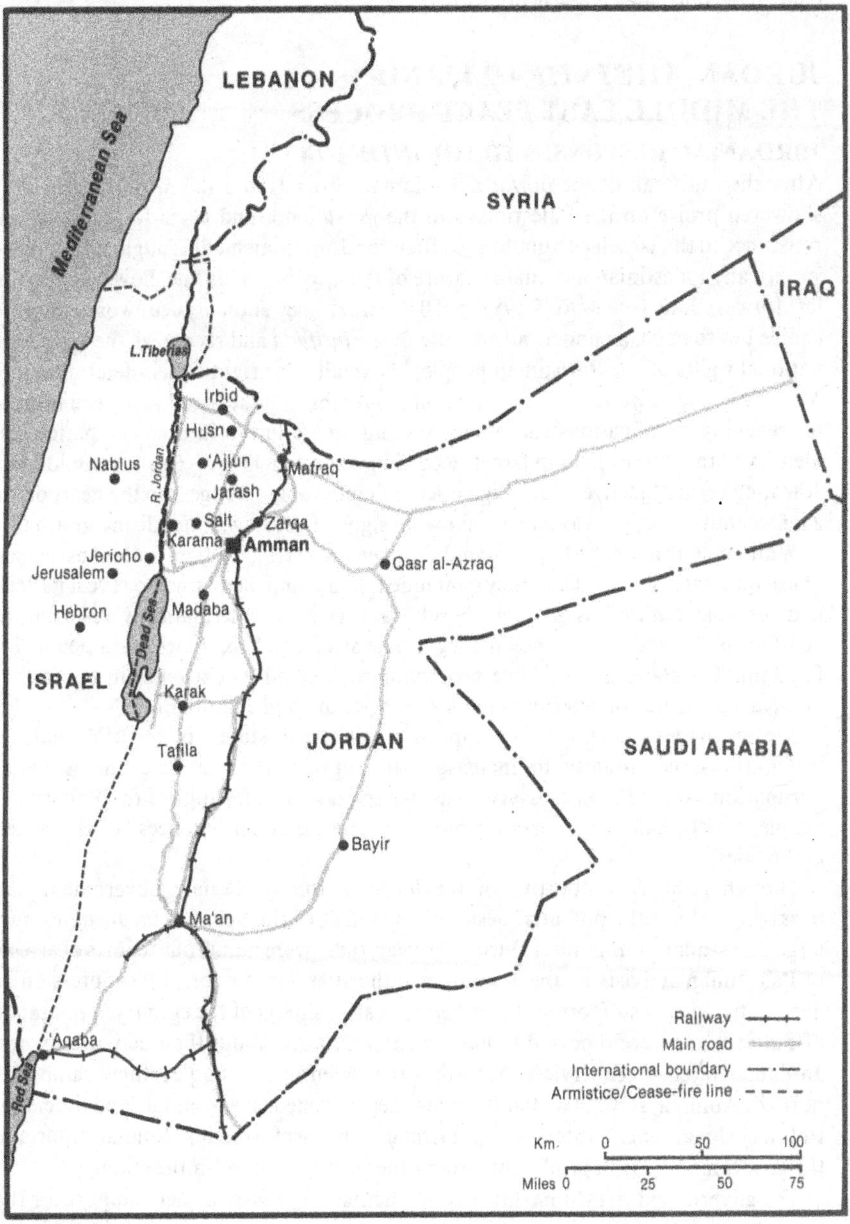
LEBANON
Mediterranean Sea
SYRIA
IRAQ
L.Tiberias
Irbid
Husn
'Ajlun
Mafraq
Nablus
Jarash
R. Jordan
Salt
Zarqa
Karama
Amman
Jericho
Jerusalem
Qasr al-Azraq
Hebron
Dead Sea
Madaba
ISRAEL
Karak
JORDAN
SAUDI ARABIA
Tafila
Bayir
Ma'an
'Aqaba
Red Sea
Railway
Main road
International boundary
Armistice/Cease-fire line
Km 0 50 100
Miles 0 25 50 75

Jordan

in the doldrums faced Jordan and the Hashemite regime with its most tormenting challenges since the civil war of 1970–71.

JORDAN, THE *INTIFADA*, AND THE MIDDLE EAST PEACE PROCESS

JORDANIAN RESPONSES TO THE *INTIFADA*

After the outbreak of the *intifada*, Jordanian officials and the media consistently showered praise on the Palestinians in the West Bank and Gaza for their valiant resistance to the Israeli occupation. At first, the Jordanian media sought to dilute the specifically Palestinian nationalist nature of the uprising. This line, however, did not last for very long (see *MECS* 1987, p. 505). Israel, they soon argued, would have no choice but to concede under the pressure of the *intifada* and recognize the legitimate national rights of the Palestinian people, above all their right to self-determination. Moreover, the *intifada* and its impact on the Arabs in Israel itself, was seen to have far-reaching ramifications for Israel's staying power in the future. The nationalist identity of the Palestinians in Israel, according to an article in *al-Dustur,* would serve "the long-term objective of driving an Arab demographic wedge into the heart of the Zionist entity," which was already showing signs of "old age...and disintegration."[1]

While encouraging the Palestinians to pursue their struggle, the Jordanians heaped abuse on Israel. The *intifada*, they contended, had compelled Israel to reveal its "evil and terrorist nature" as a "racist" and "fascist" state systematically resorting to "barbarous...practices" to quell the legitimate struggle of the Palestinian people for freedom. The Palestinian people was trying to "defend its existence in the face of neo-Nazi measures of destruction, murder, eviction, and intimidation."[2]

Jordan made frequent public appeals to the Arab states, to the UN, and the international community to increase their support for the Palestinians under occupation, to take the necessary measures to end the sufferings of the Palestinian people, and to halt the "repressive measures and inhuman practices" of the Israeli authorities.[3]

Though publicly supportive of the *intifada*, the Jordanian Government had misgivings about the potential destabilizing effect of the uprising on Jordan's own large Palestinian community. During the year, there were numerous reports of arrests of Palestinian activists by the Jordanian authorities and the forceful suppression of demonstrations in support of the *intifada* in various parts of the country. Thousands of Palestinians were reported to have been questioned about their activities by the Jordanian intelligence services. According to residents of the Baq'a refugee camp, just north of Amman, some 300–400 Jordanian security men closely monitored the camp. Political slogans were absent and political debate was forbidden. Similar reports of the government's "iron grip" came from other refugee camps in the country.[4]

The government denied having arrested activists because of their support for the *intifada*. People arrested, according to the minister of interior, "were subversive elements."[5] Other cabinet ministers, however, admitted that the government did not permit "expressions of sympathy that go beyond speeches to spill into the streets." According to the minister of information, "the kingdom was not opposed to peaceful displays of support, such as public rallies." Demonstrations were "not the only way" to support the *intifada*.[6]

On the initiative of the Professional Associations' Union, a body in which PLO sympathizers were heavily represented, local "popular committees" were established in the various parts of the country. They organized public activities in support of the *intifada* and collected donations for the people in the occupied territories. Various voluntary associations, universities, businesses, and banks made donations to the fund. Reports on the fund-raising were intensive in the early months of the *intifada*. They steadily subsided from April onward. The funds collected were used to provide aid to the families of people killed or wounded in the *intifada*.[7]

A separate government fund-raising campaign was sponsored by the Ministry of Religious Endowments (*Awqaf*) and Religious Affairs. It also supported bereaved families, as well as students from the occupied territories in Jordanian universities. Though the ministry opposed the parallel private-sector effort, no attempt was made to curb its activity. Both funds combined were said to have collected $5m.[8] How much of this money was actually transferred is unknown. The Israeli authorities introduced severe restrictions on the flow of funds to the West Bank and Gaza. Even the Jordanians were reported to have limited the flow of funds through Jordanian banks.[9]

Fund-raising, however, was not an attractive outlet for the more politically active sectors of the population. The Shultz initiative (see below) gave rise to added domestic tension in Jordan. Opposition groups published statements attacking the US initiative. Hundreds of Palestinian nationalists and Islamic fundamentalists demonstrated in Amman against Shultz and the US when Shultz toured the area in early April.[10] Bombs exploded in Amman twice in April. "Black September," operated by the Abu Nidal faction, claimed responsibility for both incidents.[11]

Despite its negative implications for domestic stability in Jordan, the Jordanian leadership perceived the *intifada* as having a number of positive consequences as well. The *intifada* prompted a renewed active US involvement in the peace process which showed some promise of ending the stalemate in Arab-Israeli negotiations. Husayn referred to the uprising as a "watershed, an historic event," which would "shake the world out of its complacency and place the Palestinian issue as a whole, and the problem of the occupation in particular, in their proper perspective."[12] The *intifada*, therefore, offered "an excellent opportunity" for peace.[13] As opposed to the euphoric mood of the local media, the regime also had a realistic appraisal of the limits of the uprising. Husayn and other senior spokesmen explained that the uprising in itself would not lead to an Israeli withdrawal, though it could serve as a catalyst for the essential process of negotiation.[14]

In the meantime, the Jordanians were wary that the *intifada* might lead to a resurgence of PLO influence.[15] They made every effort in the first three to four months of the uprising to deny the PLO credit, and to publicly discount any PLO role in the *intifada*. The uprising was portrayed as a purely spontaneous internal phenomenon.[16] It not only had nothing to do with outsiders, but was an expression of frustration with the Arab states and with the PLO. The PLO, in the words of a top palace adviser, had brought the Palestinians "nothing during the last two decades."[17] The *intifada*, according to Husayn, had created a new situation, because the people in the West Bank and Gaza had "chosen to lessen their reliance on others outside to speak for them."[18] The PLO, he contended, was now required to ask itself whether it still understood "the wishes and feelings of the Palestinian people. If not, new realities may emerge very soon, realities that would take the PLO and the entire Arab world by surprise." There was a "new dynamism" in the occupied territories, which had given "precedence to the role of the people [there] over that of any party concerned...including the PLO."[19]

The attempt to portray the uprising as an expression of popular disenchantment with the PLO soon proved to be an exercise in deception, or in wishful thinking. From mid-January onward, the leaflets of the Unified National Leadership of the uprising were invariably published in the name of the PLO and on its behalf (see chapter on the West Bank and the Gaza Strip). Moreover, they assumed an increasingly anti-Jordanian tone, frequently accusing Jordan and its supporters in the West Bank of power-sharing and collaboration with Israel.[20] The Jordanians were particularly perturbed by one of the versions of "call number 10," circulated in mid-March, which appealed to the West Bank representatives in the Jordanian parliament to resign. This the Jordanians interpreted as a frontal assault on the concept of unity between the two banks. The Jordanian Government delivered an official protest to the PLO representative in Amman. The PLO replied that the "true text" of the leaflet did not include "clauses prejudicing the national unity of the one Arab people."[21] Husayn, however, was said to have been "truly stung" by the willingness of many Palestinian deputies living on the East Bank to consider the appeal, before it had been partially rescinded.[22]

PLO explanations notwithstanding, this incident finally dispelled any illusions the Jordanians might still have had about the nature of the *intifada*. From then onward, the Jordanian perception and portrayal of the uprising began to change. This had an immediate effect on Jordan's perception of its own role in the peace process, culminating eventually in Jordan's decision to disengage from the West Bank (see below).

Jordan's argument made since the 1974 Rabat resolutions — that the PLO had, in effect, been imposed on the people of the occupied territories by an Arab League decision about which they had not been consulted — had clearly been disproved by the *intifada*. Husayn now admitted that the Palestinian people had "elected the PLO" as their representative. "From this premise," he concluded, Jordan could "not carry any more burdens."[23]

Jordan finally accepted the fact that the *intifada* was a Palestinian national phenomenon, founded not only on a deep sense of identification with the PLO,[24] but also upon the rejection of Jordan as a desirable partner with the PLO in representing the Palestinians.[25]

JORDAN AND THE SHULTZ INITIATIVE

During the first few months of the *intifada*, Jordan's position on the ME peace process remained basically unchanged. The destabilizing effect of the uprising only served to reinforce Jordan's long-standing sense of urgency (cf. *MECS* 1987, p. 496). Husayn stressed the need to "take action at once, before time runs out and before the fatal psychological moment comes when all hope is lost."[26] He observed that if no action was taken, the Arab and Jewish populations in Palestine would approach equilibrium by the turn of the century. This was a "recipe for disaster." Husayn spoke of a trend in Israel "toward greater extremism," which, he argued, resulted from the "fear that Israeli Palestinians and Palestinians in the occupied territories [were] getting together."[27]

Jordanian spokesmen emphasized the pressing need to convene an international conference, citing the *intifada* both as further proof of the necessity to reactivate the peace process and also as a means to set the stage for the desired international conference. The conference, under UN auspices, was to be attended by all parties to the conflict, including the PLO, and the five permanent members of the UN Security Council, to negotiate the implementation of UN Resolutions 242 and 338 and to solve the Palestinian question in all its aspects.[28] Husayn continued to emphasize the need for the participation of the European powers as an essential means to avoid polarization between the two superpowers and their respective regional clients.[29]

As for the authority of the conference, Jordanian spokesmen restated their rejection of what they regarded as symbolic substitutes for an ongoing conference, in which the "moral weight"[30] of the powers would be brought to bear on the negotiations. Jordan's interpretation of the April 1987 London agreement between Husayn and Shimon Peres, Israel's deputy premier and foreign minister, continued to differ from that of Peres and his supporters in Israel (see *MECS* 1987, pp. 496–98). In January, Prime Minister Zayd al-Rifa'i went so far as to deny that such a document existed.[31]

Husayn conceded that in the conference direct negotiations would take place in geographic groups[32] and Rifa'i reaffirmed Jordan's acceptance of a conference that would not impose a settlement or veto an agreement reached by the parties.[33] But as the Jordanian daily *al-Ra'y* clarified, Jordan did not accept "the bogus protocol role" which, it maintained, Peres wished to impose upon the conference.[34] Rifa'i stated emphatically that Jordan was not "after a photo opportunity." It would not agree to any international "opening" that fell short of a full-scale conference with a continuing role until peace was achieved. Each delegation would have to be entitled to refer any impasse to the conference and, thereby, to allow for the "moral weight of the world" to "assist the parties" to reach agreement.[35]

On the subject of Palestinian representation at the conference, Jordan continued to suggest, though less assertively than before, that the Palestinians participate in a joint Jordanian-Palestinian delegation. Jordan explained, as it had done before, that this Jordanian preference resulted not from its own opposition to independent PLO representation, but from the realistic assumption that Israel's opposition to the PLO and to independent Palestinian statehood made such an alternative a pragmatic imperative. Rifa'i stated that Jordan would not object to the PLO being represented in an independent delegation or as part of an all-Arab delegation but, he added, "we deal with the possible."[36] The Jordanians still contended that the PLO would be required to accept Resolutions 242 and 338 and renounce violence as a precondition for its participation in the conference.[37] But they simultaneously reaffirmed that, in any event, they would not negotiate on the PLO's behalf.[38]

As for the objectives of the peace process, what was paramount in the Jordanian view was the acceptance by Israel of the principle of territory in exchange for peace. Israel had to accept the principle of withdrawal from all the territories occupied in 1967, including Arab Jerusalem, before Jordan would join negotiations. Interim arrangements for autonomy in the West Bank and Gaza were of little importance, in Jordan's view. It therefore expressed opposition to "partial solutions" and projects dealing with self-rule. What mattered was agreeing upon the final status of the occupied territories.[39]

Prompted by the outbreak of the *intifada*, US Secretary of State George Shultz launched a new peace initiative in early 1988. Shultz's plan attempted to address Jordanian prerequisites by proposing direct negotiations to be launched by an international conference and an explicit "interlock" between the negotiations over an interim settlement and negotiations over the final status of the occupied territories (see chapters on the United States and the Middle East, and the Middle East peace process). Even so, when Shultz visited Jordan at the end of February, he was received with calculated caution. The Jordanians welcomed the revitalization of the peace process, but they had already clarified publicly prior to Shultz's ME tour that Jordan was wary of any moves designed to "defuse" or "contain" the *intifada*.[40] The Jordanians clearly did not want to appear to be pulling the chestnuts out of the fire for the sake of Israel and the US, by cooperating in what could be seen by the Palestinians as an exercise to frustrate their national aspirations. Husayn chose to be in London when Shultz visited Amman. The talks in Jordan were held with Crown Prince Hasan at the head of the Jordanian team, followed by further talks between Shultz and Husayn in London at the beginning of March. Jordanian statements during and after the visit stressed Jordan's adherence to the Arab consensus, its opposition to separate or partial settlements, and its belief that an international conference, including the PLO, was the "only route" to a peaceful settlement.[41]

For Jordan, the most sensitive issue was that of Palestinian representation. The Shultz plan envisaged negotiations between Israel and a joint Jordanian-Palestinian delegation. Jordan still favored a joint delegation; but with the *intifada* steadily enhancing the PLO's status, the Jordanians no longer had the confidence nor the leverage to continue to pressure the PLO to accept such coordination.[42] Nevertheless. they continued to emphasize that PLO involvement was imperative. It was the Jordanians who claimed credit for having introduced an amendment to the Shultz proposals, replacing the word "states" (to be involved in the negotiations) with the word "parties," in order to pave the way for PLO participation.[43]

Jordan welcomed the US endorsement of the idea of an international conference though it still required clarifications on the role and powers of the conference, which Jordan and other Arab diplomatic sources regarded as a vague part of the Shultz plan.[44]

From the Jordanian point of view, the most encouraging facet of the Shultz plan was the proposal to start final-status negotiations by the end of 1988, irrespective of the measure of progress made in negotiations on the interim phase of autonomy for the Palestinians that was also part of the plan. Husayn, however, made any commitment conditional upon Israel's acceptance of the principle of territory in exchange for peace.[45]

Having made the above points, the Jordanians were frustrated by the positions Shultz presented when he toured the area again in early April. Following talks with Husayn in Amman on 5 April, "informed [Jordanian] sources" complained that Shultz had not conveyed anything new on Israel's position on withdrawal, nor had he clarified other questions raised by the Jordanians.[46] Shultz went on to commit a diplomatic *faux pas* which severely irritated the Jordanians.[47] In an interview with the chief editors of the Jordanian newspapers, Shultz repeated statements he had previously made in a similar interview in Israel. He noted that the US opposed negotiations with the PLO, the establishment of a Palestinian state, and Israel's withdrawal to the 1967 boundaries. The Jordanians did not permit the publication of

Shultz's remarks in the government-controlled media.[48] They presumably believed that such publication would only embarrass Jordan by creating the impression that it was negotiating with the US on a plan that did not address Palestinian national rights. The Shultz approach, according to the *Jordan Times* , was "too partial to Israeli concerns" and Shultz's claim to be "fair and balanced [was] hard to swallow."[49] A Jordanian journalist was quoted as having said that Shultz's remarks in Amman "were insulting and biased."[50]

In another round of talks with Husayn on 6 April, the king handed Shultz a document outlining the basic principles which governed the Jordanian position. These were:

A. The inadmissability of the acquisition of territory by war. Israeli withdrawal from the occupied territories is the basis for the settlement of the Arab-Israeli conflict, and the establishment of a just and durable peace.

B. The settlement of the Arab-Israeli conflict requires the settlement of the Palestinian problem in all its aspects, including the right of the Palestinian people to self-determination.

C. The settlement of the Arab-Israeli conflict and the Palestinian problem must be a comprehensive one. Negotiations to arrive at a comprehensive settlement can only take place in an international conference.

D. The international conference will not be only a ceremonial gathering designed to launch direct negotiations. It should reflect the moral and constant weight of the five permanent members of the Security Council in assisting all the parties to the conflict to arrive at a comprehensive, just, and lasting peace.

E. The principles of Security Council Resolution 242 apply to all occupied Arab territories and are the basis for negotiations in the bilateral committees.

F. In exercising its sovereign right, Jordan is prepared to attend the international conference with the other involved parties. Jordan will not represent the Palestinian people at the conference, nor will it negotiate the settlement of the Palestinian problem on behalf of the PLO. Jordan is also prepared to attend the conference in a joint Jordanian-Palestinian delegation if the concerned parties accept this arrangement.[51]

Particularly noteworthy were the shifting tone and emphasis in Jordan's Palestinian policy. Rifa'i told journalists that Jordan had "reminded the Americans" that it favored Palestinian self-determination as a "sacred and natural right." The US, he said, had been asked to acknowledge the Palestinians' right to self-determination.[52] Jordan had for long recognized this right of the Palestinians, but during negotiations with the Americans in the more recent past they had deliberately refrained from pressing the US on this issue (see *MECS* 1984–85, p. 516). However, remnants of Jordan's own reservations on this question were still evident. Rifa'i noted that Jordan differed with the PLO over the organization's demand that self-determination be exercised in an independent state led by the PLO. If the PLO insisted that it lead the Palestinian state "then what happens to the principle of self-determination?" he asked. "We must stop at the right to self- determination and the rest could be left for later," he suggested. As for the US, it ought to accept self-determination "and object to a PLO-led Palestinian state if it wishes to do so."[53] This, in essence, without Rifa'i actually saying so, was Jordan's own position. It corresponded with a distinction Jordan had been making for years between the PLO and the Palestinians' right to self-determination, which Jordan still preferred to leave ultimately to the people of the occupied territories rather than to the PLO.

The most salient shift, however, was on the question of representation. Jordan no longer insisted on a joint Jordanian-Palestinian delegation. According to Rifa'i, Jordan did "not insist on any particular form of representation," but Syria and the PLO had to attend any proposed international conference. Jordan was ready to attend independently, within a joint Arab delegation or in a joint Jordan-PLO delegation. It was impossible to have a conference without the PLO. "We [the Jordanians] are not the only ones to decide," he added.[54] Indeed, so far as the joint Jordan-PLO delegation was concerned, this was now entirely up to the PLO and other Arab parties involved. In the past, Jordan had argued consistently that it would not substitute or deputize for the PLO, which had to be represented. Simultaneously, however, Jordan had applied pressure on the PLO to accept a joint delegation. This pressure had now disappeared. This change related not simply to procedure, but to substance as well. Independent Palestinian representation in the negotiations, as the PLO and Jordan well understood, could pave the way for the creation of an independent Palestinian state as the logical conclusion of any future negotiations.

Rifa'i noted that differences related to the questions of Israeli withdrawal, the role and the authority of the proposed international conference, and Palestinian representation had emerged between the Jordanians and the Americans during their talks. Jordan's principles in regard to the peace process were, however, "nonnegotiable." Jordan's position, Rifa'i noted, had been coordinated with other Arab states; moreover, it accorded with the positions of all the permanent members of the UN Security Council save for the US. But, more importantly, Jordan's principles were "declared to remove doubts" that Jordan might be competing with the PLO at the expense of the Palestinian people. "All such skepticism [was] unfounded," Rifa'i stressed.[55]

Though the Jordanians were frustrated and discouraged by Shultz's apparent reluctance to exert pressure on Israel,[56] Rifa'i declared that Jordan "would not reject the initiative." Jordan was prepared to "continue the dialogue indefinitely." At the same time, Jordan would "not accept any initiative that [did] not secure the rights of the Palestinian people." Jordan's position on the initiative would be determined by the extent to which it corresponded with Jordan's principles, as presented to Shultz.[57]

Jordan's unwillingness to reject the Shultz initiative derived from considerations of both substance and tactics. The Jordanians were genuinely interested in the revitalization of the peace process for which US involvement was imperative. The American position on the international conference and on the Palestinian question, though unsatisfactory, was evolving. Arab rejection was, therefore, seen as potentially damaging to this positive trend. The Shultz initiative was also positive in the centrality it accorded to Jordan (though negative in the sense that it expected too much of the Jordanians on matters in which they could not deliver independently). On the purely tactical level, the Jordanians did not want the Arabs "to take the blame for [the] failure" of the US initiative. Arab rejection, the Jordanians believed, would let Israel off the hook and preclude any chance of the US eventually exerting pressure on Israel to concede.[58]

As time elapsed, Jordanian skepticism and pessimism[59] in respect to the Shultz initiative increased. Jordanian sources expressed mounting criticism of Shultz's apparent unwillingness to press Israel to agree to withdraw from the occupied territories. According to Premier Rifa'i, the US could not make any progress unless it revised its pro-Israeli policy. The US, he said, was the "armorer, the banker, the political protector, and the economic savior of Israel. As such, surely it must be in a position to exert influence on Israel to accept a peaceful settlement."[60] As for the specifics of the Shultz plan, Jordan's main reservations were that it did not include the PLO in the process; that it did not endorse an international conference that would have considerably more than a ceremonial role; and that it did not provide for simultaneous negotiations on an interim settlement and final status talks.[61] In such circumstances, Husayn believed that it would have been "suicidal to accept" the initiative. Shortly before Shultz's previous visit to Jordan in early June, Jordan informed the US secretary of state that any attempt to apply further pressure on Jordan would be "a waste of time."[62] Shultz had talks with Husayn in Amman on 4 June. From the tone of the Jordanian press, which continued to criticize Shultz for "being so partial to Israeli and Zionist positions,"[63] it was obvious that the initiative was not making much headway in Jordan. Even so, in his address to the Arab summit in Algiers only a few days later, Husayn still refrained from rejecting the initiative, expressing the hope that it would still develop to conform with the bases of the Arab position.[64]

Husayn's decision, in July, to disengage from the West Bank (see below) was, at least in part, an attempt to force the US to restructure its political initiative to conform with the Arab consensus on the PLO. It made the Shultz initiative, with its emphasis on Jordanian centrality and PLO exclusion, inoperative.

JORDAN'S DEFENSIVE POSTURE

During the initial phase of the *intifada*, Jordanian statements on the Palestinian question reflected the ambiguity that had characterized Jordan's position since the Rabat resolutions of 1974. These resolutions had not only recognized the PLO as the "sole legitimate representative of the Palestinian people," but had called for the transfer of any Palestinian territory retrieved from Israel to PLO control. These resolutions had essentially disqualified Jordan from playing any substantial role in the determination of the political fate of the West Bank and Gaza. Officially, Jordan had accepted the Rabat resolutions. But, in practice, it had systematically sought to undermine them and to retain its position as a chief negotiator over the fate of these territories, together with the PLO.

During the first few months of the *intifada*, Jordanian statements supporting independent Palestinian statehood[65] were still accompanied by others reaffirming Jordan's unique historical and legal link to Palestine. Minister for Occupied Territory Affairs Marwan Dudin noted that the West Bank remained a constitutionally inseparable part of the Hashemite Kingdom over which Jordan still enjoyed the right of sovereignty.[66] Husayn restated his long-standing view that Palestinians and Jordanians were "all members of one family" and asserted that he himself was "as much a Palestinian as every Palestinian."[67] Rifa'i suggested that a future Palestinian state would be linked to Jordan in a confederation. The two states on the East and West Banks of the Jordan would have a "very special relationship," he said, because "they were really one people."[68]

From early April, however, a shift of emphasis in Jordanian policy was becoming increasingly discernible. Shortly after the publication of Jordan's policy principles in respect to the Shultz initiative (see above), a flurry of Jordanian statements was issued, apparently designed to dispel any Palestinian doubts or suspicions about Jordan's position on Palestinian representation. On 11 April, a "Jordanian official" clarified that it was the PLO, in its capacity as the sole legitimate representative of the Palestinian people, that would negotiate Palestinian-Israeli issues at a future international conference. Jordan was prepared to attend such a conference in a joint delegation with the Palestinians, but the Jordanians would take part only in negotiations to regain Jordanian and not Palestinian territories. The Jordanian territories involved, according to the spokesman, were an area of some 5 sq. km., at the confluence of the Jordan and the Yarmuk rivers (which Israel was said to have occupied in the 1948–49 war), and another area of some 20 sq. km., south of the Dead Sea (which Israel was said to have taken "in the wake of" the 1967 war).[69] In late April and early May, in a series of speeches at *iftar* banquets throughout the country, Husayn made an unusual effort to stress that Jordan had no ambitions in Palestine. Its involvement in the issue, he contended, was motivated solely by Jordan's sense of duty toward the Palestinians and their cause. Jordan, Husayn reiterated, would not substitute for the PLO and would not represent the Palestinians. Jordan would attend a future international conference as a sovereign state with the longest line of confrontation with Israel,[70] i.e., not as one with territorial claims in Palestine. Jordan was still willing to consider the idea of a joint delegation, if this was acceptable to the PLO and the Palestinian people. But what Jordan now had in mind was a joint delegation in which half the members would be from Jordan and half from the PLO; the former team would concentrate on the "Jordanian dimension" of the problem, while the latter would deal with the "Palestinian dimension." This, in effect, would amount to two delegations.[71]

As senior Jordanian spokesmen explained, the new Jordanian position was intended to convince all and sundry that Jordan was not competing with the PLO in any manner or form. According to Minister of Court 'Adnan Abu 'Awda, Jordan had discovered that the PLO, which had rejected the idea of a joint delegation with Jordan, was quite willing to enter into a joint delegation with Egypt. Jordan, therefore, concluded that it was not the principle of a joint delegation that bothered the PLO, but rather its mistrust of Jordan's intentions in regard to the Palestinian question. Husayn's statements were designed, therefore, to "finally dispel" from the minds of Palestinians and non-Palestinians "the impression that Jordan was competing with the organization, i.e., that it had ambitions in the occupied Palestinian territory, or that it had ambitions or aspirations for hegemony over the Palestinian people."[72]

Jordan's new posture was accompanied by emphatic statements to the effect that Jordan had "absolutely nothing to do" with the issue of Palestinian representation,[73] or that it had any desire whatsoever to discuss anything concerning the Palestinian question.[74] This was a rather radical departure from previous Jordanian positions, which had tended to emphasize the need for *partnership* between Jordan and the PLO in matters related to the future of Palestine (see *MECS* 1984–85, pp. 513–14; 1987, pp. 499–501). Yet it did not signify a total Jordanian renunciation of any role in Palestinian affairs. Instead, it seemed to be an attempt to establish a new mode of coordination with the PLO, that would at least appear to be founded on mutual trust and equality rather than on Jordanian supremacy and constant rivalry.

At the Arab summit held in Algiers in early June (for details, see chapter on inter-Arab relations), Husayn made a final effort to regain Arab and Palestinian recognition of Jordan's special status in Palestinian affairs, that, at least in theory, would not undermine the representative status of the PLO. Husayn's speech at the summit was a classical Hashemite exposé and defense of Jordan's historical role in Palestine from the days of the Arab Revolt in World War I until the present. Since Jordan's establishment in 1921, Husayn noted, it had been closely associated with the Palestine question. This inseparable bond (*talazum*) was reinforced by the unification of the West Bank with Jordan in 1950. Husayn went to great lengths to dismiss the notion put forward by many Arabs and Israelis alike that this "historical [Arab] national event" was in effect an act of Jordanian annexation or occupation. He urged his audience to recall that it was an elected parliament, equally representing the East and West Banks, which had decided on the act of unification and that it was the then representatives of the Palestinian people who had initiated the demand for the union.[75] Moreover, the period of unity of the two banks preceding the 1967 war was "a living model" of a greater Arab union to which all Arabs aspired at that time. That was an age when identity with the territorial state (*qutriyya*) was far less pervasive. Now, however, if the representatives of the Palestinian people sought separation (*infisal*) from Jordan, their desire would be welcomed and respected by Jordan, just as the Palestinians' decision to unite with Jordan had been welcomed in 1950. But, Husayn added, this legitimate desire to secede was no justification for denigrating the unity that had existed prior to 1967, by portraying it as some form of hegemony exercised by one Arab state over another for the sake of greed and profit.[76]

Husayn similarly rejected the notion that Jordan's continued political and financial support for the people of the occupied territories after the 1967 war, was motivated by a desire for political or territorial gain at the PLO's expense. Jordan, he noted, was often asked why it continued to maintain such a high level of involvement in the Palestinian question by dealing with political initiatives, by drawing up development plans for the occupied territories, and simultaneously upholding the constitutional and institutional links that solidified the unity of the East and West Banks. In Jordan itself and in the Arab world, there were those who wondered why Jordan did not confine itself to expressing its support for the PLO instead of taking action that generated suspicion about its true intentions. Jordan's answer to these questions, Husayn contended, was that its relationship with Palestine was unique and not merely one of pan-Arab commitment, as was the case with the other Arab states. Jordan had a distinctive association with Palestine, which was the product not of ambition but of "geographical proximity, the intermix of population (*al-tamazuj al-sukkani*), cultural integration, economic integration, and a common historical experience."[77]

In his effort to portray Jordan's record of involvement in the Palestinian question in the best possible light, Husayn indulged in some rather coarse distortions of history. He contended that Jordan had for long been aware of the PLO's "sensitivity" (*hassasiyya*) resulting from its perception of Jordan as a competitor. Therefore, already in 1972, two years before the Rabat resolutions, Jordan had offered the Palestinians a choice of three options as the basis for the future Jordanian-Palestinian relationship: (1) a return to the pre-1967 unitary formula, (2) a federation between the two autonomous "regions" (*qutrayn*) of Jordan and Palestine, and (3) an independent Palestinian state.[78]

In fact, the historical record was rather different. In March 1972, in the aftermath of the civil war in Jordan (of which Husayn, understandably, made no mention in his speech), Jordan did indeed publish the federation ("United Arab Kingdom") plan, but its publication was in no way intended to assuage PLO sensitivities. It was an outright challenge to the organization and its representative status, and was fully understood as such by the PLO. The choice among the three options was only put forward consistently by Jordan after the October War. At that time, it was an integral facet of Jordan's struggle against the growing recognition of the PLO in the Arab world. By its offer of the three options, Jordan had sought to portray itself as the protector of the Palestinians' right to self-determination. This effort had failed, however, to prevent the adoption of the Rabat resolutions of 1974, which, in effect, disqualified Jordan as a legitimate negotiator over the future of the West Bank.

Shortly before the Algiers summit, Husayn restated the position he had taken in 1974 — that Jordan sought the retrieval of the occupied territories to enable the people there to exercise their right of self-determination, by allowing them a free choice among these three possibilities.[79] In his speech at the Algiers summit, Husayn pointed out that of the three, the federation option had been "the most acceptable at that time," because it reaffirmed "the outstanding historical relationship" between the Jordanian and Palestinian peoples.[80] This was certainly true of Jordan's position and still remained so.[81]

Husayn's last effort to convince his Arab brethren to maintain a special role for Jordan in Palestinian affairs was of no avail. He urged the Arab states to support PLO participation in an "effective international conference" that would negotiate peace in the ME, without "binding ourselves as to the details on the form of participation." Jordan, he said, would nevertheless abide by an Arab decision to pose the establishment of an independent Palestinian state as a precondition for such a conference as it would accept Arab insistence on an independent PLO delegation to the conference "even if this did not lead to the convening of the conference."[82] In other words, Jordan would bow to the Arab consensus, even if it believed the consensus to be unrealistic, and, therefore, undesirable. Husayn's advocacy of more flexible formulas that would not deny Jordan's role in questions related to Palestinian representation and statehood was followed up by another appeal in regard to the channeling of financial aid to the occupied territories. Husayn urged the summit to recognize Jordan as a legitimate conduit of funds to support the *intifada*. By this he "did not mean that [Jordan] should be the [sole] channel for the delivery of this support, to the exclusion of all others."[83] Aid ought to be delivered through all possible channels — international organizations, Jordan, and the PLO. But Husayn went on to point out that Jordan was especially qualified for this role. Jordan, he said, had consistently been providing various forms of support to the West Bank since 1967. Moreover, Husayn thought it "useful to recall" that in "practical terms, the unity of the two banks remained intact after the occupation." Jordanian law was still applied in the West Bank, Jordanian currency and passports were still used, Jordanian state institutions continued to function there, and Jordan still paid salaries to 18,000 civil servants in the West Bank and even to another 6,000 in the Gaza Strip.[84]

The *Jordan Times*, commenting on Husayn's speech at the summit, highlighted the king's emphasis on the "inexorable link between the Palestinians and Jordanians." Attempts would continue on finding a permanent solution to the Palestine problem.

But, in the end, Jordan was confident that "an arrangement will emerge which will express the distinct political identity of both Palestinians and Jordanians, while simultaneously affirming the close demographic, economic, social, and nationalistic impulses, which have kept Jordanians and Palestinians so deeply intertwined for so many years. The truth of this relationship shall also triumph in the end."[85]

If Husayn had sought to obtain recognition for Jordan's special role in Palestine, the resolutions of the Algiers summit were a sore disappointment. The resolutions (see chapter on inter-Arab relations) reaffirmed the right of the Palestinians to independent statehood under the leadership of the PLO, stressed the commitment of the Arab states to provide the necessary aid to the Palestinian people "in all forms and by all means," and supported the participation of the PLO at an international conference on an equal footing with the other parties.[86] No mention was made of Jordan, certainly not of any special role for the kingdom in matters pertaining to Palestine. Moreover, according to a PLO source, the summit had adopted a number of resolutions on the Palestine question, in addition to the final communiqué, in which the rejection of Jordan's plea was even more obvious. These additional resolutions clearly stated that support for the uprising would be channeled through the PLO, as the "sole legitimate representative" of the Palestinian people, as well as "available international channels"; and that one of the guiding principles of a future international conference would be the establishment of an independent Palestinian state under the PLO.[87]

JORDAN'S DISENGAGEMENT FROM THE WEST BANK

THE PRELUDE TO DISENGAGEMENT

Prior to the Algiers summit there were rumors that Husayn intended to announce Jordan's disengagement from the West Bank. In his speech at the summit Husayn alluded to pressure from within the Jordanian establishment to resort to such action, but the overall tone and essence of his speech was a final plea for recognition of Jordan's historic role in Palestine. The Jordanians had little to show for their effort at the summit. They could draw some consolation from the fact that the summit had neither condemned nor flatly rejected the Shultz initiative. But they had failed in practically every other respect. Jordan had faced Arab censure, orchestrated by the PLO, for seeking to "impose itself" on the Palestinian people.[88] For Husayn, the Algiers summit was "the last straw."[89]

After the summit, Crown Prince Hasan was particularly outspoken in his criticism of the Arab states' handling of the Palestinian question. He said that the way it had been dealt with "was ineffective and impractical in terms of chances of implementation."[90] During the summit, Jordan and the PLO had clashed over two issues: Palestinian representation and the channeling of aid to the occupied territories. The Jordanians took exception to the PLO claim that it represented the Palestinians inside and outside the occupied territories, i.e., in Jordan as well. It was agreed to delete from the summit resolutions any specific reference to Palestinians outside the occupied territories.[91] The Jordanians, however, had no satisfaction on the aid issue. Hasan spoke of a "genuine feeling of resentment" that no explicit recognition was given at the summit to Jordan's role in this matter.[92] Moreover, "for Jordan to shoulder such responsibilities [for providing aid] and be attacked sometimes by the same people who ask for our support, is something we totally reject."[93]

Jordanian indignation was compounded by a sense of humiliation. In Algiers, Husayn had been on the receiving end of the kind of treatment he had given 'Arafat at the Amman summit in November 1987 (see *MECS* 1987, pp. 502–3). 'Arafat had taunted Husayn several times, repeatedly rubbing in the Rabat resolutions on the PLO's exclusive representative status. He reminded the king at one point that only three countries, Britain, Pakistan, and Iraq, had ever formally recognized Jordan's annexation of the West Bank.[94]

Pique and resentment were clearly a factor in the creation of the mood that eventually brought about the decision to disengage from the West Bank. However, the king and those included in his "political kitchen" (Prime Minister Zayd al-Rifa'i, Chief of the Royal Court Marwan al-Qasim, Minister of Court 'Adnan Abu 'Awda, Commander in Chief of the Armed Forces Zayd Ibn Shakir and Foreign Minister Tahir al-Masri),[95] appear to have gone through an agonizing process of internal debate and deliberation that reflected a sense of reluctance, uncertainty, and even confusion, before finally making their historic decision. Palestinians close to the king argued that he could not relinquish his role in Palestinian affairs, primarily because of the large Palestinian community on the East Bank and the need to keep the moderate wing of the Israeli Government engaged in some form of peace process. Hard-line East Bankers replied that the king had already stuck his neck out far enough for minimal political gain and it was time the government turned its attention to its East Bank constituency and its own domestic problems.[96]

Shortly before and immediately after the Algiers summit, reports that Husayn was planning to restructure the Jordanian State or to "Jordanize" the kingdom were emphatically denied by senior Jordanian spokesmen. Thus, in late May, Minister of Court 'Adnan Abu 'Awda reiterating Jordan's historical association with Palestine, stated quite categorically that, "no one" in Jordan was even thinking about dissolving the parliament that equally represented the East and the West Banks.[97] In early June, Minister of Information Hani al-Khasawna similarly rejected reports on disengagement plans, emanating from the West Bank, as part of a hostile campaign against Jordan. Jordan, he explained, had only clarified that it would in no way compete with the PLO on the question of Palestinian representation. He deplored "the suspect claim by hostile circles" that Jordan intended to "wash its hands of the West Bank."[98]

Crown Prince Hasan even went so far as to publicly criticize the "parochial school of East Jordanianism," noting that Jordan had a fundamental interest in "safeguarding the geopolitical stability of the area called the Hashemite Kingdom of Jordan,"[99] i.e., both the East and West Banks. It was particularly significant that these statements were made at this juncture by Hasan who, in the more distant past, had himself been described by some Arab and other observers as a leading figure in this "parochial school of East Jordanianism." Jordan, Hasan said, had a responsibility for the West Bank by virtue of Security Council Resolutions 242 and 338. Forfeiting this responsibility could play into the hands of those Israelis who claimed the territory for themselves. At the same time, he was fully aware of the fact that the majority of Palestinians in the occupied territories did not look to Jordan for political leadership. But Jordan, Hasan said, was "not in the business of currying favor with the young, justifiably angry population." He personally would not be at all perturbed, he said, even if support for Jordan "was zero per cent" in the West Bank and Gaza.[100]

According to the crown prince, the PLO and Israel could very well handle "partial and bilateral issues" between them at a future international conference. However, in an apparent allusion to the large Palestinian population in Jordan, he suggested that they alone could not deal with the "demographic dimension" of the Palestinian question. Jordan would remain the "window to the east" for the occupied territories,[101] and would have to be involved in the ultimate political settlement of the Palestinian question.

Early in July, Minister for Occupied Territory Affairs Marwan Dudin announced that Jordan intended to continue with its development plan for the West Bank and Gaza.[102] As late as mid-July, the director-general of Jordan's Foreign Ministry still chose to reject any talk of disengagement, arguing that the links between Jordan and Palestine were so organic that they could not possibly be severed.[103] Minister of Interior Raja'i al-Dajani stated that Jordan had no intention of changing the status of the people in the West Bank who were Jordanian citizens.[104]

However, by mid-July there were also clearer indications that Jordan was about to adopt some extraordinary measures. Addressing the fourth annual conference of Jordanian expatriates, Foreign Minister Tahir al-Masri referred to Jordan's long-standing fear that Israel might attempt in the future to solve its demographic problems by expelling Palestinians to Jordan, as part of the "alternative homeland" philosophy, according to which Jordan was in fact Palestine. Masri noted that this Israeli thinking compelled Jordan to take some "daring steps" that would "emphasize the Palestinian identity in Palestine."[105]

Husayn's apparent wavering was a function of the inherent tension between short-term and long-term considerations. There were a number of such short-term considerations: the mood of resentment toward the Arab states and the PLO, particularly after the Algiers summit; Husayn's deeply felt disappointment with the Israelis, and the Labor Party in particular, for having failed to make more of an effort to achieve a peaceful settlement before the outbreak of the *intifada*;[106] disillusionment and frustration with the US for not having applied sufficient pressure on Israel and for having expected Jordan to negotiate instead of the PLO,[107] at a time when the Jordanians were convinced that they were unable to do so; the final realization that nothing could be gained by overt competition with the PLO and that Jordan had to lend credibility to its declared abandonment of such competition; the realization that the aid to the West Bank and Gaza was not producing any political advantage; and, finally, the conviction that, in light of the political stalemate, Jordan had to make an extra effort to put to rest the Israeli notion of Jordan becoming the "alternative homeland" for the Palestinians. For the long term, Jordan still remained interested in some form of special link to a future Palestinian entity or state. It was the short-term calculations that prevailed, but in Husayn's words and deeds one can detect a concerted effort to reconcile the two.

FAKK AL-IRTIBAT — THE SEVERANCE OF LEGAL AND ADMINISTRATIVE TIES

On 28 July, the government canceled Jordan's not very effective development plan (1986–90) for the occupied territories (for details of the plan and its execution, see *MECS* 1986, pp. 455–57; 1987, pp. 503–5). Two days later, a royal decree dissolved the Chamber of Deputies. On 31 July, in a speech to the nation, Husayn announced his intention to sever Jordan's legal and administrative ties with the West Bank. The speech was followed by a series of measures designed to implement the disengagement decision. On 4 August, the government decided to retire almost all the Jordanian civil servants employed in the West Bank. The decision came into effect on 16 August and affected 18,000 civil servants in the various government departments and institutions. It applied mainly to teachers, health workers, and municipal employees, most of whom also received salaries from Israel. They were all to receive different forms of pension and compensation depending on the length of their service. However, the decision did not apply to over 3,000 employees of the Ministry of Religious Endowments (*Awqaf*) and Religious Affairs, including the Islamic religious court system. These would be exempted because, according to the government statement, they embodied the "Islamic cultural presence in the occupied Palestinian territory."[108]

It was not expected that the economic impact of these measures would be particularly severe. Retired employees were to be compensated and the development plan had not actually introduced any more than a fraction of the sums originally planned for the West Bank and Gaza.

On 6 August, the king issued a royal decree abolishing the Supreme Committee for West Bank Affairs, a body that had been formed in 1980 to formulate administrative, financial, and social policy on the West Bank (see *MECS* 1979–80, p. 581). On the same day, the Ministry for Occupied Territory Affairs, also established in 1980, was similarly abolished. The duties of the ministry were now transferred to a newly formed department for Palestinian Affairs in the Foreign Ministry. Jordan radio and television also dropped special programming aimed at the West Bank.

However, the most significant step taken by the Jordanian authorities to implement the disengagement decision related to the rights of citizenship of the West Bank population. On 20 August, the prime minister issued new instructions to the Ministry of Interior's Civil Registration Department and the Department of Passports, according to which all Jordanian citizens residing in the West Bank prior to 31 July 1988 would henceforth be considered Palestinians, and not Jordanian nationals. West Bankers would still be allowed to obtain "temporary" Jordanian passports. These, however, would be valid only for renewable two-year periods, as opposed to the regular five-year duration. They would be considered solely as travel documents, which would neither entitle the bearer to the rights of citizenship nor require him/her to fulfill the obligations deriving therefrom, such as military service. This placed West Bankers on a par with people from the Gaza Strip who had received such "temporary" passports in the past, without becoming Jordanian citizens. Residents of the Gaza Strip who had previously obtained Jordanian passports would be allowed to renew them for two years, but no new passports were to be issued in the future to Gazans.[109]

Family Cards (*daftar al-'a'ila*), which had been issued to all Jordanian citizens since 1979 (see *MECS* 1979–80, p. 581) both as a means of identification and as proof of eligibility for various government services, were now to be canceled for West Bankers. West Bankers were to retain their canceled cards as an identification document accepted by the Jordanian Government.

Various restrictions on West Bankers taking up residence on the East Bank had already been in force prior to the disengagement. However, the new regulations, being more stringent, were clearly designed to make Palestinian emigration to the East Bank all the more difficult. Palestinians who were not actually residing on the West

Bank prior to 31 July, such as those working in the Gulf and elsewhere, would have to return to their "natural place of residence" upon returning home. For all those who had originally left from there to seek employment outside the country, this meant the West Bank.[110] For similar reasons, the number of students from the West Bank who were to be allowed to study in East Bank universities was to be reduced to the same level as that applicable to students from other Arab states.[111] On the other hand, no measures were to be taken in respect to property owned by West Bankers on the East Bank.[112] Bearers of two-year passports would continue to enjoy the rights of other Jordanian citizens regarding travel, the purchase of goods and property, and the use of their money without restriction.[113]

The measures adopted were unprecedented and far-reaching, but not all of Jordan's ties with the West Bank were severed. According to Minister of Interior Raja'i al-Dajani, Jordan had no intention of erecting a "Great Wall of China" between the two banks.[114] The bridges across the Jordan were to remain open as before, and West Bankers were still allowed to cross without having to obtain visas or present passports. Jordan maintained an overt administrative, and no doubt political, link with the West Bank through the West Bank religious establishment. Since the officials of the Ministry of Religious Endowments (*Awqaf*) and Religious Affairs continued to receive their salaries from the Jordanian Government, they now assumed a series of new functions as the remaining representatives of the Jordanian Administration in the West Bank. Only documents endorsed by the Department of *Awqaf* in the West Bank were to be accepted by the Jordanian authorities for the purpose of issuing temporary Jordanian passports. The Department of *Awqaf* was similarly to endorse documents for purposes of land registration. Birth, death, marriage, divorce, and inheritance certificates would be accepted by the Jordanian authorities only when endorsed by the office of the Chief Islamic Justice in the West Bank and by the newly established Department for Palestinian Affairs at the Jordanian Foreign Ministry.[115] The religious courts in the West Bank were to register all forms of power of attorney for the conduct of transactions on the East Bank.[116]

According to Minister of *Awqaf* and Religious Affairs 'Abd al-'Aziz al-Khayyat, his ministry continued to spend 4m. Jordanian dinars (JD) p.a. on religious institutions and mosques in the West Bank. This included the upkeep of 750 mosques, the most important of these being al-Aqsa mosque in Jerusalem, and the payment of salaries to 3,500 employees of the ministry. These included 1,800 *Awqaf* employees, 200 officials in the religious courts, about 420 teachers, and other functionaries in various Islamic institutions.[117]

In the economic sphere, Jordan was to continue to import agricultural and industrial products from the West Bank and Gaza. The extent of such imports would be determined by "market needs."[118] This seems to suggest that Jordan would no longer commit itself to buying certain quantities of produce from the West Bank and Gaza as it had done at times in the past. In December, in what was widely understood in the West Bank as a form of political pressure, Jordan banned the import of olive oil from the area. The Jordanians, however, explained that the decision was motivated by economic and not political considerations, following surplus production in the East Bank.[119] The Agricultural Cooperative Union in in the West Bank and the Gaza Charitable Association would continue to issue certificates of origin (i.e., that the produce was not from Israel). Branches of the Cairo-Amman Bank, reopened in 1986 (see *MECS* 1986, p. 456), were also to continue their operations.

Schools in the West Bank, until such time as they (or the PLO) chose otherwise, were to continue to follow the Jordanian system and curriculum. The Jordanian Ministry of Education would continue to arrange matriculation (*tawjihi*) examinations for West Bank schools and issue the necessary certificates.

Most significantly, however, the disengagement measures left a series of constitutional questions in abeyance. In his speech of 31 July, Husayn spoke of severing Jordan's legal (*qanuni*) and administrative (*idari*) ties with the West Bank. He made no mention of Jordan's constitutional (*dusturi*) links, which were actually left intact, at least for the time being. No amendment was made to the constitution even though Article One, as formulated in 1952 (i.e., after the annexation of the West Bank), specified that Jordan's territory was "indivisible" and that "no portion of it" could be ceded.[120] Indeed, Minister of Information Hani al-Khasawna denied reports that Jordanian maps were to be modified to exclude the West Bank.[121] Well into 1989, Jordan television continued to show on the evening news a map of Jordan that included the West Bank.

The resolution adopted by the Jordanian parliament in April 1950 on the unification of the East and West Banks was neither amended nor abrogated. The Chamber of Deputies did not even discuss the matter; Husayn dissolved the chamber the day before his disengagement speech, thus effectively avoiding any such debate. He preferred not to use unambiguous terms, such as abrogation or nullification, in response to questions on this issue. In a press conference on 7 August, he was only prepared to say that the 1950 resolution had been "affected in one dimension" when the PLO opted for an independent state, a desire to which Jordan had responded positively. When asked whether Jordan had irrevocably renounced sovereignty over the West Bank he replied with a question of his own: "Did I say that?"[122] The minister of information flatly denied that the disengagement meant the abolition of the 1950 resolution.[123]

Another issue of constitutional significance was related to the Chamber of Deputies and the question of future elections. The king had a number of constitutional options following the dissolution of the chamber: to call for new elections within four months, to postpone elections indefinitely, or do neither and have the dissolved parliament automatically reconvened four months after the dissolution. On 2 October a royal decree was issued, postponing parliamentary elections indefinitely.[124] General elections were to be held after the amendment of the 1986 Election Law, which, like its predecessor of 1960, included representation for the West Bank (see *MECS* 1986, pp. 425–27). The Election Law could easily have been amended in time to hold elections in November 1988. Husayn, however, chose to bide his time. He was in no rush to hold elections for a parliament that would only represent the East Bank and thus lend a stamp of finality to the disengagement. He seemed to be waiting for the results of the forthcoming meeting of the PLO's Palestine National Council (PNC), as well as the results of the elections in Israel, before making any decisions of this nature.

In August, a committee was set up in the Interior Ministry to draw up recommendations for the revision of the Election Law.[125] In early November, Minister of Interior Raja'i al-Dajani revealed that the committee had already covered most of the material related to the amendments. What remained was the part that was "the state's [i.e., the king's] decision." However, as Dajani himself observed, to have "a decent law," there was no need to hurry.[126]

The appointed upper house of parliament, the Senate, was not dissolved after the disengagement. On 13 August, four senators, three of whom were Palestinians, including Hikmat al-Masri who resided on the West Bank, were replaced. All the new senators were residents of the East Bank and only one of them was of Palestinian extraction.[127] Thus, the Palestinian representation in the Senate was reduced and residents of the West Bank were excluded. This situation was similar to the one prevailing after the Rabat resolutions of 1974, until the revival of parliament in early 1984 (see *MECS* 1983–84, pp. 511–13). As opposed to the lower house, there was no legally required representation of West Bankers in the Senate. By maintaining the Senate, even though it was unable to exercise its legislative functions without the lower house, the continuity of the bicameral parliament representing both banks was preserved. This would remain so until the dissolved Chamber of Deputies was replaced by one that was representative of the East Bank alone. The Senate held occasional meetings to issue statements or to hear government briefings and also represented the Jordanian parliament at the meeting of the International Parliamentary Union held in Sofia in September.

JORDAN'S ROLE IN THE PEACE PROCESS IN THE WAKE OF DISENGAGEMENT

In his disengagement speech, Husayn made it quite clear that the severance of Jordan's legal and administrative ties with the West Bank ought not to be construed as Jordanian dissociation from the Palestinian question and the Arab-Israeli peace process. Husayn repeatedly made the point that the disengagement was not of Jordan's own choosing, but rather a response to the Palestinian and overall Arab consensus on Palestine.[128] It was the PLO, he noted, that had decided on secession (*infisal*) from Jordan in an independent Palestinian state, as part of the Palestinian and overall Arab tendency to highlight the Palestinian identity. Jordan, for its part, had never imagined that the preservation of its legal and administrative ties with the West Bank could be an impediment to the liberation of the occupied territories. In light of the Arab consensus Jordan was simply fulfilling its duty by doing "what [had] been demanded" of it.[129]

At the Algiers summit, Husayn had already expressed his reservations about this Arab consensus and its lack of realism (see above). But he was now indignantly suggesting that if this was what the Arabs wanted, then so be it. Jordan, however, would never "relinquish its commitment to participation in the peace process, in accordance with the six points"[130] it had presented to Shultz in April (see above). Jordan, Husayn continued, was a "major party" to the Arab-Israeli conflict and it would consequently assume both its particularly Jordanian and overall pan-Arab (*al-wataniyya wal-qawmiyya*) responsibility on that basis.[131]

Jordan had been a long-standing supporter of an international conference as the only suitable forum for negotiations for a comprehensive settlement. This support remained the case following the disengagement. Husayn, other Jordanian spokesmen, and the media repeatedly reaffirmed their position that Jordan, as a confrontation state with the longest border with Israel, still had an indispensable role, which it was "prepared to play to the fullest extent" under the auspices of such a conference in the future.[132] The conflict with Israel was "not only a Palestinian-Israeli conflict, but an Arab-Israeli conflict."[133] However, the option that Jordan would speak in the name of, or along with the Palestinians did not exist "at the moment," according to Husayn. Jordan's efforts to form a joint Jordanian-Palestinian delegation had not led anywhere; that effort, the king said, was "behind us now." Jordan and the PLO would both have to attend any future peace conference, but they would each do so independently unless the PLO "categorically" requested a different formula.[134]

In the wake of the *intifada* and Jordan's disengagement, the international conference assumed a significantly different role in Jordan's strategy regarding the ME peace process. Previously, the international conference had been intended by the Jordanians to serve as a vehicle for Palestinian, Arab, and international support for the central role that Jordan expected to play. If in the not too distant past the Jordanians had seen the conference as a useful framework for the necessary inclusion of the PLO alongside Jordan, it was now becoming a vital mechanism to prevent a PLO monopoly of the negotiating process and possible Jordanian exclusion.

The Jordanians admitted that they no longer pursued their former dualist approach, which held that Jordan's role in the peace process, as a state whose territory in the West Bank was occupied, did not conflict with PLO's role as the sole legitimate representative of the Palestinian people.[135] The Jordanians now reaffirmed, time and again, their lack of territorial ambition and their acceptance of the PLO's recognized representative status. Simultaneously, however, they also consistently condemned the notion of bilateral Palestinian-Israeli negotiations. This, they contended, was a form of "unilateral action" that contradicted the Arab consensus. Only negotiations in an international conference, where both Jordan and the PLO would be represented, were likely to "remove any possible apprehensions."[136] In the aftermath of the PNC (see also below) Jordan welcomed the notion of direct dialogue between the US and the PLO, but only as a necessary preparatory step for an international conference,[137] and certainly not as a substitute for it. The Jordanians, therefore, continued to urge the US, the USSR, the EEC, and the Arab states to work for the convening of an international conference, which, in their view, was "the only way to proceed" to establish comprehensive peace in the ME.[138] They were equally concerned to remind all and sundry of Jordan's "pivotal" role in the maintenance of regional stability, because of its proximity to the West Bank.[139]

Indeed, Jordan's unique association with Palestine continued to be highlighted after the disengagement in much the same terms as before. In his disengagement speech, Husayn stated that Jordan would never give up its support for the Palestinian cause, since "no one outside Palestine had, or could have," a closer association with Palestine than Jordan or the Hashemite family.[140] The Jordanians still maintained that a "special historic relationship," or "sacred historic unity" bound Jordan and the Palestinians, to the extent that it would be difficult even to contemplate separating the two peoples.[141] This immutable link would remain intact, because Jordan was a "natural demographic and geographic extension of the West Bank" and because Jordanians and Palestinians were "one people regardless of what is said."[142] This reality could not be affected by the fact that the PLO had now to assume complete responsibility for representing the Palestinians.[143] According to Crown Prince Hasan, the disengagement measures, however justified politically, were "not...aimed at the fiber of the relationship between Jordanians and Palestinians, either in the context of

Jordanian pluralism [on the East Bank] or in the context of East-West Bank relations."[144]

Moreover, the unity between Jordanians and Palestinians in Jordan's pluralistic society was, in Husayn's words, "a living example of the fusion (*indimaj*) between different Arab groups," which gave credence to the belief in the inevitable attainment of Arab unity. In the modern era, as the European model suggested, national self-expression (*al-dhat al-wataniyya*) did not conflict with the realization of "formulas of institutional unity" that could eventually unite all Arabs.[145] Husayn's vision of the future was based on the establishment of a "very close relationship" between Jordan and a Palestinian state and certainly did not exclude a Jordanian-Palestinian confederation.[146] However, in their hour of relative weakness, the Jordanians refrained from committing themselves in advance to the confederation formula.

The idea of confederation between two independent states was not a Jordanian idea but a PLO proposal. According to Raja'i al-Dajani this was a concept that encouraged regionalism rather than unity and Jordan believed only in "unionist formulas."[147] Since confederation was a contractual agreement between two states, detailed discussions of the matter would only be possible after the establishment of the independent Palestinian state.[148] Whether or not Jordan would enter into a confederation with a Palestinian state depended on the future balance of power between the two entities. Despite Jordanian statements in favor of independent Palestinian statehood, it would be safe to assume that Jordanian reservations and apprehensions in this regard had not disappeared. Jordan would presumably prefer a federation or confederation with an emasculated Palestinian entity rather than with a fully independent state, which could pose a serious irredentist threat to the kingdom.

The effect of Husayn's disengagement, however, was to shift the major onus of preemption and containment onto the shoulders of Israel and the US.

JORDAN, THE PLO, AND THE PNC RESOLUTIONS

Jordan's disengagement was a move directed at all the key players in the ME peace process, primarily the PLO, Israel, and the US.

As far as Israel and the US were concerned, the Jordanian objective was to finally convince them that the "Jordanian option" as they perceived it, i.e., a negotiating process that would circumvent the PLO, was unrealistic.[149] The Jordanians did not expect their decision to have any significant impact on the forthcoming US presidential elections. They did, however, entertain hopes that it would compel Israeli voters to recognize "the Palestinian number," and realize that they would have to talk to the PLO.[150]

But it was the PLO and the Palestinians in general who were the main target of the Jordanian decision. Jordan explained that it had to remove, once and for all, any remaining doubts and suspicions about its intentions regarding the West Bank and Jordan's commitment to the PLO's representative status. The Jordanians were, however, quick to point out that the PLO would henceforth be solely responsible for the consequences of the measures taken.[151] After all, as Husayn had noted repeatedly, and quite contemptuously, in his disengagement speech, Jordan's decision had been made according to the wishes of the PLO. This was not really the case. It could be argued, as the Jordanians did, that Jordan was simply abiding by the Arab consensus on the PLO, as reaffirmed at the behest of the PLO in Algiers. Husayn, however, had not consulted the PLO on the disengagement decision. Indeed, Husayn subsequently admitted that, since this decision pertained to Jordanian sovereignty, there was no need to consult anyone else about it.[152] Zayd al-Rifa'i remarked, with noticeable disdain, that Jordan had only offered the PLO what it had always insisted upon. "Consultation about what? Had we consulted the organization...would [the PLO] have refused?"[153] The lack of consultation with the PLO before a decision as momentous as the disengagement was as clear an indication as any of Jordan's ingrained hostility toward, and mistrust of the Palestinian leadership.

The Jordanians were obviously challenging the PLO to prove its diplomatic mettle and "live up to" its responsibility as the "sole legitimate representative" of the Palestinians. In the words of *Sawt al-Sha'b,* Jordan would support the PLO "as long as it faithfully and honestly serves the Palestinian cause. But [it] would not do so if the PLO became a burden on the people of Palestine."[154] Husayn expressed the hope that "the pressure of the events, particularly in the occupied territories, and the responsibilities that [Jordan had] chosen to give" the PLO, would contribute to the organization's "ability to come up with the right answers."[155] Jordan, he said, was waiting for the PLO's response to the disengagement decision. There would be "no quarter to blame but the PLO, if they fail to make up their minds and assume their responsibilities."[156]

The "right answers" from the Jordanian perspective were those that would give momentum to the peace process. These should include the acceptance by the PLO of the principle of partition, the acceptance of UN Resolution 242, and the recognition of Israel.[157] Shortly before the PNC in Algiers, a Jordanian official let it be known that Jordan expected a "positive attitude" from the PLO, especially in reference to UN Resolution 242.[158]

Jordan's position toward the PLO remained ambiguous after the disengagement. On the one hand, the Jordanians had resigned themselves to the PLO's reinforced status created by the *intifada.* On the other hand, they resented the rejection and denial of Jordan's role in Palestinian affairs by the PLO, by the leadership of the *intifada* and, consequently, by the Arab summit in Algiers. This duality in the Jordanian position led to inconsistencies, which suggested that the Jordanians themselves were in two minds about the desired PLO response to disengagement. Meeting Jordan's challenge by adopting the kind of resolutions that would pave the way for PLO involvement in the peace process would seemingly have been as welcome to the Jordanians as a PLO failure to live up to its new responsibility: the former could lead to a breakthrough in the peace process and a corresponding alleviation of Jordanian anxieties resulting from the prolonged stalemate; the latter would portray the PLO as an ineffective empty vessel, and give the Palestinians and the Arab world reason to reconsider their support for the organization. Husayn made a subtle allusion to this possibility in his disengagement speech. He explained that "as long as there was a collective [Arab] conviction" that Jordanian disengagement would serve the Palestinian cause, Jordan had no choice but to bow to this consensus.[159] This suggested that Jordan might adopt a different policy if this consensus proved impractical. Immediately after the disengagement, Husayn complained that Jordan had been "taken for granted by so many in this world."[160] These statements seemed to indicate that Jordan's move was motivated by expectations that a PLO failure to meet Jordan's challenge might eventually prove the importance of Jordan's role to those who had hitherto ignored it. Husayn himself, at the Algiers summit, had expressed his doubts about the wisdom of the Arab consensus (see above). After the disengagement, senior advisers to the king expressed similar reservations and "strongly hinted they had little faith in the ability of the PLO to do the job of negotiating an Israeli withdrawal or arriving at the creation of an independent Palestinian state."[161]

Moreover, in the initial phase following the disengagement, the Jordanians made a concerted effort to discredit and embarrass the PLO. Husayn himself set the tone in his speech by referring to the PLO's desire for "secession" (*infisal*) from Jordan.[162] In the political lexicon of Arab nationalism terms such as secessionism, regionalism, and isolationism were particularly derogatory. After the disengagement these were all hurled at the PLO, whose "tune had reached its secessionist peak" at the Algiers summit.[163] The government-controlled press abounded with articles accusing Yasir 'Arafat and the PLO of corruption, fickle leadership, confusion, indecision, deception, and even excessive moderation toward Israel.[164] At a time when senior Jordanian spokesmen were urging the PLO to adopt a more flexible policy toward Israel, the rather strident press campaign was, at least in part, a cynical exercise in obstructionism. But it may also have been deliberately designed as a form of pressure on the PLO not to be too flexible by agreeing, for example, to direct negotiations between the PLO and Israel, which could exclude Jordan altogether from the peace process.

Jordanian-PLO relations remained uncongenial. Husayn, nevertheless, had an interest in renewed coordination with the organization, albeit on a new, more symmetrical foundation than he had previously envisaged. The disengagement and the subsequent pressure tactics employed by the Jordanians were also intended to induce the PLO to recognize the relevance of Jordan to the day-to-day affairs of West Bankers, the peace process, and the ultimate solution of the Palestinian question. Hence, after the disengagement, Jordanian spokesmen frequently noted the need for renewed Jordanian-PLO political coordination. This, they explained, would be necessary for channeling support to the people in the West Bank and Gaza, but more so "for the sake of the Palestinian cause" in general.[165]

The tone of Jordanian statements on coordination with the PLO had changed radically in comparison to the period preceding the outbreak of the *intifada*. Jordan began to court the PLO, whereas previously Husayn had scornfully rejected 'Arafat's overtures (see *MECS* 1987, p. 502). In March, Husayn extended an invitation to 'Arafat to visit Jordan. 'Arafat would not bother, he had no intention whatsoever of assisting Husayn in extricating Jordan from its post-*intifada* predicament.

All the same, senior Jordanian and PLO officials held fairly regular meetings in Amman during the first half of the year. Consultations focused on the *intifada* and the Shultz initiative, but there was no sign of any new agreement. The Jordanian-PLO Joint Committee to Support the Steadfastness of the Occupied Territories also met on one occasion. But it was only after the disengagement that more substantive talks were held between the two parties.

The disengagement caught the PLO by surprise. It took the organization a few days to regain its composure before it dispatched a delegation to Amman to consult with the Jordanians on how to proceed with the implementation of the new decision. The delegation, headed by Mahmud 'Abbas (Abu Ma'zin) of the PLO Executive Committee, held talks in Amman from 11–14 August with the king, Rifa'i, and other cabinet ministers. Agreement was reached with relative ease on the measures to be taken with regard to such matters as passports, the open bridges, the freedom of travel, the export of goods from the West Bank to Jordan, and other administrative matters relating to the daily life of the people in the occupied territories. It was also agreed that the Jordanian-PLO Joint Committee to Support the Steadfastness of the Occupied Territories would continue to function.[166] Jordan had obtained PLO sanction not only for the disengagement steps to be taken, but also for the residual ties Jordan was to maintain with the West Bank.

One important and very sensitive problem, however, remained unsolved — the status of Jordanians of Palestinian origin who lived on the East Bank. In 1978, when Jordan and the PLO first resumed their formal dialogue after the Rabat resolutions, they arrived at an understanding according to which the PLO had agreed to respect "the principle of the state's sovereignty over its territories and people" (see *MECS* 1978–79, p. 640). To whom the Palestinians in Jordan owed their ultimate allegiance — to their government or to the PLO, their "sole legitimate representative" — was a latent question that arose yet again after the disengagement. Jordan and the PLO agreed that Jordanians of Palestinian origin were to be regarded as full Jordanian citizens in terms of rights and duties. This agreement, however, only papered over what remained a thorny and potentially explosive issue. For the PLO this understanding with Jordan was essentially a temporary arrangement. It did not infringe upon the Palestinian identity of these people, upon their right to return to Palestine, or to exercise self-determination — a right which applied to all Palestinians wherever they were, and not only to those in the occupied territories. Accepting the "Jordanization" of these Palestinians, in the PLO view, was tantamount to acquiescence in their permanent resettlement (*tawtin*) outside Palestine and the abandonment of their national rights. As for Jordan, despite the lip service it paid to the notion that Jordanian citizenship for these Palestinians did not compromise their legitimate rights as Palestinians, it regarded their Jordanian identity and loyalty to the Jordanian State as a permanent and essential prerequisite for its national unity and domestic stability.[167]

Both Jordan and the PLO preferred, at this juncture, to avoid open conflict over this delicate question. They therefore agreed, in effect, to disagree and let the matter rest for the time being.

In the first few months after the disengagement, an air of tension characterized the generally cool relationship between Jordan and the PLO. But it soon gave way to a marked improvement as the PLO launched its new diplomatic offensive. At the end of October, 'Arafat joined President Husni Mubarak of Egypt, on a visit to 'Aqaba for talks with Husayn. This was 'Arafat's first visit to Jordan in nearly a year (see also chapters on Egypt and the Palestine Liberation Organization).

According to Jordanian sources, Husayn had laid special emphasis in the talks on the need to convene an international conference as the only way to achieve comprehensive, just, and lasting peace in the area. The talks had also stressed the importance of enhancing "the special distinguished relationship between the Jordanian and Palestinian peoples."[168] 'Arafat expressed the PLO's support for a confederation between Jordan and an independent Palestine; Husayn, however, remained noncommittal. He contended that any discussion of a confederation between Jordan and a future Palestinian state was "premature until the situation crystallizes in a better way to enable us to discuss relations between members of the Palestinian and Jordanian family."[169]

The resolutions of the PNC, held in Algiers in November, and the declaration of Palestinian independence (see chapter on the Palestine Liberation Organization) were well received in Jordan. The PLO, according to Husayn, was "shouldering its responsibilities" and had demonstrated its willingness to join in an "historic reconciliation between Arabs and Israelis."[170] Jordan immediately declared its support for the resolutions and recognized the independent Palestinian state.[171] The PLO's acceptance of the principle of partition and its endorsement of Resolutions 242 and 338 had paved the way for convening an international conference.[172] The PNC, according to Husayn, had finally accepted the US conditions for the incorporation of the organization into the peace process. The ball was now in the US and Israeli court, and it was incumbent upon them to respond positively to the PLO move.[173] The initial US response, which described the PNC resolutions as inadequate, and the subsequent American refusal to grant 'Arafat an entry visa to the US (see chapter on the United States and the Middle East), were condemned by Husayn as an attempt at "stifling the voice of Palestinian moderation."[174]

In late November 'Arafat held talks with Husayn in Amman and, at the same time, Jordan and Egypt agreed to spearhead a collective Arab bid to move the session of the UN General Assembly from New York to Geneva to enable 'Arafat to address the UN body.[175] Following 'Arafat's Geneva speech and press conference, and the US decision to enter into a "substantive dialogue" with the PLO, Jordan, with certain justification, claimed credit for having played a major role in bringing this new reality into being.[176]

Husayn maintained that relations with the PLO were now "extremely close" and "probably better than they [had] ever been, without the suspicions and doubts of the past."[177] This was probably more than a slight exaggeration, yet it truly reflected Jordan's fears of exclusion and its interest in coordination with the PLO. Such coordination, according to *al-Ra'y*, was extremely important, because of the "bonds uniting the two peoples" and because both Jordan and the PLO were essential parties to any peace settlement.[178]

THE DOMESTIC RAMIFICATIONS OF THE *INTIFADA* AND THE DISENGAGEMENT

THE ATTEMPTED INVIGORATION OF JORDANIAN CONSCIOUSNESS

The *intifada* "raised the political temperature within Jordan itself, reigniting old tensions"[179] between Jordanians and the large Palestinian community, which constituted about half of the entire population.[180] The Jordanian authorities were consequently concerned that rising Palestinian national sentiment could "undermine the sense of Jordanian identity," which Jordan had tried to foster by blurring the distinction between East Bankers and West Bankers.[181]

During the year, the Jordanians appeared to be making a concerted effort to reinforce the distinctive sense of Jordanian national pride and consciousness. The new Cabinet formed by Rifa'i in January (see below) included a new portfolio for "culture and national heritage." The series of speeches made by Husayn in April and May, outlining Jordan's new positions on Palestine (see above), contained numerous references to the achievements of the Jordanian State in all walks of life despite the adverse circumstances in which Jordan had had to function over the years. Husayn placed special emphasis on the impressive development of Jordan's armed forces, but also elaborated upon Jordan's achievements in other spheres such as education,[182] health care, and other public services. All Jordanians, "regardless of where any person who joined this family came from or [where] his fathers and forefathers [had come from]," were expected to work as a "united family" to preserve this Jordanian entity.[183]

In an effort to discredit his domestic opponents, Husayn denounced the use of the term "patriotic forces" to denote politically active groups in the country. Since this was a term employed by predominantly Palestinian opposition groups, Husayn contended that no group had the right to insinuate that others in the country were unpatriotic. Moreover, he suggested, activism and patriotism were not necessarily synonymous, and some of these self-styled patriots might very well be serving foreign forces.[184]

Jordanian anxieties resulting from the *intifada* were exacerbated by Husayn's fears that Israel, under the persistent pressure of the Palestinian uprising, might be tempted to carry out a "transfer" of hundreds of thousands of Palestinians as openly advocated by the extreme right wing in the Israeli political spectrum (see chapter on Israel). Jordanians conceded that the idea of such a "transfer" to Jordan "haunted" them. It would upset the demographic balance in Jordan and could pose a very serious threat to the regime.[185]

The disengagement was intended, at least in part, to clarify to Palestinians, Israelis, and everyone else that Jordan was not Palestine and that Palestinian national aspirations could only be satisfied west of the river, in Palestine itself.[186] Without denying their historic association with Palestine, the Jordanians sought to emphasize that Jordan was a legitimate entity in its own right and not an "alternative homeland" for the Palestinians. Jordan, according to Crown Prince Hasan, was "not the alternative repository for the Palestinian people." It was "not waste land."[187] Opening a coin museum in Amman in November, Husayn maintained that the collection of "coins minted in Jordan from the dawn of history" was testimony to the fact that Jordan, throughout the ages, had been "a wellspring of civilization, development, and prosperity."[188]

In his disengagement speech, Husayn stressed that the new measures in regard to the West Bank would have no effect on "Jordanian citizens of Palestinian extraction" on the East Bank. They would continue to enjoy all the rights and be bound by all the obligations of citizenship, as an integral part of the Jordanian State.[189] National unity (*al-wahda al-wataniyya*), the king continued, was the very foundation of Jordan's stability and security. Any attempt to infringe upon it, under whatever pretense, would only assist the "enemy to implement his expansionist policy at the expense of Palestine and Jordan."[190] In the same vein, Crown Prince Hasan asserted that "through joint action, commitment and dedication, and [the promotion of] a true sense of national belonging," the "Jordanian family" would be able to "attain the national goals and aspirations of the Great Arab Revolt,"[191] led by the Hashemites in the First World War.

In an effort to dismiss the notion that Jordan was actually a Palestinian state with a Palestinian majority, Husayn repeatedly disputed the figures. He argued that Jordanians of Palestinian extraction were less than 40% of the East Bank population.[192] Moreover, these Palestinians, the Jordanians insisted, were represented solely by the Jordanian Government and not by the PLO.[193] In accordance with this logic, the Jordanian Interior Ministry reportedly decided in October to issue two-year "temporary" passports to all Palestinian deportees from the West Bank and members of the PNC who resided in Jordan, i.e., placing them on the same footing as West Bankers who were no longer Jordanian citizens.[194]

Following the disengagement, the Jordanians also gave unprecedented publicity to the fact that Palestinian refugee camps were being integrated into the cities. The policy itself was not new, but the publicity was a novelty, which lent added emphasis to the Jordanian line that all Palestinians in Jordan were Jordanian citizens in the full sense of the word. According to UN Relief Works Agency figures, the number of refugees actually residing in camps was c. 250,000.[195] This figure included refugees (*laji'in*) from 1948 and displaced persons (*nazihin*) from 1967, and was less than a third of the overall number of refugees in Jordan. Over the years, the majority had resettled outside the camps.

Jordan's new approach was not free of internal contradiction. It was difficult to maintain, at one and the same time, that Palestinians were Jordanians if they happened to live on the East Bank, and that they were not if they resided on the West Bank. This distinction was particularly difficult to uphold in the case of the numerous families, whose members lived on different sides of the river. It was equally complicated to disengage from the West Bank, with the declared objective of promoting a Jordanian consciousness, while simultaneously reiterating the historic and inseparable bond uniting Palestinians and Jordanians as one people.

It was this confusion that tended, at least initially, to erode the confidence of Palestinians in their future in Jordan. Tensions between East Bankers and Palestinians were not alleviated. In mid-December, they surfaced in the form of violent clashes between Palestinian and Jordanian students at the University of Jordan in Amman. Palestinians marching in support of the *intifada* were confronted by Jordanians chanting slogans in favor of Husayn. At least one student was injured in the ensuing brawl.[196]

If the disengagement was intended to further the "building [of] the contemporary Jordanian State...[as] an oasis for security and stability for all its citizens,"[197] in the short term at least it was having a questionable effect.

DOMESTIC TENSIONS AND THE TIGHTENING GRIP OF GOVERNMENT

During the year, Jordan's economy, which had been in the throes of recession since the early 1980s, plunged into a deep crisis characterized by a falling dinar, rising unemployment, and a massive foreign debt. (For a detailed analysis, see chapter "Jordan's Economy: From Prosperity to Crisis.") Tensions arising from the *intifada*, coupled with a depressed economy, thrust Jordan into its worst domestic crisis since the civil war of 1970–71.

Jordan was a more open society than its Arab neighbors, and its government was usually less intrusive and repressive than in countries like Syria or Iraq. However, under the premiership of Zayd al-Rifa'i the heavy hand of government became increasingly visible, tightening its control over the press and political life in general (see *MECS* 1984–85, pp. 510–12; 1986, pp. 427–28, 437–38; 1987, pp. 492–93), by exploiting the existence of martial law, in force since 1967.[198] Under the impact of the *intifada* and Jordan's economic woes, the systematic effort of the government to reinforce its control became all the more evident.

In August, in order "to bolster the national role" of Jordan's press, the government dissolved the boards of directors of the three dailies, *al-Dustur, al-Ra'y*, and *Sawt al-Sha'b*. Temporary administrative committees were appointed to run the papers for the next two years.[199] In meetings with representatives of the press, Crown Prince Hasan and Prime Minister Rifa'i emphasized the role of the press in "increasing public participation in building the homeland" and the consequent need for "constructive criticism," a "responsible [sense of] freedom and genuine patriotism," and "accuracy in publishing news" that would avoid "sensationalism and unreliable reports or those attributed to irresponsible sources."[200] At the end of October, Husayn visited the offices of each of the three dailies where he "gave his directives to develop the journalistic process."[201]

Nor was the government very tolerant toward the foreign press. NBC's Rick Davis was ordered to leave the country at the end of April after having filed a report in which he compared Israeli and Jordanian treatment of the Palestinians. Davis had also referred to Jordan as a "tightly controlled and at times even repressive society." Two local journalists, who also worked for American news organizations, had their credentials withdrawn.[202]

Government intrusion, however, did not stifle public discussion. In the aftermath of the disengagement, the debate was said to have been "unusually vigorous...among an anxious local elite."[203] Husayn's decision to disengage from the West Bank met with criticism from left-wing intellectuals, members of the various professional associations, and the banned political parties in Jordan. More than 200 people affiliated with these generally pro-PLO groups signed a statement passed on to Reuters in early October, criticizing Husayn for having made a decision that could jeopardize the chances of all Palestinians to exercise their national rights. Jordan's decision, they said, had paved the way for the final resettlement of the Palestinians in Jordan, outside of their homeland. Furthermore, Husayn had failed to consult the public before making his historic decision. They took this opportunity to renew their long-standing demand for democratization of the political system, joining others who were calling for the revival of political parties banned since 1957.[204]

The measures adopted by the government to implement the disengagement decision fanned uncertainty amongst Palestinians in Jordan and the West Bank about their future relationship with the Jordanian State. Economic jitters resulted in flight from the Jordanian dinar and large withdrawals of savings from Jordanian banks. According to a Western official, the king's announcement came when the economy was "already going down." It was "really the last thing they needed in terms of the effect on confidence."[205] It was estimated that West Bankers withdrew between $200m.–$300m. from Jordanian banks shortly after the disengagement. With reserves at the Central Bank down to $28m., the government was unable to intervene effectively to save the plummeting dinar, which lost about half of its dollar value during 1988. Remittances from Jordanians of Palestinian extraction, who were the majority of Jordan's expatriate work force, also dropped. This was due to a combination of factors, the most important of which was the recession in the Arab oil states, but the disengagement had a negative impact as well.[206]

Jordan's severe domestic crisis was reflected in the frequent reshuffling of Rifa'i's Cabinet (see Table 1). Rifa'i himself became the target of growing public censure, which focused on the corruption and financial mismanagement of his government.[207]

Husayn, however, unwilling to appear to be bowing to pressure from below, kept his good boyhood friend in office. In a reshuffle in January, three new portfolios were created: for water and irrigation, culture and national heritage, and housing, which was added to the portfolio for public works. In August, following the disengagement, a minor reshuffle took place with the abolition of the Ministry for Occupied Territory Affairs and the division of the Ministry of Labor and Social Development and the Ministry of Supply, Industry, and Trade, each into two separate ministries (see Table 1). The ratio of Palestinians in the Cabinet, just below half, was maintained in the August reshuffle. However, when the Cabinet was reshuffled again in December, the

TABLE 1: JORDANIAN CABINET CHANGES IN 1988*

Portfolio	*9 January*	*6 August*	*19 December*
Prime Minister and Defense	Zayd al-Rifa'i	Zayd al-Rifa'i	Zayd al-Rifa'i
Deputy Prime Minister and Education	Dhuqan al-Hindawi	Dhuqan al-Hindawi	Dhuqan al-Hindawi
Minister of State for Premiership Affairs	Fa'iz al-Tarawna	Fa'iz al-Tarawna	Zuhayr al-'Ajluni
Minister of State for Premiership Affairs	—	—	'Abd al-Salam Kan'an (P)
Minister of State for Parliamentary Affairs	Sami Jawda (P)	Sami Jawda (P)	—
Interior	Raja'i al-Dajani (P)	Raja'i al-Dajani (P)	Raja'i al-Dajani (P)
Labor)[a]	Rashid 'Urayqat (P)	Marwan Dudin (P)	Marwan Dudin (P)
Social Development)	Rashid 'Urayqat (P)	Fawwaz Tuqan (P)	Fawwaz Tuqan (P)
Foreign Affairs	Tahir al-Masri (P)	Tahir al-Masri (P)	Marwan al-Qasim[d]
Municipal, Rural, and Environmental Affairs	Yusuf Hamdan	Yusuf Hamdan	Marwan al-Humud
Awqaf, Religious Affairs, and Holy Places	'Abd al-'Aziz al-Khayyat (P)	'Abd al-'Aziz al-Khayyat (P)	'Abd al-'Aziz al-Khayyat (P)
Public Works and Housing	Shafiq Zuwayda	Shafiq Zuwayda	Shafiq Zuwayda
Supply)[a]	Hamdi al-Tabba'	'Abd al-Salam Kan'an (P)	Fa'iz al-Tarawna
Industry and Trade)	Hamdi al-Tabba'[a]	Hamdi al-Tabba'	Hamdi al-Tabba'
Transport and Communications	Khalid al-Hajj Hasan	Khalid al-Hajj Hasan	Khalid al-Hajj Hasan
Finance (and Customs)[b]	Hanna 'Awda (P)	Hanna 'Awda (P)	Hanna 'Awda (P)
Energy and Mineral Wealth	Hisham al-Khatib (P)	Hisham al-Khatib (P)	Hisham al-Khatib (P)
Planning	Tahir Kan'an (P)	Tahir Kan'an (P)	Tahir Kan'an (P)
Higher Education	Nasir al-Din al-Asad	Nasir al-Din al-Asad	Nasir al-Din al-Asad
Agriculture	Marwan al-Humud	Marwan al-Humud	Yusuf Hamdan
Information	Hani al-Khasawna	Hani al-Khasawna	Hani al-Khasawna
Culture and National Heritage	Muhammad al-Hammuri	Muhammad al-Hammuri	Muhammad al-Hammuri
Tourism	Zuhayr al-'Ajluni	Zuhayr al-'Ajluni	Yanal Hikmat
Justice	Riyad al-Shak'a (P)	Riyad al-Shak'a (P)	Riyad al-Shak'a (P)
Health	Zayd Hamza	Zayd Hamza	Zuhayr Malhas
Occupied Territory Affairs[c]	Marwan Dudin (P)	—	—
Youth	'Awad Khulayfat	'Awad Khulayfat	'Awad Khulayfat
Water and Irrigation	Ahmad Dakhqan	Ahmad Dakhqan	Ahmad Dakhqan

* For previous reshuffles, see *MECS* 1986, pp. 459–60.

(P) Palestinian origin.

[a] One portfolio divided into two in August.

[b] Customs added in December Cabinet.

[c] Abolished in August.

[d] Also deputy prime minister.

number of Palestinian ministers was reduced to about one third, probably as an indication of Jordan's realization, after the PNC, that the PLO was indeed "shouldering its responsibilities."

The December reshuffle was accompanied by important changes in the palace, which were also a sign of the times. The king's cousin, FM Zayd Ibn Shakir, the commander in chief of the armed forces since 1976, was appointed chief of the royal court, replacing Marwan al-Qasim who became deputy premier and foreign minister. The position of commander in chief was abolished. Chief of Staff, Fathi Abu Talib now became the senior officer responsible for the armed forces, while Ibn Shakir assumed the additional and new post of adviser to the king for armed forces affairs. Another former senior officer, 'Amir Khammash, Jordan's chief of staff in the 1967 war, and subsequently a minister of defense, minister of court, and member of the Senate, was appointed as special adviser to the king. The position of minister of court was abolished and 'Adnan Abu 'Awda, who had held this title since 1984, assumed the new post of adviser for political affairs. The appointment of the Palestinian Abu 'Awda, who had been a very close adviser to the king for many years and a supporter of Jordan's involvement in Palestinian affairs, was an indication of Husayn's continued interest in the peace process and the ultimate settlement of the Palestinian question. However, the elevation of the two senior military men to positions in the palace reflected the king's more immediate concern with matters pertaining to the security of the East Bank kingdom in its hour of domestic trial.

JORDAN IN THE ARAB ARENA

As in other spheres, the *intifada* also had a negative impact on Jordan's inter-Arab stature. This was clearly evident in June at the Arab summit in Algiers (see above, and chapter on inter-Arab relations), where Husayn failed to make any headway in his quest for Arab recognition for a Jordanian role in the Palestinian question. Jordan's humiliation at Algiers stood in stark contrast to Husayn's sense of satisfaction at the previous Arab summit held in Amman, only weeks before the outbreak of the *intifada* (see *MECS* 1987, pp. 506–7). After years of decline, the uprising had clearly reestablished the PLO's inter-Arab position, very much at Jordan's expense.

Well aware of the group dynamics of Arab summitry, Jordan showed little enthusiasm for an Arab summit dedicated solely to the *intifada*. The Jordanians suggested that there was no pressing need for another summit so soon after the one held in Amman in November 1987. What was needed, they argued, was Arab consultation that would allow the Arab states and the PLO to formulate a common stand on the Shultz initiative,[208] and this did not necessarily require a summit. Needless to say, the Jordanians did not have their way.

Husayn's disengagement decision was accompanied by Jordanian resolve to assume a leading role in Arab efforts toward greater political unity. Husayn, who believed that there was "nothing harder than isolation,"[209] seemed to have come to the conclusion that, if constrained on Palestine, Jordan should bolster its Hashemite legitimacy on the Arab unity front as the geopolitical pivot of inter-Arab cooperation. In his disengagement speech, Husayn had already alluded to the EEC as the example the Arabs ought to follow.[210] In the ensuing months there was a flurry of reports and statements emanating from Jordan on the need for a new grouping of Arab states in the *Mashriq,* along the lines of the Gulf Cooperation Council or the proposed alignment of *Maghrib* states. In December, Husayn revealed that Jordan was negotiating with Iraq, Egypt, North Yemen, and Syria on a cooperation formula.

One of Jordan's major objectives in fostering greater Arab cooperation was to extricate itself from its economic crisis. Husayn noted that Arab economic coordination would "undoubtedly improve the distribution of Arab wealth and raise the standard of living in the Arab world."[211] The Jordanians often complained that their enormous foreign debt amounted to less than the unhonored pledges of aid made to Jordan at the Baghdad summit in 1978. Only Saudi Arabia had fulfilled its commitments.[212]

Jordan's reduced room for maneuver on the Palestine question did not affect its bilateral relations with the various Arab states. Jordan continued to maintain good relations with all the key Arab states — Egypt, Iraq, Syria,and Saudi Arabia.

Jordan had developed a close liaison with Egypt. Husayn and Mubarak conferred frequently to coordinate their positions on the ME peace process and other regional affairs such as the Gulf War. Mubarak's consistent support for Jordanian-PLO coordination in the peace process was appreciated by Husayn. Jordan's relentless effort to have Egypt readmitted to the Arab League was a clear indication of Husayn's belief that Egypt's assumption of a leading role in Arab politics would benefit Jordan. A steady trade relationship was also developing between the two countries. In May, they signed a trade protocol for 1988, according to which the volume of bilateral trade was to reach $250m. Studies were also undertaken for the linking of the national grids of the two countries by 1993 (see also chapter on Egypt).

Jordan had consistently supported Iraq throughout the Gulf War and a firm rapport had developed over the years between King Husayn and President Saddam Husayn. The cessation of the Gulf War, however, was a mixed blessing for Jordan. On the one hand, the Jordanians were finally relieved of their fears of Iranian revolutionary expansionism. Moreover, Iraqi military power could now be seen by the Jordanians as an effective deterrent against Israel. Jordan profited immediately from Iraqi goodwill, in the form of a gift of over 200 tanks and armored personnel carriers captured from Iran and handed over to the Jordanian armed forces. On the other hand, it meant reduced Iraqi dependence on Jordan's logistic facilities and the potential development of Iraq into a regional superpower with aspirations of domination in the Fertile Crescent. King Husayn's dismissal of the fears that "some people" in the West had of Iraqi power and his reference to Iraqi assurances of commitment to those who had supported Iraq in the war,[213] spoke for themselves.

The potential economic impact of the Gulf cease-fire was also not uniform. The Jordanians hoped that Iraqi rehabilitation would pave the way for new outlets for Jordanian manpower, more exports to Iraq, and for Iraqi investment in Jordan, not to mention the payment of an Iraqi debt to Jordan of over JD200m. However, on the negative side, Jordanian anxieties were aroused by early indications that the Iraqis were to cut back on their use of 'Aqaba port and the related transit business that had developed in leaps and bounds during the war years, to Jordan's benefit. In December, it was reported that Jordan and Iraq had set up a standing committee to ensure the continuous flow of Iraqi goods to and from 'Aqaba. The Iraqis, nevertheless, decided shortly thereafter to cease the export of crude oil through 'Aqaba and the idea of laying a pipeline from Iraqi oil fields to 'Aqaba was dropped.

The relationship with Syria was somewhat less intensive than that nurtured by Jordan with Egypt and Iraq. Asad and Husayn conferred less regularly, but Prime Minister Rifa'i made frequent trips to Damascus. Relations remained correct despite Jordan's close alliance with Iraq and Egypt. Jordan's efforts to mediate between Syria, Iraq, and Egypt, and thus release itself from the dangers of potential confrontation with Syria, did not bear much fruit.

At the end of the year, Jordan resumed its efforts to have the Arab League abandon the practice of consensus and opt for majority decision making.[214] This move suggested Jordanian disappointment with Syrian obstructionism and veto power in the Arab arena.

Jordan and Syria continued their preparatory negotiations and joint planning for the construction of the Wahda Dam on the Yarmuk River that was intended to serve both countries. The 100-meter-high dam was planned to store 225m. cu. meters of water to be used for drinking, irrigation, and the generation of electricity.[215] Construction of the $440m. project[216] was expected to be completed in the early 1990s. Jordan was to exploit most of the dam's water supply while Syria was to have 75% of the hydroelectric power generated. Jordan and Syria were also involved in negotiations for the linking of their national grids.

As with his other Arab neighbors, Husayn also regularly consulted with Saudi Arabia's King Fahd on regional issues. Jordan's traditionally friendly ties with Saudi Arabia assumed growing importance as Jordan's economic woes increased. Saudi Arabia was Jordan's most reliable source of financial support in the Arab world. It was the only Arab state that had actually paid up its annual commitments to Jordan, as decided upon at the Baghdad summit in 1978. Jordan had received $300m. a year from the Saudis.

Jordan was also fostering an important economic link, though of a different sort, with North Yemen. Rising unemployment, particularly severe amongst Jordan's professionals, prompted Jordan to seek new outlets for its skilled manpower. One of these was North Yemen. In February, agreement was reached on a Yemeni request for the services of 500 Jordanian teachers, 60 engineers, and some 300 doctors and specialists.

JORDAN AND THE GREAT POWERS

As in recent years, Jordan, though still a regional ally of the US, continued to express deep disappointment with US policy in the ME (see *MECS* 1987, p. 508). Jordanian spokesmen and media repeatedly accused the Reagan Administration not only of siding with Israel, but also of being under the influence of the right wing of the divided Israeli Government. The Jordanians urged the US to put pressure on Israel rather than on the Arabs, if progress was to be achieved in the peace process. The US, Husayn contended, had lost its credibility in the eyes of the Arabs,[217] because of its pro-Israeli bias. A wide-ranging memorandum of agreement, signed in April between Israel and the US, was described by Husayn as "disturbing, shocking, and disappointing."[218] Jordan also criticized the US decision in March to close down the offices of the PLO mission to the UN in New York and condemned US vetoes of anti-Israeli resolutions in the Security Council.

The US aid package to Jordan of $100m. ($60m. for military purchases and $40m.

for economic aid) was approved by the US Senate Appropriations Committee in June for the forthcoming fiscal year. The level of aid was seen in Jordan as yet another example of Washington's bias in Israel's favor, considering that Israel received $3bn. annually from the US.[219]

As he had done in 1987 (see *MECS* 1987, p. 508), Husayn again declined a US invitation to visit Washington. However, toward the end of the year, a certain improvement was discernible in the troubled relationship. US Secretary of Defense Frank Carlucci visited Jordan in October for what were described by a US official as "warm and cordial" talks. Both sides were said to be interested in "maintaining a long and close relationship."[220] There was no question of Jordan changing its basically pro-US orientation.

The election of George Bush as President was welcomed in Jordan. The consensus in Israel, that the new Administration was likely to be less sympathetic toward it, was seen in Jordan as a good cause for "relative Arab satisfaction."[221]

Jordan's relations with the Soviet Union continued to improve. Husayn had received an "excellent impression" of the new leadership in the Kremlin during his visit to Moscow in December 1987 (see *MECS* 1987, pp. 509–10). Husayn spoke highly of the "new dynamic leadership" that was willing to give and take and to play a constructive role in the achievement of world peace.[222]

The steadily improving relationship with the Soviet Union was a function of a growing Jordanian sense of reassurance that Soviet objectives in the area were not subversive. As 'Adnan Abu 'Awda observed, the policy of the Soviet Union in the area had evolved from one which appeared to be based on dealings with parties to one of dealing with existing governments.[223]

The Jordanians often drew attention to the fact that Soviet policy on the ME conflict was considerably more supportive of the Arab position than that of the US. Crown Prince Hasan even went so far as to suggest that the Soviet Union ought to have "veto and arbitration" powers at a future international conference.[224] Both Jordan and the Soviet Union welcomed the PNC resolutions for having removed the obstacles to an international conference. They seemed to be equally concerned that the US-PLO dialogue might lead to a negotiation process from which they could be excluded. Jordan and the Soviet Union were now probably the two parties most interested in an international conference.

Though Jordan's relations with the Soviet Union had improved steadily since the 1970s, including the conclusion of some important arms deals, the Jordanians were still reluctant to become overdependent on the USSR. Jordan had considered purchasing the Mig-29 fighter aircraft but eventually opted for a European alternative.

Jordan's relations with Western Europe revolved around two key issues: the role of the West Europeans in bringing about a shift in US policy in the ME, and arms procurement.

During the year, Husayn paid visits to major European capitals — Paris, Rome, London, Bonn, and Vienna — in a concerted effort to secure European support for an international conference and to encourage European pressure on the US to do likewise.

Following Jordan's failure to purchase advanced fighter aircraft from the US (see *MECS* 1984–85, p. 521) and its reluctance to purchase such systems from the USSR, Western Europe was becoming an increasingly important arms supplier to Jordan. In

February, agreement was reached between Jordan and France for the sale of 12 *Mirage* 2000 fighter aircraft (with an option to purchase another eight) and for the modernization of 15 *Mirage* F-1 fighters already in service with the Jordanian Air Force. In September, it was reported that Jordan had also signed an agreement with Britain to purchase *Tornado* ground-attack aircraft, manufactured jointly by Britain, West Germany, and Italy.

NOTES

For the place and frequency of publications cited here, and for the full name of the publication, news agency, radio station, or monitoring service where an abbreviation is used, please see "List of Sources." Only in the case of more than one publication bearing the same name is the place of publication noted here.

1. *Al-Dustur,* Amman, 28 January 1988.
2. E.g., *al-Dustur,* Amman, 6, 13, 18 January; JNA, 7 January — SWB, 11 January; Jordan TV, 13 January — DR, 14 January; *JT,* 19 January, 19 April 1988.
3. *JT,* 26 January, 30 March; *Akhbar al-Usbu',* 11 February; R. Amman, 12 April — DR, 14 April 1988.
4. E.g., *al-Nashra,* Athens, 11 January, 22 February, 21 March; *NYT,* 25 January, 7 February, 9 May; *Ma'ariv,* 26 January; *Yedi'ot Aharonot,* 18 March 1988.
5. R. Monte Carlo, 18 December — DR, 19 December 1988.
6. *NYT,* 7 February; *JT,* 9 February 1988.
7. *JT,* 4 December 1988.
8. *JT,* 15 March, 12 July 1988.
9. *Ha'aretz,* 27 October 1988.
10. *Al-Dustur,* Amman, 26 February; *The Guardian,* 8 April 1988.
11. R. Monte Carlo, 11 April — DR, 11 April 1988.
12. *JT,* 10 February 1988.
13. Tahir al-Masri to *El Pais,* 5 June — DR, 23 June 1988.
14. Husayn to *al-Qabas,* 11 May; Crown Prince Hasan on Jordan TV, 24 May — DR, 27 May 1988.
15. *NYT,* 8 January 1988.
16. Zayd al-Rifa'i quoted in *JT,* 4 January; Husayn on Jordan TV, 14 January — DR, 15 January 1988.
17. *NYT,* 8 January 1988.
18. Jordan TV, 29 January — DR, 1 February 1988.
19. Husayn to *Der Spiegel,* 1 February — DR, 3 February; Marwan Dudin in *JT,* 23 February 1988.
20. Shaul Mishal with Reuben Aharoni, *Speaking Stones; The Words behind the Palestinian Intifada* (Tel Aviv: HaKibbutz Hameuchad, 1989; in Hebrew).
21. R. Amman, 13 March — DR, 14 March 1988.
22. *IHT,* 12 August 1988.
23. R. Amman, 3 May — DR, 6 May; JNA, 10 May — DR, 11 May 1988.
24. Hani al-Khasawna to *al-Dustur,* London, 8 August 1988.
25. *Al-Mustaqbal,* 6 August 1988.
26. *Der Spiegel,* 1 February — DR, 3 February 1988.
27. *Time,* 2 May 1988.
28. Rifa'i in *JT,* 4 January; Husayn on Jordan TV, 14 January — DR, 15 January; Tahir al-Masri in *al-Ra'y*, 25 January 1988.
29. Husayn on Jordan TV, 29 January — DR, 1 February 1988.
30. Husayn on Jordan TV, 14 January — DR, 15 January 1988.
31. *JT,* 4 January 1988.
32. Jordan TV, 14 January — DR, 15 January 1988.
33. *The Times,* 12 February 1988.

34. *Al-Ra'y*, 24 January 1988.
35. *The Times*, 12 February 1988.
36. Rifa'i in *JT*, 6 February; similarly *The Times*, 12 February 1988.
37. Husayn to *Der Spiegel*, 1 February — DR, 3 February 1988.
38. Rifa'i in *JT*, 6 February 1988.
39. Rifa'i in *The Times*, 12 February and in *JT*, 17 February 1988.
40. E.g., Rifa'i in *JT*, 6 February; editorial in *al-Ra'y*, 7 February 1988.
41. R. Amman, 27 February — DR, 29 February 1988.
42. *NYT*, 1 March; *Al-Sharq al-Awsat*, 27 March 1988.
43. R. Monte Carlo, 11 March — DR, 14 March; *JT*, 15 March 1988.
44. *JT*, 15 March 1988.
45. *NYT*, 1 March; R. Monte Carlo, 1 March — DR, 2 March 1988.
46. *JT*, 6 April 1988.
47. *Al-Sharq al-Awsat*, 7 April 1988.
48. R. Monte Carlo, 6 April — DR, 6 April 1988.
49. *JT*, 6 April 1988.
50. *Al-Sharq al-Awsat*, 7 April 1988.
51. *JT*, 9 April 1988.
52. Ibid.
53. Ibid.
54. Ibid; R. Amman, 11 April — DR, 12 April 1988.
55. Ibid.
56. *FT*, 7 April; *al-Mustaqbal*, 9 April 1988.
57. *JT*, 9 April 1988.
58. *JT*, 15 March, 6 April 1988.
59. *NYT*, 9 May 1988.
60. *JT*, 26-27 May 1988.
61. *NYT*, 9 May; *al-Qabas*, 25 May; R. Monte Carlo, 26 May — DR, 27 May 1988.
62. *FT*, 25 May 1988.
63. *JT*, 8 June 1988.
64. Official Arabic text of Husayn's speech given at the Algiers summit on 7 June 1988, p. 29 (Dayan Center Archives).
65. E.g., 'Abdallah Salah, Jordan's representative at the UN, in *JT*, 28–29 January; Minister of Information Hani al-Khasawna quoted by GNA, 20 February — DR, 22 February 1988.
66. *Al-Tadamun*, 2 January 1988.
67. Jordan TV, 29 January — DR, 1 February; *Der Spiegel*, 1 February — DR, 3 February 1988.
68. *The Times*, 12 February 1988.
69. R. Monte Carlo, 11 April — DR, 12 April 1988.
70. E.g., Husayn in *iftar* speech at Mafraq on 4 May — *al-Ra'y*, 5 May 1988.
71. Husayn in *iftar* speeches at Salt on 2 May and Mafraq on 4 May — *JT*, 3 May, *al Ra'y*, 5 May 1988.
72. *Al-Majalla*, 25–31 May 1988; similarly Minister of Information Hani al-Khasawna in *al-Dustur*, Amman, 21 May 1988.
73. Husayn quoted by JNA, 10 May — DR, 11 May 1988.
74. Abu 'Awda in *al-Majalla*, 25–31 May 1988.
75. Official Arabic text of Husayn's speech given at the Algiers summit on 7 June 1988, pp. 11–13 (Dayan Center Archives). Needless to say, Husayn's discussion of this issue is partisan, making no mention, of course, of Jordanian manipulation of the Palestinians at that juncture.
76. Ibid., pp. 13–15.
77. Ibid., p. 31.
78. Ibid., p. 33.
79. *Al-Qabas*, 11 May 1988.
80. Husayn's speech at Algiers, ibid., p. 34.
81. In statements made shortly before the summit, Husayn referred repeatedly to the federation formula as "the ideal pattern for what we seek to achieve." *Al-Dustur*, Amman, 9 May; similarly, *al-Qabas*, 11 May 1988.

82. Husayn's speech at Algiers, ibid., pp. 38–39.
83. Ibid., pp. 40–41.
84. Ibid., pp. 41–42.
85. *JT,* 9–10 June 1988.
86. Algiers TV, 9 June — SWB, 11 June 1988.
87. VoP, San'a, 10 June — SWB, 13 June 1988.
88. *Al-Mustaqbal,* 6 August 1988.
89. *IHT,* 12 August 1988.
90. *JT,* 15 June 1988.
91. *Al-Dustur,* London, 13 June; *al-Qabas,* 16 June 1988.
92. *JT,* 28 June 1988.
93. *JT,* 15 June 1988.
94. *IHT,* 12 August 1988.
95. *Al-Mustaqbal,* 6 August 1988.
96. *FT,* 25 May 1988.
97. *Al-Majalla,* 25–31 May 1988.
98. *Al-Sharq al-Awsat,* 9 June 1988.
99. *JT,* 15, 28 June 1988.
100. *JT,* 28 June 1988.
101. *JT,* 15 June 1988.
102. *JT,* 5 July 1988.
103. *Al-Yawm,* 15 July 1988.
104. *Sawt al-Sha'b,* 16 July 1988.
105. *Al-Dustur,* Amman, 13 July 1988.
106. *IHT,* 11 August 1988.
107. Husayn at press conference on 7 August, Jordan TV, 7 August — DR, 8 August; Khasawna quoted by MENA, 20 August — DR, 23 August 1988.
108. R. Amman, 4 August — DR, 5 August; *FT,* 5 August; *JT,* 6 August 1988.
109. *JT,* 21 August; *Sawt al-Sha'b,* 30 August 1988.
110. Interview with Minister of Interior Raja'i al-Dajani in *al-Ra'y,* 10 September 1988.
111. *Al-Dustur,* Amman, 23 August 1988.
112. *Al-Dustur,* Amman, 3 September 1988.
113. *Al-Ra'y,* 10 September 1988.
114. Ibid.
115. *JT,* 21 August 1988.
116. *Al-Nahar,* E. Jerusalem, 1 December 1988.
117. *JT,* 17 September, 10 October 1988.
118. JNA, 20 August — DR, 22 August 1988.
119. *JP,* 9, 13 December; *JT,* 12 December 1988.
120. For text of constitution see Muhammad Khalil (ed.), *The Arab States and the Arab League,* Vol. 1 (Beirut: Khayats, 1962), pp. 55–75.
121. MENA, 31 August — DR, 1 September 1988.
122. Jordan TV, 7 August — DR, 8 August 1988.
123. *Sawt al-Sha'b,* 3 August 1988.
124. Amman, 2 October — DR, 3 October 1988.
125. *Al-Dustur,* Amman, 22 August 1988.
126. *JT,* 10–11 November 1988.
127. R. Amman, 13 August — DR, 17 August 1988. The Senate had been appointed anew in January 1988.
128. For the full Arabic text of Husayn's speech, see *al-Ra'y,* 1 August 1988.
129. Ibid.
130. Ibid.
131. Ibid.
132. E.g., *al-Dustur,* Amman, 4 August; Husayn at press conference on 7 August, Jordan TV, 7 August — DR, 8 August 1988.
133. 'Adnan Abu 'Awda in *al-Majalla,* 10–16 August 1988.
134. Husayn at press conference, Jordan TV, 7 August — DR, 8 August, and in an interview

with *CSM* quoted on Jordan TV, 20 September — DR, 21 September; *JT,* 23 October 1988.
135. Hani al-Khasawna in *Sawt al-Sha'b,* 5 August; Tahir al-Masri in *Sawt al-Sha'b,* 4 October 1988.
136. *Sawt al-Sha'b,* 25 June; similarly *al-Dustur,* Amman, 10 August 1988.
137. Rifa'i quoted in *al-Dustur,* Amman, 12 December; *al-Ra'y,* 16 December 1988.
138. Husayn quoted in *JT,* 4 December; Tahir al-Masri in speech to UN General Assembly, *JT,* 14 December 1988.
139. Hasan to *JT,* 11 December 1988.
140. *Al-Ra'y,* 1 August 1988.
141. *Sawt al-Sha'b,* 29 July; Hani al-Khasawna quoted by R. Abu Dhabi, 30 July — DR, 1 August; *JT,* 1 August; *al-Dustur,* Amman, 10 August 1988.
142. Raja'i al-Dajani to *al-Ra'y,* 10 September 1988.
143. Khasawna quoted in *Sawt al-Sha'b,* 3 August 1988.
144. *JT,* 11 December 1988.
145. *Al-Ra'y,* 1 August 1988.
146. Husayn on "Face the Nation," 20 November — WF, 20 November; Jordan TV, 9 December — DR, 12 December 1988.
147. *Sawt al-Sha'b,* 30 August 1988.
148. Rifa'i quoted on Jordan TV, 1 November — DR, 2 November 1988.
149. *JT,* 31 July; 'Adnan Abu 'Awda in *al-Majalla,* 10-16 August; Rifa'i in *al-Anba,* 10 September 1988.
150. Zayd al-Rifa'i in *al-Anba,* 10 September; Tahir al-Masri in *al-Dustur,* Amman, 24 September 1988.
151. *Sawt al-Sha'b,* 29 July; Khasawna quoted by R. Abu Dhabi, 30 July — DR, 1 August; *Sawt al-Sha'b,* 3 August 1988.
152. *Sawt al-Sha'b,* 12 August 1988.
153. *Al-Anba,* 10 September 1988.
154. *Sawt al-Sha'b,* 29 July; *JT,* 31 July 1988.
155. Husayn's press conference, 7 August, Jordan TV, 7 August — DR, 8 August 1988.
156. Jordan TV, 20 September — DR, 21 September; R. Amman, 21 October — DR, 24 October 1988.
157. Tahir al-Masri in *al-Dustur,* Amman, 24 September 1988.
158. AFP, 6 November — DR, 10 November 1988.
159. *Al-Ra'y,* 1 August 1988.
160. Press conference, 7 August, Jordan TV, 7 August — DR, 8 August 1988.
161. *NYT,* 8 August 1988.
162. *Al-Ra'y,* 1 August 1988.
163. *Al-Dustur,* Amman,10 August; Raja'i al-Dajani in *al-Ra'y,* 10 September 1988.
164. *Al-Ra'y,* 25, 27 September, 2, 4, 5, 7, 27 October 1988.
165. Khasawna in *Sawt al-Sha'b,* 3 August and *al-Ra'y,* 8 December; Abu 'Awda in *al-Majalla,* 10–16 August; Tahir al-Masri in *al-Dustur,* Amman, 24 September 1988.
166. MENA, 15 August — DR, 17 August 1988.
167. Jordan TV, 14 August — DR, 15 August; MENA, 15 August — DR, 17 August; *al-Mustaqbal,* 20 August; *al-Majalla,* 24–30 August, 21–27 September 1988.
168. R. Amman, 23 October — DR, 24 October 1988.
169. JNA, 27 October — DR, 28 October 1988.
170. *JT,* 4 December 1988.
171. R. Amman, 15 November — DR, 16 November 1988. Immediately after the disengagement, Jordan had already announced that the PLO mission in Jordan would have diplomatic status.
172. Rifa'i quoted by JNA, 15 December — DR, 16 December 1988.
173. *JT,* 21 November 1988.
174. *JT,* 28 November 1988.
175. *JT,* 28 November 1988.
176. *Sawt al-Sha'b,* 16 December 1988.
177. Jordan TV, 16 December — DR, 19 December 1988.

178. *Al-Ra'y*, 28 December 1988.
179. *FT*, 25 May 1988.
180. Figures are disputed. For a brief but cogent discussion of this issue see Valerie Yorke, "Jordan is not Palestine: the demographic factor," *MEI*, 16 April 1988.
181. *FT*, ibid.
182. Jordan's achievements in this sphere were particularly impressive. In 1961, 67% of the population were illiterate. In 1987 this figure was down to 26% (*JT*, 9 January 1988). Jordan had 56,000 students in its own universities and colleges and 40,000 studying abroad. (*JT*, 3 February 1988).
183. E.g., *al-Ra'y*, 25 April; R. Amman, 3 May — DR, 6 May; *al-Dustur*, Amman, 9 May 1988.
184. *Al-Ra'y*, 5 May; *al-Qabas*, 11 May 1988.
185. *FT*, ibid.; *al-Dustur*, Amman, 10 August 1988.
186. Husayn to *al-Anba*, 6 September and in *JT*, 4 December; Tahir al-Masri in address to UN General Assembly, *Sawt al-Sha'b*, 4 October 1988.
187. *JT*, 28 June 1988.
188. R. Amman, 12 November — DR, 14 November 1988.
189. *Al-Ra'y*, 1 August 1988.
190. Ibid.
191. *JT*, 11 September, 6-7 October 1988.
192. Husayn at press conference of 7 August, Jordan TV, 8 August — DR, 8 August; *Le Monde*, 16 December 1988.
193. *Ha'aretz*, 17 August 1988.
194. *Al-Bayan*, Dubai, 11 October 1988.
195. *JT*, 21 September, 17 October 1988.
196. *JP*, 11 December 1988.
197. Khasawna in *JT*, 17 July 1988.
198. For a detailed account of human rights violations in Jordan, see report of The Arab Organization for Human Rights published in *al-Nashra*, Athens, 26 September 1988.
199. *Sawt al-Sha'b*, 26 August 1988.
200. *Al-Dustur*, Amman, 1 September; *JT*, 3 October 1988.
201. R. Amman, 25 October — DR, 25 October 1988.
202. *NYT*, 1, 6 May; *al-Majalla*, 18–24 May 1988.
203. *FT*, 18 October 1988.
204. *Ha'aretz*, 4 October; *FT*, 18 October 1988.
205. *FT*, 18 October 1988.
206. *FT*, 18 October; *Le Monde* translated in *Ha'aretz*, 16 November 1988.
207. *JP*, 28 December 1988.
208. *Al-Mustaqbal*, 27 February; Khasawna in *JT*, 24 May; *al-Majalla*, 1-7 June 1988.
209. R. Amman, 8 December — DR, 9 December 1988.
210. *Al-Ra'y*, 1 August 1988.
211. R. Amman, 8 December — DR, 9 December 1988.
212. JNA, 15 December — DR, 16 December; *al-Hawadith*, 30 December 1988.
213. R. Amman, 8 December — DR, 9 December 1988.
214. Husayn to *al-Hawadith*, 30 December 1988.
215. *JT*, 21–22 July 1988.
216. *JT*, 11 October 1988.
217. Husayn on Jordan TV, 29 January — DR, 1 February 1988.
218. *JT*, 9 May 1988.
219. *WT*, 25 April; *al-Dustur*, Amman, 4 July 1988.
220. *FT*, 31 October 1988.
221. *JT*, 12 November 1988.
222. Jordan TV, 14, 16 January — DR, 15, 19 January; R. Amman, 21 October — DR, 24 October 1988.
223. *Al-Majalla*, 25–31 May 1988.
224. *JT*, 19 March 1988.

Lebanon
(Al-Jumhuriyya al-Lubnaniyya)

WILLIAM W. HARRIS

The primary marker on the Lebanese political calendar for 1988 was the termination of President Amin Jumayyil's six-year term on 23 September. In the event, owing to the unyielding positions of the main Christian leadership, on the one side, and the Syrians and West Beirut, on the other, the presidency became vacant and competing governments emerged in East and West Beirut. After 14 years of sectarian strife and deepening geopolitical splintering, Lebanon finally stood on the brink of a formal partition.

Syrian determination to make the presidential transition the occasion for a decisive imposition of Syria's will on the Lebanese arena, a determination stiffened rather than weakened by a lengthening procession of frustrations, provided an important dynamic for the year's various happenings. As in the past, Damascus had to face opposition or spoiling tactics from a motley and shifting assortment of Lebanese and foreign factors in 1988, including Christians, Shi'i fundamentalists, Druzes, pro-'Arafat Palestinians, Iraq, Iran, and Israel. These ranged from a "strategic ally" of Syria to an array of sworn enemies of both Hafiz al-Asad and each other, but all had some interest against Syrian strategic hegemony in Lebanon. Together, and in some cases singly, Syria's "friends," rivals, and enemies possessed the capacity to block Syrian ambitions, a capacity successfully exercised through 1988 despite partially productive efforts by Damascus to secure an understanding with the US.

As for the evolution of domestic communal affairs in 1988, the two main communities — the Christians and the Shi'is — moved in different directions. Although the approach to the presidential transition complicated the already Byzantine interactions between the Maronite power centers, East Beirut in general responded to the continued pressures from Damascus with minimal understandings, at least on the Syrian issue, between major leadership elements — before 23 September meaning the presidency and the Lebanese forces militia and thereafter, the army command and the militia.

In contrast, tensions in the Shi'i sector between the secular centrist Amal movement and the religious fundamentalists of Hizballah erupted into violent hostilities from March onward, in part reflecting the maneuverings for a Syrian-American "deal" and its implications for the balance of Syrian and Iranian influences amongst the Shi'is. The clashes, persisting into early 1989, caused many hundreds of casualties in the southern suburbs of Beirut and the villages of South Lebanon and shattered the Shi'i community, with detrimental implications regarding immediate Shi'i aspirations for increased weight in the central political arena.

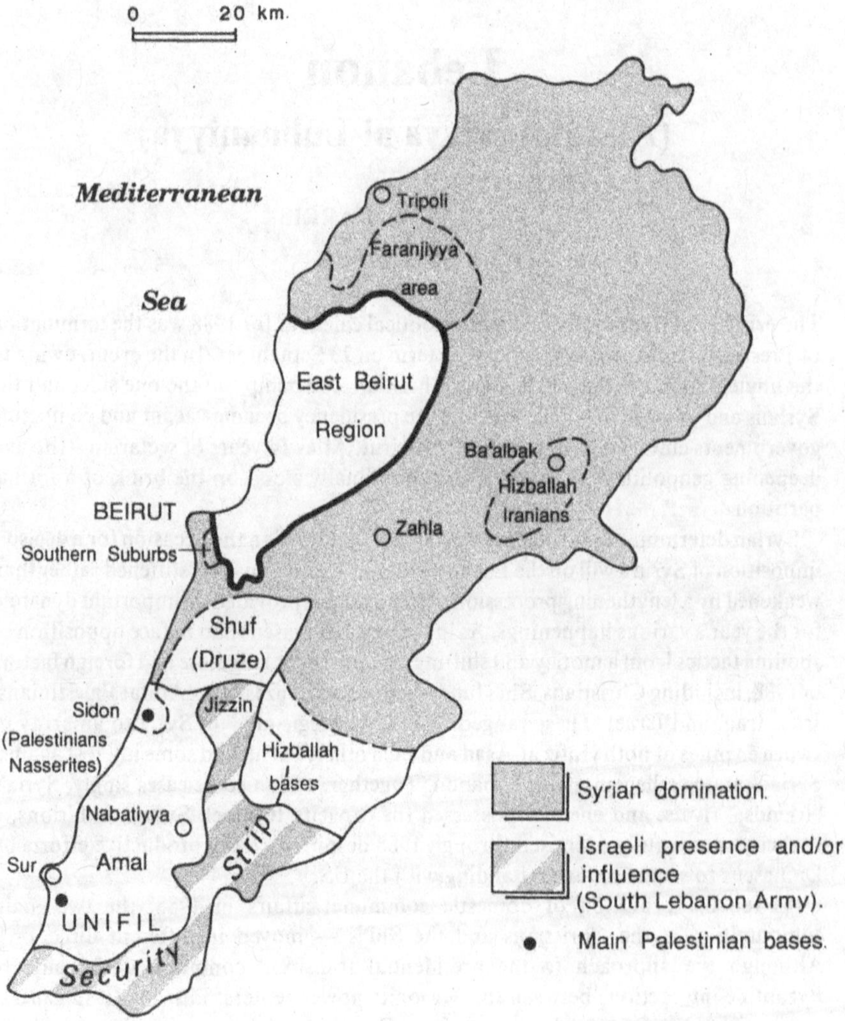

Lebanon: Geographicla Divisions, 1988

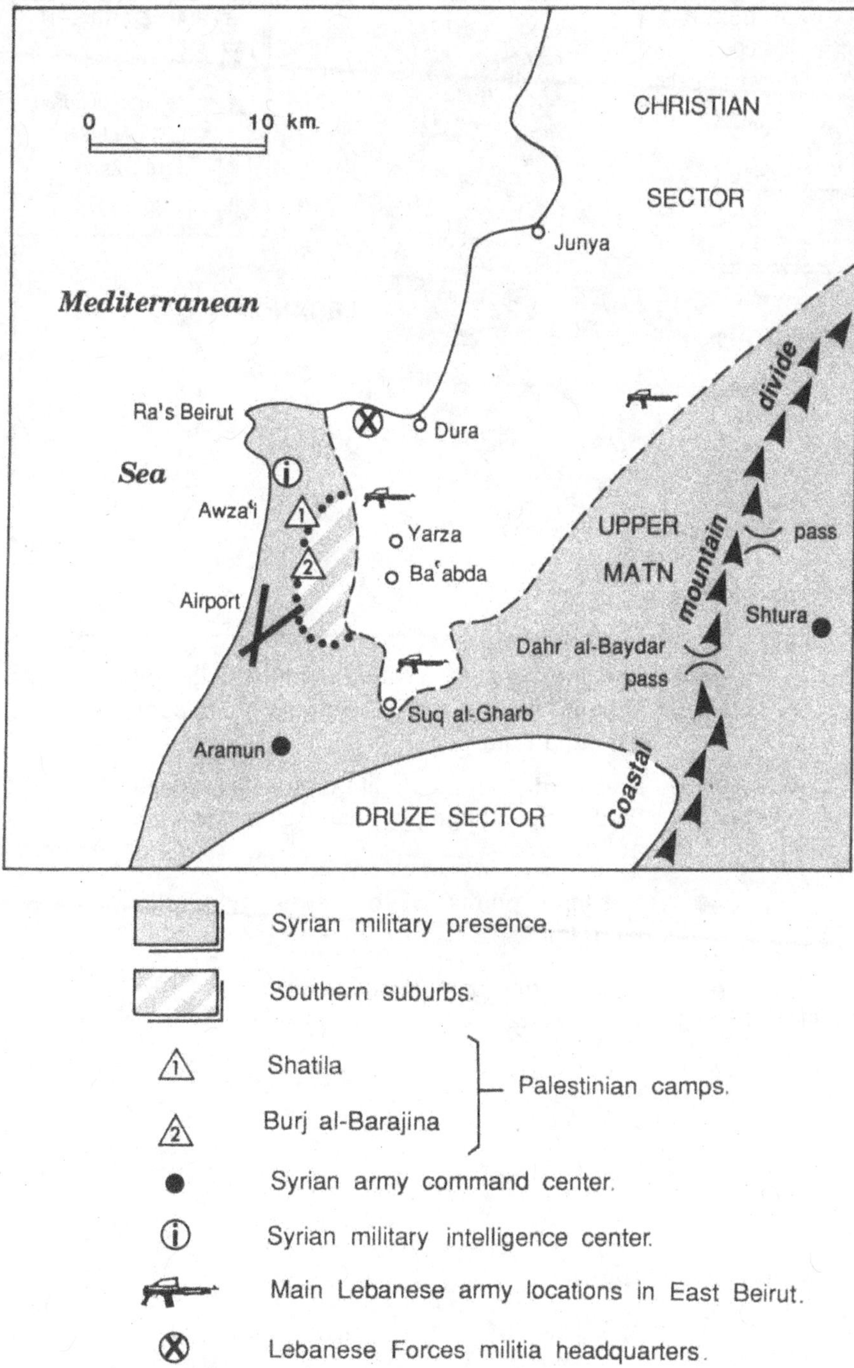

Beirut Region: Areas Control, 1988

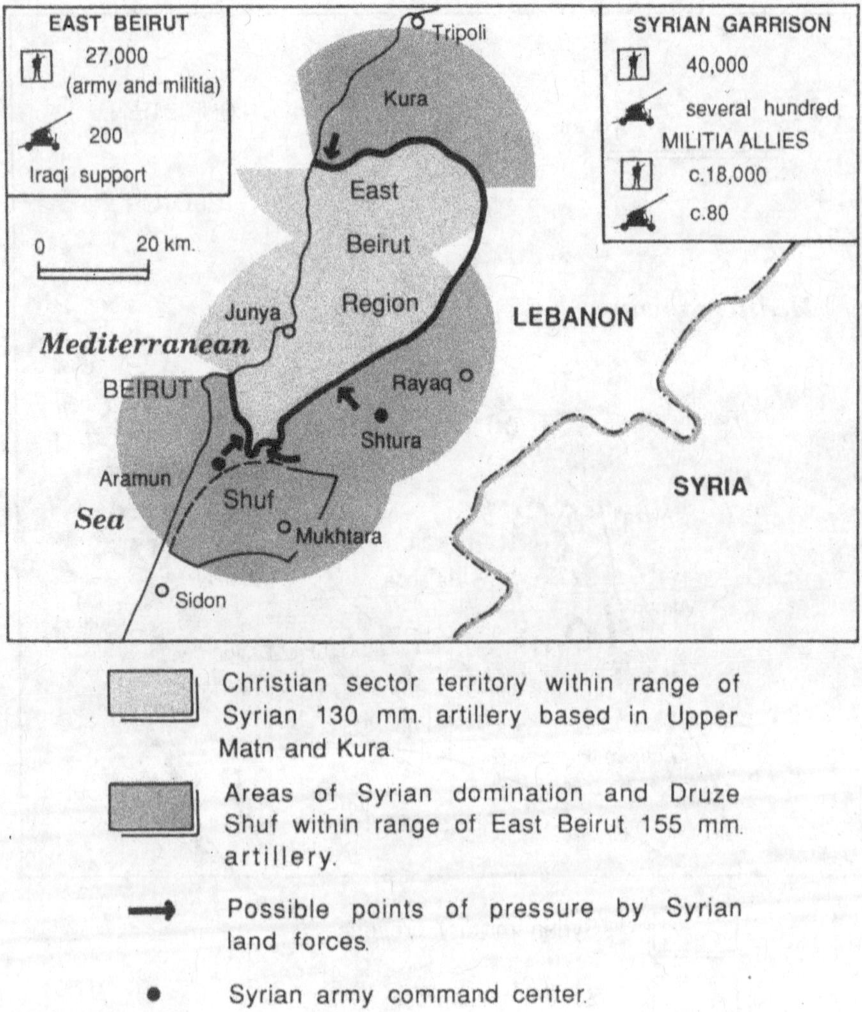

East Beirut/Syria Confrontation, March 1989

Lebanon's economy in 1988 continued to exhibit the features increasingly evident since the onset of the currency collapse in 1985: dramatic infrastructural decay and the division between the "dollar society" of a large minority and the impoverished "lira [pound] society" of the majority, though with a substantial "gray zone" linking the two as the American dollar gradually superseded the local currency in internal economic operations. Degradation of public facilities — electricity, roads, telephones, education — and a renewed fall in the value of the pound with the presidential vacancy (from £L428 to the dollar in September to £L513 in December) after stabilization in the first half of the year, brought a further deterioration in living standards for many. Nonetheless, financial inputs from the Lebanese diaspora, the intervening foreign forces, agricultural and drug trading in the Biqa', light industrial exports assisted by the collapsed exchange rate, and smuggling activities exploiting Beirut's residual entrepôt potential all combined to ensure that the various territorial fragments could maintain a ramshackle viability.

This review considers 1988 political and military developments in Lebanon as a set of interdependent themes: the contest over the presidential transition, encompassing an intensification of the perennial tussle between East Beirut and Syria regarding the orientation of the Lebanese regime; maneuvers and perturbations associated with Syrian efforts to coordinate West Beirut factors, coordination essential to the credibility of Syrian bargaining with Washington; and the vagaries of anarchy and stalemate in South Lebanon, dominated by the interactions of Israeli power with a variety of other local and foreign elements.

AL-ISTIHQAQ AL-DUSTURI (THE CONSTITUTIONAL CONJUNCTION): EAST BEIRUT, THE PRESIDENCY, AND SYRIA

From the beginning of the year, beneath the superficialities of an already vigorous bazaar of competing Maronite hopefuls, deep pessimism prevailed amongst informed opinion regarding the prospects for any understanding between East Beirut and Syria, the primary powers in Lebanese domestic affairs, on a new president to succeed Amin Jumayyil.[1] The East Beirut weekly, *al-Nahar al-'Arabi wal-Duwali,* still a serviceable source of gossip, even referred to the "inconceivability of agreement on a political solution and election of a president."[2] Expectations of a comprehensive standoff related to the virtual impossibility of compromise between the existing Christian leadership and the "Islamic and nationalist" positions proffered through Damascus, the ability of the sides to destroy any process not to their taste, and the incapacity of either main block to override the other by force, considering the multiplicity of external interests in Lebanon.

Increased American diplomatic intervention, opening with a visit by Under Secretary of State for Middle East Affairs Richard Murphy to Damascus in early February, mainly served to excite Syrian ambitions and to reinforce Christian truculence. The American concern was to avoid the prospect of Jumayyil's departure from office bringing unpredictable upheavals, with possible regional implications, at a time of renewed concentration on developments in the Arab-Israeli conflict as the Palestinian *intifada* continued. Washington envisaged its role as that of an "honest broker," engaged in the thankless task of trying to extract reasonable compromises from unreasonable people — seeking a formula which would acknowledge Syria's interests on its western flank while safeguarding Lebanon's independence and would protect the communities, while establishing a fairer distribution of powers in the political system. American officials exuded a qualified sympathy for non-Christian aspirations and for the Syrian strategic position.

Asad accepted American mediation with East Beirut, specifically Amin Jumayyil, on condition that discussions centered on comprehensive internal political reform: shifting executive authority from the presidency to the Cabinet and abolishing political sectarianism. The Syrians refused to open the subject of *'alaqat mumayyaza* (privileged relations) to link Lebanon and Syria, indicating that this was a bilateral Syrian-Lebanese matter for implementation after the reforms created an amenable Lebanese political environment. Damascus still viewed basic change in Lebanon's internal structure as inseparable from its long-standing requirements for "strategic integration," meaning limitation of Lebanese sovereignty in the foreign, defense, cultural, and economic spheres; the former would remove obstacles to the latter.[3]

On reforms, the most that the Christian leadership, here including Syria's ally Sulayman Faranjiyya, would countenance did not yet go beyond mild adjustment of the existing structure and left the Maronite political advantage substantially intact. Jumayyil's final "constitutional proposal" of early 1988, transferred to Damascus for discussion and built on a Christian consensus arrived at with the assistance of the Maronite Patriarchate, contained such old ideas as Christian/non-Christian equality in parliament (change from the 6/5 Christian advantage), suggested reduction of sectarianism in the allocation of official functions over a long period and tinkerings with the balance between the presidency and the Cabinet; but it did not budge on a perpetuated Maronite presidency with political centrality.[4]

Despite the usual chorus of "moderate" Maronite protestations supporting *ta'ayush* (communal coexistence in a new Lebanon), West Beirut correctly perceived a lack of will for fundamental change. In addition, the non-Christians themselves could not evolve a unified concept for a new Lebanon, only agreeing on claims that the Christian constitutional advantage no longer fairly reflected demographic realities. West Beirut's disarray stemmed from personal hostilities and sectarian suspicions amongst Sunnis, Shi'is, and Druzes as deep as those between Christian and non-Christian. This disarray itself guaranteed a certain fatuousness in the "Damascus shuttle" of West Beirut personalities and Lebanese presidential advisers intensified under Syrian patronage from January onward.

It is doubtful whether Syria anticipated such improbabilities as an accord amongst the Lebanese. For the Syrian regime, accelerated Syrian-Lebanese and Syrian-American diplomatic activity in the run-up to the Lebanese presidential transition had a quite different immediate purpose: to demonstrate Syria's role as power broker in Lebanese affairs to buttress a push for a Syrian-American arrangement over the heads of the Lebanese. Positive Syrian interest in American involvement in Lebanese affairs was a relative novelty, based on a cold assessment of the proven impracticality of every other route to establishing credible Syrian overlordship in Lebanon.

The Syrian vision of the potential bargain was clear, limited, and hard-headed, with a separation between Lebanon and wider regional compromise in the mind of Hafiz al-Asad[5] if not in the expectations of Washington. In exchange for Syrian efforts to control "terror" and religious fundamentalism, to free foreign hostages, and to discourage provocations against Israel — the appearance of such things being for the moment in Syria's own interests anyway — the US would tacitly accept the supremacy of Syrian influence in all Lebanon north of the Zahrani River, would support Lebanese presidential candidates with "programs" acceptable to Damascus, and would exert more pressure to restrict Israeli room for maneuver in South Lebanon. Syrian leaders hoped that the combination of heightened strain within East Beirut over the presidential succession and forceful American mediation with Christian bosses might at last crack open the Christian sector, producing a Syrian-inclined president who would then act as a conduit for reforms and *'alaqat mumayyaza.*

In April, Jumayyil and the Lebanese Forces (LF) together rejected emerging joint American-Syrian ideas for reforms to be implemented by the incoming presidency,[6] viewing such ideas as cover for a phased imposition of the hated Tripartite Agreement sponsored by Syria in 1985–86. It seems Jumayyil hoped that the Syrian opposition to American proposals regarding the Arab-Israeli conflict would erode American interest in pressing the matter. Notwithstanding their contempt for each other, the three East Beirut power centers — the militia, the Jumayyil presidency at Ba'abda, and the army command at Yarza — united in their hostility to one aspect or another of Syria's maneuverings. Similarly, although most of the more than 1m. people resident in the East Beirut enclave resented the militia and its exactions, had no respect for self-appointed "Christian leaders," and opposed the effective cantonization foisted upon them, a large majority also perceived Damascus as devious and arrogant and remained firmly attached to entrenched Christian privileges in the Lebanese State, still fearing West Beirut aspirations as an unknown and threatening quantity.[7]

East Beirut thus presented a complex and often misinterpreted face to the outside. Undoubtedly it was an unattractive entity, its structure riven with competing mafias, its so-called leaders relying tacitly or openly on popular insecurities to maintain sectarianism, and its anarchic features given only a strange respectability by comparison with the more dismal conditions prevailing elsewhere in Lebanon. In March 1988, for example, successive security incidents causing a number of casualties[8] indicated continued frictions between followers of Jumayyil and militia chief Samir Ja'ja'. For several reasons, however, attention paid in Damascus and West Beirut to the production of armed conflict amongst the East Beirut power centers and possible elevation of a "moderate" power center (meaning the Maronite Patriarchate, parliamentary deputies, and some older traditional leaders) could not be said to reflect the pre-September reality of East Beirut.

First, Jumayyil's ambitions to continue as a Maronite "effective" after his presidency imposed caution regarding a personal deal with the Syrians. For example, after a June encounter with Asad at the Arab summit in Algiers, Jumayyil tried to exploit a flurry of contacts with Damascus concerning a security plan and a new government to regain his old primacy — but it all came to nothing due to the usual Syrian preconditions regarding reform of the regime. Second, Jumayyil's autonomy was increasingly limited by the steady sapping of his already shrunken militia following and Kata'ib (Phalange) party base by the Lebanese forces. Third, despite commitment to a united Lebanon and scorn for militias, the army commander, Michel 'Awn, had been alienated by Syrian designs on the Lebanese military institutions, as expressed in the Tripartite Agreement. Fourth, because its respectability and influence depended on a sensitive balancing role in the Christian sector, the Maronite Patriarchate wherever possible avoided involvement in political initiatives and preferred the more passive role of offering a safety valve between factions.

In 1987 and early 1988, the presidency itself emerged as a communications channel amongst power centers, with regular meetings of personalities at Ba'abda and constant efforts by presidential advisers to sustain consensus regarding Syrian maneuvers. The limited *ad hoc* alignment thus established proved adequate to preserve strategic cohesion above the details of jealousies and leadership collisions up to the September presidential transition.

In July, at the outset of the three-month electoral period, East Beirut appeared in a relatively strong position. On the one hand, Syria's credibility in Lebanon had suffered a blow with the May collapse of the Shi'i community into savage internecine fighting (see below). This major complication for Syria's affairs in West Beirut seemed likely to persist and Ba'abda reacted with an airy confidence, one presidential source now dismissing any consideration of political reforms in the immediate future.[9] With 25 of the 77 surviving parliamentary deputies resident in the Christian sector, any attempt to impose a Syrian-oriented new presidency would be instantly aborted.

On the military level, East Beirut had little to fear in the existing circumstances: no combination of opposition militias possessed the resources to override the joint strength of the army brigades located in East Beirut and the LF militia, whereas the Syrians would need to mount the equivalent of a full-scale war to ensure a decisive impact, which was not a realistic possibility in the prevailing regional and international climate. As for the implicit threat that no president suitable to Syria meant no president at all, the LF relished the partitionary implications of such a vacuum; far from being a deterrent, it was an alluring prospect for Syria's main local enemy.

Events during the critical August-September period followed a tortuous path toward the shabby ending of the Jumayyil presidency. The coolness in American-Syrian exchanges after nonactivation of "understandings" reached in April persisted until mid-September, then was suddenly succeeded by the curious farce of Richard Murphy's final expedition to Damascus. East Beirut's bosses engaged in their penultimate round of jockeyings for survival and advantage, while simultaneously locked into common rejection of West Beirut and Syrian challenges to "Maronite privileges." In particular, Jumayyil's last bid to use his office to service future aspirations provoked fascinating Christian gyrations; Jumayyil had long lost the capability to overturn the East Beirut power structure, but his final acts as president were enough to determine his rivals on his political elimination.

Syria made its preliminary move in early August when ex-president Sulayman Faranjiyya put forward his candidacy for the presidency. East Beirut and the US rejected Faranjiyya and there is little doubt that Syria's promotion of the old Zgharta *za'im* represented a bargaining card to assist acceptance of a second candidate, at least by Washington. Signs already indicated that Syria's real choice was Aqar deputy Mikha'il Dahir,[10] whose "program" satisfied Syrian and West Beirut requirements. Apparent American preference for a conciliation candidate rather than the Syrian vision of a "strong" president who would brush aside Christian opposition to "reform" angered Damascus, which saw Washington as reneging on earlier arrangements.[11]

A parliamentary session summoned to elect Faranjiyya on 18 August failed to achieve a quorum, owing to an East Beirut boycott tacitly backed by the US Embassy.

In the meantime, Gen. 'Awn tried to raise his own credibility as a candidate with rumors about the Army taking over "security" in urban East Beirut and with sharp public criticism of the Christian militia.[12] 'Awn had reason to hope for American patronage,[13] but this merely drew Jumayyil and Ja'ja' together to thwart him. More significantly, the frigid Syrian reaction ensured 'Awn's open collaboration in sabotaging the 18 August electoral bid, provoking Syrian fury and leading on to virtual endorsement by the LF in early September. This effectively finished 'Awn's immediate prospects, as militia chief Samir Ja'ja' well knew.

Reemphasized Syrian support for Faranjiyya in September amounted to a deliberate Syrian ploy to face Washington with the options of either negotiating under pressure or accepting a constitutional void in Lebanon. Both East and West Beirut prepared for a vacant presidency, with Jumayyil, watched suspiciously by Ja'ja' and 'Awn, maneuvering for the role of godfather of a "transitional government" and with Acting Prime Minister Salim al-Huss withdrawing the year-old "resignation" of the existing government, which opened the way for its perpetuation.

On 13 September, an American delegation headed by Murphy arrived in Damascus only nine days before the end of Jumayyil's term, after appeals by the Vatican, Saudi Arabia, and even the Soviet Union for an effort to break the deadlock. The Americans were plainly tired and exasperated with both the Syrians and the Lebanese, but maintained their long-held view regarding the necessity of change in the Lebanese political system and wanted to avoid a break with the Syrian regime. In short, they were ready for a concord which would demonstrate American commitment to a "new Lebanon," which might shock East Beirut into a serious consideration of the Christian future, yet which would probably give Syria little concrete advantage.

After three days of discussions, Murphy indicated to Syrian Vice President 'Abd al-Halim Khaddam that if Damascus gave up Faranjiyya it could have whatever presidential candidate it wanted, at the same time reaffirming American support for broad principles of reform and promising to press the Syrian-American "name" on East Beirut.[14] The Syrians quickly proposed Mikha'il Dahir following an extraction of reassurances concerning his "program" and the Americans departed to inform the Christian bosses.

It is difficult to believe that Murphy did not anticipate the ferocious Maronite response to the Syrian-American agreement, a response guaranteeing that Asad's gains would remain theoretical while Washington, at small cost, could virtuously claim having tried. The entire East Beirut leadership — Patriarchate, army command, presidency, and militia — attacked the "imposition" as a transgression of Lebanon's sovereignty, intending to wreck Dahir's candidacy by boycotting the 22 September parliamentary assemblage.[15] Al-Huss and other West Beirut personalities declared their astonishment, observing that East Beirut had never raised such a chorus against foreign steerage of earlier presidential elections, for example regarding Elias Sarkis and Bashir Jumayyil.

Several Arab states, particularly Iraq and Egypt, encouraged East Beirut rejectionism. More free to pursue its vendetta against "the traitor" Asad following the August cease-fire in the Gulf, Iraq sponsored a public alignment with the LF and 'Arafat to cause trouble for Syria in Lebanon. The first major Iraqi arms shipment for the LF, including multiple rocket launchers and 20 tanks, was unloaded in Beirut port on 16 August, immediately before the first electoral session.[16] As for Cairo, President

Mubarak made a personal attack on Syrian policy in mid-September, asserting that "Syrian intervention has brought the present state of fragmentation."[17]

Substantial Arab support assisted the establishment of a linkage between Gen. 'Awn, affronted by what he saw as an American snub to his own candidacy, and Samir Ja'ja' on 21 September, which was a noteworthy development considering the history of tension between Yarza and the militia. This temporarily stabilized relations between the primary military elements in the Christian sector.

The one major breaking of ranks came from Jumayyil, who made a surprise journey to Damascus the day before leaving office. Jumayyil evidently saw the crisis over the Syrian-American agreement as an opportunity to make a dramatic move as a "broker,"[18] salvaging his personal position for the future. Jumayyil had been careful not to antagonize Dahir, promptly labeled a Syrian agent by the LF, and one story is that he proposed to Asad a transitional government headed by Dahir as prime minister as a device to reconcile "moderate" East Beirut and Syria. The Syrians, however, claimed that he came fully accepting a Dahir presidency and that he would never have been received otherwise.[19] Whatever the case, the mission flopped in the face of Syrian suspicion and the generally hostile East Beirut reaction on Jumayyil's return. 'Awn and Ja'ja' dismissed the affair out-of-hand and even the Patriarchate responded coldly.

Failure of the 22 September electoral session was a foregone conclusion. Thereafter, the last hours of the Jumayyil presidency witnessed a scramble for a transitional regime, Jumayyil desperately seeking to avoid calling on 'Awn by sounding out various Maronite civilians and Salim al-Huss. Each avenue was closed by successive vetoes from West or East Beirut and literally at 10 minutes to midnight Jumayyil had no option, in the East Beirut context, but to issue a decree appointing a temporary military administration headed by 'Awn. With Huss asserting the continuing legitimacy of his Cabinet, Lebanon now had no president and two governments.

For the remainder of 1988 paralysis prevailed at the national level, though both Huss and 'Awn sought to limit steps likely to institutionalize partition and proclaimed the holding of presidential elections as their sole priority. Each "government" naturally refused to recognize the legality of the other. 'Awn's military council, entirely Christian due to the refusal of the three appointed non-Christian officers to participate, based its authority on presidential decree. Huss's Cabinet, minus two of its three remaining Christian ministers (Joseph al-Hashim and Victor Qasir) because they did not dare to continue, asserted that the decree flouted custom and constitutional requirements: the prime minister must be a Sunni under the unwritten "National Pact," the basis of Lebanon's confessional order, and the president could not by exclusive fiat either create a government or have the same person simultaneously army commander and prime minister.

Within East Beirut, the new army-militia relationship became the central political reality. 'Awn had created a difficult dilemma for himself; for the moment the understanding with Ja'ja' secured his power base for facing Syria and West Beirut, but it also badly damaged his reputation, particularly outside the Christian sector, and greatly restricted his room for maneuver. 'Awn still aspired to be president, as indicated by such remarks as "generals are the best presidents,"[20] and could hope to use his blocking capacity and his new central role in East Beirut as a bargaining chip.

Much depended, however, on subordination of militia influence and here the tactical alignment with the LF created problematic circumstances. The LF had exhibited aggressiveness and some ingenuity in penetrating and partially subverting army brigades on several occasions since 1986 while the army command's response, though not without effect, had hitherto been defensive. More important, the militia had deliberately built up a structure for the social and economic manipulation of East Beirut which the army, despite its advantages in public popularity and military weight, would find it difficult to contain.

A majority of LF leaders viewed the presidential vacancy and the likely further fragmentation of central institutions as strengthening the "federalism" option for Lebanon's future[21] and therefore as positive trends. Some, perhaps including deputy leader Karim Bakraduni, had fears about ultimate internal and external isolation if the militia appeared too openly to espouse concepts beyond the bounds of Arab and international acceptability, but such people had a minor restraining effect.

Nonetheless, Ja'ja' rejected as undesirable any standard reformist notion that the communities could interact in mutual self-respect under a new powerful unitary central government. Lebanon should become a patchwork of autonomous cantons under loose "federal" coordination; only in this way could Christian power be preserved when Christians were no longer more than a large minority. Naturally, cantons ensured a happy future for militias and here the LF looked to the Druze-dominated Progressive Socialist Party (PSP) and the Shi'i fundamentalist Hizballah as *de facto* allies, regardless of their public orientations, because of their sectarian character and usurpation of state functions.

Ja'ja' and his circle, which included a significant section of the Maronite religious institution, had nothing but contempt for the *ta'ayush* ("coexistence") formula of 'Awn, Jumayyil, the Patriarchate, and traditional Christian leaders — the idea that the 1943 confessional system could be adjusted in such a way as to maintain a Christian political advantage while gaining acceptance from West Beirut and Syria. The "federalists" regarded the East Beirut version of *ta'ayush* as dangerous to the Christian sectarian future, though many leveled precisely the same accusation against the militia outlook. In any event, Ja'ja' had no reason to assist the presidential ambitions of 'Awn, a centralist and a competitor; on the contrary, the LF had every interest in exploiting their East Beirut power base to erode 'Awn's credibility and to imprison him in their camp.

First the militia turned to liquidate Amin Jumayyil's area of influence in the Upper Matn hinterland of East Beirut and to settle accounts with the ex-president. Already before 23 September, the militia command had put pressure on Jumayyil's local lieutenants in the mountain suburbs, while Jumayyil had weakened himself by dismissing some of his armed entourage without compensation.[22] In the days after leaving office, Jumayyil pursued contacts with both Damascus and West Beirut, especially complimenting Salim al-Huss, and in consequence was immediately placed under virtual house arrest by the LF. The *coup de grâce* came in early October when Ja'ja' ordered the incorporation of the autonomous armed elements of the Upper Matn into the LF, formidable intimidation discouraging any resistance, a step which gave him an unprecedented control over all irregular military units in East Beirut. The LF also moved to seize other Jumayyil establishments, including two radio stations, the newspapers *al-'Amal* and *Réveille,* and the Bikfaya "palace."

Representations to 'Awn received little attention, the military council terming the affair a party matter irrelevant to the Army. Jumayyil found himself isolated; the Patriarchate ignored his plight and the primary East Beirut news magazine referred approvingly to a "unification of the sector's weaponry forestalling a security disruption."[23] Stories circulated alleging massive financial gains by the ex-president during his term and on 22 October Jumayyil left for indefinite residence abroad, paying a large "tax" for unimpeded passage. Personal threats reportedly hastened his departure.[24]

By November, two main features could be identified as characterizing the political trend in East Beirut. First, despite continuation of the *détente* between the Army and the militia, the longer-term conflict of interests, concepts and ambitions remained undiminished. 'Awn derived strength from his status as head of the locally acknowledged "legitimacy" and some public acceptability in the Arab and international arenas. Against this, as the period of "two governments" lengthened, as the two Beiruts became more estranged and as partitionary provocations multiplied, the LF were perceptibly gaining ground; Iraqi aid strengthened the militia's military dimension while absorption of Jumayyil's apparatus expanded its structure. Much depended here on personal fortunes and evolutions in external relations as the militia was still vulnerable to disruptions resulting from blows to its leadership or from shifts in the regional balance.

Second, contrary to some wishful thinking in West Beirut, the Maronite Patriarch Nasrallah Butrus Sufayr and with him many Christian parliamentary deputies showed every sign of genuine hostility to the American-Syrian deal. Defense of Maronite "rights" and Christian positions did not necessarily require militia arm-twisting. "Moderate" East Beirut opinion did not identify with the LF, but the above attitude, supplemented by militia pressure, was solid enough to ensure that the projected October election for the parliamentary chairman met the same fate as its presidential counterpart.

Thereafter, the West Beirut daily *al-Safir* abruptly suspended hopeful commentary about East Beirut "moderates" and "damaged parties" and referred to Sufayr's demands for changes in the Murphy-brokered accord as arousing "rancor amongst Islamic and Syrian-allied political forces." Further, "Syrian officials no longer express their interest as before in discussing ideas put to them concerning cooperation with the Patriarch and encouraging him to visit Damascus; some Syrian officials repeatedly observe that Sufayr is in one front with Kaslik and is taking a decisive position rejecting change in the Lebanese regime and any concessions on [Christian] privileges and there is no hope from him in this domain."[25]

Syrian leaders, having hoped for a relatively smooth American imposition of the Syrian-American agreement on the "isolationists," had taken 'Awn's "coup" as a personal insult. The Syrian media called on the Lebanese "to overthrow this government, and so destroying the Zionist project which it carries and works to implement"[26] and ignored 'Awn's request that they receive an envoy. In his turn, after attempting to establish a dialogue, with references to Syria as the "nearest neighbor" whose interests Lebanon was "committed to guard,"[27] 'Awn drifted into equalizing the Syrian and Israeli presences in Lebanon, which was an anathema to Damascus. In December, following the Syrian-promoted institution of a new army command in West Beirut, an acrimonious dispute over Central Bank allocations to Yarza and unilateral official appointments by 'Awn's military council, the reconstruction of the Lebanese State seemed a distant dream.

At the end of the year East Beirut's bipolar power distribution between Army and militia was visibly less stable than the tripolar arrangement which had disappeared with the demise of the Jumayyil presidency. In a December interview with the international Arab weekly *al-Majalla*, 'Awn asserted that LF leaders had accepted a "total [national] solution" encompassing an end to militias and separate political projects.[28] This indicated 'Awn's distaste for an intolerable reality; the military council, which claimed sole legitimacy not just in East Beirut but in all Lebanon and looked ahead to disbandment of militias with absorption of militiamen into regular army units was being forced to coexist, even in East Beirut, with a militia which controlled the ports, collected taxes,and generally behaved like a state apparatus. For the LF, the future of the "canton" depended on reduction of the army brigades to militia appendages; for army personnel from 'Awn down to common soldiers the militia represented "the enemy within."

Significantly, the buffer and communications interchange which Jumayyil's advisers had provided had gone. The increased political interventions of the Patriarchate, demonstrating inexperience, exposure to pressure, and lack of fixed purpose, were so far no substitute. For example, after a visit to the Vatican in November, Sufayr patronized discussions concerning a "list" of presidential candidates to be submitted to West Beirut and Damascus. The exercise became a fiasco; West Beirut condemned the absence of a political reform program while within East Beirut Sufayr found himself exploited by Ja'ja' and at odds with the military council. The LF supported the initiative, obviously anticipating its failure, to embarrass and restrict 'Awn, whereas the general boycotted the maneuver, suspecting it to be a device to destroy his own presidential candidacy.

AL-KHANDAQ AL-WAHID (THE ONE TRENCH): WEST BEIRUT AND "NATIONALIST LEBANON"

In the best of hypothetical worlds, "Islamic and nationalist" West Beirut ought to have provided a reliable base for Syrian operations. Certainly by the late 1980s the two other major areas of Syrian military domination — the zones buffering Syrian metropolitan territory encompassing the central Biqa' and North Lebanon — were satisfactorily subordinated to Syrian Ba'thist purposes.

The Shi'i fundamentalist enclave in Ba'albak and its surroundings, still the location of several hundred Iranian Revolutionary Guards as well as assorted militia elements, was overawed by the primary Syrian military concentration in Lebanon (which was aligned to confront any Israeli thrust up the Biqa') and was closely monitored and infiltrated by Syrian army intelligence from its headquarters in the nearby Armenian settlement of 'Anjar. The formerly recalcitrant cities of Zahla and Tripoli, respectively Christian and Sunni Muslim and regarded as potential channels of Israeli and Arab troublemaking close to the Syrian borders, had been effectively neutralized since late 1985 by Syrian "security plans."

Otherwise, a maze of mutual antagonisms existed within and between the Christian, Shi'i, and Sunni populations of the Biqa' and the north and long experience had made Syrian intelligence expert at exploiting these antagonisms to cement an image of Syrian indispensability as patron, protector, and mediator amongst the myriad factions. In 1988, the most prominent case requiring Syrian intervention involved a land dispute between Maronite and Shi'i clans near Qubbayat, which degenerated into artillery exchanges. Only limited insubordination in Ba'albak and sporadic terrorist incidents in Tripoli, variously blamed on 'Arafat and the LF, disturbed the impression of Syrian mastery, though the popular view of Syrian personnel, many of whom behaved like Lebanese militiamen in their extraction of "cuts" from business-protection rackets, was inevitably cool.

For Asad, however, overlordship in Beirut remained critical to reduce dangers of subversion of Syrian authority in the Biqa' and northern buffer areas and for the regulation of foreign influences on Syria's flank. East Beirut was the final target but the full, stable coordination of West Beirut's factions to Syrian policy and the ending of diversions in the "Islamic and nationalist" arena counted as a prerequisite. Despite some successes 1988 proved another inconclusive year for Syria in the shifting sands of West Beirut. Before examining the 1988 trends in detail it is useful to assess Syria's balance of assets and liabilities in the "Islamic and nationalist" core in the late 1980s.

One could summarize Syria's advantages in relation to West Beirut as proximity, familiarity, and military weight. No other external factor dealing with West Beirut possesses this combination to the same degree. In geographical terms Syria's supreme asset has been its access to and domination of the Beirut metropolitan area via control of a fat wedge of mountain terrain extending coastward from Zahla and Shtura and containing the main axis of communications between Beirut and the Biqa'. This wedge gives the Syrian Army a secure hinterland and transport links for its operations in West Beirut, separates the Christian and Druze "cantons," constraining undesirable interchange, and has provided an excellent platform for artillery harassment of East Beirut. As for familiarity, Syria has since 1983 patronized an uninterrupted flow of "sisterly" contacts with all West Beirut's main political and religious leaders, has subordinated the largest West urban militia — the Shi'i Amal movement — and has reconstructed its multilocal intelligence apparatus.

The military-weight element deserves special comment in the context of direct Syrian military supervision of West Beirut from February 1987. In 1987 and 1988 perhaps one quarter of Syria's garrison force in Lebanon — about 8,000 out of more than 30,000 troops — has been deployed west of the Dahr al-Baydar mountain pass towards Beirut and the Awali River, a marked change compared with the preceding five years. Following the initial display of armed might in the West Beirut streets this greatly enhanced capacity in the environs of Beirut has been carefully managed. First, the direct military presence in the urban area was quickly lowered to lessen exposure to attack, but with concentrations at critical points such as Awza'i (entry to Ra's Beirut from the south) and the airport and "observer" units scrutinizing movement at the crossings to East Beirut and around the Palestinian camps and the Shi'i southern suburbs. Second, the main mass was drawn back into the 'Aramun hills from where it could promptly reinforce the Beirut units when necessary, intimidate the Druze "canton" in the Shuf by gnawing at its fringes, and project some force south to the outskirts of Sidon, the location of the main surviving pro-'Arafat forces' base. The distribution has vulnerabilities in regard to its spread and single primary supply line across Dahr al-Baydar, but these really apply only in the case of hostilities with Israel, and much less in dealing with local subversive factors.

Why then has Syria so often found itself floundering? On the local level, the multitudinous sectarian and factional divisions have so far proved a match for Syria's management capacities, especially in view of economic, Arab, and international constraints on the direct use of force. The Syrian regime must bear a measure of responsibility for its difficulties, because since 1983 Damascus has often operated on the dubious assumption that encouraging factional conflict is a cheap means of exhausting the local parties, thus easing later imposition of outside authority. The year 1988 saw hostilities in West Beirut as healthy as ever; Syria proved able to manipulate events and to sustain its strategic position, but still not equal to final imposition and suppression.

Much of the vitality of local conflict has, of course, had non-Lebanese sources; 1988 was yet another year in which Syrian assets, however formidable, could not override the interests of Syria's non-Lebanese competitors. Syria aside, two major ME actors — revolutionary Iran and the pro-'Arafat Palestinians — continued to maintain aspirations in Lebanon which precluded acceptance of Syrian hegemony while two other powers — Iraq and Israel — had both reasons and resources to frustrate Syrian ambitions.

For 'Arafat's mainstream portion of the PLO, "Islamic and nationalist Lebanon," containing 350,000 Palestinian refugees, remained the chief geographical base for autonomous power; for Asad, exclusive control of Syria's western flank and determination to steer Palestinian politics demanded final reduction of this autonomy. In early 1988, despite one year of Syrian deployment in West Beirut and encirclement by Amal and the Syrian-promoted Palestinian National Salvation Front (PNSF), 'Arafat's Fath kept a residual foothold in the urban Palestinian camps of Shatila and Burj al-Barajina (up to 1,000 fighters). As an extension of the major PLO apparatus in the Sidon camps (dominated by Fath with over 5,000 fighters) this was a persistent irritant to the Syrian presence, also assisting 'Arafatist linkage with Shi'i fundamentalists and disgruntled Sunnis and Druzes.

Through the 1980s, Iran and Syria have been strategic allies on the regional level, also cooperating in Lebanon after 1982 against the Israeli and American presences. The two countries, however, have had a basic conflict of interests centered on the orientation of the Shi'i community, Lebanon's largest single sect and making up perhaps 60% of the non-Christian population. For revolutionary Iran, credible steerage of its coreligionists in Lebanon, involving promotion of Islamic republican sentiments, remains important for Tehran's projection of influence beyond its own borders. For the secular Ba'thists in Damascus, Shi'i fundamentalism has proved a convenient tool for manipulation against Western and Israeli interests (paralleling the use of Amal against the Palestinians), but to be curbed when the time came for a deal with the Americans. Khaddam, as the official responsible for Syria's "Lebanese file," defined the parameters of the Syrian-Iranian interaction in Lebanon in May 1988:

> We greatly value our alliance with Iran, but our regional allies must respect our position; our role [in Lebanon] is above all other considerations and in their operations, our allies should pay attention to our interests and to those of our [Lebanese] friends. The movements of some have become a threat to the Syrian role. We shall not allow the creation of complications in the Lebanese arena.[29]

Friction between Iranian and Syrian influences increased after the Syrian armed "entry" to West Beirut in February 1987. A strange sort of equilibrium survived into 1988, with the irritations consequent on "cheek by jowl" patronage of mutually antagonistic militias (Syria with Amal and Iran with the fundamentalist Hizballah), each militia itself seeking supremacy amongst the Shi'is, balanced by sensitive appreciations of the mutual benefits arising from the broader strategic connection between the two states. Within the Shi'i community a major upheaval loomed, the indicators including Syrian discomfort with the security vacuum arising from exclusion of the Shi'i southern suburbs from West Beirut "security plans," the incompatibility of the secular and religious fundamentalist visions for the Shi'i future, the enhancement of Amal-Hizballah suspicions by interpenetrations of Iranian and Syrian intelligence activities, and different concepts held by Syria, Iran, and the fundamentalist kidnappers concerning the "return" for freeing foreign hostages.

Early in 1988, encouraged by positive diplomatic indications from Washington, Syria evolved its lines of approach for reducing competitors in the West Beirut arena while quietening the US, and by implication Israel, as preparation for the presidential transition. As had been the case since 1983, Syria's main partner in Lebanon, the Shi'i Amal movement under Minister Nabih Barri, was closely involved in proceedings, partly through its own interests in local power equations and partly through Syrian stimulation. The approach, as evidenced by subsequent expectations and comments expressed by "persons close to Damascus" in the Lebanese press,[30] linked the south, West Beirut and, ultimately, East Beirut.

Amal had ample reason for action on its own account in South Lebanon. Here Hizballah posed an increasingly serious threat to Amal's main geographical base; in late 1987 the fundamentalists for the first time received buttressing by a contingent of Iranian Revolutionary Guards from Ba'albak. Hizballah looked to intensify the assault on Amal's authority both directly, through challenges in the villages, and indirectly, through provoking Israel into retaliatory strikes on the area, disrupting local life and demonstrating Amal's incapacity to provide security. In 1987, Syria played its usual double game, agreeing with the fundamentalists regarding some increase in pressure on Israel and encouraging the Iranian move southward, thus diverting attention from Beirut and assisting Syria's confrontationalist credentials, but relying on Amal to keep matters from getting out of control, which was an unfair but typical Syrian imposition on an ally already sorely pressed by local Lebanese and Palestinian groups.

In February 1988, the kidnapping by fundamentalists operating within Amal territory of an American officer serving with Unifil finally made the situation intolerable for Amal's southern command. At this point, it also suited Syria to adjust its tactical posture; a squeeze on the fundamentalists whom Syrian army intelligence had so recently been promoting might assist progress with the Americans on the more important issue of the presidency. For the moment, the military outlook was relatively advantageous for Amal, as a prolonged pause in the intermittent fighting with the pro-'Arafat Palestinians, ironically mediated by the Iranians, had cooled the Amal-'Arafat fronts in Beirut and Sidon. Damascus intended reopening accounts with 'Arafat a little later.

On 4–7 April Amal struck at Hizballah positions around Nabatiyya, quickly achieving exclusive mastery of the area in shoot-outs costing some 50 dead. The blow gave Amal a decisive edge in the south and after a few days, scores of Hizballahis, including clerics, were expelled to the Biqa'. Amal enabled Syria to indicate flexibility to the Americans and Israelis concerning security matters in the south in the case of acknowledgment of Syrian overlordship of Lebanon. The fact that the operation was entirely an Amal concern outside the zone of Syrian deployment obviated any perturbation in the Syrian-Iranian strategic relationship.

Attention now shifted to West Beirut. The Syrian approach comprised two distinct elements. With regard to the Palestinian camps, Damascus aimed at the conclusive military neutralization of the surviving Palestinian pockets, mainly using Syrian-aligned Palestinians under tight supervision. 'Arafat's supporters had been substantially worn down in three years of attrition and were boxed in by the Syrian army, but their continued open presence in the Lebanese capital nagged at Asad. The Syrian leader's assent to a meeting with 'Arafat, the first since the latter's expulsion from Damascus in 1983, on the occasion of Abu Jihad's funeral in early April, resulted from external Arab and Soviet prodding and had no relevance to conditions on the ground in Lebanon.

With regard to the southern suburbs beyond Syria's West Beirut "security plan" and where Hizballah and Iran enjoyed considerable freedom, Syria expected Amal to hold the situation and to prevent security infractions from spilling into areas of Syrian deployment. Damascus wished to freeze the matter of the suburbs, the fundamentalists, and the foreign hostages until the most favorable moment for an arrangement with the Americans, thus dangling the prospect of a Syrian police operation to curb the West's *bête noire* in exchange for the removal of the LF from urban East Beirut and a satisfactory imposition concerning the presidency. Until such a price was extracted, everything would sit, with Asad avoiding risks to his Iranian connection. Unfortunately for the Syrian leader, Hizballah, enraged by events in the south, was evolving a quite different project for the suburbs.

Coordinating with powerful radicals in Tehran through the Iranian embassy, Hizballah plotted to respond to Amal's Nabatiyya assault by a coup to seize control of Beirut's Shi'i areas, then demanding a restoration in the south. Although Hizballah and its Iranian friends carefully aimed their project only against Amal, a basic challenge to Syrian credibility was unavoidable. In mid-1988, Syria thus had to face a major crisis, calling on all Asad's skills for the simultaneous preservation of Syria's Iranian and Western openings.

Hizballah opened its campaign on 6 May.[31] After only three days Amal — complacent, poorly disciplined and organized, and with its local structure internally subverted by the fundamentalists — was virtually eliminated from all central and southern parts of the suburbs. Hizballah pursued a methodical and well-prepared advance: substantial reinforcements had infiltrated from the Biqa' over preceding weeks, exposing a slackening of Syrian vigilance; Amal was crippled in some areas by wholesale desertion of the Biqa' clans to the other side, and 'Arafat's network in Burj al-Barajina and elsewhere willingly assisted the fundamentalists. In the following two weeks, punctuated by innumerable cease-fires as Iranian negotiators sought to delay Syrian intervention, Hizballah crept forward against the residual Amal presence in the northern quarters of Ghubayra and al-Shiyya. By 28 May, on the eve of an agreed "Syrian entry," up to 500 had been killed and 2,000 injured,[32] the majority civilians, with many quarters severely damaged by ruthless bombardments and looting. It ranked as by far the worst episode of hostilities in Lebanon since the comparable West Beirut affair of February 1987.

Initial Syrian and Iranian moves aimed at containment of each other without confrontation. Syria made a bid to turn its predicament to advantage, using the Hizballah upsurge to try to stampede the US into forcing changes in East Beirut, after which Damascus would supposedly do everyone the favor of squashing fundamentalism.[33] To postpone any hasty choice between the West and Iran and to juggle each as pressure on the other, Syria held back on direct armed intervention to sustain Amal. This certainly suited Hizballah's Iranian allies, who, alarmed by Syrian gropings for an arrangement with the Americans, had viewed the Amal move in the south as part of an emerging "conspiracy" and wanted time to create new realities strengthening the fundamentalist hand with the Syrian Army kept as much as possible on the sidelines. In an emergency consultation, Asad and Iranian President Khameneh'i agreed on a four-party committee, but this was immediately doomed as anything other than a time-wasting device by divergent interpretations of restoring the status quo ante: for Hizballah this applied to South Lebanon as well as the suburbs, while for Amal and Syria it meant only Beirut.[34]

Within a week, the Syrian attempt to brazen things out disintegrated into near panic. On 13 May Amal, wearied and with some of its leaders reportedly embittered by the lack of Syrian back-up,[35] abdicated any responsibility for the outer perimeter of the southern suburbs; Hizballah fighters surged onto the airport autostrade, entering the area of Syrian deployment and stimulating street disturbances in Awza'i, adjacent to a Syrian encampment and checkpoints.[36] Also, Washington now seemed indifferent to Syria's scheme and East Beirut responded to the Syrian maneuvering to link treatment of the Shi'i and Christian sectors with a confident rejection. Khaddam wildly accused the Americans of betrayal and of encouraging extremism against Syria in the southern suburbs as well as in East Beirut, this while Syria had "stood by its obligations when it acted to restrain extremist activities in Lebanon."[37] Faced with the real possibility of subversion of its general position in West Beirut, Damascus now committed itself to an early military entry into the southern suburbs unconnected to any change in East Beirut.

Iran and Hizballah held off the intervention for a further two weeks, gradually inserting conditions to protect the fundamentalists. The task was eased by a fervent Syrian desire, despite forceful posturing, for a peaceable outcome; in the absence of imminent compensation from other quarters Asad had no stomach for a costly showdown. Rumors also circulated about a threat to kill the foreign hostages if Syria made any hasty move; the fundamentalists were well aware that this would badly embarrass the Syrians with the West. Both the Iranian negotiators and Hizballah spokesmen repeatedly offered full cooperation with "our Syrian brothers" and asserted no opposition "in principle" to a Syrian entry in order to "separate forces" and deal with the parties in an equal manner. Hizballah, however, indicated that acceptance of Syrian entry depended on preservation of the armed fundamentalist presence in the suburbs and satisfaction in the south, while Iranian envoy Besharati advanced the idea of a joint Iranian-Syrian security force and requested an extended opportunity for the four-party committee to reach a "political settlement."

After intensified hostilities on 25 May coupled with warning signs of an outbreak in the south, Syria felt impelled to take action. Asad took the extraordinary step of inviting Hizballah leaders to Ladhiqiyya, where an agreement was reached allowing a quiet Syrian entry to the suburbs, but preserving Hizballah assets. The entry would undoubtedly enable a closer Syrian supervision of local events, but could not be compared with the West Beirut "security plan," under which Syria's only constraint was its own capacity. Syrian troops would spread throughout the suburbs, "armed manifestations" would disappear from the streets, and militia offices would become "political" offices, but Hizballah would not be disarmed and would maintain a potent military presence at its Hayy al-Madi barracks and along the contact line with East Beirut. Most important, within a few weeks the bulk of Syrian troops would withdraw, with the ineffectual Lebanese internal security force taking their place.[38]

On returning to Beirut, Hizballah spokesman Ibrahim Amin quoted Asad as having told the delegation that "you represent the true Islam in Lebanon as against the Islam deputed by imperialism to hit Islam; you are the Islamic struggle in Lebanon which I have remembered in my speeches."[39] This contrasted interestingly with the quite different comments on fundamentalism intended for American and Christian ears and can only have been deeply offensive to many in Amal; thus Asad ran with the hares and hunted with the hounds.

When, on 27–28 May, 3,500 Syrian soldiers moved into the suburbs, Syria superficially appeared to make a considerable gain: the inter-Shi'i conflict subsided with Syria's role as an indispensable interlocutor reinforced, increased Syrian authority in the suburbs was achieved while preserving the strategic connection with Iran, and Syria presented an image of forcefulness for pursuing its dialogue with the West. In significant respects, however, appearance failed to coincide with reality, threatening further troubles. First, far from being patched up, the split in the Shi'i community had deepened, compromising Syria's immediate management prospects. Venomous propaganda exchanges continued between Amal and Hizballah, the former making accusations of "satanic" fundamentalist collaboration with the LF and the latter alleging brutal torture and referring to Amal as a "gang" of American hirelings employed to wipe out the Islamic resistance. Traditional Shi'i leaders such as Qabalan and Shams al-Din attacked Hizballah while the fundamentalists refused any longer to respect the "Higher Shi'i Council." Hizballah also warned that it soon intended to return to the unresolved matter of South Lebanon.

At the same time, because of the exhaustion of Amal's Beirut apparatus, Syria lost much of the buffer through which it could steer and monitor Shi'i affairs without seeming to be involved. The thinning-out of Syrian forces in the suburbs in June-July, with interposition of a Lebanese "internal security" screen, could not alter the fact that further local difficulties promised more direct implications for Syrian prestige. In advance of substantial reconstruction, Amal only retained a leading role in the south, as the test of Biqa' orientations had not been in its favor, and here the Syrian entry into the suburbs actually increased pressures. Syria made a gain in Beirut, in the service of the struggle for the central regime, at the price of diverting fundamentalist energies southward, and many Hizballah fighters moving to Sidon to link up with Palestinians and Sunni fundamentalists.

Even before the quietening of the Shi'i suburbs, a new round of hostilities began in and around the Beirut Palestinian camps, this time a bitter struggle amongst the Palestinians themselves without Amal involvement. Preliminary clashes followed 'Arafat's April visit to Damascus, ending several months of calm for Shatila and Burj al-Barajina. In contrast to the Shi'i matter, the origins of these clashes were obscure, principally because on issues connected with 'Arafat the West Beirut media, including the leading daily *al-Safir,* had to be especially careful not to wander far from the

Syrian line. The novel feature was Syrian success in isolating 'Arafat's followers from other Palestinian and Lebanese groups; participation in the hostilities only involved 'Arafat's "Fath central committee" and the Syrian-sustained Fath rebels, under Abu Musa, in Damascus. One interpretation, obviously favored by Syria, accused 'Arafat of initiating the fighting and of using the meeting with Asad as cover for a quick blow to Palestinian opponents, this to maintain bargaining strength by sabotaging Syria's position in West Beirut during an important stage of Syria's maneuverings in relation to the Americans. The opposed interpretation, supported by 'Arafat's new friends in East Beirut, accused Syria of organizing everything as a standard proxy assault on a competitor, driven by the Syrian ambition finally to monopolize West Beirut before the presidential conjunction.[40]

Whatever the truth, or mix of truth, Damascus lost little time in steering events toward the long-sought-after elimination of the pro-'Arafat presence in the Beirut camps. After the intervention in the suburbs, Syria was in a temporarily favorable position while from mid-June the Syrian leadership took a markedly more critical stance regarding the PLO command, following the Bassam Abu Sharif article and other new signs of 'Arafat's readiness for dealings with the "Zionist entity." For once, Syria had no need for Amal; 'Arafat's "peace strategy" ensured that Palestinian dissidents could be relied on for this last push. More important, the massive Syrian armed presence in the surroundings of Beirut created a quite different military environment from that which existed in pre-1987 phases of the "Camps War." 'Arafat could expect little from Walid Junblat's Druzes or from the Communists; both had been thoroughly intimidated over the previous year by the Syrians, furious at their past spoiling tactics. Syrian tanks now squatted on the hillsides from which Palestinian artillery had formerly operated against Amal, supported from the Druze canton.

For Junblat, maintenance of Druze interests in the Shuf and his own survival for the moment required a calculated subservience to Damascus. As Abu Musa's cohorts, stiffened as never before by the close presence of Syrian power, ate into 'Arafat's strong points the PSP hastened to condemn "the 'Arafat rightist deviation" and "the calumnies against Syria and personal attacks on President Asad," also carefully referring to Abu Sharif's publication as "a traitorous document."[41] With Syrian troops patrolling his coastal access[42] and uncomfortably conscious of Syrian suspicions regarding his connection both to Israeli-influenced territory and to Palestinians in Sidon, Junblat could not afford even the faintest appearance of crossing Syria in Beirut during the lead-up to the presidential conjunction.

On 28 June, after more than a month of intermittent fighting, Shatila fell to Abu Musa's forces. Without any respite, hostilities then intensified in Burj al-Barajina, urgently targeted by Damascus as a source of pro-'Arafat collaboration with fundamentalists in neighboring Shi'i quarters. By this stage, Shatila was reduced to rubble and only a quarter of the dwellings in the Burj remained habitable, most civilians having fled both camps. In early July the Libyans suspended mediation attempts and withdrew their observers, commenting on "signs of a plot which they do not wish to be a party to,"[43] which is difficult to interpret as other than a veiled reference to Syria. The end came in the Burj on 8 July, when an agreement was reached for the evacuation of the last 175 'Arafat supporters and their families to Sidon, following the hundreds who had preceded them in the final few days.[44] On arrival in Sidon, the Fath commander from the Burj made bitter remarks about the neutral stand of such PLO affiliates as the Popular Front for the Liberation of Palestine (PFLP) and the Democratic Front for the Liberation of Palestine (DFLP): "We fought alone as our allies had their own calculations — until now they were not aware of the full dimensions of the conspiracy."[45]

Thus, Syria stabilized its West Beirut base for concentration on the tussle with East Beirut in the last two months of Jumayyil's term, but the advantage gained was in some measure illusory. On the one hand, as long as East Beirut maintained its cohesion on central matters, enjoyed the attentions of Iraq and Israel,and did not face determined pressure from the US, Syria would find it difficult to translate West Beirut assets into concrete advantage in the struggle regarding the central regime. In 1988, West Beirut had only limited weight in the power equation. Trouble in West Beirut could wreck Syrian maneuvering in relation to the Christian sector, but quiet could not decisively assist. On the other hand, concerning Hizballah and the pro-'Arafat elements, Syria had not so much solved its problems as deferred them or relocated them geographically. The cost of a "cheap" quietening of West Beirut was a reinforcement of the 'Arafat bastion in Sidon, a reception center for a stream of Palestinians and fundamentalists.

In the three months after the 23 September failure of the Syrian-American arrangement for a new president, two main streams of events affected West Beirut: renewed turbulence in the Shi'i community and interactions between Syria and local factors for facing the new reality between West and East Beirut.

The Amal-Hizballah matter resurfaced dramatically on the very day of the presidential conjunction, with the assassination in Awza'i of Da'ud Da'ud, the Amal military commander and southern warlord, and two senior subordinates. There was no doubt, certainly not for Amal and Syrian intelligence, that this represented a revenge blow by fundamentalist elements. Amal swiftly identified three persons and demanded their handover to the Syrians; Hizballah made no response. At first, leading clerics associated with Hizballah tried to deflect the issue by a violent verbal assault on East Beirut, with Subhi Tufayli railing against "the vipers of the Sharqiyya,"[46] but tension enveloped the southern suburbs leading to armed clashes in mid-October in both Shiyah and the West Biqa'. Hizballah accelerated preparations on its project to attack Amal in the south, using Sidon as a base for organization and allegedly buying weaponry from the Palestinians.[47]

On 21 November, four leading Hizballah personalities, including Tufayli and Ibrahim Amin, narrowly escaped a car bomb on returning to Ba'albak from talks in Damascus. Mystery shrouded the event, but in the prevailing atmosphere it was enough to cause an explosion of hostilities in Beirut. For the first time since February 1987, street fighting erupted in quarters covered by Syria's West Beirut "security plan," spilling out from the suburbs to many parts of Ra's Beirut. Only after 30 deaths on 27 November did the Syrians take any serious action, ending the episode with a parade of power and weapons seizures from both Amal and Hizballah units. Shi'i notables reacted with embarrassment, Fadlallah, for example, blaming unspecified "foreign intelligence services" which "manufacture incidents and wars."[48] The fundamentalist stance became more openly belligerent, including hints that if Amal did not allow "strugglers" to wage war on Israel in the south, Amal would be expelled from the suburbs regardless of the Syrian presence.[49]

In contrast to the near hysteria of May, Syria here responded phlegmatically to a far more serious geographical infraction of the West Beirut "security plan." This related to a fortuitous change in the Iranian-Syrian balance arising from Iran's summer defeat in the Gulf War and to greater Syrian confidence about being able to stand above the inter-Shi'i conflict, even using further local crises to increase influence with Hizballah while losing nothing with other Shi'i elements. For the moment, Iran's internal preoccupations following the cease-fire and new diplomatic openings to the West and the Arabs to outflank Iraq meant less patience and sympathy for perturbations caused by Lebanese fundamentalists;[50] the passive "holding operation" approach to Lebanon of those ascendant in Tehran, though probably temporary, suited Syria. In such conditions, Damascus could hope that the connections established within Hizballah by Syrian army intelligence — the responsibility of 'Alawites Ghazi Kan'an and 'Ali Duba — might be built on for greater coordination to Syrian purposes. One new Syrian idea involved the creation and manipulation of a joint Amal-Hizballah "operations room" for South Lebanon (see next section). For the longer term, however, incompatibilities remained unaltered; the ultimate fundamentalist agenda diverged from that of Damascus and no "Islamic regime" in Tehran would acknowledge Syrian Ba'thi hegemony over Lebanese Shi'is.

Apart from the inter-Shi'i aspect, three groups of political factors interacted in West Beirut after September 1988 under the umbrella of the Huss Cabinet: Syria's direct allies, including Amal, the Ba'th and the rival wings of the Syrian Social Nationalists; the "leftists," including Junblat's PSP, the Communists and assorted Nasserites, such as Mustafa Sa'd's Popular Army based in Sidon; and traditionalist "poles," chiefly the Sunni "Higher Islamic Council" under Mufti Hasan Khalid, but with extensions to Shi'i notables like Defense Minister 'Adil 'Usayran. The autonomist tendencies of the latter two groups and their non-Syrian Arab links — for the "left" meaning Palestinians, Libya, and Algeria and for the traditionalists Saudi Arabia and conservative regimes — especially irritated Damascus when an extraordinary challenge like the presidential vacuum required total coordination between West Beirut and Syrian policy.

Given the likelihood of a long stalemate after the September events, Syria looked both to create additional physical support for its presence in "Islamic and nationalist Lebanon" and to fashion more efficient instruments for pressure on East Beirut; the obvious initial step was a reorganization of the Lebanese army brigades in Syrian-dominated areas with their increased separation from Michel 'Awn's command in Yarza. 'Awn's problematic position with the institution of the military administration gave the appropriate excuse. Enthusiastic backing came from Syria's allies and the "left," each for its own reasons, but the traditionalist leaders resisted, suspecting that the main effects would be partitionary and destructive of established legitimacy rather than assisting the emergence of a new Lebanon. Syria hoped that reequipped, reoriented Lebanese army units under an amenable new West Beirut command would enable the Syrian Army to economize on its deployment while maintaining undiminished domination, would buttress demands for a unified Greater Beirut "security plan" — with Syrian withdrawals sapping East Beirut's grounds for objection — and might provide a nucleus for later Syrian supervision of the whole Lebanese military structure, as envisaged in the Tripartite Agreement. A senior Syrian official observed to *al-Safir* that the preliminary Syrian objective was "a reduction of the Syrian forces distributed around the streets of Beirut which are a target for the aims of

Syria's enemies in Lebanon, also bearing in mind the considerable expenses forced on Syria by the presence of its Army in the Lebanese capital."[51]

The army question furnished a convenient meeting point for the different outlooks of the Syrians and Druze leader Walid Junblat. For Junblat, the effective partition of the Army reduced the chances for the eventual emergence of a new central authority, thus holding off prospective submergence of the relatively small Druze community. Druze demographic fears, particularly regarding possible Shi'i encroachment on the Shuf, also received expression in Junblat's renewed proposals in December for a return of Christian refugees since 1985 seen less as a threat than a demographic buffer.[52] On the Army, Junblat could demonstrate "loyalty" to the Syrians while the favor was useful to Damascus in furthering its project. Junblat presumably gambled that the more far-reaching Syrian goals were impracticable; for their part, the Syrians had long experience of Junblat's gyrations for the survival of his autonomous region.

Damascus strongly disapproved of the hesitations of conservative Sunni personalities, chiefly grouped in the Higher Islamic Council, to adopt the requisite hostile stance against 'Awn and was suspicious of some West Beirut contacts with the Maronite Patriarchate, though Syria returned to a more open attitude toward Sufayr in late November. Through October, Acting Prime Minister Salim al-Huss, supported by conservative *zu'ama,* stalled on pressures for the al-Huss Cabinet to appoint a new army commander. Al-Huss viewed this as an unnecessary partitionary escalation which would only ease partitionary measures by East Beirut.[53] The acting prime minister had no patience with 'Awn's political performance, but conceived his responsibility as trying to end the constitutional impasse, not to prolong it, and apparently had hopes concerning Arab mediation efforts, unwanted by Syria. Barri and Junblat pushed the army proposal, with a vociferous Junblati media offensive against the mufti and the Higher Islamic Council. Isolated and intimidated by militias, al-Huss and the traditionalist group had no choice but to fall into line with Syrian wishes. In mid-November, the al-Huss Cabinet made Brig. Sami Khatib provisional army chief, 'Adil 'Usayran technically avoiding a formal dismissal of 'Awn. The wriggling made no difference: 'Awn's military council responded angrily and Syria had made clear the sort of West Beirut alignment it desired for 1989.

THE SOUTH: ISRAELI POWER AND LOCAL DEVELOPMENTS

Despite frequent outbreaks of fighting involving Israel, Palestinian groups, and local militias, the main geostrategic division of Lebanon south of the 'Awali in 1988 remained the alignment which had emerged after the 1985 Israeli withdrawals. Israel both guarded its northern border and projected itself into Lebanese affairs by maintaining a buffer zone in the form of a narrow arc from the sea to the Jizzin hills and the South Biqa'. This arc incorporated the so-called "security strip," the base for a fluctuating Israeli military presence and the 2,500 members of the Israeli proxy militia known as the South Lebanese Army (SLA), and an extension of Israeli influence into the mainly Christian Jizzin area, directly controlled by the SLA. The arc gave Israel topographic domination of all South Lebanon with a minimal inclusion of hostile population. In 1988, as in previous years, Lebanese and Palestinian fighters were able to make occasional shock incursions, for example the suicide car bombing which killed eight Israelis in October, but not to threaten the viability of the buffer zone.

The rest of the south comprised a patchwork of influences, confronting the Israelis and competing with one another, which can be considered as three geographical complexes. In the South Biqa' around Lake Qar'un, split from other "liberated" areas by the finger of Israeli influence reaching from Marj 'Ayun up to Jizzin, Hizballah established local primacy and a congenial operations center for assaults on the Israeli buffer zone. Eastward, in the Shi'i rural core of Nabatiyya and Jabal Aamel, Amal struggled to maintain a precarious supremacy, with a qualified suppression of Hizballah in 1988 being made possible only by truce arrangements with the Palestinians. On the coast, in the Tyre refugee camps, and around Sidon the Palestinian organizations held sway. Sidon's 'Ayn al-Hilwa and Miya Miya camps housed the Lebanese command center for 'Arafat's Fath, but also contained important facilities for a number of Palestinian radical groups antagonistic to 'Arafat's new political strategy. In mainly Sunni Sidon, 'Arafat had a strong connection with Sa'd's Popular Army, which helped to limit Syrian intelligence probing. Superimposed on the southern extensions of this patchwork and parts of the Israeli arc was the Unifil deployment of 5,500 men, coexisting uncomfortably with the factions and giving some local security, but ineffectual in its main task of holding the line between the Israelis and their opponents.

Through 1988, changes in Syrian and Palestinian priorities, related to Arab-Israeli developments, had implications for events in the south. Early in the year, Syria showed signs of wanting to help Syrian-American discussions by restraining radicalism and encouraging the Amal assault on Hizballah; after September, with the nonimplementation of the Syrian-American understanding regarding the presidency and 'Arafat's dramatic maneuvers for talks with the Israelis, Syria appeared to alter its approach. Damascus now had a renewed interest in instigating radical Palestinians to attack the Israelis and in playing with Shi'i fundamentalism. 'Arafat's achievement of direct contacts with the Americans in December greatly annoyed both the Syrians and many Palestinians, ranging from George Habash's PFLP to such extreme militants such as Ahmad Jibril and Abu Nidal. Proxy provocations on Israel's northern border were an obvious means to create an atmosphere of violence, discredit 'Arafat's "peace" offensive and reassert radical and Syrian weight. The trend of hostilities in the buffer zone from the October car bomb attack to December activities by the Syrian aligned PNSF fitted with such an approach, as observed by the IDF chief of staff.[54]

Strategies of the Palestinian organizations in South Lebanon increasingly diverged through 1988. Up to about October, competition to support the *intifada* made perseverance with efforts to penetrate the buffer zone *de rigueur* for all, regardless of local problems in Lebanon. 'Arafat's Fath, however, had an unfortunate summer, its reversals in Beirut being paralleled by a succession of failures against Israel. Israeli sources noted the elimination or apprehension of 10 Fath raiding units in the summer months, an attrition which retarded the organization's activities despite training of replacements.[55] Thereafter, 'Arafat's opening to the US following the November session of the Palestine National Council (see chapter on the Palestine Liberation Organization) was accompanied by a virtual suspension of military operations against the "security strip." In contrast, Palestinian radicals who repudiated 'Arafat's diplomacy had more incentive to pursue the "armed struggle."

The Syrian and Palestinian shifts complicated Amal's position, giving little time for the movement to use its March blow to Hizballah for consolidation in the south. The September assassination of Da'ud Da'ud, a central personality in Amal's southern structure, gravely damaged prospects for organizational coordination, already constantly threatened by Hizballah infiltration.[56] In this sphere, Syria's late-year drift toward a new look at exploiting fundamentalism could hardly have come at a more inconvenient juncture; it coincided with Hizballah moves to attack Amal in the Iqlim-al-Tuffah villages above Sidon in January 1989 and publicly surfaced in the subsequent Syrian-Iranian-sponsored "agreement" between the two parties by which Hizballah openly returned to Amal territory. An unfavorable trend in the Syrian-Iranian-Hizballah dimension increased the importance to Amal of maintaining the truce with the Palestinians, for example as reflected in a surprise 22 December agreement with the 'Arafat supporters for removing the "front" near 'Ayn al-Hilwa.[57] Amal's relations with the Palestinians were no longer dominated by geographical competition, but their management was made more intricate by Amal's need to cope with the fact that, at the end of 1988, Palestinian factions had entirely contradictory outlooks not just toward Syria but also toward the local confrontation with Israel.

Amal had always faced conflicting demands from other forces active in the south. The situation by early 1989, however, was particularly problematic: a forced link with Hizballah for provoking Israel, a continued tacit desire for quiet with Israel, a truce with Palestinians, some of whom wanted access to the border strip to provoke hostilities to derail the strategy of others who had an undeclared "cease-fire" regarding Israel, a Syrian ally juggling options, and the continuing "dance" for influence between Iran and Syria. Small wonder that different Amal fragments looked in different directions.

From the Israeli perspective, the level of challenge to the border zone in 1988 was about the same as that of 1987, again with Hizballah responsible for the majority but without the large-scale fundamentalist frontal assaults which had been mounted in the previous year.[58] (See also chapter on armed operations.) Israel viewed the development of the Hizballah infrastructure in the South Biqa' with special concern. This was the target for the only substantial Israeli land operation of the year, a preemptive incursion in early May to demolish the Hizballah bases in Maydun and other locations. The timing, following closely the Amal attack on Hizballah in Nabatiyya and paralleling Syrian-American discussions, stimulated fundamentalist suspicions and perhaps had implications for the hostilities in the southern suburbs, which began within days of the Israeli raid. In any case, Hizballah promptly replaced its losses in the Lake Qar'un vicinity, ideal as a base area because of the broken topography, the covering Shi'i population in such villages as Mashghara, the relative freedom from Syrian interference, and the proximity of targets. Israeli troops made further raids in July and August, but there were no illusions about lasting effects.[59]

Israel also launched 24 air strikes during 1988, concentrated against Hizballah in the South Biqa' and against a range of Palestinian command centers and installations around Sidon and above Damur, in the coastal hills of the Shuf. The main group of attacks came between the 19 October car bomb and the early November attempt to assassinate Antoine Lahad, the SLA commander. In this period, Israeli planes struck Mashghara, Fath and DFLP facilities near Sidon, and Jibril's Shuf base; these attacks accounted for about 30 of the c. 85 deaths caused by air raids in 1988.[60] On 8 December, Israeli forces made their deepest penetration of Lebanon for some years, with a combined air-sea night operation landing troops near Damur to assault the mountain headquarters of Jibril's PFLP-GC. With 20 of Jibril's followers killed, this helped settle scores for the 1987 hang-glider raid on northern Galilee (see *MECS* 1987, chapter on armed operations). Despite the fact that the Israeli operation took place within the Syrian deployment around Beirut, close to Syrian command points, and Jibril's status under direct Syrian patronage, the Syrian Army ignored the proceedings. Israel and Syria, as the main external powers with territorial presences in Lebanon, thus maintained their cautious avoidance of direct confrontation with one another, preferring to pursue conflicts of interest through proxies. (For more details on the military activity in this zone, see chapter on armed operations.)

NOTES

For the place and frequency of publications cited here, and for the full name of the publication, news agency, radio station, or monitoring service where an abbreviation is used, please see "List of Sources." Only in the case of more than one publication bearing the same name is the place of publication noted here.

1. Author's interview with a senior presidential adviser, Beirut, January 1988.
2. *NAD,* 22 February 1988.
3. *Al-Majalla,* 24 September 1988. Regarding Syrian-Lebanese relations the magazine claims Murphy agreed with Asad on 17 September that "the understanding on the character and quality of *'alaqat mumayyaza* between Lebanon and Syria will be reached in coming Syrian-Lebanese discussions, but the United States acknowledges that Syria has interests in Lebanon." *Al-Safir,* 6 December 1988, puts forward the blunt Syrian position (according to a Muslim parliamentary "pole") that "it is not possible to isolate the presidential elections from the agreement with Syria which doesn't care whether or not the elections take place as its overriding concern is its security beginning from Lebanon."
4. Text outlined in *al-Safir,* 4 March 1988.
5. On the occasion of the Shultz visit to the ME in March, the Syrians carefully separated failure to reach a regional understanding from Lebanese issues.
6. *Al-Safir,* 23 April 1988.
7. See W. W. Harris, *The Christian Camp on the Eve of the 1988 Lebanese Presidential Elections,* Occasional Paper Series (Tel Aviv University, Dayan Center, November 1988).
8. *Al-Safir,* 23 March 1988.
9. Ibid., 16 June 1988.
10. Ibid., 5 August 1988.
11. Ibid., 11 August 1988.
12. Ibid., 11 August 1988.
13. Ibid., 5 August 1988.
14. Ibid., 19 September. Also see *al-Nahar,* 28 October 1988. Sarkis Na'um on Murphy in Damascus, and *al-Majalla,* 24 September 1988.
15. The Syrians insisted on the elections taking place in the old parliament building in Sahat al-Nijma, across the confrontation line from East Beirut. Christian deputies found this a convenient excuse for not appearing, citing security arguments. East Beirut leaders demanded that the elections be held in the temporary parliament house on the Museum crossing, considered "neutral" territory.
16. *Al-Majalla,* 7 September 1988.
17. *Al-Safir,* 21 September 1988.
18. Ibid., 22 September 1988. (Walid Shuqayr's commentary, plausible despite bias.)
19. Ibid., 22 September 1988.
20. Ibid., 1 October; *al-Nahar,* 1 October 1988, does not quote the remark, merely referring to 'Awn's "indication" that he was still a presidential candidate.
21. Ja'ja' reemphasized the viability of federalism after the September events.

22. *Al-Safir,* 6 October 1988.
23. *NAD,* 10 October 1988.
24. *Al-Nahar,* 24 October 1988, quotes Jumayyil in an interview with the Kuwaiti daily *al-Anba* as alleging a telephone threat by Bakraduni.
25. *Al-Safir,* 21 October 1988. Kaslik, the university associated with the Maronite religious institution, is known for hard-line political standpoints.
26. *Al-Thawra,* Damascus, 25 September (quoted in *al-Safir,* 26 September 1988.)
27. *Al-Nahar,* 29 September 1988.
28. *Al-Majalla,* 12 October 1988.
29. *Al-Safir,* 27 May 1988.
30. The columns of Sarkis Na'um in *al-Nahar* and Walid Shuqayr in *al-Safir* are interesting sources for this sort of thing.
31. The following account is based on reports in *al-Safir,* 6-28 May 1988 and in *NAD,* 23, 30 May 1988.
32. *Al-Safir,* 28 May 1988 refers to "more than" 350 dead and "roughly" 1,800 wounded. The newspaper reported 525 casualties for the first three days.
33. Ibid., 16 May 1988. Reference to a "senior Syrian personality" (perhaps Asad) warning Shultz during his April talks in Damascus about the "hegemony of extremism in Lebanon." The personality is quoted: "Mr. Shultz, if you decide to come here another time to talk with us, I hope you will not be surprised to find your conversation partner wearing a turban, growing a beard, carrying his beads, and turning his eyes away from you as he speaks, because, in his fundamentalist way, he treats with you as with an infidel." This report also indicates that the Syrians emphasized to Shultz that "hesitation in agreeing to a Lebanese settlement with Syria will put developments in the constitutional conjunction in the hands of the fundamentalists." Syria's line, if accurately represented here, presumably reflected both cunning calculation in trying to stampede Washington and a touch of real worry. (Muwaffaq Madani column.)
34. Ibid., 16 May 1988.
35. *NAD,* 6 June 1988.
36. *Al-Safir,* 14 May 1988.
37. Ibid., 16 May 1988, as quoted by Muwaffaq Madani.
38. Ibid., 27 May 1988. (Five-point plan outlined.)
39. Ibid., 28 May 1988, comments by Ibrahim Amin.
40. See, for example, *NAD,* 4 July 1988 (includes observations by Abu Iyad).
41. *Al-Safir,* July 1988.
42. Author's observations on passing the PSP port at Khalda (installations surrounded by Syrian troops) on way to Sidon, November 1987.
43. *Al-Safir,* 6 July 1988.
44. Ibid., 6, 9 July 1988.
45. Ibid., 9 July 1988.
46. *Al-Nahar,* 26 September 1988.
47. *NAD,* 14 November 1988.
48. *Al-Safir,* 26 November 1988.
49. *NAD,* 26 November 1988.
50. Appeal from Iranian Foreign Minister Velayati to Hizballah for restraint (*al-Safir,* 25 November 1988). Khameneh'i calls for an end to inter-Shi'i problems (*al-Safir,* 29 November 1988).
51. *Al-Safir,* December 1988.
52. *NAD,* 26 December 1988. A Christian return was also important for the economic future of the Shuf.
53. *Al-Nahar,* 22 October 1988. Sarkis Na'um's comment on "the al-Huss Government and tough decisions."
54. *Ha'aretz,* 29–30 December 1988. "'Arafat's opponents have increased penetration attempts in order to derail his policies."
55. Ibid., 11–12 August 1988 (overseas weekly edition).
56. Apparently those responsible for the kidnapping of the American Untso officer in February were formerly Amal personnel.

57. *Al-Safir*, 23 December 1988.
58. *Ha'aretz*, 29–30 December 1988.
59. Ibid., 14–15 July, 25–26 August 1988.
60. Numbers derived from *al-Safir* and *Ha'aretz* reports.

Libya
(Al-Jamahiriyya al-'Arabiyya al-Libiyya al-Sha'biyya al-Ishtirakiyya al-'Uzma)

YEHUDIT RONEN

Libya's domestic and foreign affairs in 1988, the regime's 19th year in power, were dominated by Mu'ammar al-Qadhdhafi's mood of reconciliation and tendency to compromise.

Domestically, the Libyan leader concentrated his efforts on rekindling the people's "revolutionary" zeal and enhancing the regime's political prestige, virtually two sides of the same coin. In principal, such efforts did not signal any new departures from Qadhdhafi's earlier engagements in domestic affairs, all primarily aimed at further ensuring the regime's political survival. Practically, however, Qadhdhafi resorted during the year to new, shrewd tactics whose dynamics and consistency created the impression of being the goals rather than the means.

Seizing upon the occasion of the annual conference of the General People's Congress (GPC), formally the *Jamahiriyya*'s highest political authority, held in Ra's al-Unuf in early March, Qadhdhafi announced, somewhat dramatically, a new campaign for ensuring the people's liberties. The release of 400 prisoners on 4 March was the harbinger of political and economic moves and guidelines proclaimed later in the year with the aim of placating the population and projecting an image of a newly tolerant regime. At that stage no one could yet gauge the real significance of these measures. Nevertheless, as propaganda and public relations, they seemed to be effective in increasing the regime's popularity while at the same time creating a refreshing, positive atmosphere at home.

Qadhdhafi's fence-mending drive also encompassed the expatriate opposition, though with limited success. In any case, the opposition continued to be ineffective and did not pose any real threat to Qadhdhafi's leadership.

On the foreign front, the most noteworthy development was the peace concluded with Chad, with whom Tripoli had hitherto been embroiled in an eight-year war. Not only had the reconciliation with Chad won Qadhdhafi personal prestige, it was also of great political significance, since it gained Tripoli Ndjamena's recognition of the former's long-professed claim of sovereignty over the Aouzou Strip. Reconciliation with Chad also paved the way for a Libyan diplomatic breakthrough in Black Africa.

Libya was also at pains to improve its political standing in the Maghrib. The political and economic *rapprochement* which developed significantly during the year between Libya and its two neighbors, Tunisia and Algeria, and the plan for a political merger between Algiers and Tripoli, were clear marks of Libya's achievements.

The strong animosity between Libya and the US cast a dark, threatening shadow on

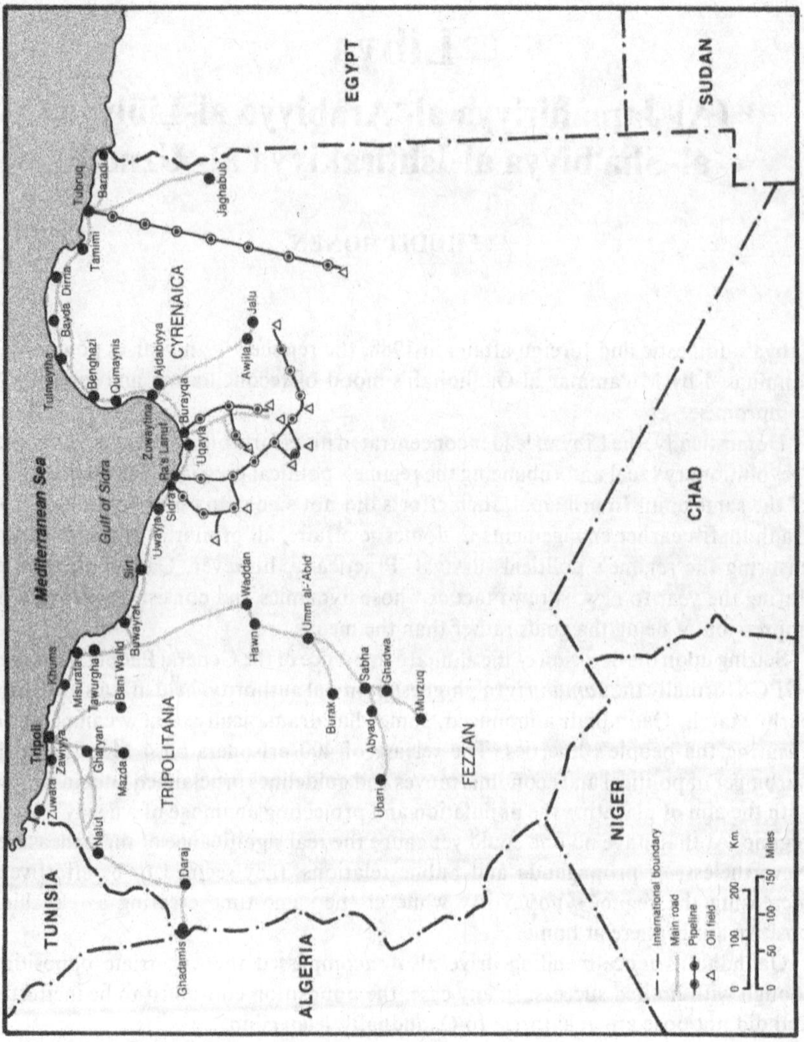
EGYPT
SUDAN
CHAD
NIGER
ALGERIA
TUNISIA
FEZZAN
TRIPOLITANIA
CYRENAICA
Mediterranean Sea
Gulf of Sidra
Tubruq
Baradi
Jaghabub
Tamimi
Darna
Bayda
Tulmaytha
Benghazi
Qumaynis
Ajdabiyya
Jalu
Awjila
Zuwaytina
Burayqa
Ra's Lanuf
'Uqayla
Sidra
'Uwayja
Sirt
Buwayrat
Waddan
Hawn
Umm al-'Abid
Khums
Misurata
Tawurgha
Bani Walid
Tripoli
Zawiyya
Zuwara
Gharyan
Mazda
Nalut
Daraj
Ghadamis
Sabha
Ghadwa
Burak
Abyad
Ubari
Murzuq
International boundary
Main road
Pipeline
Oil field
0 100 200 Km
0 50 100 150 Miles

Libya

the former's foreign affairs, offsetting much of the atmosphere of euphoria which prevailed on its other external fronts. Especially worrisome for Qadhdhafi was the new heightening of tension at the end of the year that evolved from Washington's accusation that Tripoli was manufacturing chemical weapons. On 4 January 1989, the mutual strain reached its peak when US navy fighters shot down two Libyan MiG-23 aircraft over the Mediterranean. In contrast to the intensive, if negative, nature of US-Libyan contacts, relations with the USSR were low-key.

Qadhdhafi's attempt to defuse tensions in foreign relations was also directed toward the regime in Cairo, albeit to a lesser degree. The attempt did not produce any tangible results, and mutual relations retained the hostile nature that had characterized them in past years. Against this background, it was not surprising that Tripoli continued to regard Sudan as a most important asset. Libya continued to provide Khartoum with political, military, and economic backing, hoping to tighten their ties to a level that would enable them to unify. In 1988, however, this did not materialize.

Libya channeled much of its energies into the issues concerning the Palestinian uprising in the West Bank and Gaza Strip and ameliorating relations with PLO chairman Yasir 'Arafat. To be more involved in these spheres fitted Qadhdhafi's interventionism and ideology and also reflected his pragmatism, since he wished in this way to achieve a more central position in inter-Arab politics.

INTERNAL AFFAIRS

ATTEMPTING TO GEAR UP THE PEOPLE'S "REVOLUTIONARY" AWARENESS

As had already become routine, the Basic People's Congresses (BPCs) held their annual meetings throughout the *Jamahiriyya* in late 1987-early 1988. (For details on the BPCs' position in the overall system of the "people's power," see *MECS* 1976–77, pp. 526–27). Formally, the BPCs were to discuss and then recommend policies to the country's highest forum, the GPC, which was to meet in March. Though Qadhdhafi could find satisfaction from the smooth and orderly functioning of the political system of the "people's power", which celebrated its 11th anniversary in 1988, he appeared to be gravely troubled by what he termed the people's "indifference" toward the "revolutionary" process. In particular, Qadhdhafi was concerned with the falling attendance at the BPCs' meetings which clearly indicated, though he did not say so explicitly, a much more dangerous process, namely the further erosion of the people's "revolutionary" zeal. While that process was not new (see chapters on Libya in earlier volumes of *MECS*), Qadhdhafi feared that continued erosion of such zeal could seriously damage his personal and political prestige and, in turn, jeopardize his regime's hold on the country.

Thus, the Libyan leader spared no effort to try to rekindle the people's "revolutionary" zeal and, in the process, attended in an unusual manner many BPCs and addressed many other popular forums. "All the masses, men and women, are required to attend the popular conferences."[1] Not attending the BPCs' sessions "cannot be allowed to continue and we must stop it," he further stated.[2]

Qadhdhafi's criticism was mainly directed at the educated, primarily doctors and the students. The BPC, Qadhdhafi stated angrily, "is now a medium which is backward to a great extent, in which illiteracy and ignorance prevail."[3] Wishing to change that situation, the Libyan leader even threatened the absent doctors with the withdrawal of their licenses should they fail to attend future meetings. Qadhdhafi also indirectly referred to student protests about conditions at the universities, emphasizing that the BPC was the only forum in which they were allowed to protest. "If anyone protests, we get hold of him, and we search for his card to find out whether he was present [in the BPC] or not. If he was not present, his alibi will not be accepted. He would be equal to an animal,"[4] he elaborated in a threatening tone.

THE ANNUAL CONFERENCE OF THE GENERAL PEOPLE'S CONGRESS

The flagging "revolutionary" enthusiasm did not disrupt the functioning of the "people's power" system. On 2–9 March, the GPC convened in Ra's al-Unuf in the Sidra Gulf, as scheduled.

The week-long deliberations of the GPC, formally the country's sole independent political decision-making body, resulted in a long list of resolutions regarding domestic and foreign affairs. None of them marked a departure from previous decisions and all clearly bore Qadhdhafi's seal, as he himself said during a long speech at the GPC's opening session. The major resolutions concerned economic development, agriculture, and administration. Most noteworthy were the resolutions to reorganize society in such a way as to ensure its productivity; and to consolidate "strategic projects" which would "generate revenue as an alternative to oil" and which would "guarantee self-sufficiency" and "agricultural wealth." The GPC also ratified the budget for 1988. The resolutions on foreign policy reiterated professed and chewed-over principles.[5] Once again, the real significance of the GPC annual conference lay mainly in the fact of its having taken place and its smooth operation rather than in having enunciated any new policies.

MINOR CHANGES IN THE GENERAL PEOPLE'S COMMITTEE

In keeping with established pattern, the GPC conference ended with an announcement of changes in the General People's Committee (GPCom, the equivalent of a cabinet). There was virtually no reshuffle and all the secretaries (equivalent to ministers) continued to hold their portfolios (for the table of the 1987 GPCom composition, see *MECS* 1987, p. 565). However, three new offices were added to the GPCom: Secretariat (equivalent to a ministry) for Marine Wealth headed by Muftah Muhammad Ku'ayba; Secretariat for Vocational Training under Ma'tuq Muhammad Ma'tuq; and Secretariat for Mass Mobilization and Revolutionary Guidance, headed by 'Ali al-Shahiri. These changes dealt only with structure, and even so only with broadening the Cabinet rather than changing its structure. This was in stark contrast to the comprehensive GPCom reshuffle of 1987, which reflected Qadhdhafi's dissatisfaction with certain developments in domestic and foreign affairs. In 1988, Qadhdhafi appeared to be more preoccupied with easing internal tensions rather than aggravating them. In any case, he could afford to feel at ease, because the new GPCom was reinforced by two hard-line revolutionaries, Ma'tuq and al-Shahiri, who, along with the other members of the Cabinet, all known for their dedication to Qadhdahfi, were expected to take a responsible care of the country's affairs.

A DECLARED COMMITMENT TO THE PEOPLE'S PERSONAL LIBERTIES

The problem of ensuring individual freedoms in the *Jamahiriyya* greatly exercised

Qadhdhafi during the year under review. "The revolution is a cry for freedom.... Consequently, what interests me is to make the state into a state of the free masses...," the Libyan leader stated on 2 March on the occasion of the GPC conference,[6] the year's main political event. The next day, 400 prisoners were reportedly released from the jails. Wishing to exploit the releases to enhance his personal and political prestige, Qadhdahfi climbed onto a bulldozer and, while the television cameras recorded the event, he personally demolished the gates of Tripoli's central prison.[7] In the weeks following, the film was replayed every evening on state-controlled television, and the state-controlled newspapers published daily lists of names of Libyans and institutions that had sent telegrams of thanks and bouquets of flowers to their leader.

On 7 March, 130 foreign prisoners were freed; it remained unclear whether they formed a part of the 400 already reported. The authorities admitted, however, that about 100 detainees, all accused of plotting against the "people's power" with foreign help, were still in jail.[8] A hostile foreign source put the number of political prisoners still jailed in Libya in the first half of 1988 at 2,200.[9] There was no independent report on the extent of the releases, the number of those still in prison, or the kind of crimes of which they had been accused.

Qadhdhafi's surprising and well-advertised move was the first in a series of measures all aimed, as he declared, at strengthening the people's personal liberties. Nevertheless, when examining more closely the release and other subsequent acts (see below), it would seem that Qadhdhafi was motivated by pragmatic considerations rather than principles. Qadhdhafi primarily wished to achieve a double aim: defusing the Libyans' grievances against the rigid control over their lives of the hated "Revolutionary Committees," while increasing his popularity at home and abroad. (The "Revolutionary Committees" are responsible both for safeguarding Qadhdhafi's personal security and political standing and for kindling "revolutionary" zeal — in other words, of ensuring the regime's future. In recent years, they had gained such dominance over internal life, that even Qadhdhafi himself was troubled. For more details, see *MECS* 1984–85, pp. 557–58). An additional motive for Qadhdahfi's release of prisoners could have been his wish to further encourage reconciliation with the expatriate Libyan opposition (see below).

On 9 March, Qadhdhafi added to his "spring surprises," as one Arab journal put it,[10] by calling for the abolition of capital punishment, except for those found guilty of crimes of violence or of conspiring with foreign states. The death sentence should be replaced by life imprisonment "with no possibility of parole or pardon," he stated.[11] "Only He who created man should be the one to interfere in his life...," said Qadhdhafi in his second, lengthy public reference to that issue.[12] (It should be recalled that only a year earlier nine Libyans accused of treason were publicly executed in Benghazi by the authorities; see *MECS* 1987, p. 550.)

Carried on the wave of his new spirit of freedom Qadhdhafi also referred to the Libyans' right to travel abroad freely. "We did not release people from prison in order to imprison them internally," he stated on 9 March, calling on all Libyans who had been banned from traveling to show up at the passport office on 12 March "to end this matter."[13] On that day Qadhahdfi himself appeared at the passport office and, again in a theatrical act, publicly tore up lists of those banned from traveling abroad.[14]

Qadhdhafi also referred to the issue of compulsory military service which was enacted in 1978 (see *MECS* 1978–79, pp. 687–88). He strongly criticized the state of affairs in which people were "conscripted off the streets" and for periods that were too long. "I want to see an end to all this. Everyone should know that when he reaches a certain age and graduates he will have to spend only 24 months in the Army. When he finishes, his place will be taken by someone else."[15]

Qadhdhafi's spirit of liberalization also encompassed the economic sphere. After more than a decade of crusading against private trade, in 1988 he began to loosen the state's hold on the economy by encouraging private enterprises. "You can import and export in complete freedom," Qadhdhafi said in one of his public appearances.[16] That reversal seemed to be the result of the authorities' urgent need to cope with the severe and chronic shortages of food and other basic commodities which, in turn, cause great discontent among the population (for Libya's economic difficulties and the consequent day-to-day hardships of the population, see chapters on Libya in recent volumes of *MECS*). Not only did Qadhdhafi urge the reopening of private shops,[17] but he also gave his approval to the black market which he had hitherto vehemently condemned. The flourishing black market, Qadhdhafi said, was a positive development because it showed the people's initiative in meeting their needs.[18] By the standards of his "social-economic revolution" (see chapters on Libya in earlier volumes of *MECS*), this was a significant deviation from the unequivocal rejection of unproductive activities.

THE ATTEMPT TO RECONCILE OPPOSITION

Qadhdhafi's reconciliatory mood was also exemplified by his attitude toward the expatriate Libyan opposition. As part of an effort to settle the dispute with the opposition, Qadhdhafi met several of its leaders while in Algeria in 1987 and invited them to return home. The main members of the opposition, 'Abd al-Mun'im al-Huni, one of the members of the Revolutionary Command Council which seized power in September 1969, and Mahmud Sulayman Maghribi, who had been Qadhdhafi's first prime minister after the 1969 coup, reportedly visited Libya,[19] but eventually decided to remain abroad. In any case, these two cases did not alter the pattern of hostile relations between Qadhdhafi and his opponents in exile. The latter refused to return home despite Qadhdhafi's repeated invitations and promises that no harm would befall them.[20]

Qadhdhafi's attempts to make peace with the opposition should be viewed especially against the background of the relatively new serious threat to the regime, the reinforcement of the expatriate opposition by senior officers imprisoned during 1987 by the Chadian Army. The most annoying case was that of the commander of the Libyan forces in Chad, Col. Khalifa Bilqasim Haftar, who defected with several hundred of his soldiers to the Libyan opposition group, the National Front for the Salvation of Libya.[21] This group, the major Libyan opposition movement, continued, however, to be more of a nuisance than a real threat to the regime.

FOREIGN AFFAIRS

THE AFRICAN ARENA

THE PEACE PROCESS WITH CHAD

The tension which dominated Libyan-Chadian relations in early 1988 was clearly reflected in mutual charges and countercharges of preparations of war. Especially vociferous were Ndjamena's complaints of Tripoli's violation of its airspace by almost daily surveillance flights over the Tibesti region.[22] Libya, however, categorically denied these "lies" and "fabrications" of "agent" Habré.[23]

Whatever the truth, the increased number of Libyan and Libyan-backed Chadian forces in western Sudan, bordering on Chad (see chapter on Sudan), together with Libya's building of major fortifications at key points in the Aouzou Strip — a 112,000 sq. km. area claimed by both countries — further inflamed relations. The Libyan defensive positions were reportedly protected by mine fields, missiles, mobile radar systems, and other weapons, manned by a total of 12,000 soldiers.[24] The building of such a defensive line did not necessarily reflect Qadhdhafi's immediate offensive intentions, though certainly no one could rule out such an option. Rather it indicated Libya's fear of being attacked once again by Chadian forces, with or without direct French and American involvement. It should be recalled that the penetration of Chadian mobile units deep into Libyan territory in fall 1987 — for the first time during Libya's war with Chad — was a trauma for the Libyan leadership.

Notwithstanding the mounting tension, the two sides were not dragged into renewed cycles of fighting. On the Libyan side, it should be noted, there was no logic in resuming clashes, at least as long as Tripoli's virtual control of the Aouzou Strip was not threatened. Also, there was no logic in Libya's resumption of the fighting considering the timing, the eve of the meeting of the *ad hoc* committee of the Organization of African Unity (OAU), that was to discuss the demand of both sides for sovereignty over the Aouzou Strip.[25]

At the same time, however, Libya did not sit idly by; shelving the military option at least temporarily, it prepared the ground for political action against Chad. On 19 March, five Chadian opposition factions met in Tripoli and signed an agreement confirming their confidence in Goukkouni Wuedei as the president of the Libyan-backed *Gouvernement d'Union Nationale de Transition* (Gunt).[26] The Libyan media which reported the event entirely ignored the other Gunt leadership, established by Qadhdhafi in 1986, with al-Shaykh Ibn 'Umar at its head (see *MECS* 1986, p. 519). Libya was also reportedly providing, along with Algeria, aid to raise a new army for Goukkouni.[27]

Nevertheless, along with declaring its support for the Goukkouni Gunt, Libya spelled out in early April, for the first time since Habré's advent to power in 1982, its conditions for recognizing his government. They were: Habré's recognition of Libyan sovereignty over the Aouzou Strip, the withdrawal of foreign forces (i.e., France and the US) from Chad, the conclusion of a cease-fire between Goukkouni and Habré, and the release of Libyans captured by the Habré Army.[28] Chad, however, totally rejected Qadhdhafi's "ultimatum."[29]

Almost two months later, Qadhdhafi made another surprise move, aimed at achieving a reconciliation with Habré's Government and other African states. On 25 May, the silver jubilee of the foundation of the OAU and the "Africa Day," the Libyan leader declared Libya's recognition of Habré's Government and the end of "all outstanding problems" between the two countries. Qadhdhafi described his one-sided move as "a present to Africa" on its festive day, hoping that "reducing the burden on the shoulders of the leaders of Africa" would enable them to devote themselves to solving the continent's problems. Qadhdhafi went on to offer Chad a "Libyan Marshall plan" to reconstruct cities damaged by Libya's "punishment raids" during its war in Chad. Libya also suggested that Chadian prisoners of war would be released to be repatriated through the OAU.[30] One should notice, however, that Qadhdhafi did not refer to the issue of the disputed Aouzou Strip. His disregard of the issue was presumably a deliberate tactic aimed at showing that the area, long annexed by Libya, was part and parcel of its territory.

Habré's reactions to Qadhdhafi's initiative were cautious. Wishing perhaps to signal further goodwill towards Chad, Qadhdhafi on 14 June arrested the Chadian leader, Ibn 'Umar, who had not joined Goukkouni's Gunt and remained an active opponent of Habré.[31]

Whether connected or not to Ibn 'Umar's arrest, a short while later Libyan-Chadian political ties improved. On 7-9 July, the foreign ministers met for direct talks in Libreville in Gabon. Though the talks failed to produce a resumption of ties or even to set a date or place for another meeting, they were important because they were the first official meeting between representatives of the two countries since the outbreak of the war.

On 22 September, additional progress was made when Libya handed over 10 Chadian prisoners of war to representatives of the OAU.[32] Five days later, another 110 Chadian prisoners were also handed over in the same way.[33]

On 3 October, Libya's policy of pressing for reconciliation led on 3 October to the restoration of diplomatic relations "at the highest level immediately."[34] The dispute over the Aouzou Strip remained unresolved, but both countries pledged in a joint communiqué to settle the issue in a peaceful way.[35]

Qadhdhafi's reconciliation with Chad reflected, first of all, his estimation that the disadvantages of perpetuating the state of war significantly outnumbered the advantages. Furthermore, Qadhdhafi's two proclaimed reasons for military intervention in Chad in 1980, the need to assure Libya's security and the commitment to Chad's Muslim population, seemed irrelevant in 1988. Libya's military presence in Chad only intensified friction with France, the US, and Habré's Chad to the point of of seriously endangering Libya's security and Qadhdhafi's political position. Helping the Muslims in Chad seemed, in any case, to be only a justification for Libya's encroachment on Chad. On the other hand, Libya's main though undeclared motive for militarily intervening in Chad — to make its *a posteriori* annexation of the Aouzou Strip a *fait accompli* — was undoubtedly achieved. Under these circumstances, a continuation of fighting was not supposed to yield any additional significant benefits, while it certainly continued to damage Libya's essential interests. Thus, considering the circumstances and being affected by Algerian pressure, Qadhdhafi had taken the optimal course.

DIPLOMATIC BREAKTHROUGH IN BLACK AFRICA

In its foreign policy, Libya in 1988 embarked on a new campaign aimed at ameliorating its political standing in the African continent. "Libya is an active state in the African family. It constitutes the northern gate of Africa....Libya is also the Mecca of African revolutionaries," Qadhdhafi stated on 25 May. He also offered to reconcile himself with Chad (see above) and to resume Libyan diplomatic ties with eight African countries, all aligned with the West: Kenya, Liberia, Zaire, Mauritius, Gabon, Senegal, Gambia, and the Ivory Coast.[36]

The Libyan offensive of conciliation chalked up significant successes. On 22

October, Libya restored its ties with Zaire, which had been frozen by Libya in May 1984 in protest against Zaire's resumption of diplomatic relations with Israel in 1983 (see *MECS* 1983–84, p. 591). The Libyans had played a major role in ousting Israel from Africa in the early 1970s; in the late 1970s and the 1980s, Libya refused to maintain diplomatic ties with any state maintaining diplomatic ties with Israel. The abandonment of that principle in 1988 reflected Qadhdhafi's new pragmatism, which meant giving up the rigid ideological line in foreign policy in general and in African policy in particular.

The hitherto troubled relations with Liberia should be mentioned. Monrovia's restoration of diplomatic ties with Israel in 1983 drew a virulent response from Tripoli. In late spring 1984 Libya decided to "freeze" its relations with Liberia (see *MECS* 1983–84, p. 591). In November, the relations of the two countries improved markedly following the visit to Liberia of the Libyan foreign liaison secretary, Jadallah 'Azuz al-Talhi, the highest ranking official to visit the Liberian capital since 1984.

Another Libyan success was the resumption of diplomatic relations with Senegal on 5 November. Exactly eight years earlier Senegal broke off its ties with Libya on the ground that it was involved in subversive activities against Senegal (see *MECS* 1979–80, p. 642).

Diplomatic relations with Nigeria, Niger, and Somalia also improved considerably.

At the same time, Libya continued to maintain its well-established ties with the "revolutionary" regimes in Burkina Faso, Ghana, and Uganda, as attested to by the visits to Tripoli of the heads of state of these three countries: Blaise Compaoré (Burkina Faso) on 2–4 January, 29–31 May, and 7–9 November; Jerry Rawlings (Ghana) on 6–7 November, and Yoweri Museveni (Uganda) on 17–18 January and 6–7 November 1988.

Other important visits by African heads of state to Tripoli were those of João Bernardo (Guinea-Bissau) on 19–21 May, of Ibrahim Babangida (Nigeria) on 30 May-1 June, of Moussa Traoré (Mali) on 27–28 October, and of Muhammad Siad Barre (Somalia) on 18–21 December 1988.

LIBYA'S STRENGTHENED POSITION IN THE MAGHRIB

IMPROVED TIES WITH ALGERIA

Despite Algeria's decision in late 1987 to postpone the union with Libya proposed by Tripoli (see *MECS* 1987, pp. 557–58), bilateral ties improved signficantly in 1988.

On 11 January, the Algerian president, Chedli Benjedid, *en route* from Tunis, arrived in Tripoli where he received an enthusiastic welcome.[37] Though Libya did not release details on the visit's aims or its results, one may assume that apart from discussing their bilateral ties, the two leaders also dealt with the improvement of inter-Maghrib relations. Since the political and economic benefits of *rapprochement* with Algeria and Tunisia were highly attractive, Qadhdhafi reciprocated with a three-day visit to Algeria on 6 February. Two days later, Qadhdhafi and Benjedid arrived together at the Tunisian-Algerian border village of Sakiet Sidi Youssef (200 km. west of Tunis), to mark the 30th anniversary of the French bombing there during the Algerian War of Independence. Qadhdhafi's participation in the ceremony was surprising since the event had hitherto been commemorated only by Algeria and

Tunisia, who considered it a symbol of their common heritage and fate. Qadhdhafi's participation was a clear indication of accelerating *rapprochement* between the three countries under the aegis of Algeria.

On 19 March, the fifth anniversary of the Treaty of Friendship and Concord signed by Algeria and Tunisia and later by Mauritania, Jallud visited Algiers and Tunis, where his talks concentrated on unifying the two countries.[38] The issue was discussed during Jallud's second visit to Algiers on 27–28 June when the two leaders decided to submit the question of Libyan-Algerian union to discussion by "the popular masses" of their two "fraternal countries." The visit also resulted in a number of agreements: implementing the "creation of a joint Libyan-Algerian Arab Company for operating an aluminum complex in the Great *Jamahiriyya,*" for the establishment of a joint bank named the "Arab Bank for Investment and Commerce," as well as other decisions on promoting various common economic activities.[39]

During the fall and winter, Libya asserted that "work is going on relentlessly in both Libya and Algeria to establish union,[40] but there was no visible sign of progress in this direction. It seemed that the issue of union had reached an impasse, apparently because of the lack of agreement on what union involved. While Libya seemed to prefer political union in one state, Algeria seemed to prefer a federal arrangement. The violent riots which swept Algeria in the winter also compelled the government to focus on domestic, rather than foreign affairs.

Jallud's visits to Algiers on 5 and 25 December may have been aimed at speeding up the process of union. He may also have been trying to mobilize Algerian political support for Libyan efforts to deter the US from attacking Libya (see below; for other intra-Maghrib activities, in which Qadhdhafi was involved during 1988, see chapter on inter-Arab relations).

IMPROVED TIES WITH TUNISIA

The amelioration in Libya's relations with Tunisia, already noticed in late 1987, continued in 1988.

On 4 February, Qadhdhafi began a three-day official visit to Tunisia, his first since the onset of the serious dispute between the two countries in 1985 (see *MECS* 1984–85, pp. 564–65). During the visit, a five-point agreement was reached on tightening cooperation in "all fields." The most noteworthy items were the decisions to cancel visa requirements from 15 February; to build the planned trans-Maghrib gas pipeline through Tunisia; to supply Algerian natural gas to West Libya, and to implement the ruling of the International Court of Justice (ICJ) regarding the border of the continental shelf.[41] The visit and its results should also be viewed within the context of Libya's place in the Maghrib. Libya put it plainly, stating that closer ties with Tunis were "a step" toward building a greater Maghrib unity,[42] wishing, thereby, to free itself of its isolation on the fringes of North Africa (see chapters on Libya in recent volumes of *MECS*).

Libyan eagerness to improve relations with Tunisia was further indicated by Qadhdhafi's visit there on his way back from Algeria on 8 February, when he came over to participate in the symbolically important memorial ceremony together with the Tunisian and Algerian heads of state (see above).

The pace of *rapprochement* was further maintained when the two countries announced on 15 February the opening of their border to "free movement" of their citizens[43] and with the return to Tunisia, on 9 March, of two dredges along with their 25-member crews. The latter had been reportedly detained earlier in Libya's territory. The same day Libya also released "all other" Tunisians who had been arrested in recent years in Libya.[44] On 19–20 March, Jallud visited Tunis at the end of a trip to Algiers. As reported by Tripoli, the issue of building up "the unity of our Arab nation" dominated the talks.[45] Less than three weeks later, the two countries signed a cooperation agreement in Tripoli, encompassing political, cultural, economic, and foreign relations.[46] On 5 April, Tripoli's cordial attitude toward Tunis was further underlined by Qadhdhafi's announcement of the withdrawal of a Libyan division from the common border with Tunisia.[47] Two days later, Qadhdhafi also announced the abolition "as of today" of the Ra's Jadir border checkpoint between the "one and only Arab people" in Libya and Tunisia. The Libyan leader even took an active role — though of a merely symbolic effect — in helping to destroy the checkpoint.[48]

On 22–23 May, Qadhdhafi paid an additional visit to Tunisia. The press statement issued at the end of the visit emphasized Libyan and Tunisian agreement to ensure the freedom of movement by providing their citizens with "a unified identity card," the unrestricted movement of goods, and the freedom of residence, work, and possession of private property.[49]

The reopening of the common border led to a substantial increase in the supplies of imported goods in Tripoli. A large number of Libyans reportedly crossed the border to buy commodities in Tunisia. According to one estimate, during the two months after frontiers were reopened, 200,000 Libyans spent c. $200m in Tunisia.[50] The increase of imported food and other goods in Libya helped ease popular grievances caused by the severe shortages of food (see above). This was another positive by-product for Qadhdhafi of the political *rapprochement* with Tunisia.

Rapprochement reached another peak at the end of May when the two countries announced the appointment of ambassadors (their decision to resume diplomatic ties had been taken in late 1987; see *MECS* 1987, p. 558). 'Abd al-'Ati 'Ubaydi, the Libyan representative to the Arab League in Tunis, was also named the new envoy.[51]

In mid-June, however, their relations ran into a drag as indicated by the repeated delays in Tunisian President Zayn al-'Abidin Ben 'Ali's state visit to Libya. The Libyans attributed the postponement to the president's "fatigue" and "illness" and denied any tension in their relations.[52] Nevertheless, it seemed that the disagreement between them mainly concerned the extent of cooperation in a broad range of economic ventures, especially over the joint prospecting for oil and its exploitation.[53] One may assume that Tunisia, which in 1988 suffered a severe drought and locust plague, was applying pressure for greater economic cooperation and revenue sharing, which Libya was not enthusiastic about meeting. But Qadhdhafi could not afford to let his ties with Tunisia be marred once again, knowing as he did that such a development would be detrimental to his *rapprochement* with Algeria. Anxious to keep up the momentum on 10–11 July, Tripoli hosted Tunisian Prime Minister Hedi Baccouche,[54] and, on 24 July, inaugurated a new sea connection between the two countries, since it had become necessary to cope with the growing demand for movement between them.

On 6–8 August, the Tunisian president visited the *Jamahiriyya,* his first visit since seizing power in November 1987. He was welcomed in a grand ceremony,[55] reflecting the importance of the visit to Qadhdhafi, personally and politically. Beyond the verbal euphoria which dominated the visit, practical decisions were adopted to "accomplish integration," as "a first step toward the attainment of unity," and as a contribution toward "the building of a great Arab Maghrib." The most important decision was an agreement on the joint exploration for offshore oil in the Gulf of Gabes.[56] In less than a month, on 3 September, the Buri oil field, 125 km. northwest of Tripoli, was festively opened to joint exploitation.[57]

The improved ties between the two countries were further exemplified by the exchange of visits of high-ranking officials. Some of the visits were connected with Tunisian attempts to reconcile Libya and Chad,[58] the US,[59] and Egypt.[60] The chief Libyan visits to Tunis were Jallud's 11-day stay in September and the four-day visit of al-Khuwaylidi al-Humaydi, a most senior member of the Libyan leadership in the same month.

On 8 December, Qadhdhafi arrived in Tunis for a four-day visit. The two countries seized the event to reiterate their "determination to continue efforts to realize their people's aspiration for unity."[61] One could also assume that Qadhdhafi used the visit to ask the Tunisian Government to exploit its contacts with Washington to influence the US to change its military policy toward Libya.

RELATIONS WITH THE UNITED STATES: FURTHER ESCALATION OF TENSION

Fears of another US attack continued to obsess Qadhdhafi throughout 1988. The US bombing of Tripoli and Benghazi in spring of 1986 nourished the Libyan leader's perception of the US as his most dangerous enemy.

Libya's fear of an imminent American assault, or any sort of "hostile scheme" against its regime was repeatedly expressed by Qadhdhafi throughout the year.[62] Libyan expressions of anxiety were colored by a barrage of virulent attacks against the "Yankee contemporary imperialist leaders' barbarism...[and] decadence [which] shows that they are real enemies of humanity, freedom, and peace...the enemies of mankind."[63]

Although White House and State Department officials claimed that the Qadhdhafi regime's threat to its neighbors in the Mediterranean region was receding,[64] Washington still found it expedient to act to further damage Qadhdhafi's position and erode his influence in the Maghrib. Around the turn of 1987, when the process of political *rapprochement* between Tripoli and Tunis was gathering momentum, Washington reportedly asked the French Government to exert pressure upon Tunisia in order to curb, or at least slow down, that process.[65] Simultaneously, the US exerted direct political and economic pressures on Tunis,[66] with the same goal in mind. As expected, the Libyan media responded angrily, denouncing the US "hypocrisy" and "poking of its colonial nose" in Maghrib affairs.[67]

In late July, the strained Libyan-US relations were further aggravated by the arrest of eight Libyan citizens in the US on the charge of running a covert intelligence operation that included planning the assassination of a senior US official (the retired Lt. Col. Oliver North) in retaliation for his role in planning the bombing raids against Libya in 1986. The Libyans were also accused of channeling funds to finance anti-American activities.[68] Libya denied the charges, claiming that the arrest of the Libyan "students," as it described them, was another American "terrorist" and "racist act of aggression" against the *Jamahiriyya*.[69] On 9 November, the Libyan "students" were deported by the US and returned home.[70]

Animosity between the two countries reached a new high in the fall-winter, following the US claim that Libya was "on the verge of full-scale production" of chemical weapons[71] in the "largest chemical weapons production plant the CIA had detected anywhere."[72] Libya categorically denied the American allegation, saying that the plant to which the US referred was a "pharmaceutical plant."[73] Simultaneously, Libya accused the US of preparing an attack on Tripoli for its alleged involvement in manufacturing chemical weapons.[74]

On 4 January, Libyan fears were substantiated when US navy fighters shot down two Libyan MiG-23 jet fighters over the Mediterranean off the Libyan coast. Libya claimed that its aircraft were on "a routine reconnaissance patrol over international waters" when the US carried out its "premeditated attack" on them. Qadhdhafi branded the incident an act of increased "American terrorism."[75] The US version was that the American pilots were acting "in self defense" in shooting down the Libyan aircraft that had "continued to close in a hostile manner" while aircraft of the Sixth Fleet were carrying out "routine operations."[76] It is also possible that the Americans provoked the Libyan aircraft or had simply attacked them. One cannot rule out the further possibility that the Libyans, who were very nervous, had initiated the clash, wishing thereby to thwart a more damaging assault on targets within their country.

Whatever the case, the new low point in Libyan-US relations came at a bad time for Qadhdhafi — the eve of the change of administration in Washington. Tripoli's oft-repeated hopes that a new era in relations with the US would begin immediately after President Reagan left the White House[77] did not seem to be, at least at the turn of 1988, very likely.

LIBYA AND THE ARAB WORLD

LIBYA AND EGYPT

Despite repeated mediation attempts by various Arab governments aimed at reconciling Tripoli and Cairo, and despite sporadic gestures of mutual goodwill, relations between the two countries remained hostile in 1988.

On 1 March, while Egyptian President Husni Mubarak was visiting Khartoum, Cairo announced that four Libyan MiG-23 fighter jets had landed in Egypt. Libya claimed, in a somewhat delayed reaction, that the landings were an "emergency," forced upon the aircraft by "bad weather conditions [and] lack of fuel."[78] Egyptian sources reported, however, that all of the Libyan pilots had asked for political asylum,[79] giving the impression that they had defected. Whatever the case, the whole affair ended 10 days later with the return of the aircraft and their crews to Libya. The release of the Libyan MiGs seemed to be a part of a deal concluded between the two countries, an impression corroborated by the release on 10 March of 36 Egyptians held in Libya on charges of espionage.[80]

Being at the height of a reconciliatory campaign at home and abroad, Qadhdhafi tried to create an atmosphere of *détente* with Egypt, if entirely on his own terms. On 28 March, he announced the withdrawal of all Libyan military forces from along the "artificial" common border and its opening to free movement of citizens of the two countries. He also proposed to Cairo a project "remote from politics" — cooperation in building a canal from al-Nubariyya (in the western Delta) to Tubruk, linking it to the Libyan "great man-made river" (for details on the latter, see *MECS* 1983–84, pp. 579–80). Qadhdhafi suggested that Libya would provide the funds and Egypt the manpower for this project, which would transform the desert between the two countries into "a paradise."[81]

Yet Qadhdhafi's reiteration, in the same breath, of his "full and firm opposition" to the Egyptian regime proved that nothing had substantially changed in his attitude toward Egypt. Qadhdhafi added that Tripoli "cannot think at all" of restoring any sort of relations with Mubarak's regime at the political level "as long as it is related to the Zionist enemy...[and to] US imperialism." He went on further to accuse Egypt of "selling out Palestine, Jerusalem, and God."[82]

Though furious with Egypt for its rejection of his "strategic, historical, and civilizational message,"[83] Qadhdhafi announced on 26 April the resumption of telephone and telegram links with Egypt.[84] Furthermore, on 8 May, Tripoli announced its decision to stop the propaganda campaign against Egypt.[85] Around midyear the atmosphere thus seemed to be improving. But then, again, the vicissitudinous pattern of these relations showed itself once more. Tripoli did not keep its promise and in the fall resumed its virulent assault upon Egypt which had "turned into a harmful area that exports poisons to the Arab homeland...."[86] Qadhdhafi's renewed indignation with Cairo could be explained by the latter's thwarting union with Sudan (see below), and by Cairo's support for 'Arafat's political moves (see chapter on Egypt). By the end of the year, Libyan-Egyptian relations had again come to be as tense and hostile as they had been at its outset (for further discussion of these relations see chapter on Egypt).

LIBYA AND SUDAN

Sudan continued to be an essential strategic and political asset for Libya, especially since the latter's strong animosity for Egypt continued unabated. That, in turn, explained the further economic and military aid Tripoli provided to Khartoum during the year. At the same time, however, bilateral ties were not free of tension. The alleged presence of Libyan and Libyan-backed forces in Darfur, within Sudan's territory, during the first half of the year, injected renewed strain into their relations, if not for long (see chapter on Sudan).

In August, the wheel had turned again when Tripoli reported that talks with the Sudanese Umma Party, headed by Prime Minister al-Sadiq al-Mahdi, had led to an agreement to work toward a political union with Khartoum.[87] But pressure within Sudan, as well as from Egypt and the US forced Khartoum a short while later to back out and the whole issue was shelved. Close relations, however, remained intact. Sudanese Prime Minister al-Mahdi visited Tripoli for two days in mid-November and the Libyan senior military figure, Abu Bakr Yunis, returned the visit in Khartoum in early December. The visits resulted in the signing of another cooperation agreement.[88]

VOCIFEROUS SUPPORT OF THE PALESTINIAN UPRISING

Events of the Palestinian uprising in the West Bank and Gaza Strip were prominently covered by the Libyan media throughout 1988. The uprising completely accorded with Qadhdhafi's perception, and hence inflammatory rhetoric was persistently directed at the Arabs in general and the Palestinians in particular to be firm in fighting the "Zionist enemy" as the only means for solving the Israeli-Arab conflict and the Palestinian problem. Moreover, the whole issue of the uprising gave Qadhdhafi a new opportunity to exert, or at least to try to exert, political influence in inter-Arab politics, while at the same time attempting to restore his shattered relations with the PLO leadership (see below).

Thus Qadhdhafi, and the Libyan media, did not miss any opportunity to declare vehement support "with all our resources"[89] for the "tremendous Palestinian revolution"[90] which "restores," as Qadhdhafi stated, "Arab dignity."[91] Qadhdhafi also reiterated his view that Israel "has no right to exist,"[92] and called on the Palestinians to extend the uprising all over the area "from the [Jordan] river to the [Mediterranean] sea and from southern Lebanon to southern Palestine....Even if the world decided to establish a state for the Jews," the Libyan leader went on, "we refuse to accept that this should be at the expense of us, the Arabs....We should not pay for the crimes of Hitler...."[93] In the same vein, Qadhdhafi presented to the world his conception of the uprising's two goals: "a political one" aimed at conveying to "the whole world the voice of the Palestinian people... who demand their independence" and a "strategic" one aimed at liberating Palestine from "the Zionist occupation."[94] Concerning the second goal, Qadhdhafi on another occasion declared that three main slogans "must be adopted from now on": popular rejection (of the Israeli occupation of Palestine from 1948–67), civil disobedience, and secret sabotage.[95]

Libya was at pains during the year under review to project the image of a devoted backer of "our brothers" the Palestinians, as the flood of references to that issue attested. Its holding on 13–14 June in Benghazi of an "international conference" in support of "the people's uprising in occupied Palestine"[96] with 'Arafat present was another indication. Qadhdhafi justified his participation in the Arab summit conference in Algiers in June (for details, see chapter on inter-Arab relations) by the urgent need to discuss how to consolidate the Palestinian uprising.[97] It should be noted that until 1988, Qadhdhafi had declined to attend the Arab summit conferences. To further display its devotion to the cause of the Palestinians, Libya reportedly allocated $4m. monthly as aid to the uprising. The first installment was reportedly paid in April as Tripoli's contribution to the pan-Arab national fund which was then being set up.[98] In August, Qadhdhafi announced that the *Jamahiriyya* would pay the salaries — estimated at $1m. per month — of the employees of the Civil Administration in the West Bank and Gaza who had gone on a collective strike (see chapter on West Bank and Gaza Strip).[99] In October, al-Fath Central Committee member Salah Khalaf (Abu Iyad) stressed that the *Jamahiriyya* was the only Arab country which had met its financial commitment to the uprising, as decided at the Algiers summit.[100] It should be noted, however, that there was no independent information regarding the scope, or actual delivery, of Libya's financial aid and the whole issue remained somewhat ambiguous.

RELATIONS WITH THE PLO

Relations between Libya and the PLO had been tense since 1982, following Qadhdhafi's not providing any significant military aid to the Palestinians in Lebanon, during their major military confrontation with the Israeli Army. Since Qadhdhafi had consistently waved the banner of Arab military struggle against Israel, his disregard of the Palestinians fighting in Lebanon created a crisis of confidence with 'Arafat's PLO mainstream.

The highly strained relations were reflected in early 1988 in Qadhdhafi's repeatedly hostile references to 'Arafat. "The Palestinians in Israeli-occupied territories felt abandoned by the PLO"; therefore, Qadhdahfi stated, 'Arafat might have to resign "as a step toward reunifying Palestinians." The PLO now meant "nothing," and the Fath group was "only one of many Palestinian factions struggling to liberate their homeland," and the PLO chairman himself "no longer had special status." 'Arafat ranked alongside Abu Musa and Ahmad Jibril, he said, adding that only a new leader could reunify the PLO.[101] In another biting attack on 'Arafat, Qadhdhafi called for his dismissal: "One person [in the PLO] is betraying in his direction [tending to direct negotiations with Israel]. Therefore, the organization must overthrow him...."[102]

Notwithstanding his strong anti-'Arafat statements, Qadhdhafi launched a new initiative in the early spring, aimed, as stated by Tripoli, at unifying the Palestinian ranks. Consequently, a stream of Palestinian leaders arrived in Libya, including 'Arafat's second in command Khalil al-Wazir (Abu Jihad), who remained in Tripoli from 2–7 April. Reconciliation with the PLO leadership was further boosted by the assassination of Abu Jihad on 16 April in Tunis. The dramatic event helped to bridge the rift between Qadhdhafi and 'Arafat. The latter visited Tripoli on 19–23 April, the first time since 1982. The removal of the barriers, at least formally, between Qadhdhafi and 'Arafat, intensified the pace of the latter's visits to Tripoli during the summer (in late May, late June, early July, and two visits in mid-August).

Tripoli was quick to seize upon 'Arafat's visits to enhance its prestige at home and in the Arab world, repeatedly quoting 'Arafat's hailing of Libya's role in halting the fighting between "the Palestinian brothers in Lebanon."[103] It should be noted that in addition to the Palestinian uprising, the camps war in Lebanon (see chapters on the PLO and on inter-Arab relations) served as another means of deepening Libya's political involvement in inter-Arab and inter-Palestinian affairs.

In August, Qadhdhafi voiced his support for the establishment of a Palestinian government-in-exile, offering his country as a base for such a government if and when the PLO decided to form it.[104] Nevertheless, Qadhdhafi soon reversed his stand and early in the fall expressed his opposition to the establishment of an interim or exiled Palestinian government, presumably fearing it might lead to the holding of direct negotiations with Israel.

Nevertheless, pressures apparently exerted on Libya by Algeria and Tunisia, as well as during 'Arafat's lobbying trips to Tripoli (more than five visits in the last quarter of 1988), convinced Qadhdhafi to declare on 15 November his recognition of the Palestinian state with "Jerusalem...as its capital,"[105] on condition that its borders be those they were during the British Mandate.[106]

NOTES

For the place and frequency of publications cited here, and for the full name of the publication, news agency, radio station, or monitoring service where an abbreviation is used, please see "List of Sources." Only in the case of more than one publication bearing the same name is the place of publication noted here.

1. Tripoli TV, 1 January — DR, 5 January 1988.
2. Tripoli TV, 4 January — DR, 6 January 1988.
3. Tripoli TV, 21 January — SWB, 23 January 1988.

4. *CR,* Libya, No. 1, 1988.
5. Tripoli TV, 9 March — DR, 9 March 1988.
6. Tripoli TV, 3 March — DR, 4 March 1988.
7. *Al-Fajr al-Jadid,* 5 March 1988.
8. Qadhdhafi's interviews with *al-Majalla,* 30 March, and *al-Tadamun,* 2-8 April 1988.
9. *Al-Ahram,* 4 July 1988.
10. *Al-Mustaqbal,* 9 April 1988.
11. Tripoli TV, 9 March — DR, 10 March 1988.
12. Tripoli TV, 2 May — DR, 5 May 1988.
13. Tripoli TV, 9 March — DR, 10 March 1988.
14. *Al-Mustaqbal,* 9 April 1988 (a report from Tripoli).
15. Tripoli TV, 2 May — DR, 5 May 1988.
16. Tripoli TV, 1 September — DR, 6 September 1988.
17. E.g., Qadhdhafi's interview with *al-Tadamun,* 2–8 April 1988.
18. Tripoli TV, 29 August — DR, 31 August 1988.
19. *Al-Watan al-'Arabi,* 22 January; *al-Shira',* 11 April 1988.
20. E.g., Tripoli TV, 2 March, 2 May — DR, 4 March, 5 May 1988.
21. AFP, 25 March — DR, 28 March 1988.
22. E.g., R. Ndjamena and R. Tripoli during January 1988.
23. JANA, 2, 16 February — 3, 17 February 1988.
24. KUNA, 3 March — DR, 4 March; *Le Nouvel Observateur,* 18–24 March — DR, 1 April 1988.
25. The *ad hoc* committee, made up of representatives of Algeria, Cameroon, Gabon, Mozambique, Nigeria, and Senegal, was scheduled to convene in early 1989, then it was delayed to April, and it was delayed once again to 24 May, to coincide with the general assembly of heads of state and government of the OAU in Addis Ababa.
26. *Al-Fajr al-Jadid,* 20 March 1988.
27. *FR,* 3 March 1988.
28. Interview with Qadhdhafi, TANJUG, 6 April — DR, 7 April 1988.
29. R. Ndjamena, 7 April — DR, 8 April 1988.
30. Qadhdhafi's speech to the diplomatic corps in Tripoli, Tripoli TV, 25 May — DR, 26 May 1988.
31. R. Paris, 15 June — DR, 16 June 1988. Later, in November, Ndjamena signed a reconciliation agreement with Ibn 'Umar.
32. JANA, 23 September — DR, 26 September 1988.
33. Tripoli TV, 27 September — DR, 28 September 1988.
34. JANA, 3 October — DR, 13 October 1988.
35. For the full text of the communiqué, *Le Monde,* 5 October 1988.
36. Tripoli TV, 25 May — DR, 26 May 1988.
37. *Al-Fajr al-Jadid,* 12 January 1988.
38. JANA, 19 March — DR, 24 March; *al-Fajr al-Jadid,* 20 March 1988.
39. JANA, 29 June — DR, 30 June; for more details on the common economic projects, *MEED,* 15 July 1988.
40. JANA, 4 October — DR, 5 October 1988.
41. *Al-Fajr al-Jadid,* 6 February 1988. For the full text of the agreement, JANA, 6 February — DR, 8 February 1988. The ruling was made by the ICJ in 1982 and confirmed in 1985. It gave Libya around 1,300 sq. km. of sea, which has hydrocarbons and other resources.
42. *Al-Fajr al-Jadid,* 6, 10 February 1988.
43. *Al-Sada,* 20-21 February 1988.
44. JANA, 9 March — DR, 10 March 1988.
45. JANA, 20 March — DR, 25 March; for more details on the visit, JANA, 21 March — DR, 25 March 1988.
46. For the agreement, R. Tripoli, 5 April — DR, 7 April 1988.
47. JANA, 5 April — DR, 5 April 1988.
48. Tripoli TV, 7 April — DR, 8 April 1988.
49. For the full text, R. Tunis, 22 May — DR, 23 May 1988.
50. *FT,* 18 June 1988. See also *MEED,* 6 May; *al-Majalla,* 21–27 September 1988.

51. AFP, 31 May 1988.
52. R. Tripoli, 14 June — DR, 15 June; interview with a senior Libyan official, R. Paris, 24 June — DR, 27 June 1988.
53. R. Paris, 24 June — DR, 27 June; *NAD,* 27 June - 3 July; *al-Muharrir,* 2 July; *al-Ittihad,* Abu Dhabi, 25 July 1988.
54. For details on the visit, see R. Tripoli, 11 July — DR, 12 July 1988.
55. JANA, 6 August, R. Tripoli, 7 August — DR, 8 August 1988.
56. For the joint communiqué issued at the end of the visit, see JANA, 8 August — DR, 9 August 1988.
57. R. Tunis, 4 September — DR, 8 September; *Memo,* 16 September 1988.
58. *Al-Majalla,* 17–23 August; *al-Watan al-'Arabi,* 9 September; *al-Mustaqbal,* 1 October 1988.
59. *Al-Ittihad,* Abu Dhabi, 7, 16 September 1988.
60. *Al-Wafd,* 4 August 1988.
61. For the full text of the communiqué, Tripoli TV, 11 December — DR, 12 December 1988.
62. E.g., JANA, 31 January, 26 May, 12 June — DR, 1 February, 27 May, 13 June; R. Tripoli, 30 April — DR, 3 May; see also Qadhdhafi's references in interviews with *al-Safir,* 1 January; *al-Tadamun,* 2–8 April 1988.
63. Qadhdhafi's address to "the international conference of the first American-Indian nation for liberation," held in Tripoli on 30 January-3 February. See Tripoli TV, 30 January — DR, 1 February 1988.
64. *NYT,* 10 January 1988.
65. *CR,* Libya, No. 1, 1988.
66. *Al-Majalla,* 2-8 March 1988.
67. JANA, 2 April, 7 May — DR, 4 April, 9 May. For many similar references, *al-Fajr al-Jadid,* 10, 11, 12, 13 May 1988.
68. *WP,* 21, 23 July 1988.
69. R. Tripoli, 20 July — DR, 21 July 1988.
70. JANA, 9 November — DR, 10 November 1988.
71. *IHT,* 15 September 1988, quoting the State Department spokesman, Charles E. Redman.
72. *IHT,* 27 October 1988, quoting the CIA director, William H. Webster.
73. E.g., JANA, 14 November, 22 December — DR, 15 November , 23 December 1988.
74. E.g., JANA, 14, 15 November, 22 December — DR, 15 November, 23 December 1988.
75. R. Tripoli, 4 January — DR, 4 January 1988.
76. USIS, 4 January 1988, quoting Defense Secretary Frank C. Carlucci.
77. E.g., Qadhdhafi's interviews with *IHT,* 9 February, 16 April; *al-Tadamun,* 2–8 April; *al-Shira',* 11 April; *NYT,* 7 September 1988.
78. JANA, 3 March — DR, 3 March 1988.
79. MENA, 1 March; *al-Masa,* 2 March 1988.
80. AFP, 10 March — DR, 11 March 1988.
81. Qadhdhafi's speech, delivered on the occasion of the 18th anniversary of the evacuation of British troops from Tubruk, Tripoli TV, 28 March — DR, 29 March 1988.
82. Ibid.
83. JANA, 1 April — DR, 1 April 1988.
84. Tripoli TV, 26 April — DR, 27 April 1988.
85. JANA, 8 May — DR, 9 May 1988.
86. E.g., JANA, 4 October — DR, 5 October 1988.
87. JANA, 31 August, 2 September — DR, 2, 8 September 1988.
88. For details, R. Tripoli, 3 December — DR, 5 December 1988.
89. R. Tripoli, 7 August — DR, 8 August 1988.
90. E.g., *al-Fajr al-Jadid,* 5, 11, 24 May 1988.
91. *Al-Jamahiriyya,* 19 February 1988.
92. E.g., his interview with *Neue Kronen-Zeitung,* 29 February — DR, 1 March 1988.
93. Qadhdhafi's speech at a banquet honoring the Tunisian president, as quoted by R. Tripoli, 7 August — DR, 8 August 1988.
94. Qadhdhafi's interview with R. Monte Carlo, 10 August — DR, 11 August 1988.

95. JANA, 16 January — DR, 19 January; also R. Tripoli, 7 August — DR, 8 August 1988.
96. For details on the conference, Tripoli TV, 13 June — DR, 15 June 1988.
97. *Al-Fajr al-Jadid,* 10 June 1988.
98. TANJUG, 6 May — DR, 9 May 1988.
99. R. Monte Carlo, 10 August — DR, 11 August 1988.
100. JANA, 25 October — DR, 25 October 1988, quoting an interview with Abu Iyad.
101. Qadhdhafi in an interview with the SWB, 10 January — DR, 14 January. *A posteriori,* Tripoli did not feel comfortable with the harsh words, claiming, therefore, that Qadhdhafi's interview was distorted by the SWB. See JANA, 16 January — DR, 19 January 1988.
102. Qadhdhafi's interview with *al-Safir,* 1 January; see another reference by Qadhdhafi to that issue in Tripoli TV, 27 January — DR, 28 January 1988.
103. E.g., JANA, 3 July — DR, 5 July; also Tripoli TV, 25 June — DR, 27 June 1988.
104. *Al-Ittihad,* Abu Dhabi, quoted by KUNA, 24 August — DR, 24 August; see also Qadhdhafi's interview with R. Monte Carlo, 10 August — DR, 11 August 1988.
105. R. Tripoli, 15 November — DR, 16 November 1988.
106. Qadhdhafi's interview with *al-Sayyad,* 18–24 November 1988.

The People's Democratic Republic of Yemen
(Jumhuriyyat al-Yaman al-Sha'biyya al-Dimuqratiyya)

JOSEPH KOSTINER

During the third year after the January 1986 civil war, the People's Democratic Republic of Yemen (PDRY) was still struggling to cope with its consequences. Plagued by factional struggles, the leadership was unable to reach consensus on a variety of issues. The flow of events in 1988 was influenced by the trials in the South Yemeni courts of 'Ali Nasir Muhammad, the deposed PDRY leader and head of the opposition who was living in the neighboring Yemeni Arab Republic (YAR), and his supporters. These trials had several aims: to establish the authority of the PDRY's new leadership, which took over after 'Ali Nasir's deposition; to symbolize their dissociation from 'Ali Nasir; and to demonstrate both their determination to bring to justice and ultimately punish those they held responsible for "bloody January" as well as their independence, unanimity, and strength in holding the trials despite general Arab protest and calls for amnesty to the accused. However, the trials, and notably the death sentence imposed upon 35 of 'Ali Nasir's followers, created new difficulties for the PDRY's leaders in asserting their rule and dealing with the results of the civil war.

Coping with 'Ali Nasir's opposition became an embarrassment and a burden for Aden. 'Ali Nasir's opposition movement attracted dissatisfied elements in the PDRY and generated disagreements among the leaders in Aden over granting amnesty to some of the sentenced members of the opposition. Some Arab states not only pleaded with Aden for amnesty, but also criticized what they called Aden's intransigence. The PDRY faced a particularly difficult period in its relations with the YAR, 'Ali Nasir's base and shelter, as the tension over the fate of the opposition leaders aggravated a crisis between the Yemens over rights in the oil-rich, but disputed border region of Ma'rib-Shabwa. In addition to problems of factional strife among the new leaders and mistrust of different Arab states who were potential financial benefactors, there was also a lack of finances and industrial development, all of which added to the PDRY's difficulties in 1988.

Factional struggles continued all year behind the scenes, occasionally coming out into the open, as was evident in the infighting over administrative appointments, and even in assassinations. The struggle sprouted within the armed forces, in the provinces, the central bureaucracy and up to the top levels of policy-makers. The only significant

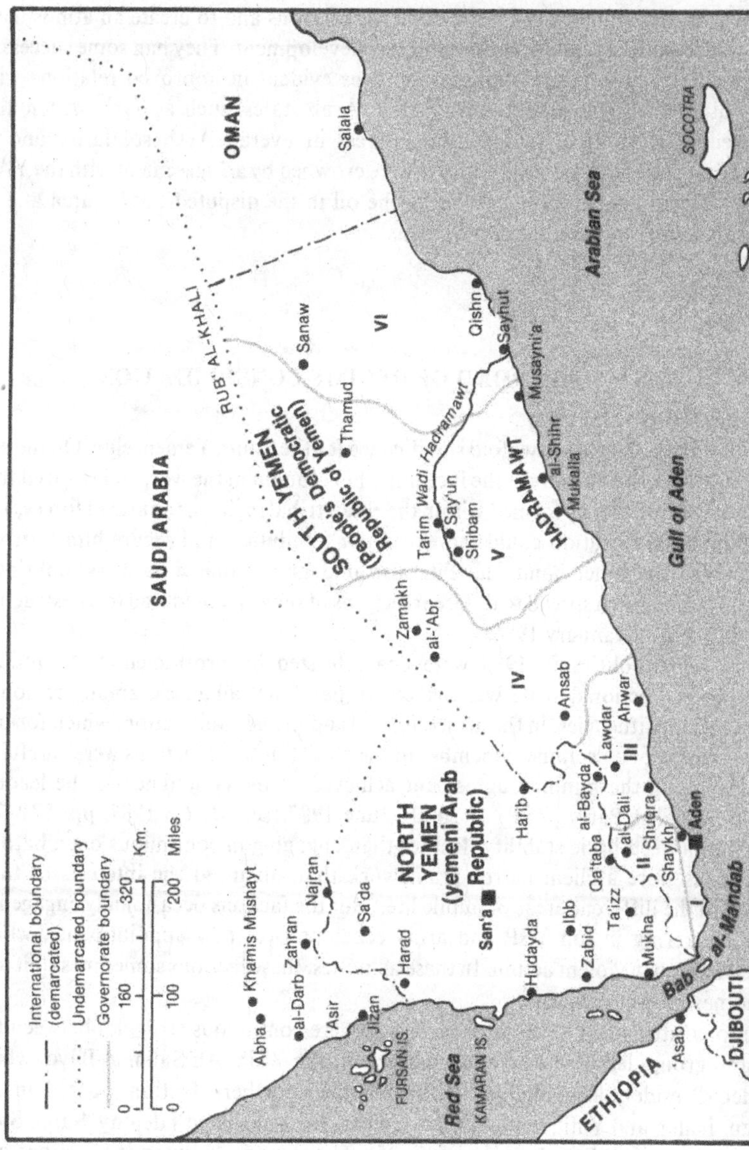

North and South Yemen

ray of light was the promising forecast of oil production in late 1989 and 1990, which could give an important boost to the troubled PDRY economy.

PDRY leaders sought to ease the domestic tensions and to create an atmosphere conducive to political stability and economic development. They had some success in conducting their foreign relations, which was evident in improved relations with Oman, other Gulf states, and more distant Arab states, such as Syria. Aden also succeeded in showing it had a keen interest in overall Arab solidarity and in cooperation with Arab states. Its efforts were crowned by an agreement with the YAR in early May to cooperate in exploiting the oil in the disputed border area and to resume the effort to unite the two Yemens.

INTERNAL AFFAIRS

DIFFICULTIES ON THE ROAD OF REGIME CONSOLIDATION

ELITE FACTIONALISM

The civil war of 1986 had a twofold significance for the South Yemeni elite. On the one hand, they took their cue from the factions which fought in the war, and realized that only a solid constituency formed within the elite's tribal regions, the armed forces, and the public administration could serve a leader's ambition and secure him a strong position. On the other hand, the elite also understood that a heedless, unbridled factional strife, which spread to different sections of society, could lead to a destructive result as it had in January 1986.

Hence, elite politics in 1988 were characterized by protracted, but cautious factionalism. Factional strife was evident in parochial alliances, among regional-peripheral constituencies, in the armed forces, and the administration, which formed the power base of a prominent member of the elite. But these factions were careful to avoid wrecking the minimal agreement achieved at the conference of the leading Yemeni Socialist Party (YSP) of 20–21 June 1987 (see *MECS* 1987, pp. 571–72) which guaranteed basic stability. Rather than engaging in continuous open battles, the factions were a client-patron framework that advanced the interests of their activists in the different areas of public life.[1] But the factions occasionally engaged in power brokering in top YSP and army echelons over new appointments, which erupted into open violent action. In these activities, these factions sometimes split and formed new power centers.[2]

Factional strife took several forms. There were continuous struggles between the Hadrami group, led by the secretary-general of the YSP, ʻAli Salim al-Bayd, which included President Khaydar al-ʻAttas, and the "northern faction," based in the Radfan, Daliʻi, and Yafiʻi mountainous regions, led by al-Bayd's deputy, Salim Salih Muhammad (see *MECS* 1986, pp. 529–35). The struggle between the factions was evident in different spheres.

The staffing of the YSP and the provincial governments during the civil war and during the subsequent persecutions was high on the new elite's list of priorities. The process of manning these positions became a focus of inter- and intra-factional rivalries. During the meeting of the YSP's Central Committee in November 1987, Salim Salih's loyalists were weakened, notably by the expulsion of the minister of housing, Muhammad Sulayman, from the committee. On the other hand, the position of al-Bayd's supporters was consolidated. On 9 December 1987, Prime Minister Yasin Sa'id Nu'man appointed new commissioners for the provincial governments of Abyan, Shabwah, Hadramawt, and Mahra,[3] regions which had been the center of fighting and had had pockets of support for the deposed PDRY president, 'Ali Nasir Muhammad, during the civil war. The new appointments undoubtedly reflected the YSP's overall attempt to eliminate support for 'Ali Nasir and to replace his people by those loyal to the new elite, but these appointments presumably also attested to the strengthened position of al-Bayd. In February 1988 the YSP's Politburo also approved the reconstitution of the YSP's Political and Technical Committee, which was placed under al-Bayd's leadership.[4]

Another expression of internal struggle was evident in the emergence of new political leaders within the factions. The army chief of staff, deputy minister of defense, and Politburo candidate-member, Brig. Gen. Haytham Qasim Tahir, enjoyed the armed forces' support and, as a descendant of Radfan, he had the support of the population which had the reputation of being rabid nationalists whose rebellion had sparked off the revolt against the British in 1963. He was regarded as a future minister of defense. Sayf Sa'il Khali, the YSP's secretary at Aden and another member-candidate of the Politburo, seemed to be 'Abd al-Fattah Isma'il's successor as the YSP's new ideologist; like Isma'il, he enjoyed support among Aden's intellectuals and Soviet leaders. Fadl Muhsin 'Abdallah, secretary of the YSP's Central Committee and a member of the Politburo, was regarded as another emerging leader.[5] It is evident that these new men did not challenge the old guard, but rather cooperated with them. They were also the main behind-the-scences strongmen in the power struggles among the elite, supporting and deposing senior leaders. Their ability to form their own factions remains to be seen.

According to a newspaper published in Cairo by South Yemeni opposition elements, another form of factional strife was evident among the middle-ranking positions of the YSP, in the armed forces, and the provincial administrations. The newspaper reported that officers from the Yafi'i tribal confederacy were killed because they were affiliated with a rising YSP activist, Jarallah 'Umar, whose activities had been opposed by the leaders. The paper also noted that the death on 30 October of Lt. Col. Sayf Muthanna Rashid was the result of interfactional strife.[6]

THE IMPACT OF THE DEATH SENTENCES: THE CHALLENGE OF 'ALI NASIR'S OPPOSITION

The death sentences imposed on 'Ali Nasir and 34 of his aides on 13 December 1987 (*MECS* 1987, p. 573) created new difficulties for the new regime in Aden. The South Yemeni determination to try the accused as conspirators and traitors and inflict the death penalty on them was aimed at solving two problems which 'Ali Nasir's opposition group created for Aden. First, the Aden elite sought to prove its unequivocal dissociation from 'Ali Nasir's group and its uncompromising and persistent policy of punishing the opposition. To paraphrase the words of Rashid Muhammad Thabit, the PDRY minister of state for union affairs, all Yemenis (and Thabit pointed at the YAR too) had to denounce "the conspiracy" of 1986.[7] Fadil Muhsin, the secretary of the YSP's Central Committee, pointed out that the sentences should teach the opposition that there was no way back for anybody who had fired at his comrades.[8] The trials thus became a symbol of the policy of the new elite who depicted themselves as victims of a cruel conspiracy, but had nevertheless emerged victorious, determined to punish the defeated perpetrators of "bloody January" and teach a lesson to whoever hoped to soften up Aden. Second, the new elite presumably sought to delegitimize 'Ali Nasir and his supporters, hoping thereby to eliminate their attractiveness to various states in the region which had attempted to mediate between the opposition and the new elite and to reinstate 'Ali Nasir as a major leader in Aden. Aden also hoped to retract the tens of thousands of fleeing South Yemeni refugees, who kept flocking to 'Ali Nasir's camp (see *MECS* 1987, pp. 572–73).

But the impact of the sentences and the subsequent behavior of Aden's leaders proved counterproductive for the PDRY, first, because the sentences drew immediate pleas of amnesty for the sentenced leaders, from many states, some of which had close relations with Aden and gave the PDRY valuable assistance. Prominent among those were the YAR, the PDRY's neighbor and interlocutor over unity (see below), and Kuwait, one of the PDRY's main financial backers. Their pressure caused major embarrassment in Aden (see further below). Moreover, 'Ali Nasir's appeal in the Arab world and among dissatisfied groups in the PDRY did not diminish, but rather increased. He was interviewed by newspapers of different Arab states, which played up his statements in their headlines. 'Ali Nasir shrewdly played the role of a reasonable, moderate leader victimized by a group of extremist, irresponsible people in Aden. He criticized the atmosphere in the new elite, as "dancing among serpents," who fight each other and ruin the state. 'Ali Nasir believed that the sentences "have finally closed the door to regional reconciliation."[9] He thereby encouraged the YAR, Egypt, and the Gulf states to persuade Aden to give up their stubbornness, while his group attracted more escapees from the PDRY, notably 37 officers who crossed the border in March 1988.[10] There were also reports that 'Ali Nasir, leading an armed group of tens of thousands, might try to attack the PDRY and that his loyalists distributed leaflets in Aden (a fact denied by the PDRY authorities).[11]

The response of Aden's leaders to these developments was rather confused. On 27 December 1987, the Supreme People's Presidium confirmed 11 of the death sentences and commuted the remaining 24 to prison terms. On 29 December, five prisoners who had been in PDRY custody (the other six were in the YAR) were executed. They included Mubrak Salim Ahmad, commander of 'Ali Nasir's presidential guard, Ahmad Husayn Musa, former commander of the Air Force, and 'Alawi Husayn Farhan, former minister of security.[12] Another 127 defendants attended the trials, the rest were with 'Ali Nasir in the YAR.

The commutation of 24 death sentences attested to Aden's misgivings over the penalties. These further increased due to the mounting criticism over the execution of the five. Intra-elite struggle reportedly intensified over the proper handling of the prisoners. President 'Attas was reported to be more lenient, and willing to grant clemency, while al-Bayd was uncompromising.[13] The deliberations between these leaders resulted in a readiness to confirm the amnesty for all "fighters" (i.e., 'Ali Nasir's supporters) who had not been sentenced and in a declaration made by 'Attas that 'Ali Nasir might get clemency only if he went into exile in Moscow or East Germany.[14]

In the coming weeks, the two sides did not get any closer to each other and the death penalty pronounced on 'Ali Nasir and six of his aides remained in force. Aden kept on reiterating that the sentences were passed in accordance with proper judicial procedures and refused to back down.[15] The tension over the sentences eased somewhat in the spring, due to the new *rapprochement* between the two Yemens (see below), but it continued to threaten stability in the PDRY.

ECONOMIC DEVELOPMENT

During the period under review, there were no major breakthroughs in the PDRY's ailing economy. The government focused on assessing the situation, planning for the future and authorizing the beginning of several construction projects. Evidently, the new elite was acutely aware of the PDRY's difficult economic situation which the five-year plan had failed to remedy and which was exacerbated by the civil war. The third development plan (1986–90) was finally launched in 1988.[16]

The most promising field for development was oil. Exports were expected to start in late 1989 or 1990, when the estimated output of the Amal, 'Ayyad, and Gharb fields in Shabwa province would reach 1.2m tons. Extraction and contracts for the construction of a center to store the oil and a pipeline from Shabwa to Bir 'Ali (200 km.) were given to the Soviet Union. But the Canadian company, Occidental, and the French company, Total, were also reported to be searching for oil.[17] The expansion of the port of Aden to facilitate the docking of heavy tankers and large ships, and of Aden's refineries, which process Iranian and Soviet crude oil, was started. The construction of new roads linking provincial cities to each other and the development of agricultural plantations were also contemplated.[18]

FOREIGN AFFAIRS

During the period under review Aden sought to tackle two main challenges in its foreign relations. It intended to influence the rich Gulf states to extend to the PDRY financial aid that would facilitate economic rehabilitation. The leaders in Aden were also interested in improving relations with the PDRY's immediate neighbors, the YAR and Oman, in the hope that this would keep the PDRY from getting entangled in complex regional disputes, which would detract Aden's attention from domestic reconstruction and worsen its relations with the Gulf states. Aden, therefore, continued to improve its relations with states in the region, a policy which had been initiated during 'Ali Nasir Muhammad's term in office. Foreign Minister 'Abd al-'Aziz al-Dali elaborated on the principles of this policy: peaceful coexistence with other states, noninterference in the affairs of other states and mutual respect for sovereignty.[19] Minister of Internal Affairs Salih Mundir al-Siyayli reiterated a foreign policy principle, most appealing to the PDRY's neighbors, that the PDRY found a way of avoiding entanglements in its neighbors' frontier areas.[20] PDRY leaders found it difficult to carry out their friendly policies, because of the criticism different Arab quarters raised against the death sentences. Several Arab papers, which promoted 'Ali Nasir's views, expressed their doubts about Aden's leaders. The latter had therefore to overcome the negative image the trials had created.[21]

At the same time the PDRY was also interested in maintaining a revolutionary posture in order to justify its Marxist ideology. It did so by befriending hard-line, radical Arab states concerning mutual interests and by maintaining a close alliance with the Soviet Union, which was the PDRY's greatest defender and the main source of economic support.[22]

RELATIONS WITH THE YEMENI ARAB REPUBLIC

The PDRY's relations with the YAR were burdened by two main problems. One was the residence in the YAR of 'Ali Nasir and his followers, a problem which had often troubled Aden (see *MECS* 1987, pp. 575–76), but which had become very difficult to handle following San'a's protest against the trial.[23] The second problem sprang from the search for oil by both states along their common border in the Ma'rib-Shabwa zone. This border was undemarcated and when the PDRY struck oil — the YAR had also started producing oil — tension developed between them, which sometimes led to armed skirmishes there — the latest in November 1987.

Both states were undoubtedly interested in solving the problems peacefully. From the PDRY's vantage point, improved relations with the YAR were the key to countering 'Ali Nasir's activities and a way of showing the Gulf states Aden's good intentions of relaxing tensions in the region. Aden was reluctant to allow the situation to deteriorate into a war which would be an unbearable burden on the PDRY's economy and a blow to its designs for reconstruction. The YAR, in its turn, had similar considerations (see chapter on the YAR).

In the past, the two Yemens often resorted to negotiations on unity between them as the best way to solve the problem of the tensions at the frontier. They had made some significant steps toward unity, which were slowed down after the 1986 civil war. The resumption of efforts aimed at unity was a worthy goal and a sufficient reason for tackling the present problems. Soviet encouragement to improve relations between the two Yemens (see below) further enabled the parties to proceed in this direction.

Between December 1987 and April 1988, representatives of the two states met several times. 'Attas met the YAR minister of petroleum and mineral resources to discuss oil issues and al-Bayd received the YAR Deputy Prime Minister Muhammad Sa'id al-'Attar to discuss economic integration, notably as concerned oil production.[24] There were meetings in San'a to discuss the above-mentioned skirmishes. Fadil Muhsin and Qasim Tahir, secretary of the YSP Central Committee and the chief of staff, also went to San'a in January to discuss economic cooperation and security issues.[25] Qasim Tahir and Muhsin 'Abdullah visited San'a again in March.[26] These initial talks served to relax the tension between the two states. During this period there was also an attempt by the PLO to mediate between the parties over the disputed Ma'rib-Shabwa region. This mediation bore no immediate fruit, but it did generate new principles for a settlement: both parties agreed to avoid clashes, to withdraw their units from the area, and to explore the possibilities of cooperation in the production of oil.[27] Qasim Tahir then presumably followed up on the military aspects of the settlement. Hence, YAR Foreign Minister 'Abd al-Karim al-Iryani could state in early January, perhaps with undue optimism, that the YAR's relations with the PDRY were "the best one could hope for. There is nothing to spoil them."[28]

The dialogue between the two states peaked in meetings in late March between PDRY Prime Minister Yasin 'Abduh Nu'man and his opposite number in the YAR, 'Abd al-'Aziz 'Abd al-Ghani in Aden. These meetings were followed by two meetings between al-Bayd and the YAR President 'Ali 'Abdallah Salih in Ta'izz on 16 April and finally in San'a on 3-4 May. An agreement was then concluded on a number of issues. As discussed in the meeting in Ta'izz according to al-Bayd, the parties decided to resort to "a peaceful dialogue" and to reduce the number of units stationed at their common borders. Fighting between the parties in the past, he said, was "dishonest and unfair" and it was the leaders' responsibility to prevent its recurrence. Al-Bayd viewed this accord as the normalization of relations after the events of January 1987.[29] According to PDRY sources, the parties also defused 'Ali Nasir's opposition by reaching an agreement over several unpublished commitments the YAR had undertaken to close the camps of 'Ali Nasir's supporters and encourage them to return to the PDRY.[30] If this accord were to prove effective, it could definitely contribute to the PDRY's stability.

The May agreement was given substance by an accord over the disputed Ma'rib-Shabwa region. The two parties agreed to establish a "joint investment" venture covering an area of 2,200 sq. km., that is, to search for oil jointly. To facilitate this goal, the parties decided to remove their military units from the region and establish a joint "topographical committee" to demarcate the region.[31] The two states thus surmounted the problem of domination in the Ma'rib-Shabwa area by deciding to operate there jointly.

The two Yemens also agreed to advance the process of achieving unity. The two leaders decided to reactivate all the previous unity agreements and the leading administrative organs for unity, the Yemen Council (comprising the presidents of both states), the Joint Ministerial Committee and other committees. The two countries also decided to implement another principle agreed upon at Ta'izz, namely, to prepare a timetable for referring the draft constitution of the united Yemen for ratification to the people's councils in both states.[32] The two leaders did not take any other steps toward unity, apparently, because they still harbored basic fears about prompt unification. But, under its slogan, a major step toward improving relations was taken.

The next few months witnessed additional progress. In late May and early June 1988, the two Yemeni ministers of internal affairs agreed to fix new crossing points along the frontier in order to facilitate free passage of citizens of both states who would have to present only identification documents, without passports.[33] Units of both armies were removed from the disputed border region;[34] PDRY Prime Minister Yasin 'Abduh Nu'man then announced that the two states would establish a joint company to prospect for minerals in the Ma'rib-Shabwa region.[35] A Lebanese paper also reported in early August that 'Ali Nasir's supporters were forced by the YAR authorities to cease their military training in their camps and to limit themselves to cultural and social activities.[36]

By the end of 1988, the PDRY authorities could sense that their relations with the YAR ceased to pose an immediate threat to Aden and held out the promise of new prospects. While complete unity was not yet in reach, the unity talks in themselves produced significant improvement in economic and political fields.

RELATIONS WITH THE GULF STATES

IMPROVED RELATIONS WITH OMAN

Aden's relations with Oman, like those with the YAR, were a test case of its good intentions toward the Gulf states. Moreover, PDRY leaders also sought to surmount any difficulties on the country's eastern frontier which could impede domestic stability. They therefore strove to improve relations with Oman, a process which had been slowed down after the 1986 civil war (see *MECS* 1987, p. 576).

The Arab summit in Amman in November 1987 offered an opportunity for the

President, Khaydar al-'Attas, to meet with Oman's leader, Sultan Qabus. 'Attas later announced that the two leaders had discussed mutual problems and the unresolved demarcation of their border. He added that both states would soon upgrade their diplomatic representations from the nonresident, to resident-envoys.[37] Relations further warmed up about a year later, when 'Attas made an official visit to Oman. He said that the PDRY hoped that this would achieve: the beginning of renewed cooperation in economic and technical fields; the resolution of mutual problems, notably the complete demarcation of the border with the help of "mutual understanding"; and the coordination of their foreign policies in order to advance "regional stability" and contribute to "Arab solidarity." 'Attas considered such multifaceted action as the beginning of a "new phase," prospecting "wide horizons."[38]

Judging by reports after the meeting, the PDRY's expectations of an improvement in relations were fulfilled. An agreement was reportedly reached on resolving most of their problems. Omani assistance to the PDRY in trade, communications, and economics was also reported.[39]

THE PEOPLE'S DEMOCRATIC REPUBLIC OF YEMEN AND OTHER GULF ISSUES

The PDRY was unwilling to align itself unequivocally with either of the antagonists in the Iraqi-Iranian War in order to avoid having them or their allies take any hostile action against the PDRY. Aden's position was that the war should terminate and that the parties should accept UN Resolution 598.[40] The cease-fire was, therefore, received by 'Attas "with optimism."[41] This position enabled the PDRY to maintain good relations with each side. 'Attas said that while Aden had developed no special relations with Iran after the war, its relations with Tehran were "good and natural." In the Amman summit of November 1987, the PDRY opposed the idea of breaking relations with Iran.[42] In October 1988, Iran's foreign minister visited Aden and met its leaders.[43] There was also an improvement of relations with Iraq: the Iraqi minister of education visited Aden in July and signed a cultural exchange agreement.[44] In the same month, 'Attas visited Baghdad and announced the turning of a new leaf in their relations, leading towards cooperation in a variety of fields.[45] However, no progress was reported beyond these declarations.

PDRY relations with the Gulf Cooperation Council (GCC) states were more tangible being based on South Yemen's dependence on economic aid from Kuwait, the United Arab Emirates (UAE) and, to a lesser extent, Saudi Arabia. 'Attas hailed the positive aspects of the GCC experience and hinted at the PDRY's hope of joining the GCC, but he stressed that Aden's immediate goal was unity with the YAR, according to the example set by the GCC.[46]

'Attas signed a decree in January 1988 ratifying a loan the PDRY had received from the Kuwait-based Arab Economic Development Fund for the construction of a ring road in Aden.[47] Kuwait also helped Aden by dispatching 30,000 barrels of oil per day for refining in Aden, which gave a boost to the PDRY economy.[48] PDRY spokesmen showed their gratitude to Kuwait in different ways. Despite Aden's policy of not alienating either of the sides in the Iraqi-Iranian War, its leaders did not hesitate to denounce Iran's assaults on Kuwait-bound ships and other targets on the Kuwaiti mainland.[49] 'Attas depicted PDRY relations with Kuwait as "a model of relationship."[50] He also hailed the relationship with the UAE by stressing its role (in conjunction with Kuwait) in generating the *rapprochement* between the PDRY and

Oman, and by emphasizing the personal commitment of UAE President Zayid Ibn Sultan al-Nuhayan to his country's relations with the PDRY.[51]

Aden's relations with Saudi Arabia were more convoluted. South Yemen's efforts to prospect for oil at the juncture of its undemarcated boundary with both the YAR and Saudi Arabia, and the growing cooperation between the two Yemens on this issue, gave Riyadh cause to suspect a possible strengthening of the PDRY's power. During a visit by Foreign Minister al-Dali to Riyadh in March 1988, issues of mutual interest were discussed, notably Saudi economic aid to the PDRY.[52] But the visit had no apparent follow-up. Moreover, occasional collisions between Saudi and South Yemeni forces were reported in the spring and summer of 1988. They revolved around a Saudi attempt to lure tribesmen (the al-Karak, al-Shakura, al-Mu'abir, and al-Sa'rifi were mentioned) at the frontier area to accept Saudi protection and even citizenship.[53] Subsequently, unspecified Saudi units crossed into PDRY territory and clashed with South Yemeni soldiers. Aden was not prepared to give in and insisted on Saudi withdrawal.[54] These clashes led both parties to seek a relaxation of tension. The minister for internal affairs, al-Siyayli, visited Riyadh in October and took up the issue with his Saudi counterpart. The results were reported to be "positive and fruitful" and leading to a "considerable improvement" in relations.[55] Saudi participation in financing the construction of a PDRY hospital, a housing project, and the renovation of the port of Aden were then reported.[56]

RELATIONS WITH OTHER ARAB STATES

The PDRY adopted a cooperative and friendly attitude toward parties belonging to the "radical" or "revolutionary" camp, attempting thereby to bridge over divisions among them and maintain a good relationship with all of them. Thus, Aden supported PLO unity under Yasir 'Arafat and was particularly supportive of the continuation of the *intifada* in the West Bank and Gaza Strip, which rendered the "Zionist entity and its friends" muted, unable to provide a proper response. Al-Dali stressed that the *intifada* "belonged to the PLO and should not be thrown at anybody else's door." Aden also supported the overall Arab assistance to the *intifada*, notably the resolution to be adopted at the Algiers summit[57] (see chapters on the Palestine Liberation Organization and inter-Arab relations). A number of PLO leaders, notably 'Arafat himself and activists of the Democratic Front for the Liberation of Palestine (whose leaders had common organizational origins with PDRY leaders in the *Qawmiyyun al-'Arab* during the 1960s) occasionally visited Aden and held talks with senior officials there.

PDRY leaders made an effort to improve relations with Syria, the leading state among the "revolutionary" bloc. Damascus differed with Aden over several issues: it sided with Iran in the Gulf War, opposed 'Arafat's leadership in the PLO, and maintained good relations with 'Ali Nasir Muhammad.[58] The PDRY leaders tried to bridge over these gaps and al-Dali visited Damascus in July 1988 to make an attempt (which was futile) to mediate between Iraq and Syria. However, 'Attas's visit led to an agreement between his country and Syria on cooperation over planning, economic, and trade issues which was ratified by the South Yemeni Government on 15 September.[59] PDRY-Syrian relations had obviously improved.

The PDRY also continued its friendly relationships with Ethiopia and Libya, as evidenced by exchanges of visits to each other's capital. One report also noted that

1,000 PDRY soldiers were fighting on the Libyan side in Chad; several were killed and several deserted.[60]

Aden also followed the Arab trend to mend fences with Egypt. Diplomatic relations which had been cut in 1979, following Egypt's signature of the Camp David Accords, were renewed with Cairo in early February 1988, and described as a manifestation of "deep bonds and historical ties."[61] Ambassadors were exchanged in early May.[62]

RELATIONS WITH THE GREAT POWERS

PDRY relations with the Soviet Union remained the cornerstone of Aden's economic and security policies. The dispatch of ships by the US and other Nato states into the Gulf prompted a Soviet response in conjunction with the PDRY. The Soviets used a naval base on Perim Island in the Red Sea and the Suqotra base, to monitor Western naval activity.[63] Moscow was also reported to have rehabilitated the South Yemeni Army, bringing itup to the size and standard it had had prior to the 1986 civil war.[64] However at the same time, in the spirit of *détente,* Moscow supported the PDRY's *rapprochement* with Gulf states and its cooperation with the YAR.

The coordination of security and political policy was carried out through visits of high-ranking officials to each others' capitals, notably 'Attas's visit to Moscow in May.[65] In August, Soviet journalists and party activists met with YSP cadres to explain the new policy of *glasnost* and *perestroika.* The Soviet Union also became the main party responsible for comprehensive development of oil production, a project which was financed by French capital.[66] The agreement included plans to construct a huge oil reservoir at Shabwa.[67] The Soviets undertook to build a thermal power plant, a plant for water desalination in the early 1990s, and economic enterprises in fisheries and farming.[68]

There were no reports of substantial contacts between the PDRY and the US. Diplomatic relations since October 1969 have been ruptured and Aden's leaders often criticized American policies in the Gulf and on Arab-Israeli issues. However, a Lebanese paper reported that in late 1988, Aden and Washington resumed initial contacts to restore diplomatic relations,[69] but it was unclear what would become of these contacts.

NOTES

For the place and frequency of publications cited here, and for the full name of the publication, news agency, radio station, or monitoring service where an abbreviation is used, please see "List of Sources." Only in the case of more than one publication bearing the same name is the place of publication noted here.

1. *Al-Majalla,* 17 February 1988.
2. *Al-Ittihad,* Abu Dhabi, 2 September 1988.
3. R. Aden, 28 December — SWB, 30 December 1987.
4. R. Aden, 7 February — DR, 12 February 1988.
5. *Al-Majalla,* 17 February 1988.
6. *Al-'Amal,* Cairo, 11 January 1989.
7. Thabit's statement was summarized by SWB's announcement, 12 January 1988.
8. Fadil Muhsin's interview, *al-Watan,* 10 December 1987.
9. 'Ali Nasir's interviews, *al-Watan al-'Arabi,* 25 December — DR, 30 December; DR announcement, 14 December; *al-Ittihad,* Abu Dhabi, 31 December 1987.

10. *Al-Shira'*, 28 March 1988.
11. Cf. Rashid Muhammad Thabit's interview, *al-Sharq al-Awsat,* 12 January 1988.
12. R. Aden, 12 December — DR, 15 December 1987; *CR,*PDRY, No. 1, 1988, pp. 32–33.
13. Ibid.
14. 'Attas's interview, *al-Majalla,* 30 December 1987.
15. *Al-Usbu' al-'Arabi,* 22 August 1988.
16. *CR,*PDRY, No. 1, 1988, p. 34; R. Aden, 25 January — DR, 29 January 1988.
17. R. Aden, 18 January — SWB, 26 January 1988.
18. *Al-Wahda,* Abu Dhabi, 15 April 1988.
19. *Al-Afaq,* 4 February 1988.
20. *Al-Afaq,* 25 February 1988.
21. *Al-Yawm al-Sabi',* 28 December; *al-'Alam,* 26 December; *al-Yamama,* 23 December 1987; *al-Dustur,* London, 4 January 1988.
22. *Al-Afaq,* 4 February 1988.
23. *Al-Yamama,* 23 December 1987.
24. R. Aden, 1 December — DR, 3 December 1987.
25. *Al-Ittihad,* Abu-Dhabi, 14 December — DR, 17 December 1987; ANA, 1 February — DR, 2 February 1988.
26. R. Aden, 6 March — DR, 9 March 1988.
27. *Al-Siyasa,* Kuwait, 20 April 1988.
28. Iryani's interview, *al-Sharq al-Awsat,* 3 January — DR, 7 January 1988.
29. Al-Bayd's interview, *al-Ittihad,* Abu Dhabi, 25 April — DR, 28 April; *al-Sharq al-Awsat,* 30 April 1988.
30. *Al-Hawadith,* 20 May 1988.
31. R. San'a, 4 May — DR, 5 May 1988.
32. Ibid.
33. R. San'a, 30 May — DR, 2 June; DR announcement, 2 June 1988.
34. *Al-Bayan,* Dubai, 16 June — DR, 3 August 1988.
35. Nu'man's interview, *al-Sharq al-Awsat,* 3 October 1988.
36. *Al-Ra'y,* 1 August 1988.
37. *Al-Anba,* Kuwait, 12 December 1987.
38. 'Attas's interview, *al-Bayan,* Dubai, 30 October 1988.
39. *Al-Usbu' al-'Arabi,* 28, 30 November 1988.
40. 'Attas's interview, *al-Anba,* Kuwait, 12 December 1987.
41. 'Attas's interview, *al-Bayan,* Dubai, 30 October 1988.
42. 'Attas's interview, *al-Majalla*, 23 March 1988.
43. ANA, 31 October — DR, 2 November 1988.
44. *Al-Thawra*, Baghdad, 11 July 1988.
45. *Fourteenth October*, 8 September 1988.
46. 'Attas's interview, *al-Ra'y al-'Amm*, 8 October 1988.
47. R. Aden, 27 January — DR, 28 January 1988.
48. *Al-Anba*, Kuwait, 3 December 1987.
49. Al-Dali quoted by KUNA, 7 December — DR, 17 December; 'Attas's interview, *al-Majalla*, 23 March 1988.
50. 'Attas's interview, *al-Ra'y al-'Amm*, 8 October 1988.
51. 'Attas's interview, *al-Bayan*, Dubai, 30 October 1988.
52. MENA, 30 March 1988.
53. *Al-Ahali*, 6 July 1988.
54. *Al-Muharrir*, 17 December 1987; *al-Ra'y al-Akhir*, 8 November 1988.
55. R. Aden, 26 October — DR, 27 October; *Iqra*, 8 December 1988.
56. Siyayli's interview, *al-Jazira*, 30 October 1988; *al-Mustaqbal*, 29 January 1989.
57. Al-Dali's interview, *al-Majalla*, 9 March 1989.
58. *Al-Watan al-'Arabi*, 14 October 1988.
59. *Al-Ittihad*, Abu Dhabi, 2 August; AFP, 14 September 1988.
60. *Al-Watan al-'Arabi*, 6 May 1988.
61. R. Aden, 5 February — DR, 10 February 1988.
62. ANA, 7 May — DR, 10 May 1988.

63. *WT*, 25 December 1988.
64. *Le Monde*, 22 January 1988.
65. DR announcement, 19 May 1988.
66. R. Aden, 10 March — DR, 16 March 1988.
67. *Al-Ittihad*, Abu Dhabi, 21 March 1988.
68. *Fourteenth October*, 20 April 1988.
69. *La Revue du Liban*, 7 January 1989.

The Saudi Arabian Kingdom
(Al-Mamlaka al-'Arabiyya al-Sa'udiyya)

JACOB GOLDBERG

The chaos surrounding the 1988 budget illustrated the economic and financial crisis plaguing the kingdom and the regime's growing confusion in handling it. The initial imposition of new taxes and the cancellation of subsidies signified a major policy shift, but the subsequent revocation of most of these revenue-raising measures represented a return to the former reluctance to alienate the population and the fear of a mass exodus of foreign professionals. The episode also reflected the extreme tensions permeating Saudi society and the royal family's failure to put across the need for austerity.

There were few signs of direction in the Saudi economy in 1988. Political and social considerations seemed to have drastically constrained the regime's ability to pursue policies justified on economic and financial grounds. The devaluation of the Saudi riyal (SR) was a case in point. Though a devaluation seemed to have become unavoidable, the leadership kept on postponing it. There was also hope that the end of the Iraqi-Iranian War would create a much more favorable investment climate in the kingdom and an opportunity for major Saudi participation in Iraqi reconstruction projects. Moreover, it seemed that the end of the war would enable the government to reduce defense expenditures, thereby cutting down the large deficit. Such expectations, however, failed to materialize; in fact, defense outlays soared to an unprecedented percentage of the budget.

There were growing doubts about the economy's ability to sustain growth without an increase in oil revenues. This assessment was reinforced by a continuing decline in 1988 of non-oil earnings, which led the leadership to increase oil revenues by raising oil production. Thus, despite a decade-long emphasis on the "development of the non-oil sectors," Saudi Arabia's dependence on oil revenues remained as strong as ever.

Consequently, the kingdom's oil policies were increasingly linked to budgetary needs and constraints. First, the Saudis were determined to avoid the "swing producer" role and to oppose any lowering of their quota. Second, the chief Saudi interest was to hold on to the kingdom's market share, even if this entailed discounts resulting in a price decline. Third, the kingdom had to expand its oil-revenue base by going into downstream investments, i.e., refining and marketing in addition to production, in order both to secure export outlets and increase revenues. These principles were translated into policies in the second half of 1988. Oil production was increased from 4.6m. barrels per day (b/d) in August to 6.8m. b/d in November (its quota was 4.35m. b/d). This increase attested to Saudi oil policy being totally subordinated to short-term revenue needs and to a growing readiness to ignore Opec arrangements.

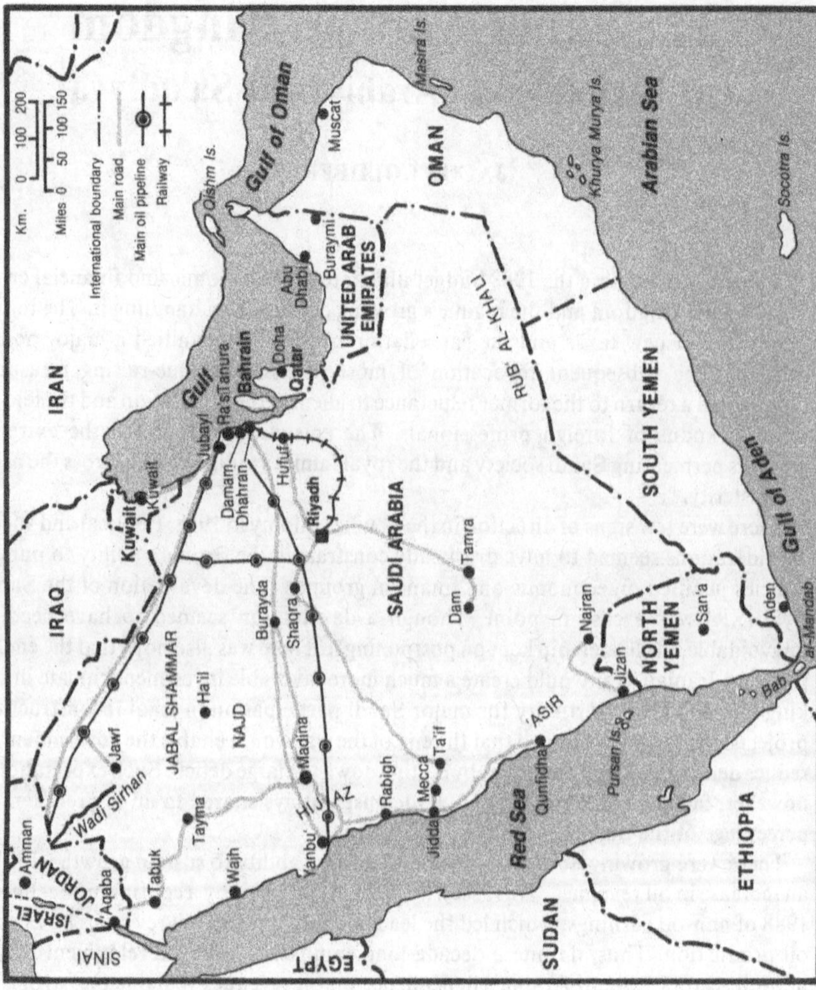

Saudi Arabia

Finally, the royal family saw its financial reserves continuing to dwindle. The need to resort to loans (through a bond offering), with all the religious sensitivities involved, demonstrated the severity of the problem, but the poor response to the bond issue made it doubtful whether the government would succeed in raising the necessary funds. With the persistent inability to decrease the budget deficit, it looked as if the drawdown on the reserves was bound to continue. Against this background, the preparation of a credible budget for 1989 (as opposed to the 1988 fiasco) assumed a high priority.

The kingdom's external environment seemed to have improved considerably in 1988. The end of the Iraqi-Iranian War with neither victor nor vanquished, created a kind of a stalemate between the two which was the best possible outcome from the perspective of Riyadh's long-term interests. Moreover, even before the war's end, Saudi Arabia improved its position *vis-à-vis* Iran. By imposing obstacles that prevented Iranian pilgrims from performing the *hajj* and threatening Saudi security, the royal family demonstrated its determination not to be intimidated by Khomeyni. The Saudi disposition to stand up to Iranian challenges was also reflected in the oil market when Riyadh increased its production by 50% thereby driving prices down and weakening the Iranian economy and war machine.

But the most significant development in 1988 was the expansion of the spectrum of Saudi foreign relations. The conclusion of the "arms deal of the 20th century" with Britain created a long-term military relationship between Riyadh and London, which seemed to have broken the near-total American monopoly on the sale of weapons to the kingdom. The Chinese-Saudi missile deal demonstrated that the royal family was not averse to purchasing arms even from Communist countries. Moreover, commercial ties with China were institutionalized with the opening of trade offices in both capitals, a move widely viewed as a prelude to diplomatic relations between Riyadh and Beijing. Relations with the USSR warmed up considerably as signaled by visits of senior Saudi leaders to Moscow, visits of two senior Soviet officials to Riyadh, and an unprecedented meeting between King Fahd and Deputy Foreign Minister Vorontsov. Finally, the practical expulsion of the American ambassador from Riyadh illustrated the growing distance between the kingdom and the US.

This higher visibility of Saudi foreign policy was viewed as reflecting King Fahd's assertiveness, activism, and desire to abandon Riyadh's former passive posture. But this more visible and less timid Saudi profile was also seen as justifying "a reassessment of the kingdom's role in the world," particularly to force Washington to view Saudi Arabia "as a mature country which is not blindly following American strategic planning in the Middle East."[1] A more balanced view, however, would interpret the Saudi moves on the Soviet, Chinese, and British fronts as aimed at improving the kingdom's position *vis-à-vis* Washington rather than at abandoning the centrality of the US in Saudi foreign policy.

DOMESTIC AFFAIRS

ECONOMIC AND BUDGETARY PROBLEMS

The 1988 budget reflected a continuation of the process of shrinking expenditures and declining revenues. Total projected spending was $37.65bn. (SR141.2bn.), down 17% from the $45.3bn. (SR170bn.) of 1987. The decline represented an across-the-board slashing of all items including social services, infrastructure, public administration, defense, and subsidies. Overall estimated revenues were $28.08bn. (SR105.3bn.), down 12% from the $31.3bn. (SR117.37bn.) of 1987. The decline in revenue represented an anticipated fall in both oil and non-oil income. The deficit, $9.57bn. (SR35.9bn.), was no less than 27% of total expenditures, second only to that of the US.[2]

In its attempt to devise a balanced budget, the royal family confronted the dilemma of having to choose between two evils — slashing expenditures even at the expense of public dissatisfaction, or running up considerable deficits even at the expense of depleting the kingdom's reserves. In previous years, the Saudi leaders opted for a combination of both: they slashed budget outlays substantially, but still maintained a high level of spending in areas deemed "vital." They were reluctant, however, to adopt any of the following three options: (1) increasing and widening the tax base; (2) slashing generous subsidies; and (3) obtaining loans at home or abroad.

The 1988 budget reflected major innovations affecting all three options.

(1) The income of foreign workers earning more than SR6,000 annually was to be taxed by 5%–30%. Customs duties were to be raised by 7%–12% on most items and by 20% on industrial items. New imposts were to be imposed: an airport tax; a 5% stamp duty on real estate deals; a flat SR10 fee on domestic airline tickets and hospital visits; a SR50 surcharge on international air tickets; and a SR200 fee for car registration. There were also substantial increases in postal rates (350%), and visa and driving license fees.

(2) The subsidy system was to be radically amended: gasoline and diesel oil went up by 50%; the wheat cultivation subsidy was cut from SR3,500 to SR2,000 per ton; subsidies on sugar, rice, oils, and milk were practically canceled; and subsidies on water, electricity, and barley were drastically reduced.

(3) The government was going to raise SR30bn. ($8bn.) through the sale of Treasury bonds as a means of covering almost 80% of the budget deficit. It was the first time since the 1950s that the kingdom — with its deep-rooted religious aversion to the concept of interest — resorted to borrowing. The government did not indicate whether the bonds would be offered overseas as well as domestically, and it forbade publication of details of the bonds, apparently out of fear of a backlash from religious circles.[3]

The budget appeared to signify a radical shift in Saudi Arabia's economic policy. The strategy of creating a competitive non-oil sector, even at the cost of substantial deficits, was abandoned in favor of correcting the balance-of-payments deficit and stemming the drain on reserves. In social and political terms, the new budget illustrated the government's readiness to reverse course, increase living costs for ordinary Saudis, and run the risk of alienating both Saudi nationals and foreign workers. This shift seems to have arisen from the precarious position of the financial reserves and from predictions of a depressed oil market.

But within days, the royal family reversed course and returned to its traditional policies. The attempt to tax foreign workers led to a considerable outcry, especially among the highly paid Western workers. Alarmed by the prospect of a mass exodus of professionals, and in the face of mass resignations by doctors, nurses, engineers, technicians, teachers, and bankers, the government canceled the new tax. But it was also a loud outcry from the influential Saudi business community, alarmed by the exodus of foreign employees and / or by the need to pay the taxes for them in order to stem the tide of resignations — that forced the royal family to rescind the tax.[4]

On 26 January, the government moved to cancel other measures as well. First, the subsidies on water and electricity were restored. Then, an array of surcharges on airport services, airline tickets, medical services and supplies, real estate sales, etc. were canceled. Finally, some of the increased customs duties on imports were revoked, probably due to protests from the local business community.[5]

The fact that the regime felt compelled to promptly rescind such large-scale revenue measures showed that its freedom of action was severely limited. It also showed that the domestic, social, economic, and political constraints were so serious that they could force the royal family to revoke measures it had deemed absolutely vital only a short while earlier. Indeed, it appeared that King Fahd himself made the decision to rescind the unpopular measures. In the past, he had often been reluctant to increase living costs for ordinary Saudis.

Revoking the new measures contributed to the irrelevancy of the budget, especially on the revenue side. Non-oil revenue fell considerably with the cancellation of the new taxes, surcharges, and customs duties, and because of a decline in the kingdom's investment revenue caused by falling overseas assets and interest rates worldwide. It appeared that whatever capital gains Saudi Arabia had on its foreign investments were used to cover extrabudgetary expenditures.[6] It was also unlikely that oil revenue targets would be met, since they were compromised by a weak oil market throughout 1988. Moreover, the decision to offer discounts and rebates to large oil customers further decreased oil revenues. One can, therefore, understand the Saudi decision to ignore the quota of 4.3m. b/d and to raise production to as high as 6.8m. b/d in late 1988 in order to maximize revenues and compensate for other lost earnings (see section on oil).

Such fundamental changes in revenue called for an adjustment of the budget. Non-oil revenue was, thus, revised from SR36.36bn. to SR31.775bn.; and oil revenue, estimated at SR68.944bn., was adjusted to SR73.525bn. Total revenue remained unchanged — SR105.3bn.[7] It was obvious, however, that the government had serious doubts about its ability to attain such a revenue level. Consequently, it ordered individual ministries to reduce outlays by unspecified amounts. The new instructions most probably followed a cabinet meeting in June in which Finance Minister Muhammad Abu al-Khail presented a midyear report on revenue and expenditure trends, and "received royal directives in this regard."[8]

It soon became apparent that almost insurmountable obstacles hampered the implementation of the third innovation — the sale of Treasury bonds, i.e., obtaining loans. The measure was vulnerable to the criticism of religious leaders unhappy with the notion of interest-bearing borrowing. There were also serious doubts as to whether the kingdom could find an acceptable borrowing mechanism to cover both budget and current account deficits. It seemed probable that the bond issue would be withdrawn like other revenue measures which had been rescinded. But with oil and non-oil revenues falling, the need to raise funds through the sale of bonds became paramount.

In February, Deputy Finance Minister Salih al-'Umayir said that the offer of SR30bn. in Treasury bonds would be announced "shortly," that it would be confined to the state's auxiliary funds and some national banks, and that the bonds would not be offered to the public. But in a very unusual move, the government publicly disavowed his statement that the bond issue was imminent.[9] It was not until the second week of June that the first block of the domestic bond issue was offered to the financial institutions of the private sector. Prior to this, an undisclosed amount had already gone to three large government funds — the Public Investment Fund, the General Organization for Social Insurance, and the Civil Service Pension Fund. Funds from these institutions were cheaper than those to be raised from the commercial banks. In what was to become a fortnight's program, the first SR1.5bn. block of development bonds carried maturities from one to five years. The yields were originally to be linked to US Treasury bonds; but in order to avoid the religiously sensitive issue of interest, this linkage was changed to the bonds paying a return based on the cash flow of certain state projects. Such returns ranged from around 7.8% for one-year maturity, to above 8.6% for three-year and over 9% for five-year maturity. Bankers said that the offer was undersubscribed and estimated that no more than SR1bn. had been taken by banks.[10]

A second issue of SR1.5bn. was announced on 26 June and a third for the same amount on 11 July. The government also introduced a repurchase program for new bonds to make them more attractive to the kingdom's banks. Starting in August, the Saudi Arabian Monetary Agency (Sama) was to repurchase up to 10% of the value of newly issued bonds in a bank portfolio. The bonds scheme had a number of obstacles: (1) the need to obscure the nature and exact level of interest; (2) rumors of a possible devaluation of the riyal; (3) rising and more attractive US interest rates; (4) more promising interest rates on the riyal interbank deposit market; and (5) questions about the banks' ability to resell the bonds. Thus, in order to broaden the market for the bonds, and in response to bankers' demands, the government allowed the banks to include the bonds in their mutual funds portfolios and to sell them directly to private individuals and to corporations.[11]

There were no firm details about the success or failure of the bond offerings. But it did appear that the banks' profits were lower than expected and that the scheme itself was still considered rather controversial. It was also impossible to judge the success of the bond issue in encouraging a repatriation of savings held abroad or in preventing new savings finding their way overseas. It was estimated that almost 50% of the entire issue — SR14bn. — might have been placed with the three governmental institutions and pension funds. No figures were available as to how much of the balance — SR16bn. — was subscribed; but according to one source, bond sales were suspended in November and the government reverted to drawing on the reserves to finance the deficit.[12]

The success of the bond offering became even more crucial given the state of the government's financial reserves. Whereas it was generally assumed that foreign reserves amounted to no more than $60bn. there were doubts about the liquidity of at least 50% of this amount. Moreover, government reserves placed with Sama fell sharply — from SR118.5bn. at the end of 1986 to SR78bn. at the end of 1987. The SR40.5bn. difference represented the actual size of the 1987 budget deficit. Thus, if the 1988 budget deficit of SR36bn. had been fully financed from reserves rather than borrowings, the reserves with Sama might have fallen to SR42bn. — slightly over $11bn. — by the end of 1988. Indeed, it was argued that given the disappointing performance of the bond offering, liquid reserves had fallen to just over $15bn. at the end of 1988.[13]

The state of the financial reserves and the bond issue was also related to the riyal's rate of exchange. Saudi currency had been weak for some time, but the prospect of a large bond issue served initially to firm riyal rates. However, when many of the new revenue-raising measures were dropped, there was immediate panic selling of riyals in anticipation of a devaluation. Such expectations created pressure on the currency, pushing up domestic interest rates.[14] The failure of the government to implement the bond offering reinforced expectations of a devaluation in the first half of 1988. The Saudi leaders thus hoped that the announcement of the bond issue in June would have, in the words of Sama's governor, Hammad Sayyari, "a calming influence" on the riyal.[15]

There were a number of factors favoring a devaluation: (1) it could increase riyal earnings from dollar-denominated oil exports; (2) an increase in riyal earnings coupled with a stable level of expenditures could reduce the budget deficit; (3) a devaluation could correct the imbalance created by the firming of the dollar on currency markets; and (4) a devaluation was likely to reduce imports and consumption in general. On the other hand, there were arguments against a devaluation: (1) the dollar-denominated salaries of the foreign workers would have to be increased; (2) Saudi workers were likely to exert pressure to adjust their salaries and keep them at real value; and (3) the past record showed that devaluations did not necessarily lead to reduced spending and imports. It was clear that by avoiding a devaluation in 1988, the royal family made the measure almost inevitable in 1989.

SAUDI OIL POLICIES

PRODUCTION AND PRICES

Saudi opposition to major increases in oil prices continued throughout 1988. The salient reason underlying such opposition has never been as clearly, frankly, and publicly spelled out as it was by Oil Minister Hisham Nazir himself in January 1988:

> Our experience with fluctuating prices dictates prudence....Increase in prices to high levels would...promote new sources of energy and the appearance of new production sites. That is what happened in 1982 after oil prices had increased in an unacceptable way...countries have turned to coal to run their power plants and industrial facilities, as coal is 50% cheaper. Oil-producing countries should move slowly on oil prices so as to avoid promoting alternative sources, and to guarantee themselves the revenue they seek without throwing the market into confusion.[16]

Thus, Nazir dismissed the arguments for a price rise to $20 a barrel and indicated that even $18 might be too high. If the market improved, Nazir observed, production rather than prices should be increased. One thing he made abundantly clear: Saudi Arabia would never be boxed into a swing-producer role again, nor would it accept lower quotas simply to correct an imbalance produced by quota violation. The kingdom would only consider quota readjustments if market forces changed or if demand increased.

Nazir also suggested that price discounting should not be considered as serious a violation as overproduction. He presumably made his comments in the knowledge that Saudi Arabia intended to return to effective netback pricing in order to maintain output at around its quota of 4.3m. b/d. Indeed, the thrust of Saudi oil policy in 1988 pointed to the overriding goals of maintaining the kingdom's market share at all costs and rejecting a swing-producer role even if prices plunged.

These principles were translated into a number of policy-lines. One was giving preferential terms to the kingdom's four major oil customers — Exxon, Chevron, Texaco, and Mobil — as an inducement to them to maintain their purchases. In April, the *Middle East Economic Survey* went as far as stating that King Fahd himself had confirmed the kingdom's practice of offering price discounts. The Saudi Government denied such allegations.[17] But news reports persisted that Saudi Arabia's policy was based on market-related pricing arrangements, and that because of such discounts to customers buying more than 100,000 b/d, the Saudis managed to increase their production in the second quarter.[18] Saudi determination to avoid acting as Opec's swing producer was also reflected in the resumption of a dormant program to store oil in ocean-going tankers. The Saudis were reportedly intent on rebuilding the huge strategic offshore stockpile that they had used to push for their market share during the 1986 oil-price collapse.

On the eve of Opec's extraordinary meeting in April, King Fahd stressed Saudi resistance to any further production cuts, asserting that non-Opec producers had to bear the brunt of the cuts. He argued that Opec, primarily Saudi Arabia, had sacrificed a substantial part of its oil output in order to strengthen prices, while non-Opec producers seized the opportunities and increased their production, thereby stealing the market share from Opec.[19] It came, therefore, as a surprise that the Saudis were suddenly willing to consider production cuts. It appeared, however, that the Saudi position was a bluff prompted by the offer of seven non-Opec producers to reduce output by 5%, i.e., 200,000 b/d, and by the heavy pressure the Saudis came under from their Opec partners.[20] In the end, the Saudis rejected the non-Opec proposal, because it would have caused a 750,000 b/d cut (5%) in Opec's production. The net result was that Saudi Arabia effectively torpedoed any chance of an Opec/non-Opec agreement on oil production cuts. Underlying such an adamant stand was the Saudi conviction that all Opec production cuts in the past (40% since 1981) had led to a surrender of their market share to non-Opec countries "which are producing approximately at full capacity." Nazir told the Opec conference that Saudi Arabia had seen its oil production drop from 10m. b/d to 4m. b/d, and had lost $110bn. in anticipated revenue. The kingdom was, consequently, determined to hold on to its market share and to guarantee itself a steady level of revenue at all costs.[21]

Between August and November, the Saudis were rapidly raising their production from the 4.3m. b/d quota to as high as 6.8m. b/d. Moreover, the Cabinet warned that "the kingdom will not accept an Opec member adding to its quota at the kingdom's expense and will not freeze its production while others increase."[22] It was only after Opec had reached a new agreement in late November (see chapter on Middle East oil developments) that Saudi production declined to its quota level. By the end of the year it seemed that Saudi oil policy became totally linked, if not subordinated, to Saudi revenue requirements. The implication was that the kingdom no longer attached major importance to its leadership of Opec nor to any long-term schemes of cooperation between oil producers and consumers.

RESTRUCTURING THE OIL INDUSTRY

Soon after being appointed oil minister in 1986, Hisham Nazir launched a campaign to restructure the whole Saudi oil industry which was split between the Arabian-American Oil Company (Aramco) and the General Organization for Petroleum and Minerals (Petromin). Founded in 1933, Aramco was acquired by the Saudi Government in 1980 and controlled all exploration and production of oil in the kingdom. Petromin was established in 1962 as a state oil corporation and it assumed responsibility for refining, domestic marketing, and distribution of petroleum products.

The industry was being reshaped primarily in order to eliminate the overlap in authority between Aramco and Petromin and to increase efficiency. Petromin, particularly, had become so inefficient that it was deprived of overseeing the Petroline pipeline, an operation that was assigned to Aramco. The idea was to establish a fully integrated holding company directing different affiliates responsible for all aspects of the oil industry: exploration, production, crude refining, lube blending, domestic marketing, export sales, and shipping. The company would probably be called the Saudi National Oil Company and would be similar in structure to the Kuwait Petroleum Corporation.[23]

But there was something else in the Kuwaiti model which the Saudis wished to emulate. They realized that the kingdom needed a permanent mechanism to secure a large portion of its oil revenues whatever the vicissitudes of Opec policies. The Saudis had long been envious of Kuwait's ability to guarantee itself a high baseload of exports, because it possessed a large downstream network. The royal family was determined to purchase downstream mechanisms overseas which would enable the kingdom to hold on to its market share and to sell as much oil as possible as refined products, which are sold at market-related prices rather than as officially priced crude.

This was precisely the role entrusted to the new Saudi oil company: "to be the vehicle for the kingdom's drive to establish a substantial presence in the downstream industry overseas by means of joint ventures with the former Aramco parents as well as with others." This effort was designed to counter oil-price instability by "providing secure outlets for Saudi crude and avoiding the bitter experience of late 1985 when Saudi production fell sharply to 2m. b/d." According to Oil Minister Nazir, the decision to find downstream facilities abroad "went hand in hand with the major reorganization of the oil industry at home."[24]

It did not come as a surprise, therefore, when on 16 June it was announced that Saudi Arabia was buying 50% of Texaco's refining and marketing network in 23 eastern and Gulf Coast states in the US. The deal included three major refineries with a combined capacity of 615,000 b/d, 49 oil terminals, 1,450 Texaco-owned or -leased service stations, and more than 10,000 others that carry the Texaco name. The assets represent some 10% of the US market. The Saudis were to pay half the working capital, amounting to $800m., and three quarters of the initial oil inventory — 30m. barrels — worth some $480m. The deal would give Saudi Arabia a much more secure market for up to 600,000 b/d and the potential to earn more money from refined products. When signing the agreement in November, Nazir expressed his hope that "other similar deals will follow." He made it clear that Saudi Arabia regarded the joint venture with Texaco as a pattern for a big push into the downstream part of the industry. Finally, he put it all into context when stating that the strategy underlying such purchases of downstream networks was aimed at "maximizing the oil revenues of the kingdom."[25]

DEFENSE AND MILITARY PRIORITIES

The economic recession also affected the largest single item in the Saudi budget — defense. Budgetary allocations for defense were cut from $19bn. in 1984–85 to $17.7bn. in 1985–86, to $16.2bn. in 1987, and to a projected $13.5bn. in 1988. As a percentage of the overall budget, however, military expenditures increased from 27% in 1984–85 to 32% in 1985–86, to 35.7% in 1987, and to an all-time record of 36% in 1988.

The very cautious spending trends in all sectors contrasted starkly with the arms procurement budget which was described as a "spending feat." There was evidence that the midyear instruction to all ministries to reduce expenditures did not apply to the defense budget.[26] Instead, in his budget address, King Fahd stressed the need for continuing high military expenditures. Moreover, government spokesmen left the impression that military expenditures would take an increasing share of the budget, given the substantial cutbacks in other sectors. In addition, the Defense Ministry had been benefiting from extrabudgetary sources of finance. The actual military outlays have always been shrouded in mystery. What made it easier to obscure the true extent of military expenditures was the growing trend of financing arms deals through oil supplies. Therefore, it was safe to assume that actual military outlays exceeded by far the figures stipulated in the budget.

The arms purchases program of 1986 and 1987 (see *MECS* 1987, pp. 587–88) continued unabated in 1988. The two most conspicuous arms deals of the year greatly exceeded past ones both qualitatively and quantitatively and introduced new dimensions into the ME arms race. In March, it was revealed that Saudi Arabia had purchased from China intermediate-range, surface-to-surface ballistic missiles. The CSS-2, *East Wind* missiles had an effective range of 1,500 miles when armed with conventional warheads and 2,200 miles when carrying nuclear warheads. Saudi-Chinese negotiations had been going on since July 1985, but the royal family managed to keep the talks secret from the Americans (see below).[27]

Then, in July, Saudi Arabia and Britain signed the biggest arms deal ever, worth some $25bn. It constituted the second phase of the *Tornado* deal signed in 1986 which had included 132 aircraft and was worth some $12bn. The 1988 deal was much more comprehensive and consisted of 48 *Tornado* jet fighters, 60 *Hawk* trainer aircraft, 80 *Black Hawk* attack helicopters, six minesweepers, and the construction of two major air bases.[28] The Saudis also signed a deal with France for 12 *Super-Dauphin* helicopters armed with *Exocet* missiles and several light patrol boats. In addition, the Saudis continued their search for eight advanced submarines, 20 maritime patrol aircraft, and 1,200 battle tanks, with the Brazilian tank *Osorio* seeming to have won the competition. Finally, the Saudis were also seeking multiple launch rockets, a highly sophisticated American artillery system that is designed for use in high intensity combat.

Such massive arms deals — in times of general recession, austerity, and contraction — again raised the question of the strategy underlying the military buildup and its targets. While public attention was focused on the Persian Gulf and the Iraqi-Iranian

War as explaining Saudi policies, some military analysts sought to link the Saudi buildup to the growing Soviet presence around the peninsula. According to these analysts, the Soviet Union had been consolidating its position in southern Arabia and had been particularly active around the Bab al-Mandab Straits. It was thought to have up to 5,000 "advisers" in South Yemen, to have full control of an air base where fighter, transport, and reconnaissance planes were stationed, and to have built a sizable command complex, invulnerable to conventional attack, inside a mountain near Aden.

But more ominous for the Saudis was the presence of the Soviet Navy on Perim Island, in the middle of the 20km.-wide Bab al-Mandab Straits, and on Socotra, off the Horn of Africa. According to this analysis, the Red Sea had become increasingly important in Saudi strategy. There was a steady flow of military and commercial traffic, including oil tankers, to and from the Suez Canal and the kingdom's oil and petrochemical terminal at Yanbu' and its largest port at Jidda. The existing Saudi military presence was insufficient to defend the Red Sea arena, especially in view of its length, 1,900 km., which is six times the length of the Saudi coast on the Gulf. The problem became more tangible after unidentified mines were discovered in the Red Sea in 1984 (see *MECS* 1984–85, pp. 188–91). This analysis explains not only the purchase of minesweepers but also the search for submarines; unsuitable in shallow waters of the Persian Gulf (less than two meters), submarines have useful roles in the at least 1,000-meter-deep Red Sea.[29]

Such an interpretation, however, fails to explain the military buildup in its entirety and to account for the purchase of and search for intermediate surface-to-surface missiles, 132 *Tornado* fighter-bomber jets, 1,200 battle tanks, etc. Also, it would appear unreasonable for the Saudi leadership to believe that it could effectively counter the Soviet presence in the Red Sea area through such arms deals. Moreover, the massive procurement was likely to exacerbate the difficulty of absorbing such a range of sophisticated and expensive weapons. On paper, they might appear to add great strength to the Saudi armed forces; in reality, they could be detrimental.

For one thing, the Saudis might have overdiversified their purchases by acquiring weapons from the US, Britain, France, Brazil, China, and other countries. Differences in the equipment make it difficult for operators and repairmen to transfer among systems. Spreading personnel thinly over different weapons systems could cause severe personnel problems, because the Saudis had no reserves in the event of sustained military operations.[30] Despite good pay, the armed forces were still highly understaffed. The perennial lack of volunteers coupled with the reluctance of the regime to impose a draft dimmed any prospects of increasing the size of the armed forces. King Fahd continued to appeal to Saudi youth "to join the armed forces because the responsibility of defending the Islamic holy places requires solid support by youths imbued with belief and equipped with science in the service of their religion, homeland, and nation."[31] Speaking to a group of army and police officers, the king stated that "if 500,000 young, educated Saudis" were to join the armed forces, this could have been "the most valuable asset to the kingdom's security."[32] The king's appeal was unlikely to be heeded. Illustrative of the problem was the half-empty housing in the huge military base at Hafar al-Batin. In fact, according to one estimate, the Army actually declined in size between 1975 and 1982.

Viewed against this background, the policy of massive arms procurement seemed highly questionable. It led one Western defense attaché to comment that "it definitely looks like the Saudis have got eyes bigger than their stomachs; this obsession with new weapons reminds us of the Shah."[33] That the level of military expenditures was going to be maintained, and even raised, became abundantly clear with the announcement of the 1989 budget: defense allocations were to rise to $14.7bn. (SR55bn.) and to constitute an all-time record — 39% of the total budget.[34]

INTERNAL CHALLENGES

THE 1988 *HAJJ*

The pilgrimage of 1988 was a turning point in Saudi policy toward the *hajj* in general and toward Iran's role in it in particular. The shift was undoubtedly rooted in the bloody *hajj* of 1987 which ended in the death of over 400 pilgrims and Saudi security men (see *MECS* 1987, pp. 172–74, 589–91). The Saudi leaders felt that their inability to control fully 150,000 Iranian pilgrims, let alone prevent them from engaging in provocative behavior, was a major source of embarrassment for the kingdom and its status as Guardian of the Holy Places.

Saudi anxieties were further heightened by Iranian statements in early 1988. In February, Deputy Foreign Minister 'Ali Muhammad Besharati announced that Iran would send more pilgrims in 1988 "without seeking the permission of the Saudi authorities to organize mass political demonstrations."[35] The head of the Iranian *hajj* delegation, Imam Jamarani, added that Iran was preparing "one of the most magnificent *hajj* ceremonies, whether in its religious dimension or in its political dimension." Khomeyni himself urged pilgrims to carry out even more vehement demonstrations than in 1987 and to denounce the enemies of Islam. Finally, Iranian leaders continued to advocate publicly the "internationalization of Mecca and Medina" by taking them away from Saudi authority and placing them under general Islamic rule.[36]

The Saudi leadership responded by blaming the "demagogic practices and sabotage of the Iranians" for "the death of hundreds of innocent people." It warned that "the kingdom will not be in the least complacent about exercising its sovereignty and in not permitting anyone to dictate conditions and undertake actions contrary to the purpose of performing the *hajj*."[37] And an official cabinet statement warned Iran that if its pilgrims "come to chant atheistic slogans, let them know that we have taken measures to stop any individual or group from demonstrating; we will deal firmly with them."[38] But secretly, the royal family sought to obtain an Iranian pledge to desist from political activities in the *hajj*. Only when this attempt led nowhere did the Saudis embark on a new course.

As recently as February, Minister of Interior Prince Na'if declared that "all Muslims, regardless of their nationality and political views, have the right to perform the *hajj*."[39] But in March, the royal family decided to limit the number of Iranian pilgrims to a manageable level. Basically, the Saudi leadership refused to go along with a situation whereby Iran would send over 150,000 pilgrims every year whereas the second largest group, of the more populous Egypt, would not exceed 60,000. Unwilling, however, to project the decision as aimed only against the Iranians, reluctant to be perceived as incapable of handling security during the *hajj*, and seeking to give their policy a stamp of all-Islamic legitimacy, the Saudis put the issue on the agenda of the Islamic

Conference Organization (ICO). At a meeting of the ICO's foreign ministers in Amman in late March, the Saudis persuaded the delegates to agree to a general pilgrim quota system for *each* country. Saudi Foreign Minister, Prince Sa'ud al-Faysal, explained that this move was necessary in view of major construction and renovation work being carried out to enlarge the holy shrines in Mecca and Medina. The quota was put at one pilgrim for every 1,000 people in each Muslim country. Iran was allocated a quota of 45,000, which it promptly rejected and vowed to ignore.[40]

The Saudi-Iranian confrontation over the *hajj* was further exacerbated by Riyadh's cutting diplomatic relations with Tehran in late April. While Iran announced in May that it would boycott the *hajj* altogether, there were news reports that Tehran was training non-Iranian Shi'is to disrupt and sabotage the *hajj*.[41] This led the Saudis to restate the set of regulations and punishments for transgressors in a most unequivocal manner: "We will deal with the misguided who are tempted to perpetrate crimes that disturb security, such as possessing weapons or explosives, or carrying out any hooligan, terrorist, or sabotage acts, such as demonstrations, slogans, carrying photographs or flags, using loudspeakers, blocking roads, or disturbing pilgrims' worship. The punishment of those who...strive for mischief is execution, or the amputation of hands and feet from opposite sides of the body, or exile from the land."[42]

The Saudis also required all pilgrims to carry identity cards with passport details and computer classification numbers. Pilgrims from the Shi'i-populated Eastern Province were allowed to perform the *hajj* only if they had not done so before. According to some reports, by a Saudi request 5,000 Egyptian troops were stationed in Mecca and Medina to handle disturbances and clashes; in addition, a seven-man team from the elite West German antiterrorist squad was training Saudi commandos. These reports were flatly denied by Interior Minister Prince Na'if.[43]

Despite one attempt by a group of pilgrims to smuggle light arms, the *hajj* passed peacefully and uneventfully in stark contrast with the violent 1987 *hajj*. The overall Saudi objective was achieved: the number of pilgrims from abroad declined to 752,000 and the absence of Iranian pilgrims assured order and tranquillity.[44] (For more details on the 1988 *hajj*, see chapter "An Uneasy Truce in Islam.")

OPPOSITION AND SUBVERSION

At the end of March, a huge explosion and fire occurred at the Sadaf petrochemical plant in Jubayl. Though described by the government as "an accident," they led to fears of sabotage by pro-Iranians among the large Shi'i community in the Eastern Province. Such fears were heightened when a large amount of explosives was found a few days later near the vast refinery area of Ras Tanura.[45] Then, in early August, the Hizballah organization in Beirut announced that members of its Saudi branch had killed three Saudi police officers who were on their way to Hizballah headquarters in Qatif, the largest Shi'i concentration in the Eastern Province. The Hizballah claimed that the Saudis had arrested three of its members and warned Riyadh against harming them.[46]

Such incidents tended to substantiate the potential for sabotage and subversion inherent in Saudi Arabia's 400,000-strong Shi'i community. But what exacerbated the dilemma were the 15,000 Shi'is employed by Aramco in the oil fields, who formed one third of its entire work force. Given the proximity of Iran, there was fear in

Riyadh that Tehran might manipulate the Saudi Shi'is in a direction detrimental to Riyadh, particularly in view of the adverse economic conditions in the Eastern Province. Such fears were confirmed when the Saudi authorities arrested four Shi'is and charged them with starting the fire at the Sadaf plant.

Alarmed, apparently, by an increasing number of incidents and hoping to deter potential saboteurs, the government appealed to the *'ulama,* seeking capital punishment for certain offenses. In late August, the 22nd session of the Council of Senior *'Ulama* in Ta'if prescribed the death penalty "as a deterrent punishment" for anyone found guilty of having perpetrated an act of sabotage or any act undermining security. These included: "attacks on people, private or public buildings — houses, mosques, schools, hospitals, factories, bridges, arms depots, reservoirs; attacks on public resources of the Treasury, such as petroleum pipelines; or blowing up planes or hijacking them."[47] Though phrased in general terms, it was clear that the Sadaf explosion was the impetus for this edict, and four weeks later, the four Shi'is were executed. But one of the most revealing passages in the council's resolution was the admission that "the Kingdom of Saudi Arabia is exposed to such acts of sabotage which result in innocent people being killed and much property and public installations being destroyed." This admission contrasted with the government's practice of denying such acts were sabotage, attributing them to "accidents."

Following the executions, the Hizballah's Saudi branch vowed to avenge the "martyrdom" of its four members. It pledged to continue to resist the attempt of "the corrupt Saudi princes to stifle Islamic momentum in the peninsula."[48] At the end of October, a Saudi diplomat was assassinated in Ankara, Turkey, and the Hizballah claimed responsibility for the murder.[49] At the same time, reports spread about a Hizballah movement in the Hijaz, whose members had been trained by the Iranians at a camp near Tehran. Following the executions, Hizballah members were reported to be pursuing Saudi princes and officials in Europe.[50]

DRUG PROBLEMS

The problem of drug smuggling continued to preoccupy the Saudi authorities throughout 1988. They said that the imposition of the death penalty on drug offenders (see *MECS* 1987, p. 594), served as "a reminder, warning, and deterrent," that led to a 40% decline in drug smuggling into the kingdom. This decline explains why the government gave such prominence to the eight separate executions of drug offenders.

Several new measures were taken in 1988. In April, Minister of Interior Prince Na'if signed a cooperation agreement with Syria aimed at "combating narcotics."[51] In May, it was announced that narcotics-combating officials from Saudi Arabia were participating in American projects designed "to test and refine new technology to interdict illicit transport of drugs." One device, already in use in the US and Saudi Arabia, was a high- and low-density X-ray unit used in ports of entry to identify marijuana, hashish, and other contraband in luggage, packages, and containers.[52] In late June, the government announced that foreign diplomats accused of using or smuggling narcotics could not claim diplomatic immunity. A senior Interior Ministry official told *al-Riyad* that diplomatic immunity would not "prevent us from imposing capital punishment on drug smugglers and pushers."[53]

FOREIGN AFFAIRS

SAUDI ARABIA, IRAN, AND THE IRAQI-IRANIAN WAR

Saudi Arabia's relations with Iran throughout the 1980s have been characterized by a peculiar ambiguity. On the one hand, there was anxiety in Riyadh because of the revolutionary character of the Iranian regime and the spillover of the Iraqi-Iranian War into Arab states of the Gulf. This anxiety became more tangible in 1987 when the Saudis feared that their most sensitive oil and military installations might become targets of Iranian attacks. On the other hand, the royal family sought to refrain from any action likely to provoke the Iranian leadership, and to maintain channels of communication with various groups in Tehran. As a result, a very confusing state of relations evolved, characterized at certain times by *rapprochement* and at other times by severe friction and tension.

The death of 400 people in the 1987 *hajj* was a turning point in Saudi-Iranian relations. The Saudis felt that Iran's goal was to destabilize the kingdom and make it appear unfit to be entrusted with the custody of the two holy shrines. Such a change in Riyadh's perception heralded a Saudi propaganda campaign unprecedented in its harshness and a new Saudi strategy predicated on the notion that efforts to accommodate Tehran had utterly failed. Instead, the royal family ceased to appease Iran and launched a two-pronged offensive aimed at weakening and isolating Khomeyni. The Saudi leadership endeavored to forge an all-Arab front which would cut ties with the Iranian regime and force it to stop the war. At the same time, the Saudis sought to generate international pressure on Khomeyni through various boycotts and particularly an arms embargo to implement Security Council Resolution 598. But by the beginning of 1988, it seemed that the offensive had failed.

GROWING CONFRONTATION: JANUARY-JULY 1988

Saudi-Iranian relations in 1988 must be divided into two distinct periods, with late July constituting a clear-cut watershed. In the first six months, the Saudi leadership, reconciled to the limits of its options against Iran, realized that it could not bring effective international or all-Arab pressure to bear on Tehran. Consequently, Riyadh confined its efforts to strengthening the kingdom's own political and military leverage *vis-à-vis* Tehran and to improving its ability to withstand Iranian challenges. Thus, first priority was accorded to the one issue which had created the turning point in 1987 — Iranian participation in the *hajj*.

The new Saudi thinking on the *hajj* was touched off at the beginning of the year by official Iranian statements. These promised not only to repeat in 1988 the "political demonstrations and denunciations with more enthusiasm and vigor," but also not to seek Saudi permission to organize such demonstrations. The Saudi Government retorted that "evil is the distinctive feature of the psychological profile of the Iranian regime" and reiterated its "determination not to allow a repetition of Iranian criminal practices."[54] Saudi anxieties heightened upon learning that 100,000 Revolutionary Guards were being trained especially for the purpose of "causing havoc in Mecca and Medina during the pilgrimage." In addition, the Saudis found evidence that Iran had contacted Pakistani Shi'i pilgrims and persuaded them to join Iranians in the demonstrations. The Saudis viewed this as an Iranian attempt to widen the confrontation in Mecca so that Tehran could claim that Muslims other than Iranians defied the Saudi authorities.[55]

A debate apparently ensued in Riyadh about what measures should be taken to prevent the recurrence of the 1987 fiasco. One school argued that the kingdom should refuse entry to Iranian pilgrims, or severely reduce their numbers. The other school called for a moderate reduction in the number of Iranian pilgrims in a way that would not alienate the Islamic world.[56] The formula finally adopted envisaged a drastic cut in the number of Iranian pilgrims, but rather than challenge Iran, the Saudis persuaded the ICO to formally adopt a general measure limiting the number of pilgrims from each Muslim country to 1,000 per 1m. population.

The only country affected by this measure was Iran, whose pilgrims were to decline by 70% — from 150,000 to 45,000. But having the ICO adopt the measure was meant to avoid provoking Khomeyni and allow him to save face. Khomeyni, however, refused to play by these rules and defiantly declared that "this year, 150,000 Iranian pilgrims will perform their obligation to denounce and disavow the infidels, the US, and Israel." He added that "denouncing the infidels is central to the political obligations of the pilgrimage; without it the pilgrimage is no pilgrimage." Khomeyni went as far as sending to Riyadh in April a delegation of pilgrims, which demanded that the Saudis accept 150,000 Iranian pilgrims and allow the staging of demonstrations and marches. The Saudi Government rejected these demands, which prompted Khomeyni to intensify his threats against the kingdom.[57]

In addition to the confrontation over the *hajj,* Saudi Arabia continued to condemn Iran for pursuing the "senseless" war against Iraq. King Fahd termed Iran's conditions for ending the war "unreasonable and unacceptable," saying that "conditions come after the war ends." The king asserted that "the war will end one day; but why wait till it annihilates everything and everybody?" Saudi leaders and media urged the Security Council to punish Iran for its refusal to implement Resolution 598 by imposing an arms embargo and economic sanctions, and by suspending Iran's UN membership. But having realized that their leverage was limited, the Saudis felt they had to rely, as a last resort, on the American military umbrella. King Fahd went as far as publicly defending the presence of foreign navies in the Persian Gulf, arguing that the Arab states "have a right to seek outside help to prevent Iran from embroiling them in the war."[58]

Saudi Arabia again accused Iran of cooperating with Israel against the Arab nation. The Saudi media argued that Israeli-Iranian contacts had created "some kind of mutual understanding and desire to deepen ties." One such alleged understanding was that Khomeyni, armed with Israeli weapons, would launch "a new offensive against Iraq so that Israel could liquidate the *intifada.*" Another alleged deal envisaged "the emigration of 30,000 Iranian Jews to Palestine in exchange for weapons and military equipment." Moreover, Israel was said to be actively supporting the Iranian war effort against Iraq. Illustrative of such support was the Israeli pilotless surveillance aircraft which was shot down by Iraqi antiaircraft forces while gathering data on Iraqi targets. The Saudi media concluded that three factors underlay the Israeli-Iranian alliance: (1) both regimes suffered from acute international and regional isolation; (2) both could use each other to promote their common goal of hurting Arab interests; and (3) both were based on "fascist-Nazi ideologies using iron and fire to repress people under their rule."[59]

The Saudis also accused the Iranian regime of fomenting trouble in various parts of the Islamic world. In Lebanon, Tehran was said to be trying to split the population, to use one faction as "a bridge to penetrate into the country," and to encourage fighting as a means of diverting public attention from its own defeats. Iran was also blamed for "marketing its revolution through aggression and international terrorism," and for supporting "terrorist movements all over the world." Finally, Iran was accused of actively training Saudi opposition forces for subversive activities both inside the kingdom and against Saudi targets abroad. Tehran was reported to have provided $60m. for training members of two groups — the Organization of the Islamic Revolution in the Arabian Peninsula and the Hijazi Revolutionary Forces.[60]

The Saudi-Iranian confrontation reached its peak in April with Khomeyni's threat to disrupt the *hajj,* the explosion in the Sadaf petrochemical complex (see above), and Iranian attacks on Saudi and Kuwaiti targets in the Gulf (see chapter on the Iraqi-Iranian War). Consequently, on 26 April the Saudi Government announced its decision to sever diplomatic relations with Iran. The official communiqué claimed that despite all Saudi efforts "to normalize relations on the basis of mutual respect stemming from Islamic ties," Tehran "persisted in its hostile acts."[61]

But rather than citing such recent "hostile acts" which could have accounted for the timing of the announcement, the communiqué referred only to the attack nine months earlier on the Saudi Embassy in Tehran. Saudi officials, likewise, referred to the general pattern of relations without any emphasis on recent events: "We have done our utmost to engage Iran in a constructive dialogue, but whatever they promised privately, Khomeyni contradicted publicly." Finally, King Fahd himself made only general references to "Iran's repeated acts of aggression against the kingdom, mistaking our patience for acquiescence." He went as far as threatening that "if obliged," Saudi Arabia would not hesitate to use its CSS-2 Chinese missiles against Iran. In the absence of any concrete, immediate reason, it appeared that the Saudi decision was designed primarily to improve the Saudi image in the US. The decision was related to the strong anti-Saudi sentiments prevailing in Washington in the aftermath of the exposure of the Chinese-Saudi missile deal (see below, section on Saudi Arabia and the US). The Saudi Foreign Ministry, therefore, made it a point to deny "the allegation that the decision to sever relations with Iran was made under foreign pressure."[62]

RELAXATION OF TENSIONS: AUGUST-DECEMBER 1988

Two events in July seemed to have marked a turning point, paving the way for a later *rapprochement:* Khomeyni's decision not to send Iranian pilgrims to Mecca and the end of the Gulf War. Khomeyni, to be sure, blamed Saudi Arabia for closing its gates to all Iranian pilgrims, ignoring the fact that 45,000 Iranians were allowed in. But his decision to boycott the pilgrimage altogether could not but please the Saudi leaders, who breathed a sigh of relief.[63] For the first time in a decade, the *hajj* passed without any demonstrations, clashes, or disturbances.

It was during the *hajj* period that Iran announced its acceptance of a cease-fire in its war against Iraq, thereby removing one of the most controversial issues between Riyadh and Tehran. Khomeyni's announcement caught the royal family by complete surprise. The initial thinking in Riyadh was that it might be "another gimmick to check the recent Iraqi advances into Iranian territory," or that it was "an offer by a moderate like [Speaker of the *Majlis,* Hujjat al-Islam] Rafsanjani which could be blasted from within by the hard-liners." The conventional wisdom in Riyadh was that

Iran accepted a cease-fire only in order "to regroup, regain power, obtain crucial arms, and be in a position to launch a new offensive, and to prepare for new conspiracies and seditions."[64] But this perception changed once Iran formally accepted Security Council Resolution 598 and the cease-fire went into effect on 20 August.

The peaceful *hajj* and the end of the war heralded a series of Saudi overtures toward the Iranian regime. Speaking to leaders of pilgrimage delegations, King Fahd declared that he regretted not having seen Iranian pilgrims and expressed hope "to settle these matters in an amicable manner." Speaking in the same spirit at a meeting in Jidda of Muslim information ministers, King Fahd held out an olive branch to Tehran saying: "Iran is an Islamic country; deep in my heart I would have loved to have seen my Iranian brothers here today."[65] Such gestures were accompanied by reports that Saudi and Iranian representatives were negotiating the resumption of diplomatic relations. The Saudis refused to comment on these reports, stating only that "the kingdom wants to maintain normal relations and not entrench enmity with Iran."[66]

The relaxation of tensions was translated also into tangible measures. In October, King Fahd ordered the Saudi media to stop all criticism of and attacks on Iran as a sign of Saudi good intentions. In December, it was reported that the Saudis were negotiating compensation for the families of the Iranians killed in the Mecca incident. The Saudis reportedly accepted the principle of compensation and the bargaining revolved around the amount to be paid and the number of Iranians killed. The Saudis offered $1.5m. for each of the 275 Iranians they said had died, while Iran demanded $2m. for the 650 people it said had been killed. There were also reports, denied by Saudi officials, that Riyadh had offered to help Iran rebuild its postwar economy. In addition, the Saudis endeavored to participate actively in the process of mediation between Iran and Iraq. On the Saudi side, both Prince Sa'ud al-Faysal, the foreign minister, and Prince Bandar, the ambassador in Washington, played a role in UN efforts to reconcile the two countries. Thus, by the end of the year, an atmosphere of *rapprochement* began to prevail between Riyadh and Tehran.[67] (For more details on Saudi-Iranian relations, see chapter "An Uneasy Truce in Islam.")

THE INTER-ARAB ARENA

At various stages in 1986 and 1987, Saudi policies in the Arab world concentrated on achieving three main goals: effecting a reconciliation between Syria and Iraq, attempting through all-Arab pressures to force Iran into terminating the war with Iraq, and convening the Arab summit conference, delayed since 1983(!), in Riyadh. Having failed to attain any of these goals and in view of the ever-increasing Iranian challenge to their own security, the Saudi leaders focused on a much more limited goal: the formation of an all-Arab front which would sever all ties with Iran.

The Amman summit of November 1987 was expected to accomplish just that. In the aftermath of the summit, a euphoric mood prevailed in Riyadh. Not only did an all-Arab front against Iran crystallize, but the apparent reconciliation of such adversaries as Syria's President Hafiz al-Asad and Iraq's President Saddam Husayn, PLO chairman Yasir 'Arafat and Jordan's King Husayn, Asad and Lebanon's President Amin Jumayyil, aroused new hopes in Riyadh that an overall Arab reconciliation was within reach. In addition, the resolution that each Arab country was entitled to resume diplomatic relations with Egypt, though not a full-fledged return of Cairo to Arab ranks, amounted nevertheless to a breakthrough.

Saudi optimism was based on the notion that the reconciliations, coupled with Egypt's return to Arab politics, produced a firm Arab consensus against Iran. This, they hoped, could diminish the threats and dangers posed by Khomeyni, and perhaps even signal the beginning of the end of the Iraqi-Iranian War. In early 1988, however, Saudi optimism faded. With the various Arab parties entrenched in their positions, no serious reconciliation ensued on any major inter-Arab issue. The Amman summit had no real follow-up; its declarations and resolutions (except those concerning relations with Egypt) remained basically nonstarters. The Saudis were back to square one.

Disappointment and disillusionment with the results of the summit led the royal family to retreat to a backstage role in inter-Arab politics. Saudi activities in, and expectations from, the Arab arena in 1988 were characterized by pessimism and unusual passivity. It seemed as if the Saudi leaders had reconciled themselves to the idea that it was not in their power to mediate splits and rivalries plaguing the Arab world since the early 1980s and to restore any semblance of Arab solidarity. Such a retreat was best expressed in the royal family's ceasing to pursue the traditional policy of convening an Arab summit in Riyadh.

Instead, the Saudi leadership confined itself to pursuing more limited objectives, primarily those connected with the security of the kingdom itself. Thus, the royal family sought, and obtained, all-Arab legitimacy and support for its decision to sever diplomatic relations with Iran. In late April, the Arab League General Secretariat justified the Saudi move on the grounds that "Iran's policy of riots, threats, and aggression intended to destabilize the region."[68] Likewise, the Saudis strove to obtain Arab political backing for their decision to reduce drastically the number of Iranian pilgrims. All in all, the Saudis kept a low profile characterized by a distinctly defensive posture devoid of any grand designs and ambitions. This new posture was best reflected in the Algiers summit in June, where King Fahd did not play a particularly significant role (see chapter on inter-Arab relations).

It was only toward the end of 1988 that the leadership's perception of Arab politics seemed to be changing, a change clearly anchored in the end of the Iraqi-Iranian War. For eight years, the war and Persian Gulf politics in general had become intertwined with and aggravated Arab politics and rivalries. The end of the war relieved inter-Arab relations of this exacerbating factor. The fact that the war did not end in Iran's favor also considerably weakened and isolated Tehran's ally, Syria. This in turn curtailed Asad's ability to play a negative role, from Riyadh's perspective, and to wield his veto power in Arab politics. On the other hand, Egypt's increasing involvement in all-Arab issues could be viewed only as a positive development by Riyadh. Finally, the uprising in the West Bank and the Gaza Strip, the declaration of Palestinian independence in November, and the opening of a US-PLO dialogue in December (see chapter on the Palestine Liberation Organization) created a new rallying point for renewed Arab solidarity. These developments revived Saudi hopes that the road was finally paved for the convening of the much-delayed Arab summit in Riyadh.

As 1988 came to a close, however, it appeared that a number of elements indispensable for the summit were still not in place. For one, despite statements pointing to an imminent Syrian-Iraqi *rapprochement,* it remained as elusive as ever. For another, the Lebanese crisis took a turn for the worse following the end of

President Jumayyil's term of office and the formation of two governments in Beirut. These further complicated Syria's standing in the Arab arena. Also, despite the general Arab support of the Palestinian uprising, there was no agreement as to the next stage in the political process and the Palestinian role in it. The net result was that Saudi Arabia continued to keep a low profile in inter-Arab relations, being reluctant to embark on any bold initiatives whose failure was bound to further embarrass the royal family. The only exception was reportedly Riyadh's efforts to have Egypt readmitted into the Arab League, i.e., to have Egypt's President Husni Mubarak participate in the Arab summit in Riyadh.

RELATIONS WITH EGYPT

The resumption of full diplomatic relations between Saudi Arabia and Egypt in late 1987 significantly broadened the range of contacts, cooperation, and coordination between the two countries. As expected, cooperation, previously limited to financial matters, considerably expanded to include strategic, military, and political issues. From a Saudi perspective, the resumption of relations rectified a decade-long anomaly in Riyadh's foreign policy.

The improvement in relations was already apparent in January when Mubarak paid an official visit to the kingdom and was given a red-carpet welcome by King Fahd. The two were reported to have discussed "a common policy on the Iran-Iraq War and the Palestinian issue." It was clear, however, that in view of Khomeyni's increasing belligerency toward Saudi Arabia, Riyadh felt it necessary to secure Egyptian support as a counterbalance. There were reports that Saudi contingency plans included calling for help from Egypt, if needed, and that Mubarak was expected to help the Gulf states with military equipment and advisers. But the visit was also an opportunity for King Fahd to state that "the kingdom and Egypt are one country and one people in solidarity since ancient times" and for Mubarak to reciprocate, "our ties are deeply rooted and eternal."[69]

Further high-level contacts between the two countries were also related to Saudi anxiety over Iran. In April, Mubarak and Fahd exchanged letters apparently in anticipation of the Saudi severance of diplomatic ties with Tehran. In late May, Interior Minister Prince Na'if and Deputy National Guard Commander Prince Badr made official visits to Cairo. While the former discussed the dispatch of 5,000 Egyptian troops for the *hajj* period, the latter had talks on military cooperation.[70]

While in Cairo, Prince Na'if announced that King Fahd "will soon visit Egypt" reciprocating Mubarak's visit in January. It was assumed that the king would stop in Cairo on his way to the Algiers summit in June, but that did not happen. In August, it was again reported that Fahd "was due in Cairo on 12 August for a four-day working visit." The visit was then postponed to 28 August. The agenda for the visit included Egyptian-Syrian reconciliation, the return of Arab League headquarters to Cairo, and a series of agreements on economic cooperation between Cairo and Riyadh. But, this visit, too, was postponed and it did not take place until the end of the year. No reasons were given (an anti-Saudi article in an Egyptian opposition paper was, reportedly, at the background of this postponement — see chapter on Egypt). Saudi spokesmen, however, continuously emphasized that relations were excellent and that the kingdom's endeavors in the Arab arena were aimed at "the readmission of Egypt to the Arab League and to all other regional and international forums."[71]

ATTITUDE TOWARD THE PALESTINIANS AND THE PLO

The *intifada* in the West Bank and the Gaza Strip gave the Saudi leadership an opportunity to demonstrate its commitment to the Palestinian cause. The Saudi media consistently praised "the heroic struggle of the Palestinian masses against the Zionist occupation" and expressed the hope that the uprising would end in "the liberation of Jerusalem and the holy places" and in "the Palestinians regaining their rights."[72] The regime also accorded prominent publicity to private donations channeled through the Popular Committee for the Support of Palestinian Freedom Fighters. Established under the slogan "give a riyal and save a Palestinian," the committee was chaired by Prince Salman, the governor of Riyadh. It was reported to have raised over SR50m., which included private donations by members of the royal family. To strengthen the campaign, the Council of Senior *'Ulama* issued a *fatwa* (religious ruling) making it mandatory to channel to the *intifada* part of the charity tax (*zakat*) paid by Saudi citizens.[73]

Saudi financial support for the PLO continued on the level of previous years. This is why the royal family was taken by complete surprise by Yasir 'Arafat's reported statement that "except for Iraq and Kuwait, no Arab state supported the Palestinian struggle." Responding promptly, a Saudi official said that since 1979, $368m. had been given for "Palestinian steadfastness in the territories" through the joint Jordanian-PLO committee; over $20m. had been donated directly to Palestinian institutions in the territories, such as hospitals, universities, municipalities, and schools; and that millions of Saudi riyals had been donated since the beginning of the *intifada* through the Popular Committee.[74]

The PLO must have detected the degree of Saudi anger, because within a day its representative in Riyadh, Rafiq al-Natsha, declared that Saudi Arabia was the only Arab country "to have fully honored its commitments undertaken at the Baghdad summit of 1978." He announced that since then, Riyadh had provided the PLO with $855m. (three annual installments of $28.5m. over a 10-year period). He also revealed that the "misunderstanding has compelled the PLO to send a message to King Fahd, emphasizing that the Palestinian leadership would not do anything to damage the kingdom or minimize the extent of its assistance to the Palestinian resistance." The Saudis were reported to have accepted the "clarifications," and relations with the PLO "returned to what they used to be."[75]

The crisis was followed by two visits of 'Arafat to Riyadh in mid-April and late May, apparently in preparation for the Algiers summit in June and in the context of the PLO's demand for $128m. in immediate assistance toward the *intifada* and a further monthly allowance of $48m. to be donated by Arab states. The Saudi leadership seized the opportunity to impress on 'Arafat the need for, and the feasibility of, a *rapprochement* with Syria in the aftermath of the assassination of Abu Jihad (see chapter on armed operations). The Saudis took credit for 'Arafat's visit to Damascus and promised "to remove all obstacles preventing a full reconciliation" between 'Arafat and Asad. But no amount of Saudi efforts could heal the rift between the two.[76]

The royal family was apparently consulted by King Husayn prior to his decision to sever ties with the West Bank (see chapter on Jordan). The Saudi leaders welcomed the move, arguing that it would "highlight Palestinian identity and strengthen the PLO's role as the sole representative of the Palestinian people." But they asserted that

Husayn's move had imposed on the PLO the duty "to adopt a political formula which is based on the new realities."[77] According to a statement attributed to Prince Bandar, the Saudi ambassador in Washington, the Saudi leadership was exerting pressure on the PLO to have the forthcoming meeting of the Palestine National Council (PNC) recognize Israel through the acceptance of UN Resolution 181 ("partition"). Once the PNC issued the declaration of Palestinian independence and adopted the PLO's new political program in mid-November (see chapter on the Palestine Liberation Organization), Saudi Arabia was among the first countries to recognize the "state" and to welcome the program.[78]

RELATIONS WITH SYRIA

Saudi-Syrian relations in 1988 were primarily affected by differences over the Lebanese crisis. Another controversial issue — Syrian support of Iran in the Gulf War — did not dominate relations between Riyadh and Damascus as much as it had in previous years. What accounted for the change was most probably the fact that the Saudi leaders gave up any hopes of the Syrians' exercising a moderating influence on Tehran.

The royal family consistently emphasized that it had no formula for solving the Lebanese crisis. Instead, the Saudis offered their mediation to both presidents — Asad and Jumayyil — and promised to support any formula they agreed upon. Meanwhile, the Saudis argued that "only the enemies of the Arabs — primarily the Zionists" — benefited from the ongoing bloodshed. They refused to be dragged into domestic Lebanese politics by supporting one faction against the others, despite being asked to do so by a number of Lebanese and Syrian leaders.[79]

The Syrian-Saudi differences peaked in October when a new Lebanese president had to be elected. Despite Syrian requests that Riyadh support "their" candidate, King Fahd refused "to interfere in the Lebanese electoral process," because Saudi policy was based on "the principle of nonintervention in the domestic affairs of any other country." There were, nevertheless, reports that the Saudis were conducting behind-the-scenes negotiations with Syrian officials and various Lebanese factions aimed at arriving at an acceptable formula. But by the end of 1988, Saudi-Syrian differences were not any closer to a resolution and figured prominently in the failure to convene an Arab summit in Riyadh.[80]

It was against this background that King Fahd summoned Asad to Riyadh in mid-December. In two days of talks, they discussed a wide spectrum of issues that deeply divided them. Essentially, Fahd tried to demonstrate to Asad that Syria was almost totally isolated on most key issues affecting the Arab world. He sought to impress on Asad the need to shift Syrian policy to make it conform to mainstream Arab positions on: (1) the readmission of Egypt to the Arab League; (2) an all-Arab solution to the Lebanese crisis "free of Syrian vetoes and obstacles"; (3) recognition of the newly declared independent Palestinian state and endorsement of the PLO's political program; and (4) acceptance of an international conference as the only way of arriving at "a settlement of the Middle East problem."[81] Fahd's success remained to be seen.

THE INTERNATIONAL ARENA

RELATIONS WITH THE UNITED STATES

The year 1988 was one of the stormiest in Saudi-American relations, a mixture of serious friction and close cooperation. There were profound policy differences covering a wide range of regional issues, but Riyadh also realized that given the severity of the challenges it was facing in the Gulf and in view of its own vulnerability, it was highly imprudent to create further strains in what was once described as "the very special relations" with Washington.

The Saudi leadership was very critical of the US positions in the Arab-Israeli conflict. In a message to President Reagan, King Fahd criticized Washington for not "shouldering its responsibility toward the *intifada,* and the Israeli actions against the Palestinian people." The Saudi media called "morally wrong" the US veto of a Security Council resolution critical of Israel's handling of the *intifada.* They condemned the US depiction of the draft as "inopportune" and called it "the most cynical statement anyone could have made at a time when Israel was butchering innocent, unarmed civilians in Palestine." Both the royal family and the media criticized the intention to close the PLO's offices in New York, describing it as "a blatant defiance of international will" and "a crime aimed at satisfying the Israeli enemy." Moreover, closing the PLO's offices was bound to undermine Washington's "credibility as an honest broker and accepted mediator" and further complicate Shultz's initiative (see chapter on the United States and the Middle East). The Saudis called on "the entire world to stand up against the US and reconsider whether New York is a suitable place for the UN."[82]

The Saudi leadership apparently refused to endorse Shultz's initiative, describing the US proposal for interim Palestinian autonomy as "utterly ignoring the popular *intifada* and the consequences and changes it has brought about." They also rejected the exclusion of the PLO from the American initiative and expressed their preference for a joint Arab stand *vis-à-vis* all peace proposals, vowing to help shape an Arab consensus on the Shultz initiative. For Washington, which expected a public Saudi endorsement of the initiative, this refusal amounted to a negative posture and Shultz's visit to Riyadh in early April ended in failure.[83]

Saudi-American relations reached a crisis in March and April after the exposure of the Saudi-Chinese missile deal. What particularly irritated Washington was "the carefully crafted, two-year deliberate and extensive Saudi effort to deceive the Administration and hide the deal." When Prince Bandar visited Beijing in late 1985 to conclude the deal, the US was told that he was trying to dissuade China from selling missiles to Iran and was offering to buy the same missiles for Iraq. It turned out that after arriving in Saudi ports, instead of being transferred to Iraq some of these missiles were trucked south into the Rub' al-Khali desert where, the Saudis told the Americans, they were building a huge "ammunition depot," which in fact was a training and storage area for the Chinese missiles.

It was only in January 1988 that US intelligence blew the Saudi cover, obtaining "irrefutable evidence" that trucks carrying CSS-2 missiles were traveling south, rather than north to Iraq, from Saudi ports. On 6 March, the US Administration confronted Ambassador Prince Bandar with satellite evidence, demanding to know whether Riyadh had obtained "nuclear missiles." The envoy confirmed the purchase of missiles, but flatly denied that the kingdom had obtained, or even sought, nuclear warheads.

On 12 March Bandar delivered a letter from King Fahd to President Reagan, conveying the assurance in writing. But the Saudi Government refused US requests to inspect the missiles, arguing that it was a matter of "strict confidentiality" between Saudi Arabia and China.[84]

The crisis reached its climax a few days later when the State Department announced that the US ambassador to Saudi Arabia, Hume Horan, had been recalled. The decision was prompted by the Saudi request to have Horan replaced after he met with King Fahd to deliver an official US complaint expressing "unhappiness and concern" over the Chinese-Saudi missile deal. But the decision was most likely rooted in personal differences between the envoy and the royal family, and a realization in Washington that high-ranking Saudi leaders refused to deal with him. According to one US official, the decision to recall Horan was made once the royal family made it clear that "he would no longer have access." Prince Bandar was apparently instrumental in shaping the Saudi attitude and in conveying it to the State Department. That Bandar disapproved of Horan was made obvious when the Prince absented himself from Horan's swearing-in ceremony.[85]

According to another version, Saudi disapproval of Horan stemmed from his practice of communicating with a wide range of Saudi groups rather than confining his contacts to government officials. As one State Department official put it, "he knew too much, he speaks Arabic too well, he knew too many Saudis who have ambivalent feelings toward the royal family, and he had a set of contacts the Palace didn't have." It was reportedly after a meeting taped by security men, at which Horan discussed with Shaykh Ibn Baz, the leading Saudi religious authority, his criticism of the kingdom, that the royal family sought Horan's replacement.[86] Still another version, quoting "Saudi sources," had it that the Saudis had found out that Horan was of Iranian descent and that his father, 'Abdallah Intizam, had been foreign minister under the Shah. Horan was reported to have incurred Fahd's anger after "he had blamed the Saudis for committing aggression against Iranian pilgrims."[87] The official Saudi version, however, was that Horan had been forced out because of Saudi displeasure at the "audacious US message" over the missile deal, simply by being the channel through which the US protest had been communicated. The Saudis, however, did not declare him *persona non grata* and they denied ever explicitly demanding his replacement.[88]

The exposure of the Chinese missile deal led 58 US senators to ask Reagan to delay plans to sell Saudi Arabia $450m. worth of military equipment intended to provide ground support for the Awacs aircraft. Expressing "deep concern" that the Saudis hid their purchase of the missiles, they said the deal "raised serious questions about the possibility of the Saudis compromising the security and technology of sensitive weapons systems." They called upon the Administration to "reconsider any new arms sales to the kingdom until the Chinese missiles are withdrawn," given that the missiles "represent a tremendous threat to regional security and peace." A more strongly worded letter was sent by 187 House members, asserting that "selling Saudi Arabia more weaponry at this time would reward Saudi deceit." Unwilling to have a showdown with Congress, the White House announced on 25 April a delay in notifying Congress of the arms sales.[89]

The royal family, aware of the strong anti-Saudi sentiments in Washington, decided to act promptly. Within hours, the Saudi Government announced that it would sign the Nuclear Non-Proliferation Treaty and that it was severing diplomatic relations with Iran. While the former decision was adopted in order to assuage Congressional anxiety and defuse criticism over the missiles, the latter was designed to improve generally the Saudi image in Washington. The Administration, for its part, sought to capitalize on the momentum created by the two Saudi decisions and within two days formally notified Congress of its intention to sell the Saudis arms worth $825m. The package included not only the Awacs equipment, but also Bradley vehicles and antitank missiles.[90] With Walter Cutler, Horan's predecessor and successor, resuming residence in Riyadh in late April, American-Saudi relations were back to normal.

But the harmony was disrupted again in July with the announcement of the huge British-Saudi arms deal (see above and below). Embodied in the deal was the underlying criticism of the US for rejecting, or placing unacceptable conditions on, arms sales to the kingdom, which forced the royal family to turn to other sources of weaponry. As one Saudi official commented, "the US is unable to sell arms to friendly Arab countries without humiliating them; we are not going to pay billions of dollars to be insulted." But the Saudi leadership was apparently pleased when rather than criticizing Riyadh, the Administration put the entire blame for the loss of the deal on Congress: "Saudi Arabia has asked us a number of times to provide her with arms, but Congress turned down the requests. This is a $30bn. loss for American companies. Our national interests are better served when we can sell legitimate self-defense items to friendly Arab countries."[91]

The consensus among Arab and Western officials following the British-Saudi deal was that it affected not only the military relations between Washington and Riyadh: "The overall relationship was damaged in the sense that it became more brittle and more susceptible to political stresses," said a State Department official. And a major commentary in *The New York Times* concluded that "Britain supplanted the US as chief arms supplier to the kingdom," and that "the 40-year-old special relationship between Riyadh and Washington has become a thing of the past."[92] Realizing that their defense and security depended ultimately on the US, and apprehensive that the fallout of such widespread commentaries could cause permanent damage, the royal family in an unprecedented move, made a major policy statement. The preface to the statement asserted that it was directed at "broadcasts...articles and commentaries on the recent deal and its effects," which "began to cast doubts" on the nature of Saudi-American relations, and that the arms deal "cannot influence these relations whose roots go back half a century."

The statement itself declared: "Believing that the stand by the hard-liners in Congress against the sale of weapons to the kingdom was not based on hostility toward us — inasmuch as Congress is subject to well-known pressures harmful to US interests — the kingdom wants to affirm its desire to fill its military needs, in the form of aircraft and advanced defensive weapons from US factories."[93]

After the end of the Iraqi-Iranian War, Saudi-American relations were increasingly affected by the US attitude toward Arab-Israeli issues, and particularly the Palestinians. The Saudi leaders frequently called on the US to play a more active role by pressuring Israel into attending an international conference and recognizing the PLO. They condemned Washington for refusing 'Arafat a visa, then welcomed the Administration's "historic decision" to open a dialogue with the PLO, for which they took much credit.[94]

RELATIONS WITH BRITAIN

British-Saudi relations improved constantly after the two countries concluded the *Tornado* arms deal in 1986 (see *MECS* 1986, pp. 568–69). The only controversial issue — the question of British offset investments in Saudi Arabia — appeared to have been resolved by the memorandum of understanding the two countries signed in late 1987 (see *MECS* 1987, p. 611). Crown Prince 'Abdallah paid an official visit to London in June at the invitation of Prime Minister Margaret Thatcher. The main purpose of the visit appeared to be London's interest in getting further acquainted with the man who was likely to succeed King Fahd. Unlike Fahd, Defense Minister Sultan and other senior members of the royal family, the crown prince was not widely traveled in Europe. During the talks, the issue of offset investments came up again and differences surfaced; but it did not seem to jeopardize the *Tornado* deal.[95]

Less than a month after 'Abdallah's visit, London announced the conclusion of "the arms deal of the 20th century" with Saudi Arabia. It was the largest Western arms and military facility deal ever signed between two countries. Worth some £15bn. ($25bn.), the deal was a follow-up to, and a new phase of, the *Tornado* agreement of 1985–86. It would give a huge boost to the British armaments industry over the next decade, guaranteeing hundreds of thousands of jobs. If transformed into specific, formal contracts, the implementation of the agreement could be stretched over two decades. The deal provided for the sale of 48 *Tornado* jets, 60 *Hawk* trainer/attack aircraft, 80 Westland *Black Hawk* helicopters, and six minesweepers. But it was the construction of two air bases and the supply of related facilities which accounted for more than half of the multibillion package. As in the 1986 deal, the weapons and facilities were to be paid for in countertraded oil. But Saudi officials claimed that there would be no change in the existing volume of 400,000 barrels a day sold to British Petroleum and Shell.[96]

The Saudis sought to remove the impression that the deal with Britain was a form of Saudi punishment of the US. The Saudi media described the deal as one that underlined "the independence of the Saudi decision-making process" and "the principle of diversification of our sources of weaponry." While Saudi leaders hoped that the deal would not damage relations with the US, they nevertheless emphasized that it injected more balance into Saudi Arabia's foreign relations.[97] It was clear, however, that if the multifaceted deal was to be implemented in its entirety, Britain would supplant the US as Saudi Arabia's major arms supplier.

RELATIONS WITH THE SOVIET UNION

The pattern of Soviet-Saudi relations throughout the 1980s was one of Soviet overtures, ambiguous Saudi responses and diplomatic contacts, replacing the vituperative propaganda campaigns of the 1970s. But despite numerous reports, rumors, and indications, the *rapprochement* between the two countries did not result in the establishment of diplomatic relations. Moreover, relations in the second half of 1987 seemed to have cooled considerably as a result of a divergence of interests over three cardinal issues: the Soviet presence in Afghanistan, Soviet policy toward the Iraqi Iranian War, and the Arab-Israeli peace process. Of these, Afghanistan was the major stumbling block.

In early 1988, contacts between Riyadh and Moscow were resumed when the former asked to send a high-level delegation for talks in Moscow. The delegation, headed by Foreign Minister Prince Sa'ud and the Ambassador in Washington Prince Bandar, ostensibly came to convey a message from King Fahd — then chairman of the Gulf Cooperation Council (GCC) — after the GCC's summit in December 1987 (see chapter on the Gulf states). The Saudi request, however, reflected Riyadh's perception of greater superpower cooperation following the Reagan-Gorbachev summit in Washington in December 1987. The Saudis hoped that Moscow could now play a more constructive role in terms of considering a withdrawal from Afghanistan, applying more effective pressure and an arms embargo on Iran and insisting on a PLO role in an international conference. The visit also prompted speculation that the two countries might be preparing to establish diplomatic relations. But a Soviet Foreign Ministry official conceded that though Moscow had "no objection to such a move, it is up to the Saudi side to make a decision."[98]

Real progress was apparently achieved in February when a Soviet delegation headed by Assistant Foreign Minister in charge of Middle East Affairs Vladimir Polyakov arrived in Riyadh for what was believed to be the first such visit by a senior Soviet official in 50 years. Polyakov had audiences with Crown Prince 'Abdallah, Foreign Minister Sa'ud, and other senior members of the royal family. The most conspicuous change was obviously the recent Soviet offer of troop withdrawal from Afghanistan. The Soviets were also inclined to support a new Security Council resolution imposing sanctions on Tehran for its failure to implement Resolution 598. They also expressed opposition to certain American ideas regarding the Arab-Israeli peace process which excluded the PLO. Thus, a Saudi official asserted that "Soviet responses on all three issues were accepted with satisfaction in Riyadh."[99]

But underlying such a positive Saudi posture were factors going beyond the immediate three issues. First, the royal family was very likely impressed with Soviet leader Gorbachev's "liberalism" and reforms and viewed him as considerably less dogmatic and doctrinaire than his predecessors. The Saudi leaders felt that Moscow was now less interested than a decade or two ago in supporting radical leftist and revolutionary movements all around the world and in exporting the Communist ideology. Second, lingering fears in Riyadh of an eventual US retreat from the Persian Gulf, possibly after the presidential elections, led the royal family to appreciate the benefits of closer contacts with the Soviets. Third, the Saudi leaders felt that they had been "taken for granted" by the US for a long time and that they needed more effective leverage *vis-à-vis* the American Administration. Kuwait's experience in playing Moscow off against Washington and obtaining both Soviet and US warship protection for Kuwaiti oil exports was said to have impressed the Saudis. They hoped that a Soviet flag in Riyadh would make the Americans "stand up and take notice of a major ally that feels it is ignored."[100] Finally, as one Saudi official said, the royal family realized that "the kingdom and the Soviet Union agree on many issues despite the absence of diplomatic relations, while US and Saudi positions differ on these issues despite such relations." These considerations converged into a desire "to diversify the kingdom's foreign relations" not only in the direction of the Soviet Union, but also of China.[101]

It was probably in response to predictions of an imminent resumption of diplomatic ties that the Saudis unofficially cautioned against excessive optimism, calling such a move "premature." They also leaked that Moscow and Riyadh could improve relations, "but do not necessarily have to exchange ambassadors."[102] But the Geneva agreement of 15 April stipulating Soviet withdrawal from Afghanistan, and the start of implementation on 15 May once again prompted news reports about diplomatic relations. Such speculation was accompanied by reports that Soviet Foreign Minister Eduard Shevardnadze was due to visit Riyadh in October, at which time the resumption of ties would be announced. What gave such speculation more credence was the exchange of ambassadors between Qatar and the Soviet Union in August, making Saudi Arabia and Bahrain the only GCC countries without diplomatic relations with Moscow.[103]

Such speculation reached its peak in December when a Soviet delegation headed by Deputy Foreign Minister Yuli Vorontsov arrived in Saudi Arabia for talks with the Afghan Mujahidin. The meeting on 5 December between King Fahd and Vorontsov was probably the highest-level public contact between Saudi Arabia and the Soviet Union since 1938 when relations had been suspended. The conventional wisdom among analysts was that the groundwork had been laid for the resumption of diplomatic relations, but the actual move was not expected until March or April 1989, i.e., after the full completion of the Soviet withdrawal from Afghanistan.[104]

It seemed, however, that other factors were at play. It appeared that senior members of the royal family, such as Defense Minister Sultan, still opposed the idea.[105] It was also not at all clear whether the royal family could obtain the vital consent of the religious leaders and *'ulama* without consensus within its own ranks. Nevertheless, it was clear by the end of 1988 that Saudi Arabia and the USSR were closer than ever to resuming diplomatic ties. The year 1988 also witnessed something of an economic paradox: the USSR emerged as by far the leading purchaser of Saudi wheat; of the total Saudi exports of 1,245,950 tons, 310,500 tons (a quarter) went to the Soviet Union.[106] Still, there was occasional friction, when, for example, Gorbachev called on the Arabs "to recognize Israel." The Saudis regarded this as "a change in the Soviet position which does not serve the Arab cause" and urged Moscow instead to pressure the US and Israel to recognize the PLO.[107]

RELATIONS WITH CHINA

It was only after the exposure of the Chinese-Saudi missile deal in March that it became known that the two countries had been negotiating the deal since 1985. The Saudi ambassador in Washington, Prince Bandar, was responsible for all negotiations with the Chinese government. In April, the Chinese Deputy Foreign Minister, Qi Huaiyuan, arrived in Riyadh, the first official visit to the kingdom by a senior Chinese leader. He delivered a message to King Fahd from China's President, Li Xiannian, and explicitly expressed his government's desire to establish diplomatic ties with Riyadh. There was also evidence that Qi's visit aimed at formalizing relations between the two countries in a way that would preempt a similar move by the USSR.[108] The Saudis had a problem with China, not only because it was a Communist country, but also because Saudi Arabia was one of Taiwan's last remaining supporters.

Such considerations did not inhibit the expansion of commercial ties. Trade talks had started in Washington in late 1987 between the ambassadors of the two countries. To Saudi Arabia, China was a market for petrochemical products which it had difficulties selling in Europe. To China, trade and commerce had an added value: they were the second best to formal, diplomatic relations. Prince Bandar's visit to China in mid-October further strengthened economic ties between the two countries and paved the way for an agreement signed in Washington in November. It provided that China and Saudi Arabia would open commercial offices in each other's capitals, that these offices would be the first permanent representations of the two countries, and this arrangement could possibly be a prelude to full diplomatic recognition.[109]

NOTES

For the place and frequency of publications cited here, and for the full name of the publication, news agency, radio station, or monitoring service where an abbreviation is used, please see "List of Sources." Only in the case of more than one publication bearing the same name is the place of publication noted here.

1. *NYT,* 11 December 1988.
2. SPA, 30 December 1987; *al-Siyasa,* Kuwait, 3 January 1988.
3. *FT,* 6, 7 January; *IHT,* 10 June 1988.
4. *The Times,* 5 January; *NYT, IHT,* 6 January 1988.
5. *WSJ,* 27 January; *MM,* 25 January; *CR:* Saudi Arabia, No. 2, 1988, p. 11.
6. *CR:* Saudi Arabia, No. 1, 1988, p. 14.
7. Ibid., No. 3, p. 12.
8. SPA, 28 June — DR, 30 June 1988.
9. *Al-Sharq al-Awsat,* 9 February; *CR:* Saudi Arabia, No. 2, 1988, p. 11.
10. *FT,* 26 May, 10, 13, 28 June; *IHT,* 27 June 1988.
11. *FT,* 13 July, 29 September 1988.
12. *CR:* Saudi Arabia, No. 4, 1988, p. 12; *Gulf States Newsletter,* 23 January 1989.
13. *CR:* Saudi Arabia, No. 4, 1988, p. 3.
14. Ibid., No. 1, pp. 15–16; *MM,* 25 January 1988.
15. *FT,* 8 June 1988.
16. SPA, 4 January — DR, 5 January 1988.
17. *MEES,* 11 January, 4 April; SPA, 4 April — DR, 5 April 1988.
18. *NYT,* 17 May; *CR:* Saudi Arabia, No. 3, 1988, p. 16.
19. *NYT,* 28, 29 April 1988.
20. *Gulf States Newsletter,* 18 April 1988.
21. R. Riyadh, 6 May — DR, 9 May; *NYT,* 2 May 1988.
22. *FT,* 5 October, 11 November 1988.
23. *NYT,* 25 February, 10 May; *FT,* 18 February, 29 June 1988.
24. *MEES,* 9 May; *NYT,* 25 February 1988.
25. *FT,* 11 November 1988.
26. *CR:* Saudi Arabia, No. 3, 1988, p. 12.
27. *WP,* 29 March 1988.
28. *FT,* 9 July 1988.
29. Ibid., 23 November 1988.
30. Ibid., 12 July 1988.
31. *Al-Mustaqbal,* 8 October 1988.
32. SPA, 26 July — DR, 27 July 1988.
33. *FT,* 12 July 1988.
34. *Gulf States Newsletter,* 23 January 1989.
35. Iranian TV, 6 February — DR, 8 February 1988.
36. *IHT,* 25 March 1988.
37. SPA, 8 February — DR, 9 February 1988.
38. SPA, 7 March — DR, 9 March 1988.
39. R. Riyadh, 8 February — DR, 10 February 1988.
40. *IHT,* 25 March 1988.
41. *CR:* Saudi Arabia, No. 3, 1988, p. 6; *MM,* 25 July 1988.
42. SPA, 28 June, 8 July — DR, 30 June, 8 July 1988, respectively.
43. *Al-Siyasa,* Kuwait, 12 July; *FT,* 22 July; SPA, 16 July — DR, 18 July 1988.
44. KUNA, 11 July — DR, 11 July; SPA, 22 July — DR, 25 July 1988.

45. *Al-Thawra al-Islamiyya,* July 1988; *CR:* Saudi Arabia, No. 2, 1988, p. 9.
46. VoL, 8 August — DR, 9 August 1988.
47. SPA, 29 August — DR, 30 August 1988.
48. AFP, 5 October — DR, 6 October 1988.
49. *WT,* 27 October 1988.
50. *CR:* Saudi Arabia, No. 4, 1988, p. 7.
51. SPA, 26 April — DR, 28 April 1988.
52. *WP,* 12 May 1988.
53. *Al-Riyad,* 27 June 1988.
54. IRNA, 8 February — DR, 9 February; R. Riyadh, 9 February — DR, 10 February 1988.
55. *The Observer,* 12 April; *NYT,* 29 April 1988.
56. *NYT,* 28 February 1988.
57. IRNA, 11 April — DR, 12 April; R. Riyadh, 19 April — DR, 20 April; *NYT, FT,* 17 June 1988.
58. *NYT, WP,* 27 December 1987; R. Riyadh, 6 February — DR, 8 February 1988.
59. R. Riyadh, 24 January — DR, 27 January; *'Ukaz,* 15 February; *al-Bilad,* 11 February 1988.
60. *Al-Riyad,* 25 May; *al-Jazira,* 7 June; *al-Muharrir,* 5 March 1988.
61. Riyadh TV, 26 April — DR, 27 April 1988.
62. *NYT,* 29 April; *al-Siyasa,* Kuwait, 28 April; R. Riyadh, 27 April 1988.
63. *NYT, FT,* 17 June 1988.
64. *Saudi Gazette,* 19 July; *al-Yawm,* 1, 2 August 1988.
65. *WP,* 26 July; R. Riyadh, 11 October — DR, 13 October; *The Observer,* 12 October 1988.
66. *Al-Muharrir,* 12 August; SPA, 5 October — DR, 6 October 1988.
67. SPA, 20 October — DR, 21 October; *The Observer,* 7 December; SPA, 27 August — DR, 29 August; *al-Muharrir,* 27 September 1988.
68. TAP, 28 April — DR, 29 April 1988.
69. R. Cairo, 10 January — DR, 12 January; *JP,* 10 January 1988.
70. MENA, 4 April — DR, 5 April; *CR:* Saudi Arabia, No. 3, 1988, p. 6; *al-Siyasa,* Kuwait, 12 July; *FT,* 22 July 1988.
71. *FT,* 10 May; SPA, 22 May — DR, 23 May; R. Amman, 5 August — DR, 7 August; *al-Usbu' al-'Arabi,* 22 August; *al-Hawadith,* 26 August; Crown Prince 'Abdallah's interview with *al-Sharq al-Awsat,* 19 June 1988.
72. *Al-Bilad, al-Madina, al-Jazira,* throughout 1988.
73. *Al-Majalla,* 27 January; *al-Mustaqbal,* 27 February; *CR:* Saudi Arabia, No. 3, 1988, pp. 6–7.
74. KUNA, 21 February — DR, 22 February; R. Riyadh, 22 February — DR, 23 February 1988.
75. *Al-Sharq al-Awsat,* 23, 29 February; R. Riyadh, 25 February — DR, 26 February 1988.
76. R. Riyadh, 16 April, 31 May — DR, 18 April, 1 June, respectively; *al-Bilad,* 26 April; *al-Tadamun,* 30 April 1988.
77. R. Monte Carlo, 16 July — DR, 18 July; R. Riyadh, 1 August — DR, 2 August; *al-Bilad,* 2 August 1988.
78. *Ha'aretz,* 17 October; *al-Riyad,* 16 November 1988.
79. SPA, 13 January — DR, 14 January; *al-Mustaqbal,* 25 June; R. Riyadh, 9 July — DR, 10 July; *'Ukaz,* 24 September 1988.
80. *Al-Mustaqbal,* 1 October; *al-Nahar,* 19 December 1988.
81. *Al-Hawadith,* 18 December; *al-Majalla,* 21 December; *al-Mustaqbal,* 24 December 1988.
82. R. Riyadh, 9 February — DR, 10 February; *Saudi Gazette,* 12 February; *'Ukaz,* 3 March; *al-Riyad,* 11 March; *al-Yawm, al-Madina,* 14 March 1988.
83. R. Riyadh, 27, 28 February — DR, 28, 29 February respectively; *al-Qabas,* 8 March; SPA, 7 April — DR, 8 April 1988.
84. *WP,* 29 March 1988.
85. *Middle East Policy Survey,* 31 March; *WP,* 1 April; *NYT,* 2 April; *al-Mustaqbal,* 9 April 1988.
86. *MM,* 27 June; *CR:* Saudi Arabia, No. 3, 1988, p. 8.
87. *October,* 3 July 1988.

88. *MM,* 27 June; SPA, 1 April — DR, 1 April 1988.
89. *NYT,* 15, 26 April 1988.
90. *WP,* 26, 28 April; *FT,* 27 April 1988.
91. *NYT,* 11, 28 July; *WP,* 10 July 1988.
92. *NYT,* ibid.
93. SPA, 30 July — DR, 1 August 1988.
94. R. Riyadh, 1 December — DR, 2 December; *al-Jazira,* 17 December 1988.
95. *FT,* 14 June 1988.
96. Ibid.; *IHT,* 9 July; *MM,* 25 July 1988.
97. *Al-Jazira, al-Riyad, al-Bilad,* 9 July 1988.
98. *FT,* 27 January; *al-Ittihad,* Abu Dhabi, 2, 3 February 1988.
99. R. Riyadh, 21 February — DR, 22 February; *al-Mustaqbal, al-Tadamun,* 27 February 1988.
100. *JP,* 26 April 1988.
101. *Al-Tadamun,* 27 February 1988.
102. SPA, 28 February — DR, 29 February; *CSM,* 1 March 1988.
103. *Al-Ra'y al-'Amm,* 16 May; *al-Watan,* 17 July; *al-Qabas,* 18 October 1988; *CR:* Saudi Arabia, No. 4, 1988, p. 8.
104. *FT,* 7 December; *al-Mustaqbal,* 10 December 1988.
105. *FR,* 2 December 1988.
106. *CR:* Saudi Arabia, No. 3, 1988, p. 12; *'Ukaz,* 4 May 1988.
107. *Al-Bilad,* 11 April 1988.
108. *The Guardian,* 4 April 1988.
109. SPA, 13 October — DR, 14 October; *FT,* 14 November 1988.

The Republic of Sudan
(Jumhuriyyat al-Sudan)

YEHUDIT RONEN

The bleakness dominating Sudan's domestic affairs in 1987 deepened in 1988. Even the formation of a broad-based coalition government in mid-May, following nearly nine months with formal government, did not improve matters substantially. The political bickering within the leadership of the two major coalition partners — the Umma Party (UP) and the Democratic Unionist Party (DUP) — as well as their squabbles with the National Islamic Front (NIF), Sudan's third major political force, which was included in the government for the first time since the renewal of democratic life in 1986, stirred up the political turbulence. The government under the premiership of al-Sadiq al-Mahdi was virtually paralyzed throughout the year, mainly reacting to events rather than leading them.

The comprehensive personnel reorganization in the top army and police commands in the summer should be viewed in this context; but the changes did not halt the security and military deterioration.

The disastrous floods in late summer only made matters worse, by adding a human dimension to the catastrophe. But, as formerly, the government proved incompetent to deal with the crisis.

The long-disputed issue of the *Shari'a* law, which surfaced with renewed vigor in the fall, threatened further political turmoil. Tension sharpened following the breach of the UP and DUP pledge to the NIF to enforce the alternative Islamic Law in place of the *Shari'a* which had been introduced by Numayri in 1983 but had been suspended in the aftermath of his downfall.

The devastating war in the south in which the Sudanese People's Liberation Army (SPLA) was overrunning more and more of the southern region, helped the government to shelve the *Shari'a* issue. Although militarily the civil war was generally fought as it had been the year before, politically the conflict witnessed a new though undramatic departure. In mid-November, the SPLA-DUP talks culminated in the signing of a "peace agreement," but it was not followed by any progress until the end of the year, because, *inter alia,* of the NIF's rejection of the agreement. It was difficult, however, to gauge how much the disputes within the SPLA leadership affected military and political events.

Thus, the end of 1988 saw the severe crisis of expectations continuing to dominate Sudan's domestic affairs, threatening the survival of al-Mahdi's Government and even perhaps of the democratic system. The foiling of a coup attempt in mid-December served as clear evidence of the crisis.

Khartoum's foreign policy in 1988 focused primarily on Sudan's immediate neighbors. The two main arenas of preoccupation were the northern-western arc,

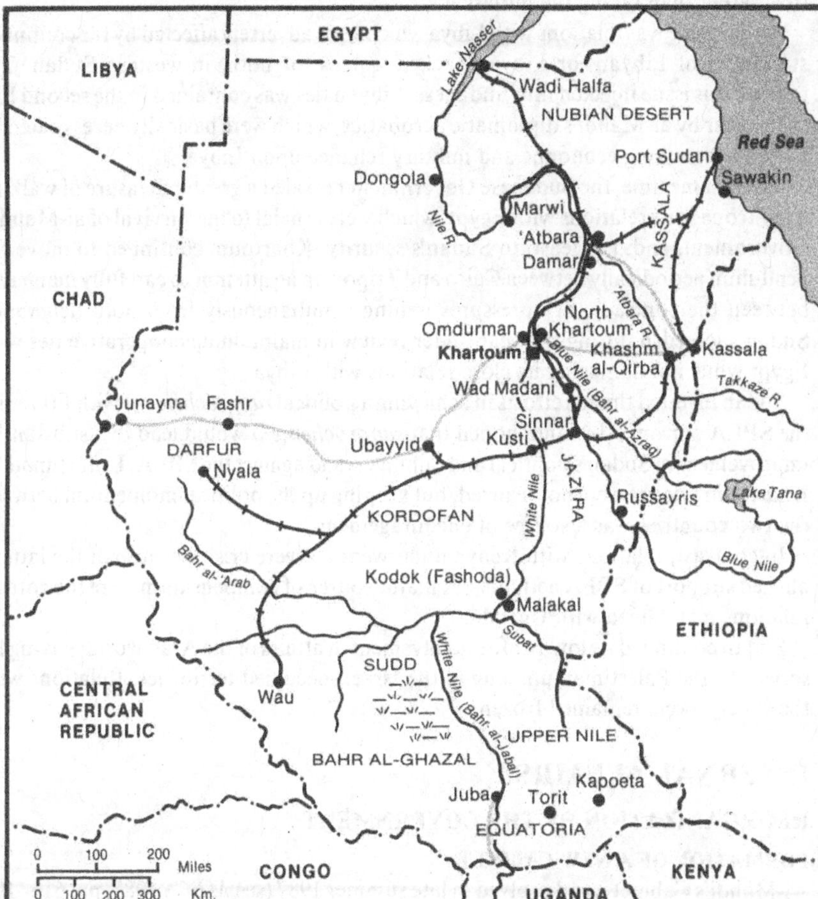

Sudan —Marshes —River —Railway —Main Road —International boundary

containing Egypt, Libya, and Chad and the eastern-southern arc, containing Ethiopia, Kenya, and Uganda. In both arcs, Khartoum's policy mostly entailed extinguishing fires rather than taking the initiative.

An example was relations with Libya which were adversely affected by the continued stationing of Libyan, or Libyan-backed, forces, or both, in western Sudan. The tension this issue injected into Sudanese-Libyan ties was contained in the second half of the year by al-Mahdi's diplomatic acrobatics, which were basically necessitated by Sudan's increasing economic and military reliance upon Libya.

At the same time, the Sudanese Government revealed a greater measure of walking a tightrope in its relations with Egypt, which were crucial to the survival of al-Mahdi's Government, and, not least, to Sudan's security. Khartoum continued to move the pendulum periodically between Cairo and Tripoli, in an attempt to carefully maneuver between the contradictory pressures issuing simultaneously from both neighbors. Sudan succeeded during the year under review in maintaining cooperative ties with Egypt while not damaging its close relations with Libya.

Sudan invested tireless efforts in achieving a political *rapprochement* with Ethiopia, the SPLA patron. Al-Mahdi hoped that *rapprochement* would lead to a substantial improvement in Sudan's political and military stand against the SPLA. Unfortunately, Khartoum's hopes were not realized, but keeping up the political momentum between the two countries was a source of encouragement.

In contrast, relations with Kenya underwent a severe crisis because of the latter's alleged support of SPLA activities. A major source of compensation were the cordial relations maintained with Uganda.

Sudan continued its low-profile involvement in affairs of the Arab world, paying lip service to the Palestinian uprising in the Israeli-occupied territories. Relations with the superpowers remained frozen.

INTERNAL AFFAIRS

REORGANIZATION OF THE GOVERNMENT

FORMATION OF A NEW CABINET

Al-Mahdi's Cabinet was dissolved in late summer 1987 (see *MECS* 1987, pp. 616–19). None was formed to replace it until late spring 1988. In practice, however, members of the dissolved Cabinet remained in office, while the prime minister was preoccupied with intensive negotiations with the major political parties in an attempt to set up a broad-based coalition government.

In mid-March, after the premier had not made any substantial progress, he presented the Constituent Assembly with an ultimatum: if the program for setting up a new government which he had presented to the assembly on 15 March was not accepted by the majority of members, he would resign. A Sudanese publication, apparently close to the UP, cited al-Mahdi sources as saying that the party would return to the opposition benches if the program was rejected.[1] The main points of al-Mahdi's program were: (1) new legislation to replace the *Shari'a* Islamic Law which Numayri had introduced in September 1983 (see *MECS* 1983–84, pp. 639–42); (2) the "general mobilization of all resources" to confront the war in the south; and (3) the "urgent convening" of the Constitutional Conference to settle the conflict in the south[2] (see below).

During the second half of March and the first half of April, Khartoum's politicians debated the proposal. On 12 April, just less than a month after al-Mahdi's ultimatum, the assembly approved the program and overwhelmingly voted for the formation of a national reconciliation government (*khukumat al-wifaq al-watani*). On 20 April, the next important step in forming a new government was taken, when Khartoum's major parties, except for the NIF, signed a statement of the "goals and policies of the new government."[3] Four days later, the NIF, too, signed after the settlement of a dispute between it and the other political parties over a timetable for replacing the *Shari'a* law with an alternative Islamic penal code[4] (see below).

Meanwhile, the formal mechanism continued to function: on 27 April, al-Mahdi was reelected prime minister by the Constituent Assembly.[5] A day later, he was sworn in as prime minister for the third time since the renewal of the democratic era in Sudan in 1986.

Nevertheless, progress was not as smooth as al-Mahdi had wished. In early May, a dispute broke out over who was to be Speaker of the assembly and who was to be interior minister, holding up the cabinet's formation. Muhammad Ibrahim Khalil, who had been Speaker since May 1986, resigned on 7 April in protest against the conduct of dozens of deputies who vociferously contested his decision to adjourn a debate on the political crisis.[6] The NIF had nominated Ahmad Sulayman, a well-known lawyer, for Speaker, but the UP and the DUP rejected the nomination on the ground that he had been a minister in the first stage of Numayri's "defunct regime."[7] Neither was there agreement on which party would get the Interior Ministry with its great clout in domestic affairs. Al-Mahdi circumvented these two controversial issues without resolving them, thus enabling him to announce on 14 May his new Cabinet, as follows:

TABLE 1: AL-MAHDI'S CABINET (MAY 1988)

Prime Minister	Al-Sadiq al-Mahdi	UP
Defense	'Abd al-Majid Hamid Khalil[e,g]	UP
Foreign Affairs	Husayn Sulayman Abu Salih[i]	DUP
Justice and Attorney General	Hasan 'Abdallah al-Turabi[e,g]	NIF
Agriculture and Natural Resources	Al-Fatih Muhammad al-Tijani[g]	DUP
Energy and Mining	Bakri Ahmad 'Adil[h,j]	UP
	Mubarak 'Abdallah al-Fadil[h,k]	UP
Irrigation and Water Resources	Muhammad Bashir[j]	UP
Higher Education and Scientific Research	Shaykh Mahjub Ja'far[g]	UP
Finance and Economic Planning	'Umar Nur al-Da'im[h]	UP
Local Government	Richard Makubi[g]	Southern Party
Health	Ahwaj Muhammad Musa[g]	DUP
Industry	'Abd al-Wahhab 'Uthman[b,g]	NIF
Internal Trade, Cooperation, and Supply	'Ali al-Hajj Muhammad Adam[b,g]	NIF
Economy and Foreign Trade	Mubarak 'Abdallah al-Fadil[h,k]	UP
Animal Wealth	Isma'il Abakir[j]	UP
Transportation	Aldo Ago Deng[f,h]	Southern Party
Public Communication	Taj al-Sirr Mustafa 'Abd al-Salam[g]	NIF
Public Works and Housing Planning	'Uthman 'Umar 'Ali[b,g]	DUP
Labor and Social Security	Matthiew Abor[b,g]	Southern Party
Culture and Information	'Abdallah Muhammad Ahmad[b,g]	UP

TABLE 1 (Contd.)

Social Welfare and Refugee Affairs[d]	Ahmad 'Abd al-Rahman Muhammad[b,e,g]	NIF
Youth and Sports	Joshua Diwal[b,g]	Southern Party
Relief and Evacuees	Hasan 'Ali Shabbu[g]	DUP
Public Service and Administrative Reform	Fadlallah 'Ali Fadlallah[b,g]	UP
Religious Affairs	'Abd al-Malik 'Abdallah al-Ja'li[b,g]	DUP
Tourism and Hotels	Amin Bashir Fallin[b,g]	SNP[l]
Cabinet Affairs	Salah al-Din 'Abd al-Salam al-Khalifa[b,g]	UP
Interior	'Abbas Abu Shamma 'Abd al-Mahmud[b,c,g]	
Minister without Portfolio	Angelo Beda[a,b,g]	Southern Party

NOTES:

a Angelo Beda, who had been appointed a speaker of the southern council on 16 May, became a cabinet member by al-Mahdi decree.

b For biographical details on the new ministers, see *al-Siyasa*, Khartoum, 20 May 1988.

c He was appointed by al-Mahdi on 14 June 1988. The new minister, aged 49 and who had studied law in Egypt and Britain, was the Khartoum chief of police; *al-Raya*, Khartoum, 15 June 1988.

d Newly created post, reflecting the growing problem of refugees displaced by famine and war.

e Held ministerial positions under the Numayri regime.

f The most important southern appointment in the new Cabinet. Aldo Ago Deng also became deputy prime minister.

g New appointment.

h Reshuffle.

i See Note 5 in cabinet table, *MECS* 1987, p. 619.

j Unchanged; see ibid.

k 'Adil resigned in early August. Al-Fadil was appointed in mid- September, in addition to his portfolio of Economy and Foreign Trade.

l Sudan National Party — a Nuba party; see *MECS* 1986, p. 579.

The new Cabinet, the third since the 1986 elections, had 27 ministers. It also included 13 ministers of state: five UP members, four from the DUP and another four from the NIF.[8] The new government was strongly Islamic, largely due to the new coalition partner, the NIF, which was led by Hasan 'Abdallah al-Turabi. The appointment of al-Turabi, the architect of the September 1983 *Shari'a* law and an ardent advocate of reapplying it to the post of justice minister and attorney general potentially created ample opportunity for formal moves in Islamic affairs. Not surprisingly, the NIF's inclusion in the government triggered the protest of the United Sudanese African Parties, the largest group of Khartoum-based southern parties. It withdrew its support from al-Mahdi and declared itself the main opposition party under the leadership of Eliaba James Surur.[9]

The new government did not undergo any substantial, structural changes. The major innovation was al-Mahdi's relinquishing the defense portfolio, for the first time since assuming the premiership in late spring 1986. The prime minister then gave the defense portfolio to a veteran UP personality and confidant, 'Abd al-Majid Hamid Khalil, realizing that the deteriorating state of affairs, above all the civil war, called for a full-time defense minister which al-Mahdi certainly could not be. Knowing that power lies with the military and concerned about the mounting unrest in the country, al-Mahdi preferred to have that crucially important position held by an efficient, well-experienced officer whose loyalty to the prime minister seemed unquestionable. (For details regarding Khalil's political activities during the Numayri regime, see *MECS* 1980–81, p. 762; 1981–82, pp. 820–21).

The relief of having formed a new cabinet was rapidly dissipated by bomb, machine-gun, and hand-grenade attacks on Westerners in the Acropole Hotel and the nearby Sudan Club in Khartoum on 15 May, killing seven people (five Westerners and two Sudanese) and injuring 21.[10] The incident brought into sharp focus the deteriorating security conditions in the capital.

Wishing to tighten security precautions and to increase the authority of the police, al-Mahdi in early June reshuffled the senior police echelon (see below). On 7 June, Muhammad Yusuf Muhammad, a political figure from the NIF and a lawyer, was elected Speaker of the Constituent Assembly.[11] A week later, al-Mahdi gave 'Abbas Abu Shamma 'Abd al-Muhammad, known as a political independent, the interior portfolio, the sole unmanned cabinet post, thus removing an obstacle to the government's day-to-day functioning.

Though the composition of the Cabinet was completed early in summer, it was soon subject to further pressures. On 5 August, Bakri 'Adil, a veteran UP politician and the minister for energy and mining, resigned. He blamed his resignation on the Cabinet's making decisions directly concerning his ministry (such as the dissolution of the board of directors of the National Institution for Electricity), without consulting him while he was abroad.[12] But apparently his rage was triggered off by power struggles within his party's leadership: he strongly opposed the appointment in the first week of August of 'Ali Hasan al-Din as UP general secretary,[13] a position hitherto held by Bakri 'Adil. The affair was soon contained, although tension gathered below the surface. On 13 September, al-Mahdi appointed another UP member and senior politician, Mubarak 'Abdallah al-Fadil to the recently vacated energy and mining portfolio, thereby ending the minor crisis. Strong rivalries within the UP and DUP leaderships, growing friction among the three major coalition partners, and the country's potentially explosive problems, threatened, at the end of 1988, to drag Khartoum's Government into a new maelstrom.

RESHUFFLE OF THE ARMY AND POLICE TOP COMMANDS

The reorganization of the top political establishment was soon followed by a shake-up of the army and the police top commands. On 6 June, the Commander in Chief Gen. Fawzi Ahmad al-Fadil and the Chief of Staff Gen. 'Abd al-'Azim Siddiq were pensioned off, after serving since the fall of 1986. The same day, Maj. Gen. (Navy) Fathi Ahmad 'Ali was promoted to lieutenant general and was appointed an acting commander in chief of the armed forces. The position of chief of staff was left vacant for about a month, when Lt. Gen. Faysal Mansur Shawir was appointed. The reorganization of the army top command also included the pensioning off of 20 senior officers.[14]

In the reshuffle of the top echelons of the police hierarchy, Commissioner General Gen. Ibrahim Ahmad 'Abd al-Karim and his deputy, Lt. Gen. 'Abd al-Latif 'Ali Ibrahim were relieved of their posts. The commander of the Police College, Maj. Gen. 'Uthman al-Shafi'i Muhammad, was raised to the rank of police lieutenant general and became the new commissioner general. Police Maj. Gen. 'Abduh Kahin, who was the director of the Central Intelligence Department, was raised to the rank of police lieutenant general and became his deputy. Other personnel changes in the key positions soon followed.[15]

The authorities did not provide any explanation for what appeared to be a sudden and comprehensive purge, which one foreign publication said took "everyone" in

Khartoum by surprise.[16] Whether the drastic reshuffle was meant to preempt a subversive move by the Army, or to inject new blood into the high commands of the key institutions responsible for the country's security, it was clear that the driving force behind the changes was the new defense minister. One may assume that Khalil wanted to be surrounded in his new office by close and loyal aides. Fathi, the new commander in chief, was said to be a personal friend and confidant,[17] having been the director of the defense minister's office when Khalil was vice president and commander in chief of the armed forces in the early 1980s, during the Numayri era.

The purge of the top police ranks could be explained by the significant deterioration in security in the country in general and in the Khartoum area in particular. The two terrorist attacks in the capital in January[18] and May (see above), and the wave of strikes and violent demonstrations which swept Khartoum and other parts of the country in late May in protest against power cuts and acute shortages of bread and drinking water, clearly reflected the seriously escalating disorder. The government's virtual helplessness in coping with the growing difficulties and the mounting restiveness of the public moved al-Mahdi to install in the key army and police posts confident and hardened men who hopefully could, if necessary, abort any subversion.

In mid-August, it became clear that more replacements were due in the army top command. On 17 August, the State Council, on the recommendation of the Army's commander in chief, announced that the four members of the Armed Forces General Staff had been relieved of their posts. Four majors general were promoted to lieutenants general and named as their successors. The most noteworthy change was the dismissal of Shawir and the appointment of Mahdi Abu Nimr as the new chief of staff. Again, the government did not provide any explanation for the purges. The commander in chief referred to them as "normal," saying they were dictated by "the need to achieve homogeneity" in the Army's command.[19]

THE FLOODS DISASTER

The torrential rains which fell at the beginning of August devastated the Khartoum area, leaving more than 1m. people homeless and an even greater number without basic foodstuffs. In addition, the floods resulted in acute shortages of drinking water and power; the cutting of telephone and telex links; and the sweeping away of roads and railway tracks. The capital was in effect paralyzed.[20] The patience of the population, which had daily been suffering great hardship, was exhausted. The accumulated bitterness erupted into massive anti-government demonstrations in Khartoum's streets early in the month.[21]

Al-Mahdi, alert to the mounting grievances, acted to assuage them by announcing drastic measures meant to create the impression that the authorities were acting determinedly to tackle the new crisis. On 8 August, the government imposed a six-month state of emergency. Al-Mahdi stated that the emergency laws would give the Government "the legal power to deal with the situation."[22] But one could not ignore the premier's exploitation of the crisis to impose the controversial state of emergency, the cancellation of which the SPLA laid down as a major precondition for beginning negotiations with Khartoum.

Meanwhile, on 12 August rain fell on the Sudanese capital and, along with the rains falling in abundance over the Ethiopian highlands, raised the water level of the Blue

Nile at Khartoum to 16.94 meters and caused floods. (In 1946, the Nile reached the level of 17.02 meters, causing Sudan's most serious floods this century.)[23]

The floods once again turned the limelight on the government's bad performance. The widespread impression of the government's inability to handle the country's domestic affairs was not dissipated even by the massive international relief campaign during the month.[24] The public's growing disappointment with the government's executive capabilities and lack of leadership was clearly reflected in the statement of Bona Malwal, a veteran southern figure who had cooperated with the Khartoum Government in the 1970s: "I do not think we can maintain this vacuum much longer....We need some authority....The government has shown itself to be nonexistent in a crisis."[25]

Al-Mahdi, aware of the public's loss of patience, addressed the Constituent Assembly on 22 August, the first time since the floods began. He attempted to calm the public by giving the impression that the difficulties were being tackled. The hardships, he stated, "are not unsolvable...we are not trying to reach Mars or the moon."[26] Nevertheless, it did not seem that he had dealt with the people's grievances or allayed their apprehensions.

FURTHER CONTROVERSY OVER THE *SHARI'A* ISSUE

The application in September 1983 of Islamic Law (*Shari'a*) as the foundation of a new Sudanese legal system, triggered the intense opposition of the non-Muslim population in the south and of various Muslim circles in the north. (For more details on the application of *Shari'a* law, see *MECS* 1983–84, pp. 639–44, 653–54.)

During the first 18 months of the application of the *Shari'a* until Numayri's downfall, the regime made it clear that the adoption of the Islamic way of life in Sudan was irrevocable. But the collapse of the Numayri regime heightened the expectations of the anti-*Shari'a* circles that the application of the *Shari'a* would be canceled. The SPLA's condition that the government cancel the *Shari'a* before a dialogue could start between them gave further vigor to the *Shari'a*'s opponents.

The transitional military government of 'Abd al-Rahman Muhammad Hasan Siwar al-Dhahab, which led the country during April 1985-April 1986, had shelved the *Shari'a* issue out of preoccupation with consolidating its power and stabilizing Khartoum's political life.

The al-Mahdi governments which followed Dahab's could not afford to resuscitate this most controversial issue either. Though opposing the reapplication of the *Shari'a*, al-Mahdi feared taking any step which might stir up political opposition. The NIF, however, which was the architect of and the driving force behind Numayri's application of the *Shari'a* in 1983, persistently demanded its reenforcement nationwide. The NIF's emergence during the April 1986 election as a significant third political force (see *MECS* 1986, pp. 576, 578) forced al-Mahdi to consider seriously the demand of the NIF in order to reduce the latter's threat to his grip on power.

The coalition crises which plagued the government during 1987–88, spurred al-Mahdi in spring 1988 to invite the NIF to join the new, broad-based coalition government. The NIF's inclusion in the government significantly strengthened its bargaining position. Indeed, al-Mahdi promised to enact the alternative laws (*al-Qawanin al-Badila*) to the *Shari'a* within 60 days of the government's formation.

Meanwhile, the country was plagued by difficulties, the foremost being the floods.

The contentious issue of the *Shari'a* was overshadowed by urgent economic and sociopolitical problems, which enabled the UP and the DUP to delay further the decision over the *Shari'a*. The NIF called the delay "unreasonable."[27] Al-Mahdi tried to appease the NIF by releasing a series of statements indicating his determination to apply the alternative Islamic laws.[28] On 11 September, a bill on the alternative laws of September 1983 was submitted to the Constituent Assembly for discussion.[29] The move provoked a parliamentary walkout by the 22 members of the United Sudanese African Parties, the main opposition.[30] Thus, the government failed to obtain a quorum for the debate and the issue was shelved once again.

The violent food riots which swept Khartoum in early November and the SPLA-DUP agreement signed later in the month, and which needed government and parliamentary approval before coming into force, pushed the *Shari'a* issue further into the margins, especially since the document called, *inter alia,* for a freeze on the reapplication of the *Shari'a* law until a national constitutional conference was held. (For the agreement see below.)

THE ABORTIVE COUP ATTEMPT

At the end of the year, Khartoum was again dragged into political turmoil, which was reflected in the authorities' foiling of a coup attempt in early December. According to the official version, the abortive coup was staged by Lt. Col. 'Abd al-Rahman Sa'id who wanted to halt the deterioration of conditions in the country.[31] He was arrested together with 16 other officers, nine of them from the Army.[32]

Though the authorities quickly played down the incident, they could not ease the atmosphere of great political and socioeconomic crisis in Khartoum. On 20 December, the authorities placed the capital under a state of emergency following reports of another coup attempt.[33] Details were not available, but the massive, stormy demonstrations in Khartoum in late December in protest against the government's announcement of steep rises in the prices of commodities[34] were an additional reminder that despite almost three years of democratic rule, nothing had basically changed for the better.

THE CIVIL WAR IN THE SOUTH

THE COURSE OF THE FIGHTING

At the turn of 1987–88, Khartoum launched a successful offensive aimed at retaking Kurmuk and Qaysan from the SPLA. The two garrison towns located on the border with Ethiopia in the Blue Nile province — outside the informal boundaries of the southern region — were captured by the SPLA in November 1987 (for details, see *MECS* 1987, p. 624). On 22 December 1987, the Army recaptured Kurmuk and, on 1 January, the 32nd anniversary of Sudan's independence, it recaptured Qaysan.

The SPLA did not sit idly by. On 12 January, it captured Kapoeta,[35] a strategic garrison town in eastern Equatoria (see map). Kapoeta controlled the routes from Juba — the capital of the southern region — to SPLA headquarters on the Boma plateau in Ethiopia (see map) and to roads to Kenya and Uganda, whence the SPLA could dispatch reinforcements to its troops inside Sudan. In addition, holding Kapoeta enabled the SPLA to strengthen its control over the east bank of the Nile in eastern Equatoria and, most important, to strengthen its gradual stranglehold on Juba. The all of Kapoeta signified a most detrimental development for Khartoum, not only nilitarily but also psychologically, since it showed that the SPLA can hold positions n Equatoria, an area not populated by the Dinka-dominated SPLA.

In early 1988, only parts of western Bahr al-Ghazal and western Equatoria were 'irtually free from sustained SPLA attacks, and the armed forces were holed up in a hrinking handful of garrison towns, primarily Juba, Wau, and Malakal[36] (see map).

Later in January, the Army suffered further military blows. On 23 January, the SPLA claimed the shooting-down of a MiG-23 fighter plane about 5 km. from Torit.[37] Khartoum admitted the loss of the plane, but said it was caused by a 'technical failure" while the plane was attempting to land at Juba airport.[38] On 20 February, the SPLA reported the destruction a day earlier of seven steamers carrying elief supplies to the famine-hit town of Malakal, the capital of the Upper Nile egion.[39] The Army, however, reported its success in repulsing the SPLA ambushes, and the killing of "105 outlaws and one European."[40]

Whatever the truth, the fighting continued unceasingly, with both sides claiming luring March and April further military successes one after the other. Especially onspicuous were the SPLA allegations of downing an "enemy" helicopter in late March, east of Juba, and of destroying on the ground a MiG-23 aircraft in mid-April while raiding the Juba airport.[41] The Army, however, ignored the first allegation and efuted the other.[42]

Meanwhile, the rainy season arrived in May. The Army was forced to retreat to its trongholds thus reducing the frequency of military confrontations. Though the rainy eason favored the SPLA, the SPLA activities against the Army did not increase luring June, July, and August. Khartoum publicly emphasized repeatedly that its orces had "complete control" of the security situation in the southern region.[43] Khartoum tried to make political capital out of the relative calm, implying that it was he result of the determination and the executive ability of the recently changed military nd political personnel (see above). Nevertheless, the relative calm should be mainly ttributed to the SPLA, which because of its internal disputes (see below) or because f Ethiopia's decreasing military aid (see below), or both, restricted its operations.

In September, clashes between the SPLA and the Army were renewed. The most ntensive fighting took place around Jabel Lado, a prominent cliff about 27 km.north f Juba, which controlled the main air routes into Juba from Khartoum. On 16 September, the SPLA announced the capture of Jabel Lado,[44] but the Army made no nention of this claim. Ten days later, the SPLA announced the capture of Keyala, nother strategic garrison town, east of Torit[45] (see map), which the Army indirectly dmitted.[46] During September and October, the SPLA announced that it had captured arrison towns around Torit.[47]

In November and December, the fighting abated somewhat, the SPLA being ngaged in a dialogue with the DUP (see below).

'OLITICAL CONTACTS

Simultaneous with the unceasing fighting, both the warring sides were engaged in the irst half of 1988 in a series of contacts which proved fruitless. Even the committee ormed early in the year to negotiate unofficially with the SPLA[48] found itself busy in acilitating the distribution of emergency relief, primarily of food supplies. (The long, evastating drought created a human catastrophe with famine and refugees in the outh.)[49]

In the summer and fall of 1988, new vigor was injected into the political deadlock. Most conspicuous were the talks in Addis Ababa between the SPLA and the DUP,[50] which ended in the signing of a "peace agreement" on 16 November.[51] The document emphasized the "keenness" of the two sides to convene the national constitutional conference in order to enhance the prospect of achieving peace. The document stated, however, that the SPLA agreed that until the constitutional conference was convened, the 1983 *Shari'a* laws would be "frozen" which was a departure from its earlier demand that they be repealed. Other clauses of the agreement called for a cease-fire, the lifting of the state of emergency (enforced by al-Mahdi earlier in the year), and the abrogation of the military agreements which had been concluded between Sudan and other countries (i.e., Libya and Egypt). The agreement stipulated that the conference would be convened on 31 December 1988 if all the preconditions were met.

The agreement was in effect a repetition of the agreement of Koka Dam signed in 1986 between the SPLA and the National Forces for the National Salvation of Sudan, a grouping which represented the professional and political elite in Khartoum in the aftermath of Numayri's downfall (see *MECS* 1986, p. 585). The only difference was the SPLA's less rigid attitude toward the issue of the *Shari'a* laws, as seen by its readiness to compromise, at least temporarily and perhaps only tactically. Although officially the UP was not involved in the SPLA-DUP rounds of talks, al-Mahdi presumably gave his blessing.

A serious obstacle in the peace talks was the NIF's flat rejection of the agreement, which threatened its efforts to reapply the *Shari'a* laws. The violent protest demonstrations staged by the NIF in central Khartoum about a week after the agreement was signed[52] clearly attested to the NIF's determination to oppose the agreement. The NIF threat to bring about the collapse of the shaky coalition government, if need be, restrained al-Mahdi from making any bold political move during the civil war until the end of the year.

DISPUTES WITHIN THE SPLA LEADERSHIP

The SPLA, formally the armed wing of the Sudanese People's Liberation Movement, but actually the dominant power among the southern rebels, suffered a series of disputes within its leadership during 1988. The absence of coherent ideology, the conflicting opinions concerning the movement's aims and means of achieving them, the personal rivalries among the leadership, and the mounting dissension in the SPLA — especially in Equatoria — all these together shook the movement's highest echelon.

The first serious rupture appeared in early January. Lt. Col. Carabino Kuanyin, the leader of the 1983 Bor mutiny (which rekindled the war between the south and Khartoum)[53] and a well-known military commander, reportedly initiated a coup against Lt. Col. John Garang, but failed.[54] Carabino and his close aides were arrested by the Ethiopians.[55] The SPLA did not refer to the Carabino affair until 10 April when a member of the SPLA's High Command admitted that Carabino had been under "protective custody" because of his "racialism and disrespect for, and attempt to destroy, the movement's leadership."[56]

Whatever Carabino's activities or threats against Garang, the conflict between them arose mainly from the following causes:

(1) Carabino's dissatisfaction because of Ethiopian dominance over the movement.

(2) Carabino's grievance because of Garang's rigid control over the SPLA which

pushed Carabino to a relatively low place in the leadership hierarchy although he was the SPLA's theoretical number two and chief of staff.

(3) Disagreement over the further conduct of the military struggle against Khartoum: while Carabino reportedly wanted to "transfer" the war to northern Sudan in line with the strategy of liberating the whole country,[57] Garang, under the patronage of Ethiopia, seemed to prefer limiting the fighting to the southern region.

(4) The dispute over Garang's reported refusal to transfer to the movement the $40m. fund, which was reportedly deposited in his name in a London bank.[58]

(5) Friction over Garang's attempts to create tribally based classes inside the SPLA, favoring his fellow Dinkas over the others.[59] Whatever the reasons for the conflict, Carabino disappeared from the SPLA stage,[60] and Nyon Bany was named chief of staff.

In late March, another strong tremor shook the SPLA leadership. Arok Thuon Arok, theoretically number five but actually number two in the rigid SPLA hierarchy, was arrested by Garang.[61] Arok was considered to be a fighter who had led major battles. He had also stood at the head of SPLA delegations seeking support abroad and had headed the "secret" talks with the Khartoum delegation in London in November 1987,[62] the first known discussions since 1986. His alleged crime was having questioned his leader's hard line on the November 1987 talks with al-Mahdi's Government.[63] As in the earlier case, Garang did not refer at all to the affair and Arok's fate remained unknown.

Another SPLA leader and a veteran southern politician, Daniel Kot Matthiew, though not considered as belonging to the core of the SPLA leadership, was reportedly killed in late May by Garang.[64] The whole picture remained vague with no details available.

Early in the summer, Garang arrested Joseph Odoho, a veteran politician from the powerful Equatorian tribe, the Latuka, and a leading member of the movement's political wing.[65] Odoho and Garang differed in their political orientations: while Garang favored a more Marxist approach, Odoho leaned toward Western-style socialism. Odoho also criticized what he considered Garang's despotic rule. In addition, Odoho accused the SPLA leader of collaborating with the Ethiopians to suppress those seeming to favor a peaceful settlement of the war.[66] The SPLA, sticking to its policy of not referring in public to dissension among its leaders, ignored this case as well.

In late July, Gordon Kong Choul, the leader of the Anya-nya II which had split early in the year, who had joined the SPLA as a member of its High Command, was jailed by Garang. Choul was accused of attempting to form a new movement in the south, rivaling Garang's.[67] As was expected, Garang made no mention of the Choul affair.

It was difficult to gauge the extent of the damage to the SPLA as a result of the struggles for power within its top hierarchy. One may assume that they weakened the SPLA's military strength and its political bargaining position *vis-à-vis* both Khartoum, and perhaps even its patron, Addis Ababa.

EXTERNAL AFFAIRS

THE ARAB WORLD

THE SUDANESE-LIBYAN-EGYPTIAN "TRIANGLE"

Libya

The stationing of Libyan troops in western Sudan, as was persistently claimed in early 1988 by political sources in Khartoum, though not officially, created new tensions in relations between the two countries. It should be recalled that friction over the same issue marred bilateral ties in the first half of 1987; the crisis subsided later in the year due to a Sudanese initiative, though the problem remained unsolved. (For details, see *MECS* 1987, pp. 625–26.)

By the beginning of 1988, however, al-Mahdi's Government could no longer ignore the presence of foreign forces in the Darfur region in the west of the country. Strong pressures were put on the government not only by Chad[68] and perhaps even by Egypt, but also by political circles at home led by the Darfurian members of parliament.[69] The Darfur region, where the Ansar religious sect and its political arm, the UP, had their roots, is a vast area with a relatively sparse population whose tribal loyalties reach across the borders to Chad and Libya. Monitoring the border area was difficult, and the Darfur region, being at a great distance from the country's political and economic centers, was hard to bring under control by the national and regional authorities. With a chronically poor, neglected, and turbulent population, the region in 1988, more than ever before, was a "bandit country,"[70] with both Libya and Chad using it to move arms and men.

Furthermore, at the turn of February-March, the estimated 1,500–2,000[71] men under the control of the Chadian dissident leader, al-Shaykh Ibn 'Umar who was backed by the Libyans, tried to take control of the Jabal Marra area in the Darfur region, which straddles the road to the frontier at Junayna.[72] But the local Fur people, to whom Jabal Marra is sacred, held off the invaders.[73]

While the Sudanese Government did not publicly attack the Libyan leader, Mu'ammar al-Qadhdhafi, it resorted unsuccessfully to quiet diplomacy to persuade the Libyans to leave as quickly as possible. The Sudanese attempt resulted in tension. In early March, the Libyan authorities presented the Sudanese with an official protest against Khartoum's allegation about the presence of the Libyan forces on its territory, which Tripoli repeatedly denied.[74] In addition, the Libyans officially requested Khartoum on that occasion to clarify the reasons for the expulsion of the Libyan student delegation from Sudan, and the closure of the Libyan cultural center in Khartoum.[75] Another Sudanese source reported several days later that Qadhdhafi even ordered Libyan diplomatic personnel in Khartoum to return home,[76] underlining thereby his protest. At that stage of the rupture, the government sent 'Ali Hasan Taj al-Din, a member of the Council of State, on an urgent "secret visit" to Libya.[77] Khartoum did not dwell on the visit's aims or its results, but it seemed, however, that after the visit Khartoum was appeased, perhaps by Libya's readiness to increase its economic and military aid. In any case, neither side referred in public during the whole of March to the sensitive issue of the presence of the Libyans or Libyan-backed forces in Darfur. The visit of 'Uthman al-Mirghani, a senior leader from the DUP and a veteran politician, to Tripoli on 13–20 March did not shed more light on that issue, but the crisis continued to subside as was clearly shown by the visit to Khartoum on

6-8 April by the Libyan commander in chief, Abu Bakr Yunis. Presumably, speeding up Libyan military assistance to Sudan was prominent in his discussions.

Meanwhile, the foreign presence in western Sudan reportedly increased. In the summer, it was estimated at 5,000: 3,000 from the forces of Chadian President Hisène Habré,[78] and a 2,000-strong contingent of what was referred to by various sources as Qadhdhafi's "Islamic Legion" which included Ibn 'Umar's men.[79] Refraining from turning directly to Qadhdhafi to tackle the increasingly acute problem, Khartoum handled it with both Chad and the forces of Ibn 'Umar, though one may assume that Tripoli was active behind the scenes. At the end of the year, the al-Mahdi Government announced that Ibn 'Umar's forces had handed over all their weapons to the Sudanese Army.[80] In mid- December, Khartoum also announced the signing of an agreement with Chad concerning the return of Ibn 'Umar's forces to Ndjamena.[81]

In addition to Khartoum's tireless efforts to end the presence of Ibn 'Umar's forces in Darfur, it spared nothing to tighten ties with Tripoli. The union plan, as presented to the public in early September (for details, see chapter on Libya), was a milestone in Sudanese-Libyan relations. But it blew up a political storm in Khartoum; it was rejected vehemently notably by the pro-Egyptian DUP[82] and even within the UP.[83] Al-Mahdi was alarmed by the new political ferment. The statement released by his foreign minister (a DUP member) in mid-October, that the unity plan was "nothing more than a call for meetings of committees to decide on special relations between Sudan and Libya,"[84] probably reflected al-Mahdi's list of priorities: neglecting the plan for union with Libya for the sake of maintaining stability in Sudan. It is possible that this was the major message delivered by al-Mahdi at his meeting with Qadhdhafi in Tripoli in mid-November.

Egypt

The *rapprochement* in Sudan's relations with Egypt in 1987 gathered further momentum in the year under review. A clear indication was the reported Egyptian military aid (experts and weapons) to Sudan at the end of 1987 to help its Army recapture Kurmuk and Qaysan from the SPLA[85] (see above). The signing in late January of the 1988 trade pact for $225m. ($25m. more than the 1987 pact),[86] was an additional indication of the growing bilateral ties.

On 1 March, relations reached a new peak: President Husni Mubarak arrived in Khartoum for a visit which lasted several hours; it was his first since 1985 and reciprocated al-Mahdi's visit to Cairo in 1987. Though the Sudanese media did not release a detailed statement regarding the visit's aims or its results, one may assume that the further implementation of the Brotherhood Charter (*Mithaq al-Ikha;* see *MECS* 1987, p. 627) concluded a year earlier was high on the list of topics the two leaders discussed. One may further assume that Sudan seized the occasion to ask Egypt to accelerate the delivery of military aid to Sudan, which was urgently needed to fend off the SPLA's increasing assaults on the Army (see above). Khartoum also possibly asked the Egyptians to intensify their mediatory efforts to improve relations between Khartoum and Addis Ababa.

Whatever the issues discussed by the two leaders, one should also view Mubarak's visit within the broader context of the complicated relations in the Sudanese-Libyan-Egyptian triangle. Sudanese-Libyan relations in early 1988 were tense (see above). Thus, Sudan's tightening ties with Egypt disturbed Qadhdhafi greatly, since close links between Khartoum and Cairo were the antithesis of the relations between Tripoli and Khartoum. By moving the pendulum toward Egypt in order to bring pressure to bear on Libya, al-Mahdi perhaps hoped to get Tripoli to increase its military and economic aid to Sudan and to evacuate its forces from the western part of the country. Sudan also exploited Mubarak's visit to persuade Egypt to return to Libya the four aircraft which had landed in Egypt on 1 March[87] (see chapter on Libya), and also to promote the Sudanese mediatory contacts aimed at reconciling Libya and Egypt,[88] tactics used by the Sudanese to ease tensions in the tripartite relationship.

Two weeks after Mubarak's visit, the arrival of Egyptian military aid to Sudan was reported.[89] No details were available with regard to the types or quantities of the aid.

On 9–10 April, a high-level Egyptian delegation, headed by Premier 'Atif Sidqi, was in Khartoum for talks on "furthering bilateral relations," which ended in the two sides signing the "final document on the implementation of the Brotherhood Charter."[90]

These growing ties were further highlighted by the visits of Sudanese Defense Minister Khalil and Chief of Staff Shawir to Cairo in mid-July. On 14 July, the two countries signed a military cooperation protocol providing for the exchange of "experience in military fields," and for helping Sudan establish "a number of advanced military industries."[91]

The fall and winter of 1988 saw the further exchange of visits by senior officials, the most noteworthy being that of the Egyptian prime minister to Khartoum on 8–9 October.[92]

The unity plan with Libya injected new tension into Sudan's relations with Egypt in the final months of 1988. The arrival in Cairo on 4 October of Idris al-Banna, the deputy chairman of Sudan's State Council, was meant to "clear the air."[93]

RECOGNITION OF THE "PALESTINIAN STATE"

Though being geographically and politically remote from the Palestinian problem, Khartoum found it important to reiterate during the year its "full support" of the "Palestinian uprising in the Israeli-occupied Arab lands."[94] Sudan's persistent wish to emphasize its being part and parcel of the Arab world was further expressed in its attendance at the Arab summit conference in Algeria on 7–9 June (for more details, see chapter on inter-Arab relations). On 2 December, Sudan announced its "full and official recognition" of the Palestinian state.[95] Khartoum's relatively delayed reaction could be explained by its highly careful policy toward controversial issues in the Arab world, trying to maneuver among the major, and sometimes contradictory, streams in that arena, without negatively provoking any of them.

SUDAN AND ITS NEIGHBORS FROM THE SOUTH

ETHIOPIA

During the year under review, Sudan spared no efforts to ease the tensions in its relations with Ethiopia. (For the sources of the strain which reached another high at the end of 1987, see *MECS* 1987, pp. 628–29.)

In early 1988, the joint committee set up a short while earlier (see *MECS* 1987, p. 629), was expected to convene, but disagreement over the venue canceled out the meeting[96] and further soured the already very troubled relations.

Meanwhile, the USSR, Egypt, Algeria, Nigeria, Somalia, and Djibouti offered Sudan and Ethiopia their reconciliatory services.[97] Whether connected to this initiative or not, on 23 March al-Mahdi and Mengistu Haile Mariam met in Djibouti for "private talks" on mutual problems. Both leaders took part in the summit meetings of the Intergovernmental Authority for Combating Drought and Desertification on 21–22 March.[98] The occasion was also utilized for the first meeting of the Sudanese-Ethiopian joint committee.[99] The meeting did not produce any tangible results, however, and its major importance was that it took place, thus breaking the deadlock between the two countries.

The second meeting of the joint committee took place in Addis Ababa on 28–30 April. It resulted in the formation of a technical committee, comprising six members of each side, to discuss "all [bilateral] issues and propose solutions."[100] On 12–15 May, the committee convened in Khartoum. An agreement was reached, which was to be submitted for further discussion to a joint ministerial committee on organizing border security and trade between the two countries.[101]

Contacts gathered further momentum when al-Mahdi, accompanied by a high-ranking entourage, arrived in Addis Ababa on 25 May for four days to attend the summit conference of the Organization of African Unity. On the sidelines, a tripartite meeting was held among al-Mahdi, Mengistu, and Mubarak. (Egypt was mediating between Sudan and Ethiopia.) As stated by Khartoum, the talks centered on reviewing "recent strides" in the development of their ties.[102] No further details were available, but one may assume that the Sudanese repeated their request that Ethiopia stop supporting the SPLA, and possibly also urged the latter to enter into negotiations with Khartoum.

Garang's reported preparations in late May to move his headquarters from Ethiopia to Kenya[103] indicated that Addis Ababa had already put pressure on the SPLA or that the SPLA was apprehensive that such an eventuality was seriously considered. Repeated statements by senior Sudanese officials on the improved ties with Addis Ababa,[104] and, much more significant, the return to Khartoum in late June of Ethiopian Ambassador Feleke Tabour,[105] contributed to the impression of growing *rapprochement* between Sudan and Ethiopia. (Hitherto, Sudan was represented in Addis Ababa by an ambassador, while Ethiopia was represented in Khartoum only by a chargé d'affaires.)

This gradual warming up of ties also became apparent by the Ethiopian foreign minister, Bayeh Berhanu, coming to Khartoum on 21 July and then Sudan, in "a goodwill gesture," announcing the decision to return to Addis Ababa three Ethiopian airplanes — two civilian and one military — in which Ethiopian pilots had defected to Sudan[106] (see *MECS* 1986, p. 593).

During 12–14 August, the Sudanese-Ethiopian technical committee met once again in Addis Ababa. The importance of the meeting lay in the fact of its having taken place; neither the matters discussed nor the decisions marked any new departures. After the meeting, there was no further improvement in relations.

KENYA

In the early spring of 1988, a serious crisis marred Sudan's relations with neighboring Kenya. Khartoum accused Nairobi of providing the SPLA with military and logistical aid.[107] More specifically, Khartoum claimed that cargo planes were flying regularly from Kenya to southern Sudan.[108] Sudan also accused Kenya of permitting the SPLA office in Nairobi, while acting under the guise of a relief organization to undermine Sudanese interests. Al-Mahdi's Government repeatedly asked Nairobi to close the SPLA office,[109] whose activities it considered "hostile" and "an interference in its internal affairs."[110] Nairobi denied extending any support to the SPLA and refused to close the office. Aware that it was unable to put military pressure on Kenya, Sudan instead carried on a war of words in the summer, threatening to retaliate in kind and to give refuge to Kenyan dissidents unless Kenya closed the office.[111] Sudan interlarded its threats with "quiet diplomacy,"[112] but to no avail. Tension between the two continued until the year's end.

UGANDA

The considerations underlying Khartoum's *rapprochement* with Kampala in 1987 (see *MECS* 1987, p. 630) continued to exist during the year under survey. In 1988, Khartoum had an even greater interest in maintaining the pattern of cooperative ties with Kampala, since it feared more than ever before that Uganda might serve as an additional base for SPLA operations against its Army. The status of the SPLA in neighboring Kenya (see above) increased Sudanese fears of a possible SPLA pincer movement from Uganda and Kenya. Garang's personal ties with the Ugandan president, Yoweri Museveni, and the SPLA efforts to extend its activities in the neighboring countries added to Khartoum's apprehension.

Thus, Sudan lost no opportunity to bolster links with Uganda. On 4–5 February, senior officials from both countries met in Arua (northwestern Uganda) to discuss common security problems and agreed on a number of measures aimed at improving border relations.[113] A further meeting, in Kampala in mid-March, ended with the signing of a memorandum providing for the return from Sudan of up to 60,000 Ugandan refugees. Ugandan refugees who opted to remain in Sudan would be moved to camps 80 km. inside Sudan to ensure that they did not engage in cross-border incursions to destabilize the Ugandan regime. In return, Kampala promised Khartoum not to allow the SPLA to use Ugandan territory as a base against Sudan.[114]

The importance which Sudan attributed to cooperation with Uganda was further reflected by Commander in Chief Fathi's arrival in Kampala in August.[115]

Meanwhile, Uganda reported that the SPLA was making violent incursions deep inside its territory.[116] Kampala's growing fears that the raids would undermine Ugandan security led Museveni to meet al-Mahdi on 20 August in Khartoum. During a three-day official visit, Museveni held talks with al-Mahdi and other Sudanese political leaders on "African issues in general and bilateral relations in particular."[117] As became known later, Museveni also made an effort at mediating between al-Mahdi's Government and the SPLA.[118]

At the end of September, the third round of talks between the two countries began, this time in Khartoum. The talks ended with the signing of three accords of cooperation.[119] The dynamics of the good ties were maintained till the end of 1988.

RELATIONS WITH THE SUPERPOWERS

No special change had marked Sudan's relations with Moscow and Washington. These continued to be low-profiled, as in earlier years.

NOTES

For the place and frequency of publications cited here, and for the full name of the publication, news agency, radio station, or monitoring service where an abbreviation is used, please see "List of Sources." Only in the case of more than one publication bearing the same name is the place of publication noted here.

1. *Al-Watan,* Khartoum, quoted by SUNA, 19 March — DR, 21 March 1988.
2. For the full text of the program, see SUNA, 15 March — DR, 16 March 1988.
3. SUNA, 20 April — DR, 21 April 1988.
4. *Al-Siyasa,* Khartoum, 25 April 1988.
5. Ibid., 28 April 1988.
6. Ibid., 8 April 1988.
7. *Alwan,* 3 May 1988.
8. *Al-Siyasa,* Khartoum, 22 June 1988.
9. *Alwan,* 14 May 1988.
10. For more details on the attacks, see the daily Sudanese press of the second half of May 1988.
11. For biographic details, see *Sawt al-Umma,* 8 June 1988.
12. *Al-Siyasa,* Khartoum, 6 August; *al-Dustur,* London, 29 August 1988.
13. *Al-Usbu',* 6 August 1988.
14. For more details on the reshuffle, see *al-Raya,* Khartoum, 6 June and *Alwan,* 21 June 1988.
15. SUNA, 6 June — DR, 6 June; *Alwan,* 13 June 1988.
16. *New African,* August 1988.
17. Ibid.
18. In what was the first terrorist murder in a long time, a leading Shi'a Muslim opponent of the Iraqi Government, Mahdi al-Hakim, was assassinated in Khartoum on 17 January. The incident departed from the context of a murder affair and it affected also Khartoum's politics. For more details, see the Sudanese press of the second half of January.
19. SUNA, 18 August — DR, 18 August 1988.
20. For details on the extent of the catastrophe, see e.g., *al-Anba,* Kuwait, 7 August; *The Times,* 9 August; *al-Wafd,* 16 August 1988 — all reported from Khartoum.
21. AFP, 3 August 1988.
22. *The Times,* 9 August 1988.
23. SUNA, 27 August — DR, 29 August 1988.
24. For details on the international relief aid, see e.g., *MEED,* 26 August, 8 September 1988.
25. An interview with the *Guardian Weekly,* 28 August 1988.
26. R. Omdurman, 22 August — DR, 24 August 1988.
27. SUNA, 6 September — DR, 9 September 1988.
28. E.g., SUNA, 12, 24 July — DR, 13, 25 July; *al-Siyasa,* Khartoum, 31 July 1988.
29. AFP, 20 September — DR, 20 September 1988.
30. *Al-Siyasa,* Khartoum, 20 September, 4 October 1988.
31. SUNA, 14 December — SWB, 20 December, and *al-Majalla,* 21–27 December 1988, quoting a senior military source.
32. SUNA, 26 December — SWB, 29 December 1988.
33. MENA, 20 December; *al-Ayyam,* 21 December 1988.
34. SUNA, 27 December — SWB, 29 December; *FT,* 29, 30 December 1988, reports from Khartoum.
35. R. SPLA, 12 January — DR, 12 January 1988.
36. *AC,* 15 April 1988.
37. R. SPLA, 25 January — DR, 26 January 1988.
38. SUNA, 24 January, 7 February — DR, 25 January, 8 February 1988.
39. R. SPLA, 20 February, 2 March — DR, 22 February, 2 March 1988.
40. *Al-Siyasa,* Khartoum, 24 February; *al-Sudani,* 1 March 1988.
41. R. SPLA, 30 March, 16 April — DR, 31 March, 20 April 1988.
42. *Al-Sudani,* 17 April 1988.
43. E.g., *al-Raya,* Khartoum, 9, 12, 21 June; *al-Siyasa,* Khartoum, 24 June, 14 July and *al-Hawadith,* 29 July 1988, an interview with Defense Minister Khalil.

44. R. SPLA, 23 September — DR, 26 September 1988.
45. R. SPLA, 26 September — DR, 26 September 1988.
46. R. Omdurman, 28 September — DR, 29 September 1988.
47. R. SPLA, 28 September, 5, 7, 31 October — DR, 29 September, 7, 11 October, 2 November 1988.
48. For details on the committee, see *al-Ayyam,* 8 February and *al-Siyasa,* Khartoum, 12 February 1988.
49. According to a "Sudanese official senior source," the number of immigrants arriving in Khartoum from the south in search of food and security, reached 1.8m. in the summer of 1988. See R. Omdurman, 1 June — DR, 3 June. The exodus of the southern Sudanese into the north coincided with their massive influx into Ethiopia. According to a Sudanese estimate, 80% of the population of the south was uprooted by war and famine. *The Guardian,* 15 May. For more details on the acute, massive starvation in the south, see reports, e.g., *NYT,* 3 October; *Guardian Weekly,* 20 November; *Time,* 5 December 1988.
50. E.g., R. SPLA, 22 April — DR, 23 August; *al-Siyasa,* Khartoum, 20 October 1988.
51. For the full text of the agreement, see R. SPLA, 17 November — SWB, 19 November 1988.
52. SUNA, 23 November — SWB, 25 November; *FT,* 23 November; *The Economist,* 26 November 1988.
53. For details on the mutiny, see *MECS* 1982–83, p. 778.
54. *Sawt al-Umma,* 4 January 1988.
55. *CR:* Sudan, No. 1, 1988.
56. *Al-Raya,* Khartoum, 10 April 1988, an interview with Joseph Qawa, a senior SPLA leader.
57. *CR:* Sudan, No. 1, 1988.
58. *Akhir al-Anba,* 5 March 1988.
59. *Al-Ittihad,* Khartoum, 22 January 1988.
60. The arrest of Carabino served as a reminder of the case of Benjamin Bol, the former representative of the SPLA in London. Bol, who was known for his opposition to Ethiopia's domination of his movement, was put under house arrest in Addis Ababa in 1984 and there, it was believed, he was beaten to death.
61. *AC,* 15 April 1988.
62. For details on the "secret" talks, see *al-Tadamun,* 6 February 1988, for an interview with State Minister for Defense Afadallah Burma Nasir.
63. *AC,* 15 April 1988.
64. *Al-Raya,* Khartoum, 31 May 1988.
65. *Al-Siyasa,* Khartoum, 2 June 1988. For Odoho's involvement in the southern anti-Numayri activities in the early 1980s, see *MECS* 1981–82, p. 825.
66. *AC,* 9 September 1988.
67. *Al-Raya,* Khartoum, 21 July 1988.
68. E.g., R. Ndjamena, 2, 11 March — DR, 2, 16, March; *al-Ayyam,* 4 March, quoting Chadian and French sources.
69. E.g., *al-Ayyam,* 2, 8 March; *al-Adwa,* Khartoum, 5 March; *al-Sudani,* 6 March 1988 — statements of senior leaders.
70. As described by the *The Economist,* 7 May 1988.
71. Ibid. and *CR:* Sudan, No. 3, 1988.
72. In 1987, al-Mahdi refused Libya's request to use Junayna airport for its attacks on Chad.
73. *The Economist,* 7 May. See also the statement of Defense Minister Khalil in *al-Siyasa,* Khartoum, 5 March 1988.
74. E.g., JANA, 5 March — DR, 7 March; SUNA, 7 March — DR, 8 March 1988, quoting Jum'a al-Fazani, the Libyan ambassador in Khartoum.
75. *Al-Sudani,* 1 March 1988.
76. *Al-Usbu',* 1 March 1988.
77. *Al-Sudani,* 3 March 1988.
78. AFP, 10 June; *CR*: Sudan, No. 3, 1988.
79. *Al-Ayyam,* 17 July; *al-Raya,* Khartoum, 28, 31 July 1988.
80. SUNA, 9 September — DR, 9 September 1988, a statement made by the defense minister.
81. SUNA, 13 December — DR, 16 December 1988.
82. *Al-Usbu',* 1 September; *Alwan,* 7 September; *al-Siyasa,* Khartoum, 17 October 1988.

83. *Al-Jumhuriyya,* Cairo, 16 September 1988, quoting Ahmad al-Mahdi's criticism.
84. *Al-Majalla,* 12–18 October; see also his interview in *al-Siyasa,* Kuwait, 20 December 1988.
85. *Al-Majalla,* 23–29 November 1988.
86. *CR:* Sudan, No. 1; *al-Usbu',* 29 July 1988.
87. *Al-Adwa,* Khartoum, 5 March 1988.
88. E.g., *al-Sudani,* 8 March; *al-Ayyam,* 13 March; *al-Sharq al-Awsat,* 29 March 1988, interviews with al-Mirghani.
89. *Al-Ayyam,* 18 March 1988.
90. *Al-Siyasa,* Khartoum, 9, 11 April 1988.
91. *Al-Ayyam,* 15 July 1988.
92. For more details, see *al-Siyasa,* Khartoum, 8, 9 October 1988.
93. MENA, 4 October — DR, 5 October 1988, quoting Idris.
94. *Al-Ayyam,* 1 April; for the intensive stream of similar references, see the Sudanese media throughout the year.
95. R. Omdurman, 2 December — DR, 6 December 1988.
96. *Al-Siyasa,* Khartoum, 8 January 1988.
97. *Al-Ayyam,* 16 February, 3, 13 March; SUNA, 20 March — DR, 21 March; SUNA, 27 January — DR, 28 January; SUNA, 14 April — DR, 15 April; and SUNA, 19 March — DR, 21 March 1988, respectively.
98. SUNA, 23 March — DR, 24 March 1988.
99. *Al-Ayyam,* 23 March 1988.
100. *Al-Siyasa,* Khartoum, 1 May 1988.
101. *Al-Ayyam,* 15 May 1988.
102. *Al-Siyasa,* Khartoum, 30 May 1988.
103. R. Omdurman, 3 May — DR, 4 May; *Sudan Times,* 25 May — JPRS, 18 July 1988.
104. E.g., *al-Siyasa,* Kuwait, 16 June; *'Ukaz,* 13 July 1988, interviews with al-Mirghani.
105. *Sawt al-Umma,* 26, 28 June; for interviews with the new ambassador, see *al-Majalla,* 10–16 August 1988.
106. SUNA, 22 July — DR, 25 July 1988.
107. E.g., *al-Sudani,* 3 March; *al-Usbu',* 24 April 1988, quoting senior officials.
108. *Al-Raya,* Khartoum, 1 June 1988, quoting a senior security source.
109. E.g., *Sawt al-Umma,* 6 June; *al-Raya,* Khartoum, 1, 14, 22 June 1988.
110. R. Omdurman, 25 June — DR, 28 June; SUNA, 6 June — DR, 7 June 1988.
111. E.g., *al-Raya,* Khartoum, 19 June; SUNA, 24 June — DR, 27 June 1988.
112. For details, see *al-Majalla,* 6–12 July; *al-Adwa,* Khartoum, 12 July 1988.
113. For further details, see *ARB,* 15 March 1988.
114. *Al-Ayyam,* 21 March; *ARB,* 15 April 1988.
115. *Al-Ayyam,* 4 August 1988.
116. *AC,* 15 July 1988.
117. *Al-Raya,* Khartoum, 23 August 1988, a report from Museveni's press conference in Khartoum.
118. *Al-Sudani,* 29 September 1988, quoting Khalil.
119. *Al-Sudani,* 27, 29 September 1988.

The Arab Republic of Syria
(Al-Jumhuriyya al-'Arabiyya al-Suriyya)

YOSEF OLMERT

During 1988, Syria's domestic and foreign relations were largely similar to those in the preceding year.

Domestically, the economic crisis and the political uncertainty surrounding relationships within the closed circle of Syria's leadership continued. The economic crisis, whose origins could be traced back for several years (see chapters on Syria in previous volumes of *MECS*) showed no signs of abating during the year under survey. Some of the economy's basic problems, such as overextended and inefficient public sectors, huge military expenditures (including funds to maintain the military presence in Lebanon), large-scale corruption, and dwindling levels of foreign aid were very much in evidence during 1988. However, there were also signs pointing to the onset of recovery: increased oil production, decreased debt to banks, lower prices for some consumer goods, improved trade balance, and a strengthened pound. The government continued its anticorruption campaign and took steps to liberalize the economy and encourage foreign investment. Agricultural production went up, boosted by favorable climatic conditions, in contrast to previous years.

Political instability in recent years had stemmed mainly from dissent within the highest echelons of the regime, and much less so from the challenge of the opposition. The man at the center of the dissent was Rif'at al-Asad, President Hafiz al-Asad's younger brother and vice president of the republic. His continued absence from the country (on his departure from Syria, see *MECS* 1986, pp. 605–7) while nominally holding the title of vice president indicated the political uncertainty as did repeated, though unconfirmed, reports about conflicts among some of the president's closest aides jockeying for better positions. These conflicts were fueled by the uncertainty regarding the president's health. Dissent and rumors, notwithstanding, Asad's personal grip over the country seemed as unchallenged in 1988 as in previous years.

During 1988, two biographies of the president were published outside Syria[1] which highlighted his long hold on the leadership of traditionally unruly Syria. Yet, even the more sympathetic (though unofficial) of the two biographies referred to Asad's achievements as "fragile,"[2] and it was in foreign policy that Syria's standing seemed particularly "fragile" during 1988.

One of Asad's biographers described his role in Arab politics thus:

> More than any Arab statesman of his day, Hafiz al-Asad represents the Arabs' aspiration to be master of their own destiny in their own region. The aspiration remains largely frustrated but he has at least ensured that the case for Arab rights and security can no longer be ignored.[3]

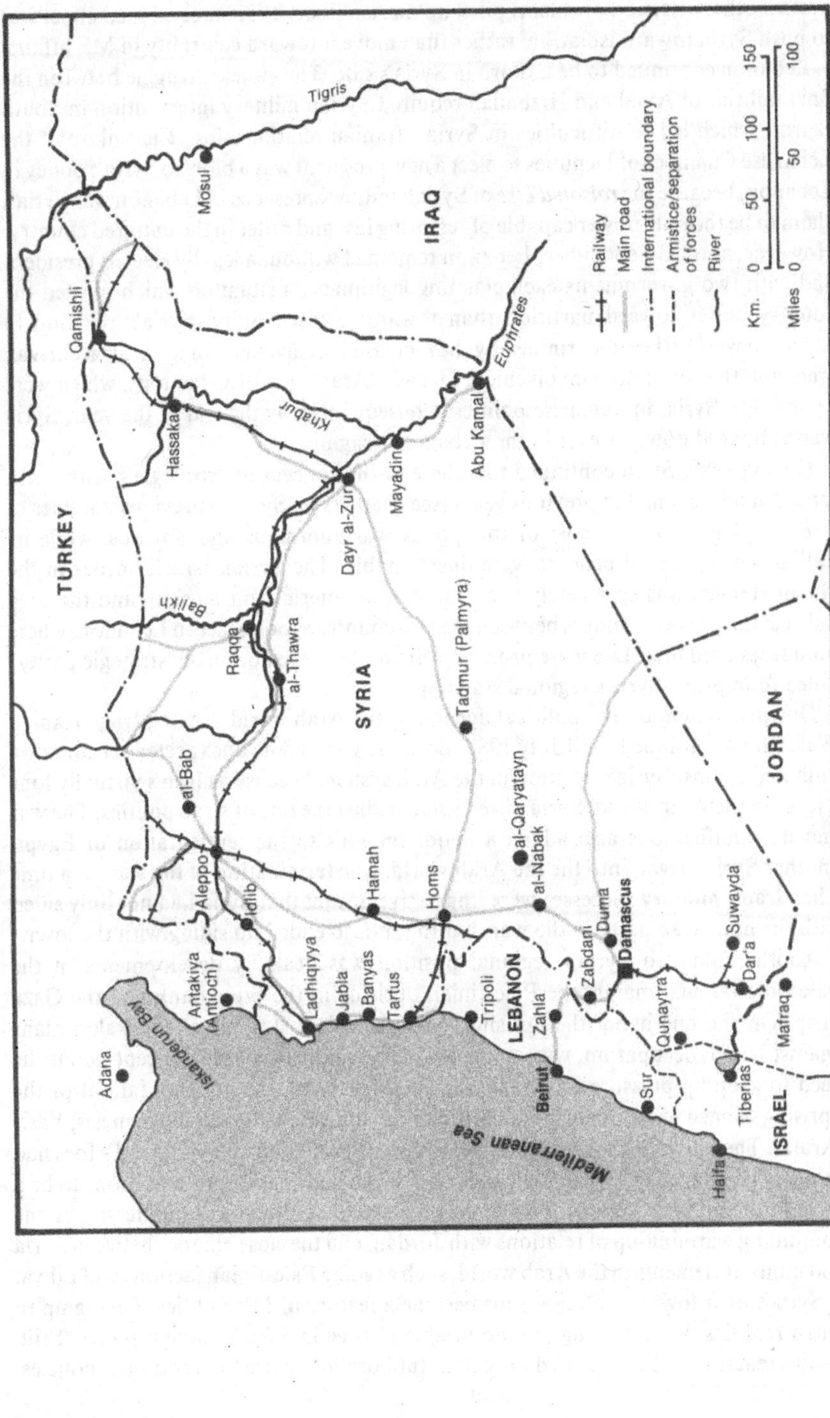
TURKEY
SYRIA
IRAQ
JORDAN
LEBANON
ISRAEL
Mediterranean Sea
Iskanderun Bay
Tigris
Euphrates
Khabur
Balikh
Adana
Antakiya (Antioch)
Aleppo
Idlib
al-Bab
al-Thawra
Raqqa
Hassaka
Qamishli
Mosul
Dayr al-Zur
Mayadin
Abu Kamal
Tadmur (Palmyra)
al-Qaryatayn
al-Nabak
Hamah
Homs
Ladhiqiyya
Jabla
Banyas
Tartus
Tripoli
Zahla
Beirut
Zabdani
Duma
Damascus
Suwayda
Dar'a
Qunaytra
Tiberias
Mafraq
Sur
Haifa
Railway
Main road
International boundary
Armistice/separation of forces
River
Km. 0 50 100 150
Miles 0 50 100

Syria

This statement reflects Syria's long-standing ambition to be a linchpin of Arab politics, a leading force in the politics of the Middle East. Reality in 1988, however, proved otherwise, and problems piled up on Asad's desk. Their combined effect was to push Syria toward isolation, rather than move it toward centrality in ME affairs.

Lebanon continued to be a thorn in Syria's side. The violent struggle between the Shi'i militias of Amal and Hizballah required Syrian military intervention in South Beirut, which led to difficulties in Syrian-Iranian relationships. The failure of the Lebanese Chamber of Deputies to elect a new president was a blow to Syria's policy in Lebanon, because the *raison d'être* of Syria's military presence in Lebanon was Syria's claim to be the only power capable of restoring law and order in the battered country. However, as of 23 September, Lebanon remained without a legally elected president and with two governments each claiming legitimacy, a situation which pushed the country closer toward partition than toward restored unity. Syria's position in Lebanon was further undermined by the increased involvement of its Arab archrival, Iraq, and the continuing involvement of Yasir 'Arafat-led PLO factions, which were opposed to Syria, in Lebanese politics. Consequently, by the end of the year, Syria was as bogged down as ever in the Lebanese quagmire.

During 1988, Syria continued to adhere to the concept of "strategic parity" with Israel, much as it had in previous years (see chapters on Syria in previous volumes of *MECS*). The economic cost of this policy was enormous and obvious, while its military and political benefits were questionable. The Syrian-Israeli border in the Golan Heights was completely peaceful, despite intermittent tension, and the only indirect military encounters between the two countries took place in Lebanon, where both sides used their Lebanese proxies. Adherence to the notion of "strategic parity" failed to improve Syria's regional standing.

One prime item on the political agenda of the Arab world was the Iraqi-Iranian War, which continued until July 1988. Both the war and its unexpected termination militated against Syria's position in the Arab system, because as Iran's virtually lone backer in the Arab world, Syria pitted itself against the tide of Arab politics. The war and its ramifications also added a major impetus to the reintegration of Egypt, another Syrian rival, into the the Arab world. The termination of the war, at a time when Iraq's military successes were impressive, meant that Syria had not only sided with the non-Arab party in the war, but that it also ended up siding with the loser.

Another blow to Syria's regional position was dealt by developments in the Palestinian arena, mainly the Palestinian uprising in the West Bank and the Gaza Strip. On the one hand, the uprising, being a violent struggle of the Palestinians against Israeli occupation, was in line with the long-held Syrian concept about the need to keep up pressure on Israel. On the other hand, the political fallout of the uprising seemed to pay many political dividends to Hafiz al-Asad's old nemesis, Yasir 'Arafat. The outcome of all this was clear: a year in which so many of Asad's foes had so many reasons to celebrate their successes was a bad year for his ambitions to be a focal figure in Arab politics. This undesirable state of affairs was unaffected by the continuing warming-up of relations with Jordan, and the close alliance between Syria and militant elements in the Arab world, such as some Palestinian factions and Libya.

Syria's drift toward isolation thus became a feature of ME politics. Facing up to harsh realities did not bring any noticeable change in Syria's foreign policy. Still, Asad's reaction was not limited only to a stubborn insistence on traditional policies.

Repeated reports about secret contacts between Syria and Egypt, designed supposedly to lead to the resumption of diplomatic relations between the two countries, served notice that Asad did not wish to place himself completely and irreversibly in a tight corner, as did his participation in the emergency Arab summit in Algiers in June, and Syria's repeated call for greater Arab solidarity against Israel.

The same was likewise true regarding Syria's position in the international arena. During the year, there were increasing signs that the Syrian leadership was displeased with and suspicious of certain facets of the USSR's foreign policy, particularly the overall conciliatory approach to regional crises including the ME as opposed to the Syrian confrontational approach. The ongoing improvement of relations between the Soviets and Israel was much to Syria's chagrin. Such was the case also with regard to Soviet overtures toward Egypt, the Soviet role in the Iraqi-Iranian War, and the Soviet encouragement of PLO moderation. However, Syria did not bring matters to a crisis: it chose to remain Moscow's closest ME ally and the recipient of some of the best weapons systems in the Soviet arsenal.

Relations between Syria and the US improved during 1988, but no major breakthrough was achieved. The policies of the two countries with regard to the ME continued to be incompatible on more issues than one.

DOMESTIC AFFAIRS

THE SYRIAN REGIME

As in previous years, Rif'at al-Asad figured prominently in press reports about Syria's domestic politics. In the early months of 1988, there was a flurry of reports about his imminent return to Damascus, possibly in order to assume the position of adviser to the president on domestic security.[4] Rif'at did not return, yet the reports seemed to cause apprehension among his adversaries in Syria. Another vice president, 'Abd al-Halim Khaddam, was rumored to have inquired about the possibility of obtaining Saudi citizenship if Rif'at al-Asad returned.[5] Yet another opponent, 'Adnan Badr Hasan, head of one of Syria's numerous intelligence agencies, detained two big businessmen known to be Rif'at's supporters.[6]

Though still in exile, Rif'at al-Asad was thus very much in the news. He reportedly established a new political organization called "Young Syria,"[7] threatened to take legal action to prevent the publication of a book about him in Paris,[8] and his bodyguards were involved in violence at a Spanish resort.[9] A Syrian journalist, working in the service of Rif'at al-Asad, was seriously wounded in an attempt on his life late in December 1988.[10] Clearly, Rif'at's activities and machinations were a source of embarrassment to his brother; still Rif'at retained his official title as vice president and his possible return to Syria remained a source of tension.

In February, there was a report that another member of the Asad clan — the president's son, Basil — had been appointed commander of the Syrian Defense Companies, an elite military unit designed to protect the regime, whose previous commander was Rif'at al-Asad himself.[11] (On Basil's past activities, see *MECS* 1986, p. 606; 1987, p. 636.) Another Syrian leader whose name was frequently linked to possible changes in the government was 'Abd al-Halim Khaddam. According to one report, Khaddam was a key figure in the government, mainly because of his role in the formulation of Syria's foreign policy. Hafiz al-Asad, according to this report, destined

Khaddam to be his successor.[12] Other reports indicated that Khaddam had lost favor with the president due to the failure of his Lebanese policies[13] (see below).

Another leader who definitely lost his position was Gen. 'Ali Haydar, the commander of the Special Forces, one of the military units entrusted with the task of defending the regime. According to one report, he was fatally wounded in an attempt on his life.[14] Another report cited poor health as the reason for Haydar's replacement as commander of the Special Forces by a nephew of Gen. 'Ali Duba, head of Syria's Military Intelligence.[15] This appointment, as well as the large number of members of the Asad family in key political and military positions, highlighted the intricate web of clan and tribal loyalties in the regime's top echelons.

By the end of the year, the following men were in key positions in Syria: Hafiz al-Asad; Rif'at al-Asad; Basil al-Asad; and Ghazi Kan'an (head of Syrian Intelligence in Lebanon and a relative of the Asad family). Other members of the Asad family who occupied political and military positions were Jamil al-Asad (Hafiz's brother) and his son Funnaz; and 'Adnan and Muhammad al-Asad (two of Hafiz's uncles). Other non-Asad key figures were: 'Abd al-Halim Khaddam; Gen. Hikmat Shihabi (chief of staff); Gen. Mustafa Talas (deputy prime minister and minister of defense); Gen. 'Ali Duba (head of Military Intelligence); Gen. 'Ali Aslan (deputy chief of staff); Gen. Shafiq Fayyad (commander of the Third Armored Division, related through marriage to Rif'at al- Asad); Gen. Muhammad Khuli (head of the Air Force Intelligence); Gen. Muhammad Nassif (head of the General Intelligence Directorate, nominally attached to, but practically enjoying much autonomy from, the Ministry of Interior); Ahmad Sa'id Salah (head of the Political Security Office); Brig. 'Adnan Makhluf (a prominent intelligence chief); and 'Abd al-Ra'uf al-Kasm[16] (former prime minister and current chief of the National Security Bureau, which liases between the Ba'th Party and the security apparatus). Hafiz al-Asad's ability to manipulate his lieutenants was one of the main reasons for his success in ruling Syria for such a long time. Ironically, though, it was the president's poor health which kept alive and fueled much of the infighting within the regime. As in 1987 (see *MECS* 1987, p. 636), during the year under survey there were reports that Asad's health was so bad that an official visit by the foreign minister of the Federal Republic of Germany (FRG), Hans Dietrich-Genscher, was postponed at 24 hours' notice, and that there were large-scale troop movements in the country.[17] Toward the end of the year, there was another report the reliability of which could not be assessed — about Asad's heart problems: that Soviet doctors treating Asad strongly recommended hospitalizing him in the USSR, but that Asad had refused to leave Syria and senior Eastern bloc doctors came to treat him in Damascus instead.[18]

THE SYRIAN OPPOSITION

Only a few years ago, the Islamic opposition in Syria appeared to pose a severe threat to the country's internal stability. Then came the Hamah events of 1982, when the regime ruthlessly eliminated thousands of Muslim activists and innocent residents (see *MECS* 1981–82, pp. 849–53). Since then the Muslim Brotherhood, the main opposition group in Syria, ceased to be a challenge to the regime. In 1986, the Brotherhood's activities had indicated a possible recovery of the organization, when dozens of Syrian security men were killed in a series of successful terror operations (see *MECS* 1986, pp. 608–10). But this success proved short-lived. The opposition, which depended largely on foreign aid, was rent by internal splits, and the government tried, to an extent successfully, to reconcile its differences with some of the opposition factions through political negotiations. In 1985, one of the fundamentalist factions, 'Adnan 'Uqla's vanguard group, had reached an agreement with the government to cease armed activities in return for a full pardon of its members (see *MECS* 1984–85, p. 648). According to another report, 'Uqla was lured back to Syria by a government agent and subsequently disappeared from sight.[19] According to this report, the Syrian Government had succeeded in causing a rift in the Muslim Brotherhood by subtly manipulating the differences between the various wings of the organization. Agents of the regime negotiated terms for a cease-fire with a group led by two prominent Muslim Brothers, Hasan Huwaydi and Munir Ghadban. These two were opposed by a militant group led by 'Adnan Sa'd al-Din and, in the process, the entire Muslim Brotherhood movement came to a virtual standstill.[20] The impasse led to attempts to establish a third wing.[21] In December 1988, there was a report about three Muslim Brothers being killed in Damascus by Syria's security forces.[22]

The Brotherhood's virtual paralysis did not remove all potential danger to the regime. There were other opposition elements with which the regime had to deal. One was the dissident Communist Labor Party, which announced that 312 of its members were being detained by the regime.[23] Another dissident Communist group, the "Political Bureau," announced that one of its members was tortured to death in his jail cell[24] (on the splits in the Syrian Communist Party, see *MECS* 1986, pp. 607–8). On a number of occasions, there were reports about large-scale operations of the Syrian security apparatus to detain opponents of the regime.[25] According to one such report, a prominent Syrian athlete, Nizar al-'Abdallah, who gained fame in the Mediterranean Games held in Syria in 1987 (see *MECS* 1987, p. 651), was detained.[26] In September, there was an unverified report about an attempted *coup d'état*, after which 40 soldiers and officers were executed.[27]

During the year, one of the regime's rivals, Dr. Ahmad Sulayman al- Ahmad, a prominent 'Alawi scholar whose father was an 'Alawi religious leader, announced from exile the formation of a new opposition body, the "National Democratic Party."[28] Another prominent opposition figure, Dr. Jihad al-Hawrani (son of Akram al-Hawrani,[29] one of the Ba'th Party's historic leaders and a bitter rival of the Asad Government), mended his fences with the regime, returned to Damascus,and met with Asad.[30]

THE ECONOMIC SITUATION

During the first half of the year under review, Syria's economy seemed to be showing its first signs of pulling out of a deep crisis, following sweeping government changes, a crackdown on corruption, and a liberalization program. According to various reports, a campaign by the new government to boost the private sector, increase oil output, and reform agriculture (see *MECS* 1987, pp. 638–40) was beginning to pay dividends. An unnamed foreign diplomat serving in Damascus said that "Syria went through a very difficult period....At times it was difficult for them to find enough hard currency to import some of their basic needs....But it looks as though things were now improving."[31] In each of the first five months of the year, the trade balance showed a surplus,[32] and this trend continued through September.[33] Syrian exports in 1988 totaled $833m., a figure highly acclaimed by the official press.[34] The improvement was largely due to increased production of light oil in the Jazira area in the northeastern corner of Syria.

Oil fields were discovered in the Jazira as early as 1956, and since then there have been more discoveries. By far the most exciting was made by Pecten, a Houston-based company, in cooperation with Royal Dutch Shell and Deminex. Discovery of the al-Tayyam field was announced in 1984; what made it particularly significant was that the oil was very light and low in sulphur, in contrast to the heavy sulphurous oil produced in Syria's other fields. After years of preparatory work, the new field started to produce, and in March 1988 the overall production from the Jazira areas was said to be running at 106,000 barrels per day (b/d). In early 1988, it was revealed that the Pecten Consortium had made another promising discovery at 'Umar, northeast of al-Tayyam field, which some reports said was the biggest of the new finds. It was thought that the new field could produce an initial 50,000 b/d, to be increased subsequently to 100,000 b/d. The success of Pecten stimulated international interest in Syrian oil potential. In March 1988, Canadian Occident Petroleum was reported to be on the point of signing for a concession to explore areas in Syria, and other companies, among them British Petroleum, Aramco, Kuwait Petroleum Company, Murphy Eastern, and the Turkish State Oil Company, were also thought to be seriously interested in exploration in Syria.[35] Another improvement in the oil industry was achieved through a resumption of the oil deal with Iran (on the origin of the deal and its changing terms, see chapters on Syria in previous volumes of *MECS*). Once again, Iran was to supply 1m. tons (20,000 b/d) of high-quality light free oil, and an unspecified amount of "contract oil" at market prices.[36] It seemed, then, that the Syrian oil industry had got into gear. As an unnamed Western official monitoring Syria's economy put it, "wherever you look closer at the oil industry in Syria, it looks a little better."[37]

Another sector which showed signs of recovery was agriculture, which enjoyed better crops because of better climatic conditions than in previous years, pushing cereal production in 1988 to 3.5m. tons, compared with an average of about 1.5m. tons in each of the previous five years. Based on a wheat consumption estimate of half a kilogram per head per day, Syria should have achieved self-sufficiency with production at about 2m. tons. Yet, Syria invited urgent tenders for the supply of 240,000 tons of wheat and 50,000 tons of flour. This urgent demand for wheat imports was caused by wastage, poor storage facilities, transport difficulties, and large-scale smuggling of wheat to Lebanon and Turkey, where market prices were significantly higher than the official prices paid to farmers in Syria. The Syrians were also exporting small quantities of hard wheat to Europe and importing less expensive varieties to earn foreign exchange.[38] In fact, the discrepancy between Syria's cereal production and the urgent imports revealed the darker side of Syria's largely government-owned economy. Shortages of basic foodstuffs, large-scale corruption, and inefficiency continued to dominate the daily life of millions of Syrians.

The official Syrian press itself was full of reports about shortages and the low quality of available foodstuffs.[39] This line of reporting started in 1987 (see *MECS* 1987, p. 639), and was clearly designed to indicate to the public that the leadership was aware of the predicament and was doing its best to confront it. Such was the case also with the anticorruption campaign. Such campaigns had become a constant feature of Syrian life in recent years, almost a yearly ritual, in which the regime made public its determination to uproot corruption. At first, it seemed that the harsh measures used by the regime yielded positive results; but soon matters returned to normal: corruption, theft, and smuggling continued unabated as the next anticorruption campaign was in the making. This year, too, the official press extensively reported the harsh penalties imposed for economic crimes.[40] However, the official press failed to tell its readers about the involvement of high-ranking military and party leaders in economic corruption. This part of the story was told by non-Syrian newspapers known to be hostile to the Syrian regime. Some of the reports named the following prominent personalities as accomplices to corruption: Vice President Zuhayr Mashariqa; Gen. Majid Sa'id, head of the office of General Intelligence;[41] Ahmad 'Abbud, a senior Intelligence officer close to 'Ali Duba[42] (see above); and Gen. Ibrahim al-Safi, commander of the First Armored Division.[43] More details on the web of corruption spun by the Syrian leadership were published by a French journalist in a book, in which Talas, Khaddam, and 'Abd al-Ra'uf al-Kasm were prominently mentioned.[44]

Military expenditures were another principal reason for Syria's economic difficulties. The adherence to the goal of "strategic parity" with Israel (see below) was not mere rhetoric, it drained Syria's economic resources and impeded progress toward significant recovery. According to an unconfirmed report, Syria cut its military budget by 15% in 1988 in order to ease the pressure;[45] the overall budget was $45bn.[46] Prime Minister Mahmud al-Zu'bi declared that the main target of the budget was to finance development projects, but he reiterated the regime's determination to allocate all the resources available to achieve the long-desired "strategic parity."[47]

In the face of these economic difficulties, there were Syrians who called upon the government to adopt a radical solution to the problems: transformation of the Syrian economy from a government-run socialist system to a capitalist one. This was the gist of a comprehensive report compiled by a group of experts and presented to President Asad.[48] During the year there was no indication that the self-styled revolutionary, Hafiz al-Asad, was ready to adopt this drastic recommendation. However, there were signs that Ba'th Party purists were concerned lest further steps of economic liberalization take place and they warned that it was vital that the state should remain in complete control of its natural resources and strictly monitor the movement of foreign currency.[49]

One source of foreign currency which even the purists did not oppose was foreign aid. Given the budgetary constraints of the Gulf oil states and their continuing displeasure at Syria's regional policies, the aid outlook for 1988 was not very bright. Official transfers dropped from $1.061bn. in 1985 to perhaps $800m. in 1986 and to $600m. in 1987. In 1988, they were estimated to be as low as $500m.[50] Syrian officials, however, were quoted as saying that the arrears to the World Bank were likely to be paid, and once done, disbursements that had been held up would be unblocked and eventually new aid programs could begin.[51]

REGIONAL AFFAIRS

STRATEGIC PARITY WITH ISRAEL

As in previous years, the dominant theme in Syria's policy toward Israel in 1988 was the need to achieve "strategic parity." From numerous speeches by Syrian leaders and commentaries by the official media, as well as information about Syria's military buildup, a picture could be drawn regarding the ideological and military dimensions of the concept of "strategic parity." The ideological dimension was based on four major assumptions deeply rooted in Syrian thinking: (1) The Arab-Israeli conflict was a clash not only between states, but also between civilizations. Syria believed that, as in previous historic clashes between civilizations in the ME, time was on the side of the indigenous Arabs and not of the invading "aggressors," i.e., Israel. The fact that time was on the side of the Arabs did not mean that the Arabs should be inactive until they achieved their final victory against Israel. Such a victory could come sooner if the Arabs sustained their pressure on Israel. (2) The Arabs should not sign any binding peace treaty with Israel, but should leave open the option of continuing the conflict until Israel was eliminated. (3) Syria had a focal role in the conflict with Israel. Asad's ideal, strategic vision was a unified Arab nation in which Syria played its rightful, traditional role at the helm of the pan-Arab movement. Moreover, Palestine was a part of "Greater Syria." Syria should not go its own way, as Egypt did, and sign a separate agreement with Israel. Hence, the Golan Heights were not a key to peace between Syria and Israel. They should be returned to Syria, lock, stock,and barrel, but even if this was done, peace would not follow because there were other unresolved problems between the Arabs and Israel. (4) Israel was an aggressive state by nature, an entity which lived by the sword. For this reason, there was only a military solution to the conflict, and such a solution was a pan-Arab responsibility. In the meantime, Syria was willing to carry the burden of the conflict by itself. The aim of the Arab use of force was to get Israel to make concessions it refused to make by diplomatic means.

The slogan of "strategic parity" enabled the Syrian regime to respond to three political needs: it underlay Syria's claim to centrality in Arab politics; offered the Syrian people a noble explanation of their economic predicament; and explained why Syria had not yet started a war against Israel.

When all these components of the concept are put together, it becomes clear that the Syrian definition of parity was multidimensional and comprehensive, and that military preparedness was only one facet. During the year, Syrian leaders, Asad among them, reiterated their loyalty to parity and outlined some of its components. Asad declared in his Revolution Day speech on 8 March that Israel would be defeated, like the Crusaders. If the Arabs cannot defeat Israel now, he asked rhetorically, why rush into capitulationist solutions? Time, he reminded his audience, as well as the rest of the Arab nation, was on the side of the Arabs.[52] A leading Syrian commentator elaborated on the president's speech and distinguished between two kinds of superiority: Israel had "temporary superiority," but the Arabs enjoyed "qualitative and historic" superiority; hence the need to avoid capitulationist solutions because the future favored the Arabs.[53] In the same vein, Mustafa Talas emphasized the "profound historic" positions of Syria, its pan-Arab commitment, and the fact that Palestine and Syria were one.[54] Another Syrian commentator stressed that the conflict was a contest of willpower; it was not only a military conflict, but a confrontation of societies.[55] The Syrian chief of staff declared that there was no hope for peace, the only choice was war with Israel.[56] Hafiz al-Asad told his soldiers that the Syrian Army had greatly improved and that political concessions to Israel were out of the question; those who made them would regret it.[57]

On numerous occasions, Syria's leaders and the media emphasized the need for Arab solidarity against Israel, as had existed in 1973. The repeated calls for Arab solidarity and a pan-Arab drive to achieve parity with Israel were partly vindicated at the Arab emergency summit conference in Algiers in early June, which mentioned the need for such "strategic parity" (see chapter on inter-Arab relations, and below).

Syrian rhetoric was matched by action. Syria's Army continued its feverish and costly preparations for a possible showdown with Israel. These preparations were threefold: (1) developing a "neutralizing response" to Israel's military strength on the ground, on the high seas, and in the air, in the form of well-equipped and heavily manned lines of defense along the border in the Golan Heights and in the Biqa' Valley in Lebanon, a very dense ground-to-air defense system, and coast-to-sea missiles; (2) developing a "retaliatory response" by amassing an impressive number of ground-to-ground missiles; and (3) developing an "offensive response" by establishing a large number of mobile and armored units, airlifted commando units, tactical ground-to-ground missiles, and possibly also chemical weapons.

To achieve all the above required heavy expenditures and foreign supplies of arms. During the year there were numerous reports about Syrian arms deals, including one about a possible sale of a new shorter-range Chinese missile to Syria, much to the consternation of Israeli and American officials.[58] The USSR supplied Syria with more SS-21 ground-to-ground missiles[59] and 30 highly sophisticated MiG-29 aircraft.[60] An unconfirmed report said that the Soviets also agreed to sell Syria Tupolev-22 planes, considered the world's best bbombers, MiG-31 planes, and the huge Antonov-124 transport planes.[61] There was also a report about Soviet agreement on selling Syria Su-24 bombers, considered to be among the best bombers in the Soviet arsenal.[62] According to another report, Syria had begun building a new defense line in the Biqa' Valley in Lebanon with the help of Soviet specialists.[63] There were also reports about Soviet-Syrian cooperation in producing chemical weapons.[64] In addition, the Soviets also expanded a warship base in Tartus on the Syrian coast[65] (see below).

This wave of reports about the Syrian buildup was bound to arouse concern in Israel. Reacting to the alleged Syrian-Chinese deal, Defense Minister Yitzhak Rabin warned, in June, that Syria "should not even contemplate" using missiles against Israel, because the latter would deal it a "death blow."[66] For Syria's part, an editorial in *al-Thawra* claimed that Israeli leaders had "fabricated" a story about the supply of "sophisticated weapons" to Syria in order to create new "pretexts" for pressuring the US Administration into supplying additional weapons and military hardware to Israel.[67] The war of words was intensified in the following months. Senior Israeli officers, including the commander of the Air Force,[68] the commander of the Northern Command,[69] and the chief of staff[70] warned that Syria was preparing for war against Israel. Civilian Israeli commentators developed a more nuanced attitude toward the Syrian buildup, ranging from a belief that the Syrians had already decided in principle to launch a war and were waiting for a pretext to make good their decision,[71] to a more optimistic analysis that Syria acknowledged Israel's military superiority, hence would be doubly careful to evade a confrontation.[72] One analyst even claimed that an Israeli-Syrian *détente* was possible.[73] Other Israeli experts, while displaying obvious concern about the Syrian buildup, expressed the opinion that Syria had invested too many resources in ground-to-ground missiles at the expense of other vital weapons systems.[74]

The Syrians likewise publicly voiced their concern about Israel's intentions. The launching of Israel's alleged "spy" satellite in September was carefully examined,[75] and Syria's minister of telecommunications sent messages to the Arab League urging discussion of this development.[76] Israel's alleged nuclear capability was also cited as a source for concern[77] (for previous Syrian references to nuclear capability, see *MECS* 1986, p. 613).

Despite all the saber rattling, there was no direct military collision between the two countries in 1988. The closest the two countries came to a confrontation was in early May, when Israeli troops numbering up to 2,500 men moved into the eastern sector of South Lebanon (see chapter on armed operations). This limited invasion came after two Israeli soldiers, one of them a senior officer, had been killed during a penetration by the Palestinians of Israel's northern border. The invading Israelis pushed to within a mile of the Syrian-held town of Mashghara, which guards the southern entrance to the strategic Biqa' Valley. Defense Minister Rabin was at pains to reassure Syria that "nothing unexpected took place. Except for a small Syrian force located in Mashghara, due to Hizballah-Amal rifts, we were very far from the Syrian forces."[78] Rabin alluded to the "red-lines" arrangement between Israel and Syria which had existed between 1976 and 1982, and which was designed to prevent an untimely and unmanageable conflict between the two countries.[79] Syria had consistently denied the existence of any such arrangement. However, whenever Israel launched retaliatory raids into Lebanon, even in close proximity to Syria's positions, Syria's response indicated that Damascus was determined to decide the timing, location, and scope of any clash with Israel, surely not until the much-desired "strategic parity" with Israel was achieved.

SYRIA IN LEBANON

The year 1988 was to be an eventful one in the history of the Lebanese civil war as well as Syria's involvement in it, because President Amin Jumayyil's term of office was to expire on 23 September 1988, and a new president was to be elected. In 1987, there was already much discussion in both Syria and Lebanon regarding the elections. The very fact that the presidency was a focal point of attention and discussion in a state as fragmented as Lebanon indicated that many Lebanese politicians still clung to the idea of a united Lebanon, whose sovereignty was personified in an elected president. For Syria, presidential elections in Lebanon amounted to a litmus test of its ability to be the ultimate arbiter in Lebanese politics. Syria's policy of military presence in Lebanon was based on historical, strategic,and political considerations, which gave ground to a claim to legitimacy. A friendly Lebanese president was, therefore, an asset to Syria; a hostile Lebanese president, whose election was legal and whose administration was recognized in the Arab world and internationally, could be a major obstacle for Syrian policy. The stakes were high, therefore, particularly since the elections attracted the attention of other regional powers, such as Israel, Iran, and Arab countries as well as external actors, such as the US. Being the main military power in Lebanon clearly gave Syria the edge over any adversary. Its intervention in the West Beirut fighting in February 1987 further enhanced its position (see *MECS* 1987, pp. 643–45, 642–45, respectively).

Syria's main objective in 1988 was to defuse potentially explosive situations in Lebanon, thus clearing the way for the election of a pro-Syrian candidate as president. First, the Syrians mediated between their Shi'i-backed Amal militia and the PLO, and helped bring an end to Amal's 32-month long military siege of the camps in

Beirut (on the siege, see chapters on Lebanon and the PLO in previous volumes of *MECS*). Syrian forces, therefore, moved to replace Amal's around the camps. The commander of the Syrian forces, 'Ali Hammud, declared that their task was to guarantee the security of the camps, not to surround them for a long time.[80] The Syrian presence in the vicinity of the camps and in other parts of West Beirut was reported to have made life more bearable and secure in the city.[81] In February, the Syrians encouraged the deployment of the all-Shi'i, pro-Amal Sixth Brigade of the Lebanese Army around the southern suburbs of Beirut, long considered the main stronghold of the pro-Iranian Hizballah.[82] This move followed the kidnapping of an American officer in the UN Interim Force in Lebanon (Unifil), Lt. Col. William Higgins, by Hizballah gunmen and the subsequent tension between al-Amal and Hizballah (see chapter on Lebanon). Syria then tried to bring about a reconciliation between two of its allies in Lebanon, the Shi'i leader Nabih Barri and the Druze leader Walid Junblat.[83] It was also reported that Syria tried to reactivate the more comprehensive alliance of the leftist and nationalist parties,[84] as well as the virtually Sunni-dominated al-Murabitun in West Beirut.[85]

Early in April, Syrian-backed Amal and Iranian-backed Hizballah forces clashed in South Lebanon. Amal had the upper hand and gained total control of Tyre, the largest Shi'i town there, after routing Hizballah. Until then, the course of events in Lebanon in the early months of 1988 had been favorable to Syria. But things started to change in early May, when the Hizballah, vanquished in the south, started an offensive against Amal in the southern suburbs of Beirut. After a few days of fighting, in which Hizballah had the upper hand, the Amal-dominated quarters of al- Shiyya, al-Ghubayra, and Harat al-Hurayk were captured by Hizballah, which thus became the sole authority in Beirut's Shi'i suburbs where hundreds of thousands of Shi'is lived, and where, so it was said, 23 foreign hostages were being held.[86] At this point, Syria threatened to intervene in order to put an end to the bloodshed and save Amal from a total humiliating defeat.[87] In fact, Syria had to save its own face. The intra-Shi'i fighting had developed into a major crisis, which confronted Syria with a serious dilemma. The clashes in Beirut as well as in South Lebanon were a new climax in the collision of Syrian and Iranian ambitions in Lebanon. The outcome of the Beirut battle meant that Iran proved superior to Syria in the capital of Lebanon, just meters away from a large concentration of Syrian troops which were there to assert Syrian hegemony in Beirut, and in the rest of Lebanon. Thus, Syria faced a dilemma in daring to deploy its troops in the southern suburbs without first reaching an understanding with Iran: Syria did not do so when it took over West Beirut in February 1987 (see above), and entering the southern suburbs now without agreement with the Iranians could lead to bloodshed and armed confrontation with Hizballah and to a major crisis with Iran. Not entering the suburbs could lead to a serious erosion in Syria's position in Lebanon.

In mid-May Syria and Iran started urgent consultations while thousands of Syrian soldiers, backed up by tanks and heavy artillery, besieged the southern suburbs. Hafiz al-Asad engaged in brinkmanship in Beirut and prevailed. Within a few days an agreement was reached between Syria and Iran by which Syrian troops, without their heavy weapons, were introduced into the southern suburbs; the population there displayed its enthusiasm at the sight of the Syrian troops.[88] Syria's handling of the situation clearly demonstrated maturity and responsibility; Syria was soon to reap the political fruits. Lebanese Prime Minister Salim al-Huss,[89] Amal leader Nabih Barri,[90] and a Hizballah delegation[91] went to Syria to confer with the Syrian leadership. Yet, Syria had some explaining to do, particularly why it had not clashed with Hizballah despite its threats to do so, and why it allowed Hizballah to remain in the southern suburbs even after the Syrian deployment there. Syrian Information Minister Muhammad Salman gave the official response: Syria was in a state of war with Israel and Hizballah was also an enemy of Israel.[92] What the minister failed to say was that Syria also did not wish to further undermine its close alliance with Iran, including its economic relations with the Islamic Republic. Be that as it may, Syria came out almost undamaged from a crisis which could have developed into a major problem.

The road was now open for another Syrian effort to prepare the ground for the Lebanese presidential elections. The Syrians simultaneously pursued four courses of action: (1) they tried to reach an agreement with President Jumayyil, thus ensuring support of at least some Maronite deputies for a Syrian-backed candidate; (2) they tried to lure other Lebanese politicians onto their side or put pressure on them; (3) they extended their military presence in Lebanon to additional areas; and (4) they tried to coordinate their policy in Lebanon with the US in order to ensure American support for a Syrian-backed candidate; such support could neutralize any Israeli objections and possibly also Lebanese Christian objections. On 10 June, Asad met Jumayyil at the Arab summit in Algiers.[93] According to one report, the two leaders reached a secret agreement regarding the reform of the Lebanese political system before the elections.[94]

The Syrian Army in Lebanon also extended its deployment to areas closer to the Israeli-controlled "security zone" in the south.[95] Late in July, Syria tried unsuccessfully to assassinate Samir Ja'ja', the commander of the Lebanese Forces (LF), and perhaps their most bitter rival among the Lebanese Christians.[96] It was also reported that the Syrians made a "deal" with Hizballah to prevent more kidnappings of Westerners in Beirut.[97]

Throughout 1988, Syria was engaged in a dialogue with the US aimed at coordinating their policy in Lebanon, particularly with regard to the presidential elections. This dialogue proved successful in so far as it brought the two sides closer (see below); still the ultimate goal of Syria's policy in Lebanon was to elect a pro-Syrian president and this goal was not achieved. The Lebanese Chamber of Deputies failed to have the required quorum for electing a president, and President Jumayyil exercised his constitutional powers and appointed an emergency cabinet led by the army commander, Gen. Michel 'Awn, himself an unofficial candidate for the presidency (see chapter on Lebanon). Syria was left empty-handed, with a candidate who not only could not possibly be elected, former president Sulayman Faranjiyya, but who also had a tarnished image. Syria's supporters had their own cabinet, which challenged 'Awn's. Thus, while the May showdown in Beirut was a Syrian success, the presidential elections were a Syrian fiasco. True, Syria remained the most powerful force in Lebanon but not powerful enough solely to determine the course of events there, because some Lebanese factions, such as the LF, Gen. 'Awn and his supporters in the Lebanese Army,and even the much discredited President Jumayyil realized that Syria was reluctant to use force when it could cost the Syrian Army dearly in human lives or run the risk of political difficulties for Syria, such as Arab pressures. The expanding relations between the LF and Iraq were just one indication of the potential troubles Syria's Christian enemies in Lebanon could cause Syria.

SYRIA, IRAN, IRAQ, AND THE GULF WAR

The Syrian-Iranian relationship, for a few years in the early 1980s a linchpin of Syria's regional policy, became strained in 1987 and this trend continued throughout 1988 for a variety of reasons: (1) rivalry between the two countries in and over Lebanon; (2) Syria's growing and troubled dependence on Iranian oil supplies (see above); (3) growing pressures on Syria from within the Arab system to abandon its support of Iran and join the overwhelmingly pro-Iraqi Arab consensus regarding the war; and (4) the dynamics of the war brought about a realignment of inter-Arab politics, particularly Egypt's improved relationships with many Arab countries, which was detrimental to Syria's regional interests (see chapter on inter-Arab relations).

The combined effect of these factors led Syria to acquiesce in anti-Iranian resolutions adopted at the Islamic conference in Kuwait in 1987 and the Arab summit conference in Amman in November 1987 (see chapter on inter-Arab relations, *MECS* 1987). Still, a complete Syrian about-face, from support of Iran to an alliance with Iraq, was impossible for three main reasons: (1) Syria did not want to ignite a full-scale conflict with Iran in Lebanon; (2) the rivalry between the two Ba'th regimes in Damascus and Baghdad still seemed to be irreconcilable despite repeated Saudi and Jordanian mediation efforts and occasional direct contacts between the two adversaries, including meetings between President Asad and Saddam Husayn (see chapter on Syria, *MECS* 1987, pp. 646–47). In addition to the deep personal animosity between the two leaders, at stake were claims for superior political legitimacy emanating from the split in the Ba'th Party, problems over the use of the Euphrates waters, and a long history of exploiting Kurdish separatists in both countries against each other — in sum an almost chronic struggle for political supremacy in the Fertile Crescent; (3) a major political volte-face was incompatible with the style of Hafiz al-Asad, who had built his reputation as a canny and shrewd political operator on his patience, resilience,and consistency. For Asad, therefore, to switch sides and endorse Iraq required a great deal of explaining to the Syrian people. He was reluctant to do so, and consequently narrowed his own scope for maneuver.

In dealing with this situation, Syria pursued three lines of action: it tried to bring about a cease-fire in the war, took part in Arab and other forums where Iran came in for condemnation, and continued the war of words with Iraq, including support for Iraqi opposition elements. Early in 1988, Syria's relations with the Gulf states, which eagerly sought a cease-fire, and with Iran were at a critical point, as Syria was playing its mediation card.[98] Syria's argument had always been that keeping on good terms with Iran would enable it to play the part of a mediator. However, Damascus had no contact with Iraq and its mediation role was confined, therefore, to an attempt at promoting a dialogue between Iran and the Gulf states. The official Syrian explanation of its mediation effort was that it was in line with Syria's policy to end the war so that all resources could be directed at Israel, while Iraq tried to distract attention from the Arabs' "major conflict" with Israel.[99]

In its early stage, the Syrian initiative seemed to have some success. On 3 January, Iranian Foreign Minister 'Ali Akbar Velayati said that Tehran welcomed Syria's initiative. It was also reported that Syria had succeeded in getting the Iranians to postpone their much-anticipated offensive. Iraq, however, seemed hostile to the Syrian effort and on 8 January it launched an air strike on Iran's Tabriz refinery, which was followed by attacks on ships off the Iranian coast on 10 and 12 January.

These attacks broke a 10-day lull in the hostilities (on the course of the war, see chapter on the Iraqi-Iranian War). On 19 January, the Iraqi press charged that Syria's mediation efforts were aimed at "whitewashing" Iran and violated the agreement reached at the Amman summit in November 1987 to form a common front against Iran.[100] Syria's fledgling mediation clearly came to an abrupt end and the war of words with Iraq intensified. Iraq was charged with responsibility for the failure;[101] the Iraqis responded by arranging a mass meeting to commemorate the massacres at Hamah in 1982.[102] The mutual recrimination continued unabated during the year.[103] Nothing was really surprising about it, considering the legacy of animosity. Late in December it was reported that the Iraqi Kurdish leader, Mas'ud Barazani (the son of the legendary Mawla Mustafa al-Barazani) was in Damascus, trying to form a united front of the Iraqi opposition against Saddam Husayn's regime.[104] This happened at a time when the Gulf War was over and Syria's leaders were reportedly worried about Iraq's encouragement of the Syrian Muslim opposition and growing support for the LF in Lebanon. It was reported that Syria's security forces stepped up their surveillance of the border areas between Syria and Iraq.[105] Saddam's involvement in Lebanon was depicted by the Syrian media as the beginning of a new axis: 'Awn-Ja'ja'-Saddam Husayn in alliance with Israel.[106] The ferocity of the verbal attacks on Iraq was no doubt motivated by Syria's concern that once Iraq was not engaged in the Gulf War, it would try to subvert Syria's regime and its regional policies.

While Syria had advocated an end to the war, the Iranian decision to accept UN Security Council Resolution 598 calling for just that caught Syria off guard. Shortly before, the two countries were on the verge of a collision in Beirut (see above), but as soon as this crisis was resolved, in late May, Syria was at pains to reassure Iran about its support. Mustafa Talas declared that there were "no disagreements whatsoever" between the two countries.[107] Still, Damascus did not object to the anti-Iranian resolution adopted at the Arab summit conference in Algiers, in June. And when the US downed the Iranian airbus civilian plane in early July, Syria was quick to condemn the US action.[108] (On the incident, see chapter on the Iraqi-Iranian War.) After Iran's acceptance of the cease-fire, the Syrians were quick to congratulate Iran and challenge Iraq to turn all its resources against the "Zionist" enemy.[109] Velayati arrived in Damascus on 13 August to confer with the Syrian leadership regarding the new situation.[110] Toward the end of the year, there was an unverified report that Syria and Iran had signed a secret agreement to coordinate terror activities against some Gulf states[111] (for further discussion of these relations, see chapter on inter-Arab relations).

SYRIA AND THE PLO

The basic parameters of the relationship between Syria and the PLO remained intact during 1988. Syria continued to object to Yasir 'Arafat's leadership and was determined to prevent any extension of the PLO's presence in Lebanon. What complicated matters for Syria regarding the PLO was that the Palestinian uprising in the West Bank and Gaza Strip seemed to enhance the PLO's pan-Arab and international prestige which was dramatically highlighted by the opening of an official dialogue between the US and the PLO (see chapters on the United States and the Middle East, and the Palestine Liberation Organization). Another burden on Syrian policy with regard to the PLO was the apparent change in PLO policy toward

Israel. Consequently, Syria's official stand toward this conflict became harsher and more militant than that of the PLO. This situation fitted Syria's desire to be the undisputed flag bearer of the Arab struggle against Israel, but it also enhanced Syria's image as a radical, uncompromising state, an image not so popular in the international arena and one which contributed to Syria's overall growing isolation in the Arab world.

At the beginning of the year, there were signs of a Syrian-PLO *rapprochement*. The pro-Syrian Amal militia decided in January to lift the siege around the Palestinian camps in West Beirut. The siege was seen as an embarrassment to Amal and Syria at a time when the plight of the Palestinians in the West Bank and Gaza Strip was attracting much Arab and international attention. Syria also wanted to ease tensions in Beirut as part of its strategy of dealing with the presidential elections in Lebanon. Soviet mediation efforts between Syria and the PLO played a role as well, and in December 1987 Damascus had already reportedly demonstrated its goodwill by releasing 150 'Arafat supporters from their detention in Syria.[112] A senior Lebanese commentator reported that nine unidentified PLO leaders had sent a letter to Syria's leaders urging a resumption of the high-level PLO-Syrian dialogue. Damascus, according to this report, had reacted positively to the suggestion, asking the PLO to forward a detailed position paper.[113] Early in March, there was a report about a meeting between Syrian Foreign Minister Faruq al-Shar' and the PLO's Faruq Qaddumi and Salah Khalaf (Abu Iyad) in Algiers, which was also attended by Algeria's foreign minister.[114] Early in April, "informed" Palestinian sources reported that a close 'Arafat associate, Hasib al-Sabbagh, had paid an unannounced visit to Damascus, during which he held talks with Khaddam, in a bid to bridge the gap between Syria and the PLO.[115]

The Syrian-PLO contacts were given a dramatic boost following the assassination of the PLO's chief of military operations, Khalil al-Wazir (Abu Jihad; see chapter on armed operations), and his subsequent funeral in Damascus on 20 April. The funeral itself, in the center of Damascus, was attended by senior pro-'Arafat and pro-Syrian Palestinian leaders and turned into a major show of support for the PLO and the Palestinian cause.[116] 'Arafat, however, failed to attend and his absence indicated that no major progress had been achieved in Syrian-PLO contacts prior to the funeral; Syria refused to assure 'Arafat that he would meet with President Asad, because it did not want to provide 'Arafat with an opportunity to demonstrate to thousands of frenzied Palestinians that he had prevailed over Syrian attempts to eliminate him.[117]

Syria, however, did not close the door on a dialogue with 'Arafat. On 24 April,[118] for the first time since his expulsion from Syria in June 1983, 'Arafat came to Damascus. The meeting was followed by a report about a Syrian decision to release 2,000 pro-'Arafat Palestinians from detention in Syria and about attempts to organize a three-way summit, attended by Asad, Jordan's King Husayn, and 'Arafat.[119] According to other reports, Syria released only a few Palestinian detainees.[120] The Gulf press reported that the Asad-'Arafat talks resulted in an agreement on the return of several al-Fath military battalions to Syria, as well as the convening of a minisummit with the participation of Asad, 'Arafat, and Libyan and Algerian leaders.[121] PLO leaders sounded optimistic about the prospects of a continuing improvement in relations with Syria and its possible implications. Na'if Hawatima of the Democratic Front for the Liberation of Palestine declared that the normalization of PLO-Syrian relations meant "drawing Jordan towards the correct joint policies of Syria and the PLO."[122] Salah Khalaf said that the meeting resulted in an agreement to preserve and escalate the uprising in the West Bank and Gaza Strip.[123] After meeting Asad once again during the Algiers summit conference, 'Arafat declared that a "new page was opened in PLO-Syrian relations."[124]

These Palestinian statements proved premature. Shortly after the Asad-'Arafat meeting in Damascus, fighting broke out again in Palestinian camps in West Beirut between 'Arafat loyalists and Syria's Palestinian supporters, mainly from the Abu Musa faction. By early July, the camps fell to the pro-Syrians, whom the Syrian troops surrounding the camps had allowed to move men and weapons into the camps during the battles. 'Arafat's men were evacuated from the camps to the Sidon area.[125] The fighting unleashed a war of words between Syria and the PLO. Bassam Abu Sharif, one of 'Arafat's closest advisers, charged that the ousting of PLO men from Beirut was "part of the Syrian-American plan."[126] A pro-Syrian source said that "involving Syria's name" in the Palestinian in-fighting was wrong, and that Syria had nothing to do with it. In fact, the Syrians claimed, the battles and 'Arafat's defeat were a sign of growing opposition to 'Arafat in the Palestinian arena.[127] This opposition, they said, focused on 'Arafat's political moves, particularly the statements made by Bassam Abu Sharif.

Clearly, the breakup of the Syrian-PLO dialogue so soon after its resumption indicated that there were unbridgeable gaps between them. To begin with, Hafiz al-Asad and Yasir 'Arafat loathed each other personally, and without personal trust between them no significant Syrian-PLO dialogue could develop. Beyond the personal factor, Syria was reluctant to give 'Arafat's loyalists any foothold in Lebanon, particularly not during a year of presidential elections. This decision was also in line with the Syrian policy of preventing the presence in Lebanon of any power which might challenge Syria's supremacy there. In addition, Syria objected to the PLO's policy of independent Palestinian decision. It resented the PLO *rapprochement* with Egypt, its good relations with Iraq and, above all, its "moderate" political posture, as was exemplified by Abu Sharif's statements and, toward the end of the year, by the resolutions of the Palestine National Council (see chapter on the Palestine Liberation Organization). The pro-Syrian Palestinian factions boycotted the meeting, and Damascus fumed over the "moderate tone" of the decisions and the opening of a dialogue between the PLO and the US. Still, even Hafiz al-Asad could not ignore the PLO's declaration: "The establishment of the Palestinian state," read an official announcement in Damascus, "is consistent with Syria's policy, with the Arab summit resolutions, and with international legitimacy."[128]

In summary, it seemed at the end of the year that Syria's rift with 'Arafat's PLO was as distant as ever from healing. Syria scored a victory over 'Arafat by expelling his men from the camps in Beirut, but 'Arafat had the last word, riding high on a wave of diplomatic recognition and supportive media coverage while Syria seemed to be isolated.

ATTEMPTS TO EVADE ISOLATION

While the cumulative effects of various developments in inter-Arab politics pushed Syria toward growing diplomatic isolation, the Syrian regime was determined to prevent it from being complete and irreversible. Syria's participation in the Amman summit of November 1987 was followed by a mediation effort in the Iraqi-Iranian War, conciliatory moves toward the PLO (see above) and the establishment of diplomatic relations with Oman,[129] a pro-Western and pro-Egyptian Arab country. Syria also attended the three-day Arab summit in Algiers in June 1988. This time Syria did not impose preconditions, as it had before the Amman summit when it insisted that the agenda contain more than only a discussion of the Gulf War. Syria's reward came when the Algiers conference "affirmed the renewal of the obligation to support the states confronting Israel to enable them to strengthen their defense capabilities and reinforce their potentialities in order to liberate the occupied Arab territories and recover usurped Arab rights." The Algiers conference also alluded favorably to the need to achieve "strategic parity" between the Arabs and Israel[130] (see chapter on inter-Arab relations).

During the year, Syria demonstrated its solidarity with Arab countries when they seemed to be threatened by Israel or by other adversaries. Two particular cases stand out. On 5 April, a Kuwaiti plane, hijacked on a flight from Bangkok to Kuwait, was flown to Mashhad in Iran. After the aircraft flew out of Mashhad on 8 April, Syrian troops in control of Beirut airport took strict measures to prevent it from landing there; the plane was finally allowed to land at Larnaca in Cyprus[131] (for details, see chapter on Kuwait). Syria had many good reasons not to allow the plane to land in Beirut, among them the desire to throw off the image of association with international terrorism, as well as a reluctance to get involved in a conflict with Iran and the pro-Iranian factions in Lebanon. In addition, the episode enabled Syria to demonstrate its support for Kuwait and improve relations with it, a point which Syrian spokesmen were quick to seize upon.[132] Syria also showed solidarity with Saudi Arabia, following an alleged Israeli warning to Riyadh regarding its purchase of Chinese missiles (see chapter on Saudi Arabia). Syria declared that any attack on Saudi Arabia would be considered an attack on Syria itself[133] and used the opportunity to renew its call for a joint Arab effort to establish "strategic parity" with Israel.[134]

An important outcome of Syria's efforts to avoid total isolation in the Arab world was the emerging informal dialogue with Egypt in which two countries, Saudi Arabia and particularly Jordan, played the role of mediator. Syria's relations with Jordan during 1988 continued to be friendly, a trend that began in late 1985 and has persisted since then (see chapters on Syria and Jordan in previous volumes of *MECS*). Jordan, which had friendly relations with both Syria and Egypt, sought to reconcile these two bitter enemies, because only Arab solidarity could face up to Israel's alleged stubbornness. Such solidarity would be "qualitative progress in the Arab struggle...mainly with regard to the Palestinian question and the continued Israeli occupation of the Golan Heights."[135] Such language appealed to Syria's rulers, and thus toward the end of 1988, there was a flurry of diplomatic activity designed to reconcile Syria with Egypt. Early in December, a Jordanian newspaper quoted an unnamed Arab diplomat as saying that King Husayn was trying to organize a Jordanian-Syrian-Egyptian summit in Amman.[136] On 4 December, Jordanian Prime Minister Zayd al-Rifa'i visited Damascus, where he discussed this issue with Asad. A Jordanian source was later quoted as saying that improvement of relations between Damascus and Cairo might be a long process.[137] This subject was also raised in Husayn's meetings with Egyptian President Mubarak in November,[138] and with Asad and King Fahd of Saudi Arabia in mid-December. Reports from Riyadh indicated that Saudi leaders were pressing for a summit between Asad and Mubarak.[139] The Syrian press did not mention the possibility of such a conference, but reiterated the call for Arab solidarity against Israel.[140] Such intensive diplomatic activity led to reports about imminent resumption of diplomatic relations between Syria and Egypt.[141] (See also chapter on Egypt).

While these relations were not restored until the end of 1988, the reports and rumors were not without foundation. Syrian and Egyptian sources were on record regarding the desirability of such a restoration, indicating that better relations were in the making. Egypt's foreign minister confirmed that there were attempts to normalize relations with Syria[142] and a senior Egyptian journalist enthusiastically discussed the possibility of restoration of "full and solid relations with Damascus."[143] A "senior Syrian official," later identified as Foreign Minister Faruq al-Shar',[144] praised Egypt publicly for recognizing the Palestinian state, in face of what Damascus called "pressures from Israel." Al-Shar' also approved of Egypt's commitment to the Joint Arab Defense Treaty which links Arab states.[145]

SYRIA IN THE INTERNATIONAL ARENA

SYRIA AND THE SOVIET UNION

Syria's relations with the Soviet Union during 1988 basically continued a trend much in evidence during 1987: they reflected both the fundamental strength of the relationship as well as difficulties emanating from conflicting interests in specific issues. During 1988, it seemed that the conflicting interests outweighed the fundamental agreements. An Arab newspaper known as a keen observer of Syria analyzed in March the state of relationships between the two countries and its conclusion was straightforward: they were at a very delicate stage. Damascus complained that the Soviets delegated junior officials to conduct the contacts with it, in contrast to the situation preceding Gorbachev's rise to power in 1985. The Soviets, for their part, complained that the Syrians did not pay regularly for their arms purchases. There were also conflicting interests regarding Lebanon and the Syrian policy toward the PLO.[146] Still, it was virtually impossible to find public Syrian pronouncements of displeasure with the Soviet Union, not even after Soviet moves designed to improve relations with Israel, such as raising the level of Israel's consular delegation in Moscow (see chapter on the Soviet Union and the Middle East).

On the occasion of the eighth anniversary of the Soviet-Syrian Treaty of Friendship and Cooperation, the Syrian press was at pains to praise the ties between the two countries and Moscow's role in the ME.[147] Nevertheless, there were signs of strain. Syria received a great deal of sophisticated Soviet arms (see above), but not everything that it desired. Hafiz al-Asad was displeased with alleged Soviet designs to convene an international peace conference on the ME, in which there would be some form of direct negotiations between the Arabs and Israel, which Syria vehemently opposed. The Syrians also expressed concern about alleged Soviet designs to arrange a direct dialogue between the PLO and Israel.[148] There was a report that the Soviets were so displeased with Syria's contacts with the US over Lebanon (see below) that they leaked details of the contacts to the Lebanese press in order to abort them.[149] According to another report, Syrian leaders, incensed with the state of their ties with the Soviet Union, called upon Syrian Communist leaders to condemn Gorbachev's policy of *glasnost*.[150]

SYRIA AND WESTERN EUROPE

During 1987, Syria was engaged in an intensive effort to restore its diplomatic and economic relations with WestEuropean countries to what they had been before 1986, when these relations were severed as a result of Syria's involvement in international terrorism (see *MECS* 1987, pp. 651–52). This Syrian effort was very visible also in 1988.

The FRG's Foreign Minister, Hans-Dietrich Genscher, arrived in Damascus on 15 January. Subjects covered in his talks with Syrian leaders included the restoration of full economic ties between Syria and the EEC, for which the FRG assumed the presidential responsibility in the first half of 1988.[151] On 2 March, Syria and the EEC signed an agreement by which Syria would receive $11m. from the EEC for its high institute for technology.[152]

Relations between Syria and France were generally shaped by the problem of French hostages in Beirut. Late in April, on the eve of the first round of France's presidential elections, the hostages were to be released, but the release was aborted. According to one report, Syria had demanded that it sponsor the release and that the hostages be freed in Damascus instead of Beirut.[153] The hostages were finally freed on 4 May when they were handed over first to the Syrian authorities in West Beirut. This action took place in the final days of the second round of the French presidential campaign. Prime Minister Jacques Chirac thanked the Iranian Government, but also praised President Asad for his personal action and interest.[154] The murky nature of the deals concerning the hostages and their release was underlined by France's decision on 3 May to expel a Syrian businessman, 'Umram Adham, from France. Adham was known to be a mediator between the French and Syrian governments and his expulsion was related to his suspected authorship of a lengthy article in a pro-Syrian Beirut newspaper, *al-Haqiqa*, which criticized Chirac's Government over the hostage issue.[155] Adham's expulsion order was canceled in July.[156]

Diplomatic relations between Syria and Great Britain remained ruptured during 1988. Britain demanded that any restoration of relations would be preceded by the release of Terry Waite from captivity, apparently in West Beirut[157] (on contacts regarding Waite's release in 1987, see *MECS* 1987, p. 651). Late in October, four British parliamentarians (two from the Labor Party and two from the Conservative Party) visited Damascus, much to the chagrin of the Thatcher Government. On this occasion, Syrian Foreign Minister Faruq al-Shar' called upon Britain to improve relations.[158] After the visit, a resumption of ties was anticipated,[159] but by the end of 1988 they had yet to materialize.

SYRIA AND THE UNITED STATES

The restoration of full diplomatic relations between the US and Syria, the partial lifting of American trade sanctions against Syria, and diplomatic contacts indicated that Syrian-American relations had improved during 1987 (see *MECS* 1987, pp. 652–53). This improvement continued during 1988. Three subjects were at the top of the list in their relationship: the question of American hostages in Lebanon; the ME peace process; and presidential elections in Lebanon, including attempts at achieving a political settlement there. In mid-February, Assistant Secretary of State for Near Eastern Affairs Richard Murphy visited Damascus and discussed the hostages issue with Asad. Asad reportedly said that Syria was not interested in a conflict with Iran and its Lebanese allies over this matter.[160] However, when an American officer, Lt. Col. Higgins who served in Unifil, was kidnapped (see above), Syria was active in trying to locate him.[161] The question of hostages resurfaced in September, following another visit by Murphy to Damascus. According to an unconfirmed report, Murphy received a written Syrian commitment to do whatever possible to bring about the release of American hostages before the American presidential elections. This commitment was part of a larger American-Syrian agreement regarding Lebanon[162] (see below). Early in October, an Indian hostage, who was a US resident and a teacher at the American University in Beirut, was released by his captors in Beirut. The State Department was publicly at pains to downplay Syria's role in securing the release, apparently because Iran claimed in public that it was secured due to its own efforts.[163] Syria's foreign minister, however, said a few days later that improvement in relations between Syria and the US now depended solely on Washington, indicating that Syria had already displayed its goodwill. The foreign minister added that the issue of the US hostages in Lebanon was unrelated to other issues.[164]

The moribund ME peace process was revived early in 1988, when US Secretary of State George Shultz, deciding personally to make an effort to solve the Palestinian problem, went to the ME on 25 February (see chapters on the United States and the Middle East, and the Middle East peace process). Shultz visited Damascus on 27 February for the first time since the ill-fated Israeli-Lebanese talks in 1983. According to some reports, the US was adopting a two-pronged approach toward Syria, in which the Golan Heights issue and the Palestinian question would be dealt with separately. Early in March, Shultz returned to the region and had another round of talks with Asad.[165] The talks failed to change Syria's basic positions; the Syrians claimed that the US initiative was designed to bring an end to the Palestinian uprising in the West Bank and Gaza Strip.[166] Vice President Khaddam maintained that the US policy was still a captive of the US-Israeli relationship. The US stand, he claimed, must be clear on the question of Israeli withdrawal from all the occupied Arab territories.[167] While Khaddam did not say so specifically, he clearly alluded to Syria's long-standing fear that the issue of the Golan Heights might be left on the back burner. Hafiz al-Asad, as usual, passed the final Syrian judgment on the US initiative, when he declared that it included the "same proposals, same spirit, same essence though the words were different...there is nothing new."[168] Additional meetings between Shultz and Asad on 5 April and 6 June failed to elicit any changed Syrian reaction. After the June meeting, Shultz said bluntly that he personally objected to an independent Palestinian state in the West Bank and Gaza Strip.[169]

The sharp difference of opinion regarding the peace process demonstrated the constraints on American-Syrian relations. There were other manifestations of these constraints. The US did not lift all trade sanctions against Syria, because of its alleged connections with the notorious Abu Nidal terrorist group.[170] Syria, for its part, traded verbal salvos with the US over the latter's downing of an Iranian plane (see above) and American threats against Libya at the end of the year.[171] Relations between the US and Syria also had a brighter side: the new US ambassador, Edward Djerjian, was esteemed by Syria's leaders.[172] American oil interests were involved in oil exploration and development in Syria (see above) and the two countries were engaged in an intensive dialogue regarding Lebanon. The dialogue failed to solve the political impasse in Lebanon, but it demonstrated the desire of both countries to exploit to the maximum areas of potential cooperation.

Early in 1988, American and Syrian officials started a dialogue regarding Lebanon. Initially, it was April Glaspie, the State Department director for Lebanon, Jordan, and Syrian affairs (who was soon to become US ambassador in Iraq) who discussed the subject with the Syrians. Then, Shultz too, in his February, March, and April talks with Asad, touched upon the Lebanese issue. Shultz also met President Jumayyil in Cyprus while on his way from Jordan to the US on 8 April. Shultz told reporters that the US and Syria were discussing written proposals for new power-sharing arrangements giving special attention to "minority rights." He said the goal was to make sure that the presidential elections took place successfully.[173] Arab sources revealed more details about the Shultz-Asad understanding: (1) Israel will withdraw from South Lebanon and the South Lebanese Army will be merged with the Lebanese Army; (2) the powers of the Speaker of the Lebanese Chamber of Deputies will be enhanced; (3) the government will not be based on a confessional status; (4) Syria will ensure the holding of the presidential elections on schedule; (5) Syria will enjoy a "special status" in Lebanon; and (6) the US will pay Syria $200m. for Syria's war against drug trafficking in Lebanon.[174] According to another report, the two countries also agreed to terminate the armed Palestinian presence, first in Beirut, then later along the coast to Sidon.[175] On the eve of the would-be elections, Syria and the US cemented their agreement by picking a joint candidate, Mikha'il Dahir, for president.[176] All this was to no avail. But even after the thwarting of the elections, American-Syrian discussions regarding Lebanon continued.[177]

NOTES

For the place and frequency of publications cited here, and for the full name of the publication, news agency, radio station, or monitoring service where an abbreviation is used, please see "List of Sources." Only in the case of more than one publication bearing the same name is the place of publication noted here. In the present chapter, however, all references to *al-Thawra*, are to the Damascus newspaper of that name, unless otherwise stated.

1. M. Ma'oz, *Asad: Sphinx of Damascus* (London: Weidenfeld & Nicolson, 1988); P. Seale, *Asad of Syria: The Struggle for the Middle East* (London: I.B.Tauris & Co. Ltd., 1988).
2. Seale, p. 493.
3. Ibid., p. 492.
4. *Kull al-'Arab*, 4 April; also, *al-Muharrir*, 2 April; *al-Thawra*, Baghdad, 17 April 1988.
5. *Kull al-'Arab*, ibid.
6. *Al-Muharrir*, ibid.
7. *Al-Sharq al-Jadid*, 8 August 1988.
8. *Al-Muharrir*, 9 July 1988.
9. *Al-Dustur*, London, 3 October 1988 (quoting a Spanish newspaper, *El Pais*).
10. AFP, 26 December 1988.
11. VoL, 18 February — DR, 19 February 1988.
12. *Al-Bayadir al-Siyasi*, 5 September 1988.
13. VoL, 5 December; *al-Watan al-'Arabi*, 16 December 1988.
14. *Al-Nashra*, Athens, 5 September 1988.
15. *MM*, 12 December 1988.
16. This list is based on ibid. and *al-Watan al-'Arabi*, 26 August 1988.
17. *Al-Masira*, 15 February 1988.
18. *Al-Watan al-'Arabi*, 2 December 1988.
19. Chris Kutschera in *ME*, April 1988.
20. Ibid.

21. *Al-Muharrir*, 23 July 1988.
22. *Al-Muharrir*, 17 December 1988.
23. *Al-Muharrir*, 27 February 1988.
24. *Al-Nashra*, 16 May 1988.
25. *Al-Jumhuriyya*, Baghdad, 8 April; *al-Dustur*, London, 18 April; INA, 25 May; *al-Yawm al-Sabi'*, 8 July 1988.
26. *Al-Nashra*, 5 September 1988.
27. *Middle East Insider*, 19 September 1988.
28. *Al-Musawwar*, 8 July 1988.
29. On Akram al-Hawrani's career, see P. Seale, *The Struggle for Syria: A Study of Post-War Arab Politics, 1945–1958* (London: Oxford University Press, 1965); I. Rabinovich, *Syria Under the Ba'th 1963–66: The Army-Party Symbiosis* (Jerusalem: Hebrew University Press, 1972).
30. *Al-Watan al-'Arabi*, 23 December 1988.
31. *JP*, 23 June 1988 (quoting from Reuters report).
32. *CR:* Syria, No. 3, 1988, p. 12.
33. *Al-Bayan*, Beirut, 28 October 1988.
34. *Al-Ba'th*, 20 November 1988.
35. *CR:* Syria, 1988–89, pp. 32–34.
36. *CR:* Syria, No. 3, 1988, p. 16.
37. *FT*, 28 September 1988.
38. Ibid.
39. *Al-Thawra*, 9 April, 3 May; *al-Ba'th*, 24 May, 29 May, 5 June; also a report to this effect in the Polish newspaper, *Tribuna Ludo*, 22 May 1988.
40. *Al-Ba'th*, 10 July, 24 October; *Nidal al-Sha'b*, quoted by *Ma'ariv*, 22 August; *Tishrin*, 21 May, 23 October; *Akhbar al-Usbu'*, 29 September 1988.
41. *Al-Muharrir*, 26 March 1988.
42. *Al-Thawra*, Baghdad, 16 April 1988.
43. *Al-Muharrir*, 7 May 1988.
44. About the book, see *al-Jumhuriyya*, Baghdad, 25 October; another report about Khaddam, see *al-Akhbar*, Cairo, 22 September 1988.
45. *Ha'aretz*, 8 May 1988.
46. *Ha'aretz*, 25 July 1988.
47. *Al-Thawra*, 25 November 1988.
48. The report was leaked to and published by *al-Yawm al-Sabi'* (an anti-Syrian publication), July-August 1988.
49. The economic editor of *Tishrin*, 15 November 1988.
50. *CR:* Syria, No. 1, 1988, p. 4.
51. *CR:* Syria, No. 3, 1988, p. 5.
52. *Al-Thawra*, 9 March 1988.
53. Muhammad Zurf, *Tishrin*, 13 March 1988.
54. R. Damascus, 12 April 1988.
55. Dr. Bahjat Bighjati, *Tishrin*, 16, 18 July 1988.
56. *Ha'aretz*, 1 August 1988.
57. *Ha'aretz*, 2 August 1988.
58. *NYT*, 22 June; *IHT*, 23 June 1988.
59. *Ha'aretz*, 6 July 1988.
60. *Al-Wafd*, 12 July 1988.
61. *Al-Ittihad al-Usbu'i*, 7 April 1988.
62. *Ha'aretz*, 30 August 1988 (quoting *al-Ittihad*).
63. Voice of Free Lebanon, 18 September — DR, 19 September 1988.
64. *Ma'ariv*, 1 July; *Ha'aretz*, 27 September 1988 (quoting the French weekly *Le Point*).
65. *FR*, 14 April; *NYT*, 28 August 1988.
66. Israeli TV, 23 June — DR, 23 June 1988.
67. *Al-Thawra*, 23 June 1988.
68. *Ha'aretz*, 18 July 1988.
69. *Ma'ariv*, 2 August 1988.
70. *Ma'ariv*, 31 August 1988.

71. Y. Olmert and A. Levite, *Ha'aretz*, 12 July 1988.
72. Z. Schiff, *Ha'aretz*, 4 August 1988.
73. A. Yaniv, *Middle East Insight*, January-February 1988, pp. 27–33.
74. *Ma'ariv*, 18 July 1988 (quoting *US News and World Report*, which quoted Israeli military and civilian experts).
75. Ilyas Khuri, *al-Ba'th*, 21 September 1988.
76. R. Damascus, 29 September — DR, 29 September 1988.
77. *Tishrin*, 27 September 1988.
78. *CR:* Syria, No. 3, 1988, p. 8.
79. On the "red-lines" arrangement, see Y. Olmert, "The Lebanese Crisis: The Dangers to Security in the Mediterranean," *Adelphi Papers*, No. 230, Part 11, Spring 1988, pp. 21–32.
80. VoL, 20 January — DR, 21 January 1988.
81. *JP*, 24 February 1988 (quoting a story in *The Observer*).
82. VoL, 28 February 1988.
83. *Al-Hawadith*, 11 March 1988.
84. *Al-Muharrir*, 12 March 1988.
85. *NAD*, 29 March 1988.
86. *Ma'ariv*, 17 May 1988.
87. *The Guardian*, 10 May 1988.
88. *IHT*, 28 May; *Ma'ariv*, 29 May 1988.
89. R. Monte Carlo, 25 May 1988.
90. R. Beirut, 17 May — DR, 18 May 1988.
91. AFP, 26 May 1988.
92. Quoted by *Ma'ariv*, 30 May 1988.
93. R. Beirut, 10 June 1988.
94. *Al-Qabas International*, 14 July 1988.
95. *Ma'ariv*, 29 June 1988 (quoting R. Beirut).
96. Middle East TV, 27 July 1988.
97. *The Times*, 23 August 1988.
98. *Al-Ba'th*, 29 January 1988.
99. R. Damascus, 3 February — DR, 3 February 1988.
100. *CR:* Syria, No. 1, 1988, p. 10.
101. *Al-Ba'th*, 11 February 1988.
102. *Al-Thawra*, Baghdad, 25 February 1988.
103. *Tishrin*, 13 July (about corruption in Iraq); R. Damascus, 19 July — DR, 19 July (about Iraqi responsibility for the war); *al-Ba'th*, 10 August; *al-Thawra*, 3 September; R. Damascus, 8 September — DR, 9 September 1988 (on alleged atrocities committed against Saddam's enemies in Iraq); JANA, 13 September — DR, 14 September 1988 (condemning Iraq's use of chemical weapons in the Gulf War).
104. Iranian TV, 21 December 1988.
105. *Ma'ariv*, 23 August 1988.
106. *Al-Thawra*, 27 October 1988.
107. R. Tehran, 19 May — DR, 20 May 1988.
108. R. Damascus, 5 July — DR, 6 July 1988.
109. *Tishrin, al-Ba'th*, 20 July 1988.
110. R. Damascus, 13 August — DR, 15 August 1988.
111. *Al-Dustur*, London, 10 October 1988.
112. *CR:* Syria, No. 1, 1988, p. 12.
113. Walid Shaqir, *al-Safir*, 4 March 1988.
114. *Al-Masira*, 14 March 1988.
115. *Al-Ittihad*, Abu Dhabi, 8 April 1988.
116. For a detailed description of the participants, see *al-Bayadir al-Siyasi*, 23 April 1988.
117. *FT*, 22 April 1988.
118. *CR:* Syria, No. 2, 1988, p. 9.
119. *Ha'aretz*, 18 April 1988.
120. *Al-Anba*, Kuwait, 3 May 1988, quoting Palestinian and Lebanese sources.
121. GNA (quoting from *al-Ittihad* and *al-Siyasa*), 2 May — DR, 2 May 1988.

122. KUNA, 2 May — DR, 2 May 1988.
123. *CR:* Syria, No. 3, 1988, p. 10.
124. R. Monte Carlo, 10 June 1988.
125. *CR:* Syria, No. 3, 1988; ibid.
126. Ibid.
127. Louis Faris, R. Monte Carlo, 1 July — DR, 1 July 1988.
128. *Tishrin*, 17 November 1988.
129. *CR:* Syria, No. 1,1988, p. 10.
130. *CR:* Syria, No. 3, 1988, p. 11.
131. *CR:* Syria, No. 2, 1988, p. 11.
132. R. Damascus, KUNA, 12 April — DR, 13 April 1988.
133. *Al-Sharq*, 6 April 1988.
134. *Al-Thawra*, 5 April 1988.
135. *Al-Dustur*, Amman, 25 December 1988.
136. *Akhbar al-Usbu'*, 1 December 1988.
137. AFP, 4 December 1988.
138. *Al-Anba*, Kuwait, 2 December 1988.
139. *FT*, 15 December 1988.
140. *Al-Ba'th, Tishrin*, 15 December 1988.
141. *Al-Shira'*, 5 December; *al-Siyasa*, Kuwait, 13 December; MENA, 23 December 1988 (quoting Arab lawyers taking part in a meeting with Asad).
142. MENA, 5 December 1988.
143. Muhsin Muhammad, *al-Jumhuriyya*, Cairo, 10 December 1988.
144. *FT*, 15 December 1988.
145. *FT*, 25 November 1988.
146. *Al-Qabas*, 20 March 1988.
147. *Al-Thawra*, 8 October 1988.
148. *Ma'ariv*, 16 October 1988 (quoting from *al-Qabas*).
149. *NAD*, 14 November 1988.
150. *al-Watan al-'Arabi*, 23 December 1988.
151. *CR:* Syria, No. 1, 1988, p. 7.
152. *Al-Ba'th*, 3 March 1988.
153. Voice of Free Lebanon, 26 April — DR, 27 April 1988.
154. *CR:* Syria, No. 3, 1988, pp. 8–9.
155. Ibid., p. 9.
156. *Al-Diyar*, 12 July 1988.
157. *Shu'un al-Sa'a*, 7 August 1988.
158. *Ha'aretz*, 25 October 1988.
159. *Al-Sharq al-Jadid*, 13 November 1988.
160. *NAD*, 15 February 1988.
161. *Al-Usbu' al-'Arabi*, 21 March 1988.
162. *Al-Muharrir*, 24 September 1988.
163. *Ha'aretz*, 5 October 1988.
164. *Al-Ittihad*, Abu Dhabi, 8 October 1988.
165. *CR:* Syria, No. 2, 1988, p. 6.
166. *Al-Ba'th*, 1 March 1988.
167. SANA, 8 March — DR, 9 March 1988.
168. Asad's speech on the 25th anniversary of the Ba'th revolution, *al-Ba'th*, 9 March 1988.
169. *Ha'aretz*, 7 June 1988.
170. *Ha'aretz*, 26 August 1988.
171. R. Damascus, 25 December 1988.
172. *Al-Safir*, 6 May; *al-Ra'y*, 16 May 1988.
173. *CR:* Syria, No. 2, 1988, p. 10.
174. *Al-Muharrir*, 16 April 1988.
175. *Al-Sharq al-Awsat*, 15 July 1988.
176. DR, 18 September; *JP*, 19 September 1988.
177. *Al-Siyasa*, Kuwait, 30 October; *al-Anwar*, 23 December 1988.

Turkey
(Türkiye Cumhuriyeti)

WILLIAM M. HALE

Nineteen-eighty-eight was a year of mixed fortunes for Turkey. Domestically, the country enjoyed relative political stability, especially when compared to the turbulent days of the 1970s. Thanks to the increased majority which he had won in the general elections of November 1987, there was no serious chance that Prime Minister Turgut Özal would be outvoted in parliament. Except in the Kurdish provinces of the southeast, public order was generally well assured, and the gradual withdrawal of the military from the political stage continued. On the other hand, the government's popularity was under severe strain. Undoubtedly, the major cause was the state of the economy — in particular, the surge in inflation to a peak of almost 90% and the painful effects of the measures which the government belatedly took to cope with it. Political life was also affected by a constitutional referendum, held in September 1988, which most Turks almost certainly regarded as unnecessary, and a tussle within the ruling Motherland Party (*Anavatan Partisi*) between Özal and his opponents. This came to a head in a governmental crisis at the very end of the year, which did not work itself out until January 1989.

Turkey's relations with Europe, and in particular with Greece, were once again the dominant theme in its foreign policy problems. The year started on an optimistic note. Özal met his Greek counterpart Andreas Papandreou in the Swiss resort of Davos at the end of January and the two premiers agreed to seek an amicable settlement of their diverse disputes. Unfortunately, this proved to be a false dawn. Before long, the "spirit of Davos" began to evaporate in the face of mutual recriminations over Cyprus. By the end of the year, a lasting *rapprochement* seemed even further away than it had at the beginning. In the Middle East, meanwhile, events took a more promising turn. The cease-fire in the Gulf War had the indirect result of facing Turkey with the task of caring for tens of thousands of Kurdish refugees, who were escaping savage retribution from the Iraqi regime. On the other hand, the cease-fire ended what could have been a serious threat to Turkey's security on its southeastern borders and opened up important economic possibilities.

DOMESTIC POLITICS

PARLIAMENT AND THE PARTIES

Unlike most ME states, Turkey is a secular democratic republic in which a number of parties compete for power in regular and fair elections. The party structure is dominated by two divisions. The first is the classic one between right and left, represented respectively by Özal's Motherland Party, and the Social Democrat

Turkey

International boundary — Main road — River

Populist Party (SDPP; *Sosyaldemokrat Halkçi Parti*) led by Erdal İnönü. The second division derives from the fact that all preexisting parties were abolished by the military regime of 1980-83. Both the Motherland Party and the SDPP are new creations, established in 1983 and 1985, respectively. However, on 6 September 1987 a national referendum allowed the pre-1980 political leaders to return to active politics (see *MECS* 1987, p. 664). Two of them, ex-premiers Süleyman Demirel and Bülent Ecevit, had formed their own parties as a personal challenge to Özal and İnönü.

In the general elections of November 1987, the Motherland Party had won 292 of the 450 seats in Turkey's unicameral parliament, the Grand National Assembly. This gave Özal's Government a handsome majority of 134 seats over the combined opposition. The Motherland Party espoused economic liberalism combined with a strongly pro-Western foreign policy and a tinge of Islamic conservatism on cultural matters. Following the elections, the SDPP became the main opposition party, with 99 seats. İnönü was challenged from the left by Ecevit, who headed a separate Democrat Left Party (DLP; *Demokratik Sol Partisi*); however, Ecevit's party had won no seats in the 1987 elections and generally appeared to be a waning force. The only other opposition party represented in parliament was the True Path Party (TPP; *Doğru Yol Partisi*), led by Demirel, which had 59 seats. The differences between Demirel and Özal were almost entirely those of personal rivalry; in terms of policies, there was little to distinguish their two parties. (For details on the elections and their repercussions, see *MECS* 1987, chapter on Turkey.)

Within the Motherland Party, Özal's main problem derived from the fact that his party contained three disparate groups. The first of these could broadly be described as liberal-conservative; it was certainly the largest and generally supported the prime minister. The second faction supported a Turkish brand of Islamic fundamentalism and was led by MehmetKeçeciler. Alongside the Islamicists was an ultranationalist or neo-fascist group, which was informally commanded by Mustafa Taşar. In 1987, Keçeciler and Taşar had formed what was known as the "Holy Alliance," designed to further their views and to prevent the liberals around Özal from gaining a monopoly of power within the party. Özal had excluded them from important positions in the government, but he could not afford to ignore them entirely since they commanded substantial support in sections of the party's grass-roots organization.

A related source of friction within the ruling party was Özal's increasing tendency toward nepotism. After the elections, Özal had promoted his younger brother, Yusuf, by appointing him to the Cabinet as a minister of state, with special responsibility for economic affairs. The prime minister's son, Ahmet, played an important role behind the scenes in the world of politics and finance, while his wife, Semra, was constantly in the headlines, both as an outspoken critic of the Islamicists and a very active president of the "Foundation for Strengthening and Publicizing Turkish Womanhood" (known for short as "the Daisies"). All this gave ample scope for the satirists, such as Melih Aşik of the *Milliyet* newspaper who, in his weekly chronicle of "The Daisy Age," reported on the doings of "the Lord Sultan Turgut," "the Heir Apparent Ahmet," and "Queen Semra," in a pastiche of the antique Ottoman court chronicles.[1]

Like most political jokes, this had a serious point. From his powerful position, Yusuf Özal began clearing out long-serving and experienced civil service mandarins from important economic posts and replacing them with his nominees, most of whom, like himself, had been trained in the US or Britain and were known collectively as "the Princes." In return, the mandarins tended to side with the Holy Alliance against the steadily increasing power of the Özal family and their entourage. The most important changes occurred in the Central Bank where the young Rüşdü Saracoğlu succeeded Yavuz Canevi, a leading mandarin, as governor. Canevi then became under secretary at the Treasury, to which the Central Bank is supposed to be subordinate; in practice, however, Saracoğlu began to treat the bank as an independent fiefdom. These changes naturally increased the suspicions of the civil service mandarins, as well as other critics, that the prime minister was trying to set up a kind of dynastic regime.

These conflicts came to a head at the Motherland Party's national congress, which was held in Ankara in June 1988. The congress began with a dramatic reminder of the bloody days of political terrorism of the 1970s, as an attempt was made on the prime minister's life by a right-wing fanatic called Kartal Demirağ. According to contemporary press reports, Demirağ had accomplices, and had evidently been trained for the job. It was also known that he had been a member of the "Grey Wolves," an ultranationalist terrorist group, before 1980, and had escaped from prison in January 1988 while serving a 10-year sentence for manslaughter. He was placed on trial and sentenced to another 20 years' imprisonment in November 1988. Despite widespread suspicions to the contrary, the court decided that he had been acting alone, and failed to shed any further light on the incident.[2]

Fortunately, Turgut Özal survived the attack with no more than a wounded hand. The incident probably won him public sympathy, but did not quieten his opponents within the Motherland Party. In local internal ballots held earlier in the spring to elect delegates to the congress, the Holy Alliance made sweeping gains, winning the support of 60% of the 2,000-odd delegates. This enabled it to capture 35 of the 50 seats in the party's Executive Committee, which drafts party policy and runs the party machine. Although Özal was confirmed as party chairman unopposed, Keçeciler and Taşar were also able to retain important positions within the party, as chief assistant to the chairman and chief deputy chairman, respectively. However, in a cabinet reshuffle which was announced on 26 June, the prime minister made no concessions to his right wing. Two ministers connected with the Holly Alliance, Justice Minister Oltan Sungurlu and Minister of State for Environment and Mining Veysel Atasoy, lost their cabinet posts. Özal replaced Atasoy with Karam İnan, a former minister in the Justice Party (*Adalet Partisi*) cabinets of the 1970s, who was generally recognized as a pro-Western liberal. Sungurlu's successor was Mehmet Topaç, a previously unknown backbencher.

One compensation for Özal in all this was that most of the opposition parties were also in a state of internal disarray. The TPP was something of an exception. At the party's annual congress, held in May, Demirel and his team retained command of the party without difficulty. On the other other hand, the DLP was shaken by the resignation of Ecevit from the party leadership on 7 March. His successor, Necdet Karababa, was a political unknown. It was generally assumed that without Ecevit the party would simply dissolve, with most of its members deserting to the SDPP. In fact, Ecevit's position continued to be highly ambiguous; he continued to give press interviews almost as though he were still leader of the party. Even if he revoked his decision, however, he seemed to have only the slenderest chance of regaining political power.

Contemporary upheavals in the SDPP were of greater significance, since the party was clearly the largest element in the opposition to the government. However, İnönü was also having difficulty in controlling his rank and file. Erdal İnönü was the son of former president İsmet İnönü, but he had only entered politics at the age of 57 in 1983, having previously been professor of physics at Istanbul's Bosphorus University. His lack of knowledge of economics was also considered a serious disadvantage;[3] nevertheless, since 1983 he had shown unexpected powers of public persuasion and leadership.

By 1988 it appeared that İnönü's main problems were not personal, but the lack of ideological cohesion within his party. Like the Motherland Party, the SDPP was a fusion of several variegated strains. On the left were a number of deputies, mostly from the eastern provinces, who were anxious to push the party in a more radical direction and were not averse to making an open appeal to supporters of Kurdish separatism — a virtually taboo topic in most of the Turkish political establishment. The SDPP also contained a number of senior members of the former Republican People's Party (RPP; *Cumhuriyet Halk Partisi*), which was led by Ecevit before its dissolution by the military regime of 1980–83. Such old hands were likely to resent the mushroom-like rise of political newcomers in the SDPP. A prominent member of this group was Deniz Baykal, once the leader of the left wing of the RPP. In recent years, Baykal had tended to gravitate toward the political center and was actually opposed by the pro-Kurdish faction; however, he had greater practical political experience than İnönü, and would be the most likely candidate for the party leadership if İnönü were to retire from the scene. Another group of the "old guard" from the former RPP was led by the Istanbul deputies Ali Topuz (another former minister in RPP governments of the 1970s) and Aytekin Kotil, a former mayor of Istanbul.

İnönü's problem with his party's convoluted factionalism came to a head at the end of February 1988. Earlier in the year, a member of the pro-Kurdish radical group, Mehmet Ali Eren (actually a deputy for Istanbul) had spoken openly in the National Assembly of the "Kurdish minority" and "minoritarian nationalism." Eren had narrowly escaped official censure by the SDPP party caucus. Meanwhile, two SDPP deputies from the Kurdish-inhabited eastern provinces, Adnan Ekmen and Mahmut Alinak, joined a hunger strike protesting against prison conditions in the eastern city of Diyarbakir. İnönü was evidently determined to bring them under control and summoned them to Ankara for a dressing-down. However, he had to face further bickering when the party's Central Management Committee reinstated two local branch officials against his wishes. At a meeting of the Party Assembly (*Parti Meclisi*) on 28 February, he threw down an open challenge to his opponents by resigning from the chairmanship, together with his secretary-general, Fikri Sağlar. He would only return to the party leadership, he vowed, if a special meeting of the Party Congress (*Kurultay*) accepted that all candidates for membership of the Party Assembly, the central policy-making body, should be approved by himself. Fortunately for the party, İnönü's opponents backed down and he withdrew his resignation on 29 February. At the annual congress of the SDPP held in the third week of July, İnönü was reelected chairman of the party by a large majority. Deniz Baykal, who was elected unopposed as secretary-general, now appeared to be working with him as part of a united team.

THE CONSTITUTIONAL REFERENDUM AND GOVERNMENT UPSETS

These internal disputes in the parties took place against the background of a political cum constitutional row over the date of municipal elections. Under Article 127 of the constitution, such elections must be held every five years; the last were held in March 1984 (see *MECS*, 1983–84, pp. 722–24) and new elections would, therefore, have become due in March 1989. However, Özal had important reasons for wishing to bring forward this date. The strongest of these was the soaring rate of inflation which, as Özal realized, was primarily due to chronic overspending in the public sector. To restore a relative degree of price stability, he would either have to reduce public expenditure or increase taxes, or adopt a mixture of both remedies. However, the prime minister realized that these measures would inevitably reduce the popularity of his party.

From the government's viewpoint there was a strong argument for getting the local elections over as soon as possible, before the nasty economic medicine had to be delivered to the public. To secure this, however, an amendment to the constitution would be necessary. This would require either (1) a two-thirds supporting majority in parliament or (2) a three-fifths majority, plus acceptance in a national referendum.[4] In parliament, the Motherland Party accounted for just under two thirds of the seats; in other words, if Özal were to achieve the change by the first method, he would have to gain the support of at least one of the opposition parties.

On 16 July, it was reported that Özal had struck a deal with the TPP to support the proposal: it thus seemed likely that a referendum would not be necessary. Unfortunately for the premier, it appears that Demirel and his supporters then changed their minds. When the constitutional amendment was put to the vote of a specially convened session of the Assembly on 6 August, both the opposition parties failed to support it. It thus became clear that if Özal persisted in his proposal, then a referendum would be necessary. The opposition naturally claimed that this would be a serious waste of time and that the government should drop the whole idea. At this stage, Özal would probably have done best to abandon his proposal and to take a risk that his party could still win the local elections in March 1989. However, he evidently decided against this, perhaps because it would have involved too great a loss of face or because he actually expected to carry the referendum. He may also have hoped that the referendum campaign would put moral pressure on the dissidents within his party to rally round the party flag and would thus reduce the infighting among his own rank and file.

Whatever the reasons for it, the referendum date was duly fixed as 25 September. Both government and opposition parties swung into action, with the opposition urging the public to vote "no," while the Motherland Party naturally campaigned for a "yes" vote. The opposition leaders claimed that if the vote went against him, Özal's Government would be forced to resign. Given the immense size of his parliamentary majority, this seemed rather farfetched; however, it does seem to have injected some life into a campaign which most of the public probably regarded as quite unnecessary. By 19 September, six days before polling was due to take place, Özal was evidently becoming worried by opinion poll results which suggested that the "noes" would carry the day by a massive majority. He therefore made the surprising announcement on television that "I can leave the prime ministry and politics depending on the result of the referendum."[5] In subsequent interviews, he declined to say what percentage of "no" votes would induce him to take this step. Nevertheless, by appearing to place his own political future on the line, he evidently hoped to rally the party faithful and to challenge wavering voters with the possibility that if they voted against the amendment they might leave Turkey with no prime minister, no obvious successor, and a political crisis of major proportions.

Whether or not it was genuine, Özal's threat seems to have worked. Before the premier's announcement, public opinion polls had put the likely "yes" vote at around 26%. When the referendum results came through, this was increased to 35% with 65% for the "noes"; (there were very few abstentions, as voting was virtually compulsory). The proportion of "yes" votes was only 1% less than the share that the Motherland Party had won in the 1987 general elections. Özal was thus able to claim that his government's popularity remained undented and that he deserved to stay in office. Nevertheless, he could hardly present the episode as anything like a total victory.

Government morale suffered a further setback when a major cabinet crisis erupted at the end of December. In September 1988, a millionaire businessman, Kemal Horzum, was extradited from Switzerland to Turkey to face charges of having defrauded the state-owned Real Estate Bank of some $80m. The story stayed on the fringes of politics until 12 December, when the *Hürriyet* newspaper alleged that Deputy Prime Minister Kaya Erdem was connected with the swindle. Until this stage, Erdem had been considered one of the pillar's of Özal's Government, and had been one of the prime minister's oldest colleagues. As deputy prime minister, he was in charge of economic affairs between 1983 and 1987. He lost this responsibility to Yusuf Özal in December 1987, but retained his post of deputy premier. However, it appears that there was no love lost between him and the Özal family as a whole and that he strongly resented the advance of Yusuf Özal and the other "Princes" since the 1987 elections.

This interpretation of events was strengthened by the fact that Erdem not only rejected the implications of the *Hürriyet* story, but also alleged that it had been leaked to the paper by Bülent Şemiler, the director of the Real Estate Bank. Şemiler, one of the "Princes" was known to be a close friend of Ahmet Özal and had been entrusted by the premier with investigating the Horzum swindle. Erdem was reported to have told Turgut Özal that either he or Şemiler must go. In the event, Şemiler resigned on 25 December in order, as he put it, to "protect the interests of the bank and in order not to push the prime minister into difficulties in the party."[6] However, Şemiler continued to enjoy the premier's approval, since he was appointed a chief adviser to the prime minister immediately afterward. Moreover, Erdem was unable to ride out the storm or suppress the apparent breach between himself and the Özal family. Accordingly, he was forced to submit his own resignation on 4 January.

The conflict did not work itself out until the early weeks of 1989. On 6 January, in the aftermath of Erdem's resignation, it was announced that Yavuz Canevi, one of the most prominent civil service mandarins, would take a month's holiday, and then resign from his command at the Treasury. At least 55 transfers of senior Treasury officials were also ordered by Yusuf Özal. All this strengthened the impression thatTurgut Özal and his family were trying to turn the top of the civil service as well as the government into what Melih Aşik referred to as the "Turgutian Empire."[7]

A worrying aspect of these events for the Motherland Party was that while Özal was apparently becoming more imperial, he was also becoming less popular. Undoubtedly, the main reason for this was the government's failure to control inflation. A poll published in *Milliyet* on 29 April showed that support for the Motherland Party had fallen to 23.3%, compared to its 36% share in the general elections the previous November. The same poll put the SDPP at 28%, and Demirel's TPP at 26.9%. A later survey by the same polling organization, published in *Milliyet* on 25 December, showed support for Özal's party virtually unchanged, at 23.1%, but a sharp rise in support for the SDPP to 33.1%, mainly gained from the TPP, which was now down to 19.3%. If correct, these figures suggested that far from all of the 35% who had voted "yes" in the September referendum were actually Motherland Party supporters. It seemed unlikely that these figures would have any immediate effects on the government's parliamentary majority, since general elections were not constitutionally due until 1992; nevertheless, it was clear that Özal would have to work hard to recoup his popularity by that date.

THE ROLE OF THE MILITARY AND KURDISH SEPARATISM

Since 1983, the Army had gradually been withdrawing from Turkish politics. Nevertheless, its political attitudes were still important — partly because ex-general Kenan Evren, the leader of the coup of 12 September 1980, continued to serve as president and could be assumed to express military attitudes, and partly because the armed forces still carried out important law-and-order functions in the restless Kurdish provinces.[8] Demands for the relaxation of supposedly anti-Communist laws were also likely to awaken military ire, granted that most army commanders continued to see Marxism, Islamic fundamentalism, and Kurdish separatism as three mortal threats to the security of Turkey and the spirit of Atatürkism.

An important aspect of the military's role in politics was the future of the presidency, which continued to be discussed during 1988. Constitutionally, Turkey is a parliamentary rather than a presidential republic; nevertheless, the president has substantial moral authority, besides important powers of appointment. Under the present constitution, the president is elected for a seven-year term by the Grand National Assembly and may not be reelected. However, Evren was declared elected unopposed when the constitution was accepted in the national referendum of 7 November 1982. Evren's term of office was thus due to expire in November 1989. Although there is no stipulation to this effect in the constitution, many army officers tended to regard it as an unwritten rule that the president should be a retired military commander (of the seven presidents of Turkey since the 1920s, only one had a civilian professional background). At the same time, there was a growing feeling that this tradition was contrary to the basic principles of democracy and that a civilian candidate should at least be treated as eligible for election in 1989.

The question came to the fore in January 1988, when Turgut Özal publicly hinted that he might himself run for the presidency when Evren retired, and that he would seek a form of direct election rather than the method of election by the Assembly. This proposal was naturally criticized by the opposition parties, who did not want to see Özal stay at the top of the political tree until 1996. The picture was further complicated by the possibility that Evren might seek to have a constitutional amendment enacted which would allow him to be reelected in 1989. For his part, Evren was quite cagey about this. It was not until February 1989 that he announced that he would "definitely" be retiring from the presidency the following November, but this left open the possibility that another ex-military candidate might be put forward. Meanwhile, it appeared that the prime minister might be backing off the idea of standing himself. The question thus remained in the air and likely to provoke more heated debate in 1989.

Whatever its eventual outcome, the argument over the future of the presidency was clearly linked to the broader question as to whether Turkey was yet a full-fledged democracy. Not surprisingly, the universities, together with the trade unions and the opposition parties, were the main source of demands for further liberalization of the regime. On 28 April, large numbers of students demonstrated in Istanbul against the tight government controls over the universities. More than 150 were arrested and 10 or more injured in clashes with police. Further demonstrations in several universities followed on 29 April. On Labor Day, 1 May, some 600 trade unionists, led by opposition members of parliament, defied an official ban on rallies to lay a wreath in Istanbul's Taksim Square. Police broke up the meeting, but some 700 students then marched on the square.

These demonstrations were accompanied by a renewed outbreak of violence in the Kurdish provinces, particularly by members of the Kurdistan Workers' Party (PKK; *Parti-ye Karkaran-i Kurdistan*), the largest Kurdish guerrilla c:ganization in Turkey. On 28 March, Kurdish insurgents killed nine civilians in two villages in Siirt province, bringing the total death toll to over 950 since the PKK launched its present campaign in 1984. Four days later, Turkish troops chanced upon a large detachment of the PKK near the town of Nusaybin, just north of Turkey's border with Syria, and killed 20 of them for the loss of two soldiers and an officer. This was followed by further raids on the weekend of 7–8 May, when 21 villagers (who were probably Kurds hostile to the PKK) also lost their lives.

The apparent fear that Turkey might be slipping back into the anarchic conditions of the late 1970s seemed exaggerated, but it evidently carried some weight with President Evren. As on previous occasions, the president displayed a worrying tendency to make unguarded remarks off the cuff. On 30 April, he told an audience in the Black Sea city of Trabzon that "there are people who want to push our country into anarchy...Turkey will not see such days again. If Turkey is in a similar situation, the force to resist this is the armed forces." The implied threat that the Army might launch another coup naturally provoked a barrage of protests from the politicians; Demirel, for instance, alleged that the president was "stirring up those eager for another coup." Evren appeared to realize his mistake on 2 May, when he reassured another Black Sea audience that "the period of fights and disputes is over. As long as unity exists, democracy will progress step by step." Özal tried to back the president up, by assuring the public that "I believe that he [Evren] seriously and sincerely supports democracy."[9] By the end of May, the row seemed to have subsided, but it inevitably left Evren's political reputation somewhat tarnished.

Meanwhile, the Kurdish provinces continued to produce problems for both the politicians and the Army. Following the fierce clashes in April and early May, a further 27 people were killed, including three soldiers, in renewed fighting between 23 and 31 May. Thereafter, direct attacks by the PKK seem to have subsided. In the wider context, the Kurds suffered a devastating blow in March 1988 when Iraqi President Saddam Husayn's regime launched a ruthless offensive against their main bases in Iraq (see chapter on Iraq). This seems to have intensified after Iran's acceptance of a cease-fire in the Gulf War, which left Iraq's forces free to mop up the Kurdish guerrillas. In the face of a draconian campaign by Iraq, which included the use of poison-gas bombs against Kurdish civilians, thousands of villagers from Iraqi Kurdistan fled north into Turkish territory during August and September.

For the first time, Turkey was faced with a major Kurdish refugee problem, which left the local authorities in a serious dilemma. On the one hand, they could hardly refuse entry to the refugees, for obvious humanitarian reasons. On the other hand, they were reluctant to import large numbers of battle-hardened Kurdish fighters, who might provoke further trouble among the native Kurdish population. The exact number of refugees in Turkey was uncertain; the official figure, as of mid-September, was around 50,000–60,000, but unofficial estimates put the total as high as 100,000–150,000. To complicate the picture, it was reported that a large number of refugees (generally put at around 20,000) moved on from Turkish territory to Iran — whether voluntarily or not was also disputed.[10]

Those refugees who remained in Turkish territory were first put in tented encampments near the Iraqi border. After some weeks, many were moved further into the interior as it became clear that they would have to be given more robust accommodation in less harsh climatic conditions. Nevertheless, many refugees (according to reports, about 10 per day) fell victim to outbreaks of gastroenteritis and the bitter cold. Such reports naturally detracted from the Turkish Government's reasonable claims that Turkey, itself a relatively poor country, had shouldered a heavy burden in caring for the refugees, and had fully carried out its international obligations. Looking to the future, it seemed likely that this latest tragic chapter in the history of the Kurds would not be the last. Even if the PKK went to ground for a period, demands by the Kurds for greater cultural rights within Turkey would almost certainly continue.

HUMAN RIGHTS

The position of the Kurds in Turkey could be seen as part of the wider question of human rights. This was a topic on which the Turkish Government had been under heavy attack from liberal groups in Western Europe, and to which it had to turn some attention. Apart from the intrinsic importance of civil rights in any democracy, it was realized in Turkey that the country could not become a full member of the EEC unless it was able to convince the present member states that human rights were at least as well protected as they were in Western Europe. The causes of complaints against Turkey's human rights record were essentially twofold: first, that existing legislation limited freedom of speech, assembly, and publication to an unacceptable degree and, second, that conditions of interrogation and trial did not meet West European norms — in particular, that torture was regularly and routinely applied to suspects under interrogation. These two points may be considered separately.

Granted the almost total breakdown of law and order in Turkey during the late 1970s, it was inevitable that very large numbers of people should have been detained on political charges after the coup of 12 September 1980; Amnesty International (AI), the London-based human rights pressure group, put the total at around 250,000, which apparently included several hundred prisoners of conscience.[11] More serious was the fact that certain statutes permitted the charging of people with crimes of conscience which did not have to involve the use of violence or incitement to violence, and that these had continued to be enforced long after the end of the military regime. The most frequently used were Sections 141 and 142 of the Penal Code, which were originally enacted in 1936. Of these, Section 141 made it a heavily punishable offense to "form, organize, or direct the activities of...any society with the aim of...establishing the hegemony or domination of a social class over the other social classes, or eliminating a social class, or overthrowing any of the fundamental economic or social orders established within the country." Section 142 specified slightly lighter punishments for those convicted of disseminating propaganda to the same effect.

These statutes had a dangerously catchall character, which enabled their usage against people expressing a wide range of oppositional views, particularly those on the left. Examples of such trials continued during the year. Notable among them were the cases of Haydar Kutlu and Nihat Sargın, two long-standing Turkish communists, who returned to Turkey from exile in November 1987 (see *MECS* 1987, p. 666). They were promptly charged under Section 141 for having established a United Communist Party of Turkey and their trial dragged on during 1988. Similar cases affected ex-ambassador Mahmut Dikerdem and 42 other members of the Turkish Peace Association (a pro-disarmament pressure group), the chairman and vice chairman of the Turkish Human Rights Association, the founders of the Socialist Party, and a number of Christian missionaries, both Turkish and foreign.

In January 1988, Turkey became one of the first signatories of the Council of Europe's Convention for the Prevention of Torture. This reinforced Article 17 of the Turkish constitution, which provides that "no one shall be subjected to torture or ill-treatment." Nevertheless, there is evidently a wide gap between word and deed. A report published in January 1989 by AI claimed that virtually all those arrested on political charges since 1980 had been tortured, as a means of extracting confessions. AI reported that this practice continued during 1987-88, and included the regular use of tortures of the most gruesome kind.[12]

Apart from this, conditions for convicted prisoners or those on remand (both political prisoners and ordinary criminals) were often very severe. This led to an 11-day hunger strike in Diyarbakir prison in February 1988. It was ended when the government made unexpected concessions of improved conditions. However, further hunger strikes against conditions were reported in no less than 22 prisons throughout the country during the rest of the year — supported in many cases by large-scale demonstrations outside the jails by relatives and supporters. These protests were evidently intensified by the introduction of new prison regulations on 1 August, which appear to have withdrawn many of the concessions made the previous February.[13]

The Turkish authorities' reply to the constant reports of torture was that most of them were groundless: that there may have been some isolated instances of the use of torture, but where these occurred they were followed up and, where charges were proved, guilty officials were brought to book. In fact, relatively few prosecutions of alleged torturers appear to have taken place. It would seem likely that a mass reeducation of the police, and new regulations which would disallow the use by the courts of confessions extracted under torture, would both be necessary if the practice was to be eliminated.[14]

On the question of Penal Code Sections 141 and 142, and other contentious statutes, developments during 1988 and early 1989 seemed slightly more encouraging. In the course of a visit to West Germany in October, President Evren remarked to journalists that he accepted that eventually the Communist Party would have to be legalized in Turkey, and the death sentence abolished; (in fact, there had been no executions since 1984). However, it was unclear how the president could oblige the government to put this commitment into effect, or when. During the year, it was reported that some revisions of Sections 141 and 142 were under consideration, but it appeared that these would leave their most contentious provisions intact. In February 1989, there were further reports that Sections 141 and 142 might eventually be abolished altogether.[15] Should this be achieved, the campaign for securing wider human rights would obviously have turned an important corner; in the meantime, Turkey still had some way to go before the EEC members were likely to accept it as a fully democratic state.

ECONOMIC TRENDS

During 1988, the Turkish economy exhibited most of the trends which had been apparent in earlier years — that is to say, a strong rate of overall economic growth combined with a high rate of inflation. Growth was also offset by a distinct industrial downturn at the end of the year. However, there was also a noticeable improvement in the balance of payments, in which a positive balance in the current account was recorded for the first time in 16 years.

According to preliminary estimates, the real growth of gross national product (GNP) in 1988 stood at 6.5%, a slight fall from the 7.4% growth rate recorded for 1987. Thanks mainly to good weather conditions, value added in the agricultural sector grew by 6.1% at constant prices, compared with a growth rate of 2.1% in the previous year. On the other hand, industrial output grew at a slower rate than in 1987 (at 7.9% compared to 9.6%). This was largely accounted for by a slowdown in demand and, hence, in industrial output at the end of the year, which is explained later. The growth rate of value added in the services sector remained roughly constant at 6.7%.[16]

The improvement in Turkey's balance of payments position was mainly accounted for by a rise in exports to around $11.7bn., from $10.3bn. in 1987. Imports, however, increased at a lower rate, from $13.6bn. in 1987 to about $14bn. in 1988. The deficit in visible trade was counterbalanced by a surplus on the invisibles account. Although interest payments on the foreign debt increased from $2.5bn. to around $3bn., there was a sharp upswing in tourist revenues to $2.1bn. (from $1.5bn. the previous year) and in other invisible earnings, such as transit trade, construction contracts, shipping, and the like (from $2.6bn. in 1987 to some $3.6bn. in 1988). Remittances from Turkish workers in Western Europe and the oil-producing states fell slightly, to around $1.7bn. Nevertheless, Turkey was able to record an overall surplus on current account of some $800m. The last time such a surplus had been achieved was in 1973. As a result, Turkey was able to reduce its total disbursed overseas debt, from $38.3bn. in December 1987 to $37.4bn. in June 1988; (in addition, it held another $9.7bn. in undisbursed credits). The debt servicing ratio (that is, total interest plus capital repayments as a percentage of exports plus invisibles) stood at around 40%. In effect, Turkey was able to meet its overseas interest payments plus part of its capital repayments from current overseas income, and borrow new money to meet its remaining capital repayments. This represented a manageable debtor situation, particularly when compared to that of many other Third World countries.[17]

On the exports side, sales to the EEC countries grew only slightly (from $4.9bn. in 1987 to $5.1bn. in 1988), but still represented about 43% of the total. Most of the growth in exports was due to increased sales to the Islamic states, whose share rose to 31%, and to other countries (26%). The share of manufactured goods in total exports fell slightly (from just under 80% in 1987 to around 77% in 1988) but this was more than compensated for by a sharp rise in the value of agricultural and mineral exports. In import trade, Turkey continued to benefit from the weakness in oil prices. As in previous years, crude oil was the single biggest item on the import list, but the bill for oil imports fell by around 11%, to represent around 17% of total imports by value. This was encouraging (especially since Turkey's exports to the ME states had actually increased during the year) and was an important factor in the improvement in the current account balance.[18]

For the government, businessmen, and ordinary wage earners alike, inflation was undoubtedly the major economic problem of 1988. Granted that there were few, if any, external inflationary pressures, there was general agreement that it had been caused primarily by overspending in the public sector — both by central government and local authorities. What made inflation particularly harmful in Turkey was the fact that wages were not index linked, so that workers were faced with the constant erosion of real wages. This had tended to worsen the already serious problem of income inequalities. It was recognized that the government could only tackle the problem by reducing public expenditure and increasing taxation. However, governments had been reluctant to take this step, since it would undoubtedly be unpopular in the short term. Instead, the Özal Government allowed a rapid increase in public expenditure in 1987, so as to create a preelection boom. Turks paid the price for this policy during 1988, as the inflationary pressures it set up worked their way through the economy.

The official figures for inflation during 1988 told their story. During the first quarter, the wholesale prices index rose by 21.4%. This was followed by a fall to 9.7% and 9.3% during the second and third quarters, respectively, but a surge back to 16.5% in the final quarter. In November, inflation touched a high point of an annualized rate of around 85%. The rate of price increases slowed during December, but the recorded wholesale prices index rise for the year as a whole was still left at 69.7%.[19] Meanwhile, the scale of overspending in the public sector was shown by the fact that the actual budget deficit, at some TL3,440bn., was almost 50% over target and about 17% of central government expenditure. The draft budget for 1989, introduced to parliament in October, aimed to hold the deficit at around TL4,480bn. (a decrease in real terms), but there was no proof that the government would succeed in sticking to this target, or in bringing inflation down to the planned 50% in 1989.[20]

During the year, the government also tried to use the banking system to squeeze excess money out of the economy. At the beginning of 1988, interest rates, which were fixed by the government, were below the rate of inflation. This induced savers to switch their funds to the unofficial foreign currency market, causing a wide gap to develop between the official and unofficial (i.e., free market) exchange rates. Accordingly, on 4 February, the government raised the rate for six-month time deposits from 38% to 52%. Unfortunately, the continuing rise in inflation meant that before long savers were again faced with a negative real rate of return. To halt another run on the lira, the government announced on 17 October that banks would be allowed to set their own interest rates up to a limit of 85% for one year and 63% for six-month deposits. For a short time, total borrowing costs shot up to around 150% p.a. At the end of the year, rates had fallen somewhat, but this brought them back to below real inflation-adjusted levels, facing the authorities with much the same problem as they had experienced at the beginning of 1988.[21]

In the meantime, there was evidence that the government's attempts to restrict demand by raising interest rates was having some effects on the level of industrial output. This was a novel experience for most industrialists, who had been able to expand output steadily for the previous seven years. Members of the Istanbul Chamber of Commerce (in other words, the main private firms in the city) reported a drop of 5.6% in manufacturing output for the third quarter of 1988, a trend which apparently continued into the final quarter. By the beginning of 1989, layoffs were being reported by a large number of firms. There were no signs of an early recovery in 1989, and it was thus likely that GNP growth would be a good deal lower than in 1988.[22] The difficult conditions were creating strain between the government and the business community, hitherto one of Özal's strongest sources of support. In a poll conducted in November by the Turkish Industrialists' and Businessmen's Association (*Tüsiad*), Turkey's most powerful business lobby, more than 90% of respondents said they were disappointed with the government's efforts to curb inflation. As the *Tüsiad* chairman, Ömer Dinçkök, put it: "Turkey is spending far beyond its available resources; inflation has increased to such an extent that we are inhaling it along with the pollution."[23]

Needless to say, shopfloor workers were equally affected by rising inflation. The existing labor legislation, which was enacted by the military regime of 1980–83, outlawed strikes in a wide range of public services and banned any kind of general strike. Despite these restrictions, almost 2.9m. work days were lost through strikes in 1988, an increase of 45% over 1987.[24] Of the total work force of around 22m., about 7.5m. were wage earners (the remainder being self-employed, or working in small family units); some 3m. of these were union members, of whom about two thirds were members of unions affiliated to *Türk-İş*, the biggest labor confederation. On 11 March, some 1.5m. *Türk-İş* members staged lunchtime protests in support of higher wages and the removal of restrictions on the unions — a fair indication of the wide scale of industrial discontent.

On 27 May, parliament enacted certain changes to the labor laws, in an attempt to avoid blacklisting by the International Labor Organization. However, these amendments were mostly cosmetic and did not remove the most contentious restrictions. Meanwhile, the available evidence suggested that real wages were continuing to decline. The State Planning Organization, the government's official planning body, estimates that real wages fell by 30% in the public sector, and by 20% in the private sector, during Özal's first term of office (1983–87).[25] Given the steady growth in GNP, the conclusion must almost certainly be that the already serious problem of the maldistribution of income has significantly worsened during the 1980s.

FOREIGN RELATIONS

TURKEY, GREECE, AND CYPRUS

As the only ME member of Nato, Turkey enjoys a unique position in the region. It is also an associate member of the EEC, and strengthened this commitment in 1987 by applying for full membership of the community. Closer to home, its relations with the West have been upset by a complex series of disputes with Greece. The tensions between the two nations have an important historical cum psychological dimension. Greeks resent the centuries of Ottoman rule, while Turks recall the disastrous Greek invasion of Asia Minor of 1919–22. On the material level, the two states have had long-standing disputes over the questions of offshore oil rights and territorial waters in the Aegean. Finally, the Cyprus problem has created a tangled web of hostility. The Greek Cypriots' failure to implement the rights which the Turkish Cypriots were granted under the Cypriot constitution of 1960 and the Turkish invasion of 1974 have effectively divided the island into mutually hostile enclaves.

In March 1987, the offshore oil rights dispute brought Greece and Turkey close to armed confrontation (see *MECS* 1987, p. 672). A series of secret diplomatic contacts then took place between the two governments. These bore unexpected fruit on 30–31 January 1988, when Özal met his Greek counterpart, Andreas Papandreou, in the Swiss resort of Davos. By this stage, Özal was clearly concerned to improve the outlook for Turkey's application for full membership of the EEC. Papandreou was also anxious to defuse the crisis with Turkey since, if it came to an armed collision, Greece would find it hard to defend its Aegean islands against the vastly superior Turkish forces.

The Davos summit produced a broad agreement under two heads. In the psychological sphere, the two premiers agreed that "rigid frames of mind have been created in various segments of their societies," and that these should be overcome. It was agreed that the crisis of March 1987 "should never be repeated and [that] both sides must concentrate their efforts for the establishment of lasting peaceful relations."[26] To this end, it was announced that contacts among civil servants, the military, the press, and businessmen would be encouraged. A joint Chamber of Commerce would be set up, together with a hot line between the two premiers, who would hold annual meetings to review progress. The two leaders also agreed to create working parties to tackle economic and political issues. The first of these would work for closer collaboration in such fields as joint business ventures and increases in trade, tourism, and cultural contacts. The second, at ambassadorial level, would attempt to identify "problem areas" between the two sides — that is, the offshore rights and territorial waters disputes. In the joint communiqué issued after the Davos meeting, Özal and Papandreou did not address the Cyprus issue directly. However, Papandreou later stated that the dispute should not become a Greek-Turkish issue, and that a solution should be sought through the UN. This left the door open for contacts between the Greek and Turkish Cypriot administrations, under UN auspices.

The disadvantage of the Davos agreement was that it did not offer any specific solutions to the issues dividing the two nations and rested excessively on the personal accord between Özal and Papandreou. These problems became clear at a meeting of the Turkey-EEC Association Council which began in Luxembourg on 25 April. The purpose of the meeting was to tackle economic issues, such as the reduction of tariffs between Turkey and the community, the Turkish request to secure free movement of Turkish workers already in the EEC states, and the release of an Ecu 600m. ($750m.) aid package from Brussels to Turkey. Just before the meeting, Greece insisted that the opening address, to be delivered by EEC Commissioner Claude Cheysson, should include a statement explicitly linking the Turkish occupation of northern Cyprus to

Turkey-EEC relations. The Turkish delegation, which was led by Foreign Minister Mesut Yılmaz, got wind of this statement in advance and refused to attend the meeting unless it was deleted. Greece refused, and the meeting was therefore blocked. Eventually, a compromise was hammered out in which the opening statement accepted merely that the Cyprus problem affected relations between Greece and Turkey. This persuaded Greece to lift its veto on the economic dialogue. However, it was clear that the two sides were still far apart on such substantive issues as Cyprus, and that Turkey was likely to encounter tough Greek opposition in its application for community membership.

Despite the setback at Luxembourg, Özal and Papandreou were too committed to the process of dialogue to abandon it entirely. Much importance was attached to a visit by Özal to Athens which began on 13 June. Greek hopes had apparently been raised by the expectation that Turkey might announce some sort of military withdrawal from Cyprus, and Papandreou was reported to have insisted on the drafting of a firm timetable for the complete demilitarization of the island as the basis for agreement on a federal Cypriot constitution. Özal, however, stuck to the predictable Turkish line that withdrawals would have to be linked to progress in negotiating a new constitution. The blockage over Cyprus prevented progress on any of the other substantive issues. Özal thus left Athens with nothing achieved, beyond a stated commitment to continue the dialogue. This situation effectively remained unchanged at the end of the year.

It was clear from the start that any real progress on the Cyprus problem would depend on agreement between the leaders of the Greek and Turkish Cypriots. A new chapter in the seemingly endless Cypriot saga appeared to have been opened in February 1988, when George Vassiliou was elected president of Cyprus, in succession to Spyros Kyprianou. Vassiliou was recognized as being more personally outgoing and affable than Kyprianou. During his election campaign, he had appeared to keep his options open on a possible settlement with the Turks. Rauf Denktaş, president of the self-proclaimed Turkish Republic of Northern Cyprus, had originally hoped that he would be able to make progress in talks with the new Greek-Cypriot leader. Subsequent experience showed that this would be very hard to achieve. On 24 August, Denktaş and Vassiliou met in Geneva at a luncheon hosted by UN Secretary-General Pérez de Cuellar. This caused a new surge of optimism and was pictured as the Cypriot counterpart to the Davos summit. However, at a series of meetings held in New York and Nicosia during the last three months of the year, the two Cypriot leaders discovered that they were still poles apart.

As a starting point, both sides accepted the principle of establishing a federal republic composed of two states, Greek and Turkish, in which the "three freedoms" agreed to by Denktaş and former president Makarios in 1977 would be guaranteed — that is to say, freedom of movement, freedom of settlement, and the right to property for citizens of both communities in each of the two federal states. On the other hand, proposals which Denktaş submitted on 22 November made it clear that he interpreted these freedoms in a very restricted sense. According to the Turkish-Cypriot proposals, the police on both sides would be entitled to control movement and could exclude or expel "undesirable persons." Freedom of settlement would also be limited for an interval of 18 years after the new federal constitution came into force. Even after this, each federal state would establish a ceiling to limit the number of citizens of the other community resident in its territory. Denktaş apparently feared that if all the Greek Cypriots who had become refugees in 1974 returned to their former homes in northern Cyprus, then his federal state would cease to be Turkish in more than name. So far as the future constitution was concerned, Denktaş also insisted on "political equality of the partner republics and peoples." It was not even clear that he would accept full withdrawal of the Turkish mainland troops from Cyprus; instead, he proposed that "non-Cypriot forces...will be brought to the level necessary for ensuring adequate and effective guarantees."[27] It was extremely unlikely that the Greek Cypriots would accept these proposals, since they would almost certainly see the proposed federal republic as a disguised form of partition, allowing some Turkish forces to remain in Cyprus indefinitely. Given this, it seemed probable that the intercommunal talks would remain stalemated unless one or both of the mainland governments intervened to break the logjam.

TURKEY, NATO, AND THE EEC

The apparent stalling of the Greek-Turkish dialogue by the middle of 1988 left the most pressing problem in Turkey's relations with its Western allies unresolved. Nevertheless, general developments in relations with the US and Western Europe were not unencouraging. By 1988, it was clear that democratic government was reasonably well established and that Turkey's economy, although beset by numerous problems, was growing at an impressive rate. Accordingly, the West European states began to abandon the reservations which they had formerly had about strengthening their relations with Ankara. British Prime Minister Margaret Thatcher visited Turkey in April, and President Evren paid official visits to Britain in July and to West Germany in October. Since these were the first visits by the head of state to West European capitals since the coup of 1980, they were treated in Turkey as an important badge of Turkey's renewed international respectability.

On the central question of Turkey's application for membership of the community, relations with Brussels obviously suffered something of a setback at the time of the Luxembourg meeting. Nevertheless, consideration of the application went ahead as planned. In accordance with the procedure applied in earlier cases, the Commission (see *MECS* 1987, p. 672) had first of all to prepare an official opinion on the proposal. In due course, this would be put to the community's Council of Ministers, which would then decide whether to open official negotiations with Turkey which could eventually result in an accession treaty. The Commission was not expected to deliver its opinion until the autumn of 1989; in the meantime, its experts visited Turkey to gather information.

Thanks to the numerous political and economic obstacles to Turkey's accession (at least in the near future) it was not expected that either the Commission or the Council of Ministers would give an enthusiastic response. Hence, most speculation centered on the question of how Turkey would react if the community gave it a blunt "no," or something close to it. The main fear in Western Europe was that it might withdraw from Nato. On its side, the Turkish Government was evidently reluctant to threaten open blackmail, partly because it did not want to provoke bad feeling and partly because it realized that withdrawal from Nato would be very costly for Turkey as well as its Western allies. On the other hand, Özal could not afford to ignore the threat option entirely, or the likely reaction of Turkish opinion if the application were turned down abruptly. Accordingly, in May 1988 he told journalists that in such a case "our public might have questions about the matter" (of Nato membership).[28] Later indications were that a full-scale withdrawal from Nato would be unlikely, but that Turkey might well drag its heels in carrying out its commitments to Nato if it were rebuffed by the community.

Among Turkey's other allies, relations with the US were of primary importance, both because Turkey was still dependent on Washington for military and some economic aid, and because it evidently hoped that the US could exercise influence in its favor in Brussels. The main problem in this context was caused by the existence of important Greek and Armenian lobbies in Congress, both of which opposed the strengthening of ties with Turkey. A Defense and Economic Cooperation Agreement (DECA) with the US had been signed in March 1987 (see *MECS* 1987, p. 673). Congressional opposition had prevented the Reagan Administration from extending as much aid as Ankara had originally requested. Accordingly, the DECA remained unratified by the Turkish Parliament. Nevertheless, both governments unofficially agreed to put it into effect. On 28 February 1988, the Turkish Cabinet officially ratified a "side letter" from Secretary of State Shultz promising a "high level of support for Turkey," within the limitations imposed by Congress, for the duration of the DECA (that is, until 1990). This cleared the air in Turkish-US relations, allowing Evren to pay a long-delayed visit to Washington in June. The election of George Bush also promised a degree of continuity in US policy which was generally to Turkey's advantage. Barring occasional upsets caused by pro-Greek or Armenian members of Congress, it seemed likely that relations with Washington would remain on a relatively even keel for the next few years.

TURKEY AND THE MIDDLE EAST

Since World War II, relations with Europe and the US have constituted by far the most important field of Turkey's foreign policy. Nevertheless, links with the other ME states have also increased in importance over the last 10 years. Economic interests have largely accounted for this. On the one side, the sharp rises in oil prices of 1973–74 and 1979–82 vastly increased the share of the ME states in Turkey's total imports. On the other, the growing ME market for Turkish exports of both food and industrial products has been exploited by Turkish firms and encouraged by the government. The result is that the ME countries have come to account for around one third of Turkey's total exports — second only to the EEC in value. Hence, the Turkish Government has to devote much attention to maintaining good relations with its ME neighbors, despite the occasionally bitter disputes between them.

In relations with Turkey's immediate neighbors — Iran, Iraq, and Syria — economic interests were offset by serious political problems. Throughout the Gulf War, Ankara maintained a policy of strict neutrality between Baghdad and Tehran, carefully balancing one side against the other. Nevertheless, Turkey had to face the possibility that if Iraq were defeated, this could have serious implications for its own security, by encouraging the Kurdish resistance in southeastern Anatolia. The importance of economic links with Iran meant that Turkey could not afford an open break with the Islamic Republic. Accordingly, Özal's Government had devoted considerable attention to maintaining good relations with Iran despite constant attacks on Turkish secularism by Tehran radio and active pro-fundamentalist propaganda by Iranian representatives in Turkey. Relations with Baghdad had been easier, since Turkey and Iraq had a common interest in suppressing the Kurdish attempts to establish an autonomous state. On a third front, relations with Syria had traditionally been cool, partly for historical reasons (in particular, Turkey's annexation of Alexandretta province in 1939), and partly because Turkey suspected Syria of being the principal source of external support for the PKK guerrillas. The Syrians, for their part, were perturbed by Turkey's construction of several large dams on the upper Euphrates, which could sharply reduce the flow of water into Syria.

Syrian-Turkish relations had appeared to take an important step forward in July 1987 when Özal had visited Damascus, and secured President Asad's agreement to end support for the PKK in return for a promised minimum flow in the Euphrates (see *MECS* 1987, p. 675). However, the new understanding with Syria made little further progress in 1988. Incidents during the year (specifically, the clash with the PKK at the beginning of April near Nusaybin — see above) suggested that the Kurdish insurgents in Turkey were still receiving help from Syria. Equally, talks among Turkish, Syrian, and Iraqi representatives aiming to reach a tripartite pact on the future division of the Euphrates waters, which were held in November 1988, broke up without any firm agreement.

In an attempt to improve Turkey's delicate relationship with Iran, Özal paid an official visit to Tehran at the end of February 1988, during which a "preliminary agreement" was signed for the construction of an oil pipeline to run from the Iranian oil center of Ahwaz to the Turkish Mediterranean coast at Dörtyol. For Iran, the main advantage of this project was that it would free it from dependence on the dangerous Gulf sea route for its oil exports. Turkey, too, could expect to earn valuable transit fees. For both sides, the principal disadvantage of the plan was its enormous cost, which was put at around $3bn.–$3.5bn. at 1988 prices. Of this, Iran would be expected to provide $2bn. leaving the remainder to Turkey. After some bargaining, it was agreed that Iran would raise the whole capital cost by oil sales to third countries; Turkey would then waive its pipeline royalties until its share had been met.[29] Nevertheless, there were grave doubts as to whether Iran would be able to provide such a huge sum, granted the slackness in the world oil market and the urgent need for reconstruction after the Gulf War. Moreover, from Iran's viewpoint, its acceptance of the UN cease-fire resolution in July 1988 substantially reduced the strategic value of the proposed pipeline.

After Özal's return from Tehran, the pipeline project dropped out of the headlines and was replaced by more predictable issues. An apparently deliberate attempt by the Iranian Air Force to bomb the Habur bridge linking Turkey with Iraq on 24 March did not serve to improve Iranian-Turkish relations. The fluctuating state of relations with Iran was demonstrated by the trade figures for 1988: Turkey's exports to Iran grew slightly, by around 13%, but its imports (largely of crude oil) dropped by 28%. Total trade with Iran stood at around $1.2bn. — well below the peak of around $3bn. which it had reached in 1985.[30]

Economically, Iraq has been of greater importance to Turkey than Iran in recent years. In 1988, Turkish exports to Iraq grew by around 19% and its imports by 25%, to reach a total of some $2.6bn.[31] Mutual trade was the major subject of discussion for Özal when he visited Baghdad at the beginning of April. There had been some speculation that he might act as mediator in the Gulf War, and the two belligerents agreed to suspend the "war of the cities" for the period of the Turkish premier's stay in Baghdad. In fact, Özal seemed reluctant to push himself forward in this role unless there were good chances of success — which, at this time, did not appear to be the case. Instead, he concentrated on commercial problems. Since the Gulf War had forced Iraq to devote most of its immediate cash resources to arms purchases, it had little remaining hard currency with which to pay its ordinary commercial creditors, such as Turkey. The result was that total Iraqi debts to Turkey were estimated to have reached \$1.5bn.–\$2.2.bn., of which only \$900m. was covered by official credit arrangements. The Iraqi authorities apparently asked Özal to extend the government credit limit, but were bluntly refused. Instead, Özal announced that no more official credits could be extended to Iraq after the end of April. The overall rise in Turkey's exports during the year can probably be attributed to the fact that once Iran had accepted a cease-fire, Iraq found it easier to provide resources to meet its ordinary commercial liabilities.

Needless to say, Iran's acceptance of UN Security Council Resolution 598, which came into effect in August, came as a welcome, if unexpected relief to Turkey, as to other countries. As the Istanbul daily *Cumhuriyet* had put it on 1 April, "the policy of active neutrality is becoming very difficult to maintain. It is very much like tightrope walking, and has certain limits."[32] Iran's sudden change of course relieved Turkey of the need to continue with the delicate tightrope act and removed the possibility that the war might have spilled over into other countries, including Turkey. The beginning of the cease-fire also awakened hopes that Turkish construction firms could benefit from their relative closeness and experience of working in the region, by winning a substantial share of the valuable reconstruction contracts which were likely to be on offer in both countries. By the end of the year, these hopes had yet to be fulfilled. Until Iran and Iraq reached an agreement on the course of their mutual border, they seemed likely to postpone large-scale reconstruction of their shattered cities in the war zone. Nevertheless, the longer-run outlook was still hopeful, and suggested that Turkey's relations with its immediate neighbors might be easier to handle than they had been in the recent past.

NOTES

For the place and frequency of publications cited here, and for the full name of the publication, news agency, radio station, or monitoring service where an abbreviation is used, please see "List of Sources." Only in the case of more than one publication bearing the same name is the place of publication noted here.

1. Melih Aşik, "Papatya Devri," published in *Milliyet* on Sundays. "The Daisy Age" is a facetious reference both to Semra Özal and the "Tulip Age" of the Ottoman Empire in the 18th century.
2. This and the following narrative is based on contemporary Turkish and British press reports. Specific references are given only for other sources, or for quotations, statistics, and exclusive stories.
3. Metin Heper, "Party Not Participating in Economics," *Dateline Turkey,* 5 March 1988, p. 8.
4. Turkish constitution of 1982, Article 175, as amended by parliament on 4 May 1987.
5. Quoted, Reuters, 19 September 1988.
6. *Milliyet,* 26 December 1988.
7. See Note 1 above.

8. Martial law was officially withdrawn throughout Turkey in July 1987. However, a "state of emergency" remained in force in the Kurdish provinces. Under this, the Army retains important law-and-order functions.
9. Quotations as reported by Reuters, 30 April, 2 May, 3 May; and *The Guardian*, 4 May 1988.
10. Figures from *MEED*, 16 September, p. 29; *Dateline Turkey*, 3 September, 1 October; *Turkey Briefing*, September and November 1988.
11. *Turkey: Brutal and Systematic Abuse of Human Rights* (London: AI, January 1989), p. 1.
12. Ibid., pp. 15–32.
13. Ibid., pp. 35–41; *Turkey Briefing*, March, May, July, November 1988.
14. AI, op. cit., pp. 51-69: *The Observer*, 19 February 1989.
15. AI, op. cit., p. 8; Reuters, 11 February 1989.
16. *Briefing*, 13 February 1989, p. 18. Figures for 1987 vary slightly from those reported in *MECS* 1987, as the latter were preliminary estimates. All figures calculated at constant (1968) prices.
17. Foreign trade figures estimated from January-November data, as published in *Briefing*, 13 February 1989, p. 22. Data on foreign debt from ibid., p. 25.
18. Ibid., pp. 20–21 (based on January-November data).
19. Ibid., p. 19.
20. *MEED*, 20 February, p. 34, and 28 October, pp. 23–24; Reuters, 2 February 1989.
21. *FT*, 5 February; *MEED*, 28 October, pp. 23–24; E. Donald Besch Jr., "Banking Sector Pulls Through Turbulent Year," *Dateline Turkey*, 31 December, p. 5; *Milliyet*, 4 January 1989.
22. *Dateline Turkey*, 31 December; *Milliyet*, 19 January 1989.
23. *FT Survey: Turkish Banking*, 8 December 1988, p. ix.
24. *Dateline Turkey*, 31 December 1988.
25. *FT*, 21 April 1988.
26. *The Independent*, 2 February 1988.
27. *New Cyprus*, December 1988, p. 9.
28. Reuters, 27 May 1988.
29. As reported in *Milliyet*, 1 March 1988.
30. Data from *Briefing*, 13 February 1989, pp. 20–21: totals for 1988 estimated from January-November data.
31. Ibid., pp. 20–21.
32. *Cumhuriyet*, 1 April 1988.

The Yemeni Arab Republic

(Al-Jumhuriyya al-'Arabiyya al-Yamaniyya)

JOSEPH KOSTINER

In 1988, the Yemeni Arab Republic (YAR) continued to exploit the relative calm at home and in the surrounding region to develop itself politically and economically. As in previous years, Yemeni leaders and notably President 'Ali 'Abdallah Salih gave the highest priority to achievements in these fields in order to compensate for the long years of internal war which were also lean years in terms of development. The maintenance of stability within and around the YAR was interrelated as in previous years. The YAR's neighbors, Saudi Arabia and the People's Democratic Republic of Yemen (PDRY), encouraged rival groups within the YAR to advance their national interests on the YAR's account. The YAR's attempts to improve relations with these two states, the *detènte* between the superpowers, and the discovery of oil all contributed to regional tranquillity and formed the basis for internal development.

In domestic affairs, Salih continued to permit different groups within the YAR to assert themselves in representative institutions. This enabled them to participate in the political process, but it also helped incorporate them within the established political structure. These aims, to widen political representation (which the regime called "democratization") and to enhance the regime's legitimacy, motivated Salih to call elections for the Consultative Assembly (*majlis al-shura*) in July. The results brought into the open both Muslim fundamentalist and leftist elements in opposition to Salih while giving his supporters a decisive majority. Salih took advantage of this situation to form a new government, change personnel in many top administrative positions, and finally, to stand for reelection, all successfully achieved by September. These political accomplishments were not matched by parallel economic steps; oil production increased slowly but the economy was plagued by inflation and the excessive import of consumer goods. The hope for a flourishing economy was put off to a later day.

In foreign affairs, the YAR surmounted difficulties which had hampered its relations with the PDRY, and signed an agreement for economic cooperation and renewed movement toward union. San'a kept on exercising a policy of nonalignment in the Arab world and reinforcing Arab solidarity by supporting widely agreed Arab interests, such as the Palestinian uprising in the Israeli-administered territories and Iraq in its war against Iran. This policy enabled the YAR to become an intermediary in regional controversies such as Egypt's rehabilitation in the Arab world. San'a's successes helped guarantee the regional tranquillity the YAR was seeking.

INTERNAL AFFAIRS

THE ELECTIONS FOR THE CONSULTATIVE COUNCIL AND THE PRESIDENCY

UNDERLYING MOTIVES AND CONCEPTS

'Ali 'Abdallah Salih's decision to hold elections for the YAR's main executive and parliamentary organs can be attributed to the following three factors.

(1) The YAR's search for internal reconciliation. It had already become evident in the early 1980s that Salih's regime, while it occasionally cracked down on the opposition, notably the leftist National Democratic Front (NDF), it realized that there was no practical way of taming all the factions in the YAR—tribal, rural or urban-based, Zaydi or Shafi'i, conservative or left-wing—through governmental coercion. Yemen's political culture of divisions, resulting from a tribal background and decades of internal war, was a barrier to establishing unity of these factions and enlisting their unequivocal loyalty to the government. Salih's regime tended rather to recognize this diversity and to encourage dialogue and cooperation among the different groups. Yemeni leaders emphasized the virtues of the tribal background of their society and the plurality of their political opinions. They stressed that their political system encouraged cooperation and common action among the different groups by enabling them to participate in government institutions (see *MECS* 1987 pp. 679–80). Elections were a logical fulfillment of this philosophy.

(2) Elections and parliamentary or quasi-parliamentary representation were practices which the Salih regime had been using for several years to both encourage conciliation and cooperation among representatives of different social groups and to reinforce popular support for his regime among the Yemeni masses. Salih established the General People's Congress (GPC), held elections for the presidency in 1983 and for provincial representatives in 1987 (cf. *MECS* 1987, p. 680). These were described as manifestations of "democratization," which served to strengthen the national dialogue and give the regime an aura of legitimacy and popularity. The elections of 1988 were the zenith of this process.[1]

(3) Several recent developments also called for elections. The beginning of oil production in the YAR and the influx of hundreds of thousands of South Yemeni refugees, both of which were likely to trigger social change in the YAR, alongside changing political conditions that were generated by unity negotiations with the PDRY, all enabled Salih to obtain further popular support for his regime that would permit him to cope with future developments. His aim was to permit both leftist and Islamic-conservative elements to elect and be elected in order to have them function overtly and under the open eye of the government. Thus, an adviser to the San'a Government, 'Abd al-'Aziz al-Muqallah, noted that there was no real intention among the San'a elite to permit the free activity of political parties, because they were "divisive" and "destructive." Neither were the leaders interested in transferring the source of political power from army ranks to civilian politicians. Muqallah stressed that the military was the only group that acted on the basis of national interests, did not cause division, and whose leaders were clean-handed.[2] The elections were, therefore, not aimed at producing sweeping political changes in the YAR, but rather at providing for Salih's regime a calm, sound body politic.

THE ELECTIONS: RESULTS AND IMPLICATIONS

The elections to the Consultative Assembly took place on 5 July. They were described by the official radio as "the biggest parliamentary general elections in the contemporary history of our country," carried out freely, by secret ballot all over the state.[3] An electorate comprised of 1.1m. people (all male citizens over 18 and 60,000 women) chose 128 representatives for the Assembly from among 1,200 candidates. Salih had the right to appoint an additional 31 deputies, to make a total of 159. As the YAR did not permit the activity of political parties, none participated in the elections, although the candidates, as individuals, could campaign in public places all over the country, including mosques. The elections at 238 balloting centers were prepared and supervised by committees of the Consultative Assembly.[4] Kuwaiti and Lebanese papers noted the absence of any governmental involvement during the elections, with the exception of security officers of the Ministry of Internal Affairs responsible for law and order. The elections were described as being as calm and orderly as possible.[5]

The results constituted a major success for Salih's regime. One third of the new deputies were identified with Salih's policies and were delegates of the GPC. They and the 31 appointed members—among them 'Abd al-Karim 'Abdallah al-'Arshi as Speaker, several ministers and tribal leaders (such as Abu Shawarib and Abu Luhum) — gave Salih a majority in the new assembly. Most of Salih's supporters were tribesmen (about 40 seats), the others being urban intellectuals and officials. Reports indicated that there was an "Islamic trend," centered on the San'a *'ulama* and other "traditional" families, who won over 20 seats. Some were reported to be adherents of the Muslim Brethren, but most were "moderates," interested in the dominance of the Islamic holy law (*Shari'a*) and in the pursuit of a pious life-style. This group won a majority in San'a and was salient in other urban centers. Leftists — Marxists, Ba'this, and Nasirites — who in one way or another advocated the NDF ideas, won c. 10 seats.[6] Salih's achievement was evident in the number of seats his supporters had won and in their role as the middle road between the Islamic and leftist extremes. Those advocating the continuation of Salih's policy of supporting "the 26 September 1962 revolution and the democratic regime" were thereby in the majority.[7]

Salih felt confident enough to exploit this achievement to introduce additional administrative-political changes. Formally resigning the presidency, he declared himself "a soldier in the service of the country" ready to serve in any position. On 17 August, 152 members of the new assembly reelected him president, a decision he "accepted." The assembly also voted to strengthen the office of the president by terminating its sharing of power with the Military Command Council.[8] Salih also moved to reform his Personal Advisory Council, which had consisted of 15 members by adding 10 more on 30 July.[9] He then appointed a new Cabinet, led by the previous prime minister, 'Abd al-'Aziz 'Abd al-Ghani, and consisting of loyal men who also had displayed professional skills. Thus, Deputy Prime Minister Hassan Muhammad Makki, Deputy Prime Minister and Minister of Foreign Affairs 'Abd al-Karim al-Iryani, Minister of Interior 'Abdallah Barakat, and others were reappointed to the new Cabinet (see Appendix I). Salih also appointed new provincial governors for San'a, 'Ibb, Ma'rib, and Dammar. Prime Minister 'Abd al-Ghani appointed new senior officials in the office of the Prime Minister, and the Ministries of Development, Legal Affairs, Justice, Foreign Affairs, Public Works, and others (see Appendix II).

To cultivate the regime's backbone, the armed forces, Salih on 24 September promoted 307 officers from the rank of major to the rank of lieutenant colonel.[10] Other reports claimed that Salih had also promoted senior officers to the ranks of colonel and brigadier general.

Violence by the opposition in the YAR in 1988 continued at a low ebb. One of the few exceptions was a rocket attack on the American Embassy in San'a in early May which caused no casualties. The authorities detained several suspects.[11]

It was a year of political institutionalization and reinforcement of the government's legitimacy. The degree of "democratization" remains to be seen: the authority of the new Consultative Assembly included the making of domestic and foreign policies, the right to express nonconfidence in the Cabinet, and the right to ratify the budget and new laws. The real value of these changes depended on the new assembly's ability to translate these rights into practice.

ECONOMIC CONDITIONS AND DEVELOPMENT

Oil revenues remained the backbone of the Yemeni economy. Annual production in the Ma'rib oil fields was c. 190,000 barrels per day (b/d) with a forecast of 400,000 b/d by the end of the decade. However, the relatively low price per barrel, a rising tide of imports, and foreign borrowing led to an estimated deficit of 22% in the gross domestic product in 1987. Private sector imports had risen by 30% since 1986 while government imports more than doubled. In 1987, the deficit in the balance of payments was $631m. in comparison to the $149m. low in 1986.[12] A government spokesman's assertion that the YAR would not have a "consumers' boom" typical of Third World oil-exporting states[13] was premature.

The government focused on utilizing enhanced imports and foreign financing to boost the development of fisheries, agriculture, industry,and oil;[14] the main thrust of development centered on infrastructure projects, such as building a new pier at Hudayda,[15] establishing 156 agricultural guidance centers,[16] prospecting for oil and gas in different parts of the YAR, including the Red Sea shore,[17] and exploiting 2,200 sq. km. of oil fields in cooperation with the PDRY (see below) along their common border.[18]

YAR leaders' hopes hinged on the establishment of new projects to utilize mineral resources in order to boost the Yemeni economy in the future. At present, however, the expenditure involved in the activation of new industrial and business enterprises and rising consumers' expenditure have only produced difficulties.

FOREIGN RELATIONS

YAR spokesmen had often reiterated that the principles of the YAR's foreign policy focused on encouraging Arab unity and solidarity, and envisaging the YAR playing the role of a catalyst for solidarity by helping Arab states overcome their differences and face their "real enemies." In practice, the YAR sought the calmness and stability in the Arab world that would keep it from becoming entangled in regional disputes and which would be conducive to internal development. This policy was most evident in its relations with the PDRY.

RELATIONS WITH THE PEOPLE'S DEMOCRATIC REPUBLIC OF YEMEN

San'a's problems involving the PDRY in previous years (see *MECS* 1987, pp. 682–83) were still evident in 1988. The undemarcated border in the YAR's southeastern parts continued to encourage more clashes among unruly tribal groups. The presence of the former PDRY leader, 'Ali Nasir Muhammad, and 40,000 of his supporters, who opposed the new elite in Aden, had threatened to draw the YAR into an undesirable dispute with its southern neighbor. The discovery of oil in the Ma'rib (YAR territory) and Shabwa (PDRY territory) regions along the undemarcated border had prompted both states to suspect each other of malevolent intentions. The YAR's position was to give 'Ali Nasir and his followers asylum as "Yemen is the country for all Yemenis."[19] San'a was also firm about preventing any infringements of its sovereignty by the PDRY in the border area. But, in 1988, the YAR faced growing difficulties in maintaining this position. Foreign Minister al-Iryani admitted that tribal clashes in the border area "did happen and may recur after one day, one week, or one month. It is an ordinary matter." The situation was aggravated, he noted, by an increased military presence and erection of fortifications in the south.[20] YAR spokesmen also displayed frustration over the unresolved status of 'Ali Nasir's group. Their pressure on the PDRY Government to lighten the verdicts passed on the sentenced opposition members won only partial success (see chapter on the People's Democratic Republic of Yemen). Political mediation between the opposition and the leaders in Aden was fruitless.[21] There was new tension between the two states, evident in the increased military activity over oil exploitation along the border area in early 1988[22] and a booby-trapped letter addressed to a former PDRY minister of justice now residing in San'a, which was successfully dismantled.[23] This prompted San'a to engage in discussions with Aden on solutions to these problems.

Both San'a and Aden regarded unity between their states as a major goal and at the same time as a tactical framework under which practical frontier issues could be resolved (on the progress of these discussions see chapter on the People's Democratic Republic of Yemen). Salih contacted the PDRY leader, 'Ali Salim al-Bayd, on 27 January to caution him about the border tension.[24] While San'a carried on the dialogue with the PDRY in meetings between their prime ministers, chiefs of staff, and political emissaries, Salih described the reports about possible armed clashes between the two states as "hostile and biased rumors."[25] On 16 April, Salih played host to al-Bayd, who came to San'a for discussions. On 4 May, an agreement was signed on the joint exploitation of oil in the Ma'rib-Shabwa region and on allowing citizens of both states to cross the border freely. The two sides also agreed to ratify the draft constitution for a united Yemen.

The Consultative Assembly Speaker, al-'Arshi, described the agreement as a manifestation of a "peaceful and democratic dialogue."[26] Minister of the Interior 'Abdallah Barakat noted that "the barriers between the north and the south have been eliminated."[27] Foreign Minister al-Iryani, however, alluded to the YAR's difficulties on the road to real unity. He admitted that there were "citizens" in both states who opposed unity, although they did not include decision makers. He also pointed out that the constitution of the United Yemen did not rule out a multiparty system, whereas the constitutions of each state did not permit parties to function.[28]

It was therefore understandable that YAR spokesmen would be primarily concerned with the practical aspects of the 4 May agreement, namely, the cooperation between the two states and improved relations. They did not contemplate immediate and full unity. Salih obviously recognized that attaining this goal required bridging over ideologically, politically, and economically different systems. He made unity a "strategic" objective, implicitly placing it as a long-term goal. Meanwhile, the YAR remained committed to "work[ing] through dialogue and continuous meetings," namely, advancing toward unity gradually.[29]

RELATIONS WITH THE GULF STATES

The YAR continued to view the Gulf states, incorporated in the Gulf Cooperation Council (GCC), as its main financial backers and partners in the attainment of tranquillity in the region. San'a supported the GCC's position on ending the Iraqi-Iranian War through acceptance of UN Security Council Resolution 598 (see chapter on the Iraqi-Iranian War). Iranian aggression against GCC states, notably Kuwait, was strongly condemned by the Yemeni media, which depicted it as a threat to regional stability and peace. YAR spokesmen on occasion objected to the superpowers' military presence in the region, a position which was somewhat incompatible with the Gulf states' reliance on the US naval armada in the Gulf, but this difference caused no open dispute. Salih even stated that the YAR, being part "of the Gulf and the Peninsula, blesses every step leading to unity among local states," a hint at San'a's hope to join the GCC,[30] which was not fulfilled.

The YAR's relations with most Gulf states were cordial. Salih visited the United Arab Emirates (UAE) on 20 December 1987 and the UAE's president, Zayid Ibn Sultan al-Nuhayan, agreed to finance the second stage of the YAR's Ma'rib dam. Kuwait remained one of the YAR's major benefactors, providing, among other things, finances for some of the YAR's oil explorations.[31]

In San'a's relations with Riyadh, the presence of c. 1m. Yemeni workers in Saudi Arabia, smuggling from Saudi territory into the YAR, and tribal skirmishes along their undemarcated border increased tension between the two states. Saudi influence on some Yemeni tribes added strain. Moreover, Saudi fears that San'a's emerging oil production might lead the YAR to new ventures, such as cooperation, if not unity, with the PDRY (see chapters on Saudi Arabia and the People's Democratic Republic of Yemen), precipitated a border crisis. An Egyptian paper reported in July that Saudi Arabia was encouraging tribal groups from both the PDRY and the YAR to be loyal to Riyadh and even to assume Saudi citizenship.[32] While this report had no follow-up, the YAR tried to allay Saudi anxiety over San'a's relations with the PDRY. Salih visited Mecca on 5 May, immediately after concluding the agreement with the PDRY and met with King Fahd,[33] presumably to inform him of the nature of this agreement. Despite this tension, Yemeni Minister of Supplies and Trade Muhammad al-Khadim went to Riyadh in February and discussed with his counterpart issues of trade and investments in the private sector.[34] During the year, Riyadh also assisted the YAR in rehabilitating regions which had been hit by earthquakes and in developing telephone lines between the main Yemeni cities.[35]

The YAR remained critical of Iran, which was seen in San'a as responsible for the continuation of the Gulf War, unwilling to embrace peace, and aggressive toward other Arab and Islamic states. Iran's acceptance of UN Resolution 598 in July was received in San'a with "deep satisfaction."[36] On the other hand, San'a had a close relationship with Iraq, since Iraq deserved support first and foremost as an Arab "fraternal" state ready for peace, and as an entity defending its independence and sovereignty against aggression.[37] Salih visited Baghdad in August[38] and several senior Iraqi ministers visited San'a during the year.

RELATIONS WITH OTHER ARAB STATES

The YAR had been one of the states most eager to renew its diplomatic relations with Egypt. Cairo's record in helping the Yemeni revolution in the 1960s, in providing teachers for the YAR school system, and in training its Army, tilted the YAR toward Egypt even during the early 1980s when it had been boycotted by the majority of Arab states. Loyal to inter-Arab commitments, San'a awaited an Arab summit decision endorsing the renewal of relations. The Amman summit of November 1987 provided this opportunity and San'a, quick to seize it, restored its ties with Cairo on 15 November 1987.[39]

The restoration of ties sparked off multifaceted cooperation with Egypt. An Egyptian military mission visited San'a in December 1987. Interviews Yemeni leaders gave after the summit indicated that military cooperation between the two states was contemplated in connection with the security of the Red Sea. Al-Iryani stressed Egypt's role in guarding against "external aggression" there;[40] Egyptian President Husni Mubarak visited San'a in May and held talks with Salih, which led to the establishment of a military committee to coordinate policies on Red Sea issues. Salih then described Mubarak as "a person with a perfect outlook...who desires the welfare of the Egyptian people and the Arab nation."[41] YAR Prime Minister 'Abd al-Ghani visited Egypt in October and concluded six agreements over cooperation in technical and economic spheres, in agriculture, health, education, science and technology, proper utilization of manpower, and in encouraging investments in both states.[42]

The YAR's relations with Egypt also concerned inter-Arab disputes. San'a, to some extent with Sudan, undertook to mediate disputes between Egypt and Libya (see chapter on Egypt) and between Egypt and Algeria. Salih phoned the Libyan President Mu'ammar al-Qadhdhafi during Mubarak's visit to San'a, and then visited Tripoli while *en route* to the Arab summit in Algiers in early June. Salih apparently sought to enable both states to renew their air traffic, reopen their border, and encourage them to stop their propaganda attacks on each other.[43] The mediation between Egypt and Algeria took place mainly during the Algiers summit in June, which led to meetings of the advisers to the Egyptian and Algerian presidents.[44] The YAR, in return, enjoyed cordial relations with Libya and even defended the Libyan position in the Iraqi-Iranian War, calling it "logical," as Tripoli was in favor of ending the war and had improved its relations with Iraq.[45]

The YAR hailed the Palestinian uprising in the Israeli administered territories. Al-Iryani explained that the uprising precipitated the end of the Israeli occupation. He stressed, however, that there was little the YAR or other Arab states could do, other than assist the uprising financially as agreed at the Algiers summit. He thought that the Algiers resolutions were good, though limited, indicating that the Arab world had no military option against Israel.[46] San'a, therefore, helped the PLO. In addition to the training camps on its soil, San'a supported the PLO's policies and resolutions on the uprising, notably the Palestinian declaration of independence on 15 November.[47] PLO leader Yasir 'Arafat found in the YAR leadership a loyal advising and sounding board, and visited San'a monthly, usually toward the end of each month. In January 1988, a GPC session established a Palestinian Support Fund to aid the uprising.[48] YAR spokesmen also rejected all claims by Israel and world Jewry that Yemeni Jews suffered from persecution, and maintained that they enjoyed all rights to live in security and to emigrate if they wished.[49]

'Abd al-Ghani visited Syria in January, which attested to San'a's continuous relationship with Damascus.[50] King Husayn of Jordan visited San'a in November 1988.[51] It was agreed in March that Jordanian physicians and technicians would work in major hospitals and provincial medical centers.[52]

ATTITUDES TOWARD THE GREAT POWERS

The Soviet Union remained a major supporter of the YAR during 1988. This was evident in the sphere of technical assistance. The meeting of the Joint Yemeni-Soviet Committee for Technical and Economic Cooperation in San'a in December 1987 led to a Soviet undertaking to study how to improve the functioning of the main Yemeni dams (notably Ma'rib and Harid) and how to develop its ports.[53] Soviet Minister of Geology Yevgeny Kozlovsky visited San'a in February to sign an agreement to help draw a geological map of the YAR.[54] Militarily, al-Iryani noted that 70% of the YAR's ammunition came from the Soviet Union, along with Soviet instructors.[55] The Soviet first deputy to the minister of defense, Gen. Peter Lutshev, visited San'a in October,[56] but the visit did not have any noticeable results. In addition, senior YAR ministers, such as Deputy Prime Minister Makki and Minister of Interior Barakat, visited Moscow during the year. There were no reports of any new strategic cooperation or military buildup between the two states during 1988.

Yemeni spokesmen stressed that the YAR sought to diversify its sources of arms and economic assistance, and generally to maintain a nonpartisan and open-minded foreign policy.[57] Hence, the YAR sought close contacts with the US, a goal it only partially achieved. Al-Iryani explained that the ties between San'a and Washington were good,[58] as was evident from Salih's meeting with the US Deputy Secretary of State Richard Murphy in San'a in June and during the UN General Assembly session in October. However, there were several barriers which, in Yemeni eyes, prevented making the Yemeni-American relationship more cordial and, perhaps, also one with strategic cooperation. Al-Iryani explained that the Soviet Union sold weapons to the YAR "on softer terms," which San'a also expected but failed to obtain from Washington. San'a also insisted that it could hardly develop comprehensive cooperation with Washington, in view of the latter's support for Israel and its policy in the Arab-Israeli conflict, which San'a regarded wrong and sterile.[59] Moreover, according to the YAR, Murphy suggested negotiations on the establishment of an American military base to oversee the Red Sea, a proposal San'a rejected , since it was opposed to any foreign presence in this region.[60]

During his trip to East Asia in late 1987, Salih also visited the People's Republic of China which agreed to give San'a a loan to help finance some of the development projects incorporated in the current Five-Year Plan.[61]

APPENDIX I: 'ABD AL-GHANI'S CABINET, JULY 1988

Article 1:

The new government shall be formed as follows:

Prime Minister — 'Abd al-'Aziz 'Abd al-Ghani
Deputy Prime Minister — Dr. Hassan Muhammad Makki
Deputy Prime Minister and Minister of Foreign Affairs — Dr. 'Abd al-Karim 'Ali al-Iryani
Deputy Prime Minister, Minister of Development, and Head of the Central Planning Organ — Dr. Muhammad Sa'id al-'Attar
Deputy Prime Minister — Mujahid Yahya Abu Shawarib
Minister of Public Works and Transportation — 'Abdallah Husayn al-Kurshumi
Minister of Interior — Dr. 'Abdallah Husayn Barakat
Minister of *Awqaf* and Guidance — 'Ali Ibn 'Ali al-Samman
Minister of Petroleum and Mineral Wealth — Ahmad 'Ali al-Muhanni
Minister of Economy, Supply, and Trade — Dr.'Abd al-Wahhab Mahmud 'Abd al-Hamid
Minister of Communications and Telecommunications — Muhammad al-Khadim al-Wajih
Minister of State for Unity Affairs — Yahya Husayn al-'Arshi
Minister of Education and Head of the General Authority of Scientific Institutes — Ahmad Muhammad al-Anisi
Minister of Legal and Consultative Council Affairs — Isma'il Ahmad al-Wazir
Minister of Justice — Muhsin Muhammad al-'Ulufi
Minister of Social Affairs and Labor — Ahmad Muhammad Luqman
Minister of Information and Culture — Hasan Ahmad al-Lawzi
Minister of Youth and Sports — Dr. Muhammad Ahmad al-Kabbab
Minister of Civil Service and Administrative Reform — Muhammad 'Abdallah al-Ja'ifi
Ministger of Finance — 'Alawi Salih al-Salami
Minister of Electricity and Water — Jamal Muhammad 'Abduh
Minister of Municipalities and Housing — Muhsin 'Ali al-Hamadani
Minister of Agriculture and Fisheries — Dr. Nasir 'Abdallah al-'Awlaqi
Minister of Health — Dr. Muhammad 'Ali Muqbil

SOURCE: R. San'a, 31 July — DR, 1 August 1988.

APPENDIX II: APPOINTMENTS OF SENIOR OFFICIALS, AUGUST 1988

Governors (appointed by President Salih)
Governor of the Province of San'a: Muhammad Hasan Dammaj
Governor of the Province of 'Ibb: Col. Salih 'Abbas al-Khulani
Governor of the Province of Ma'rib: Gen. 'Abdallah Naji Daris
Governor of the Province of Damar: Lt. Col. Dirham 'Abduh Nu'man

Senior Officials in the Ministries (appointed by Prime Minister 'Abd al-Ghani)
Director, Office of the Prime Minister — Muhammad Sa'id Zafir
Deputy Minister, Ministry of Development — Dr. Muthir 'Abdallah al-Sa'idi
Deputy Minister, Ministry of Legal Affairs and Affairs of the Consultative Council — 'Abdallah 'Awad Ahmad
Deputy Minister, Ministry of Public Works and Transport — Muhammad Muhammad al-Tayyib
Deputy Minister, Ministry of *Awqaf* and Guidance — Ahmad 'Abdallah al-Hajari
Under Secretary, the Ministry of Justice: Ahmad Salih Farhan
Assistant Under Secretary, the Ministry of Justice—Muhammad Muhammad al-Durabi
General Deputy: Col. 'Ali Muhammad al-Yana'i
Deputy Chief Justice of the Supreme Judicial Council and Chief Justice of the Supreme Court of Cassation at the Ministry of Justice — Muhammad Isma'il al-Hajji
Deputy Chief Justice of Supreme Court of Cassation — Muhammad Ahmad al-Jarrafi
Deputy Chief Justice of the Supreme Court of Cassation — Ahmad Muhammad 'Ali al-Wazir
Under Secretary, Ministry of Youth and Sports — 'Abd al-Rahman Muhammad al-Akwa'
President of the Council of the Administration of the Bank for Agricultural Cooperative Loans, the Ministry of Agriculture and Fisheries — 'Abdallah al-Burkani
Assistant Under Secretary, Ministry of Foreign Affairs — Sharaf Salih al-Sa'idi
President, Central Agency for Oversight and Accounting — 'Abd al-Malik Mansur
President, Office for the Eradication of Legal Injustices — Judge Muhammad Lutf al-Sabahi

SOURCE: *Al-Jumhuriyya*, Ta'izz, 17 August — DR, 17 October 1988.

NOTES

For the place and frequency of publications cited here, and for the full name of the publication, news agency, radio station, or monitoring service where an abbreviation is used, please see "List of Sources." Only in the case of more than one publication bearing the same name is the place of publication noted here.

1. Interview with Secretary General of the Consultative Assembly 'Ali Muqbil Ghathim, *al-Shira'*, 31 October 1988.
2. Al-Muqallah's interview with *al-Mustaqbal*, 1 August 1988.
3. *Al-Watan al-'Arabi*, 19 February 1988.
4. R. San'a, 4 June — DR, 6 June 1988.
5. *Al-Siyasa*, Kuwait, 10 July 1988.
6. *Al-Mustaqbal*, 9, 12 July; *al-Dunya*, 18 August; *CR*, YAR, No. 3, 1988.
7. *Al-Siyasa*, Kuwait, 10 July; *al-Ra'y*, 9 July 1988.
8. R. San'a, 18 July — DR, 22 July; Reuters, 17 July; Salih's interview with *al-Tadamun*, 7 August 1988.
9. R. San'a, 13, 30 July — DR, 15 July, 3 August 1988.
10. R. San'a, 24 September — DR, 26 September 1988.
11. Isma'il al-Makki's interview with MENA, 17 January — DR, 21 January; *MEED*, 13 May 1988.
12. Ibid.; *CR*, YAR, No. 4, 1988.
13. Al-Iryani's interview with *al-Watan al-'Arabi*, 1 January 1988.
14. 'Abd al-Ghani's speech, R. San'a, 25 August — DR, 29 August 1988.
15. *Al-Siyasa*, Kuwait, 31 December 1988.
16. Minister of Agriculture Husayn al-'Amri's interview, *al-Ittihad*, Abu Dhabi, 8 April 1988.
17. *Al-Shira'*, 21 September 1988.
18. *CR*, YAR, No. 4, 1988-89.
19. *Al-Yawm al-Sabi'*, 20 December 1987.
20. Al-Iryani's interview with *al-Watan al-'Arabi*, 1 January 1988.
21. *Al-Hawadith*, 22 January 1988.
22. *Al-Ahali*, 3 February 1988.
23. *Al-Ittihad*, Abu Dhabi, 2 February 1988.
24. *Al-Ahali*, 3 February 1988.
25. Salih's interview with *al-Siyasa*, Kuwait, 29 February 1988.
26. Al-'Arshi's interview with *al-Majalla*, 26 June 1988.
27. Barakat's interview with *al-Sharq al-Awsat*, 16 October 1988.
28. Al-Iryani's interview with *al-Sharq al-Awsat*, 15 October 1988.
29. Salih's interview with *al-Ra'y al-'Amm*, 11 October 1988.
30. Ibid.
31. *Al-Yamama*, 6 January 1988.
32. *Al-Ahali*, 6 July 1988.
33. R. Riyadh, 5 May — DR, 9 May 1988.
34. *'Ukaz*, 9, 10 February 1988.
35. *Al-Madina*, 2 September 1988.
36. R. San'a, 19 July — DR, 20 July 1988.
37. Salih's interview with *al-Ahram*, 27 May 1988.
38. INA, 4 August — DR, 9 August 1988.
39. R. San'a, 15 November — DR, 16 November 1987.
40. Al-Iryani's interview with *al-Tadamun*, 19 December 1987.
41. Salih's interview with *al-Ahram*, 27 May 1988.
42. *Al-Ahram*, 20 October; *Akhir Sa'a*, 26 October 1988.
43. *Al-Ittihad*, Abu Dhabi, 9 June 1988.
44. *Al-Ittihad*, Abu Dhabi, 17 July 1988.
45. Al-Iryani's interview with *al-Tadamun*, 19 December 1987.
46. Al-Iryani's interview with *al-Yaqza*, 25 March 1988.
47. R. San'a, 15 November — DR, 16 November 1988.
48. *Al-Watan*, 15 January 1988.

49. *Al-Musawwar,* 6 January 1989.
50. *Al-Shira',* 29 January 1988.
51. R. San'a, 30 November — DR, 30 November 1988.
52. R. San'a, 17 March — DR, 18 March 1988.
53. R. San'a, 15 December — DR, 17 December 1988.
54. R. San'a, 10 February — DR, 12 February 1988.
55. Al-Iryani's interview with *al-Usbu' al-'Arabi,* 28 November 1988.
56. R. San'a, 22 October — DR, 25 October 1988.
57. Al-Iryani's interview with *al-Usbu' al-'Arabi,* 28 November 1988.
58. Al-Iryani's interview with *al-Siyasa,* Kuwait, 11 July 1988.
59. Ibid.
60. *Al-Majalla,* 29 June 1988.
61. *Al-Yamama,* 6 January 1988.

INDEX

NOTE

Most political parties, organizations, public bodies, and institutions have been indexed by name rather than by country, and where it is not otherwise obvious the name of the country is shown in parentheses at the end of the entry. Page numbers in bold type indicate principal references. Alphabetical order is word-by-word.

About the Book and Editors

A unique annual record of political developments in the Middle East, the *Middle East Contemporary Survey* (*MECS*) is acknowledged as the standard reference work on events and trends in the region. Designed to be a continuing, up-to-date reference for scholars, researchers and analysts, policymakers, students, and journalists, it examines in detail the rapidly changing Middle Eastern scene in all its complexity.

Each volume is divided into two parts: the first provides a series of essays on broad regional issues and on the region's foreign relations; the second offers country-by-country surveys of all the Arab states, as well as Turkey, Israel, and Iran. They elucidate the inner dynamics of each country's polity and society.

Volume XII covers the year 1988—an eventful and in many ways momentous year in the Middle East. In the West Bank and Gaza, the *intifada* grew and conflict intensified, creating profound changes for all Palestinians, for Israel, and for the region at large. In 1988, the civilian uprising paved the way for the Palestinian declaration of independence and the concomitant boost in the PLO's international standing, generating new impetus for the long-stalemated Middle East peace process. The *intifada* also led to King Hussein's dissociation from the West Bank in word and deed.

Among the other major themes covered in this volume are the sudden termination of the eight-year Iran-Iraq War with its domestic and regional repercussions; the Soviet withdrawal from Afghanistan after nine years of occupation; the impact of glasnost on Moscow's new political style, specifically its Middle Eastern policy; the ongoing disintegration of Lebanon; and the general elections in Israel, whose results led again to the formation of a National Unity Government.

Ami Ayalon is Senior Lecturer in the Department of Middle Eastern and African History and Senior Research Fellow at the Moshe Dayan Center at Tel Aviv University. **Haim Shaked** is Professor of Middle Eastern and African History and Senior Research Fellow at the Moshe Dayan Center, and Director, Middle East Studies Institute, Graduate School of International Studies, University of Miami.